D1302829

GLENCOE LITERATURE

The Reader's Choice

Teacher Reviewers

Bill Beyer
General Wayne Middle School
Malvern, Pennsylvania

Sister Marian Christi
St. Matthew School
Philadelphia, Pennsylvania

Christine Ferguson
North Buncombe Middle School
Asheville, North Carolina

Elizabeth Fischer
Tower Heights Middle School
Centerville, Ohio

Diane Gerrety
Bridgetown Junior High
Cincinnati, Ohio

Susan Giddings
Marble Falls Middle School
Marble Falls, Texas

Denise Goeckel
Magsig Middle School
Centerville, Ohio

Debbie Hampton
Central Davidson Middle School
Lexington, North Carolina

Tammy Harris
Walnut Springs Middle School
Columbus, Ohio

Marlene Henry
Northwood Elementary
Troy, Ohio

Brian Hinders
Tower Heights Middle School
Centerville, Ohio

Cheryl Keffer
Fayette County Schools Gifted Program
Oak Hill, West Virginia

Sheryl Kelso
Oldtown School
Oldtown, Maryland

Gail Kidd
Center Middle School
Azusa, California

Karen Mantia
Northmont City Schools
Clayton, Ohio

Nancy Mast
Hobart Middle School
Hobart, Indiana

Chiyo Masuda
Albany Middle School
Albany, California

Kim Mistler
Delhi Junior High School
Cincinnati, Ohio

Wilma Jean Nix
Baldwin Junior High School
Montgomery, Alabama

Joe Olague
Alder Junior High
Fontana, California

Bonita Rephann
Musselman Middle School
Bunker Hill, West Virginia

Marie Rinaudo
St. John Berchman's Cathedral School
Shreveport, Louisiana

Carol Schowalter
El Roble Intermediate School
Claremont, California

Karen Shannon
Davis Drive Middle School
Apex, North Carolina

Joan Slater
Strack Intermediate
Klein, Texas

Joyce Stakem
St. Catherine of Siena School
Wilmington, Delaware

Elizabeth Struckman
Bridgetown Junior High School
Centerville, Ohio

Debbie Trepanier
Jenkins Middle School
Chewelah, Washington

Sarah Vick
Central Davidson Middle School
Lexington, North Carolina

Erin Watts
Albright Middle School
Houston, Texas

Anne Welch
Huntsville Middle School
Huntsville, Alabama

James Zartler
Centennial Middle School
Portland, Oregon

Senior Program Consultants

Beverly Ann Chin is Professor of English, Director of the English Teaching Program, Director of the Montana Writing Project, and former Director of Composition at the University of Montana in Missoula. In 1995–1996, Dr. Chin served as President of the National Council of Teachers of English. She currently serves as a Member of the Board of Directors of the National Board for Professional Teaching Standards. Dr. Chin is a nationally recognized leader in English language arts standards, curriculum, and assessment. Formerly a high school English teacher and adult education reading teacher, Dr. Chin has taught in English language arts education at several universities and has received awards for her teaching and service.

Denny Wolfe, a former high school English teacher and department chair, is Professor of English Education, Director of the Tidewater Virginia Writing Project, and Director of the Center for Urban Education at Old Dominion University in Norfolk, Virginia. For the National Council of Teachers of English, he has served as Chairperson of the Standing Committee on Teacher Preparation, President of the International Assembly, member of the Executive Committee of the Council on English Education, and editor of the SLATE Newsletter. Author of more than seventy-five articles and books on teaching English, Dr. Wolfe is a frequent consultant to schools and colleges on the teaching of English language arts.

Program Consultants

Jeffrey S. Copeland is Professor and Head of the Department of English Language and Literature at the University of Northern Iowa, where he teaches children's and young adult literature courses and a variety of courses in English education. A former public school teacher, he has published many articles in the professional journals in the language arts. The twelve books he has written or edited include *Speaking of Poets: Interviews with Poets Who Write for Children and Young Adults* and *Young Adult Literature: A Contemporary Reader.*

Mary Ann Dudzinski is a former high school English teacher and recipient of the Ross Perot Award for Teaching Excellence. She also has served as a member of the core faculty for the National Endowment for the Humanities Summer Institute for Teachers of Secondary School English and History at the University of North Texas. After fifteen years of classroom experience in grades 9–12, she currently is a language arts consultant.

William Ray has taught English in the Boston Public Schools; at Lowell University; University of Wroclaw, Poland; and, for the last fourteen years, at Lincoln-Sudbury Regional High School in Sudbury, Massachusetts. He specializes in world literature. He has worked on a variety of educational texts, as editor, consultant, and contributing writer.

Jacqueline Jones Royster is Professor of English and Associate Dean of the College of Humanities at The Ohio State University. She is also on the faculty of the Bread Loaf School of English at Middlebury College in Middlebury, Vermont. In addition to the teaching of writing, Dr. Royster's professional interests include the rhetorical history of African American women and the social and cultural implications of literate practices.

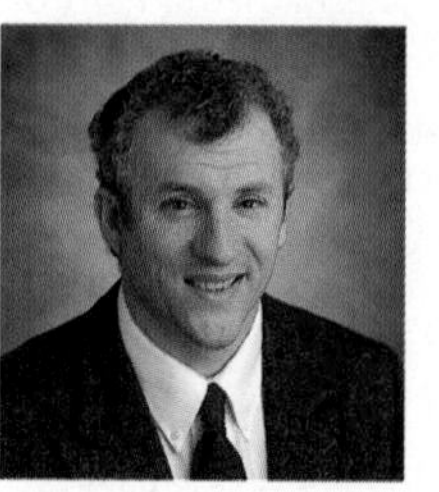

Jeffrey Wilhelm, a former English and reading teacher, is currently an assistant professor at the University of Maine where he teaches courses in middle and secondary level literacy. He is the author or co-author of several books on the teaching of reading and literacy, including *You Gotta BE the Book* and *Boys and Books.* He also works with local schools as part of the fledgling Adolescent Literacy Project and is the director of two annual summer institutes: the Maine Writing Project and Technology as a Learning Tool.

Acknowledgments

Grateful acknowledgment is given authors, publishers, photographers, museums, and agents for permission to reprint the following copyrighted material. Every effort has been made to determine copyright owners. In case of any omissions, the Publisher will be pleased to make suitable acknowledgments in future editions.

Acknowledgments continued on page R152.

The Standardized Test Practice pages in this book were written by The Princeton Review, the nation's leader in test preparation. Through its association with McGraw-Hill, The Princeton Review offers the best way to help students excel on standardized assessments.

The Princeton Review is not affiliated with Princeton University or Educational Testing Service.

Glencoe/McGraw-Hill

A Division of The ***McGraw·Hill*** *Companies*

Printed in the United States of America

Send all inquiries to:
Glencoe/McGraw-Hill
8787 Orion Place
Columbus, OH 43240-4027

ISBN 0-07-825106-0
(Student Edition)

ISBN 0-07-825137-0
(Teacher Wraparound Edition)

3 4 5 6 7 8 9 10 027/055 05 04 03

Teacher Wraparound Edition

GLENCOE LITERATURE

The Reader's Choice

Program Consultants

Beverly Ann Chin
Denny Wolfe
Jeffrey Copeland
Mary Ann Dudzinski
William Ray
Jacqueline Jones Royster
Jeffrey Wilhelm

Course 2

New York, New York   Columbus, Ohio   Woodland Hills, California   Peoria, Illinois

Book Overview

Contents

THEME ❦ ONE

🌍 *indicates world literature*

THEME TWO

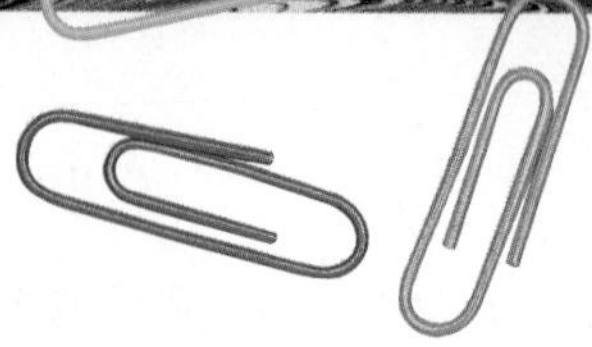

THEME THREE

Facing Challenge

THEME FOUR

Where the Heart Is

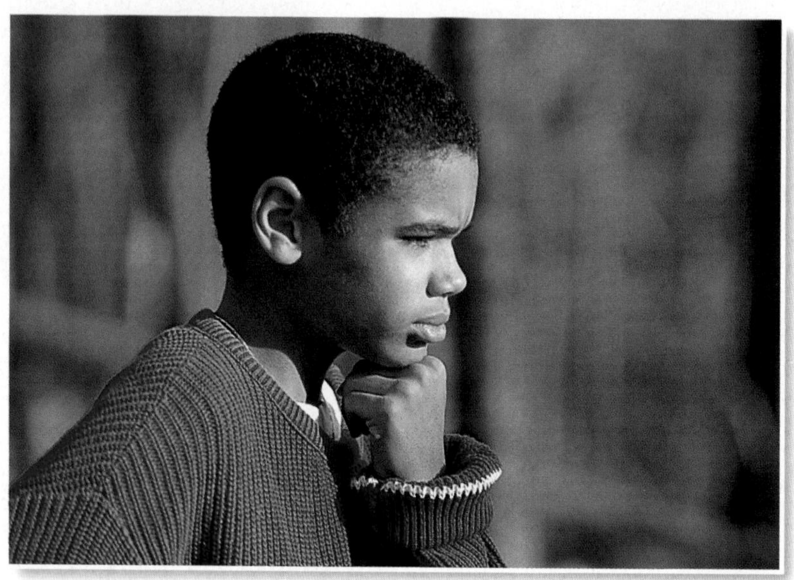

THEME FIVE

At the Crossroads

THEME SIX

THEME SEVEN

A Different Dimension

THEME EIGHT

A Delicate Balance 768

Reference Section

Features

MEDIA Connection

COMPARING SELECTIONS

GENRE FOCUS

Active Reading Strategies

Interdisciplinary Connection

Writing WORKSHOP

Skills

Grammar Link

Listening, Speaking, and Viewing

Reading and Thinking Skills

Technology Skills

Vocabulary Skills

Writing Skills

Skill Minilessons

GRAMMAR AND LANGUAGE

READING AND THINKING

VOCABULARY

Selections by Genre

Fiction

Nonfiction

Poetry

Drama

Myths, Legends, Folktales

Electronic Media

Songs

Comic Strips

Comedy Script

PROFESSIONAL ARTICLES

Program Philosophy

What are the goals of *Glencoe Literature*?

by Denny Wolfe

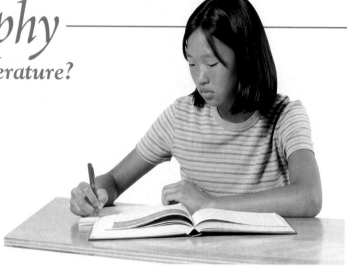

Glencoe Literature was inspired by the belief that all students—from all cultures, of all abilities—can benefit from reading rewarding literature. We recognize, however, that in order for students to be well read in today's information society, they need also to read well. With diverse and visually appealing anthologies and instructive resources, **Glencoe Literature** helps students meet both goals.

Presenting quality literature for all students To reflect our increasingly diverse society, each book presents as wide an array of selections as possible. A rich mix of classic and contemporary selections unites old voices with new. Authors from many cultures address a wide range of topics and themes. And through informed exposure to a variety of reading material—from creative genres, such as poems, songs, stories, plays, myths, and folktales, to expository texts, such as biographies, oral histories, letters, essays, magazine articles, and editorials—students learn to recognize the purpose and structural features of different kinds of text. **Glencoe Literature** enables teachers and students to share a wealth of literary experiences and to explore together the many voices of modern society.

Improving reading skills of all students **Glencoe Literature** fosters universal access to the language arts curriculum. Average students, advanced learners, students with special needs, English Language Learners (ELL)—all can be successful in meeting or exceeding state and local teaching objectives. In the following ways, **Glencoe Literature** helps all students develop skills as readers, writers, listeners, speakers, and viewers:

- **Three-Part Instructional Format**
  A well-organized and logical teaching strategy promotes reading comprehension and language development for each selection in **Glencoe Literature**. The **Before You Read** section sparks interest, builds background knowledge, and previews key vocabulary words from the selection. Next, the **selection pages** include definitions and pronunciation guides for vocabulary words, footnotes for unfamiliar words or concepts, and visual illustrations of other terms mentioned in the text. Finally, the **Responding to Literature** section asks questions that encourage comprehension and higher-order thinking, then follows up with listening, speaking, and writing activities that develop students' comprehension and skills.

- **Systematic Language Instruction**
  To complement instruction of the reading selections, **Glencoe Literature** provides several resources to systematically teach and assess spelling, vocabulary, and conventions of language:
  - ***Spelling Power***
  - ***Vocabulary Power***
  - ***Grammar and Composition Handbook***

  These resources allow teachers to move methodically through instruction in skills and strategies.

- **English Language Learners and Students with Special Needs/Strategic Intervention**
  The **Teacher Wraparound Edition,** as well as a wide assortment of print and electronic resources, provides further reading support and activities for ELL students and students with special needs. Every selection is accompanied by specific strategies to make the basic program of instruction accessible to all. Activities for advanced learners are also included to challenge these students to perform to their potential.

- **Striking Design and Considerate Text**
  The engaging design of the text and resources helps students focus attention and read. Clear labels, colored headings, and numbered and bulleted lists frame ideas and highlight key points. Photos and fine art in many styles and from many cultures enhance text and allow students to make connections to the selections. Maps, charts, and graphic organizers make information visual and easy to grasp.

Through its varied and active instructional strategies, **Glencoe Literature** welcomes all students to learn the power of literacy and to develop a lifelong love of reading.

How do we honor diverse voices in the classroom?

by William Ray

The classroom in which a diverse group of students meets a diverse curriculum is perhaps the happiest of all, but all students need to be exposed to a culturally diverse literature program. Even in the most homogeneous school, hearing a rich mixture of literary voices is crucial not only to a literary education but also to a democratic society. In the following statement, Sandra Cisneros describes her participation in a discussion of "the house of the imagination" at the University of Iowa; reading these words to students can be a lesson in both metaphor and democracy:

> Everyone seemed to have some communal knowledge which I did not have—and then I realized that the metaphor of house was totally wrong for me. Suddenly I was homeless. There were no attics and cellars and crannies. I had no such house in my memories. As a child I had read of such things in books, and my family had promised such a house, but the best they could do was offer the miserable bungalow I was embarrassed with all my life. This caused me to question myself, to become defensive. What did I, Sandra Cisneros, know? My classmates were from the best schools in the country. They had been bred as fine hothouse flowers. I was a yellow weed among the city's cracks.

Literature as a cultural mirror

Many of us are fortunate enough to teach students of diverse backgrounds and so have witnessed some of our students experiencing special moments of recognition when they see their culture reflected in a piece of literature. As a student of mine, some years ago, put it, "I like this book—it feels like home." Using literature of many cultures not only can be a revelation for students who are not of the dominant culture but also can be a springboard for students who wish to share their own experiences. Here are two examples from my classroom:

- One of my urban African-American students, during a discussion of Sandra Cisneros's *House on Mango Street*, educated her white, suburban classmates out of their stereotypical views of urban life.
- A student of Nigerian descent explained to his classmates how Igbo customs have been maintained or changed since the time of Chinua Achebe's novel *Things Fall Apart*.

Cultural awareness and global respect Democracy demands that the voices of everyone be heard. ***Glencoe Literature: The Reader's Choice*** includes representative voices from many corners of the world and from many cultures. For students to develop their own voices, views, and values—grounded in families and communities that schools serve—they must hear and consider the voices of others. Through students' own responses and their classmates' responses to literature contained in these pages, students extend their own world views and take important steps toward becoming responsible thinkers and citizens.

Resources for the Teacher

- *Theme Planning Guide*
- *Interactive Reading Sourcebook*
- *Interactive Lesson Planner*
- *Interactive Teacher's Edition*
- *Presentation Plus!*
- *Testmaker: ExamView Pro*
- *Literature Classics CD-ROM*
- *Block Scheduling Guide*
- *Vocabulary PuzzleMaker*

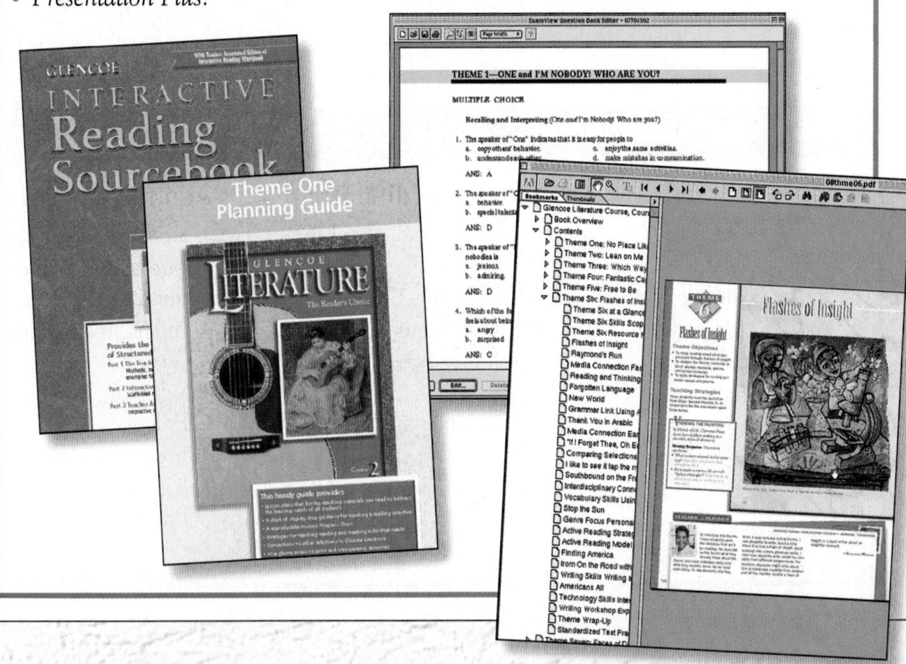

Reading

How do we engage students through critical and creative reading?

by Jeffrey Wilhelm

Reading is a very complex act, and its complexity is largely invisible. When I studied how young readers became engaged with text, I found that proficient readers flexibly used a variety of strategies depending on the text and the reading purpose. Yet less involved readers did not understand that they were supposed to "do" anything at all beyond decoding words. When I asked one student what he saw when he read, he replied, "Words, man. I see nothing but words!" The best readers, on the other hand, could richly describe characters, settings, and situations—often including details that went far beyond the implied meanings of the text.

Active reading In ***Glencoe Literature: The Reader's Choice,*** we base instructional activities on the notion that reading is interactive—that is, a conversation between a reader and a text that results in the creation of meaning. We also base our activities on knowledge of engagement—that is, that readers use a wide range of strategic reading behaviors to personally connect to text and to creatively and critically reflect upon their reading experiences. Key research tells us that visualizing a text enhances comprehension. So the first order of business in assisting reading performance is to carefully model for students our own visualizing process and then to encourage students in their own efforts to "see" and "relate" to characters, forces, and ideas. ***Glencoe Literature: The Reader's Choice*** guides students to use response journals, art, drama, and other creative activities to support this level of reading.

Higher-level thinking skills Once students have visualized and related to text, they can then begin to make inferences, draw conclusions, and evaluate critically the selections they read. Far from being extras, these higher-level thinking skills are essential to synthesizing ideas and to connecting larger ideas and themes across selections. Because students are better able to understand, interpret, and evaluate topics, ideas, and themes that they have related to their own prior knowledge and experiences, ***Glencoe Literature: The Reader's Choice*** introduces critical reading after a rich experiential reading has been supported.

Reading for comprehension Crucial to teaching readers is the notion of reading for meaning. In ***Glencoe Literature: The Reader's Choice,*** students

- consider how the structure of each text supports its meaning
- learn how literary conventions, vocabulary knowledge, and comprehension strategies aid understanding
- develop and practice specific, strategic reading behaviors
- receive direct instruction in how to read in creative and critical ways and through a variety of response dimensions

Our goal is to help students not only develop a powerful repertoire of reading strategies but also consider reading a personally meaningful social pursuit.

Resources for Reading

Student Edition/Teacher Wraparound Edition:

- Active Reading Strategies
- Active Reading Models
- Before You Read
- Reading the Selection
- Responding to Literature
- Comparing Selections
- Media Connections
- Reading and Thinking Skills
- Vocabulary Skills
- Genre Focus
- Reading Handbook
- Glossary
- Skill Minilessons
- Critical Thinking
- Author's Craft

Additional resources:

- *Active Reading Guide*
- *Interactive Reading Sourcebook*
- *Interactive Reading Workbook*
- *Selection Vocabulary Practice*
- *Vocabulary Power*
- *Reading Skills Practice Workbook*
- *Inclusion Strategies Sourcebook*
- *inTIME* magazine
- *Glencoe Literature Library*
- *Five-Star Stories*
- *The Contemporary Readers*
- *Literature Classics CD-ROM*
- Glencoe Literature Web Site (http://www.lit.glencoe.com)

How do we effectively teach literacy?

by Jane Fell Greene

As educators we know a lot more about how students learn to read than we did in the days of *Dick and Jane*. Reading research has informed us that the complex act of reading is neither automatic nor passive, but is rather a highly interactive process in which students must rapidly, fluently, and automatically process print, and then bring their own experiences and knowledge of the world to construct meaning from text.

We know that the following are the common critical elements of all good reading instruction:

- **Word Analysis** Students need to acquire phonemic awareness and to learn sound-symbol correspondence (phonics) as they practice decoding (word identification) and encoding (spelling). The ***Interactive Reading Sourcebook*** provides guidance for the teacher and practice for the student working to acquire these skills. ***Spelling Power*** provides systematic spelling instruction, practice, and assessment.
- **Vocabulary Development** Students need opportunities to develop their knowledge of individual words and morphologic relationships as well as larger concepts. ***Glencoe Literature*** offers many opportunities for rich classroom discussions and for practice using context clues, figurative language, and other language devices (such as idioms and analogies) to help develop students' vocabulary. ***Vocabulary Practice*** provides additional practice and assessment of in-text vocabulary. In addition, ***Vocabulary Power*** provides systematic instruction, practice, and assessment.
- **Comprehension Skills and Strategies** Students need to bolster comprehension skills and strategies. The **Student Edition,** the ***Active Reading Guide,*** and other resources teach and model essential reading and thinking skills (including summarizing, clarifying, questioning, and predicting) and give students opportunities to practice, re-apply, and connect these skills to other tasks both in and out of the classroom.
- **Independent Reading** Students need to read independently. There is no greater way to develop comprehension, vocabulary, writing, and spelling than to encourage students to read widely and voraciously. ***Glencoe Literature*** offers an abundance of appropriate and engaging materials for outside reading. See page T96 for a comprehensive list of titles.
- **Assessment Tools** Students need to be met where they are. Because assessment informs instruction, we know it is important for teachers to have access to assessment tools that can be administered quickly and easily and that will provide an ongoing picture of students' reading growth. The ***Initial Screening and Fluency Assessment*** book provides tools to help you gauge your students' proficiency and progress. For more about screening and placement, see page T39 in this book. For more about assessment, see page T36.

Universal access ***Glencoe Literature*** and its ancillary resources provide universal access to the reading selections and deliver solid, research-based literacy instruction. For example, the ***English Language Learners Sourcebook*** and other program components provide reading support for students learning English. ***The Interactive Reading Sourcebook,*** the ***Inclusion Strategies Sourcebook,*** and other materials offer additional help for students with diverse special needs or who need strategic intervention.

For those students functioning two or more years below grade level, or those functioning below the thirtieth percentile on SAT-9 and other standardized tests, ***LANGUAGE!,*** our comprehensive literacy intervention curriculum, puts struggling readers back on track. In addition, ***Speaking and Listening to the English LANGUAGE!,*** a teachers' book of 270 sequential, cumulative lessons for English Learners, provides scripted daily lessons and practice in producing sentences in spoken English.

Please see **The Teaching of Reading** beginning on page T86 of this book and the ***Interactive Reading Sourcebook*** for strategic intervention instruction and activities.

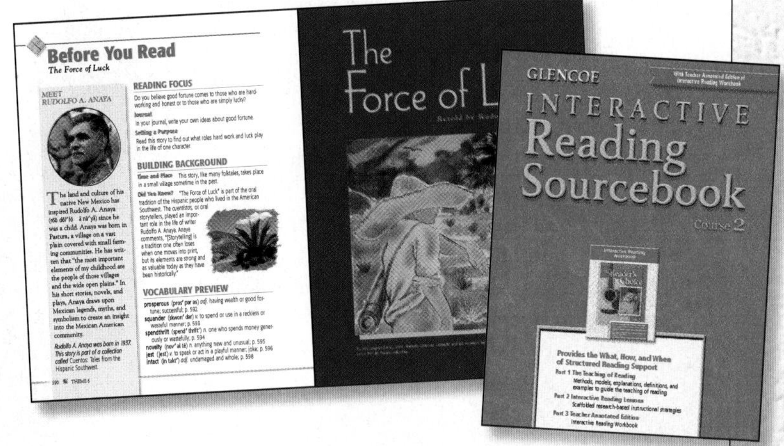

Writing

How does writing enhance learning in the language arts classroom?

by Jacqueline Jones Royster

We think of the language arts classroom as a language-rich environment, made all the richer by the collection of texts and activities in ***Glencoe Literature.*** As both art and artifact, writing is a flexible tool that can work dynamically with other elements of instruction to enhance both learning and performance. From this point of view, writing activities are generously incorporated throughout each thematic unit for a variety of purposes.

Writing to make personal connections with reading selections Through journaling and other writing activities, students have a mechanism for responding to whatever they read and making sense of the details. Writing can help students express personal connections with ideas, images, and experiences; see ways to go beyond their own connections toward broader implications; and note critical distinctions between their own experiences and the content of the reading selections.

Writing to experiment as creative thinkers We as teachers accomplish an important cultural task when we help students move from viewing themselves as just consumers of other people's writing to seeing themselves also as producers of writing. The creative writing activities in ***Glencoe Literature*** encourage students to write in many genres and to compose and present their work through various media. With these writing activities, students can explore varied roles and diverse points of view as a way to think seriously about what it means to produce literature.

Writing to understand form and function Through the **Writing Workshops** in ***Glencoe Literature,*** students gain direct experience producing various forms and genres of writing. The genre knowledge students build helps them to see writing as having structure and organization as shaped by audience, purpose, and context. Throughout ***Glencoe Literature*** writing activities reinforce students' understanding of form and function by asking them to try their own hand at writing essays, sonnets, narratives, autobiographical sketches, business documents, satires, parodies, soliloquies, and other distinctive forms.

Writing to develop higher order thinking skills

Writing helps students think about what a text says and does and whether it is successful. Students can sort through ideas, weigh the impact and consequences of language choices, and use these assessments to make informed judgments about what works in written expression and why.

The writing activities in ***Glencoe Literature*** foster students' ability to think like literary critics. Through writing, students can express what appeals to them as readers and explain how authors achieve particular effects, justifying their interpretations by providing examples and evidence from the text. Students may also investigate broader meaning of texts through research and writing. By gathering and synthesizing information from primary and secondary sources, students can discover the historical, political, or cultural context of a literary work.

Writing to communicate effectively The act of writing itself—writing frequently for many purposes and in various genres—hones students' abilities as writers and communicators. Through activities, workshops, and assessments, ***Glencoe Literature*** provides ample practice for developing writing skills. For example, **Writing Workshops** at the end of each thematic unit guide students recursively through the writing process, focusing on particular moments of engagement—prewriting, drafting, revising, editing/proofreading, and publishing/presenting.

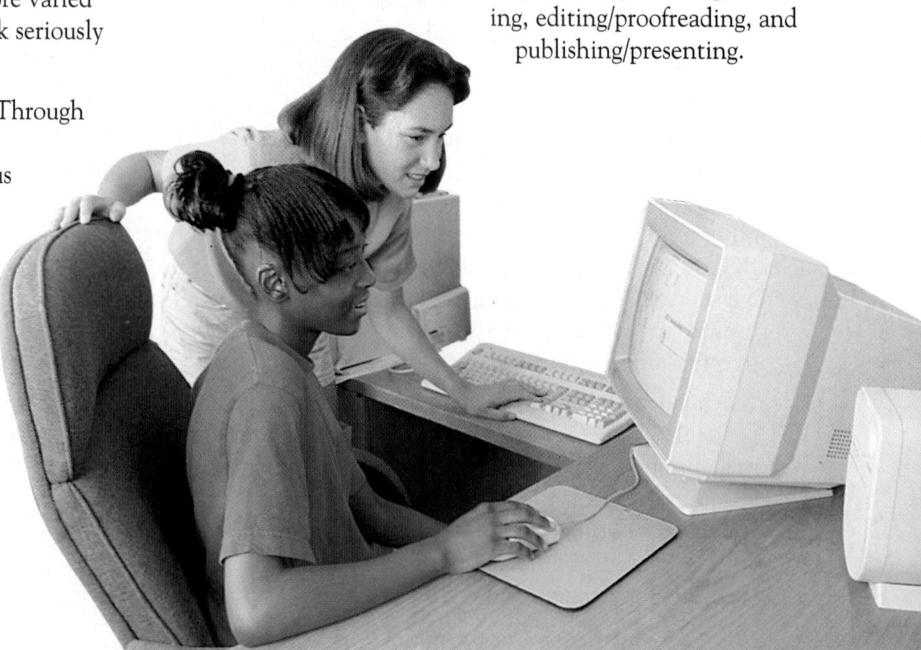

In addition, complete annotated **Writing Workshop Models** of student writing help teachers and students focus on the **6+1 Traits™** of effective writing:

- **Ideas:** Focused, coherent message with relevant supporting details
- **Organization:** Clear, logical arrangement of main points and supporting details
- **Voice**: Writer's distinctive expression of individuality and sense of audience
- **Word Choice:** Vivid, precise diction appropriate to the writing purpose
- **Sentence Fluency:** Well-structured sentences of varying lengths
- **Conventions:** Correct spelling, grammar, usage, and mechanics
- **Presentation:** Engaging visual layout of words and design elements

Writing to master standard English conventions *Glencoe Literature* provides two paths for achieving mastery of grammar, usage, and mechanics:

- **Point-of-Use Approach** In both the Student and Teacher Wraparound editions, **Grammar and Language Minilessons** help teachers review or reteach a skill in grammar, usage, or mechanics while linking that skill to an author's application of it in a literary work, thus giving students a "real-world" example from which to learn.
- **Systematic Approach** Teachers may use the ***Grammar and Composition Handbook*** to study systematically English language conventions, moving methodically through instruction in such skills as identifying parts of speech, using modifiers correctly, and enhancing sentence fluency through sentence combining.

Writing to prepare for the world of work Many writing activities in ***Glencoe Literature*** ask students to draft career-related documents in response to the reading selections. For example, students might write a fictional character's résumé or application letter. In addition, at least one **Writing Workshop** focuses on a business or technical document, such as a business letter or problem-solution report. These kinds of writing help to sharpen students' understanding of audience and purpose, and to enhance their abilities to write clearly and coherently for the world of work.

With such varied purposes for using writing in the company of the other language arts, we believe that students will be well prepared to perform at high levels of quality and excellence.

Resources for Writing

Student Edition/Teacher Wraparound Edition:

- Personal Writing
- Creative Writing
- Writing About Literature
- Comparing Selections
- Writing Skills
- Grammar Links
- Writing Workshops
- Theme Assessments
- Writing Workshop Models with annotations
- Writing Minilessons
- Grammar and Language Minilessons

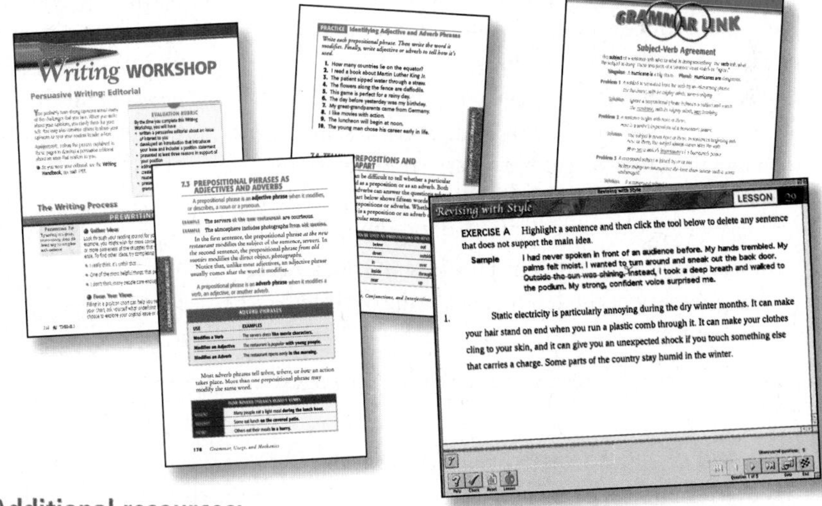

Additional resources:

- *Grammar and Composition Handbook*
- *Grammar and Language Workbook*
- *Interactive Grammar and Language Workbook*
- *Grammar and Language Transparencies*
- *Writing and Proofreading Practice*
- *Writing and Proofreading Transparencies*
- *Research and Report Writing*
- *Writer's Assistant CD-ROM*
- *Revising with Style*

Integrated Language Arts

What are the benefits of an integrated language arts program, such as *Glencoe Literature: The Reader's Choice*?

by Beverly Ann Chin

Current research confirms that integrating the English language arts is an effective way to help students improve their comprehension as well as their communication and thinking skills. Reading, writing, listening, speaking, viewing, and representing—when taught in conjunction and through a variety of classroom and home-based activities—enhance students' critical and creative thinking abilities, and allow real learning to occur. In addition, integrating language arts instruction respects students' individual interests and strengths.

The following discussion outlines the ways in which the ***Glencoe Literature: The Reader's Choice*** anthology and its additional resources effectively and imaginatively integrate the related and reciprocal processes of reading, writing, listening, speaking, viewing, and representing.

Reading and writing Students' reading and writing skills develop when they

- read, analyze, and respond to a wide array of texts—high-quality literature in various genres as well as engaging informational materials
- engage in a variety of writing activities before and after reading, such as writing journal entries and developing graphic organizers; answering questions about the selection; and writing analytical, personal, or creative responses to a variety of prompts
- write and revise for different purposes and audiences and in a variety of modes by completing **Writing Workshops**

For more information on reading and writing, see pages T30–T33.

Listening and speaking Students' listening and speaking skills develop when they

- participate in class discussions, give oral responses to literature, make presentations, and respectfully listen and respond to other viewpoints
- participate in role playing, readers' theater, choral reading, storytelling, and other creative drama activities as an avenue for understanding and interpreting reading selections

Viewing and representing Students' viewing and representing skills develop when they

- complete graphic organizers as well as art and multimedia projects, visually and graphically representing their opinions, ideas, and responses to the reading
- examine the fine art and photographs within selections by responding to viewing questions
- respond to **Selection Focus Transparencies,** which provide visual cues that activate personal associations to the reading selections
- use design principles to format writing assignments and display information on charts, maps, and graphs for written reports and oral presentations

Each language arts skill depends on another for its full expression. How can you know, for example, that students have comprehended what they have read if they do not share their responses to the text through talking, writing, or representing their ideas visually? The language arts skills have been woven together into the fabric of ***Glencoe Literature: The Reader's Choice.*** As a result, you can better meet the needs of all the students in your classroom by encouraging the development of their learning styles and multiple modes of expression.

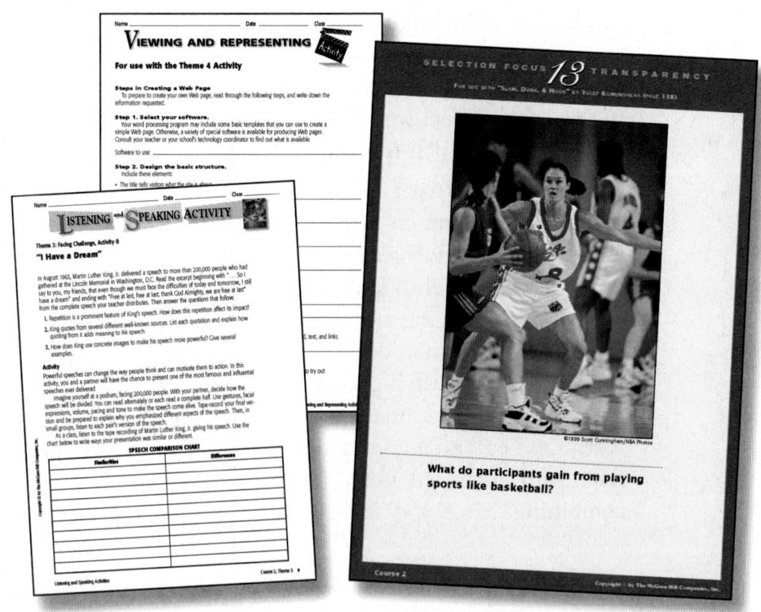

Technology & Media Literacy

What roles do technology and media literacy play in the language arts classroom?

by Jeffrey Wilhelm

Technology is a tool that extends human abilities. The technology components of the ***Glencoe Literature*** program can be integrated into your language arts instruction and used to extend students' abilities to read, write, and think critically and express themselves creatively. The program's wide variety of technology tools includes videos; audiotapes; software; the Glencoe Literature Web site (http://www.lit.glencoe.com); and various technology features, exercises, and activities that are integral to the **Student Edition** and the **Teacher Wraparound Edition.**

Technology as a reading, writing, and research tool

Students may use technology to develop their reading, writing, and research skills. For example, the ***Glencoe Literature*** program includes

- **Technology Skills** features, which offer instruction in such skills as formatting documents, drafting e-mail messages, and creating spreadsheets
- **Internet Connections** activities, which prompt students to conduct research on the selections' authors, themes, or subject matter, using a search engine on the Internet
- **Multimedia projects,** which encourage students to express themselves using a variety of non-print media
- **Writing Workshops,** which encourage students to use word processors to draft their work and provide technology tips for greater success
- ***Writer's Assistant*** and ***Revising with Style*** CD-ROMs and other software programs, which enhance reading, writing, and other language arts skills

You may find that students with special needs are particularly excited by and responsive to the use of technology in the classroom and at home.

Teaching media literacy When students learn to interpret, analyze, and evaluate media messages as well as create their own, they can exert some control over the way such messages shape their thinking and their lives. Students who are media savvy understand the variety of ways in which different technologies organize and represent information.

Because of the growing importance of media literacy, ***Glencoe Literature*** integrates the study of media into its language arts instruction. Students are asked to

- study various literary genres and informational text types and to consider how the medium affects the message
- apply knowledge gleaned from the study of various media (e.g., television and radio advertisements and interviews) to verbal and visual responses to literary selections
- analyze how opinions, biases, and agendas may be communicated through various media forms

The ***Glencoe Literature*** **Student Edition** includes **Media Connection** activities and **Listening, Speaking, and Viewing** features to enhance students' media literacy. Additional program resources include ***Media Connections Activities, inTIME*** magazine, and ***Humanities Across TIME.*** These tools can help students understand the nature and techniques of mass media and critique various media messages. In addition, they help students learn to produce their own media messages in a variety of aural, visual, and textual formats.

Assessment

How can we use assessment to enhance instruction?

by Beverly Ann Chin

Assessment is an essential part of the teaching and learning process. Assessments, both formal and informal, enable you to reflect on the way you teach and on the way your students learn. When used frequently and effectively, assessment tools provide you and your students with feedback and opportunities to set goals for the future and to modify instruction.

When you use assessment not only as an evaluation of students' knowledge and skills but also as an opportunity for communication—both with students and their parents or guardians—you can enhance and improve the quality of your instruction and curriculum.

Integrating instruction and assessment with *Glencoe Literature* Assessment tools for ***Glencoe Literature*** support the belief that the most effective way to monitor and assess students' progress in a language arts classroom is to use a variety of approaches and procedures: formal tests, informal assessments, writing assessments, performance assessments, and portfolios. All of these types of assessments are designed to be used throughout the school year to help you document students' progress and assess the effectiveness of instruction.

On-going and summative assessment The following components, found in the **Student Edition (SE),** are integral parts of your assessment program:

- **Theme Projects** The **Theme Projects** outlined at the beginning of each thematic unit allow students to develop their understanding of the theme through structured performance-based activities. The projects are reprinted in the ***Performance Assessment*** book along with guidelines and rubrics for evaluation.
- **Responding to Literature** The Responding to Literature activities, including **Analyzing Literature, Literary Elements, Extending Your Response,** and **Skill Minilessons,** provide a varied set of tasks for students to complete. Sample answers and rubrics for evaluation are available in the **Teacher Wraparound Edition (TWE).**
- **Writing Workshops** Near the end of each thematic unit, the **Writing Workshop** engages students in creating an extended piece of writing. Models, strategies, and tips help students develop their writing through the recursive stages of prewriting, drafting, revising, editing/proofreading, and publishing/presenting. A complete **student model** for each workshop appears in the SE, and annotations and **6+1™ evaluation guidelines** are provided in the TWE. In addition, detailed rubrics for the workshops can be found in ***Writing Assessment and Portfolio Management.*** These rubrics can help you evaluate students' command of ideas, organization, voice, word choice, sentence fluency, conventions, and presentation.
- **Theme Assessment** At the conclusion of each thematic unit, the **Theme Assessment** enables students to evaluate their own work and to set goals for future learning. The Theme Assessment also provides an opportunity for portfolio-building. ***Writing Assessment and Portfolio Management*** provides guidelines to evaluate students' portfolios.

In addition to these on-going in-text assessments, ***Glencoe Literature*** provides the following assessment tools:

- **Selection Quick Checks** Each **Selection Quick Check** quiz provides three to five short-answer questions, enabling you to quickly and easily assess basic reading comprehension.
- **Selection and Theme Assessment**
    - **Selection Tests** are formal one- or two-page tests designed to assess students' comprehension of the reading selections. Each test has up to four parts—**Recalling and Interpreting, Using Vocabulary, Interpreting and Evaluating,** and **Evaluating and Connecting**—which include multiple-choice questions, graphic organizers, and essay questions.

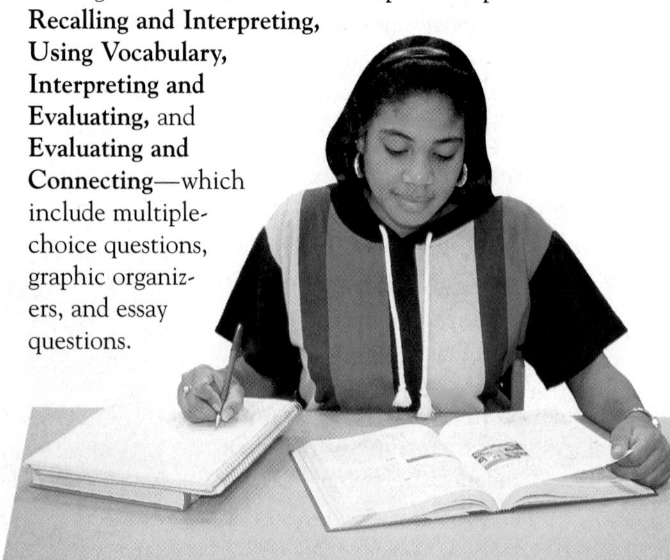

- The **Theme Test** is a two-page summative assessment with short-answer and essay questions designed to evaluate students' summative understanding of the selections in a thematic unit.

For your convenience, these selection tests and summative assessments are also available on the ***Testmaker: ExamView Pro*** CD-ROM. This CD-ROM allows you to modify the order, content, and number of questions to meet the particular needs of all your students.

- ***Performance Assessment*** The ***Performance Assessment*** book provides an alternative means for evaluating students' comprehension of each literature selection and each theme as a whole. The book includes an **Assessment Checklist** for most types of speaking and listening or other performance-based activities, as well as detailed rubrics for evaluating specific kinds of student activities.
- ***Grammar and Composition Handbook*** This handbook provides extensive instruction, practice, and assessment for the systematic teaching of oral and written language conventions. The handbook can also be used as a supplement to writing instruction.
- ***Vocabulary Power*** **and** ***Spelling Power*** These workbooks provide systematic teaching, practice, and assessment of vocabulary and spelling. Reviews, tests, and oral quizzes offer a means for frequent assessment, and an annotated teacher's edition is provided for each level.

Using *Initial Screening and Fluency Assessment* At the start of the school year, you may want to administer the entry-level assessment available in the ***Initial Screening and Fluency Assessment*** book. This quick and informal screening tool for basic reading proficiency will help you determine whether ***Glencoe Literature*** is appropriate for your students or whether certain students would be better served by the intensive intervention program ***LANGUAGE!*** Oral reading fluency assessments may be administered once per theme to monitor students' oral reading proficiency. (For more about entry-level screening and placement, see page T39 in this book.)

Charting student progress and communicating with parents As you work through a thematic unit, you can photocopy the **Student Progress Chart,** found in the ***Theme Planning Guide,*** and use copies to record scores or grades and comments on each student's progress. As you meet regularly with students and their parents or guardians, you can share this information and set goals for future learning. Also see page T44 in this book for more information about how to use the **Student Progress Chart.**

Resources for Assessment

Student Edition/Teacher Wraparound Edition:

- Theme Projects
- Responding to Literature
- Comparing Selections
- Writing Workshops
- Theme Assessments
- Skill Minilessons

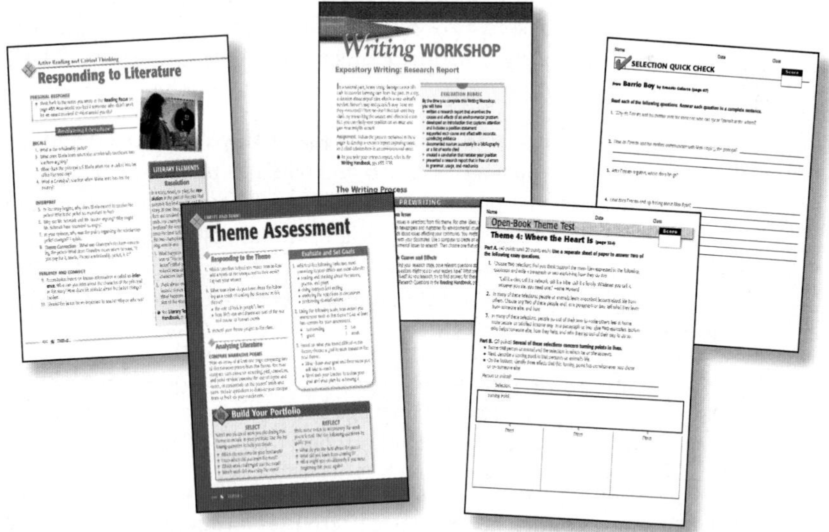

Additional resources:

- *Selection Quick Checks*
- *Selection and Theme Assessment*
- *Performance Assessment*
- *Grammar and Composition Handbook*
- *Vocabulary Power*
- *Spelling Power*
- *Writing Assessment and Portfolio Management*
- *Interactive Tutor: Self-Assessment*
- *MindJogger Videoquizzes*
- *Testmaker: ExamView Pro*
- *Initial Screening and Fluency Assessment*

Instructional Planning and Support

Road Map to Success

The materials in the following pages provide a clear road map for you to follow when planning instruction.

- **Screening and Placement** This feature explains how to determine whether your students are ready to work with the ***Glencoe Literature: The Reader's Choice*** program—or whether they might need an intervention reading program, help in developing English language skills, or special needs instruction. (p. T39)
- **How to Manage a Classroom** These pages suggest various useful ways to group students in a classroom setting to meet the instructional needs of each student. (p. T40)
- **How to Teach a Lesson** These pages provide step-by-step guidance for how to teach a typical reading selection in ***Glencoe Literature: The Reader's Choice,*** using the materials available in the **Student Edition, Teacher Wraparound Edition,** and other resources. (p. T42)
- **Monitoring Student Progress** This segment explains how to use the **Student Progress Chart** to record assessment results and to monitor students' progress through each of the eight thematic units of ***Glencoe Literature: The Reader's Choice.*** (p. T44)
- **Pacing Chart** This extensive chart breaks instruction into a detailed day-by-day plan, showing you what to teach and when to teach it. The chart highlights the components of the program that are essential for helping all students successfully meet or exceed state and local teaching objectives. The chart also lists materials for extra instructional time for English Language Learners and Special Needs students as well as additional resources available to you as you teach each lesson. (p. T46)
- **Teaching English Language Learners** This feature provides background support for teachers of English Language Learners and contrasts several of the most common languages heard in classrooms today. (p. T78)
- **The Teaching of Reading & Strategic Intervention** This section provides instruction, guidelines, and suggested activities for teaching reading. A bibliography of current confirmed research in the teaching of reading concludes this section. (p. T86)
- **Glencoe Resources for Independent Reading** This feature lists the program resources available to support independent reading. (p. T96)

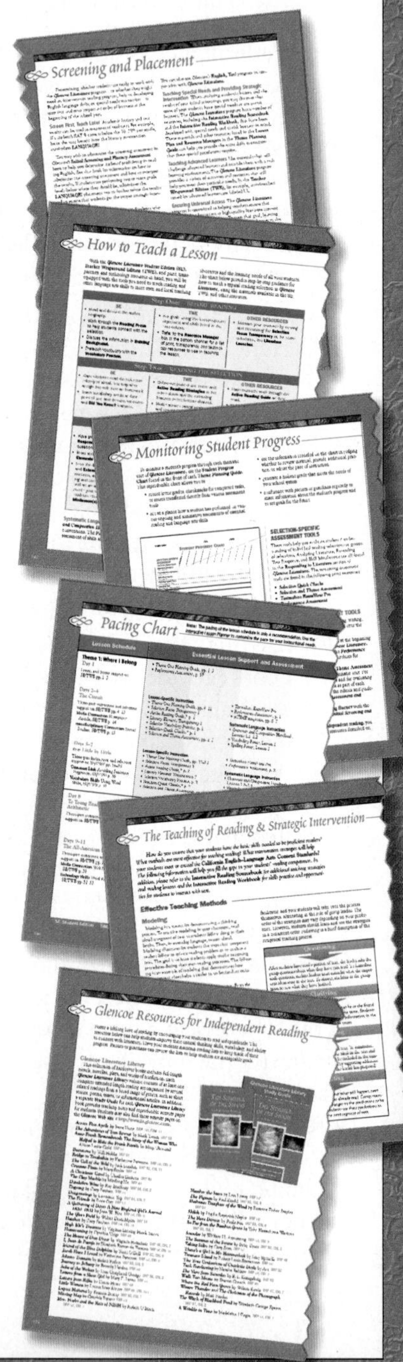

Screening and Placement

Determining whether students are ready to work with the *Glencoe Literature* program—or whether they might need an intervention reading program, help in developing English language skills, or special needs instruction—is your first and most important order of business at the beginning of the school year.

Screen First, Teach Later Academic history and test results can be used as measures of readiness. For example, if a student's SAT 9 score is below the 30–35th percentile, he or she may benefit from the literacy intervention curriculum ***LANGUAGE!***

You may wish to administer the screening assessment in Glencoe's ***Initial Screening and Fluency Assessment*** book to help you determine students' proficiency in reading English. See that book for information on how to administer the screening assessment and how to interpret the results. If students are performing two or more grade levels below where they should be, administer the ***LANGUAGE!*** placement test to further refine the results and to ensure that students get the proper strategic intervention they need.

Teaching English Language Learners Students who are reading one or two grades below level and whose first language is not English would benefit from the ELL support offered as part of the ***Glencoe Literature*** program. The **Lesson Plan and Resource Managers,** located in each ***Theme Planning Guide,*** include lists of selection-specific resources you can use to provide an additional 30–45 minutes of daily instruction for English Language Learners. In addition, the feature ***Teaching English Language Learners,*** beginning on page T78 contrasts English with several of the most common languages heard in classrooms today and provides background for working with the students who speak those languages. Lastly, the introduction to the ***English Language Learners Sourcebook*** has teaching ideas and suggestions for how to assist those who are struggling to learn English while also learning language arts content. You can also use Glencoe's ***English, Yes!*** program in conjunction with ***Glencoe Literature: The Reader's Choice.***

Teaching Special Needs and Providing Strategic Intervention When analyzing academic history and the results of your initial screenings, you may discover that some of your students have special needs or are at-risk learners. The ***Glencoe Literature*** program has a number of resources, including the ***Interactive Reading Sourcebook*** and the ***Interactive Reading Workbook,*** that have been developed with special needs and at-risk learners in mind. These materials and other resources listed in the **Lesson Plan and Resource Managers** in the ***Theme Planning Guide*** can help you provide the extra daily instruction that these special populations require.

Teaching Advanced Learners Use materials that will challenge advanced learners and provide them with a rich learning environment. The ***Glencoe Literature*** program provides a variety of activities and resources that will help you meet their particular needs. In the **Teacher Wraparound Edition (TWE),** for example, activities best suited for advanced learners are labeled L3.

Ensuring Universal Access The ***Glencoe Literature*** program is committed to helping teachers ensure that every student has access to high-quality literature content and language arts instruction. To meet that goal, learning activities and various instructional notes in the TWE are labeled L1, L2, and L3 for Basic, Average, and Advanced learners. In addition, in the TWE interleaf pages preceding each thematic unit, all reading selections are labeled with DRP® (Degrees of Reading Power) and Lexile® readability measures. These measures can assist you in determining which selections are developmentally suited to your students' reading abilities.

How to Manage a Classroom

As a teacher, your primary focus will likely be on the content and quality of your instruction. But you will also want to consider how to organize your classroom to best meet the needs of your students. The Consortium on Reading Excellence (CORE) recommends ***instructional grouping*** *to manage your classroom more effectively. As you teach* **Glencoe Literature: The Reader's Choice,** *you may find it helpful to use the CORE Flexible-Grouping Model below. The model describes several strategies for organizing students into an assortment of groups to address different learning needs. Implementing the model can help your students make great strides toward meeting or exceeding state and local teaching objectives.*

CORE Flexible-Grouping Model

(Adapted and reprinted with permission from CORE *Teaching Reading Sourcebook*)

Whole Class

Whole-class instruction is most beneficial when the instructional objectives are appropriate for the entire mixed-level group. For example, all students may profit when you have the whole class together to read and discuss a short story.

As a pre-reading activity you might discuss the ***Reading Focus*** *with the whole class, or you might have the class view a short* **Literature Launchers** *video segment.*

Individual or Partner

Individual or partner arrangements provide practice and independent application of an acquired skill. Partners may be at different learning levels, as in a peer-tutoring relationship, or at the same level working on a commonly needed skill.

The ***Responding to Literature*** *section provides opportunities for individual and paired learning. You might also choose to have students act as peer reviewers as they work through each* ***Writing Workshop.***

Teacher-Directed Small Groups

Teacher-directed small groups provide direct instruction to students who share commonly needed skills. During such small-group time, the teacher can closely monitor students and provide structured feedback.

Refer to the **Literature Groups Sourcebook** *for reproducible student activities and strategies for scheduling, forming, managing, and assessing literature discussion groups. In addition, the* **Inclusion Strategies Sourcebook** *provides a broad range of strategies and small group activities designed for strategic intervention.*

Independent Small Groups or Learning Centers

Independent small groups or learning centers are appropriate for interest-based and theme-organized instruction, as well as for cooperative-learning experiences. Learning centers free the teacher to work directly with students who need special attention. Learning center activities should be aligned with specific instructional outcomes. The group composition may be either heterogeneous, representing mixed skill levels and instructional needs, or homogenous, in which students share common skill levels and instructional needs. Homogeneous (same-level) groupings, sometimes termed *needs-based groups*, are used to meet individual needs identified by formal and informal assessment. In order to keep the groups flexible, frequent assessment is necessary.

Theme Projects *or various subject-area activities described in the* **Interdisciplinary Activities** *booklet are especially appropriate for independent small groups or learning center work.*

CORE Flexible-Grouping Model *(continued)*

Cross-Class Regrouping
In some schools, students may be scheduled into another class for skill-based (homogeneous) instruction. This model is often termed *regrouping and replacement* because the regular mixed class is reconstituted into several other classes for targeted instruction. In this regrouping model, teachers in a given grade or even across grades divide up the students based on assessment information and deploy them among groups of teachers. Such grouping maximizes the teacher's ability to focus instruction on a group of students who share common learning needs. Students then return to their heterogeneous home classes for literature-based instruction.

You might divide students into groups to focus on specific areas such as English language conventions, spelling, and vocabulary before gathering in the main classroom for literature-based learning.

Dedicated Reading Classes
An effective method for meeting students' needs in middle school is to enhance the regular, mixed-group literature class with a dedicated reading class that focuses on reading instruction at various skill levels. It is important that students in dedicated reading classes are also scheduled into regular, heterogeneous literature classes. In this way, students receive the skills they need to catch up while also getting the literature they need to develop grade-level concepts and vocabulary.

Use the **Interactive Reading Sourcebook** *and the* **Interactive Reading Workbook** *for dedicated reading skills instruction.*

How to Teach a Lesson

With the *Glencoe Literature* **Student Edition (SE), Teacher Wraparound Edition (TWE),** and print, transparency, and technology resources in hand, you will be equipped with the tools you need to teach reading and other language arts skills to meet state and local teaching objectives and the learning needs of all your students. The chart below provides step-by-step guidance for how to teach a typical reading selection in ***Glencoe Literature,*** using the materials available in the SE, TWE, and other resources.

SE	TWE	OTHER RESOURCES
Step One: BEFORE READING		
• Read and discuss the author biography. • Work through the **Reading Focus** to help students connect with the selection. • Discuss the information in **Building Background.** • Preteach vocabulary with the **Vocabulary Preview.**	• Set goals using the lesson-specific objectives and skills listed in the side column. • Refer to the **Resource Manager** box in the bottom channel for a list of print, transparency, and technology resources to use in teaching the lesson.	• Motivate your students by viewing and discussing the **Selection Focus Transparency** or, for some selections, the **Literature Launcher.**
Step Two: READING THE SELECTION		
• Have students read the selection silently or aloud. You may also assign the selection as homework. • Teach vocabulary words at their point of use and discuss footnotes and **Did You Know?** features.	• Utilize the point-of-use notes and **Active Reading Strategies** in the side column and the extending features in the bottom channel. • Model active reading strategies and critical thinking skills at every opportunity.	• Have students work through the **Active Reading Guide** as they read. • Refer to the **Lesson Plan and Resource Manager** in the ***Theme Planning Guide*** for a list of resources that support, reteach, and enhance the TWE activities.
Step Three: RESPONDING TO THE SELECTION		
• Have students answer the **Personal Response** and **Analyzing Literature** questions. • Read and discuss the **Literary Elements** feature. • From the **Literature and Writing** and **Extending Your Response** sections, assign at least one writing and one discussion activity, as well as an alternate activity that meets your students' needs. All students should complete the **Skill Minilesson(s).**	• The **Analyzing Literature** items are scaffolded to provide reading and critical thinking support. TWE annotations make this scaffolding clear. Sample answers may be shared with students. • Make use of the teaching tips for the **Extending Your Response** activities. • Use the rubrics for writing and the answer keys for the **Skill Minilesson(s)** to monitor students' progress.	• Assess students' understanding and skills development by using a variety of assessment resources, including ***Selection Quick Checks, Selection and Theme Assessment, Performance Assessment,*** and ***Testmaker: ExamView Pro.*** • Refer to the **Lesson Plan and Resource Manager** for additional resources for extending and enriching instruction.

Systematic Language Instruction ***Vocabulary Power*** and ***Spelling Power*** workbooks and the ***Grammar and Composition Handbook*** provide for the systematic teaching of vocabulary, spelling, and English language conventions. The **Pacing Chart** and ***Theme Planning Guide*** show how to schedule the instruction and assessment of skills and strategies covered in these materials.

Universal Access

Your classroom is a miniature community that includes special populations of students. The **Lesson Plan and Resource Manager** for each selection (found in the ***Theme Planning Guide***) will help you plan your instruction to best serve the needs of all your students and to help them meet or exceed state and local teaching objectives.

Various teaching strategies and student activities found at point-of-use throughout the **Teacher Wraparound Edition** help make the text accessible to all students during the course of regular classroom study. In addition, a comprehensive assortment of print and electronic resources provides the additional instructional support needed to devote specific attention to individual students beyond the regular classroom time to foster their optimal achievement.

English Language Learners (ELL) Do some of your students need more extensive instruction in vocabulary or other English language skills? The **Lesson Plan and Resource Manager** for each selection includes a list of materials specifically created for English Language Learners. These materials may be used daily to provide additional instruction.

- The ***English Language Learners Sourcebook*** provides general teaching strategies for English Language Learners and blackline masters with selection-specific teaching strategies.
- The **Audio Library** includes an oral reading in English of nearly every selection. (Also available in Spanish.)
- Each volume of ***English, Yes!*** contains adaptations of contemporary and classic short stories followed by a comprehensive three-part skills check; it is especially suited for students who need help improving basic English skills.
- The ***Performance Assessment*** booklet may provide the best means of assessment for your ELL students.
- **Spanish Summaries** and **Spanish Translations** are available for nearly every selection.

Special Needs/Strategic Intervention Do some of your students have reading or learning difficulties? The **Lesson Plan and Resource Manager** for each selection also includes a list of materials designed especially for strategic intervention with special needs learners. These materials may be used daily to provide additional instruction.

- The ***Interactive Reading Sourcebook*** provides reading lessons and strategies for teaching reading, and the ***Interactive Reading Workbook*** offers skills practice and opportunities for students to interact with text.
- The ***Inclusion Strategies Sourcebook*** includes general teaching strategies for less-proficient readers and learning disabled and special needs students, along with reproducible student pages with teaching options for meeting individual needs.
- The **Audio Library** includes an oral reading in English of nearly every selection.
- The ***Performance Assessment*** booklet may provide the best means of assessment for your special needs students.

Advanced Learners Do some of your students need acceleration or enrichment activities? Assign these students the challenging activities presented in the TWE and additional resources.

- TWE activities labeled **L3** and point-of-use notes labeled **Advanced Learners** provide opportunities for enrichment.
- The ***Interdisciplinary Activities*** booklet offers ways to explore a topic in more depth and to reinforce content-area standards in mathematics, science, and social studies.
- You may assign additional readings, such as works in the ***Glencoe Literature Library,*** to encourage your students to broaden their study of a particular author, theme, or concept. See page T96 in this book for a list of Glencoe resources for independent reading.

Student Progress As you work through a thematic unit, use photocopies of the **Student Progress Chart** found in the ***Theme Planning Guide*** to record scores or grades and comments on each student's progress and performance. Meet regularly with students and their parents or guardians to share this information and to set goals for future learning.

Monitoring Student Progress

To monitor a student's progress through each thematic unit of *Glencoe Literature,* use the **Student Progress Chart** found in the front of each ***Theme Planning Guide.*** This reproducible chart allows you to

- record letter grades, checkmarks for completed tasks, or scores transferred directly from various assessment tools
- see at a glance how a student has performed on various ongoing and summative assessments of essential reading and language arts skills
- use the information recorded on the chart in judging whether to review material, provide additional practice, or adjust the pace of instruction
- generate a holistic grade that meets the needs of your school system
- conference with parents or guardians regularly to share information about the student's progress and to set goals for the future

Student Name ______________ Class ________ Theme ________

STUDENT PROGRESS CHART

SELECTION-SPECIFIC ASSESSMENT On-Going Assessment	Selections									
Analyzing Literature in Student Edition										
Extending Your Response in Student Edition										
Skill Minilesson(s) in Student Edition										
Selection Quick Check in Selection Quick Checks										
Selection Test in Selection and Theme Assessment										
Performance Assessment in Performance Assessment										

THEME-LEVEL ASSESSMENT

Summative Assessment	Score/Grade	Comments
Theme Projects in Student Edition		
Writing Workshop in Student Edition		
Theme Assessment in Student Edition		
Theme Test in *Selection and Theme Assessment* and *Testmaker: ExamView Pro*		
Reading Fluency in *Initial Screening and Fluency Assessment*		
Independent Reading		

SYSTEMATIC LANGUAGE ASSESSMENT

Vocabulary Power Unit ___	Lesson ___	Lesson ___	Lesson ___	Lesson ___	Lesson ___	Review Test

Spelling Power Unit ___	Lesson ___	Lesson ___	Lesson ___	Lesson ___	Review/Proofreading

Grammar and Composition Handbook	Lessons													
	Pre-test	1	2	3	4	5	6	7	8	9	10	11	12	Post-test
Chapter ___														
Chapter ___														
Chapter ___														

Signature of Parent or Guardian ______________

17

SELECTION-SPECIFIC ASSESSMENT TOOLS

These tools help you evaluate students' understanding of individual reading selections or groups of selections. Analyzing Literature, Extending Your Response, and Skill Minilessons are all found in the **Responding to Literature** section of ***Glencoe Literature.*** The remaining assessment tools are found in the following print resources:

- ***Selection Quick Checks***
- ***Selection and Theme Assessment***
- ***Testmaker: ExamView Pro***
- ***Performance Assessment***

THEME-LEVEL ASSESSMENT TOOLS

These tools help you evaluate reading, writing, and critical thinking skills developed over the course of one thematic unit.

- **Theme Projects** can be found at the beginning of each thematic unit in ***Glencoe Literature.*** They are also reprinted in the ***Performance Assessment*** book along with rubrics for evaluation.
- A **Writing Workshop** and **Theme Assessment** appear at the end of each thematic unit. For scoring Writing Workshops and for evaluating students' writing portfolios as part of each Theme Assessment, use the rubrics and guidelines found in ***Writing Assessment and Portfolio Management.***
- Monitor students' **reading fluency** with the fluency assessments in ***Initial Screening and Fluency Assessment.***
- To track students' **independent reading,** you may want to use the resources described on pages T96–T97.

SYSTEMATIC LANGUAGE ASSESSMENT TOOLS

The ***Vocabulary Power*** and ***Spelling Power*** workbooks and the ***Grammar and Composition Handbook*** systematically guide students through a sequence of lessons in vocabulary, spelling, and conventions of language. Pretests, posttests, and reviews help you determine whether students are successfully building on skills they have already learned.

Using the Pacing Chart

The **Pacing Chart** on pages T46–T77 suggests a timetable for teaching lessons in ***Glencoe Literature: The Reader's Choice.*** Designed for a 175-day school year where one-and-a-half to two hours a day are devoted to reading and language arts instruction, the pacing chart offers a manageable schedule for teaching all students all the essential reading and language arts skills. It also lists all the instructional materials you need to help all students meet or exceed state and local teaching objectives.

Pacing Essential Instruction and Assessment for All Students In addition to the many teaching notes, activities, and minilessons within the **Student Edition (SE)** and **Teacher Wraparound Edition (TWE),** the following resources are essential for all students, including average and advanced learners. The **lesson-specific resources** provide point-of-use support and assessment to help you introduce or reteach reading and language arts skills germane to each reading lesson. The **systematic resources** provide a sequence of lessons in vocabulary, spelling, and English language conventions that help you assist your students in learning specific skills and in building on skills they have already learned. These resources include tests to help you assess students' progress.

ESSENTIAL LESSON SUPPORT AND ASSESSMENT

Lesson-Specific Instruction

- *Selection Focus Transparencies*
- *Active Reading Guide**
- *Literary Elements Transparencies*
- *Selection Vocabulary Practice*
- *Selection Quick Checks**
- *Selection and Theme Assessment*
- *Testmaker: ExamView Pro CD-ROM*
- *Performance Assessment*
- *Writing Assessment and Portfolio Management*
- *Initial Screening and Fluency Assessment*
- *inTIME* magazine

Systematic Language Instruction

- *Grammar and Composition Handbook*
- *Vocabulary Power*
- *Spelling Power*

SE: Student Edition TWE: Teacher Wraparound Edition

*Also available in Spanish

Pacing for English Language Learners and Special-Needs Students For English Language Learners and for students with special needs, you may want to offer more intensive instruction. Use the following additional instructional materials and add thirty to forty-five minutes a day to your lesson schedule.

ENGLISH LANGUAGE LEARNERS

- English Language Learners (TWE)
- *English Language Learners Sourcebook*
- *Theme Planning Guide*
- *Spanish Summaries*
- *Spanish Translations*
- *Audio Library**
- *English, Yes!*

SPECIAL NEEDS/STRATEGIC INTERVENTION

- *Interactive Reading Sourcebook*
- *Interactive Reading Workbook*
- Special Needs (TWE)
- *Inclusion Strategies Sourcebook*
- *Theme Planning Guide*
- *Audio Library**

Pacing with Essential Teaching Tools With every lesson on the pacing chart, you will want to use the following essential teaching tools and resources to help you organize lessons, activities, and assessment.

ESSENTIAL TEACHING TOOLS AND RESOURCES

- *Theme Planning Guide*
  provides detailed lesson plans for each lesson, strategies to teach reading and to meet individual needs, connections to other selections, and facsimiles of all related print and transparency resource pages
- *Literature Groups Sourcebook*
  includes reproducible student activity sheets and strategies for directing and managing literature groups
- *Interactive Lesson Planner CD-ROM*
  allows you to see a day-by-day breakdown of all instructional activities, create your own plan of instruction, and print lesson plans
- *Interactive Teacher Edition CD-ROM*
  gives you point-and-click access to teaching resources and the convenience of editing and printing to suit your needs

Pacing Chart

Note: The pacing of the lesson schedule is only a recommendation. Use the *Interactive Lesson Planner* to customize the pace for your instructional needs.

Lesson Schedule	Essential Lesson Support and Assessment	
Theme 1: What I Am, What I Want to Be Day 1 Lesson and lesson support on SE/TWE pp. 1–3	• *Theme One Planning Guide*, pp. 1–3 • *Performance Assessment*, p. 69	
Days 2–3 Names/Nombres Three-part instruction and selection support on SE/TWE pp. 4–11 **Grammar Link** Avoiding Sentence Fragments, SE/TWE p. 12	**Lesson-Specific Instruction** • *Theme One Planning Guide*, pp. 4–11 • *Selection Focus Transparency 1* • *Active Reading Guide*,* p. 1 • *Literary Elements Transparency 1* • *Selection Vocabulary Practice*, p. 1 • *Selection Quick Checks*,* p. 1 • *Selection and Theme Assessment*, pp. 1–2	• *Testmaker: ExamView Pro* • *Performance Assessment*, p. 1 **Systematic Language Instruction** • *Grammar and Composition Handbook*, Lessons 1.1–1.2 • *Vocabulary Power*, Lesson 1 • *Spelling Power*, Lesson 1
Day 4 One and I'm Nobody! Who are you? Three-part instruction and selection support on SE/TWE pp. 13–17	**Lesson-Specific Instruction** • *Theme One Planning Guide*, pp. 12–16 • *Selection Focus Transparency 2* • *Active Reading Guide*,* p. 2 • *Literary Elements Transparency 2* • *Selection Quick Checks*,* p. 2 • *Selection and Theme Assessment*, pp. 3–4	• *Testmaker: ExamView Pro* • *Performance Assessment*, p. 2 **Systematic Language Instruction** • *Grammar and Composition Handbook*, Lessons 1.3–1.4
Days 5–6 Face It and Almost Ready Three-part instruction and selection support on SE/TWE pp. 18–22 **Writing Skills** Using Dialogue in a Narrative, SE/TWE p. 23	**Lesson-Specific Instruction** • *Theme One Planning Guide*, pp. 17–21 • *Selection Focus Transparency 3* • *Active Reading Guide*,* p. 3 • *Literary Elements Transparency 3* • *Selection Quick Checks*,* p. 3 • *Selection and Theme Assessment*, pp. 5–6	• *Testmaker: ExamView Pro* • *Performance Assessment*, p. 3 **Systematic Language Instruction** • *Grammar and Composition Handbook*, Lesson 1.5 • *Vocabulary Power*, Lesson 2 • *Spelling Power*, Lesson 2
Days 7–8 Strong Men Weep Three-part instruction and selection support on SE/TWE pp. 25–33 **Media Connection** Newspaper Column, SE/TWE p. 24	**Lesson-Specific Instruction** • *Theme One Planning Guide*, pp. 22–29 • *Selection Focus Transparency 4* • *Active Reading Guide*,* p. 4 • *Literary Elements Transparency 4* • *Selection Vocabulary Practice*, p. 2 • *Selection Quick Checks*,* p. 4	• *Selection and Theme Assessment*, pp. 7–8 • *Testmaker: ExamView Pro* • *Performance Assessment*, p. 4 • *inTIME* magazine, pp. 30–31 **Systematic Language Instruction** • *Grammar and Composition Handbook*, Lesson 1.6
Days 9–10 from Wait Till Next Year Three-part instruction and selection support on SE/TWE pp. 34–39 **Comparing Selections** SE/TWE p. 40	**Lesson-Specific Instruction** • *Theme One Planning Guide*, pp. 30–37 • *Selection Focus Transparency 5* • *Active Reading Guide*,* p. 5 • *Literary Elements Transparency 5* • *Selection Vocabulary Practice*, p. 3 • *Selection Quick Checks*,* p. 5 • *Selection and Theme Assessment*, pp. 9–10	• *Testmaker: ExamView Pro* • *Performance Assessment*, p. 5 • *inTIME* magazine, pp. 30–31 **Systematic Language Instruction** • *Grammar and Composition Handbook*, Lesson 2.1 • *Vocabulary Power*, Lesson 3 • *Spelling Power*, Lesson 3

SE: Student Edition **TWE:** Teacher Wraparound Edition ***Also available in Spanish**

English Language Learners (Add 30–45 Minutes a Day)	Special Needs/Strategic Intervention (Add 30–45 Minutes a Day)
• *English Language Learners Sourcebook*, pp. 1–13 • *English, Yes!*	• *Inclusion Strategies Sourcebook*, pp. vii–xii
• Naming a Child, TWE p. 6 • *English Language Learners Sourcebook*, p. 17 • *Theme One Planning Guide*, p. 6 • *Spanish Summaries*, p. 1 • *Spanish Translations*, pp. 1–4 • *Audio Library** • *English, Yes!*	• *Interactive Reading Sourcebook*, pp. T47–T49 • *Interactive Reading Workbook*, pp. 1–3 • *Inclusion Strategies Sourcebook*, pp. 5–6, 55–56 • *Audio Library**
• Compound Words, TWE p. 14 • *English Language Learners Sourcebook*, p. 18 • *Spanish Summaries*, p. 2 • *Audio Library** • *English, Yes!*	• *Interactive Reading Sourcebook*, pp. T50–T52 • *Interactive Reading Workbook*, p. 4 • *Inclusion Strategies Sourcebook*, pp. 55–56 • *Theme One Planning Guide*, p. 14 • *Audio Library**
• Dramatic Reading, TWE p. 19 • *English Language Learners Sourcebook*, p. 19 • *Spanish Summaries*, p. 3 • *Audio Library** • *English, Yes!*	• *Interactive Reading Sourcebook*, pp. T53–T55 • *Interactive Reading Workbook*, p. 5 • *Inclusion Strategies Sourcebook*, pp. 39–40, 55–56, 77–78 • *Theme One Planning Guide*, p. 19 • *Audio Library**
• Baseball Terms, TWE p. 27 • *English Language Learners Sourcebook*, p. 20 • *Spanish Summaries*, p. 4 • *Spanish Translations*, pp. 5–8 • *Audio Library** • *English, Yes!*	• *Interactive Reading Sourcebook*, pp. T55–T58 • *Interactive Reading Workbook*, pp. 6–7 • *Inclusion Strategies Sourcebook*, pp. 39–40, 55–56 • *Theme One Planning Guide*, p. 24 • *Audio Library**
• The Art of Storytelling, TWE p. 36 • *English Language Learners Sourcebook*, p. 21 • *Theme One Planning Guide*, p. 32 • *Spanish Summaries*, p. 5 • *Spanish Translations*, pp. 9–10 • *Spanish Audio Library* • *English, Yes!*	• *Interactive Reading Sourcebook*, pp. T58–T60 • *Interactive Reading Workbook*, pp. 8–9 • *Inclusion Strategies Sourcebook*, pp. 7–8, 27–28, 69–70 • *Theme One Planning Guide*, p. 32

Lesson Schedule	Essential Lesson Support and Assessment	
Days 11–13 **Broken Chain** Three-part instruction and selection support on SE/TWE pp. 43–55 **Media Connection** Television Script, SE/TWE pp. 41–42 **Technology Skills** Word Processing, SE/TWE pp. 56–57	**Lesson-Specific Instruction** • *Theme One Planning Guide*, pp. 38–45 • *Selection Focus Transparency* 6 • *Active Reading Guide*,* p. 6 • *Literary Elements Transparency* 6 • *Selection Vocabulary Practice*, p. 4 • *Selection Quick Checks*,* p. 6	• *Selection and Theme Assessment*, pp. 11–12 • *Testmaker: ExamView Pro* • *Performance Assessment*, p. 6 **Systematic Language Instruction** • *Grammar and Composition Handbook*, Lessons 2.2–2.3
Day 14 **Without Commercials** Three-part instruction and selection support on SE/TWE pp. 58–61	**Lesson-Specific Instruction** • *Theme One Planning Guide*, pp. 46–50 • *Selection Focus Transparency 7* • *Active Reading Guide*,* p. 7 • *Literary Elements Transparency 7* • *Selection Quick Checks*,* p. 7 • *Selection and Theme Assessment*, pp. 13–14 • *Testmaker: ExamView Pro* • *Performance Assessment*, p. 7	**Systematic Language Instruction** • *Grammar and Composition Handbook*, Lesson 2.4 • *Vocabulary Power*, Lesson 4 • *Spelling Power*, Lesson 4
Days 15–16 from **Barrio Boy** Three-part instruction and selection support on SE/TWE pp. 66–74 **Genre Focus** Autobiography, SE/TWE pp. 62–63 **Active Reading Strategies** Tips for Reading Autobiographical Writing, SE/TWE pp. 64–65 **Vocabulary Skills** Base Words, SE/TWE p. 75	**Lesson-Specific Instruction** • *Theme One Planning Guide*, pp. 51–58 • *Selection Focus Transparency* 8 • *Active Reading Guide*,* p. 8 • *Literary Elements Transparency* 8 • *Selection Vocabulary Practice*, p. 5 • *Selection Quick Checks*,* p. 8 • *Selection and Theme Assessment*, pp. 15–16	• *Testmaker: ExamView Pro* • *Performance Assessment*, p. 8 **Systematic Language Instruction** • *Grammar and Composition Handbook*, Lesson 2.5
Days 17–18 **Fish Cheeks** Three-part instruction and selection support on SE/TWE pp. 76–81 **Interdisciplinary Connection** Social Studies, SE/TWE p. 82 **Reading and Thinking Skills** Sequencing, SE/TWE p. 83	**Lesson-Specific Instruction** • *Theme One Planning Guide*, pp. 59–66 • *Selection Focus Transparency* 9 • *Active Reading Guide*,* p. 9 • *Literary Elements Transparency* 9 • *Selection Vocabulary Practice*, p. 6 • *Selection Quick Checks*,* p. 9 • *Selection and Theme Assessment*, pp. 17–18	• *Testmaker: ExamView Pro* • *Performance Assessment*, p. 9 **Systematic Language Instruction** • *Grammar and Composition Handbook*, Lessons 3.1–3.2 • *Vocabulary Power*, Lesson 5
Days 19–21 from **Rosa Parks: My Story** Three-part instruction and selection support on SE/TWE pp. 84–103	**Lesson-Specific Instruction** • *Theme One Planning Guide*, pp. 67–74 • *Selection Focus Transparency* 10 • *Active Reading Guide*,* p. 10 • *Literary Elements Transparency* 10 • *Selection Vocabulary Practice*, p. 7 • *Selection Quick Checks*,* p. 10 • *Selection and Theme Assessment*, pp. 19–20 • *Testmaker: ExamView Pro*	• *Performance Assessment*, p. 10 • *in*TIME magazine, pp. 22–23 **Systematic Language Instruction** • *Grammar and Composition Handbook*, Lesson 3.3 • *Vocabulary Power*, Unit 1 Review/Test • *Spelling Power*, Unit 1 Review/Proofreading

SE: Student Edition TWE: Teacher Wraparound Edition *Also available in Spanish

English Language Learners (Add 30–45 Minutes a Day)	Special Needs/Strategic Intervention (Add 30–45 Minutes a Day)
• Ethnic Foods, TWE p. 45 • *English Language Learners Sourcebook*, p. 22 • *Spanish Summaries*, p. 6 • *Spanish Translations*, pp. 11–17 • *Audio Library** • *English, Yes!*	• *Interactive Reading Sourcebook*, pp. T61–T63 • *Interactive Reading Workbook*, pp. 10–11 • Emotional, TWE p. 50 • Physically Challenged, TWE p. 56 • *Inclusion Strategies Sourcebook*, pp. 23–24, 53–54 • *Theme One Planning Guide*, p. 40 • *Audio Library**
• Cultural Concepts of Beauty, TWE p. 60 • *English Language Learners Sourcebook*, p. 23 • *Spanish Summaries*, p. 7 • *Audio Library** • *English, Yes!*	• *Interactive Reading Sourcebook*, pp. T63–T65 • *Interactive Reading Workbook*, p. 12 • *Inclusion Strategies Sourcebook*, pp. 1–2 • *Theme One Planning Guide*, p. 48 • *Audio Library**
• Elements of Autobiography, TWE p. 62 • Description, TWE p. 68 • Using Prefixes, TWE p. 75 • *English Language Learners Sourcebook*, pp. 24, 25 • *Theme One Planning Guide*, p. 53 • *Spanish Summaries*, p. 8 • *Spanish Translations*, pp. 18–22 • *Audio Library** • *English, Yes!*	• *Interactive Reading Sourcebook*, pp. T66–T68 • *Interactive Reading Workbook*, pp. 13–14 • Less-Proficient Readers, TWE p. 70 • *Inclusion Strategies Sourcebook*, pp. 33–34 • *Theme One Planning Guide*, p. 53 • *Audio Library**
• Comparing Customs, TWE p. 78 • *English Language Learners Sourcebook*, p. 26 • *Spanish Summaries*, p. 9 • *Audio Library** • *English, Yes!*	• *Interactive Reading Sourcebook*, pp. T68–T71 • *Interactive Reading Workbook*, pp. 15–16 • Learning Disabled, TWE p. 83 • *Inclusion Strategies Sourcebook*, pp. 57–58, 69–70, 81–82 • *Theme One Planning Guide*, p. 61 • *Audio Library**
• Figures of Speech, TWE p. 86 • *English Language Learners Sourcebook*, pp. 27, 28 • *Spanish Summaries*, p. 10 • *Spanish Translations*, pp. 22–34 • *Audio Library** • *English, Yes!*	• *Interactive Reading Sourcebook*, pp. T71–T73 • *Interactive Reading Workbook*, pp. 17–20 • Less-Proficient Readers, TWE p. 88 • Visually Impaired, TWE p. 94 • *Inclusion Strategies Sourcebook*, pp. 3–4 • *Theme One Planning Guide*, p. 69 • *Audio Library**

<table>
<tr><th>Lesson Schedule</th><th colspan="2">Essential Lesson Support and Assessment</th></tr>
<tr><td>Days 22–23
Writing Workshop Narrative Writing: Autobiographical Anecdote
Lesson and lesson support on SE/TWE pp. 104–107</td><td colspan="2">• Writing Assessment and Portfolio Management, pp. 1–13, 14–16, 38–44</td></tr>
<tr><td>Day 24
Theme Assessment
Lesson and lesson support on SE/TWE pp. 108–109</td><td>• Selection and Theme Assessment, pp. 125–126
• Testmaker: ExamView Pro
• Performance Assessment, p. 96</td><td>• Writing Assessment and Portfolio Management, pp. 1–12, 38–44
• Initial Screening and Fluency Assessment, Theme One Reading Fluency</td></tr>
<tr><td>Theme 2: Winds of Change
Day 25
Lesson and lesson support on SE/TWE pp. 112–115</td><td colspan="2">• Theme Two Planning Guide, pp. 1–3
• Performance Assessment, p. 70</td></tr>
<tr><td>Days 26–28
Hollywood and the Pits
Three-part instruction and selection support on SE/TWE pp. 116–129
Interdisciplinary Connection Science, SE/TWE p. 130</td><td>Lesson-Specific Instruction
• Theme Two Planning Guide, pp. 4–11
• Selection Focus Transparency 11
• Active Reading Guide,* p. 11
• Literary Elements Transparency 11
• Selection Vocabulary Practice, p. 8
• Selection Quick Checks,* p. 11</td><td>• Selection and Theme Assessment, pp. 21–22
• Testmaker: ExamView Pro
• Performance Assessment, p. 11
Systematic Language Instruction
• Grammar and Composition Handbook, Lesson 3.4</td></tr>
<tr><td>Day 29
Growing Pains
Three-part instruction and selection support on SE/TWE pp. 132–135
Media Connection Song, SE/TWE p. 131</td><td>Lesson-Specific Instruction
• Theme Two Planning Guide, pp. 12–16
• Selection Focus Transparency 12
• Active Reading Guide,* p. 12
• Literary Elements Transparency 12
• Selection Quick Checks,* p. 12
• Selection and Theme Assessment, p. 23</td><td>• Testmaker: ExamView Pro
• Performance Assessment, p. 12
Systematic Language Instruction
• Grammar and Composition Handbook, Lessons 3.5–3.6
• Vocabulary Power, Lesson 6
• Spelling Power, Lesson 5</td></tr>
<tr><td>Days 30–31
Slam, Dunk, & Hook
Three-part instruction and selection support on SE/TWE pp. 137–141
Media Connection Magazine Article, SE/TWE p. 136
Reading and Thinking Skills Identifying Main Idea and Supporting Details, SE/TWE p. 142
Vocabulary Skills Context Clues, SE/TWE p. 143</td><td>Lesson-Specific Instruction
• Theme Two Planning Guide, pp. 17–21
• Selection Focus Transparency 13
• Active Reading Guide,* p. 13
• Literary Elements Transparency 13
• Selection Quick Checks,* p. 13
• Selection and Theme Assessment, p. 24
• Testmaker: ExamView Pro</td><td>• Performance Assessment, p. 13
• inTIME magazine, p. 26
Systematic Language Instruction
• Grammar and Composition Handbook, Lesson 3.7</td></tr>
<tr><td>Days 32–33
A Crush
Three-part instruction and selection support on SE/TWE pp. 148–159
Genre Focus Fiction, SE/TWE pp. 144–145</td><td>Lesson-Specific Instruction
• Theme Two Planning Guide, pp. 22–29
• Selection Focus Transparency 14
• Active Reading Guide,* p. 14
• Literary Elements Transparency 14
• Selection Vocabulary Practice, p. 9</td><td>• Selection Quick Checks,* p. 14
• Selection and Theme Assessment, pp. 25–26
• Testmaker: ExamView Pro
• Performance Assessment, p. 14
Systematic Language Instruction
• Grammar and Composition Handbook,</td></tr>
</table>

SE: Student Edition TWE: Teacher Wraparound Edition *Also available in Spanish

English Language Learners (Add 30–45 Minutes a Day)	Special Needs/Strategic Intervention (Add 30–45 Minutes a Day)
• An Autobiographical Anecdote, TWE p. 104 • *English Language Learners Sourcebook*, p. 9 • *English, Yes!*	• *Inclusion Strategies Sourcebook*, pp. 73–74
• *English Language Learners Sourcebook*, pp. 1–13 • *English, Yes!*	• Special Needs, TWE p. 109 • *Inclusion Strategies Sourcebook*, p. xii
• *English Language Learners Sourcebook*, pp. 1–13 • *English, Yes!*	• *Inclusion Strategies Sourcebook*, pp. vii–xii
• Little Princess, TWE p. 118 • *English Language Learners Sourcebook*, pp. 29, 30 • *Spanish Summaries*, p. 11 • *Spanish Translations*, pp. 35–42 • *Audio Library** • *English, Yes!*	• *Interactive Reading Sourcebook*, pp. T74–T77 • *Interactive Reading Workbook*, pp. 21–22 • Less-Proficient Readers, TWE pp. 124, 128 • *Inclusion Strategies Sourcebook*, pp. 9–10 • *Theme Two Planning Guide*, p. 6 • *Audio Library**
• Relationships, TWE p. 133 • *English Language Learners Sourcebook*, p. 31 • *Spanish Summaries*, p. 12 • *Spanish Translations*, p. 43 • *Audio Library** • *English, Yes!*	• *Interactive Reading Sourcebook*, pp. T77–T79 • *Interactive Reading Workbook*, p. 23 • *Inclusion Strategies Sourcebook*, pp. 11–12 • *Theme Two Planning Guide*, p. 14 • *Audio Library**
• Basketball Slang, TWE p. 138 • Creating Context, TWE p. 143 • *English Language Learners Sourcebook*, p. 32 • *Spanish Summaries*, p. 13 • *Spanish Translations*, pp. 44–45 • *Audio Library** • *English, Yes!*	• *Interactive Reading Sourcebook*, pp. T80–T82 • *Interactive Reading Workbook*, p. 24 • Less-Proficient Readers, TWE p. 142 • *Inclusion Strategies Sourcebook*, pp. 67–68 • *Theme Two Planning Guide*, p. 19 • *Audio Library**
• Multicultural Stories, TWE p. 144 • Rites of Passage, TWE p. 150 • *English Language Learners Sourcebook*, pp. 34, 35 • *Theme Two Planning Guide*, p. 24 • *Spanish Summaries*, p. 14 • *Spanish Translations*, pp. 46–51	• *Interactive Reading Sourcebook*, pp. T82–T85 • *Interactive Reading Workbook*, pp. 25–26 • Less-Proficient Readers, TWE p. 147 • *Inclusion Strategies Sourcebook*, pp. 29–30 • *Theme Two Planning Guide*, p. 24 • *Audio Library**

Lesson Schedule	Essential Lesson Support and Assessment	
Day 44 Theme Assessment Lesson and lesson support on SE/TWE pp. 212–213	• *Selection and Theme Assessment*, pp. 127–128 • *Testmaker: ExamView Pro* • *Performance Assessment*, p. 96	• *Writing Assessment and Portfolio Management*, pp. 1–12, 38–44 • *Initial Screening and Fluency Assessment*, Theme Two Reading Fluency
Theme 3: Facing Challenge Day 45 Lesson and lesson support on SE/TWE pp. 216–219	• *Theme Three Planning Guide*, pp. 1–3 • *Performance Assessment*, p. 71	
Days 46–47 New Directions Three-part instruction and selection support on SE/TWE pp. 220–224 **Vocabulary Skills** Using Homophones, SE/TWE p. 225	**Lesson-Specific Instruction** • *Theme Three Planning Guide*, pp. 4–8 • *Selection Focus Transparency 19* • *Active Reading Guide*,* p. 19 • *Literary Elements Transparency 19* • *Selection Vocabulary Practice*, p. 13 • *Selection Quick Checks*,* p. 19 • *Selection and Theme Assessment*, pp. 33–34	• *Testmaker: ExamView Pro* • *Performance Assessment*, p. 18 • *inTIME* magazine, pp. 6–7 **Systematic Language Instruction** • *Grammar and Composition Handbook*, Lesson 4.4 • *Vocabulary Power*, Lesson 10 • *Spelling Power*, Lesson 9
Days 48–49 The Wreck of the Hesperus and I'll Walk the Tightrope Three-part instruction and selection support on SE/TWE pp. 226–233	**Lesson-Specific Instruction** • *Theme Three Planning Guide*, pp. 9–14 • *Selection Focus Transparency 20* • *Active Reading Guide*,* p. 20 • *Literary Elements Transparency 20* • *Selection Quick Checks*,* p. 20 • *Selection and Theme Assessment*, pp. 35–36	• *Testmaker: ExamView Pro* • *Performance Assessment*, p. 19 • *inTIME* magazine, pp. 12–13, 22–23 **Systematic Language Instruction** • *Grammar and Composition Handbook*, Lesson 4.5
Days 50–51 Too Soon a Woman Three-part instruction and selection support on SE/TWE pp. 234–241	**Lesson-Specific Instruction** • *Theme Three Planning Guide*, pp. 15–22 • *Selection Focus Transparency 21* • *Active Reading Guide*,* p. 21 • *Literary Elements Transparency 21* • *Selection Vocabulary Practice*, p. 14 • *Selection Quick Checks*,* p. 21 • *Selection and Theme Assessment*, pp. 37–38	• *Testmaker: ExamView Pro* • *Performance Assessment*, p. 20 **Systematic Language Instruction** • *Grammar and Composition Handbook*, Lessons 4.6–4.7 • *Vocabulary Power*, Lesson 11 • *Spelling Power*, Lesson 10
Days 52–53 A Boy and His Dog Three-part instruction and selection support on SE/TWE pp. 242–248 **Comparing Selections** SE/TWE p. 249 **Reading and Thinking Skills** Visualizing, SE/TWE p. 250	**Lesson-Specific Instruction** • *Theme Three Planning Guide*, pp. 23–30 • *Selection Focus Transparency 22* • *Active Reading Guide*,* p. 22 • *Literary Elements Transparency 22* • *Selection Vocabulary Practice*, p. 15 • *Selection Quick Checks*,* p. 22 • *Selection and Theme Assessment*, pp. 39–40	• *Testmaker: ExamView Pro* • *Performance Assessment*, p. 21 • *inTIME* magazine, p. 2 **Systematic Language Instruction** • *Grammar and Composition Handbook*, Lessons 5.1–5.2
Days 54–55 The Women's 400 Meters and To James Three-part instruction and selection support on SE/TWE pp. 251–256 **Interdisciplinary Connection** Math, SE/TWE p. 257	**Lesson-Specific Instruction** • *Theme Three Planning Guide*, pp. 31–36 • *Selection Focus Transparency 23* • *Active Reading Guide*,* p. 23 • *Literary Elements Transparency 23* • *Selection Quick Checks*,* p. 23 • *Selection and Theme Assessment*, pp. 41–42	• *Testmaker: ExamView Pro* • *Performance Assessment*, p. 22 • *inTIME* magazine, p. 27 **Systematic Language Instruction** • *Grammar and Composition Handbook*, Lessons 5.3–5.4 • *Vocabulary Power*, Lesson 12

SE: Student Edition TWE: Teacher Wraparound Edition *Also available in Spanish

English Language Learners (Add 30–45 Minutes a Day)	Special Needs/Strategic Intervention (Add 30–45 Minutes a Day)
• *English Language Learners Sourcebook*, pp. 1–13 • *English, Yes!*	• Special Needs, TWE p. 213 • *Inclusion Strategies Sourcebook*, p. xii
• *English Language Learners Sourcebook*, pp. 1–13 • *English, Yes!*	• *Inclusion Strategies Sourcebook*, pp. vii–xii
• Pair Pictures, TWE p. 225 • *English Language Learners Sourcebook*, p. 41 • *Theme Three Planning Guide*, p. 6 • *Spanish Summaries*, p. 19 • *Spanish Translations*, pp. 64–65 • *Audio Library** • *English, Yes!*	• *Interactive Reading Sourcebook*, pp. T97–T99 • *Interactive Reading Workbook*, pp. 36–37 • *Inclusion Strategies Sourcebook*, pp. 39–40 • *Theme Three Planning Guide*, p. 6 • *Audio Library**
• Weather Proverbs, TWE p. 227 • *English Language Learners Sourcebook*, p. 42 • *Spanish Summaries*, p. 20 • *Audio Library** • *English, Yes!*	• *Interactive Reading Sourcebook*, pp. T100–T102 • *Interactive Reading Workbook*, pp. 38–39 • Learning Disabled, TWE p. 229 • *Theme Three Planning Guide*, p. 11 • *Audio Library**
• Past Perfect Verbs, TWE p. 236 • *English Language Learners Sourcebook*, p. 43 • *Spanish Summaries*, p. 21 • *Spanish Translations*, pp. 66–69 • *Audio Library** • *English, Yes!*	• *Interactive Reading Sourcebook*, pp. T103–T105 • *Interactive Reading Workbook*, pp. 40–41 • *Inclusion Strategies Sourcebook*, pp. 53–54, 61–62 • *Theme Three Planning Guide*, p. 17 • *Audio Library**
• Unusual Expressions, TWE p. 244 • *English Language Learners Sourcebook*, p. 44 • *Spanish Summaries*, p. 22 • *Spanish Translations*, pp. 70–73 • *Audio Library** • *English, Yes!*	• *Interactive Reading Sourcebook*, pp. T106–T108 • *Interactive Reading Workbook*, pp. 42–43 • Less-Proficient Readers, TWE pp. 247, 250 • *Inclusion Strategies Sourcebook*, pp. 59–60 • *Theme Three Planning Guide*, p. 25 • *Audio Library**
• Track and Field, TWE p. 252 • *English Language Learners Sourcebook*, p. 45 • *Spanish Summaries*, p. 23 • *Spanish Translations*, pp. 74–75 • *Audio Library** • *English, Yes!*	• *Interactive Reading Sourcebook*, pp. T108–T110 • *Interactive Reading Workbook*, p. 44 • *Audio Library**

Lesson Schedule	Essential Lesson Support and Assessment	
Day 67 Theme Assessment Lesson and lesson support on SE/TWE pp. 320–321	• *Selection and Theme Assessment*, pp. 129–130 • *Testmaker: ExamView Pro* • *Performance Assessment*, p. 97	• *Writing Assessment and Portfolio Management*, pp. 1–12, 38–44 • *Initial Screening and Fluency Assessment*, Theme Three Reading Fluency
Theme 4: Where the Heart Is Day 68 Lesson and lesson support on SE/TWE pp. 324–327	• *Theme Four Planning Guide*, pp. 1–3 • *Performance Assessment*, p. 72	
Day 69 Bums in the Attic Three-part instruction and selection support on SE/TWE pp. 328–331 **Interdisciplinary Connection** Technology, SE/TWE p. 332	**Lesson-Specific Instruction** • *Theme Four Planning Guide*, pp. 4–8 • *Selection Focus Transparency* 29 • *Active Reading Guide*,* p. 29 • *Literary Elements Transparency* 29 • *Selection Quick Checks*,* p. 29 • *Selection and Theme Assessment*, p. 53 • *Testmaker: ExamView Pro*	• *Performance Assessment*, p. 28 **Systematic Language Instruction** • *Grammar and Composition Handbook*, Lessons 7.1–7.2 • *Vocabulary Power*, Lesson 15 • *Spelling Power*, Lesson 13
Day 70 En un Barrio de Los Angeles/ In a Neighborhood in Los Angeles Three-part instruction and selection support on SE/TWE pp. 333–337 **Technology Skills** Internet, SE/TWE pp. 338–339	**Lesson-Specific Instruction** • *Theme Four Planning Guide*, pp. 9–13 • *Selection Focus Transparency* 30 • *Active Reading Guide*,* p. 30 • *Literary Elements Transparency* 30 • *Selection Quick Checks*,* p. 30 • *Selection and Theme Assessment*, p. 54	• *Testmaker: ExamView Pro* • *Performance Assessment*, p. 29 • *inTIME* magazine, pp. 8–9 **Systematic Language Instruction** • *Grammar and Composition Handbook*, Lesson 7.3
Days 71–72 The Courage That My Mother Had and Mother to Son Three-part instruction and selection support on SE/TWE pp. 340–344	**Lesson-Specific Instruction** • *Theme Four Planning Guide*, pp. 14–19 • *Selection Focus Transparency* 31 • *Active Reading Guide*,* p. 31 • *Literary Elements Transparency* 31 • *Selection Quick Checks*,* p. 31	• *Selection and Theme Assessment*, pp. 55–56 • *Testmaker: ExamView Pro* • *Performance Assessment*, p. 30 **Systematic Language Instruction** • *Grammar and Composition Handbook*, Lesson 7.4
Days 73–74 Antaeus Three-part instruction and selection support on SE/TWE pp. 346–359 **Media Connection** Newspaper Story, SE/TWE p. 345	**Lesson-Specific Instruction** • *Theme Four Planning Guide*, pp. 20–27 • *Selection Focus Transparency* 32 • *Active Reading Guide*,* p. 32 • *Literary Elements Transparency* 32 • *Selection Vocabulary Practice*, p. 20 • *Selection Quick Checks*,* p. 32 • *Selection and Theme Assessment*, pp. 57–58	• *Testmaker: ExamView Pro* • *Performance Assessment*, p. 31 **Systematic Language Instruction** • *Grammar and Composition Handbook*, Lesson 7.5 • *Vocabulary Power*, Lesson 16 • *Spelling Power*, Lesson 14

SE: Student Edition **TWE: Teacher Wraparound Edition** ***Also available in Spanish**

English Language Learners (Add 30–45 Minutes a Day)	Special Needs/Strategic Intervention (Add 30–45 Minutes a Day)
• *English Language Learners Sourcebook*, pp. 1–13 • *English, Yes!*	• Special Needs, TWE p. 321 • *Inclusion Strategies Sourcebook*, p. xii
• Understanding the Theme's Title, TWE p. 326 • *English Language Learners Sourcebook*, pp. 1–13 • *English, Yes!*	• *Inclusion Strategies Sourcebook*, pp. vii–xii
• Symbolism, TWE p. 329 • *English Language Learners Sourcebook*, p. 52 • *Theme Four Planning Guide*, p. 6 • *Spanish Summaries*, p. 29 • *Spanish Translations*, p. 92 • *Audio Library** • *English, Yes!*	• *Interactive Reading Sourcebook*, pp. T126–T128 • *Interactive Reading Workbook*, p. 54 • *Inclusion Strategies Sourcebook*, pp. 65–66 • *Audio Library**
• Shades of Meaning, TWE p. 334 • *English Language Learners Sourcebook*, p. 53 • *Spanish Summaries*, p. 30 • *Spanish Translations*, pp. 93–94 • *Audio Library** • *English, Yes!*	• *Interactive Reading Sourcebook*, pp. T128–T130 • *Interactive Reading Workbook*, p. 55 • Less-Proficient Readers, TWE p. 338 • *Theme Four Planning Guide*, p. 11 • *Audio Library**
• Building Fluency, TWE p. 341 • *English Language Learners Sourcebook*, p. 54 • *Spanish Summaries*, p. 31 • *Spanish Translations*, pp. 95–96 • *Audio Library** • *English, Yes!*	• *Interactive Reading Sourcebook*, pp. T130–T133 • *Interactive Reading Workbook*, p. 56 • *Theme Four Planning Guide*, p. 16 • *Audio Library**
• Dialogue That Mimics Speech, TWE p. 348 • *English Language Learners Sourcebook*, p. 55 • *Theme Four Planning Guide*, p. 22 • *Spanish Summaries*, p. 32 • *Audio Library** • *English, Yes!*	• *Interactive Reading Sourcebook*, pp. T133–T135 • *Interactive Reading Workbook*, pp. 57–60 • Learning Disabled, TWE p. 353 • *Inclusion Strategies Sourcebook*, pp. 13–14, 41–42, 67–68, 79–80 • *Theme Four Planning Guide*, p. 22 • *Audio Library**

Lesson Schedule	Essential Lesson Support and Assessment	
Day 75 **Home and the 1st** Three-part instruction and selection support on SE/TWE pp. 360–365 **Reading and Thinking Skills** Making Connections, SE/TWE p. 366	**Lesson-Specific Instruction** • *Theme Four Planning Guide*, pp. 28–33 • *Selection Focus Transparency 33* • *Active Reading Guide*,* p. 33 • *Literary Elements Transparency 33* • *Selection Vocabulary Practice*, p. 21 • *Selection Quick Checks*,* p. 33	• *Selection and Theme Assessment*, pp. 59–60 • *Testmaker: ExamView Pro* • *Performance Assessment*, p. 32 **Systematic Language Instruction** • *Grammar and Composition Handbook*, Lesson 7.6
Days 76–77 **The Teacher Who Changed My Life** Three-part instruction and selection support on SE/TWE pp. 367–375	**Lesson-Specific Instruction** • *Theme Four Planning Guide*, pp. 34–41 • *Selection Focus Transparency 34* • *Active Reading Guide*,* p. 34 • *Literary Elements Transparency 34* • *Selection Vocabulary Practice*, p. 22 • *Selection Quick Checks*,* p. 34 • *Selection and Theme Assessment*, pp. 61–62	• *Testmaker: ExamView Pro* • *Performance Assessment*, p. 33 **Systematic Language Instruction** • *Grammar and Composition Handbook*, Lesson 7.7 • *Vocabulary Power*, Lesson 17 • *Spelling Power*, Lesson 15
Days 78–79 **How I Learned English** Three-part instruction and selection support on SE/TWE pp. 376–379 **Comparing Selections** SE/TWE p. 380 **Grammar Link** Using Irregular Verbs Correctly, SE/TWE p. 381	**Lesson-Specific Instruction** • *Theme Four Planning Guide*, pp. 42–46 • *Selection Focus Transparency 35* • *Active Reading Guide*,* p. 35 • *Literary Elements Transparency 35* • *Selection Quick Checks*,* p. 35 • *Selection and Theme Assessment*, pp. 61–62	• *Testmaker: ExamView Pro* • *Performance Assessment*, p. 33 **Systematic Language Instruction** • *Grammar and Composition Handbook*, Lesson 8.1
Days 80–82 **Oh Broom, Get to Work** and **Anansi and His Visitor, Turtle** Three-part instruction and selection support on SE/TWE pp. 382–393 **Vocabulary Skills** Roots, SE/TWE p. 394 **Writing Skills** Describing with Sensory Details, SE/TWE p. 395	**Lesson-Specific Instruction** • *Theme Four Planning Guide*, pp. 47–52 • *Selection Focus Transparency 36* • *Active Reading Guide*,* p. 36 • *Literary Elements Transparency 36* • *Selection Vocabulary Practice*, p. 23 • *Selection Quick Checks*,* p. 36	• *Selection and Theme Assessment*, pp. 63–64 • *Testmaker: ExamView Pro* • *Performance Assessment*, p. 34 **Systematic Language Instruction** • *Grammar and Composition Handbook*, Lesson 8.2
Days 83–84 **The Night the Bed Fell** Three-part instruction and selection support on SE/TWE pp. 398–408 **Genre Focus** Essay, SE/TWE p. 396 **Active Reading Strategies** Tips for Reading an Essay, SE/TWE p. 397	**Lesson-Specific Instruction** • *Theme Four Planning Guide*, pp. 53–60 • *Selection Focus Transparency 37* • *Active Reading Guide*,* p. 37 • *Literary Elements Transparency 37* • *Selection Vocabulary Practice*, p. 24 • *Selection Quick Checks*,* p. 37 • *Selection and Theme Assessment*, pp. 65–66	• *Testmaker: ExamView Pro* • *Performance Assessment*, p. 35 **Systematic Language Instruction** • *Grammar and Composition Handbook*, Lesson 8.3 • *Vocabulary Power*, Lesson 18 • *Spelling Power*, Lesson 16
Days 85–86 **The Dog Diaries** Three-part instruction and selection support on SE/TWE pp. 410–419 **Media Connection** Comic Strip, SE/TWE p. 409	**Lesson-Specific Instruction** • *Theme Four Planning Guide*, pp. 61–68 • *Selection Focus Transparency 38* • *Active Reading Guide*,* p. 38 • *Literary Elements Transparency 38* • *Selection Vocabulary Practice*, p. 25 • *Selection Quick Checks*,* p. 38 • *Selection and Theme Assessment*, pp. 67–68	• *Testmaker: ExamView Pro* • *Performance Assessment*, p. 36 • *inTIME* magazine, p. 2 **Systematic Language Instruction** • *Grammar and Composition Handbook*, Lesson 8.4 • *Vocabulary Power*, Unit 4 Review/Test • *Spelling Power*, Unit 4 Review/Proofreading

SE: Student Edition **TWE: Teacher Wraparound Edition** ***Also available in Spanish**

English Language Learners (Add 30–45 Minutes a Day)	Special Needs/Strategic Intervention (Add 30–45 Minutes a Day)
• Understanding Poetry, TWE p. 363 • *English Language Learners Sourcebook*, p. 56 • *Theme Four Planning Guide*, p. 30 • *Spanish Summaries*, p. 33 • *Audio Library** • *English, Yes!*	• *Interactive Reading Sourcebook*, pp. T136–T138 • *Interactive Reading Workbook*, p. 61 • Learning Disabled, TWE p. 366 • *Inclusion Strategies Sourcebook*, pp. 19–20, 37–38 • *Theme Four Planning Guide*, p. 30 • *Audio Library**
• Connecting, TWE p. 369 • *English Language Learners Sourcebook*, p. 57 • *Theme Four Planning Guide*, p. 36 • *Spanish Summaries*, p. 34 • *Audio Library** • *English, Yes!*	• *Interactive Reading Sourcebook*, pp. T138–T141 • *Interactive Reading Workbook*, pp. 62–63 • *Inclusion Strategies Sourcebook*, pp. 39–40 • *Theme Four Planning Guide*, p. 36 • *Audio Library**
• How Did You Learn English? TWE p. 377 • *English Language Learners Sourcebook*, p. 58 • *Spanish Summaries*, p. 35 • *Spanish Translations*, pp. 97–98 • *Audio Library** • *English, Yes!*	• *Interactive Reading Sourcebook*, pp. T141–T143 • *Interactive Reading Workbook*, p. 64 • *Theme Four Planning Guide*, p. 44 • *Audio Library**
• Behavior of Hosts and Guests, TWE p. 383 • Searching for Our Roots, TWE p. 394 • *English Language Learners Sourcebook*, pp. 59, 60, 61 • *Theme Four Planning Guide*, p. 49 • *Spanish Summaries*, p. 36 • *Spanish Translations*, pp. 99–102 • *Audio Library** • *English, Yes!*	• *Interactive Reading Sourcebook*, pp. T143–T146 • *Interactive Reading Workbook*, pp. 65–66 • Learning Disabled, TWE p. 385 • *Inclusion Strategies Sourcebook*, pp. 79–80 • *Audio Library**
• Idiomatic Expression, TWE p. 400 • *English Language Learners Sourcebook*, p. 62 • *Theme Four Planning Guide*, p. 55 • *Spanish Summaries*, p. 37 • *Spanish Translations*, pp. 103–106 • *Audio Library** • *English, Yes!*	• *Interactive Reading Sourcebook*, pp. T146–T148 • *Interactive Reading Workbook*, pp. 67–68 • Learning Disabled, TWE p. 396 • *Inclusion Strategies Sourcebook*, pp. 47–48 • *Theme Four Planning Guide*, p. 55 • *Audio Library**
• Pets Across Cultures, TWE p. 412 • *English Language Learners Sourcebook*, p. 63 • *Theme Four Planning Guide*, p. 63 • *Spanish Summaries*, p. 38 • *Audio Library** • *English, Yes!*	• *Interactive Reading Sourcebook*, pp. T149–T151 • *Interactive Reading Workbook*, pp. 69–70 • *Theme Four Planning Guide*, p. 63 • *Audio Library**

Lesson Schedule	Essential Lesson Support and Assessment	
Days 87–88 **Writing Workshop** Descriptive Writing: A Photo in Words Lesson and lesson support on SE/TWE pp. 420–423	• *Writing Assessment and Portfolio Management*, pp. 1–13, 23–25, 38–44	
Day 89 **Theme Assessment** Lesson and lesson support on SE/TWE pp. 424–425	• *Selection and Theme Assessment*, pp. 131–132 • *Testmaker: ExamView Pro* • *Performance Assessment*, p. 97 • *Writing Assessment and Portfolio Management*, pp. 1–12, 38–44	• *Initial Screening and Fluency Assessment*, Theme Four Reading Fluency
Theme 5: At the Crossroads Day 90 Lesson and lesson support on SE/TWE pp. 428–431	• *Theme Five Planning Guide*, pp. 1–3 • *Performance Assessment*, p. 73	
Days 91–92 **Amigo Brothers** Three-part instruction and selection support on SE/TWE pp. 432–443	**Lesson-Specific Instruction** • *Theme Five Planning Guide*, pp. 4–11 • *Selection Focus Transparency* 39 • *Active Reading Guide*,* p. 39 • *Literary Elements Transparency* 39 • *Selection Vocabulary Practice*, p. 26 • *Selection Quick Checks*,* p. 39 • *Selection and Theme Assessment*, pp. 69–70	• *Testmaker: ExamView Pro* • *Performance Assessment*, p. 37 **Systematic Language Instruction** • *Grammar and Composition Handbook*, Lesson 8.5 • *Vocabulary Power*, Lesson 19 • *Spelling Power*, Lesson 17
Day 93 **Your World** Three-part instruction and selection support on SE/TWE pp. 444–446 **Comparing Selections** SE/TWE p. 447 **Interdisciplinary Connection** Health, SE/TWE p. 448 **Listening, Speaking, and Viewing** Small-Group Discussions, SE/TWE p. 449	**Lesson-Specific Instruction** • *Theme Five Planning Guide*, pp. 12–16 • *Selection Focus Transparency* 40 • *Active Reading Guide*,* p. 40 • *Literary Elements Transparency* 40 • *Selection Quick Checks*,* p. 40 • *Selection and Theme Assessment*, pp. 69–70	• *Testmaker: ExamView Pro* • *Performance Assessment*, p. 37 **Systematic Language Instruction** • *Grammar and Composition Handbook*, Lesson 8.6 • *Vocabulary Power*, Lesson 20
Days 94–95 **The Scholarship Jacket** Three-part instruction and selection support on SE/TWE pp. 450–458	**Lesson-Specific Instruction** • *Theme Five Planning Guide*, pp. 17–24 • *Selection Focus Transparency* 41 • *Active Reading Guide*,* p. 41 • *Literary Elements Transparency* 41 • *Selection Vocabulary Practice*, p. 27 • *Selection Quick Checks*,* p. 41 • *Selection and Theme Assessment*, pp. 71–72	• *Testmaker: ExamView Pro* • *Performance Assessment*, p. 38 **Systematic Language Instruction** • *Grammar and Composition Handbook*, Lesson 9.2 • *Vocabulary Power*, Lesson 21 • *Spelling Power*, Lesson 18
Days 96–97 **All Summer in a Day** Three-part instruction and selection support on SE/TWE pp. 460–469 **Media Connection** Web Site, SE/TWE p. 459	**Lesson-Specific Instruction** • *Theme Five Planning Guide*, pp. 25–32 • *Selection Focus Transparency* 42 • *Active Reading Guide*,* p. 42 • *Literary Elements Transparency* 42 • *Selection Vocabulary Practice*, p. 28 • *Selection Quick Checks*,* p. 42	• *Selection and Theme Assessment*, pp. 73–74 • *Testmaker: ExamView Pro* • *Performance Assessment*, p. 39 • *inTIME* magazine, pp. 24–25 **Systematic Language Instruction** • *Grammar and Composition Handbook*,

SE: Student Edition TWE: Teacher Wraparound Edition *Also available in Spanish

English Language Learners (Add 30–45 Minutes a Day)	Special Needs/Strategic Intervention (Add 30–45 Minutes a Day)
• Describing the Topic, TWE p. 420 • *English Language Learners Sourcebook*, p. 9 • *English, Yes!*	• *Inclusion Strategies Sourcebook*, pp. 69–70
• *English Language Learners Sourcebook*, pp. 1–13 • *English, Yes!*	• Special Needs, TWE p. 425 • *Inclusion Strategies Sourcebook*, p. xii
• *English Language Learners Sourcebook*, pp. 1–13 • *English, Yes!*	• *Inclusion Strategies Sourcebook*, pp. vii–xii
• Spanish Words, TWE p. 434 • *English Language Learners Sourcebook*, p. 64 • *Spanish Summaries*, p. 39 • *Spanish Translations*, pp. 107–114 • *Audio Library** • *English, Yes!*	• *Interactive Reading Sourcebook*, pp. T152–T155 • *Interactive Reading Workbook*, pp. 71–74 • Emotional, TWE p. 436 • *Inclusion Strategies Sourcebook*, pp. 53–54 • *Theme Five Planning Guide*, p. 6 • *Audio Library**
• Group Discussion Tips, TWE p. 449 • *English Language Learners Sourcebook*, p. 65 • *Theme Five Planning Guide*, p. 14 • *Spanish Summaries*, p. 40 • *Audio Library** • *English, Yes!*	• *Interactive Reading Sourcebook*, pp. T155–T156 • *Interactive Reading Workbook*, p. 75 • *Inclusion Strategies Sourcebook*, pp. 73–74 • *Theme Five Planning Guide*, p. 14 • *Audio Library**
• Visualizing Words, TWE p. 452 • *English Language Learners Sourcebook*, p. 66 • *Theme Five Planning Guide*, p. 19 • *Spanish Summaries*, p. 41 • *Spanish Translations*, pp. 115–118 • *Audio Library** • *English, Yes!*	• *Interactive Reading Sourcebook*, pp. T157–T159 • *Interactive Reading Workbook*, pp. 76–77 • *Inclusion Strategies Sourcebook*, pp. 35–36, 43–44 • *Theme Five Planning Guide*, p. 19 • *Audio Library**
• Sunny Day and Rainy Day Activities, TWE p. 462 • *English Language Learners Sourcebook*, p. 67 • *Spanish Summaries*, p. 42 • *Spanish Translations*, pp. 119–122 • *Audio Library** • *English, Yes!*	• *Interactive Reading Sourcebook*, pp. T159–T162 • *Interactive Reading Workbook*, pp. 78–79 • Less-Proficient Readers, TWE p. 470 • *Theme Five Planning Guide*, p. 27 • *Audio Library**

Lesson Schedule	Essential Lesson Support and Assessment	
Days 96–97 (continued) **Reading and Thinking Skills** Drawing Conclusions, SE/TWE p. 470	Lesson 9.3 • *Vocabulary Power*, Lesson 22 • *Spelling Power*, Lesson 19	
Days 98–99 **Primer Lesson** and **The Bird Like No Other** Three-part instruction and selection support on SE/TWE pp. 471–479 **Technology Skills** Becoming an Active Viewer, SE/TWE pp. 480–481	**Lesson-Specific Instruction** • *Theme Five Planning Guide*, pp. 33–38 • *Selection Focus Transparency 43* • *Active Reading Guide*,* p. 43 • *Literary Elements Transparency 43* • *Selection Vocabulary Practice*, p. 29 • *Selection Quick Checks*,* p. 43	• *Selection and Theme Assessment*, pp. 75–76 • *Testmaker: ExamView Pro* • *Performance Assessment*, p. 40 **Systematic Language Instruction** • *Grammar and Composition Handbook*, Lesson 10.1
Days 100–101 **The Old Demon** and **The Boy and His Grandfather** Three-part instruction and selection support on SE/TWE pp. 482–498 **Grammar Link** Using Pronouns, SE/TWE p. 499	**Lesson-Specific Instruction** • *Theme Five Planning Guide*, pp. 39–44 • *Selection Focus Transparency 44* • *Active Reading Guide*,* p. 44 • *Literary Elements Transparency 44* • *Selection Vocabulary Practice*, p. 30 • *Selection Quick Checks*,* p. 44 • *Selection and Theme Assessment*, pp. 77–78	• *Testmaker: ExamView Pro* • *Performance Assessment*, p. 41 **Systematic Language Instruction** • *Grammar and Composition Handbook*, Lesson 10.2 • *Vocabulary Power*, Lesson 23 • *Spelling Power*, Lesson 20
Days 102–105 **The Monsters Are Due on Maple Street** Three-part instruction and selection support on SE/TWE pp. 504–527 **Genre Focus** Drama, SE/TWE pp. 500–501 **Active Reading Strategies** Tips for Reading a Drama, SE/TWE pp. 502–503 **Media Connection** Web Site, SE/TWE p. 528 **Vocabulary Skills** Idioms, SE/TWE p. 529	**Lesson-Specific Instruction** • *Theme Five Planning Guide*, pp. 45–52 • *Selection Focus Transparency 45* • *Active Reading Guide*,* p. 45 • *Literary Elements Transparency 45* • *Selection Vocabulary Practice*, p. 31 • *Selection Quick Checks*,* p. 45 • *Selection and Theme Assessment*, pp. 79–80 • *Testmaker: ExamView Pro* • *Performance Assessment*, p. 42 • *inTIME* magazine, pp. 24–25	**Systematic Language Instruction** • *Grammar and Composition Handbook*, Lesson 10.3 • *Vocabulary Power*, Unit 5 Review/Test • *Spelling Power*, Unit 5 Review/Proofreading
Days 106–107 **Writing Workshop** Expository Writing: Definition Essay Lesson and lesson support on SE/TWE pp. 530–533	• *Writing Assessment and Portfolio Management*, pp. 1–13, 26–28, 38–44	
Day 108 **Theme Assessment** Lesson and lesson support on SE/TWE pp. 534–535	• *Selection and Theme Assessment*, pp. 133–134 • *Testmaker: ExamView Pro* • *Performance Assessment*, p. 98 • *Writing Assessment and Portfolio Management*, pp. 1–12, 38–44	• *Initial Screening and Fluency Assessment*, Theme Five Reading Fluency

SE: Student Edition **TWE:** Teacher Wraparound Edition *Also available in Spanish

English Language Learners (Add 30–45 Minutes a Day)	Special Needs/Strategic Intervention (Add 30–45 Minutes a Day)
• Forms of Address, TWE p. 472 • *English Language Learners Sourcebook*, p. 68 • *Spanish Summaries*, p. 43 • *Audio Library** • *English, Yes!*	• *Interactive Reading Sourcebook*, pp. T163–T165 • *Interactive Reading Workbook*, p. 80 • Less-Proficient Readers, TWE p. 474 • *Theme Five Planning Guide*, p. 35 • *Audio Library**
• Describing a Setting, TWE p. 483 • *English Language Learners Sourcebook*, p. 69 • *Theme Five Planning Guide*, p. 41 • *Spanish Summaries*, p. 44 • *Spanish Translations*, p. 123 • *Audio Library** • *English, Yes!*	• *Interactive Reading Sourcebook*, pp. T165–T168 • *Interactive Reading Workbook*, pp. 81–84 • Less-Proficient Readers, TWE p. 490 • *Inclusion Strategies Sourcebook*, pp. 21–22 • *Audio Library**
• Understanding Drama, TWE p. 500 • Idioms, TWE pp. 506, 529 • Symbolism in Names, TWE p. 512 • Nonverbal Language, TWE p. 521 • *English Language Learners Sourcebook*, pp. 70, 71, 72, 73 • *Spanish Summaries*, p. 45 • *Spanish Translations*, pp. 124–138 • *Audio Library** • *English, Yes!*	• *Interactive Reading Sourcebook*, pp. T169–T171 • *Interactive Reading Workbook*, pp. 85–88 • Less-Proficient Readers, TWE pp. 503, 510, 519 • *Inclusion Strategies Sourcebook*, pp. 75–76 • *Theme Five Planning Guide*, p. 47 • *Audio Library**
• Preparing for Definition Essays, TWE p. 530 • *English Language Learners Sourcebook*, p. 9 • *English, Yes!*	
• *English Language Learners Sourcebook*, pp. 1–13 • *English, Yes!*	• Special Needs, TWE p. 535 • *Inclusion Strategies Sourcebook*, p. xii

Lesson Schedule	Essential Lesson Support and Assessment
Theme 6: Twists and Turns Day 109 Lesson and lesson support on SE/TWE pp. 538–541	• *Theme Six Planning Guide*, pp. 1–3 • *Performance Assessment*, p. 74
Days 110–111 Charles and No News Three-part instruction and selection support on SE/TWE pp. 543–552 **Media Connection** Comic Strip, SE/TWE p. 542 **Grammar Link** Using Commas Correctly, SE/TWE p. 553	**Lesson-Specific Instruction** • *Theme Six Planning Guide*, pp. 4–9 • *Selection Focus Transparency* 46 • *Active Reading Guide*,* p. 46 • *Literary Elements Transparency* 46 • *Selection Vocabulary Practice*, p. 32 • *Selection Quick Checks*,* p. 46 • *Selection and Theme Assessment*, pp. 81–82 • *Testmaker: ExamView Pro* • *Performance Assessment*, p. 43 **Systematic Language Instruction** • *Grammar and Composition Handbook*, Lesson 10.4 • *Vocabulary Power*, Lesson 24 • *Spelling Power*, Lesson 21
Days 112–113 Who's on First Three-part instruction and selection support on SE/TWE pp. 554–561 **Technology Skills** Multimedia, SE/TWE pp. 562–563	**Lesson-Specific Instruction** • *Theme Six Planning Guide*, pp. 10–17 • *Selection Focus Transparency* 47 • *Active Reading Guide*,* p. 47 • *Literary Elements Transparency* 47 • *Selection Quick Checks*,* p. 47 • *Selection and Theme Assessment*, p. 83 • *Testmaker: ExamView Pro* • *Performance Assessment*, p. 44 **Systematic Language Instruction** • *Grammar and Composition Handbook*, Lesson 10.5
Day 114 After Twenty Years Three-part instruction and selection support on SE/TWE pp. 564–570 **Listening, Speaking, and Viewing** Storytelling, SE/TWE p. 571	**Lesson-Specific Instruction** • *Theme Six Planning Guide*, pp. 18–25 • *Selection Focus Transparency* 48 • *Active Reading Guide*,* p. 48 • *Literary Elements Transparency* 48 • *Selection Vocabulary Practice*, p. 33 • *Selection Quick Checks*,* p. 48 • *Selection and Theme Assessment*, pp. 84 • *Testmaker: ExamView Pro* • *Performance Assessment*, p. 48 **Systematic Language Instruction** • *Grammar and Composition Handbook*, Lesson 11.1 • *Vocabulary Power*, Lesson 25 • *Spelling Power*, Lesson 22
Days 115–117 The Million-Pound Bank Note Three-part instruction and selection support on SE/TWE pp. 572–589	**Lesson-Specific Instruction** • *Theme Six Planning Guide*, pp. 26–33 • *Selection Focus Transparency* 49 • *Active Reading Guide*,* p. 49 • *Literary Elements Transparency* 49 • *Selection Vocabulary Practice*, p. 34 • *Selection Quick Checks*,* p. 49 • *Selection and Theme Assessment*, pp. 85–86 • *Testmaker: ExamView Pro* • *Performance Assessment*, p. 46 **Systematic Language Instruction** • *Grammar and Composition Handbook*, Lesson 11.2
Days 118–119 The Force of Luck Three-part instruction and selection support on SE/TWE pp. 590–599 **Comparing Selections** SE/TWE p. 600 **Interdisciplinary Connection** Social Studies, SE/TWE p. 601	**Lesson-Specific Instruction** • *Theme Six Planning Guide*, pp. 34–41 • *Selection Focus Transparency* 50 • *Active Reading Guide*,* p. 50 • *Literary Elements Transparency* 50 • *Selection Vocabulary Practice*, p. 35 • *Selection Quick Checks*,* p. 50 • *Selection and Theme Assessment*, pp. 87–88 • *Testmaker: ExamView Pro* • *Performance Assessment*, p. 47 **Systematic Language Instruction** • *Grammar and Composition Handbook*, Lesson 11.3 • *Vocabulary Power*, Lesson 26 • *Spelling Power*, Lesson 23
Days 120–121 Beware of the Dog Three-part instruction and selection support on SE/TWE pp. 602–615	**Lesson-Specific Instruction** • *Theme Six Planning Guide*, pp. 42–49 • *Selection Focus Transparency* 51 • *Active Reading Guide*,* p. 51 • *Literary Elements Transparency* 51 • *Selection Vocabulary Practice*, p. 36 • *Selection Quick Checks*,* p. 51 • *Selection and Theme Assessment*, pp. 89–90 • *Testmaker: ExamView Pro* • *Performance Assessment*, p. 48

SE: Student Edition TWE: Teacher Wraparound Edition *Also available in Spanish

English Language Learners (Add 30–45 Minutes a Day)	Special Needs/Strategic Intervention (Add 30–45 Minutes a Day)
• *English Language Learners Sourcebook*, pp. 1–13 • *English, Yes!*	• *Inclusion Strategies Sourcebook*, pp. vii–xii
• Cultural Differences, TWE p. 544 • *English Language Learners Sourcebook*, p. 74 • *Spanish Summaries*, p. 46 • *Audio Library** • *English, Yes!*	• *Interactive Reading Sourcebook*, pp. T172–T174 • *Interactive Reading Workbook*, pp. 89–90 • *Inclusion Strategies Sourcebook*, pp. 71–72 • *Theme Six Planning Guide*, p. 6 • *Audio Library**
• Understanding Humor, TWE p. 556 • *English Language Learners Sourcebook*, p. 75 • *Spanish Summaries*, p. 47 • *Audio Library** • *English, Yes!*	• *Interactive Reading Sourcebook*, pp. T175–T177 • *Interactive Reading Workbook*, pp. 91–92 • *Inclusion Strategies Sourcebook*, pp. 43–44 • *Theme Six Planning Guide*, p. 12 • *Audio Library**
• Language from Another Era, TWE p. 566 • Group Storytelling, TWE p. 571 • *English Language Learners Sourcebook*, pp. 76, 77 • *Theme Six Planning Guide*, p. 20 • *Spanish Summaries*, p. 48 • *Spanish Translations*, pp. 139–141 • *Audio Library** • *English, Yes!*	• *Interactive Reading Sourcebook*, pp. T177–T179 • *Interactive Reading Workbook*, pp. 93–94 • *Inclusion Strategies Sourcebook*, pp. 51–52, 95–96 • *Theme Six Planning Guide*, p. 20 • *Audio Library**
• Using a Flowchart, TWE p. 574 • *English Language Learners Sourcebook*, p. 78 • *Spanish Summaries*, p. 49 • *Spanish Translations*, pp. 142–157 • *Audio Library** • *English, Yes!*	• *Interactive Reading Sourcebook*, pp. T180–T183 • *Interactive Reading Workbook*, pp. 95–98 • Learning Disabled, TWE p. 576 • *Inclusion Strategies Sourcebook*, pp. 83–84 • *Theme Six Planning Guide*, p. 28 • *Audio Library**
• Folktales, TWE p. 592 • *English Language Learners Sourcebook*, p. 79 • *Spanish Summaries*, p. 50 • *Audio Library** • *English, Yes!*	• *Interactive Reading Sourcebook*, pp. T183–T185 • *Interactive Reading Workbook*, pp. 99–100 • Less-Proficient Readers, TWE p. 594 • *Inclusion Strategies Sourcebook*, pp. 85–86 • *Audio Library**
• Creating a Map, TWE p. 604 • *English Language Learners Sourcebook*, p. 80 • *Spanish Summaries*, p. 51 • *Spanish Translations*, pp. 158–165 • *Audio Library** • *English, Yes!*	• *Interactive Reading Sourcebook*, pp. T186–T188 • *Interactive Reading Workbook*, pp. 101–102 • Less-Proficient Readers, TWE p. 606 • Learning Disabled, TWE p. 610 • *Inclusion Strategies Sourcebook*, pp. 87–88

Lesson Schedule	Essential Lesson Support and Assessment
Days 120–121 (continued)	**Systematic Language Instruction** • *Grammar and Composition Handbook*, Lesson 11.4 • *Vocabulary Power*, Lesson 27 • *Spelling Power*, Lesson 24
Days 122–123 The Highwayman Three-part instruction and selection support on SE/TWE pp. 620–627 **Genre Focus** Poetry, SE/TWE pp. 616–617 **Active Reading Strategies** Tips for Reading Poetry, SE/TWE pp. 618–619	**Lesson-Specific Instruction** • *Theme Six Planning Guide*, pp. 50–57 • *Selection Focus Transparency* 52 • *Active Reading Guide,** p. 52 • *Literary Elements Transparency* 52 • *Selection Quick Checks,** p. 52 • *Selection and Theme Assessment*, pp. 91–92 • *Testmaker: ExamView Pro* • *Performance Assessment*, p. 49 **Systematic Language Instruction** • *Grammar and Composition Handbook*, Lesson 11.5 • *Vocabulary Power*, Lesson 28
Days 124–125 Annabel Lee Three-part instruction and selection support on SE/TWE pp. 628–632 **Vocabulary Skills** Multiple-Meaning Words, SE/TWE p. 633	**Lesson-Specific Instruction** • *Theme Six Planning Guide*, pp. 58–62 • *Selection Focus Transparency* 53 • *Active Reading Guide,** p. 53 • *Literary Elements Transparency* 53 • *Selection Quick Checks,** p. 53 • *Selection and Theme Assessment*, p. 93 • *Testmaker: ExamView Pro* • *Performance Assessment*, p. 50 **Systematic Language Instruction** • *Grammar and Composition Handbook*, Lesson 11.6
Days 126–127 The Cremation of Sam McGee Three-part instruction and selection support on SE/TWE pp. 635–642 **Media Connection** Oral History, SE/TWE p. 634 **Reading and Thinking Skills** Identifying Cause-and-Effect Relationships, SE/TWE p. 643	**Lesson-Specific Instruction** • *Theme Six Planning Guide*, pp. 63–70 • *Selection Focus Transparency* 54 • *Active Reading Guide,** p. 54 • *Literary Elements Transparency* 54 • *Selection Quick Checks,** p. 54 • *Selection and Theme Assessment*, p. 94 • *Testmaker: ExamView Pro* • *Performance Assessment*, p. 51 **Systematic Language Instruction** • *Grammar and Composition Handbook*, Lesson 11.7 • *Vocabulary Power*, Unit 6 Review/Test • *Spelling Power*, Unit 6 Review/Proofreading
Days 128–129 Writing Workshop Narrative Writing: Short Story Lesson and lesson support on SE/TWE pp. 644–647	• *Writing Assessment and Portfolio Management*, pp. 1–13, 29–31, 38–44
Day 130 Theme Assessment Lesson and lesson support on SE/TWE pp. 648–649	• *Selection and Theme Assessment*, pp. 135–136 • *Testmaker: ExamView Pro* • *Performance Assessment*, p. 98 • *Writing Assessment and Portfolio Management*, pp. 1–12, 38–44 • *Initial Screening and Fluency Assessment*, Theme Six Reading Fluency
Theme 7: A Different Dimension Day 131 Lesson and lesson support on SE/TWE pp. 652–655	• *Theme Seven Planning Guide*, pp. 1–3 • *Performance Assessment*, p. 75

SE: Student Edition TWE: Teacher Wraparound Edition *Also available in Spanish

English Language Learners (Add 30–45 Minutes a Day)	Special Needs/Strategic Intervention (Add 30–45 Minutes a Day)
	• *Theme Six Planning Guide*, p. 44 • *Audio Library**
• World Poetry, TWE p. 616 • Picture the Highwayman, TWE p. 622 • *English Language Learners Sourcebook*, p. 81 • *Spanish Summaries*, p. 52 • *Audio Library** • *English, Yes!*	• *Interactive Reading Sourcebook*, pp. T188–T190 • *Interactive Reading Workbook*, pp. 103–104 • *Inclusion Strategies Sourcebook*, pp. 43–44, 45–46 • *Theme Six Planning Guide*, p. 52 • *Audio Library**
• Multiple-Meaning Words, TWE p. 633 • *English Language Learners Sourcebook*, p. 82 • *Theme Six Planning Guide*, p. 60 • *Spanish Summaries*, p. 53 • *Audio Library** • *English, Yes!*	• *Interactive Reading Sourcebook*, pp. T191–T193 • *Interactive Reading Workbook*, pp. 105–106 • Less-Proficient Readers, TWE p. 629 • *Theme Six Planning Guide*, p. 60 • *Audio Library**
• Ancient Burial Rites, TWE p. 637 • *English Language Learners Sourcebook*, p. 83 • *Spanish Summaries*, p. 54 • *Spanish Translations*, pp. 166–170 • *Audio Library** • *English, Yes!*	• *Interactive Reading Sourcebook*, pp. T193–T196 • *Interactive Reading Workbook*, pp. 107–108 • Less-Proficient Readers, TWE p. 643 • *Inclusion Strategies Sourcebook*, pp. 25–26, 67–68 • *Theme Six Planning Guide*, p. 65 • *Audio Library**
• Elements of Poems, TWE p. 644 • *English Language Learners Sourcebook*, p. 9 • *English, Yes!*	• *Inclusion Strategies Sourcebook*, pp. 73–74
• *English Language Learners Sourcebook*, pp. 1–13 • *English, Yes!*	• Special Needs, TWE p. 649 • *Inclusion Strategies Sourcebook*, p. xii
• *English Language Learners Sourcebook*, pp. 1–13 • *English, Yes!*	• *Inclusion Strategies Sourcebook*, pp. vii–xii

Lesson Schedule	Essential Lesson Support and Assessment	
Days 132–134 **Lob's Girl** Three-part instruction and selection support on SE/TWE pp. 658–671 **Media Connection** Magazine Article, SE/TWE pp. 656–657 **Reading and Thinking Skills** Monitoring Comprehension, SE/TWE p. 672 **Writing Skills** Using Sentence Variety, SE/TWE p. 673	**Lesson-Specific Instruction** • *Theme Seven Planning Guide*, pp. 4–11 • *Selection Focus Transparency* 55 • *Active Reading Guide*,* p. 55 • *Literary Elements Transparency* 55 • *Selection Vocabulary Practice*, p. 37 • *Selection Quick Checks*,* p. 55	• *Selection and Theme Assessment*, pp. 95–96 • *Testmaker: ExamView Pro* • *Performance Assessment*, p. 52 **Systematic Language Instruction** • *Grammar and Composition Handbook*, Lesson 11.8
Days 135–136 **Key Item** Three-part instruction and selection support on SE/TWE pp. 674–680 **Interdisciplinary Connection** Communication, SE/TWE p. 681	**Lesson-Specific Instruction** • *Theme Seven Planning Guide*, pp. 12–19 • *Selection Focus Transparency* 56 • *Active Reading Guide*,* p. 56 • *Literary Elements Transparency* 56 • *Selection Vocabulary Practice*, p. 38 • *Selection Quick Checks*,* p. 56 • *Selection and Theme Assessment*, pp. 97–98	• *Testmaker: ExamView Pro* • *Performance Assessment*, p. 53 • *inTIME* magazine, pp. 18–20 **Systematic Language Instruction** • *Grammar and Composition Handbook*, Lesson 11.9 • *Vocabulary Power*, Lesson 29 • *Spelling Power*, Lesson 25
Days 137–139 **The Smallest Dragonboy** Three-part instruction and selection support on SE/TWE pp. 682–697	**Lesson-Specific Instruction** • *Theme Seven Planning Guide*, pp. 20–27 • *Selection Focus Transparency* 57 • *Active Reading Guide*,* p. 57 • *Literary Elements Transparency* 57 • *Selection Vocabulary Practice*, p. 39 • *Selection Quick Checks*,* p. 57	• *Selection and Theme Assessment*, pp. 99–100 • *Testmaker: ExamView Pro* • *Performance Assessment*, p. 54 **Systematic Language Instruction** • *Grammar and Composition Handbook*, Lesson 11.10
Days 140–141 **Aunty Misery** Three-part instruction and selection support on SE/TWE pp. 700–705 **Genre Focus** Legends, Myths, and Folklore, SE/TWE p. 698 **Active Reading Strategies** SE/TWE p. 699	**Lesson-Specific Instruction** • *Theme Seven Planning Guide*, pp. 28–32 • *Selection Focus Transparency* 58 • *Active Reading Guide*,* p. 58 • *Literary Elements Transparency* 58 • *Selection Vocabulary Practice*, p. 40 • *Selection Quick Checks*,* p. 58 • *Selection and Theme Assessment*, p. 101	• *Testmaker: ExamView Pro* • *Performance Assessment*, p. 55 **Systematic Language Instruction** • *Grammar and Composition Handbook*, Lesson 12.1 • *Vocabulary Power*, Lesson 30
Days 142–143 **Strawberries** Three-part instruction and selection support on SE/TWE pp. 706–711 **Grammar Link** Capitalization, SE/TWE p. 712	**Lesson-Specific Instruction** • *Theme Seven Planning Guide*, pp. 33–40 • *Selection Focus Transparency* 59 • *Active Reading Guide*,* p. 59 • *Literary Elements Transparency* 59 • *Selection Vocabulary Practice*, p. 41 • *Selection Quick Checks*,* p. 59	• *Selection and Theme Assessment*, p. 102 • *Testmaker: ExamView Pro* • *Performance Assessment*, p. 56 **Systematic Language Instruction** • *Grammar and Composition Handbook*, Lesson 12.2
Days 144–145 **Atalanta's Race** and **Atalanta** Three-part instruction and selection support on SE/TWE pp. 713–724	**Lesson-Specific Instruction** • *Theme Seven Planning Guide*, pp. 41–46 • *Selection Focus Transparency* 60 • *Active Reading Guide*,* p. 60 • *Literary Elements Transparency* 60 • *Selection Vocabulary Practice*, p. 42 • *Selection Quick Checks*,* p. 60 • *Selection and Theme Assessment*, pp. 103–104	• *Testmaker: ExamView Pro* • *Performance Assessment*, p. 57 • *inTIME* magazine, p. 27 **Systematic Language Instruction** • *Grammar and Composition Handbook*, Lesson 12.3 • *Spelling Power*, Lesson 26

SE: Student Edition **TWE: Teacher Wraparound Edition** ***Also available in Spanish**

English Language Learners (Add 30–45 Minutes a Day)	Special Needs/Strategic Intervention (Add 30–45 Minutes a Day)
• Life in a Fishing Village, TWE p. 660 • *English Language Learners Sourcebook*, p. 84 • *Theme Seven Planning Guide*, p. 6 • *Spanish Summaries*, p. 55 • *Audio Library** • *English, Yes!*	• *Interactive Reading Sourcebook*, pp. T197–T199 • *Interactive Reading Workbook*, pp. 109–110 • Physically Disabled, TWE p. 657 • Less-Proficient Readers, TWE pp. 662, 672 • *Inclusion Strategies Sourcebook*, pp. 91–92 • *Theme Seven Planning Guide*, p. 6 • *Audio Library**
• Computer Terminology, TWE p. 676 • *English Language Learners Sourcebook*, p. 85 • *Spanish Summaries*, p. 56 • *Audio Library** • *English, Yes!*	• *Interactive Reading Sourcebook*, pp. T199–T202 • *Interactive Reading Workbook*, pp. 111–112 • *Inclusion Strategies Sourcebook*, pp. 93–94 • *Theme Seven Planning Guide*, p. 14 • *Audio Library**
• Dragon Stories, TWE p. 684 • *English Language Learners Sourcebook*, p. 86 • *Spanish Summaries*, p. 57 • *Spanish Translations*, pp. 171–182 • *Audio Library** • *English, Yes!*	• *Interactive Reading Sourcebook*, pp. T202–T204 • *Interactive Reading Workbook*, pp. 113–116 • Less-Proficient Readers, TWE p. 686 • *Inclusion Strategies Sourcebook*, pp. 97–98 • *Theme Seven Planning Guide*, p. 22 • *Audio Library**
• *Theme Seven Planning Guide*, p. 30 • *Spanish Summaries*, p. 58 • *Spanish Translations*, pp. 183–184 • *Audio Library** • *English, Yes!*	• *Interactive Reading Sourcebook*, pp. T205–T207 • *Interactive Reading Workbook*, pp. 117–118 • *Audio Library**
• Folktales, TWE p. 708 • *English Language Learners Sourcebook*, p. 87 • *Spanish Summaries*, p. 59 • *Spanish Translations*, pp. 185–186 • *Audio Library** • *English, Yes!*	• *Interactive Reading Sourcebook*, pp. T208–T210 • *Interactive Reading Workbook*, pp. 119–120 • *Theme Seven Planning Guide*, p. 35 • *Audio Library**
• Women in Society, TWE p. 714 • *English Language Learners Sourcebook*, p. 88 • *Theme Seven Planning Guide*, p. 43 • *Spanish Summaries*, p. 60 • *Audio Library** • *English, Yes!*	• *Interactive Reading Sourcebook*, pp. T210–T213 • *Interactive Reading Workbook*, pp. 121–122 • Less-Proficient Readers, TWE p. 718 • *Inclusion Strategies Sourcebook*, pp. 81–82, 89–90 • *Audio Library**

Lesson Schedule	Essential Lesson Support and Assessment	
Days 146–147 Cat and Rat: The Legend of the Chinese Zodiac Three-part instruction and selection support on SE/TWE pp. 725–734 **Vocabulary Skills** Analyzing Word Parts, SE/TWE p. 735	**Lesson-Specific Instruction** • *Theme Seven Planning Guide*, pp. 47–54 • *Selection Focus Transparency* 61 • *Active Reading Guide*,* p. 61 • *Literary Elements Transparency* 61 • *Selection Vocabulary Practice*, p. 43 • *Selection Quick Checks*,* p. 61	• *Selection and Theme Assessment*, pp. 105–106 • *Testmaker: ExamView Pro* • *Performance Assessment*, p. 58 **Systematic Language Instruction** • *Grammar and Composition Handbook*, Lesson 12.4 • *Vocabulary Power*, Lesson 31
Day 148 Icarus and Daedalus Three-part instruction and selection support on SE/TWE pp. 736–741	**Lesson-Specific Instruction** • *Theme Seven Planning Guide*, pp. 55–62 • *Selection Focus Transparency* 62 • *Active Reading Guide*,* p. 62 • *Literary Elements Transparency* 62 • *Selection Vocabulary Practice*, p. 44 • *Selection Quick Checks*,* p. 62	• *Selection and Theme Assessment*, pp. 107–108 • *Testmaker: ExamView Pro* • *Performance Assessment*, p. 59 **Systematic Language Instruction** • *Grammar and Composition Handbook*, Lesson 13.1 • *Spelling Power*, Lesson 27
Days 149–150 Prometheus Three-part instruction and selection support on SE/TWE pp. 742–746 **Comparing Selections** SE/TWE p. 747	**Lesson-Specific Instruction** • *Theme Seven Planning Guide*, pp. 63–70 • *Selection Focus Transparency* 63 • *Active Reading Guide*,* p. 63 • *Literary Elements Transparency* 63 • *Selection Vocabulary Practice*, p. 45 • *Selection Quick Checks*,* p. 63 • *Selection and Theme Assessment*, pp. 107–108	• *Testmaker: ExamView Pro* • *Performance Assessment*, p. 59 **Systematic Language Instruction** • *Grammar and Composition Handbook*, Lesson 13.2 • *Vocabulary Power*, Lesson 32 • *Spelling Power*, Lesson 28
Days 151–152 The Bunyans and Brer Rabbit and Brer Lion Three-part instruction and selection support on SE/TWE pp. 749–759 **Media Connection** Opera Libretto, SE/TWE p. 748	**Lesson-Specific Instruction** • *Theme Seven Planning Guide*, pp. 71–76 • *Selection Focus Transparency* 64 • *Active Reading Guide*,* p. 64 • *Literary Elements Transparency* 64 • *Selection Vocabulary Practice*, p. 46 • *Selection Quick Checks*,* p. 64 • *Selection and Theme Assessment*, pp. 109–110	• *Testmaker: ExamView Pro* • *Performance Assessment*, p. 60 **Systematic Language Instruction** • *Grammar and Composition Handbook*, Lesson 13.3–13.4 • *Vocabulary Power*, Unit 7 Review/Test • *Spelling Power*, Unit 7 Review/Proofreading
Days 153–154 Writing Workshop Expository Writing: Book Review Lesson and lesson support on SE/TWE pp. 760–763	• *Writing Assessment and Portfolio Management*, pp. 1–13, 32–34, 38–44	
Day 155 Theme Assessment Lesson and lesson support on SE/TWE pp. 764–765	• *Selection and Theme Assessment*, pp. 137–138 • *Testmaker: ExamView Pro* • *Performance Assessment*, p. 99 • *Writing Assessment and Portfolio Management*, pp. 1–12, 38–44	• *Initial Screening and Fluency Assessment*, Theme Seven Reading Fluency
Theme 8: A Delicate Balance Day 156 Lesson and lesson support on SE/TWE pp. 768–771	• *Theme Eight Planning Guide*, pp. 1–3 • *Performance Assessment*, p. 76	

SE: Student Edition **TWE: Teacher Wraparound Edition** ***Also available in Spanish**

English Language Learners (Add 30–45 Minutes a Day)	Special Needs/Strategic Intervention (Add 30–45 Minutes a Day)
• Beastly English, TWE p. 728 • Word Families, TWE p. 735 • *English Language Learners Sourcebook*, pp. 89, 90 • *Spanish Summaries*, p. 61 • *Spanish Translations*, pp. 187–189 • *Audio Library** • *English, Yes!*	• *Interactive Reading Sourcebook*, pp. T213–T215 • *Interactive Reading Workbook*, pp. 123–124 • *Inclusion Strategies Sourcebook*, pp. 99–100 • *Theme Seven Planning Guide*, p. 49 • *Audio Library**
• Prefixes, TWE p. 739 • *English Language Learners Sourcebook*, p. 91 • *Spanish Summaries*, p. 62 • *Spanish Translations*, pp. 190–191 • *Audio Library** • *English, Yes!*	• *Interactive Reading Sourcebook*, pp. T216–T218 • *Interactive Reading Workbook*, pp. 125–126 • *Inclusion Strategies Sourcebook*, pp. 25–26 • *Theme Seven Planning Guide*, p. 57 • *Audio Library**
• Multiple-Meaning Words, TWE p. 745 • *English Language Learners Sourcebook*, p. 92 • *Spanish Summaries*, p. 63 • *Spanish Translations*, pp. 192–194 • *Audio Library** • *English, Yes!*	• *Interactive Reading Sourcebook*, pp. T218–T221 • *Interactive Reading Workbook*, pp. 127–128 • *Theme Seven Planning Guide*, p. 65 • *Audio Library**
• Dialect, TWE p. 755 • *English Language Learners Sourcebook*, p. 93 • *Theme Seven Planning Guide*, p. 73 • *Spanish Summaries*, p. 64 • *Audio Library** • *English, Yes!*	• *Interactive Reading Sourcebook*, pp. T221–T224 • *Interactive Reading Workbook*, pp. 129–131 • Less-Proficient Readers, TWE p. 752 • *Inclusion Strategies Sourcebook*, pp. 77–78 • *Theme Seven Planning Guide*, p. 73 • *Audio Library**
• Creating Book Jackets, TWE p. 760 • *English Language Learners Sourcebook*, p. 9 • *English, Yes!*	• Learning Disabled, TWE p. 762 • *Inclusion Strategies Sourcebook*, pp. 67–68
• *English Language Learners Sourcebook*, pp. 1–13 • *English, Yes!*	• Special Needs, TWE p. 765 • *Inclusion Strategies Sourcebook*, p. xii
• *English Language Learners Sourcebook*, pp. 1–13 • *English, Yes!*	• *Inclusion Strategies Sourcebook*, pp. vii–xii

Lesson Schedule	Essential Lesson Support and Assessment	
Day 157 **We Are All One** Three-part instruction and selection support on SE/TWE pp. 772–779	**Lesson-Specific Instruction** • *Theme Eight Planning Guide*, pp. 4–11 • *Selection Focus Transparency* 65 • *Active Reading Guide*,* p. 65 • *Literary Elements Transparency* 65 • *Selection Vocabulary Practice*, p. 47 • *Selection Quick Checks*,* p. 65 • *Selection and Theme Assessment*, pp. 111–112	• *Testmaker: ExamView Pro* • *Performance Assessment*, p. 61 **Systematic Language Instruction** • *Grammar and Composition Handbook*, Lesson 13.5 • *Vocabulary Power*, Lesson 33 • *Spelling Power*, Lesson 29
Days 158–159 **Birdfoot's Grampa and Miracles** Three-part instruction and selection support on SE/TWE pp. 782–786 **Media Connection** Journal, SE/TWE p. 780 **Vocabulary Skills** Dictionary Skills, SE/TWE p. 781	**Lesson-Specific Instruction** • *Theme Eight Planning Guide*, pp. 12–16 • *Selection Focus Transparency* 66 • *Active Reading Guide*,* p. 66 • *Literary Elements Transparency* 66 • *Selection Quick Checks*,* p. 66 • *Selection and Theme Assessment*, pp. 113–114	• *Testmaker: ExamView Pro* • *Performance Assessment*, p. 62 • *inTIME* magazine, pp. 8–9 **Systematic Language Instruction** • *Grammar and Composition Handbook*, Lesson 13.6
Days 160–162 **Rikki-tikki-tavi** Three-part instruction and selection support on SE/TWE pp. 788–804 **Media Connection** Movie Review, SE/TWE p. 787 **Interdisciplinary Connection** Science, SE/TWE p. 805	**Lesson-Specific Instruction** • *Theme Eight Planning Guide*, pp. 17–24 • *Selection Focus Transparency* 67 • *Active Reading Guide*,* p. 67 • *Literary Elements Transparency* 67 • *Selection Vocabulary Practice*, p. 48 • *Selection Quick Checks*,* p. 67 • *Selection and Theme Assessment*, pp. 115–116	• *Testmaker: ExamView Pro* • *Performance Assessment*, p. 63 **Systematic Language Instruction** • *Grammar and Composition Handbook*, Lesson 13.7 • *Spelling Power*, Lesson 30
Days 163–165 **Uncle Tony's Goat** Three-part instruction and selection support on SE/TWE pp. 806–815 **Grammar Link** Using Apostrophes to Show Possession, SE/TWE p. 816 **Listening, Speaking, and Viewing** Critical Viewing, SE/TWE p. 817	**Lesson-Specific Instruction** • *Theme Eight Planning Guide*, pp. 25–32 • *Selection Focus Transparency* 68 • *Active Reading Guide*,* p. 68 • *Literary Elements Transparency* 68 • *Selection Vocabulary Practice*, p. 49 • *Selection Quick Checks*,* p. 68 • *Selection and Theme Assessment*, pp. 117–118	• *Testmaker: ExamView Pro* • *Performance Assessment*, p. 64 **Systematic Language Instruction** • *Grammar and Composition Handbook*, Lesson 13.8 • *Vocabulary Power*, Lesson 34
Day 166 **Loo-Wit** Three-part instruction and selection support on SE/TWE pp. 818–821	**Lesson-Specific Instruction** • *Theme Eight Planning Guide*, pp. 33–37 • *Selection Focus Transparency* 69 • *Active Reading Guide*,* p. 69 • *Literary Elements Transparency* 69 • *Selection Quick Checks*,* p. 69 • *Selection and Theme Assessment*, pp. 119–120	• *Testmaker: ExamView Pro* • *Performance Assessment*, p. 65 • *inTIME* magazine, pp. 12–13 **Systematic Language Instruction** • *Grammar and Composition Handbook*, Lesson 13.9
Day 167 **The Flower-Fed Buffaloes** Three-part instruction and selection support on SE/TWE pp. 822–824 **Comparing Selections** SE/TWE p. 825	**Lesson-Specific Instruction** • *Theme Eight Planning Guide*, pp. 38–42 • *Selection Focus Transparency* 70 • *Active Reading Guide*,* p. 70 • *Literary Elements Transparency* 70 • *Selection Quick Checks*,* p. 70 • *Selection and Theme Assessment*, pp. 119–120 • *Testmaker: ExamView Pro*	• *Performance Assessment*, p. 65 • *inTIME* magazine, pp. 10–11, 16–17 **Systematic Language Instruction** • *Grammar and Composition Handbook*, Lesson 13.10 • *Vocabulary Power*, Lesson 35 • *Spelling Power*, Lesson 31

SE: Student Edition **TWE: Teacher Wraparound Edition** ***Also available in Spanish**

English Language Learners (Add 30–45 Minutes a Day)	Special Needs/Strategic Intervention (Add 30–45 Minutes a Day)
• Folktales, TWE p. 774 • *English Language Learners Sourcebook*, p. 94 • *Spanish Summaries*, p. 65 • *Spanish Translations*, pp. 195–198 • *Audio Library** • *English, Yes!*	• *Interactive Reading Sourcebook*, pp. T225–T227 • *Interactive Reading Workbook*, pp. 132–133 • *Audio Library**
• Sound/Symbol Correlation, TWE p. 781 • Indirect Quotations, TWE p. 783 • *English Language Learners Sourcebook*, pp. 95, 96 • *Spanish Summaries*, p. 66 • *Audio Library** • *English, Yes!*	• *Interactive Reading Sourcebook*, pp. T228–T230 • *Interactive Reading Workbook*, p. 134 • *Theme Eight Planning Guide*, p. 14 • *Audio Library**
• Understanding Long Sentences, TWE p. 790 • Predators, TWE p. 798 • *English Language Learners Sourcebook*, pp. 97, 98 • *Theme Eight Planning Guide*, p. 19 • *Spanish Summaries*, p. 67 • *Spanish Translations*, pp. 199–211 • *Audio Library** • *English, Yes!*	• *Interactive Reading Sourcebook*, pp. T230–T233 • *Interactive Reading Workbook*, pp. 135–138 • Visually Impaired, TWE p. 792 • *Theme Eight Planning Guide*, p. 19 • *Audio Library**
• Possessives, TWE p. 808 • Focus Groups, TWE p. 817 • *English Language Learners Sourcebook*, pp. 99, 100 • *Theme Eight Planning Guide*, p. 27 • *Spanish Summaries*, p. 68 • *Audio Library** • *English, Yes!*	• *Interactive Reading Sourcebook*, pp. T234–T237 • *Interactive Reading Workbook*, pp. 139–140 • *Theme Eight Planning Guide*, p. 27 • *Audio Library**
• *English Language Learners Sourcebook*, p. 101 • *Spanish Summaries*, p. 69 • *Audio Library** • *English, Yes!*	• *Interactive Reading Sourcebook*, pp. T237–T239 • *Interactive Reading Workbook*, p. 141 • *Theme Eight Planning Guide*, p. 35 • *Audio Library**
• *Theme Eight Planning Guide*, p. 40 • *Spanish Summaries*, p. 70 • *Spanish Translations*, p. 212 • *Audio Library** • *English, Yes!*	• *Interactive Reading Sourcebook*, pp. T240–T241 • *Interactive Reading Workbook*, p. 142 • *Audio Library**

Lesson Schedule	Essential Lesson Support and Assessment	
Days 168–169 Turkeys Three-part instruction and selection support on SE/TWE pp. 826–832 **Reading and Thinking Skills** Making Inferences, SE/TWE p. 833	**Lesson-Specific Instruction** • *Theme Eight Planning Guide*, pp. 43–49 • *Selection Focus Transparency 71* • *Active Reading Guide*,* p. 71 • *Literary Elements Transparency 71* • *Selection Vocabulary Practice*, p. 50 • *Selection Quick Checks*,* p. 71 • *Selection and Theme Assessment*, pp. 121–122	• *Testmaker: ExamView Pro* • *Performance Assessment*, p. 66 • in*TIME* magazine, pp. 16–17 **Systematic Language Instruction** • *Grammar and Composition Handbook*, Lessons 14.1–14.2 • *Vocabulary Power*, Lesson 36 • *Spelling Power*, Lesson 32
Day 170 The Pasture Three-part instruction and selection support on SE/TWE pp. 834–837	**Lesson-Specific Instruction** • *Theme Eight Planning Guide*, pp. 50–54 • *Selection Focus Transparency 72* • *Active Reading Guide*,* p. 72 • *Literary Elements Transparency 72* • *Selection Quick Checks*,* p. 72	• *Selection and Theme Assessment*, p. 123 • *Testmaker: ExamView Pro* • *Performance Assessment*, p. 67 **Systematic Language Instruction** • *Grammar and Composition Handbook*, Lesson 14.3
Days 171–172 Short Poems Three-part instruction and selection support on SE/TWE pp. 840–845 **Genre Focus** Short Forms of Poetry, SE/TWE pp. 838–839	**Lesson-Specific Instruction** • *Theme Eight Planning Guide*, pp. 55–59 • *Selection Focus Transparency 73* • *Active Reading Guide*,* p. 73 • *Literary Elements Transparency 73* • *Selection Quick Checks*,* p. 73 • *Selection and Theme Assessment*, p. 124 • *Testmaker: ExamView Pro*	• *Performance Assessment*, p. 68 **Systematic Language Instruction** • *Grammar and Composition Handbook*, Lessons 14.4–14.5 • *Vocabulary Power*, Unit 8 Review/Test • *Spelling Power*, Unit 8 Review/Proofreading
Days 173–174 Writing Workshop Expository Writing: Research Report Lesson and lesson support on SE/TWE pp. 846–849	• *Writing Assessment and Portfolio Management*, pp. 1–13, 35–37, 38–44	
Day 175 Theme Assessment Lesson and lesson support on SE/TWE pp. 850–851	• *Selection and Theme Assessment*, pp. 139–140 • *Testmaker: ExamView Pro* • *Performance Assessment*, p. 99 • *Writing Assessment and Portfolio Management*, pp. 1–12, 38–44	• *Initial Screening and Fluency Assessment*, Theme Eight Reading Fluency

SE: Student Edition **TWE: Teacher Wraparound Edition** ***Also available in Spanish**

English Language Learners (Add 30–45 Minutes a Day)	Special Needs/Strategic Intervention (Add 30–45 Minutes a Day)
• *Theme Eight Planning Guide*, p. 45 • *Spanish Summaries*, p. 71 • *Spanish Translations*, pp. 213–214 • *Audio Library** • *English, Yes!*	• *Interactive Reading Sourcebook*, pp. T242–T244 • *Interactive Reading Workbook*, pp. 143–144 • Learning Disabled, TWE p. 828 • Less-Proficient Readers, TWE p. 833 • *Audio Library**
• *Theme Eight Planning Guide*, p. 52 • *Spanish Summaries*, p. 72 • *Spanish Translations*, p. 215 • *Audio Library** • *English, Yes!*	• *Interactive Reading Sourcebook*, pp. T244–T247 • *Interactive Reading Workbook*, p. 145 • *Theme Eight Planning Guide*, p. 52 • *Audio Library**
• Translation, TWE p. 838 • *Spanish Summaries*, p. 73 • *Spanish Translations*, p. 216 • *Audio Library** • *English, Yes!*	• *Interactive Reading Sourcebook*, pp. T247–T249 • *Interactive Reading Workbook*, p. 146 • *Theme Eight Planning Guide*, p. 57 • *Audio Library**
• Discussing the Issue, TWE p. 846 • *English Language Learners Sourcebook*, p. 9 • *English, Yes!*	• *Inclusion Strategies Sourcebook*, pp. 75–76
• *English Language Learners Sourcebook*, pp. 1–13 • *English, Yes!*	• Special Needs, TWE p. 851 • *Inclusion Strategies Sourcebook*, p. xii

Teaching English Language Learners

by Dr. Jane Fell Greene

Helping English language learners succeed in your language arts classroom requires an understanding of the problems and roadblocks they face, as well as a knowledge of strategies that can help such students gain competence and confidence in using English. The following material is provided as background support for you as you work with your students who are learning English.

Language/Dialect

Nearly 7,500 distinct languages are known to be spoken in the 191 countries of the world. Fewer than 2,000 of those languages have invented orthographic (writing) systems. Linguists have identified distinct families of languages from which modern languages have emerged. Some languages are technically not distinct languages since they are mutually intelligible. These languages are categorized as different languages based on their countries' geographic boundaries, but linguists would say that such languages are really dialects of the same language. Other languages have dialects that are so distinct that they are not mutually intelligible.

Every speaker speaks a dialect, or a particular version of a language. Dialects may be ethnic or regional. In the United States, speakers of English are almost always able to code-switch; that is, they are able to change from one dialect to another. The English dialect that is most widely used by educated speakers and writers is called Standard English.

Phonology

Phonology is the study of sounds produced in spoken language. In each language, each isolated speech sound is called a phoneme. Phonology examines how phonemes interact with each other. Phonology explains the phonological processes in a language as they are related to the rules of production.

Orthography

Orthography is the study of writing systems. The English writing system is alphabetic, so its orthographic system is spelling, a sound-to-symbol code. Speakers of various languages have invented various orthographic systems to map speech to print. Most of the world's spoken languages have no orthographic systems; that is, they have no written forms.

Morphology

Morphology is the study of word formation and structure. In each language, the smallest units of meaning are called morphemes. Morphology studies how words are put together from their smaller parts and the rules governing this process. The English word *cats*, for example, contains the free morpheme *cat* and the bound morpheme for plural, *-s*. Students whose languages do not have these kinds of suffixes can be predicted to have difficulty conceptualizing them linguistically. They will need to understand the linguistic process of adding or altering meaning via morphology before they can be expected to understand and apply the meanings of English morphemes.

Syntax

Syntax is the study of sentence structure. All languages are rule-governed; sentence structure rules differ among languages. Syntax describes how sentences may be grammatically structured in a particular language. In some languages, the rules of syntax are simple; only a few possibilities exist. In English, syntax is complex. For example, while English typically has a subject-verb-object sentence order (e.g., *Juan threw the ball.*), the transformational process permits alteration of word order to produce sentences with similar meanings (e.g., *The ball was thrown by Juan.*) or to ask questions (e.g., *Did Juan throw the ball?*). In each transformation, the word order is altered.

INSTRUCTIONAL SUPPORT AND STRATEGIES

The following resources provide instructional support for teaching students who are learning English.

- ***English Language Learners Sourcebook*** This book provides strategies for teachers to use in helping English language learners, as well as student worksheets that relate to specific selections in ***Glencoe Literature: The Reader's Choice.*** The worksheets are designed for students from all language backgrounds who have had some instruction in English. In addition, suggestions are included for ways to adapt the materials for use with less-proficient students.
- ***English, Yes!*** This literature-based program is for readers who need help improving their basic English skills. Each book offers readability-controlled stories by famous writers, and the stories are presented with illustrations and other features that assist readers in understanding the selection.
- ***Speaking and Listening to the English LANGUAGE!*** This book, by Dr. Jane Fell Greene, provides spiraled lessons in English language structure and functions that are essential for students learning English.

In addition to the resources listed above, the charts that follow can help you grasp the main differences between the English language and the first languages spoken by many of your students. To be sensitive to your students' needs, you will want to understand the challenges they face as they study reading, writing, listening, and speaking in the English language.

Contrastive Analysis of English Learners' First Languages

(Used with permission of Dr. Jane Fell Greene)

English contrasts with CANTONESE		
Phonology	**Orthography**	**Morphology/Syntax**
Cantonese is one of the most widely spoken dialects of Chinese, behind Mandarin. Differences in phonology and vocabulary make oral communication between speakers of Cantonese, Mandarin, and other Chinese dialects difficult. Even within the Cantonese dialect, such varieties as those spoken in Hong Kong and Guangzhou (Canton City) have different phonologies. Nevertheless, the language is mutually intelligible through a common written language. English phonemes that do not exist in Cantonese include /b/, /ch/, /d/, /g/, /j/, /sh/, /th/, /v/, and /z/. English phonemes that can be projected to be difficult for native speakers of Cantonese are /b/, /ch/, /d/, /f/, /g/, /j/, /l/, /m/, /n/, /ng/, /o/, /sh/, /th/, /v/, /z/, *l*-clusters, and *r*-clusters.	People from different regions of China speak different dialects of Chinese. But as the hundreds of Chinese dialects look the same when written, written communication is possible between speakers of different dialects. The Chinese orthographic system is based on image (form), sound, and meaning. Its thousands of distinctive characters, called ideographs, have six symbol types: pictographs, indicatives, ideatives, harmonics, transmissives, and borrowed words.	Cantonese words are single-syllable. Each word carries at least one meaning, but meaning can change based upon the four *tones* in which the words are uttered. Each tone may provide a large number of homonyms. Cantonese has no inflectional suffixes (such as English *-s*, *-ed*, *-ing*, and *-est*) that can add to or modify a word's meaning

For more detailed information about strategies for teaching English language learners, see ***Speaking and Listening to the English LANGUAGE!***

English contrasts with HMONG		
Phonology	**Orthography**	**Morphology/Syntax**
The Hmong language has 13 vowels and 56 consonants. Like Cantonese and Vietnamese, Hmong is a tonal language, one in which the same word can be produced with various tones, which give the word several different meanings. Production of phonemes is complex.	Hmong has an alphabetic orthographic system. In the sense that phoneme-grapheme associations determine production, Hmong's orthography is like that of English. Hmong consonant letters related to English include the following: *m* Bilabial nasal *n* Dental-alveolar nasal *ng* Velar nasal *ny* Alveo-palatal nasal *p* Bilabial stop *b* Implosive *p/b* *ph* *p* with aspiration *t* Dental-alveolar stop *d* Implosive *t/d* *th* Aspirated *t* *k* Velar stop *kh* Aspirated *k* *7* Glottal stop *c* Alveo-palatal affricate *ch* Aspirated *c* *s* Dental-alveolar fricative *sh* Voiceless alveolar-palatal fricative *h* Laryngeal fricative *l* Dental-alveolar lateral approximate *r* Dental-alveolar central flap	Because Hmong has been so recently coded, and because of the difficult recent history of its speakers, relatively little has been written regarding the grammar, morphology, and syntax rules of Hmong. Hmong is an isolating language; that is, it has no inflection in its nouns or verbs, no endings such as *-ed* or *-ing* to indicate verb tense, and no endings such as *-s* or *-'s* to extend meanings of nouns. In Hmong, each syllable carries a meaning of its own. In speech, however, some syllables are produced more closely than others. Each syllable has a tone that is represented by a consonant letter written at the close of the syllable. This causes no confusion to Hmong speakers, since the only consonant permitted at the end of a syllable is *ng*. The ordinary syllable pattern is CV (consonant-vowel). However, the consonant may be represented by two, three, or even four consonant letters, and the vowel by one or two letters. Hmong's basic sentence structure is SVO (subject-verb-object).

- Ask students to identify through their reading the main problem in a passage or selection.
- Ask students how that problem is defined. Is the problem part of an academic task (such as a math problem) or the beginning of the explanation of a process (such as a science experiment)?
- What logical steps or actions may be taken to solve the problem? What possible or partial solutions are presented?
- What happens as a result of the steps or actions taken?
- What other actions may be taken to provide a final solution?
- Ask students to evaluate why a solution did or did not work. How might they have solved the problem differently?

Additional Professional Resources

For more information about the topics, skills, and strategies discussed here, consult the following resources. You may also refer to the additional resources listed in the ***Interactive Reading Sourcebook.***

Anders, P., C. Bos, and D. Filip. 1984. The effect of semantic feature analysis on the reading comprehension of learning-disabled students. In J. A. Niles and L. A. Harris (eds.), *Changing perspectives on research in reading/language processing and instruction*. Rochester, NY: National Reading Conference.

Anderson, R. C., and P. Freebody. 1981. Vocabulary knowledge. In J. T. Guthrie (ed.), *Comprehension and teaching: Research reviews* (pp. 77–117). Newark, DE: International Reading Association.

Anderson, R. C., and P. D. Pearson. 1984. A schema-theoretic view of basic processes in teaching comprehension. In P. D. Pearson (ed.) *Handbook of reading research* (pp. 225–353). New York: Longman.

Armbruster, B., and T. H. Anderson. 1985. Producing "considerate" expository text: Or easy reading is damned hard writing. *Journal of Curriculum Studies* 17(3), pp. 247–252.

Armbruster, B. B., T. H. Anderson, and J. Ostertag. 1989. Teaching text structure to improve reading and writing. *The Reading Teacher* (1989, November), pp. 130–158.

Bear, D., M. Invernizzi, S. Templeton, and F. Johnston. 2000. *Words their way: Word study for phonics, vocabulary, and spelling instruction*. Upper Saddle River, NJ: Prentice Hall.

Beck, I. L., and M. G. McKeown. 1983. Learning words well—A program to enhance vocabulary and comprehension. *The Reading Teacher* 36, pp. 622–625.

Brown, A. L., A. S. Palincsar, and B. B. Armbruster. 1984. Instructing comprehension-fostering activities in interactive learning situations. In R. B. Ruddell, M. R. Ruddell, and H. Singer (eds.), *Theoretical models and processes of reading* (4th ed.). Newark, DE: International Reading Association.

Caine. R. and G. Caine. 1994. *Making connections: Teaching and the human brain*. Menlo Park, CA: Addison-Wesley.

Coté, N., S. R. Goldman, and E. U. Saul. 1998. Students making sense of informational text: Relations between processing and representation. *Discourse Processes* 25(1), pp. 1–53.

Duffy, G. G., L. Roehler, and B. A. Herrmann. 1988. Modeling mental processes helps poor readers become strategic readers. In R. L. Allington (ed.), *Teaching struggling readers: Articles from* The Reading Teacher. International Reading Association.

Fry, E., J. Kress, and D. Fountoukidis. 1993. *The reading teacher's book of lists*. Paramus, NJ: Prentice Hall.

Heller, M. F. 1986. Modeling critical thinking in the English classroom. *Highway One* (1986, Spring), pp. 87–90.

Honig, B., L. Diamond, L. Gutlohn, and J. Mahler. 2000. *CORE: Teaching reading sourcebook*. Novato, CA: Arena Press.

Marks, M., M. Pressley, J. D. Coley, S. Craig, R. Gardner, T. DePinto, and W. Rose. 1993. Three teachers' adaptations of reciprocal teaching in comparison to traditional reciprocal teaching. *Elementary School Journal* 94(2), pp. 267–283.

Meyer, B. J. F., and R. O. Freedle. 1984. Effects of discourse type on recall. *American Educational Research Journal* 21(1), pp. 121–143.

Nagy, W. E. 1988. *Teaching vocabulary to improve reading comprehension*. Newark, DE: International Reading Association.

Ogle, D. 1986. K-W-L: A teaching model that develops active reading of expository text. *The Reading Teacher* 39, pp. 564–570.

Palincsar, A. S., and A. L. Brown. 1984. Reciprocal teaching of comprehension-fostering and comprehension-monitoring activities. *Cognition and Instruction* 1, pp. 117–175.

Pinnell, G., and I. Fountas. 1998. *Word matters: Teaching phonics and spelling in the reading/writing classroom*. Portsmouth, NH: Heinemann.

Richards, J. C., and J. P. Gipe. 1995. What's the structure? A game to help middle school students recognize common writing patterns. *Journal of Reading* 38(8), pp. 667–669.

Rosenblatt, L. 1994. The transactional theory of reading and writing. In R. Ruddell, M. R. Ruddell, and H. Singer (eds.), *Theoretical models and processes of reading* (4th ed., pp. 996–1056). Newark, DE: International Reading Association.

Schumm, J. S., D. S. Haager, and A. G. Leavell. 1991. Considerate and inconsiderate text instruction in postsecondary developmental reading textbooks: A content analysis. *Reading Research and Instruction* 30(4), pp. 42–51.

Schwartz, R. M., and T. E. Raphael. 1985. Concept of definition: A key to improving students' vocabulary. *The Reading Teacher* 39, pp. 198–205.

Guide to Text Readability: DRP® and Lexile® Measures

The **Degrees of Reading Power®** (DRP) program for reading provides a measure for determining the readability of texts. Throughout the teacher materials in your **Teacher Wraparound Edition,** you will encounter DRP readability measures assigned to the reading selections in ***Glencoe Literature: The Reader's Choice*** as well as the readability measures for additional works offered to your students. You will also find readability scores based on the Lexile Framework® for Reading. You can use these to effectively inform your classroom instruction by identifying reading materials that are suitable for individual students. You may also find these readability measures on the ***Glencoe BookLink*** CD-ROM.

Degrees of Reading Power® (DRP)

DRP values indicate the readability of prose text. The higher the value, the more difficult the text. The scale ranges from 0 to 100; commonly encountered English text tends to fall somewhere between 25 and 85. Although middle school texts have an average difficulty of 56 and high school texts have an average difficulty of 62, no single readability level is appropriate for each grade level. Rather, a typical classrom has materials with a range of readability levels available for use—some intended for less-proficient readers, some for average readers, and some for stronger readers. The following chart shows the average DRP readability range for materials widely available for use at each grade. Some materials you might use, however, will certainly fall outside of the range for your particular grade.

Grade	DRP Readability Ranges
6	51–61
7	52–62
8	53–64
9	53–65
10	51–68
11	56–67
12	57–68

The Lexile® Framework

A Lexile measure assigned to a text is the specific number that describes the reading demands of the text. The typical Lexile Scale ranges from 200 to 1700 Lexiles. As with the DRP measures, there is not a direct translation from a specific Lexile measure to a specific grade level. Within any classroom, there will be a range of readers and a range of materials to be read. The levels shown on the following chart indicate the approximate range of Lexile scores for 50 percent of the materials found in a typical grade-level classroom. For example, the middle half of the instructional materials typically found in a sixth-grade classroom range in difficulty from about 850L to 1050L.

Grade	Text Measures (from Lexile Framework Map)
6	850L to 1050L
7	950L to 1075L
8	1000L to 1100L
9	1050L to 1150L
10	1100L to 1200L
11 and 12	1100L to 1300L

*Degrees of Reading Power, DRP, and TASA are registered trademarks of Touchstone Applied Science Associates, Inc. (TASA). Lexile is a registered trademark of MetaMetrics, Inc.

Glencoe Resources for Independent Reading

Foster a lifelong love of reading by encouraging your students to read independently. The resources below can help students improve their critical thinking skills, vocabulary, and ability to connect with literature. Have your students maintain reading lists to keep track of their progress. Parents or guardians can review the lists to help students set manageable goals.

Glencoe Literature Library

This collection of hardcover books includes full-length novels, novellas, plays, and works of nonfiction. Each ***Glencoe Literature Library*** volume consists of at least one complete extended-length reading accompanied by several related readings from a broad range of genres, such as short stories, poems, essays, or informational articles. In addition, a separate **Study Guide** for each ***Glencoe Literature Library*** book provides teaching notes and reproducible activity pages for students. Students may also find these activity pages on the **Glencoe Literature Web site** <http://www.lit.glencoe.com>.

- ***Across Five Aprils*** by Irene Hunt DRP[1] 59
- ***The Adventures of Tom Sawyer*** by Mark Twain DRP 55
- ***Anne Frank Remembered: The Story of the Woman Who Helped to Hide the Frank Family*** by Miep Gies and Alison Leslie Gold DRP 57
- ***Bearstone*** by Will Hobbs DRP 51
- ***Bridge to Terabithia*** by Katherine Paterson DRP 50
- ***The Call of the Wild*** by Jack London DRP 62
- ***Cezanne Pinto*** by Mary Stoltz DRP 54
- ***A Christmas Carol*** by Charles Dickens DRP 60
- ***The Clay Marble*** by Minfong Ho DRP 49
- ***Dandelion Wine*** by Ray Bradbury DRP 56
- ***Dogsong*** by Gary Paulsen DRP 51
- ***Dragonwings*** by Lawrence Yep DRP 54
- ***The Friends*** by Rosa Guy DRP 51
- ***A Gathering of Days: A New England Girl's Journal 1830–1832*** by Joan W. Blos DRP 56
- ***The Glory Field*** by Walter Dean Myers DRP 51
- ***Hatchet*** by Gary Paulsen DRP 54
- ***High Elk's Treasure*** by Virginia Driving Hawk Sneve
- ***Homecoming*** by Cynthia Voigt DRP 48
- ***The House of Dies Drear*** by Virginia Hamilton DRP 49
- ***I, Juan de Pareja*** by Elizabeth Borton de Treviño DRP 58
- ***Island of the Blue Dolphins*** by Scott O'Dell DRP 53
- ***Jacob Have I Loved*** by Katherine Paterson DRP 52
- ***Johnny Tremain*** by Esther Forbes DRP 55
- ***Journey to Jo'burg*** by Beverly Naidoo DRP 50
- ***Julie of the Wolves*** by Jean Craighead George DRP 55
- ***Letters from a Slave Girl*** by Mary E. Lyons DRP 51
- ***Letters from Rifka*** by Karen Hesse DRP 49
- ***Little Women*** by Louisa May Alcott DRP 60
- ***Lupita Mañana*** by Patricia Beatty DRP 53
- ***Missing May*** by Cynthia Rylant DRP 53
- ***Mrs. Frisby and the Rats of NIMH*** by Robert O'Brien DRP 52
- ***Number the Stars*** by Lois Lowry DRP 52
- ***The Pigman*** by Paul Zindel DRP 55
- ***Shabanu: Daughter of the Wind*** by Suzanne Fisher Staples DRP 54
- ***Shiloh*** by Phyllis Reynolds Naylor DRP 50
- ***The Slave Dancer*** by Paula Fox DRP 55
- ***So Far from the Bamboo Grove*** by Yoko Kawashima Watkins DRP 50
- ***Sounder*** by William H. Armstrong DRP 53
- ***The Summer of the Swans*** by Betsy Byars DRP 50
- ***Taking Sides*** by Gary Soto DRP 52
- ***There's a Girl in My Hammerlock*** by Jerry Spinelli DRP 46
- ***Treasure Island*** by Robert Louis Stevenson DRP 56
- ***The True Confessions of Charlotte Doyle*** by Avi DRP 52
- ***Tuck Everlasting*** by Natalie Babbitt DRP 56
- ***The View from Saturday*** by E. L. Konigsburg DRP 53
- ***Walk Two Moons*** by Sharon Creech DRP 49
- ***Where the Red Fern Grows*** by Wilson Rawls DRP 47
- ***Winter Thunder*** and ***The Christmas of the Phonograph Records*** by Mari Sandoz
- ***The Witch of Blackbird Pond*** by Elizabeth George Speare DRP 57
- ***A Wrinkle in Time*** by Madeleine L'Engle DRP 51

inTIME magazine

This lively collection of articles drawn from issues of *TIME* helps students develop the skills they need to interact with informational text in a meaningful way. Each of the news stories, feature articles, reviews, profiles, and essays in the magazine connects to an author, work, or theme in ***Glencoe Literature: The Reader's Choice*** as well as to a lesson in ***Glencoe Writer's Choice***. In addition, a separate **Teacher's Guide,** including lessons and reproducible student worksheets designed to develop students' reading and critical thinking skills, accompanies each magazine.

Five-Star Stories

This collection of anthologies features well-known short stories organized by theme and adapted and abridged for a variety of reading levels. You may use the ***Glencoe BookLink*** CD-ROM to identify the exact readability level for each selection. Exercises included in the anthologies help to increase students' vocabulary and improve their reading comprehension, critical thinking, and understanding of literary elements. Themes include the following:

- Travels
- Adventures
- Chills
- Surprises
- Shocks
- Twists
- Encounters
- Conflicts

The Contemporary Readers

Each volume of ***The Contemporary Readers*** consists of six nonfiction books designed for developing readers from a wide range of backgrounds. The selections included in each book range from eight hundred to twelve hundred words and are linked to such themes as human interest, science and nature, or current issues. A set of audiocassettes and a ***Teacher's Resource Book,*** comprised of a Teacher's Guide and reproducible activity pages, complement each volume. You may use the ***Glencoe BookLink*** CD-ROM to identify the exact readability level for each selection in ***The Contemporary Readers.***

Glencoe BookLink CD-ROM

This CD-ROM provides a database that you can use to identify specific readings for students. The software shows **Degrees of Reading Power® (DRP)** readability scores for all the prose fiction and nonfiction selections in ***Glencoe Literature: The Reader's Choice,*** as well as for the ***Five-Star Stories, The Contemporary Readers,*** books in the ***Glencoe Literature Library***, and a number of other titles. Using ***Glencoe BookLink*** CD-ROM, you can search for specific selections by author and title or create reading lists sorted by range, genre (fiction, nonfiction, poetry, or drama), Glencoe theme, or special areas of interest. To further help you guide students to readings that interest them, ***Glencoe BookLink*** CD-ROM provides brief summaries of reading selections as well as **Lexile®** measures of readability.

Literature Classics CD-ROM

This interactive CD-ROM collects over four hundred assorted classic literature selections that may be used to extend students' reading. You may access selections on the CD-ROM by author, title, date, genre, theme, country, and course/grade level. The **Genre Focus Lesson Plans** and **blackline masters** included with the CD-ROM may be used to monitor students' reading.

[1] Degrees of Reading Power® DRP values indicate the readability of prose text. The higher the value, the more difficult the text. Though the scale ranges from 0 to 100, texts widely available for use at grades six through eight typically range from 51 to 64. Some materials, however, may certainly fall outside of this range.

Theme 1 At a Glance
What I Am, What I Want To Be

THEME OPENING

- **Introducing the Theme** (p. 1)
- **Exploring the Theme** (p. 2)
- **Theme Projects** (p. 3)

Theme 1: WHAT I AM, WHAT I WANT TO BE

SELECTIONS

Names/Nombres (p. 4)

One (p. 13)

I'm Nobody! Who are you? (p. 13)

Face It (p. 18)

Almost Ready (p. 18)

Media Connection: Heroes (p. 24)

Strong Men Weep (p. 25)

***from* Wait Till Next Year** (p. 34)

Media Connection: *from* The Wonder Years (pp. 41–42)

Broken Chain (p. 43)

Without Commercials (p. 58)

Active Reading Model: *from* Barrio Boy (p. 66)

Fish Cheeks (p. 76)

***from* Rosa Parks: My Story** (p. 84)

SKILL FEATURES

Grammar Link (p. 12)

Writing Skills (p. 23)

Technology Skills (pp. 56–57)

Genre Focus: Autobiography (pp. 62–63)

Active Reading Strategies (pp. 64–65)

Vocabulary Skills (p. 75)

Interdisciplinary Connection (p. 82)

Reading and Thinking Skills (p. 83)

WRITING WORKSHOP

Narrative Writing: Autobiographical Anecdote (pp. 104–107)

THEME ASSESSMENT

- **Responding to the Theme, Analyzing Literature, Evaluate and Set Goals** (p. 108)
- **Build Your Portfolio** (p. 108)
- **Reading on Your Own** (p. 109)
  The Witch of Blackbird Pond by Elizabeth George Speare
  Baseball in April and Other Stories by Gary Soto
  Where You Belong by Mary Ann McGuigan
- **Standardized Test Practice** (pp. 110–111)

KEYS TO LITERARY CONNECTIONS

Comparing Selections

The **Comparing Selections** feature in this theme provides opportunities for addressing diverse aspects of the reading and literature curriculum.

For example, in Comparing Selections on page 40, students compare their responses to "Strong Men Weep" and to the excerpt from *Wait Till Next Year*. Students also have the opportunity to discuss their feelings about sports, which will help them identify with ideas Cosgrove and Goodwin shared in these selections.

World Literature

The Student Edition contains a variety of literature that represents cultures from around the world. World literature selections are highlighted with the icon above.

TEACHING SUPPORT

The Teaching Support offers a wealth of interactive instructional support:

Meeting Individual Needs
- Special Needs
- English Language Learners
- Multiple Modes of Expression
- Advanced Learners

Internet Connection

Assessment

Portfolio Options

Minilessons
- Grammar and Language
- Reading
- Writing
- Listening and Speaking

Connecting to Other Selections

Real-World Connection

Interdisciplinary Connection

Life Skills Connection

Family and Community Activity

Key to Ability Levels

The activities throughout this theme have been coded for students of various abilities.

L1 **BASIC** activities for all students

L2 **AVERAGE** activities for average to above-average students

L3 **ADVANCED LEARNERS** activities for above-average students

Block Scheduling

Activities that are particularly suited to use within a block scheduling framework are identified with this icon.

Teaching Today

The Glencoe *Teaching Today* professional development Web site at www.teachingtoday.glencoe.com features daily teaching tips, free downloads, annotated Web resources, educational news, and a wealth of information on a wide range of topics.

Theme 1 At a Glance

What I Am, What I Want To Be

Reading Skills in this theme

Variety of Texts

In addition to autobiographical selections, this theme includes the following text types:

- poetry
- essay
- memoir
- short story
- newspaper column
- television script

Comprehension Skills

The following instructional support for comprehension skills appears in this theme of the Student Edition:

- **Reading and Thinking Minilessons** (pp. 17, 22, 55, 103)
- **Active Reading Strategies and Model** (pp. 64–74)
- **Sequencing** (p. 83)

See also the **Reading Minilessons** throughout the theme in this Teacher Wraparound Edition.

For strategies for reading longer works, such as novels and novellas, see "Tips for Independent Reading" on page 109.

Reading Resources

Active Reading Guide The ***Active Reading Guide*** provides graphic organizers and study guide questions to support students' reading of each selection. (***Active Reading Guide***, pp. 1–10)

Interactive Reading Sourcebook and **Interactive Reading Workbook** The ***Interactive Reading Sourcebook*** and ***Interactive Reading Workbook*** offer focused comprehension strategies and lessons on critical thinking skills as well as fluency practice and activities to teach and support phonics, decoding, spelling, and vocabulary development.

Vocabulary Power The ***Vocabulary Power*** workbook (Lessons 1-5) provides systematic teaching, practice, and assessment of vocabulary for better reading comprehension.

Audio Library Available on audiocassette and on CD, the ***Audio Library*** provides valuable comprehension support.

Glencoe Literature Library Each title in the ***Glencoe Literature Library*** includes a full-length work plus related readings. A separate Study Guide is available for each title.

Five–Star Stories These anthologies of familiar short stories adapted and abridged for a variety of reading levels include exercises to help increase students' vocabulary and improve their reading comprehension.

The Contemporary Readers ***The Contemporary Readers*** are nonfiction books linked to various themes and designed for developing readers from a wide range of backgrounds.

Literature Classics CD-ROM The selections on this CD-ROM can be searched by author, theme, or genre.

inTIME and **Humanities Across TIME** Coproductions of Glencoe and Time, Inc., these resources include a wealth of high-interest nonfiction related to the selections in this theme.

Assessment in this theme

Assessment in the Student Edition

This program offers a number of diverse ways to evaluate student understanding and skill proficiency. In the Student Edition, use the following:

- **Responding to Literature**
  Following each selection, students are asked to recall facts, interpret ideas, and evaluate concepts as they answer a variety of questions and complete activities to extend their understanding.
- **Theme Assessment (pp. 108–109)**
  Here students respond to the selections on personal and analytical levels. They also assume ownership of their learning by setting and evaluating goals and by selecting work for their portfolios.

See also the many **Assessment Resources** listed on the facing page.

Standardized Test Practice

The Princeton Review has developed the Standardized Test Practice pages found at the end of this thematic unit (pp. 110–111). For additional practice, direct students to the following resources:

- ITBS Preparation and Practice
- SAT-9 Preparation and Practice
- TerraNova Preparation and Practice

Writing Skills in this theme

Writing Skills

The Student Edition of Theme One offers strong instructional support for writing skills:

In **Extending Your Response**, which follows each selection:

- **Writing About Literature**
- **Personal/Creative Writing**

See also the **Writing Minilessons** throughout the theme in this Teacher Wraparound Edition.

Writing Workshops

Theme One concludes with a **Writing Workshop** that guides students through the process of writing an autobiographical anecdote (pp. 104–107).

Writing Resources

Writer's Assistant CD-ROM Each **Writing Workshop** is supplemented by an interactive writing guide on the ***Writer's Assistant*** CD-ROM. This easy- to-use writing guide provides prompts, templates, and other tools that lead students through the writing process.

Grammar and Composition Handbook The ***Grammar and Composition Handbook*** (Lessons 1.1–3.3) provides systematic instruction in English language conventions.

Spelling Power The ***Spelling Power*** workbook (Lessons 1–4) provides systematic teaching, practice, and assessment of spelling to help students become better spellers and thus enhance their writing.

Writing and Proofreading Practice Blackline masters present in-depth instruction and practice on a specific step in the writing process and proofreading (pp. 1–7, 8–14).

Writing and Proofreading Transparencies Transparencies provide graphic organizers and proofreading exercises for whole-class instruction (pp. 1–6, 7–8, 25–26).

Research and Report Writing Guide This resource provides extensive tips and activities to guide students in their writing projects in the literature classroom as well as in classes across the curriculum.

Style and Documentation Sourcebook for Writers This sourcebook is a combination reference and workbook, giving students the most up-to-date information and guidance regarding traditional as well as technological research strategies and documentation.

Revising with Style This resource offers instruction and exercises focusing on the revision process and covering topics from proofreading and correcting common grammatical errors to sentence combining and reordering.

Assessment Resources

Selection Quick Checks For each selection, a **Quick Check** of three to five short-answer questions measures students' literal comprehension.

Selection and Theme Assessment The ***Selection and Theme Assessment*** instrument tests students' abilities to recall, interpret, and evaluate what they've read. The tests consist of multiple-choice, short answer, and essay questions.

Performance Assessment Alternative assessment instruments and rubrics for Theme One are found in the ***Performance Assessment*** ancillary.

Writing Assessment and Portfolio Management These notes and strategies, student models, and assessment tools assist with the task of measuring students' progress as writers and as monitors of their own writing.

Testmaker: ExamView Pro Teachers can customize selection and Theme One tests by accessing the ***Testmaker*** database.

Interactive Tutor: Self-Assessment The ***Interactive Tutor: Self-Assessment*** software provides multiple-choice tests with immediate feedback to help students evaluate their knowledge and understanding of each literature selection.

MindJogger Videoquizzes Using a popular game show format, ***MindJogger Videoquizzes*** on videocassettes enable teachers to evaluate student understanding of Theme One in a quick and fun manner.

Theme 1 Skills Scope and Sequence

Lessons	Literary Elements	Reading and Thinking	Writing
Names/Nombres Julia Alvarez DRP:57 Lexile:960	Theme, SE p. 10 *Theme, TWE pp. 6, 8* *Plot: Internal Conflict, TWE p. 7* *Mood, TWE p. 9*	*Inferring, TWE p. 6* *Classifying, TWE p. 7* *Evaluating, TWE p. 7*	Sensory Imagery, SE p. 11 Journal Entry, SE p. 11 *Descriptive Detail, TWE p. 12*
One James Berry I'm Nobody! Who are you? Emily Dickinson	Visual Imagery, SE p. 16 *Visual Imagery, TWE pp. 14, 15*	Comparing and Contrasting, SE p. 17 *Logical Reasoning, TWE p. 14* *Drawing Conclusions, TWE p. 15* *Summarizing, TWE p. 15*	Paragraph About Theme, SE p. 17 Self-Portrait, SE p. 17
Face It Janet S. Wong **Almost Ready** Arnold Adoff	Irony, SE p. 21 *Repetition, TWE p. 19* *Irony, TWE p. 20* *Free Verse, TWE p. 20*	Visualizing, SE p. 22 *Generalizing, TWE p. 20* *Paraphrasing, TWE p. 20*	Poem's Speaker, SE p. 22 Short Poem, SE p. 22 Using Dialogue, SE p. 23
Strong Men Weep Benedict Cosgrove DRP:61 Lexile:1150	Author's Purpose, SE p. 32; *TWE pp. 27, 29* *Genre, TWE p. 27* *Irony, TWE p. 31*	Newspaper Column, SE p. 24 *Comparing and Contrasting, TWE pp. 24, 28* *Distinguishing Fact from Opinion, TWE pp. 29, 30*	Critical Review, SE p. 33 Persuasive Paragraph, SE p. 33
from Wait Till Next Year Doris Kearns Goodwin DRP:61 Lexile:1230	Memoir, SE p. 39; *TWE p. 37* *Narrator, TWE p. 36* *Concrete Lang., TWE p. 37* *Memoir, TWE p. 37*	Comparing Selections, SE p. 40 *Elaborating, TWE p. 37* *Monitoring Comprehension, TWE p. 37* *Supporting Details, TWE p. 37*	
Broken Chain Gary Soto DRP:55 Lexile:740	Conflict, SE p. 53; *TWE pp. 45, 47, 48, 49, 50* *Character, TWE pp. 46, 51* *Plot, TWE pp. 50, 52*	Television Script, SE p. 41 Prior Knowledge, SE p. 55 *Sequence of Events, TWE p. 41* *Author's Purpose, TWE p. 46* *Connotation/Denotation, TWE p. 54*	Paragraph (Details), SE p. 54 Advice Column, SE p. 54 Explanation, SE p. 54 *Writing to Show, TWE p. 47*
Without Commercials Alice Walker	Speaker, SE p. 61 *Point of View, TWE p. 60*	*Drawing Conclusions, TWE p. 59* *Summarizing, TWE p. 59* *Evaluating, TWE p. 60*	
from Barrio Boy Ernesto Galarza DRP:57 Lexile:980	Autobiography, SE p. 62 Description, SE p. 73 *Description, TWE pp. 68, 69, 70, 72*	Autobiography, SE p. 64 *Informational Text, TWE p. 63* *Distinguishing Fact from Opinion, TWE p. 69* *Inferring, TWE p. 71*	Paragraph (Setting), SE p. 74 Personal Letter, SE p. 74
Fish Cheeks Amy Tan DRP:58 Lexile:850	Sensory Imagery, SE p. 80 *Sensory Imagery, TWE p. 79*	Interdisciplinary Connection, SE p. 82 Sequencing, SE p. 83 *Evaluating, TWE p. 79* SN *Learning Disabled, TWE p. 83*	Summary, SE p. 81 Story, SE p. 81 Summary, SE p. 82
from Rosa Parks: My Story Rosa Parks DRP:50 Lexile:880	Sequence, SE p. 101; *TWE pp. 86, 87, 89, 90, 94, 96* *Dialogue, TWE p. 87* *Setting, TWE p. 89* *Tone, TWE p. 96* *Mood, TWE p. 100*	Cause and Effect, SE p. 103 *Judging a Source, TWE p. 88* *Analyzing Arguments, TWE p. 91* *Propaganda Tech., TWE p. 91* *Logical Reasoning, TWE p. 92* *Generalizing, TWE p. 99*	Summary, SE p. 102 Text for Children's Picture Book, SE p. 102 Narrative, SE p. 104 *Maintaining Consistency in Verb Tenses, TWE p. 93*
Writing Workshop Narrative Writing: Autobiographical Anecdote			*Logical Sequence, TWE p. 106*

Key: Student material is in roman. *Teacher material is in italic.* Technology ELL English Language Learners

	Vocabulary and Spelling	Grammar and Language	Listening, Speaking, and Viewing	Life Skills; Study and Research; Technology
	Antonyms, SE p. 11	Sentence Fragments, SE p. 12 *Proper Nouns and Proper Adjectives, TWE p. 8*	Literature Groups, SE p. 11 Interviewing, SE p. 11 Readers Theater, SE p. 11 ELL *Naming a Child, TWE p. 6*	*Foreign Names, TWE p. 9* *Family Tree, TWE p. 9*
	ELL *Compound Words, TWE p. 14*		Literature Groups, SE p. 17 Musical Brochure, SE p. 17	
		Punctuating Dialogue, TWE p. 23	Literature Groups, SE p. 22 Listening to Poetry, SE p. 22 ELL *Dramatic Reading, TWE p. 19*	
	Owning a Word, SE p. 33 *Root Words, TWE p. 27* ELL *Baseball Terms, TWE p. 27*	*Main Verbs and Helping Verbs, TWE p. 30*	Literature Groups, SE p. 33 *Announcing, TWE p. 29* *Videotape, TWE p. 31*	*Perspectives on the Hero, TWE p. 31* *English Pronunciation, TWE p. 33*
	Etymology, TWE p. 36	*Prepositional Phrases, TWE p. 38*	*Videotape, TWE p. 37* ELL *The Art of Storytelling, TWE p. 36*	
	Synonyms, SE p. 55 ELL *Ethnic Foods, TWE p. 42* *Prefixes, TWE p. 47*	Subject-Verb Agreement, SE p. 55 *Mechanics: Brackets, TWE p. 42* *Pronouns Used as Objects, TWE p. 52*	Literature Groups, SE p. 54 Improv., SE p. 54 *Debating, TWE p. 49*	Word Processing, SE p. 56 SN *Emotional, TWE p. 50* SN *Physically Challenged, TWE p. 56*
				ELL *Cultural Concepts of Beauty, TWE p. 60*
	Compound Words, SE p. 74 Base Words, SE p. 75 ELL *Description; Word Meanings; Using Prefixes; TWE pp. 18, 70, 75* SN *Less-Proficient Readers; TWE p. 70*	*Subject-Verb Agreement, TWE p. 72*	ELL *Elements of Autobiography, TWE p. 62*	*Immigration and Citizenship, TWE p. 71*
	Analogies, SE p. 81 *Etymology, TWE p. 79*	*Adjectives, TWE p. 79*	Literature Groups, SE p. 81 *Interviewing, SE p. 82* ELL *Comparing Customs, TWE p. 78*	Traditional Chinese Cooking, SE p. 81
	Unlocking Meaning, SE p. 103 SN *Less-Proficient Readers, TWE p. 88* ELL *Figures of Speech, TWE p. 86* *Jargon, TWE p. 93* *Etymology, TWE p. 97* *Antonyms, TWE p. 100*	Nouns, SE p. 103 *Quotation Marks, TWE p. 89* *Commas, TWE p. 91* *Capitalization of Proper Nouns, TWE p. 100*	Literature Groups, SE p. 102; Skit, SE p. 102 SN *Visually Impaired, TWE p. 94* *Effective List., TWE p. 95* *Video, TWE p. 97* *Documentary, TWE p. 99*	*Supporting and Contributing, TWE pp. 90, 96* *Boycott, TWE p. 92; Rosa Parks, Civil Rights Movement, TWE p. 98* *Key Events, TWE p. 92; Working For a Cause, TWE p. 97*
			ELL *Autobiographical Anecdote, TWE p. 104*	

SN **Special Needs/Strategic Intervention**

Theme 1 RESOURCE MANAGER

Lessons	Essential Resources		English Language Learners
Names/Nombres JULIA ALVAREZ PACING: 2 DAYS	**Lesson-Specific Instruction** Selection Focus Transp. 1 Active Reading Guide,* p. 1 Literary Elements Transp. 1 Vocabulary Practice, p. 1 Quick Checks,* p. 1 Selection and Theme Assessment, pp. 1–2 Testmaker: ExamView Pro Performance Assessment, p. 1	**Systematic Language Instruction** Grammar and Comp. Hbk, L.1.1–1.2 Vocabulary Power, Lesson 1 Spelling Power, Lesson 1	English Language Learners Sourcebook, p. 17 Theme One Planning Guide, p. 6 Spanish Summaries, p. 1 Spanish Translations, pp. 1–4 Audio Library* English, Yes!
One JAMES BERRY **I'm Nobody! Who are you?** EMILY DICKINSON PACING: 1 DAY	**Lesson-Specific Instruction** Selection Focus Transp. 2 Active Reading Guide,* p. 2 Literary Elements Transp. 2 Quick Checks,* p. 2	Selection and Theme Assessment, pp. 3–4 Testmaker: ExamView Pro Performance Assessment, p. 2 **Systematic Language Instruction** Grammar and Comp. Hbk., L.1.3–1.4	English Language Learners Sourcebook, p. 18 Spanish Summaries, p. 2 Audio Library* English, Yes!
FACE IT JANET S. WONG **ALMOST READY** ARNOLD ADOFF PACING: 2 DAYS	**Lesson-Specific Instruction** Selection Focus Transp. 3 Active Reading Guide,* p. 3 Literary Elements Transp. 3 Quick Checks,* p. 3 Selection and Theme Assessment, pp. 5–6	Testmaker: ExamView Pro Performance Assessment, p. 3 **Systematic Language Instruction** Grammar and Comp. Hbk., L. 1.5 Vocabulary Power, Lesson 2 Spelling Power, Lesson 2	English Language Learners Sourcebook, p. 19 Spanish Summaries, p. 3 Audio Library* English, Yes!
Strong Men Weep BENEDICT COSGROVE PACING: 2 DAYS	**Lesson-Specific Instruction** Selection Focus Transp. 4 Active Reading Guide,* p. 4 Literary Elements Transp. 4 Vocabulary Practice, p. 2 Quick Checks,* p. 4 Selection and Theme Assessment, pp. 7–8 Testmaker: ExamView Pro	Performance Assessment, p. 4 TIME *inTIME* magazine, pp. 30–31 **Systematic Language Instruction** Grammar and Comp. Hbk., L. 1.6	English Language Learners Sourcebook, p. 20 Spanish Summaries, p. 4 Spanish Translations, pp. 5–8 Audio Library* English, Yes!
***from* Wait Till Next Year** DORIS KEARNS GOODWIN PACING: 2 DAYS	**Lesson-Specific Instruction** Selection Focus Transp. 5 Active Reading Guide,* p. 5 Literary Elements Transp. 5 Vocabulary Practice, p. 3 Quick Checks,* p. 5 Selection and Theme Assessment, pp. 9–10	Testmaker: ExamView Pro Performance Assessment, p. 5 TIME *inTIME* magazine, pp. 30–31 **Systematic Language Instruction** Grammar and Comp. Hbk., L. 2.1 Vocabulary Power, Lesson 3 Spelling Power, Lesson 3	English Language Learners Sourcebook, p. 21 Theme One Planning Guide, p. 32 Spanish Summaries, p. 5 Spanish Translations, pp. 9–10 Spanish Audio Library English, Yes!

Key: Workbook · Blackline Masters · Textbook · Transparency · CD-ROM · Videodisk (also available in videocassette)

Special Needs/ Strategic Intervention	Reteaching and Enrichment
Interactive Reading Sourcebook, pp. T47–T49 Interactive Reading Workbook, pp. 1-3 Inclusion Strategies Sourcebook, pp. 5-6, 55-56 Audio Library*	Fine Art Transparency 4 Reading Skills Practice Workbook, pp. 1-20 Grammar and Language Transp. 1 Gr. and Lang. Wkbk., pp. 61-62, 119-120 Grammar and Comp. Hbk., L.2.1, 5.1, 12.4 TIME *Humanities Across TIME,* Cover 8 Interactive Tutor: Self-Assessment Vocabulary PuzzleMaker Web Site (lit.glencoe.com)
Interactive Reading Sourcebook, pp. T50–T52 Interactive Reading Workbook, p. 4 Inclusion Strategies Sourcebook, pp. 55-56 Theme One Planning Guide, p. 14 Audio Library*	Reading Skills Practice Workbook, pp. 3-4 Interactive Tutor: Self-Assessment Vocabulary PuzzleMaker Web Site (lit.glencoe.com)
Interactive Reading Sourcebook, pp. T53–T55 Interactive Reading Workbook, p. 5 Inclusion Strategies Sourcebook, pp. 39-40, 55-56, 77-78 Theme One Planning Guide, p. 19 Audio Library*	Fine Art Transparency 31 Grammar and Language Transparency 2 Gr. and Lang. Wkbk., pp. 267-270 Grammar and Comp. Hbk., L. 13.6 Interactive Tutor: Self-Assessment Vocabulary PuzzleMaker Web Site (lit.glencoe.com)
Interactive Reading Sourcebook, pp. T55–T58 Interactive Reading Workbook, pp. 6-7 Inclusion Strategies Sourcebook, pp. 39-40, 55-56 Theme One Planning Guide, p. 24 Audio Library*	Literature Launchers, Side A, Segment 2 Reading Skills Practice Workbook, pp. 5-6 Grammar and Language Transp. 3 Gr. and Lang. Wkbk., pp. 87–88 Grammar and Comp. Hbk., L. 3.6 Media Connection Activities, p. 1 TIME *Humanities Across TIME,* Covers 3, 9 Interactive Tutor: Self-Assessment Vocabulary PuzzleMaker Web Site (lit.glencoe.com)
Interactive Reading Sourcebook, pp. T58–T60 Interactive Reading Workbook, pp. 8-9 Inclusion Strategies Sourcebook, pp. 7-8, 27-28, 69-70 Theme One Planning Guide, p. 32	Reading Skills Practice Workbook, pp. 7-8 Grammar and Language Transp. 4 Gr. and Lang. Wkbk., pp. 141–142 Grammar and Comp. Hbk., L. 7.1 Interactive Tutor: Self-Assessment Vocabulary PuzzleMaker Web Site (lit.glencoe.com)

Web　Audiocassette　Diskette　*Also available in Spanish

INDEPENDENT READING

Encourage students to spend thirty minutes each day in independent reading. The following Glencoe components and outside resources provide opportunities for reading related to this theme.

The Glencoe Literature Library

You may want to assign one or more of these titles for independent reading. For a complete listing of titles available in the Glencoe Literature Library, see page T96 of this book.

- *Taking Sides* by Gary Soto
- *The Witch of Blackbird Pond* by Elizabeth George Speare
- *Bearstone* by Will Hobbs
- *There's a Girl in My Hammerlock* by Jerry Spinelli
- *I, Juan de Pareja* by Elizabeth Borton de Treviño

inTIME News stories, feature articles, reviews, profiles, and essays in the magazine connect to an author, work, or theme in the Student Edition. See the **inTIME Teacher's Guide** for specific connections to this theme.

Resources for Less-Proficient Readers

For reading especially created for less-proficient readers, suggest

- *Five-Star Stories*
- *The Contemporary Readers*

Additional Resources for Independent Reading

The following titles are listed with specific reading selections throughout this theme. You may want to suggest that students look for these in your local or school library.

- *In the Year of the Boar and Jackie Robinson* by Bette Bao Lord
- *Going Home* by Nicholasa Mohr
- *Emily Dickinson* by Victoria Olsen
- *All the Colors of the Race* by Arnold Adoff
- *Dreams into Deeds: Nine Women Who Dared* by Linda Peavy and Ursula Smith
- *The Random House Book of Sports Stories* by L. M. Schulman
- *Baseball in April and Other Stories* by Gary Soto
- *Homesick: My Own Story* by Jean Fritz
- *The Moon Lady* by Amy Tan
- *They Had a Dream* by Jules Archer
- *Where* by Fred Powledge
- *Where You Belong* by Mary Ann McGuigan

Lessons	Essential Resources	English Language Learners
Broken Chain Gary Soto Pacing: 3 Days	**Lesson-Specific Instruction** Selection Focus Transp. 6 Active Reading Guide,* p. 6 Literary Elements Transp. 6 Vocabulary Practice, p. 4 Quick Checks,* p. 6 Selection and Theme Assessment, pp. 11–12 Testmaker: ExamView Pro Performance Assessment, p. 6 **Systematic Language Instruction** Grammar and Comp. Hbk., L.2.2–2.3	English Language Learners Sourcebook, p. 22 Spanish Summaries, p. 6 Spanish Translations, pp. 11–17 Audio Library* English, Yes!
Without Commercials Alice Walker Pacing: 1 Day	**Lesson-Specific Instruction** Selection Focus Transp. 7 Active Reading Guide,* p. 7 Literary Elements Transp. 7 Quick Checks,* p. 7 Selection and Theme Assessment, pp. 13–14 Testmaker: ExamView Pro Performance Assessment, p. 7 **Systematic Language Instruction** Grammar and Comp. Hbk., L. 2.4 Vocabulary Power, Lesson 4 Spelling Power, Lesson 4	English Language Learners Sourcebook, p. 23 Spanish Summaries, p. 7 Audio Library* English, Yes!
from Barrio Boy Ernesto Galarza Pacing: 2 Days	**Lesson-Specific Instruction** Selection Focus Transp. 8 Active Reading Guide,* p. 8 Literary Elements Transp. 8 Vocabulary Practice, p. 5 Quick Checks,* p. 8 Selection and Theme Assessment, pp. 15–16 Testmaker: ExamView Pro Performance Assessment, p. 8 **Systematic Language Instruction** Grammar and Comp. Hbk., L. 2.5	English Language Learners Sourcebook, pp. 24, 25 Theme One Planning Guide, p. 53 Spanish Summaries, p. 8 Spanish Translations, pp. 18–22 Audio Library* English, Yes!
Fish Cheeks Amy Tan Pacing: 2 Days	**Lesson-Specific Instruction** Selection Focus Transp. 9 Active Reading Guide,* p. 9 Literary Elements Transp. 9 Vocabulary Practice, p. 6 Quick Checks,* p. 9 Selection and Theme Assessment, pp. 17–18 Testmaker: ExamView Pro Performance Assessment, p. 9 **Systematic Language Instruction** Grammar and Comp. Hbk., L.3.1–3.2 Vocabulary Power, Lesson 5	English Language Learners Sourcebook, p. 26 Spanish Summaries, p. 9 Audio Library* English, Yes!
from Rosa Parks: MY STORY Rosa Parks Pacing: 3 Days	**Lesson-Specific Instruction** Selection Focus Transp. 10 Active Reading Guide,* p. 10 Literary Elements Transp. 10 Vocabulary Practice, p. 7 Quick Checks,* p. 10 Selection and Theme Assessment, pp. 19–20 Testmaker: ExamView Pro Performance Assessment, p. 10 TIME *inTIME* magazine, pp. 22-23 **Systematic Language Instruction** Grammar and Comp. Hbk., L. 3.3 Vocabulary Power, Unit 1 Review/Test Spelling Power, Unit 1 Review/ Proofreading	English Language Learners Sourcebook, pp. 27, 28 Spanish Summaries, p. 10 Spanish Translations, pp. 22–34 Audio Library* English, Yes!
Writing WORKSHOP Narrative Writing: Autobiographical Anecdote Pacing: 2 Days	Writing Assessment and Portfolio Management, pp. 1–13, 14–16, 38–45	English Language Learners Sourcebook, p. 9 English, Yes!

Key: Workbook Blackline Masters Textbook Transparency CD-ROM Videodisk (also available in videocassette)

Special Needs/ Strategic Intervention	Reteaching and Enrichment
Interactive Reading Sourcebook, pp. T61–T63 Interactive Reading Workbook, pp. 10–11 Inclusion Strategies Sourcebook, pp. 23–24, 53–54 Theme One Planning Guide, p. 40 Audio Library*	Literature Launchers, Side A, Segment 1 Fine Art Transparency 1 Reading Skills Practice Workbook, pp. 9–10 Grammar and Language Transp. 5 Gr. and Lang. Wkbk., pp. 107–108, 143–144, 183–192 Grammar and Comp. Hbk., L.4.2, 10.1–10.5 Media Connection Activities, p. 2 Interactive Tutor: Self-Assessment Vocabulary PuzzleMaker Web Site (lit.glencoe.com)
Interactive Reading Sourcebook, pp. T63–T65 Interactive Reading Workbook, p. 12 Inclusion Strategies Sourcebook, pp. 1–2 Theme One Planning Guide, p. 48 Audio Library*	Reading Skills Practice Workbook, pp. 11–12 Interactive Tutor: Self-Assessment Vocabulary PuzzleMaker Web Site (lit.glencoe.com)
Interactive Reading Sourcebook, pp. T66–T68 Interactive Reading Workbook, pp. 13–14 Inclusion Strategies Sourcebook, pp. 33–34 Theme One Planning Guide, p. 53 Audio Library*	Fine Art Transparency 32 Grammar and Language Transp. 6 Gr. and Lang. Wkbk., pp. 183–184 Grammar and Comp. Hbk., L. 10.1 Interactive Tutor: Self-Assessment Vocabulary PuzzleMaker Web Site (lit.glencoe.com)
Interactive Reading Sourcebook, pp. T68–T71 Interactive Reading Workbook, pp. 15–16 Inclusion Strategies Sourcebook, pp. 57–58, 69–70, 81–82 Theme One Planning Guide, p. 61 Audio Library*	Grammar and Language Transp. 7 Gr. and Lang. Wkbk., pp. 7–8, 117–118 Grammar and Comp. Hbk., L. 5.1 Interactive Tutor: Self-Assessment Vocabulary PuzzleMaker Web Site (lit.glencoe.com)
Interactive Reading Sourcebook, pp. T71–T73 Interactive Reading Workbook, pp. 17–20 Inclusion Strategies Sourcebook, pp. 3–4 Theme One Planning Guide, p. 69 Audio Library*	Literature Launchers, Side A, Segment 3 Grammar and Language Transparencies 8–10 Gr. and Lang. Wkbk., pp. 237–238, 259–260, 267–270 Gr. and Comp. Hbk., L.2.1, 12.2–12.4, 13.2–13.4, 13.6 Interactive Tutor: Self-Assessment Vocabulary PuzzleMaker Web Site (lit.glencoe.com)
Inclusion Strategies Sourcebook, pp. 73–74	Writing and Proofreading Practice, pp. 1–7, 8–14 Writing and Proofreading Transparencies 1–6, 7–8, 25–26 Revising with Style Writer's Assistant

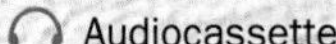

Web Audiocassette Diskette *Also available in Spanish

Theme RESOURCES

To explore the theme further you may want to use these resources:

- Listening and Speaking Activities (pp. 1–3)
- Viewing and Representing Activities (pp. 1–6, 7–9)
- Critical Thinking Skills (pp. 2–4)
- Media Connection Activities, (pp. 1–2)
- Interdisciplinary Activities (pp. 2–5)
- Family and Community Activities (p. 11)
- Selection and Theme Assessment (pp. 125–126)
- Performance Assessment (pp. 69, 96)

TIME Humanities Across TIME

See also these additional theme planning resources:

- Theme One Planning Guide
- Interactive Reading Sourcebook
- Literature Groups Sourcebook
- Interactive Lesson Planner
- Interactive Teacher Edition
- Glencoe Web Site <lit.glencoe.com>

Use Glencoe's ***Presentation Plus!*** This multimedia teaching tool lets you present dynamic lessons that will engage your students. Using Microsoft PowerPoint®, you can customize the presentation to create your own personalized lessons.

What I Am, What I Want to Be

Theme Objectives

- To enjoy reading about people and their unique experiences
- To analyze the literary elements in nonfiction, poetry, and short story selections
- To apply strategies for reading autobiographical writing

Viewing the Art

Norman Rockwell (1894–1978) was one of the most popular illustrators of his time. His homespun pictures of American life were seen regularly on the covers of such magazines as *Colliers*, *Life*, and *The Saturday Evening Post*.

Responding to the Art Discussion Questions:

- What do you think the girl in the painting is thinking about? *(probably wondering about her appearance)*
- What connection do you see between the art and the title of this theme? *(The girl appears to be comparing her appearance to the picture in her lap, perhaps wondering if she'll become like her adult idol.)*

What I Am, What I Want to Be

Girl at Mirror, 1954. Norman Rockwell. Printed by permission of the Norman Rockwell Family Trust. ©1954 the Norman Rockwell Family Trust.

Teacher to Teacher

Pojoaque Middle School • New Mexico

Our school is located within a trilingual district composed of Anglo, Hispanic American, and Native American students. So, when opening the theme "What I Am, What I Want to Be," I use each student's native culture as a starting point. We discuss who we are and what makes us who we are from a cultural standpoint, and students write an essay on this topic from the perspective of their own cultural backgrounds. They share their essays in class, and we talk about cultural differences. Then students create a pictorial autobiography using pictures of themselves growing up. They put these pictures on a poster or some other background; list all their hobbies, interests, and activities; and describe their likes and dislikes. They include information about various personal attitudes and use adjectives to describe their qualities.

Gerald J. Romero

> **"*Only one of me and nobody can get a second one from a photocopy machine.*"**
>
> —*James Berry, "One"*

THEME CONTENTS

GENRE FOCUS AUTOBIOGRAPHY

RESOURCE MANAGER

See the ***Theme One Planning Guide*** for additional teaching notes, strategies, and resources for introducing the theme "What I Am, What I Want to Be."

Teaching Strategies

Have students read the quotation from "One" by James Berry in preparation for the discussion of the theme "What I Am, What I Want to Be."

Introducing the Theme

Direct your students' attention to the **Theme Contents.** Ask them to read through the list of selections. Present these questions for discussion:

- Have you ever read anything by these writers before? *(Students might recognize names such as Amy Tan and Rosa Parks.)*
- From the titles, which selection do you think you will relate to best?
- What do you notice about the variety of writing in this theme? *(Students may note that there are several poems and autobiographical selections in the contents.)*
- If you had your choice, which selection would you read first? Why?

LITERATURE & HUMANITIES

Have students examine the painting *Figuera (1971)*, Transparency 49 from *World History in Art*, and determine how many figures they see. Then have them discuss what comment the artist might be making about a person's identity.

GLENCOE TECHNOLOGY

LITERATURE CLASSICS CD-ROM

Search for other selections related to the theme of "What I Am, What I Want to Be."

Exploring the Theme

What I Am, What I Want to Be

- Students may place themselves in their age, cultural, gender, and socioeconomic groups in describing how others see them.
- Students may see themselves very differently than how they feel they are perceived. Some may think that outward appearances are not reliable clues when it comes to discovering who a person really is.

Have students write two-sentence responses to these questions: *Who are you? Who do you want to be?*

Starting Points

One Among Many
Write the word *conformity* on the board and ask students to give examples of what the word means to them. Mention that for many animals, like the penguins pictured here, conforming to a group helps ensure their safety and survival. *(Students may feel that each penguin thinks it is unique, yet each likes belonging to a crowd.)*

- Find out if students think conformity is necessary for humans to survive.
- Prompt with questions such as: What are the advantages and disadvantages of *conforming to society's norms?*

You Are the Only You
Invite students to write as many words as they can think of. Encourage them to be generous with themselves and to remember that while other students may have similar adjectives in their word-sketches, it is the combination of these words that will reveal individuality. No two students will have exactly the same self-portrait.

FINE ART TRANSPARENCY 15

You may wish to use ***Fine Art Transparency 15*** to help students think about their self-portraits.

Exploring the Theme

What I Am, What I Want to Be

How do other people see you? More importantly, how do you see yourself? In this theme, you will explore what makes you who you are and what it will take to become who you want to be. To begin, try one of the options below.

Starting Points

ONE AMONG MANY

What do you think makes each of these penguins stand out in a crowd?

- Write a short conversation between two of the penguins. Imagine they are introducing themselves.

YOU ARE THE ONLY YOU

You are the only you. Think about yourself for a minute, and get ready to sketch yourself in words.

- Draw a name tag. Write your name in the center of it. What are the first words that come to mind when you read your name? Around the name tag, list several words that describe what makes you unique. You may also wish to include photos or drawings on your name tag.

Drawing by Chas. Addams; ©1977. The New Yorker Magazine, Inc.

interNET CONNECTION

Personality Suggest that students use *temperament, character, personality,* or *identity* as keywords on a search engine to find out more about what makes a person unique, what makes a person an individual. Have them share their results with the class.

Theme Projects

As you read the selections in this theme, choose one of the projects below. Work on your own, with a partner, or in a group.

LEARNING FOR LIFE

Writing a Job Description

What do you dream of doing when you grow up? Do you think about being a dancer, or a veterinarian, or a designer of video games? Think about your dream job. Then write a description of your job.

1. When you have made your choice, do some library research to find out more about it. Talk to people in your community who have similar jobs. Take notes about their job descriptions.
2. Write your job description, and contribute it to a classroom Career Notebook. As you learn about other interesting careers, add new descriptions to the notebook.

MULTIMEDIA PROJECT

A Self-Portrait

Create a multimedia self-portrait.

1. Gather information about yourself. Create a summary of interesting facts about your life, perhaps using a visual format such as a timeline or a graph to chart these highlights.
2. Gather photos or drawings of you and your family or friends. Try to include music, videos, and taped interviews to showcase your life.
3. Present your self-portrait to your class.

interNET CONNECTION

Check out the Web for more project ideas. Use your favorite search engine to find other job-related ideas or other topics related to the "What I Am, What I Want to Be" theme. Key words such as *jobs, employment*, and career fields like *medicine* and *aviation* can get you started.

CRITICAL LISTENING

Musical Notes

Your taste in music reflects who you are, as well as your interests.

1. Do you enjoy popular music, oldies, jazz, reggae, rap, or some other type of music? Bring in examples of different kinds of music you enjoy.
2. Talk to older family members about the kinds of music they listened to when they were your age. Research their favorite kinds of music, and bring examples, photographs, or articles about that music to class. You might even create a musical timeline showing the kinds of music young people have enjoyed over time.
3. Plan a musical tour through history. Display your research and photographs. Using tapes or CDs, play examples of a wide variety of music. Invite another class or family members to your classroom to participate in your musical tour.

Theme Projects

Teaching Strategies

The following suggestions may help your students plan and carry out their theme projects.

Learning for Life

- Before they write, ask students to close their eyes and think of what they are happiest doing.
- Ask students to help one another identify jobs and professions connected to what they enjoy doing.
- Encourage students to ask professionals in the community which hobbies would be good preparation for careers in their chosen fields.

Multimedia Project

- Encourage students to create a self-portrait that reflects their present thoughts and feelings as well as dreams and plans for the future.
- You may wish to set a time limit for the final presentations.

Critical Listening

- Encourage students to seek out partners who are interested in the same kind of music.
- Invite student musicians to perform and to talk about songwriters or composers they admire.

Additional Resources

- ***Interdisciplinary Activities,*** pp. 2–5
- ***Viewing and Representing Activities,*** pp. 7–9
- ***Listening and Speaking Activities,*** pp. 1–3
- ***Critical Thinking Skills,*** pp. 2–4
- ***Selection and Theme Assessment,*** pp. 125–126
- ***Performance Assessment,*** p. 69

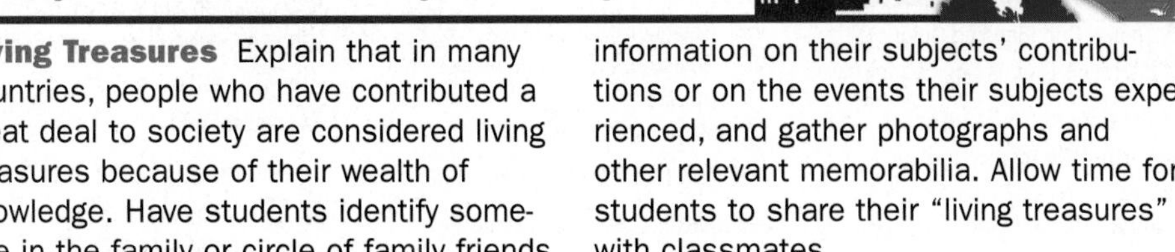

Family and Community Activity

Living Treasures Explain that in many countries, people who have contributed a great deal to society are considered living treasures because of their wealth of knowledge. Have students identify someone in the family or circle of family friends who could be considered a living treasure and create a short documentary film or report about this person. Encourage students to conduct interviews, research information on their subjects' contributions or on the events their subjects experienced, and gather photographs and other relevant memorabilia. Allow time for students to share their "living treasures" with classmates.

Additional Resources

- ***Family and Community Activities,*** p. 11

Before Reading

Objectives

- To read and analyze a short story about a girl torn between her Dominican and American identities
- To recognize and state an implied theme in a short story
- To identify and discuss sensory details in a story

Skills

Reading/Thinking: Inferring; Evaluating; Classifying
Writing: Journal Entry
Vocabulary: Antonyms
Grammar/Language: Proper Nouns and Proper Adjectives
Listening/Speaking: Interviewing
Collaboration: Literature Groups; Readers Theater

Motivating STUDENTS

Selection Focus Transparency 1: Encourage students to discuss how they might feel if someone changed their name for convenience.

Reading Focus: As an extension of the Reading Focus, have small groups of students discuss times when a nickname can make a person feel proud or uncomfortable.

Before You Read

Names/Nombres

MEET JULIA ALVAREZ

Asked where she finds the ideas for her richly detailed stories, Julia Alvarez says, "I think when I write, I write out of who I am and the questions I need to figure out. A lot of what I have worked through has to do with coming to this country and losing a homeland and a culture, as a way of making sense." Alvarez has written several novels, including *How the Garcia Girls Lost Their Accents*, *Yo!*, and *In the Time of the Butterflies*.

Julia Alvarez was born in 1950. This selection was published in 1985.

READING FOCUS

Have you ever stopped to think about your name? What does your name tell others about you?

Sharing Ideas
In small groups, talk about what names mean to you. Does your own name seem to capture any of the real you?

Setting a Purpose
Read the selection to find out what names mean to Julia Alvarez.

BUILDING BACKGROUND

The Time and Place
This selection is set in the early 1960s in New York City. Julia Alvarez was born in New York, but she lived in the Dominican Republic until the age of ten.

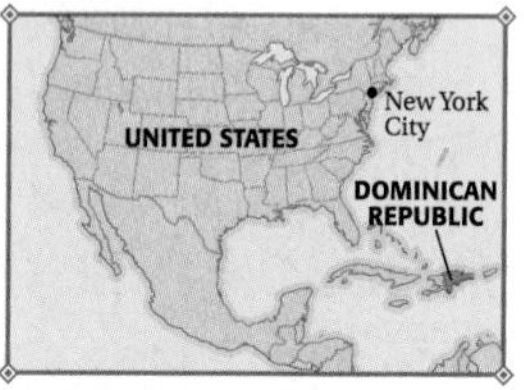

VOCABULARY PREVIEW

ironically (ī ron′ i kəl ē) *adv.* in a way that is different from what would be expected; p. 6
initial (i nish′ əl) *adj.* at the beginning; first; p. 7
merge (murj) *v.* to join together so as to become one; unite; p. 7
inevitably (i nev′ ə tə blē) *adv.* in a way that cannot be avoided or prevented; p. 7
vaguely (vāg′ lē) *adv.* in a way that is not clear, exact, or definite; p. 7
specify (spes′ ə fī′) *v.* to state or describe in detail; p. 7
exotic (ig zot′ ik) *adj.* strangely attractive; foreign; p. 8
chaotic (kā ot′ ik) *adj.* confused and disorganized; in great disorder; p. 8
commencement (kə mens′ mənt) *n.* a beginning; start; graduation ceremonies; p. 9

RESOURCE MANAGER

Teaching Tools and Resources
- Theme One Planning Guide
- Literature Groups Sourcebook

Essential Lesson Support

Lesson-Specific Instruction
- Selection Focus Transparency 1
- Literary Elements Transparency 1
- Active Reading Guide,* p. 1
- Selection Vocabulary Practice, p. 1
- TIME *inTIME* magazine, pp. 3–5, 6–7, 27

Assessment
- Selection Quick Checks,* p. 1
- Selection and Theme Assessment, pp. 1–2
- Testmaker: ExamView Pro
- Performance Assessment, p. 1

Systematic Language Instruction
- Grammer & Composition Handbook, Lessons 1.1–1.2
- Vocabulary Power, Lesson 1
- Spelling Power, Lesson 1

English Language Learners
- ELL Sourcebook, p. 17
- Spanish Summaries, p. 1
- Spanish Translations, pp. 1–4
- Audio Library*
- English, Yes!

Spec. Needs/Strat. Interven.
- Interactive Reading Sourcebook, pp. T47–T49
- Interactive Reading Workbook, pp. 1–3
- Inclusion Strategies Sourcebook, pp. 5–6, 55–56

*Also available in Spanish

Names/Nombres

Julia Alvarez

When we arrived in New York City, our names changed almost immediately. At Immigration, the officer asked my father, *Mister Elbures*, if he had anything to declare. My father shook his head, "No," and we were waved through. I was too afraid we wouldn't be let in if I corrected the man's pronunciation, but I said our name to myself, opening my mouth wide for the organ blast of the *a*, trilling my tongue for the drumroll of the *r*, *All-vah-rrr-es!* How could anyone get *Elbures* out of that orchestra of sound?

Nombres is a Spanish word for "names."

Portrait of Virginia, 1929. Frida Kahlo. Fundacion Dolores Olmedo, Mexico City, D.F., Mexico.

Reading the Selection

SUMMARY

In this short autobiographical work, Julia Alvarez discusses the many names—family names, nicknames, school names, American names, and Spanish names—she has had and how her feelings about her names changed at different periods in her life.

Spanish Summaries, p. 1

A Active Reading Strategies

CONNECT Ask students how they feel when their names are mispronounced. Are they proud of their names? Would they change their names if possible?

VOCABULARY If you haven't previewed the selection vocabulary with students, stop and remind them to use context clues to unlock the meanings of new vocabulary words.

Additional Resources

Active Reading Guide, p. 1

Audio Library

Spanish Audio Library

Teaching Support

CONNECTING TO OTHER SELECTIONS

The chart at the right shows three ways to connect "Names/Nombres" to other selections in this book.

For specific teaching strategies, see the ***Theme One Planning Guide.***

Connection	Title
Life Skills: Adapting	→ "Fish Cheeks," p. 77
Thematic: Changing Identity	→ "Bums in the Attic," p. 329
Literary: Theme	→ "One," p. 14

B Literary Elements

THEME Julia's teachers and friends mispronounce her name, and Julia wonders if she should correct them. Ask students what point they think Alvarez might be making about her identity. *(She suggests that because people are having a difficult time with an unfamiliar name, she feels more like an outsider.)*

C Critical Thinking

INFERRING Have students suggest what they think Julia's mother means when she responds, "A rose by any other name would smell as sweet?" *(Julia's mother means that no matter what Julia's friends call her, she is the same person.)*

D Literary Elements

THEME Here Alvarez creates an alternate identity for herself. Ask students what they think Alvarez is saying about the connection between one's name and one's identity. *(It seems the author believes that even a fake name cannot change one's true identity.)*

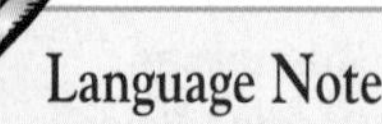

Language Note

Rich Noisy Name Ask students what they think the speaker means by *rich noisy name*. *(It has interesting sounds that stand out.)* Have students think of people or places that have rich noisy names.

Teaching Support

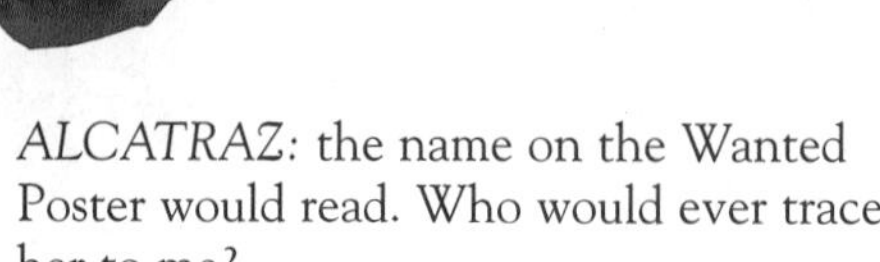

At the hotel my mother was *Missus Alburest*, and I was *little girl*, as in, "Hey, little girl, stop riding the elevator up and down. It's *not* a toy!"

When we moved into our new apartment building, the super called my father *Mister Alberase*, and the neighbors who became mother's friends pronounced her name *Jew-lee-ah* instead of *Hoo-lee-ah*. I, her namesake, was known as *Hoo-lee-tah* at home. But at school, I was *Judy* or *Judith*, and once an English teacher mistook me for *Juliet*.

B It took awhile to get used to my new names. I wondered if I shouldn't correct my teachers and new friends. But my mother argued that it didn't matter. "You know what your friend Shakespeare said, C '*A rose by any other name would smell as sweet.*'"[1] My family had gotten into the habit of calling any literary figure "my friend" because I had begun to write poems and stories in English class.

By the time I was in high school, I was a popular kid, and it showed in my name. Friends called me *Jules* or *Hey Jude*, and once a group of troublemaking friends my mother forbid me to hang out with called me *Alcatraz*.[2] I was *Hoo-lee-tah* only to Mami and Papi and uncles and aunts who came over to eat *sancocho*[3] on Sunday D afternoons—old world folk whom I just as soon would go back to where they came from and leave me to pursue whatever mischief I wanted to in America. *JUDY ALCATRAZ*: the name on the Wanted Poster would read. Who would ever trace her to me?

My older sister had the hardest time getting an American name for herself because Mauricia did not translate into English. Ironically, although she had the most foreign-sounding name, she and I were the Americans in the family. We had been born in New York City when our parents had first tried immigration and then gone back "home," too homesick to stay. My mother often told the story of how she had almost changed my sister's name in the hospital.

After the delivery, Mami and some other new mothers were cooing over their new baby sons and daughters and exchanging names and weights and delivery stories. My mother was embarrassed among the Sallys and Janes and Georges and Johns to reveal the rich, noisy name of *Mauricia*, so when her turn came to brag, she gave her baby's name as *Maureen*.

"Why'd ya give her an Irish name with so many pretty Spanish names to choose from?" one of the women asked her.

My mother blushed and admitted her baby's real name to the group. Her mother-in-law had recently died, she apologized,

1. This line is from William Shakespeare's play *Romeo and Juliet.*
2. *Alcatraz* is an island in San Francisco Bay that once was the home of a very tough federal prison.
3. *Sancocho* (sän kō′ chō) is a meat stew.

Vocabulary

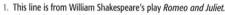

ironically (ī ron′ i kəl ē) *adv.* in a way that is different from what would be expected

MEETING INDIVIDUAL NEEDS: ENGLISH LANGUAGE LEARNERS

Naming a Child At the top of page 7 is an explanation of how Mauricia got her name. This provides an opportunity for students to share customs or traditions relating to naming a child.

Activity Have English language learners gather in small groups to share how they got their names and tell about some of the naming customs of their cultures. Invite students to share their information with other groups and with the class. After students read page 8, ask those students with Hispanic surnames to share their complete names with the class.

Additional Resources

English Language Learners Sourcebook, p. 17

and her husband had insisted that the first daughter be named after his mother, *Mauran*. My mother thought it the ugliest name she had ever heard, and she talked my father into what she believed was an improvement, a combination of *Mauran* and her own mother's name *Felicia*.

"Her name is *Mao-ree-chee-ah*," my mother said to the group.

"Why that's a beautiful name," the new mothers cried. "*Moor-ee-sha, Moor-ee-sha*," they cooed into the pink blanket.

Moor-ee-sha it was when we returned to the States eleven years later. Sometimes, American tongues found even that mispronunciation tough to say and called her *Maria* or *Marsha* or *Maudy* from her nickname *Maury*. I pitied her. What an awful name to have to transport across borders!

E My little sister, Ana, had the easiest time of all. She was plain *Anne*—that is, only her name was plain, for she turned out to be the pale, blond "American beauty" in the family. The only Hispanic-seeming thing about her was the affectionate nickname her boyfriends sometimes gave her, *Anita*, or as one goofy guy used to sing to her to the tune of the Chiquita Banana advertisement, *Anita Banana*.

Later, during her college years in the late '60s, there was a push to pronounce Third World[4] names correctly. I remember calling her long distance at her group house and a roommate answering.

"Can I speak to Ana?" I asked, pronouncing her name the American way.

"Ana?" The man's voice hesitated. "Oh! you mean *Ah-nah!*"

F Our first few years in the States, though, ethnicity[5] was not yet "in." Those were the blond, blue-eyed, bobby socks years of junior high and high school before the '60s ushered in peasant blouses, hoop earrings, serapes. G My initial desire to be known by my correct Dominican name faded. I just wanted to be Judy and merge with the Sallys and Janes in my class. But inevitably, my accent and coloring gave me away. "So where are you from, Judy?"

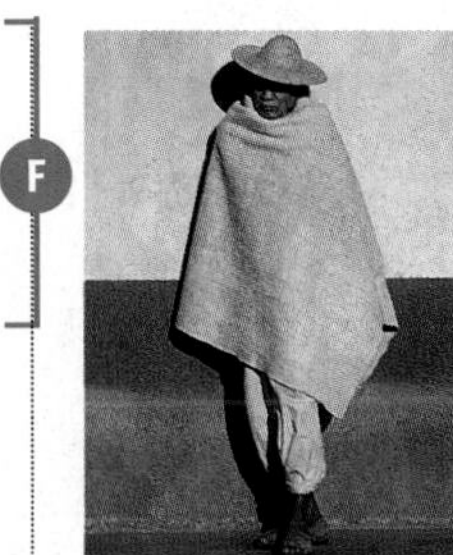

Did You Know?
A *serape* (sə rä′ pā) is a blanketlike outer garment similar to a shawl. It is often woven with bright colors and patterns and is worn chiefly by men in Latin American countries.

"New York," I told my classmates. After all, I had been born blocks away at Columbia Presbyterian Hospital.

"I mean, *originally*."

"From the Caribbean," I answered vaguely, for if I specified, no one was quite sure what continent our island was on.

4. *Third World* refers to poorer, less developed countries, mainly in Latin America, Africa, and Asia.

5. *Ethnicity* is a word for certain things that a group of people share, such as language, culture, history, race, and national origin. U.S. citizens come from many different ethnic backgrounds.

Vocabulary
initial (i nish′ əl) *adj.* at the beginning; first
merge (murj) *v.* to join together so as to become one; unite
inevitably (i nev′ ə tə blē) *adv.* in a way that cannot be avoided or prevented
vaguely (vāg′ lē) *adv.* in a way that is not clear, exact, or definite
specify (spes′ ə fī′) *v.* to state or describe in detail

E Active Reading Strategies

EVALUATE Have students discuss why Julia Alvarez put *American beauty* in quotation marks. Was it appropriate to do so? *(The quotation marks emphasize the stereotype. What is American and what passes for beauty are too limited, too narrowly defined.)*

F Critical Thinking

EVALUATING Ask students what they think the author means by the phrase "...ethnicity was not yet 'in.'" *(Until recently it was not fashionable to be proud of ethnic identity; pressure was applied to "blend in.")*

G Literary Elements

PLOT: *Internal Conflict* Have students discuss why they think Julia tells others she is from New York, even though she has lived mostly in the Dominican Republic. *(Julia wants to fit in, not to be thought of as a foreigner.)*

FYI

The Dominican Republic is part of the West Indies and is part of the continent of North America. The West Indies is an archipelago that extends from Florida to Venezuela and separates the Caribbean Sea from the Atlantic Ocean. The Dominican Republic, along with Haiti, is located on the island of Hispaniola.

Reading Minilesson

Classifying Remind students that classifying words means putting them into groups that have common characteristics. Point out that the very title of this selection "Names/Nombres" presents two classifications: words in English/words in Spanish.

Activity Work as a class to complete a table like the one here. Have students suggest additional English and Spanish first names to add to the chart. (Change category headings as necessary to suit the ethnicity of your class.) L2

English Names		Spanish Names	
Female	Male	Female	Male
Kate	George	Mauricia	Alfonso

Additional Resources

 ***Reading Skills Practice Workbook***

VIEWING THE PAINTING

Fernando Botero is a contemporary artist from Colombia. He often paints cheerful, balloon-shaped, not quite true-to-life people.

Viewing Response *Students may suggest that musicians like these would be appropriate for the birthday party scene, but Botero's satiric style would fit almost any part of the story.*

H Active Reading Strategies

EVALUATE Help students identify the proper spelling of Puerto Rico. Ask them why they think this spelling is given, considering the pronunciations are the same. *(Help students understand that the author seems to be poking fun at Americans' knowledge of the language and geography of the Caribbean.)*

I Literary Elements

THEME Point out to students the connection between the story's title and theme and this passage. *(The author reveals her entire name—all of her "official" names.)* Ask students how a name this long could define one's identity. *(Students should realize that by including all middle names and family surnames for four generations back, one would have a greater sense of familial identity.)*

The Musicians, 1979. Fernando Botero. Oil on canvas, 85¾ x 74¾ in. Private collection.

Viewing the painting: Which scene from the story would you like to see painted in the style of Botero?

"Say your name in Spanish, oh please say it!" I had made mouths drop one day by rattling off my full name, which according to Dominican custom, included my middle names, mother's and father's surnames for four generations back.

"Julia Altagracia Maria Teresa Alvarez Tavares Perello Espaillat Julia Pérez Rochet González," I pronounced it slowly, a name as chaotic with sounds as a Middle Eastern bazaar or market day in a South American village.

I suffered most whenever my extended family attended school occasions. For my graduation, they all came, the whole noisy, foreign-looking lot of old, fat aunts in their dark mourning dresses and hair nets, uncles with full, droopy mustaches and baby-blue or salmon-colored suits and white pointy shoes and fedora[6] hats, the many little cousins who

H "Really? I've been to Bermuda. We went last April for spring vacation. I got the worst sunburn! So, are you from Portoriko?"

"No," I shook my head. "From the Dominican Republic."

"Where's that?"

"South of Bermuda."

I They were just being curious, I knew, but I burned with shame whenever they singled me out as a "foreigner," a rare, exotic friend.

6. A *fedora* is a soft felt hat with a curved brim and a crease along the top.

Vocabulary

exotic (ig zot′ ik) *adj.* strangely attractive; foreign

chaotic (kā ot′ ik) *adj.* confused and disorganized; in great disorder

Teaching Support

Grammar and Language Minilesson

Proper Nouns and Proper Adjectives Remind students that proper nouns name a specific person, place, thing, or idea, such as *Bill, Utah, Ford,* or *June*. Proper adjectives are formed from proper nouns, as in *Texas chili.* Both proper nouns and proper adjectives begin with capital letters. Encourage students to look over pages 8–9 and list the proper nouns and proper adjectives they see.

Activity Have students change all of the listed words so that they relate to an experience they have had. If they once went to Florida on vacation, they would change *Bermuda* to *Florida.* Then have each student use several of the words they have listed to write a brief paragraph about a trip, the family, or an important event. **L2**

Additional Resources

- ***Grammar and Language Transparency 1***
- ***Grammar and Language Workbook,*** pp. 61–62, 119–120
- ***Grammar and Composition Handbook,*** Lessons 2.1, 5.1, 12.4
- ***Writer's Choice,*** Lessons 9.1, 12.2

J snuck in without tickets. They sat in the first row in order to better understand the Americans' fast-spoken English. But how could they listen when they were constantly speaking among themselves in florid-sounding phrases, rococo[7] consonants, rich, rhyming vowels. Their loud voices carried . . .

How could I introduce them to my friends? These relatives had such complicated names and there were so many of them, and their relationships to myself were so convoluted. There was my Tía Josefina, who was not really an aunt but a much older cousin. And her daughter, Aída Margarita, who was adopted, *una hija de crianza*. My uncle of affection, Tío José, brought my *madrina* Tía Amelia and her *comadre* Tía Pilar.[8] My friends rarely had more than their nuclear family[9] to introduce.

7. *Florid* and *rococo* both mean "very showy, highly decorated, or flowery."
8. Something that is *convoluted* is all twisted, coiled, and wound around. The rest of this paragraph identifies some of the writer's convoluted family relationships. *Tía* (tē′ ə) and *Tío* (tē′ ō) mean "Aunt" and "Uncle." *Una hija de crianza* (o͞o′ nə ē′ hə dā krē än′ zə) is an adopted daughter. *Madrina* (mə drē′ nə) and *comadre* (kō mä′ drā) both mean "godmother." Later, the writer mentions *primas* (prē′ məs) and *hermanas* (ār män′ əs), her female cousins and sisters.
9. Parents and their children make up what is called a *nuclear family.* An *extended family* includes other close relatives, such as grandparents, aunts, uncles, and cousins.

After the commencement ceremony my family waited outside in the parking lot while my friends and I signed yearbooks with nicknames which recalled our high school good times: "Beans" and "Pepperoni" and "Alcatraz." We hugged and cried and promised to keep in touch.

Our good-byes went on too long. I heard my father's voice calling out across the parking lot, *"Hoo-lee-tah! Vámonos!"*[10]

Back home, my *tíos* and *tías* and *primas*, Mami and Papi, and *mis hermanas* had a party for me with *sancocho* and a storebought *pudín*,[11] inscribed with *Happy Graduation, Julie*. There were many gifts—that was a plus to a large family! I got several wallets and a suitcase with my initials and a graduation charm from my godmother and money from my uncles. K The biggest gift was a portable typewriter from my parents for writing my stories and poems.

Someday, the family predicted, my name would be well-known throughout the United States. I laughed to myself, wondering which one I would go by.

10. *"Vámonos!"* (vä′ mə nōs) means "Let's go!"
11. A *pudín* (po͞o dēn′) is a pudding.

Vocabulary
commencement (kə mens′ mənt) *n.* a beginning; start; graduation ceremonies

J Author's Craft

MOOD Ask students to describe the mood or atmosphere of this scene and explain how the author helps readers picture the scene. *(The scene is noisy and filled with anticipation. She uses vivid descriptions: "florid-sounding phrases," "rococo consonants," "rich, rhyming vowels," and "loud voices carried.")*

K Active Reading Strategies

EVALUATE Have students discuss this question: Although this selection is autobiographical, do you think it is entirely believable? Explain why you think so. *(Some students will say yes, because it is what could possibly have happened. Others will say no, because she did not include some of the strong negative feelings she might have had.)*

Thematic Focus

What I Am, What I Want to Be
Have students compare Julia's feelings of not wanting to be a "foreigner" or a "rare, exotic friend" with how they would feel in a similar situation. Are Julia's feelings typical of someone her age? Have students share their experiences with those of other readers and provide examples to support their ideas.

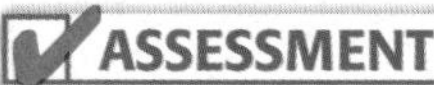

Quick Checks, p. 1

interNET CONNECTION

Names Students can use a search engine to find out more about names in different countries. They can use such keywords as *names, pronunciations, Spanish, English.* Encourage them to look for names that are distinctive in particular cultures, as well as names that are common or similar in many cultures. Discuss possible reasons for the similarities.

Real-World Connection

Family Tree A student can gain a better understanding of the author's concerns by researching the names in his or her family's history or the history of a family friend.

Activity Have each student interview a grandparent or an older relative to create a family tree. Encourage them to note whether a family name was changed or modified in any way. **L2**

You may wish to display ***Fine Art Transparency 4*** to enrich the discussion of feelings.

Responding to the Selection

PERSONAL RESPONSE

Students may question her protected feelings, feel a strong connection to some of her experiences, or raise issues they wished she had addressed.

Analyzing Literature

1. The immigration officer cannot pronounce *Alvarez*. He pronounces it *Elbures*.
2. As a teenager, Julia wants to be called Judy because she wants to fit in and be like other American teens.
3. Julia suffers most when her extended family attends school functions. Julia describes her relatives as a noisy, foreign-looking bunch.
4. The Alvarez family predicts that Julia's name will be well-known throughout the United States.
5. Julia doesn't like the immigration officer's pronunciation, but she doesn't say anything for fear he won't let the family into the United States.
6. A passage that shows Alvarez's desire to be like her classmates: *I just wanted to be Judy and merge with the Sallys and Janes in my class.* As Julia grows up, she seems to become proud of her Spanish heritage.
7. Alvarez is embarrassed by her relatives because they are so different from those of her American friends. They dress differently, act differently, and have different manners and customs. Alvarez would prefer them to be quiet and unobtrusive.
8. Alvarez's professional name is Julia Alvarez. It signifies her pride in her Dominican heritage.
9. The title represents the importance to her of both English and Spanish names.
10. Students should correctly identify the ethnic or cultural group or groups they belong to. They should also tell whether and when they identify with one group or another. You might identify your own background to get them started.

Active Reading and Critical Thinking

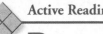

Responding to Literature

PERSONAL RESPONSE

- Describe your impressions as you read about the writer's problems and triumphs living in two very different cultures.

Analyzing Literature

RECALL

1. How is the Alvarez family name changed when they go through immigration?
2. Why does the teenage Alvarez just want to be called Judy?
3. Which occasions make Alvarez suffer the most? Find a **description** from the story to help explain your answer.
4. What does the Alvarez family predict about Julia's future career?

Brackets connect questions that are paired to develop higher-level thinking skills.

INTERPRET

5. How do you think Julia Alvarez feels about the change made to her family's name at the immigration office? Support your opinion with evidence from the selection.
6. Find a passage showing Alvarez's wish to be just like her classmates. How do you think her attitude changes as she grows up?
7. Why does Alvarez feel the way she does when her relatives appear at school functions? How would you feel?
8. Which of Alvarez's many names does she choose to use as a professional writer? In your opinion, why does she choose that one?

EVALUATE AND CONNECT

9. In your opinion, why does Alvarez give this story the title of "Names/Nombres"?
10. **Theme Connection** What different cultures or groups do you belong to? When do you choose to identify with one group versus another?

LITERARY ELEMENTS

Theme

The main idea of a written work is usually expressed as a general statement called a **theme.** Sometimes a piece of writing has a **stated theme**—one that is expressed directly. More often, a piece of writing has an **implied theme,** which is not stated directly but is revealed gradually as the piece unfolds.

1. What do you think is the theme of "Names/Nombres"? Is the theme stated directly, or is it implied? Support your opinion with examples and quotations from the story.
2. How does the title of the story relate to its theme?

- See **Literary Terms Handbook,** p. R11.

LITERARY ELEMENTS

1. The implied theme has to do with how names relate to personal identity. One example occurs when Julia thinks that if she were to become a criminal named Judy Alcatraz, surely no one could trace that name to her.
2. The title represents Julia's conflicting feelings about her different names.

Additional Resources

Literary Elements Transparency 1

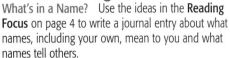

Extending Your Response

Writing About Literature

Sensory Imagery Julia Alvarez uses imagery that appeals to the senses. You can hear "the drumroll of the *r*," taste *sancocho,* and see "uncles with full, droopy mustaches." Find other sensory imagery in the selection. Name the senses they appeal to.

Literature Groups

Debating Shakespeare Julia's mother quotes Shakespeare—"a rose by any other name would smell as sweet." Do names affect how people are treated in this story? In your life? Is this fair? Share your ideas with your group.

Performing

Readers Theater Work with two or three other students to prepare a readers theater presentation of a scene from "Names/Nombres." Choose a scene that relates to the theme of the selection.

Personal Writing

What's in a Name? Use the ideas in the **Reading Focus** on page 4 to write a journal entry about what names, including your own, mean to you and what names tell others.

Listening and Speaking

Conducting an Interview Pick three people to interview about their names. Be sure to ask people to explain how they got these names. Record their answers and share your results.

Reading Further

For more about living in two cultures, try these:

In the Year of the Boar and Jackie Robinson by Bette Bao Lord

Going Home by Nicholasa Mohr

Child of the Owl by Laurence Yep

Save your work for your portfolio.

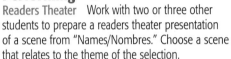

Skill Minilesson

Reteach • Review

VOCABULARY • ANTONYMS

Many words have antonyms—words that mean the opposite. For example, antonyms for *happy* include *sad, miserable, gloomy,* and *unhappy.* Choosing among antonyms helps you think about the exact meaning of a word.

PRACTICE Match each word with its antonym.

1. ironically	a. final
2. chaotic	b. clearly
3. merge	c. separate
4. initial	d. predictably
5. vaguely	e. orderly

Literature and Writing

Writing About Literature

Students' lists should

- include details that clearly appeal to the senses
- indicate which senses the details appeal to

Personal Writing

Students' journal entries should

- express clear opinions about what their own names mean to them
- explain what names tell other people and support their ideas with logical reasons

Extending Your Response

Literature Groups Encourage students to give each group member time to express an idea about the meaning of the quotation before they agree or disagree. Then have students review the ideas and add to their original thoughts. COLLAB. LEARN.

Performing Encourage students to act with their voices by using changes in volume, pitch, rhythm, stress patterns, and speed to express anger, fear, excitement, exhaustion, uncertainty, or other emotions.

Listening and Speaking Remind students to ask questions that require the person being interviewed to think and give detailed answers. COLLAB. LEARN.

Skill Minilesson

VOCABULARY • ANTONYMS

1. d 2. e 3. c 4. a 5. b

Additional Resources

Vocabulary Practice, p. 1

ASSESSMENT

- ***Quick Checks,*** p. 1
- ***Selection and Theme Assessment,*** pp. 1–2
- ***Performance Assessment,*** p. 1
- ***Testmaker: ExamView Pro***
- ***Interactive Tutor: Self-Assessment***

Objective

- To recognize and correct sentence fragments

Teaching Strategies

Explain that a sentence fragment is a group of words that does not contain both a subject and a predicate. *Wrote stories and poems* leaves one wondering who wrote them. Ask each student to write a sentence about something that happened yesterday. Write a few of the sentences on the board and have volunteers identify the subject and the predicate in each.

Activity

One acceptable solution: At school, Julia's friends called her Judy, Judith, Jules, Jude, or Alcatraz. The nicknames did not bother her because they meant she was popular.

Students should

- write in complete sentences
- use correct punctuation

Additional Resources

- ***Grammar and Language Workbook,*** p. 55
- ***Grammar and Composition Handbook,*** Lesson 1.2
- ***Writer's Choice,*** Lessons 7.1, 8.9

Teaching Support

Avoiding Sentence Fragments

A complete sentence contains both a subject and a predicate. The **subject** tells who or what the sentence is about. The **predicate** tells what is happening or being done. The predicate always includes a **verb.**

Morris sniffed.

In this complete sentence, *Morris* is the subject, and *sniffed* is the verb.
A **sentence fragment** is incomplete. It leaves out the subject or the verb or both.

Problem 1 The subject is missing.
Wrote stories and poems.

Solution Add a subject.
Julia Alvarez wrote stories and poems.

Problem 2 The verb is missing.
Julia's obvious talent as a writer.

Solution Add a verb to the fragment.
Julia's obvious talent as a writer soon became apparent to her parents.

Problem 3 The subject and verb are missing.
Her parents bought her a portable typewriter. As a graduation gift.

Solution Combine the fragment with another sentence.
Her parents bought her a portable typewriter as a graduation gift.

For more about sentence fragments, see **Language Handbook,** p. R12.

ACTIVITY

Rewrite the following paragraph, correcting any sentence fragments you find. You may be able to combine a fragment with another sentence, or you may need to add a subject or a verb.

At school, Julia's friends called her Judy. Or sometimes Judith or Jules or Jude. Some troublemaking friends. They called her Alcatraz. These nicknames didn't bother her. Just showed her popularity with other kids.

Writing Minilesson

Writing Descriptive Detail Encourage each student to draw or paint a picture of a favorite relative that includes as many details about the person as possible.

Activity Suggest that students work in pairs or in small groups to write character sketches that are based on their drawings and paintings. Sketches should be written in complete sentences, not in the fragments sometimes used in dialogue. You may want ot brainstorm to develop a list of descriptive words and phrases on the board first.
L2 COLLAB. LEARN.

Additional Resources

- ***Writer's Choice,*** Lessons 3.1–3.3

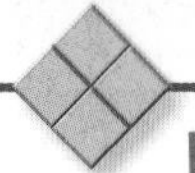

Before You Read

One and *I'm Nobody! Who are you?*

MEET JAMES BERRY

When James Berry looked around the British classroom where he was teaching and saw no books about African and Caribbean children, he began to write about his Caribbean homeland. He describes his poems as "scooped bits of the times I've lived in."

James Berry was born in Jamaica in 1925. "One" is from When I Dance: Poems, *published in 1988.*

MEET EMILY DICKINSON

Emily Dickinson has been called a private poetic genius. Of the 1,775 poems she wrote, only seven were published during her lifetime, and none with her consent.

Emily Dickinson was born in 1830 and died in 1886. "I'm Nobody! Who are you?" was first published in 1891.

READING FOCUS

What is it that makes you unique, or special, in this world?

QuickWrite

Reflect on your unique qualities. Then jot down these qualities, and tell how they set you apart from all others.

Setting a Purpose

Read to find out what these two poems have in common.

BUILDING BACKGROUND

James Berry and Emily Dickinson lived in different centuries and on different continents. Although their paths never crossed, these two poets shared a sense of "otherness," of what it is like to be a unique individual. In his writing, James Berry often explores what it means to be part of a racial minority, something he experienced firsthand when he immigrated to Great Britain from Jamaica in 1948 at the age of 23.

A shy woman, Emily Dickinson seldom left her home in Amherst, Massachusetts. On the surface, her life seemed uneventful. She lived a quiet life, seeing few people outside of her own family. Dickinson's poetry, however, reveals a lively, sensitive, and original human being, committed to writing about the world from her own unique perspective.

Emily Dickinson's home in Amherst.

Before Reading

Objectives

- To read and compare two poems that express each poet's sense of self
- To identify and appreciate visual imagery in poetry
- To write a comparison of poetic themes

Skills

Reading/Thinking: Logical Reasoning; Drawing Conclusions; Summarizing; Comparing and Contrasting

Writing: Self-Portrait

Collaboration: Literature Groups

Motivating STUDENTS

Selection Focus Transparency 2: Have students view and discuss Andy Warhol's *Marilyn.*

Reading Focus: To extend the Reading Focus, you may want to pair each student with a friend and ask the partners to list each other's special qualities.

RESOURCE MANAGER

Teaching Tools and Resources

- Theme One Planning Guide
- Literature Groups Sourcebook

Essential Lesson Support

Lesson-Specific Instruction

- Selection Focus Transparency 2
- Literary Elements Transparency 2
- Active Reading Guide,* p. 2

Assessment

- Selection Quick Checks,* p. 2
- Selection and Theme Assessment, pp. 3–4
- Testmaker: ExamView Pro
- Performance Assessment, p. 2

Systematic Language Instruction

- Grammer & Composition Handbook, Lessons 1.3, 1.4

English Language Learners

- ELL Sourcebook, p. 18
- Spanish Summaries, p. 2
- Audio Library*
- English, Yes!

Spec. Needs/Strat. Interven.

- Interactive Reading Sourcebook, pp. T50–T52
- Interactive Reading Workbook, p. 4
- Inclusion Strategies Sourcebook, pp. 55–56
- Audio Library*

*Also available in Spanish

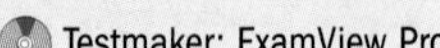

Reading the Selection

A Active Reading Strategies

Help students notice the great number of images in the poem. Ask them which are the most vivid. Then ask students to describe how the images add up to a picture of the speaker.

B Critical Thinking

LOGICAL REASONING Do students agree that they are originals? Ask those who disagree to explain. *(Most students will agree on the basis of the examples Berry provides. Others may cite clones or twins as examples of people who are not originals.)*

C Literary Elements

VISUAL IMAGERY Read these lines aloud: *and mirrors can show me multiplied many times, say, dressed up in green, or dressed up in blue.* Ask students to describe what they see and to discuss how the image helps readers understand that the speaker is only "One."

Additional Resources

- ***Active Reading Guide,*** p. 2
- ***Audio Library***
- ***Spanish Audio Library***
- ***Spanish Summaries,*** p. 2

One

James Berry

Only one of me
and nobody can get a second one
from a photocopy machine.

Nobody has the fingerprints I have.
Nobody can cry my tears, or laugh my laugh
or have my expectancy° when I wait.

But anybody can mimic° my dance with my dog.
Anybody can howl how I sing out of tune.
And mirrors can show me multiplied
many times, say, dressed up in red
or dressed up in grey.

Nobody can get into my clothes for me
or feel my fall for me, or do my running.
Nobody hears my music for me, either.

I am just this one.
Nobody else makes the words
I shape with sound, when I talk.

But anybody can act how I stutter in a rage.
Anybody can copy echoes I make.
And mirrors can show me multiplied
many times, say, dressed up in green
or dressed up in blue.

6 An *expectancy* is the feeling one has while expecting something.
7 To *mimic* is to copy, or imitate.

Teaching Support

CONNECTING TO OTHER SELECTIONS
For a teaching strategy that connects "One" to "Names/Nombres," turn to the *Theme One Planning Guide*.

MEETING INDIVIDUAL NEEDS — ENGLISH LANGUAGE LEARNERS

Compound Words On the board, write *somebody, photocopy,* and *fingerprints*. Explain that often the meaning of a compound word can be figured out by combining the meanings of the words that form it. For example:

somebody = some + body (a person; someone who is important)
photocopy = photo + copy (a copy created by a photographic process)
fingerprints = finger + prints (unique impressions made by the fingertips)

Activity Have students look for other examples of compound words. You may wish to have them list and define them in their vocabulary notebooks.

Additional Resources

- ***English Language Learners Sourcebook,*** p. 18

I'm Nobody! Who are you?

Emily Dickinson

I'm Nobody! Who are you?
Are you—Nobody—Too?
Then there's a pair of us!
Don't tell! they'd advertise—you know!

How dreary°—to be—Somebody!
How public—like a Frog—
To tell one's name—the livelong June°—
To an admiring Bog!°

5 *Dreary* means "sad; depressing; dull; uninteresting."
7 The *livelong June* would be the whole month.
8 A *bog* is the swampy sort of ground where frogs live.

"Sun Shower," 1995. Diana Ong. Computer graphic, 5 x 4 in. Chrome.

D Active Reading Strategies

CONNECT Ask students what they think Emily Dickinson might say to James Berry about being "One." *(If everyone is "one," she would like to be "one" in a quiet and private way.)*

E Critical Thinking

DRAWING CONCLUSIONS Ask students why Dickinson chooses a frog to make her point. *(A frog's croaking is monotonous, and nobody cares to hear it.)*

F Literary Elements

VISUAL IMAGERY Have students describe the picture Dickinson paints using *the livelong June—To an admiring Bog!* *(These words create images of water, mud, reeds, nice weather, and a lone frog.)*

LITERATURE & HUMANITIES

Display *Green Coca Cola Bottles,* in *American Art History and Culture*, page 574. Have students examine how the images, though repeated, still reinforce the idea of individuality.

Thematic Focus

What I Am, What I Want to Be
The speakers in both poems make strong statements about who they are and who they want to be.

ASSESSMENT

Quick Checks, p. 2

Reading Minilesson

Summarizing Remind students that the purpose of summarizing is to provide a brief, easily understood restatement of the most important ideas of a text.

Activity Ask students to work individually to summarize "I'm Nobody! Who are you?" by completing the graphic organizer. Invite a few volunteers to share their work with the class and discuss whether their summaries have included the right information. **L2**

Additional Resources
Reading Skills Practice Workbook

Question Used to Discover Important Facts	Answer
What does the speaker say about himself/herself?	*He or she is "nobody."*
Whom does the speaker meet?	*He or she meets another "nobody."*
What does the speaker think about his/her situation?	*It is better to be "nobody" than "somebody."*
Summary: *The speaker, who calls himself or herself "nobody," meets another "nobody" and says that it is better to be "nobody" than "somebody."*	

Responding to the Selection

PERSONAL RESPONSE

Student responses should indicate how the poems helped them reflect on what they are and what they want to be. Writing should include supporting passages and ideas from the poems.

Analyzing Literature

1. The author mentions fingerprints, feelings, experiences, actions, perceptions, and ways of thinking and speaking.
2. In the category of Nobodies, people are private and quiet. In the category of Somebodies, people are public and talk about themselves to anyone who will listen.
3. It lists the many things that make any person unique.
4. The speaker is a private person and feels that telling one's name in public would be dull and repetitive.
5. The speaker most values his private feelings and experiences. He finds the things that people can see him do—dress up, act angry, or show off—less valuable.
6. Students can express personal preferences for being Nobody or Somebody. Some may think that being Nobody is what makes you Somebody.
7. He would want to be appreciated for his words and for simply being who he is.
8. Some students may choose "One" because it is a confident poem that celebrates the poet's belief in his individuality. Other students may choose "I'm Nobody! Who are You?" because in it the poet asserts that she is more comfortable with herself than with others.
9. There would be no politicians, actors, musicians, or other public figures.
10. She writes in a conversational tone, addressing the reader as "you" and asking direct questions.

Active Reading and Critical Thinking

Responding to Literature

PERSONAL RESPONSE

- What did you realize about yourself while reading these poems?
- What do the poems say about promoting yourself?

Analyzing Literature

RECALL

1. In what ways does the speaker in James Berry's poem feel unique? In what ways is he not unique?
2. Into what two categories does the speaker in Emily Dickinson's poem divide people, including herself? Describe each category.

Brackets connect questions that are paired to develop higher-level thinking skills.

INTERPRET

3. How does "One" celebrate the uniqueness of individuals?
4. Why does the speaker in Emily Dickinson's poem feel that being "Nobody" is preferable to being "Somebody"?

EVALUATE AND CONNECT

5. Which aspects of being human do you think the speaker in "One" values most? Which aspects are less valuable?
6. If you had to decide to be Dickinson's Nobody or Somebody, which would you choose? Explain.
7. What lasting impression do you imagine the speaker in "One" would want to leave on people he has known?
8. Theme Connection Which of these poems better expresses how you feel about yourself? Explain.
9. How would the world change if everyone decided to be a "Nobody"?
10. What is it about Emily Dickinson's writing **style** that makes you feel as if she is actually talking to you?

LITERARY ELEMENTS

Visual Imagery

Visual imagery is the collection of details that writers use to help readers visualize scenes. Visual imagery makes writing come to life. In "One," James Berry repeats, "And mirrors can show me multiplied / many times. . . ." These lines help readers "see" a young man preening as he looks at himself in a mirror in different-colored clothes.

1. Reread "I'm Nobody! Who are you?" and "One." Find an example of visual imagery that helps you "see" what the speaker is describing in each poem.
2. How does Berry's use of the image of a photocopy machine reflect his thoughts about individuality?

● See **Literary Terms Handbook,** p. R11.

LITERARY ELEMENTS

1. Some examples include Dickinson's lines about a frog that croaks repetitively in a deserted bog or the line in "One" about dancing with his dog.
2. It implies that unlike paper, which can be replicated, the speaker is multidimensional and unique.

Additional Resources

 ***Literary Elements Transparency 2***

Extending Your Response

Writing About Literature

Theme The **theme** of a poem is its central idea or message. Write a paragraph identifying the message of each of these two poems.

Personal Writing

New Thoughts About Myself Return to the notes you wrote in the **Reading Focus** on page 13. Would you change the qualities you listed after reading these two poems? Write a short self-portrait that shows who you are. Explore your unique character traits and personality more than your appearance.

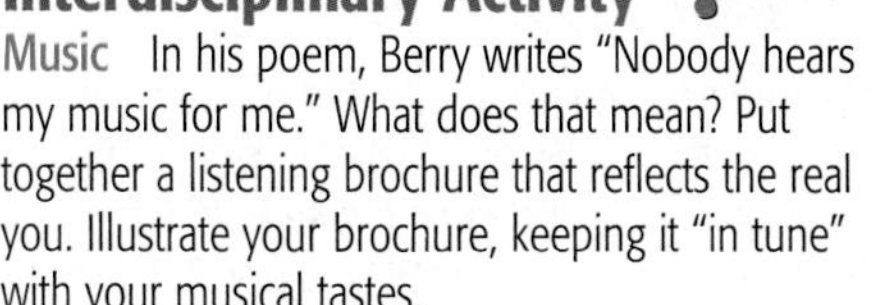

Interdisciplinary Activity

Music In his poem, Berry writes "Nobody hears my music for me." What does that mean? Put together a listening brochure that reflects the real you. Illustrate your brochure, keeping it "in tune" with your musical tastes.

Literature Groups

Present Yourself! Read each poem line by line. Identify the line that is the most thought provoking. How does the line challenge or confirm your own thoughts about yourself? Does it make you reconsider what makes a person unique? Does it give you a strong visual image? With your group, choose the line that provokes the most interest. Write the line on a banner to present to the class. Be ready to defend your choice in a larger group discussion.

Reading Further

If you enjoyed the work of these poets, you might like to check out these other works:

Short Stories: *A Thief in the Village and Other Stories* by James Berry

Biography: *Emily Dickinson* by Victoria Olsen

Save your work for your portfolio.

Skill Minilesson

Reteach · Review

READING AND THINKING • COMPARING AND CONTRASTING

In the poems "One" and "I'm Nobody! Who are you?" the speakers share private thoughts and feelings about their own identities with you, the reader. In some ways the poems are similar. In other ways they are very different.

PRACTICE Try your hand at comparing and contrasting.

1. Write one paragraph that compares the poems, describing how they are alike.
2. Write a second paragraph that contrasts the poems, showing how they are different. Think about the structure, rhyme, rhythm, and punctuation in each poem. Pay special attention to imagery, meaning, and word choice. You might begin by examining how each poet uses the word *nobody.* They both use the word several times, but the intended meaning is quite different.

 For more about comparing and contrasting, see **Reading Handbook,** p. R93.

Extending Your Response

Writing About Literature

Students' paragraphs should
- clearly state the theme of each poem
- list the similarities and differences in the poems' themes

Personal Writing

Students' self-portraits should
- describe their unique character traits and personality
- include personal details from the QuickWrite activity on page 13

Interdisciplinary Activity You may want to invite students to bring in a few sample recordings of the music listed on their brochures to play for the class.

Literature Groups Encourage students to begin by deciding upon a method of coming to an agreement. COLLAB. LEARN.

Skill Minilesson

READING AND THINKING
- **COMPARING AND CONTRASTING**

1. Each expresses thoughts about the poet's sense of self.
2. "One" is longer, has no rhyme, uses repetition, expresses ideas in complete sentences. The speaker's main idea is that no matter who or what mimics him, he will remain one of a kind. "I'm Nobody! Who are you?" is shorter, uses rhyme and invented capitalization. The speaker says she would rather remain anonymous than bear the burden of fame.

Additional Resources

Reading Skills Practice Workbook

ASSESSMENT

- ***Quick Checks,*** p. 2
- ***Selection and Theme Assessment,*** pp. 3–4
- ***Performance Assessment,*** p. 2
- ***Testmaker: ExamView Pro***
- ***Interactive Tutor: Self-Assessment***

Before Reading

Objectives

- To read and analyze two poems about personal characteristics and self-confidence
- To identify and understand irony in poetry
- To write a description of the speaker in a poem

Skills

Reading/Thinking: Generalizing; Paraphrasing; Visualizing
Writing: Short Descriptive Poem
Listening/Speaking: Reading and Listening to Poetry
Collaboration: Literature Groups; Partner Reading

Motivating STUDENTS

Selection Focus Transparency 3: Have students view and discuss *Girl in Mirror* by Roy Lichtenstein.

Reading Focus: To extend the Reading Focus, ask students to draw self-portraits. They can draw realistic portraits or create caricatures that exaggerate their most striking features.

Before You Read

Face It and *Almost Ready*

MEET JANET S. WONG

Janet Wong's mother is Korean, her father Chinese. "Growing up, I never felt very Korean," Wong says. "Lately I have been wanting to know more about my mother, and for the first time I find myself craving Korean beef bone soup and kimchi, which I used to hate."

"Face It" is from an anthology called A Suitcase of Seaweed and Other Poems, *published in 1996.*

MEET ARNOLD ADOFF

Arnold Adoff believes that "writing a poem is making music with words and space." The award-winning poet, teacher, and lecturer is married to writer Virginia Hamilton.

"Almost Ready" is from an anthology, Slow Dance Heart Break Blues, *published in 1995.*

READING FOCUS

What is the real *you* like? Do you have your father's chin or your grandmother's sense of humor? Think about your physical characteristics and your personality traits. Do you know which ones are family traits?

Chart It!

Make a chart showing some of your personality traits and physical characteristics. Label the ones you think are family traits and those that are unique to you.

Setting a Purpose

Read to find out what the speakers in these poems think about how they look.

BUILDING BACKGROUND

Our cultural and ethnic heritage is also part of what makes each of us unique. Janet S. Wong writes: "Sometimes the first question a stranger will ask me, even before learning my name, is 'What are you?' or 'Where are you from?' These kinds of people usually stare hard at my face, as if they are testing themselves on how well they can tell the difference between Chinese and Korean and Japanese."

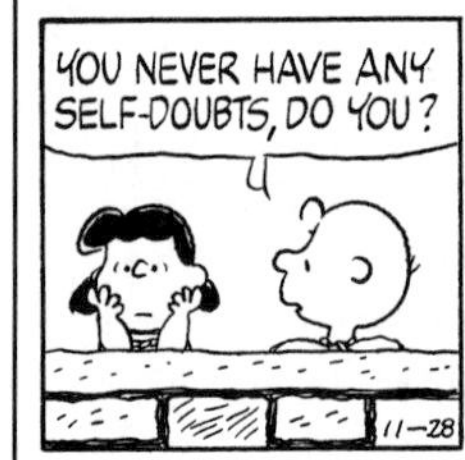

RESOURCE MANAGER

Teaching Tools and Resources
- Theme One Planning Guide
- Literature Groups Sourcebook

Essential Lesson Support

Lesson-Specific Instruction
- Selection Focus Transparency 3
- Literary Elements Transparency 3
- Active Reading Guide,* p. 3

Assessment
- Selection Quick Checks,* p. 3
- Selection and Theme Assessment, pp. 5–6
- Testmaker: ExamView Pro
- Performance Assessment, p. 3

Systematic Language Instruction
- Grammer & Composition Handbook, Lesson 1.5
- Vocabulary Power, Lesson 2
- Spelling Power, Lesson 2

English Language Learners
- ELL Sourcebook, p. 19
- Spanish Summaries, p. 3
- Audio Library*
- English, Yes!

Spec. Needs/Strat. Interven.
- Interactive Reading Sourcebook, pp. T53–T55
- Interactive Reading Workbook, p. 5
- Inclusion Strategies Sourcebook, pp. 39–40, 55–56, 77–78
- Audio Library*

*Also available in Spanish

FACE IT

Janet S. Wong

My nose belongs
to Guangdong, China—
short and round, a Jang family nose.

My eyes belong
to Alsace, France—
wide like Grandmother Hemmerling's.

But my mouth, my big-talking mouth, belongs
to me, alone.

Reading the Selection

A Active Reading Strategies

EVALUATE The first part of this statement is not literally true. Have students explain what larger idea it implies. *(Her nose looks just like the noses of her Chinese ancestors.)*

B Literary Elements

REPETITION Ask students to point out examples of repetition that lend rhythm to the poem. *(The word* belong *occurs in all three stanzas, and the word* mouth *is repeated in the last stanza.)*

C Active Reading Strategies

EVALUATE Ask students why the speaker feels she is responsible for her mouth. *(What she says with her mouth is not hereditary like the shape of her nose and her eyes.)*

Additional Resources

- ***Active Reading Guide,*** p. 3
- ***Audio Library***
- ***Spanish Audio Library***
- ***Spanish Summaries,*** p. 3

Teaching Support

MEETING INDIVIDUAL NEEDS — ENGLISH LANGUAGE LEARNERS

Dramatic Reading Performing "Almost Ready" with its repeated language pattern gives English language learners a rewarding experience in English pronunciation, inflection, and phrasing.

Activity Read the poem aloud as students follow. Then have students read aloud with you at least twice. Concentrate on phrasing and emphasize the rhythmic lines. Then have them read the poem aloud. Coach them on pronunciation and phrasing until their delivery is fluent. After students have mastered reading the poem, invite them to give a dramatic reading for the class.

Additional Resources

- ***English Language Learners Sourcebook,*** p. 19

D Literary Elements

IRONY Ask students whether the speaker in "Almost Ready" sounds self-assured. Invite a discussion of what the phrase "I am going to her birthday party as..." brings to mind. *(Students may be reminded of going to a costume party, which suggests concealing one's real self.)*

E Critical Thinking

GENERALIZING Have students consider whether they think people in real life who act hip and cool are usually as self-confident as they appear.

F Literary Elements

FREE VERSE Ask students to take a close look at the way the lines are arranged on the page and how the physical arrangement of lines might help deliver the poem's main idea. *(The lines may be like a list of things to do. This shows how many people think about one thing at a time and helps readers understand the speaker's growing panic.)*

Thematic Focus

What I Am, What I Want to Be In "Face It" and "Almost Ready," the speakers focus on particular personal traits. Ask students to consider how a person's vulnerability, shyness, or talkativeness is an important part of who they are.

ASSESSMENT

 ***Quick Checks,*** p. 3

ALMOST READY

Arnold Adoff

I
am
going
to
her
birth-
day
party

as
this
cool
and
in-
control
young
dude:

as
soon
as
I
find
my
new
shirt,

as
soon
as
I
find
my
hip
shoes,

as
soon
as
I
find
my
deep
voice,

as
soon
as
I
find
my
right
mask.

Teaching Support

CONNECTING TO OTHER SELECTIONS
For a teaching strategy that connects "Almost Ready" to "The Dog Diaries," see the ***Theme Four Planning Guide.***

FINE ART TRANSPARENCY 31

You may wish to use ***Fine Art Transparency 31*** to enrich the discussion.

Reading Minilesson

Paraphrasing Help students recall that paraphrasing is restating something in your own words. Remind students that a summary should contain only the most important ideas, whereas a *paraphrase* should include virtually the same information as the original, including the author's opinion.

Activity Help students paraphrase "Almost Ready" by telling what the poem's speaker really means. If necessary, model the first one or two items for your students. **L2**

Additional Resources
Reading Skills Practice Workbook

Responding to Literature

PERSONAL RESPONSE

- What is your response to these two poems?
- Which lines from each poem did you find most memorable? Why?

Analyzing Literature

RECALL

1. What images does the poem "Face It" focus on?
2. Summarize what happens in "Almost Ready."

Brackets connect questions that are paired to develop higher-level thinking skills.

INTERPRET

3. How do you think the images and the title of the poem "Face It" relate to the poem's **theme?**
4. What inner **conflict** is the speaker of "Almost Ready" feeling? How does the conflict relate to the poem's title? Explain.

EVALUATE AND CONNECT

5. Do you agree with the speaker of "Face It" that people are a combination of their ancestors' characteristics and their own unique traits? Why or why not?
6. Do you agree that young people often show an exterior that is "cool and in-control," while their inner feelings are quite different? Explain.
7. How does the arrangement of the lines of "Almost Ready" relate to the meaning of the poem? How does this special structure affect the actual reading of the poem?
8. How do *you* prepare to go to a birthday party? In what ways are you like the speaker in "Almost Ready"? In what ways are you different?
9. Theme Connection What did you discover or realize about yourself as you read these poems? Explain.
10. Did you find these poems humorous, serious, or both? Explain.

LITERARY ELEMENTS

Irony

When something awful happens and you say "Oh, great!" you are being ironic. In literature, **verbal irony** exists when the writer, or a character the writer creates, says the opposite of what he or she really means. Similarly, **situational irony** exists when what actually happens in a situation is the opposite of what we expect.

Irony may be used for humorous purposes, as when someone says "Nice weather" during a blizzard. It also can be used in a serious, or even bitter, way. For example, you might mutter "Nice guy" after someone has done something rude.

Watch for irony in literature. If you don't see when a writer is using irony, you may misunderstand what that author is trying to say.

1. Find and explain an example of irony in either poem.
2. Is the title of one of these poems an example of irony? Why or why not?

● See **Literary Terms Handbook,** p. R6.

Responding to the Selection

PERSONAL RESPONSE

Students may say that they know how the speakers in these poems feel because they have had similar feelings.

Analyzing Literature

1. It focuses on the speaker's facial features, especially the nose, the eyes, and the mouth.
2. A boy likes a girl and wants to impress her, but he feels he has to change everything about himself to do so. At first the reader thinks the speaker is self-confident but soon realizes that he is really insecure.
3. "Face It" is a pun. It refers to the speaker's face, which is described in the poem, and it refers to being honest with oneself.
4. The speaker is in conflict about his identity. He does not have the confidence to go as himself.
5. Most students will agree and will cite examples of relatives who look like them. Students will also agree that everyone's face is unique.
6. Most students will agree and say that they often feel they need to hide strong feelings.
7. The lines are written like lists of things to do to get ready. This arrangement makes the rhythm of the poem and the repetitions more obvious.
8. Student responses should include some comparisons to the poem.
9. Students will express varied thoughts about their appearance and self-confidence.
10. Most students will find serious ideas and possibly humor in both poems. Both speakers are expressing serious thoughts and feelings. The reference to the "big-talking mouth" in "Face It" and to the incongruity between the overconfidence and the dissolving self-confidence in "Almost Ready" are humorous.

LITERARY ELEMENTS

1. In "Almost Ready," there is irony in the speaker's view of himself.
2. "Almost Ready" is an example of irony. The speaker in the poem is clearly not ready.

Additional Resources

Literary Elements Transparency 3

Extending Your Response

Writing About Literature

Students' paragraphs should

- describe the character and personality of one of the speakers
- use lines from the poem to support their conclusions

Creative Writing

Students' poems should

- describe themselves or people they know
- use exact words

Literature Groups Encourage students to recognize the honesty in each poem and ask them to discuss how honesty in poetry is an important element. COLLAB. LEARN.

Listening and Speaking Suggest that readers practice reading the poem several times before sharing it with their partners. Remind students to speak slowly and clearly. Encourage them to pay attention to the musical quality of the words so that listeners can more fully enjoy the reading.

Skill Minilesson

READING AND THINKING
- **VISUALIZING**

Students' paragraphs should contain accurate descriptions of the images in the two poems.

Additional Resources

Reading Skills Practice Workbook

Extending Your Response

Writing About Literature

Character The speakers in both poems reveal a great deal about themselves in very few words. Write a paragraph describing the speaker from either poem as you picture that person.

Literature Groups

Poet's Corner Both of these poems offer surprise endings. In "Almost Ready," the speaker says "as soon as I find my right mask." What does this line mean? Do you agree or disagree that clothing and "put-on" airs such as a "deep voice" can be a mask? The poem "Face It" also ends with a surprise. When the speaker refers to her "big-talking mouth," what is she revealing about herself?

Girl with a Red Hat, 1940. Raphael Soyer. Oil on canvas, 76.8 x 43.2 cm. Fundacion Coleccion Thyssen-Bornemisza, Madrid.

Creative Writing

Who Am I? Write a short poem that describes you or a person you know, such as a friend or a relative. Try to include as much information as possible, using exact words. If you are writing about yourself, review your chart from the **Reading Focus** on page 18 before you begin.

Listening and Speaking

Listening to Poetry To be fully enjoyed, a poem is best read aloud. Listeners can close their eyes and picture the images as they hear the rhythm of the lines. With a partner, take turns reading these poems to each other.

Reading Further

If you would like to read more by these poets, try these books:

All the Colors of the Race by Arnold Adoff

Good Luck Gold and Other Poems by Janet S. Wong

Save your work for your portfolio.

Skill Minilesson

Reteach · Review

READING AND THINKING • VISUALIZING

Visualizing a story or a poem is a skill that can help you enjoy and understand that piece of writing better. As you read or listen, try to re-create images or scenes in your mind. Pay close attention to the details the writer chooses. Ask yourself: what does this image or scene look like, smell like, feel like? What is going on here?

PRACTICE Reread each of the poems. As you do, try to visualize the images in each poem.

Write a paragraph describing some of the images that come to mind as you read or listen to each poem. You might want to sketch some of the images to accompany your paragraph.

- For more about visualizing, see **Reading Handbook**, p. R87.

ASSESSMENT

- ***Quick Checks,*** p. 3
- ***Selection and Theme Assessment,*** pp. 5–6
- ***Performance Assessment,*** p. 3
- ***Testmaker: ExamView Pro***
- ***Interactive Tutor: Self-Assessment***

Writing Skills

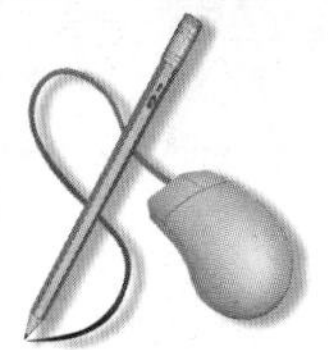

Using Dialogue in a Narrative

Dialogue, or conversation quoting the exact words of characters, is an effective narrative technique. It can rivet the reader's attention. And no wonder. Dialogue can bring characters to life and dramatically show them reacting to one another.

When you use dialogue in your writing, try to weave it in smoothly. Dialogue may be introduced in several ways—at the beginning, middle, or end of a sentence. Sometimes a block of conversation can continue for several lines. Following are some examples of how dialogue can be used. As you read, notice how the writer has used capitalization and punctuation marks.

How Dialogue Can Be Used in Writing	
At the beginning of a sentence: "It's a polite Chinese custom to show you are satisfied," explained my father to our astonished guests. —Amy Tan, "Fish Cheeks" **In the middle of a sentence:** He said, "Let me have those front seats," because they were the front seats of the black section. —Rosa Parks, from *Rosa Parks: My Story* **At the end of a sentence:** Ernie groaned and said, "Ah, man." —Gary Soto, "Broken Chain"	**As a block of conversation:** . . . inevitably, my accent and coloring gave me away. "So where are you from, Judy?" "New York," I told my classmates. After all, I had been born blocks away at Columbia Presbyterian Hospital. "I mean, *originally.*" "From the Caribbean," I answered vaguely, for if I specified, no one was quite sure what continent our island was on. —Julia Alvarez, "Names/Nombres" **Mechanics Tip:** Indent each time the speaker changes. **An interrupted quotation:** "Children," Miss Ryan called for attention. "Ernesto has learned how to pronounce butterfly!" —Ernesto Galarza, from *Barrio Boy*

ACTIVITIES

1. Write at least three sentences of dialogue about a childhood memory. Use dialogue to begin one sentence, to form the middle of another, and to end a third.
2. Write a paragraph in which one friend tells a joke to another. Include a block of dialogue and indent correctly.

Writing Skills

Objective

- To recognize and use dialogue in narrative writing

Teaching Strategies

To dramatize the difference between indirect speech and dialogue, read the following passage aloud to the class.

Kim told her sister she didn't want to paint their bedroom yellow because it would be too sunny and energetic. Kim's sister, Maria, said that yellow was the color of the moon and could be a soothing color. Kim couldn't imagine who'd want to live on the moon. She certainly didn't.

Ask students to take the parts of Kim and Maria and role-play this conversation. Encourage them to improvise and add emotion.

Activities

1. Students' sentences should adhere to the punctuation guidelines in their books.
2. Students may want to include an interrupted quotation in their blocks of dialogue.

Additional Resources

 ***Writer's Choice,*** Lessons 4.4, 20.6

Teaching Support

Grammar and Language *Minilesson*

Punctuating Dialogue Have students find a paragraph in "Names/Nombres" that includes dialogue. Ask a few volunteers to read dialogue from the story aloud, including punctuation and capitalization, as if they were dictating it to a typist.

Activity Have small groups of students conduct an informal meeting to discuss one of the four poems in this theme. They should tape-record five minutes of the discussion and transcribe a small portion, using the sample dialogue on page 23 as a model for punctuating it. Have them check for accuracy of content and punctuation. **L3** COLLAB. LEARN.

Additional Resources

 ***Grammar and Language Transparency 2***

Gr. & Lang. Wkbk., pp. 267–270

Gr. & Comp. Hbk., Lesson 13.6

Writer's Choice, Lessons 4.4, 20.6

MEDIA *Connection*

Objective

- To read and understand a newspaper column

Literature LINK

Strong Men Weep This newspaper column connects to the literature selection that follows this lesson. Point out the connection: Like the disabled but victorious mountain climbers, Lou Gehrig of the New York Yankees faced one of life's great challenges with courage, determination, and grace.

Analyzing Media

1. Some students may say that the author writes short paragraphs because people skim for information in newspapers. Others may say that the short paragraphs make the article move along quickly.
2. Responses may include stories of popular figures who have accomplished great feats but behaved poorly in their personal lives.

Informational Text

For more examples of informational text, direct students to the articles in the *InTIME* magazine.

Additional Resources

Media Connections, p. 1

Teaching Support

MEDIA *Connection*

NEWSPAPER COLUMN

This column was written in 1981, after John McEnroe won the tennis championship at Wimbledon, England. The young McEnroe had a reputation for behaving badly on the tennis court. Do you think Erma Bombeck's comments are relevant today?

Heroes

by Erma Bombeck—Syndicated Newspaper Column, August 2, 1981

On the first Saturday of last month, a 22-year-old U.S. tennis player hoisted a silver bowl over his head at Centre Court at Wimbledon.

The day before, five blind mountain climbers, a man with an artificial leg, an epileptic, and two deaf adventurers stood atop the snowcapped summit of Mount Rainier.

It was a noisy victory for the tennis player, who shared it with thousands of fans, some of whom had slept on the sidewalks outside the club for six nights waiting for tickets.

It was a quiet victory for the climbers, who led their own cheering, punctuated by a shout from one of them that echoed on the winds: "There's one for the epileptics!"

There was a lot of rhetoric exchanged at Wimbledon regarding "bad calls."

At Mount Rainier they learned to live with life's bad calls a long time ago. The first man to reach the mountaintop tore up his artificial leg to get there.

Somehow, I see a parallel here that all Americans are going to have to come to grips with. In our search for heroes and heroines, we often lose our perspective.

We applaud beauty pageant winners; we ignore the woman without arms who paints pictures with a brush in her teeth. We extol the courage of a man who will sail over 10 cars on a motorcycle; we give no thought (or parking place) to the man who threads his way though life in a world of darkness or silence.

The care and feeding of heroes is solely in the hands of the public. Not all winners are heroes. Not all people with disabilities are heroes. "Hero" is a term that should be awarded to those who, given a set of circumstances, will react with courage, dignity,

decency, and compassion—people who make us feel better for having seen or touched them.

I think the crowds went to the wrong summit and cheered the wrong champion.

Analyzing Media

1. The author writes mostly very short paragraphs. Why do you suppose she does so?
2. Do you agree that we cheer the wrong heroes? Give examples to support your opinion.

Reading *Minilesson*

Comparing and Contrasting In this section, Bombeck contrasts an often-rude athlete with a group of handicapped achievers—to persuade readers that society often cheers for the wrong heroes.

Activity Have the class complete this Venn diagram that will show the two types of heroes compared and contrasted. L2

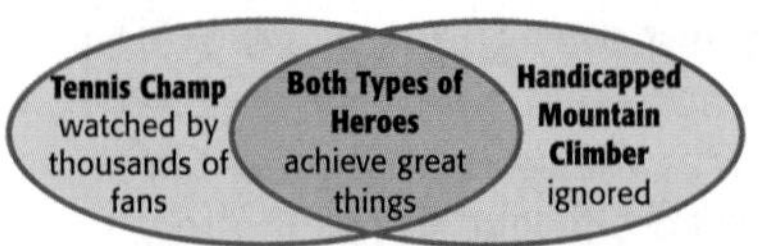

Additional Resources

Reading Skills Practice Workbook

Before You Read

Strong Men Weep

MEET BENEDICT COSGROVE

A lifetime sports fan, journalist, and writer, Benedict Cosgrove is also the co-editor of *Gluttony*, an anthology of short stories and essays. Cosgrove's most recent book, *Covering the Bases*, from which this selection is taken, is a collection of sports writing, radio transcripts, and photographs of the most unforgettable moments in baseball, as recorded by the writers and broadcasters who were there.

Benedict Cosgrove lives in San Francisco, California. This work was published in 1996.

READING FOCUS

Do you have a hero? Why do you consider this person a hero?

Sharing Ideas

In small groups, discuss the qualities you think heroes share. Then make a list of people you think are heroes, and explain why each person is on the list. Do heroes have to be famous?

Setting a Purpose

Read to find out why Lou Gehrig is considered a hero.

BUILDING BACKGROUND

This essay is about an event that took place at Yankee Stadium, New York City, in 1939. The author sets the scene for Shirley Povich's account.

Shirley Povich (1905–1998) was, at age twenty, the youngest sports reporter in the U.S. Considered the *Washington Post*'s "most revered sports columnist," he wrote for that paper for 75 years. His approach to writing was simply stated: "I write what I like to read."

Shirley Povich

VOCABULARY PREVIEW

consecutive (kən sek′ yə tiv) *adj.* following one after another in order without interruption; p. 26

discrepancy (dis krep′ ən sē) *n.* a lack of agreement, as between facts; p. 27

eloquent (el′ ə kwənt) *adj.* expressive, effective, and stirring in speech or writing; p. 29

esteem (es tēm′) *n.* favorable opinion; high regard; p. 29

elicit (i lis′ it) *v.* to draw forth or bring out; p. 29

hindrance (hin′ drəns) *n.* something that holds back progress or movement; obstacle; p. 30

Before Reading

Objectives

- To read and analyze an article
- To identify the author's purpose in writing an article
- To write a critical review

Skills

Reading/Thinking: Comparing and Contrasting; Distinguishing Fact from Opinion

Writing: Review; Persuasive Paragraph

Vocabulary: Root Words; Owning a Word

Grammar/Language: Main Verbs and Helping Verbs

Listening/Speaking: Announcing a Game

Collaboration: Literature Groups

Motivating STUDENTS

Literature Launchers: "The Story of Lou Gehrig"

Videodisc Side A, Segment 2

Also available in VHS.

Selection Focus Transparency 4: Have students discuss the graph of attendance at baseball games from 1900 to 1994.

Reading Focus: As an extension of the Reading Focus, have students tell the class what public figures they think are overpraised.

RESOURCE MANAGER

Teaching Tools and Resources
- Theme One Planning Guide
- Literature Groups Sourcebook

Essential Lesson Support

Lesson-Specific Instruction
- Selection Focus Transparency 4
- Literary Elements Transparency 4
- Active Reading Guide,* p. 4
- Selection Vocabulary Practice, p. 2
- TIME *inTIME* magazine, pp. 30-31

Assessment
- Selection Quick Checks,* p. 4
- Selection and Theme Assessment, pp. 7-8
- Testmaker: ExamView Pro
- Performance Assessment, p. 14

Systematic Language Instruction
- Grammer & Composition Handbook, Lesson 1.6

English Language Learners
- ELL Sourcebook, p. 20
- Spanish Summaries, p. 4
- Spanish Translations, pp. 5-8
- Audio Library*
- English, Yes!

Spec. Needs/Strat. Interven.
- Interactive Reading Sourcebook, pp. T55-T58
- Interactive Reading Workbook, pp. 6-7
- Inclusion Strategies Sourcebook, pp. 39-40, 55-56
- Audio Library*

*Also available in Spanish

Reading the Selection

SUMMARY

In 1995, Cal Ripken Jr. of the Baltimore Orioles broke the record for consecutive games played, a record set by Lou Gehrig 56 years earlier. Many fans said Ripken was a more skilled player, but Gehrig transcended statistics when he said goodbye at Yankee Stadium on July 4, 1939. His speech was eloquent, touching, and filled with appreciation for his fans and colleagues. Strong men wept because Gehrig, still at the top of his game, had developed a fatal illness.

Spanish Summaries, p. 4

Active Reading Strategies

PREDICT Ask students to predict what the "disturbing thread" in the discussions is. *(Students may guess that it is an unkind rumor about one of the players or about the record.)*

VOCABULARY If you haven't previewed the selection vocabulary with students, stop and remind them to use context clues to unlock the meanings of new vocabulary words.

Additional Resources

Active Reading Guide, p. 4

Audio Library

Spanish Audio Library

Strong Men Weep

Lou Gehrig's Famous Farewell

July 4, 1939

Benedict Cosgrove

Cal Ripken breaking Lou Gehrig's streak of 2,130 consecutive games might have been the best thing that could have happened to the old Yankee captain's reputation.

For months and weeks leading up to that great night in September 1995, when Ripken finally passed Gehrig, a disturbing thread began to weave through the endless discussions surrounding The Streak.

Vocabulary

consecutive (kən sek′ yə tiv) *adj.* following one after another in order without interruption

Teaching Support

CONNECTING TO OTHER SELECTIONS

COMPARING *selections*

This selection is compared with "Wait Till Next Year" on page 35. A lesson for teaching a comparison of the two selections appears on page 40.

The chart at the right shows three ways to connect "Strong Men Weep" to other selections in this book.

For specific teaching strategies, see the ***Theme One Planning Guide.***

Connection	Title
Life Skills: Supporting and Contributing	"Too Soon a Woman," p. 235
Thematic: Farewells	"There Is No Word for Goodbye," p. 179
Literary: Sequence of Events	"A Crush," p. 149

Among all the factions[1] that had formed as it became clear that Ripken was going to just keep on going (factions that seemed to dissolve—along with everyone else who cared at all about the record—into a mass, warm embrace of the man the moment he began his spontaneous, lump-in-the-throat jog around the field at Camden Yards),[2] there was, it seemed, a small but nonetheless significant group of voices that appeared bent on pointing out the questionable discrepancies in Gehrig's original record.

B Gehrig played first base, as opposed to Cal, who played a far more demanding shortstop. Gehrig often played only an inning or two when he wasn't feeling 100 percent—or when he was on the road, in order to keep the streak going—while Ripken played in something insane, like eight and two-thirds of every nine innings during his streak. Gehrig never had to deal with coast-to-coast airplane travel or Astroturf or blah blah blah. The point, it seemed, was that Gehrig's legendary streak, while kind of impressive, was really nothing compared to Ripken's *more genuine* streak.

C And I'll buy that. Ripken's is the more amazing streak. By far. Hands down. No question.

With his streak broken, though, perhaps Gehrig can be fully appreciated as the great, great ballplayer that he was, the ballplayer whose career was cut short when he still had some good years left in him, rather than as the guy whose tainted consecutive-game streak Cal Ripken finally obliterated.[3]

But no matter how Gehrig is remembered as a player, no matter how fine or fearsome a hitter the man was (a .340 lifetime average; a .632 slugging percentage; the career mark for grand slams; 1,990 RBIs), or how loyal a teammate, or how worthy a leader as the captain of the awesome Yankee teams of the 1920s, he

Lou Gehrig poses with another baseball legend, his teammate Babe Ruth.

1. *Factions* are small groups of people, within a larger group, who disagree on an issue or set of issues.
2. The home field of Ripken's team, the Baltimore Orioles, is named *Camden Yards.*
3. *Tainted* means "spoiled or made inferior." To *obliterate* something is to destroy it completely.

Vocabulary

discrepancy (dis krep′ ən sē) *n.* a lack of agreement, as between facts

Vocabulary Skills

Word Roots Making a connection to the root of *obliterate* can help students remember its meaning. In Latin, *littera* means "letter," and one of the meanings of the prefix *ob-* is "against." Originally *obliterate* referred to the wearing away of letters carved in stone until they could not be read.

Ask students to think of other words with the prefix *ob-* (*oblivious, obsolete, obstacle*).

B Literary Elements

GENRE: *Informational Text* Encourage students to identify Benedict Cosgrove's introduction as informational text. Point out that he both provides players' statistics and describes the discrepancies between their schedules and playing conditions. He keeps to the facts.

C Literary Elements

AUTHOR'S PURPOSE After comparing Gehrig's and Ripken's streaks and concluding that Ripken's was the more amazing, Cosgrove makes his point: Lou Gehrig was a "great, great ballplayer." Ask students whether they think this approach is the best way to prepare readers for Gehrig's speech.

MEETING INDIVIDUAL NEEDS — ENGLISH LANGUAGE LEARNERS

Baseball Terms For English language learners who are unfamiliar with baseball, discuss the following:

inning: a division of the game in which teams alternate batting and fielding. There are nine innings in a game.

streak: an unbroken series of events

grand slam: a home run hit while there are players on all three bases. It brings in four runs.

Activity Pair students who are familiar with baseball with those who are not to find and define baseball terms in the selection. Students can listen to the selections being read aloud and add new terms to their notebooks.

COLLAB. LEARN.

Additional Resources

English Language Learners Sourcebook, p. 20

G Critical Thinking

DISTINGUISHING FACT FROM OPINION Some of Povich's statements are opinions, not facts. You may wish to share the following model to illustrate the thinking process involved in distinguishing facts from opinions.

Model: As I read, I noticed that the sportswriter makes statements that may be true but can't be proved. For instance, unless he could read Gehrig's mind, he couldn't be sure Gehrig was grateful for Barrow's supporting arm or know for sure that Gehrig was choking back emotions that threatened to silence him. I think he was using his opinions to make the story more dramatic.

H Active Reading Strategies

VISUALIZE Ask students to choose a moving scene on this page, visualize it, and describe it or draw a picture of it. *(They might choose the star athlete leaning on his 70-year-old boss or his tough-as-nails manager crying at the microphone.)*

Have students find out more about the disease that killed Lou Gehrig. Tell them to use *Lou Gehrig's disease* or *ALS* as keywords on a search engine.

ago, stepped out of the background halfway through the presentation ceremonies, and draped his arm across Gehrig's shoulder. But he was doing more than that. He was holding Gehrig up, for Big Lou needed support.

As he leaned on Barrow, Gehrig said, "Thanks, Ed." He bit his lip hard, was grateful for the supporting arm, as the Yankees of 1927 stepped to the microphone after being introduced. Babe Ruth, Bob Meusel, Waite Hoyt, Herb Pennock, Benny Bengough, Bob Shawkey, Mark Koenig, Tony Lazzeri, all of the class of '27 were there. And Gehrig had been one of them, too. He had been the only one among them to bestride both eras.

Still leaning on Barrow, Gehrig acknowledged gifts from his Yankee mates, from the Yankee Stadium ground crew, and the hot dog butchers, from fans as far as Denver, and from his New York rivals, the Giants. There was a smile through his tears, but he wasn't up to words. He could only shake the hands of the small army of officials who made the presentations.

He stood there twisting his doffed baseball cap into a braid in his fingers as Manager Joe McCarthy followed Mayor La Guardia and Postmaster General Farley in tribute to "the finest example of ball player, sportsman, and citizen that baseball has ever known," but Joe McCarthy couldn't take it that way, either. The man who has driven the highest-salaried prima donnas[8] of baseball into action, who has baited a thousand umpires, broke down.

McCarthy openly sobbed as he stood in front of the microphone and said, "Lou, what else can I say except that it was a sad day in the life of everybody who knew you when you came to my hotel room that day in Detroit and told me you were quitting as a ball player because you felt yourself a hindrance to the team. My God, man, you were never that."

And as if to emphasize the esteem in which he held Gehrig though his usefulness to the Yankees as a player was ended, McCarthy, too, stepped out of the fringe full into the circle where Gehrig stood and half embraced the big fellow.

Now it was Gehrig's turn to talk into the microphone, to acknowledge his gifts. The 60,000 at intervals had set up the shout, "We want Lou!" even as they used to shout "We want Ruth"—yells that they reserved for the only two men at Yankee Stadium for which the crowd ever organized a cheering section.

But Master of Ceremonies Sid Mercer was anticipating Gehrig. He saw the big fellow choked up. Infinitesimally[9] Gehrig shook his head, and Mercer announced: "I shall not ask Lou Gehrig to make a speech. I do not believe that I should."

They started to haul away the microphones. Gehrig half turned toward the dugout, with the ceremonies apparently at an end. And then he wheeled suddenly, strode back to the loud-speaking apparatus, held up his hand for attention, gulped, managed a smile, and then spoke.

8. Originally, a *prima donna* was the leading female singer of an opera company. Now, the term is applied to any "star" who is overly proud or demanding.

9. *Infinitesimally* means "in such a small way as to be almost unnoticeable."

Vocabulary
hindrance (hin′ drəns) *n.* something that holds back progress or movement; obstacle

Teaching Support

Grammar and Language Minilesson

Main Verbs and Helping Verbs Write on the board the four principal parts that are used to form a verb's tenses.

base form: *break*
present participle: *breaking*
past form: *broke*
past participle: *broken*

Explain that a principal part of a verb is often combined with a helping verb to form a verb phrase. In the verb phrase *are breaking*, the helping verb is *are*, and the main verb is *breaking*. The most common helping verbs are *be, have,* and *do*.

Activity Have students list verb phrases from page 30 and identify the main and helping verbs in each. Examples:

he *was doing*
Gehrig *had been* one of them **L2**

Additional Resources

- ***Grammar and Language Transparency 3***
- ***Grammar and Language Workbook,*** pp. 85–86, 87–88
- ***Grammar and Composition Handbook,*** Lesson 3.6
- ***Writer's Choice,*** Lesson 10.6

Gehrig is overcome with emotion at his final appearance in Yankee Stadium.

"For weeks," said Gehrig, "I have been reading in the newspapers that I am a lucky fellow who got a tough break. I don't believe it. I have been a lucky guy. For 16 years, into every ballpark in which I have ever walked, I received nothing but kindness and encouragement. Mine has been a full life."

He went on, fidgeting with his cap, pawing the ground with his spikes as he spoke, choking back emotions that threatened to silence him, summoning courage from somewhere. He thanked everybody. He didn't forget the ballpark help; he told of his gratitude to newspapermen who had publicized him. He didn't forget the late Miller Huggins, or his six years with him; or Manager Joe McCarthy, or the late Col. Ruppert,[10] or Babe Ruth, or "my roommate, Bill Dickey."

And he thanked the Giants— "The fellows from across the river, who we would give our right arm to beat"—he was more at ease in front of the mike now, and he had a word for Mrs. Gehrig and for the immigrant father and mother who had made his education, his career, possible. And he denied again that he had been the victim of a bad break in life. He said, "I've lots to live for, honest."

And thousands cheered.

10. When Gehrig first joined the Yankees, *Huggins* managed the team and helped Gehrig develop his baseball skills. *McCarthy* became manager after Huggins. Jacob *Ruppert* was the owner or co-owner of the Yankees from 1914 to 1939.

I Active Reading Strategies

EVALUATE What words would describe Lou Gehrig's character and how fans feel about him? *(He is brave, shy, and emotional. He seems to be loved and admired by his fans.)*

J Literary Elements

IRONY Explain that situational irony exists when the outcome of a situation is the opposite of one's expectations. Point out that Gehrig's saying "I've lots to live for, honest" is ironic because he's just been diagnosed with a terminal illness. Challenge students to find other ironies in the selection.

Thematic Focus

What I Am, What I Want to Be Encourage students to extend their discussion of what it means to be a hero. Why is Lou Gehrig considered a hero? Is Cal Ripken a hero? Ask students for examples.

At the MOVIES

- *Pride of the Yankees* (1942, 128 minutes, NR), a Hollywood biography of Lou Gehrig re-creates the tribute to Gehrig at Yankee Stadium. Preview the video to decide whether it is appropriate for your class.

Real-World Connection

Heroes To help students gain perspective on the word *hero*, they can compare stories of different kinds of heroes.

Activity Have each student find a magazine or newspaper article about a true hero who reacts with courage, dignity, and compassion to a difficult personal or social challenge. Encourage them to look for heroes from different countries or cultural backgrounds, if possible. In small groups, students should share and discuss their articles and pose and answer questions like *What challenges did this person face? How did he or she handle those challenges?* Then ask a member of each group to share the story of his or her hero with the class. **L2** **COLLAB. LEARN.**

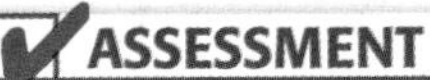

ASSESSMENT

Quick Checks, p. 4

Responding to the Selection

PERSONAL RESPONSE

- Students may say they wondered why good people die young or how Gehrig found the courage to remain optimistic and focus on others.
- Most students will probably agree that Gehrig was a hero because of his selflessness and courage in the face of death.

Analyzing Literature

1. Cal Ripken. The discussions focused on the ways in which Ripken's feat was more impressive than Gehrig's.
2. He will be most associated with his farewell speech on July 4, 1939.
3. He was referring to baseball fans, umpires, photographers, and everyone else who heard Gehrig's speech.
4. They cheered throughout his speech, especially when he said, "I've lots to live for, honest."
5. Ripken "played a far more demanding shortstop," "Gehrig often played only an inning or two when he wasn't feeling 100 percent," and "Gehrig never had to deal with coast-to-coast airplane travel or Astroturf."
6. It is ironic that Gehrig, who has just been diagnosed with a terminal disease, considers himself lucky. He shows dignity and class by being so grateful for the chance to play baseball.
7. He wanted to grab readers' emotions immediately and to emphasize that this was not a usual day at the stadium.
8. Gehrig was brave, upbeat, humble, and appreciative of others.
9. Students may say it has more impact because it's true. It is more impressive to find such an admirable man in real life than it is in fiction.

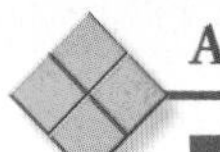

Active Reading and Critical Thinking

Responding to Literature

PERSONAL RESPONSE

- What thoughts and feelings did you have at the end of this selection?
- Think back to the discussion in the **Reading Focus** on page 25. Do you think that Lou Gehrig was a hero? Why or why not?

Analyzing Literature

RECALL

1. What player broke Lou Gehrig's streak of 2,130 consecutive games? What was the focus of the "endless discussions surrounding The Streak"?
2. With what event does Cosgrove believe Gehrig will always be most associated?
3. To whom was the journalist Shirley Povich referring when he wrote, "I saw strong men weep this afternoon"?
4. What did Gehrig say that July day that made people cheer?

Brackets connect questions that are paired to develop higher-level thinking skills.

INTERPRET

5. According to Cosgrove, what were the main points of discussion concerning the differences between the streaks of Cal Ripken and Lou Gehrig? Support your ideas with quotations from the selection.
6. "Today I consider myself the luckiest man on the face of the earth." Explain the significance of this statement.
7. The opening image in Povich's piece is emotional and powerful. Why do you think Povich chose this image? Explain.
8. What did you learn about Lou Gehrig's character from reading some of his farewell words?

EVALUATE AND CONNECT

9. "Strong Men Weep" is an example of **nonfiction.** It is about real events and a real person. Does knowing that this is a true story affect your experience of this man's character? Explain.
10. In your opinion, was Gehrig "the luckiest man on the face of the earth"? Explain.

LITERARY ELEMENTS

Author's Purpose

All writers have a purpose or goal they want to achieve in their writing. To **entertain** is one purpose for writing. To **describe** something is another purpose. Sometimes writers want to **inform** the reader or to **explain** something. Sometimes writers want to **persuade** their readers to believe something. A strong piece of writing often combines purposes: A persuasive essay, for example, may include description and information.

1. What was Shirley Povich's purpose in writing his memorable piece in the *Washington Post*? Support your opinion with examples from the account.
2. How would Povich's piece have been different if his purpose had been to describe Gehrig's batting statistics?

See **Literary Terms Handbook,** p. R2.

32 THEME 1

10. Students will probably say no, because he was dying young. Some may agree with his perception that he had already had a wonderful life.

LITERARY ELEMENTS

1. He wanted readers to understand the esteem and affection everyone had for Gehrig.
2. He would have focused on facts and numbers only, leaving out the emotional details.

Additional Resources

Literary Elements Transparency 4

Extending Your Response

Writing About Literature

Critical Review Write a paragraph reviewing "Strong Men Weep." Consider these questions: What did you learn from this selection? What kinds of details did Cosgrove and Povich include? How did these details affect your opinion of Gehrig?

Personal Writing

My Hero "Strong Men Weep" recounts the famous farewell of a legendary sports hero. Who is one of your heroes? Think about the people you listed in the **Reading Focus** on page 25. Write a paragraph using effective details to convince your reader that the person you chose is a true hero.

Literature Groups

A Sporting Debate Benedict Cosgrove and Shirley Povich wrote about a good and courageous man who happened to be a great baseball player. Does a reader have to love the game of baseball to be affected by this account of Lou Gehrig? Why or why not? Support your opinion with examples from the selection and other stories about heroes.

Reading Further

For more about sports, try these:

Dreams into Deeds: Nine Women Who Dared by Linda Peavy and Ursula Smith

The Random House Book of Sports Stories by L. M. Schulman

Save your work for your portfolio.

Skill Minilesson

Reteach · Review

VOCABULARY • OWNING A WORD

Reading the definition of a word doesn't make the word yours, but it's a first step. Words become truly part of your vocabulary when you understand how they're used and you start using them yourself.

PRACTICE Use what you know about the meanings of the underlined words to complete the sentences.

1. Tainted meat is likely to contain
   a. fat c. germs
   b. ice crystals
2. The response to an eloquent speech would be
   a. applause c. yawns
   b. boos
3. You would obliterate an answer by
   a. choosing it c. erasing it
   b. repeating it
4. A _____ could be a hindrance to a driver.
   a. seat belt c. store
   b. traffic jam
5. Two consecutive days are Saturday and
   a. Sunday c. the next Saturday
   b. Monday

Extending Your Response

Writing About Literature

Students' reviews should

- tell what they learned, including both facts and opinions
- give appropriate examples of Cosgrove's and Povich's details and explain how they differ
- explain clearly how each detail affects their opinions of Gehrig

Personal Writing

Students' paragraphs should

- name one of their heroes
- explain why he or she is a hero
- use details to persuade readers of the subject's heroism

Literature Groups Point out to students that they should think about Lou Gehrig separately from his role as a baseball player. Remind them to use examples from both the selection and their own knowledge. COLLAB. LEARN.

Skill Minilesson

VOCABULARY • OWNING A WORD

1. c 2. a 3. c 4. b 5. a

Additional Resources

Vocabulary Practice, p. 2

*inter*NET CONNECTION

English Pronunciation Readers who need practice sounding out English words may search the Internet for helpful sites using the keywords "English pronunciation." You might also direct students to the *Web of Online Dictionaries*, whose searchable database contains definitions and pronunciations as well as a detailed pronunciation guide.

ASSESSMENT

- ***Quick Checks,*** p. 4
- ***Selection and Theme Assessment,*** pp. 7–8
- ***Performance Assessment,*** p. 4
- ***Testmaker: ExamView Pro***
- ***Interactive Tutor: Self-Assessment***

Before Reading

Objectives

- To read and analyze a true story about how baseball helps a girl build her relationship with her father
- To define a memoir
- To write an advertisement for a baseball or a softball team

Skills

Reading/Thinking: Elaborating; Inferring; Monitoring Comprehension
Vocabulary: Etymology
Grammar/Language: Prepositional Phrases

Motivating STUDENTS

Selection Focus Transparency 5: Have students view and discuss the Jacques Barzun quote about baseball.

Reading Focus: As an extension of the Reading Focus, have pairs of students use precise language and sensory imagery to share their past enthusiasm for a celebrity and tell how it affected them.

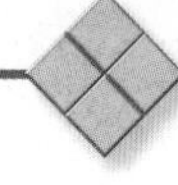

Before You Read

from *Wait Till Next Year*

MEET DORIS KEARNS GOODWIN

Doris Kearns Goodwin became a baseball fan at the age of six, when her father taught her to keep score as she listened to the Brooklyn Dodgers games. This early training in summarizing baseball games for her father helped her develop the storytelling skills she continues to use as an adult. In addition to *No Ordinary Time*, her Pulitzer Prize–winning book about Franklin and Eleanor Roosevelt, she has written books about other American presidents, taught at Harvard University, and appears frequently on TV news programs.

Wait Till Next Year, *Doris Kearns Goodwin's memories of growing up in the 1950s, was published in 1997.*

READING FOCUS

Sports heroes need not always be a single person. They can be an entire team. You can also find a hero closer to home, as young Doris Kearns Goodwin did.

Sharing Ideas

Have you ever become very enthusiastic about a group, such as a sports team or a musical group? What effect did that enthusiasm have on you? How do you feel about it now?

Setting a Purpose

As you read, think about why the young Doris became such a loyal fan of the Dodgers.

BUILDING BACKGROUND

The Time and Place This selection is set in a Long Island, New York, suburb in 1949. This was ten years after Lou Gehrig said his farewell to the New York Yankees.

Did You Know? The period 1949–1956 was a glorious period for New York baseball fans. Each year, one or two of the city's three baseball teams—the Yankees, the Giants, and the Brooklyn Dodgers—competed in the World Series. The Yankees won the championship in six of those years.

VOCABULARY PREVIEW

juncture (jungk′ chər) *n.* a critical point of time; p. 36
agitated (aj′ ə tāt′ ed) *adj.* upset; disturbed; p. 36
narrative (nar′ ə tiv) *n.* story; storytelling; p. 37
ritual (rich′ o͞o əl) *n.* an established form of doing something; ceremony; p. 37
naive (nä ēv′) *adj.* simple in nature; childlike; p. 37
divulge (di vulj′) *v.* to make known; give away; p. 38
staple (stā′ pəl) *adj.* important; main; p. 38

RESOURCE MANAGER

Teaching Tools and Resources
- Theme One Planning Guide
- Literature Groups Sourcebook

Essential Lesson Support

Lesson-Specific Instruction
- Selection Focus Transparency 5
- Literary Elements Transparency 5
- Active Reading Guide,* p. 5
- Selection Vocabulary Practice, p. 3

Assessment
- Selection Quick Checks,* p. 5
- Selection and Theme Assessment, pp. 9–10
- Testmaker: ExamView Pro
- Performance Assessment, p. 5

Systematic Language Instruction
- Grammer & Composition Handbook, Lesson 2.1
- Vocabulary Power, Lesson 3
- Spelling Power, Lesson 3

English Language Learners
- ELL Sourcebook, p. 21
- Spanish Summaries, p. 5
- Spanish Translations, pp. 9–10
- Spanish Audio Library
- English, Yes!

Spec. Needs/Strat. Interven.
- Interactive Reading Sourcebook, pp. T58–T60
- Interactive Reading Workbook, pp. 8–9
- Inclusion Strategies Sourcebook, pp. 7–8, 27–28, 69–70

*Also available in Spanish

from

Wait Till Next Year

Doris Kearns Goodwin

WHEN I WAS SIX, my father gave me a bright-red scorebook that opened my heart to the game of baseball. After dinner on long summer nights, he would sit beside me in our small enclosed porch to hear my account of that day's Brooklyn Dodger[1] game. A

1. Until 1958, when they moved to Los Angeles, the *Dodgers* were based in Brooklyn, a part of New York City.

Reading the Selection

SUMMARY

Doris's father introduces her to baseball when she is six and teaches her to keep score. She listens to every Dodger game on the radio while he is at work and gives him a play-by-play account after dinner. Doris thinks her narratives are the only way her father can follow the games; she doesn't know he reads the box scores in the daily paper.

Spanish Summaries, p. 5

A Active Reading Strategies

PREDICT Ask students to use clues in this paragraph to predict whether Doris will enjoy listening to baseball games and reporting them to her father. *("Opened my heart to the game of baseball," suggests that this is something Doris will enjoy.)*

VOCABULARY If you haven't previewed the selection vocabulary with students, stop and remind them to use context clues to unlock the meanings of new vocabulary words.

Additional Resources

Active Reading Guide, p. 5

Audio Library

Spanish Audio Library

Teaching Support

CONNECTING TO OTHER SELECTIONS

COMPARING *selections*

This selection is paired with "Strong Men Weep" on page 26. A lesson for teaching a comparison of the two selections appears on page 40.

The chart at the right shows three other ways to connect "Wait Till Next Year" to selections in this book.

For specific teaching strategies, see the ***Theme One Planning Guide.***

Connection		Title
Life Skills: Setting Reasonable Expectations	→	"A Crush," p. 149
Thematic: Home	→	"How I Learned English," p. 377
Literary: Character	→	"The Women's 400 Meters," p. 252

B Active Reading Strategies

CONNECT Ask students what activities they have learned to enjoy because their parents enjoy them.

Etymology Explain that the word *fan* is short for *fanatic*, a person who is excessively enthusiastic about something. *Fanatic* comes from the Latin *fanaticus*, which means "frenzied." Ask whether students know the meaning (specific to baseball) of the verb *fan*. *(A pitcher who fans a batter strikes the batter out.)*

Historical Note

Women in Baseball In 1963, Nancy Lotsey of New Jersey became the first girl to play in an organized baseball competition with boys. In 1974, Little League was officially opened to girls. In 1980, Crystal Fields of Maryland became the first girl to win the national Pitch, Hit, and Run Championship. In 1989, Julie Croteau was the first woman to play on a men's college varsity baseball team.

C Literary Elements

NARRATOR Who is telling the story? *(The author, Doris Kearns Goodwin, looks back on her childhood.)*

Teaching Support

from
Wait Till Next Year

Night after night he taught me the odd collection of symbols, numbers, and letters that enable a baseball lover to record every action of the game. Our score sheets had blank boxes in which we could draw our own slanted lines in the form of a diamond as we followed players around the bases. Wherever the baserunner's progress stopped, the line stopped. He instructed me to fill in the unused boxes at the end of each inning with an elaborate checkerboard design which made it absolutely clear who had been the last to bat and who would lead off the next inning. By the time I had mastered the art of scorekeeping, a lasting bond had been forged among my father, baseball, and me. B

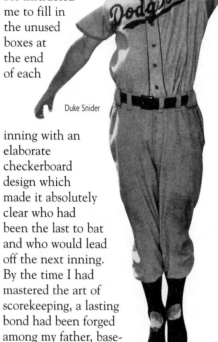

Duke Snider

All through the summer of 1949, my first summer as a fan, I spent my afternoons sitting cross-legged before the squat Philco radio which stood as a permanent fixture on our porch in Rockville Centre, on the South Shore of Long Island, New York. With my scorebook spread before me, I attended Dodger games through the courtly voice of Dodger announcer Red Barber. As he announced the lineup, I carefully printed each player's name in a column on the left side of my sheet. Then, using the standard system my father had taught me, . . . I recorded every play. I found it difficult at times to sit still. As the Dodgers came to bat, I would walk around the room, talking to the players as if they were standing in front of me. At critical junctures, I tried to make a bargain, whispering and cajoling while Pee Wee Reese or Duke Snider[2] stepped into the batter's box: "Please, please, get a hit. If you get a hit now, I'll make my bed every day for a week." Sometimes, when the score was close and the opposing team at bat with men on base, I was too agitated to listen. C Asking my mother to keep notes, I left the house for a walk around the block, hoping that when I returned the enemy threat would be over, and once again we'd be up at bat. Mostly, however, I stayed at my post, diligently recording each inning so that, when my father returned from his

2. *Pee Wee Reese* and *Duke Snider* were two of the star players on the Dodgers team during the 1950s.

Vocabulary
juncture (jungk′ chər) *n.* a critical point of time
agitated (aj′ ə tāt′ ed) *adj.* upset; disturbed

MEETING INDIVIDUAL NEEDS — ENGLISH LANGUAGE LEARNERS

The Art of Storytelling Goodwin's impulse to tell stories is rooted in human nature. Every culture tells stories and myths, from the German fairy tale "The Goose Girl" to the Norse story of the Tree of Life to the Nigerian myth of how the god Obatala created humans.

Activity Pair native and nonnative speakers. Have them tell each other fairy tales or myths from their own cultures and discuss themes that cross cultures. If they wish, they may research the mythology of their native cultures at the library. Remind students to explain unfamiliar terms to their listeners. COLLAB. LEARN.

Additional Resources

English Language Learners Sourcebook, p. 21

job as bank examiner for the State of New York, I could re-create for him the game he had missed.

D When my father came home from the city, he would change from his three-piece suit into long pants and a short-sleeved sport shirt. . . . Then my parents would summon me for dinner from my play on the street outside our house. All through dinner I had to restrain myself from telling him about the day's game, waiting for the special time to come when we would sit together on the couch, my scorebook on my lap.

"Well, did anything interesting happen today?" he would begin. And even before the daily question was completed I had eagerly launched into my narrative of every play, and almost every pitch, of that afternoon's contest. It never crossed my mind to wonder if, at the close of a day's work, he might find my lengthy account the least bit tedious. For there was mastery as well as pleasure in our nightly ritual. E Through my knowledge, I commanded my father's undivided attention, the sign of his love. It would instill in me an early awareness of the power of narrative, which would introduce a lifetime of storytelling, fueled by the naive confidence that others would find me as entertaining as my father did. . . .

These nightly recountings of the Dodgers' progress provided my first lessons in the narrative art. From the scorebook, with its tight squares of neatly arranged symbols, I could unfold the tale of an entire game and tell a story that seemed to last almost as long as the game itself. At first, I was unable to resist the temptation to skip ahead to an important play in later innings. At times, I grew so excited about a Dodger victory that I blurted out the final score before I had hardly begun. But as I became more experienced in F my storytelling, I learned to build a dramatic story with a beginning, middle, and end. Slowly, I learned that if I could recount the game, one batter at a time, inning by inning, without

Pee Wee Reese

Vocabulary
narrative (nar′ ə tiv) *n.* story; storytelling
ritual (rich′ o͞o əl) *n.* an established form of doing something; ceremony
naive (nä ēv′) *adj.* simple in nature; childlike

D Author's Craft

SUPPORTING DETAILS Have students identify the details the author uses to paint a vivid picture of the nightly ritual of telling her father about the latest Dodger game. *(He would change clothes, they would have dinner, and then they would sit on the couch while she described every play, using her scorebook as a source.)*

E Literary Elements

MEMOIR Ask students to discuss some of the clues in this passage that let readers know this selection is a memoir. *(In this passage, Doris Kearns Goodwin looks back on her childhood memories through the eyes of an adult. She evaluates the effect past events have had on her life.)*

F Critical Thinking

ELABORATING Ask students to think about the storytelling process Doris used to tell her father about a game. What is the first bit of information Doris would have given her father about a game? *(She might name the opposing team and tell him who the starting pitcher was.)*

® *The following videotape program is available from Glencoe:*

- **Biography: Jackie Robinson***

**Also available in the Glencoe Literature Video Library.*

Reading Minilesson

Monitoring Comprehension When students have trouble understanding what they read, they can use a "fix-up" strategy, such as asking themselves questions to check their comprehension.

Activity Work as a class to complete the graphic organizer. Ask students to suggest self-monitoring questions about the content of page 37. *(Some samples are provided.)*

Finally, ask students to explain why Goodwin's father's reaction was important to her. **L2**

Additional Resources

Reading Skills Practice Workbook

DID I UNDERSTAND WHAT I JUST READ?
What questions can I ask to check myself?
Why is Goodwin so eager to tell her father about the game?
Why doesn't she wonder whether she is being tedious?
Personal experience that can help me answer:
When you are listened to, you feel interesting.
When you want urgently to tell something, you may not notice that you are boring the listener.

Active Reading Strategies

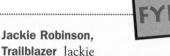

VISUALIZE Help students visualize how commuters followed baseball games. You may wish to model the process.

Model: The author says that the daily papers carried box scores that were the first thing her father and the other commuters read on the train in the morning. I can see a bunch of businessmen, all reading newspapers as they ride the train. The men are talking about the game, perhaps making jokes about the losing team.

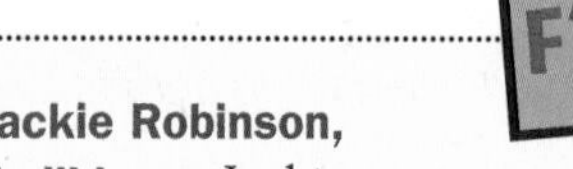

Jackie Robinson, Trailblazer Jackie Robinson broke the color barrier in baseball in 1947. Signed by the Brooklyn Dodgers, he was the first African American player in the major leagues.

Thematic Focus

What I Am, What I Want to Be Doris masters the science of baseball scorekeeping and the art of storytelling. Encourage students to discuss the ways Doris learns these skills and the rewards they bring her throughout her life.

ASSESSMENT

Quick Checks, p. 5

Teaching Support

Jackie Robinson

divulging the outcome, I could keep the suspense and my father's interest alive until the very last pitch. . . .

All through that summer, my father kept from me the knowledge that running box scores appeared in the daily newspapers. He never mentioned that these abbreviated histories had been a staple feature of the sports pages since the nineteenth century and were generally the first thing he and his fellow commuters turned to when they opened the *Daily News* and the *Herald Tribune* in the morning. I believed that, if I did not recount the games he had missed, my father would never have been able to follow our Dodgers the proper way, day by day, play by play, inning by inning. In other words, without me, his love of baseball would be forever unfulfilled.

Vocabulary

divulge (di vulj′) *v.* to make known; give away

staple (stā′ pəl) *adj.* important; main

Grammar and Language Minilesson

Prepositional Phrases Have students list some phrases such as "sitting on the floor" to describe where they are when they talk on the phone. Review *preposition,* a word that relates a noun or a pronoun to some other word in a sentence. Prepositional phrases usually answer the questions *where, when,* or *how.*

Activity Have students make a list of prepositions, choose three, and write a sentence using each one. **L2**

Additional Resources

- ***Grammar and Language Transparency 5***
- ***Grammar and Language Workbook,*** pp. 141–142
- ***Grammar and Composition Handbook,*** Lesson 7.1
- ***Writer's Choice,*** Lesson 13.1

Responding to Literature

PERSONAL RESPONSE

- Think back to the group discussion in the **Reading Focus** on page 34. Do you think the kind of devoted team loyalty the author describes is a good thing? Why or why not?

Analyzing Literature

Brackets connect questions that are paired to develop higher-level thinking skills.

RECALL

1. What triggers Doris Kearns Goodwin's interest in baseball?
2. How does Doris learn about the games she describes to her father?
3. What does Doris learn from her experience in re-creating games for her father?
4. From what other source could Doris's father have gotten the information?

INTERPRET

5. Why do you think Doris's father never tells her that he could have read about the games in the daily newspaper?
6. Why do you suppose her father never complains about her lengthy accounts of the games? Use details from the story to support your opinion.
7. In what ways did her experience in describing baseball games help Doris develop her writing skills? Explain.
8. What did you learn about the relationship between Doris and her father from the selection? Use references to the selection to back up your answer.

EVALUATE AND CONNECT

9. Considering this selection, who do you think was Doris's greatest childhood hero? Explain why you think so.
10. Doris Kearns Goodwin writes, "I learned to build a dramatic story with a beginning, middle, and end." Do you think that's a good idea for a young writer? Is it the only way to tell a story? Is it the best way? Explain.

LITERARY ELEMENTS

Memoir

Goodwin's *Wait Till Next Year* is a personal **memoir**—a record of her own experiences, related from her own memories. In a memoir, the author describes events for us as he or she recalls them. It usually expresses the author's opinions about events and people. In this selection, Goodwin writes from the point of view of an adult author looking back at herself as a child.

1. How do you think Doris Kearns Goodwin feels about her younger self? Use examples from the selection to support your answer.
2. How would this selection differ if it had been written in the late 1950s by a teenaged Doris rather than in the 1990s by the adult author? How would it differ if it had been written by Doris's father? Explain your answers with examples from the selection.

- See **Literary Terms Handbook**, p. R6.

Responding to the Selection

PERSONAL RESPONSE

Some students may say that team loyalty is good because it brings people together and gives them something to care about. Others may disagree because they do not think baseball is very important.

Analyzing Literature

1. Her father gave her a scorebook when she was six years old.
2. She listened to Red Barber announce them on the radio on summer afternoons.
3. She learned how to tell a story and how to get his undivided attention.
4. He could have read the box scores in the newspapers.
5. He wanted her to feel important and needed—to think he was relying on her.
6. He loved her and enjoyed spending time with her: "I commanded my father's undivided attention" and "others would find me as entertaining as my father did."
7. It taught her to build suspense and craft a narrative with a beginning, middle, and end.
8. They love and respect each other: "a lasting bond had been forged among my father, baseball, and me," "waiting for the special time to come when we would sit together on the couch," and "I believed . . . without me, his love of baseball would be forever unfulfilled."
9. Her greatest hero was her father. He inspired her lifelong hobby and her career. As an adult, she appreciates the time he took to teach her the game and hear her stories.
10. It is often the best way to tell a story, and writers should know the rules before they break them.

LITERARY ELEMENTS

1. She looks back fondly. She may be amused by her innocence at that time.
2. Teenaged Doris may not have appreciated the extent of her father's love and patience/nor realized that storytelling could turn into a career. Her father would probably have explained what the game and their ritual meant to him.

Additional Resources

Literary Elements Transparency 5

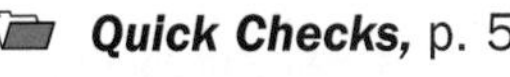

ASSESSMENT

- ***Quick Checks,*** p. 5
- ***Selection and Theme Assessment,*** pp. 9–10
- ***Performance Assessment,*** p. 5
- ***Testmaker: ExamView Pro***
- ***Interactive Tutor: Self-Assessment***

COMPARING *selections*

Objective

- To compare two nonfiction selections that deal with heroes and the sport of baseball

COMPARE **RESPONSES**

- **Alike:** Both are true stories about baseball. The authors love baseball. Cosgrove/Povich: "an eloquent and tremendously moving few minutes." Goodwin: "I was too agitated to listen." **Different:** Povich's was written right after the event, Goodwin's years later.
- Some students may prefer the immediacy or the raw emotion of the first selection; others may like the nostalgia of the second.
- Students may say they learned more facts from the first selection and more about relationships from the second.

COMPARE **EXPERIENCES**

Groups' responses should

- give pros and cons of each sport
- indicate favorites chosen on the basis of group discussion and evaluation **COLLAB. LEARN.**

Additional Resources

Literature Groups Sourcebook

COMPARE **CREATIONS**

Students' ads should

- be lively and appealing
- keep their audience in mind
- reveal knowledge about the team and the sport

Teaching Support

Critical Thinking

COMPARING SELECTIONS

Strong Men Weep and from Wait Till Next Year

COMPARE **RESPONSES**

Both "Strong Men Weep" and the selection from *Wait Till Next Year* deal with the topic of baseball.

- How are the selections alike? How are they different? Support your responses with examples from the selections.
- Which selection did you prefer? Why?
- Which piece did you learn more from, and which challenged you more as a reader? Explain.

COMPARE **EXPERIENCES**

Think about your own experiences with sports and games. Do you prefer participating, like Lou Gehrig, or are you happy to be just an observer, like the young Doris Kearns Goodwin? Do you like solitary sports such as running, or do you prefer team sports? Do you prefer to be a spectator or to read about the events?

- Consider your feelings about sports and games. What is it that you really enjoy about different games? Is it the team effort of soccer or the individual positions in baseball or softball? Do you like a challenge on your own, as in chess, or do you prefer close interaction, as in volleyball? Try to figure out exactly what it is you enjoy most about your favorite sports and games.
- In small groups, take turns discussing your favorite sports and games. Respond to questions and comments from your group members.
- In your group, take a poll of favorite sporting events. Share a graph of the results of your polls in a class discussion.

COMPARE **CREATIONS**

Write a radio, television, or newspaper advertisement for a school or local baseball or softball team. The team may be an imaginary one or an actual team you know about. Use language and sensory details in your ad that will excite the public about the team's upcoming season.

PORTFOLIO OPTIONS

Select and Reflect Have students ask themselves the following questions as they reflect on the ads they wrote:

- Does my ad include sensory details that convey the experience of being at a baseball game?
- How will my ad motivate people to come to the game? Students should clip their reflections to their ads and place them in their portfolios. Later, they may consider using the comments to revise their ads as portfolio showcase pieces.

Additional Resources

Writing Assessment and Portfolio Management, pp. 37–44

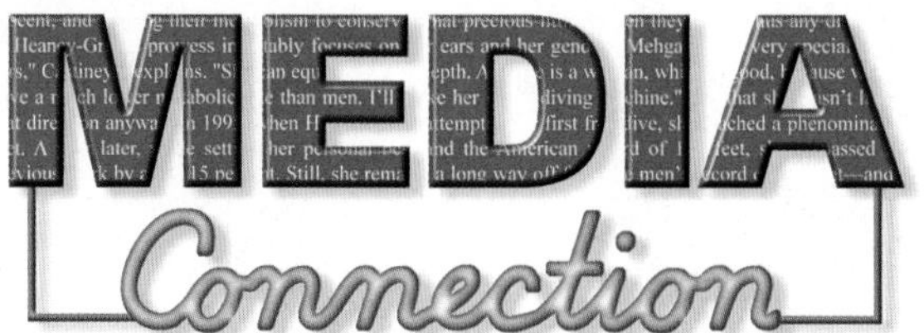

TELEVISION SCRIPT

These scenes from the first episode of the TV series *The Wonder Years* first aired January 31, 1988. In this episode, it is fall 1968 and the first day of junior high for Kevin, his best friend Paul, and Winnie. Wayne is Kevin's older brother, who likes to torment Kevin. The Narrator is the adult Kevin, looking back on his "wonder years."

from *The Wonder Years* Episode 1: "The Wonder Years"

—by Neal Marlens and Carol Black

[Exterior. Day. Bus stop.
Kevin and Paul stand beside one another at the bus stop. Wayne and others are there.]

KEVIN

[To Paul.] Don't worry about it, you look fine.

PAUL

Let me see our class schedule one more time.

KEVIN

No.

NARRATOR

He was gonna have to get a grip on himself. This was the junior high bus stop and if we were gonna hold our own with the older kids we were gonna have to act mature. We seemed to have something of a height disadvantage, but we did our best to fit in.

[Kevin and Paul stick their tongues out, mimicking the older kids. They spot Winnie who is walking toward the bus stop.]

NARRATOR

What an incredible stroke of luck, a new kid. A helpless waif would be even more lost than we were, a helpless waif in fishnet tights and gogo boots.

WINNIE

Hi Kevin. Hi Paul.

PAUL

[Amazed.] Winnie Cooper?

WINNIE

Gwendolyn. I don't want to be called Winnie anymore, my real name is Gwendolyn.

NARRATOR

Well, there was no question now, we were entering uncharted territory. Even the familiar was cloaked in the vestments of the devil. Junior high school was a whole new ball of wax.

MEDIA Connection

Objective

- To read and understand a television script

Literature LINK

Broken Chain This television script connects to "Broken Chain," the short story that follows this lesson. Point out the connection by telling students that Kevin feels vulnerable on his first day of junior high and tries hard to be "cool." Alfonso, the main character in "Broken Chain," also wants very much to make a good impression while everything—including his teeth and his bicycle chain—work against him.

Historical Note

In 1968, both Martin Luther King Jr. and Robert F. Kennedy were assassinated, American troops were fighting in Vietnam, and police and antiwar demonstrators clashed at the Democratic National Convention in Chicago.

Teaching Support

Reading *Minilesson*

Sequence of Events In a drama, a reader or viewer must pay attention to the sequence of events to understand cause-and-effect relationships and characters' motives.

Activity Have students complete the graphic organizer to track the sequence of events on pp. 41–42. Then discuss how Kevin feels about his first day of school. **L2**

Kevin and Paul are nervous about their first day of junior high. ➡

➡

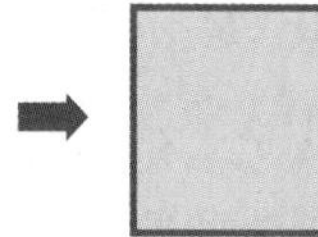

Kevin leaves the cafeteria.

Additional Resources

Reading Skills Practice Workbook

Pop Culture

Who's Who in 1968

- *Sgt. Pepper's Lonely Hearts Club Band* by the Beatles won the Grammy Award for best album.
- Peggy Fleming won the only U.S. gold medal in the Olympics in Grenoble, France.
- The Green Bay Packers won the Super Bowl; the Boston Celtics won the NBA championship; and the Detroit Tigers won the World Series.

Analyzing Media

1. Kevin exits the cafeteria quickly because his brother has embarrassed and infuriated him.
2. Some students may have felt nervous, others not. Responses may include students' stories about how they overcame nervousness or how someone else put them at ease in a new setting.

Additional Resources

Media Connections, p. 2

[Later that day.

Interior. Day. Cafeteria.

Kevin and Paul carry their trays and look for a table to sit at in the cafeteria.]

NARRATOR
Lunch, at last, something I figured even I couldn't screw up.

PAUL
Where do you want to sit?

KEVIN
Anywhere. Let's just sit here.

[Kevin and Paul sit down at a table.]

NARRATOR
A suburban junior high school cafeteria is like a microcosm of the world. The goal is to protect yourself, and safety comes in groups. You have your cool kids, you have your smart kids, you have your greasers, and in those days, of course, you had your hippies. In fact, in junior high school, who you are is defined less by who you are than by who's the person sitting next to you—a sobering thought.

KEVIN
[To Paul.] Try to look like you're having fun.

[Winnie approaches the table at which Kevin and Paul are sitting.]

WINNIE
Hi. Do you guys mind if I sit with you?

KEVIN
Sure, Winnie.

NARRATOR
We were on our way. Our group was forming. And Winnie, I mean, Gwendolyn, was not chopped liver. Who knows, maybe we even had an outside chance to become the cool seventh grade group, if we could just remain inconspicuous until we picked up a few more members.

[Wayne, at another table with friend Steve, spots Kevin, Paul and Winnie and approaches them.]

WAYNE
Hey Steve, it looks like my baby brother and his girlfriend have found each other.

KEVIN
She's not my girlfriend.

WAYNE
[To Winnie.] He thinks you are so cute.

KEVIN
I don't think she's cute.

WAYNE
He wants to give you a big wet kiss.

[Wayne makes a sucking noise.]

WAYNE
He told me.

KEVIN
You liar, I never said that! I don't want to kiss her, I don't even like her!

[Kevin picks up his apple and walks briskly to exit the cafeteria.]

Analyzing Media

1. Why do you think Kevin exits the cafeteria so quickly?
2. Did you ever have a nervous first day at a new school or in a new grade? What do you think about it now?

Teaching Support

Grammar and Language Minilesson

Mechanics: Brackets Draw students' attention to the use of brackets around the italicized stage directions. Point out that the brackets help to separate the stage directions from the spoken dialogue.

Activity Write the following sentences on the board and ask students to explain the use of brackets in each one.

1. He [Kevin] seems to be afraid to show others that he likes Winnie.
2. The word *microcosm* (from two Greek word parts: *micro* [small] and cosmos [world or universe]) refers to a smaller version or copy of the larger universe.

Before You Read

Broken Chain

MEET GARY SOTO

Gary Soto's experiences growing up in a Spanish-speaking neighborhood inspire much of his work. Like his parents and grandparents, Soto labored for a time as a migrant farm worker picking fruit. His love of literature came later, when he went to college. "Writing is my one talent," he says. "There are a lot of people who never discover what their talent is. . . . I am very lucky to have found mine." His writing includes award-winning poetry, novels, memoirs, essays, and films for both young people and adults.

Gary Soto was born in 1952. This story was published in 1990.

READING FOCUS

Why are some people so concerned about their appearance?

Discuss
Discuss with the class why teenagers are often so concerned about how they look, how they dress, and what others think of them.

Setting a Purpose
Read to find out what concerns the main character has about his appearance.

BUILDING BACKGROUND

The Time and Place A Mexican American neighborhood in Fresno, California, in the 1980s is the setting for this selection.

Did You Know? "Broken Chain" takes place in a Spanish-speaking neighborhood in Fresno, California, a neighborhood where Mexican American families have made their homes for many decades.

VOCABULARY PREVIEW

sullen (sul′ ən) *adj.* stubbornly withdrawn or gloomy; sulky; p. 45
swagger (swag′ ər) *v.* to walk or behave in a bold, rude, or overly proud way; p. 45
wince (wins) *v.* to draw back slightly, as in pain; p. 48
impulse (im′ puls) *n.* an internal force that causes one to act without thinking; p. 50
retrieve (ri trēv′) *v.* to locate and bring back; recover; fetch; p. 50
desperation (des′ pə rā′ shən) *n.* distress caused by great need or loss of hope; p. 50
emerge (i murj′) *v.* to come out; p. 52

Before Reading

Objectives

- To read and analyze a short story about a boy who is concerned about his appearance
- To identify conflict in a short story
- To write a paragraph analyzing the use of details

Skills

Reading/Thinking: Identifying Author's Purpose; Activating Prior Knowledge; Inferring; Identifying Assumptions
Writing: Advice Column; Describing a Character
Vocabulary: Synonyms; Prefixes
Grammar/Language: Subject-Verb Agreement; Pronouns
Listening/Speaking: Debating
Collaboration: Literature Groups; Improvisation

Motivating STUDENTS

Literature Launchers: Play "Getting to Know Gary Soto."

Videodisc Side A, Segment 1

Also available in VHS.

Selection Focus Transparency 6: Have students view the transparency and answer the question.

Reading Focus: As an extension of the Reading Focus, have students discuss when care with one's appearance might be important.

RESOURCE MANAGER

Teaching Tools and Resources
- Theme One Planning Guide
- Literature Groups Sourcebook

Essential Lesson Support

Lesson-Specific Instruction
- Selection Focus Transparency 6
- Literary Elements Transparency 6
- Active Reading Guide,* p. 6
- Selection Vocabulary Practice, p. 4

Assessment
- Selection Quick Checks,* p. 6
- Selection and Theme Assessment, pp. 11–12
- Testmaker: ExamView Pro
- Performance Assessment, p. 6

Systematic Language Instruction
- Grammer & Composition Handbook, Lessons 2.2, 2.3

English Language Learners
- ELL Sourcebook, p. 22
- Spanish Summaries, p. 6
- Spanish Translations, pp. 11–17
- Audio Library*
- English, Yes!

Spec. Needs/Strat. Interven.
- Interactive Reading Sourcebook, pp. T61–T63
- Interactive Reading Workbook, pp. 10–11
- Inclusion Strategies Sourcebook, pp. 23–24, 53–54
- Audio Library*

*Also available in Spanish

Reading the Selection

SUMMARY

On Saturday, Alfonso, who is painfully self-conscious, meets a girl when he rescues her little brother. He asks her to go bike riding with him on Monday. Alfonso asks his older brother, Ernie, to lend him his bike for Sandra to use, but Ernie refuses. On Monday, Alfonso breaks his bike chain and he is left with no bike at all. At the last minute, Ernie shows up and lends his bike to Alfonso after all. Sandra doesn't mind riding on the crossbar. She and Alfonso have fun anyway.

Spanish Summaries, p. 6

A Active Reading Strategies

CONNECT Ask students if they can identify with how Alfonso feels. What advice would they give Alfonso?

VOCABULARY If you haven't pre-viewed the selection vocabulary with students, stop and remind them to use context clues to unlock the meanings of new vocabulary words.

Additional Resources

Active Reading Guide, p. 6

Audio Library

Spanish Audio Library

Broken Chain

Gary Soto

Alfonso sat on the porch trying to push his crooked teeth to where he thought they belonged. He hated the way he looked. Last week he did fifty sit-ups a day, thinking that he would burn those already apparent ripples on his stomach to even deeper ripples, dark ones, so when he went swimming at the canal next summer, girls in cut-offs would notice. And the guys would think he was tough, someone who could take a punch and give it back. He wanted "cuts"[1] like those he had seen on a calendar of an Aztec warrior standing on a pyramid with a woman in his arms. (Even she had cuts he could see beneath her thin dress.) The calendar hung above the cash register at La Plaza. Orsua, the owner, said Alfonso could have the calendar at the end of the year if the waitress, Yolanda, didn't take it first.

1. Here, *cuts* is slang for "good, solid abdominal muscles."

Teaching Support

CONNECTING TO OTHER SELECTIONS

The chart at the right shows three ways to connect "Broken Chain" to other selections in this book. For specific teaching strategies, see the ***Theme One Planning Guide***.

Connection	Title
Life Skills: Self-Image	→ "Without Commercials," p. 59
Thematic: Family	→ "Growing Pains," p. 133
Literary: Conflict	→ "Antaeus," p. 347

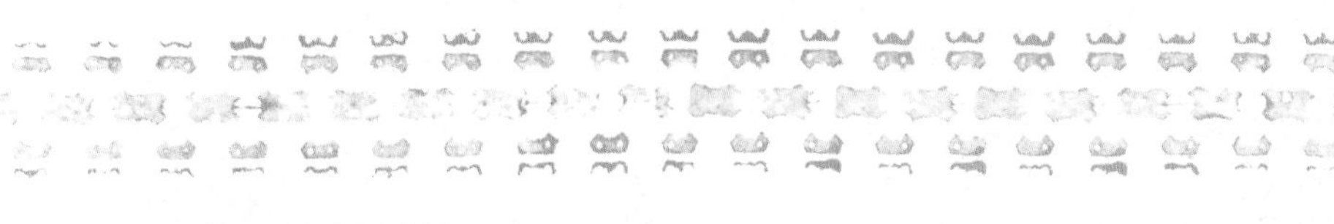

Alfonso studied the magazine pictures of rock stars for a hairstyle. He liked the way Prince looked—and the bass player from Los Lobos.[2] Alfonso thought he would look cool with his hair razored into a V in the back and streaked purple. But he knew his mother wouldn't go for it. And his father, who was *puro Mexicano,*[3] would sit in his chair after work, sullen as a toad, and call him "sissy."

Alfonso didn't dare color his hair. But one day he had had it butched on the top, like in the magazines. His father had come home that evening from a softball game, happy that his team had drilled four homers in a thirteen-to-five bashing of Color Tile. He'd swaggered into the living room, but had stopped cold when he saw Alfonso and asked, not joking but with real concern, "Did you hurt your head at school? *Qué pasó?*"[4]

B Alfonso had pretended not to hear his father and had gone to his room, where he studied his hair from all angles in the mirror. He liked what he saw until he smiled and realized for the first time that his teeth were crooked, like a pile of wrecked cars. He grew depressed and turned away from the mirror. He sat on his bed and leafed through the rock magazine until he came to the rock star with the butched top. His mouth was closed, but Alfonso was sure his teeth weren't crooked.

Alfonso didn't want to be the handsomest kid at school, but he was determined to be better-looking than average. The next day he spent his lawn-mowing money on a new shirt, and, with a pocketknife, scooped the moons of dirt from under his fingernails.

He spent hours in front of the mirror trying to herd his teeth into place with his thumb. He asked his mother if he could have braces, like Frankie Molina, her godson, but he asked at the wrong time. She was at the kitchen table licking the envelope to the house payment. She glared up at him. "Do you think money grows on trees?" C

His mother clipped coupons from magazines and newspapers, kept a vegetable garden in the summer, and shopped at Penney's and K-Mart. Their family ate a lot of *frijoles,* which was OK because nothing else tasted so good, though one time Alfonso had had Chinese pot stickers[5] and thought they were the next best food in the world.

2. *Prince* is the former name of a rock star. *Los Lobos* (lōs lō′ bōs), "The Wolves," is a Mexican American band.
3. *Puro Mexicano* (pōō′ rō me′ hē kä′ nō) means "pure Mexican."
4. *"Qué pasó?"* (kā pä sō′) translates as "What happened?"

5. *Frijoles* (frē hō′ les) are beans—pinto bean, kidney beans, or black beans—that are cooked until very tender, mashed, and fried. A *pot sticker* is a kind of Chinese dumpling.

Vocabulary
sullen (sul′ ən) *adj.* stubbornly withdrawn or gloomy; sulky
swagger (swag′ ər) *v.* to walk or behave in a bold, rude, or overly proud way

Cultural Note

Historically, attitudes toward hairstyles have varied from culture to culture. A young Aztec man wore his hair in a distinctive short cut with a single long lock at the nape of his neck that he was not allowed to cut off until he had captured his first prisoner in battle. However, for centuries in Japan, Africa, and ancient Greece, only warriors were allowed to wear long hair.

B Literary Elements

PLOT: *Internal Conflict* Guide students to see that Alfonso's obsession with his appearance is an internal conflict. For example, "He liked what he saw until he smiled and realized... his teeth were crooked." Alfonso yearns to be good-looking; but every time he fixes one flaw, he notices another, so he is never happy with himself.

C Literary Elements

PLOT: *External Conflict* Ask students what Alfonso's mother's response to his request for braces represents. *(It represents a conflict between what each thinks is important. It also hints at the family's financial status. Alfonso's mother cares more about his character than his looks. Paying the bills for necessities is about all they can manage.)*

MEETING INDIVIDUAL NEEDS — ENGLISH LANGUAGE LEARNERS

Ethnic Foods Write these words on the board: *frijoles, pot stickers, tortillas.* Point out that names for foods from other cultures become part of the English language as those foods become popular.

Activity Have students discuss some of their favorite foods and then set up a chart showing these foods and their countries of origin.

Country	Food
Mexico	tortilla
Greece	baklava
France	croissant
China	pot stickers

Additional Resources

English Language Learners Sourcebook, p. 22

Ⓜ Critical Thinking

INFERRING Ask students whether Alfonso's family has money. How do they know? You may wish to share the following model to illustrate the thinking process involved in making inferences.

Model: I remember that Alfonso's mother said they could not afford braces. She clips coupons, grows her own vegetables, and feeds the family beans to save money. Alfonso's and Ernie's bikes are both cheap. Their father's truck has an unmatched fender. These things lead me to infer that Alfonso's family does not have a lot of money.

N Literary Elements

FIGURES OF SPEECH A simile compares two things by using *like* or *as*, and a metaphor establishes a comparison by saying one thing *is* another thing. "The chain lay in his hand like a dead snake" is a simile. Ask students to find another simile and a metaphor on page 50. (*Simile:* slicing his hand like a snake's fang. *Metaphor:* a paper boy with dollar signs in his eyes.)

O Literary Elements

PLOT: *Climax* Ask students why Alfonso's breaking his bike chain brings the story to a climax. (*Now he doesn't even have one bike for his date. His brother is angry with him, he doesn't know what to say to Sandra, and he has no idea how to achieve his goal of going out with her.*)

Teaching Support

wasn't looking. Ernie punched Alfonso in the arm, and Alfonso, his eyes wide with anger, punched back.

Monday morning they hurried to school on their bikes, neither saying a word, though they rode side by side. In first period, Alfonso worried himself sick. How would he borrow a bike for her? He considered asking his best friend, Raul, for his bike. But Alfonso knew Raul, a paper boy with dollar signs in his eyes, would charge him, and he had less than sixty cents, counting the soda bottles he could cash.

Between history and math, Alfonso saw Sandra and her girlfriend huddling at their lockers. He hurried by without being seen.

During lunch Alfonso hid in metal shop[9] so he wouldn't run into Sandra. What would he say to her? If he weren't mad at his brother, he could ask Ernie what girls and guys talk about. But he *was* mad, and anyway, Ernie was pitching nickels with his friends.

Alfonso hurried home after school. He did the morning dishes as his mother had asked and raked the leaves. After finishing his chores, he did a hundred sit-ups, pushed on his teeth until they hurt, showered, and combed his hair into a perfect butch. He then stepped out to the patio to clean his bike. On an impulse, he removed the chain to wipe off the gritty oil. But while he was unhooking it from the back sprocket, it snapped. The chain lay in his hand like a dead snake.

Did You Know?
A *sprocket* is a wheel that has teeth around its edge to grab the links of a chain. A bicycle has a small sprocket on the rear wheel and a larger one between the two wheels.

Alfonso couldn't believe his luck. Now, not only did he not have an extra bike for Sandra, he had no bike for himself. Frustrated, and on the verge of tears, he flung the chain as far as he could. It landed with a hard slap against the back fence and spooked his sleeping cat, Benny. Benny looked around, blinking his soft gray eyes, and went back to sleep.

Alfonso retrieved the chain, which was hopelessly broken. He cursed himself for being stupid, yelled at his bike for being cheap, and slammed the chain onto the cement. The chain snapped in another place and hit him when it popped up, slicing his hand like a snake's fang.

"Ow!" he cried, his mouth immediately going to his hand to suck on the wound.

After a dab of iodine, which only made his cut hurt more, and a lot of thought, he went to the bedroom to plead with Ernie, who was changing to his after-school clothes.

"Come on, man, let me use it," Alfonso pleaded. "Please, Ernie, I'll do anything."

Although Ernie could see Alfonso's desperation, he had plans with his friend Raymundo. They were going to catch frogs at the Mayfair canal. He felt sorry for

9. The *metal shop* is a room where students learn the skills of working with metals. Schools often also have wood shops and car shops to teach similar skills.

Vocabulary
impulse (im′ puls) *n.* an internal force that causes one to act without thinking
retrieve (ri trēv′) *v.* to locate and bring back; recover; fetch
desperation (des′ pə rā′ shən) *n.* distress caused by great need or loss of hope

MEETING INDIVIDUAL NEEDS — SPECIAL NEEDS

Emotional Ask students whether they can relate to how upset Alfonso gets when his bike chain breaks—and then, to make matters worse, he cuts his hand. Discuss how Alfonso handles his frustration. Point out that throwing the chain doesn't work but talking to Ernie does (ultimately).

Activity Have students complete a chart about Alfonso's two ways of dealing with frustration, listing *Ways That Work* in one column and *Ways That Don't Work* in the other. **L2**

Additional Resources
Inclusion Strategies

his brother, and gave him a stick of gum to make him feel better, but there was nothing he could do. The canal was three miles away, and the frogs were waiting.

Alfonso took the stick of gum, placed it in his shirt pocket, and left the bedroom with his head down. He went outside, slamming the screen door behind him, and sat in the alley behind his house. A sparrow landed in the weeds, and when it tried to come close, Alfonso screamed for it to scram. The sparrow responded with a squeaky chirp and flew away.

At four he decided to get it over with and started walking to Sandra's house, trudging slowly, as if he were waist-deep in water. Shame colored his face. How could he disappoint his first date? She would probably laugh. She might even call him *menso*.[10]

He stopped at the corner where they were supposed to meet and watched her house. But there was no one outside, only a rake leaning against the steps.

10. *Menso* (men′ sō) means "ignorant or foolish."

Sibling Rivals, 1989. Phoebe Beasley. Collage, 32 x 41 in. Stella Jones Gallery, New Orleans.

Viewing the collage: What does this collage say to you about rivalry? Could these figures be Alfonso and Ernie? Why or why not?

Active Reading Strategies

PREDICT Ask students if they can predict whether Ernie will somehow help his brother. *(Some students may think he will. He feels sorry for Alfonso and gives him a stick of gum to make him feel better.)*

Literary Elements

CONFLICT: *Character* Ask students to think about the way Alfonso handles this conflict. What do his thoughts and actions say about his character? *(At first Alfonso is angry and frustrated, but he calms down and decides to face an embarrassing situation. This shows that Alfonso needs to learn effective ways to deal with his anger but that he is mature enough to face Sandra and explain the situation.)*

Viewing the Collage

While teaching art in a high school, Phoebe Beasley ran out of supplies and had her students work on collages with whatever materials were available. She became fascinated with the medium and soon became widely known as a collage artist herself. The family is one of her favorite themes.

Viewing Response *Students will bring a variety of personal interpretations to the collage, most likely noting more differences than similarities between the collage siblings and Alfonso and Ernie, whose rivalry doesn't seem to be very serious.*

Real-World Connection

Create a TV Show Students may benefit from drawing upon their own experiences and knowledge to help each of them create an episode about the life of someone like Alfonso. This will help them connect to the selection and to Alfonso's concerns.

Activity Have the class work in groups to develop ideas for a TV show based on the life of someone like Alfonso. The show should be set in the present in an average urban neighborhood. Students should answer questions like these: *Is the show a situation comedy or a drama? What will the title be? Who are the characters, both main and secondary? What is the series about in general? What will be the plot of one episode? What common theme will the episode contain that will connect with many cultures?* **L2** COLLAB. LEARN.

R Literary Elements

PLOT: *Falling Action* Remind students that falling action presents the results of the climax. Ask them what events here result from the climax. *(Ernie is no longer angry; he lends Alfonso his bike.)*

S Literary Elements

PLOT: *Conflict Resolution* Help students realize that Alfonso achieves his goal in the last paragraph of the story. Ask them how this paragraph resolves the tension. *(Alfonso gets together with Sandra, who seems to like him and not mind his crooked teeth. He feels comfortable with her.)*

You may wish to use ***Fine Art Transparency 1*** before students discuss the story's theme.

Thematic Focus

What I Am, What I Want to Be
Have students compare Alfonso with themselves and other readers their age. Are his thoughts, feelings, words, actions, and experiences typical of people his age? Do they apply to young people from other cultural backgrounds besides Alfonso's? Ask for examples.

Quick Checks, p. 6

Why did he have to take the chain off? he scolded himself. He always messed things up when he tried to take them apart, like the time he tried to repad his baseball mitt. He had unlaced the mitt and filled the pocket with cotton balls. But when he tried to put it back together, he had forgotten how it laced up. Everything became tangled like kite string. When he showed the mess to his mother, who was at the stove cooking dinner, she scolded him but put it back together and didn't tell his father what a dumb thing he had done.

Now he had to face Sandra and say, "I broke my bike, and my stingy brother took off on his."

He waited at the corner for a few minutes, hiding behind a hedge for what seemed like forever. Just as he was starting to think about going home, he heard footsteps and knew it was too late. His hands, moist from worry, hung at his sides, and a thread of sweat raced down his armpit.

He peeked through the hedge. She was wearing a sweater with a checkerboard pattern. A red purse was slung over her shoulder. He could see her looking for him, standing on tiptoe to see if he was coming around the corner.

What have I done? Alfonso thought. He bit his lip, called himself *menso*, and pounded his palm against his forehead. Someone slapped the back of his head. He turned around and saw Ernie.

"We got the frogs, Alfonso," he said, holding up a wiggling plastic bag. "I'll show you later."

Ernie looked through the hedge, with one eye closed, at the girl. "She's not the one who messed with Frostie and me," he said finally. "You still wanna borrow my bike?" R

Alfonso couldn't believe his luck. What a brother! What a pal! He promised to take Ernie's turn next time it was his turn to do the dishes. Ernie hopped on Raymundo's handlebars and said he would remember that promise. Then he was gone as they took off without looking back.

Free of worry now that his brother had come through, Alfonso emerged from behind the hedge with Ernie's bike, which was mud-splashed but better than nothing. Sandra waved.

"Hi," she said.

"Hi," he said back.

She looked cheerful. Alfonso told her his bike was broken and asked if she wanted to ride with him. S

"Sounds good," she said, and jumped on the crossbar.

It took all of Alfonso's strength to steady the bike. He started off slowly, gritting his teeth, because she was heavier than he thought. But once he got going, it got easier. He pedaled smoothly, sometimes with only one hand on the handlebars, as they sped up one street and down another. Whenever he ran over a pothole, which was often, she screamed with delight, and once, when it looked like they were going to crash, she placed her hand over his, and it felt like love.

❖

Vocabulary
emerge (i murj′) *v.* to come out

Teaching Support

Grammar and Language *Minilesson*

Pronouns Used as Objects Write the following on the board: Personal pronouns used as objects: (singular) *me, you, him, her, it,* (plural) *us, you, them*
Remind students that personal pronouns are used to replace nouns that refer to people or things. The sentence will still mean the same thing.
Alfonso borrowed a bike from Ernie.
Alfonso borrowed a bike from *him*.

Activity Have students substitute the correct pronoun for the underlined word(s).

1. Alfonso met Sandra at four-thirty. Since he only had one bike, he asked Sandra to sit on the crossbar. *(her)*
2. My mother kept our baby pictures in a small blue box. Yesterday she gave those pictures to my brother and me. *(us)*
3. Alfonso was angry because the chain broke when he removed *the chain*. *(it)* **L2**

Additional Resources

- ***Grammar and Language Transparency 5***
- ***Grammar and Language Workbook,*** pp. 107–108, 143–144
- ***Grammar and Composition Handbook,*** Lesson 4.2
- ***Writer's Choice,*** Lessons 11.1, 13.2

Responding to Literature

PERSONAL RESPONSE

- What thoughts and feelings did you have at the end of the story? Describe your reactions in your journal.
- In what ways did you identify with Alfonso? Explain in detail.

Analyzing Literature

RECALL

1. What aspects of his appearance would Alfonso like to change?
2. Describe the difference between Alfonso's and Ernie's bikes.
3. How does Alfonso break his bicycle chain?
4. What is Sandra's reaction to Alfonso's appearing with just one beat-up bike?

Brackets connect questions that are paired to develop higher-level thinking skills.

INTERPRET

5. Why is Alfonso unhappy with the way he looks?
6. How does the author show that Alfonso cares very much about the appearance of his bike?
7. Why is Alfonso so upset when he breaks his bicycle chain? Do you think he is overreacting? Why or why not?
8. At the end of the story, Alfonso is different. How has he changed? What caused the change? Use examples to support your answers.

EVALUATE AND CONNECT

9. Alfonso is always trying to straighten his teeth. What does the **repetition** of this image show you about his state of mind throughout the story?
10. Theme Connection Does reading a story about someone your own age make you feel more connected to the character? Why or why not?

Spokes, 1983. John D. Wibberley. Acrylic on canvas, 16 x 24 in. Artist's collection.

LITERARY ELEMENTS

Conflict

The struggle between two opposing forces that lie at the center of a plot in a story is called the **conflict.** An **external conflict** exists when a character struggles against an outside force—another person, nature, society, or fate. An **internal conflict** exists within the mind of the character who is torn between opposing feelings or goals. In "Broken Chain" Alfonso struggles with both kinds of conflicts.

1. What are the external conflicts that seem to prevent Alfonso from reaching his goal of meeting Sandra for a "date"? Find two or more examples.
2. Alfonso is desperately searching for his own style. Describe how his lack of confidence about his looks could be interpreted as an internal conflict.

● See **Literary Terms Handbook,** p. R3.

Responding to the Selection

PERSONAL RESPONSE

- Some students may say that they were glad the story turned out happily and that Alfonso grew as a person.
- Students may say they know how it feels not to fit in, to be critical of their looks, or to fight with their siblings.

Analyzing Literature

1. Alfonso would like to change his teeth, his muscles, and his hair.
2. Alfonso's bike is so clean it gleams; Ernie's is dirty.
3. He unhooks the chain to clean it.
4. She is content to sit on the crossbar.
5. He feels insecure and is afraid girls will not like him.
6. He describes in great detail the care Alfonso takes to clean his bike.
7. He needed two bikes and now he has none, so he'll have to break his date. Most students will say he's overreacting because Sandra won't judge him by his bike (as the end of the story proves).
8. He is more confident and mature because he has overcome a crisis and learned not to worry so much: "Free of worry now" and "once he got going, it got easier."
9. It shows how obsessed he is with straightening out his teeth and, by implication, his physical appearance.
10. Most students feel more connected to characters their own age because they have similar concerns and they are easier to identify with and understand.

LITERARY ELEMENTS

1. The external conflicts in the story include Alfonso's fight with Ernie, Ernie's denying Alfonso the use of his bike, and the broken chain on Alfonso's bike.
2. His desire to see Sandra conflicts with his fear that she will think he is ugly.

Additional Resources

Literary Elements Transparency 6

Literature and Writing

Writing About Literature

Students' paragraphs should
- give appropriate examples of Soto's descriptive details
- explain clearly how each detail helps readers understand Alfonso's life

Creative Writing

Students' letters should
- spell out Alfonso's concerns clearly

Students' advice columns should
- reassure Alfonso that he is normal
- address his concerns in order
- provide reasons for their conclusions

Extending Your Response

Literature Groups Tell students that the chart can have as many rows as they wish, as long as they find support in the story for each item. COLLAB. LEARN.

Interdisciplinary Activity

Remind students to make sure their explanations proceed in a logical sequence and match their diagrams.

Performing Encourage students to spend time planning and rehearsing their improvisations. If possible, videotape each pair's performance and make the tapes available for viewing.

Literature and Writing

Writing About Literature

Details In "Broken Chain," Gary Soto includes many details about Alfonso's family and neighborhood. Write a paragraph or two about how Soto's use of details helps you understand what his life at home and at school must have been like. Choose details from the story to prove your point.

Creative Writing

Dear Advice Columnist Recall your discussion in the **Reading Focus** on page 43 about peoples' concern with their appearance. Alfonso is self-conscious about his appearance. Imagine that he has written to an advice column. What questions might Alfonso ask? What advice might a helpful person give him? Write the letter and the response.

Extending Your Response

Literature Groups

Comparing Alfonso with Himself Together, read the first and last paragraphs in the story. Then have a discussion comparing how Alfonso feels at the beginning of the story with how he feels at the end. Make a comparison chart that shows the results of your discussion.

	AT THE BEGINNING	AT THE END
ALFONSO'S FEELINGS ABOUT HIMSELF		

Interdisciplinary Activity

Science Why does a bicycle need a chain? Can a bike work without one? With a partner, examine a bike scientifically. Write your own explanation of how a bicycle works. Use diagrams to illustrate your ideas. Check with a reference book or your science teacher to see whether your explanation is correct and revise it as needed.

Performing

Improvisation Work with a partner to improvise a scene between Alfonso and Sandra after their bike ride at the end of the story. What would the two say to each other? Would they be nervous or shy? What would their body language look like? Perform your improvised scene in front of the class.

Reading Further

Check out these books by Gary Soto:

Poetry: *Neighborhood Odes*

Novel: *Taking Sides*

Short Stories: *Baseball in April and Other Stories*

Save your work for your portfolio.

Teaching Support

Reading Minilesson

Distinguishing Between Connotative and Denotative Meanings Remind students that the dictionary definition of a word is called its denotation. An emotional or cultural association that a word may have is called a connotation. A word can have a negative or a positive connotation. For example, the dictionary definition of *attractive* is "arousing interest or pleasure." In addition to this meaning, the word *attractive* has a positive connotation of something beautiful, pretty, or handsome. Explain that words with neutral connotations may have synonyms with positive or negative connotations.

Activity Ask students to review "Broken Chain," looking for words that have positive or negative connotations. Help them to identify these words and discuss the denotations and connotations. Words with negative connotations include *crooked* (imperfect), *tough* (mean, rough), and *average* (boring, unspectacular). L2

Additional Resources

Reading Skills Practice Workbook

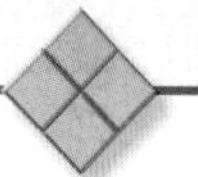

Skill Minilessons

Reteach · Review

GRAMMAR AND LANGUAGE • SUBJECT-VERB AGREEMENT

A subject and a verb are basic parts of a sentence. The subject and its verb must agree in number. A singular noun used as a subject of a sentence calls for a singular form of the verb:

Alfonso rides his bike after school.

A plural noun used as the subject calls for a plural form of the verb:

Alfonso and Ernie ride their bikes after school.

PRACTICE For each sentence, write the subject and the correct form of the verb.

1. Gary Soto (writes, write) stories about teens.
2. The book *Baseball in April and Other Stories* (is, are) an award winner.
3. There (is, are) eleven short stories, most about Latino young people.
4. The stories, like "Broken Chain," (focuses, focus) on the difficulties of growing up.
5. The end of the book (contains, contain) a list of Spanish words and their English translations.

• For more about subject-verb agreement, see **Language Handbook,** pp. R14–R15.

READING AND THINKING • ACTIVATING PRIOR KNOWLEDGE

Things you already know can help you understand what you read. Even if you read about an adventure in another galaxy, you will understand some parts easily because of knowledge you acquired previously. All the life experiences you have had contribute to your prior knowledge.

PRACTICE What have you read or experienced that helped you better understand the characters' thoughts and feelings in "Broken Chain"? Write a paragraph describing how this prior knowledge helped you understand the story.

• For more about this and related reading strategies, see **Reading Handbook,** p. R86.

VOCABULARY • SYNONYMS

Synonyms are words that mean nearly the same thing. When you know synonyms for a word, you can decide which one best expresses the exact meaning you want. For example, *desperation* expresses a more frantic feeling than *hopelessness.* A hopeless person might just sit and do nothing. But a desperate person would try something–anything! Still, *desperation* and *hopelessness* are synonyms, because they are close in meaning. A **thesaurus,** a book that lists and defines synonyms, can help you understand how synonyms differ in meaning.

PRACTICE Write a synonym for each word below. Then write one sentence using each word and another sentence using its synonym.

1. sullen
2. retrieve
3. swagger
4. wince
5. impulse

Skill Minilessons

GRAMMAR AND LANGUAGE
SUBJECT-VERB AGREEMENT

1. Gary Soto writes
2. book is
3. are stories
4. stories focus
5. end contains

READING AND THINKING
ACTIVATING PRIOR KNOWLEDGE

Students' paragraphs should
- give examples from their own lives and their reading
- tie the examples to the story

VOCABULARY
SYNONYMS

Examples
1. sullen, *gloomy*
   The *sullen* clerk didn't answer.
   When it rained, he felt *gloomy*.
2. retrieve, *fetch*
   I had to *retrieve* the lost ring.
   My dog likes to *fetch* sticks.
3. swagger, *strut*
   The models *strut* down the runway.
   The winners *swagger* proudly.
4. wince, *flinch*
   The shot made him *wince*.
   Most people *flinch* from pain.
5. impulse, *whim*
   She had an *impulse* to buy it.
   He took the ride on a *whim*.

Additional Resources

- ***Gr. & Lang. Wkbk,*** pp. 183–192
- ***Gr. & Comp. Hbk,*** L.10.1–10.5
- ***Writer's Choice,*** L.16.1–16.5
- ***Reading Skills Practice Workbook***
- ***Vocabulary Practice,*** p. 4

ASSESSMENT

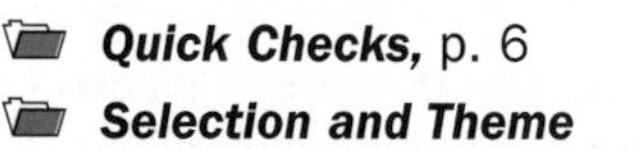

- ***Quick Checks,*** p. 6
- ***Selection and Theme Assessment,*** pp. 11–12
- ***Performance Assessment,*** p. 6
- ***Testmaker: ExamView Pro***
- ***Interactive Tutor: Self-Assessment***

Bicycle Repair
Have students use a search engine and such keywords as *bicycle repair* to learn how to repair a broken bicycle chain (or make another kind of bicycle repair). Ask them to write, in their own words, step-by-step directions for the process.

Technology Skills

Objectives

- To use desktop publishing software to publish an autobiographical anecdote
- To investigate how desktop publishing techniques are used to produce a school newspaper

Teaching Strategies

Help students learn about the possibilities of desktop publishing by demonstrating the kinds of design and layout they can create on their computers. Show students how to do the following:

- set up a multiple-column page
- format text in various ways
- use such design features as drop caps and shading
- number pages automatically and create headers and footers
- create banner headlines
- create a table of contents
- use various fonts
- resize and position photos and artwork

Adapting to Available Technology

The appearance and layout of menu items and tools may differ slightly from those illustrated and discussed here, depending on which word processing software is installed on your school's computers. If necessary, adapt the lesson to match your software.

Teaching Support

Word Processing: Desktop Publishing

With a small group, examine several books, magazines, and newspapers. Notice how text and illustrations are arranged on the page. Can you tell who the intended readers are just by the way a page is designed? How do book, magazine, and newspaper pages differ? Summarize what your examination tells you about page design.

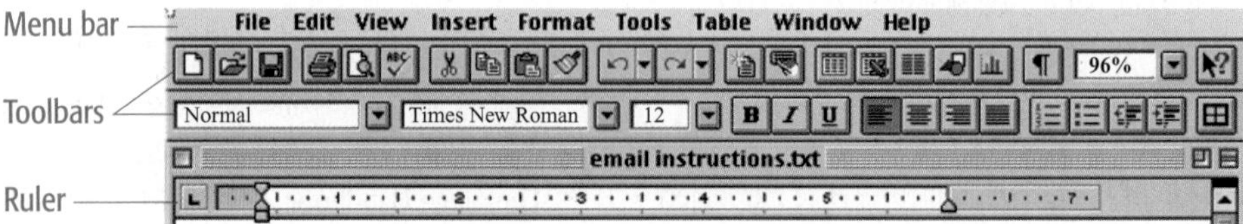

Getting Oriented

Get to know some important features of your word processing software. Start with a document that has some text in it. Experiment with each feature by selecting a portion of text before choosing a menu command or clicking an icon.

1. Pull down the **View** menu, and select **Page Layout.** Use this view for the remaining items in this list.
2. Pull down the **Format** menu, and select **Columns.** Locate the columns icon in the toolbar.
3. Find the **Font Box** in the toolbar. Locate the **Font** feature in the **Format** menu. Experiment with some fonts. (See the **TYPOGRAPHY** chart on the next page for more information about fonts, or typefaces.)
4. Find the **Font Size** box in the toolbar. Select **Font** in the **Format** menu.
5. On the toolbar, find the buttons for align left, align right, center, and align left and right (also called justification).
6. Look under **Tools** to find the feature **Hyphenation.** (It may be in a Tools submenu under **Language.**)
7. Find the buttons that automatically create numbered and bulleted lists.
8. Locate the buttons that will decrease or increase indentations.
9. On the ruler, find the button that controls tab stops, or locate its feature in the **Format** menu.
10. Experiment with the margin markers on the ruler.

Sample Typefaces (all in 12 pt. size)

Serif Faces
Bookman Old Style
Courier New
Garamond
Times New Roman

Sans-Serif Faces
Ariel
Avant Garde Book
Helvetica Condensed Light

Meeting Individual Needs: SPECIAL NEEDS

Physically Challenged If students are not proficient keyboarders or have muscular difficulties, they may want to investigate using voice-activation software. Such software is easy to set up and use, but each student must spend about thirty minutes training the program to recognize his or her particular speech patterns.

Activity Invite students who are interested in voice-activation technology to do research on how it works and where it is available. L2

Additional Resources

Inclusion Strategies

TYPOGRAPHY

Typeface	Type size
Many different typefaces—each with unique roman, *italic,* and **bold** styles—are available on computers. A few are illustrated on page 56.	Type size is measured in points. One point equals about 1⁄72 inch. The main text in most publications is between ten and twelve points.
Serif type	**Sans-serif type**
On serif type, the main strokes of letters are embellished with little strokes, or "feet," that are thought to make words more readable.	Sans-serif type lacks "feet." Traditionally used only for headings, sans-serif type is also used for the main text in many contemporary designs.
Headings	**Display typefaces**
Headings are often bold and usually larger than the main text. Different levels of heading may have different "weights," or sizes.	Display typefaces are typically large and eye-catching and often quite unusual. This book uses display type for its selection and feature titles.

Creating an Autobiographical Sketch

1. In the selection from *Wait Till Next Year,* Doris Kearns Goodwin tells how her relationship with her father led to a lifelong fascination with baseball. Think about the major events in your own life. Was there a particular person or incident that had a strong or lasting effect on you? Focus on a particular experience that you can describe. Try to recall the experience and the feelings you had at the time. Ask yourself: What other people were involved? What writing elements will I use—humor? irony? suspense?
2. Use your computer and word processing software to plan, draft, revise, and edit a brief autobiographical sketch relating that experience.
3. Before presenting your sketch, prepare a design for it that will be appropriate to your subject. Share your designed sketch with a partner, and ask for suggestions for improvement.
4. Prepare a final version, and print your document.

The Title

The Title

The Title

The Title

ACTIVITIES

1. Use the word processing features you learned about to complete the **Writing Workshop** in this theme.
2. In a group, interview your school's newspaper sponsor (if there is one) to determine how word processing is used in the production of the school newspaper.

Activities

All word processing programs can be used to create newsletters, fliers, brochures, posters, and the like. They easily integrate images with text, and their text prints at a high resolution. You may wish to bring in an outside expert to demonstrate techniques.

Create a buddy system, pairing proficient and less-proficient students. Before beginning, invite the class as a whole to create a list of suggestions that might make the publishing process easier. Encourage students to suggest solutions and alternate approaches to each other, both in class discussion and separately. After the assignment is complete, come together one last time for a whole-class discussion of what students learned, what problems they faced, and how they might solve those problems next time.

Student anecdotes should

- demonstrate an ability to lay out text in an organized page design
- contain graphic elements, such as rules, banner headlines, clip art, photos, or other illustrations
- use more than one font and type size

Invite groups of students to share what they found out about how the school newspaper is produced.

INTERDISCIPLINARY CONNECTION

Journalism Students may want to use their desktop publishing skills to create a newsletter, magazine article, brochure, or poster about a science or social studies topic.

Activity Invite students to choose a topic, conduct research (possibly over the Internet), write an article or essay, scan photos and illustrations or create graphics, and lay out a page about their chosen topic. Students may also want to include "Did You Know?" lists or sidebars to highlight interesting tidbits they discover. If a color printer is available, students may want to experiment with colorful heads and illustrations. Before students present their published work, encourage them to reflect on their research and knowledge to raise additional unanswered questions about their topic. L3

Before Reading

Objectives

- To read and analyze a poem about human diversity and acceptance
- To think about point of view in relation to a poem

Skills

Reading/Thinking: Drawing Conclusions; Summarizing; Evaluating
Collaboration: Summarizing

Motivating STUDENTS

Selection Focus Transparency 7: Have students view and discuss the quotation by Martin Luther King Jr.

Reading Focus: To extend the Reading Focus, invite students to look at photographs of people in books and magazines. Have them compare images presented in books about world cultures with images presented in current magazine advertisements.

Before You Read

Without Commercials

MEET ALICE WALKER

From the time she was eight, Alice Walker kept a notebook of poetry. Today her writings include novels, poems, short stories, and essays. As the youngest of eight children in a Georgia sharecropping family, Walker says, "I always seemed to need more peace and quiet than anybody else. . . . Books became my world, because the world I was in was very hard." Walker is the first African American woman to win the Pulitzer Prize for a novel. Much of her writing focuses on the difficult lives of poor, heroic, African American women.

Alice Walker was born in 1944. This poem was published in 1984.

READING FOCUS

How many different kinds of people are there in the world? Think about the variety of faces you see in a large crowd at a parade or a sports event.

Sharing Ideas

With a small group, discuss the variety of people you see in advertisements. Do ads reflect the broad diversity of human beings in the world?

Setting a Purpose

Read the poem to find out what the speaker thinks about ads.

BUILDING BACKGROUND

Alice Walker grew up attending all-black schools that "gave us a feeling that they really belonged to us. There was a lot of self-help and community." Even in this supportive environment, however, Walker felt like an outcast after an older brother accidentally shot her in the eye with a BB gun. Her blinded eye was covered with scar tissue. "I used to pray every night that I would wake up and somehow it would be gone. I couldn't look people in the eye because I thought I was ugly." It was this experience that first inspired Walker to record her observations and feelings. Later, surgery repaired much of the scar tissue. This change helped improve her self-image considerably.

Walker is considered one of the major American writers of this century. She is active in both the Civil Rights and women's rights movements. She helped reintroduce readers to the author Zora Neale Hurston, another important African American writer.

RESOURCE MANAGER

Teaching Tools and Resources
- Theme One Planning Guide
- Literature Groups Sourcebook

Essential Lesson Support

Lesson-Specific Instruction
- Selection Focus Transparency 7
- Literary Elements Transparency 7
- Active Reading Guide,* p. 7

Assessment
- Selection Quick Checks,* p. 7
- Selection and Theme Assessment, pp. 13–14
- Testmaker: ExamView Pro
- Performance Assessment, p. 7

Systematic Language Instruction
- Grammer & Composition Handbook, Lesson 2.4
- Vocabulary Power, Lesson 4
- Spelling Power, Lesson 4

English Language Learners
- ELL Sourcebook, p. 23
- Spanish Summaries, p. 7
- Audio Library*
- English, Yes!

Spec. Needs/Strat. Interven.
- Interactive Reading Sourcebook, pp. T63–T65
- Interactive Reading Workbook, p. 12
- Inclusion Strategies Sourcebook, pp. 1–2
- Audio Library*

*Also available in Spanish

Without Commercials

Alice Walker

Listen,
stop tanning yourself
and talking about
fishbelly
white.
The color white
is not bad at all.
There are white mornings
that bring us days.
Or, if you must,
tan only because
it makes you happy
to be brown,
to be able to see
for a summer
the whole world's
darker
face
reflected
in your own.

⁂

Stop unfolding
your eyes.
Your eyes are
beautiful.
Sometimes
seeing you in the street
the fold zany°
and unexpected
I want to kiss
them
and usually
it is only
old
gorgeous
black people's eyes
I want
to kiss.

⁂

Stop trimming
your nose.
When you
diminish°
your nose
your songs
become little
tinny, muted°
and snub.
Better you should
have a nose
impertinent°
as a flower,
sensitive

27 A thing that's *zany* is odd or crazy in a comical way.

41 To *diminish* means "to make smaller in size."
45 In this context, *muted* means "muffled, softened, or less strong."
49 Something *impertinent* is improperly bold or rude.

Reading the Selection

A Active Reading Strategies

QUESTION The poet uses words such as *listen, stop, must,* and *should*. Ask students to discuss the poet's feelings toward the topic. *(The poet feels that people should stop trying to change their appearances. She feels that a natural look is beautiful.)*

B Critical Thinking

DRAWING CONCLUSIONS Ask students to think about what these lines say about Walker's attitude toward race. *(Since Walker compares these eyes to "black people's eyes," we can assume that the people are not black people. By saying that she wants to kiss these eyes, we can conclude that Walker sees beauty in other races.)*

C Active Reading Strategies

QUESTION The speaker says that all colors, eyes, and noses are wonderful. Ask students what underlying belief this opinion expresses.

Additional Resources

- ***Active Reading Guide,*** p. 7
- ***Audio Library***
- ***Spanish Audio Library***
- ***Spanish Summaries,*** p. 7

Teaching Support

CONNECTING TO OTHER SELECTIONS
For a teaching strategy that connects "Without Commercials" to "Broken Chain," turn to the ***Theme One Planning Guide.***

Reading Minilesson

Summarizing Write the following summary of the first stanza on the board: *It's fine to tan yourself if it makes you happy and tanning helps you get a different perspective on life. But don't do it because you think it's bad to be white. White is a good color.*

Activity Have students work in pairs to reread the poem and create summaries of each stanza using the following checklist:

- Does the summary cover the main idea of the stanza?
- Does it consider all supporting details?
- Are the details and main idea combined so that the summary is clear but brief?

L2 **COLLAB. LEARN.**

Additional Resources

- ***Reading Skills Practice Workbook***

Interdisciplinary Connection

Objectives

- To practice reading skills in a content area—social studies
- To gain insight into culturally linked attitudes toward foods

Teaching Strategies

Informational Text

Discuss how the captions and photos on the page support each other. Then ask students to find and bring to class examples of illustrations with captions. Discuss the effectiveness of each example. What can a photo do better than written words? What can a caption do better than a photo? Ask students to suggest other graphic aids they might find in a social studies text. Discuss the kinds of information each can add to a text.

Activity Students may describe food or meal traditions that are specific to their families but which may or may not be traced to their cultural heritage. Point out that interviews, surveys, and polls are important tools in the social sciences. Stress the importance of framing good questions, keeping an open mind, and recording responses accurately.

Teaching Support

Interdisciplinary Connection

SOCIAL STUDIES

Food with Attitude

The young Amy Tan had a tense Christmas Eve dinner. Her mother had prepared all of her favorite foods–tofu, squid, dried mushrooms, and fish cheeks–but Amy was too embarrassed to enjoy them. She worried that these foods and her family's meal customs would be strange and unappetizing to her non-Chinese guests.

Today, a young Amy Tan might not have to worry as much. Americans have become much more sophisticated in their dining habits. You'll probably find tofu, squid, and many other once-exotic items in almost any large supermarket. Still, some dishes popular elsewhere have not yet made it into the American mainstream, and maybe never will. Here are a few of them.

Insects (including termites, ants, and grasshoppers) have been, and still are, eaten by people all over the world. They are an excellent source of protein–even better than beef. Depending on the insect and the location, insects may be eaten raw, cooked, or ground up and used as a spice or a medicine.

Headcheese is not really a cheese, but it is made from a head–a calf's head, including the brain. You can find the recipe in many cookbooks.

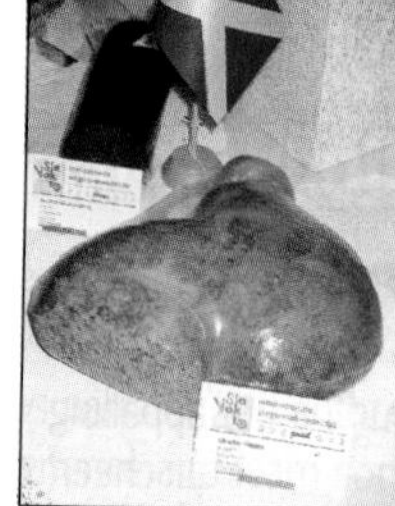

Haggis is a Scottish dish containing the chopped heart, liver, and lungs of a sheep mixed with suet (hard fat), oatmeal, onions, and spices. All this is stuffed into a cleaned sheep's stomach and boiled.

Fugu is a dish of puffer fish, or blowfish, so-called because the fish pumps itself full of air or water to appear larger when in danger. Highly prized in Japan, fugu must be cleaned and prepared by specially trained chefs because the fish's internal organs contain a very powerful poison. The danger seems to add to its popularity.

ACTIVITY

Pretend you are a social scientist trying to understand your family's eating customs. Interview family members, especially older ones, about foods. Ask questions such as:

- What food or meal traditions do we have in our family?
- Where did these traditions come from?
- What dishes from other countries or from other parts of our country do you enjoy?
- What foods did you enjoy as a child?
- How have your food likes and dislikes changed over the years?

Write a report summarizing the results of your survey.

MEETING INDIVIDUAL NEEDS — MULTIPLE MODES OF EXPRESSION

Intrapersonal Encourage students to share their experiences of interviewing, being interviewed, and watching interviews on TV news programs and talk shows. What do they think makes a good interviewer? List students' answers on the board. You may want to offer a few of these suggestions:

- Ask questions that encourage the other person to talk.
- Listen closely to all answers.
- Ask follow-up questions based on what the person says.
- Query what you do not understand.

Activity Have small groups prepare lists of questions they think will get people talking. Ask the groups to give each other feedback on their interviewing techniques. **L2** **COLLAB. LEARN.**

Sequencing

Sequencing is organizing things into some kind of order, or sequence. Writers often use chronological order, or time order, to sequence their stories. Events take place one after another in time order. A skillful reader looks for clues that tell the order in which events actually occurred. Consider these passages from "Fish Cheeks."

> On Christmas Eve I found out that my mother had outdone herself in creating a strange menu. . . .
>
> And then they arrived—the minister's family and all my relatives in a clamor of doorbells and rumpled Christmas packages. . . .
>
> Dinner threw me deeper into despair. . . .
>
> At the end of the meal my father leaned back and belched loudly, thanking my mother for her fine cooking. . . .
>
> After everyone had gone, my mother said to me, "You want to be the same as American girls on the outside."

As you can see, each new paragraph moves the story a little further along in time. Author Amy Tan lets you know when each event happened. She makes use of words and phrases such as *on Christmas Eve, at the end of the meal, then,* and *after.* Not all stories contain clues as specific as these. Sometimes a story moves backward as well as forward in time. Still, you can usually figure out the order in which events occur. Watch especially for words and phrases such as *meanwhile, before, after, first, second, last, eventually, then, next, earlier,* and *later.*

● For more about sequencing, see **Reading Handbook,** p. R91.

ACTIVITY

Look through a short story of your choice. List all the words you find that provide clues to the time order of the events in the story. Then make a chart sequencing at least five events from the story in their correct time order.

Objective

- To recognize sequencing and identify time order in stories

Teaching Strategies

Encourage students to use the events of the preceding day as the basis for stories they would like to write. They should begin by thinking about and making notes on the characters involved, the event or events they will describe (the plot), and the place where the actions will occur (the setting). Next, have them list sentences, such as the following, that could be used to start their stories.

- It all began when my alarm didn't go off.
- Things started off as usual.
- The first thing I did when I got to school yesterday was...

Have students write brief summaries of their stories, using some of the sequencing words suggested in their books.

Activity

Students' responses should

- list the words that provide clues to the sequence of events
- list five events in their proper sequence

Additional Resources

Reading Skills Practice Workbook

Teaching Support

MEETING INDIVIDUAL NEEDS

SPECIAL NEEDS

Learning Disabled Help students sequence by asking them to arrange the events in proper order.

Activity Write the following event summaries on the board:

1. While Alfonso was cleaning his bike, the chain broke.
2. Sandra hopped on the crossbar and off they went.
3. The kid's sister, Sandra, agreed to go bike riding with Alfonso.

Encourage them to check the selection as a way of verifying the sequence. **L1**

Additional Resources

Inclusion Strategies

Before Reading

SUMMARY

In 1955, Rosa Parks refused to give her seat on a bus to a white person. She was taken to jail and found guilty of violating a segregation law in Montgomery, Alabama. The black community boycotted the buses while a legal team and Mrs. Parks fought the segregated bus laws in court. After an eventful year, the Supreme Court's ruling that segregation on the Montgomery buses was unconstitutional marked the beginning of the Civil Rights movement.

Spanish Summaries, p. 10

Objectives

- To read and analyze an autobiographical excerpt
- To identify a sequence of events
- To write a summary of key events

Skills

Reading/Thinking: Inferring; Identifying Cause-and-Effect Relationships; Drawing Conclusions; Judging the Credibility of a Source; Evaluating; Analyzing Arguments; Identifying Propaganda Techniques; Logical Reasoning; Synthesizing; Generalizing
Writing: Consistency in Verb Tenses; Summary; Script; Narrative
Vocabulary: Jargon; Etymology; Antonyms; Unlocking Meaning
Grammar/Language: Quotation Marks; Commas; Capitalization of Proper Nouns; Nouns
Listening/Speaking: Effective Listening Techniques; Skit
Life Skills: Supporting and Contributing
Collaboration: Literature Groups; Performance

Before You Read

from *Rosa Parks: My Story*

MEET ROSA PARKS

Rosa Parks experienced the injustice of segregation on a daily basis growing up in Alabama. In the 1930s, she became active in Civil Rights, focusing on voter registration. Despite much effort, little had changed for African Americans in the South. Then one day in the 1950s, Rosa Parks refused to give up her bus seat. Without planning it, she became "the mother of the Civil Rights movement."

Rosa Parks was born in 1913. This story is part of her autobiography, first published in 1992.

READING FOCUS

When something in the world seems unjust, what can an ordinary person do about it?

List Ideas

Work with a partner and think of a situation that seems to affect people unfairly. Then make a list of actions that ordinary people might take to improve the situation.

Setting a Purpose

Find out what Rosa Parks did to improve a situation.

BUILDING BACKGROUND

The Time and Place This selection begins on December 1, 1955, in racially segregated Montgomery, Alabama.

Did You Know? Until the 1960s, Southern states had laws to separate the races. African Americans fought in the courts and through organized protests to end such discrimination.

VOCABULARY PREVIEW

comply (kəm plī′) *v.* to go along with a request; p. 86
resigned (ri zīnd′) *adj.* giving in without resistance; p. 88
boycott (boi′ kot) *n.* an organized protest in which the participants refuse to buy, sell, or use a product or service; p. 90
mobilize (mō′ bə līz′) *v.* to become prepared, as for war or an emergency; p. 91
inconvenience (in′ kən vēn′ yəns) *v.* to cause someone difficulty, bother, or hassle; p. 93
indignity (in dig′ nə tē) *n.* an offense against one's pride or dignity; humiliation; p. 94
oppression (ə presh′ ən) *n.* the act of controlling or governing by the cruel and unjust use of force or authority; p. 95
negotiate (ni gō′ shē āt′) *v.* to discuss in order to bring about an agreement; p. 97
impose (im pōz′) *v.* to apply legally; enforce; p. 100

84 THEME 1

RESOURCE MANAGER

Teaching Tools and Resources
- Theme One Planning Guide
- Literature Groups Sourcebook

Essential Lesson Support

Lesson-Specific Instruction
- Selection Focus Transparency 10
- Literary Elements Transparency 10
- Active Reading Guide,* p. 10
- Selection Vocabulary Practice, p. 7
- TIME *inTIME* magazine, pp. 22-23

Assessment
- Selection Quick Checks,* p. 10
- Selection and Theme Assessment, pp. 19-20
- Testmaker: ExamView Pro
- Performance Assessment, p. 10

Systematic Language Instruction
- Grammer & Composition Handbook, Lesson 3.3
- Vocabulary Power, Unit 1 Review/Test
- Spelling Power, Unit 1 Review/Proofreading

English Language Learners
- ELL Sourcebook, pp. 27-28
- Spanish Summaries, p. 10
- Spanish Translations, pp. 22-34
- Audio Library*
- English, Yes!

Spec. Needs/Strat. Interven.
- Interactive Reading Sourcebook, pp. T71-T73
- Interactive Reading Workbook, pp. 17-20
- Inclusion Strategies Sourcebook, pp. 3-4

*Also available in Spanish

"You're Under Arrest"

When I got off from work that evening of December 1, I went to Court Square as usual to catch the Cleveland Avenue bus home. I didn't look to see who was driving when I got on, and by the time I recognized him, I had already paid my fare. It was the same driver who had put me off the bus back in 1943, twelve years earlier. He was still tall and heavy, with red, rough-looking skin. And he was still mean-looking. I didn't know if he had been on that route before—they switched the drivers around sometimes. I do know that most of the time if I saw him on a bus, I wouldn't get on it. A

from Rosa Parks: MY STORY

Rosa Parks
with Jim Haskins

Reading the Selection

Motivating STUDENTS

Literature Launchers: "Taking a Seat, Making a Stand"

Videodisc Side A, Segment 3

Also available in VHS.

Selection Focus Transparency 10: Ask students for their interpretations of the quotation by Dr. Martin Luther King Jr.

Reading Focus: Have students discuss ways of righting unfair social situations.

A Active Reading Strategies

PREDICT Ask students to think about the relationship between Rosa Parks and the bus driver. Have them predict what role he may play in the predicament she will describe. *(Because the driver has given Parks trouble before, he may do it again.)*

Teaching Support

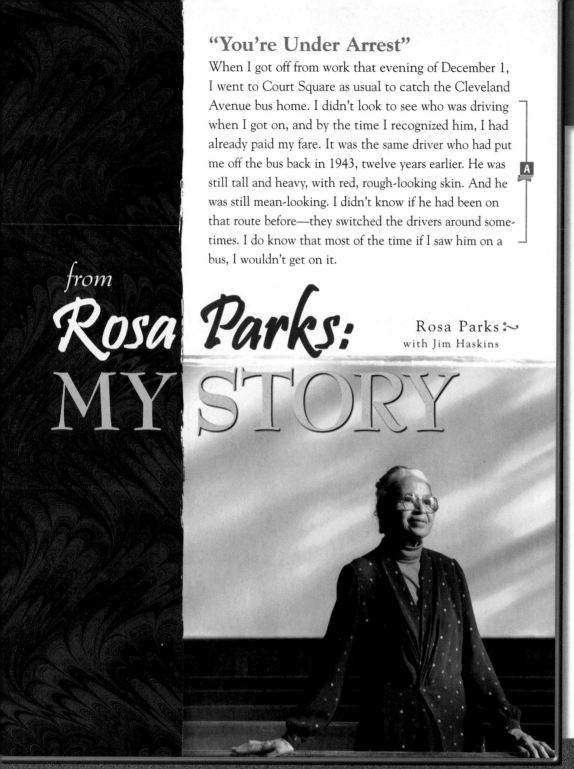

CONNECTING TO OTHER SELECTIONS

The chart at the right shows three ways to connect *Rosa Parks: My Story* to other selections in this book.

For specific teaching strategies, see the ***Theme One Planning Guide.***

Connection	Title
Life Skills: Taking Action	→ "New Directions," p. 221
Thematic: At the Crossroads	→ "Atalanta's Race," p. 714
Literary: Tone	→ "We Are All One," p. 773

LITERATURE & HUMANITIES

We Shall Not Be Moved

Play "We Shall Not Be Moved," on volume 2, track 18 of the CD *American Music: Cultural Traditions*. Have students discuss the role such songs can play in social and political change.

VOCABULARY If you haven't previewed the selection vocabulary with students, stop and remind them to use context clues to unlock the meanings of new vocabulary words.

B Literary Elements

SEQUENCE This passage describes the first step of Rosa Parks's ordeal. Ask students how Parks uses sequencing within this passage to bring the events to life. *(The minute-by-minute description helps readers picture the events as they happened.)*

Additional Resources

- ***Active Reading Guide,*** p. 10
- ***Audio Library***
- ***Spanish Audio Library***
- ***Spanish Summaries,*** p. 10

I saw a vacant seat in the middle section of the bus and took it. I didn't even question why there was a vacant seat even though there were quite a few people standing in the back. If I had thought about it at all, I would probably have figured maybe someone saw me get on and did not take the seat but left it vacant for me. There was a man sitting next to the window and two women across the aisle.

The next stop was the Empire Theater, and some whites got on. They filled up the white seats, and one man was left standing. The driver looked back and noticed the man standing. Then he looked back at us. He said, "Let me have those front seats," because they were the front seats of the black section. Didn't anybody move. We just sat right where we were, the four of us. Then he spoke a second time: "Y'all better make it light on yourselves and let me have those seats." **B**

The man in the window seat next to me stood up, and I moved to let him pass by me, and then I looked across the aisle and saw that the two women were also standing. I moved over to the window seat. I could not see how standing up was going to "make it light" for me. The more we gave in and complied, the worse they treated us.

I thought back to the time when I used to sit up all night and

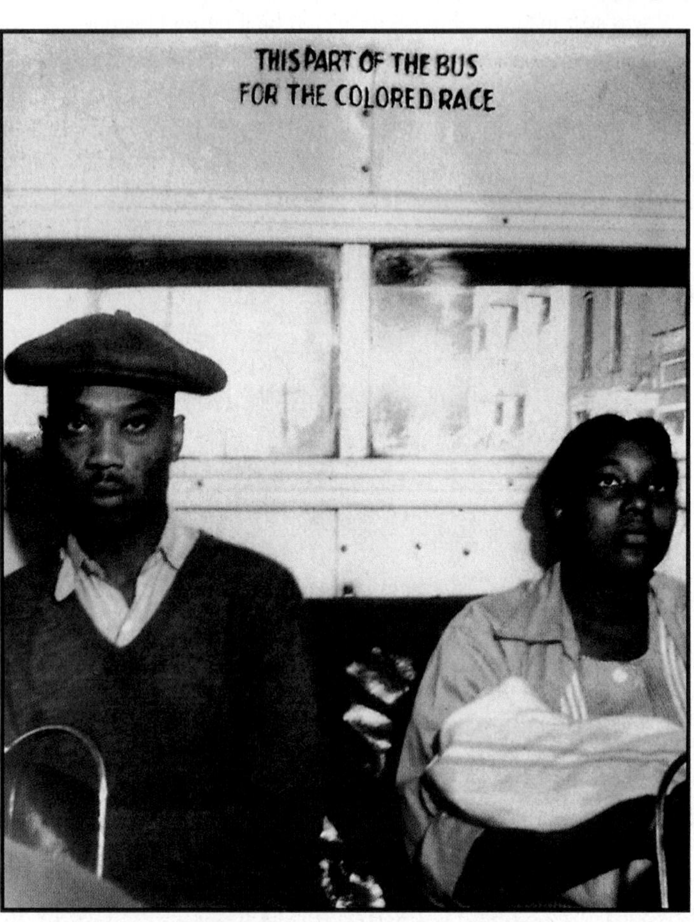

African Americans usually had to sit in the back of the bus in the segregated South.

Vocabulary
comply (kəm plī′) *v.* to go along with a request

Teaching Support

MEETING INDIVIDUAL NEEDS: ENGLISH LANGUAGE LEARNERS

Figures of Speech Write *make it light on yourselves* on the board. Ask English language learners what they think these words mean. Explain that *light* in this context is not the opposite of *dark* but means "easy" and that in English, words can take on meanings other than their literal ones. Offer other examples, such as *It's raining cats and dogs* and *running water.*

Activity Have students look for other examples of idioms in the selection or have students volunteer other examples they may have come across.

Additional Resources

- ***English Language Learners Sourcebook,*** p. 27

didn't sleep, and my grandfather would have his gun right by the fireplace, or if he had his one-horse wagon going anywhere, he always had his gun in the back of the wagon. People always say that I didn't give up my seat because I was tired, but that isn't true. I was not tired physically, or no more tired than I usually was at the end of a working day. I was not old, although some people have an image of me as being old then. I was forty-two. No, the only tired I was, was tired of giving in.

The driver of the bus saw me still sitting there, and he asked was I going to stand up. I said, "No." He said, "Well, I'm going to have you arrested." Then I said, "You may do that." These were the only words we said to each other. I didn't even know his name, which was James Blake, until we were in court together. He got out of the bus and stayed outside for a few minutes, waiting for the police.

As I sat there, I tried not to think about what might happen. I knew that anything was possible. I could be manhandled or beaten. I could be arrested. People have asked me if it occurred to me then that I could be the test case the NAACP[1] had been looking for. I did not think about that at all. In fact if I had let myself think too deeply about what might happen to me, I might have gotten off the bus. But I chose to remain.

Meanwhile there were people getting off the bus and asking for transfers, so that began to loosen up the crowd, especially in the back of the bus. Not everyone got off, but everybody was very quiet. What conversation there was, was in low tones; no one was talking out loud. It would have been quite interesting to have seen the whole bus empty out. Or if the other three had stayed where they were, because if they'd had to arrest four of us instead of one, then that would have given me a little support. But it didn't matter. I never thought hard of them at all and never even bothered to criticize them.

Eventually two policemen came. They got on the bus, and one of them asked me why I didn't stand up. I asked him, "Why do you all push us around?" He said to me, and I quote him exactly, "I don't know, but the law is the law and you're under arrest." One policeman picked up my purse, and the second one picked up my shopping bag and escorted me to the squad car. In the squad car they returned my personal belongings to me. They did not put their hands on me or force me into the car. After I was seated in the car, they went back to the driver and asked him if he wanted to swear out a warrant. He answered that he would finish his route and then come straight back to swear out the warrant. I was only in custody, not legally arrested, until the warrant was signed.

As they were driving me to the city desk, at City Hall, near Court Street, one of them asked me again, "Why didn't you stand up when the driver spoke to you?" I did not answer. I remained silent all the way to City Hall.

As we entered the building, I asked if I could have a drink of water, because my throat was real dry. There was a fountain, and I was standing right next to it. One of the policemen said yes, but by the time

1. *NAACP* stands for National Association for the Advancement of Colored People. It wanted an opportunity to test *segregation* laws in federal court. Such laws required *discrimination* against, or unfair treatment of, African Americans.

C Active Reading Strategies

EVALUATE Ask students to evaluate Rosa Parks's intentions when she refused to give up her seat. Although she says she had not planned this act of defiance, do students think she was aware of the consequences of the act?

D Critical Thinking

INFERRING Ask students what they think these words reveal about Rosa Parks's character. How does her being "an ordinary person" make her act more courageous? *(These words reveal that Parks was more courageous because, acting as an ordinary citizen, she had no organization behind her at the time.)*

E Literary Elements

DIALOGUE Though this piece is nonfiction, the author includes the words spoken by various individuals, as if they were characters in a story. Ask students what effect this "storylike" dialogue has on the selection. *(Dialogue like this makes for easier reading, moves the events along, and reveals much about characters.)*

F Literary Elements

SEQUENCE In autobiographical narratives, writers often present events in the order in which they occurred. The writer signals movement from one event or place to the next by using transition words and phrases, such as *"In the squad car"* and *"After I was seated."*

Reading Minilesson

Identifying Cause-and-Effect Relationships Rosa Parks's explanation of why she refused to give up her seat on the bus illustrates a cause-and-effect relationship. Parks not only identifies the main cause for her action but also addresses some of the *false* causes—reasons other people have given for her action that she says are not true.

Activity Present this graphic organizer to help students grasp the true and false causes of Parks's action as she explains it on page 87. Have students work individually, using information from the text to complete the organizer. *(Answers are provided in italics.)* **L2**

True Cause
- *Parks was tired of giving in to racism.*

False Cause
- *She was tired.*
- *She was old.*
- *She wanted to be the test case for the NAACP.*

Effect
- Parks did not give up her seat on the bus.

Additional Resources

Reading Skills Practice Workbook

G Critical Thinking

DRAWING CONCLUSIONS Rosa Parks does not always explain why she does or does not do certain things or how she feels. Readers must draw their own conclusions. Ask students for their thoughts on why she did not respond to being denied water even though she was angry. *(Perhaps it was because she was afraid or just didn't want the situation to get worse or strain her emotions any further.)*

H Critical Thinking

JUDGING THE CREDIBILITY OF A SOURCE An autobiography is an author's own story, which the reader is expected to accept as completely true. Ask students what Rosa Parks does to make her story as truthful and authentic as possible. *(She keeps to the facts and even reveals some that seem complimentary to her captors. For example: "They didn't search me or handcuff me.")* Discuss with students the difference between an autobiography and historical fiction. *(An autobiography tells a true story in the writer's own words. Historical fiction is set in a specific time and place, but it may contain some fictionalized characters and events.)*

Rosa Parks, civil rights leader Edgar Daniel Nixon (center), and her attorney, Fred Gray (right), photographed after Parks was fined $10 for breaking Montgomery's segregation laws.

I bent down to drink, another policeman said, "No, you can't drink no water. You have to wait until you get to the jail." So I was denied the chance to drink a sip of water. I was not going to do anything but wet my throat. I wasn't going to drink a whole lot of water, even though I was quite thirsty. That made me angry, but I did not respond. **G**

At the city desk they filled out the necessary forms as I answered questions such as what my name was and where I lived. I asked if I could make a telephone call and they said, "No." Since that was my first arrest, I didn't know if that was more discrimination because I was black or if it was standard practice. But it seemed to me to be more discrimination. Then they escorted me back to the squad car, and we went to the city jail on North Ripley Street.

I wasn't frightened at the jail. I was more resigned than anything else. I don't recall being real angry, not enough to have an argument. I was just prepared to accept whatever I had to face. I asked again if I could make a telephone call. I was ignored. **H**

They told me to put my purse on the counter and to empty my pockets of personal items. The only thing I had in my pocket was a tissue. I took that out. They didn't search me or handcuff me.

I was then taken to an area where I was fingerprinted and where mug shots were taken. A white matron[2] came to escort me to my jail cell, and I asked again if I might

2. A *matron* is a female guard who supervises female prisoners.

Vocabulary

resigned (ri zīnd′) *adj.* giving in without resistance

Teaching Support

MEETING INDIVIDUAL NEEDS: SPECIAL NEEDS

Less-Proficient Readers Have students share with the class English slang words and expressions they know of. For example, the word *mug shot* refers to a police photo taken of a prisoner's face. The word is derived from *mug,* a slang word for *face.*

Activity Give each student a list of other slang expressions that appear in the selection, such as *manhandled.* Then have partners work together to define the expressions. **L1** **COLLAB. LEARN.**

Additional Resources

Inclusion Strategies

I use the telephone. She told me that she would find out.

She took me up a flight of stairs (the cells were on the second level), through a door covered with iron mesh, and along a dimly lighted corridor. She placed me in an empty dark cell and slammed the door closed. She walked a few steps away, but then she turned around and came back. She said, "There are two girls around the other side, and if you want to go over there with them instead of being in a cell by yourself, I will take you over there." I told her that it didn't matter, but she said, "Let's go around there, and then you won't have to be in a cell alone." It was her way J of being nice. It didn't make me feel any better.

As we walked to the other cell, I asked her again, "May I use the telephone?" She answered that she would check.

There were two black women in the cell that the matron took me to, as she had said. One of them spoke to me and the other didn't. One just acted as if I wasn't there. The one who spoke to me asked me what had happened to me. I told her that I was arrested on the bus.

She said, "Some of those bus drivers sure are mean. You married?"

I said, "Yes," and she said, "Your husband ain't going to let you stay in here."

She wanted to know if there was anything she could do, and I said, "If you have a cup, I could drink a little water." She had a dark metal mug hanging above the toilet, and she caught a little water from the tap, and I took two swallows of that. She then started telling me about her problems. I became interested in her story and wondered how I could assist her. . . .

When the matron returned she told me to come out of the cell. I did not know where I was going until we reached the telephone booth. She gave me a card and told me to write down who I was calling and the telephone number. She placed a dime in the slot, dialed the number, and stayed close by to hear what I was saying.

I called home. My husband and mother were both there. She answered the telephone. I said, "I'm in jail. See if Parks will come down here and get me out."

She wanted to know, "Did they beat you?"

I said, "No, I wasn't beaten, but I am in jail."

She handed him the telephone, and I said, "Parks, will you come get me out of jail?"

He said, "I'll be there in a few minutes." He didn't have a car, so I knew it would be longer. But while we were still on the phone, a friend came by in his car. He'd heard about my being in jail and had driven to our place on Cleveland Court to see if he could help. He said he'd drive Parks to the jail. K

The matron then took me back to the cell.

As Parks' friend had indicated, the word was already out about my arrest. Mr. [E. D.] Nixon [of the Montgomery NAACP] had been notified by his wife, who was told by a neighbor, Bertha Butler, who had seen me escorted off the bus. Mr. Nixon called the jail to find out what the charge was, but they wouldn't tell him. Then he had tried to reach Fred Gray, one of the two black lawyers in Montgomery, but he wasn't home. So finally Mr. Nixon called Clifford Durr, the white lawyer who was Mrs. Virginia Durr's husband. Mr. Durr called the jail and found out that I'd

Language Note

Roots In this context, *matron* refers to a female prison guard. In other contexts, *matron* refers to a woman mature in age, character, or bearing. The word comes from the Latin word *mater*, meaning "mother." The words *mother, maternity*, and *maternal* come from this root.

I Author's Craft

SETTING Ask students to find some sensory details the author uses to help readers visualize the setting. *("dimly lighted corridor," "empty dark cell," "slammed the door.")*

J Critical Thinking

EVALUATING The matron refers to the other two prisoners as "two girls." Rosa Parks refers to them as "two black women." Ask students what this reveals about the speakers. *(Students may say that the matron does not look upon the women as social peers. Rosa Parks does.)*

K Literary Elements

SEQUENCE Review the sequence of events that enables Parks to get to the jail quickly. *(Parks's friend hears about Rosa's trouble, stops by her house to see if he can help, and drives Parks to the jail.)*

Grammar and Language *Minilesson*

Quotation Marks In stories, quotation marks signal a person's exact words, distinguishing dialogue from narrative. Write the following sentence on the board: *She handed him the telephone, and I said, "Parks, will you come get me out of jail?"* Point out to students that the quotation marks signal a break between the narrative and Rosa Parks's exact words to her husband.

Activity Ask students to insert quotation marks properly in the following sentences:

1. As we walked to the other cell, I asked her again, "May I use the telephone?"
2. I said, "Yes," and she said, "Your husband ain't going to let you stay in here."
3. I said, "No, I wasn't beaten, but I am in jail." **L2** **COLLAB. LEARN.**

Additional Resources

- ***Grammar and Language Transparency 8***
- ***Grammar and Language Workbook,*** pp. 267–270
- ***Grammar and Composition Handbook,*** Lesson 13.6
- ***Writer's Choice,*** Lesson 20.6

L Literary Elements

SEQUENCE Ask students to identify the many actions described in this short passage. *(Some examples include the matron's coming; Rosa Parks's being released; and Mrs. Durr's hugging her.)* Have students identify the words used to signal a movement from one action to another, such as *"As soon as they released me"* and *"By the time I got home"* *(Another transitional phrase is "As we were going down the stairs.")*

M Active Reading Strategies

EVALUATE Ask students to suggest words that describe Rosa Parks's attitude at this point in her experience. *(She is anxious but determined.)*

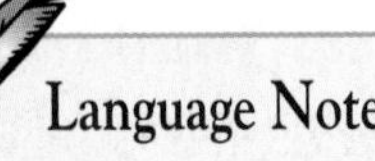

Language Note

The word *boycott* comes from Captain Charles C. Boycott (1832-1897), an English land agent in Ireland whose tenants and neighbors boycotted him (refused to associate with him) when he refused to lower rents. The Pullman, or sleeping car, gets its name from its inventor, George M. Pullman.

been arrested under the segregation laws. He also found out what the bail was.

Meanwhile Parks had called a white man he knew who could raise the bail. His friend took him over to the man's house to pick him up. I don't remember how much the bail was. . . .

The matron came to let me know that I was being released. Mrs. Durr was the first person I saw as I came through the iron mesh door with matrons on either side of me. There were tears in her eyes, and she seemed shaken, probably wondering what they had done to me. As soon as they released me, she put her arms around me, and hugged and kissed me as if we were sisters.

I was real glad to see Mr. Nixon and Attorney Durr too. We went to the desk, where I picked up my personal belongings and was given a trial date. Mr. Nixon asked that the date be the following Monday, December 5, 1955, explaining that he was a Pullman[3] porter and would be out of Montgomery until then. We left without very much conversation, but it was an emotional moment. I didn't realize how much being in jail had upset me until I got out.

As we were going down the stairs, Parks and his friends were driving up, so I got in the car with them, and Mr. Nixon followed us home.

By the time I got home, it was about nine-thirty or ten at night. My mother was glad to have me home and wanted to know what she could do to make me comfortable. I told her I was hungry (for some reason I had missed lunch that day), and she prepared some food for me. Mrs. Durr and my friend Bertha Butler were there, and they helped my mother. I was thinking about having to go to work the next day, but I knew I would not get to bed anytime soon.

Everyone was angry about what had happened to me and talking about how it should never happen again. I knew that I would never, never ride another segregated bus, even if I had to walk to work. But it still had not occurred to me that mine could be a test case against the segregated buses.

Then Mr. Nixon asked if I would be willing to make my case a test case against segregation. I told him I'd have to talk with my mother and husband. Parks was pretty angry. He thought it would be difficult to get people to support me as a test case. We discussed and debated the question for a while. In the end Parks and my mother supported the idea. They were against segregation and were willing to fight it. And I had worked on enough cases to know that a ruling could not be made without a plaintiff.[4] So I agreed to be the plaintiff.

"They've Messed with the Wrong One Now"

Meanwhile Fred Gray, the black attorney, had called Jo Ann Robinson and told her about my arrest. She got in touch with other leaders of the Women's Political Council, and they agreed to call for a boycott of the

3. Mr. Nixon was an attendant on a passenger train. The *Pullman* Company was a major manufacturer of railroad cars.

4. The *plaintiff* is the "injured party" who brings a case to court. If no one claims to have been harmed by a *defendant's* actions, a judge is not likely to allow a trial.

Vocabulary

boycott (boi′ kot) *n.* an organized protest in which the participants refuse to buy, sell, or use a product or service

Teaching Support

Life Skills Connection

Supporting and Contributing

Encourage students to discuss the fact that people deal with difficult situations more effectively when they have input and support from people they know, love, and trust, just as Rosa Parks did.

Activity Have small groups each create a three-column table to outline plans for dealing with a situation or decision they may have to face, such as moving to a new town or helping a friend in trouble. The table should include the situations or decisions, the issues to be resolved, and the people to be consulted.

L2 COLLAB. LEARN.

Situation	Issues	Consultants
1.		
2.		
3.		

buses starting Monday, December 5, the day of my trial. So on the Thursday night I was arrested, they met at midnight at Alabama State, cut a mimeograph stencil,[5] and ran off 35,000 handbills. The next morning she and some of her students loaded the handbills into her car, and she drove to all the local black elementary and junior high and high schools to drop them off so the students could take them home to their parents.

This is what the handbill said:

> This is for Monday, December 5, 1955.
>
> Another Negro woman has been arrested and thrown into jail because she refused to get up out of her seat on the bus and give it to a white person.
>
> It is the second time since the Claudette Colvin case that a Negro woman has been arrested for the same thing. This has to be stopped.
>
> Negroes have rights, too, for if Negroes did not ride the buses, they could not operate. Three-fourths of the riders are Negroes, yet we are arrested, or have to stand over empty seats. If we do not do something to stop these arrests, they will continue. The next time it may be you, or your daughter, or mother.
>
> This woman's case will come up on Monday. We are, therefore, asking every Negro to stay off the buses Monday in protest of the arrest and trial. Don't ride the buses to work, to town, to school, or anywhere on Monday.
>
> You can afford to stay out of school for one day. If you work, take a cab, or walk. But please, children and grown-ups, don't ride the bus at all on Monday. Please stay off all buses Monday.

Early that Friday morning, Mr. Nixon called the Reverend Ralph David Abernathy, minister of the First Baptist Church. Mr. Nixon had decided that black ministers could do more to mobilize support in the community than anyone else. He also called eighteen other ministers and arranged a meeting for that evening. Mr. Nixon had to work as a porter on the Montgomery–Atlanta–New York route, so he would be unable to attend, but he talked to them all about what he wanted them to do.

Then he called a white reporter for the *Montgomery Advertiser* named Joe Azbell and arranged a meeting down at Union Station to show him one of the handbills. Mr. Nixon wanted the story on the front page. Joe Azbell said he would see what he could do. Meanwhile, the story of my arrest was reported in a small article in that day's paper.

On the morning of Friday, December 2, I called Felix Thomas, who operated a cab company, and took a cab to work. I was not going to ride the bus anymore. Mr. John Ball, who was in charge of men's alterations[6] at Montgomery Fair, was surprised to see me. He said, "I didn't think you would be here. I thought you would be a nervous wreck." I said, "Why should going to jail make a nervous wreck out of

5. Before the photocopier, a *mimeograph* machine could be used to print copies from an original called a *stencil.*

6. Mr. Ball supervises the *alterations,* or changes necessary for proper fit, of men's clothes at a local store.

Vocabulary
mobilize (mō′ bə līz′) *v.* to become prepared, as for war or an emergency

N Critical Thinking

DRAWING CONCLUSIONS The people in this story moved into action quickly. Ask students what the speed of their action suggests about their feelings on the issue of bus segregation. *(People were tired of bus segregation and were ready to protest.)*

O Critical Thinking

ANALYZING ARGUMENTS Ask students whether they think it is logical to say that if African Americans did not ride the buses, the bus lines could not operate. You may wish to share the following model to illustrate the thinking process in analyzing arguments.

Model: We have learned that African Americans rode the buses. The bus companies, therefore, made most of their money from their African American customers. No company could operate without making money.

P Critical Thinking

IDENTIFYING PROPAGANDA TECHNIQUES The purpose of the handbill was to persuade people to boycott the buses. Ask students to explain the impact of personalizing the appeal by saying "The next time it may be you, or your daughter, or mother." *(Personalizing the message reminded people they had a personal stake in the issue.)*

Grammar and Language *Minilesson*

Commas Explain that commas are used before and after the year when it is used with the month and the day and to separate the day of the week from the date. They are not used when only the month and year are given. Write the following on the board:

On May 24, 1992, we moved to Alabama.
Thursday, February 16, is my birthday.
My dad bought a new car in July 1998.

Activity Write these sentences on the board:

Rosa's ordeal began in December 1956.
On December 1, 1956, she was arrested.
On the morning of Friday, December 2, she called Felix Thomas.

Ask volunteers to add the commas and have others explain whether the sentences are punctuated properly. **L2**
COLLAB. LEARN.

Additional Resources

- ***Grammar and Language Transparency 9***
- ***Grammar and Language Workbook,*** pp. 259–260
- ***Grammar and Composition Handbook,*** Lessons 13.2–13.4
- ***Writer's Choice,*** Lesson 20.4

me?" And then as soon as I got off for lunch, I went to Fred Gray's office.

Ever since Fred had opened his law practice in Montgomery, I had often done that. I'd pick up something from the store for my lunch. He usually brought his lunch. We would eat lunch together, and then sometimes I would answer the telephone while he ran out and did an errand or something, and then it was time for me to go back to work. Fred didn't have a secretary, and I often helped him out. The day after I was arrested, Fred Gray's office was like a beehive. People were calling and dropping by to ask about the boycott and the meeting the ministers had called for that night.

After work, I went to that meeting at the Dexter Avenue Baptist Church. I explained how I had been arrested, and then there were long discussions about what to do. Some of the ministers wanted to talk about how to support the protest, but others wanted to talk about whether or not to have a protest. Many of them left the meeting before any decisions were made. But most of those who stayed agreed to talk about the protest in their Sunday sermons and to hold another meeting on Monday evening to decide if the protest should continue.

On Sunday the *Montgomery Advertiser* ran a copy of Jo Ann Robinson's handbill on the front page, and that helped spread the word to people who might have missed the leaflets or didn't go to church. But no one could be sure if the protest would be successful. Just because they read a leaflet or heard about it in church, it didn't mean that people would stay away from the buses. All eighteen black-owned cab companies in Montgomery had agreed to make stops at all the bus stops and charge only ten cents, the same fare as on the buses. But people would have to wait for a cab that had room for them. To make matters worse, it looked like rain for Monday.

The sky was dark on Monday morning, but that didn't make any difference. Most black people had finally had enough of segregation on the buses. They stayed off those buses. They waited at the bus stops for the black-owned cabs to come along. Or they

Bus boycotters wait at one of the volunteer cab stops.

VIEWING THE PHOTO

The photo shows African Americans in Montgomery waiting for a cab during the bus boycott. Call attention to the expressions on the faces of the various individuals and discuss what those expressions seem to imply.

Viewing Response *The woman in the center and the one to her right display expressions of concern. The woman to the far right, however, seems at ease.*

Language Note

Discuss Rosa Parks's comparison of an office to a beehive. In what ways are the two alike? Help students understand why the author would use this simile. *(Parks probably uses it to help readers picture the situation without using a lot of words.)*

Q Critical Thinking

LOGICAL REASONING Parks explains the overwhelming support of the boycott with this sentence: "Most people had finally had enough of segregation on the buses." Ask students if this is a logical explanation for why so many stayed off the buses. Could there have been other reasons? *(Some people may have been afraid of what other African Americans would think of them if they rode the buses.)*

Teaching Support

interNET CONNECTION

Have students use the Internet to learn more about the Montgomery bus boycott, Rosa Parks, Martin Luther King Jr., the NAACP, or other topics connected with the beginnings of the Civil Rights movement in the 1950s. Suggest they use appropriate keywords on a search engine to find sources of information.

REAL-WORLD CONNECTION

The Media Encourage students to discuss the role of the news media during the boycott in regard to the handbill, the ministers' sermons, and the newspaper coverage. Discuss the role of the media today in political campaigns, protests, and public awareness programs. Ask students to mention the involvement in and impact of the news media on current national and local events.

Activity Have students work in small groups to research articles that may themselves attempt to influence public opinion or that reflect the media's influence on public opinion. Then have them draw conclusions about the power of the media and possible results of the media's influence on people. **L2** COLLAB. LEARN.

walked or got a ride. As a result, the Montgomery city buses were practically empty. Oh, a few black people took the buses, but they were mostly people who had not heard about the protest. Some of them were scared away from the buses. The city police had vowed to protect anyone who wanted to ride, and each bus had two motorcycle escorts. But some of the people who didn't know what was going on thought the police were there to arrest them for riding the buses, not to protect them. And then there were those few who didn't want to be inconvenienced. When the bus they were on passed a bus stop full of black people waiting for cabs, they ducked down low so nobody would see them.

That day I had no idea what the result was going to be, but I think everybody was quite amazed at that demonstration of people staying off the buses. It was a surprise to everybody, I think. As Mr. Nixon said, "We surprised ourselves." Never before had black people demonstrated so clearly how much those city buses depended on their business. More important, never before had the black community of Montgomery united in protest against segregation on the buses.

I didn't go to work that Monday. Instead that morning I went down to the courthouse for my trial. Parks went with me. I did not spend a lot of time planning what to wear, but I remember very clearly that I wore a straight, long-sleeved black dress with a white collar and cuffs, a small black velvet hat with pearls across the top, and a charcoal-gray coat. I carried a black purse and wore white gloves. I was not especially nervous. I knew what I had to do.

A lot of folks were down at the courthouse. Some people couldn't get in. Parks was almost prohibited from entering the courthouse. But when he said he was my husband, he was permitted to enter. You could hardly see the street for the crowds. Many members of the NAACP Youth Council were there, and they were all shouting their support.

There was a girl in the crowd named Mary Frances. She had a high-pitched voice, and it just came through the air: "Oh, she's so sweet. They've messed with the wrong one now." She said it like a little chant, "They've messed with the wrong one now."

It wasn't a long trial. The bus driver [James Blake] was the main prosecution witness.

I was not called to testify in my own behalf. Although my lawyers, Charles Langford and Fred Gray, entered a plea of "Not Guilty" for me, they did not intend to try to defend me against the charges. The point of making mine a test case was to allow me to be found guilty and then to appeal the conviction to a higher court. Only in higher courts could the segregation laws actually be changed, because the judges in the local courts were not going to do anything to change the way things were. So I was found guilty of violating the segregation laws and given a suspended sentence.[7] I was fined $10.00, plus $4.00 in court costs. The

7. In giving a *suspended sentence,* the judge has ordered Mrs. Parks to serve time in jail but, at least temporarily, will not actually require her to do so.

Vocabulary

inconvenience (in′ kən vēn′ yəns) *v.* to cause someone difficulty, bother, or hassle

Active Reading Strategies

EVALUATE The author says that people on the buses ducked down to avoid being seen by those waiting for cabs. Ask students what they think of the African Americans who rode the buses during the boycott.

Active Reading Strategies

PREDICT Have students consider the significance of this great show of support. Ask what effect they think it had on the community. *(This show of support sent a message that the African American community could work together and be a powerful force.)*

Vo•cab•u•lar•y Skills

Jargon Have students share with the class what they know about jargon, the specialized language used in a specific field like medicine, sports, computer science, and law. Note the various legal terms in this passage—*prosecution, witness, testify, plea, test case, appeal, conviction.* Ask students to volunteer other legal terms they know.

Writing Minilesson

Maintaining Consistency in Verb Tenses Work with students to identify the use of past tense in this selection. Explain that when writing about events that occurred in the past, writers must be sure that all the verbs they use are in the past tense. Students should understand that there is no shift in tense unless there is a shift in the time of the story's action.

Activity Have students each write a paragraph about something interesting they did yesterday. Remind them to use the past tense for verbs that describe past actions. Partners can check each other's paragraphs for consistency in verb tense. **L2** COLLAB. LEARN.

Additional Resources

Writer's Choice, Lesson 10.5

T **Critical Thinking**

INFERRING Call attention to the fact that Rosa Parks did not tell callers who she was. What does that fact say about her? *(It shows Parks was not interested in being a celebrity.)*

U **Literary Elements**

SEQUENCE Point out that Parks uses transitional words and phrases like *Earlier that day* and *that afternoon* to help readers follow the story's sequence of events. Ask students to find other examples. (They include *then, that night, and first.*)

FYI

Martin Luther King Jr.
The Reverend King was ordained a Baptist minister at the age of 17. In college he studied the works of Indian nationalist Mohandas K. Gandhi, whose ideas became the core of King's own philosophy of nonviolent protest. The bus boycott is an example of nonviolent protest.

V **Active Reading Strategies**

EVALUATE Have students evaluate the importance of the points raised regarding the continuation of the boycott. *(These points have merit. If the boycott failed, the African American community would be worse off than before. As bad as things had been, the white community could make them worse.)*

Teaching Support

crowd reacted angrily, but there was no organized protest.

I didn't go home after my trial was over. Instead I stayed downtown. I wanted to know what I could do. Fred Gray said he would appreciate it if I would stay in his office and answer the telephone, so I did. As soon as I got there, the telephone started ringing, because people had heard the news. I never did tell anybody who called that I was the one they were calling about. I just answered the phone and took messages. When Fred came back, Mr. Nixon took me home. It was getting pretty close to night, and I had to go home to get ready for the meeting at the Holt Street Baptist Church that evening.

Earlier that day Reverend Abernathy, who was about twenty-nine years old at the time, and some other ministers had met and decided to form the Montgomery Improvement Association (MIA). Mr. Nixon was there, and so was Fred Gray. The reason they wanted to form a brand-new organization was that they thought it would be better than just leaving the organizing to an established group like the NAACP. The NAACP was a relatively weak organization in Alabama; it was not a mass organization. Membership was kind of small, and you could hardly get people to join. They also wanted to rule out the NAACP so that the powers that be could not charge that this demonstration, this show of strength, was being led by outside agitators.

So they met that afternoon, and then they decided they should elect a president, and they elected the Reverend Martin Luther King, Jr., pastor of the Dexter Avenue Baptist Church. . . .

That night they had the meeting at the Holt Street Baptist Church, which was right in the black community so people wouldn't be afraid to attend. They didn't know how many people to expect, and they were not prepared for how many showed up. People filled that church, and hundreds more stood outside, so they set up a loudspeaker system so those people outside could hear what was going on inside. The meeting was already on when I got there, and I had a hard time getting into the church because there were so many people, inside and outside. I made it to the platform, and they gave me a seat.

The main thing they wanted to decide at that meeting was whether to continue the boycott. Some people thought we should quit while we were still ahead. And hardly anybody thought the boycott could go longer than the end of the week, which was four more days. If it did, it could be very dangerous, because everyone knew the whites wouldn't stand for it.

Mr. Nixon spoke first, as I recall. He was probably worried that people wouldn't really support a long boycott. He remembered all those years when it had been impossible to get black people to stand together. He said, "You who are afraid, you better get your hat and coat and go home. This is going to be a long-drawn-out affair. I want to tell you something: For years and years I've been talking about how I didn't want the children who came along behind me to have to suffer the indignities that I've suffered all these years. Well, I've

Vocabulary
indignity (in dig′ nə tē) *n.* an offense against one's pride or dignity; humiliation

MEETING INDIVIDUAL NEEDS **SPECIAL NEEDS**

Visually Impaired Visually impaired students may benefit from having a vivid description read aloud to them.

Activity Pair visually impaired students with students who can read with expression for a reading of the description of the ministers' meeting at the Holt Street Baptist Church. Have students begin with the paragraph starting "So they met that afternoon..." and end with "He received loud cheers and *Amens*..." on page 95. Discuss the various oral interpretations and the effects of each style on the listener.
L2 **COLLAB. LEARN.**

Additional Resources
Inclusion Strategies

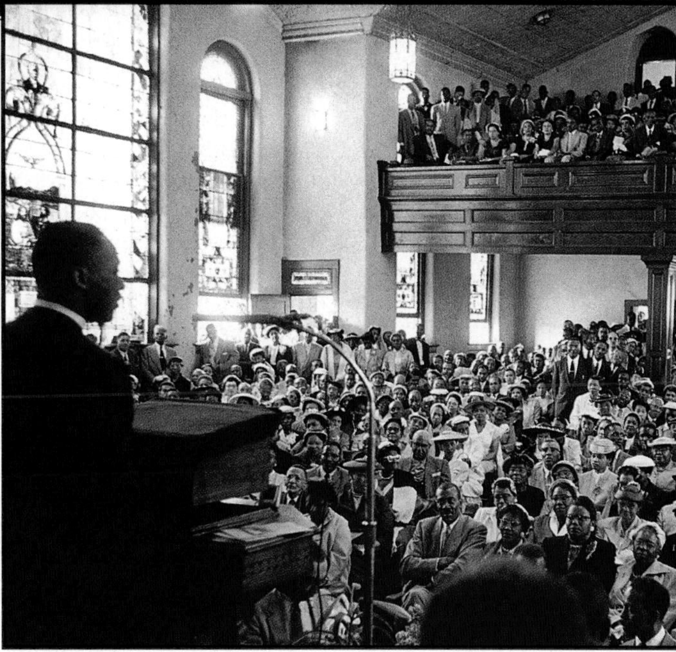

The Reverend Martin Luther King Jr. addresses supporters of the bus boycott at the Holt Street Baptist Church, December 5, 1955.

changed my mind—I want to enjoy some of that freedom myself."

Dr. King was introduced to the audience as the president of the new Montgomery Improvement Association. He was a fine speaker, and he gave a speech that really got the crowd excited. This is part of what he said:

> There comes a time that people get tired. We are here this evening to say to those who have mistreated us so long that we are tired—tired of being segregated and humiliated; tired of being kicked about by the brutal feet of oppression. . . . For many years we have shown amazing patience. We have sometimes given our white brothers the feeling that we like the way we are being treated. But we come here tonight to be saved from that patience that makes us patient with anything less than freedom and justice. One of the great glories of democracy is the right to protest for right. . . . [I]f you will protest courageously and yet with dignity and Christian love, when the history books are written in future generations the historians will pause and say, "There lived a great people—a black people—who injected new meaning and dignity into the veins of civilization." That is our challenge and our overwhelming responsibility.
>
> (*Eyes on the Prize: America's Civil Rights Years 1954–1965*, page 76)

He received loud cheers and applause and *Amens*. . . .

After that the Reverend Ralph Abernathy read the list of demands that the Montgomery Improvement Association was going to present to the bus company and the city's white leaders. There were three demands: 1) Courteous treatment on the buses; 2) First-come, first-served seating, with whites in front and blacks in back; 3) Hiring of black drivers for the black bus routes. Then he asked the audience to vote on these demands by standing

Vocabulary

oppression (ə presh′ ən) *n.* the act of controlling or governing by the cruel and unjust use of force or authority

W Literary Elements

FIGURES OF SPEECH: *Personification* This figure of speech speaks of an inanimate object or an idea in terms of a person. In the phrase "*brutal feet of oppression,*" the idea of oppression is given *feet,* a human characteristic. Challenge students to find another example of personification in King's talk. *(King speaks of "the veins of civilization.")*

X Active Reading Strategies

EVALUATE On this page, there is a contrast of leadership styles. Each is valuable in a different way. Guide students to recognize the merits of both. Encourage students to review the roles of King and of Abernathy in this event and examine their leadership styles. You may wish to model the thinking process involved in evaluating.

Model: In this event, I see King motivating the audience with his eloquent words. He drives the emotions of the audience with phrases like *"tired of being kicked about"* and *"there lived a great people."* I see that Abernathy, on the other hand, works on the practical side, explaining the demands and asking people to vote on them. One man leads by exciting emotions; the other leads by organizing a plan of action.

Listening and Speaking *Minilesson*

Effective Listening Techniques Play a recording of a speech by Martin Luther King Jr. Have students listen for the eloquence, the use of figurative language, and the appeal to people's emotions.

Activity Have students listen in small groups with these questions in mind.

- Which words or phrases stirred them most?
- Did they notice the rise and fall of the speaker's voice?
- Which part of the speech won them over to the speaker's point of view?

Ask them to discuss their emotional response to the speech. Students who enjoy public speaking may wish to present a portion of the speech to the class. **L2** **COLLAB. LEARN.**

Y

Literary Elements

TONE Discuss Rosa Parks's tone—her attitude about what she is describing. Point out that though the bus company and city officials were being totally unreasonable and unfair, Parks's tone is not complaining or bitter. Instead it is matter-of-fact, or reportorial. With very little comment, she simply tells what happened. Ask students to comment on the impact such a tone has on them as readers. *(They may say that this reportorial tone makes the account more believable because they sense that it is being told by a person whose emotions are in check.)*

Z

Active Reading Strategies

QUESTION Have students discuss Rosa Parks's and the African American community's attitude toward attempts to thwart the boycott. *(They kept their focus and worked together to find ways to move forward.)*

AA

Literary Elements

SEQUENCE Ask students to scan the page and list the words and phrases that signal time order. *(Examples include the following:* Thursday, through that week, then through the next, how long, after that, then, *and* when.*)*

X

if they wanted to continue the boycott and make the demands. People started getting up, one or two at a time at first, and then more and more, until every single person in that church was standing, and outside the crowd was cheering "Yes!"

Stride Toward Freedom

The following Thursday, December 8, Dr. King and Attorney Fred Gray and others met with the three Montgomery city commissioners and representatives of the bus company. They presented the three demands. The bus company people denied that the drivers were discourteous to black riders and would not hear of hiring any black drivers on the predominantly[8] black routes. They also said the first-come, first-served seating arrangement was in violation of the city's segregation laws. Fred Gray said that wasn't true and that the same bus company allowed that type of arrangement in the city of Mobile, Alabama. But they wouldn't change their minds.

The city commissioners wouldn't go along with any of the demands either. They didn't want to give an inch, not even to reasonable demands. They were afraid of compromising in any way with black people.

The boycott lasted through that week, and then through the next. No one had any idea how long it would last. Some people said it couldn't last, but it seemed like those who said that were the white people and not us. The whites did everything they could do to stop it.

The police started getting after the groups of blacks who were waiting at the bus stops for the black-owned cabs to pick them up. Then they threatened to arrest the cab drivers if they did not charge their regular fare, which I think was forty-five cents, to go downtown instead of ten cents like the buses charged. White private citizens resisted the boycott too.

A lot of people lost their jobs because they supported the boycott. Both Parks and I lost our jobs. . . .

After that I worked at home, taking in sewing. I started traveling quite a bit, making appearances because of my arrest and the boycott. And then I did work for the MIA.

I was on the executive board of directors of the MIA and I did whatever was needed. I dispensed clothing and shoes to people who needed them. We had an abundance of clothing and shoes sent to us from all parts of the country. Many people needed those things because they were out of work and unable to buy clothing. Those who had jobs wore out many pairs of shoes walking to and from work. I also worked for a short while as a dispatcher for the MIA Transportation Committee.

When the police started arresting cab drivers for not charging full fare, the MIA asked for volunteer drivers. Jo Ann Robinson was one. The churches collected money and bought several station wagons. Ordinary black people contributed, and so did some important white people in Montgomery, like the Durrs. As a dispatcher, I was responsible for taking calls from people who needed rides and then making calls to the drivers of private cars and the church station wagons to see that the people were picked up wherever they were.

8. Here, *predominantly* means "chiefly; for the most part."

96 THEME 1

Teaching Support

LIFE SKILLS CONNECTION

Supporting and Contributing Parks reveals that she lost her job because of the boycott. In 1968 Martin Luther King Jr. was gunned down because of his role in the Civil Rights movement. Help students understand that a protest is more than speeches, rallies, and TV cameras. Protesters often have to make sacrifices, sometimes major ones, for the cause.

Activity Have students work in small groups to list causes, such as those affecting their families, friends, town, and country for which they would be willing to make major sacrifices. Have them identify the sacrifices they would be willing to make and those they would not. **L2** COLLAB. LEARN.

After a while quite a sophisticated[9] system was developed. There were twenty private cars and fourteen station wagons. There were thirty-two pickup and transfer sites, and scheduled service from five-thirty in the morning until twelve-thirty at night. About 30,000 people were transported to and from work every day. . . .

The Montgomery Improvement Association held regular meetings, every Monday and Thursday night, to keep the people inspired and to talk about the latest problems and what to do about them. January came. The white people were getting angrier and angrier. . . .

Now Mayor Gayle announced that he would no longer negotiate with the boycotters, although we didn't see that he'd been doing much negotiating anyhow. He called the leaders of the boycott a bunch of Negro radicals.[10] There was real violence against the people by this time. Dr. King's home was bombed at the end of January. Two days later Mr. Nixon's home was bombed. Nobody tried to bomb my home, but I did get a lot of threatening telephone calls. They'd say things like, "You're the cause of all this. You should be killed." It was frightening to get those calls, and it really bothered me when Mama answered the telephone and it was one of those calls.

In early February Fred Gray filed suit in U.S. District Court saying that bus segregation was unconstitutional. By that time the appeal of my case had been thrown out on a technicality,[11] meaning my conviction was upheld. The new suit was our way of getting tough. The City Commission and the bus company and the mayor wouldn't even agree that bus drivers were not polite. Fred Gray wanted to challenge the whole bus-segregation system and go all the way to the Supreme Court. Clifford Durr offered to assist him. The suit was filed on behalf of five women who had been mistreated on the buses.

Meanwhile, the boycott was costing the bus company money. Every day bus after bus would go by with only one or two white riders. Then they stopped running the buses altogether. The boycott was also hurting downtown businesses, and so a group of white businessmen calling themselves Men of Montgomery decided to try to negotiate with the MIA themselves. But nothing came of those meetings.

Around the middle of February a group of white attorneys came up with an old law that prohibited boycotts, and on February 21 a grand jury handed down eighty-nine indictments[12] against Dr. King, more than twenty other ministers, leaders of the MIA, and other citizens. I was reindicted. BB

We were all fingerprinted. News photographers had heard about the indictments and were there to photograph us being fingerprinted. The picture of me CC

9. A *sophisticated* system is one that is developed to a high degree.
10. A *radical* is someone who supports or demands extreme change.
11. In legal terms, a *technicality* is a very small detail.
12. A *grand jury* is a special jury that hears accusations in criminal cases. If its members decide that there is enough evidence for a trial, they issue an *indictment,* which is the formal legal charge against the accused.

Vocabulary
negotiate (ni gō′ shē āt′) *v.* to discuss in order to bring about an agreement

Vo•cab•u•lar•y Skills

Etymology Explain that the word *inspire* means "to fill with a thought or feeling." The word is derived from the Latin *inspirare*, "to breathe into." When a speaker inspires an audience, he or she breathes not air but a thought or feeling into its members. Have students try to figure out the meaning of the word *expire,* which is built on the same root. If they need help, remind them that the prefix *ex-* means "out of," as in *exclude*. (*Expire* means "to breathe out, die.")

BB Critical Thinking

DRAWING CONCLUSIONS Ask students why they think this old law suddenly turned up. What does the unearthing of this law suggest about the attitude of the white attorneys at this point? *(The old law probably came up because the white attorneys were desperately searching for something they could use against the black community.)*

At the MOVIES

The following video puts the events of Rosa Parks's story into a larger context. Be sure to preview the video for appropriateness for your class.

- ***The Fateful Decade: From Little Rock to the Civil Rights Bill****

* Also available in the *Glencoe Literature Video Library*

Real-World Connection

Causes Students may have a better understanding of Rosa Parks's fight in the 1950s if they learn about someone who is working for a cause today.

Activity Have each student locate a magazine or newspaper article about an individual who shows unusual determination in working for a cause. Students may choose current civil rights activists, environmentalists, consumer advocates, or defenders of other causes. Have them consider these questions: *What cause is the person working for? What challenges have to be faced? How does the person demonstrate determination in working for the cause?* Have the class work in small groups to share their findings and encourage students to use their knowledge to raise additional questions for further exploration. **L2** COLLAB. LEARN.

GG Literary Elements

MOOD At this point in the story, the boycott has been a success and Rosa is enjoying it. How does Rosa convey that mood? *(She uses the word* honors *sarcastically.)*

Vo•cab•u•lar•y Skills

Antonyms Write the words *segregate* and *integrate* on the board. Explain that *segregate* means "apart from the flock," from the Latin *se* (apart) and *grex* (flock). *Integrate* comes from the Latin *integrare*, meaning "made whole." Have students define the words *segregate* and *integrate* in English, using a dictionary if necessary.

VIEWING THE ART

Viewing Response *Students should recognize that the artist is portraying Parks sympathetically. She is the central figure, dressed in bright red, white, and blue, while the figures of authority beside her appear weaker because of their drab colors, their flatness, and the odd perspective that seems to diminish them in spite of their greater height.*

Thematic Focus

What I Am, What I Want to Be
Every person must face challenges. Some involve doing what is right, even when it is difficult.

ASSESSMENT

Quick Checks, p. 10

Supreme Court would not arrive for another month or so. We stayed off the buses until it was official.

The written order from the U.S. Supreme Court arrived on December 20, and the following day we returned to the buses. The boycott had lasted more than a year. Dr. King, the Reverend Abernathy, Mr. Nixon, and Glen Smiley, one of the few white people in Montgomery who had supported the boycott, made a great show of riding the first integrated bus in Montgomery. . . . Three reporters from *Look* magazine . . . had me get on and off buses so they could take pictures.

GG James Blake, the driver who'd had me arrested, was the driver of one of the buses I got on. He didn't want to take any honors, and I wasn't too happy about being there myself. I really could have done without that. I got on two different buses, I guess, and each time they took pictures until they were satisfied. The reporter sat behind me each time while the photographer took pictures. . . .

Integrating the Montgomery buses did not go smoothly. Snipers[13] fired at buses, and the city imposed curfews on the buses, not letting them run after five P.M., which meant that people who worked from nine to five couldn't ride the buses home. A group of whites tried to form a whites-only bus line, but that didn't work. The homes and churches of some ministers were bombed, as I mentioned. But eventually most of the violence died down. Black people were not going to be scared off the buses any more than they were going to be scared onto them when they refused to ride.

African Americans in other cities, like Birmingham, Alabama, and Tallahassee, Florida, started their own boycotts of the segregated buses.

The direct-action civil-rights movement had begun.

Civil Rights Activist, 1983. Marshall D. Rumbaugh. Painted limewood, height: 33 in. National Portrait Gallery, Washington, D.C. Gift of Barry Bingham.

Viewing the sculpture: How do you think the artist feels about what the sculpture shows? How can you tell?

13. *Snipers* are people who shoot at others from concealed places.

Vocabulary
impose (im pōz′) *v.* to apply legally; enforce

Teaching Support

Grammar and Language Minilesson

Capitalization of Proper Nouns Call students' attention to the capitalized words on this page. Remind them that the first letter of a proper noun is capitalized; for example, months, proper names, and specific organizations (such as *U.S. Supreme Court* and *City Commission*). Nouns that are generic are not capitalized; for example, *bus company* and *mayor.*

Activity Write the following on the board, omitting capitalization. Ask students to tell which words should be capitalized and why they should be.

1. montgomery improvement association *(name of a particular group)*
2. dr. king *(name of person)*
3. attorneys *(generic noun)*
4. december 20 *(name of the month)*
5. boycotts *(generic noun)* **L2** COLLAB. LEARN.

Additional Resources

- ***Grammar and Language Transparency 10***
- ***Grammar and Language Workbook,*** pp. 237–248
- ***Grammar and Composition Handbook,*** Lessons 12.2–12.4
- ***Writer's Choice,*** Lesson 19.2–19.4

GRAMMAR AN

A *common noun* nam
idea. A *proper noun* n
thing, or idea. Proper

PRACTICE Write ea
below in one of two li
mon nouns. Capitalize
1. The story of rosa
2. Rosa parks show

READING AND

When historians study
think in terms of **cause**
caused by other events
Montgomery bus boyc
give up her seat. The e
arrested. Her arrest cau
movement to start the

PRACTICE Answer t
causes and effects in *R*
1. What caused Afric
stop at all the bus

VOCABULARY

Sometimes a new word
with a prefix or suffix at
a root with a familiar w
example, now that you
lize means, you can gue
tion means an effort to
and resources for action

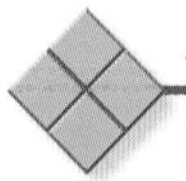

Responding to Literature

PERSONAL RESPONSE

- What questions would you like to ask Rosa Parks about the courage she showed? Record your questions in your journal.
- Which part of Rosa Parks's experience affected you more as a reader? What details about historic events did you find most surprising? Write your response in your journal.

Analyzing Literature

RECALL

1. Why did Rosa Parks decide not to give up her seat on the bus?
2. Who did Rosa Parks consult before deciding to become a test case for desegregation of buses?
3. How did Dr. Martin Luther King Jr. contribute to the success of the bus boycott?
4. How did the bus boycott make life difficult for local African Americans?

Brackets connect questions that are paired to develop higher-level thinking skills.

INTERPRET

5. Why do you think Rosa Parks chose to include so many details about the incident on the bus?
6. Why did Parks agree to become a test case and support the boycott? Was she right to be concerned about the results? Explain your answer.
7. Why was Dr. King a good leader for the boycott?
8. In what ways did the African American community show its courage during the boycott?

EVALUATE AND CONNECT

9. Rosa Parks does not reveal very much about her emotions during the difficult year that began with her arrest. Why do you think she chose to use this factual **tone** in her autobiography?
10. If you were living in Alabama during the time of segregation, what do you imagine you would have thought about segregated buses?

LITERARY ELEMENTS

Sequence of Events

In nonfiction, when the writer is describing actual events, **sequence** is extremely important. If the article or book is about important moments in history, having the correct sequence is essential. Rosa Parks helps the reader keep track of sequence by using dates and words that indicate time, such as *then, earlier, eventually, meanwhile,* and *after.*

1. How well does Rosa Parks help the reader keep track of the events during the Montgomery bus boycott? Support your opinion with examples.
2. Find three examples of the use of sequence words in the selection.

● See **Literary Terms Handbook**, p. R10.

Responding to the Selection

PERSONAL RESPONSE

- Questions students might ask include the following: Did Rosa Parks ever feel like giving up the struggle? What sustained her?
- Some students might have been affected most by Parks's determination and courage.

Analyzing Literature

1. She was "tired" of bus segregation and would not put up with it any more.
2. She consulted her husband and her mother.
3. Dr. Martin Luther King Jr. contributed to the success of the boycott by inspiring the people to support it, by enlisting the aid of others who could challenge the issue in court, and by helping to bring national attention to it.
4. Unwilling to use buses, local African Americans had to find other means of transportation. They had to walk, carpool, or wait for cabs.
5. By including so many details about the incident on the bus, Rosa enables the readers to see exactly what happened.
6. Rosa Parks agreed to become a test case because she was tired of bus segregation. Her concern was justified because things could be worse than before if the boycott failed.
7. Dr. King was a good leader because of his belief in nonviolent protest and his ability to persuade the community to keep committed to the cause.
8. The African American community supported the boycott, resisted the pressures to go back to riding the buses, and stood behind Parks publicly.
9. The factual tone makes the telling more believable and generates more sympathy from the reader than an emotional outpouring might.
10. Students may focus on the unfairness and injustice of bus segregation, the strength of the leaders and the community, and the restraint they showed in keeping the fight nonviolent.

LITERARY ELEMENTS

1. Parks does a good job by using such phrases as *next* and *in the morning*, giving dates, and mentioning the seasons (as in *"Summer came and went").*
2. Examples include *"By the time I got home it was nine-thirty," "On the morning of Friday, December 2,"* and *"In June."*

Additional Resources

Literary Elements Transparency 10

Extending You

Writing About L

Students' summaries

- touch upon the m with minimal deta
- mention those eve their Reading Focu a general way the the Civil Rights lea

Have students read to a partner and list ner reads his or her students to be sure words unless they us tation from the selec

Creative Writing

Students' texts shoul

- explain the main e
- re-create those eve sentences and lan can understand
- omit complicated i

Literature Group students that the ske require little or no ex Viewers should be ab understand the entire message just by look pictures and the few posters. COLLAB. LEARN.

Interdisciplinary Remind students to i the major events in t lines.

Performing Sugge students use script f Each character's nam stated, followed by th character is to speak

Standardized Test Practice

TEST-TAKING TIP

Certain reading passages may include charts, tables, signs, graphs, or other graphic materials. In these cases, some or all of the questions will be based on information contained in the material. You should remind students that they do not need to memorize information; they only need to refer to it to find an answer to a question.

The Princeton Review **TEST-TAKING TIP**

Remind students to use their test booklets to help solve problems. They should write as much as they can in the booklets rather than try to figure out problems in their heads. When they eliminate an answer choice, they should cross it out in the booklet. This will help them focus on the remaining answer choices.

The Princeton Review **TEST-TAKING TIP**

Encourage students to pay special attention to the parts of the test that are most difficult for them. Promote these sections as challenges that can be overcome with work and practice.

TEST-TAKING TIP

Emphasize that students should read all material carefully and not move on to the questions until they understand the information that is included in a chart, table, or other graphic material.

Standardized Test Practice

Read the following passage. Then read each question on page 111. Decide which is the best answer to each question. Mark the letter for that answer on your paper.

Taking Inventory

Mr. Krauzer seemed pleased with Randy's application for a job as stock boy. He gestured toward the aisles of groceries. "We need an accurate inventory," he said. "Are you up to it? Here's an instruction page. Look it over, and we'll talk about it."

Inventory Instructions

Fill out all parts of the inventory page. Accuracy is very important.

1 Fill in the appropriate information at the top of the inventory sheet.

2 List the items and the price per unit. Record the number of units on the shelf in the TALLY column.

3 If an item is on sale, put an X in the appropriate column.

4 Do not record more than one aisle's inventory on a single sheet. Do not use two sheets to record the inventory of a single aisle.

5 Double-check all information.

6 When you are satisfied that the report is accurate, sign your name and write your employee number at the bottom before <u>submitting</u> it to the manager on duty.

7 Bring your finished inventory sheets to the manager on duty.

INVENTORY SHEET

Date May 5, 1999
Aisle 3

Item	Tally	Price	Sale
Juicy O's 8 oz. Cans	25	$0.99	X
Jalapeño Rings	35	1.09	
Stewed Tomatoes in Water	15	0.89	
Miller's Premium Sardines	20	1.99	X

Joe Johnson
Employee Number 410

Tested Objectives

Item	Reading Objective
1, 2	Understand and analyze the differences among types of informational materials Locate information using a variety of document types
3, 6	Read and understand grade-level-appropriate material
4	Distinguish between fact and opinion
5	Clarify word meaning through use of context

1 An inventory sheet is most like —
A a schedule.
B an article.
C a list.
D a brochure.

2 If all the numbers in the tally column were added up, the total wold show —
J the price of each item.
K the number of items in the store.
L the number of employees.
M the number of items in Aisle 3.

3 There is enough information in the passage to conclude that —
A Randy has never had a job before.
B Jalapeno rings cost more than stewed tomatoes.
C Mr. Krauzer is the owner of the grocery store.
D Juicy O's costs the same as stewed tomatoes when on sale.

4 Which is a FACT in this passage?
J The inventory system at Krauzer's is remarkably efficient.
K Double-checking your tallies is a sure-fire way to avoid making mistakes.
L It is necessary to note when items are on sale.
M More than one aisle's inventory is supposed to be recorded on a single regular Inventory Sheet.

5 In this passage, the word submitting means —
A giving.
B being defeated.
C hiding.
D recording.

6 All finished sheets should be —
J filed in the office at the end of each day.
K brought to the manager on duty.
L given to Mr. Krauzer.
M filled out in triplicate.

STOP

Answers and Analyses

1. C This question requires a basic understanding of what a list is and what it looks like. While the entire page may look like a brochure, the Inventory Sheet itself is most like a list. The best answer is C.
2. M Students should use the process of elimination for this question. The total number of items cannot equal an individual price or be used to figure out the number of employees, so choices J and L can be eliminated. Finding the number of items in the store requires knowing the inventory in all aisles, not just one aisle; therefore, choice K is wrong. Since the Inventory Sheet notes that all the items are from aisle 3, choice M is the best answer.
3. B Since there is no information in the passage or the inventory sheet to indicate that Randy has never had a job, choice A can be eliminated. Mr. Krauzer could be the owner of the store, but he could also be the manager, so choice C can be eliminated. Finally, Juicy O's and stewed tomatoes have different prices, so choice D can be eliminated. That leaves choice B.
4. L Choice L is listed in the inventory directions under item 3. Neither J or K is stated anywhere in the passage. Choice M is the opposite of what is mentioned in item 4 of the directions. Choice L is the only answer supported by the passage.
5. A Choices A and B are both possible meanings for *submitting,* so students need to use context to determine the correct answer. Item 7 of the directions mentions that people should *bring* inventory sheets to the manager. *Bring* is used in the same manner as *submitting* in item 6. Nothing in the passage gives context clues for being defeated. Therefore, the best choice is A.
6. K According to item 7 in the directions, inventory sheets must be brought to the manager on duty. Of all the answer choices, choice K is the only proven fact in the passage.

Theme 2 At a Glance

Winds of Change

THEME OPENING

- **Introducing the Theme** (p. 113)
- **Exploring the Theme** (p. 114)
- **Theme Projects** (p. 115)

Theme 2: WINDS OF CHANGE

SELECTIONS

Hollywood and the Pits (p. 116)

Media Connection: Time to Change (p. 131)

Growing Pains (p. 132)

Media Connection: *from* The N.B.A.'s Sister Act (p. 136)

Slam, Dunk, and Hook (p. 137)

Active Reading Model: A Crush (p. 148)

Last Cover (p. 162)

Birthday Box (p. 174)

There Is No Word for Goodbye (p. 174)

Rip Van Winkle (p. 184)

old age sticks (p. 204)

SKILL FEATURES

Interdisciplinary Connection (p. 130)

Reading and Thinking Skills (p. 142)

Vocabulary Skills (p. 143)

Genre Focus: Short Story (pp. 144–145)

Active Reading Strategies (pp. 146-147)

Technology Skills (pp. 160–161)

Grammar Link (p. 182)

Writing Skills (p. 183)

WRITING WORKSHOP

Expository Writing: Compare-and-Contrast Essay (pp. 208–211)

THEME ASSESSMENT

- **Responding to the Theme, Analyzing Literature, Evaluate and Set Goals** (p. 212)
- **Build Your Portfolio** (p. 212)
- **Reading on Your Own** (p. 213)
  So Far from the Bamboo Grove by Yoko Kawashima Watkins
  Come Sing, Jimmy Jo by Katherine Paterson
  Things Change by Troy Aikman
  The Autobiography of Miss Jane Pittman by Ernest J. Gaines
- **Standardized Test Practice** (pp. 214–215)

KEYS TO LITERARY CONNECTIONS

Comparing Selections

The **Comparing Selections** feature in this theme provides opportunities for addressing diverse aspects of the reading and literature curriculum.

For example, in Comparing Selections on page 207, students look closely at the journeys from youth to old age in Washington Irving's "Rip Van Winkle" and E. E. Cummings's "old age sticks." Through this comparison, students can gain insight about attitudes toward aging.

World Literature

The Student Edition contains a variety of literature that represents cultures from around the world. World literature selections are highlighted with the icon above.

TEACHING SUPPORT

The Teaching Support offers a wealth of interactive instructional support:

Meeting Individual Needs
- Special Needs
- English Language Learners
- Multiple Modes of Expression
- Advanced Learners

Internet Connection

Assessment

Portfolio Options

Minilessons
- Grammar and Language
- Reading
- Writing
- Listening and Speaking

Connecting to Other Selections

Real-World Connection

Interdisciplinary Connection

Life Skills Connection

Family and Community Activity

Key to Ability Levels

The activities throughout this theme have been coded for students of various abilities.

L1 BASIC activities for all students

L2 AVERAGE activities for average to above-average students

L3 ADVANCED LEARNERS activities for above-average students

Teaching Today

The Glencoe *Teaching Today* professional development Web site at www.teachingtoday.glencoe.com features daily teaching tips, free downloads, annotated Web resources, educational news, and a wealth of information on a wide range of topics.

Reading Skills in this theme

Variety of Texts

In addition to a group of short stories, this theme includes the following text types:

- autobiographical story
- poetry
- cartoon
- song
- magazine article

Comprehension Skills

The following instructional support for comprehension skills appears in this theme of the Student Edition:

- **Reading and Thinking Minilessons** (pp. 129, 135, 159, 173, 203)
- **Main Idea and Supporting Details** (p. 142)
- **Active Reading Strategies and Model** (pp. 146–159)

See also the **Reading Minilessons** throughout the theme in this Teacher Wraparound Edition.

For strategies for reading longer works, such as novels and novellas, see "Tips for Independent Reading" on page 213.

Reading Resources

Active Reading Guide The ***Active Reading Guide*** provides graphic organizers and study guide questions to support students' reading of each selection. (***Active Reading Guide***, pp. 11–18)

Interactive Reading Sourcebook and **Interactive Reading Workbook** The ***Interactive Reading Sourcebook*** and ***Interactive Reading Workbook*** offer focused comprehension strategies and lessons on critical thinking skills as well as fluency practice and activities to teach and support phonics, decoding, spelling, and vocabulary development.

Vocabulary Power The ***Vocabulary Power*** workbook (Lessons 6–9) provides systematic teaching, practice, and assessment of vocabulary for better reading comprehension.

Audio Library Available on audiocassette and on CD, the ***Audio Library*** provides valuable comprehension support.

Glencoe Literature Library Each title in the ***Glencoe Literature Library*** includes a full-length work plus related readings. A separate Study Guide is available for each title.

Five–Star Stories These anthologies of familiar short stories adapted and abridged for a variety of reading levels include exercises to help increase students' vocabulary and improve their reading comprehension.

The Contemporary Readers ***The Contemporary Readers*** are nonfiction books linked to various themes and designed for developing readers from a wide range of backgrounds.

Literature Classics CD-ROM The selections on this CD-ROM can be searched by author, theme, or genre.

inTIME and Humanities Across TIME Coproductions of Glencoe and Time, Inc., these resources include a wealth of high-interest nonfiction related to the selections in this theme.

Assessment in this theme

Assessment in the Student Edition

This program offers a number of diverse ways to evaluate student understanding and skill proficiency. In the Student Edition, use the following:

- **Responding to Literature**
  Following each selection, students are asked to recall facts, interpret ideas, and evaluate concepts as they answer a variety of questions and complete activities to extend their understanding.
- **Theme Assessment (pp. 212–213)**
  Here students respond to the selections on personal and analytical levels. They also assume ownership of their learning by setting and evaluating goals and by selecting work for their portfolios.

See also the many **Assessment Resources** listed on the facing page.

Standardized Test Practice

The Princeton Review has developed the Standardized Test Practice pages found at the end of this thematic unit (pp. 214–215). For additional practice, direct students to the following resources:

- ITBS Preparation and Practice
- SAT-9 Preparation and Practice
- TerraNova Preparation and Practice

Writing Skills in this theme

Writing Skills

The Student Edition of Theme Two offers strong instructional support for writing skills:

In **Extending Your Response**, which follows each selection:
- **Writing About Literature**
- **Personal/Creative Writing**

See also the **Writing Minilessons** throughout the theme in this Teacher Wraparound Edition.

Writing Workshops

Theme Two concludes with a **Writing Workshop** that guides students through the process of writing a compare-and-contrast essay (pp. 208–211).

Writing Resources

Writer's Assistant CD-ROM Each **Writing Workshop** is supplemented by an interactive writing guide on the ***Writer's Assistant*** CD-ROM. This easy- to-use writing guide provides prompts, templates, and other tools that lead students through the writing process.

Grammar and Composition Handbook The ***Grammar and Composition Handbook*** (Lessons 3.4–4.3) provides systematic instruction in English language conventions.

Spelling Power The ***Spelling Power*** workbook (Lessons 5–8) provides systematic teaching, practice, and assessment of spelling to help students become better spellers and thus enhance their writing.

Writing and Proofreading Practice Blackline masters present in-depth instruction and practice on a specific step in the writing process and proofreading (pp. 1–7, 15–21).

Writing and Proofreading Transparencies Transparencies provide graphic organizers and proofreading exercises for whole-class instruction (pp. 1–6, 9–10, 27–28).

Research and Report Writing Guide This resource provides extensive tips and activities to guide students in their writing projects in the literature classroom as well as in classes across the curriculum.

Style and Documentation Sourcebook for Writers This sourcebook is a combination reference and workbook, giving students the most up-to-date information and guidance regarding traditional as well as technological research strategies and documentation.

Revising with Style This resource offers instruction and exercises focusing on the revision process and covering topics from proofreading and correcting common grammatical errors to sentence combining and reordering.

Assessment Resources

Selection Quick Checks For each selection, a **Quick Check** of three to five short-answer questions measures students' literal comprehension.

Selection and Theme Assessment The ***Selection and Theme Assessment*** instrument tests students' abilities to recall, interpret, and evaluate what they've read. The tests consist of multiple-choice, short answer, and essay questions.

Performance Assessment Alternative assessment instruments and rubrics for Theme Two are found in the ***Performance Assessment*** ancillary.

Writing Assessment and Portfolio Management These notes and strategies, student models, and assessment tools assist with the task of measuring students' progress as writers and as monitors of their own writing.

Testmaker: ExamView Pro Teachers can customize selection and Theme Two tests by accessing the ***Testmaker*** database.

Interactive Tutor: Self-Assessment The ***Interactive Tutor: Self-Assessment*** software provides multiple-choice tests with immediate feedback to help students evaluate their knowledge and understanding of each literature selection.

MindJogger Videoquizzes Using a popular game show format, ***MindJogger Videoquizzes*** on videocassettes enable teachers to evaluate student understanding of Theme Two in a quick and fun manner.

Theme 2 Skills Scope and Sequence

Lessons	Literary Elements	Reading and Thinking	Writing
Hollywood and the Pits Cherylene Lee DRP:53 Lexile:830	Symbol, SE p. 127 *Flashback,* TWE p. 118 *Character,* TWE pp. 118, 124 *Symbol,* TWE pp. 119, 121, 122, 125 *Point of View,* TWE p. 119 *Figures of Speech,* TWE p. 121	Cause and Effect, SE p. 129 *Inferring,* TWE pp. 119, 124 *Evaluating,* TWE pp. 120, 122 *Identifying Author's Purpose,* TWE p. 121 *Drawing Conclusions,* TWE pp. 125, 126 *Less-Proficient Readers,* TWE p. 142	Point of View, SE p. 128 Letter, SE p. 128 *Compare-and-Contrast Paragraph,* TWE p. 119
Growing Pains Jean Little	Mood, SE p. 134 *Mood,* TWE p. 133	Sequence of Events, SE p. 135 Song, SE p. 131 *Varying Reading Rate,* TWE p. 131 *Relationships,* TWE p. 133	Rhythm in Poetry, SE p. 135 Poetry, SE p. 135
Slam, Dunk, & Hook Yusef Komunyakaa	Alliteration, SE p. 140 *Alliteration,* TWE p. 138 *Multicultural Stories,* TWE p. 144	Magazine Article, SE p. 136 Main Idea and Sup. Details, SE p. 142 *Inferring,* TWE p. 138 *Monitoring Comprehension,* TWE p. 139 *Informational Text,* TWE p. 136 SN *Less-Proficient Readers,* TWE p. 142	Paragraph: Sensory Imagery, SE p. 141 Poem or Paragraph: Opinion, SE p. 141
A Crush Cynthia Rylant DRP:59 Lexile:1070	Fiction, SE p. 144 First- and Third-Person Point of View, SE p. 157 *Third-Person Point of View,* TWE pp. 150, 151, 154	Fiction, SE p. 146 Inference, SE p. 159 *Activating Prior Knowledge,* TWE p. 151 *Drawing Conclusions,* TWE p. 152 *Inferring,* TWE p. 153	Paragraph: Character Description, SE p. 158 Letter of Advice, SE p. 158
Last Cover Paul Annixter DRP:51 Lexile:880	Plot, SE p. 171; *TWE pp. 164, 167, 168, 170* *Foreshadowing,* TWE p. 164 *Character,* TWE p. 166 *Flashback,* TWE p. 166 *Mood,* TWE p. 170	Predicting, SE p. 173 *Identifying Cause-Effect Relationships,* TWE p. 165 *Drawing Conclusions,* TWE p. 167 *Inferring,* TWE pp. 168, 170 *Sequencing,* TWE p. 169	Paragraph: Characterization, SE p. 172 Journal Entry, SE p. 172 *Descriptive Details,* TWE p. 169
Birthday Box Jane Yolen DRP:49 Lexile:590 **There Is No Word for Goodbye** Mary TallMountain	Character, SE p. 180 *Character,* TWE pp. 176, 178 *Description,* TWE p. 177 *Symbol,* TWE p. 177 *Metaphor,* TWE p. 179	*Verifying Predictions,* TWE p. 177 *Monitoring Comp.,* TWE p. 177 *Focusing on a Question,* TWE p. 179 SN *Less-Proficient Readers,* TWE p. 179	Paragraph: Setting, SE p. 181 Symbolic Gift, SE p. 181 *Poem,* TWE p. 182
Rip Van Winkle Washington Irving DRP:64 Lexile:1230	Setting, SE p. 201; *TWE pp. 186, 189, 190, 191, 194, 195* *Style,* TWE pp. 186, 200 *Tone,* TWE pp. 187, 193, 200 *Characterization,* TWE pp. 187, 198 *Author's Purpose,* TWE p. 193 *Dialogue,* TWE p. 198	Evaluating, SE p. 203 *Making Critical Judgments,* TWE p. 187 *Identifying Bias,* TWE p. 189 *Inferring,* TWE pp. 192, 199 *Drawing Conclusions,* TWE pp. 194, 199 *Logical Reasoning,* TWE p. 197 *Identifying Assumptions,* TWE p. 199	Paragraph: Theme, SE p. 202 Diary Entry, SE p. 202 *Describing a Person,* TWE p. 187 *Setting a Mood,* TWE p. 193 *Describing with Detail,* TWE p. 195
old age sticks E.E. Cummings	Style, SE p. 206 *Free Verse,* TWE p. 205	Company Selections, SE p. 207 *Less-Proficient Readers,* TWE p. 213	Advice Column, SE p. 206
Writing Workshop Expository Writing: Compare-and-Contrast Essay			*Paragraph Development,* TWE p. 210

Key: Student material is in roman. *Teacher material is in italic.* Technology ELL English Language Learners

Vocabulary and Spelling	Grammar and Language	Listening, Speaking, and Viewing	Life Skills; Study and Research; Technology
Related Forms of Words, SE p. 129 *Sound-Letter Cues, TWE p. 122* SN *Less-Proficient Readers, TWE pp. 124, 128*	Italics, SE p. 129 *Intensifiers, TWE p. 126*	Literature Groups, SE p. 128 ELL *Little Princess, TWE p. 118* *Music, TWE p. 125*	Science, SE p. 130 News Broadcast, SE p. 128 Internet Connection, SE p. 128 *Collective Variety Shows, TWE p. 120* *Geologic Era, TWE p. 122* *Music, TWE p. 125*
Context Clues, SE p. 143		Literature Groups, SE p. 135 Set Words to Music, SE p. 135 ELL *Relationships, TWE p. 133*	
ELL *Basketball Slang, TWE p. 138* ELL *Creating Context, TWE p. 143* SN *Less-Proficient Readers, TWE p. 147*	Vivid Verbs, SE p. 141	Literature Groups, SE p. 141 Group Dramatization, SE p. 141 *Viewing, TWE p. 139* ELL *Creating Context, TWE p. 143*	
The Suffix *-ly*, SE p. 159 *Previewing, TWE p. 147*	Adverb Clauses, SE p. 159 *Capitalization, TWE p. 156*	Literature Groups, SE p. 158 ELL *Multicultural Stories, TWE p. 144* *Role-Playing a Conversation, TWE p. 154*	Letter Writing: SE p. 158 Community Services, SE p. 158 Creating a Spreadsheet, SE p. 160 *Fiction Table, TWE p. 145* ELL *Rites of Passage, TWE p. 150* *Child Development, TWE p. 152* *Science, TWE p. 153* *Human Interest Articles, TWE p. 155*
Roots, SE p. 173 *Word Meanings, TWE p. 164* ELL *Animal Characteristics, TWE p. 164* SN *Less-Proficient Readers, TWE p. 166*	Commas Used with Words in a Series, SE p. 173 *Commas and Conjunctions, TWE p. 168*	Literature Groups, SE p. 172 Dramatizing a Scene, SE p. 172	*Foxes, TWE p. 167*
Negative Prefixes, SE p. 181	Using Adjectives and Adverbs Correctly, SE p. 182 *Appositives, TWE p. 178*	Literature Groups, SE p. 181 ELL *Birthdays, TWE p. 175*	Speech for Support Group, SE p. 181
Synonyms and Antonyms, SE p. 203 *Prefixes, TWE p. 187* *Context Clues, TWE p. 191* *Synonyms, TWE p. 196* *Word Meanings, TWE p. 198*	Adverbs, SE p. 203 *Semicolons, TWE p. 190* *Hyphens, TWE p. 192* *Capitalizing Proper Nouns, TWE p. 200*	Literature Groups, SE p. 202 ELL *Cultural Changes, TWE p. 186* SN *Less-Proficient Readers, TWE p. 189* *Interviewing, TWE p. 198*	Writing a Newspaper Article, SE p. 202 *Hudson River, TWE p. 199*
ELL *Former and Latter, TWE p. 191* SN *Less-Proficient Readers, TWE pp. 194, 202*	ELL *Sentences Without Punctuation, TWE p. 205*	Literature Groups, SE p. 206	
		ELL *Speaking Before Writing, TWE p. 208*	

SN **Special Needs/Strategic Intervention**

Theme 2 RESOURCE MANAGER

Lessons	Essential Resources		English Language Learners
Hollywood and the Pits CHERYLENE LEE PACING: 3 DAYS	**Lesson-Specific Instruction** Selection Focus Transp. 11 Active Reading Guide,* p. 11 Literary Elements Transp. 11 Vocabulary Practice, p. 8 Quick Checks,* p. 11 Selection and Theme Assessment, pp. 21–22	Testmaker: ExamView Pro Performance Assessment, p. 11 **Systematic Language Instruction** Grammar and Comp. Hbk., L. 3.4	English Language Learners Sourcebook, pp. 29, 30 Spanish Summaries, p. 11 Spanish Translations, pp. 35–42 Audio Library* English, Yes!
Growing Pains JEAN LITTLE PACING: 1 DAY	**Lesson-Specific Instruction** Selection Focus Transp. 12 Active Reading Guide,* p. 12 Literary Elements Transp. 12 Quick Checks,* p. 12 Selection and Theme Assessment, p. 23	Testmaker: ExamView Pro Performance Assessment, p. 12 **Systematic Language Instruction** Grammar and Comp. Hbk., L. 3.5-3.6 Vocabulary Power, Lesson 6 Spelling Power, Lesson 5	English Language Learners Sourcebook, p. 31 Spanish Summaries, p. 12 Spanish Translations, p. 43 Audio Library* English, Yes!
Slam, Dunk, & Hook YUSEF KOMUNYAKAA PACING: 2 DAYS	**Lesson-Specific Instruction** Selection Focus Transp. 13 Active Reading Guide,* p. 13 Literary Elements Transp. 13 Quick Checks,* p. 13 Selection and Theme Assessment, p. 24 Testmaker: ExamView Pro	Performance Assessment, p. 13 TIME *inTIME* magazine, p. 26 **Systematic Language Instruction** Grammar and Comp. Hbk., L. 3.7	English Language Learners Sourcebook, p. 32 Spanish Summaries, p. 13 Spanish Translations, pp. 44–45 Audio Library* English, Yes!
A Crush CYNTHIA RYLANT PACING: 2 DAYS	**Lesson-Specific Instruction** Selection Focus Transp. 14 Active Reading Guide,* p. 14 Literary Elements Transp. 14 Vocabulary Practice, p. 9 Quick Checks,* p. 14 Selection and Theme Assessment, pp. 25–26	Testmaker: ExamView Pro Performance Assessment, p. 14 **Systematic Language Instruction** Grammar and Comp. Hbk., L. 3.8–3.9 Vocabulary Power, Lesson 7 Spelling Power, Lesson 6	English Language Learners Sourcebook, pp. 34, 35 Theme Two Planning Guide, p. 24 Spanish Summaries, p. 14 Spanish Translations, pp. 46-51 Audio Library* English, Yes!
Last Cover PAUL ANNIXTER PACING: 2 DAYS	**Lesson-Specific Instruction** Selection Focus Transp. 15 Active Reading Guide,* p. 15 Literary Elements Transp. 15 Vocabulary Practice, p. 10 Quick Checks,* p. 15 Selection and Theme Assessment, pp. 27–28	Testmaker: ExamView Pro Performance Assessment, p. 15 **Systematic Language Instruction** Grammar and Comp. Hbk., L. 3.10-3.12	English Language Learners Sourcebook, p. 36 Spanish Summaries, p. 15 Audio Library* English, Yes!

Key: Workbook · Blackline Masters · Textbook · Transparency · CD-ROM · Videodisk (also available in videocassette)

Special Needs/ Strategic Intervention	Reteaching and Enrichment
Interactive Reading Sourcebook, pp. T74–T77 Interactive Reading Workbook, pp. 21-22 Inclusion Strategies Sourcebook, pp. 9-10 Theme Two Planning Guide, p. 6 Audio Library*	Literature Launchers, Side A, Segment 6 Fine Art Transparency 17 Reading Skills Practice Workbook, pp. 19-20 Grammar and Language Transp. 11 Gr. and Lang. Wkbk., pp. 129-130, 271-272 Grammar and Comp. Hbk., L. 6.2, 13.6 TIME *Humanities Across TIME,* Cover 14 Interactive Tutor: Self-Assessment Vocabulary PuzzleMaker Web Site (lit.glencoe.com)
Interactive Reading Sourcebook, pp. T77-T79 Interactive Reading Workbook, p. 23 Inclusion Strategies Sourcebook, pp. 11-12 Theme Two Planning Guide, p. 14 Audio Library*	Media Connection Activities, p. 3 TIME *inTIME* magazine, p. 30 TIME *Humanities Across TIME,* Cover 4 Interactive Tutor: Self-Assessment Vocabulary PuzzleMaker Web Site (lit.glencoe.com)
Interactive Reading Sourcebook, pp. T80-T82 Interactive Reading Workbook, p. 24 Inclusion Strategies Sourcebook, pp. 67-68 Theme Two Planning Guide, p. 19 Audio Library*	Literature Launchers, Side A, Segment 5 Gr. and Lang. Wkbk., pp. 73-74 Grammar and Comp. Hbk., L. 3.1 Media Connection Activities, p. 4 TIME *inTIME* magazine, p. 27 TIME *Humanities Across TIME,* Cover 18 Interactive Tutor: Self-Assessment Vocabulary PuzzleMaker Web Site (lit.glencoe.com)
Interactive Reading Sourcebook, pp. T82-T85 Interactive Reading Workbook, pp. 25-26 Inclusion Strategies Sourcebook, pp. 29-30 Theme Two Planning Guide, p. 24 Audio Library*	Reading Skills Practice Workbook, pp. 23-24 Grammar and Language Transp. 12 Gr. and Lang. Wkbk., pp. 159-160, 235-248 Grammar and Comp. Hbk., L. 8.5, 12.1-12.4 Interactive Tutor: Self-Assessment Vocabulary PuzzleMaker Web Site (lit.glencoe.com)
Interactive Reading Sourcebook, pp. T85-T87 Interactive Reading Workbook, pp. 27-28 Inclusion Strategies Sourcebook, pp. 15-16, 51-52 Theme Two Planning Guide, p. 32 Audio Library*	Reading Skills Practice Workbook, pp. 25-26 Grammar and Language Transp. 13 Gr. and Lang. Wkbk., pp. 255-256, 257-258 Grammar and Comp. Hbk., L. 13.2, 13.3 Interactive Tutor: Self-Assessment Vocabulary PuzzleMaker Web Site (lit.glencoe.com)

Web Audiocassette Diskette *Also available in Spanish

INDEPENDENT READING

Encourage students to spend thirty minutes each day in independent reading. The following Glencoe components and outside resources provide opportunities for reading related to this theme.

The Glencoe Literature Library

You may want to assign one or more of these titles for independent reading. For a complete listing of titles available in the Glencoe Literature Library, see page T96 of this book.

- *So Far From the Bamboo Grove* by Yoko Kawashima Watkins
- *Letters from Rifka* by Karen Hesse
- *Across Five Aprils* by Irene Hunt
- *Johnny Tremain* by Esther Forbes

inTIME News stories, feature articles, reviews, profiles, and essays in the magazine connect to an author, work, or theme in the Student Edition. See the ***inTIME* Teacher's Guide** for specific connections to this theme.

Resources for Less-Proficient Readers

For reading especially created for less-proficient readers, suggest

- *Five-Star Stories*
- *The Contemporary Readers*

Additional Resources for Independent Reading

The following titles are listed with specific reading selections throughout this theme. You may want to suggest that students look for these in your local or school library.

- *Shirley Temple Black* by James Haskins
- *Death Trap: The Story of the La Brea Tar Pits* by Sharon Elaine Thompson
- *Mama's Going to Buy You a Mockingbird* and *Little by Little: A Writer's Education* by Jean Little
- *A Couple of Kooks and Other Stories About Love* and *Waiting to Waltz* by Cynthia Rylant
- *Pride of Lions and Other Stories* and *The Best Nature Stories of Paul Annixter* by Paul Annixter
- *Here There Be Dragons* by Jane Yolen
- *Diedrich Knickerbocker's History of New York* by Washington Irving
- *Things Change* by Troy Aikman

Theme 2 RESOURCE MANAGER (continued)

Lessons	Essential Resources	English Language Learners
Birthday Box Jane Yolen There Is No Word for Goodbye Mary TallMountain Pacing: 2 Days	**Lesson-Specific Instruction** Selection Focus Transp. 16 Active Reading Guide,* p. 16 Literary Elements Transp. 16 Vocabulary Practice, p. 11 Quick Checks,* p. 16 Selection and Theme Assessment, pp. 29–30 Testmaker: ExamView Pro Performance Assessment, p. 16 **Systematic Language Instruction** Grammar and Comp. Hbk., L. 4.1–4.2 Vocabulary Power, Lesson 8 Spelling Power, Lesson 7	English Language Learners Sourcebook, p. 37 Spanish Summaries, p. 16 Audio Library* English, Yes!
Rip Van Winkle Washington Irving Pacing: 3 Days	**Lesson-Specific Instruction** Selection Focus Transp. 17 Active Reading Guide,* p. 17 Literary Elements Transp. 17 Vocabulary Practice, p. 12 Quick Checks,* p. 17 Selection and Theme Assessment, pp. 31–32 Testmaker: ExamView Pro Performance Assessment, p. 17 **Systematic Language Instruction** Grammar and Comp. Hbk., L. 4.2 Vocabulary Power, Lesson 9 Spelling Power, Lesson 8	English Language Learners Sourcebook, pp. 38, 39 Spanish Summaries, p. 17 Spanish Translations, pp. 52–63 Audio Library* English, Yes!
old age sticks E. E. Cummings Pacing: 1 Day	**Lesson-Specific Instruction** Selection Focus Transp. 18 Active Reading Guide,* p. 18 Literary Elements Transp. 18 Quick Checks,* p. 18 Selection and Theme Assessment, pp. 31–32 Testmaker: ExamView Pro Performance Assessment, p. 17 **Systematic Language Instruction** Grammar and Comp. Hbk., L. 4.3 Vocabulary Power, Unit 2 Review/Test Spelling Power, Unit 2 Review/ Proofreading	English Language Learners Sourcebook, p. 40 Spanish Summaries, p. 18 Audio Library* English, Yes!
Writing Workshop Expository Writing: Compare-and-Contrast Essay Pacing: 2 Days	Writing Assessment and Portfolio Management, pp. 1–13, 17–19, 38–45	English Language Learners Sourcebook, p. 9 English, Yes!

Key: Workbook · Blackline Masters · Textbook · Transparency · CD-ROM · Videodisk (also available in videocassette)

Special Needs/ Strategic Intervention	Reteaching and Enrichment
Interactive Reading Sourcebook, pp. T88–T90 Interactive Reading Workbook, pp. 29-30 Inclusion Strategies Sourcebook, pp. 45-46 Theme Two Planning Guide, p. 40 Audio Library*	Fine Art Transparency 30 Reading Skills Practice Workbook, pp. 27-28 Grammar and Language Transp. 14 Gr. and Lang. Wkbk., pp. 69-70, 121-124, 131-132, 133-134 Grammar and Comp. Hbk., L. 2.5, 5.3, 5.4, 6.3, 6.4 Interactive Tutor: Self-Assessment Vocabulary PuzzleMaker Web Site (lit.glencoe.com)
Interactive Reading Sourcebook, pp. T91–T93 Interactive Reading Workbook, pp. 31-34 Inclusion Strategies Sourcebook, pp. 49-50, 89-90 Theme Two Planning Guide, p. 46 Audio Library*	Literature Launchers, Side A, Segment 4 Fine Art Transparency 14 Reading Skills Practice Workbook, pp. 29-30 Grammar and Language Transparencies 16-18 Gr. and Lang. Wkbk., pp. 127-128, 235-236, 265-266, 275-276 Grammar and Comp. Hbk., L. 6.1, 6.2, 12.1-12.4, 13.5, 13.8 Interactive Tutor: Self-Assessment Vocabulary PuzzleMaker Web Site (lit.glencoe.com)
Interactive Reading Sourcebook, pp. T94–T96 Interactive Reading Workbook, p. 35 Theme Two Planning Guide, p. 54 Audio Library*	Interactive Tutor: Self-Assessment Vocabulary PuzzleMaker Web Site (lit.glencoe.com)
	Writing and Proofreading Practice, pp. 1-7, 15-21 Writing and Proofreading Transparencies 1-6, 9-10, 27-28 Revising with Style Writer's Assistant

Theme RESOURCES

To explore the theme further, you may want to use these resources:

- Listening and Speaking Activities (pp. 4-6)
- Viewing and Representing Activities (pp. 1-6, 7-9)
- Critical Thinking Skills (pp. 5-6)
- Media Connection Activities, (pp. 3-4)
- Interdisciplinary Activities (pp. 6-9)
- Family and Community Activities (p. 12)
- Selection and Theme Assessment (pp. 127-128)
- Performance Assessment, pp. 70, 96

TIME Humanities Across TIME

See also these additional theme planning resources:

- Theme Two Planning Guide
- Interactive Reading Sourcebook
- Literature Groups Sourcebook
- Interactive Lesson Planner
- Interactive Teacher Edition
- Glencoe Web Site <lit.glencoe.com>

Use Glencoe's ***Presentation Plus!*** This multimedia teaching tool lets you present dynamic lessons that will engage your students. Using Microsoft PowerPoint®, you can customize the presentation to create your own personalized lessons.

Web Audiocassette Diskette *Also available in Spanish

Winds of Change

Theme Objectives

- To enjoy reading about the excitement, growth, and wisdom brought about by change
- To analyze the literary elements in poetry and short story selections
- To apply strategies for reading short stories

Teaching Strategies

Have students read the quotation from "I Know Why the Caged Bird Sings," by Maya Angelou in preparation for the discussion questions below.

VIEWING THE ART

Diane Griffiths is a British artist, printmaker, and ceramicist.

Responding to the Art

Discussion questions:

- How does this piece of art reflect the theme? *(It illustrates a wind that will bring a change.)*
- What kind of change does it illustrate? *(It seems to illustrate a change of seasons.)*

Winds of Change

"The need for change bulldozed a road down the center of my mind."

—Maya Angelou, *I Know Why the Caged Bird Sings*

Hawthorne Dusk, 1996. Diane Griffiths. Watercolor and crayon, 60 x 75 cm. The Grand Design Gallery, Leeds, England.

112

TEACHER to TEACHER

TIOSPAYE TOPA CHEYENNE RIVER AGENCY • EAGLE BUTTE, SOUTH DAKOTA

Our school is located in an isolated region, and for my students, the theme "Winds of Change" is often represented by changes in technology, which they have little exposure to. However, cultural heritage and traditions play an important role in their lives, so it is natural for me to talk about Native American history and the changes that occurred in Native American cultures over the past 200 years. The concept of directions has significance in our way of thinking, so using North, South, East, and West, I talk about how things were long ago, how they were not so long ago, how they are today, and where we are headed in the future. I use a circle and point out that things in our lives have a way of going around, but we never return to the beginning and the circle never ends, so there is constant change.

BRANDI THOMAS

THEME CONTENTS

Introducing the Theme

Direct your students' attention to the **Theme Contents.** Ask them to read through the list of selections. Present these questions for discussion:

- Considering the titles, what do you think this theme will focus on? *(Students may say age or growing up.)*
- Does any one title catch your interest? Which one, and why? *(Students who are interested in sports may point out "Slam, Dunk, & Hook," a title that consists of basketball terms.)*
- Have you ever read the story of Rip Van Winkle before? If so, how might it relate to other titles in the theme's contents? *(Students might note that many changes occur while Rip Van Winkle is asleep and that some of the other titles also suggest growth, change, and transition.)*

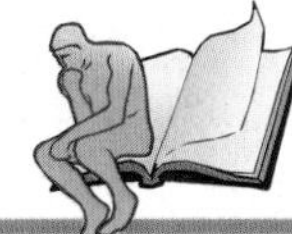

LITERATURE & HUMANITIES

Have students examine *The Red Stairway* from *U. S. History and Art*, Transparency 2, a painting of an area that has been devastated by a disaster. Then have them discuss whether the actions of the figure on the stairs are hopeful or hopeless.

GLENCOE TECHNOLOGY

LITERATURE CLASSICS CD-ROM

Search for other short selections related to the theme "Winds of Change."

RESOURCE MANAGER

See the ***Theme Two Planning Guide*** for additional teaching notes, strategies, and resources for introducing the theme "Winds of Change."

Exploring the Theme

Winds of Change

Ask students to think of quotations, sayings, song lyrics, proverbs, or phrases they have heard that express people's attitudes toward change. You may wish to offer examples, such as

- *Change is gonna do you good; Don't go changing.* (song lyrics)
- *The more things change, the more they stay the same.* (French proverb)
- *Fear No Change.* (popular expression)
- *Everything changes. Nothing stays the same. That's life.* (Buddhist teaching)
  Or, you may wish to offer Fine Art Transparency 18 as an example of a visual expression.

Have each student make up a saying or proverb that expresses his or her attitude toward change.

Starting Points

Times Change

Students might mention things Calvin's father may have done as a child, such as playing sports, hiking and swimming, or riding his bike.

- Activities could include Rollerblading (in-line skating), video and computer games, or going to the mall.
- Encourage students to name the specific time periods to which they traveled in their time machines.
- Suggest that teenagers from their parents' generations would not be as shocked by television, video, and computer activities as would teenagers living a few hundred years ago or in prehistoric times.

Change Is in the Air

Students may note changes in their school activities, family life, attitudes, and friendships. Students might like to change aspects of themselves or their situations that are problems for them, and might like to have the most positive parts of their lives and the people they love stay the same.

Ask students to list three strategies for changing something they would like to change and another three strategies for preserving something they want to stay the same. Have them discuss their strategies with partners.

Changing Times Students can use a search engine to find out more about change over the centuries. They might use keywords such as *history, music, dress,* or any other point of interest.

Exploring the Theme

Winds of Change

Life never stays the same. The world is constantly changing. In this theme, you will meet people who learn to deal with changes within themselves and in their lives. Try one of the options below to start thinking about the theme of change.

Starting Points

TIMES CHANGE

Think of several things Calvin's father may have done as a child on a nice day. Then think about an invention, a game, or another activity you enjoy that did not exist when your parents were your age.

- Work with a partner. Role-play a trip in a time machine. Introduce your invention, game, or activity to a teenager from the past.

CHANGE IS IN THE AIR

Think about the changes in your own life. Write a few notes to answer these questions.

- What has changed in your life in the last few years? What effect have these changes had?
- What would you like to change about your life? What would you like to always stay the same?

Calvin and Hobbes

by Bill Watterson

Theme Projects

As you read the selections in this theme, try out one of these projects. Work on your own, with a partner, or with a group.

LEARNING FOR LIFE

Writing a Proposal

How can your school be improved? Develop a proposal addressed to the board of education. Think about improvements that could be made without spending a huge amount of time or money. Suggest ideas for ways to accomplish your goals. Draft your proposal and share it with your class.

CRITICAL VIEWING

Picturing Myself in the Future

What will you be doing ten years from now? Where will you live? How will your life be different?

1. List changes you think might happen to you in the next ten years. Will you go to college? Have a job? Travel? Have a family?
2. Draw a picture or make a collage showing how your life may change in the future.

Search the Web for more project ideas. Also, learn more about the authors and ideas featured in this theme by visiting lit.glencoe.com.

MULTIMEDIA PROJECT

Create a Visual History Exhibit

Use collected photographs and objects to create a history exhibit of your city, town, or neighborhood that shows how it has changed over the years.

1. Find and copy pictures that show the oldest buildings and the people who lived or worked in them. Gather objects from your local historical society, historians, neighbors, and your local government.
2. Design an exhibit that compares then and now. Include photographs, documents, and objects from the past and present.

Theme Projects

Teaching Strategies

These ideas may help students carry out their theme projects.

Learning for Life

- Help students develop a list of realistic improvements.
- Suggest students poll other students to find out whether the change would be popular.
- Invite students to attend a school board meeting and observe how issues and proposals are handled.

Critical Viewing

- When creating their portraits of the future, students should include many aspects of their lives: work, home, school, friends, and family.
- As an alternative to drawing pictures or making collages, students could paint murals for their portraits of the future.

Multimedia Project

- Suggest that students interview longtime residents of the towns or cities they live in to gather reminiscences for their project.
- Encourage students to locate old family-owned businesses and find out how changing economic times have affected them.
- You may wish to have students do this project as a class, with different groups focusing on different parts of the project.

Additional Resources

- ***Interdisciplinary Activities,*** pp. 6–9
- ***Viewing and Representing Activities,*** pp. 10–12
- ***Listening and Speaking Activities,*** pp. 4–6
- ***Critical Thinking Skills,*** pp. 5–6
- ***Selection and Theme Assessment,*** pp. 127–128
- ***Performance Assessment,*** p. 70

Family and Community Activity

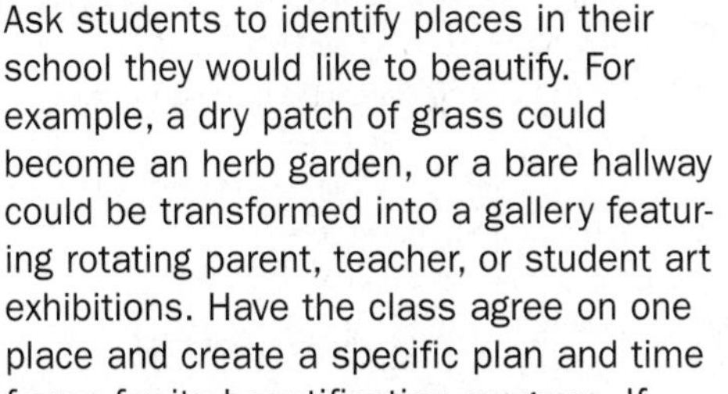

Ask students to identify places in their school they would like to beautify. For example, a dry patch of grass could become an herb garden, or a bare hallway could be transformed into a gallery featuring rotating parent, teacher, or student art exhibitions. Have the class agree on one place and create a specific plan and time frame for its beautification program. If they need materials, encourage them to have a fund-raiser or seek donations of the materials from their community. Take pictures before, during, and after the beautification program. Invite students to chronicle the change in a class journal. L1

Additional Resources

- ***Family and Community Activities,*** p. 12

Before Reading

Objectives

- To read and analyze an autobiographical story of a young girl
- To explain a story's symbols
- To write an explanation of effective use of first-person point of view

Skills

Reading/Thinking: Inferring; Evaluating; Drawing Conclusions; Identifying Author's Purpose; Cause and Effect
Writing: Compare and Contrast Paragraph; Letter
Vocabulary: Related Words
Grammar/Language: Intensifiers; Italics
Collaboration: Literature Groups

Motivating STUDENTS

Literature Launchers: "Something Different in L.A."

Videodisc Side A, Segment 6

Also available in VHS.

Selection Focus Transparency 11: Have students read and discuss the quote about Hollywood.

Reading Focus: As an extension of the Reading Focus, have partners use precise language and sensory details to discuss how and why their interests may change in five years.

Before You Read

Hollywood and the Pits

MEET CHERYLENE LEE

It's hard to imagine a successful stage, movie, and TV performer becoming a paleontologist, but that's just what Cherylene Lee did. Like the narrator in "Hollywood and the Pits," Lee was a child performer in her hometown of Los Angeles. After earning degrees in paleontology and geology, she began writing stories, poetry, and plays.

"Hollywood and the Pits" appears in the collection American Dragons: Twenty-Five Asian American Voices, *edited by Laurence Yep and published in 1995.*

READING FOCUS

Are there parts of your childhood self that you have left behind in the past few years?

Journal
Describe how your interests and hobbies have—or have not—changed in the last year or two. Write about how becoming a teenager has affected your childhood interests.

Setting a Purpose
Read to discover one teen's view on change.

BUILDING BACKGROUND

The Time and Place It is 1968 in Los Angeles, California. In the middle of the city, close to the glamour of Hollywood, is an archaeological site filled with the skeletons of prehistoric creatures.

VOCABULARY PREVIEW

obsessed (əb sesd′) *adj.* overly concentrated or focused on a single emotion or idea; p. 118
bewildered (bi wil′ dərd) *adj.* very confused; p. 118
barrage (bə räzh′) *n.* a heavy concentration or great outpouring, as of words; p. 119
excavated (eks′ kə vāt′ əd) *adj.* uncovered or removed by digging; unearthed; p. 119
immobilize (i mō′ bə līz′) *v.* to make unable to move; fix in place; p. 119
painstaking (pānz′ tā′ king) *adj.* requiring close, careful labor or attention; p. 123
predator (pred′ ə tər) *n.* an animal, such as a lion or hawk, that kills other animals for food; p. 125
deception (di sep′ shən) *n.* that which fools or misleads; p. 125
scavenger (skav′ in jər) *n.* an animal, such as a hyena or vulture, that feeds on dead, decaying animals; p. 125

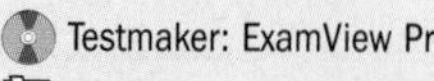

RESOURCE MANAGER

Teaching Tools and Resources
- Theme Two Planning Guide
- Literature Groups Sourcebook

Essential Lesson Support

Lesson-Specific Instruction
- Selection Focus Transparency 11
- Literary Elements Transparency 11
- Active Reading Guide,* p. 11
- Selection Vocabulary Practice, p. 8

Assessment
- Selection Quick Checks,* p. 11
- Selection and Theme Assessment, pp. 21-22
- Testmaker: ExamView Pro
- Performance Assessment, p. 11

Systematic Language Instruction
- Gr. & Comp. Hbk., Lesson 3.4

English Language Learners
- ELL Sourcebook, pp. 29-30
- Spanish Summaries, p. 11
- Spanish Translations, pp. 35-42
- Audio Library*
- English, Yes!

Spec. Needs/Strat. Interven.
- Interactive Reading Sourcebook, pp. T74-T77
- Interactive Reading Workbook, pp. 21-22
- Inclusion Strategies Sourcebook, pp. 10-11
- Audio Library*

*Also available in Spanish

HOLLYWOOD AND THE PITS

Cherylene Lee

In 1968 when I was fifteen, the pit opened its secret to me. I breathed, ate, slept, dreamed about the La Brea[1] Tar Pits. I spent summer days working the archaeological dig[2] and in dreams saw the bones glistening, the broken pelvises, the skulls, the vertebrae looped like a woman's pearls hanging on an invisible cord. I welcomed those dreams. I wanted to know where the next skeleton was, identify it, record its position, discover whether it was whole or not. I wanted to know where to dig in the coarse, black, gooey sand. I lost myself there and found something else. 

1. *La Brea* (lə brā′ ə)
2. An *archaeological* (är′ kē ə loj′ i kəl) *dig* is a place where objects such as ancient bones are dug up for study.

Reading the Selection

SUMMARY

The narrator, a childhood star in television and on stage, discovers at age 15 that she no longer "has what it takes." When she can no longer get parts to perform, she discovers a new reality by working at the La Brea tar pits. She is attracted by this oily, messy place where she is accepted simply for her interest and willingness to work. It teaches her about the survival of the fittest and life in Hollywood.

Spanish Summaries, p. 11

A Active Reading Strategies

PREDICT Encourage students to think about the story title and the last line on this page. Considering the title and the narrator's statement, what do students think the story will be about?

VOCABULARY If you haven't previewed the selection vocabulary with students, stop and remind them to use context clues to unlock the meanings of new vocabulary words.

Additional Resources

Active Reading Guide, p. 11
Audio Library
Spanish Audio Library

Teaching Support

CONNECTING TO OTHER SELECTIONS

The chart at the right shows three ways to connect "Hollywood and the Pits" to other selections in this book.

For specific teaching strategies, see the ***Theme Two Planning Guide.***

Connection	Title
Life Skills: Lifelong Learning	→ "Bums in the Attic," p. 329
Thematic: Growing Up	→ "The Teacher Who Changed My Life," p. 368
Literary: Irony	→ "Names/Nombres," p. 5

Cultural Note

Explain to students that, since 1911, Hollywood has been the center of the film industry in the United States. Then ask them to suggest what the narrator means by "a place where dreams and nightmares can often take the same shape." *(Anything can happen in the movies.)*

B Active Reading Strategies

RESPOND Invite students to put themselves in the narrator's place. How do they think she feels as she passes the other girls? *(She must feel disappointed about not getting work and envious of the others who are working.)*

C Literary Elements

FLASHBACK Help students see how learning about the narrator's past helps them understand the changes she is experiencing in the present. *(She was always the one to be chosen at auditions and interviews and now she is never chosen.)*

D Literary Elements

CHARACTER Have students tell what they have learned about the main character at this point. *(She is Asian American, has grown up in Hollywood, and has been a successful child actor. At age fifteen, she feels she is disappointing her mother because she can no longer get parts.)*

Hollywood and the Pits

My mother thought something was wrong with me. Was it good for a teenager to be fascinated by death? Especially animal death in the Pleistocene?[3] Was it normal to be so obsessed by a sticky brown hole in the ground in the center of Los Angeles? I don't know if it was normal or not, but it seemed perfectly logical to me. After all, I grew up in Hollywood, a place where dreams and nightmares can often take the same shape. What else would a child actor do?

"Thank you very much, dear. We'll be letting you know."

I knew what that meant. It meant I would never hear from them again. I didn't get the job. I heard that phrase a lot that year.

I walked out of the plush office, leaving behind the casting director, producer, director, writer, and whoever else came to listen to my reading for a semiregular role on a family sit-com.[4] The carpet made no sound when I opened and shut the door.

B I passed the other girls waiting in the reception room, each poring over her script. The mothers were waiting in a separate room, chattering about their daughters' latest commercials, interviews, callbacks, jobs. It sounded like every Oriental[5] kid in Hollywood was working except me.

C My mother used to have a lot to say in those waiting rooms. Ever since I was three, when I started at the Meglin Kiddie Dance Studio, I was dubbed "The Chinese Shirley Temple"—always the one to be picked at auditions and interviews, always the one to get the speaking lines, always called "the one-shot kid," because I could do my scenes in one take—even tight close-ups. My mother would only talk about me behind my back because she didn't want me to hear her brag, but I knew that she was proud. In a way I was proud too, though I never dared admit it. I didn't want to be called a show-off. But I didn't exactly know what I did to be proud of either. I only knew that at fifteen I was now being passed over at all these interviews when before I would be chosen.

D My mother looked at my face hopefully when I came into the room. I gave her a quick shake of the head. She looked bewildered. I felt bad for my mother then. How could I explain it to her? I didn't understand it myself. We left saying polite good-byes to all the other mothers.

We didn't say anything until the studio parking lot, where we had to search for our old blue Chevy among rows and rows of parked cars baking in the Hollywood heat.

"How did it go? Did you read clearly? Did you tell them you're available?"

"I don't think they care if I'm available or not, Ma."

"Didn't you read well? Did you remember to look up so they could see your eyes? Did they ask you if you could play the piano? Did you tell them you could learn?"

3. *Pleistocene* (plīs′ tə sēn′) is the name of the period that began about two million years ago, when glaciers covered much of North America and Europe.
4. *Sit-com* is short for "situation comedy," the most common type of TV comedy series.
5. People of eastern Asia and their descendants are sometimes referred to as being *Oriental,* which means "of the East."

Vocabulary
obsessed (əb sesd′) *adj.* overly concentrated or focused on a single emotion or idea
bewildered (bi wil′ dərd) *adj.* very confused

Teaching Support

Meeting Individual Needs: ENGLISH LANGUAGE LEARNERS

Little Princess Explain that Shirley Temple was a world-famous child movie star during the 1930s. Her singing, dancing, curly hair, and dimples captured the hearts of millions of fans. Like Cherylene, Shirley Temple did not have a major movie career as an adult. She became a California politician, an ambassador, and a cancer-research spokesperson.

Activity Having students compare photos of Shirley Temple to the photos of Cherylene on page 120 will give them a better understanding of the author's reference, as will watching all or part of a Shirley Temple movie.

Additional Resources

English Language Learners Sourcebook, pp. 29–30

The barrage of questions stopped when we finally spotted our car. I didn't answer her. My mother asked about the piano because I lost out in an audition once to a Chinese girl who already knew how to play.

My mother took off the towel that shielded the steering wheel from the heat. "You're getting to be such a big girl," she said, starting the car in neutral. "But don't worry, there's always next time. You have what it takes. That's special." She put the car into forward and we drove through a parking lot that had an endless number of identical cars all facing the same direction. We drove back home in silence.

F E *In the La Brea Tar Pits many of the excavated bones belong to juvenile mammals. Thousands of years ago thirty young animals in the area were drawn to watering holes, not knowing they were traps. Those inviting pools had false bottoms made of sticky tar, which immobilized its victims and preserved their bones when they died. Innocence trapped by ignorance. The tar pits record that well.*

I suppose a lot of my getting into show business in the first place was a matter of luck—being in the right place at the right time. My sister, seven years older than me, was a member of the Meglin Kiddie Dance Studio long before I started lessons. Once during the annual recital held at the Shrine Auditorium, she was spotted by a Hollywood agent who handled only Oriental performers. The agent sent my sister out for a role in the CBS *Playhouse 90* television show *The Family Nobody Wanted.* The producer said she was too tall for the part. But true to my mother's training of always having a positive reply, my sister said to the producer, "But I have a younger sister . . ." which started my show-biz career at the tender age of three.

G My sister and I were lucky. We enjoyed singing and dancing, we were natural hams, and our parents never discouraged us. In fact they were our biggest fans. My mother chauffeured us to all our dance lessons, lessons we begged to take. She drove us to interviews, took us to studios, went on location with us, drilled us on our lines, made sure we kept up our schoolwork and didn't sass back the tutors hired by studios to teach us for three hours a day. She never complained about being a stage mother. She said that we made her proud.

My father must have felt pride too, because he paid for a choreographer[6] to put together our sister act: "The World Famous Lee Sisters," fifteen minutes of song and dance, real vaudeville stuff. We joked about that a

6. A *choreographer* creates or directs dance movements.

Vocabulary

barrage (bə räzh′) *n.* a heavy concentration or great outpouring, as of words
excavated (eks′ kə vāt′ əd) *adj.* uncovered or removed by digging; unearthed
immobilize (i mō′ bə līz′) *v.* to make unable to move; fix in place

E Literary Elements

SYMBOL Students should note how the description of the tar pits connects to or is symbolic of Cherylene's life. *(It is easy to innocently assume that something that is attractive is good when in fact it may have negative effects. Cherylene is a successful actor who is trapped by her success.)*

F Literary Elements

POINT OF VIEW Have students compare and state the point of view of the italicized passage and of the rest of the writing. *(The italicized passage has an unknown narrator—it seems like a passage from an encyclopedia or science book. In the rest of the text, the narrator is the main character, Cherylene Lee.)*

G Critical Thinking

INFERRING Ask students why they think Cherylene's mother is dedicated. Do they think she has motives other than just being helpful? *(Students may think she simply wants to support her daughters. Some may suggest that she is very proud and that her daughters' success also makes her feel better about herself.)*

Writing Minilesson

Compare and Contrast Writing a short compare-and-contrast paragraph can help students understand and evaluate the different bits of information they receive when reading a story.

Activity Review the information the narrator has provided about herself. Have each student write a short paragraph about a personal experience at a younger age and how that experience compares with his or her interests now. Review some important compare-and-contrast words, such as *same as, different from, although, still, then,* and *now.* **L2**

Additional Resources

Writer's Choice, Lesson 5.3

VIEWING THE PHOTOS

The photographs can give the viewer insights into the characters that are not included in the writing. Ask students to discuss how these photographs help them understand Cherylene better.

Responding to the Photos *Both photographs show Cherylene with famous entertainers. In the top photo, she is dancing with Gene Kelly. The lower photo gives a real sense of the differences in age and size between Cherylene and her sister.*

H Critical Thinking

EVALUATING Ask students to think about the long, difficult hours that Cherylene and her sister work. Encourage them to consider how the Lee sisters' lives are different from those of most children. *(Students might question whether it was fair for Cherylene and her sister to work so hard at such young ages. They live in a hotel and may not have a lot of friends their age or time to play.)*

I Active Reading Strategies

PREDICT Have students read the last paragraph on this page and then predict what they think might happen when the girls grow. *(Some students may say that when Cherylene grows she will no longer be as cute as she was at seven. She may lose her audience appeal.)*

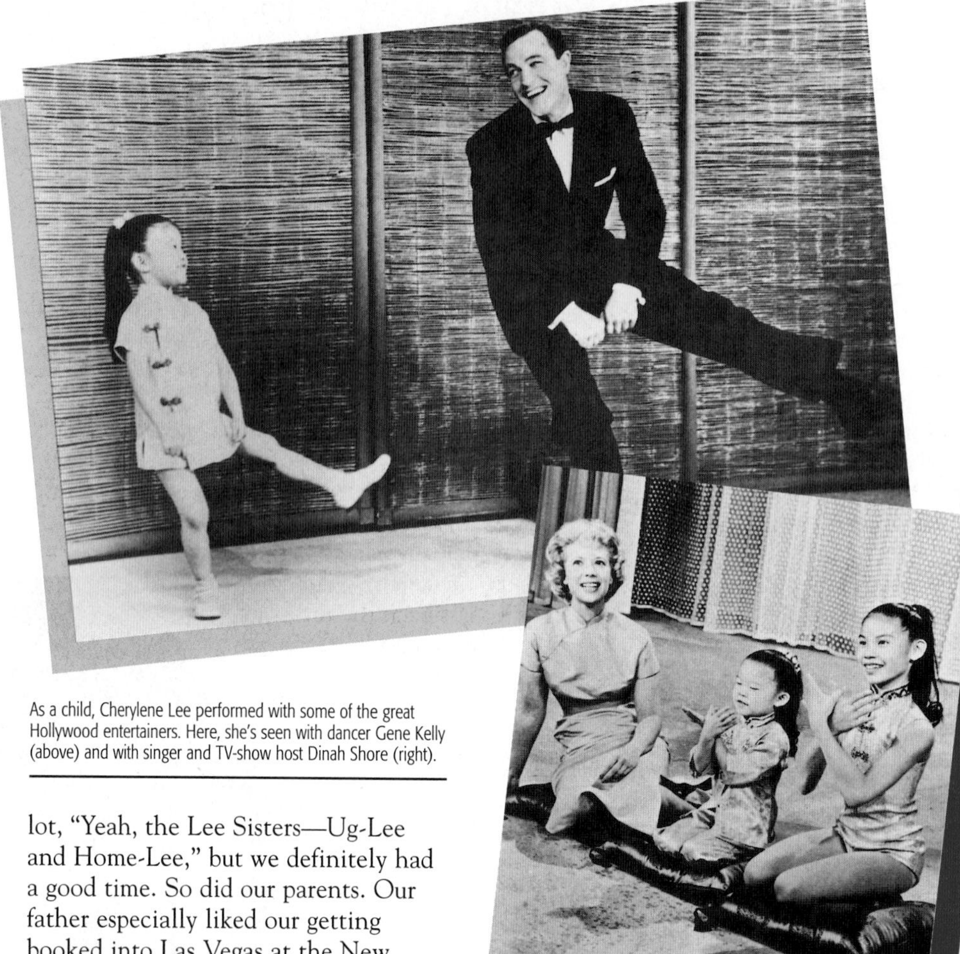

As a child, Cherylene Lee performed with some of the great Hollywood entertainers. Here, she's seen with dancer Gene Kelly (above) and with singer and TV-show host Dinah Shore (right).

lot, "Yeah, the Lee Sisters—Ug-Lee and Home-Lee," but we definitely had a good time. So did our parents. Our father especially liked our getting booked into Las Vegas at the New Frontier Hotel on the Strip. He liked to gamble there, though he said the craps tables in that hotel were "cold," not like the casinos in downtown Las Vegas, where all the "hot" action took place.

In Las Vegas our sister act was part of a show called "Oriental Holiday." The show was about a Hollywood producer going to the Far East, finding undiscovered talent, and bringing it back to the U.S. We did two shows a night in the main showroom, one at eight and one at twelve, and on weekends a third show at two in the morning. It ran the entire summer often to standing-room-only audiences—a thousand people a show.

Our sister act worked because of the age and height difference. My sister then was fourteen and nearly five foot two; I was seven and very small for my age—people thought we were cute. We had song-and-dance routines to old tunes like

Teaching Support

MEETING INDIVIDUAL NEEDS: ADVANCED LEARNERS

Old-Time Variety Shows *Vaudeville* is a term for a type of entertainment popular in the United States from the 1890s through the 1930s. Shows consisted of acts that included comedians, dancers, jugglers, and singers. The narrator and her sister worked in a later tradition—the TV variety shows and Hollywood musicals of the 1950s.

Activity Have partners research common vaudeville or variety show techniques. Ask them to prepare short vaudeville comedy acts, including stage names and costumes. Then have pairs perform their skits for the class. **L3** COLLAB. LEARN.

"Ma, He's Making Eyes at Me," "Together," and "I'm Following You," and my father hired a writer to adapt the lyrics to "I Enjoy Being a Girl," which came out "We Enjoy Being Chinese." We also told corny jokes, but the Las Vegas audience seemed to enjoy it. Here we were, two kids, staying up late and jumping around, and getting paid besides. To me the applause sometimes sounded like static, sometimes like distant waves. It always amazed me when people applauded. The owner of the hotel liked us so much, he invited us back to perform in shows for three summers in a row. That was before I grew too tall and the sister act didn't seem so cute anymore.

Many of the skeletons in the tar pits are found incomplete—particularly the skeletons of the young, which have only soft cartilage connecting the bones. In life the soft tissue allows for growth, but in death it dissolves quickly. Thus the skeletons of young animals are more apt to be scattered, especially the vertebrae protecting the spinal cord. In the tar pits, the central ends of many vertebrae are found unconnected to any skeleton. Such bone fragments are shaped like valentines, disks that are slightly lobed—heart-shaped shields that have lost their connection to what they were meant to protect.

I never felt my mother pushed me to do something I didn't want to do. But I always knew if something I did pleased her. She was generous with her praise, and I was sensitive when she withheld it. I didn't like to disappoint her.

I took to performing easily, and since I had started out so young, making movies or doing shows didn't feel like anything special. It was part of my childhood—like going to the dentist one morning or going to school the next. I didn't wonder if I wanted a particular role or wanted to be in a show or how I would feel if I didn't get in. Until I was fifteen, it never occurred to me that one day I wouldn't get parts or that I might not "have what it takes."

When I was younger, I got a lot of roles because I was so small for my age. When I was nine years old, I could pass for five or six. I was really short. I was always teased about it when I was in elementary school, but I didn't mind because my height got me movie jobs. I could read and memorize lines that actual five-year-olds couldn't. My mother told people she made me sleep in a drawer so I wouldn't grow any bigger.

But when I turned fifteen, it was as if my body, which hadn't grown for so many years, suddenly made up for lost time. I grew five inches in seven months. My mother was amazed. Even I couldn't get used to it. I kept knocking into things, my clothes didn't fit right, I felt awkward and clumsy when I moved. Dumb things that I had gotten away with, like paying children's prices at the movies instead of junior admission, I couldn't do anymore. I wasn't a shrimp or a small fry any longer. I was suddenly normal.

Before that summer my mother had always claimed she wanted me to be normal. She didn't want me to become spoiled by the attention I received when I was working at the studios. I still had chores to do at home, went to public school when I wasn't working, was punished severely when I behaved badly. She didn't want me to feel I was different just because I was in the movies. When I was eight, I was interviewed by a reporter who wanted to know if I thought I had a big head.

J Literary Elements

FIGURES OF SPEECH Draw students' attention to how Lee compares the applause to static and distant waves. Remind them that this is called a *simile,* a comparison using the words *like* or *as*. Encourage students to find other examples of similes in this story or to make up their own. Discuss the effects of such aesthetic language on the listener, such as presenting an unusual or memorable image of a common object or idea.

K Literary Elements

SYMBOL Discuss how the description of scattered young skeletons and disconnected bone fragments relates to Cherylene's story. *(The image presents a picture of the young as vulnerable and unprotected.)*

L Active Reading Strategies

CONNECT Ask students if they have ever felt clumsy and uncomfortable with the way they look. Ask them to think of examples of things they did when they were younger but can no longer get away with. *(Students might say they can no longer pay children's prices at certain events, go on children's rides at a fair, or be excused from certain activities and responsibilities because they are too young.)*

Reading Minilesson

Identifying Author's Purpose

Understanding why the author included the italicized sections in this piece can help students understand it as a whole.

Activity Work with students to make a list of questions that can help determine Lee's reasons for including the italicized paragraph on page 121. For example:

Q. Why is the author telling me about the La Brea Tar Pits? *A. She wants me to compare the Tar Pits to the life of a child star.*

Q. How is the information on the skeletons similar to the information about Hollywood? *A. In both cases, young creatures are tempted to places that are traps.* **L2**

Additional Resources

Reading Skills Practice Workbook

M Critical Thinking

EVALUATING Ask students to state whether they think Cherylene's mother is completely accurate when she tells the reporter "I don't do that—I'm not that way." *(Some students may think that she is "that way"; others may point out that she seems to be very emotionally involved in the situation and just wants the best for her daughters.)*

N Literary Elements

SYMBOL Discuss how the image of the churning tar pits relates to or is symbolic of the confusion Cherylene is experiencing about her life. *(The tar pits create a situation in which the normal order of things is skewed. This is how Cherylene feels as she faces rejection where she once had success.)*

Vo•cab•u•lar•y Skills

Sound-Letter Cues As students come across an unfamiliar word, invite them to try sounding it out. They may recognize the spoken word. Suggest that they look at the letter or group of letters at the beginning, middle, and end of each word. What is the beginning syllable? Does the middle or end of the word contain words that students already know? Students can ask themselves these questions and then try pronouncing the whole word. If they have trouble, suggest that they look up the pronunciation in their dictionary or their textbook's glossary.

Teaching Support

Hollywood and the Pits

"Sure," I said.

"No you don't," my mother interrupted, which was really unusual, because she generally never said anything. She wanted me to speak for myself.

I didn't understand the question. My sister had always made fun of my head. She said my body was too tiny for the weight—I looked like a walking Tootsie Pop. I thought the reporter was making the same observation.

"She better not get that way," my mother said fiercely. "She's not any different from anyone else. She's just lucky and small for her age."

M The reporter turned to my mother, "Some parents push their children to act. The kids feel like they're used."

"I don't do that—I'm not that way," my mother told the reporter.

But when she was sitting silently in all those waiting rooms while I was being turned down for one job after another, I could almost feel her wanting to shout, "Use her. Use her. What is wrong with her? Doesn't she have it anymore?" I didn't know what I had had that I didn't seem to have anymore. My mother had told the reporter that I was like everyone else. But when my life was like everyone else's, why was she disappointed?

N *The churning action of the La Brea Tar Pits makes interpreting the record of past events extremely difficult. The usual order of deposition—the oldest on the bottom, the youngest on the top—loses all meaning when some of the oldest fossils can be brought to the surface by the movement of natural gas. One must look for an undisturbed spot, a place untouched by the action of underground springs or natural gas or human interference. Complete skeletons become important, because they indicate areas of least disturbance. But such spots of calm are rare. Whole blocks of the tar pit can become displaced, making false sequences of the past, skewing the interpretation[7] for what is the true order of nature.*

That year before my sixteenth birthday, my mother seemed to spend a lot of time looking through my old scrapbooks, staring at all the eight-by-ten glossies of the shows that I had done. In the summer we visited with my grandmother often, since I wasn't working and had lots of free time. I would go out to the garden to read or sunbathe, but I could hear my mother and grandmother talking.

"She was so cute back then. She worked with Gene Kelly when she was five years old. She was so smart for her age. I don't know what's wrong with her."

"She's fifteen."

"She's too young to be an ingenue[8] and too old to be cute. The studios forget so quickly. By the time she's old enough to play an ingenue, they won't remember her."

"Does she have to work in the movies? Hand me the scissors."

My grandmother was making false eyelashes using the hair from her hairbrush. When she was young she had incredible hair. I saw an old photograph of her when it flowed beyond her waist like a cascading black waterfall. At seventy, her hair was still black as night, which made her few strands of silver look like shooting stars. But her hair had thinned greatly with age. It sometimes fell out in clumps.

7. *Skewing* (skū′ ing) *the interpretation* is twisting it so that it is wrong or off the mark.
8. An *ingenue* (än′ jə nōō′) is an actress who plays innocent, inexperienced young women.

Interdisciplinary Connection

Science Scientists learn a great deal about the natural history of an area by carefully digging up and preserving animal and plant fossils. In a typical archaeological site, the deeper one digs, the older the fossils will be.

Activity There are names for the geologic eras spanning millions of years of Earth's history. Ask students to work in pairs or small groups to research information about geologic eras and to create timelines that show their names and dates. They may wish to list each era's distinct life forms and climate. Ask students to list any additional, unanswered questions they raised in the course of their research that they might explore at a later date. **L2** COLLAB. LEARN.

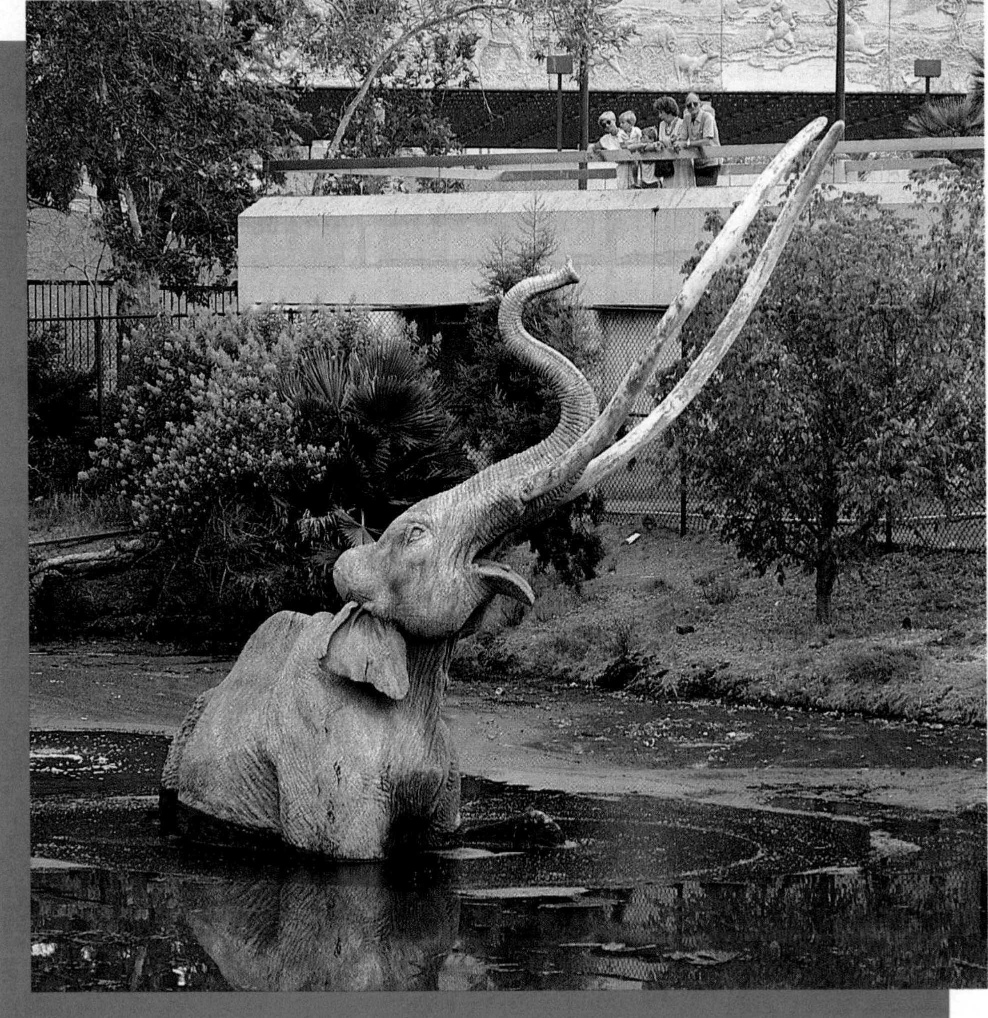

Oil seeping up through the earth's surface evaporated, leaving soft tar that trapped Ice Age animals in the area now called the La Brea Tar Pits.

She wore it brushed back in a bun with a hairpiece for added fullness. My grandmother had always been proud of her hair, but once she started making false eyelashes from it, she wasn't proud of the way it looked anymore. She said she was proud of it now because it made her useful.

It was painstaking work—tying knots into strands of hair, then tying them together to form feathery little crescents.

Vocabulary
painstaking (pānz′ tā′ king) *adj.* requiring close, careful labor or attention

The La Brea Tar Pits
This site lies within an area designated as Hancock Park in Los Angeles, California. These pits are an important archaeological site for information about the Pleistocene epoch.

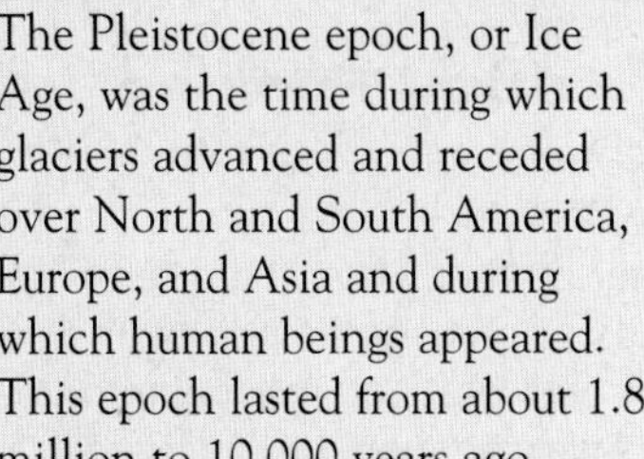

Historical Note

The Pleistocene epoch, or Ice Age, was the time during which glaciers advanced and receded over North and South America, Europe, and Asia and during which human beings appeared. This epoch lasted from about 1.8 million to 10,000 years ago.

Active Reading Strategies

RESPOND Discuss how Cherylene's grandmother changes her reasons for feeling proud of her hair. *(At one time she was proud of the way it looked; now she is proud because it makes her feel useful.)* Ask students how this kind of change relates to Cherylene. *(Cherylene once succeeded because of her looks; now she must make herself useful.)*

MEETING INDIVIDUAL NEEDS: MULTIPLE MODES OF EXPRESSION

Spatial Some students may benefit from creating a sketch that illustrates the sequence of an elephant's sinking into the tar. Their classmates may gain a better understanding of the process by looking carefully at these drawings.

Activity Have students make six drawings that show the elephant in the photograph approaching, stepping into, sinking, and disappearing into the tar. When students have finished their drawings, have them share them with the class or display them on posters. **L2**

P Active Reading Strategies

EVALUATE Work with students to evaluate the grandmother's intent in telling the narrator that her hair is too young to make false eyelashes. Do they think the grandmother meant to frustrate her even more? *(Students will probably realize that the grandmother is trying to point out that even though the narrator's entertainment career is ending, she is still very young. Her life is just beginning.)*

Q Critical Thinking

INFERRING Ask students to state how Cherylene feels as she listens to her mother. Have them tell what words or phrases helped them infer their answers. You may wish to use the following model to guide students in the process of inferring.

Model: I've read that Cherylene is very confused about the changes going on in her life. I think Cherylene is uncomfortable listening to her mother talk about how cute she once was. The words *going on and on* make me think that Cherylene has heard enough about this topic.

R Literary Elements

CHARACTER Have students compare the mother's and the grandmother's reactions to the changes taking place in Cherylene's life. *(The grandmother seems to be accepting the changes, while the mother is unable to do so.)*

Teaching Support

Hollywood and the Pits

Her glamorous false eyelashes were much sought after. Theatrical make-up artists waited months for her work. But my grandmother said what she liked was that she was doing something, making a contribution, and besides it didn't cost her anything. No overhead. "Till I go bald," she often joked.

She tried to teach me her art that summer, but for some reason strands of my hair wouldn't stay tied in knots.

"Too springy," my grandmother said. "Your hair is still too young." And because I was frustrated[9] then, frustrated with everything about my life, she added, "You have to wait until your hair falls out, like mine. Something to look forward to, eh?" She had laughed and patted my hand.

My mother was going on and on about my lack of work, what might be wrong, that something she couldn't quite put her finger on. I heard my grandmother reply, but I didn't catch it all: "Movies are just make-believe, not real life. Like what I make with my hair that falls out—false. False eyelashes. Not meant to last."

The remains in the La Brea Tar Pits are mostly of carnivorous animals. Very few herbivores are found—the

9. To be *frustrated* is to be kept from doing something or achieving some goal.

MEETING INDIVIDUAL NEEDS — SPECIAL NEEDS

Less-Proficient Readers Write *carnivore* and *herbivore* on the board. Explain that the ending *-vore* comes from a Latin word that means "to devour or eat," *carni-* from a Latin word that means "flesh or meat," and *herbi-* from a Latin word that means "a flowering plant."

Activity Give students a list of word parts and definitions, such as *carne (meat)* and *vore (eat),* and a word bank. Have them create a chart matching the words with the word parts and their definitions. **L1**

Additional Resources

Inclusion Strategies

ratio is five to one, a perversion of the natural food chain. The ratio is easy to explain. Thousands of years ago a thirsty animal sought a drink from the pools of water only to find itself trapped by the bottom, gooey with subterranean[10] oil. A shriek of agony from the trapped victim drew flesh-eating predators, which were then trapped themselves by the very same ooze which provided the bait. The cycle repeated itself countless times. The number of victims grew, lured by the image of easy food, the deception of an easy kill. The animals piled on top of one another. For over ten thousand years the promise of the place drew animals of all sorts, mostly predators and scavengers—dire wolves, panthers, coyotes, vultures—all hungry for their chance. Most were sucked down against their will in those watering holes destined to be called the La Brea Tar Pits in a place to be named the City of Angels, home of Hollywood movie stars.

S

I spent a lot of time by myself that summer, wondering what it was that I didn't have anymore. Could I get it back? How could I if I didn't know what it was?

T

That's when I discovered the La Brea Tar Pits. Hidden behind the County Art Museum on trendy[11] Wilshire Boulevard, I found a job that didn't require me to be small or cute for my age. I didn't have to audition. No one said, "Thank you very much, we'll call you." Or if they did, they meant it. I volunteered my time one afternoon, and my fascination stuck—like tar on the bones of a saber-toothed tiger.

My mother didn't understand what had changed me. I didn't understand it myself. But I liked going to the La Brea Tar Pits. It meant I could get really messy and I was doing it with a purpose. I didn't feel awkward there. I could wear old stained pants. I could wear T-shirts with holes in them. I could wear disgustingly filthy sneakers and it was all perfectly justified. It wasn't a costume for a role in a film or a part in a TV sit-com. My mother didn't mind my dressing like that when she knew I was off to the pits. That was okay so long as I didn't track tar back into the house. I started going to the pits every day, and my mother wondered why. She couldn't believe I would rather be groveling[12] in tar than going on auditions or interviews.

U

While my mother wasn't proud of the La Brea Tar Pits (she didn't know or care what a fossil was), she didn't discourage me either. She drove me there, the same way she used to drive me to the studios.

"Wouldn't you rather be doing a show in Las Vegas than scrambling around in a pit?" she asked.

"I'm not in a show in Las Vegas, Ma. The Lee Sisters are retired." My older sister

10. *Carnivorous* (kär niv′ ər əs) animals eat meat; *herbivores* (hur′ bə vôrz′) eat mainly plants. So, the remains in the pits are a *perversion* because they give a false picture of reality. *Subterranean* means "underground."

11. *Trendy* describes what is currently popular, and Wilshire Boulevard is loaded with trendy shops, stores, and restaurants.

12. *Groveling* is lying or crawling facedown in a demeaning manner.

Vocabulary

predator (pred′ ə tər) *n.* an animal, such as a lion or hawk, that kills other animals for food
deception (di sep′ shən) *n.* that which fools or misleads
scavenger (skav′ in jər) *n.* an animal, such as a hyena or vulture, that feeds on dead, decaying animals

S Literary Elements

SYMBOL Discuss with students how this description symbolizes the dark side of the movie-making industry in Hollywood. Encourage them to see how both the tar pits and Hollywood have attracted many who were doomed to failure, "sucked down against their will."

T Active Reading Strategies

EVALUATE Ask students why they think Cherylene decides to work at the tar pits. *(The job does not require her to be small or cute, and she finds the pits very interesting.)*

U Critical Thinking

DRAWING CONCLUSIONS Although Cherylene's mother would prefer to have her go to auditions instead of the tar pits, she drives Cherylene to work every day. Discuss with students what her mother is telling Cherylene through her actions. *(Students may understand that Cherylene's mother is giving the same support and approval now that she gave when Cherylene was acting, even though she is not saying it aloud.)*

interNET CONNECTION

Music Students can search the Internet for sites connected with particular types of music in either of two ways. Using a subject directory, they can follow a path such as music > genres > a particular genre (such as classical, country, jazz, hip hop, pop/rock). Using a search engine, they can use the genre as a keyword.

Real-World Connection

Music of the Times Throughout the years, music has chronicled not only the changes occurring in the world but also the more personal changes that occur in people's lives. Initiate a discussion with students about songs that deal with the theme of change.

Activity Students can work in pairs or small groups and write songs about change in their own or other people's lives. The lyrics, or words, should tell a story. Encourage students to create their own melodies or, if necessary, use a melody all group members know. When each group has written a song and practiced it, invite the groups to perform for the class. **L2** COLLAB. LEARN.

Active Reading Strategies

EVALUATE Ask students which character, Cherylene or her mother, has the more realistic outlook on what is happening. Why? *(Cherylene does because she accepts the fact that her career in show business is over. Her mother is still hoping that somehow things will return to the way they had been.)*

Critical Thinking

DRAWING CONCLUSIONS Discuss with students how Cherylene's feelings about the changes in her life might be affected by what she is learning at the pits. *(She is gaining a mature perspective of time and gaining a better understanding of Hollywood.)*

Thematic Focus

Winds of Change Cherylene Lee faced a major change in her life when she was no longer chosen for acting, singing, or dancing parts.

FINE ART TRANSPARENCY 17

You may want to use ***Fine Art Transparency 17*** to enrich a discussion of how Cherylene Lee adjusts to the change in her life and uses it to grow.

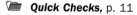

ASSESSMENT

Quick Checks, p. 11

Teaching Support

had married and was starting a family of her own.

"But if you could choose between . . ."

"There isn't a choice."

"You really like this tar-pit stuff, or are you just waiting until you can get real work in the movies?"

I didn't answer.

My mother sighed. "You could do it if you wanted, if you really wanted. You still have what it takes."

I didn't know about that. But then, I couldn't explain what drew me to the tar pits either. Maybe it was the bones, finding out what they were, which animal they belonged to, imagining how they got there, how they fell into the trap. I wondered about that a lot.

At the La Brea Tar Pits, everything dug out of the pit is saved—including the sticky sand that covered the bones through the ages. Each bucket of sand is washed, sieved, and examined for pollen grains, insect remains, any evidence of past life. Even the grain size is recorded—the percentage of silt to sand to gravel that reveals the history of deposition, erosion, and disturbance. No single fossil, no one observation, is significant enough to tell the entire story. All the evidence must be weighed before a semblance[13] *of truth emerges.*

The tar pits had its lessons. I was learning I had to work slowly, become observant, to concentrate. I learned about time in a way that I would never experience—not in hours, days, and months, but in thousands and thousands of years. I imagined what the past must have been like, envisioned Los Angeles as a sweeping basin, perhaps slightly colder and more humid, a time before people and studios arrived. The tar pits recorded a warming trend; the kinds of animals found there reflected the changing climate. The ones unadapted disappeared. No trace of their kind was found in the area. The ones adapted to warmer weather left a record of bones in the pit. Amid that collection of ancient skeletons, surrounded by evidence of death, I was finding a secret preserved over thousands and thousands of years. There was something cruel about natural selection and the survival of the fittest.[14] Even those successful individuals that "had what it took" for adaptation still wound up in the pits.

I never found out if I had what it took, not the way my mother meant. But I did adapt to the truth: I wasn't a Chinese Shirley Temple any longer, cute and short for my age. I had grown up. Maybe not on a Hollywood movie set, but in the La Brea Tar Pits.

13. A *semblance* of truth would be the slightest likeness of truth.

14. *[Natural . . . fittest]* refers to natural selection, the theory that the plants and animals best suited to their environment tend to survive and pass on their characteristics to their offspring.

Grammar and Language *Minilesson*

Intensifiers Write the following words on the chalkboard: *almost, extremely, just, nearly, practically, quite, rather, really, so, somewhat, too,* and *very*. Explain to students that these words are called *intensifiers,* adverbs that emphasize or intensify an adjective or another adverb.

Activity Write the following sentences on the board; then have students identify the intensifiers in each sentence.

1. I remember the child performer Cherylene Lee. *(none)*
2. She was very small and extremely cute. *(very; extremely)*
3. Cherylene and her sister were a rather successful act. *(rather)*
4. Cherylene became quite frustrated when she was too old to get parts. *(quite; too)* **L2**

Additional Resources

- ***Grammar and Language Transparency 11***
- ***Grammar and Language Workbook,*** pp. 129–130
- ***Grammar and Composition Handbook,*** Lesson 6.2
- ***Writer's Choice,*** Lesson 12.7

Active Reading and Critical Thinking

Responding to Literature

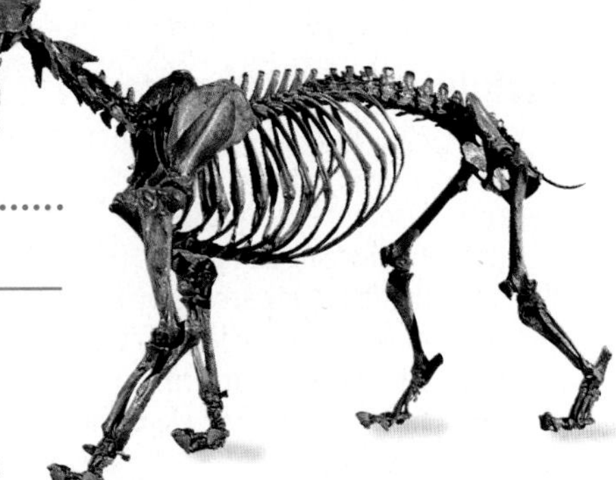

PERSONAL RESPONSE

- If you were the main character, would you have continued to pursue your career as a performer? Discuss your opinions with a partner.

Analyzing Literature

RECALL

1. Describe the narrator's career as a successful child star.
2. What begins to happen to the narrator's success after she turns fifteen?
3. What does the narrator do in the tar pits?
4. How does the narrator's mother react to her daughter's lack of jobs as she becomes a teenager and her newfound interest in the tar pits?

Brackets connect questions that are paired to develop higher-level thinking skills.

INTERPRET

5. In your opinion, why was "The World Famous Lee Sisters" act so successful?
6. In your opinion, how does the narrator feel about the slump in her Hollywood career?
7. In your opinion, why does the narrator find working in the tar pits so rewarding?
8. How does the narrator's relationship with her mother change over the course of the story?

EVALUATE AND CONNECT

9. Why is the story of the narrator's life interrupted from time to time with factual material about the tar pits? What connection do you think the author is making between Hollywood and the La Brea Tar Pits?
10. Theme Connection "Hollywood and the Pits" describes the changes in one person's life from childhood to adolescence. Does the story remind you about changes in your own life? Add these ideas to your journal entry from the **Reading Focus.**

LITERARY ELEMENTS

Symbol

A **symbol** is any object, person, place, or experience that stands for more than what it is. In "Hollywood and the Pits," the narrator uses the animals trapped in the La Brea Tar Pits to symbolize her experience as a child actor.

1. On page 119, find the statement "Innocence trapped by ignorance." How does this phrase help you understand Lee's use of symbolism in the story?
2. Find and explain another example of symbolism from a section of the selection printed in slanted, or italic, type.

- See **Literary Terms Handbook,** p. R11.

Responding to the Selection

PERSONAL RESPONSE

Most students will probably feel that Cherylene made the right choice to quit acting. Others may say that she should have persisted.

Analyzing Literature

1. At age three, she began working in television and on the stage, even in Las Vegas. She and her sister told jokes, sang, and danced.
2. She is no longer able to get acting parts.
3. She works to help recover and classify the animal bones that are found there.
4. She doesn't really understand how her daughter has changed and wants her to keep pursuing her acting career.
5. People thought they were very cute because of their age and height difference. They sang old, familiar songs and told corny jokes.
6. She seems to be confused. She wonders whether she can get back whatever she has lost; yet, she seems to be able to accept the change.
7. She doesn't have to worry about auditioning for the job, she can be as messy as she likes, and most importantly, she feels that the work has a real purpose.
8. In the beginning, they are close and share a purpose. When Cherylene begins to work at the tar pits, her mother drives her there but really wants Cherylene to stay in show business.
9. The information about the tar pits reflects what is happening to the narrator. The tar pits are a strong reminder that all living things must die and that Hollywood is insignificant compared to millions of years of time.
10. Students should identify aspects of change in their own lives and show how the story reminded them of these.

LITERARY ELEMENTS

1. She is pointing out how she was trapped in her acting career.
2. The passage on page 121 states that the heart-shaped bone fragments were disconnected from any skeleton. This image suggests that Hollywood can "tear the heart out" of a young, innocent person.

Additional Resources

Literary Elements Transparency 11

Extending Your Response

Writing About Literature

Students' explanations should

- state clearly whether the story's point of view was the most effective possible
- explain why they think this or another point of view would be the most effective

Personal Writing

Students' letters should

- reflect a clear understanding of the narrator's experience
- compare the narrator's experience with events from their own lives
- follow the format and tone of a friendly letter

Internet Connection Students can find more information on the La Brea Tar Pits and the Pleistocene Epoch on the Web by entering these words as search terms on a search engine.

Literature Groups Point out to students that they should use the text to create and answer the questions and that they should include answers for both Cherylene and her mother. COLLAB. LEARN.

Learning for Life Encourage students to choose animals about which they know little or nothing. Be sure that students write their news reports in an appropriate style.

Extending Your Response

Writing About Literature

Point of View Most fiction is written from one of two points of view. The events are described from the point of view of either a character in the story or an unknown, all-seeing narrator. In "Hollywood and the Pits," Cherylene Lee uses the point of view of her main character. The reader sees the events as the main character saw them. Do you think this was the most effective point of view to use for this story? Explain your opinion.

Personal Writing

Moving On Look back at your journal entry for the **Reading Focus** on page 116. Write a letter to Cherylene Lee, comparing the narrator's experience of becoming a teenager and abandoning her childhood interests with your own experience.

interNET CONNECTION

You can find out more about prehistoric animals at many sites on the World Wide Web. Just type *"prehistoric animals"* in the subject window of your browser or search engine. Don't forget the quotation marks. They help to narrow the number of choices.

Literature Groups

Follow-up Interview The narrator tells about being interviewed when she was in the movies at age eight. Imagine that the reporter has come back ten years later to interview the narrator, again in the presence of her mother. What questions might the reporter ask, and how might the narrator's responses differ from her mother's? Devise questions and answers using details from the story.

Learning for Life

News Broadcast Imagine that you are a science news reporter, and a complete skeleton of a prehistoric animal has just been discovered at the La Brea Tar Pits. First, research animals that have been found at the pits during the last ninety years. Then choose one animal, research its characteristics, and write a news story about the finding of its skeleton. Add illustrations to your story.

Reading Further

If you would like to read more about life as a child actor or about the La Brea Tar Pits, try these books:

Shirley Temple Black by James Haskins

Death Trap: The Story of the La Brea Tar Pits by Sharon Elaine Thompson

Save your work for your portfolio.

MEETING INDIVIDUAL NEEDS — SPECIAL NEEDS

Less-Proficient Readers Explain to students that every word has a history, called its etymology. Knowing something about the history of a word can help less-proficient readers better understand how the word is used today. Invite students to read the section on etymology in their dictionary. Then examine a few dictionary entries with students and help them to read the etymological information in each entry.

Activity Ask students to research the word orgins of the following words: *obsess, bewilder, barrage, excavate, immobilize, painstaking, predator, deception,* and *scavenger.* Encourage them to share interesting or surprising facts with the class. L1

Skill Minilessons

Reteach · Review

GRAMMAR AND LANGUAGE • ITALICS

Italic type is a special *slanted* type used to set off titles of books, plays, movies, CDs, magazines, newspapers, and other long works. Italic type is also used to call out a foreign word or a word used as a word. In handwritten work, underline the words you want read as italic.

PRACTICE Write each sentence, underlining for italics where needed.

1. I read an article about fossils in National Geographic.
2. My teacher said that I overused terrifying in my review of the movie Jurassic Park.
3. Ed learned that the book Dinosaur Defeat was made into a play called The End of Their World.
4. I can't believe that the Times misspelled the word riot as rot in this morning's headline.
5. I learned from the local newspaper, Our Town, about the future filming of a movie in our city.

● For more about using italics, see **Language Handbook,** pp. R39–R40.

READING AND THINKING • CAUSE AND EFFECT

A **cause** is a condition or event that makes something happen. What happens as the result of a cause is an **effect.** Many events in stories are connected by cause-and-effect relationships. In "Hollywood and the Pits," when the narrator's older sister is too tall for a part in a TV show, the narrator gets the part. This begins her acting career.

Cause
Older sister is too tall

Effect
Younger sister gets part

PRACTICE Answer these questions about other causes and effects in "Hollywood and the Pits."

1. What causes the narrator's mother to worry that her daughter is fascinated by death?
2. What is a possible cause of the narrator's lack of acting work?
3. What led prehistoric mammals to become trapped in the tar pits?
4. What effect did the screaming of trapped animals in the pits have on predators in the area?

● For more about cause and effect, see **Reading Handbook,** p. R89.

VOCABULARY • RELATED FORMS OF WORDS

If you know the meaning of *happy* (an adjective), you probably also know the meaning of *happiness* (a noun) and *happily* (an adverb). If you know the meaning of one form of a word, you can usually figure out the meanings of its other forms. For example, if you know that a *predator* hunts its food, you can figure out what *predatory* behavior is.

PRACTICE Use what you know about the vocabulary words in "Hollywood and the Pits" to write definitions of the underlined words below.

1. to have an obsession
2. the child's bewilderment
3. the car's immobilization
4. to work painstakingly
5. a deceptive statement

Skill Minilessons

GRAMMAR AND LANGUAGE
ITALICS

1. *National Geographic*
2. *terrifying; Jurassic Park*
3. *Dinosaur Defeat; The End of Their World*
4. *Times; riot; rot*
5. *Our Town*

READING AND THINKING
CAUSE AND EFFECT

1. The daughter begins spending every day at the tar pits where they study the skeletons of ancient dead animals.
2. She has grown and is no longer cute.
3. Predators came to drink and were trapped by the gooey, sticky tar and oil.
4. They came to feed on the trapped animals, only to become trapped themselves.

VOCABULARY
RELATED FORMS OF WORDS

1. something that draws a great deal of one's attention or focus
2. confusion
3. state of being unable to move
4. with great care and attention to detail
5. misleading

Additional Resources

- ***Grammar and Language Workbook,*** pp. 271–272
- ***Grammar and Composition Handbook,*** Lesson 13.6
- ***Writer's Choice,*** Lesson 20.6
- ***Reading Skills Practice Workbook***
- ***Vocabulary Practice,*** p. 8

ASSESSMENT

- ***Quick Checks,*** p. 11
- ***Selection and Theme Assessment,*** pp. 21–22
- ***Performance Assessment,*** p. 11
- ***Testmaker: ExamView Pro***
- ***Interactive Tutor: Self-Assessment***

Interdisciplinary Connection

Objective

- To practice reading skills in a content area—science

Teaching Strategies

Classifying Ask students to brainstorm a list of items that might be unearthed in an archaeological dig. Have them seperate items that would contain carbon-14 from items that would not. *(Any fossils containing matter that belonged to a living plant or animal would contain it.)*

Reading Informational Text Ask students to skim the selection to identify words that are particularly important for understanding a science passage. Write their suggestions on the board and ask volunteers to define each word, using a dictionary for help if necessary.

Then ask groups of students to examine a chapter or lesson in a science textbook to compile a list of words that are particularly important in that discipline.

Activity Students can begin their research on the Internet, using *state fossils* as keywords. They can continue research through conventional library resources. If your state lacks a state fossil or dinosaur, they may choose another state's fossil (about three fifths of the states have one) and report their results to the class.

Additional Resources

Interdisciplinary Activities, pp. 6–9

Teaching Support

Interdisciplinary Connection SCIENCE

Radiocarbon Dating

If you're a scientist who wants to know the age of a fossil you dug up, radiocarbon dating might help you. This type of dating tells us that the bone and plant fossils found in the La Brea Tar Pits range from 8,000 to 40,000 years old.

Only a small sample of a fossil, as little as a few grams, is needed for radiocarbon dating. Before dating the sample, a scientist cleans it by placing the sample in a jar filled with a chemical solution. Every tool the scientist uses to handle the fossil must also be clean and dry to prevent inaccurate results. Data about where the object was found can help confirm a dating.

Radiocarbon dating works by measuring the level of a radioactive form of carbon called carbon-14 inside a fossil. All living things contain carbon-14. Plants constantly absorb this element from the atmosphere. Human beings and other animals absorb it mainly through food provided by plants. Once an organism dies, however, it stops absorbing carbon-14. The carbon-14 remaining in its body begins to decay, or break down. Scientists know that carbon-14 decays at a particular rate, or speed. It takes 5,730 years for carbon-14 to reach what scientists call a half-life. By measuring the amount of carbon-14 left in an object, scientists can get an accurate idea of its age.

Radiocarbon dating doesn't work with every found object. Metal objects, such as ancient coins, tools, or weapons, were never alive, so scientists must use other methods to date them. Objects less than 50,000 years old qualify best for radiocarbon dating. That's pretty young for a fossil when you consider that scientists have uncovered the skeletal remains of sea animals that lived more than 500 million years ago!

ACTIVITY

Some states have an official state fossil or dinosaur. Find out which fossil or dinosaur, if any, represents your state. Locate a picture of the creature or its fossilized remains. During which time period was it alive? What do scientists know about it? Do research and share what you learned with your class.

If your state doesn't have an official state fossil, you might plan a campaign to have one adopted. Begin by finding out what fossils have been found in your state. Then choose the one you think would best represent the state.

MULTIPLE MODES OF EXPRESSION

Spatial A timeline can help students understand where the La Brea fossils fit into Earth's history.

Activity Have students work in small groups to create a prehistory timeline. Suggest that they begin 500 million years ago—the time of the fossilized sea creatures—and end 8,000 years ago—the last period "recorded" by the La Brea Tar Pits. Encourage students to make their time lines proportional. *(Time line: 5,370 years = half-life of carbon-14; 8,000 years ago = latest La Brea Tar Pit remains; 40,000 years ago = earliest tar pit remains; 50,000 years ago = outer limit of radiocarbon dating; and 500 million years ago = time when fossilized sea creatures lived)* **L2** COLLAB. LEARN.

MEDIA Connection

SONG

This song was written for the January 14, 1972, episode of the TV show *The Brady Bunch.* In the episode, the oldest brother, Greg, writes the song for the Brady Six to record after Peter's voice unexpectedly starts to change.

Time to Change

Words and Music by Raymond Bloodworth, Chris Welch, and Billy Meshel

Sha na na na na na na na na
Sha na na na na
Sha na na na na na na na na
Sha na na na na

Autumn turns to winter,
and then winter turns
to spring.
It's not just the seasons,
you know; it goes for
everything.
It's even true for voices as
boys begin to grow.
You gotta take a lesson
from Mother Nature,
and if you do you'll
know
When it's time to change,
then it's time to change.

Don't fight the tide, come
along for the ride.
Don't you see?
When it's time to change,
you've got to rearrange
Who you are into what
you're going to be.
Sha na na na . . . [repeat]

Day by day it's hard to see
the changes you've
been through.
A little bit of livin', a little
bit of growin' all adds
up to you.

Every boy's a man inside,
a girl's a woman too.
And if you want to reach
your destiny, here's
what you've got to do.
When it's time to change,
then it's time to change.
Don't fight the tide, come
along for the ride.
Don't you see?
When it's time to change,
you've got to rearrange
Who you are into what
you're going to be.

Sha na na na . . .
[repeat]

Analyzing Media

1. What does the song mean by "you've got to rearrange / Who you are into what you're going to be"? Explain in your own words.
2. Describe a time when you've had to rearrange yourself into "what you're going to be" or a time when you expect you'll need to.

Objective

- To read and understand song lyrics

Literature LINK

Growing Pains This song connects to "Growing Pains," the literature selection that immediately follows this lesson. Point out the connection by telling students that "Time to Change" could be giving advice to the narrator of "Growing Pains." The song offers a positive perspective on changes that take place in the course of growing up. The poem focuses on the mixed feelings people have about change.

Analyzing Media

1. Some students may say that the lyric means that we shouldn't be afraid of change. Others may say it means we need to be flexible and "go with the flow."
2. Responses may refer to school- or home-related situations in which students were called upon to face up to challenges or were confronted by something new.

Additional Resources

Media Connections p. 3

*in*TIME **magazine**

Teaching Support

Reading Minilesson

Varying Reading Rate Reading a poem or a song often requires readers to slow down enough to appreciate the rhythm and rhyme or even to sing the song aloud or in their heads. The "feel" of a song—the way that the music, rhythm, and rhyme interact—is often as important as, or even more important than, the actual words.

Activity Have small groups create rhythmic, dramatic readings of the song. Encourage them to take turns with different lines, clapping along to the rhythm or chanting the "Sha na na" chorus. Have each group perform its rendition; then discuss what the class enjoyed about each interpretation. **L2** COLLAB. LEARN.

Additional Resources

Reading Skills Practice Workbook

Brady Bunch Have students use a search engine to look for additional information about *The Brady Bunch*.

Responding to the Selection

PERSONAL RESPONSE

Many students will probably identify with the speaker, relating the poem to their own experiences. Some students may suggest ways to comfort the mother.

Analyzing Literature

1. The speaker is a young person, probably a girl, who is upset because she and her mother are fighting.
2. She cries and asks for understanding.
3. The title suggests that growing up can sometimes be painful.
4. She feels embarrassed about it, and watching her mother cry makes her feel uncomfortable.
5. No, because her mother apologizes, saying that she had had a very bad day.
6. The speaker has mixed feelings and seems very human. She is upset but understands that her mother's anger will pass. She hates to see her mother cry and does not want to have to take care of her.
7. No, the poem is written from the daughter's point of view. We hear the mother's side only through the daughter's words.
8. When people are hurt or upset, they are more likely to lose their tempers.
9. The speaker is probably twelve or thirteen. Her mother may suddenly confide in her because she is becoming a teenager and seems grown up.
10. Teenagers may not enjoy being expected to behave like adults. Even though they are growing up, they are not adults yet.

Active Reading and Critical Thinking

Responding to Literature

PERSONAL RESPONSE

◆ What went through your mind as you read this poem? What, if anything, would you have done differently?

Analyzing Literature

RECALL

1. Who is the **speaker** in the poem, and what is she feeling?
2. What does the main character do that she wishes her mother would not do?

Brackets connect questions that are paired to develop higher-level thinking skills.

INTERPRET

3. Why do you think the author chose "Growing Pains" as the title for this poem?
4. How do you think the speaker's feelings about her own crying in front of people affect how she feels about her mother's crying?

EVALUATE AND CONNECT

5. Does the speaker think she deserved to be "bawled out"? How can you tell?
6. How do the main character's feelings about her mother's behavior seem true to life? Support your opinion with examples.
7. Do you think the poet showed both sides of the conflict between the mother and the daughter? Why or why not?
8. What does the poem tell you is one common reason that people often lose their tempers?
9. Theme Connection About how old do you think the speaker might be? Why do you think her mother suddenly confides in her?
10. How does the poem express feelings about the new responsibilities that come with growing up?

LITERARY ELEMENTS

Mood

The emotional atmosphere, or feeling, of a story or poem is called the **mood**. Writers choose details to create a mood or feeling that brings a scene to life. Descriptive words, setting, dialogue, and characters' actions can all contribute to the mood of a piece of writing. In "Growing Pains," the poet uses such lines as, "It was horrible" and "I was glad to be by myself" to express the mood of the poem.

1. Reread "Growing Pains." How would you describe the mood of the poem?
2. Find two other examples of details that express the mood of the poem.
3. Compare the mood of the first two stanzas with the mood of the last stanza.

● See **Literary Terms Handbook**, p. R7.

LITERARY ELEMENTS

1. Some words to describe the mood of the poem are *tense, angry,* and *sad.*
2. Possible answers: "She went on and on until I began to cry" and "Dad had done something to hurt her."
3. The mood in the first two stanzas is self-assured and angry; in the last stanza it is one of sadness and confusion.

Additional Resources

Literary Elements Transparency 12

Extending Your Response

Writing About Literature

Appreciating Rhythm "Growing Pains" is an example of a poem that does not rhyme but that has a rhythm most easily grasped if you read the poem aloud. Working with a partner, read the poem aloud to each other, and then write about how the rhythm affects the listener or contributes to the effect of the poem.

Creative Writing

Expressing Yourself Return to your notes from the **Reading Focus** on page 132. Write a short poem telling about a time when you were angry or confused because someone had hurt your feelings. Use details that describe why you were angry or confused.

Performing

Words Set to Music Work with a small group to find instrumental music that evokes the mood of "Growing Pains." Then make a tape of the music to use as background during a group reading of the poem. Try various effects–for example, by grouping low and high voices or single and group voices.

Literature Groups

Problem Solving The speaker in the poem is having trouble communicating with her mother. Find examples from the poem that describe how the two characters are not getting along. Then work together to come up with a list of recommendations to help them better understand each other. Write a plan with suggestions for both characters, and share it with the class.

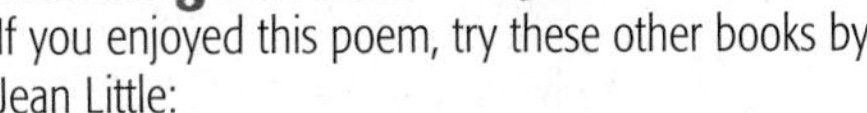

Reading Further

If you enjoyed this poem, try these other books by Jean Little:

Mama's Going to Buy You a Mockingbird

Little by Little: A Writer's Education

Save your work for your portfolio.

Skill Minilesson

Reteach · Review

READING AND THINKING • SEQUENCE OF EVENTS

Jean Little divided "Growing Pains" into four stanzas. The first three tell a story that is a sequence of events. The events appear in the order they happened. Paying attention to the sequence of events in a story or poem helps you better understand the piece of literature. How would "Growing Pains" be different if the poem began with the mother crying?

PRACTICE Reread "Growing Pains," paying special attention to the events that happen in each stanza. Then write one paragraph that explains the sequence of events in the poem.

- For more about sequencing, see **Reading Handbook,** p. R91.

Extending Your Response

Writing About Literature

Students' explanations should

- tell ways that the rhythm of the poem affects the listener
- explain how they think the poem's rhythm contributes to its meaning

Creative Writing

Students' poems should

- describe a time when they were angry because someone hurt their feelings
- include details that clearly show why they were angry or confused

Performing Encourage students to try several different pieces of music and choose the one that works best. When students perform, be sure that the music never obscures the spoken text.

Literature Groups Have students carefully reread the poem, looking for examples. Then encourage students to use their own experience to brainstorm recommendations. COLLAB. LEARN.

Skill Minilesson

READING AND THINKING

- **SEQUENCE OF EVENTS**

Possible answer:

A mother got mad at her daughter and bawled her out. Then the daughter left and went to her room. The mother went to the daughter's room and apologized and cried. This made the daughter uncomfortable. She was not an adult yet and didn't want to have to understand her mother or handle her sadness.

Additional Resources

Reading Skills Practice Workbook

ASSESSMENT

- ***Quick Checks,*** p. 12
- ***Selection and Theme Assessment,*** p. 23
- ***Performance Assessment,*** p. 12
- ***Testmaker: ExamView Pro***
- ***Interactive Tutor: Self-Assessment***

Objective

- To read and understand a magazine article

Literature LINK

Slam, Dunk, and Hook This magazine article connects to "Slam, Dunk, and Hook," the literature selection that immediately follows it. Point out the connection by telling students that women's basketball, the subject of the article, has reached new heights of success in the world of professional sports. The article focuses on the early excitement generated by the W.N.B.A. In "Slam, Dunk, and Hook," we see the game from a poet's point of view.

Analyzing Media

1. Students may mention the exciting pace of the game, the finesse and skill of the players, or the competition between teams.
2. For the first time in American history, there is a national women's basketball league. This represents a significant change in a male-dominated sport.

Additional Resources

Media Connections, p. 4

inTIME **magazine**

Teaching Support

MEDIA Connection

MAGAZINE ARTICLE

This article comes from the business section of a weekly newsmagazine. In your opinion, why did it appear in the business section?

from "The N.B.A.'s Sister Act"

by Steve Wulf—*Time*, August 4, 1997

An hour and a half before the tip-off last Wednesday, the doors of the Charlotte Coliseum swung open, and America came pouring in. Charlotte was about to play New York, and the excitement was as palpable as it would be before any game between the Hornets and the Knicks.

Except this was July, the teams were called the Sting and the Liberty, and the players that the fans were beseeching for autographs were not Ewing and Rice but Lobo and Bullett. One of the hottest items at the souvenir stands was a T-shirt that read

INVENTED BY MAN,
PERFECTED BY WOMAN.

"This is phenomenal," said a woman who drove 65 miles from South Carolina to bring her daughter to the game. "My daughter thinks I'm the best mama in the world." Following the laser lights and loud music required of every N.B.A. pregame show, the announcer thundered, "O.K., Charlotte, We Got Next!"

Welcome to the W.N.B.A., the Women's National Basketball Association, or the N.B.A.'s baby sister. On the court, the sneakers squeak with the same urgency as they do in the N.B.A., the coaches yell, "Why isn't that a foul?" at the refs, and the players get fined for roughhousing—though the $500 recently assessed Nancy Lieberman-Cline of the Phoenix Mercury for holding Jamila Wideman of the Los Angeles Sparks by the neck equals what Dennis Rodman spends in a year for eyeliner.

Backed by the N.B.A., the W.N.B.A. has exceeded all expectations midway through its two-month inaugural season, averaging 8,766 in attendance, and occasionally eclipsing Major League Soccer and P.G.A. golf in television ratings. W.N.B.A. games are televised nationally. Viewers watching the N.B.A. playoffs in June were besieged with the W.N.B.A. slogan, "We Got Next." The phrase is commonly used on playgrounds to reserve the next game, but in light of the early success of the league, it takes on a new meaning. "We are building a first-class operation that appeals to fans, players, television, corporate sponsors," says Val Ackerman, W.N.B.A.'s president. "Our dream is to become the fifth major league."

1. What do you think makes basketball such a popular sport?
2. How is the W.N.B.A. a sign of the "winds of change" during our time?

Reading Minilesson

Informational Text Remind students that the main purpose of most magazine articles is to inform. Ask students to summarize in one sentence what this article attempts to tell readers. Then discuss how the article differs from other types of informational materials—e.g., textbooks or encyclopedia articles.

Activity Have students work in groups to make a chart comparing two or more types of informational material. Display the completed charts for the class and discuss the advantages of each type. **L2**

Additional Resources

Reading Skills Practice Workbook

Before You Read

Slam, Dunk, & Hook

MEET YUSEF KOMUNYAKAA

The poet and educator Yusef Komunyakaa (ū' sef kō mun yä' kä) uses his Louisiana childhood and his time in Vietnam as an Army correspondent as resources for the material in his poetry. A winner of the Pulitzer Prize for Poetry in 1994, Komunyakaa writes poems on a wide variety of subjects, including jazz, racial prejudice, and war.

Yusef Komunyakaa was born in 1947. "Slam, Dunk, & Hook" was published in 1992 in a collection of his poetry called Magic City.

READING FOCUS

What do you like about sports? Which games do you prefer, and why?

QuickWrite

Make a quick list of your feelings about sports. Tell which games you love and which games you hate. Then explain your own role in sports: do you prefer to play or to watch? Which do you value more–fierce competition between teams or intense loyalty among team members? Describe your feelings.

Setting a Purpose

Read this poem to appreciate the speaker's love of basketball.

BUILDING BACKGROUND

Did You Know? Basketball was invented in 1891 by James Naismith, an instructor in physical education who lived in Springfield, Massachusetts. In need of an indoor game for the winter months, Naismith used a soccer ball and two peach baskets, one hung at each end of a gym. The rules Naismith made up for that game form the basis of today's game.

Before Reading

Objectives

- To read and analyze a poem about playing basketball
- To recognize and identify examples of alliteration in a poem and write a short poem using alliteration
- To write about sensory imagery

Skills

Reading/Thinking: Inferring
Writing: Short Poem
Grammar/Language: Vivid Verbs
Listening/Speaking: Debate; Dramatic Reading
Collaboration: Literature Groups; Listening and Speaking

Motivating → STUDENTS

Literature Launchers: "Playing Basketball"

Videodisc Side A, Segment 5

Also available in VHS.

Selection Focus Transparency 13: Have students look at the photos and discuss what they notice about the physical intensity of basketball.

Reading Focus: As an extension of the Reading Focus, encourage students to use precise language and sensory details to discuss how people have very different reactions to sports—there is no one right way to feel.

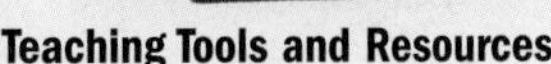

RESOURCE MANAGER

Teaching Tools and Resources
- Theme Two Planning Guide
- Literature Groups Sourcebook

Essential Lesson Support

Lesson-Specific Instruction
- Selection Focus Transparency 13
- Literary Elements Transparency 13
- Active Reading Guide,* p. 13
- TIME *inTIME* magazine, p. 26

Assessment
- Selection Quick Checks,* p. 13
- Sel. and Theme Assmt., p. 24
- Testmaker: ExamView Pro
- Performance Assessment, p. 13

Systematic Language Instruction
- Gr. & Comp. Hbk, L. 3.7

English Language Learners
- ELL Sourcebook, p. 32
- Spanish Summaries, p. 13
- Spanish Translations, pp. 44–45
- Audio Library*
- English, Yes!

Spec. Needs/Strat. Interven.
- Interactive Rdg. Sbk, pp. T80–T82
- Interactive Rdg. Wkbk, p. 24
- Inclusion Strat. Sbk, pp. 67–68
- Audio Library*

*Also available in Spanish

Reading the Selection

A Active Reading Strategies

PREDICT Have students read the first four lines of the poem and predict what the speaker's attitude toward basketball is. *(The speaker is a player who loves the sport.)*

Additional Resources

- ***Active Reading Guide,*** p. 13
- ***Audio Library***
- ***Spanish Audio Library***
- ***Spanish Summaries,*** p. 13

B Literary Elements

ALLITERATION Ask students to identify the sound device in lines 5 and 10. *(It is alliteration created by the repetition of the s sound.)*

C Critical Thinking

INFERRING What is the speaker saying about the power of the sport? *(Basketball can be used to impress young girls [lines 18–19], comfort someone [lines 24–26], and help kids stay out of trouble [lines 29–31].)*

D Active Reading Strategies

VISUALIZE Ask students to visualize a basketball game and imagine some sounds one could hear. *(One could hear whistles, squeaking tennis shoes, and a ball being dribbled.)*

Teaching Support

Slam, Dunk, & Hook

Yusef Komunyakaa

Fast breaks. Lay ups. With Mercury's°
Insignia on our sneakers,
We outmaneuvered the footwork
Of bad angels. Nothing but a hot
Swish of strings like silk
Ten feet out. In the roundhouse°
Labyrinth° our bodies
Created, we could almost
Last forever, poised in midair
Like storybook sea monsters.
A high note hung there
A long second. Off
The rim. We'd corkscrew
Up & dunk balls that exploded
The skullcap of hope & good
Intention. Bug-eyed, lanky,
All hands & feet . . . sprung rhythm.
We were metaphysical° when girls
Cheered on the sidelines.
Tangled up in a falling,
Muscles were a bright motor
Double-flashing to the metal hoop
Nailed to our oak.
When Sonny Boy's mama died
He played nonstop all day, so hard
Our backboard splintered.
Glistening with sweat, we jibed°
& rolled the ball off our
Fingertips. Trouble
Was there slapping a blackjack°
Against an open palm.
Dribble, drive to the inside, feint,°
& glide like a sparrow hawk.
Lay ups. Fast breaks.
We had moves we didn't know
We had. Our bodies spun
On swivels of bone & faith,
Through a lyric slipknot
Of joy, & we knew we were
Beautiful & dangerous.

1 In ancient Roman mythology, *Mercury* was the swift messenger of the gods. He was often portrayed wearing winged sandals.

6–7 *Roundhouse* is a slang term for a sweeping movement—in this case, wide, swinging arm movements. A *labyrinth* is any confusing, complicated arrangement.

18 Here, *metaphysical* means that the players seemed to go beyond the limits of the physical world.

27 To *jibe* is to be in harmony with one another.

30 A *blackjack* is a weighted, flexible, leather-covered weapon.

32 A *feint* is a movement intended to "fake out" an opponent.

MEETING INDIVIDUAL NEEDS — ENGLISH LANGUAGE LEARNERS

Basketball Slang English language learners may be familiar with the game but not with its American slang.

Activity Have English language learners work in small groups with English-proficient students. Ask a student from each group to read a few lines of "Slam, Dunk, and Hook." Then invite the group to paraphrase them. Model by reading aloud and paraphrasing lines 1–4: *We made fast breaks and lay ups. Our cool shoes made us feel as fast as the messenger of the gods. We played more skillfully than our super-powerful opponents.* Have volunteers identify and demonstrate some of the moves. COLLAB. LEARN.

Additional Resources

- ***English Language Learners Sourcebook,*** p. 32

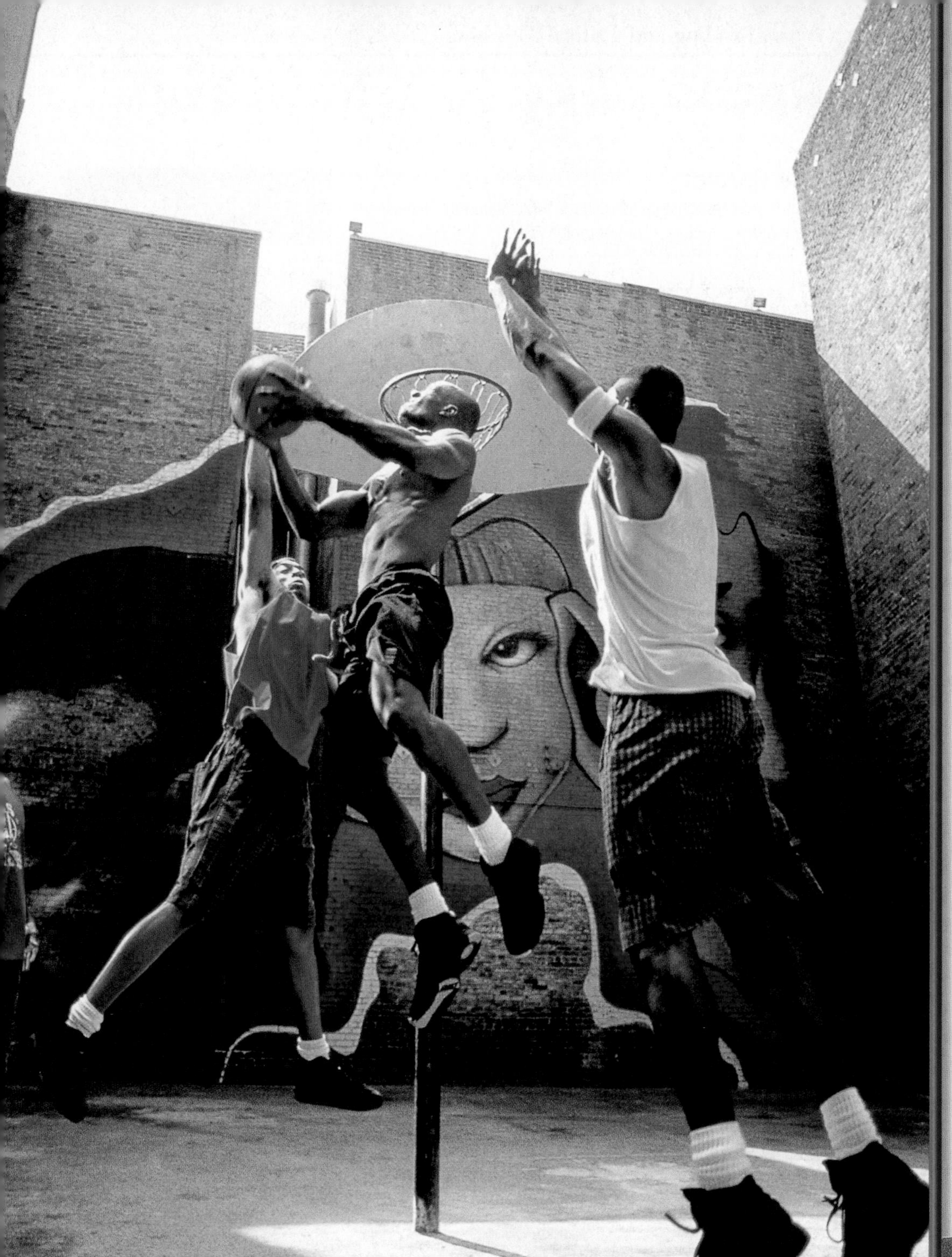

FYI

Michael Jordan dominated the National Basketball Association in scoring from 1987 to 1993 and led his team, the Chicago Bulls, to six NBA championships between 1991 and 1998. Jordan's career in basketball began slowly: he was cut from his tenth-grade junior varsity team. He worked hard to earn a spot on the team the following year and succeeded. His story is told through words, photographs, and statistics in the book *For the Love of the Game* written by Jordan himself.

At the MOVIES

- ***Hoosiers*** (1986, 115 min., PG) will appeal to basketball fans and to those who enjoy cheering for the underdog. This drama concerns a small-town high school basketball team and a coach trying to make a comeback. Preview the movie to decide whether it is appropriate for your students.

Reading Minilesson

Monitoring Comprehension This poem uses many sensory images to convey the fast-paced excitement of a basketball game and what it means to the players. Encourage students to be sure they understand these sensory images by comparing them with actual basketball terms they are familiar with.

Activity Have students work in small groups. Ask them to reread the poem in sections and prepare graphic organizers for comparing the sensory images from the poem to commonly used terms. **L2** COLLAB. LEARN.

Images from the Poem	Commonly Used Terms
the footwork of bad angels	the opposite team
roundhouse labyrinth	A complicated sweeping movement

Additional Resources

Reading Skills Practice Workbook

Responding to the Selection

PERSONAL RESPONSE

Some students will identify strongly with the poem, while others may not. Most should connect the rhythm and feeling of the poem to the fast-paced action of basketball. Students should explain their choice of lines.

Analyzing Literature

1. These terms include *fast breaks, lay ups, footwork, swish, ten feet out, roundhouse, off the rim, dunk, metal hoop, backboard, ball, dribble, drive to the inside, feint,* and *moves.*
2. People are playing basketball. They move quickly, running, jumping, and shooting the ball. A shot just misses off the rim, and someone dunks the ball. The narrator describes Sonny Boy, who played the whole day through when his mother died. The players keep going, sweating, making moves, and feeling joyful.
3. These are all basketball terms, and they convey the dramatic, fast pace of the poem.
4. They are strenuous and joyful, a way to connect with other people and a way to work off emotions.
5. Students should speak from their own experience and explain their responses.
6. The poem is presented, like a basketball game, in two halves. The language contains short words and phrases, which give the poem a very fast rhythm. It also shifts quickly, almost stopping and starting up again, the way basketball players move.
7. Students should describe a personal experience and explain how it reminds them of the poem.
8. The game connects the players to one another.
9. Students should understand that basketball is a fast-paced, strenuous, exciting sport that demands a lot of strength, stamina, and physical coordination. It is also a way for players to work together and connect with each other.
10. Through the game he becomes aware of his own strength, power, and beauty. Some students may say that sports have helped them become strong, learn to cooperate with others, and learn to keep going even when they are fatigued.

Active Reading and Critical Thinking

Responding to Literature

PERSONAL RESPONSE

- What is your response to this poem? Which line from the poem did you find most memorable? Why?

Analyzing Literature

RECALL

1. What are some of the terms in "Slam, Dunk, & Hook" that are directly related to the game of basketball? Make a list of terms.
2. Summarize the action in "Slam, Dunk, & Hook."

INTERPRET

3. Why is "Slam, Dunk, & Hook" a good title for this poem?
4. What message about team sports does "Slam, Dunk, & Hook" express?

EVALUATE AND CONNECT

5. According to "Slam, Dunk, & Hook," team sports are dramatic, emotional, and exhilarating. Do you agree or disagree? Explain.
6. How do the structure and the rhythm of the poem help to create the feel of an actual game of basketball? Explain.
7. Does this poem remind you of an experience of your own? Explain.
8. What is Komunyakaa saying about the connection between participation in basketball and friendship? Do you agree or disagree? Explain.
9. What did you learn about basketball, or about the attitude of the players, from reading this poem? Explain.
10. Theme Connection How do you think playing basketball might have changed the speaker of the poem? Has participation in sports or other activities changed you? How?

Brackets connect questions that are paired to develop higher-level thinking skills.

LITERARY ELEMENTS

Alliteration

Alliteration is the repetition of sounds, most often consonant sounds, at the beginnings of words. Writers often use alliteration in their poetry to enhance the sounds of the lines as a poem is read aloud. Consider the example of alliteration in these lines from "Slam, Dunk, & Hook":

Our bodies spun
On swivels of bone & faith

The words *bodies* and *bone* both begin with *b;* the words *spun* and *swivels* both begin with *s.*

1. Find another example of alliteration in this poem or in another poem in this book. Read the example aloud and point out the alliteration.
2. Write your own short poem or paragraph about a real or imaginary sports event. Use images to help your readers see, hear, and feel what you describe in your writing. Try to use alliteration appropriate to your subject.

• See **Literary Terms Handbook**, p. R1.

LITERARY ELEMENTS

1. Other examples of alliteration are *A high note hung there; Dribble, drive to the inside; We were metaphysical when girls/Cheered.*
2. Students' poems should describe a sports event, use clear, strong images, and contain examples of alliteration.

Additional Resources

Literary Elements Transparency 13

Extending Your Response

Writing About Literature

Sensory Imagery "Slam, Dunk, & Hook" is filled with **sensory imagery,** or words that appeal to our senses. Pick out your favorite image, and write a paragraph explaining why it is memorable.

Creative Writing

Sports: Up Close and Personal What do you like best about sports in general? What specific sport do you like best? Do you prefer to play or to watch? Review your response to the **Reading Focus** on page 137. Then write a short poem or a paragraph or two that describes your feelings about sports.

Literature Groups

Hooray for Sports! "Slam, Dunk, & Hook" strongly endorses participation in team sports. What about the win-at-all-costs attitude that sometimes comes with competition? Should amateur teams feel and act differently than professional teams? Debate the issue. Support your opinions with examples from the poem and from your own experience.

Listening and Speaking

Appreciating Poetry In small groups, choose the most dramatic and exhilarating images from the poem. One group member should read the lines aloud while the remaining members dramatize the scene. Share your dramatization with your classmates.

Reading Further

If you would like to read more poems about basketball or other sports, try these books:

Slam Dunk: Basketball Poems, compiled by Lillian Morrison

American Sports Poems, edited by R. R. Knudson and May Swenson

Jump Ball: Basketball A Basketball Season in Poems by Mel Glenn

Save your work for your portfolio.

Skill Minilesson

Reteach · Review

GRAMMAR AND LANGUAGE • VIVID VERBS

"Slam, Dunk, & Hook" is filled with colorful, **vivid verbs** that help readers visualize the quick action taking place on the basketball court. For example, think about this description:

"We'd corkscrew
Up & dunk balls that exploded"

The vivid verbs help you visualize the scene. The image is much more effective than just saying, "We'd jump up and throw balls that went into the basket." A **thesaurus,** a book of synonyms, can help you find vivid verbs.

PRACTICE Reread the poem. As you do, pick out some of the vivid verbs that helped you visualize the images in the poem. Keep a list of vivid verbs in your journal, and add verbs to the list as you find them in your reading.

- For more about verbs, see **Language Handbook,** p. R33.

Extending Your Response

Writing About Literature

Students' paragraphs should
- describe an image from the poem
- explain why it is memorable

Creative Writing

Students' writing should
- describe their feelings about all sports and their favorites
- focus on whether they prefer to play or watch

Literature Groups Have students prepare for the debate by making notes about their own experiences and those of people they know. COLLAB. LEARN.

Listening and Speaking

Have students rehearse a scene several times, working to create an effective dramatization.

Skill Minilesson

GRAMMAR AND LANGUAGE
- **VIVID VERBS**

Examples of vivid verbs from the poem include *outmaneuvered, poised, hung, corkscrew, exploded, cheered, tangled, double-flashing, nailed, splintered, jibed, rolled, slapping, dribble, drive, feint, glide,* and *spun.*

Additional Resources

- ***Grammar and Language Workbook,*** pp. 73–74
- ***Grammar and Composition Handbook,*** Lesson 3.1
- ***Writer's Choice,*** Lesson 10.1

ASSESSMENT

- ***Quick Checks,*** p. 13
- ***Selection and Theme Assessment,*** p. 24
- ***Performance Assessment,*** p. 13
- ***Testmaker: ExamView Pro***
- ***Interactive Tutor: Self-Assessment***

Objective

- To understand the elements of prose fiction
- to distinguish the major forms of prose fiction: novel, novella, short story

Teaching Strategies

Ask each student to think of his or her favorite childhood story. Prompt a discussion about what the stories were, whether they were told or read to them, and what students liked about them.

Setting Since most students are familiar with Hollywood through the movies, ask them to call out the first word that comes to mind when they hear the word *Hollywood*. Create a word collage of student responses on the board. Explain that these ideas, images, and perceptions could all be included in the setting of a story about Hollywood.

Characters Ask students to use their imaginations to come up with a list of characters for a work of fiction about Hollywood. These could be movie stars or other people they would expect to find in Hollywood. Encourage a discussion about how we often learn something unexpected about human nature through fiction.

Teaching Support

FICTION

Fiction—writing about imaginary people and events—can be divided into three types, based on length. You can read a **short story** in a single session lasting between several minutes to an hour or two. A **novel** (usually well over a hundred pages) might take you several days or a few weeks to get through. A **novella** is longer than a short story but shorter than a novel. Some novellas and most novels feature more characters, plot developments, and settings than would be included in a short story.

Novels, novellas, and short stories all share the elements described below. The models demonstrate those elements in the short story "Hollywood and the Pits."

Stages in Plot Development

The main character is a teenage girl who has worked as a child actor but now is interested only in her work on an archaeological dig at the La Brea Tar Pits. Her mother doesn't understand her new interest.

1 **EXPOSITION** is background information about characters and setting. It sets the scene for the conflict.

ELEMENTS OF PROSE FICTION

	MODEL: "Hollywood and the Pits"
SETTING is the time and place of the story's action. Setting also includes the customs, values, and beliefs of a place or a time. A short story or novella usually has a limited setting. A novel is likely to stretch across different locations and a long period of time.	"Hollywood and the Pits" opens in Los Angeles in 1968 and, in **flashbacks,** moves through the 1950s and 1960s.
CHARACTERS are the actors in the story. They can be people, animals, robots, or whatever the writer chooses. The main character is called the **protagonist.** A short story or novella usually has a single protagonist. A novel may include more than one.	The characters include the two Lee sisters, their mother, and various unnamed minor characters. The younger Lee sister is the protagonist.

MEETING INDIVIDUAL NEEDS: ENGLISH LANGUAGE LEARNERS

Multicultural Stories Storytelling is a wonderful way to expose all students to the richness of other cultures.

Activity Ask each English language learner to prepare to tell a folktale or a legend that is popular in his or her native culture and involves an interesting protagonist. Create a storytelling atmosphere by having students sit in small circles to tell one another their stories. Make sure students give their stories titles. Have them join different story circles during the week. At the end of the week, you may wish to play a game of charades. Write the story titles on slips of paper and have students pick one to act out for classmates to guess.

Additional Resources

English Language Learners Sourcebook, p. 33

3 CLIMAX is the point of highest interest, conflict, or suspense in the story.
4 FALLING ACTION shows what happens to the character after the climax.
As the main character grows up, demand for her at the Hollywood studios declines. No longer a novelty, she's become an average, awkward teenager. She grows discouraged, but her mother keeps taking her to auditions.
In the summer of 1968, she works on a dig at the La Brea Tar Pits and decides to give up show business.
The main character's mother is disappointed by her decision. Although she doesn't understand it, she accepts it and drives her daughter to the tar pits rather than to auditions.
Working in the tar pits, the main character realizes the cruelty of what happened there. She sees the pits as a symbol of what happens to many performers who are used and then discarded by the Hollywood studios.
As young children, the main character and her older sister develop a song-and-dance act and become successful. The main character gets roles in Hollywood films because she is cute and can do her scenes in one take. Her mother encourages her career.
2 RISING ACTION develops the conflict.
5 RESOLUTION gives the final outcome.

PLOT is the basic structure of the story. It is a series of related events in which a problem is explored and then solved. Plot is created through **conflict**–a struggle between people, ideas, or forces.

> The conflict is between the younger Lee sister and her mother. The diagram on these pages shows how the plot develops.

POINT OF VIEW is the vantage point from which a story is told. The person telling the story is the **narrator.** In **first-person** point of view, the narrator is a character in the story. In **third-person** point of view, the narrator is someone outside the story. In some longer works of fiction, the author may use more than one narrator, telling a story from different points of view.

> "Hollywood and the Pits" is told from the first-person point of view. The narrator is the younger Lee sister. She is probably an adult looking back at herself between the ages of three and fifteen.

THEME is the main message that the reader can take from the story. A theme may be stated directly in the story or in its title. However, most stories have **implied** themes, suggested by what the characters learn or by what their experiences illustrate. Readers' ideas about implied themes may vary.

> The theme of "Hollywood and the Pits" is implied. A reader might state its theme this way: Hollywood can trap and destroy young performers just as the La Brea Tar Pits trapped many young animals.

Point of View Encourage a discussion of how students feel about the point of view in "Hollywood and the Pits." Ask if they can relate to the feelings the narrator expresses. Invite them to share their own points of view on the situation of child actors and parents who want their children to be stars.

Theme Explain to students that the writer has used italics to help her express the theme of the story. She interjects italicized information about the tar pits to give the reader deeper insight into how she is feeling about herself as a performer. Have students locate passages in italics and describe what the passages tell them about the theme.

Plot Students may associate plot with the action of the story. In this case, the plot works up to a climax over the conflicting ambitions of a mother and her daughter.

Forms of Fiction Ask students to name some fiction they have read and enjoyed or would like to read. Categorize the titles and their authors on the board as short stories or novels. Students may be uncertain about whether they have read or can name a novella. Point out that one novella they almost certainly know, if only from seeing one of its many adaptations for film or television, is Charles Dickens's *A Christmas Carol.* Some of Stephen King's longer stories are novellas.

Technology

Fiction Table

Students can use word-processing software to create a table of the five elements of fiction. Have each student open a new document and insert a six-column table with the headings shown below.

Title	Setting	Characters	Plot	Point of View	Theme

For each new work of fiction that students read, have them add a new row and complete the table with information about each of the work's five elements. Students can use their tables to review the various stories they read or to help them compare and contrast the various texts. **L2**

Active Reading Strategies

Objective

- To understand and apply strategies for reading and comprehending short stories

Teach the Strategies

Ask students to think of their favorite jokes. Encourage each of them to jot down a joke—preferably one with characters and a setting. Have students work in small groups to tell their jokes. Apply active reading strategies: Could students predict the outcome? Visualize the setting? Connect the joke to their own experience?

Predict

Remind students that a skillful reader pays attention to the details of a story when predicting its outcome. Writers often use "trivial" details to foreshadow greater events.

Visualize

Point out that visualizing can help students remember what they have read.

Review

Reviewing the sequence of events can sometimes interfere with a reader's pace, but it can help prevent confusion and frustration.

Teaching Support

ACTIVE READING MODEL

Active Reading Strategies

Tips for Reading Fiction

How do you approach reading fiction? You can begin by sorting out the basic elements: the characters, setting, plot, point of view, and theme. A short story or novella will usually have fewer characters than a novel–in some cases as few as one or two. Often a story will have a single setting. Since a short story is usually meant to be read in one sitting, the plot and theme usually revolve around how the characters respond to a single event. Looking for these elements and using the strategies below can help you read works of fiction with greater understanding.

- For more about reading strategies, see **Reading Handbook,** pp. R73–R102.

PREDICT

At certain points in your reading, take time to wonder what will happen next.

Ask Yourself . . .

- Can I tell from the title if this story is going to be humorous or dramatic?
- How will these characters respond to this development?
- How will the story end?

VISUALIZE

Keep the characters and the setting in your mind's eye as you read.

Ask Yourself . . .

- What does this character look like? Has the author given me hints or specific details?
- Have I ever seen a setting like this? Can I picture it?

REVIEW

If you are reading a novel, a novella, or a long short story, it might help to stop from time to time to review what you have found out so far.

Ask Yourself . . .

- Who are the main characters?
- How would I summarize the plot up to this point?

Reading Journal

Quirky Characters

Cynthia Rylant in "A Crush" tells the story of two unique, interesting characters. Invite students to describe physical features and personality traits of unusual characters they have read about.

Activity As they read, invite students to create two webs, one for Ernie and one for Dolores. Around each web have students record details about each character. After reading, have students review their webs and then write a brief epilogue to the story telling what the lives of Ernie and Dolores are like one, five, or ten years in the future. **L2**

CONNECT

As you read, keep trying to make connections. How does the work of fiction connect to your current life or to your past or future?

Ask Yourself . . .

- Does this character remind me of someone I know or another character I have read about?
- Have I ever felt like this character?
- Would I have responded in this way if this event had happened to me?

EVALUATE

As you read, form opinions about how the work is written and how you feel about the characters and their actions. Don't wait until the end to decide if you like it. Make judgments from the very beginning, but feel free to change your opinions as you read.

Ask Yourself . . .

- Has the author made this character believable?
- Has this story grabbed me? Do I want to find out what happens?
- Are these characters people I care about?

APPLYING THE STRATEGIES

Practice applying the strategies to the following short story, "A Crush." Use the Active Reading Model notes in the margins as you read. Write your responses on a separate piece of paper or use stick-on notes.

Connect

Remind students that most authors write in order to connect with their readers. As characters develop and the plot unfolds, the students should be aware of how they are feeling about a story and whether it is relevant to their lives. Challenge students to find something or someone in each story they read that makes them feel connected to the selection.

Evaluate

Encourage students to think of reading a work of fiction as making a new friend. There will be things they like and things they don't like. Aspects of the story may seem strange, exciting, dull, or even confusing. It is important for students to realize that their own opinions are important and will help determine the kinds of literature they may be drawn to later in their lives. Remind them that judging a work should enhance, not interfere with, the experience of reading.

MEETING INDIVIDUAL NEEDS: SPECIAL NEEDS

Less-Proficient Readers Previewing and reviewing important words and concepts can enhance less-proficient readers' comprehension of any reading selection. In addition, previewing provides an opportunity to learn new vocabulary in a meaningful context.

Activity Before students read a selection, ask them to copy a list of words you consider vital to understanding the selection. Invite them to sound out the unfamiliar words using their knowledge of sound-letter cues to see if they recognize the spoken word. Then have students look up the words in a dictionary. Encourage students to use each new word in a sentence. **L2**

Before Reading

Objectives

- To read and analyze a short story about a change in feelings
- To identify point of view in a short story
- To write a character description

Skills

Reading/Thinking: Activating Prior Knowledge; Drawing Conclusions; Inferring
Writing: Letter of Advice
Vocabulary: Suffix *-ly*
Grammar/Language: Capitalization; Adverb Clauses
Listening/Speaking: Role Playing a Conversation
Life Skills: Writing a Job Description
Collaboration: Literature Groups

Motivating STUDENTS

Selection Focus Transparency 14: Have students view and discuss the quote about love from Dr. Karl Menninger.

Reading Focus: As an extension of the Reading Focus, have pairs of students share their ways of meeting people and use precise language and sensory details to tell how new friends have changed them.

ACTIVE READING MODEL

Before You Read

A *Crush*

MEET CYNTHIA RYLANT

Cynthia Rylant (rī′ lənt) grew up poor in the Appalachian Mountains of West Virginia in a home without electricity or running water. In her early writings, she drew on this experience to describe ordinary characters in difficult situations. "I get a lot of personal gratification," says Rylant, "thinking of those people who don't get any attention in the world and making them really valuable in my fiction—making them absolutely shine with their beauty. . . . I want to deal with people who don't have what they want."

Cynthia Rylant was born in 1954. This story was first published in 1990.

READING FOCUS

Think about someone your age you wish you knew better. How could you let that person know you are interested?

List Ideas
List ways you might quietly let someone know you'd like to get to know him or her better.

Setting a Purpose
Read "A Crush" to discover how one person decides to show interest in another.

BUILDING BACKGROUND

The Time and Place It is the late 1900s in a small town in the United States.

VOCABULARY PREVIEW

excess (ek′ ses) *adj.* more than usual or necessary; p. 149
speculation (spek′ yə lā′ shən) *n.* the act of forming an opinion or conclusion based on guesswork; p. 150
taut (tôt) *adj.* stretched tight; p. 150
improbable (im prob′ ə bəl) *adj.* not likely; p. 151
illuminated (i lo͞o′ mə nāt id) *adj.* lit up; p. 152
venture (ven′ chər) *v.* to do something in spite of possible risk or danger; p. 152
eventually (i ven′ cho͞o ə lē) *adv.* in the end; finally; p. 153
intently (in tent′ lē) *adv.* in a firmly focused way; with concentration; p. 154
discreetly (dis krēt′ lē) *adv.* in a manner showing good judgment; cautiously; p. 155
hardy (här′ dē) *adj.* able to endure hardship; strong and healthy; p. 155

RESOURCE MANAGER

Teaching Tools and Resources
- Theme Two Planning Guide
- Literature Groups Sourcebook

Essential Lesson Support

Lesson-Specific Instruction
- Selection Focus Transparency 14
- Literary Elements Transparency 14
- Active Reading Guide,* p. 14
- Selection Vocabulary Practice, p. 9

Assessment
- Selection Quick Checks,* p. 14
- Sel. and Theme Assmt., pp. 25–26
- Testmaker: ExamView Pro
- Performance Assessment, p. 14

Systematic Language Instruction
- Gr. & Comp. Hbk, L. 3.8, 3.9
- Vocabulary Power, Lesson 7
- Spelling Power, Lesson 6

English Language Learners
- ELL Sourcebook, pp. 34–35
- Spanish Summaries, p. 14
- Audio Library*
- English, Yes!

Spec. Needs/Strat. Interven.
- Interactive Rdg. Sbk, pp. T82–T85
- Interactive Rdg. Wkbk, pp. 25–26
- Inclusion Strat. Sbk, pp. 29–30
- Audio Library*

*Also available in Spanish

A Crush

Cynthia Rylant

When the windows of Stan's Hardware started filling up with flowers, everyone in town knew something had happened. Excess flowers usually mean death, but since these were all real flowers bearing the aroma of nature instead of floral preservative,[1] and since they stood bunched in clear mason jars instead of impaled on styrofoam crosses, everyone knew nobody had died. So they all figured somebody had a crush and kept quiet.

ACTIVE READING MODEL

QUESTION What is the author telling us about the size of the town? [A]

1. *Floral preservative* is a chemical that helps cut flowers stay fresh looking.

Vocabulary
excess (ek′ ses) *adj.* more than usual or necessary

Reading the Selection

SUMMARY

Ernie is a shy, mentally disabled man who moves to a group home when his mother dies. Jack becomes his friend and teaches him to garden. Jack also begins taking Ernie to breakfast at a restaurant across the street from a hardware store. When Ernie sees Dolores, the tough manager of the store, he falls in love with her. He begins leaving flowers in front of the store before it opens. Although she doesn't find out who is giving her the flowers, they make her happy.

Spanish Summaries, p. 14

[A] Active Reading Strategies

QUESTION *(Students can infer that this is a small town. The phrase* everyone in town *is a clue that the town must be very small if everyone pays attention to the hardware store.)*

VOCABULARY If you haven't previewed the selection vocabulary with students, stop and remind them to use context clues to unlock the meanings of new vocabulary words.

Additional Resources

Active Reading Guide, p. 14
Audio Library
Spanish Audio Library

Teaching Support

CONNECTING TO OTHER SELECTIONS

The chart at the right shows three ways to connect "A Crush" to other selections in this book.

For specific teaching strategies, see the ***Theme Two Planning Guide.***

Connection		Title
Life Skills: Teaching and Mentoring	→	"The Scholarship Jacket," p. 451
Thematic: At the Crossroads	→	"The Boy and His Grandfather," p. 495
Literary: Plot	→	"Charles," p. 544

B Literary Elements

THIRD-PERSON POINT OF VIEW Ask students to evaluate the narrator's viewpoint. Who is telling the story? *(Students might suggest that the narrator is someone outside the story; that is, he or she is not a named character.)* Explain to students that this story is told from the third-person point of view. The words *he, she,* and *they* signal a third-person narrator.

C Active Reading Strategies

PREDICT *(Students may guess that the tattoo is an ordinary object, such as a rose, or an object that is unique and personal.)*

D Active Reading Strategies

VISUALIZE Ask students to describe their images aloud, or encourage them to draw sketches of Dolores's tattoo.

Cultural Note

Magical Coyotes Many Native American legends feature the coyote as a magical being. Some say that Coyote created the first humans out of feathers, mud, and straw. Others say he brought death because he knew that if everyone lived forever, we would run out of food. Many cultures told tales of Coyote bringing fire to people.

Teaching Support

ACTIVE READING MODEL

B

There wasn't really a Stan of Stan's Hardware. Dick Wilcox was the owner, and since he'd never liked his own name, he gave his store half the name of his childhood hero, Stan Laurel in the movies. Dick had been married for twenty-seven years. Once, his wife Helen had dropped a German chocolate cake on his head at a Lion's Club dance, so Dick and Helen were not likely candidates for the honest expression of the flowers in those clear mason jars lining the windows of Stan's Hardware, and speculation had to move on to Dolores.

Did You Know?
Stan Laurel was the thin man with the long face; Oliver Hardy was his not-so-thin partner. The popular comedy team of Laurel and Hardy made movies together from the late 1920s to 1951.

Dolores was the assistant manager at Stan's and had worked there for twenty years, since high school. She knew the store like a mother knows her baby, so Dick—who had trouble keeping up with things like prices and new brands of drywall compound[2]—tried to keep himself busy in the back and give Dolores the run of the floor. This worked fine because the carpenters and plumbers and painters in town trusted Dolores and took her advice to heart. They also liked her tattoo.

C **PREDICT** What do you think the tattoo might be?

Dolores was the only woman in town with a tattoo. On the days she went sleeveless, one could see it on the taut brown skin of her upper arm: "Howl at the Moon." The picture was of a baying coyote which must have been a dark gray in its early days but which had faded to the color of the spackling paste Dolores stocked in the third aisle. Nobody had gotten out of Dolores the true story behind the tattoo. Some of the men who came in liked to show off their own, and they'd roll up their sleeves or pull open their shirts, exhibiting bald eagles and rattlesnakes, and they'd try to coax out of Dolores the history of her coyote. All of the men had gotten their tattoos when they were in the service, drunk on weekend leave and full of the spitfire[3] of young soldiers. Dolores had never been in the service and she'd never seen weekend leave and there wasn't a tattoo parlor anywhere near. They couldn't figure why or where

D **VISUALIZE** Can you picture what this tattoo would look like?

2. *Drywall compound* and *spackling paste* (mentioned in the next paragraph) are used to prepare walls before painting.
3. When soldiers are off duty and allowed to go off base, they're on *leave.* When they're full of *spitfire,* they're quick-tempered and ready to fight.

Vocabulary
speculation (spek′ yə lā′ shən) *n.* the act of forming an opinion or conclusion based on guesswork
taut (tôt) *adj.* stretched tight

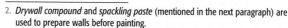

MEETING INDIVIDUAL NEEDS — ENGLISH LANGUAGE LEARNERS

Rites of Passage Point out to English language learners that getting a tattoo is a rite of passage to adulthood in some cultures. The combination of withstanding physical pain and making a permanent decision implies commitment. Brainstorm to develop a list of rites of passage common to the American culture: learning to drive, getting a job, and so on.

Activity Have students research and then make lists of rites of passage from their cultures. Do their communities still use these rituals? Do they follow some American traditions as well?

Additional Resources

English Language Learners Sourcebook, p. 34

any half-sober woman would have a howling coyote ground into the soft skin of her upper arm. But Dolores wasn't telling.

That the flowers in Stan's front window had anything to do with Dolores seemed completely improbable. As far as anyone knew, Dolores had never been in love nor had anyone ever been in love with her. Some believed it was the tattoo, of course, or the fine dark hair coating Dolores's upper lip which kept suitors away. Some felt it was because Dolores was just more of a man than most of the men in town, and fellows couldn't figure out how to court someone who knew more about the carburetor of a car or the back side of a washing machine than they did. Others thought Dolores simply didn't want love. This was a popular theory among the women in town who sold Avon and Mary Kay cosmetics. Whenever one of them ran into the hardware for a package of light bulbs or some batteries, she would mentally pluck every one of the black hairs above Dolores's lip. Then she'd wash that grease out of Dolores's hair, give her a good blunt cut, dress her in a decent silk-blend blouse with a nice Liz Claiborne skirt from the Sports line, and, finally, tone down that swarthy, longshoreman[4] look of Dolores's with a concealing beige foundation, some frosted peach lipstick, and a good gray liner for the eyes.

Dolores simply didn't want love, the Avon lady would think as she walked back to her car carrying her little bag of batteries. If she did, she'd fix herself up.

H The man who was in love with Dolores and who brought her zinnias and cornflowers and nasturtiums[5] and marigolds and asters and four-o'clocks in clear mason jars did not know any of this. He did not know that men showed Dolores their tattoos. He did not know that Dolores understood how to use and to sell a belt sander. He did not know that Dolores needed some concealing beige foundation so she could get someone to love her. The man who brought flowers to Dolores on Wednesdays when the hardware opened its doors at 7:00 A.M. didn't care who Dolores had ever been or what anyone had ever thought of her. He loved her and he wanted to bring her flowers.

Ernie had lived in this town all of his life and had never before met Dolores. He was thirty-three years old, and for thirty-one of those years he had lived at home with his mother in a small, dark house on the edge of town near Beckwith's Orchards. Ernie had been a beautiful baby, with

ACTIVE READING MODEL

EVALUATE E
Does Rylant do a good job of supplying you with enough details to picture the character of Dolores?

RESPOND F
Would you like to live in the same town with women like the Avon and Mary Kay ladies?

QUESTION G
How could someone be in love with Dolores and know so little about her?

4. A *swarthy longshoreman* is a dark or sunburned dockworker.
5. *nasturtiums* (nä stur′ shəms)

Vocabulary
improbable (im prob′ ə bəl) *adj.* not likely

E Active Reading Strategies

EVALUATE Ask students which of these details paints the most vivid picture of Dolores. *(Students might choose the description of her facial hair or her knowledge of machines.)*

F Active Reading Strategies

RESPOND *(Students might respond negatively because these ladies seem too judgmental and concerned with people's looks.)*

G Active Reading Strategies

QUESTION Encourage students to think about the nature of a crush when answering this question.

FYI

Bachelor's Button
The cornflower is also known as the bachelor's button. This is partly because rural bachelors used to carry this flower in their pockets. If it stayed fresh, it meant the girlfriend still cared. If it shriveled up, it meant "she loves me not."

H Literary Elements

THIRD-PERSON POINT OF VIEW Ask students to list some of the characters' thoughts revealed on this page by the narrator. *(People think Dolores hasn't had a suitor because of her tattoo or facial hair; the Avon lady believes Dolores doesn't want love; Ernie loves Dolores no matter what people think about her.)*

Reading *Minilesson*

Activating Prior Knowledge Readers often have to draw on knowledge from previous reading or from their own experience. For example, in order to understand the townspeople's perception of Dolores, readers need to be aware of common stereotypes concerning men and women.

Activity Draw the following chart on the board, and work with students to create a list of common male and female stereotypes. Discuss with students why Dolores, as the narrator describes her, does not match many of the ideas about women on your list. Finally, ask students how their own prior knowledge of male and female stereotypes helped them understand this part of the story. **L2**

Men	Women
have facial hair	wear makeup
work with their hands fixing and building things	are homemakers—caring for their homes and families
have tattoos	do not have tattoos

Additional Resources

 ***Reading Skills Practice Workbook***

A Crush

ACTIVE READING MODEL

CONNECT

I Do you know of any children or adults whose mental development happened this slowly?

REVIEW

J Who are the major characters you have met so far?

VISUALIZE

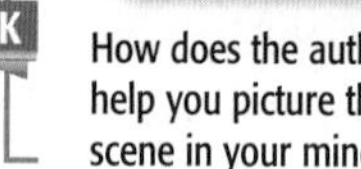

K How does the author help you picture this scene in your mind?

a shock of shining black hair and large blue eyes and a round, wise face. But as he had grown, it had become clearer and clearer that though he was indeed a perfectly beautiful child, his mind had not developed with the same perfection. Ernie would not be able to speak in sentences until he was six years old. He would not be able to count the apples in a bowl until he was eight. By the time he was ten, he could sing a simple song. At age twelve, he understood what a joke was. And when he was twenty, something he saw on television made him cry.

Ernie's mother kept him in the house with her because it was easier, so Ernie knew nothing of the world except this house. They lived, the two of them, in tiny dark rooms always illuminated by the glow of a television set, Ernie's bags of Oreos and Nutter Butters littering the floor, his baseball cards scattered across the sofa, his heavy winter coat thrown over the arm of a chair so he could wear it whenever he wanted, and his box of Burpee seed packages sitting in the middle of the kitchen table.

These Ernie cherished. The seeds had been delivered to his home by mistake. One day a woman wearing a brown uniform had pulled up in a brown truck, walked quickly to the front porch of Ernie's house, set a box down, and with a couple of toots of her horn, driven off again. Ernie had watched her through the curtains, and when she was gone, had ventured onto the porch and shyly, cautiously, picked up the box. His mother checked it when he carried it inside. The box didn't have their name on it but the brown truck was gone, so whatever was in the box was theirs to keep. Ernie pulled off the heavy tape, his fingers trembling, and found inside the box more little packages of seeds than he could count. He lifted them out, one by one, and examined the beautiful photographs of flowers on each. His mother was not interested, had returned to the television, but Ernie sat down at the kitchen table and quietly looked at each package for a long time, his fingers running across the slick paper and outlining the shapes of zinnias and cornflowers and nasturtiums and marigolds and asters and four-o'clocks, his eyes drawing up their colors. L

Vocabulary

illuminated (i loo′ mə nāt id) *adj.* lit up

venture (ven′ chər) *v.* to do something in spite of possible risk or danger

I Active Reading Strategies

CONNECT Encourage students to write in their journals about someone each knows who fits this description.

J Active Reading Strategies

REVIEW *(The major characters introduced so far are Dick Wilcox, Dolores, Ernie, and Ernie's mother.)*

K Active Reading Strategies

VISUALIZE *(Students may mention the author's use of descriptive details, such as Ernie watching through the curtains, shyly and cautiously picking up the box, and examining each little package of seeds.)*

L Critical Thinking

DRAWING CONCLUSIONS Ask students what they conclude about Ernie's mother. *(She provides no stimulus or encouragement for him to exercise his mind or his social skills.)*

Historical Note

W. Atlee Burpee & Co. is the world's largest mail-order seed company. It was founded in Pennsylvania more than one hundred years ago by eighteen-year-old W. Atlee Burpee, who borrowed $1,000 from his mother to start the business.

Teaching Support

MEETING INDIVIDUAL NEEDS

ADVANCED LEARNERS

Child Development Some students might be interested in doing further research on the stages of normal child development. This will help them better understand the description of Ernie's development on this page.

Activity Have students work in pairs to research the developmental stages that children typically go through as they mature. If possible, have them interview child psychologists, school counselors, or pediatricians to gather information. Ask each of them to make a chart showing abilities and the ages at which most children acquire them. Have them share their charts and their findings with the class. As an extension of the activity, suggest that students ask their parents at what ages they mastered various skills. **L3** COLLAB. LEARN.

152 THEME 2

Two months later Ernie's mother died. A neighbor found her at the mailbox beside the road. People from the county courthouse came out to get Ernie, and as they ushered him from the home he would never see again, he picked up the box of seed packages from his kitchen table and passed through the doorway.

Eventually Ernie was moved to a large white house near the main street of town. This house was called a group home, because in it lived a group of people who, like Ernie, could not live on their own. There were six of them. Each had his own room. When Ernie was shown the room that would be his, he put the box of Burpee seeds—which he had kept with him since his mother's death—on the little table beside the bed and then he sat down on the bed and cried.

Ernie cried every day for nearly a month. And then he stopped. He dried his tears and he learned how to bake refrigerator biscuits and how to dust mop and what to do if the indoor plants looked brown.

Ernie loved watering the indoor plants and it was this pleasure which finally drew him outside. One of the young men who worked at the group home—a college student named Jack—grew a large garden in the back of the house. It was full of tomato vines and the large yellow blossoms of healthy squash. During his first summer at the house, Ernie would stand at the kitchen window, watching Jack and sometimes a resident of the home move among the vegetables. Ernie was curious, but too afraid to go into the garden.

O Then one day when Ernie was watching through the window, he noticed that Jack was ripping open several slick little packages and emptying them into the ground. Ernie panicked and ran to his room. But the box of Burpee seeds was still there on his table, untouched. He grabbed it, slid it under his bed, then went back through the house and out into the garden as if he had done this every day of his life.

He stood beside Jack, watching him empty seed packages into the soft black soil, and as the packages were emptied, Ernie asked for them, holding out his hand, his eyes on the photographs of red radishes and purple eggplant. Jack handed the empty packages over with a smile and with that gesture became Ernie's first friend.

Jack tried to explain to Ernie that the seeds would grow into vegetables but Ernie could not believe this until he saw it come true. And when it did, he looked all the more

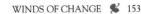

Vocabulary
eventually (i ven′ cho͞o ə lē) *adv.* in the end; finally

ACTIVE READING MODEL

PREDICT M
Do you think someone like Ernie could live alone?

PREDICT N
How long do you think it will take Ernie to go outdoors?

QUESTION P
Do you think Ernie usually talks much to Jack or the other people in the group home?

M Active Reading Strategies

PREDICT *(Students should recognize that Ernie could probably not live alone because he is mentally handicapped and has spent most of his life inside his mother's house.)*

N Active Reading Strategies

PREDICT *(Students might suggest that Ernie will go outside when he makes a connection between the garden and the pictures on his most prized possessions—the Burpee seeds.)*

O Critical Thinking

INFERRING Ask students what Ernie thinks when he first sees Jack ripping open seed packages. What good effect does this misunderstanding have? *(He thinks Jack has taken his flower seeds and is planting them. It gives him the courage to go out to the garden for the first time.)*

P Active Reading Strategies

QUESTION *(It seems that Ernie is extremely shy, probably because the only person he has talked to has been his mother. Also, the narrator tells us that Jack is Ernie's first friend.)*

Interdisciplinary Connection

Science Explain to students how seeds grow into vegetables and flowers. Tell them that a seed is the embryo of a plant and carries the genetic information it needs to grow into that kind of plant. The seed also contains the nutrients the plant needs to begin to grow. All the gardener must add is light, water, and soil.

Activity Have students plant seeds (indoors or out, depending on the time of year and climate). Suggest that they try growing different batches of seeds under different conditions: some with fertilizer and others without, some with six hours of light per day and others with twelve, and so on. Have them record which plants grow best under which conditions. L1

WINDS OF CHANGE 153

VIEWING THE PAINTING

Suggest that students take note not only of the diner but also the neighborhood around it as they study the painting.

Viewing Response *Students may suggest that young people or working-class people would probably be the customers at a diner like this.*

Q Active Reading Strategies

EVALUATE Encourage students to explain their opinions using examples from the story. *(Students might suggest that the use of transitional words and phrases, such as* Wednesday morning *and* the first time, *help readers follow the passage of time.)*

R Active Reading Strategies

CONNECT Explain to students that although going to breakfast might seem easy to them, it is very scary for Ernie. Encourage them to write about scary first experiences in their journals.

S Literary Elements

THIRD-PERSON POINT OF VIEW Discuss with students how and what readers learn about Jack's personality from the narrator. *(Because we learn Jack's thoughts from the narrator, we know that he is a kind and patient person. When Jack takes Ernie to breakfast, he leaves very early to avoid the crowds that frighten Ernie.)*

Teaching Support

Boulevard Diner–Worcester, MA, 1992. John Baeder. Oil on canvas, 30¼ x 48¼ in. O. K. Harris Works of Art, New York.

Viewing the painting: While Ernie was eating breakfast at the Big Boy restaurant, his life was changed. Whose life might be changed at the diner in this painting?

intently at the packages of zinnias and cornflowers and the rest hidden beneath his bed. He thought more deeply about them but he could not carry them to the garden. He could not let the garden have his seeds.

That was the first year in the large white house.

The second year, Ernie saw Dolores, and after that he thought of nothing else but her and of the photographs of flowers beneath his bed.

Jack had decided to take Ernie downtown for breakfast every Wednesday morning to ease him into the world outside that of the group home. They left very early, at 5:45 A.M., so there would be few people and almost no traffic to frighten Ernie and make him beg for his room. Jack and Ernie drove to the Big Boy restaurant which sat across the street from Stan's Hardware. There they ate eggs and bacon and French toast among those whose work demanded rising before the sun: bus drivers, policemen, nurses, mill workers. Their first time in the Big Boy, Ernie was too nervous to eat. The second time, he could eat but he couldn't look up. The third time, he not only ate everything on his

EVALUATE

Q Do you think the author has done a good job of showing the passage of time?

CONNECT

R Have you ever been really frightened to try a new experience?

Vocabulary

intently (in tent′ lē) *adv.* in a firmly focused way; with concentration

Listening and Speaking Minilesson

Role-Playing a Conversation Post these guidelines for role-playing:

- Discuss with your partner what the characters are like and what situation they are in.
- Be spontaneous. React as you think your character would react.
- Use facial expressions and gestures to reinforce what you say.

Activity Have students work with partners to role-play a conversation between Ernie and Jack the first time they go to breakfast together. Remind them that Ernie is shy, has a small vocabulary, and usually speaks slowly, while Jack is self-confident and friendly. After students practice, have them perform their conversations for the class. **L2** COLLAB. LEARN.

plate, but he lifted his head and he looked out the window of the Big Boy restaurant toward Stan's Hardware across the street. There he saw a dark-haired woman in jeans and a black T-shirt unlocking the front door of the building, and that was the moment Ernie started loving Dolores and thinking about giving up his seeds to the soft black soil of Jack's garden.

Love is such a mystery, and when it strikes the heart of one as mysterious as Ernie himself, it can hardly be spoken of. Ernie could not explain to Jack why he went directly to his room later that morning, pulled the box of Burpee seeds from under his bed, then grabbed Jack's hand in the kitchen and walked with him to the garden where Ernie had come to believe things would grow. Ernie handed the packets of seeds one by one to Jack, who stood in silent admiration of the lovely photographs before asking Ernie several times, "Are you sure you want to plant these?" Ernie was sure. It didn't take him very long, and when the seeds all lay under the moist black earth, Ernie carried his empty packages inside the house and spent the rest of the day spreading them across his bed in different arrangements.

That was in June. For the next several Wednesdays at 7:00 A.M. Ernie watched every movement of the dark-haired woman behind the lighted windows of Stan's Hardware. Jack watched Ernie watch Dolores, and discreetly said nothing.

When Ernie's flowers began growing in July, Ernie spent most of his time in the garden. He would watch the garden for hours, as if he expected it suddenly to move or to impress him with a quick trick. The fragile green stems of his flowers stood uncertainly in the soil, like baby colts on their first legs, but the young plants performed no magic for Ernie's eyes. They saved their shows for the middle of the night and next day surprised Ernie with tender small blooms in all the colors the photographs had promised.

The flowers grew fast and hardy, and one early Wednesday morning when they looked as big and bright as their pictures on the empty packages, Ernie pulled a glass canning jar off a dusty shelf in the basement of his house. He washed the jar, half filled it with water, then carried it to the garden where he placed in it one of every kind of flower he had grown. He met Jack at the car and rode off to the Big Boy with the jar of flowers held tight between his small hands. Jack told him it was a beautiful bouquet.

Vocabulary

discreetly (dis krēt′ lē) *adv.* in a manner showing good judgment; cautiously

hardy (här′ dē) *adj.* able to endure hardship; strong and healthy

ACTIVE READING MODEL

REVIEW [T] Go over in your mind what has happened so far in the story.

RESPOND [U] What would you like to ask the writer about this scene? Do you imagine that she knows someone like Ernie?

EVALUATE [V] Does Jack's behavior in the restaurant reflect what you know about him so far?

T Active Reading Strategies

REVIEW Encourage students to list not only events but also character descriptions. Prompt students with questions if they omit an important event or description.

U Active Reading Strategies

RESPOND *(Students might suggest that the author knows someone like Ernie because she captures his personality so well.)*

V Active Reading Strategies

EVALUATE You may wish to share the following model to guide students in the process of evaluating.

Model: From what I've read so far, I know that Jack seems to care about Ernie's well-being. He takes Ernie to breakfast once a week to help Ernie develop social skills. I think Jack knows Ernie has a crush on Dolores, but doesn't say anything because he has patience. He knows that Ernie does things carefully. That's why he doesn't say anything to Ernie about Dolores.

Real-World Connection

Love Stories Students might enjoy reading and discussing real-life stories about love. Have each student find a magazine or newspaper article about love. It can be about romantic love or about love of family, friends, pets, an activity, an idea, or a place.

Activity Have the class work in groups to discuss their articles. Students should answer such questions as *Who is the subject of the article? Who or what does this person love? What has he or she learned from this experience? How does the person describe his or her feelings?* After reading and discussing the articles, invite students to draw conclusions about love in real life. **L2** COLLAB. LEARN.

Objectives

- To create a simple spreadsheet
- To calculate averages using a spreadsheet
- To create a bar graph from spreadsheet data

Teaching Strategies

Demonstrate how to do some or all of the following spreadsheet tasks:

- edit column and row headings
- change column widths
- add and delete columns and rows
- enter data into cells
- create formulas using functions
- copy formulas across rows or down columns
- print a spreadsheet
- create bar, pie, and line graphs from spreadsheet data

Adapting to Available Technology

Many computers come with a spreadsheet program already installed. Some common spreadsheet programs are

- Microsoft Excel
- Lotus 1-2-3
- Quatro Pro
- AppleWorks

While there are minor differences between programs, they can all be used to perform complex calculations using formulas and functions. Data in these spreadsheets can easily be converted into graphs.

Teaching Support

Technology Skills

Spreadsheets: Creating a Spreadsheet

Accountants use spreadsheet software for budgets and other kinds of financial planning and record keeping. You can use one to help with your own financial planning and for other purposes. The terrific thing about electronic spreadsheets is that the mathematical work is all done by the computer.

When you open a new spreadsheet document, you'll see a worksheet and menus and toolbars similar to those on a word-processing document. Some of the icons, however, are found only on spreadsheet programs. Data is entered into small cells that make up rows and columns on the worksheet. A cell carries one piece of information. A column contains a category of data—for example, persons' names. A row contains a complete record for one person or thing. For example, a row might contain one person's name, address, job title, weekly salary, and other data.

	A	B	C
1	Gift List	Estimated Cost	Actual Cost
2	New CD	$ 15.00	$ 12.95
3	Mall gift certificate	$ 25.00	$ 25.00
4	Scarf	$ 25.00	$ 27.50
5	Book	$ 10.00	$ 12.50
6	Movie gift certificate	$ 20.00	$ 20.00
7			
8	Totals	$ 95.00	$ 97.95

This shows a simple example of a spreadsheet. After the data was typed in, the computer found the total (or sum) of the costs. With a spreadsheet, you can do even difficult calculations quickly and easily.

You can also convert spreadsheet data into various kinds of graphs. (Spreadsheet software programs usually refer to graphs as charts.) The example on page 161 shows a bar graph that compares the estimated costs of the gifts listed on the left with their actual costs.

Technology Tip

Be sure you check with your teacher or lab instructor about the spreadsheet program you are using. You may need to change these directions somewhat. In one popular spreadsheet program, for example, the formula for adding a group of cells uses two periods in place of a colon: =SUM(B2..B6).

Practice

1. Open your spreadsheet software.
2. Select **New** from the **File** menu. This will open a blank worksheet.
3. Without clicking, move your cursor over each item on the toolbars to get an idea of what functions are available. Use the program's Help if you want additional information about any of the tools.
4. Enter the gifts and estimated prices shown in the first spreadsheet example.
5. To get the computer to figure the sum, click in the cell where you want the sum to appear, but don't enter a figure into the cell.
6. Look at the top of your screen, and find the formula bar (look for an equal sign). Click on the = to begin the formula. An equal sign will appear in the space to the right of the formula bar. Without leaving any spaces, complete the

Meeting Individual Needs — MULTIPLE MODES OF EXPRESSION

Logical/Mathematical These learners may find the activities on page 161 relatively easy, whereas other students may find them more challenging.

Activity Have students work in groups whose members have various learning styles. Invite each student to identify something he or she is good at that might help the group complete the activities on page 161. Before the groups begin their tasks, have them discuss how each student's particular talent can contribute to the group's work. Invite groups to discuss this again about halfway through the assignment and then to evaluate their group's process after the assignment has been completed. **L2**

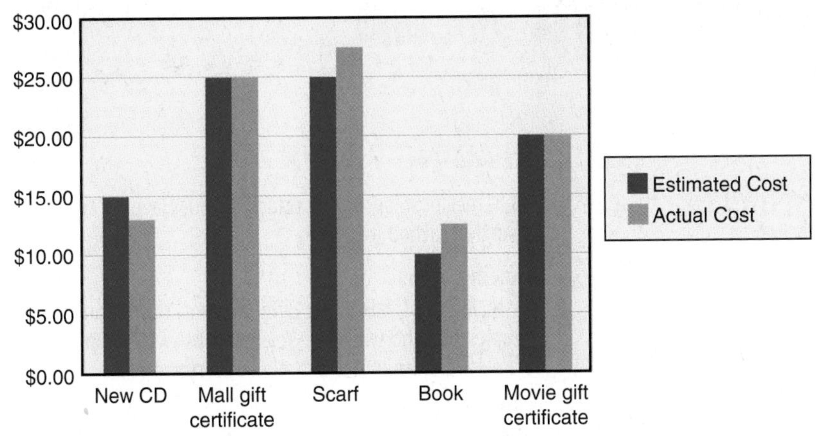

formula so that it looks like this: **=SUM(B2:B6)**. This tells the program that you want to add all the cells from B2 to B6. Hit the **Enter** key on your keyboard (the **Return** key on a Mac) when you finish your formula. The sum of the figures will appear in the highlighted cell.

ACTIVITIES

1. Working with a small group, find out how many hours per week each member spends: (a) studying for school and (b) watching television. Record the figures on a spreadsheet that looks something like this:

	A	B	C
1	**Student**	**Hours Studying**	**Hours Watching TV**
2	name		
3	name		
4	name		
5	name		
6			
7	**Averages**		

2. Have the spreadsheet figure the group's average time spent on studying for school and the average time spent watching television. The formula for computing an average is =SUM followed by the range of cells to be added, followed by a slash mark and the total number of students–for example, (B2:B5)/4.
3. Open a new worksheet. Add your data with the data of all the other groups in class. Have the computer calculate the class averages. Then make a bar graph to compare the averages for your class. Most programs will walk you through the steps in creating a chart. Use the Help feature if you need more help.

Activities

Invite students to identify questions and concerns they have as they read the directions for the three activities on this page. Encourage students to offer one another suggestions and answers to their questions.

Each group's first spreadsheet should

- properly list all the students in the group and the amount of time they study and watch TV per week.
- use formulas to calculate the group's average studying time and TV-watching time per week.

Each group's second spreadsheet should list and sum up each group's average times to find the average times for the class. Student bar graphs should accurately show the data from the group's second spreadsheet.

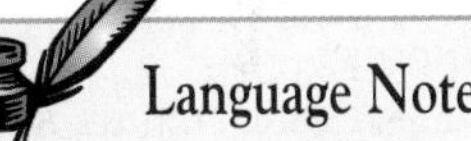

Language Note

Old and New Cells The English word *cell* was first used in the 1100s to mean a "small religious house." It came from the Latin word *cella*, meaning "small room." The word evolved over time to mean a "small compartment" or "bounded space." Invite students to explain how modern uses for the word *cell* still fit in with its original meaning. *(A prison cell is a small room; a cell in biology is a small organism bounded by a membrane; a cell in a spreadsheet is a small unit bounded by row and column edges.)*

REAL-WORLD CONNECTION

Budget Help Spreadsheets can be used to keep track of all kinds of financial information, including stock portfolios.

Activity Have each student use a set amount of imaginary money (say $50,000) to buy shares of several stocks and then use a spreadsheet to track the stocks' performance over several weeks. One column can be for the price paid, another for each day's closing price. They can find closing prices in newspapers and on many Internet sites. Encourage students to create formulas to calculate the profit or loss for each stock based on the day's closing price. Also have students calculate their percent profit or loss for each stock. Finally, let students calculate the total profit/loss and percent profit/loss for their portfolios. **L3**

Before Reading

Objectives

- To read and analyze a short story about trust between two brothers and a pet fox
- To understand and restate the plot of a short story
- To write a critical review

Skills

Reading/Thinking: Identifying Cause-Effect Relationships; Drawing Conclusions; Inferring; Logical Reasoning; Analyzing; Predicting; Sequencing
Writing: Another Point of View; Descriptive Details
Vocabulary: Roots
Grammar/Language: Commas and Conjunctions; Commas Used with Words in a Series
Listening/Speaking: Debate; Performing a Scene
Collaboration: Literature Groups

Motivating STUDENTS

Selection Focus Transparency 15: Have students view the transparency and answer the question provided.

Reading Focus: As an extension of the Reading Focus, have students use precise language and sensory details to discuss how differences of opinion can lead to tension in a family or among friends. Invite volunteers to recall a time when they have changed an opinion about something and what caused them to change.

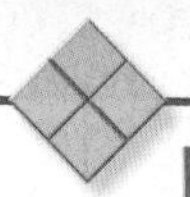

Before You Read

Last Cover

MEET PAUL ANNIXTER

Paul Annixter (a niks′ tər) is the pseudonym, or pen name, of Howard Sturtzel. Best known for his stories about nature and animal life, Sturtzel began writing at the age of nineteen. Asked why he became a writer, Sturtzel responded, "As a very young man I took up a timber claim in northern Minnesota. It was while proving up on the land that I began writing, mostly nature stories about the animals and elements I was up against." By 1950 he had written more than five hundred short stories.

Paul Annixter was born in 1894 in Minneapolis, Minnesota. He died in 1985.

READING FOCUS

What relationships are important to you? Have you ever felt strongly attached to a pet?

Sharing Ideas
In small groups, talk about different kinds of relationships people have and why close relationships—with people and animals—play an important role in everyone's life.

Setting a Purpose
Read to discover the relationships shared by the characters in this story.

BUILDING BACKGROUND

Did You Know? Stories and fables have long portrayed the red fox as a clever and sly creature, always ready to trick an unsuspecting animal out of its food—or its life. Red foxes hunt small prey and do not hunt in packs. They are quick, solitary hunters.

VOCABULARY PREVIEW

bleak (blēk) *adj.* cheerless; depressing; p. 164
surly (sur′ lē) *adj.* rude and bad tempered; gruff; p. 164
invalid (in′ və lid) *n.* one who is disabled by disease or injury; p. 165
passive (pas′ iv) *adj.* not participating or active; p. 166
instinct (in′ stingkt) *n.* a way of knowing, behaving, or reacting that comes naturally rather than through learning; p. 167
sanction (sangk′ shən) *v.* to give support or encouragement to; approve; p. 168
wily (wī′ lē) *adj.* full of tricks; crafty; sly; p. 170
sanctuary (sangk′ cho͞o er′ ē) *n.* a place of safety or protection; p. 170
incredulous (in krej′ ə ləs) *adj.* unwilling or unable to believe something; p. 170

162 THEME 2

RESOURCE MANAGER

Teaching Tools and Resources
- Theme Two Planning Guide
- Literature Groups Sourcebook

Essential Lesson Support

Lesson-Specific Instruction
- Selection Focus Transparency 15
- Literary Elements Transparency 15
- Active Reading Guide,* p. 15
- Selection Vocabulary Practice, p. 10

Assessment
- Selection Quick Checks,* p. 15
- Sel. and Theme Assmt., pp. 27-28
- Testmaker: ExamView Pro
- Performance Assessment, p. 15

Systematic Language Instruction
- Gr. & Comp. Hdbk., L. 3.10-3.12

English Language Learners
- ELL Sourcebook, p. 36
- Spanish Summaries, p. 15
- Audio Library*
- English, Yes!

Spec. Needs/Strat. Interven.
- Interactive Rdg. Sbk., pp. T85-T87
- Interactive Rdg. Wkbk., pp. 27-28
- Inclusion Strat. Sbk., pp. 15-16, 51-52
- Audio Library*

*Also available in Spanish

Last Cover

Paul Annixter

I'm not sure I can tell you what you want to know about my brother; but everything about the pet fox is important, so I'll tell all that from the beginning.

It goes back to a winter afternoon after I'd hunted the woods all day for a sign of our lost pet. I remember the way my mother looked up as I came into the kitchen. Without my speaking, she knew what had happened. For six hours I had walked, reading signs, looking for a delicate print in the damp soil or even a hair that might have told of a red fox passing that way—but I had found nothing.

"Did you go up in the foothills?" Mom asked.

A I nodded. My face was stiff from held-back tears. My brother, Colin, who was going on twelve, got it all from one look at me and went into a heartbroken, almost silent, crying.

Three weeks before, Bandit, the pet fox Colin and I had raised from a tiny kit,[1] had disappeared, and not even a rumor had been heard of him since.

"He'd have had to go off soon anyway," Mom comforted. "A big, lolloping fellow like him, he's got to live his life same as us. But he may come back. That fox set a lot of store by[2] you boys in spite of his wild ways."

1. Although it's a shortened form of kitten, *kit* refers to any young, fur-bearing animal, especially one that's smaller than normal.
2. *Lolloping* means "leaping or bounding," and to *set store by* means to "have trust or confidence in."

Reading the Selection

SUMMARY

In this short story, Stan and his brother Colin rescue and raise a baby fox. When the fox matures, it leaves the boys. Because it is familiar with humans and their ways, the fox kills chickens belonging to area farmers. Colin often observes the fox in the wild and knows of its special hiding place. The fox hides there when local farmers band together to hunt it down.

Spanish Summaries, p. 15

A Active Reading Strategies

PREDICT Ask students to predict whether the brothers will find the missing pet. Which brother seems more attached to the pet? Why? *(Some students may say both brothers; some may say Stan, because he looks for the fox; and some may say Colin, because he cries when Stan has no news.)*

VOCABULARY If you haven't previewed the selection vocabulary with students, stop and remind them to use context clues to unlock the meanings of new vocabulary words.

Additional Resources

- *Active Reading Guide,* p. 15
- *Audio Library*
- *Spanish Audio Library*

Teaching Support

CONNECTING TO OTHER SELECTIONS

The chart at the right shows three ways to connect "Last Cover" to other selections in this book.

For specific teaching strategies, see the ***Theme Two Planning Guide.***

Connection	Title
Life Skills: Teaching and Mentoring	→ "Birthday Box," p. 175
Thematic: Animal Nature	→ "Uncle Tony's Goat," p. 807
Literary: Short Story	→ "Broken Chain," p. 44

B Literary Elements

PLOT: *Conflict* Have students describe in their own words how the father and the brothers feel about the fox. *(The father thinks of the fox as an egg thief and chicken killer; the boys think of the fox as their pet.)*

C Active Reading Strategies

PREDICT Have students discuss whether they think the fox will attack the chickens. You may wish to use the following model to guide students in the process of predicting.

Model: I know that it's the middle of winter, and most animals are hibernating. There may not be much food for the fox. Since the fox knows where the chickens are and has killed at least one chicken already, I think the fox will return to his old ways and steal chickens.

D Author's Craft

FORESHADOWING Have students list things the father says that hint at what the fox may do in the future. *(The father says, "We'll be seeing a lot more of that fellow," "That fox learned to...not likely to forget that," "Late winter's a high time...they're out deviling.")*

Vo•cab•u•lar•y Skills

Word Meanings Draw students' attention to the phrase *the seven sleepers are under cover*. Explain that *under cover* means that these seven animals are "sheltered, hidden, or covered over for protection."

Teaching Support

B "He set a lot of store by our food, anyway," Father said. He sat in a chair by the kitchen window mending a piece of harness. "We'll be seeing a lot more of that fellow, never fear. That fox learned to pine for table scraps and young chickens. He was getting to be an egg thief, too, and he's not likely to forget that."

"That was only pranking[3] when he was little," Colin said desperately.

From the first, the tame fox had made tension in the family. It was Father who said we'd better name him Bandit, after he'd made away with his first young chicken.

C "Maybe you know," Father said shortly. "But when an animal turns to egg sucking he's usually incurable. He'd better not come pranking around my chicken run again."

It was late February, and I remember the bleak, dead cold that had set in, cold that was a rare thing for our Carolina hills. Flocks of sparrows and snowbirds had appeared to peck hungrily at all that the pigs and chickens didn't eat.

"This one's a killer," Father would say of a morning, looking out at the whitened barn roof. "This one will make the shoats[4] squeal."

A fire snapped all day in our cookstove and another in the stone fireplace in the living room, but still the farmhouse was never warm. The leafless woods were bleak and empty, and I spoke of that to Father when I came back from my search.

"It's always a sad time in the woods when the seven sleepers are under cover," he said.

"What sleepers are they?" I asked. Father was full of woods lore.[5]

"Why, all the animals that have got sense enough to hole up and stay hid in weather like this. Let's see, how was it the old rhyme named them?

Surly bear and sooty bat,
Brown chuck and masked coon,
Chippy-munk and sly skunk,
And all the mouses
'Cept in men's houses.

"And man would have joined them and made it eight, Granther Yeary always said, if he'd had a little more sense."

"I was wondering if the red fox mightn't make it eight," Mom said.

Father shook his head. "Late winter's a high time for foxes. Time when they're out deviling, not sleeping." D

My chest felt hollow. I wanted to cry like Colin over our lost fox, but at fourteen a boy doesn't cry. Colin had squatted down on the floor and got out his small hammer and nails to start another new frame for a new picture. Maybe then he'd make a drawing for the frame and be able to forget his misery. It had been that way with him since he was five.

I thought of the new dress Mom had brought home a few days before in a heavy cardboard box. That box cover would be fine for Colin to draw on. I spoke of it, and Mom's glance thanked me as she went to

3. Here, *pranking* means "playfulness; mischief."
4. The *shoats* are young pigs.
5. The accumulated stories and beliefs about a subject are called *lore*.

Vocabulary
bleak (blēk) *adj.* cheerless; depressing
surly (sur′ lē) *adj.* rude and bad tempered; gruff

MEETING INDIVIDUAL NEEDS — ENGLISH LANGUAGE LEARNERS

Animal Characteristics Draw English language learners' attention to the different animals named on this page. As they read or listen to the selection being read aloud, have them write down each animal's name. Explain that *coon* is short for *raccoon, chuck* is short for *woodchuck, chippy-munk* refers to a *chipmunk,* and the normal plural for *mouses* is *mice.*

Activity Have students create posters or dictionaries that list each animal name. Next to each name have students draw a picture to illustrate it. They can use dictionaries or illustrated dictionaries to locate meanings, pronunciations and usage notes.

Additional Resources

English Language Learners Sourcebook, p. 36

get it. She and I worried a lot about Colin. He was small for his age, delicate and blond, his hair much lighter and softer than mine, his eyes deep and wide and blue. He was often sick, and I knew the fear Mom had that he might be predestined.[6] I'm just ordinary, like Father. I'm the sort of stuff that can take it—tough and strong—but Colin was always sort of special.

Mom lighted the lamp. Colin began cutting his white cardboard carefully, fitting it into his frame. Father's sharp glance turned on him now and again.

6. Mom fears that Colin has been chosen by God to die at a very young age.

"There goes the boy making another frame before there's a picture for it," he said. "It's too much like cutting out a man's suit for a fellow that's, say, twelve years old. Who knows whether he'll grow into it?"

Mom was into him then, quick. "Not a single frame of Colin's has ever gone to waste. The boy has real talent, Sumter, and it's time you realized it."

"Of course he has," Father said. "All kids have 'em. But they get over 'em."

"It isn't the pox we're talking of," Mom sniffed.

"In a way it is. Ever since you started talking up Colin's art, I've had an invalid for help around the place."

Vocabulary

invalid (in′ və lid) *n.* one who is disabled by disease or injury

Fox Hunt, 1893. Winslow Homer. Oil on canvas, 38 x 68½ in. Museum of American Art, Pennsylvania Academy of Fine Art.

Viewing the painting: Do you think the painting captures Father's explanation that "winter's a high time for foxes"? Explain.

E Active Reading Strategies

EVALUATE Have students compare the ways the mother and the father view Colin. *(The mother worries about Colin because he is small and sickly. She also encourages his artistic nature. The father thinks Colin should get over his artistic phase and become a better helper.)*

Viewing the Painting

Winslow Homer (1836–1910) was a self-taught American painter who often portrayed struggles for existence between humans and nature. Many of his paintings showed heroic dramas at sea, but others showed animals and men fighting for survival in the snowy woods near his home in Maine.

Viewing Response *This painting captures that idea well. The fox seems to be hunting. With the snow on the ground, it is easy for the fox to see its prey. At other times of the year, its prey is camouflaged and can be hidden by grasses and shrubs.*

Reading Minilesson

Identifying Cause-Effect Relationships

If students are to understand the cause-effect relationships in "Last Cover," they need to know both the spoken and the unspoken reasons why the mother and father say the things they do on page 165.

Activity Have students answer the following questions in order to grasp the reasons behind the parents' differing reactions to Colin's art: Why is Father critical of Colin's art? *(He says Colin wastes frames and doesn't help enough because of his art. He doesn't like it that Colin is "delicate" and "sort of special" instead of "tough and strong" like him.)*

Why is Mom supportive of Colin's art? *(She says Colin has real talent. She is worried about his being "delicate" and wants to support him any way she can. She wants him to go to the city to study art someday, not only because he has talent but because farming would be too strenuous for him.)* **L2**

Additional Resources

Reading Skills Practice Workbook

F Literary Elements

CHARACTER Have students describe the father's character. Invite them to explain why the father doesn't like "white-livered" interpretations of nature or soft ways. *(The father has to be tough to survive on the land. He is also a protector—of his animals and his family. He can't let foxes kill his animals or the family won't eat.)*

G Author's Craft

FLASHBACK Remind students that flashbacks take readers back to events that happened earlier. Ask students to explain how they think readers can tell when these flashbacks have ended. *(The time shifts back to the present with the phrase "at supper that night." When the second flashback ends, there is a line space on the page—top of the left column, p. 167.)*

H Active Reading Strategies

CONNECT Guide students to realize that the father understands the realities and harshness of nature. Ask students why they think the father doesn't want the boys to become too attached to the fox. *(The father knows the fox will leave the boys one day. He doesn't want the boys to feel hurt when that day comes.)* Ask students if they have experienced this kind of protectiveness in their families.

Teaching Support

Father wasn't as hard as he made out, I knew, but he had to hold a balance against all Mom's frothing. For him the thing was the land and all that pertained to it. I was following in Father's footsteps, true to form, but Colin threatened to break the family tradition with his leaning toward art, with Mom "aiding and abetting[7] him," as Father liked to put it. For the past two years she had had dreams of my brother becoming a real artist and going away to the city to study.

It wasn't that Father had no understanding of such things. I could remember, through the years, Colin lying on his stomach in the front room making pencil sketches, and how a good drawing would catch Father's eye halfway across the room, and how he would sometimes gather up two or three of them to study, frowning and muttering, one hand in his beard, while a great pride rose in Colin, and in me too. Most of Colin's drawings were of the woods and wild things, and there Father was a master critic. He made out to scorn what seemed to him a passive "white-livered" interpretation of nature through brush and pencil instead of rod and rifle.

At supper that night Colin could scarcely eat. Ever since he'd been able to walk, my brother had had a growing love of wild things, but Bandit had been like his very own, a gift of the woods. One afternoon a year and half before, Father and Laban Small had been running a vixen through the hills with their dogs. With the last of her strength the she-fox had made for her den, not far from our house. The dogs had overtaken her and killed her just before she reached it. When Father and Laban came up, they'd found Colin crouched nearby holding her cub in his arms.

Father had been for killing the cub, which was still too young to shift for itself, but Colin's grief had brought Mom into it. We'd taken the young fox into the kitchen, all of us, except Father, gone a bit silly over the little thing. Colin had held it in his arms and fed it warm milk from a spoon.

"Watch out with all your soft ways," Father had warned, standing in the doorway. "You'll make too much of him. Remember, you can't make a dog out of a fox. Half of that little critter has to love, but the other half is a wild hunter. You boys will mean a whole lot to him while he's a kit, but there'll come a day when you won't mean a thing to him and he'll leave you shorn."[8]

For two weeks after that Colin had nursed the cub, weaning it from milk to bits of meat. For a year they were always together. The cub grew fast. It was soon following Colin and me about the barnyard. It turned out to be a patch fox, with a saddle of darker fur across its shoulders.

I haven't the words to tell you what the fox meant to us. It was far more wonderful owning him than owning any dog. There was something rare and secret like the spirit of the woods about him, and back of his calm, straw-gold eyes was the sense

7. *Abetting* means "encouraging."

8. To be left *shorn* is to be cut off, like hair, and left alone.

Vocabulary
passive (pas′ iv) *adj.* not participating or active

MEETING INDIVIDUAL NEEDS — SPECIAL NEEDS

Less-Proficient Readers Explain that the characters in this story use a regional dialect when they speak.

Activity Write the following phrases and sentence on the board:

- *pine for table scraps*
- *that was only pranking*
- *animals that have got the sense to hole up and stay hid in weather like this*
- *out deviling*
- *Late winter's a high time for foxes.*

Have students offer simpler, more modern ways of restating each example. **L1**

Additional Resources

Inclusion Strategies

of a brain the equal of a man's. The fox became Colin's whole life.

Each day, going and coming from school, Colin and I took long side trips through the woods, looking for Bandit. Wild things' memories were short, we knew; we'd have to find him soon or the old bond would be broken.

Ever since I was ten I'd been allowed to hunt with Father, so I was good at reading signs. But, in a way, Colin knew more about the woods and wild things than Father or me. What came to me from long observation, Colin seemed to know by instinct.

I It was Colin who felt out, like an Indian, the stretch of woods where Bandit had his den, who found the first slim, small fox-print in the damp earth. And then, on an afternoon in March, we saw him. I remember the day well, the racing clouds, the wind rattling the tops of the pine trees and swaying the Spanish moss. Bandit had just come out of a clump of laurel; in the maze of leaves behind him we caught a glimpse of a slim red vixen, so we knew he had found a mate. She melted from sight like a shadow, but Bandit turned to watch us, his mouth open, his tongue lolling as he smiled his old foxy smile. On his thin chops, I saw a telltale chicken feather.

Colin moved silently forward, his movements so quiet and casual he seemed to be standing still. He called Bandit's name, and the fox held his ground, drawn to us with all his senses. For a few moments he let Colin actually put an arm about him. It was then I knew that he loved us still, for all of Father's warnings. He really loved us back, with a fierce, secret love no tame thing ever gave. But the urge of his life just then was toward his new mate. Suddenly, he whirled about and disappeared in the laurels.

Colin looked at me with glowing eyes. "We haven't really lost him, Stan. When he gets through with his spring sparking[9] he may come back. But we've got to show ourselves to him a lot, so he won't forget."

"It's a go," I said.

J "Promise not to say a word to Father," Colin said, and I agreed. For I knew by the chicken feather that Bandit had been up to no good.

A week later the woods were budding and the thickets were rustling with all manner of wild things scurrying on the love scent. Colin managed to get a glimpse of Bandit every few days. He couldn't get close though, for the spring running was a lot more important to a fox than any human beings were.

K Every now and then Colin got out his framed box cover and looked at it, but he never drew anything on it; he never even picked up his pencil. I remember wondering if what Father had said about framing a picture before you had one had spoiled something for him.

I was helping Father with the planting now, but Colin managed to be in the woods every day. By degrees he learned Bandit's range, where he drank and rested and where he was likely to be according to the time of day. One day he told me how

9. *Spring sparking* refers to the mating season.

Vocabulary

instinct (in′ stingkt) *n.* a way of knowing, behaving, or reacting that comes naturally rather than through learning

I Literary Elements

PLOT: *Rising Action* Point out to students that the events that occur and the information readers receive here all add to the rising action, or building, of the story. Ask students to identify the events and information. *(The boys see Bandit, they learn that Bandit has a mate, and Colin touches Bandit.)*

J Active Reading Strategies

EVALUATE Ask students to explain why the boys don't want to tell their father they have seen Bandit. *(Bandit has a chicken feather on his mouth. He has been stealing chickens. The boys know their father would not approve of their continuing to see Bandit.)*

K Critical Thinking

DRAWING CONCLUSIONS Every once in a while, Colin looks at his framed blank page. Have students explain why he doesn't draw anything on it. You may wish to use the following model to guide students in the process of drawing conclusions.

Model: I know Colin draws the woods and wild things, and I know he is observant and sensitive. Maybe Colin doesn't draw anything yet because he is hoping for Bandit's return after the spring running. Or maybe Colin is waiting for inspiration or a more powerful feeling before he draws.

Interdisciplinary Connection

Science Explain that foxes frequently live near farms because they eat rodents, which are easy to hunt in fields. When foxes are killed off in an area, rodent populations can grow out of control. Even though foxes often live near humans, they are rarely seen because their sharp hearing, sight, and sense of smell alert them to humans before humans are aware of them.

Activity Have students work in groups to conduct research and use what they find to write reports about foxes. They might want to investigate the red fox or other types of foxes, fox territories or ranges, or how parents care for fox cubs. They can also research the differences between foxes and their relatives, such as wolves, coyotes, jackals, and dogs. **L2**

COLLAB. LEARN.

FYI

Red foxes live about 12 years, and they mate for life. People in Australia imported foxes to control the population of rabbits, an introduced species without natural enemies that had grown out of control.

L Literary Elements

PLOT: ***Rising Action*** Have students identify the important events that build the story's tension and suspense. *(Bandit has been raiding barns and hen runs, so the farmers are banding together to hunt him down with dogs—or to shoot him on sight.)*

M Critical Thinking

INFERRING Even though the father has made threats against Bandit, he doesn't join the fox hunt. Later, he smiles with satisfaction when the dogs lose Bandit's trail. Have students explain what this shows about Father. *(Father likes Bandit, too, and does not want to see him killed. On the other hand, the father and the boys both know they can't stop the farmers from protecting their poultry.)*

he had petted Bandit again, and how they had walked together a long way in the woods. All this time we had kept his secret from Father.

As summer came on, Bandit began to live up to the prediction Father had made. Accustomed to human beings he moved without fear about the scattered farms of the region, raiding barns and hen runs that other foxes wouldn't have dared go near. And he taught his wild mate to do the same. Almost every night they got into some poultry house, and by late June Bandit was not only killing chickens and ducks but feeding on eggs and young chicks whenever he got the chance.

Stories of his doings came to us from many sources, for he was still easily recognized by the dark patch on his shoulders. Many a farmer took a shot at him as he fled and some of them set out on his trail with dogs, but they always returned home without even sighting him. Bandit was familiar with all the dogs in the region, and he knew a hundred tricks to confound[10] them. He got a reputation that year beyond that of any fox our hills had known. His confidence grew, and he gave up wild hunting altogether and lived entirely off the poultry farmers. By September the hill farmers banded together to hunt him down.

It was Father who brought home that news one night. All time-honored rules of the fox chase were to be broken in this hunt; if the dogs couldn't bring Bandit down, he was to be shot on sight. I was stricken and furious. L I remember the misery of Colin's face in the lamplight. Father, who took pride in all the ritual of the hunt, had refused to be a party to such an affair, though in justice he could do nothing but sanction any sort of hunt, for M

10. Here, *confound* means "confuse."

Vocabulary
sanction (sangk′ shən) *v.* to give support or encouragement to; approve

Teaching Support

Grammar and Language *Minilesson*

Commas and Conjunctions Write these sentences on the board, underlining the subjects once and the verbs twice:

1. He called Bandit's name, and the fox held his ground.
2. Colin got out his framed box cover and looked at it.

Explain that a clause has both a subject and a verb and can stand alone as a sentence. Commas are used when *and, or,* or *but* join more than one main clause. In the second sentence, there is only one main clause, so a comma is not used.

Activity Have students find other story sentences that use commas before conjunctions. Students should copy each sentence, underlining each subject once and each verb twice. **L2**

Additional Resources

- ***Grammar and Language Transparency 13***
- ***Grammar and Language Workbook,*** pp. 257–258
- ***Grammar and Composition Handbook,*** Lesson 13.3
- ***Writer's Choice,*** Lesson 20.3

Bandit, as old Sam Wetherwax put it, had been "purely getting in the Lord's hair."

The hunt began next morning, and it was the biggest turnout our hills had known. There were at least twenty mounted men in the party and as many dogs. Father and I were working in the lower field as they passed along the river road. Most of the hunters carried rifles, and they looked ugly.

Twice during the morning I went up to the house to find Colin, but he was nowhere around. As we worked, Father and I could follow the progress of the hunt by the distant hound music on the breeze. We could tell just where the hunters first caught sight of the fox and where Bandit was leading the dogs during the first hour. We knew as well as if we'd seen it how Bandit roused another fox along Turkey Branch and forced it to run for him, and how the dogs swept after it for twenty minutes before they sensed their mistake.

N

Noon came, and Colin had not come in to eat. After dinner Father didn't go back to the field. He moped about, listening to the hound talk. He didn't like what was going on any more than I did, and now and again I caught his smile of satisfaction when we heard the broken, angry notes of the hunting horn, telling that the dogs had lost the trail or had run another fox.

I was restless, and I went up into the hills in midafternoon. I ranged the woods for miles, thinking all the time of Colin. Time lost all meaning for me, and the short day was nearing an end, when I heard the horn talking again, telling that the fox had put over another trick. All day he had deviled the dogs and mocked the hunters. This new trick and the coming night would work to save him. I was wildly glad, as I moved down toward Turkey Branch and stood listening for a time by the deep, shaded pool where for years we boys had gone swimming, sailed boats, and dreamed summer dreams.

Suddenly, out of the corner of my eye, I saw the sharp ears and thin, pointed mask of a fox—in the water almost beneath me. It was Bandit, craftily submerged there, all but his head, resting in the cool water of the pool and the shadow of the two big beeches that spread above it. He must have run forty miles or more since morning. And he must have hidden in this place before. His knowing, crafty mask blended perfectly with the shadows and a mass of drift and branches that had collected by the bank of the pool. He was so still a pair of thrushes flew up from the spot as I came up, not knowing he was there.

O

Bandit's bright, harried[11] eyes were looking right at me. But I did not look at him direct. Some woods instinct, swifter than thought, kept me from it. So he and I met as in another world, indirectly, with feeling but without sign or greeting.

Suddenly I saw that Colin was standing almost beside me. Silently as a water snake, he had come out of the bushes and stood there. Our eyes met, and a quick and secret smile passed between us. It was a rare moment in which I really "met" my brother, when something of his essence[12] flowed into me and I knew all of him. I've never lost it since.

P

My eyes still turned from the fox, my heart pounding. I moved quietly away, and Colin moved with me. We whistled softly

11. Bandit's eyes show that he is troubled *(harried)*.
12. Colin's *essence* is his most basic nature or spirit.

N Critical Thinking

SEQUENCING Have students state in what order the fox hunt events take place and what words in the passage indicate this. *(Events are ordered by time. The writer uses words such as* morning, first hour, twenty minutes, noon, after dinner, midafternoon, *and* day was nearing an end.*)*

O Active Reading Strategies

VISUALIZE Ask students to use the descriptive details in this passage to visualize Bandit's hiding place. Ask them to describe what they see and what they imagine about smells and sounds.

P Active Reading Strategies

EVALUATE Ask students what they think about the relationship between Stan and Colin and what this hunt does to their understanding of each other. *(Stan is protective of Colin. The boys are close, but the hunt makes them grow closer. It helps them understand each other better—a bond that is never broken.)*

Writing Minilesson

Descriptive Details Guide students to understand that when writing descriptive passages, writers organize descriptive details in different ways, including *placement* (describing a scene from left to right or top to bottom), *time* (describing events in the order they occur), and *importance* (describing the most important details first or last).

Activity Have each student write a short descriptive paragraph using one method of ordering the details—by placement, by time, or by importance. **L2**

Additional Resources

Writer's Choice, Lesson 2.4

Q Literary Elements

MOOD Ask students how they feel about the way the boys protect Bandit. Encourage them to describe the emotional quality of the story. *(There is a feeling of magic, warmth, and caring.)*

R Critical Thinking

INFERRING Have students suggest ideas about why Colin finally makes his drawing. *(Colin feels compelled to share the secret of how Bandit fooled them all.)*

S Literary Elements

PLOT: *Resolution* Ask students to describe how Bandit helps Colin and his father resolve their conflict over Colin's artwork. *(Colin draws a picture of Bandit in his final hiding place. The father realizes that Colin knew where the fox was all along. He finally accepts and approves of Colin's artwork.)*

Thematic Focus

Winds of Change Discuss the changes that took place in the boys, their parents, the community, and Bandit himself as the baby fox matured.

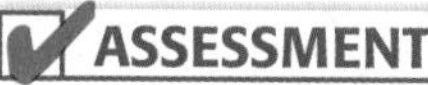

ASSESSMENT

Quick Checks, p. 15

Teaching Support

Q as we went, pretending to busy ourselves along the bank of the stream. There was magic to it, as if by will we wove a web of protection about the fox, a ring-pass-not that none might penetrate. It was so, too, we felt, in the brain of Bandit, and that doubled the charm. To us he was still our little pet that we had carried in our arms on countless summer afternoons.

Two hundred yards upstream, we stopped beside slim, fresh tracks in the mud where Bandit had entered the branch. The tracks angled upstream. But in the water the wily creature had turned down.

We climbed the far bank to wait, and Colin told me how Bandit's secret had been his secret ever since an afternoon three months before, when he'd watched the fox swim downstream to hide in the deep pool. Today he'd waited on the bank, feeling that Bandit, hard pressed by the dogs, might again seek the pool for sanctuary.

We looked back once we turned homeward. He still had not moved. We didn't know until later that he was killed that same night by a chance hunter, as he crept out from his hiding place.

R That evening Colin worked a long time on his framed box cover that had lain about the house untouched all summer. He kept at it all the next day too. I had never seen him work so hard. I seemed to sense in the air the feeling he was putting into it, how he was *believing* his picture into being. It was evening before he finished it. Without a word he handed it to Father. Mom and I went and looked over his shoulder.

It was a delicate and intricate pencil drawing of the deep branch pool, and there was Bandit's head and watching, fear-filled eyes hiding there amid the leaves and shadows, woven craftily into the maze of twigs and branches, as if by nature's art itself. Hardly a fox there at all, but the place where he was—or should have been. I recognized it instantly, but Mom gave a sort of incredulous sniff.

"I'll declare," she said, "It's mazy as a puzzle. It just looks like a lot of sticks and leaves to me."

Long minutes of study passed before Father's eye picked out the picture's secret, as few men's could have done. I laid that to Father's being a born hunter. That was a picture that might have been done especially for him. In fact, I guess it was.

S Finally he turned to Colin with his deep, slow smile. "So that's how Bandit fooled them all," he said. He sat holding the picture with a sort of tenderness for a long time, while we glowed in the warmth of the shared secret. That was Colin's moment. Colin's art stopped being a pox to Father right there. And later, when the time came for Colin to go to art school, it was Father who was his solid backer.

❖

Vocabulary

wily (wī′ lē) *adj.* full of tricks; crafty; sly

sanctuary (sangk′ cho͞o er′ ē) *n.* a place of safety or protection

incredulous (in krej′ ə ləs) *adj.* unwilling or unable to believe something

MEETING INDIVIDUAL NEEDS

MULTIPLE MODES OF EXPRESSION

Spatial Some students respond well to text that describes spatial relationships. Other learners can benefit from observing these students' depictions of spatial relationships. Work with students to outline the locations of the events in the fox hunt.

Activity Have students work in pairs. Have them use the outline of the locations and the description of the fox hunt to draw diagrams or maps of Bandit's escape during the hunt. Encourage students to use arrows or numbers to show the sequence of events. **L2** COLLAB. LEARN.

Responding to Literature

PERSONAL RESPONSE

- Were you surprised by the outcome of the story? Explain.
- Think back to the group discussion in the **Reading Focus** on page 162. What, if any, new ideas did the story give you about relationships? Record your thoughts in your journal.

Analyzing Literature

RECALL

1. Who named Bandit? What does the name tell about this person's attitude toward the fox?
2. What is Colin's talent? At the beginning of the story, what is his father's attitude toward this talent?
3. According to the narrator, what are some differences between the two brothers?
4. Why does the hunt take place and what happens to Bandit?

Brackets connect questions that are paired to develop higher-level thinking skills.

INTERPRET

5. At the beginning, what effect does the fox have on the relationship between family members? Explain.
6. Why does Colin's father feel threatened by his son's talent? What tradition is Colin threatening? Explain.
7. What do the narrator's feelings about his brother and about the pet fox reveal about the narrator? Use details from the story to support your ideas.
8. Why does the father's attitude about Bandit change during the course of the story?

EVALUATE AND CONNECT

9. Trust is one of the **themes** of "Last Cover." What role do you think trust plays in the story? Explain.
10. **Theme Connection** How does the relationship between Colin and his father change over the course of the story? How does the relationship between the brothers change? Explain.

LITERARY ELEMENTS

Plot

The sequence of events in a story, novel, or play is called a **plot.** A good writer uses each event in a plot to cause or lead to the next event. The plot begins by introducing the story's characters, setting, and situation. This is called the **exposition.** It captures the reader's attention with a strong **conflict** between opposing forces. **Rising action** in the plot adds complications to the conflict that lead to a **climax,** or point when the reader's interest is at its highest. A **resolution** reveals the final outcome of the plot.

1. Briefly outline the plot of "Last Cover."
2. Use examples from the plot to show how Bandit at first causes tensions in the family but finally helps bring the family together.

● See **Literary Terms Handbook,** p. R8.

Responding to the Selection

PERSONAL RESPONSE

Even though students may feel sad that Bandit is killed at the end of the story, they might have predicted that "his bad habits would get him into trouble." Students' journal entries might describe an awareness that relationships grow and change over time.

Analyzing Literature

1. Father named Bandit. The name tells readers that Father thinks Bandit is up to no good.
2. Colin is artistic and likes to draw. The father thinks Colin's drawing is just a passing fancy that keeps him from more useful farm chores.
3. Colin is small, delicate, sickly, and artistic. Stan is tough and strong, more like their father.
4. The hunt takes place because Bandit and his mate have been raiding the chicken coops of local farmers. Bandit gets killed, but not by the members of the hunt.
5. The fox creates tension in the family because the boys think of him as a pet, but the father knows he is wild and will, in time, act like a wild animal.
6. Colin's father feels threatened by Colin's talent because he thinks Colin will not learn to be a farmer like his brother Stan.
7. Stan, the narrator, feels protective and supportive of Colin. This is shown when he suggests Colin draw on a cardboard box cover. Stan cares strongly for the fox. He shows this when he looks for it for six hours.
8. The father's attitude toward Bandit changes as Bandit cleverly raids farms all summer but skillfully avoids being killed by farmers or their dogs. The father respects Bandit's skill and knowledge of the land.
9. Bandit learns to trust the boys when he is a kit. On the day the farmers hunt him, the boys do not give away Bandit's secret hiding place.
10. Colin and his father come to understand each other better. Stan and Colin become closer, too, especially as they both observe Bandit hiding from the hunters and share the secret.

LITERARY ELEMENTS

1. Two boys raise a fox. It grows up, it leaves them, and kills chickens to live. It evades farmers who hunt it but is killed by a chance hunter.
2. Bandit's chicken-killing causes tension in the family, but Colin's skill at drawing Bandit's hiding place reconciles them.

Additional Resources

 ***Literary Elements Transparency 15***

Extending Your Response

Writing About Literature

Students' reviews should

- include details from the story to support their opinions
- use appropriate quotations and examples from the story to show how the characters change
- flow logically from one thought to another and have a clear conclusion

Creative Writing

Students' journal entries should

- clearly present Colin's thoughts, ideas, and viewpoints
- interpret the actions of Stan, Bandit, and the father through Colin's eyes
- relate some events in the story from Colin's perspective

Literature Groups Point out to students that they should list arguments to support Colin's ideas and arguments to support the farmers' ideas. Then they should consider counterarguments to both points of view. COLLAB. LEARN.

Performing Once students understand each character's motivation, have them convey the characters vocally by changing the volume, pitch, and tone of their voices and the rate at which they speak.

Reading Further Anna Sewell's *Black Beauty* is written at a level simple enough to be suitable for less-proficient readers. In addition, it presents an opportunity to review both autobiography and point of view; the book is written as an autobiography of the horse from its point of view.

Extending Your Response

Writing About Literature

Characterization The manner in which a writer develops the characters in a story is called **characterization.** Authors characterize in several ways. A narrator may describe each character at length as he or she is introduced. We also learn about characters through their actions and interactions with other characters, through what they say or think, and through what other characters say about them. Write a few paragraphs about the characters in "Last Cover." What does the author reveal to readers about his characters? How? Do the characters seem true to life? How do the characters change during the story? Which character do you like the most? Why? Use examples and quotations from the story to support your opinions.

Creative Writing

Changing Point of View How would this story be different if Colin had narrated it? Imagine that you are Colin. Write a journal entry about Bandit's life, what happens to him, and your feelings about the whole situation. Be sure to include your attitude toward the other members of your family.

Literature Groups

Problem Solving Imagine that Colin, his brother, his father, and several local farmers are sitting down to discuss the problems Bandit has caused. What are the problems? Are there solutions other than the hunt? Debate the issue. From Colin's point of view, offer suggestions to resolve the problems. Support your ideas with details from the story.

Performing

With a small group, choose an important scene from the story and dramatize it for your classmates. Reread the section of the story several times and discuss each character's actions and feelings so that you understand what motivates each character in that scene.

Reading Further

If you would like to read more stories by Paul Annixter, try these books:

Pride of Lions, and Other Stories
The Best Nature Stories of Paul Annixter

For an animal story that has been popular for more than a hundred years, try:
Black Beauty by Anna Sewell

Save your work for your portfolio.

Skill Minilessons

Reteach • Review

GRAMMAR AND LANGUAGE • COMMAS USED WITH WORDS IN A SERIES

Commas make sentences easier to understand by signaling a pause or separation between parts of a sentence. Use commas to separate three or more words, phrases, or clauses in a series.

Example: Colin carried his pens, his pencils, and his paper to his desk.

PRACTICE Review "Last Cover" to find an example of a sentence that uses commas to separate three or more words or phrases in a series. Write this sentence in your journal, and then make up one of your own.

- For more about using commas in a series, see **Language Handbook,** p. R37.

READING AND THINKING • PREDICTING

Good readers make many types of inferences as they read. One type involves predicting outcomes. Readers may use details to predict the outcomes of conversations, actions, or events within a story. In other words, you may be able to figure out what will happen next in a story. Then, as you read, you can check your predictions by finding out what actually happened.

PRACTICE Reread "Last Cover" and find two examples of details that could help a reader predict what will happen next in the story. Share your findings with your classmates and see how many different details were found.

- For more about predicting, see **Reading Handbook,** pp. R86–R87.

VOCABULARY • ROOTS

The root of a word is the word part that is used as the base in making other words. Knowing the meaning of a root helps you understand other words with the same root. For example, *invalid* contains the root *val,* meaning "strong or well." An *invalid* is not strong or well. A *valid* argument is one that's well supported. *Valor* is the kind of bravery that comes from inner strength.

The word *incredulous* contains the root *cred,* which comes from a Latin word meaning "to believe." *Credit* can mean "approval or acknowledgment," but it can also mean "belief or trust." If you *credit* someone's statement, you believe it. By combining your understanding of the root *cred* with any context clues that may exist, you can probably figure out the meaning of words in which this root appears.

PRACTICE Briefly state what you'd guess is the meaning of each underlined word.

1. I doubted his credibility.
2. She told an incredible story.
3. Don't give credence to such a ridiculous statement.
4. It's not fair to lie to an innocent, credulous child.
5. His lawyer tried to discredit the witnesses for the other side.

Skill Minilessons

GRAMMAR AND LANGUAGE
COMMAS USED WITH WORDS IN A SERIES

Sentences should show that students understand how to use commas with words in a series correctly.

READING AND THINKING
PREDICTING

Students should be able to state their predictions and give examples of details that support them.

VOCABULARY
ROOTS

1. believability
2. unbelievable
3. trust
4. believing
5. destroy trust in

Additional Resources

- ***Grammar and Language Workbook,*** pp. 255–256
- ***Grammar and Composition Handbook,*** Lesson 13.2
- ***Writer's Choice,*** Lesson 20.2
- ***Reading Skills Practice Workbook,*** pp. 25–26
- ***Vocabulary Practice,*** p. 10

ASSESSMENT

- ***Quick Checks,*** p. 15
- ***Selection and Theme Assessment,*** pp. 27–28
- ***Performance Assessment,*** p. 15
- ***Testmaker: ExamView Pro***
- ***Interactive Tutor: Self-Assessment***

Before Reading

Objectives

- To read and analyze a story and a poem about characters dealing with separation
- To identify and explore major and minor characters in a story or poem
- To explain how the setting of the story contributes to its effect

Skills

Reading/Thinking: Verifying Predictions; Monitoring Comprehension; Drawing Conclusions; Focusing on a Question
Writing: Short Story; Speech
Vocabulary: Negative Prefixes
Grammar/Language: Appositives
Life Skills: Speech for Support Group
Collaboration: Literature Groups

Motivating STUDENTS

Selection Focus Transparency 16: Have students read the quote from Jane Yolen and discuss the ways in which readers can make a story their own.

Reading Focus: As an extension of the Reading Focus, have students make a list of their favorite presents and then use precise language and sensory details to discuss the ones that cannot be held in one's hands.

Before You Read

Birthday Box and *There Is No Word for Goodbye*

MEET JANE YOLEN

Jane Yolen wrote her first two books before she was in high school. One was about pirates and the other about the pioneer west. Since then she has written more than 150 books.

Jane Yolen was born in 1939. This story was first published in 1995.

MEET MARY TALLMOUNTAIN

Mary TallMountain was born into the Koykon-Athabaskan tribe in Nulato, Alaska. It wasn't until she was in her fifties that TallMountain began to write poetry, sometimes for sixteen hours a day! Her poems recapture her Athabaskan childhood.

Mary TallMountain was born in 1918. "There Is No Word for Goodbye" was published in Continuum: Poems by Mary TallMountain *in 1988.*

READING FOCUS

What's the most memorable gift you ever unwrapped? Have you ever thought about the gifts you have been given that you can't hold in your hands—gifts like time, friendship, or love?

QuickWrite

Make a quick list of your favorite gifts—the kind you can and cannot hold in your hands.

Setting a Purpose

Read these selections to discover two views on love and separation.

BUILDING BACKGROUND

Sometimes writers don't have to spend days and weeks coming up with an idea for a story. In 1995 an editor named Johanna Hurwitz decided to invite ten writers, including Jane Yolen, to write about a child who receives a beautifully wrapped empty box for a birthday present. The writers were inspired to write fairy tales, fantasy, poetry, and realistic stories. Each writer's imagination was sparked by the same idea, and each writer wrote a completely original piece of literature.

VOCABULARY PREVIEW

insistent (in sis′ tənt) *adj.* demanding attention or notice; p. 176
stark (stärk) *adv.* completely; harshly or grimly; p. 177
infinite (in′ fə nit) *adj.* boundless; limitless; extremely great; p. 177
subtle (sut′ əl) *adj.* not open or direct; not obvious; p. 178

RESOURCE MANAGER

Teaching Tools and Resources
- Theme Two Planning Guide
- Literature Groups Sourcebook

Essential Lesson Support

Lesson-Specific Instruction
- Selection Focus Transparency 16
- Literary Elements Transparency 16
- Active Reading Guide,* p. 16
- Selection Vocabulary Practice, p. 11

Assessment
- Selection Quick Checks,* p. 16
- Sel. and Theme Assmt., pp. 29–30
- Testmaker: ExamView Pro
- Performance Assessment, p. 16

Systematic Language Instruction
- Gr. & Comp. Hbk., L. 4.1, 4.2
- Vocabulary Power, Lesson 8
- Spelling Power, Lesson 7

English Language Learners
- ELL Sourcebook, p. 37
- Spanish Summaries, p. 16
- Audio Library*
- English, Yes!

Spec. Needs/Strat. Interven.
- Interactive Rdg. Sbk., pp. T88–T90
- Interactive Rdg. Wkbk, pp. 29–30
- Inclusion Strat. Sbk., pp. 45–46
- Audio Library*

*Also available in Spanish

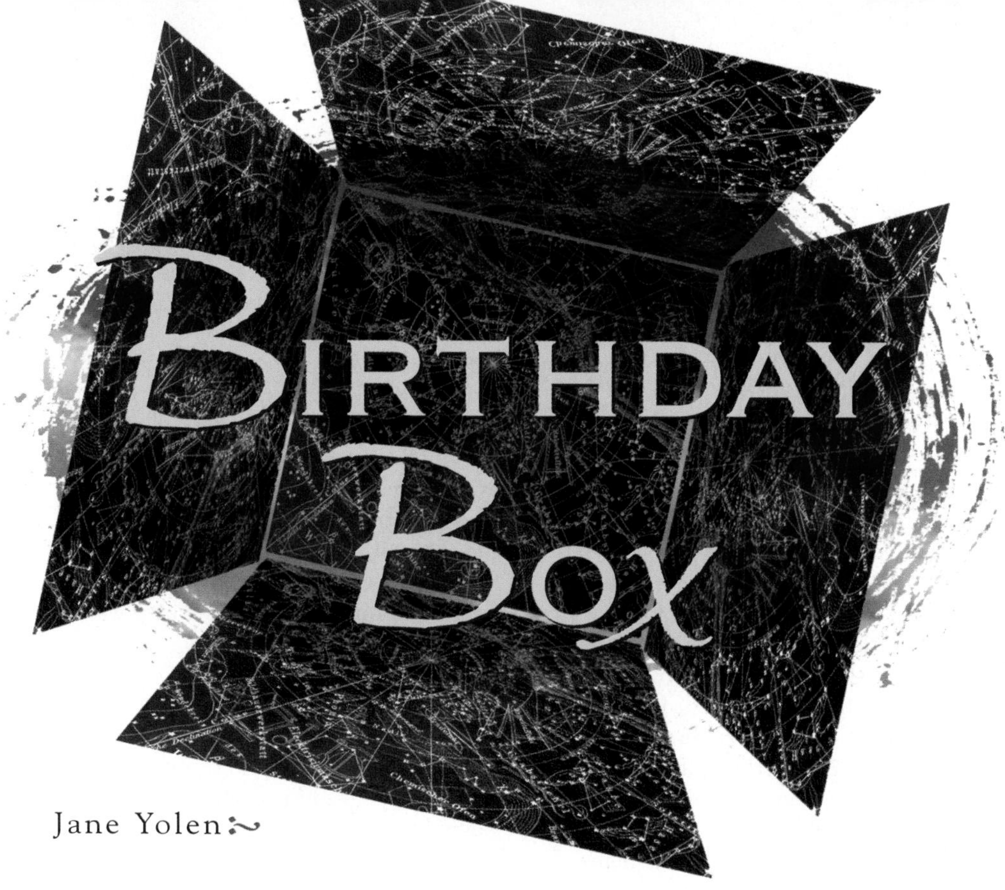

Jane Yolen

I was ten years old when my mother died. Ten years old on that very day. Still she gave me a party of sorts. Sick as she was, Mama had seen to it, organizing it at the hospital. She made sure the doctors and nurses all brought me presents. We were good friends with them all by that time, because Mama had been in the hospital for so long.

The head nurse, V. Louise Higgins (I never did know what that V stood for), gave me a little box, which was sort of funny because she was the biggest of all the nurses there. I mean she was tremendous. And she was the only one who insisted on wearing all white. Mama had called her the great white shark when she was first admitted, only not to V. Louise's face. "All those needles," Mama had said. "Like teeth." But V. Louise was sweet, not sharklike at all, and she'd been so gentle with Mama.

Reading the Selection

SUMMARY

In "Birthday Box," Katie has her tenth birthday in her dying mother's hospital room. Her mother gives her a beautifully wrapped empty box, but dies before Katie can ask why. A year later, Katie realizes that she must fill the box with her writing. In "There Is No Word for Goodbye," an older person tells a young one that there is no word for *goodbye* in Athabaskan, because they never really ever leave one another.

Spanish Summaries, p. 16

A Active Reading Strategies

PREDICT Ask students to use clues from the first paragraph to predict what the title of the story means. *(The author states that her mother died on her tenth birthday. Perhaps the birthday box is something her mother said or gave to her that day.)*

VOCABULARY If you haven't previewed the selection vocabulary with students, stop and remind them to use context clues to unlock the meanings of new vocabulary words.

Additional Resources

- ***Active Reading Guide,*** p. 16
- ***Audio Library***
- ***Spanish Audio Library***

Teaching Support

CONNECTING TO OTHER SELECTIONS
For a teaching strategy that connects "Birthday Box" to "Last Cover," see the ***Theme Two Planning Guide.***

MEETING INDIVIDUAL NEEDS — ENGLISH LANGUAGE LEARNERS

Birthdays You might want to explore the various ways different cultures celebrate birthdays. In the United States, the years are calculated from the day of birth, and birthday parties usually include giving presents to the birthday person and having a cake. Point out that, unless it is meant as a joke, it would be very unusual to be given an empty box as a birthday present.

Activity Have students read and think about how birthdays are celebrated in their own cultures. Then have students work with partners or in small groups to compare birthday celebrations in different cultures. COLLAB. LEARN.

Additional Resources

English Language Learners Sourcebook, p. 37

B Literary Elements

CHARACTER Ask students what they have learned about Katie up to this point. *(Katie is ten years old; her mother is very sick; her parents are separated; her father is not very involved in her life; she is very responsive to her mother; she's polite—her Mama was "real big on politeness.")*

C Active Reading Strategies

PREDICT Ask students to evaluate Katie's interests. What seems to be her favorite thing to do? Encourage them to support their ideas with examples. *(Katie loves paperback books, writing paper, and pens. These details help us recognize that she is creative and likes to write.)*

D Literary Elements

SETTING Remind students to use the descriptions of the setting to help them gather information about the characters. Discuss with students the significance of the breathing machine. *(It shows that Katie's mother is very sick. She cannot even breathe by herself.)*

I opened the little present first. It was a fountain pen, a real one, not a fake one like you get at Kmart.

"Now you can write beautiful stories, Katie," V. Louise said to me.

I didn't say that stories come out of your head, not out of a pen. That wouldn't have been polite, and Mama—even sick—was real big on politeness.

"Thanks, V. Louise," I said.

The Stardust Twins—which is what Mama called Patty and Tracey-Lynn because they reminded her of dancers in an old-fashioned ballroom—gave me a present together. It was a diary and had a picture of a little girl in pink, reading in a garden swing. A little young for me, a little too cute. I mean, I read Stephen King[1] and want to write like him. But as Mama always reminded me whenever Dad finally remembered to send me something, it was the thought that counted, not the actual gift.

"It's great," I told them. "I'll write in it with my new pen." And I wrote my name on the first page just to show them I meant it.

They hugged me and winked at Mama. She tried to wink back but was just too tired and shut both her eyes instead.

Lily, who is from Jamaica, had baked me some sweet bread. Mary Margaret gave me a gold cross blessed by the pope, which I put on even though Mama and I weren't churchgoers. That was Dad's thing.

Then Dr. Dann, the intern[2] who was on days, and Dr. Pucci, the oncologist (which is the fancy name for a cancer doctor), gave me a big box filled to the top with little presents, each wrapped up individually. All things they knew I'd love—paperback books and writing paper and erasers with funny animal heads and colored paper clips and a rubber stamp that printed FROM KATIE'S DESK and other stuff. They must have raided a stationery store.

There was one box, though, they held out till the end. It was about the size of a large top hat. The paper was deep blue and covered with stars; not fake stars but real stars, I mean, like a map of the night sky. The ribbon was two shades of blue with silver threads running through. There was no name on the card.

"Who's it from?" I asked.

None of the nurses answered, and the doctors both suddenly were studying the ceiling tiles with the kind of intensity they usually saved for X rays. No one spoke. In fact the only sound for the longest time was Mama's breathing machine going in and out and in and out. It was a harsh, horrible, insistent sound, and usually I talked and talked to cover up the noise. But I was waiting for someone to tell me.

At last V. Louise said, "It's from your mama, Katie. She told us what she wanted. And where to get it."

I turned and looked at Mama then, and her eyes were open again. Funny, but sickness had made her even more beautiful than good health had. Her skin was like that old paper, the kind they used to write on with quill pens, and stretched out over her bones so she looked like a model. Her

1. An extremely popular novelist, *Stephen King* writes mainly tales of horror and the supernatural.
2. An *intern* is a recent medical school graduate who works under the supervision of experienced doctors.

Vocabulary
insistent (in sis′ tənt) *adj.* demanding attention or notice

Teaching Support

REAL-WORLD CONNECTION

Life-Changing Incidents Ask students how they would cope with a life-changing incident. How might such an event change their day-to-day lives?

Activity Ask students to work in small groups to discuss how they would feel if they were to lose someone they know or someone they love. If some students have experienced such a loss, they may wish to share their personal experiences and how they came to terms with the loss. You may wish to have a school counselor address the class and discuss constructive ways to manage the anger, the frustration, and the sense of helplessness a person feels when faced by such circumstances. **L2** COLLAB. LEARN.

E

eyes, which had been a deep, brilliant blue, were now like the fall sky, bleached and softened. She was like a faded photograph of herself. She smiled a very small smile at me. I knew it was an effort.

"It's you," she mouthed. I read her lips. I had gotten real good at that. I thought she meant it was a present for me.

"Of course it is," I said cheerfully. I had gotten good at that, too, being cheerful when I didn't feel like it. "Of course it is."

I took the paper off the box carefully, not tearing it but folding it into a tidy packet. I twisted the ribbons around my hand and then put them on the pillow by her hand. It made the stark white hospital bed look almost festive.

Under the wrapping, the box was beautiful itself. It was made of a heavy cardboard and covered with a linen material that had a pattern of cloud-filled skies.

I opened the box slowly and . . .

F

"It's empty," I said. "Is this a joke?" I turned to ask Mama, but she was gone. I mean, her body was there, but she wasn't. It was as if she was as empty as the box.

Dr. Pucci leaned over her and listened with a stethoscope,[3] then almost absently patted Mama's head. Then, with infinite care, V. Louise closed Mama's eyes, ran her hand across Mama's cheek, and turned off the breathing machine.

"Mama!" I cried. And to the nurses and doctors, I screamed, "Do something!" And because the room had suddenly become so silent, my voice echoed back at me. "Mama, do something."

❖ ❖ ❖ ❖ ❖

I cried steadily for, I think, a week. Then I cried at night for a couple of months. And then for about a year I cried at anniversaries, like Mama's birthday or mine, at Thanksgiving, on Mother's Day. I stopped writing. I stopped reading except for school assignments. I was pretty mean to my half brothers and totally rotten to my stepmother and Dad. I felt empty and angry, and they all left me pretty much alone.

G

And then one night, right after my first birthday without Mama, I woke up remembering how she had said, "It's you." Not, "It's for you," just "It's you." Now Mama had been a high school English teacher and a writer herself. She'd had poems published in little magazines. She didn't use words carelessly. In the end she could hardly use any words at all. So—I asked myself in that dark room—why had she said, "It's you"? Why were they the very last words she had ever said to me, forced out with her last breath?

I turned on the bedside light and got out of bed. The room was full of shadows, not all of them real.

Pulling the desk chair over to my closet, I climbed up and felt along the top shelf, and against the back wall, there was the birthday box, just where I had thrown it the day I had moved in with my dad.

3. A *stethoscope* (steth′ ə skōp′) is an instrument used to listen to sounds made by the internal organs of the body, especially the lungs and heart. The French doctor who invented the stethoscope in 1817 got the idea after seeing children making sounds through a hollow log.

Vocabulary
stark (stärk) *adv.* completely; harshly or grimly
infinite (in′ fə nit) *adj.* boundless; limitless; extremely great

E Literary Elements

DESCRIPTION Point out to students the way the author describes Katie's mother. Then ask students how each of these images relates to her situation. *(Old paper conveys the look of her skin; fall sky refers to the fall season, a time of dying; and faded photograph suggests someone who is very old, sick, or dead.)*

F Literary Elements

SYMBOL Ask students to think about why Katie's mother gives her an empty box. Encourage them to keep their hunches in mind as they read to the end of the selection. *(Some students may understand that it has a meaning that Katie must discover.)*

G Critical Thinking

VERIFYING PREDICTIONS Ask students what they think Mama means when she says, "It's you," to Katie. Remind them to keep in mind the title of the story. You might share the following model to guide students in the thinking process involved in drawing conclusions.

Model: The story shows that Katie's mother is very caring and thoughtful. If she wants to give Katie a beautiful empty box, it must be for a reason. She knows Katie well enough to understand how "empty" she will feel without her. By saying "It's you," she is telling Katie that she, like the box, is beautiful on the outside and needs to fill herself with her writings, her thoughts, and her memories.

Reading Minilesson

Monitoring Comprehension Students might have trouble understanding the significance the narrator finds in the few words her mother uses on page 177.

Activity To monitor their comprehension and relate that part of the story to their own experience, have groups answer the following questions as they read: *Did I understand what I just read? What questions can I ask to check myself? Why does the narrator wake up suddenly? What is the difference between saying "It's for you" and "It's you"? What does Mama's being an English teacher and a writer have to do with anything?* **L2** COLLAB. LEARN.

Additional Resources

Reading Skills Practice Workbook

VIEWING THE PAINTING

A professional artist for more than thirty years, John S. Bunker is also director of the Jacksonville (Florida) Art Museum.

Viewing Response *Like the angel, who is a spirit, Katie's spirit is just beginning to emerge and manifest itself in her writing.*

H Critical Thinking

DRAWING CONCLUSIONS Have students explain why Katie stops crying. *(She realizes that her mother wanted her to write and fill the box with her work. She knows that it is time to stop crying and begin writing.)*

I Literary Elements

CHARACTER Ask students what the last two lines of the story emphasize about Katie. What change in her character might this point out? *(After she begins writing, Katie is very aware of her feelings, her energies, and her abilities.)*

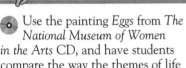

LITERATURE & HUMANITIES

Use the painting *Eggs* from *The National Museum of Women in the Arts* CD, and have students compare the way the themes of life and death are represented in the story and the painting.

Emerging Angel. John S. Bunker. Mixed media, 8 x 11 in.
Viewing the painting: How is the subject of the painting like Katie? How is it like her writing?

I pulled it down and opened it. It was as empty as the day I had put it away.

"It's you," I whispered to the box.

And then suddenly I knew.

Mama had meant *I* was the box, solid and sturdy, maybe even beautiful or at least interesting on the outside. But I had to fill up the box to make it all it could be. And I had to fill me up as well. She had guessed what might happen to me, had told me in a subtle way. In the two words she could manage.

I stopped crying and got some paper out of the desk drawer. I got out my fountain pen. I started writing, and I haven't stopped since. The first thing I wrote was about that birthday. I put it in the box, and pretty soon that box was overflowing with stories. And poems. And memories. H

And so was I.

And so was I. I

Vocabulary
subtle (sut′ əl) *adj.* not open or direct; not obvious

Teaching Support

Grammar and Language *Minilesson*

Appositives Write the following on the board: *The doctor used a stethoscope, a device for listening.* Point out that the underlined phrase is an appositive, a word or phrase, usually after a noun, that gives additional information about the noun. Appositives identify, define, or rename nouns and are set off by commas.

Activity Ask students to rewrite the following sentences using the phrases in parentheses as appositives.

1. Katie had a difficult birthday. (a ten-year-old girl) *(Katie, a ten-year-old girl, had …)*
2. V. Louise's gift was Katie's favorite. (a fountain pen) *(V. Louise's gift, a fountain pen, was Katie's favorite.)*
3. I put the letters into a special box. (all handwritten) *(I put the letters, all handwritten, into a special box.)* **L2**

Additional Resources

- ***Grammar and Language Transparency 14***
- ***Grammar and Language Workbook,*** pp. 69–70
- ***Grammar and Composition Handbook,*** Lesson 2.5
- ***Writer's Choice,*** Lesson 9.6

There Is No Word for Goodbye

Mary TallMountain

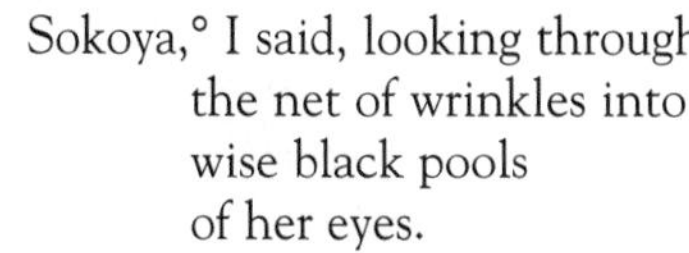

Sokoya,° I said, looking through
the net of wrinkles into
wise black pools
of her eyes.

What do you say in Athabaskan
when you leave each other?
What is the word
for goodbye?

A shade of feeling rippled
the wind-tanned skin.
Ah, nothing, she said,
watching the river flash.

She looked at me close.
We just say, Tlaa. That means,
See you.
We never leave each other.
When does your mouth
say goodbye to your heart?

She touched me light
as a bluebell.
You forget when you leave us,
You're so small then.
We don't use that word.

We always think you're coming back,
but if you don't,
we'll see you some place else.
You understand.
There is no word for goodbye.

1 *Sokoya* means "aunt."

Female Figure, 1830. Haida, Queen Charlotte Islands, British Columbia. Hardwood (possibly crab apple), wool, red and black paint, 11 x 5 x 2⅞ in. The Thaw Collection, Fenimore House Museum, Cooperstown, NY.

J Literary Elements

FIGURES OF SPEECH: *Metaphor* Help students identify two metaphors for Sokoya's face. *(TallMountain uses the metaphors* net of wrinkles *and* wise black pools of her eyes.*)*

K Critical Thinking

FOCUSING ON A QUESTION Ask students to compare the meanings of *goodbye* and *see you*. *(They may say that* goodbye *implies a permanent parting, while* see you *suggests another meeting.)*

LITERATURE & HUMANITIES

Have students listen to "Rain Dance" from the CD *American Music and Cultural Traditions*, Vol. 1, Track 1. The selection is based on a Native American creation myth.

Thematic Focus

Winds of Change Coping with the loss of someone important is a difficult lesson to learn.

ASSESSMENT

Quick Checks, p. 16

FINE ART TRANSPARENCY 30

You may want to use ***Fine Art Transparency 30*** to enrich a discussion on trying to find something positive in the loss of a loved one.

MEETING INDIVIDUAL NEEDS — SPECIAL NEEDS

Less-Proficient Readers Explain to students that poets often use relatively few words to say a lot. The fun of reading a poem is discovering the poet's message and how it is delivered. Often, poets use figures of speech, including smiles and metaphors, to express their ideas and feelings.

Activity Assign small groups two or three smiles or metaphors that create vivid images. Then have students make titled posters that illustrate them. **L1** **COLLAB. LEARN.**

Additional Resources

Inclusion Strategies

CONNECTING TO OTHER SELECTIONS

For a teaching strategy that connects "There Is No Word For Goodbye" to "Strong Men Weep," see the ***Theme One Planning Guide.***

Responding to the Selection

PERSONAL RESPONSE

Have students share with the class their ideas about gifts. Be sure they understand that Sokoya lovingly gives the gift of wisdom.

Analyzing Literature

1. She explained to the nurses what she wanted and had them get it for her.
2. Katie goes to live with her father and stepmother.
3. She asks what the Athabaskan word for *goodbye* is.
4. She was a very caring person who thought a lot about the needs of other people, especially her daughter.
5. She doesn't ever say goodbye because she feels that people never really leave each other.
6. By telling the reader what happens, she sets the mood right at the beginning. The reader knows that this is going to be a serious story.
7. Writing her thoughts and feelings helps her better understand and express her emotions. Expressing her feelings will allow Katie eventually to move beyond her angry and empty feelings.
8. Students may say that it would depend on the situation. If they received an empty box as a joke, they might be angry.
9. Encourage students to talk about their own experiences or to think of a specific person each may have to say goodbye to in the future.
10. Both selections say that family members have a great deal to give each other. Also, the selections show that there is a strong bond between family members—a bond that remains even if people are separated.

Active Reading and Critical Thinking

Responding to Literature

PERSONAL RESPONSE

- Recall the list of gifts you made for the **Reading Focus** on page 174. Before reading the story did you imagine a gift that you both can and cannot hold?
- What kind of gift did the aunt in "There Is No Word for Goodbye" give the speaker of the poem?

Analyzing Literature

RECALL

1. How did Katie's mother manage to buy her the birthday box?
2. What happens to the family after Katie's mother dies?
3. What question does the speaker in "There Is No Word for Goodbye" ask the aunt in the beginning of the poem?

Brackets connect questions that are paired to develop higher-level thinking skills.

INTERPRET

4. What can you **infer** about the character of Katie's mother when you realize that, in spite of her serious illness, she had planned a party and presents for Katie?
5. How does the aunt in TallMountain's poem feel about saying goodbye to the people she loves?

EVALUATE AND CONNECT

6. Why do you think Jane Yolen tells the reader what happens to Katie's mother in the first sentence?
7. How does filling the box with her writing help Katie deal with her grief?
8. How would you react if someone you loved gave you an empty box? Explain your answer.
9. Think about a relationship you have with an older friend or relative. How would you feel if you had to say goodbye to each other?
10. Theme Connection What do both "Birthday Box" and "There Is No Word for Goodbye" have to say about love between family members?

LITERARY ELEMENTS

Character

Characters are the actors in a work of literature. They can be people, animals, or whatever the writer chooses. In "Birthday Box," Katie and her mother are the main characters. The minor characters are the nurses and doctors in the hospital. In "There Is No Word for Goodbye," the characters are the speaker and the speaker's aunt.

1. Katie's mother hardly speaks in "Birthday Box." In what other ways does the author tell the reader about this character?
2. What do the aunt in "There Is No Word for Goodbye" and Katie's mother have in common?

- See **Literary Terms Handbook,** p. R2.

180 THEME 2

LITERARY ELEMENTS

1. She describes how she looks; she tells about her through Katie's thoughts and through her own actions.
2. They both care about a younger person and help her grow; they both give valuable gifts of the spirit.

Additional Resources

Literary Elements Transparency 16

Extending Your Response

Writing About Literature

Setting Most of the action in "Birthday Box" takes place in a hospital room. What details can you visualize about the hospital room from Yolen's description? Write a paragraph explaining how the hospital setting contributes to the effect of the story.

Creative Writing

Symbolic Gifts Katie's box is a symbol of Katie herself and of her mother's love. The language lesson received by the speaker in "There Is No Word for Goodbye" is also a symbol of love. Write a short story about a character who receives a symbolic gift.

Literature Groups

The Empty Box When Katie receives the empty box she thinks it is a joke. It takes her a year to understand what her mother meant by this gift. Do you think Katie's mother should have made sure Katie understood the meaning of the box from the beginning? Discuss your ideas and draw a conclusion. Be prepared to share your group's opinion with the whole class.

Learning for Life

Writing a Speech Sometimes people who have lived through a painful experience want to help others in a similar situation. Imagine that five years after her mother has died, Katie is asked to speak to a group of children who have lost a parent. Write a speech for Katie that expresses what she has learned about overcoming grief and finding meaning in life after such a loss.

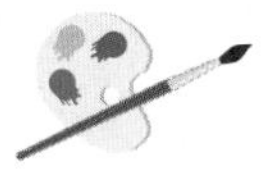

Art Activity

Wrap It! Design your own wrapping paper. Decide what special occasion your paper will be used for. Then design a paper to suit that occasion. Draw your design at a smaller scale on regular 8½ x 11-inch paper, and share it with your class.

Reading Further

Check out these other books by Jane Yolen:
The Devil's Arithmetic
Here There Be Dragons

Save your work for your portfolio.

Skill Minilesson

Reteach · Review

VOCABULARY • NEGATIVE PREFIXES

How do you change *active, moral, regular,* and *legal* into words that mean the exact opposite? Add a prefix to each one, making *inactive, immoral, irregular,* and *illegal.* The basic prefix is *in-,* but its spelling changes to *im-, ir-,* or *il-* before certain letters. Be careful, though, because these prefixes have other meanings, and they don't always change a word into its opposite. When in doubt, use a dictionary for help.

PRACTICE Write the five words from this list in which you think *in-, im-, ir-,* or *il-* is a negative prefix.

impress	income	inconsiderate
impure	injustice	impractical
irritate	indeed	irresponsible
	illustrate	

ASSESSMENT

- ***Quick Checks,*** p. 16
- ***Selection and Theme Assessment,*** pp. 29–30
- ***Performance Assessment,*** p. 16
- ***Testmaker: ExamView Pro***
- ***Interactive Tutor: Self-Assessment***

Extending Your Response

Writing About Literature

Students' paragraphs should
- explain how they think the setting of the story contributes to its effect
- include details from the story that support their ideas about the effect of the setting

Creative Writing

Students' stories should
- include a character who receives a symbolic gift
- reflect an understanding of how the gifts in these two pieces are symbolic

Literature Groups Encourage students to express their ideas and to listen to those of other people. Be sure they understand that there is no single "right" answer in this kind of situation. COLLAB. LEARN.

Learning for Life Encourage students to prepare by first putting themselves in Katie's place. Then have them write down how she eventually begins to deal with her loss.

Art Activity Encourage students to sketch several possible designs and then choose the one they think best suits the occasion.

Skill Minilesson

VOCABULARY
• NEGATIVE PREFIXES

1. impure
2. injustice
3. inconsiderate
4. impractical
5. irresponsible

Point out that the prefix *in-* and its variants are of Latin origin, while the negative prefixes *un-* and *mis-* are Anglo-Saxon. Ask students to give examples of words with the Anglo-Saxon negative prefixes.

Additional Resources
- ***Vocabulary Practice,*** p. 11

Objective

- To recognize comparative and superlative forms of adjectives and adverbs and apply strategies for using the forms correctly

Teaching Strategies

Begin by making sure that students are able to distinguish between adjectives and adverbs. Ask them to think of a list of descriptive words. Write them on the board. Categorize the words into adjectives and adverbs. Ask students to use the words in sentences. Create situations in which comparative and/or superlative forms come naturally. For example, you might wish to ask students to compare sixth grade with seventh.

Exercise

1. more slowly
2. better/more
3. most fond, fondest
4. more strongly
5. most curious

Additional Resources

- ***Grammar and Language Workbook,*** pp. 133–134
- ***Grammar and Composition Handbook,*** Lesson 6.4
- ***Writer's Choice,*** Lesson 12.9

Teaching Support

Using Adjectives and Adverbs Correctly

Adjectives describe nouns or pronouns. The **comparative** form of an adjective compares two nouns or pronouns; the **superlative** form compares more than two.

Comparative: Maria is younger than Ricardo.

Superlative: Maria is her parents' youngest child.

Adverbs describe verbs, adjectives, or other adverbs. The comparative form of an adverb compares two actions; the superlative form compares more than two.

Comparative: Susan runs faster than Jeff.

Superlative: Of all the runners on the team, Susan runs the fastest.

The endings *-er* and *-est* are used to form the comparative and superlative forms of most short adjectives and adverbs. For longer adjectives and adverbs, the words *more* and *most* are usually used.

Adjectives: dark hair, darker hair, darkest hair
curious student, more curious student, most curious student

Adverbs: works hard, works harder, works hardest
smiles happily, smiles more happily, smiles most happily

Some adjectives and adverbs are *irregular.* Irregular adjectives and adverbs do not follow the same rules for forming comparatives and superlatives. Examples: good, better, best; badly, worse, worst.

- For more about using adjectives and adverbs, see **Language Handbook,** p. R27.

EXERCISE

Write the correct comparative or superlative form of the modifier shown in parentheses.

1. Ernie learned (slowly) than an average child.
2. Jack knew him (well) than anyone else and helped him (much) than anyone.
3. Of all the things in the world, Ernie was (fond) of his seed packets.
4. Ernie started feeling (strongly) about Dolores than he felt about his seeds.
5. Who was (curious) about the flowers—Dolores, Dick, or the Avon lady?

Writing *Minilesson*

Writing a Poem Encourage students to talk about some of the older people in their lives. What are some of the differences between youth and old age? Create a list of ideas using the comparative form. (For example: *Elderly people often have more experience but less energy than young people.*)

Activity Have each student write a short poem to an elderly person who has influenced him or her and imagine reading it to the person for whom it was written. How might that person react? **L2**

Additional Resources

- ***Writer's Choice,*** Lesson 1.1

Writing Skills 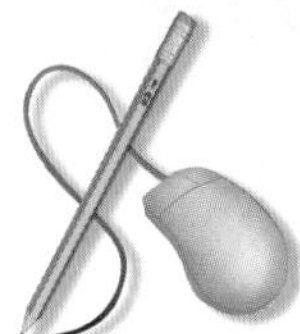

Organizing Ideas for Comparison and Contrast

When you write to explore likenesses and differences, you are using **comparison and contrast**. Diagrams can help you organize a comparison-and-contrast essay.

Venn Diagram The Venn diagram below organizes details about Alfonso and his brother Ernie, from "Broken Chain" in Theme 1, pages 44–52. Each oval shows traits of one character. Traits shared by both characters appear where the ovals overlap.

Alfonso
seventh grade
smaller, with crooked teeth
wants to look good
considers others' feelings
keeps his things neat

Both
have bikes
want to impress girls
are easily embarrassed

Ernie
ninth grade
bigger and tougher
wants to be in charge
puts himself first
lets his things get messy

Comparison Chart A comparison chart helps when you know which features you will compare. List features as headings along the left side. List subjects as headings across the top. In the example, the features are literary elements of the Theme 1 stories "Broken Chain" and "Fish Cheeks."

	BROKEN CHAIN	FISH CHEEKS
SETTING	Fresno, California, in the 1980s	Oakland, California, in 1966
MAIN CHARACTERS	Alfonso, his brother Ernie, Sandra	Amy, her parents, Robert, and his parents

EXERCISES

1. Make a Venn diagram comparing and contrasting the main characters from two different stories in this theme. Then make a chart comparing the plots and themes of the stories.
2. Use information from your diagram and chart to write an essay comparing and contrasting the two stories.

Writing Skills

Objective

- To organize ideas for exploring likenesses and differences

Teaching Strategies

Have students review the use of the Venn diagrams and create their own. Encourage students to compare their looks, feelings, and actions in sixth grade and now. Headings for their diagrams might be *Sixth Grade; Seventh Grade; Both Grades.*

Discuss the differences between the Venn diagram and the comparison chart. Ask students what other kinds of information could be organized on a comparison chart.

Exercises

1. Examples might include Dolores and Ernie from "A Crush":

Dolores
woman works in a hardware store seems experienced in life

Both
live in the same town
are seen as outsiders
are unmarried

Ernie
man
lives in a group home
has led a sheltered life

2. Headings may include *Title, Actors, Setting, Genre, Favorite Scene,* and *Rating.*

Additional Resources

- ***Writer's Choice,*** Lessons 5.3, 5.11

Teaching Support

Grammar and Language *Minilesson*

The Superlative Form This form of an adjective or adverb is used to compare three or more people, things, or events.

Activity Have students list things for which someone might hold a record. Have each student use at least three superlatives in writing a short paragraph describing a record holder and explaining why that person holds the record. **L2**

Additional Resources

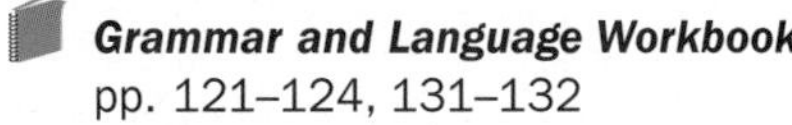

- ***Grammar and Language Workbook*** pp. 121–124, 131–132

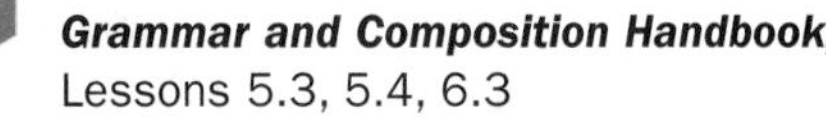

- ***Grammar and Composition Handbook,*** Lessons 5.3, 5.4, 6.3
- ***Writer's Choice,*** Lessons 12.3, 12.4, 12.8

Before Reading

Objectives

- To read and enjoy a short story
- To visualize the setting
- To write about the story's theme

Skills

Reading/Thinking: Making Critical Judgments; Identifying Main Idea; Identifying Bias; Drawing Conclusions; Logical Reasoning; Inferring; Evaluating; Identifying Assumptions
Writing: Describing a Person; Setting a Mood; Diary Entry
Vocabulary: Prefixes; Context Clues; Synonyms and Antonyms
Grammar/Language: Semicolons; Hyphens; Capitalizing; Adverbs
Listening/Speaking: Interviewing; Debating Stereotypes

Motivating → STUDENTS

Literature Launchers: "Washington Irving's New York"

Videodisc Side A, Segment 4 

Also available in VHS.

Selection Focus Transparency 17: Have the class discuss communication changes in their lifetime.

Reading Focus: Have groups use precise language and sensory details to discuss and then list things that have come into being since they were born.

Before You Read

Rip Van Winkle

MEET WASHINGTON IRVING

Washington Irving was the first American writer to win international fame. *The Sketch Book* (1820), a collection of stories admired throughout Europe, included Irving's two most famous tales, "Rip Van Winkle" and "The Legend of Sleepy Hollow." Like his famous fictional character Rip Van Winkle, Washington Irving was a born wanderer. Even as a child, he later wrote, "I began my travels, and made many tours into foreign parts and unknown regions of my native city, to the frequent alarm of my parents."

Washington Irving was born in New York City in 1783 and died in 1859.

READING FOCUS

How has the world changed since you were born? What about since your parents were born?

Think/Pair/Share
Take a moment to jot down your responses to the questions above. Then share your thoughts and feelings with a partner.

Setting a Purpose
Read this selection for the pleasure of discovering a story that readers have enjoyed for almost two hundred years.

BUILDING BACKGROUND

The Time and Place
The setting is the Hudson River valley and the Catskill Mountains, in southeastern New York State. The story takes place in the eighteenth century.

VOCABULARY PREVIEW

impunity (im pū′ nə tē) *n.* freedom from punishment, harm, or bad effects; p. 187
perseverance (pur′ sə vēr′ əns) *n.* continuation despite difficulty; determination; p. 187
incessantly (in ses′ ənt lē) *adv.* endlessly; constantly; p. 188
muse (mūz) *v.* to think or reflect; p. 190
singularity (sing′ gyə lar′ ə tē) *n.* that which is remarkable or out of the ordinary; unusualness; p. 191
incomprehensible (in′kom prē hen′ sə bəl) *adj.* not understandable; p. 191
perplexity (pər plek′ sə tē) *n.* doubt or uncertainty; puzzlement; p. 194
invariably (in vār′ ē ə blē) *adv.* without exception; p. 194
faltering (fôl′ tər ing) *adj.* shaky because of uncertainty; p. 199

RESOURCE MANAGER

Teaching Tools and Resources
- Theme Two Planning Guide
- Literature Groups Sourcebook

Essential Lesson Support
Lesson-Specific Instruction
- Selection Focus Transparency 17
- Literary Elements Transparency 17
- Active Reading Guide,* p. 17
- Selection Vocabulary Practice, p. 12

Assessment
- Selection Quick Checks,* p. 17
- Sel. and Theme Assmt., pp. 31-32
- Testmaker: ExamView Pro
- Performance Assessment, p. 17

Systematic Language Instruction
- Gr. & Comp. Hbk., L. 4.2
- Vocabulary Power, Lesson 9
- Spelling Power, Lesson 8

English Language Learners
- ELL Sourcebook, pp. 38-39
- Spanish Summaries, p. 17
- Spanish Translations, pp. 52-63
- Audio Library*
- English, Yes!

Spec. Needs/Strat. Interven.
- Interactive Rdg. Sbk., pp. T91–T93
- Interactive Rdg. Wkbk., pp. 31-34
- Inclusion Strat. Sbk., pp. 49-50, 89-90
- Audio Library*

*Also available in Spanish

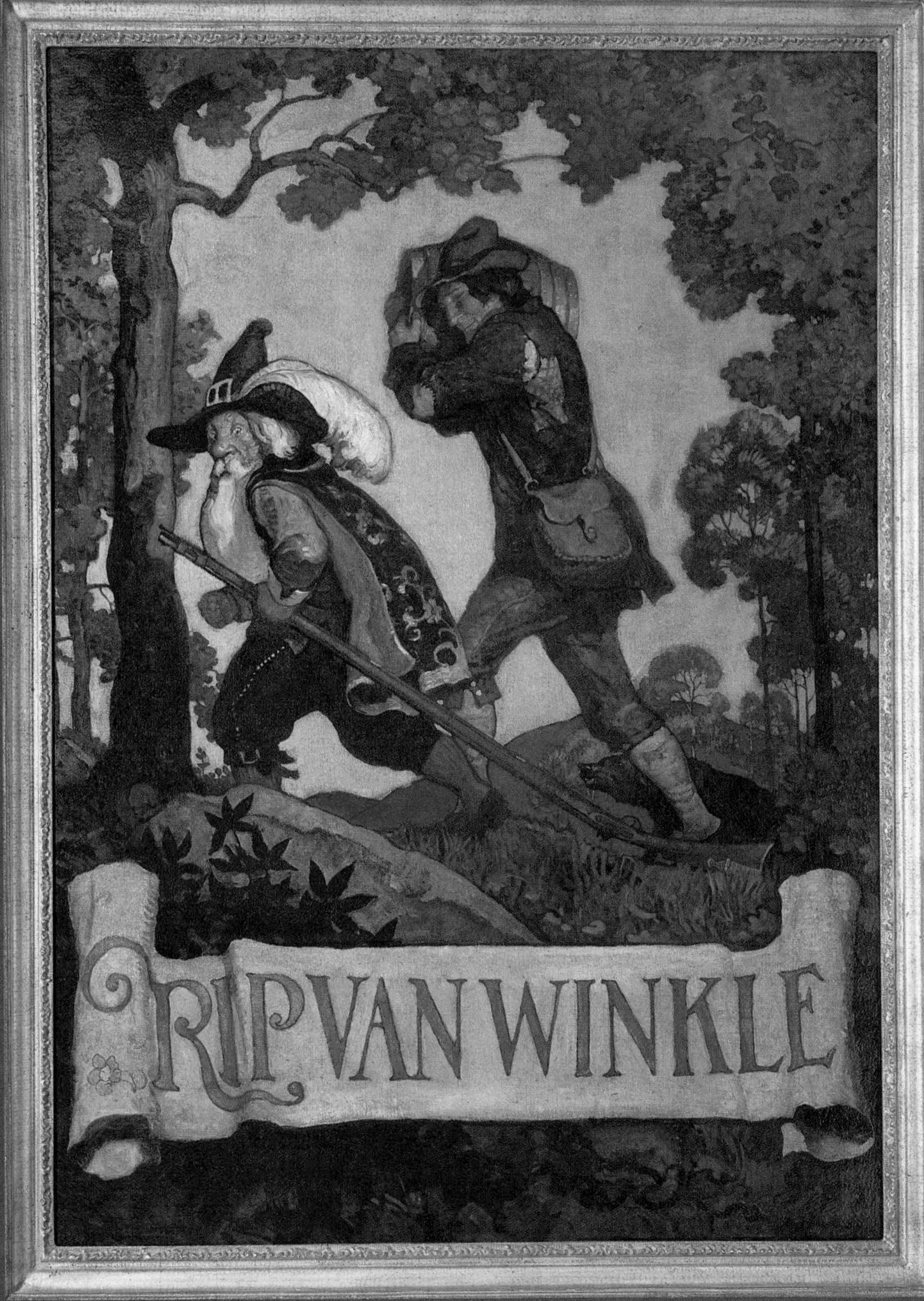

Title page from *Rip Van Winkle,* 1921. N. C. Wyeth. Oil on canvas. Millport Conservancy, Lititz, PA.

Washington Irving

Reading the Selection

SUMMARY

Rip Van Winkle, a man always ready to help with anybody's work but his own, avoids his wife's scolding by escaping into the mountains. There he plays ninepins with strange companions, falls asleep, and wakes to find that his world has changed. Back in his village, Rip discovers that what seemed to be a single night was actually twenty years.

Spanish Summaries, p. 17

A Active Reading Strategies

PREDICT Ask students to use the story's title and this illustration to make some predictions about the setting of the story. *(Because of the odd title and the fairy tale quality of the illustration, students may suggest that the story will take place in a time and place very different from this one.)*

VOCABULARY If you haven't pre-viewed the selection vocabulary with students, stop and remind them to use context clues to unlock the meanings of new vocabulary words.

Additional Resources

Active Reading Guide, p. 17
Audio Library
Spanish Audio Library

Teaching Support

CONNECTING TO OTHER SELECTIONS

COMPARING selections

This selection is paired with "old age sticks" on page 205. A lesson for teaching a comparison of the two selections is on page 207.

The chart at the right shows three ways to connect "Rip Van Winkle" to other selections in this book.

For specific teaching strategies, see the ***Theme Two Planning Guide.***

Connection		Title
Life Skills: Lifelong Learning	→	"The Old Demon," p. 483
Thematic: Family	→	"The Boy and His Grandfather," p. 495
Literary: Plot Twist	→	"After Twenty Years," p. 565

B Literary Elements

SETTING After reading the first paragraph, ask students to point out passages that help the reader visualize the setting. *(The students may provide the following suggestions:* every hour of the day, produces some change in the magical hues and shapes of these mountains; they are clothed in blue and purple, and print their bold outlines on the clear evening sky; they will gather a hood of gray vapors about their summits, which, in the last rays of the setting sun, will glow and light up like a crown of glory.*)*

The colony of New Netherland was founded by the Dutch West India Company in 1624. Fort Orange (now Albany, NY) was the colony's first permanent settlement.

C Author's Craft

STYLE Ask students to observe how Washington Irving makes the reader think well of Rip Van Winkle. *(Washington Irving presents all the character's good qualities while downplaying his weaknesses. He is setting the stage for the reader to be sympathetic to Rip's character.)*

Teaching Support

Whoever has made a voyage up the Hudson must remember the Kaatskill Mountains. They are a dismembered branch of the great Appalachian[1] family, and are seen away to the west of the river, swelling up to a noble height, and lording it over the surrounding country. Every change of season, every change of weather, indeed, every hour of the day, produces some change in the magical hues and shapes of these mountains, and they are regarded by all the good wives, far and near, as perfect barometers. When the weather is fair and settled, they are clothed in blue and purple, and print their bold outlines on the clear evening sky; but sometimes, when the rest of the landscape is cloudless, they will gather a hood of gray vapors about their summits, which, in the last rays of the setting sun, will glow and light up like a crown of glory. **B**

At the foot of these fairy mountains, the voyager may have descried[2] the light smoke curling up from a village, whose shingled roofs gleam among the trees, just where the blue tints of the upland melt away into the fresh green of the nearer landscape. It is a little village, of great antiquity, having been founded by some of the Dutch colonists, in the early times of the province, just about the beginning of the government of the good Peter Stuyvesant[3] (may he rest in peace!) and there were some of the houses of the original settlers standing within a few years, built of small yellow bricks brought from Holland, having latticed windows and gable fronts, surmounted with weathercocks.

Did You Know?

A *latticed* (lat′ ist) window has small panes separated by crossed strips of wood or metal. A gable is the triangular section of wall between the sides of a sloping roof.

In that same village and in one of these very houses (which, to tell the precise truth, was sadly timeworn and weather-beaten), there lived many years since, while the country was yet a province of Great Britain, a simple good-natured fellow, of the name of Rip Van Winkle. He was a descendant of the Van Winkles who figured so gallantly in the chivalrous[4] days of Peter Stuyvesant. He inherited, however, but little of the martial[5] character of his ancestors. I have observed that he was a simple good-natured man; he was, moreover, a kind neighbor, and an obedient henpecked husband. Indeed, to the latter circumstance might be owing that meekness of spirit which gained him such universal popularity; for those men are most apt to be obsequious and conciliating abroad, who are under the discipline of shrews at home. **C** Their tempers, doubtless, are rendered pliant and malleable in the fiery furnace of domestic tribulation, which

1. The Hudson is a river in New York, and the *Kaatskill* (now spelled *Catskill*) Mountains are part of the *Appalachian* mountain range.
2. *Descried* means "caught sight of."
3. *Peter Stuyvesant* (stī′ və sənt) was the last governor of the Dutch colony of New Netherland, which included parts of what are now Connecticut, Delaware, New Jersey, and New York. The narrator is poking fun at Stuyvesant, who was unpopular with the colonists.
4. A *chivalrous* (shiv′ əl rəs) person has the qualities of a knight, such as honor, courage, and skill in battle. The narrator again mocks Stuyvesant, who surrendered New Netherland to England in 1664, allowing it to become the British colony of New York.
5. *Martial* (mär′ shəl) means "warlike."

MEETING INDIVIDUAL NEEDS — ENGLISH LANGUAGE LEARNERS

Cultural Changes Cultural references change over time as well as from place to place, country to country. Explain that the author wrote this story in the early 1800s, so many of its phrases are outdated or are culturally different from today's. For example:

1. Women were called *good wives.*
2. The houses resembled those in Holland with yellow brick, *latticed* windows, and *gable* fronts.
3. Rip's gun is called a *fowling piece.*

Activity Have pairs of students think about and discuss cultural changes they have experienced in their communities and share their lists with the class.

Additional Resources

English Language Learners Sourcebook, p. 38

D is worth all the sermons in the world for teaching the virtues of patience and long-suffering. A nagging wife may, therefore, in some respects, be considered a tolerable blessing; and if so, Rip Van Winkle was thrice blessed.[6]

E Certain it is that he was a great favorite among all the good wives of the village, who took his part in all family squabbles; and never failed, whenever they talked those matters over in their evening gossipings, to lay all the blame on Dame[7] Van Winkle. The children of the village, too, would shout with joy whenever he approached. He assisted at their sports, made their playthings, taught them to fly kites and shoot marbles, and told them long stories of ghosts, witches, and Indians. Whenever he went dodging about the village, he was surrounded by a troop of them hanging on his coat skirts, clambering on his back, and playing a thousand tricks on him with impunity; and not a dog would bark at him throughout the neighborhood.

The great error in Rip's composition was an insuperable aversion[8] to all kinds of profitable labor. It could not be from the want of perseverance; for he would sit on a wet rock, with a rod as long and heavy as a Tartar's lance,[9] and fish all day without a murmur, even though he should not be encouraged by a single nibble. He would carry a fowling piece[10] on his shoulder for hours together, trudging through woods and swamps, and up hill and down dale, to shoot a few squirrels or wild pigeons. F He would never refuse to assist a neighbor even in the roughest toil, and was a foremost man at all country frolics for husking Indian corn, or building stone fences. The women of the village, too, used to employ him to run their errands, and to do such little odds jobs as their less obliging husbands would not do for them. In a word, Rip was ready to attend to anybody's business but his own; but as to doing family duty, and keeping his farm in order, he found it impossible.

In fact, he declared it was of no use to work on his farm; it was the most pestilent little piece of ground in the whole country. Everything about it went wrong, and would go wrong, in spite of him. His fences were continually falling to pieces; his cow would either go astray or get among the cabbages; weeds were sure to grow quicker in his fields than anywhere else; the rain always made a point of setting in just as he had some outdoor work to do; so that though his estate had dwindled away under his management, acre by acre, until there was little more left than a mere patch of Indian corn and potatoes, yet it was the worst conditioned farm in the neighborhood.

His children, too, were as ragged and wild as if they belonged to nobody. His son Rip, an urchin begotten in his own

6. *[Indeed, to the latter . . . blessed]* The narrator suggests that dealing with nagging, bad-tempered wives makes men become better, more popular people. Rip, then, is especially blessed.
7. *Dame* is a title formerly used for the woman in charge of a household.
8. An *insuperable aversion* is a great dislike that cannot be overcome.
9. A *Tartar's lance* was a twelve-foot spear carried by thirteenth-century warriors in what is now Turkey.

10. A *fowling piece* is a shotgun used to hunt wild birds.

Vocabulary
impunity (im pū′ nə tē) *n.* freedom from punishment, harm, or bad effects
perseverance (pur′ sə vēr′ əns) *n.* continuation despite difficulty; determination

D Literary Elements

TONE Ask students if they catch the playful tone in Irving's writing. Explain that even when he criticizes Dame Van Winkle's nagging, he does so in a playful way, saying Rip is "thrice blessed."

E Literary Elements

CHARACTERIZATION Explain that one way an author can delineate a character is by showing how other characters act toward him or her. Elicit from students that the favorable attitude that the children, women, and animals show toward Rip suggests that he is a likable person, despite his wife's opinion to the contrary.

F Critical Thinking

MAKING CRITICAL JUDGMENTS Ask students whether they think Rip is a good man or a deadbeat. *(Students might have a difficult time deciding how they feel about Rip, since he is helpful to everyone in town but does not take good care of his family.)*

Vo•cab•u•lar•y Skills

Prefixes Call attention to the word *insuperable* and discuss its meaning. Explain that the prefix *in-* often means "not," as in *insufficient*, *inattentive*, and *inaccurate*. Ask students for other examples of words using this prefix. *(Other examples include* insincere, inseparable, insane, *and* ineffective.*)*

Writing Minilesson

Describing a Person Throughout the story, the author uses vivid sensory details to describe Rip Van Winkle and to help the reader visualize him. Sensory details involve all the senses—taste, hearing, touch, smell, and sight.

Activity Have students work in small groups. Each group should think of a well-known person to use as the subject of a descriptive paragraph. Have them brainstorm to develop a list of sensory details about that person and then write a paragraph about him or her that includes the sensory details they like best. **L2**

COLLAB. LEARN.

Additional Resources

Writer's Choice, Lesson 3.5

VIEWING THE PAINTING

Call attention to the look on Dame Van Winkle's face, her arm bent at the elbow, her hand in a fist, the broom in her other hand. Call attention, also, to Rip's face. Ask students to identify other aspects that might reflect ideas already presented in the story. For example, the window shutter is hanging from one hinge.

Viewing Response *From her stance and facial expression, it appears that the woman is angry with the man. The woman holds a broom and seems to be working hard, but the house is falling apart and the man is walking away.*

G Literary Elements

FIGURES OF SPEECH: *Simile* Explain that a comparison of two unlike things using the words *like* or *as* is called a simile. Ask students to identify a simile in this paragraph. *(The simile is "He was...trooping like a colt.")* Ask students how Rip's son is "like a colt." *(He follows his mother closely, as a colt would his mare.)*

H Active Reading Strategies

EVALUATE Ask students to explain in their own words Rip and Dame Van Winkle's relationship. *(Although Rip seems to be a good man, he is lazy and makes life difficult for Dame Van Winkle. She constantly yells at him, hoping to motivate him, but to no avail.)*

Teaching Support

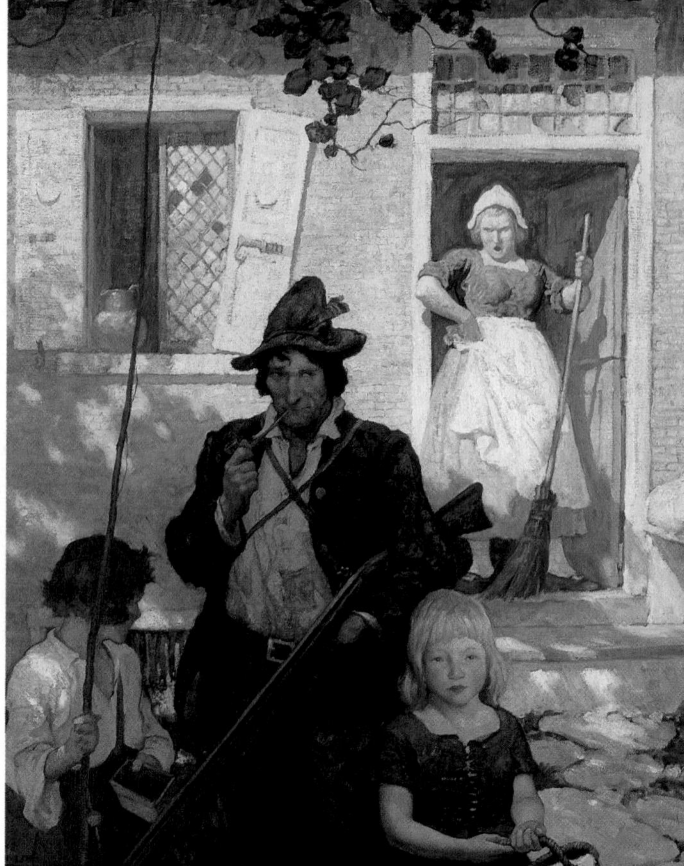

Termagant Wife, 1921. N. C. Wyeth. Oil on canvas. Millport Conservancy, Lititz, PA.

Viewing the painting: How does the painting reflect the relationship between Rip Van Winkle and his wife?

G likeness, promised to inherit the habits, with the old clothes of his father. He was generally seen trooping like a colt at his mother's heels, equipped in a pair of his father's cast-off galligaskins[11], which he had much ado to hold up with one hand, as a fine lady does her train in bad weather.

Rip Van Winkle, however, was one of those happy mortals, of foolish, well-oiled dispositions, who take the world easy, eat white bread or brown, whichever can be got with least thought or trouble, and would rather starve on a penny than work for a pound. H If left to himself, he would have whistled life away in perfect contentment; but his wife kept continually dinning in his ears about his idleness, his carelessness, and the ruin he was bringing on his family. Morning, noon, and night, her tongue was incessantly going, and everything he said or did was sure to produce a torrent of household eloquence. Rip had but one way of replying to all lectures of the kind, and that, by frequent use, had grown into a habit. He shrugged his shoulders, shook his head, cast up his eyes, but said nothing. This, however, always provoked a fresh volley from his wife; so that he would take to the outside of the house—the only side which, in truth, belongs to a henpecked husband.

11. *Galligaskins* are the loose, baggy, knee-length trousers worn in the sixteenth and seventeenth centuries.

Vocabulary

incessantly (in ses′ ənt lē) *adv.* endlessly; constantly

Reading Minilesson

Identifying Main Idea and Supporting Details A main idea is the most important idea given about a topic, while supporting details are words, phrases, or sentences that tell something about the main idea.

Activity Work with the class to fill in the following chart about the character of Rip Van Winkle and his relationship with his wife. **L2**

Main Idea About Rip: He is lazy and easy-going.
Supporting Details: • "foolish, well-oiled disposition" • "takes the world easy" • "eats white bread or brown," whichever is the least trouble • "would rather starve on a penny than work for a pound"
Main Idea About Rip's Relationship with His Wife: She nags him all the time, and he avoids her.
Supporting Details: • her tongue goes "incessantly" • he shrugs but says nothing • he retreats from the house

Additional Resources

Reading Skills Practice Workbook

Rip's sole domestic adherent[12] was his dog Wolf, who was as much henpecked as his master; for Dame Van Winkle regarded them as companions in idleness, and even looked upon Wolf with an evil eye, as the cause of his master's going so often astray. True it is, in all points of spirit befitting an honorable dog, he was as courageous an animal as ever scoured the woods—but what courage can withstand the ever-during and all-besetting terrors of a woman's tongue? The moment Wolf entered the house, his crest fell, his tail drooped to the ground, or curled between his legs, he sneaked about with a gallows air,[13] casting many a sidelong glance at Dame Van Winkle, and at the least flourish of a broomstick or ladle, he would fly to the door, yelping.

Times grew worse and worse with Rip Van Winkle as years of matrimony rolled on; a tart temper never mellows with age, and a sharp tongue is the only edged tool that grows keener with constant use. For a long while he used to console himself, when driven from home, by frequenting a kind of perpetual club of the sages, philosophers, and other idle personages[14] of the village; which held its sessions on a bench before a small inn, designated by a rubicund portrait of his Majesty George the Third. Here they used to sit in the shade through a long lazy summer's day, talking listlessly over village gossip, or telling endless sleepy stories about nothing. But it would have been worth any statesman's money to have heard the profound discussions that sometimes took place, when by chance an old newspaper fell into their hands from some passing traveler. How solemnly they would listen to the contents, as drawled out by Derrick Van Bummel, the schoolmaster, a dapper learned little man, who was not to be daunted by the most gigantic word in the dictionary; and how sagely they would deliberate upon public events some months after they had taken place.

The opinions of this junto[15] were completely controlled by Nicholas Vedder, a patriarch of the village, and landlord of the inn, at the door of which he took his seat from morning till night, just moving sufficiently to avoid the sun and keep in the shade of a large tree; so that the neighbors could tell the hour by his movements as accurately as by a sundial. It is true he was rarely heard to speak, but smoked his pipe incessantly. His adherents, however (for every great man has his adherents), perfectly understood him, and knew how to gather his opinions. When anything that was read or related displeased him, he was observed to smoke his pipe vehemently, and to send forth short, frequent, and angry puffs, but when pleased he would inhale the smoke slowly and tranquilly, and emit it in light and placid clouds. Sometimes, taking the pipe from his mouth, and letting the fragrant vapor curl about his nose, he would gravely nod his head in token of perfect approbation.[16]

From even this stronghold the unlucky Rip was at length routed by his wife, who would suddenly break in upon the tranquillity of the assemblage and call the members

12. An *adherent* is a firm supporter.
13. Having a *gallows air* is looking like one who is about to be hanged.
14. *Idle personages* are lazy persons.
15. A *junto* (jun′ tō) is a group with a common purpose.
16. *Approbation* means approval.

I Critical Thinking

IDENTIFYING BIAS Ask students to evaluate Irving's writing style. Do they think his representation of Dame Van Winkle is biased? Ask students to offer opinions as to why he speaks of her so harshly. *(Students might suggest that Irving speaks of her this way because he is trying to build sympathy for Rip. This, indeed, indicates bias toward Rip.)*

J Active Reading Strategies

EVALUATE Ask students if they think the people in this "perpetual club" are actually "sages and philosophers," or if Irving is just being playful again. *(Help students recognize that Irving is being playful.)*

Language Note

In this context, the word *patriarch* refers to the leader of the village. The word comes from the Latin *pater,* which means "father." *Patriarch* can refer to the father or head of a family, the founder of an organization, or sometimes to a bishop. *Paternal* is an adjective based on the same root.

K Literary Elements

SETTING Carefully chosen details can help readers visualize a person. Have students describe how they picture Vedder, adding details not in the story.

MEETING INDIVIDUAL NEEDS — SPECIAL NEEDS

Less-Proficient Readers To help readers understand Irving's use of exaggeration and humor, explain that people often exaggerate for emphasis; for example, "I'm so hungry I could eat a horse."

Activity Help students understand the author's actual intent in these lines: *could tell the hour by his movements as accurately as by a sundial* and *would rather starve on a penny than work for a pound.* Invite proficient readers to read passages aloud while others listen and develop vocabulary. **L1**

Additional Resources

Inclusion Strategies

VIEWING THE ART

Have students consider the "interaction" taking place between the man and dog in the picture. Ask them to study particular aspects of the subjects, such as their posture and their steady gaze at one another.

Viewing Response *The sketch here shows Rip and his dog resting atop "a green knoll," as described on this page. Their titles describe where each of the later sketches fits into the story.*

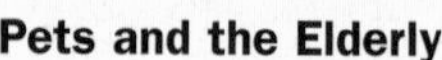

FYI

Pets and the Elderly
Studies have shown the positive effects pets have on people who live alone, particularly older people. Discuss why having a pet to care for and to talk to can keep older people healthier and happier.

L Literary Elements

SETTING: *Detail* Call attention to the details Irving uses to convey this peaceful scene. Have students identify words and phrases that emphasize the tranquillity of the scene. (*Some examples include* silent, reflection of a purple cloud, lagging bark, *and* sleeping on its glassy bosom.)

Rip With Dog Under Tree, 1921. N. C. Wyeth. Ink on paper. Stuart Kingston Gallery, Wilmington, DE.

Viewing the art: This drawing and those on pages 201–203 and 207 come from N. C. Wyeth's sketch books. They are early studies for the artist's Rip Van Winkle paintings. What parts of the story do they illustrate?

all to naught; nor was that august personage, Nicholas Vedder himself, sacred from the daring tongue of this terrible virago,[17] who charged him outright with encouraging her husband in habits of idleness.

Poor Rip was at last reduced almost to despair; and his only alternative, to escape from the labor of the farm and clamor of his wife, was to take gun in hand and stroll away into the woods. Here he would sometimes seat himself at the foot of a tree, and share the contents of his wallet[18] with Wolf, with whom he sympathized as a fellow sufferer in persecution. "Poor Wolf," he would say, "thy mistress leads thee a dog's life of it; but never mind, my lad, whilst I live thou shalt never want a friend to stand by thee!" Wolf would wag his tail, look wistfully in his master's face, and if dogs can feel pity, I verily believe he returned the sentiment with all his heart.

In a long ramble of the kind on a fine autumnal day, Rip had unconsciously scrambled to one of the highest parts of the Kaatskill Mountains. He was after his favorite sport of squirrel shooting, and the still solitudes had echoed and reechoed with the reports of his gun. Panting and fatigued, he threw himself, late in the afternoon, on a green knoll, covered with mountain herbage, that crowned the brow of a precipice.[19] From an opening between the trees he could overlook all the lower country for many a mile of rich woodland. He saw at a distance the lordly Hudson, far, far below him, moving on its silent but majestic course, with the reflection of a purple cloud, or the sail of a lagging bark,[20] here and there sleeping on its glassy bosom, and at last losing itself in the blue highlands. **L**

On the other side he looked down into a deep mountain glen, wild, lonely, and shagged, the bottom filled with fragments from the impending[21] cliffs, and scarcely lighted by the reflected rays of the setting sun. For some time Rip lay musing on this

17. A *virago* (və rä′ gō) is a scolding woman.
18. In Rip's time, *wallet* referred to a knapsack.
19. A *green knoll . . . precipice* (pres′ ə pis) refers to a high, steep cliff topped with a grassy hill.
20. A *lagging bark* is a slow-moving sailboat.
21. In this context, *impending* means overhanging.

Vocabulary
muse (mūz) *v.* to think or reflect

Teaching Support

Grammar and Language *Minilesson*

Semicolons Point out that Irving is fond of writing long sentences, many of them being a collection of shorter statements joined by semicolons. Guide students to understand that the semicolon is used in this way to join two or more independent clauses. Each clause could stand on its own as a separate sentence. The author combines them into one because the thoughts are closely related.

Activity Call attention to the paragraph that begins on page 189 and continues to page 190. Ask how many sentences make up this paragraph. Have students explain why each clause in the sentence is an independent clause. *(Each clause has a subject and a verb.)* Then have each student write a sentence joining two independent clauses with a semicolon. **L2**

Additional Resources

- ***Grammar and Language Transparency 16–18***
- ***Grammar and Language Workbook,*** pp. 265–266
- ***Grammar and Composition Handbook,*** Lesson 13.5
- ***Writer's Choice,*** Lesson 20.5

scene; evening was gradually advancing; the mountains began to throw their long blue shadows over the valleys; he saw that it would be dark long before he could reach the village, and he heaved a heavy sigh when he thought of encountering the terrors of Dame Van Winkle.

M As he was about to descend, he heard a voice from a distance, hallooing, "Rip Van Winkle! Rip Van Winkle!" He looked round, but could see nothing but a crow winging its solitary flight across the mountain. He thought his fancy must have deceived him, and turned again to descend, when he heard the same cry ring through the still evening air: "Rip Van Winkle! Rip Van Winkle!"—at the same time Wolf bristled up his back, and, giving a loud growl, skulked to his master's side, looking fearfully down into the glen. Rip now felt a vague apprehension stealing over him; he looked anxiously in the same direction, and perceived a strange figure slowly toiling up the rocks, and bending under the weight of something he carried on his back. He was surprised to see any human being in this lonely and unfrequented place; but supposing it to be some one of the neighborhood in need of his assistance, he hastened down to yield it.

On nearer approach he was still more surprised at the singularity of the stranger's appearance. He was a short, square-built old fellow, with thick bushy hair and a grizzled beard. His dress was of the antique Dutch fashion—a cloth jerkin, strapped round the waist—several pair of breeches, the outer one of ample volume, decorated with rows of buttons down the sides, and bunches at the knees. He bore on his shoulder a stout keg, that seemed full of liquor, and made signs for Rip to approach and assist him with the load. Though rather shy and distrustful of this new acquaintance, Rip complied with his usual alacrity;[22] and mutually relieving each other, they clambered up a narrow gully, apparently the dry bed of a mountain torrent. As they ascended, Rip every now and then heard long rolling peals, like distant thunder, that seemed to issue out of a deep ravine, or rather cleft,[23] between lofty rocks, toward which their rugged path conducted. He paused for an instant, but supposing it to be the muttering of one of those transient thundershowers which often take place in mountain heights, he proceeded. Passing through the ravine, they came to a hollow, like a small amphitheater,[24] surrounded by perpendicular precipices, over the brinks of which impending trees shot their branches, so that you only caught glimpses of the azure sky and the bright evening cloud. N During the whole time Rip and his companion had labored on in silence, for though the former marvelled greatly what could be the object of carrying a keg of liquor up this wild mountain; yet there was something strange and incomprehensible about the unknown, that inspired awe and checked familiarity.

22. *Alacrity* (ə lak′ rə tē) means "eager willingness."
23. A *cleft* is a wide crack or opening, as in a rock.
24. An *amphitheater* is a circular structure with rising rows of seats around a central open space.

Vocabulary

singularity (sing′ gyə lar′ ə tē) *n.* that which is remarkable or out of the ordinary; unusualness

incomprehensible (in′ kom prē hen′ sə bəl) *adj.* not understandable

M Active Reading Strategies

CONNECT Ask students whether they would have gone to the stranger if they were in Rip's place. *(Most students will say they would not because he startled both Rip and Wolf.)*

N Literary Elements

SETTING Draw students' attention to this description of the hollow. Point out how this description contrasts with the descriptions of more pleasant settings in the story. Ask students to identify a few words or phrases that make the hollow seem eerie. *(Examples include* long rolling peals, like distant thunder; deep ravine; rugged path; *and* impending trees.*)*

Vocabulary Skills

Context Clues Remind students that when they come across a word they do not know, they should try to figure out the meaning from the context—the surrounding words and sentences. For example, to understand the meaning of *apprehension*, ask students to look at the sentences immediately preceding and following. Does the dog's looking down *fearfully* suggest a meaning for apprehension? What about the following sentence: "He looked anxiously in the same direction"? *(Both suggest a sense of fear and caution, approximate meanings for* apprehension.*)*

MEETING INDIVIDUAL NEEDS — ENGLISH LANGUAGE LEARNERS

Former and Latter Write this on the board: *My sister and my friend each gave me an opinion: the former agreed with me, but the latter did not.* Explain that *former* refers to the first person mentioned, *My sister; latter* refers to the last, *my friend.*

Activity Ask students to identify who in the following example sentences agreed with the speaker.

1. John and Mr. Stone disagreed. The *former* thought he should play soccer; the *latter* thought he should not.
2. Susan and Pat want to see the play. The *former* has band practice. The *latter* is free.

Additional Resources

English Language Learners Sourcebook, p. 39

Active Reading Strategies

VISUALIZE You might want to have students examine closely the description of each of the three personages presented. Ask students to close their eyes and try to visualize them. Do they remind them of some other characters they know in literature? *(One possible example is the seven dwarfs in Snow White.)*

Language Note

The word *Flemish* refers to the area of Flanders, its people, and their language. Flanders is a historic region comprising parts of Belgium, France, and the Netherlands.

Critical Thinking

INFERRING Ask students to determine the author's purpose in describing these men as being extremely solemn and grave as they are playing a game. *(Perhaps the solemnity and gravity contribute to the strangeness of the entire scene.)*

On entering the amphitheater, new objects of wonder presented themselves. On a level spot in the center was a company of odd-looking personages playing at ninepins.[25] They were dressed in a quaint outlandish fashion; some wore short doublets, others jerkins,[26] with long knives in their belts, and most of them had enormous breeches, of similar style with that of the guide's. Their visages, too, were peculiar; one had a large head, broad face, and small piggish eyes; the face of another seemed to consist entirely of nose, and was surmounted by a white sugar-loaf hat, set off with a little red cock's tail. They all had beards, of various shapes and colors. There was one who seemed to be the commander. He was a stout old gentleman, with a weather-beaten countenance; he wore a laced doublet, broad belt and hanger, high-crowned hat and feather, red stockings, and high-heeled shoes, with roses in them. The whole group reminded Rip of the figures in an old Flemish painting, in the parlor of the village parson, which had been brought over from Holland at the time of the settlement.

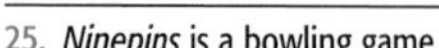

What seemed particularly odd to Rip was, that though these folks were evidently amusing themselves, yet they maintained the gravest faces, the most mysterious silence, and were the most melancholy party of pleasure he had ever witnessed. Nothing interrupted the stillness of the scene but the noise of the balls, which, whenever they were rolled, echoed along the mountains like rumbling peals of thunder.

As Rip and his companion approached them, they suddenly desisted from their

25. *Ninepins* is a bowling game.
26. A *jerkin* is the close-fitting, hip-length jacket, usually sleeveless and collarless, worn by men in the sixteenth and seventeenth centuries. It was often worn over a *doublet,* a close-fitting, waist-length jacket, with or without sleeves.

Teaching Support

Grammar and Language Minilesson

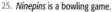

Hyphens On the board, write the following hyphenated phrases:

odd-looking personages
sugar-loaf hat
high-heeled shoes

Explain that when two words are combined to form an adjective and the adjective precedes the noun it modifies, the words are usually joined by a hyphen.

Activity Provide students with the following phrases and have them add hyphens if needed.

- wind blown hair *(wind-blown hair)*
- wide eyed reaction *(wide-eyed reaction)*
- large head *(correct)*
- moth eaten clothes *(moth-eaten clothes)* **L2**

Additional Resources

Grammar and Language Transparency 16–18

Grammar and Language Workbook, pp. 275–276

Grammar and Composition Handbook, Lesson 13.8

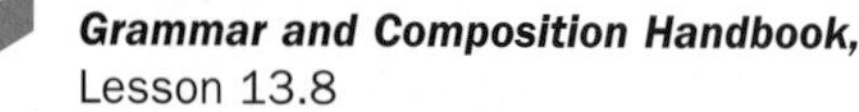

Writer's Choice, Lesson 20.8

Gnomes Bowling, 1921. N. C. Wyeth. Oil on canvas. Millport Conservancy, Lititz, PA.

Viewing the painting: How does the mood of the painting relate to the mood of Rip's night on the mountain?

play, and stared at him with such fixed, statue-like gaze, and such strange, uncouth, lackluster countenances,[27] that his heart turned within him, and his knees smote together. His companion now emptied the contents of the keg into large flagons,[28] and made signs to him to wait upon the company. He obeyed with fear and trembling; they quaffed the liquor in profound silence, and then returned to their game.

By degrees Rip's awe and apprehension subsided. He even ventured, when no eye was fixed upon him, to taste the beverage, which he found had much of the flavor of excellent Holland ale. He was naturally a thirsty soul, and was soon tempted to repeat the draft. One taste provoked another; and he repeated his visits to the flagon so often, that at length his senses were overpowered, his eyes swam in his head, his head gradually declined, and he fell into a deep sleep.

On waking, he found himself on the green knoll whence he had first seen the old man of the glen. He rubbed his eyes—it was a bright sunny morning. The birds were hopping and twittering among the bushes, and the eagle was wheeling aloft, and breasting the pure mountain breeze. "Surely," thought Rip, "I have not slept here all night." He recalled the occurrences before he fell asleep. The strange man with a keg of liquor—the mountain ravine—the wild retreat among the rocks—the woebegone[29] party at ninepins—the flagon—"Oh! that flagon! that wicked flagon!" thought Rip; "what excuse shall I make to Dame Van Winkle?"

27. *Uncouth, lackluster countenances* means "crude and dull faces."

28. *Flagons* are containers with handles and spouts, used to hold liquids.

29. *Woebegone* means "sorrowful or mournful."

Viewing the Painting

N. C. (Newall Convers) Wyeth (1882–1925) was one of the most admired and successful illustrators of his time. He is probably best remembered for his illustrations for such works as *Treasure Island, Robin Hood,* and, of course, "Rip Van Winkle."

Viewing Response *Students may mention the deep shadows and strange figures illuminated by the flash of lightning as contributing to a mood of mystery.*

Q Author's Craft

AUTHOR'S PURPOSE Ask students to think about the "odd-looking personages." How does their silence affect both Rip and the reader? How would the effect be different if they did speak? *(Their silence makes them and the event seem even more mysterious. If they spoke, Rip would probably ask who they are, and a response would end the mystery and suspense of this scene.)*

R Literary Elements

TONE Remind students of Irving's playful tone. Ask students what these words "he repeated his visits to the flagon so often" actually mean. *(They imply that he kept going back to drink more and more ale.)*

Writing Minilesson

Setting a Mood Review a passage in which the author provides much detail to set a mood. For example, on page 193, "The birds were hopping and twittering among the bushes, and the eagle was wheeling aloft, and breasting the pure mountain breeze." Remind students that though other details could be seen, the writer omitted them because they would have upset the mood.

Activity Have students write a description of a favorite place at a specific time of the day or year using details that contribute to a particular mood they wish to create. Have them read their work aloud or post it for the class to enjoy. **L2**

Additional Resources

Writer's Choice, Lesson 3.3

CC Literary Elements

DIALOGUE Call attention to the dialogue in this passage. Explain to students that writers try to make dialogue sound authentic—much like the language spoken by real people similar to the characters in the story. Have students identify conversational aspects of the dialogue here. *(Students may point to the broken sentences:* Well—who are they?—Name them. *Students may also mention the rambling sentence:* He went off to the wars too, was a great militia general.)

Vo•cab•u•lar•y Skills

Word Meanings Point to Irving's use of two adverbs, *apparently* and *certainly*. Ask students how Rip would be able to see that *certainly* the man was just as ragged as he, while he would only be able to guess that *apparently* the man was just as lazy. If necessary, have students look up the meanings of the words in a dictionary.

DD Literary Elements

CHARACTERIZATION Ask students what Rip's words reveal about his personality and state of mind. What does Rip's rambling suggests about his mental state at the moment? *(They should see his rambling as a sign of his nervousness and confusion.)*

Here a general shout burst from the bystanders—"A Tory! a Tory! a spy! a refugee![38] hustle him! away with him!" It was with great difficulty that the self-important man in the cocked hat restored order; and demanded again of the unknown culprit, what he came there for, and whom he was seeking? The poor man humbly assured him that he meant no harm, but merely came there in search of some of his neighbors, who used to keep about the tavern.

CC "Well—who are they?—name them."

Rip bethought himself a moment, and inquired, "Where's Nicholas Vedder?"

There was a silence for a little while, when an old man replied in a thin piping voice, "Nicholas Vedder! why, he is dead and gone these eighteen years! There was a wooden tombstone in the churchyard that used to tell all about him, but that's rotten and gone too."

"Where's Brom Dutcher?"

"Oh, he went off to the army in the beginning of the war; some say he was killed at the storming of Stony Point—others say he was drowned in a squall at the foot of Antony's Nose.[39] I don't know—he never came back again."

"Where's Van Bummel, the schoolmaster?"

"He went off to the wars too, was a great militia general, and is now in Congress."

Rip's heart died away at hearing of these sad changes in his home and friends, and finding himself thus alone in the world. Every answer puzzled him too, by treating of such enormous lapses of time, and of matters which he could not understand; war—Congress—Stony Point;—he had no courage to ask after any more friends, but cried out in despair, "Does nobody here know Rip Van Winkle?"

"Oh, Rip Van Winkle!" exclaimed two or three. "Oh, to be sure! that's Rip Van Winkle yonder, leaning against the tree."

Rip looked, and beheld a precise counterpart[40] of himself, as he went up the mountain: apparently as lazy, and certainly as ragged. The poor fellow was now completely confounded. He doubted his own identity, and whether he was himself or another man. In the midst of his bewilderment, the man in the cocked hat demanded who he was, and what was his name?

"God knows," exclaimed he, at his wits' end; "I'm not myself—I'm somebody else—that's me yonder—no—that's somebody else got into my shoes—I was myself last night, but I fell asleep on the mountain, and they've changed my gun, and everything's changed, and I'm changed, and I can't tell what's my name, or who I am!" DD

The bystanders began now to look at each other, nod, wink significantly, and tap their fingers against their foreheads. There was a whisper, also, about securing the gun, and keeping the old fellow from doing mischief, at the very suggestion of which the self-important man in the cocked hat retired quickly. At this critical moment a fresh, comely woman pressed through the throng to get a peep at the gray-bearded man. She had a chubby child in her arms, which, frightened at his looks, began to

38. A *Tory* was a person who supported the British during the Revolution. A *refugee* was a member of a group of British supporters who attacked the American revolutionaries.
39. *Stony Point* is a small bay on the Hudson River, and *Antony's Nose* is a mountain. Both are in southeastern New York.
40. A *precise counterpart* is a person who looks exactly like another.

Teaching Support

Listening and Speaking Minilesson

Interviewing Have students interview an older person about some event, historical or personal, that he or she recalls. Suggest events that involved some kind of change, such as the introduction of the computer or television. They might ask such questions as *What is one of the most memorable changes or periods of change you recall? What were the circumstances of the change? What brought it about? How did the change affect society or you personally?*

Activity Have students take notes during the interviews or capture them on tape. Then have each of them present a short oral report to the class, playing portions of the tape or reading excerpts from the interview. **L2** **COLLAB. LEARN.**

EE cry. "Hush, Rip," cried she, "hush you little fool; the old man won't hurt you." The name of the child, the air of the mother, the tone of her voice, all awakened a train of recollections in his mind.

"What is your name, my good woman?" asked he.

"Judith Gardenier."

"And your father's name?"

"Ah, poor man, Rip Van Winkle was his name, but it's twenty years since he went away from home with his gun, and never has been heard of since—his dog came home without him; but whether he shot himself, or was carried away by the Indians, nobody can tell. I was then but a little girl."

FF Rip had but one question more to ask; but he put it with a faltering voice,—

"Where's your mother?"

"Oh, she too had died but a short time since; she broke a blood vessel in a fit of passion at a New England peddler."

There was a drop of comfort, at least, in this intelligence. The honest man could contain himself no longer. He caught his daughter and her child in his arms. "I am your father!" cried he—"Young Rip Van Winkle once—old Rip Van Winkle now!—Does nobody know poor Rip Van Winkle?"

All stood amazed, until an old woman, tottering out from among the crowd, put her hand to her brow, and peering under it in his face for a moment, exclaimed, "Sure enough! it is Rip Van Winkle—it is himself! Welcome home again, old neighbor—Why, where have you been these twenty long years?"

Rip's story was soon told, for the whole twenty years had been to him but as one night. The neighbors stared when they heard it; some were seen to wink at each other, and put their tongues in their cheeks; and the self-important man in the cocked hat, who, when the alarm was over, had returned to the field, screwed down the corners of his mouth, and shook his head—upon which there was a general shaking of the head throughout the assemblage. GG

It was determined, however, to take the opinion of old Peter Vanderdonk, who was seen slowly advancing up the road. He was a descendant of the historian of that name, who wrote one of the earliest accounts of the province. Peter was the most ancient inhabitant of the village, and well versed in all the wonderful events and traditions of the neighborhood. He recollected Rip at once, and corroborated[41] his story in the most satisfactory manner. He assured the company that it was a fact, handed down from his ancestor the historian, that the Kaatskill Mountains had always been haunted by strange beings. That it was affirmed that the great Henry Hudson, the first discoverer of the river and country, kept a kind of vigil there every twenty years, with his crew of the *Half-Moon*; being permitted in this way to revisit the scenes of his enterprise and keep a guardian eye upon the river and the great city called by his name. That his father had once seen them in their old Dutch dresses playing at ninepins in a hollow of the mountain; and that he himself

41. Something *corroborated* (kə rob′ ə rāt əd) is supported, or confirmed.

Vocabulary
faltering (fôl′ tər ing) *adj.* shaky because of uncertainty

EE Critical Thinking

IDENTIFYING ASSUMPTIONS Ask students to discuss how the "air of the mother, the tone of her voice" struck a chord with Rip. *(Students may realize that this woman's voice and manner reminded Rip of someone in his family, perhaps his wife.)*

FF Critical Thinking

DRAWING CONCLUSIONS Discuss with students the meaning of the word *faltering.* Then ask why Rip might have asked about his wife in a "faltering voice." You may wish to share the following model to illustrate the thinking process involved in drawing conclusions.

Model: From what I've read so far, I know that Rip fears his wife and that one of his first thoughts upon waking was what his wife's reaction to his absence would be. So his voice may be faltering, or wavering, because he is dreading the reunion with her that might be coming. It is also possible that he assumes she is dead, and for that reason his voice is unsteady.

GG Critical Thinking

INFERRING Ask students to think about the townspeople's reaction to Rip. What do the winks and other gestures suggest about the people's reaction to Rip's story? *(Students should see that these people don't believe Rip. They may think he is an old man who has "lost it.")*

Interdisciplinary Connection

Social Studies Students may be interested in learning more about the Hudson River and/or the area through which it flows, the setting of this story. Researching this geographical area can give students deeper insight into the story of Rip Van Winkle.

Activity Have students work in pairs or small groups to research the Hudson River, particularly from its discovery to the years around the Revolutionary War. Students may write or deliver oral reports on the flow of the river, its role in the economic growth of the region, or its role in the war. Students may want to concentrate their study on the person for whom the river is named, Henry Hudson. Remind students that once they have chosen their topic, they should develop several relevant questions they want their reports to answer and use those answers to organize and focus their reports. Remind them also to keep track of their sources and to cite them (in writing or orally) when they present their reports. Direct them to pages R55–R59 of the **Writing Handbook** to review methods of documenting research information. **L2** COLLAB. LEARN.

HH Author's Craft

STYLE Help students understand that Irving modifies his storytelling style here by presenting all these facts in summarized form.

II Critical Thinking

INFERRING Ask students why they think Rip prefers the younger generation to his older cronies. *(Rip has lost 20 years.)*

JJ Author's Craft

TONE Point out that the terms Irving uses in speaking of Rip's wife deal with forms of government: *despotism, petticoat government, tyranny.* Have students look up the meanings of these words and explain why they are funny when used in connection with Rip's wife.

Thematic Focus

Winds of Change Many changes took place as Rip slept through an important period in our history.

FINE ART TRANSPARENCY 30

You may want to use ***Fine Art Transparency 30*** to discuss the kinds of changes that might take place in our country in the next 20 years.

ASSESSMENT

Quick Checks, p. 17

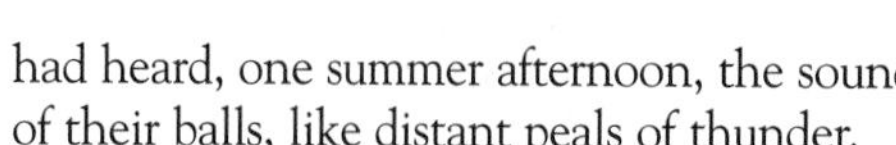

had heard, one summer afternoon, the sound of their balls, like distant peals of thunder.

HH To make a long story short, the company broke up, and returned to the more important concerns of the election. Rip's daughter took him home to live with her; she had a snug, well-furnished house, and a stout cheery farmer for her husband, whom Rip recollected for one of the urchins that used to climb upon his back. As to Rip's son and heir, who was the ditto of himself, seen leaning against the tree, he was employed to work on the farm; but showed an hereditary disposition to attend to anything else but his business.

II Rip now resumed his old walks and habits; he soon found many of his former cronies, though all rather the worse for the wear and tear of time; and preferred making friends among the rising generation, with whom he soon grew into great favor.

Having nothing to do at home, and being arrived at that happy age when a man can be idle with impunity, he took his place once more on the bench at the inn door, and was reverenced as one of the patriarchs of the village, and a chronicle of the old times "before the war." It was some time before he could get into the regular track of gossip, or could be made to comprehend the strange events that had taken place during his sleep. How that there had been a Revolutionary War—that the country had thrown off the yoke of Old England—and that, instead of being a subject of His Majesty George the Third, he was now a free citizen of the United States. Rip, in fact, was no politician; the changes of states and empires made but little impression on him; but there was one species of despotism[42] under which he had long groaned, and that was—petticoat government. Happily that was at an end; he had got his neck out of the yoke of matrimony, and could go in and out whenever he pleased without dreading the tyranny of Dame Van Winkle. Whenever her name was mentioned, however, he shook his head, shrugged his shoulders, and cast up his eyes; which might pass either for an expression of resignation to his fate, or joy at his deliverance. JJ

He used to tell his story to every stranger that arrived at Mr. Doolittle's hotel. He was observed at first to vary on some points every time he told it, which was, doubtless, owing to his having so recently awaked. It at last settled down precisely to the tale I have related, and not a man, woman, or child in the neighborhood but knew it by heart. Some always pretended to doubt the reality of it, and insisted that Rip had been out of his head, and that this was one point on which he always remained flighty. The old Dutch inhabitants, however, almost universally gave it full credit. Even to this day they never hear a thunderstorm of a summer afternoon about the Kaatskills, but they say Henry Hudson and his crew are at their game of ninepins; and it is a common wish of all henpecked husbands in the neighborhood, when life hangs heavy on their hands, that they might have a quieting draft out of Rip Van Winkle's flagon.

42. A *despotism* (des′ pə tiz′ əm) is a government under a ruler who has unlimited authority.

Teaching Support

Grammar and Language *Minilesson*

Capitalizing Proper Nouns Review the concept that proper nouns are names of particular persons, places or things. Proper nouns are capitalized.

Activity Have students capitalize proper nouns in the following list as needed. If a word should not be capitalized, have them write *correct.* **L2**

1. atlantic ocean *(Atlantic Ocean)*
2. cellular phone *(correct)*
3. amusement park *(correct)*
4. general washington *(General Washington)*
5. paris, france *(Paris, France)*
6. dame van winkle *(Dame Van Winkle)*
7. dutch inhabitants *(Dutch inhabitants)*
8. revolutionary war *(Revolutionary War)*

Additional Resources

Grammar and Language Transparency 16–18

Grammar and Language Workbook, p. 235–236

Grammar and Composition Handbook, Lesson 12.1–12.4

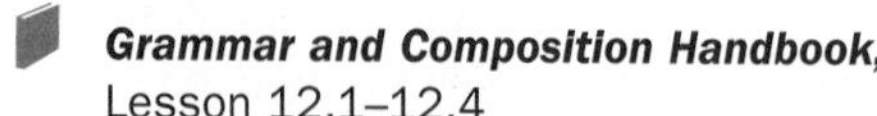

Writer's Choice, Lesson 19.1–19.4

Responding to Literature

PERSONAL RESPONSE

- What was your reaction to this story? Did you find it amusing, suspenseful, mysterious, or all three? Describe your impressions in your journal.

Analyzing Literature

RECALL

1. According to the narrator, what is the chief flaw in Rip's character? What is the chief flaw in his wife's character?
2. Briefly describe the strangers Rip meets in the mountains. What happens to him after he drinks their beverage?
3. What is the first change Rip notices after he wakes up? Describe one other change he notices once he returns to town.
4. According to the narrator, what is Rip's life like after his return?

Brackets connect questions that are paired to develop higher-level thinking skills.

INTERPRET

5. What sort of person is Rip Van Winkle? What conflict exists between him and his wife? Support your ideas with examples from the story.
6. The details used to describe the men and the atmosphere in the hollow intensify the mysterious **mood** Irving created in this part of the story. List details that helped you sense the mood of this scene.
7. In what way does Peter Vanderdonk confirm Rip's explanation of his absence?
8. In your opinion, is Rip's life better or worse after his twenty-year sleep? Explain.

EVALUATE AND CONNECT

9. Theme Connection What historical events occurred during Rip's absence? Why do you think Irving chose that twenty-year period for Rip's long nap? Explain.
10. What is your reaction to what happens to Rip and his wife in this story? Explain.

LITERARY ELEMENTS

Setting

A **setting** is the time and place in which the events of a story, novel, or play occur. For example, the setting of "Rip Van Winkle" is the Hudson River valley in the late 1700s. Strong writers often use the setting to help create an atmosphere or mood for a story. Carefully chosen details help readers visualize the place being described.

1. Pick out details from "Rip Van Winkle" that helped you picture the setting in your mind. Explain how the details helped transport you into the time and place of the story.
2. Choose another story you've read, and describe its setting.

- See **Literary Terms Handbook**, p. R10.

Dog With Broom Thrown at Him, 1921. N. C. Wyeth. Ink on paper. Stuart Kingston Gallery, Wilmington, DE.

Responding to the Selection

PERSONAL RESPONSE

Some students may have found humor in the way Irving describes Rip and his overbearing wife. Others may have enjoyed trying to figure out the meaning of the changes.

Analyzing Literature

1. Rip's chief flaw is his reluctance to work on his own property. His wife's is her nagging.
2. The strangers are short older men who seem very serious though they are playing a game. After he drinks their beverage, Rip falls asleep.
3. Rip notices that his rifle is rusty, the town's buildings and people are different, and the tree at the inn has been replaced by a flagpole.
4. Life after Rip's return is like it was before except that he is no longer being nagged.
5. Rip is a happy-go-lucky man. His wife nags him constantly about his aversion to work.
6. The details include the men's strange clothes, peculiar faces, and beards of various shapes and colors and the long knives in their belts.
7. Vanderdonk says that his ancestor the historian told of the vigil of Henry Hudson and his crew in the Kaatskills every 20 years.
8. Rip's life may be better because he can enjoy his life of leisure without being nagged. He is, however, 20 years older.
9. The American colonies have declared their independence from England and fought the Revolutionary War. George Washington is now president, and the people are living under a democratic form of government. Irving probably chose this period because it contains so many important historical events.
10. Some students may feel everything works out well for Rip and be content with Dame Van Winkle's demise. Others may feel she was not as bad as she was made out to be.

LITERARY ELEMENTS

1. The writer's descriptive details about the village and its river valley help readers visualize a quiet way of life long ago before modern conveniences, transportation, and communication.
2. Descriptions should include vivid details about the story's setting.

Additional Resources

Literary Elements Transparency 17

Literature and Writing

Writing About Literature

Students' paragraphs should

- have a clear theme statement
- support that theme with references to the text

Personal Writing

Students' diary entries should

- consider specific aspects of their world, such as communication, transportation, and food
- give details about the changes
- show that the writer is coming upon these changes suddenly, not gradually

Extending Your Response

Literature Groups Remind students there are basically two questions. One is whether the characters are stereotypes. The other is whether Irving could have made the characters more believable. Remind students that each answer must be supported by details from the story. COLLAB. LEARN.

Learning for Life Remind students to probe for details and to move from surface issues to feelings and emotions. Students should have some questions prepared to ask others in response to what they say.

Art Activity Suggest that, in addition to important political events, students might include important cultural events and entertainment milestones.

Literature and Writing

Writing About Literature

Thinking About a Theme What does "Rip Van Winkle" say about the passage of time and human nature? Write a paragraph or two explaining your ideas about the theme of this well-known story.

Personal Writing

Sweet Dreams Imagine if you were to fall asleep for the next twenty years. How do you think the world would change during that time? When you discovered these changes, how would you feel? Write a diary entry explaining what has happened, how things have changed, and how you feel.

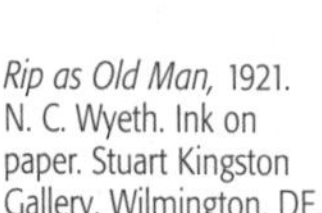

Rip as Old Man, 1921. N. C. Wyeth. Ink on paper. Stuart Kingston Gallery, Wilmington, DE.

Extending Your Response

Literature Groups

Debating Stereotypes A stereotype has only a few, highly exaggerated character traits. Stereotypes are never fully believable. For example, the strong, silent cowboy is a stereotype; so is the wicked villain or the innocent heroine. Stereotypes often appear in folktales, legends, and literature that is meant to teach a lesson. Are both Rip and his wife stereotypes? Why or why not? How might Irving have made these two characters more believable? Debate the issue. Support your opinions with examples and quotations from the story.

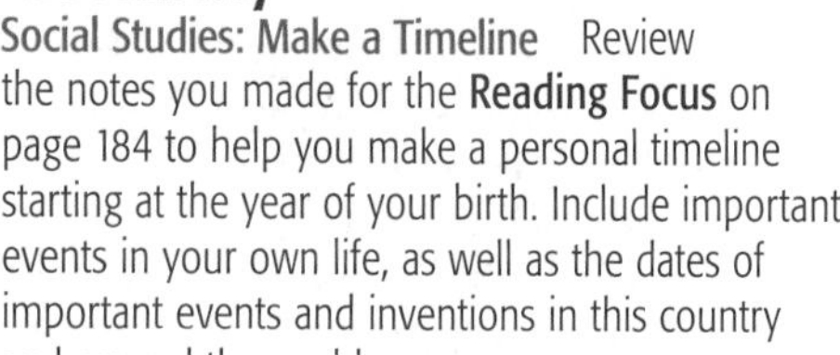

Learning for Life

A Newspaper Account Imagine that you are a journalist sent to interview Rip for the *Hudson River Valley Gazette.* Write an article about his mysterious experience. Include quotations and descriptions from Rip as well as other villagers.

Art Activity

Social Studies: Make a Timeline Review the notes you made for the **Reading Focus** on page 184 to help you make a personal timeline starting at the year of your birth. Include important events in your own life, as well as the dates of important events and inventions in this country and around the world.

Reading Further

If you would like to read more by Washington Irving, try these works:

Diedrich Knickerbocker's History of New York

"The Legend of Sleepy Hollow" in *The Sketch Book of Geoffrey Crayon, Gent.*

Save your work for your portfolio.

MEETING INDIVIDUAL NEEDS — SPECIAL NEEDS

Less-Proficient Readers Some students may have little practice in using a thesaurus or a synonym finder. Explain that a thesaurus such as *Roget's* groups related words into topical categories with numbered subdivisions. This type of thesaurus also includes an index that can be referenced quickly. A synonym finder, on the other hand, arranges word entries alphabetically with a list of synonyms for each word.

Activity Pair less-proficient readers with students who are familiar with using thesauri and synonym finders. Give them access to these reference books and have them look up synonyms for the following words and discuss their meanings: *faltering, incessantly, aversion, malleable, tribulation,* and *vehemently*. **L2** COLLAB. LEARN.

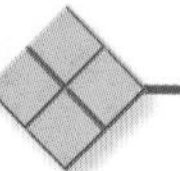

Skill Minilessons

Reteach · Review

GRAMMAR AND LANGUAGE • ADVERBS

An adverb is a word that modifies, or describes, a verb, an adjective, or another adverb. When modifying a verb, an adverb gives information about *when, where,* or *how* the action of a sentence takes place. Examples:
Rip slept **soundly.** (How?)
Later Rip woke up. (When?)
Rip looked **everywhere** for his dog. (Where?)

PRACTICE Write an adverb to modify the underlined word in each sentence.

1. Rip walked through the woods.
2. He looked into a deep mountain glen.
3. He listened to the voice in the distance.
4. The strange men stared at Rip.
5. Being quite thirsty, Rip drank the beverage.

• For more about adverbs, see **Language Handbook,** p. R27.

READING AND THINKING • EVALUATING

Evaluating characters and events in a story involves forming opinions and making judgments about what you read. Remember to evaluate *while* you are reading—not just after you have finished. As you read, ask yourself questions such as the following:

- Does this event make sense?
- Would this character really say or do this?

PRACTICE Review "Rip Van Winkle" and think about what happens to Rip once he wakes up from his sleep. Write questions about the events and trade your questions with a partner. Answer each other's questions and then talk about your answers.

• For more about reading strategies, see **Reading Handbook,** pp. R85–R100.

VOCABULARY • SYNONYMS AND ANTONYMS

As you probably know, *synonyms* are words with similar meanings, and *antonyms* are words with opposite meanings. A synonym for *loud* is *noisy,* and an antonym for *loud* is *quiet.* Although some words have no synonyms and some have no antonyms, many words have several of each.

PRACTICE Match each word below with its synonym and its antonym from the lists at the right.

Word
1. likely
2. delicate
3. invariably
4. incomprehensible
5. uncouth

Synonym	Antonym
A. fragile	a. doubtful
B. confusing	b. considerate
C. rude	c. never
D. probable	d. tough
E. constantly	e. clear

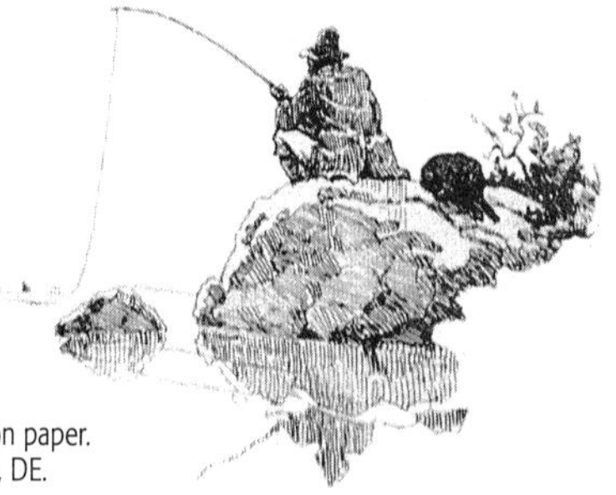

Rip Fishing, 1921. N. C. Wyeth. Ink on paper. Stuart Kingston Gallery, Wilmington, DE.

Skill Minilessons

GRAMMAR AND LANGUAGE
ADVERBS

Possible answers:

1. slowly; happily; nervously; casually
2. steadily; longingly; intently
3. eagerly; anxiously; closely
4. bewilderingly; intently
5. quickly; sloppily; shockingly

READING AND THINKING
EVALUATING

Suggest that students ask these questions as if they did not know the outcome. Questions might include: *Why didn't he notice his long beard or the changes in the skin on his hands and arms?*

VOCABULARY
SYNONYMS AND ANTONYMS

1. D, a
2. A, d
3. E, c
4. B, e
5. C, b

Additional Resources

- ***Grammar and Language Workbook,*** pp. 127–128
- ***Grammar and Composition Handbook,*** Lessons 6.1, 6.2
- ***Writer's Choice,*** Lesson 12.6
- ***Reading Skills Practice Workbook***
- ***Vocabulary Practice,*** p. 12

ASSESSMENT

- ***Quick Checks,*** p. 17
- ***Selection and Theme Assessment,*** pp. 31–32
- ***Performance Assessment,*** p. 17
- ***Testmaker: ExamView Pro***
- ***Interactive Tutor: Self-Assessment***

Theme 3 At a Glance

Facing Challenge

THEME OPENING

- **Introducing the Theme** (p. 217)
- **Exploring the Theme** (p. 218)
- **Theme Projects** (p. 219)

Theme 3: FACING CHALLENGE

SELECTIONS

New Directions (p. 220)

The Wreck of the Hesperus (p. 226)

I'll Walk the Tightrope (p. 226)

Too Soon a Woman (p. 234)

A Boy and His Dog (p. 242)

The Women's 400 Meters (p. 251)

To James (p. 251)

a poem (for langston hughes) (p. 258)

Dreams (p. 258)

Media Connection: Why 'Possum Has a Large Mouth (p. 266)

Racing the Great Bear (p. 267)

***from* Beyond the Limits** (p. 280)

Active Reading Model: The Fish Crisis (p. 294)

Media Connection: Americans Continue to Worry About the Decline of the Oceans (p. 304)

Hurricanes (p. 305)

SKILL FEATURES

Vocabulary Skills (p. 225)

Reading and Thinking Skills (p. 250)

Interdisciplinary Connection (p. 257)

Technology Skills (pp. 264–265)

Listening, Speaking, and Viewing (p. 279)

Genre Focus: Nonfiction (pp. 290–291)

Active Reading Strategies (pp. 292–293)

Grammar Link (p. 315)

WRITING WORKSHOP

Persuasive Writing: Editorial (pp. 316–319)

THEME ASSESSMENT

- **Responding to the Theme, Analyzing Literature, Evaluate and Set Goals** (p. 320)
- **Build Your Portfolio** (p. 320)
- **Reading on Your Own** (p. 321)
  Where the Red Fern Grows by Wilson Rawls
  Hostage by Edward P. Myers
  Reach Higher by Scottie Pippen
  The Outsiders by S. E. Hinton
- **Standardized Test Practice** (pp. 322–323)

KEYS TO LITERARY CONNECTIONS

Comparing Selections

The **Comparing Selections** feature in this theme provides opportunities for addressing diverse aspects of the reading and literature curriculum.

For example, in Comparing Selections on page 249, students are asked to examine the way the characters in "Too Soon a Woman" and "A Boy and His Dog" were affected by loss.

World Literature

The Student Edition contains a variety of literature that represents cultures from around the world. World literature selections are highlighted with the icon above.

TEACHING SUPPORT

The Teaching Support offers a wealth of interactive instructional support:

Meeting Individual Needs
- Special Needs
- English Language Learners
- Multiple Modes of Expression
- Advanced Learners

Internet Connection

Assessment

Portfolio Options

Minilessons
- Grammar and Language
- Reading
- Writing
- Listening and Speaking

Connecting to Other Selections

Real-World Connection

Interdisciplinary Connection

Life Skills Connection

Family and Community Activity

Key to Ability Levels

The activities throughout this theme have been coded for students of various abilities.

L1 BASIC activities for all students

L2 AVERAGE activities for average to above-average students

L3 ADVANCED LEARNERS activities for above-average students

Teaching Today

The Glencoe *Teaching Today* professional development Web site at www.teachingtoday.glencoe.com features daily teaching tips, free downloads, annotated Web resources, educational news, and a wealth of information on a wide range of topics.

Theme 3 At a Glance
Facing Challenge

Reading Skills in this theme

Variety of Texts

In addition to autobiographical selections, this theme includes the following text types:

- narrative essay
- poetry
- short story
- legend
- cartoon
- Web site
- public opinion poll

Comprehension Skills

The following instructional support for comprehension skills appears in this theme of the Student Edition:

- **Reading and Thinking Minilessons** (pp. 233, 263, 278, 314)
- **Visualizing** (p. 250)
- **Active Reading Strategies and Model** (pp. 292–303)

See also the **Reading Minilessons** throughout the theme in this Teacher Wraparound Edition.

For strategies for reading longer works, such as novels and novellas, see "Tips for Independent Reading" on page 321.

Reading Resources

Active Reading Guide The ***Active Reading Guide*** provides graphic organizers and study guide questions to support students' reading of each selection. (***Active Reading Guide***, pp. 19–28)

Interactive Reading Sourcebook and **Interactive Reading Workbook** The ***Interactive Reading Sourcebook*** and ***Interactive Reading Workbook*** offer focused comprehension strategies and lessons on critical thinking skills as well as fluency practice and activities to teach and support phonics, decoding, spelling, and vocabulary development.

Vocabulary Power The ***Vocabulary Power*** workbook (Lessons 10–14) provides systematic teaching, practice, and assessment of vocabulary for better reading comprehension.

Audio Library Available on audiocassette and on CD, the ***Audio Library*** provides valuable comprehension support.

Glencoe Literature Library Each title in the ***Glencoe Literature Library*** includes a full-length work plus related readings. A separate Study Guide is available for each title.

Five–Star Stories These anthologies of familiar short stories adapted and abridged for a variety of reading levels include exercises to help increase students' vocabulary and improve their reading comprehension.

The Contemporary Readers ***The Contemporary Readers*** are nonfiction books linked to various themes and designed for developing readers from a wide range of backgrounds.

Literature Classics CD-ROM The selections on this CD-ROM can be searched by author, theme, or genre.

inTIME and Humanities Across TIME Coproductions of Glencoe and Time, Inc., these resources include a wealth of high-interest nonfiction related to the selections in this theme.

Assessment in this theme

Assessment in the Student Edition

This program offers a number of diverse ways to evaluate student understanding and skill proficiency. In the Student Edition, use the following:

- **Responding to Literature**
  Following each selection, students are asked to recall facts, interpret ideas, and evaluate concepts as they answer a variety of questions and complete activities to extend their understanding.
- **Theme Assessment (pp. 320–321)**
  Here students respond to the selections on personal and analytical levels. They also assume ownership of their learning by setting and evaluating goals and by selecting work for their portfolios.

See also the many **Assessment Resources** listed on the facing page.

Standardized Test Practice

The Princeton Review has developed the Standardized Test Practice pages found at the end of this thematic unit (pp. 322–323). For additional practice, direct students to the following resources:

- ITBS Preparation and Practice
- SAT-9 Preparation and Practice
- TerraNova Preparation and Practice

Writing Skills in this theme

Writing Skills

The Student Edition of Theme Three offers strong instructional support for writing skills:

In **Extending Your Response**, which follows each selection:

- **Writing About Literature**
- **Personal/Creative Writing**

See also the **Writing Minilessons** throughout the theme in this Teacher Wraparound Edition.

Writing Workshops

Theme Three concludes with a **Writing Workshop** that guides students through the process of writing an editorial (pp. 316–319).

Writing Resources

Writer's Assistant CD-ROM Each **Writing Workshop** is supplemented by an interactive writing guide on the ***Writer's Assistant*** CD-ROM. This easy- to-use writing guide provides prompts, templates, and other tools that lead students through the writing process.

Grammar and Composition Handbook The ***Grammar and Composition Handbook*** (Lessons 4.4–6.5) provides systematic instruction in English language conventions.

Spelling Power The ***Spelling Power*** workbook (Lessons 9–12) provides systematic teaching, practice, and assessment of spelling to help students become better spellers and thus enhance their writing.

Writing and Proofreading Practice Blackline masters present in-depth instruction and practice on a specific step in the writing process and proofreading (pp. 1–7, 22–28).

Writing and Proofreading Transparencies Transparencies provide graphic organizers and proofreading exercises for whole-class instruction (pp. 1–6, 11–14, 29–30).

Research and Report Writing Guide This resource provides extensive tips and activities to guide students in their writing projects in the literature classroom as well as in classes across the curriculum.

Style and Documentation Sourcebook for Writers This sourcebook is a combination reference and workbook, giving students the most up-to-date information and guidance regarding traditional as well as technological research strategies and documentation.

Revising with Style This resource offers instruction and exercises focusing on the revision process and covering topics from proofreading and correcting common grammatical errors to sentence combining and reordering.

Assessment Resources

Selection Quick Checks For each selection, a **Quick Check** of three to five short-answer questions measures students' literal comprehension.

Selection and Theme Assessment The ***Selection and Theme Assessment*** instrument tests students' abilities to recall, interpret, and evaluate what they've read. The tests consist of multiple-choice, short answer, and essay questions.

Performance Assessment Alternative assessment instruments and rubrics for Theme Three are found in the ***Performance Assessment*** ancillary.

Writing Assessment and Portfolio Management These notes and strategies, student models, and assessment tools assist with the task of measuring students' progress as writers and as monitors of their own writing.

Testmaker: ExamView Pro Teachers can customize selection and Theme Three tests by accessing the ***Testmaker*** database.

Interactive Tutor: Self-Assessment The ***Interactive Tutor: Self-Assessment*** software provides multiple-choice tests with immediate feedback to help students evaluate their knowledge and understanding of each literature selection.

MindJogger Videoquizzes Using a popular game show format, ***MindJogger Videoquizzes*** on videocassettes enable teachers to evaluate student understanding of Theme Three in a quick and fun manner.

Theme 3 SKILLS SCOPE AND SEQUENCE

Lessons	Literary Elements	Reading and Thinking	Writing
New Directions MAYA ANGELOU DRP:61 Lexile:810	Biography, SE p. 223 *Biography, TWE p. 222* *Imagery, TWE p. 222*	*Distinguishing Fact from Opinion, TWE p. 222* *Problem and Solution, TWE p. 222*	Finding Solutions, SE 224 Journal Entry, SE p. 224
The Wreck of the Hesperus HENRY WADSWORTH LONGFELLOW I'll Walk the Tightrope MARGARET DANNER	Narrative Poetry, SE p. 232 *Character, TWE p. 227* *Setting, TWE p. 228* *Dialogue, TWE p. 228* *Narrative Poetry, TWE p. 230* *Plot, TWE p. 230*	Identifying Spatial Relationships, SE p. 233 *Sequence of Events, TWE p. 228* *Inferring, TWE p. 229*	Describing Imagery, SE p. 233 Writing an Article, SE p. 233 *Personal Poems, TWE p. 231*
Too Soon a Woman DOROTHY M. JOHNSON DRP:50 Lexile:580	Dialect, SE p. 240 *Setting, TWE p. 236* *Dialect, TWE pp. 236–238* *Character, TWE pp. 236, 239*	*Inferring, TWE p. 237* *Cause and Effect, TWE p. 237* *Draw. Conclusions, TWE pp. 238, 239*	Surprise Ending, SE p. 241 An Introduction, SE p. 241
A Boy and His Dog MARTHA BROOKS DRP:51 Lexile:670	Foreshadowing, SE p. 248; *TWE p. 247* *Point of View, TWE p. 244* *Tone, TWE p. 244*	Comparing Selections, SE p. 249 Visualizing, SE p. 250 *Sequence of Events, TWE p. 245* *Inferring, TWE p. 247* *Draw. Conclusions, TWE p. 247*	
The Women's 400 Meters LILLIAN MORRISON To James FRANK HORNE	Free Verse, SE p. 255 *Alliteration, TWE p. 252* *Free Verse, TWE pp. 252, 253, 254*	*Evaluating, TWE p. 252* *Inferring, TWE p. 254* *Drawing Conclusions, TWE p. 254*	Theme, SE p. 256 Journal Entry, SE p. 256
a poem (for langston hughes) NIKKI GIOVANNI DREAMS LANGSTON HUGHES	Rhyme Scheme, SE p. 262 *Rhyme Scheme, TWE p. 259* *Rhythm, TWE p. 259* *Repetition, TWE p. 261*	Identifying Assumptions, SE p. 263 *Analyzing Arguments, TWE p. 260*	Sensory Images, SE p. 263 Short Poem, SE p. 263 *Collaborative Dream Poems, TWE p. 261*
Racing the Great Bear JOSEPH BRUCHAC DRP:52 Lexile:640	Oral Tradition, SE p. 276; *TWE pp. 269, 270, 271, 272, 273, 274, 275* *Character, TWE pp. 270, 272, 273*	Web Site, SE p. 266 Setting a Purpose, SE p. 278 *Using Graphic Aids, TWE p. 266* *Focusing on a Question, TWE p. 269* *Monitoring Comp., TWE p. 271*	Dialogue, SE p. 277 Journal Entry, SE p. 277 *Persuading the Public, TWE p. 279*
from Beyond the Limits STACY ALLISON DRP:58 Lexile:790	Autobiography, SE p. 288; *TWE p. 282* *Description, TWE p. 282*	ELL *Emphasize and Organize, TWE p. 282* *Main Idea/Details, TWE p. 283* *Generalizing, TWE p. 285* *Crit. Judgment, TWE p. 287*	Challenges, SE p. 289 Journal Entry, SE p. 289 *Using Detail, TWE p. 284*
The Fish Crisis J. MADELEINE NASH DRP:70 Lexile:1240	Nonfiction, SE p. 290 Essay, SE p. 302; *TWE p. 298* *Author's Purpose, TWE p. 300*	Nonfiction, SE p. 292 *Using Text Structures, TWE p. 297* *Identifying Propaganda, TWE p. 299* *Problem and Solution, TWE p. 304*	Evaluating Sources, SE p. 303 Letter to the Editor, SE p. 303 *Interview, TWE p. 298*
Hurricanes PATRICIA LAUBER DRP:59 Lexile:860	Informational Text, SE p. 312; *TWE pp. 307, 308, 309* *Suspense, TWE p. 308* *Repetition, TWE pp. 309*	Fact/Opinion, SE p. 314 *Summarizing, TWE p. 308* *Evaluating, TWE p. 310* SN *Learning Disabled, TWE p. 311*	Summary, SE p. 313 Postcard, SE p. 313 *Dramatic Account, TWE p. 315*
Writing WORKSHOP Persuasive Writing: Editorial			*Power Words, TWE p. 318*

Key: Student material is in roman. Teacher material is in italic.  Technology ELL English Language Learners

Vocabulary and Spelling	Grammar and Language	Listening, Speaking, and Viewing	Life Skills; Study and Research; Technology
Analogies, SE p. 224 Using Homophones, SE p. 225 ELL *Pair Pictures,* TWE p. 225		Literature Groups, SE p. 224	
Etymology, TWE p. 229	ELL *Weather Proverbs,* TWE p. 227 *Identifying Adjectives,* TWE p. 230	Literature Groups, SE p. 233 Reading Aloud, SE p. 233 SN *Learning Disabled,* TWE p. 229	
Antonyms, SE p. 241 *Homophones,* TWE p. 237	ELL *Past Perfect Verbs,* TWE p. 236 *Punctuating Dialogue,* TWE p. 238	Literature Groups, SE p. 241 SN *Less-Proficient Readers,* TWE p. 250	Learning for Life: Report, SE p. 241 Research: Report, SE p. 241 Internet Connection, SE p. 241 *Mushrooms,* TWE p. 239
ELL *Unusual Expressions,* TWE p. 244 SN *Less-Proficient Readers,* TWE p. 247	*Usage:* Lie *and* Lay, TWE p. 246	Literature Groups, SE p. 248 Invited Speaker, SE p. 248	Interview, SE p. 248
ELL *Track and Field,* TWE p. 252 *Prefixes,* TWE p. 253	Ellipsis, SE p. 256 *Present and Past Participles,* TWE p. 253	Literature Groups, SE p. 256 Interview, SE p. 256 *Sports Broadcast,* TWE p. 254	Math, SE p. 257
ELL *Word Meanings,* TWE p. 259	*Prepositional Phrases,* TWE p. 260	Literature Groups, SE p. 263 Appreciating Poetry, SE p. 263	E-mail: Online Safety, SE p. 264 SN *Learning Disabled,* TWE p. 264
Multiple-Meaning Words, SE p. 278 ELL *Multiple-Meaning Words,* TWE p. 269 SN *Less-Proficient Readers,* TWE p. 272	Possessive Pronouns, SE p. 278 *Comparative and Superlative Adjectives,* TWE p. 274	Literature Groups, SE p. 277 Analyzing Persuasion, SE p. 279 *Radio Play,* TWE p. 270 ELL *Persuading the Public,* TWE p. 279	Internet Connection, SE p. 277 Iroquois Longhouse, SE p. 277 *Bears,* TWE p. 275
Base Words and Suffixes, SE p. 289 *Connotation and Denotation,* TWE p. 284 *Less-Proficient Readers,* TWE p. 287	*Apostrophe,* TWE p. 286 SN *Less-Proficient Readers,* TWE p. 287	Literature Groups, SE p. 289 *Documentary,* TWE p. 286	Internet Connection, SE p. 289 Create a Map, SE p. 289 *Planning and Designing,* TWE p. 285
Suffixes, SE p. 303 *Prefixes,* TWE p. 296	ELL *Phrasal Verbs,* TWE p. 296 *Using Quotation Marks,* TWE p. 300	Literature Groups, SE p. 303 ELL *Cultural Observations,* TWE p. 290	Interdisciplinary Activity: Diagram, SE p. 303
Prefixes that Express Number, SE p. 314 *Word Origins,* TWE p. 309	Subject-Verb Agreement, SE p. 315 Spelling Plurals, SE p. 314 *Compound Predicates,* TWE p. 310	Literature Groups, SE p. 313 News Broadcast, SE p. 313 *Video,* TWE p. 311	News Broadcast, SE p. 313 Mural, SE p. 313 ELL *Weather,* TWE p. 307
		ELL *Now Hear This,* TWE p. 316	

SN Special Needs/Strategic Intervention

Theme 3 RESOURCE MANAGER

Lessons	Essential Resources	English Language Learners
New Directions MAYA ANGELOU PACING: 2 DAYS	**Lesson-Specific Instruction** Selection Focus Transp. 19 Active Reading Guide,* p. 19 Literary Elements Transp. 19 Selection Vocabulary Practice, p. 13 Quick Checks,* p. 19 Selection and Theme Assessment, pp. 33–34 Testmaker: ExamView Pro Performance Assessment, p. 18 TIME *inTIME* magazine, pp. 6–7 **Systematic Language Instruction** Grammar and Comp. Hbk., L. 4.4 Vocabulary Power, Lesson 10 Spelling Power, Lesson 9	English Language Learners Sourcebook, p. 41 Theme Three Planning Guide, p. 6 Spanish Summaries, p. 19 Spanish Translations, pp. 64–65 Audio Library* English, Yes!
The Wreck of the Hesperus HENRY WADSWORTH LONGFELLOW **I'll Walk the Tightrope** MARGARET DANNER PACING: 2 DAYS	**Lesson-Specific Instruction** Selection Focus Transp. 20 Active Reading Guide,* p. 20 Literary Elements Transp. 20 Quick Checks,* p. 20 Selection and Theme Assessment, pp. 35–36 Testmaker: ExamView Pro Performance Assessment, p. 19 TIME *inTIME* magazine, pp. 12–13, 22–23 **Systematic Language Instruction** Grammar and Comp. Hbk., L. 4.5	English Language Learners Sourcebook, p. 42 Spanish Summaries, p. 20 Audio Library* English, Yes!
Too Soon a Woman DOROTHY M. JOHNSON PACING: 2 DAYS	**Lesson-Specific Instruction** Selection Focus Transp. 21 Active Reading Guide,* p. 21 Literary Elements Transp. 21 Vocabulary Practice, p. 14 Quick Checks,* p. 21 Selection and Theme Assessment, pp. 37–38 Testmaker: ExamView Pro Performance Assessment, p. 20 **Systematic Language Instruction** Grammar and Comp. Hbk., L. 4.6–4.7 Vocabulary Power, Lesson 11 Spelling Power, Lesson 10	English Language Learners Sourcebook, p. 43 Spanish Summaries, p. 21 Spanish Translations, pp. 66–69 Audio Library* English, Yes!
A Boy and His Dog MARTHA BROOKS PACING: 2 DAYS	**Lesson-Specific Instruction** Selection Focus Transp. 22 Active Reading Guide,* p. 22 Literary Elements Transp. 22 Vocabulary Practice, p. 15 Quick Checks,* p. 22 Selection and Theme Assessment, pp. 39–40 Testmaker: ExamView Pro Performance Assessment, p. 21 TIME *inTIME* magazine, p. 2 **Systematic Language Instruction** Grammar and Comp. Hbk., L. 5.1–5.2	English Language Learners Sourcebook, p. 44 Spanish Summaries, p. 22 Spanish Translations, pp. 70–73 Audio Library* English, Yes!
The Women's 400 Meters LILLIAN MORRISON **To James** FRANK HORNE PACING: 2 DAYS	**Lesson-Specific Instruction** Selection Focus Transp. 23 Active Reading Guide,* p. 23 Literary Elements Transp. 23 Quick Checks,* p. 23 Selection and Theme Assessment, pp. 41–42 Testmaker: ExamView Pro Performance Assessment, p. 22 TIME *inTIME* magazine, p. 27 **Systematic Language Instruction** Grammar and Comp. Hbk., L. 5.3–5.4 Vocabulary Power, Lesson 12	English Language Learners Sourcebook, p. 45 Spanish Summaries, p. 23 Spanish Translations, pp. 74–75 Audio Library* English, Yes!

Key: Workbook · Blackline Masters · Textbook · Transparency · CD-ROM · Videodisk (also available in videocassette)

Special Needs/ Strategic Intervention	Reteaching and Enrichment
Interactive Reading Sourcebook, pp. T97–T99 Interactive Reading Workbook, pp. 36–37 Inclusion Strategies Sourcebook, pp. 39–40 Theme Three Planning Guide, p. 6 Audio Library*	Fine Art Transparency 8 Reading Skills Practice Workbook, pp. 31-32 Interactive Tutor: Self-Assessment Vocabulary PuzzleMaker Web Site (lit.glencoe.com)
Interactive Reading Sourcebook, pp. T100–T102 Interactive Reading Workbook, pp. 38–39 Theme Three Planning Guide, p. 11 Audio Library*	Literature Launchers, Side A, Segment 7 Reading Skills Practice Workbook, pp. 33–34 Grammar and Language Transp. 19 Gr. and Lang. Wkbk., pp. 117–119 Grammar and Comp. Hbk., L. 5.1 TIME *Humanities Across TIME*, Cover 16 Interactive Tutor: Self-Assessment Vocabulary PuzzleMaker Web Site (lit.glencoe.com)
Interactive Reading Sourcebook, pp. T103–T105 Interactive Reading Workbook, pp. 40–41 Inclusion Strategies Sourcebook, pp. 53–54, 61–62 Theme Three Planning Guide, p. 17 Audio Library*	Fine Art Transparency 21 Reading Skills Practice Workbook, pp. 35–36 Grammar and Language Transp. 20 Gr. and Lang. Wkbk., pp. 267–270 Grammar and Comp. Hbk., L. 13.6 Interactive Tutor: Self-Assessment Vocabulary PuzzleMaker Web Site (lit.glencoe.com)
Interactive Reading Sourcebook, pp. T106–T108 Interactive Reading Workbook, pp. 42–43 Inclusion Strategies Sourcebook, pp. 59–60 Theme Three Planning Guide, p. 25 Audio Library*	Reading Skills Practice Workbook, pp. 37–38 Grammar and Language Transp. 21 Gr. and Lang. Wkbk., pp. 223–224 Grammar and Comp. Hbk., L. 3.11, 3.12 Interactive Tutor: Self-Assessment Vocabulary PuzzleMaker Web Site (lit.glencoe.com)
Interactive Reading Sourcebook, pp. T108–T110 Interactive Reading Workbook, p. 44 Audio Library*	Grammar and Language Transp. 22 Gr. and Lang. Wkbk., pp. 167–168 Grammar and Comp. Hbk., L. 9.1 TIME *Humanities Across TIME*, Cover 11 Interactive Tutor: Self-Assessment Vocabulary PuzzleMaker Web Site (lit.glencoe.com)

Web Audiocassette Diskette *Also available in Spanish

INDEPENDENT READING

Encourage students to spend thirty minutes each day in independent reading. The following Glencoe components and outside resources provide opportunities for reading related to this theme.

The Glencoe Literature Library

You may want to assign one or more of these titles for independent reading. For a complete listing of titles available in the Glencoe Literature Library, see page T96 of this book.

- *Where the Red Fern Grows* by Wilson Rawls
- *Island of the Blue Dolphins* by Scott O'Dell
- *The View from Saturday* by E. L. Konigsburg
- *Lupita Mañana* by Patricia Beatty
- *Dogsong* by Gary Paulsen

inTIME News stories, feature articles, reviews, profiles, and essays in the magazine connect to an author, work, or theme in the Student Edition. See the **inTIME Teacher's Guide** for specific connections to this theme.

Resources for Less-Proficient Readers

For reading especially created for less-proficient readers, suggest

- *Five-Star Stories*
- *The Contemporary Readers*

Additional Resources for Independent Reading

The following titles are listed with specific reading selections throughout this theme. You may want to suggest that students look for these in your local or school library.

- *The Down of a Thistle* by Margaret Danner
- *Selected Poems* by Henry Wadsworth Longfellow
- *Paradise Café and Other Stories* by Martha Brooks
- *Two Moons in August* by Martha Brooks
- *Sprints and Distances* by Lillian Morrison
- *At the Crack of the Bat* by Lillian Morrison
- *The Iroquois* by Craig and Katherine Doherty
- *Fish* by Steve Parker
- *Threatened Oceans* by Jenny T. Tesar
- *The Outsiders* by S. E. Hinton

Theme 3 RESOURCE MANAGER (continued)

Lessons	Essential Resources		English Language Learners
a poem (for langston hughes) NIKKI GIOVANNI DREAMS LANGSTON HUGHES PACING: 1 DAY	**Lesson-Specific Instruction** Selection Focus Transp. 24 Active Reading Guide,* p. 24 Literary Elements Transp. 24 Quick Checks,* p. 24 Selection and Theme Assessment, pp. 43–44	Testmaker: ExamView Pro Performance Assessment, p. 23 **Systematic Language Instruction** Grammar and Comp. Hbk., L. 6.1	English Language Learners Sourcebook, p. 46 Spanish Summaries, p. 24 Audio Library* English, Yes!
Racing the Great Bear JOSEPH BRUCHAC PACING: 2 DAYS	**Lesson-Specific Instruction** Selection Focus Transp. 25 Active Reading Guide,* p. 25 Literary Elements Transp. 25 Vocabulary Practice, p. 16 Quick Checks,* p. 25 Selection and Theme Assessment, pp. 45–46	Testmaker: ExamView Pro Performance Assessment, p. 24 **Systematic Language Instruction** Grammar and Comp. Hbk., L. 6.2 Vocabulary Power, Lesson 13 Spelling Power, Lesson 11	English Language Learners Sourcebook, p. 47 Theme Three Planning Guide, p. 45 Spanish Summaries, p. 25 Spanish Translations, pp. 76–81 Audio Library* English, Yes!
from Beyond the Limits STACY ALLISON PACING: 2 DAYS	**Lesson-Specific Instruction** Selection Focus Transp. 26 Active Reading Guide,* p. 26 Literary Elements Transp. 26 Selection Vocabulary Practice, p. 17 Quick Checks,* p. 26	Selection and Theme Assessment, pp. 47–48 Testmaker: ExamView Pro Performance Assessment, p. 25 **Systematic Language Instruction** Grammar and Comp. Hbk., L. 6.3	English Language Learners Sourcebook, p. 49 Spanish Summaries, p. 26 Spanish Translations, pp. 82–87 Audio Library* English, Yes!
The Fish Crisis J. MADELEINE NASH PACING: 2 DAYS	**Lesson-Specific Instruction** Selection Focus Transp. 27 Active Reading Guide,* p. 27 Literary Elements Transp. 27 Vocabulary Practice, p. 18 Quick Checks,* p. 27 Selection and Theme Assessment, pp. 49–50	Testmaker: ExamView Pro Performance Assessment, p. 26 TIME *inTIME* magazine, pp. 14–15 **Systematic Language Instruction** Grammar and Comp. Hbk., L. 6.4 Vocabulary Power, Lesson 14 Spelling Power, Lesson 12	English Language Learners Sourcebook, p. 50 Spanish Summaries, p. 27 Spanish Translations, pp. 88–91 Audio Library* English, Yes!
Hurricanes PATRICIA LAUBER PACING: 2 DAYS	**Lesson-Specific Instruction** Selection Focus Transp. 28 Active Reading Guide,* p. 28 Literary Elements Transp. 28 Selection Vocabulary Practice, p. 19 Quick Checks,* p. 28 Selection and Theme Assessment, pp. 51–52	Testmaker: ExamView Pro Performance Assessment, p. 27 TIME *inTIME* magazine, pp. 12–13 **Systematic Language Instruction** Grammar and Comp. Hbk., L. 6.5 Vocabulary Power, Unit 3 Review/Test Spelling Power, Unit 3 Review/ Proofreading	English Language Learners Sourcebook, p. 51 Theme Three Planning Guide, p. 69 Spanish Summaries, p. 28 Audio Library* English, Yes!
Writing WORKSHOP Persuasive Writing: Editorial PACING: 2 DAYS	Writing Assessment and Portfolio Management, pp. 1–13, 20–22, 38–45		English Language Learners Sourcebook, p. 9 English, Yes!

Key: 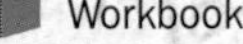 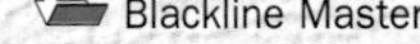 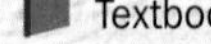 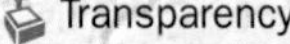  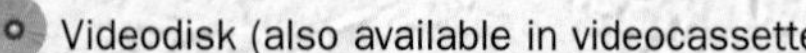

Special Needs/ Strategic Intervention	Reteaching and Enrichment
Interactive Reading Sourcebook, pp. T111–T114 Interactive Reading Workbook, p. 45 Theme Three Planning Guide, p. 39 Audio Library*	Literature Launchers, Side A, Segment 8 Grammar and Language Transp. 23 Gr. and Lang. Wkbk., pp. 141–142 Grammar and Comp. Hbk., L. 7.1 TIME *Humanities Across TIME*, Cover 13 Interactive Tutor: Self-Assessment Web Site (lit.glencoe.com)
Interactive Reading Sourcebook, pp. T114–T116 Interactive Reading Workbook, pp. 46–47 Inclusion Strategies Sourcebook, pp. 63–64 Theme Three Planning Guide, p. 45 Audio Library*	Grammar and Language Transparencies 24 Gr. and Lang. Wkbk., pp. 109–110, 121–124 Grammar and Comp. Hbk., L. 4.4, 5.3, 5.4 Media Connection Activities, p. 5 Interactive Tutor: Self-Assessment Vocabulary PuzzleMaker Web Site (lit.glencoe.com)
Interactive Reading Sourcebook, pp. T117–T119 Interactive Reading Workbook, pp. 48–49 Inclusion Strategies Sourcebook, pp. 17–18 Audio Library*	Fine Art Transparency 7 Grammar and Language Transp. 25 Gr. and Lang. Wkbk., pp. 273–274 Grammar and Comp. Hbk., L. 13.7 Interactive Tutor: Self-Assessment Vocabulary PuzzleMaker Web Site (lit.glencoe.com)
Interactive Reading Sourcebook, pp. T119–T122 Interactive Reading Workbook, pp. 50–51 Inclusion Strategies Sourcebook, pp. 41–42 Theme Three Planning Guide, p. 61 Audio Library*	Grammar and Language Transp. 26 Gr. and Lang. Wkbk., pp. 267–270 Grammar and Comp. Hbk., L. 13.6 Media Connection Activities, p. 6 TIME *Humanities Across TIME*, Cover 10 Interactive Tutor: Self-Assessment Vocabulary PuzzleMaker Web Site (lit.glencoe.com)
Interactive Reading Sourcebook, pp. T122–T125 Interactive Reading Workbook, pp. 52–53 Inclusion Strategies Sourcebook, pp. 31–32, 37–38, 43–44, 77–78, 89–90 Audio Library*	Literature Launchers, Side A, Segment 9 Reading Skills Practice Workbook, pp. 47–48 Grammar and Language Transp. 27 Gr. and Lang. Wkbk., pp. 53–54, 297–300 Grammar and Comp. Hbk., L. 1.5, 15.1 TIME *Humanities Across TIME*, Cover 15 Interactive Tutor: Self-Assessment Vocabulary PuzzleMaker Web Site (lit.glencoe.com)
	Writing and Proofreading Practice, pp. 1–7, 22–27 Writing and Proof. Transp. 1–6, 11–14, 29–30 Revising with Style Writer's Assistant

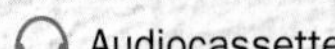
Web

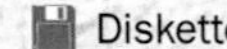
Audiocassette

Diskette

*Also available in Spanish

Theme RESOURCES

To explore the theme further you may want to use these resources:

- Listening and Speaking Activities (pp. 7-9)
- Viewing and Representing Activities (pp. 1-6, 13-15)
- Critical Thinking Skills (pp. 7-8)
- Media Connection Activities, (pp. 5-6)
- Interdisciplinary Activities (pp. 10-13)
- Family and Community Activities (p. 13)
- Selection and Theme Assessment (pp. 129-130)
- Performance Assessment, pp. 71, 97

TIME Humanities Across TIME

See also these additional theme planning resources:

- Theme Three Planning Guide
- Interactive Reading Sourcebook
- Literature Groups Sourcebook
- Interactive Lesson Planner
- Interactive Teacher Edition
- Glencoe Web Site <lit.glencoe.com>

Use Glencoe's ***Presentation Plus!*** This multimedia teaching tool lets you present dynamic lessons that will engage your students. Using Microsoft PowerPoint®, you can customize the presentation to create your own personalized lessons.

Facing Challenge

Theme Objectives

- To enjoy reading about ways in which people cope with and prevail over difficult circumstances
- To analyze the literary elements in nonfiction, legends, poetry, and short story selections
- To apply strategies for reading informative nonfiction

Teaching Strategies

Have students read the quotation by Joseph Bruchac in preparation for the discussion questions below.

VIEWING THE ART

Responding to the Art Discussion questions:

- What challenge is the woman in the photograph facing? *(the challenge of doing her best in a soccer game)*
- How does the photo relate to the Bruchac quotation? *(Both deal with challenges people must face.)*
- What does Bruchac mean by "monsters"? *(problems, demands, or trials people must face)*

Facing Challenge

"Sooner or later, each of us must . . . challenge our own monsters, with our survival in the balance."

–Joseph Bruchac, *Flying with the Eagle, Racing the Great Bear*

216

TEACHER to TEACHER

WEIS MIDDLE SCHOOL TEXAS CITY, TEXAS

The newspaper is a valuable instrument in the classroom because there is a reality to newspapers that forces students to confront possibilities in their own lives that they may think they can ignore in fiction. When introducing the theme "Facing Challenge," I bring in a number of newspaper articles and let students each select one that personally represents a challenge. We discuss how students might face these challenges, focusing on both the positive and negative aspects of reality. I like to include inspirational stories of real people who have faced and overcome challenges and apply these real-life stories to students. I ask, "What would you do if you were the person in this newspaper story?" We discuss what students may have to face and overcome one day in order to become the people they want to be.

LINDA I. RODRIGUEZ

THEME CONTENTS

GENRE FOCUS *NONFICTION*

RESOURCE MANAGER

See the ***Theme Three Planning Guide*** for additional teaching notes, strategies, and resources for introducing the theme "Facing Challenge."

Introducing the Theme

Direct your students' attention to the **Theme Contents.** Ask them to read through the list of selections. Present these questions for discussion:

- What does the title of the first selection, by Maya Angelou, tell you about the theme of facing challenge? *(A challenging situation prompts a change in direction for a character in the story.)*
- Which titles seem to have something in common? *(Among other similarities, students may suggest that two of the titles mention women, three mention athletic feats, two are related to Langston Hughes, and three mention animals.)*
- Which titles interest you most among the poems? among the short stories?

LITERATURE & HUMANITIES

Have students examine the painting *Fair Weather* on the *National Museum of Women in the Arts* CD and discuss why a mountain is often used as a metaphor for a challenge. Have them discuss ways people might get to the other side of this mountain in relation to ways people might deal with a problem.

GLENCOE TECHNOLOGY

LITERATURE CLASSICS CD-ROM

Search for other selections related to the theme "Facing Challenge."

Exploring the Theme

Facing Challenge

Ask that each student first write a few sentences about a challenging situation he or she has faced and then a few sentences about a challenge from within.

Starting Points

Facing the Monster

Have students explain what is happening in the Gary Larson cartoon and what they find humorous about it. *(Students may think that George Miller's normal response to the absurd situation is funny and that the humor comes from the fact that the Millers have found themselves in the middle of* The Three Little Pigs *story and need to find a way out.)*

- Encourage students to role-play the story of *The Three Little Pigs* from the wolf's point of view. Challenge them to make the wolf a sympathetic character.
- In addition to role-playing what may happen next in the cartoon, have students improvise the conversation between the Millers and the pigs before the wolf arrived.
- Encourage students to role-play other well-known stories in which humans and animals interact, such as *Little Red Riding Hood* and *Goldilocks and the Three Bears.*

Personal Challenges

On the board, list a few of the common challenges students could face in daily life. Create another list of major challenges in life, such as losing a loved one or experiencing a serious health problem.

- Discuss with students which of these problems are within our ability to control and which are not. Direct their responses with questions. For example, ask *How do people face problems that are not within their power to solve, such as the death of a loved one?*
- Before students write their journal entries, encourage them each to focus on a personal problem, either large or small, that was successfully solved or faced. *(Students may write journal entries that include advice for others who face similar problems.)*

Exploring the Theme

Facing Challenge

We face challenges every day. Sometimes, outside forces put us in challenging situations. Sometimes, the challenges are inside ourselves. In this theme, you will meet real and imaginary characters who face a wide range of challenges. Try one of the options below to start your own thinking about the theme.

Starting Points

FACING THE MONSTER

If you remember the story of *The Three Little Pigs,* you'll appreciate Gary Larson's cartoon about the pigs' unlucky visitors.

- Role-play the situation in the cartoon, showing what happens next. Then expand your performance by role-playing a parody of another well-known story in which the characters face a challenge.

PERSONAL CHALLENGES

Think about a problem you faced in the past year and about how you prepared yourself for the challenge.

- Write a journal entry about a challenge you faced and what you learned from the experience.

The Far Side

"Listen out there! We're George and Harriet Miller! We just dropped in on the pigs for coffee! We're coming out!... We don't want trouble!"

FINE ART TRANSPARENCY 24

You may wish to display ***Fine Art Transparency 24*** to help students think about facing challenge.

interNET CONNECTION

Challenges Students can use a search engine to find out more about challenging issues they are interested in. They might use such keywords as *health, environment,* and *global warming.*

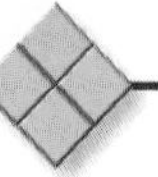

Theme Projects

As you read the selections in this theme, try your hand at one of these projects. Work on your own, with a partner, or with a group.

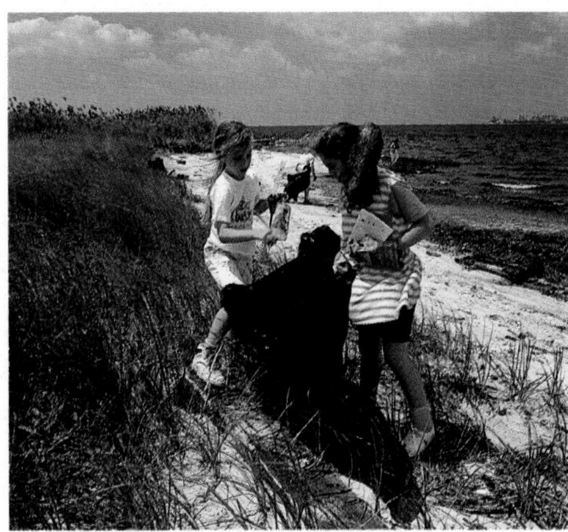

CRITICAL READING

Challenges in Fiction

1. Think about the main characters in your favorite books. Choose one character who faced a big challenge. You will pretend you are that character.
2. Plan how to portray your character. Take notes about the character's life and the special challenge that he or she faced.
3. Meet with four or five classmates for a chat. Stay in character as you talk about the ups and downs of your fictional life.
4. Compare your character's challenges and outcomes with those of your classmates. What similarities and differences did you notice?

interNET CONNECTION

Check out the Web for more project ideas. Brainstorm some keywords about facing challenges that you can enter in your search engine to locate suitable sites. You can also check out the Glencoe Literature site at lit.glencoe.com.

LEARNING FOR LIFE

Writing a Persuasive Memo

What are some challenges your community faces? Is there a park that needs repair, a river that is polluted, or a dangerous intersection that needs a stop sign?

1. Choose one problem that you feel strongly about solving, and brainstorm ways to involve the community in the solution.
2. Draft a memo to your town or city government that will persuade officials to help organize community volunteers to solve the problem.

MULTIMEDIA PROJECT

Newsmakers Facing Challenges

1. Read magazines and newspapers, browse the Web, listen to the radio, and watch television news to learn about people facing challenges.
2. Choose one person and write a make-believe interview with her or him about life's challenges.
3. With a small group, produce a news video or a radio news show using the interview as the basis for a presentation to the class.

Theme Projects

Teaching Strategies

The following suggestions may help your students plan and carry out their theme projects.

Critical Reading

- Suggest that students bring the books in to share with classmates and explain to them why they chose their characters.
- Invite students to become the characters by wearing costumes, speaking in the characters' voices, and imagining the characters' thoughts.

Learning for Life

- Direct students' attention to potential challenges to the school community.
- Write the names of local officials on the board and make a local telephone book available.
- Encourage students to focus on solutions in their memos.

Multimedia Project

- Have students use real news or radio shows as models for theirs. Encourage them to credit group members at the end of the show for their contributions.
- During the presentation, have students write questions they might ask if they could interview this person.

Additional Resources

- ***Interdisciplinary Activities,*** pp. 10–13
- ***Viewing and Representing Activities,*** pp. 13–15
- ***Listening and Speaking Activities,*** pp. 7–9
- ***Critical Thinking Skills,*** pp. 7–8
- ***Selection and Theme Assessment,*** pp. 129–130
- ***Performance Assessment,*** p. 71

Family and Community Activity

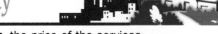

Have students choose a community organization or agency that helps people cope with challenges. Have them work in groups and ask each group to prepare a pamphlet for the class that includes

- the name, address, and phone number of the organization.
- who the organization helps or serves.
- a list of services the organization provides.
- the price of the services.
- statements from agency workers about the help they offer.
- statements from people who have benefited from the services. **L2**

Additional Resources

- ***Family and Community Activities,*** p. 13

Before Reading

Objectives

- To read and analyze a biography about facing and overcoming a challenge
- To recognize characteristics of biographies
- To write a problem-solution paragraph

Skills

Reading/Thinking: Distinguishing Fact from Opinion; Problem and Solution
Writing: Journal Entry
Vocabulary: Analogies
Collaboration: Literature Groups

Motivating → STUDENTS

Selection Focus Transparency 19: Have students read the quote by Gilbert Ware. Encourage them to discuss how overcoming small challenges can eventually lead to great accomplishment.

Reading Focus: As an extension of the Reading Focus, have small groups of students use precise language and sensory details to discuss how they can arrive at creative solutions to a problem.

Before You Read

New Directions

MEET MAYA ANGELOU

Author, poet, playwright, editor, educator, professional stage and screen performer, and singer—each of these words describes Maya Angelou (mī yə an′ jel ō). Angelou's extraordinary career has taken her to many places around the world, including Egypt and Ghana. She read her poem "On the Pulse of Morning," commissioned by President Clinton, at the 1993 inauguration.

Maya Angelou was born in 1928. "New Directions" was published in Wouldn't Take Nothing for My Journey Now *in 1993.*

READING FOCUS

Each person has his or her own method of problem solving. How do you go about solving a problem?

Think/Pair/Share
Think about a problem you recently solved. Share your problem-solving method with a partner. With your partner, put together a list of three to five words that describe an approach to solving a problem.

Setting a Purpose
As you read the selection, try to discover a problem and its solution.

BUILDING BACKGROUND

The Time and Place This selection is set in Arkansas in the early 1900s.

Did You Know? Many of Maya Angelou's most famous books are autobiographical. Although Angelou spent some of her childhood with her mother in large cities, she was raised mainly by her grandmother in the small town of Stamps, Arkansas. "New Directions" is based on the life of Angelou's grandmother, a determined woman who had a vision and then worked hard to reach her goal.

VOCABULARY PREVIEW

concede (kən sēd′) *v.* to admit to be true or proper; p. 221
meticulously (mi tik′ yə ləs lē) *adv.* in a way that shows careful attention to details; p. 221
balmy (bä′ mē) *adj.* mild; soothing; p. 222
assess (ə ses′) *v.* to determine the meaning or importance of; analyze; p. 222
loom (lo͞om) *v.* to appear to the mind as threatening; p. 222
ominous (om′ ə nəs) *adj.* threatening harm or evil; p. 222
unpalatable (un pal′ ə tə bəl) *adj.* not agreeable to the taste, mind, or feelings; unacceptable; p. 222

RESOURCE MANAGER

Teaching Tools and Resources
- Theme Three Planning Guide
- Literature Groups Sourcebook

Essential Lesson Support

Lesson-Specific Instruction
- Selection Focus Transparency 19
- Literary Elements Transparency 19
- Active Reading Guide,* p. 19
- Selection Vocabulary Practice, p. 13
- TIME inTIME magazine, pp. 6–7

Assessment
- Selection Quick Checks,* p. 19
- Sel. and Theme Assmt., pp. 33–34
- Testmaker: ExamView Pro
- Performance Assessment, p. 18

Systematic Language Instruction
- Grammer & Composition Handbook, Lesson 4.4
- Vocabulary Power, Lesson 10
- Spelling Power, Lesson 9

English Language Learners
- ELL Sourcebook, p. 41
- Theme Three Planning Guide
- Spanish Summaries, p. 19
- Spanish Translations, pp. 64–65
- Audio Library*
- English, Yes!

Spec. Needs/Strat. Interven.
- Interactive Reading Sourcebook, pp. T97–T99
- Interactive Reading Workbook, pp. 36–37
- Inclusion Strategies Sourcebook, pp. 39–40
- Audio Library*

*Also available in Spanish

New Directions

Maya Angelou

In 1903 the late Mrs. Annie Johnson of Arkansas found herself with two toddling sons, very little money, a slight ability to read and add simple numbers. To this picture add a disastrous marriage and the burdensome fact that Mrs. Johnson was a Negro.

When she told her husband, Mr. William Johnson, of her dissatisfaction with their marriage, he conceded that he too found it to be less than he expected, and had been secretly hoping to leave and study religion. He added that he thought God was calling him not only to preach but to do so in Enid, Oklahoma. He did not tell her that he knew a minister in Enid with whom he could study and who had a friendly, unmarried daughter. They parted amicably,[1] Annie keeping the one-room house and William taking most of the cash to carry himself to Oklahoma.

Annie, over six feet tall, big-boned, decided that she would not go to work as a domestic[2] and leave her "precious babes" to anyone else's care. There was no possibility of being hired at the town's cotton gin or lumber mill, but maybe there was a way to make the two factories work for her. In her words, "I looked up the road I was going and back the way I come, and since I wasn't satisfied, I decided to step off the road and cut me a new path." She told herself that she wasn't a fancy cook but that she could "mix groceries well enough to scare hungry away and from starving a man."

She made her plans meticulously and in secret. One early evening to see if she was ready, she placed stones in two five-gallon pails and carried them three miles to the cotton gin. She rested a little, and then, discarding some rocks, she walked in the darkness to the saw mill five miles farther along the dirt road. On her way back to her little house and her babies, she dumped the remaining rocks along the path.

That same night she worked into the early hours boiling chicken and frying ham. She made dough and filled the rolled-out pastry with meat. At last she went to sleep.

1. Mr. and Mrs. Johnson parted on friendly terms *(amicably)*.
2. A *domestic* (də mes′ tik) is a household servant.

Vocabulary
concede (kən sēd′) *v.* to admit to be true or proper
meticulously (mi tik′ yə ləs lē) *adv.* in a way that shows careful attention to details

Reading the Selection

SUMMARY

In this brief essay, Annie Johnson, a single mother in Arkansas in 1903, decides to build a better life for herself and her two sons. Annie doesn't like the job options available to her, so she decides to create her own opportunity. Annie begins a small business selling meat pies to factory workers. Annie eventually builds a permanent stall, which she later turns into a successful store.

Spanish Summaries, p. 19

A Active Reading Strategies

PREDICT Ask students what Annie's options are at this point. What "new path" might Annie take? *(Annie will create a job for herself instead of choosing one that already exists.)*

VOCABULARY If you haven't previewed the selection vocabulary with students, stop and remind them to use context clues to unlock the meanings of new vocabulary words.

Additional Resources

Active Reading Guide, p. 19
Audio Library
Spanish Audio Library

Teaching Support

CONNECTING TO OTHER SELECTIONS

For a teaching strategy that connects "New Directions" to "The Fish Crisis," see the ***Theme Three Planning Guide***.

LITERATURE & HUMANITIES

Have students listen to volume 2, track 7, of the CD *American Music: Cultural Traditions* to hear "The Downhearted Blues," which might have been sung around the time Maya Angelou's story takes place.

B Literary Elements

BIOGRAPHY Ask students what a biography is. *(It is a true story about a person that conveys information about the subject's personality, attitudes, and surroundings.)*

C Author's Craft

IMAGERY Have students list images that help readers visualize rural Arkansas. *(Some vivid images include dirt road, blistering summer noons, and cold, wet, and wintry middays.)*

D Critical Thinking

DISTINGUISHING FACT FROM OPINION Ask students to review the difference between fact and opinion and to give examples of both in this passage. *(Fact is verifiable; opinion is what a person or group believes or feels. The details about Annie are presented as fact. The last paragraph of the essay presents Angelou's opinions.)*

Thematic Focus

Facing Challenge Have students think about how they would respond to Annie's challenges.

FINE ART TRANSPARENCY 8

Use *Fine Art Transparency 8* to enrich students' thinking.

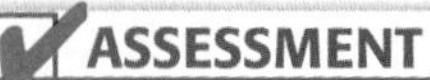

ASSESSMENT

Quick Checks, p. 19

Teaching Support

Did You Know?
A *brazier* (brā' zhər) is a metal container that holds burning coals. It is used for cooking food.

The next morning she left her house carrying the meat pies, lard, an iron brazier, and coals for a fire. Just before lunch she appeared in an empty lot behind the cotton gin. As the dinner noon bell rang, she dropped the savors into boiling fat and the aroma rose and floated over to the workers who spilled out of the gin, covered with white lint, looking like specters.[3]

Most workers had brought their lunches of pinto beans and biscuits or crackers, onions and cans of sardines, but they were tempted by the hot meat pies which Annie ladled out of the fat. She wrapped them in newspapers, which soaked up the grease, and offered them for sale at a nickel each. Although business was slow, those first days Annie was determined. She balanced her appearances between the two hours of activity.

So, on Monday if she offered hot fresh pies at the cotton gin and sold the remaining cooled-down pies at the lumber mill for three cents, then on Tuesday she went first to the lumber mill presenting fresh, just-cooked pies as the lumbermen covered in sawdust emerged from the mill.

For the next few years, on balmy spring days, blistering summer noons, and cold, wet, and wintry middays, Annie never disappointed her customers, who could count on seeing the tall, brown-skin woman bent over her brazier, carefully turning the meat pies. When she felt certain that the workers had become dependent on her, she built a stall between the two hives of industry and let the men run to her for their lunchtime provisions.

She had indeed stepped from the road which seemed to have been chosen for her and cut herself a brand-new path. In years that stall became a store where customers could buy cheese, meal, syrup, cookies, candy, writing tablets, pickles, canned goods, fresh fruit, soft drinks, coal, oil, and leather soles for worn-out shoes.

Each of us has the right and the responsibility to assess the roads which lie ahead, and those over which we have traveled, and if the future road looms ominous or unpromising, and the roads back uninviting, then we need to gather our resolve and, carrying only the necessary baggage, step off that road into another direction. If the new choice is also unpalatable, without embarrassment, we must be ready to change that as well.

❖

3. A *specter* (spek' tər) is a ghost.

Vocabulary
balmy (bä' mē) *adj.* mild; soothing
assess (ə ses') *v.* to determine the meaning or importance of; analyze
loom (lo͞om) *v.* to appear to the mind as threatening
ominous (om' ə nəs) *adj.* threatening harm or evil
unpalatable (un pal' ə tə bəl) *adj.* not agreeable to the taste, mind, or feelings; unacceptable

Reading Minilesson

Problem and Solution In the story, Annie is faced with the problem of supporting her children while caring for them herself. To reach the solution, she has to take several intermediate steps.

Activity Have small groups of students review story details and record their information in a two-column chart with the headings *Action* and *Result*. **L2**

Action	Result

Additional Resources

Reading Skills Practice Workbook

Responding to Literature

PERSONAL RESPONSE

- What went through your mind as you finished reading this selection?
- Think back to the **Reading Focus** on page 220. What words would you use to describe Mrs. Annie Johnson's method of problem solving? How does your method of problem solving compare with hers? Record your responses in a journal.

The Storyteller, 1995. Christian Pierre (b. 1962). Acrylic on Masonite, 48 x 32 in. Private collection.

Analyzing Literature

RECALL

1. What is the problem facing Mrs. Annie Johnson at the beginning of the narrative?
2. According to the narrator, what were Johnson's options for employment?
3. List the steps Johnson took to start her own business.
4. What became of Annie Johnson's stall?

Brackets connect questions that are paired to develop higher-level thinking skills.

INTERPRET

5. What is Johnson's attitude toward her problem? Explain.
6. Explain what Johnson means by the statement "I looked up the road I was going and back the way I come, and since I wasn't satisfied, I decided to step off the road and cut me a new path."
7. What does the title of the selection mean? How does it relate to Johnson's new career? Use quotations from the selection to support your ideas.
8. How did Annie Johnson's original vision become a thriving business?

EVALUATE AND CONNECT

9. The **theme** of a piece of writing is the message the writer hopes to communicate. What is the theme of this selection? Explain.
10. Theme Connection Think of someone you know who faced a challenge and set out boldly in a new direction. Tell about the result of that person's action.

LITERARY ELEMENTS

Biography

A **biography** is a true story written by an author about the life of another person. The writer researches the person's life by conducting interviews and by reading letters, books, and diaries. A good biography tells more than what the subject said or did. A good biography makes its subject come alive for readers. A biography may cover a person's entire life, or it may focus on one period of time.

1. What details did you learn about Annie Johnson's life from reading this biographical essay?
2. What else would you like to learn about Annie Johnson's life?

- See **Literary Terms Handbook,** p. R2.

Responding to the Selection

PERSONAL RESPONSE

Students may have thought about their road, or life path, as they read this selection. Students should explain how their problem-solving methods are similar to, or different from, Mrs. Annie Johnson's.

Analyzing Literature

1. Mrs. Johnson needs a job to support herself and her two young sons.
2. Mrs. Johnson's options were to work as a household servant, while leaving her sons in someone else's care, or to make the local factories work for her.
3. First, Mrs. Johnson practiced walking and carrying two pails of stones eight miles. Next, she cooked the meat and filled the pies. Then she walked to one factory, where she cooked and sold hot pies. After that, she walked to the other factory and sold the remaining cooled-down pies.
4. Over time, Mrs. Johnson's stall became a store.
5. Mrs. Johnson is quite determined. She doesn't give up, even though her business is not greatly successful at first. Over time, she builds a customer base.
6. Mrs. Johnson's future didn't look promising, and she didn't want to continue what she had been doing, so she decided to try something completely different.
7. The title refers to the new direction Mrs. Johnson took. She was a single mother supporting two sons. She didn't like the direction in which she was headed, so she stepped "off the road" in a new direction.
8. Mrs. Johnson's original vision was bringing meat pies to factory workers. Once she had enough steady customers, she built a stall from which to sell the pies. Over time it grew into a store.
9. One of the themes of this essay is that we should not be afraid to take risks and to try new things. Another theme is that persistence can take you far in life.
10. Answers should clearly state what the challenge was and how the person responded to it.

LITERARY ELEMENTS

1. To support herself and her two sons after her husband leaves, Annie walks to and from the factories to sell meat pies. As her business improves, she builds a stall and then a store.
2. Students may want to know more about how the stall becomes a store or about the narrator's connection to Annie.

Additional Resources

Literary Elements Transparency 19

Extending Your Response

Writing About Literature

Students' paragraphs should
- explain how to approach and solve a problem step by step
- include relevant examples from the selection to support ideas about how to solve a problem

Literature Groups Groups should create their lists of five important qualities only after all ideas have been discussed. Students may want to assign roles, such as a leader who keeps the discussion on the topic, a clarifier who makes sure everyone understands, and a recorder who writes down the main points covered.

Creative Writing

Students' journal entries should
- present Annie's feelings, thoughts, and fears about what could happen the next day
- be clearly written from Annie's perspective

Art Activity If students want to design a menu on a computer, have them use a font they like in a size that will show up well from a distance. They may want to use clip art to add visual appeal to the menu. Students may want to try several different layouts before completing a final menu.

Skill Minilesson

VOCABULARY • ANALOGIES

1. a 2. b 3. c

Additional Resources

Vocabulary Practice, p. 13

Extending Your Response

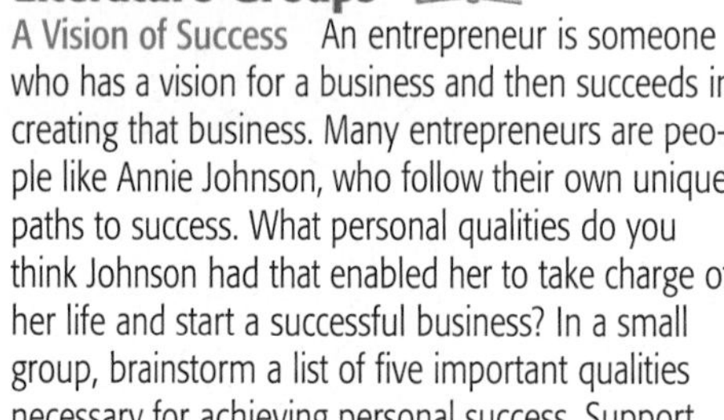

Writing About Literature

Finding Solutions "New Directions" focuses on one woman's imaginative solution to a difficult problem. Use the story and ideas you came up with in the **Reading Focus** on page 220 to write a paragraph about how to deal with a personal problem. Use examples from "New Directions" to support your ideas.

Literature Groups

A Vision of Success An entrepreneur is someone who has a vision for a business and then succeeds in creating that business. Many entrepreneurs are people like Annie Johnson, who follow their own unique paths to success. What personal qualities do you think Johnson had that enabled her to take charge of her life and start a successful business? In a small group, brainstorm a list of five important qualities necessary for achieving personal success. Support your ideas with details from the selection.

Creative Writing

A Journal Entry Imagine that you are Mrs. Annie Johnson the night before your first day selling food to the workers. How might you feel? What might you think? Describe your thoughts and feelings in a journal entry.

Art Activity

Design a Menu Design a menu for Mrs. Annie Johnson to hang on her food stall. Make your own drawings or cut out photographs of food from old magazines. Be sure to make up a catchy name for Johnson's food business.

Save your work for your portfolio.

Skill Minilesson

Reteach • Review

VOCABULARY • ANALOGIES

Analogies compare relationships. Analogies are usually written in this form:

balmy : mild :: ominous : threatening

This analogy is read:

balmy is to *mild* as *ominous* is to *threatening.*

In this example, the words in each pair are synonyms, words that are similar in meaning. Analogies can state other kinds of relationships, such as antonyms (cold : hot); cause and effect (determination : success); or part and a whole (wheel : automobile). The relationship between the second pair of words must be the same as the relationship between the first pair.

PRACTICE Decide on the relationship of the first two words. Then apply that relationship to the second set of words.

1. smile : friendly :: frown : ______
   a. hostile b. balmy c. frighten
2. grumble : complain :: concede : ______
   a. refuse b. acknowledge c. assess
3. delicious : unpalatable :: meticulous : ______
   a. tasty b. attentive c. careless

ASSESSMENT

- ***Quick Checks,*** p. 19
- ***Selection and Theme Assessment,*** pp. 33–34
- ***Performance Assessment,*** p. 18
- ***Testmaker: ExamView Pro***
- ***Interactive Tutor: Self-Assessment***

Vo•cab•u•lar•y Skills

Using Homophones

Words that sound the same but have different meanings and spellings are called **homophones.** There are hundreds of homophones in the English language. A bad bird is a foul fowl. Rabbit fur might be called hare hair. A forbidden musical group is a banned band. A string that won't stay tied will not knot.

You have to be careful to write the right word. Even if you work on a computer that can check your spelling, you need to watch for homophone mistakes. If you type *brake* when you mean *break,* no computer spell-check program can fix your mistake because both *brake* and *break* are correctly spelled words.

EXERCISES

A. Read the passage below. If the underlined word is the correct one to use, write *Correct.* If it is a homophone for the correct word, write the correct word.

> When Annie Johnson's husband left her, she needed to billed (1) a new (2) life. She did not have a job, but she did have two (3) children to take care of. Instead of feeling trapped by the passed (4), she moved with energy toward the future. With little education, she wondered if anyone wood (5) higher (6) her, so (7) she created her own business. Every day, Annie maid (8) food to cell (9) to workers at nearby factories. The scent (10) of the cooking pies guaranteed her success.

B. Complete each sentence by using two homophones. An example is provided.

Example: The bigger, better grinder could be called the *greater grater.*

1. A king's tossed chair is a _______.
2. If people take metal without paying for it, they _______.
3. If you chewed up seven grapes and then one more, you _______.
4. What the group of cows listened to is what the _______.
5. Buttons, snaps, and zippers are used to _______.

Vo•cab•u•lar•y Skills

Objective

- To recognize homophones and apply strategies for using them correctly

Teaching Strategies

After students read the explanation in their books, have them help create a list of homophones on the board. Ask students to work individually or in small groups to create definitions for each pair of homophones by following the examples given in their books. Additional homophones might include *stair/stare; boar/bore;* and *wait/weight.* Have students read their definitions aloud. Classmates can guess the answers.

Exercises

A.

1. build
2. correct
3. correct
4. past
5. would
6. hire
7. correct
8. made
9. sell
10. correct

B.

1. thrown throne
2. steal steel
3. ate eight
4. herd heard
5. close clothes

Additional Resources

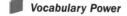

Vocabulary Power

Teaching Support

MEETING INDIVIDUAL NEEDS — ENGLISH LANGUAGE LEARNERS

Pair Pictures Write the following words on the board: *tail/tale; wait/weight;* and *flower/flour.* Use each word in the pairs in a sentence. Explain to English language learners that they can tell which meaning is intended by thinking about how the word is used.

Activity Have students work in small groups to illustrate three pairs of homophones. Help each group choose words. Then ask the students to illustrate them on posterboard or large sheets of paper. Post the illustrations so students can look at classmates' work.

Additional Resources

English Language Learners Sourcebook, p. 41

Responding to the Selection

PERSONAL RESPONSE

Students may find any of several images in "Hesperus" most striking: perhaps when the skipper wraps his daughter in his coat and ties her to the mast, or when he dies, or when the sun rises on the sight of her body. From "Tightrope," they are likely to choose the tightrope walker without a net.

Analyzing Literature

1. The ship sank, and both the skipper and his daughter died.
2. She says she'll walk the tightrope without any help and without envying other people's easier paths.
3. The central conflict is humans versus nature. It's resolved when nature wins: the storm kills both the captain and the girl and wrecks their ship.
4. The central image is the speaker as high-wire walker. The tightrope represents the challenges she must face in her life.
5. The skipper feels superior to nature ("I can weather the roughest gale."). The old sailor respects nature's power.
6. Many students will say the skipper is selfish to risk his daughter's life. Some may say it's nice they are so close, and it isn't his fault that the storm came up.
7. She'll do whatever it takes to meet life's challenges. Some students will agree with her goal-centered attitude. Others may think that people like her burn out early and don't have enough fun along the way.
8. She's trying hard and is troubled by demands from all sides. The main contrasting image is "the earth-propped stride of others." Not only must she walk on the tightrope instead of the ground, but she must do it without help or protection—no parasol, net, or balance stick.
9. Some may say they like the story or adventure or third-person point of view of "Hesperus." Others may prefer the personal tone, emotional subject, and first-person point of view of "Tightrope."
10. "Hesperus" is about the challenge of facing a physical danger. "Tightrope" is about the challenge of balancing all the many demands of one's life.

Active Reading and Critical Thinking

Responding to Literature

PERSONAL RESPONSE

- Which image from each poem did you find the most dramatic or striking? Why?

Analyzing Literature

RECALL AND INTERPRET

1. According to the speaker of "The Wreck of the Hesperus," what happened to the ship, the skipper, and the skipper's young daughter?
2. Summarize what the speaker tells you in "I'll Walk the Tightrope."
3. What is the central **conflict** in the plot of "The Wreck of the Hesperus"? How is the conflict resolved?
4. What is the central image in the poem "I'll Walk the Tightrope"? What do you think the tightrope represents?

EVALUATE AND CONNECT

5. What attitude toward nature does the skipper express in "The Wreck of the Hesperus"? How does his attitude contrast with that of the old sailor? Explain.
6. Describe the relationship between the skipper and his daughter in "The Wreck of the Hesperus." Do you think the skipper should have taken his daughter on the voyage? Explain.
7. In "I'll Walk the Tightrope," what is the speaker's attitude about facing the challenges of life? Do you agree with that point of view? Explain.
8. How do you think the speaker in "I'll Walk the Tightrope" sees herself? What images are used to compare or contrast the speaker with other people?
9. Which poem do you prefer? Why?
10. **Theme Connection** How is each of these poems related to the theme of facing challenges? Explain.

LITERARY ELEMENTS

Narrative Poetry

Narrative poetry is poetry that tells a story. "The Wreck of the Hesperus" is an example of a narrative poem. Like a short story or a novel, a narrative poem usually includes a setting, some characters, and a plot. The events in a narrative poem are often told in chronological order, the order in which they happen. In a narrative poem, the theme unfolds as the story is told.

1. Describe the setting, the plot, and the main characters of "The Wreck of the Hesperus."
2. Find another example of a narrative poem in this book or in another book. Tell why the poem is an example of narrative poetry.

• See **Literary Terms Handbook,** p. R7.

First Rate Man of War Foundering in a Gale, late 19th century. George Philip Reinagle. Oil on canvas. Royal Albert Memorial Museum, Exeter, England.

LITERARY ELEMENTS

1. The setting is the coast of New England on a cold winter night; the plot is the tale of a shipwreck; and the characters include the ship's skipper, his daughter, his crew, an old sailor, and a fisherman.
2. The poems in Theme 6 are examples of narrative poetry.

Additional Resources

 ***Literary Elements Transparency 20***

Extending Your Response

Writing About Literature

Looking at Imagery Both poems contain strong images that help readers "see" what is happening in the poems and understand the themes of the poems. Pick out an image from each poem. Then, describe how each image helps you understand the poem's message.

Creative Writing

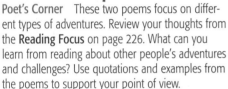

News Flash Turn the plot of "The Wreck of the Hesperus" into a newspaper article. Add any details you need, including eyewitness interviews with other sailors and weather reports about the storm.

Literature Groups

Poet's Corner These two poems focus on different types of adventures. Review your thoughts from the **Reading Focus** on page 226. What can you learn from reading about other people's adventures and challenges? Use quotations and examples from the poems to support your point of view.

Listening and Speaking

The Drama of Poetry Poetry should be read aloud to be fully appreciated. As a poem is read, listeners may close their eyes, picture the images, and hear the natural rhythm of the lines. With a partner or in a small group, choose one of the poems to read aloud. Perform your reading for the class.

Reading Further

If you would like to read more by these poets, try these books:

Selected Poems by Henry Wadsworth Longfellow, edited by Laurance Buell (many other editions available)

The Down of a Thistle by Margaret Danner

Save your work for your portfolio.

Skill Minilesson

Reteach · Review

READING AND THINKING • IDENTIFYING SPATIAL RELATIONSHIPS

One way to organize details is to use **spatial order**–that is, showing where things are located. When you read a poem, try to visualize where things are in relation to other things. For example, in the first scene of "The Wreck of the Hesperus," the skipper is standing by the helm. As you read, ask:

- What does this scene or image look like?
- Where is each thing in relation to the other things in the scene?

PRACTICE Reread each of the poems. As you do, try to think about the spatial order in the different scenes and images in each poem. For each poem, make a simple diagram (with labels) to illustrate one important scene or image. Show where each thing is in relation to the other things mentioned.

- For more about spatial order, see **Reading Handbook,** p. R91.

Extending Your Response

Writing About Literature

Students' descriptions should

- describe the image clearly
- explain the image's relation to the poem's meaning

Creative Writing

Students' articles should

- explain the most important facts first
- include direct quotes from eyewitnesses and family members
- describe the extent of the storm's damage

Literature Groups Point out to students that both external, life-threatening events and internal thoughts can be adventures.

Listening and Speaking Encourage students to spend time rehearsing their poetry readings. If possible, videotape readers' performances and make the tapes available to the class.

Skill Minilesson

READING AND THINKING

• IDENTIFYING SPATIAL RELATIONSHIPS

Students' diagrams should

- include the level of detail needed for clarity (more for "Hesperus")
- estimate the sizes and distances of things in the poems

Additional Resources

Reading Skills Practice Workbook

ASSESSMENT

- ***Quick Checks,*** p. 20
- ***Selection and Theme Assessment,*** pp. 35–36
- ***Performance Assessment,*** p. 19
- ***Testmaker: ExamView Pro***
- ***Interactive Tutor: Self-Assessment***

Before Reading

Objectives

- To read and analyze a short story about the challenges of a pioneer family
- To understand dialect and recognize how dialect reflects periods and cultures
- To write a paragraph that analyzes the story's surprise ending

Skills

Reading/Thinking: Inferring; Cause and Effect; Drawing Conclusions
Writing: Introduction
Vocabulary: Homophones; Antonyms
Grammar/Language: Punctuating Dialogue
Collaboration: Literature Groups

Motivating STUDENTS

Selection Focus Transparency 21: Have students discuss the quote by Depression-era photographer Dorothea Lange.

Reading Focus: As an extension of the Reading Focus, have small groups of students use precise language and sensory details to discuss what they would need to bring with them if they were starting a new life in a different location.

Before You Read

Too Soon a Woman

MEET DOROTHY M. JOHNSON

Dorothy M. Johnson was born in Iowa, but her experiences at the University of Montana inspired a lifelong love of the scenery and history of the American West. An honorary member of the Blackfoot Tribe, Johnson wrote vividly about Native Americans and cowboys, sheriffs and outlaws. Three of her short stories—"The Hanging Tree," "The Man Who Shot Liberty Valance," and "A Man Called Horse"—were made into classic Western movies.

Dorothy M. Johnson was born in 1905 and died in 1984.

READING FOCUS

What traits do you think pioneers needed to survive?

Think/Pair/Share
With a partner, list survival characteristics for a pioneer family traveling west 150 years ago.

Setting a Purpose
Read this story to discover what one family learns about survival.

BUILDING BACKGROUND

The Time and Place This story takes place sometime in the 1800s, on the way west across the American prairie.

Did You Know?
Pioneers traveled west on overland routes such as the Oregon Trail. Pioneer wagon trains began traveling the Oregon Trail in the 1840s. The difficult trip lasted four to six months.

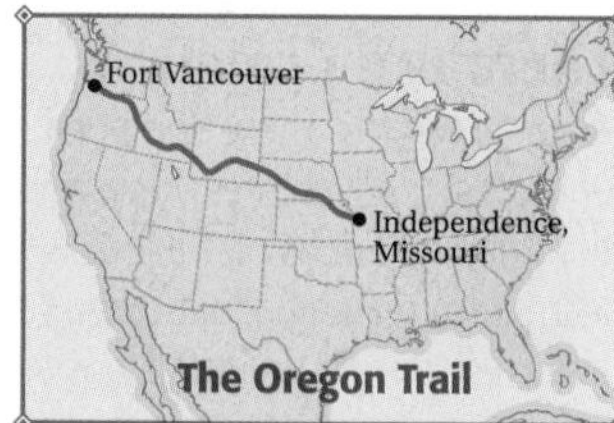

VOCABULARY PREVIEW

skimpy (skim′ pē) *adj.* lacking in quantity, fullness, or size; barely enough or not quite enough; p. 236
grudging (gruj′ ing) *adj.* given or allowed unwillingly or resentfully; p. 236
gaunt (gônt) *adj.* looking like skin and bones; p. 237
grim (grim) *adj.* fierce; severe; stern; forbidding; p. 237
endure (en door′) *v.* to put up with; undergo, as pain, stress, or other hardship; p. 238
savor (sā′ vər) *v.* to take great delight in; p. 239
gruffly (gruf′ lē) *adv.* in a rough, stern manner; p. 239
sedately (si dāt′ lē) *adv.* in a quiet, restrained style or manner; calmly; p. 239

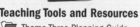

RESOURCE MANAGER

Teaching Tools and Resources
- Theme Three Planning Guide
- Literature Groups Sourcebook

Essential Lesson Support

Lesson-Specific Instruction
- Selection Focus Transparency 21
- Literary Elements Transparency 21
- Active Reading Guide,* p. 21
- Selection Vocabulary Practice, p. 14

Assessment
- Selection Quick Checks,* p. 21
- Selection and Theme Assessment, pp. 37–38
- Testmaker: ExamView Pro
- Performance Assessment, p. 20

Systematic Language Instruction
- Gr. & Comp. Hbk., L. 4.6, 4.7
- Vocabulary Power, Lesson 11
- Spelling Power, Lesson 10

English Language Learners
- ELL Sourcebook, p. 43
- Spanish Summaries, p. 21
- Spanish Translations, pp. 66–69
- Audio Library*
- English, Yes!

Spec. Needs/Strat. Interven.
- Interactive Rdg. Sbk., pp. T103–T105
- Interactive Rdg. Wkbk., pp. 40–41
- Inclusion Strat. Sbk., pp. 53–54, 61–62
- Audio Library*

*Also available in Spanish

Too Soon a Woman

Dorothy M. Johnson

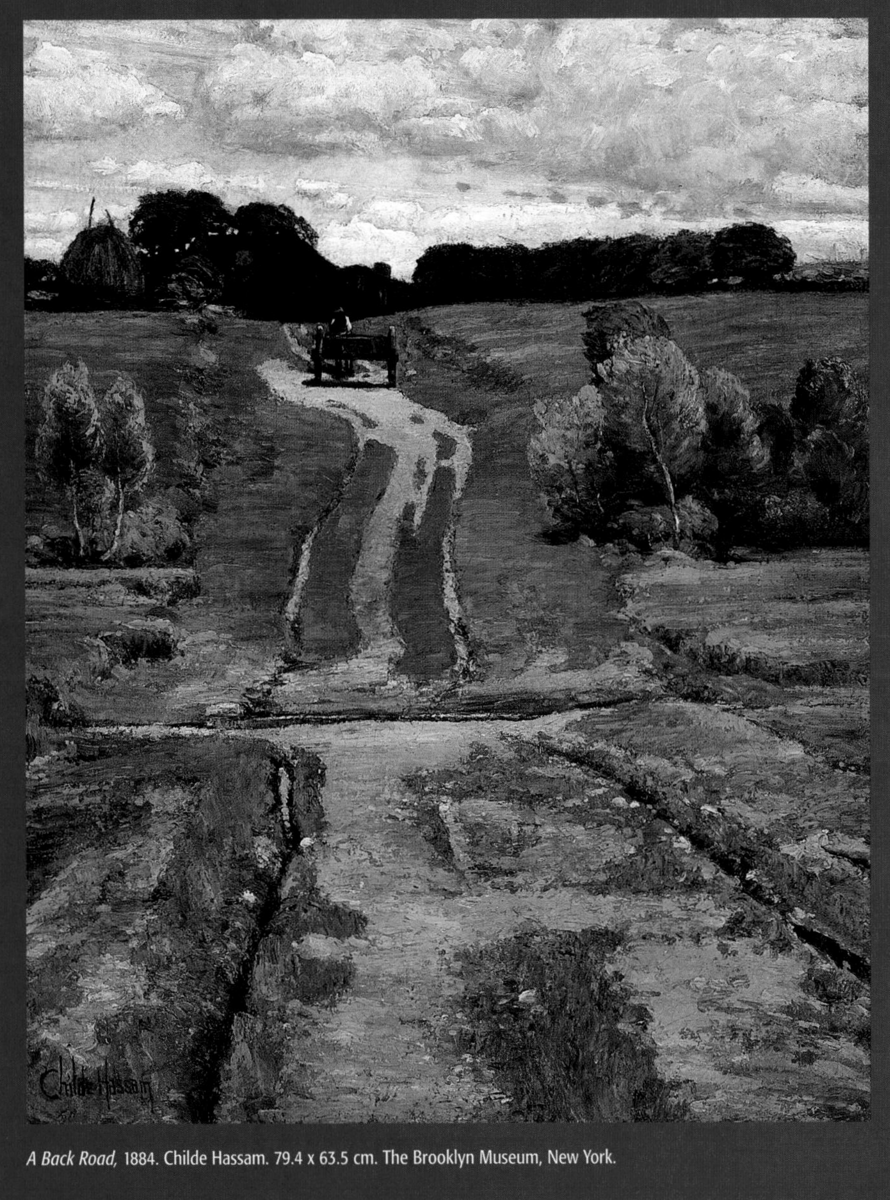

A Back Road, 1884. Childe Hassam. 79.4 x 63.5 cm. The Brooklyn Museum, New York.

Reading the Selection

SUMMARY

When an eleven-year-old boy, his sisters, and their father head west in the 1800s, they meet an eighteen-year-old woman whom the father grudgingly allows to join them. While he is away getting food, their supplies run out. The woman finds a giant mushroom, which she bravely samples to see whether it is poisonous. When she doesn't get sick, she feeds the rest of it to the children.

Spanish Summaries, p. 21

A Active Reading Strategies

PREDICT Ask students to consider the painting by Childe Hassam and the title to predict the subject of the story. *(Students may suggest that the story will be about a young woman who must act like an adult while on a difficult journey.)*

VOCABULARY If you haven't previewed the selection vocabulary with students, stop and remind them to use context clues to unlock the meanings of new vocabulary words.

Additional Resources

Active Reading Guide, p. 21

Audio Library

Spanish Audio Library

Teaching Support

CONNECTING TO OTHER SELECTIONS

COMPARING selections

This selection is paired with "A Boy and His Dog" on page 243. A lesson for teaching a comparison of the two selections appears on page 249.

The chart at the right shows three ways to connect "Too Soon a Woman" to other selections in this book.

For specific teaching strategies, see the ***Theme Three Planning Guide.***

Connection		Title
Life Skills: Problem Solving	→	from *Rosa Parks: My Story,* p. 85
Thematic: Growing Up	→	"old age sticks," p. 205
Literary: Dialogue	→	"Broken Chain," p. 44

H Literary Elements

PLOT: *Conflict* Have students describe Mary's problem and how she feels about it. *(She doesn't know whether this mushroom is poisonous, but the children need food. She could either save them or hurt them with the mushroom. She needs time to find out whether it's poisonous.)*

I Literary Elements

DIALECT Remind students that they can sometimes figure out the meaning of dialect by substituting more familiar phrases and then checking them for sense. (For example: *It hefts ten pounds* means "It weighs ten pounds"; *I don't set up to know all about everything* means "I don't pretend to know all about everything.")

J Active Reading Strategies

EVALUATE Why does the narrator use the word *cruel* here, when readers already know that Mary is testing the mushroom. *(It reflects how the children feel about Mary's keeping the food from them. They don't know that she is protecting them.)*

K Critical Thinking

DRAWING CONCLUSIONS Have students explain what Mary means when she says, "By tomorrow morning, I guess you can tell whether you want any." *(By tomorrow morning, it should be clear whether the mushroom is poisonous or safe to eat.)*

Teaching Support

Mary didn't have the horse—we never saw hide nor hair of that old horse again—but she was carrying something big and white that looked like a pumpkin with no color to it.

She didn't say anything, just looked around and saw Pa wasn't there yet, at the end of the fifth day.

"What's that thing?" my sister Elizabeth demanded.

"Mushroom," Mary answered. "I bet it hefts ten pounds."

"What are you going to do with it now?" I sneered. "Play football here?"

"Eat it—maybe," she said, putting it in a corner. Her wet hair hung over her shoulders. She huddled by the fire.

My sister Sarah began to whimper again. "I'm hungry!" she kept saying.

"Mushrooms ain't good eating," I said. "They can kill you."

"Maybe," Mary answered. "Maybe they can. I don't set up to know all about everything, like some people."

"What's that mark on your shoulder?" I asked her. "You tore your dress on the brush."

"What do you think it is?" she said, her head bowed in the smoke.

"Looks like scars," I guessed.

"'Tis scars. They whipped me. Now mind your own business. I want to think."

Elizabeth whimpered, "Why don't Pa come back?"

"He's coming," Mary promised. "Can't come in the dark. Your pa'll take care of you soon's he can."

She got up and rummaged around in the grub box.

"Nothing there but empty dishes," I growled. "If there was anything, we'd know it."

Mary stood up. She was holding the can with the porcupine grease.

"I'm going to have something to eat," she said coolly. "You kids can't have any yet. And I don't want any squalling,[3] mind."

It was a cruel thing, what she did then. She sliced that big, solid mushroom and heated grease in a pan.

The smell of it brought the little girls out of their quilt, but she told them to go back in so fierce a voice that they obeyed. They cried to break your heart.

I didn't cry. I watched, hating her.

I endured the smell of the mushroom frying as long as I could. Then I said, "Give me some."

"Tomorrow," Mary answered. "Tomorrow, maybe. But not tonight." She turned to me with a sharp command: "Don't bother me! Just leave me be."

She knelt there by the fire and finished frying the slice of mushroom.

If I'd had Pa's rifle, I'd have been willing to kill her right then and there.

She didn't eat right away. She looked at the brown, fried slice for a while and said, "By tomorrow morning, I guess you can tell whether you want any."

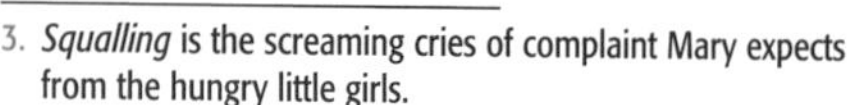

3. *Squalling* is the screaming cries of complaint Mary expects from the hungry little girls.

Vocabulary
endure (en door′) *v.* to put up with; undergo, as pain, stress, or other hardship

Grammar and Language *Minilesson*

Punctuating Dialogue Review with students some basic rules to follow when punctuating dialogue:

- Quotation marks enclose the exact words a speaker says.
- Commas separate a phrase, such as *he said,* from the speaker's actual words.
- Periods go inside quotation marks.
- Question marks go inside quotation marks if the dialogue is a question.

Activity Have students punctuate the following quotations from page 238 without referring to the story.

1. What's that thing my sister Elizabeth demanded
2. Elizabeth whimpered Why don't Pa come back
3. Mushroom Mary answered I bet it hefts ten pounds. **L2**

Additional Resources

- ***Grammar and Language Transparency 20***
- ***Grammar and Language Workbook,*** pp. 267–270
- ***Grammar and Composition Handbook,*** Lesson 13.6
- ***Writer's Choice,*** Lesson 20.6

The little girls stared at her as she ate. Sarah was chewing an old leather glove.

When Mary crawled into the quilts with them, they moved away as far as they could get.

L I was so scared that my stomach heaved, empty as it was.

Mary didn't stay in the quilts long. She took a drink out of the water bucket and sat down by the fire and looked through the smoke at me.

She said in a low voice, "I don't know how it will be if it's poison. Just do the best you can with the girls. Because your pa will come back, you know. . . . You better go to bed, I'm going to sit up."

M And so would you sit up. If it might be your last night on earth and the pain of death might seize you at any moment, you would sit up by the smoky fire, wide-awake, remembering whatever you had to remember, savoring life.

We sat in silence after the girls had gone to sleep. Once I asked, "How long does it take?"

"I never heard," she answered. "Don't think about it."

I slept after a while, with my chin on my chest. Maybe Peter dozed that way at Gethsemane[4] as the Lord knelt praying.

4. The New Testament of the Christian Bible says that Jesus, knowing his death was near, went to the Garden of *Gethsemane* (geth sem′ ə nē) to pray. Although *Peter* and other disciples had come to pray with him, they all fell asleep.

Mary's moving around brought me wide-awake. The black of night was fading.

"I guess it's all right," Mary said. "I'd be able to tell by now, wouldn't I?"

I answered gruffly, "I don't know."

Mary stood in the doorway for a while, looking out at the dripping world as if she found it beautiful. Then she fried slices of the mushroom while the little girls danced with anxiety.

We feasted, we three, my sisters and I, until Mary ruled, "That'll hold you," and would not cook any more. She didn't touch any of the mushroom herself.

That was a strange day in the moldy cabin. Mary laughed and was gay; she told stories, and we played "Who's Got the Thimble?" with a pine cone.

In the afternoon we heard a shout, and my sisters screamed, and I ran ahead of them across the clearing.

The rain had stopped. My father came plunging out of the woods leading a packhorse—and well I remember the treasures of food in that pack.

N He glanced at us anxiously as he tore at the ropes that bound the pack.

"Where's the other one?" he demanded.

Mary came out of the cabin then, walking sedately. As she came toward us, the sun began to shine.

My stepmother was a wonderful woman. O

Vocabulary

savor (sā′ vər) *v.* to take great delight in

gruffly (gruf′ lē) *adv.* in a rough, stern manner

sedately (si dāt′ lē) *adv.* in a quiet, restrained style or manner; calmly

L Active Reading Strategies

EVALUATE Ask students to explain why they think the narrator is so frightened. *(He knows the mushroom Mary ate could be poisonous.)*

M Literary Elements

CHARACTER Ask students why Mary would risk her life for people she hardly knows. *(They are Mary's only family. They've treated her better than she has ever been treated.)*

N Critical Thinking

DRAWING CONCLUSIONS The father is gruff with Mary, yet he puts her in charge of the family. What does this say about his true feelings?

Model: The father acts tough, but he must value her, or he wouldn't trust his children to her.

O Active Reading Strategies

REVIEW Have students describe the surprise ending in their own words. *(Pa eventually marries Mary, so she becomes the narrator's stepmother.)*

Thematic Focus

Facing Challenge Have students discuss how the characters's challenge changes them and what prompts the change.

Fine Art Transparency 21 may help students pull their thoughts together about why the family now thinks highly of Mary.

Real-World Connection

Poisonous Mushrooms Explain to students that, even today, people must be very careful when choosing wild mushrooms to eat. Students may better understand Mary's sacrifice if they do some research on poisonous mushrooms.

Activity Have students use the library or the Internet to research mushrooms. Ask them to gather information about how many types of poisonous mushrooms there are, what some of their names are, what they look like, and where they grow. Students can share their results with the class. To extend this activity, ask students to choose one type of poisonous mushroom to use as the subject of a thorough report. **L2**

Assessment

Quick Checks, p. 21

Responding to the Selection

PERSONAL RESPONSE

Students' drawings should represent the anticipation of the scene—the girls dancing "with anxiety" while Mary fries the mushroom strips.

Analyzing Literature

1. The original group was a father, his eleven-year-old son, and his two little girls.
2. The most pressing problem is getting food to eat.
3. Mary finds a large, white mushroom.
4. After the story ends, Mary becomes the narrator's stepmother.
5. The mother must be dead, because she isn't traveling with the family and because the father marries Mary.
6. Crops have failed, so local homesteaders have already killed most of the game.
7. Mary makes the children wait to eat until she sees whether the mushroom makes her sick. Mary's actions reveal that she is willing to take great risks to save the children.
8. The last line of the story makes readers realize that good times lie ahead. Even though events seemed hopeless in the beginning, if these events hadn't occurred, the family would not have met Mary.
9. Mary is only eighteen, but she takes responsibility and risks her life for the children. This is a very adult course of action—one that a teenager shouldn't have to take.
10. Students might crave the excitement of the pioneer journey. Students might respond that technology has made today's challenges different but no less challenging.

Active Reading and Critical Thinking

Responding to Literature

PERSONAL RESPONSE

- Draw a picture that shows your interpretation of the situation in the cabin before the children eat the mushroom.

Analyzing Literature

RECALL

1. Who were the members of the original group who left the "home place"?
2. What is the most pressing problem the family and Mary have to solve?
3. What does Mary finally find to feed the children?
4. What do you find out about Mary at the very end of the story?

Brackets connect questions that are paired to develop higher-level thinking skills.

INTERPRET

5. What can you infer about the mother of the family?
6. In your opinion, why does Pa have such a hard time providing food for the family?
7. Why does Mary make the children wait so long before she lets them eat the mushroom? What does Mary's way of testing the mushroom reveal about her?
8. How does the last line of the story make you rethink the beginning?

EVALUATE AND CONNECT

9. Why, do you think, did Johnson choose "Too Soon a Woman" for her title?
10. Theme Connection Would you have liked to experience a trek across the prairie? Does this story change the way you think about the challenges in your own life? Explain your answer.

LITERARY ELEMENTS

Dialect

In certain regions of America, particular groups speak variations of English called **dialects.** Dialects differ from Standard English because they contain different pronunciations, word forms, and meanings. The conversational language in "Too Soon a Woman" represents the author's idea of the dialect of Midwestern pioneers in the mid-1800s.

1. What do the phrases "We're prid'near out of grub" and "Just leave me be" mean?
2. Does the author's use of dialect add to the story? Why or why not?

- See **Literary Terms Handbook,** p. R3.

LITERARY ELEMENTS

1. They mean "We're almost out of food" *or* "We're pretty near out of food" and "Just leave me alone."
2. The author's use of dialect adds to the story because it makes the story seem more realistic and true to the period.

Additional Resources

Literary Elements Transparency 21

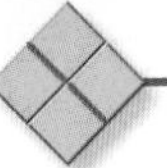

Extending Your Response

Writing About Literature

Surprise Ending The last sentence in "Too Soon a Woman" comes as a surprise to the reader. Mary is a recent and, at first, unwelcome addition to the family. Then, suddenly, the narrator tells us she became his stepmother. Write a paragraph analyzing the effectiveness of the ending of the story.

Creative Writing

A Learning Experience Recall the list you made for the **Reading Focus** on page 234. Using your list and what you learned from the story, write an introduction that explains the courage and survival techniques pioneers needed.

Literature Groups

A Caretaker's Responsibility When Mary cooked the mushroom, she had no idea if she would survive eating it. Did she take too great a risk? What would have happened to the children if she became sick or died? Would you have eaten the mushroom? Discuss these questions, and be prepared to share your group's opinions with the whole class.

interNET CONNECTION

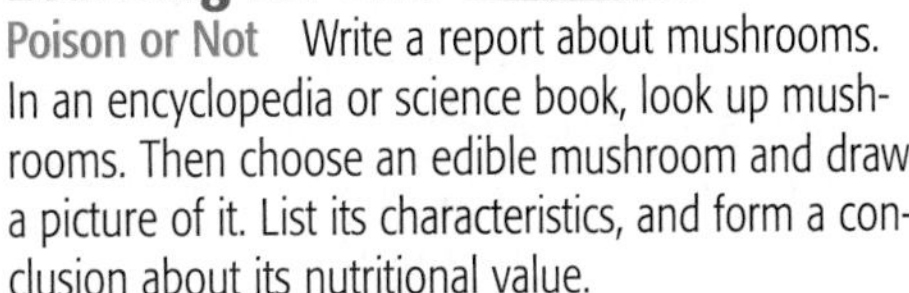

Use the Web to learn more about pioneer life. Try typing words and phrases such as *Oregon Trail* and *Conestoga* into a search engine.

Learning for Life

Poison or Not Write a report about mushrooms. In an encyclopedia or science book, look up mushrooms. Then choose an edible mushroom and draw a picture of it. List its characteristics, and form a conclusion about its nutritional value.

Save your work for your portfolio.

Skill Minilesson

Reteach · Review

VOCABULARY • ANTONYMS

Antonyms are words with opposite, or nearly opposite, meanings.

PRACTICE In each blank, write an antonym for the underlined word.

1. She had been plump before her illness, but afterwards she was quite _______.
2. The losers looked _______, but the winners looked delighted.
3. Some people react _______ to good news, while others jump up and down excitedly.
4. The portions that were served weren't generous at all; they were downright _______.
5. Successful salespeople treat customers politely, not _______.

Extending Your Response

Writing About Literature

Students' paragraphs should

- explain the effect of the surprise ending on readers
- analyze the effectiveness of the ending
- flow logically from one thought to another and have a clear conclusion

Creative Writing

Students' introductions should

- evaluate survival techniques from their earlier lists or those they learned in the story
- show an understanding of courageous actions
- contain a topic sentence and a conclusion

Literature Groups Encourage each member to list questions and ideas about the topic before coming together as a group. Have groups assign one person to take notes while the group discusses the topic.

Learning for Life Remind students that a good report contains an introductory paragraph with a strong lead, a body (several paragraphs, each built around one main idea), and a conclusion that sums up the main points of the report.

Skill Minilessons

VOCABULARY • ANTONYMS

Example antonyms:

1. gaunt
2. grim
3. sedately
4. skimpy
5. gruffly

Additional Resources

Vocabulary Practice, p. 14

ASSESSMENT

- ***Quick Checks,*** p. 21
- ***Selection and Theme Assessment,*** pp. 37–38
- ***Performance Assessment,*** p. 20
- ***Testmaker: ExamView Pro***
- ***Interactive Tutor: Self-Assessment***

Before Reading

Objectives

- To read and analyze a short story about the challenge a teenage boy must face
- To recognize how writers foreshadow coming events

Skills

Reading/Thinking: Sequence of Events; Inferring; Drawing Conclusions
Grammar/Language: Usage: *Lie* and *Lay*
Listening/Speaking: Interviewing
Collaboration: Literature Groups

Motivating → STUDENTS

Selection Focus Transparency 22: Have students discuss the quote by American novelist Agnes Sligh Turnbull.

Reading Focus: As an extension of the Reading Focus, have students use precise language and sensory details to discuss what special care ill pets might need from their owners.

Before You Read

A Boy and His Dog

MEET MARTHA BROOKS

Martha Brooks writes mainly about teenagers and their joys and disappointments. Her own childhood was spent at a tuberculosis sanatorium in rural Canada, where her parents were part of the medical staff. She and her sister grew up on the grounds with just a few other children. In her writing, Brooks has said that "what is important is that I try to be true to the characters I invent—listening to them, letting them tell their stories, and respecting the lives they live on the page."

Martha Brooks was born in 1944. This story was first published in 1988.

READING FOCUS

Human beings and their pets can become very dependent on each other. Do you have, or wish you had, a pet?

Chart It!

Choose a pet. Then create a two-column chart that shows what a pet needs from its owner and what the owner receives from the pet.

Setting a Purpose

Read this story to find out how one person feels about his dog.

BUILDING BACKGROUND

Did You Know?

Veterinary medicine deals with the diseases and injuries of animals. Animals can suffer from many of the same diseases that affect people, including heart disease and cancer.

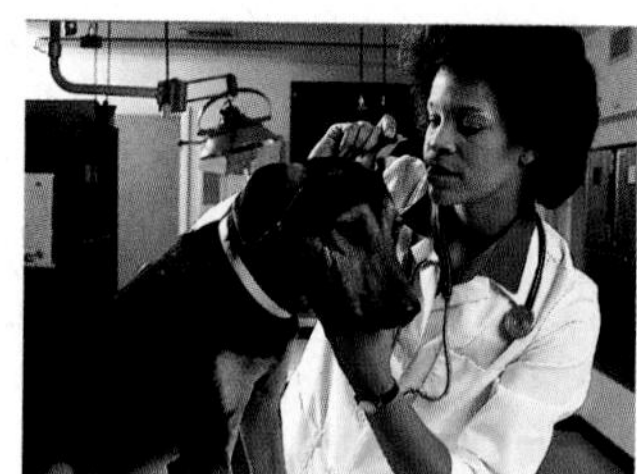

VOCABULARY PREVIEW

spasm (spaz′ əm) *n.* a sudden uncontrollable tightening of a muscle; p. 243
obligingly (ə blī′ jing lē) *adv.* helpfully; agreeably; p. 244
slither (slith′ ər) *v.* to move along with a sliding or gliding motion, as a snake; p. 246
frenzy (fren′ zē) *n.* a state of intense excitement or disturbance; p. 246
vigor (vig′ ər) *n.* strength and energy; p. 246
lolling (lol′ ing) *adj.* hanging down loosely; drooping; p. 246
saunter (sôn′ tər) *v.* to walk in a relaxed way; p. 246
reluctantly (ri luk′ tənt lē) *adv.* unwillingly; p. 247

RESOURCE MANAGER

Teaching Tools and Resources
- Theme Three Planning Guide
- Literature Groups Sourcebook

Essential Lesson Support

Lesson-Specific Instruction
- Selection Focus Transparency 22
- Literary Elements Transparency 22
- Active Reading Guide,* p. 22
- Selection Vocabulary Practice, p. 15
- TIME *inTIME* magazine, p. 2

Assessment
- Selection Quick Checks,* p. 22
- Sel. and Theme Assmt., pp. 39–40
- Testmaker: ExamView Pro
- Performance Assessment, p. 21

Systematic Language Instruction
- Gr. & Comp. Hbk., L. 5.1, 5.2

English Language Learners
- ELL Sourcebook, p. 44
- Spanish Summaries, p. 22
- Spanish Translations, pp. 70–73
- Audio Library*
- English, Yes!

Spec. Needs/Strat. Interven.
- Interactive Rdg. Sbk., pp. T106–T108
- Interactive Rdg. Wkbk., pp. 42–43
- Inclusion Strat. Sbk., pp. 59–60
- Audio Library*

*Also available in Spanish

A Boy and His Dog

Martha Brooks

A My dog is old. His eyes are constantly runny on account of he's going blind. Sometimes when we go for his walk he falls down. We'll be moving right along, I'll feel an unexpected tug at his leash, and bingo! he's over. The first time it happened he cried, sort of whimpered, and looked at his leg, the back one, the one that had betrayed him. I crouched in the tall grass (we take our walks in a sky-filled prairie field near the townhouses where we live) and felt the leg, which was in a spasm. I told him if it didn't work too well to just give up for a while. He seemed to know what I was telling him because he looked at me, whimpered some more, and finally flopped his head back on my leg. That's what kills me about dogs. They figure you're in charge of everything. Like if you pointed your finger, you could make a house fall down. Or if you told them everything's going to be okay, it would be.

After a couple of minutes he stood up and took off again in that businesslike, let's-get-the-show-on-the-road manner of his, sniffing, squatting to pee (he doesn't lift his leg anymore) near every bush in sight. Later, I found out he fell over because of arthritis. "Nothing you can do, really," said the vet, patting Alphonse's broad flat head. "He's just getting old, Buddy." She gave me some red pellet-shaped arthritis pills and sent us home.

Vocabulary
spasm (spaz′ əm) *n.* a sudden uncontrollable tightening of a muscle

Reading the Selection

SUMMARY

In this short story, a fourteen-year-old boy cares for his thirteen-year-old dog, who is arthritic and going blind. The dog becomes lethargic and doesn't eat much. The boy takes the dog to the vet, who tells the boy the dog has cancer. The boy must come to terms with losing his best friend.

Spanish Summaries, p. 22

A Active Reading Strategies

PREDICT Ask students why the narrator might have told readers that his dog is old to begin the story. What might this story be about? *(Students might suggest that the narrator is about to tell a story that revolves around his dog's old age.)*

VOCABULARY If you haven't previewed the selection vocabulary with students, stop and remind them to use context clues to unlock the meanings of new vocabulary words.

Additional Resources

Active Reading Guide, p. 22

Audio Library

Spanish Audio Library

Teaching Support

CONNECTING TO OTHER SELECTIONS

COMPARING *selections*

This selection is paired with "Too Soon a Woman" on page 235. A lesson for teaching a comparison of the two selections appears on page 249.

The chart at the right shows three other ways to connect "A Boy and His Dog" to selections in this book.

For specific teaching strategies, see the ***Theme Three Planning Guide.***

Connection	Title
Life Skills: Lifelong Learning	→ "Last Cover," p. 163
Thematic: Loss	→ "Birthday Box," p. 175
Literary: Foreshadowing	→ "Broken Chain," p. 44

B Author's Craft

POINT OF VIEW Ask students to discuss why this piece seems so personal. *(Buddy talks directly to the reader and shares his personal thoughts and feelings.)*

C Active Reading Strategies

EVALUATE Have students explain the meaning of this sentence: *Around our house, nobody put their hands over my ears.* *(Family members allow Buddy to hear whatever they say.)*

D Literary Elements

TONE Ask students to explain how Buddy's conversational style affects the story. *(It makes the story seem as if it really is being told by a fourteen-year-old.)*

E Active Reading Strategies

REVIEW Ask students to review what they know about Alphonse up to this point. *(Alphonse is very old and his health is failing. He is Buddy's confidante and companion.)*

F Literary Elements

CHARACTER Ask students what Buddy reveals about himself in this speech. *(He's thoughtful, logical, and takes responsibility seriously.)*

Teaching Support

After that, whenever he fell, he'd look quite cheerful. He'd lick the leg a bit, hang out his tongue, pant, and patiently wait. Just before stumbling to his feet, he'd look up like he was saying thank you—when I hadn't done anything!

B I couldn't let him see how bad all this made me feel. He's so smart sometimes you have to put your hands over his ears and spell things so he won't know what you're talking about. Things like cheese, cookie, walk. All his favorites.

Mom said, "He can't last forever. Everybody dies sooner or later. It's the natural course of events. And big dogs don't live as long as little dogs."

C Around our house, nobody put their hands over my ears.

D Alphonse was a present for my first birthday. Dad brought him home, just a scruffy little brown pup someone was giving away. No special breed. I still have a snapshot of him and me at the party. I was this goopy-looking blond kid in blue corduroy overalls and a Donald Duck T-shirt. Alphonse was all over me in the way of puppies. I'd been startled by Dad's flash and also by Alphonse, who'd chosen that exact moment to paw me down and slurp strawberry ice cream off my face and hands. Dad says I didn't cry or anything! Just lay bug-eyed on the shag rug with Alphonse wiggling and slopping all over me. We got on like a house on fire after that.

Which is why it's so unfair that I'm fourteen going on fifteen and he's thirteen going on ninety-four.

I guess I thought we'd just go on forever with Alphonse being my dog. Listening when I tell him stuff. When he goes, who am I going to tell my secrets to? I tell him things I wouldn't even tell Herb Malken, who is my best friend now that we've been in this city a year. E My dad's always getting transferred. He's in the army. When I grow up that's one thing I'm not going to be. In the army. I won't make my kids move every three years and leave all their friends behind. Which is one thing I *am* going to do: have more than one kid when I get married.

F There's a big myth that only children are selfish and self-centered. I can say from personal experience that only children are more likely to feel guilty and be too eager to please. It's terrible when you are one kid having to be everything to two parents.

Which is why Alphonse is more than just a dog, you see. Mom even sometimes calls him "Baby." Like he's my brother. Which it sometimes feels like.

Last week he had bad gas. I always sleep with the windows open. Even so, it got pretty awful in my bedroom.

Alphonse doesn't make much sound when he has gas. Just a little "phhhht" like a balloon with a slow leak and there's no living with him. I swear when he gets like that it would be dangerous to light a match.

I sent him out. He went obligingly. He's always been a polite dog. I listened, first to his toenails clicking over the hardwood floors, then to the scratching of his dry bristly fur as he slumped against the other side of the bedroom door. When you can't be in the same room with someone who's shared your dreams for thirteen years, it's hard to get properly relaxed. It isn't the

Vocabulary

obligingly (ə blī′ jing lē) *adv.* helpfully; agreeably

MEETING INDIVIDUAL NEEDS — ENGLISH LANGUAGE LEARNERS

Unusual Expressions List on the board the following expressions from the story: *hang out his tongue, goopy-looking blond kid, Alphonse was all over me, bug-eyed, we got on like a house on fire, he's thirteen going on ninety-four.* Explain to students that this story is told as if Buddy is talking to the reader. The style is informal and conversational. It uses expressions, often idioms, that English language learners may not be familiar with.

Activity Have students work in pairs or small groups to discuss these words and to use context to figure them out.

Additional Resources

English Language Learners Sourcebook, p. 44

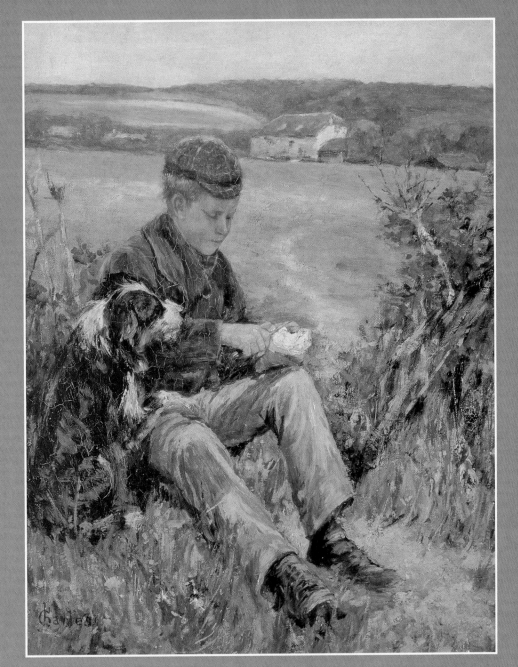

Companions. James Charles (1851–1906). Oldham Art Gallery, Manchester, England.

Viewing the painting: How do you think the lives of this boy and his dog differ from the lives of the boy and dog in the story?

VIEWING THE PAINTING

Viewing Response *Although the boy and his dog in the painting lived on a farm about a century ago and Alphonse and Buddy live in a townhome in the present day, the essential part of their lives, their relationship, seems just as close and sharing.*

FYI

Dogs and people have been companions for thousands of years. In Idaho, scientists found the remains of a dog estimated to be from 10,500 years ago. Asian, African, European, and North and South American cultural groups all bred dogs to use as companions, guards, workers, hunters, or protectors. Ancient cave paintings, artifacts, and writings show people and dogs living together the world over.

Dog Years The ratio of dog years to human years is approximately seven to one. This means that dogs age seven times as quickly as humans.

Reading *Minilesson*

Sequence of Events Ask volunteers to tell briefly what they have done since they walked into school today. As they speak, record any time words they use; for example, *first, next, then, after that, when, now, while, during, earlier, before,* and *after.* Remind students that they can keep the order of events in a story straight by charting them.

Activity Ask students to work in small groups to compile lists of time words from the story. Then have students create charts that track the story's sequence of events. They can use their lists of time words to provide clues to the sequencing. **L2**

Additional Resources

Reading Skills Practice Workbook

Active Reading Strategies

G

PREDICT Have students predict what the vet might say about Buddy's condition. *(The dog seems to be in a general decline; this latest event might indicate a severe illness.)*

H Literary Elements

IMAGERY Have students notice the sensory images the author uses to describe the fall day. Ask students why they think the author uses so many color words. *(This provides strong contrast to the fact that Alphonse cannot see. It brings out the growing sense of sadness.)*

On The Lighter Side

Generally, dogs are lovable pets, so it is hard to understand why so many dog expressions have negative connotations: "You ain't nothing but a *hound dog*" (Elvis Presley) refers to a mean and contemptible person; *hound* means "nag" or "pursue"; *dog-eared* means "damaged and worn"; *in the doghouse* means "in trouble, disfavor"; and *dogged* means "plodding."

I Literary Elements

CHARACTER Ask students to describe the kind of person the vet is. *(She seems dedicated and emotionally involved in the lives of the animals, and she cares deeply for them.)*

Teaching Support

same when they aren't near you, breathing the same air.

G For the next few days he lay around more than usual. I thought perhaps he was just overtired (even though I hadn't been able to stand it and had begun to let him back into my room, gas and all). By Sunday, Mom cocked her head at him and said to Dad and me, "I don't like the way Alphonse looks. Better take him back to the vet, Buddy."

Mom works at the army base too. It's late when she and Dad get home and by that time the vet is closed for the day. So I always take Alphonse right after school. It isn't far—three blocks past the field.

H Monday was the kind of fall day that makes you breathe more deeply—the field all burning colors, far-off bushes little flames of magenta[1] and orange, dry wavy grass a pale yellow, and the big sky that kind of deep fire blue you see only once a year, in October. Alphonse didn't fall down once. Eyes half closed, he walked slowly, sniffing the air to take in messages.

A young ginger-colored cat slithered under a wooden fence and into the field. It saw Alphonse and suddenly crouched low, eyes dark, motionless. For a minute there I didn't think he would notice it. Then his ears went up and his head shot forward. Next thing, he was hauling me along at the end of his leash, barking himself into a frenzy. The cat parted the grass like wildfire and, reaching the fence, dug its body gracelessly under at a spot where there seemed hardly an inch between wood and solid earth.

Alphonse has that effect on cats. They must think he's death on wheels the way they scatter to get out of his way. He stared proudly in the direction of the fence; his nose hadn't failed him. He walked on, a little more vigor in his step, his tongue lolling out, his ears nice and perky.

We reached the edge of the field where we usually turn around on our walks. This time, of course, we didn't. He lost some of his bounce and trailed slightly behind. I looked back. He lowered his head. "She's not going to do anything to you, you crazy dog," I told him. "She's going to shake her head again, and tell us to go home." He kept pace with me after that. Like I said, dogs believe everything you tell them.

The vet is the kind of person whose job runs her life. One minute she's smiling over a recovering patient, or one who's come in just for shots; the next, she's blowing her nose like the place is a funeral parlor. It must be murder to become so involved with your patients. She always looks as if she needs some place to hole up for a good sleep. And her legs are magnets for strays who are forever up for adoption. I

At the clinic, I sat down with Alphonse resignedly backed up between my knees. To my astonishment, a resident cat sauntered over and actually rubbed against him. Alphonse sniffed its head and then ignored

1. *Magenta* is a purplish-red color.

Vocabulary

slither (sli*th*′ ər) *v.* to move along with a sliding or gliding motion, as a snake
frenzy (fren′ zē) *n.* a state of intense excitement or disturbance
vigor (vig′ ər) *n.* strength and energy
lolling (lol′ ing) *adj.* hanging down loosely; drooping
saunter (sôn′ tər) *v.* to walk in a relaxed way

Grammar and Language *Minilesson*

Usage: Lie and Lay Copy this chart on the board. Explain that the verb *lie* means "to recline" (I will lie down for a nap), while *lay* means "to put" or "to place" (I will lay the pen on the desk).

Present	Past	Past Participle	Present Participle
lie	lay	lain	lying
lay	laid	laid	laying

Activity Have students choose a form of *lie* or *lay* to complete the following:

1. Yesterday the cat *(lay, laid)* on my father's favorite chair all day.
2. When he came into the classroom, he *(lay, laid)* the booklets on the floor.
3. You will have to *(lie, lay)* down to reach under the car. **L2**

Additional Resources

- ***Grammar and Language Transparency 21***
- ***Grammar and Language Workbook,*** pp. 223–224
- ***Grammar and Composition Handbook,*** Lessons 3.11, 3.12
- ***Writer's Choice,*** Lessons 10.9, 17.2

it (he only likes cats who run). He watched the door to the examining room and trembled. I wondered if his eyesight was improving. With one hand I held his leash; the other I bit away at because of hangnails.

When the vet, smiling, summoned us, I got to my feet and Alphonse reluctantly pattered after me. Inside the examining room he pressed against the door, willing it to open. I picked him up and lugged him over to the table.

"He's lost weight," said the vet, stroking, prodding gently.

"He was too fat," I said, patting his stomach.

She laughed, continuing her way down his body. "Has he been on a diet?"

"No. I guess older dogs don't eat as much—like older people."

She looked at his rectum. "How long has this been here?" she said softly, more to herself than to me.

"This what?" I looked.

"It's quite a small lump," she said, pressing it hard.

Alphonse stood politely on the table, shaking and puffing.

"Sometimes," she said, with a reassuring smile, "older dogs get these lumps and they usually aren't anything to worry about, Buddy."

Usually? What did she mean, *usually?* My heart began to race.

"Older neutered dogs," she continued, in the same even tone, "very often get benign[2] lumps in the anal region. But we'd better check this out, anyway. . . ."

My dog has cancer. What do I tell him now? What am I going to do? Mom and Dad have left it up to me. The vet, with strained sad eyes, says the little lump is just a symptom of what's going on inside. Why didn't I notice that he was so short of breath? That he was peeing more than usual? That he didn't eat much? That his bowels weren't working? She tells me that when dogs are old all of these things become a problem, it's the usual progress of aging. Except not in Alphonse's case. But how would I know that? I shouldn't blame myself. She says there was nothing I could have done to stop it, anyway.

So what do I tell him? Is he in pain? I couldn't stand it if he were in pain. Tonight Mom wanted to give me a sleeping pill. I refused it. Alphonse is here with me on my bed. He's going to sleep with me one last time. I'll hold him and tell him about me and what I plan to do with my life. I'll have to lie a little, fill in a few places, because I'm not *exactly* sure. But he has a right to know what he'll be missing. I'll have a good life, I know it, just like he's had. I'm going to tell him about it now, whisper it in his ear, and I won't leave out a single detail.

2. A *neutered* animal is one from which certain reproductive organs have been surgically removed, usually to prevent breeding. A *benign* (bi nīn′) lump is an abnormal growth that is not cancerous and, therefore, not usually dangerous.

Vocabulary
reluctantly (ri luk′ tənt lē) *adv.* unwillingly

J Active Reading Strategies

EVALUATE Ask students how they know that Buddy is more worried than he lets on. *(He bites his nails nervously as he waits for the vet.)*

K Critical Thinking

INFERRING The vet says she'd better check out Alphonse's lump. Then there is a break in the text. The next words are *My dog has cancer.* *(It means time has passed.)*

L Critical Thinking

DRAWING CONCLUSIONS Have students explain how they know that Buddy thinks of Alphonse more as a friend than a dog. *(Buddy asks, "So what do I tell him?" as if Alphonse could really understand the whole concept.)*

M Author's Craft

FORESHADOWING Have students discuss how the author has led up to this moment. *(The story details focus on Alphonse's failing stamina and the vet's inability to give any reassurance that Alphonse will recover.)*

Thematic Focus

Facing Challenge Have students discuss the challenge Buddy faces with Alphonse. Do they think he handles the situation maturely? Do they think Alphonse, if he could, might consider Buddy his hero?

ASSESSMENT

 ***Quick Checks,*** p. 22

MEETING INDIVIDUAL NEEDS

SPECIAL NEEDS

Less-Proficient Readers Selecting an appropriate word or phrase to complete a sentence helps promote understanding and effective communication.

Activity Have students work in pairs to complete the following sentences. Encourage them to reread page 247 for clues. **L1**

1. Buddy picked Alphonse up and lugged him over to the _____. *(table)*
2. The vet found that Alphonse had lost a lot of _____. *(weight)*
3. The boy told Alphonse all about his _____. *(future plans)*

Additional Resources

Inclusion Strategies

Responding to the Selection

PERSONAL RESPONSE

Answers should show a deeper understanding of the relationship between humans and their pets.

Analyzing Literature

1. Alphonse is arthritic and going blind. He has spasms in his leg and he stumbles.
2. The dog has become lethargic, and Buddy's mother doesn't like the way Alphonse looks.
3. Alphonse will be put to sleep.
4. They have been together almost their entire lives.
5. Buddy needs to tell Alphonse his plans because Alphonse won't be around to see them work out.
6. The author uses the first-person point of view to make readers feel what it is like to be Buddy.
7. Buddy will have to take Alphonse to the vet one last time. Then he will have to deal with the loss of Alphonse.

Extending Your Response

Literature Groups Encourage each group member to list several ideas. Have groups assign one person to take notes while the group discusses the topic and another to share the group's final ideas with the rest of the class.

Interdisciplinary Activity You may want to have several students work together to create the career-path chart. One student can show the steps a student needs to take in middle and high school; another, the steps to take in college.

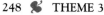

Active Reading and Critical Thinking

Responding to Literature

PERSONAL RESPONSE

- Think back to the chart about humans and their pets you made in the **Reading Focus** on page 242. How would you change the chart now that you have read "A Boy and His Dog"?

Analyzing Literature

RECALL AND INTERPRET

1. What are some of the signs of old age in Alphonse?
2. Why did Buddy take Alphonse back to the vet?
3. What will happen to Alphonse after the story ends?
4. What is significant about the amount of time the boy and his dog have been together?
5. Why does the boy need to tell his dog about his future plans?

EVALUATE AND CONNECT

6. Why did the author choose the first-person point of view?
7. Theme Connection What challenges will Buddy face after the story ends?

LITERARY ELEMENTS

Foreshadowing

Clues that prepare readers for events that will happen later in a story are called **foreshadowing.** Foreshadowing can build suspense. For example, a weapon found in a drawer might foreshadow a future crime.

1. Does Alphonse's first visit to the vet foreshadow a later event? Explain your answer.
2. Find the paragraph in which Alphonse's death is foreshadowed by a casual statement.

See **Literary Terms Handbook,** p. R5.

Extending Your Response

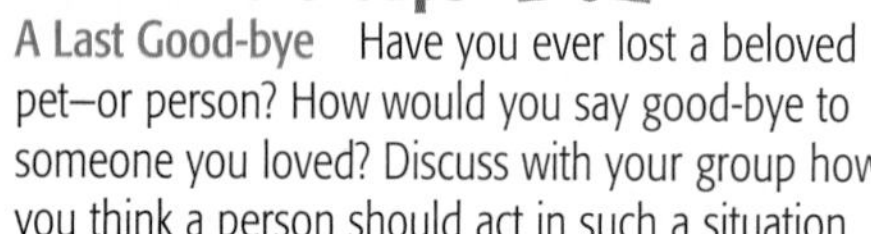

Literature Groups

A Last Good-bye Have you ever lost a beloved pet—or person? How would you say good-bye to someone you loved? Discuss with your group how you think a person should act in such a situation.

Interdisciplinary Activity

Science Invite a veterinarian or a vet student to your class. Prepare questions to ask—for example:
- Why did you choose to become a vet?
- How are vets trained?
- What subjects should students who are interested in a veterinary career study?

Then design a career-path chart that shows the steps a person needs to take to become a vet.

Reading Further

If you would like to read other stories written by Martha Brooks, try these:

Paradise Cafe and Other Stories

Two Moons in August

Save your work for your portfolio.

ASSESSMENT

- ***Quick Checks,*** p. 22
- ***Selection and Theme Assessment,*** pp. 39–40
- ***Performance Assessment,*** p. 21
- ***Testmaker: ExamView Pro***
- ***Interactive Tutor: Self-Assessment***

LITERARY ELEMENTS

1. Yes. The first visit to the vet sets the stage for later visits. Readers learn that Alphonse is old and feeble; more problems may arise.
2. Buddy's mother says, "He can't last forever. Everybody dies sooner or later. It's the natural course of events."

Additional Resources

Literary Elements Transparency 22

Critical Thinking

COMPARING SELECTIONS

Too Soon a Woman and A Boy and His Dog

COMPARE CHARACTERS

The boy narrator and Mary, in "Too Soon a Woman," and Buddy, in "A Boy and His Dog," are young people who must deal with loss in their lives. Present a skit in which, through time travel, the two boys and Mary meet to talk about how life's challenges have changed them and helped them grow. Present two acts, a first act that takes place when the characters are the same ages as they are in the stories, and a second act that takes place ten years later.

COMPARE TONE

Both selections are written from the first-person point of view, but they differ greatly in tone. Discuss these questions in small groups.

1. Which story uses elements of humor? Why do you think one writer chose to include humor and the other didn't?
2. How would you describe the tone of each story?
3. In what ways does the tone of each story suit the events the author is describing?

COMPARE DESCRIPTIONS

You probably noticed that Martha Brooks tells very little about how Buddy looks, and that Dorothy M. Johnson tells almost nothing about her narrator's appearance. Can you explain why these two writers did so little to describe how their main characters look? Write a paragraph or two explaining what you think these writers were most interested in telling us about their characters. Use examples from the story to back up your ideas.

COMPARING selections

Objective

- To compare two short stories about facing challenge

COMPARE CHARACTERS

Students' skits should

- show differences in how the characters feel and behave.
- be well rehearsed before they are presented.

COMPARE TONE

1. "A Boy and His Dog" uses humor. "Too Soon a Woman" doesn't use humor because the author wants readers to realize how serious and desperate the situation is.
2. In "Too Soon a Woman," the tone is one of quiet happiness. At the beginning of "A Boy and His Dog," the tone is lighthearted, but it becomes increasingly serious after the second trip to the vet.
3. In both stories the tone is cheerful or serious to match the events being described.

Additional Resources

Literary Groups Sourcebook

COMPARE DESCRIPTIONS

Students' paragraphs should

- contain a clear topic sentence and conclusion.
- present facts from the stories to support their ideas.

Teaching Support

PORTFOLIO OPTIONS

Select and Reflect Have students reflect on the paragraphs they wrote for the activity above by asking themselves these questions:

- Do my paragraphs explain why the writers did not describe how the characters look?
- Do my paragraphs explain what the writers most wanted to tell?
- Do I use examples from the stories to support my ideas?

Students should clip their reflections to their paragraphs and place them in their portfolios. At a later time, they might consider using the comments to revise their paragraphs as portfolio showcase pieces. **L2**

Additional Resources

Writing Assessment and Portfolio Management, pp. 38–45

Reading and Thinking Skills

Objective

- To recognize details in a literary work and use strategies for visualizing a story

Teaching Strategies

Before asking students to read the passage in their books, you may wish to have them close their eyes as you read it aloud to them. Ask them to visualize the scene and then to share the images of the woman in the story that come to mind. To extend the activity, encourage students to draw the scene or a detail from it.

Exercises

1. The characters are in and around a horse-drawn wagon on a prairie. Students may pick out words and details from the first paragraph to place the characters.
2. Students' responses may include details of the setting: the prairie, the mountain, the long road, the one-horse wagon, the father, the son, and two small daughters. Students may also jot down emotions and observations about the characters in this situation even though the words *poor, lonely,* and *homeless* are not directly stated.

Additional Resources

Reading Skills Practice Workbook

Teaching Support

Visualizing

Good writers use exact, vivid words and strong, colorful details so that their readers can **visualize,** or picture, what is going on as they read. For example, consider the following passage from "New Directions." As you read the passage, notice how the exact words and the vivid details add to your ability to picture the scene.

> The next morning she left her house carrying the meat pies, lard, an iron brazier, and coals for a fire. Just before lunch she appeared in an empty lot behind the cotton gin. As the dinner noon bell rang, she dropped the savors into boiling fat and the aroma rose and floated over to the workers who spilled out of the gin, covered with white lint, looking like specters.

As a skillful reader, use your own experiences to help you understand as well as imagine the scene. For example, have you ever felt the weight of a heavy load, such as your schoolbooks as you walked to school?

- For more about visualizing, see **Reading Handbook,** pp. R87–R88.

EXERCISES

Read the opening paragraphs from "Too Soon a Woman" by Dorothy M. Johnson. Then answer the questions at the right.

> We left the home place behind, mile by slow mile, heading for the mountains, across the prairie where the wind blew forever.
>
> At first there were four of us with the one-horse wagon and its skimpy load. Pa and I walked, because I was a big boy of eleven. My two little sisters romped and trotted until they got tired and had to be boosted up into the wagon bed.

1. Where are the characters in relation to one another and their surroundings in this scene? Pick out the words and details that tell where they are.
2. Find another descriptive passage in the story. Write a paragraph describing how the author's use of details helps readers visualize the scene. Quote examples from the story.

MEETING INDIVIDUAL NEEDS

SPECIAL NEEDS

Less-Proficient Readers The technique of visualization is particularly beneficial to less-proficient readers.

Activity Have students listen to and visualize the first sentence of "Too Soon a Woman." Ask students to describe the image brought to mind by each part of the sentence: *We left the home place behind, mile by slow mile, heading for the mountains, across the prairie where the wind blew forever.* Have students identify the words or phrases in this sentence that create visual images. Ask each student to write a sentence that contains at least two visual images. **L1**

Additional Resources

Inclusion Strategies

Before You Read

The Women's 400 Meters and *To James*

MEET LILLIAN MORRISON

A full-time author and poet, Lillian Morrison is an avid sports fan who has written entire collections of poems about sports. Morrison's connection to teenagers comes from her experience as coordinator of young adult services at the New York Public Library. She has also collected and published collections of folk rhymes and folk sayings.

Lillian Morrison was born in 1917.

MEET FRANK HORNE

Frank Horne's love of track began when he ran the quarter mile as a college student. Later, after becoming an optometrist, he coached a championship high school track team. "To James" was inspired by his coaching experiences.

Frank Horne was born in 1899. "To James" is from a 1963 collection of Horne's poetry titled Haverstraw.

READING FOCUS

Have you ever tried to run as fast and as long as you could or push your body all the way to the edge in some other way? How did it feel?

Journal

Write an entry about how your body and mind feel when you test your physical endurance. If you have ever been in a race, write about that experience.

Setting a Purpose

The first time through, just read to enjoy the poems and get an idea of what they are about. Read them aloud and listen to their sounds. Then you can read the poems more carefully to see how the poets use sounds and images to express their ideas.

BUILDING BACKGROUND

Track-and-field events, held since the Olympic Games in 776 B.C., are the oldest organized sports. These athletic meets include running and walking races, and jumping and throwing events. Track meets are usually held in a field or stadium built around a 400-meter (437-yard) oval track. The fastest, shortest races are dashes that range from 50 to 400 meters. The racers begin in a crouch at the starting line. When the starter fires a pistol, the runners leap into a full stride and run at top speed to the finish line. A fast start can often mean the difference between winning and losing the race.

Before Reading

Objectives

- To read and analyze two poems about runners and races
- To recognize the use of free verse in a poem
- To write a short essay describing the theme "Facing Challenge"

Skills

Reading/Thinking: Evaluating; Inferring; Drawing Conclusions
Writing: Journal Entry
Vocabulary: Prefixes
Grammar/Language: Present and Past Participles; Ellipsis
Listening/Speaking: Sports Broadcast; Interview
Collaboration: Literature Groups

Motivating STUDENTS

Selection Focus Transparency 23: Have students comment on Samuelson's experience and compare it to their own. Encourage them to see how her statement applies to all parts of life.

Reading Focus: As an extension of the Reading Focus, have partners use precise language and sensory details to discuss ways that people push themselves to the limits of their endurance.

RESOURCE MANAGER

Teaching Tools and Resources
- Theme Three Planning Guide
- Literature Groups Sourcebook

Essential Lesson Support

Lesson-Specific Instruction
- Selection Focus Transparency 23
- Literary Elements Transparency 23
- Active Reading Guide,* p. 23

Assessment
- Selection Quick Checks,* p. 23
- Sel. and Theme Assmt., pp. 41–42
- Testmaker: ExamView Pro
- Performance Assessment, p. 22

Systematic Language Instruction
- Gr. and Comp. Hbk., L. 5.3, 5.4

English Language Learners
- ELL Sourcebook, p. 45
- Spanish Summaries, p. 23
- Spanish Translations, pp. 74–75
- Audio Library*
- English, Yes!

Spec. Needs/Strat. Interven.
- Interactive Rdg. Sbk., pp. T108–T110
- Interactive Rdg. Wkbk., pp. 44
- Audio Library*

*Also available in Spanish

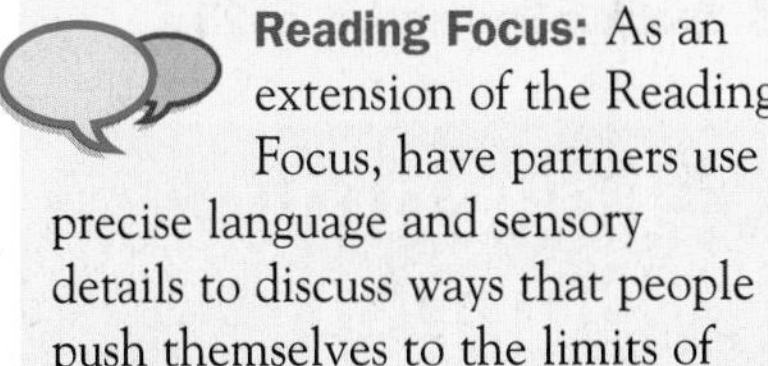

Reading the Selection

A **Literary Elements**

ALLITERATION Have students identify alliteration in the first stanza. *(It is the s sound in* skittish *and* starting.*)* Draw their attention also to the consequence of the final s sounds in *flex, knees,* and *heels*.

B **Active Reading Strategies**

VISUALIZE Have students visualize this starting scene. You might ask them to sketch it.

C **Critical Thinking**

EVALUATING Ask students to compare the runners in the first and third stanzas. *(At first, they are nervous; their energy is pent up, waiting for release. Later they are focused, propelling themselves at great speed.)*

D **Literary Elements**

FREE VERSE Free verse has no fixed pattern of rhyme, rhythm, line length, or stanza arrangement. Ask students whether this poem is written in free verse.

Additional Resources

Active Reading Guide, p. 23

 ***Audio Library***

Spanish Summaries, p. 23

The Women's 400 Meters

Lillian Morrison

Skittish,°
they flex knees, drum heels and
shiver at the starting line

waiting the gun
to pour them over the stretch
like a breaking wave.

Bang! they're off
careening° down the lanes,
D each chased by her own bright tiger.

1 The word *skittish* means "easily frightened or excited."
8 *Careening* is rushing along, perhaps swaying from side to side as if out of control.

Teaching Support

CONNECTING TO OTHER SELECTIONS
For a teaching strategy that connects "The Women's 400 Meters" to "Wait Till Next Year," see the ***Theme One Planning Guide.***

ENGLISH LANGUAGE LEARNERS

Track and Field Some English language learners might not be familiar with track events as they are organized in the United States. Tell students that the gun in the poem is used to signal the start of the race. When the gun goes off, the racers leave the starting line. Explain that the gun uses cartridges called blanks to provide a loud noise that all the racers can hear.

Activity If possible, show a video of a race or display photos of runners. Point out the cinders on the track and the way the runners lurch out of the starting blocks. Have students create word webs of track-and-field words.

Additional Resources

English Language Learners Sourcebook, p. 45

To James

Frank Horne

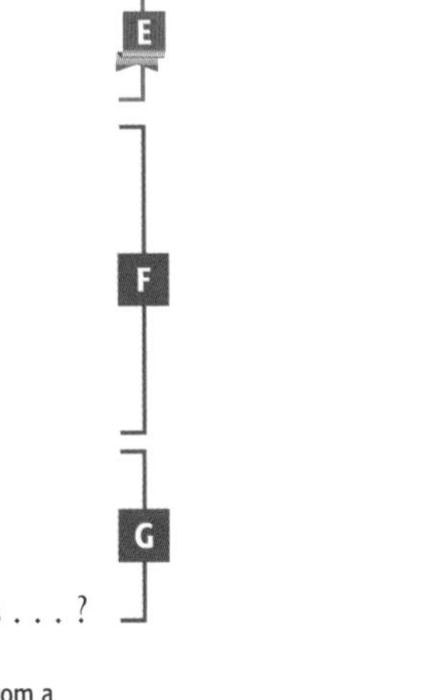

Do you remember
how you won
that last race . . . ?
how you flung your body
at the start . . .
how your spikes
ripped the cinders
in the stretch . . .
how you catapulted°
through the tape . . .
do you remember . . . ?
Don't you think
I lurched° with you
out of those starting holes . . . ?

9 To *catapult* is to leap or hurl oneself, as if from a giant slingshot.
13 To *lurch* is to plunge forward suddenly in a jerky manner.

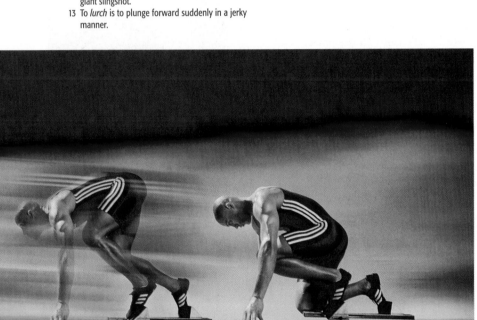

E Active Reading Strategies

EVALUATE Ask students whom the speaker is addressing in this poem. *(Students will probably understand that the person being spoken to is a runner; however, they might not be able to be more specific until they finish reading the poem.)*

F Literary Elements

VISUALIZE Have students take a moment to picture each detail of the race as it is described in this first stanza. *(Students might choose the image of the runner flinging his or her body forward at the start or catapulting through the tape.)*

Vo•cab•u•lar•y Skills

Prefixes Point out that the prefix *cata-* in *catapulted* comes from a Greek word that means "down." *Catapult* literally means "to throw down." Explain that other words begin with *cata-*, including *catalog* (literally "to count down"); *catas-trophe* (literally "to turn down"); and *cataclysm* (literally "to wash down").

G Literary Elements

FREE VERSE Have students read the poem, noting rhyme or other repeated patterns. Ask them whether they think "To James" is written in free verse. Have them explain their reasoning. *("To James" is written in free verse. It has no fixed rhyme or other repeated patterns.)*

Grammar and Language Minilesson

Present and Past Participles Review with students that participles function as main verbs and as adjectives. With regular verbs, the present participle is formed by adding *-ing*. The past participle is formed by adding *-ed*. Write the following lines from "To James" on the board:

1. Dig your starting holes deep and firm *(present participle, adjective)*
2. finish with an ecstatic burst that carries you hurtling through the tape to victory *(present participle, adjective)*
3. how your spikes ripped the cinders *(past participle, main verb)*

Activity Ask students to identify the participles in the lines on the board. Have them tell whether the participles are main verbs or adjectives and whether they are in the present or the past tense. **L2**

Additional Resources

- ***Grammar and Language Transparency 22***
- ***Grammar and Language Workbook,*** pp. 167–168
- ***Grammar and Composition Handbook,*** Lessons 9.1
- ***Writer's Choice,*** Lesson 15.1

Literary Elements

FREE VERSE In what ways are lines 1–28 and lines 29–51 of the poem similar? How are they different? *(Neither section contains rhymes or other repeated patterns. Lines 1–28 ask a series of questions; lines 29–51 make a series of statements.)*

H Critical Thinking

INFERRING Ask students what they think the poet means when he says "it's a short dash." *(He means that we don't have a long time to live.)*

I Critical Thinking

DRAWING CONCLUSIONS Have students discuss the meaning of the final lines of the poem. Ask them to explain what victory means. *(The end of the race of life is death; the victory is living life to the fullest.)*

LITERATURE & HUMANITIES

Have students examine the poster *Study for the Munich Olympic Games* in *Art Talk*, page 114. Encourage them to discuss the feelings expressed by each of the runners. What is the artist suggesting about the importance of races and other competitions in the lives of the competitors?

ASSESSMENT

Quick Checks, p. 23

Don't you think
my sinews° tightened
at those first
few strides . . .
and when you flew into the stretch
was not all my thrill
of a thousand races
in your blood . . . ?
At your final drive
through the finish line
did not my shout
tell of the
triumphant ecstasy°
of victory . . . ?

Live
as I have taught you
to run, Boy—
it's a short dash.
Dig your starting holes
deep and firm
lurch out of them
into the straightaway
with all the power
that is in you
look straight ahead
to the finish line
think only of the goal
run straight
run high
run hard
save nothing
and finish
with an ecstatic burst
that carries you
hurtling
through the tape
to victory . . .

16 The cords of tissue that connect muscles to bones are called tendons or *sinews* (sin′ ūz).
27 *Ecstasy* is a state of overwhelming joy or delight.

Teaching Support

CONNECTING TO OTHER SELECTIONS
For a teaching strategy that connects "To James" to "After Twenty Years," see the ***Theme Six Planning Guide.***

Listening and Speaking *Minilesson*

Sports Broadcast Students might gain a deeper understanding of the track-and-field images presented in these two poems if they develop a sports broadcast describing those images.

Activity In small groups, have students choose one of the poems to broadcast. Have students describe the race as a sportscaster would. Encourage them to create characters, describe the setting and the crowd, and dramatize the action of the race. Finally, have groups present their broadcasts to the class, using their voices, facial expressions, and gestures to dramatize the suspense and excitement. **L2**

Responding to Literature

PERSONAL RESPONSE

- Choose an image from each poem that stays in your mind's eye. How did the poetry affect the way you picture a track event?

Analyzing Literature

RECALL

1. What part of a race is described in "The Women's 400 Meters"?
2. Who are the two characters in the poem "To James"?

Brackets connect questions that are paired to develop higher-level thinking skills.

INTERPRET

3. How does the rhythm of "The Women's 400 Meters" make you feel as if you are at the start of a race?
4. How does the speaker in "To James" feel about the runner? How can you tell?

EVALUATE AND CONNECT

5. What does the first stanza of "The Women's 400 Meters" compare the racers to? Why is this an effective comparison?
6. Describe the image in the second stanza of "The Women's 400 Meters." How effective is this image?
7. In the third stanza of "The Women's 400 Meters," the poet suggests that each runner is being chased by a tiger. What does she mean by that?
8. Imagine that the speaker in "To James" had given you similar advice before a race. Would you agree or disagree? Explain.
9. Much of the advice in "To James" applies to life as well as to running. Find one line from the poem that you think people your age could use to help them succeed in school.
10. Theme Connection How do you think the runners in each poem could use their experience to inspire other young people?

LITERARY ELEMENTS

Free Verse

Poetry without a fixed pattern of rhyme, rhythm, line length, or stanza arrangement is called **free verse.** Both "To James" and "The Women's 400 Meters" are written in free verse. Some poets use free verse to give their poems the natural, realistic rhythms of conversation. Repetition and strong images are often the main poetic devices in free verse poetry.

1. Read the first stanza of "To James" aloud. Notice how Horne uses repetition to give some rhythm to the free verse. Write the phrases that are repeated.
2. Describe three examples of strong imagery in "The Women's 400 Meters."

- See **Literary Terms Handbook,** p. R5.

Responding to the Selection

PERSONAL RESPONSE

Students will choose different images. Some may say that the poems gave them the feeling of being a runner or a coach. Others may now see a foot race as a metaphor for life.

Analyzing Literature

1. The moments just before the race and the beginning of the race are described.
2. The characters are a runner and either his coach or his father.
3. At first, the rhythm is short and choppy; it seems a bit tense. With the word *bang,* the rhythm shifts and becomes smoother.
4. The speaker is very close to the runner; lines 12–28 describe different ways the speaker has experienced what the racer is experiencing.
5. The word *skittish* is often used to describe horses, which behave similarly before they race.
6. The author compares the group of racers to a breaking wave. Most students should think this is effective because the racers will break forward and flood the track.
7. Students should understand that the women are racing as if their lives depend on it. Also, the idea of a "bright tiger" conveys a sense of grace, great strength, and power.
8. Most students should see that the advice is sound if they want to run well.
9. Possible responses include *Dig your starting holes deep and firm, look straight ahead to the finish line,* or *think only of the goal.*
10. Runners must work hard, practice consistently and diligently, and focus on a goal. The runners could share with young people the ways in which discipline and focusing on a goal have helped them achieve their ambitions.

LITERARY ELEMENTS

1. *Do you remember, how you,* and *don't you think* are repeated.
2. Possible answers: *skittish, pour them over the stretch like a breaking wave,* and *each chased by her own bright tiger.*

Additional Resources

Literary Elements Transparency 23

Extending Your Response

Writing About Literature

Students' essays should

- describe different ways that people face challenges in their lives.
- clearly explain the challenge that is involved in each example.
- include references to or questions from the poem

Personal Writing

Students' journal entries should

- compare descriptions of their own experiences with those in the poem
- include a description that contains poetic images

Literature Groups Have students quickly jot down their impressions as soon as they have finished their runs and encourage them to compare their experiences with those in the poem.

Listening and Speaking To encourage productive interviews, suggest that students prepare questions that cannot be answered yes or no.

Skill Minilesson

GRAMMAR AND LANGUAGE • ELLIPSIS

Possible answers: "do you remember…?" This implies the speaker is waiting for the runner to remember; "at those first few strides . . ." The ellipses indicate time between the beginning of the race and the stretch.

Extending Your Response

Writing About Literature

Theme Consider how these poems connect to the theme of "Facing Challenge." What are some other ways in which people face challenge in their everyday lives? What can each poem teach people about facing challenges? What have the poems taught you about facing your own challenges? Write a short essay answering these questions. Include specific references to or quotations from the poems.

Personal Writing

Journal Recall your response to the **Reading Focus** on page 251. How does your description of pushing your body to the edge compare with the descriptions in the two poems? Write a more poetic description of your experience in your journal.

Literature Groups

Experience the Words! Run once around the schoolyard or the sports field with your group. Then sit down and compare your experiences with the descriptions of running in each poem.

Listening and Speaking

Why Run? Interview a student athlete about the reasons he or she chooses to run. Be sure to ask about the physical and psychological benefits and any negative aspects of running and competing.

Reading Further

If you would like to read more poems about sports, try these books by Lillian Morrison:

Sprints and Distances

At the Crack of the Bat

Other books of poetry you might like are:

Don't You Turn Back by Langston Hughes

On City Streets: An Anthology of Poetry edited by Nancy Larrick

Save your work for your portfolio.

Skill Minilesson

Reteach • Review

GRAMMAR AND LANGUAGE • ELLIPSIS

An **ellipsis** is the omission, or leaving out, of one or more words. In writing, three spaced periods are used to show an ellipsis. These periods are called *ellipses* (the plural of *ellipsis*). For example, the sentence "The team, without a great deal of talent or effort, won the track-and-field event" could be shortened (if you were interested only in the *result* of the event) to "The team . . . won the track-and-field event." Ellipsis marks are also used to indicate a pause in dialogue, such as: "The reason I was late for practice, Coach, is that I . . . uh . . . I needed to go home and . . . check on my sick dog."

PRACTICE Reread "To James," and find two places where the poet has used an ellipsis. Write the examples and then explain why, in your opinion, the poet has used them.

ASSESSMENT

- ***Quick Checks,*** p. 23
- ***Selection and Theme Assessment,*** pp. 41–42
- ***Performance Assessment,*** p. 22
- ***Testmaker: ExamView Pro***
- ***Interactive Tutor: Self-Assessment***

Interdisciplinary Connection

Measurement Systems

In Lillian Morrison's poem, runners anxiously wait at the starting line of a 400-meter race. The meter is the primary unit of measure for length in the metric system. However, before standardized measurements were invented, people used their bodies to measure distances and lengths.

Systems of Measure—Length	
Metric Unit	**U.S. Equivalent**
1 kilometer = 1000 meters	0.62 mile
1 meter = 10 decimeters	39.37 inches
1 decimeter = 10 centimeters	3.94 inches
1 centimeter = 10 millimeters	0.39 inch

Kingly Feet

Hundreds and hundreds of years ago, the width of a man's thumb and the length of his foot were commonly used as standard measurements for the inch and the foot. Of course, not many thumbs or feet were of equal length, which caused great frustration between merchants and buyers in the marketplace.

In Egypt, one king attempted to set a standard for the foot by distributing official measuring sticks of his own foot length. Each new king, however, wanted to use the length of *his* foot for the official standard, so the problem continued. In the fourteenth century, an English king set the standard for the length of the yard based upon the measurement of his rather rotund waist. During Queen Elizabeth's reign, the standard for the yard was the measurement from the queen's nose to the tip of her longest finger.

All Thumbs

People still sometimes use a thumb's width to guess the equivalent of an inch. Measure the width of your desktop with your thumb. Then share your answer with a classmate. Do your estimates match? Probably not.

Although your thumb won't measure an inch very accurately, it can help you estimate distances you might not be able to judge accurately with your eyes. For instance, look at the two lines drawn below. Which line is longer? Take a guess, then measure each line in thumb widths to see if you were right.

ACTIVITY

Walking heel to toe, count the "feet" between opposite walls of your classroom. Now measure the same distance with a reliable tool for measuring feet. How do the two units of measurement—your own foot versus a standard "foot"—compare?

Interdisciplinary Connection

Objective

- To understand and calculate units of measure

Teaching Strategies

Review with students (especially English language learners) the English measurement system used in the United States; then list countries that use the metric system. *(virtually every country except the United States)* After students have read the chart in their books, ask them to calculate their height in meters. Ask them to think of household items that utilize the metric system, such as measuring sticks, scales, and car speedometers.

Activity

Students may find great variation in the number of "feet" they measure by walking. They should not, however, find any discrepancy in the number of feet each measures when using a reliable tool.

Informational Text

Point out to students that the terms used for units of measure are important in the study of mathematics.

Activity

Have students look through a mathematics textbook and compile a list of other specialized vocabulary words that that they would need to become familiar with as they study math.

Teaching Support

MULTIPLE MODES OF EXPRESSION

Logical and Mathematical Students with strong logical-mathematical abilities will appreciate an opportunity to create a measurement-conversion resource sheet. Begin by asking them to list the ways in which things are measured in the United States. For example: distance is measured in inches, feet, yards, and miles; temperature is measured in Fahrenheit degrees; weight is measured in pounds and ounces.

Activity Have students research and list how distance, temperature, and weight are measured in countries that use the metric system. Ask them to organize the information on a resource sheet that could be used by tourists from their town traveling to Paris. **L2**

VIEWING THE PHOTO

Viewing Response *In the photograph, high winds are ripping snow from the slopes and blowing a trail of white off the mountaintops. The conditions seem to be similar to those that signalled defeat for Allison's group.*

N Active Reading Strategies

EVALUATE Point out the contrast between the climbers' high-tech clothing and the primitive image of *crawled out of the cave.* Ask students how this contrast helps readers learn about mountain climbing. *(Even though the climbers benefit from technology, they must perform their task in a very primitive way.)*

O Active Reading Strategies

PREDICT Ask students if they can predict what will happen from this descriptive paragraph. *(The news is probably not good because Wes' s shoulders slump, and the author says, "I saw it in Scott's eyes....")*

At the MOVIES

Everest (1998, 44 minutes, NR) will give students some idea of the mountain's grandeur and the difficulties that are faced by climbers. Preview it for suitability before showing or recommending it.

Viewing the photograph: How are the conditions here similar to those faced by the climbers in the selection?

N When dawn finally came we got dressed for the summit—pulling our down climbing suits over the layers of polypropylene long underwear, polypro socks, plastic climbing boots, polypro and down gloves, a heavy pile hat, a neoprene[10] face mask—then crawled out of the cave, pulled along by a fine thread of hope, and walked gingerly[11] to the side of the ice tower that stood above our cave. Above us we'd see the summit, that great crooked pyramid on top of the world, the crown for the Mother Goddess. If she rose straight into a clean blue sky, we could try to push ourselves higher. But if she sent off a tail of white, if the winds were still ripping the snow from the hillside, we had to go down.

Wes turned the corner first. I didn't have to look up. I could read it in his shoulders. Wes slumped, then turned to see Scott, coming around the corner after us. I saw it in Scott's eyes, then heard his voice, shouting above the constant roar of the wind. O

"Well, that's the ballgame."

Scott stomped back toward the snow cave, anguished, shaking his head. Wes stayed, staring into the sky. I turned my face

10. *Polypropylene, pile,* and *neoprene* are human-made fabrics that provide insulation from cold temperatures.

11. *Gingerly* (jin′ jər lē) means "with extreme caution; carefully."

Vocabulary

anguished (ang′ gwisht) *adj.* having or showing extreme mental or physical suffering

Teaching Support

Grammar and Language *Minilesson*

Apostrophe Write the following words on the board: *cannot = can't; he would = he'd.* Remind students that the apostrophe has two primary functions: to signal possession and to form a contraction indicating the omission of letters.

Activity Ask students to identify other words on pages 286–287 that use an apostrophe to form a contraction. Have students list the words that make up the contraction. *(Sample answers are listed below.)* **L2**

we'd *(we had)*
didn't *(did not)*
that's *(that is)*
can't *(cannot)*
don't *(do not)*
I'm *(I am)*
we're *(we are)*
couldn't *(could not)*
I'd *(I had)*

Additional Resources

- ***Grammar and Language Transparency 25***
- ***Gr. and Lang. Wkbk,*** pp. 273–274
- ***Gr. and Comp. Hbk,*** Lesson 13.7
- ***Writer's Choice,*** Lesson 20.7

P upward and saw it, too. The thick plume of spindrift sailing from the mountain-top. The jet stream had not lifted. It was slamming against the mountain at 150 miles an hour for the third day in a row. And the thin thread of hope snapped.

Back in the cave Scott's blond hair hung lank over dim eyes, his usually rosy cheeks looked pale and sunken. His chest caved in beneath his shoulders.

Q "If you guys want to wait another day," I said, "I can wait." Q looked up dimly and coughed. I was grasping at thin air. We had failed. It was over. Even so, Scott flashed a look at the rest of us, measuring reactions.

"One more day? Give it a shot?"

R Q shook his head. The Death Zone was wreaking its havoc[12] on him. He was losing wattage with every passing hour. "I can't stay up here another day," Q said. He'd been barely able to eat breakfast that morning. "If I don't go down today, I'm not going to get down."

Now just the sound of breathing, and outside the wind and then occasionally a light cloud of spindrift, floating through the tunnel and down into the cave. The cold drifted down my spine until I could feel it in my toes.

Scott picked up the walkie-talkie and called to our expedition mates waiting at base camp. *We're finished. We're coming down.* The message was received, tenderly, and we started packing. Sleeping bags, Thinsulate[13] pads, ice screws, rope, and cook gear over here, stoves, food, fuel over there. We'd carry the fragile gear, but the really soft and really hard gear could take the fast way down the Great Couloir, the chutelike valley just to the left of our route on the North Face. Camp 1 was just below the bottom of the chute; once the gear rocketed down, the other climbers would try to collect it.

We went back to the cave entry and slung on our packs. And we stood there for a moment, not looking at each other. Just stood there in the cold and the wind before taking the first step down. And then Wes moved, and Q followed, and then we were all moving. After two long years of planning and working and hoping, we were walking away from the summit. I could barely fathom[14] the disappointment. I couldn't, not with the descent ahead of us. I still had to focus on getting down in one piece.

S I turned to take a last look and my eyes fell on Scott's face. Tears were sliding down his cheeks. Did he see me watching him? It was only a moment, and he was wearing reflecting shades so it was impossible to tell. I turned around again and continued down dry-eyed. Whatever anguish I felt, I'd deal with it when we got down to safe terrain.[15]

12. The expression *wreaking havoc* means "causing destruction."

13. *Thinsulate* is the brand name of an insulating material.

14. Here, *fathom* (fath′ əm) means "to understand fully."

15. Scott Fischer successfully reached Everest's peak in 1994. Two years later, he and seven other climbers died in another attempt to reach the top.

P Literary Elements

METAPHOR Ask students to find a metaphor in this paragraph. *(It is The thin thread of hope snapped.)*

Q Critical Thinking

MAKING CRITICAL JUDGMENTS Ask how the climbers may react to the idea of failing. *(They may consider themselves failures or acknowledge that their attempt has failed.)*

R Literary Elements

CONNOTATION Ask students the literal meaning of *losing wattage. (It means "losing power.")* Ask them to explain the use of the phrase here. *(It means "losing physical strength.")*

S Active Reading Strategies

CONNECT Ask students each to recall a major disappointment in life. Can they understand what the author might be feeling?

Thematic Focus

Facing Challenge Discuss the fact that facing a physical challenge is as much a test of emotional strength as it is of physical endurance.

You may use ***Fine Art Transparency 7*** to develop the discussion further.

Quick Checks, p. 26

MEETING INDIVIDUAL NEEDS: SPECIAL NEEDS

Less-Proficient Readers Explain that the expression *Well, that's the ballgame* is sometimes used to signal the conclusion of an event. Suggest that sports expressions are used in many situations; for example, a person who is said to have hit a *grand slam* has had great success, and one who is said to have *covered all the bases* has been thorough.

Activity Have students work with partners to find other examples of words or phrases used in an unusual way on page 287. Ask students to write the expressions down and then define them. **L2**

Additional Resources

Inclusion Strategies

Responding to the Selection

PERSONAL RESPONSE

Some students may ask what "soured" her life and exactly how mountain climbing helped "sweeten" it. Others may ask if the small number of women in mountain climbing was a motivating factor in her choosing this hobby.

Analyzing Literature

1. The climbers faced the problems of the fierce wind and the thin air, which made breathing and digesting food difficult.
2. The writer is reassured by the fact that the objective is "unambiguous." The climber knows exactly what the objective is, and there are no conflicting objectives.
3. The fierce wind and the fact that one member of the team was in a weakened condition kept the team from the top.
4. At that altitude, one should expect fierce conditions of high winds and cold.
5. The writer believes the climb is a test of her personal strength and endurance and is very disappointed when she can't finish it.
6. If the mountain is not "kind," the climbers will run out of time and have to end the expedition.
7. She uses climbing as a means of testing the extent of her courage, strength, and endurance.
8. The conflict was between waiting another day to try for the top or returning that day to ensure the safety of their weakened companion.
9. The account might have been restricted to the external part of the challenge rather than the mental and emotional aspects of the climb as well.
10. Some students may mention the challenge of getting better grades in school, winning a sports event, overcoming personal fears or limitations, or helping people in need.

Active Reading and Critical Thinking

Responding to Literature

PERSONAL RESPONSE

- Suppose you had a chance to interview Stacy Allison. What questions would you like to ask her about the challenges she faced? Record your questions in your journal.

Analyzing Literature

RECALL

1. What problems did the climbers face as they sat stranded in their snow cave?
2. What does the writer find reassuring about climbing a mountain?
3. Why didn't the team of climbers reach the summit?

Brackets connect questions that are paired to develop higher-level thinking skills.

INTERPRET

4. According to the writer, "Kindness was a lot to hope for this high in the world." Explain what she means.
5. How would you describe the writer's attitude about the challenge she and the other climbers faced?
6. Why was it so important that the mountain be "kind" to the climbers?
7. According to the writer, mountain climbing was "an exploration of myself." What do you think she means?
8. What was the conflict the climbers faced on their final morning at Camp 3? How did they resolve it?

EVALUATE AND CONNECT

9. How might the account of this adventure be different if it had been written by someone who wasn't a part of the expedition? Explain.
10. Theme Connection What "summit" would you like to face? Why is that particular goal important to you?

LITERARY ELEMENTS

Autobiography

Have you ever written an account of your own life? If so, you have written an autobiography. The word part *auto* means "self," *bio* means "life," and *graphy* means "something written." A **biography** is the story of someone's life. An **autobiography** is the story of a person's life written by that person. An autobiography may cover a person's entire life, or it may focus on one aspect of that life, such as an important event or a childhood experience. Such works are sometimes called **memoirs.** Autobiography is almost always written from the first-person point of view.

1. What details did you learn about Stacy Allison's life from reading this autobiographical selection?
2. What else would you like to learn about her life?

- See **Literary Terms Handbook,** p. R2.

LITERARY ELEMENTS

1. Details about her life include these facts: she is physically and mentally strong; something went "sour" in her life; and she cares about opportunities for women.
2. Students might be interested in learning how her life turned out after this climb and later, after she did conquer Everest.

Additional Resources

Literary Elements Transparency 26

Extending Your Response

Writing About Literature

Comparing Challenges *Beyond the Limits* is an account of one person's experience in facing a difficult challenge. Think about the challenges you discussed for the **Reading Focus** on page 280. Write a paragraph comparing your or your group's challenges with those of the author.

interNET CONNECTION

If you are interested in learning more about mountain climbing, use a Web browser, and type in the phrase "mountain climbing" to search for Web sites about this challenging sport.

Creative Writing

Entry from the Top of the World Imagine that you are one of the members of the 1987 North Face expedition. You are stranded in a sleeping bag in a snow cave at Camp 3. Think about how you would feel. Write a journal entry describing your thoughts and feelings.

Literature Groups

Debate It! Mountain climbing demands physical fitness, skill, self-discipline, and courage. Critics of the sport claim that climbing is costly, dangerous, and often destructive to the natural environment. Choose one point of view, and defend your position in a small group discussion.

Interdisciplinary Activity

Social Studies/Art Reread the selection, and take notes on each place in the expedition. Use a real map to give you an outline of the journey. Then draw your own map of the area and label each site. Use your map to retell the story to a family member or a friend.

Save your work for your portfolio.

Skill Minilesson

Reteach · Review

VOCABULARY • GREEK WORD PARTS

Allison describes team member Samuel "Q" Belk as *hyperkinetic*. That word, like many scientific, technical, and medical words, is made up of Greek roots—*hyper* (meaning "more" or "excessive") and *kinetic* ("motion" or "energy"). Belk was a person who couldn't stay still. Following are some additional Greek roots and their meanings.

bio (life)	*phone* (sound, speak)
gram, graph (write)	*psych* (mind)
log, logy (study of)	*scope* (view)
meter (measure)	*tele* (far, distant)
micro (small)	*thermo* (heat)

PRACTICE Combine the Greek roots above to make ten English words.

ASSESSMENT

- ***Quick Checks,*** p. 26
- ***Selection and Theme Assessment,*** pp. 47–48
- ***Performance Assessment,*** p. 25

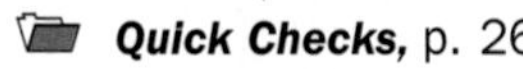

Testmaker: ExamView Pro

Interactive Tutor: Self-Assessment

Extending Your Response

Writing About Literature

Students' responses should

- identify the specific challenges
- explain similarities and differences

Creative Writing

Students' writing should

- consider what would run through one's mind, including present matters and past memories
- write as if speaking to a diary or a trusted friend
- be specific in identifying feelings and give details

Literature Groups Remind students to support their positions with specific facts and details from the selection or research sources.

Interdisciplinary Activity

Remind students that creating the map will enhance their appreciation of the autobiography.

Skill Minilesson

VOCABULARY

• GREEK WORD PARTS

Warn students that sometimes they will need to change the spelling a bit when putting Greek word parts together—for example, adding an *o* in *psychology*.

Students should combine the supplied Greek roots into at least ten acceptable words. Examples:

biology	telegram
psychology	telegraph
microgram	telemeter
micrograph	telephone
micrometer	telescope
microphone	thermograph
microscope	thermometer

Additional Resources

Vocabulary Practice, p. 17

Objective

- To understand the elements of nonfiction

Teaching Strategies

Explain that one of the appeals of nonfiction is that through it we learn about real life. Have students talk about the kinds of nonfiction they like to read. Ask for examples of people and events they have read about that interested them. Encourage students to think about what aspects of their lives they would most enjoy writing about.

Narrative Nonfiction

Ask students to give examples of narrative nonfiction they have read. Direct them to look at earlier selections in their book for examples. (They can use the part of the book's contents headed Selections by Genre on page xxvi to find a list of all the nonfiction in the book.) They should recall that the autobiographical selections in Theme 1 are examples of narrative nonfiction. Talk about other textbooks they use. They may recognize, for example, that the parts of a social studies textbook that relate chronological events are narrative whereas the parts that deal with geography are most likely expository.

Teaching Support

NONFICTION

Nonfiction is writing that tells about real-life people, places, events, and ideas. Fiction, too, can deal with real-life stories, but authors of fiction can invent characters, situations, and dialogue. Writers of nonfiction, on the other hand, write about real people, events, and situations. To do so, they use special text structures that help them organize their material for readers.

Narrative Nonfiction

Some nonfiction follows a narrative text structure similar to that used by writers of fiction. Autobiography, biography, and historical accounts are the main types of narrative nonfiction. They tell stories that have settings, characters, plots, and themes. The stories are most often told in chronological (time) order. Unlike fiction, however, the stories of narrative nonfiction are true, and the people are real.

Expository Writing

The main purpose of expository writing is to explain or to inform. Newspaper and magazine articles, how-to books, instruction manuals, and books on topics such as science and technology are some types of expository writing. The textbooks you use in science, math, or social studies classes are familiar examples of exposition.

MODEL

Breathing and Respiration

People often get the terms *breathing* and *respiration* mixed up. Breathing is the process whereby fresh air moves into and stale air moves out of lungs. Fresh air contains oxygen, which passes from the lungs into your circulatory system. Blood then carries the oxygen to your individual cells. At the same time, your digestive system has prepared a supply of glucose in your cells from digested food. Now the oxygen plays a key role in the chemical action that releases energy from glucose. This chemical reaction is called respiration. Carbon dioxide is a waste product of respiration. At the end of this reaction, carbon dioxide wastes are carried back to your lungs in your blood. There, it is expelled from your body in the stale air.

290 THEME 3

MEETING INDIVIDUAL NEEDS — ENGLISH LANGUAGE LEARNERS

Cultural Observations Have students talk in small groups or with partners about experiences that taught them something about another culture. Encourage English language learners to think of something that surprises or interests them about American culture.

Activity Pair English language learners with English-proficient students. Have students practice listening and retelling by asking them to share their cultural observations with their partners and then retell their partners' stories to the class. Finally, ask each partner whether the story has been told correctly.

Additional Resources

- ***English Language Learners Sourcebook***

To help readers understand their ideas, writers of exposition use one or more text structures to organize their writing. The following are the most common of these text structures.

- **Description** Writers of expository nonfiction often draw on description to help readers understand their topics. The writer of a book on astronomy, for example, needs to describe planets, satellites, stars, nebulas, and so on, as well as provide explanations about how the universe works.
- **Time Order** Writers often help readers by using time order to show the stages in which something happened or should be done. A history book, for example, will present events in chronological order. A how-to book will give a series of directions in the order in which they must be done.
- **Compare-Contrast** Comparing looks at how two or more things are similar. Contrasting examines how things are different. The compare-contrast text structure might be used in a science book to show the similarities and differences in two particular animals. A social studies book might compare regions, cultures, presidents, or the views of two political parties or candidates.
- **Cause-Effect** In this structure, the text is arranged to show the relationship between outcomes and their causes. For example, a drop in temperature (cause) results in the freezing of water (effect). A long drought results in decreased crops. That decrease, in turn, may lead to higher food prices. Cause-effect structures are used often in science, social science, and history materials.
- **Problem-Solution** In this text structure, a writer presents a problem and offers one or more solutions to it. Books and articles on science often make use of the problem-solution structure.

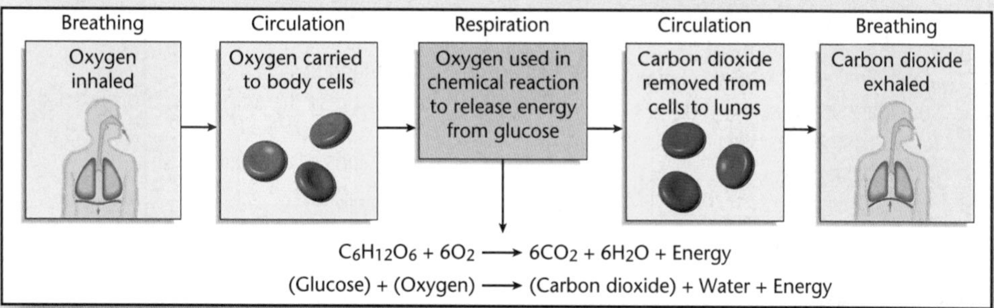

What is the main text structure used in this passage from a science textbook? What key words can you find in the passage that point to that particular text structure? Does the diagram have the same organizational structure?

Expository Writing

Ask students to examine the excerpt from a science book at the bottom of these pages to see which text structures are used there. (Examples of description, time order, compare-contrast, and cause-effect are all present in the excerpt.) Use this opportunity to stress that writers of expository text often employ more than a single structure to accomplish their goals. In answering the question in the caption accompanying the passage and illustration, most students should recognize that although the passage begins by contrasting breathing and respiration, the main text structure is probably time order (or sequencing), which the illustration reinforces.

Ask students to discuss and, if possible, to show examples of the five identified text structures in other textbooks they use. In addition, ask them to identify other techniques used in their textbooks or in other nonfiction writing, such as newspaper and magazine articles, with which they are familiar. Help them see how headings and various types of graphics (e.g., photos, diagrams, charts, graphs, tables, icons) are used to help writers of nonfiction get their ideas across to readers.

Technology

NONFICTION TABLE

Students can use word processing or spreadsheet software to create tables on which to record their analyses of text structures used in nonfiction. Have each student open a new document and insert a four-column table with the headings shown below. For each new piece of nonfiction students read, have them add a new row and complete their tables with their analysis of the text structures used by the author. **L2**

Title	Author	Main Text Structure	Other Structures Used

Active Reading Strategies

Objective

- To understand and apply strategies for reading and comprehending informative nonfiction

Teach the Strategies

Ask students to name a few of the places they get their information. Find out whether they receive news by word of mouth from family members and friends or from newspapers, magazines, and television. Prompt a discussion about whether they believe everything they hear or read. Find out what they consider reliable sources of information in their lives.

Preview

Remind students to preview what they are about to read, whether it is fiction or nonfiction. Previewing helps prepare the reader to absorb information—it gives him or her a head start.

Question

The process of questioning what we read as we go along is especially important when reading informative nonfiction. Remind students that they are the guardians of their own minds and beliefs—they need to question in order to judge and discern the accuracy of what they read.

Teaching Support

ACTIVE READING MODEL

Active Reading Strategies

Strategies for Informative Nonfiction

Do you enjoy reading about real life, about factual events in the past or present? Nonfiction writing deals with real people, places, and events. Literary nonfiction includes autobiography, biography, and essays. Informative nonfiction includes encyclopedias, textbooks, books on topics such as history and science, and most articles in newspapers and magazines. Informative nonfiction is written primarily to inform readers. Facts, therefore, are extremely important.

When reading informative nonfiction, active readers use strategies like those below to increase their understanding.

- For more about these and other reading strategies, see **Reading Handbook,** pp. R82–R101.

PREVIEW

Previewing a selection by looking at the title, headings, boldfaced terms, illustrations, and any diagrams or charts will give you an idea of what it will be about. Previewing may also help you figure out what text structure the author has used to organize the work.

Ask Yourself . . .

- How has the author organized this information? How can I use the text structure to find the most important ideas?
- Will I need to understand this chart (or other graphic) before I read the article?
- What do the photographs or illustrations tell me about the subject?

QUESTION

Questioning helps you clarify the facts in the text.

Ask Yourself . . .

- What do I know about this subject that will help me understand this information?
- Can I turn these section headings into questions that will guide my reading?
- Do I understand why the writer has included this specific information?

Reading Journal

The Scary Truth

J. Madeleine Nash's informative nonfiction article "The Fish Crisis" presents surprising and alarming facts about the depletion of fish in the world's oceans. Invite students to discuss what they already know about fishing controversies in their region and throughout the world.

Activity As they read "The Fish Crisis," invite students to list in their reading journals information that surprises or worries them. After reading, have each student write a brief summary of the part of the selection that was most alarming or comforting and why he or she found it so. **L2**

REVIEW

Think about what you read. Summarize and rephrase the information. Look back at bold-faced terms and section headings.

Say to Yourself . . .

- In other words, the author means ________.
- So far in this work ________.
- The most important information I have learned about this subject is ________.

EVALUATE

Form opinions and make judgments about what you have read.

Ask Yourself . . .

- Is this writer qualified to write on this topic?
- Are the sources for these facts reliable?
- Is this actually an opinion that the writer is presenting as a fact?
- If I wrote an essay on this subject, what would I include that this author hasn't included?

APPLYING THE STRATEGIES

Read "The Fish Crisis." Use the Active Reading Model notes in the margins as you read. Write your own responses on a separate piece of paper or use self-stick notes.

Review

Students may want to jot down notes as they read the informative nonfiction in this unit. Keeping track of names, numbers, dates, distances, and other statistics can be challenging. In some students, however, this kind of information promotes further interest in the subject matter. Students should be encouraged to review the material in a manner that contributes to their understanding and interest.

Evaluate

Encourage students to be mindful of the evaluation process while they are reading a piece of informative nonfiction—and afterward. Their opinions and judgments are important tools for participating in the information age. Have each of them keep on the desk a note card with the four evaluation questions as a reminder when reading. As a follow-up to the questions, ask students to explain where their opinions come from. For example, if a student does not believe a writer is qualified to write on a certain topic, he or she should be able to give reasons for the opinion and to cite aspects of the essay or article that led to that conclusion.

Teaching Support

Real-World Connection

Everyday Reading To extend the topic of informative nonfiction, discuss with students all the kinds of informative reading necessary in everyday life—such as various types of signs, food labels and other packaging, posters and billboards, television schedules, instructions on vending machines, and so on.

Activity Have students bring to class examples (or photos) of the many different kinds of informational reading they are likely to encounter in their everyday lives. Select a few key items and have students discuss which of the strategies mentioned on these pages would be appropriate and useful for each type of reading. **L2**

Before Reading

Objectives

- To read a work of nonfiction and understand the challenge in preserving the world's fisheries
- To recognize the persuasive techniques in an essay
- To list and evaluate the major sources used in an essay

Skills

Reading/Thinking: Using Text Structures; Evaluating; Identifying Propaganda Techniques; Distinguishing Fact from Opinion
Writing: Letter to the Editor; Interview
Vocabulary: Prefixes; Suffixes
Grammar/Language: Using Quotation Marks
Collaborating: Literature Groups

Motivating STUDENTS

Selection Focus Transparency 27: Ask students how the quotation by Edward Young might relate to the title of the selection.

Reading Focus As an extension of the Reading Focus, have students work in small groups to research in which seas tunas can be found.

ACTIVE READING MODEL

Before You Read

The Fish Crisis

MEET J. MADELEINE NASH

Starting her career in journalism in 1966 as a researcher at *Time* magazine, J. Madeleine Nash went on to become a reporter for the magazine. Nash has also used her experience as a journalist to research and write a book about parent involvement in education called *Schools Where Parents Make a Difference*.

J. Madeleine Nash was born in 1943. This article was published in the August 11, 1997, issue of Time.

READING FOCUS

When you eat a tuna sandwich for lunch, do you ever think about where the tuna fish came from?

List Ideas

Work in a small group to list all the edible fish you have heard about or tasted. Then try to guess where the fish originate—in fresh water (lakes, rivers) or the ocean.

Setting a Purpose

Read the following article to learn about the world's supply of fish.

BUILDING BACKGROUND

Did You Know? The waters where fishing takes place are called *fisheries.* The most productive fisheries are in oceans, especially areas near coastlines.

VOCABULARY PREVIEW

contemplate (kon′ təm plāt′) *v.* to give intense attention to; consider carefully; p. 296
plummet (plum′ it) *v.* to fall or drop straight downward; plunge; p. 296
depleted (di plēt′ id) *adj.* greatly reduced in amount; p. 296
undermine (un′ dər mīn′) *v.* to weaken, wear away, or destroy slowly; p. 298
exploit (iks ploit′) *v.* to use or develop for profit, often in a selfish, unjust, or unfair way; p. 299
converge (kən vurj′) *v.* to come together at a place; p. 299
amplify (am′ plə fī′) *v.* to increase; extend; p. 300
indiscriminately (in′ dis krim′ ə nit lē) *adv.* in a way that does not pay attention to differences; carelessly; p. 300
diligently (dil′ ə jənt lē) *adv.* in a way that shows great attention, care, and effort; p. 301
subsidize (sub′ sə dīz′) *v.* to aid or support with a contribution of money; p. 301

RESOURCE MANAGER

Teaching Tools and Resources
- Theme Three Planning Guide
- Literature Groups Sourcebook

Essential Lesson Support

Lesson-Specific Instruction
- Selection Focus Transparency 27
- Literary Elements Transparency 27
- Active Reading Guide,* p. 27
- Selection Vocabulary Practice, p. 18
- TIME *inTIME* magazine, pp. 14–15

Assessment
- Selection Quick Checks,* p. 27
- Sel. and Theme Assmt., pp. 49–50
- Testmaker: ExamView Pro
- Performance Assessment, p. 26

Systematic Language Instruction
- Gr. and Comp. Hbk., L. 6.4
- Vocabulary Power, Lesson 14
- Spelling Power, Lesson 12

English Language Learners
- ELL Sourcebook, p. 50
- Spanish Summaries, p. 27
- Spanish Translations, pp. 88–91
- Audio Library*
- English, Yes!

Spec. Needs/Strat. Interven.
- Interactive Rdg. Sbk., pp. T119–122
- Interactive Rdg. Wkbk., pp. 50–51
- Inclusion Strat. Sbk., pp. 41–42
- Audio Library*

*Also available in Spanish

The Fish Crisis

J. Madeleine Nash

ACTIVE READING MODEL

PREVIEW A
Page through the article. What are your first impressions?

PREDICT B
As you read, see how the article is organized. Will it be difficult to understand?

THICK SWORDFISH STEAKS. Orange roughy fillets. Great mounds of red-fleshed tuna. Judging from the seafood sections of local supermarkets, there would seem to be plenty of fish left in the oceans. But this appearance of abundance is an illusion, says Sylvia Earle, former chief scientist for the National Oceanic and Atmospheric Administration.

295

Reading the Selection

SUMMARY

Some species of fish are dying out because the fishing industry is not giving nature enough time to replenish its losses. Local and international officials are trying to set limits on the industry, but their efforts have not been completely successful.

Spanish Summaries, p. 27

A Active Reading Strategies

PREVIEW *(Students may assume that the article deals with various kinds of fish. The chart on page 298, however, may suggest that the article also deals with a problem.)*

VOCABULARY If you haven't previewed the selection vocabulary with students, stop and remind them to use context clues to unlock the meanings of new vocabulary words.

B Active Reading Strategies

PREDICT Point out that the article has no subheads to identify key ideas but that the first sentence in most paragraphs is a topic sentence.

Additional Resources

Active Reading Guide, *p. 27*

Audio Library

Spanish Audio Library

Teaching Support

CONNECTING TO OTHER SELECTIONS

The chart at the right shows three ways to connect "The Fish Crisis" to other selections in this book.

For specific teaching strategies, see the ***Theme Three Planning Guide.***

Connection		Title
Life Skills: Problem Solving	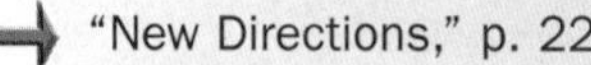 →	"New Directions," p. 221
Thematic: Interdependence	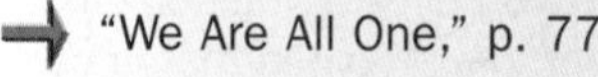 →	"We Are All One," p. 773
Literary: Author's Purpose	 →	"The Dog Diaries," p. 411

C Active Reading Strategies

QUESTION *(The opinion seems to be not that of the author of the essay but of the Natural Resources Defense Council. One would assume their "sobering report" has facts to back up their opinion, but we are not sure of that.)*

D Active Reading Strategies

PREDICT *(Students may suggest that a worse threat could be the deliberate elimination of a species or something unknown that causes the population of a species to plummet.)*

Vo•cab•u•lar•y Skills

PREFIXES The prefix *over-* signifies an excess or too much of something, as in *overfishing*. The meaning of the word can be understood by combining *over-* with the root word. Some examples are *overabundant*, *overanimated*, *overflow*, *overstuffed*, and *overmatched*.

Teaching Support

The Fish Crisis

Already, Earle fears, an international armada of fishing vessels is on the verge of exhausting a storehouse of protein so vast that it once appeared to be infinite. "It's a horrible thing to contemplate," shudders Earle. "What makes it even worse is that we know better. Yet here we go, making the same mistake over and over again."

If fishermen around the world soon start hauling back empty nets and fishing lines, it will not be for lack of warning. In the 1990s, after increasing for nearly four decades, the wild catch of marine fish leveled off worldwide and in some years actually declined. "We are reaching, and in many cases have exceeded, the oceans' limits," declare the authors of a sobering report released by the Natural Resources Defense Council earlier this year. "We are no longer living off the income but eating deeply into the capital."[1]

QUESTION C Is the author stating a fact here, or her opinion?

Fights have already started to break out over the dwindling supply. Two weeks ago, hundreds of Canadian fishermen blockaded a British Columbia port for several days to keep an Alaskan ferry from leaving. The reason for their protest? Alaskan trawlers[2] were sweeping up the salmon that spawn in Canada's rivers. Now the Canadians are threatening to do to the salmon runs of Washington State what U.S. fishermen have done to theirs.

Of course, overfishing is not the only human activity that is jeopardizing life in the oceans. Coastal pollution and habitat destruction—filling in wetlands, building dams—are contributing to the crisis. But it is overfishing, the NRDC report makes plain, that constitutes[3] the most urgent threat and demands the most immediate action.

PREDICT D What could be a worse threat than this?

Until now, the worst threat most creatures of the sea had faced at fishermen's hands was so-called commercial extinction.[4] Whenever local populations of a particular fish plummeted, boats simply targeted some other species or moved to more distant waters. The depleted stocks almost always recovered. But now, experts warn,

1. In financial terms, *capital* is wealth that is used to produce more wealth. A savings account, for example, adds to your income by earning interest. However, if you spend the savings (your capital), you earn less interest and gradually use up all your savings.
2. *Trawlers* are boats that catch fish by towing strong, bag-shaped nets across the ocean bottom.
3. Here, *constitutes* means "forms; makes up."
4. An *extinction* is the permanent elimination of something.

Vocabulary

contemplate (kon′ təm plāt′) *v.* to give intense attention to; consider carefully
plummet (plum′ it) *v.* to fall or drop straight downward; plunge
depleted (di plēt′ id) *adj.* greatly reduced in amount

MEETING INDIVIDUAL NEEDS — ENGLISH LANGUAGE LEARNERS

Phrasal Verbs Point out to English language learners the following phrasal verbs in the second and third paragraphs on page 296: *leveled off, break out,* and *sweep up.* Explain that these verbs all have a particle attached that is considered part of the verb. Elicit other examples from students, such as to *look up* or *run across* a friend, to *put* someone *down,* or to *get away* with something.

Activity Have students work with partners to continue reading the selection. Ask them to look for more examples of phrasal verbs to add to their vocabulary notebooks.

Additional Resources

English Language Learners Sourcebook, p. 50

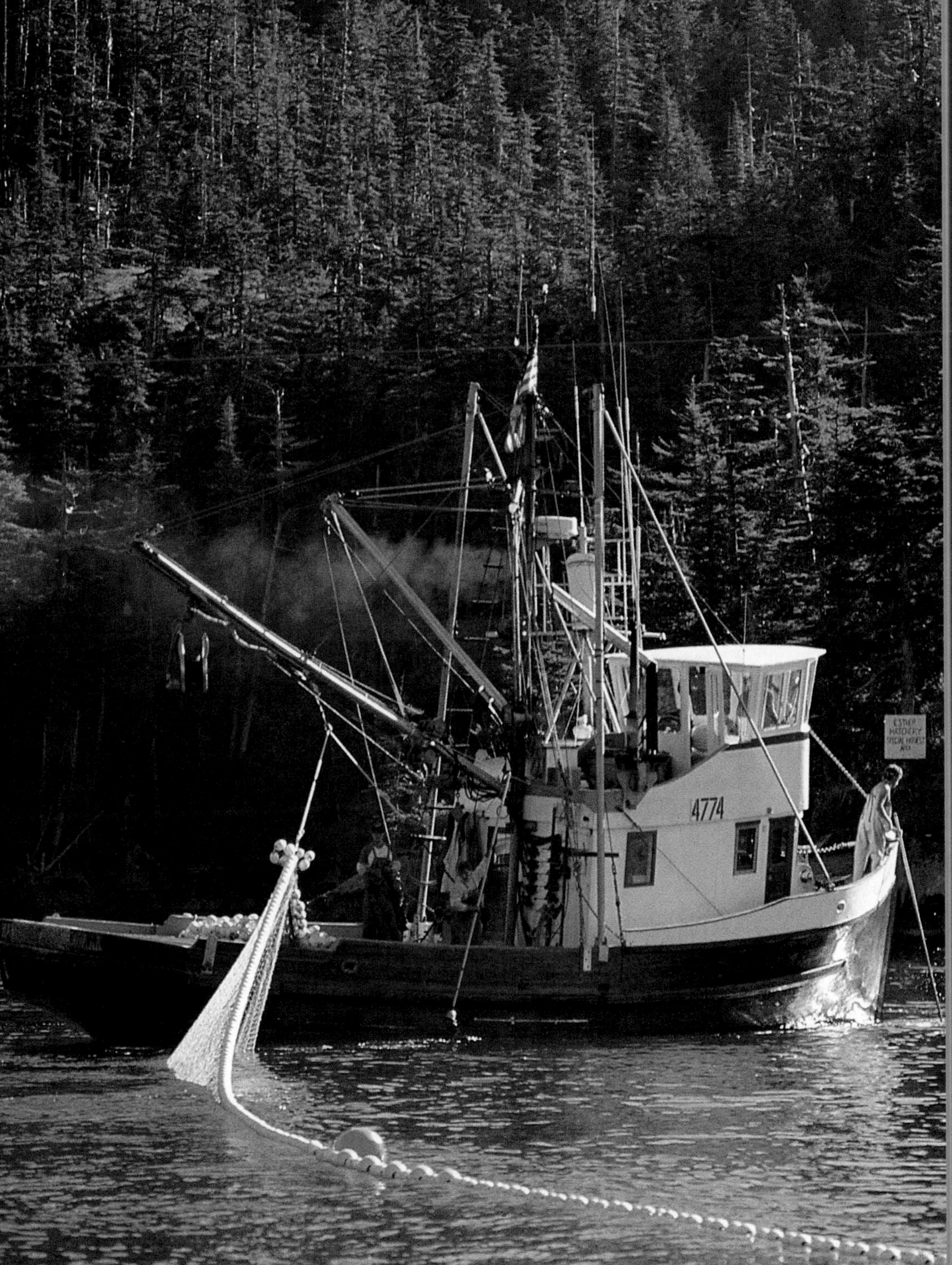

FYI

The U.S. National Marine Fisheries Service is the government agency that supports the domestic and international conservation efforts of fisheries. This agency offers statistics on fisheries and related legislation.

FYI

Tuna travel in the open waters of the tropics and in the warm seas of the world. Sometimes they travel the entire Pacific Ocean from the California coast to Japan in order to spawn. Tuna can swim at high speed, and their body temperature is a few degrees higher than the surrounding waters. There are forty species with the common name *tuna*.

Reading Minilesson

Using Text Structures Explain to students that when reading a nonfiction article, they can benefit from taking notes. A Who-What-Why chart can help them keep track of the facts.

Activity Have students work in small groups or in pairs. Suggest that they read or reread the text one paragraph at a time and write down the information they gather in a chart like the one below. **L2** COLLAB. LEARN.

Who	What	Why
Fishing industry	Overfishing	Consumer demand

Additional Resources

Reading Skills Practice Workbook

E Literary Elements

ESSAY Explain to students that authors of essays often use different techniques to communicate their ideas or opinions. Here the author presents a chart displaying some fishing facts and explaining in simple terms how readers can help.

F Critical Thinking

EVALUATING Explain to students that when detailed information is presented in graphic form, their understanding will be enhanced by evaluating the way it is organized. Suggest that students start with the heading, note the larger elements, and work down to the smaller elements. Ask them if they think the chart is an effective visual aid and companion to the selection. *(Some students might feel it is simple enough to understand and provides important supporting information to the selection. Others might think the chart is confusing and poorly organized.)*

G Active Reading Strategies

PREDICT *(It is likely that the author will explain more about fishing gear because of the statement that "technological barriers that have kept overfishing within bounds" are "shaky.")*

Teaching Support

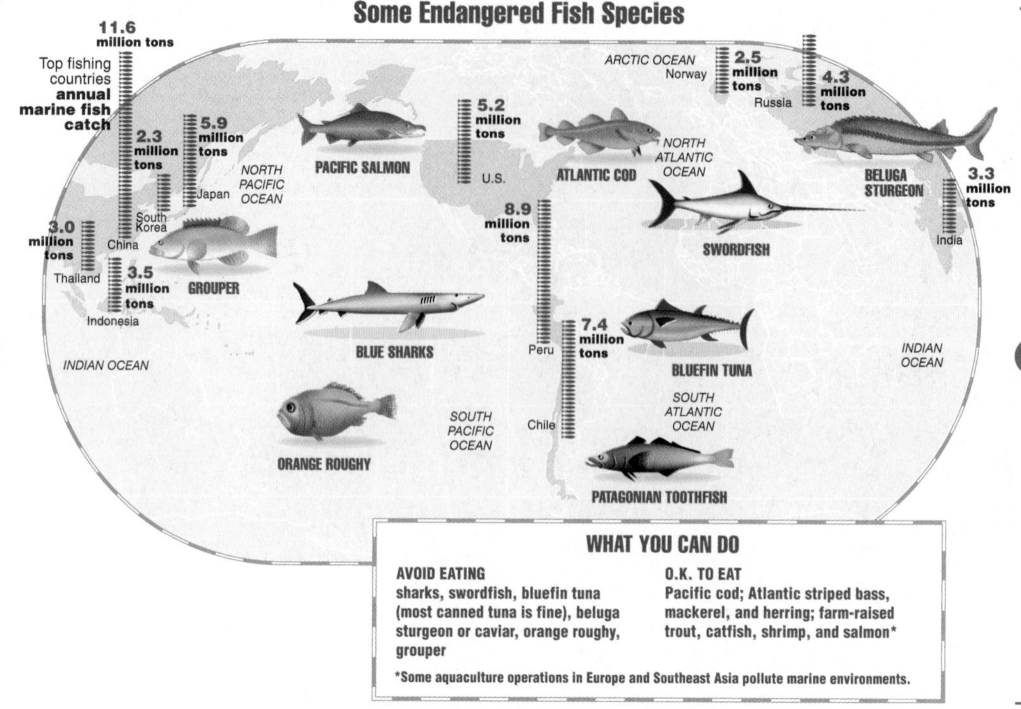

WHAT YOU CAN DO

AVOID EATING
sharks, swordfish, bluefin tuna (most canned tuna is fine), beluga sturgeon or caviar, orange roughy, grouper

O.K. TO EAT
Pacific cod; Atlantic striped bass, mackerel, and herring; farm-raised trout, catfish, shrimp, and salmon*

*Some aquaculture operations in Europe and Southeast Asia pollute marine environments.

PREDICT

Do you think the author will explain more about the kind of fishing gear that is depleting fish?

unprecedented forces—among them, industrial-scale fishing gear and a burgeoning[5] global seafood market—are altering this age-old cycle. The economic and technological barriers that have kept overfishing within bounds appear increasingly shaky, like dikes along a river that floodwaters have undermined. Should these barriers collapse, commercial extinction could escalate into biological catastrophe.[6]

In most imminent peril[7] are the giant predators of the oceans—sharks, of course, but also marlin, sailfish, swordfish, and bluefin tuna, the magnificent swimming machines that have earned the nickname "Porsches of the sea." In the western Atlantic, the breeding population of northern bluefin, the largest tuna species, is thought to consist of perhaps 40,000

5. When something is *unprecedented,* there has never before been anything like it. When something is *burgeoning,* it is growing rapidly.
6. The gradual wiping out of food fish could increase by stages *(escalate)* into a sudden, terrible disaster for all sea creatures *(biological catastrophe)*.
7. *In most imminent peril* could be restated as: "Likely to be in danger first."

Vocabulary
undermine (un′ dər mīn′) *v.* to weaken, wear away, or destroy slowly

Writing *Minilesson*

Interview Explain to students that one of the best ways to obtain more information about an issue is to interview the people involved.

Activity Have students work in pairs and take the roles of interviewer and interviewee. Have them choose a role: the fisherman or the conservationist. Suggest that they use the information they gathered in reading the selection to write the questions they will use. Then have students write a few paragraphs explaining what they have learned about each side of the overfishing issue. **L2**

Additional Resources

Writer's Choice, Lesson 26.2

adults, down from some 250,000 two decades ago. Reason: the flourishing airfreight industry that allows fish brokers to deliver Atlantic Ocean bluefin overnight to Tokyo's sashimi[8] market, where a single fish can fetch $80,000 or more at auction. "To a fisherman, catching a bluefin is a lot like winning the lottery," sighs Stanford University marine biologist Barbara Block.

The crash of commercially important fisheries is not new. What is new is how quickly fisheries arise and how quickly they are exploited. In recent years, piked dogfish, a small spiny shark, has begun to stand in for cod in the fish and chips served by British pubs, and the Patagonian toothfish has become a popular substitute for sablefish in Japan. But environmental groups are concerned about the long-term viability of the fisheries that are serving up these quaintly named piscine[9] treats. This year, for example, ships from around the world have converged on the Southern Ocean, where the toothfish makes its home. "At this rate," predicts Beth Clark, a scientist with the Antarctica Project, "the entire fishery will be gone in 18 months."

Unfortunately, it takes longer to rebuild a fishery than it does to ruin one. Consider the present state of the orange roughy on New Zealand's Challenger Plateau. Discovered in 1979, this deep-water fishing hole took off in the 1980s when the mild-tasting, white-fleshed fish became popular with U.S. chefs. Happy to stoke the surging demand, fishermen are believed to have reduced the biomass of orange roughy as much as 80% before officials stepped in. Now, says Yale University ichthyologist[10] Jon Moore, it may take centuries before the fishery rebounds. As scientists have belatedly learned, orange roughy grow extremely slowly, live 100 years or more and take 25 to 30 years to reach sexual maturity.

How can a fishing fleet do so much damage so quickly? Until recently, many fish, especially deep-water fish, were too hard to find to make tempting commercial targets. But technical advances have given fishermen the power to peer beneath the waves and plot their position

8. This is the market where Tokyo's restaurants buy their fish. *Sashimi* is raw fish.
9. To have *viability* is to be able both to survive and to work as intended. *Piscine* (pī′ sēn) means "of or relating to fish."
10. *Biomass* is the total amount of living matter within a given environmental area. It's a term that might be used by an *ichthyologist,* a scientist who specializes in the study of fish.

Vocabulary

exploit (iks ploit′) *v.* to use or develop for profit, often in a selfish, unjust, or unfair way

converge (kən vurj′) *v.* to come together at a place

ACTIVE READING MODEL

EVALUATE H

How does the author's use of the word *sighs* affect your sense of the scientist's statement?

REVIEW I

Try to rephrase this paragraph in your own words.

QUESTION J

Why is the author referring to the slow growth rate of these fish? K

H Active Reading Strategies

EVALUATE *(The word sighs implies sadness, that the speaker is not happy saying these words.)* Ask students for words meaning "says" that might describe how someone of the opposite opinion, such as a bluefin fisherman, might say the same words. *(Some possibilities include the words shouts and exclaims.)*

I Active Reading Strategies

REVIEW *(Though new types of fish replace others in use and popularity, the new types are often depleted very quickly by overfishing.)*

J Active Reading Strategies

QUESTION *(The author is referring to the slow growth rate of fish to emphasize the dangers of depleting the sea. The slow growth rate increases the possibility that endangered fish species may become extinct.)*

K Critical Thinking

IDENTIFYING PROPAGANDA TECHNIQUES The last paragraph on the page begins with a question. Ask students how they would analyze its use here. Does the author expect the reader to answer it, or is she using it to call attention to a specific idea? *(The author is not expecting an answer; she is using the question to set the reader's mind to wondering, and then she will reveal the devastating answer.)*

MEETING INDIVIDUAL NEEDS — MULTIPLE MODES OF EXPRESSION

Spatial Point out to students that the article's use of a chart to present factual information is very helpful.

Activity Have small groups each create a table, chart, graph, or some other graphic presenting detailed factual information on a topic in which they are interested, such as art, history, science, or sports. One group might create a bar graph showing the number of people from various countries represented in the town or school. Another might create a timeline tracing the development of a medium such as television or the computer. Still another might create a pie chart showing the percentages of pages in a local newspaper devoted to national news, local news, or sports. **L2**

L Active Reading Strategies

EVALUATE *(Yes, the author describes in simple terms how the technology works and is used. She does not overexplain.)*

M Literary Elements

AUTHOR'S PURPOSE Ask students why they think the author uses such descriptions as "ships as large as football fields." Why doesn't she just say the fishermen use large ships? Challenge them to find another example of this type of description. *(The author wants the reader to visualize the overwhelming challenge the fishing industry poses to fish populations, and she can do that effectively with these kinds of images.)*

N Active Reading Strategies

QUESTION *(Yes, this is some of the industrial fishing gear mentioned above.)* Explain to students that the technological aspect of the equipment is secondary to its size, which is the key idea in this paragraph.

O Active Reading Strategies

RESPOND *(Some students may feel encouraged by the fact that something positive can be done. Others, however, may feel that the positive steps already taken are quite small in comparison to the problem.)*

Teaching Support

ACTIVE READING MODEL

EVALUATE

L Does the author do a good job describing how these technical advances work?

QUESTION

N Is this some of the industrial fishing gear the author mentioned earlier?

RESPOND

O How did you feel when you read that something positive could be done to help solve part of the overfishing problem?

with unprecedented accuracy. Sonar makes it possible to locate large shoals of fish that would otherwise remain concealed beneath tens, even hundreds of feet of water. And once a fishing hot spot is pinpointed by sonar, satellite-navigation systems enable vessels to return unerringly to the same location year after year. In this fashion, fishermen from New Zealand to the Philippines have been able to home in on orange roughy and giant groupers as they gather to spawn, in some cases virtually eliminating entire generations of reproducing adults.

But what has amplified the destructive power of modern fishing more than anything else is its gargantuan[11] scale. Trawling for pollock in the Bering Sea and the Gulf of Alaska, for example, are computerized ships as large as football fields. Their nets—wide enough to swallow a dozen Boeing 747s—can gather up 130 tons of fish in a single sweep. M Along with pollock and other groundfish, these nets indiscriminately draw in the creatures that swim or crawl alongside, including halibut, Pacific herring, Pacific salmon, and king crab. In similar fashion, so-called longlines—which stretch for tens of miles and bristle with thousands of hooks—snag not just tuna and swordfish but also hapless sea turtles and albatrosses, marlin and sharks.

What happens to the dead and dying animals that constitute this so-called "by-catch"? Most are simply dumped overboard, either because they are unwanted or because fishery regulations require it. In 1993, for example, shrimp trawlers in the Gulf of Mexico caught and threw away an estimated 34 million red snappers, including many juveniles. By contrast, the annual catch of red snapper from the Gulf averages only around 3 million fish. Indeed, so many snappers are being scooped up as by-catch that the productivity of the fishery has been compromised. Fortunately, there is a solution. Shrimp nets can be outfitted with devices that afford larger animals like snappers and sea turtles a trapdoor escape hatch.

To a surprising extent, solutions to the problem of overfishing also exist, at least on paper, and that's what critics of the fishing industry find so encouraging—and so frustrating. Last year, for example, Congress passed landmark legislation that requires fishery managers to crack down on overfishing in U.S. waters. Perhaps even more impressive, the

11. From the name of a fictional giant, Gargantua, *gargantuan* means "enormous; huge."

Vocabulary

amplify (am′ plə fī′) *v.* to increase; extend

indiscriminately (in′ dis krim′ ə nit lē) *adv.* in a way that does not pay attention to differences; carelessly

Grammar and Language Minilesson

Using Quotation Marks Write the following sentence on the board: *"The number of fish is dwindling," sighed Carl. "We need to do something about it."* When a person's exact words are quoted, those words are placed within quotation marks. When the quotation is interrupted, it is closed and then reopened with quotation marks.

Activity Ask students to identify quotations in the following sentences and to place quotation marks where necessary.

1. We are reaching the limits, declared the official. We must end this crisis. *("We are reaching the limits," declared the official. "We must end this crisis.")*
2. Soon all the nets will be empty, warned the fisherman. *("Soon all the nets will be empty," warned the fisherman.)* **L2**

Additional Resources

- ***Grammar and Language Transparency 26***
- ***Grammar and Language Workbook,*** pp. 267–270
- ***Grammar and Composition Handbook,*** Lesson 13.6
- ***Writer's Choice,*** Lesson 20.6

U.N. has produced a tough-minded treaty that promises to protect stocks of fish that straddle the coastal zones of two or more countries or migrate, as bluefin tuna and swordfish do, through international waters in the wide-open oceans. The treaty will take effect, however, only after 30 or more nations ratify[12] it—and even then, some question how diligently its provisions will be enforced.

What has been missing is a willingness to take action. Consumers no less than politicians bear some of the blame. Simply by refusing to buy bluefin tuna in Tokyo, grouper in Hong Kong or swordfish in Chicago, consumers could relieve the pressure on some of the world's most beleaguered[13] fisheries and allow them the time they need to recover. To help shoppers become more selective about what they put on the dinner table, the Worldwide Fund for Nature and Unilever, one of the world's largest purveyors of frozen seafood, have launched a joint venture[14] that in 1998 will start putting labels on fish and fish products caught in environmentally responsible ways.

R A sign that consumers are worried about the world's fisheries could provide the jolt political leaders need. For the past half-century, billions of dollars have been spent by maritime nations to expand their domestic fishing fleets, subsidizing everything from fuel costs to the construction of factory trawlers. And until countries like Canada, China, Japan, South Korea, New Zealand, Norway, Spain, and, yes, the U.S. are willing to confront this monster of their own making, attempts to control overfishing are likely to prove ineffectual.[15] The problem, as Carl Safina, director of the National Audubon Society's Living Oceans Program, observes, is this: there is just too much fishing power chasing too few fish.

12. To *ratify* means to approve a document and agree to obey its rules.
13. The most *beleaguered* fisheries are those in the greatest trouble.
14. These food suppliers *(purveyors)* have formed a partnership *(joint venture)*.
15. If the attempts are *ineffectual*, they will fail to produce the desired result.

❖

Vocabulary
diligently (dil′ ə jənt lē) *adv.* in a way that shows great attention, care, and effort
subsidize (sub′ sə dīz′) *v.* to aid or support with a contribution of money

ACTIVE READING MODEL

QUESTION

Why didn't the author tell us how many nations have ratified the treaty so far? P

CONNECT

Would you or your family be willing to take a stand about these fish? Q

EVALUATE

Does Nash supply you with enough information to form your own opinion about overfishing? S

P Active Reading Strategies

QUESTION *(Perhaps the author feels the treaty will not matter anyhow. Her next words might imply that,* even then, some question how diligently its provisions will be enforced.*)*

Q Active Reading Strategies

CONNECT *(Some students may feel that their families should take a stand. Others may feel that the government should step in.)*

R Critical Thinking

DISTINGUISHING FACT FROM OPINION
Ask students if they accept the detail in the first sentence as fact or if they suspect that some of the information is really the author's opinion.
(Students might use the word could *as a clue that the author is predicting what might happen in the future. This is her interpretation—her opinion.)*

S Active Reading Strategies

EVALUATE *(Some students may feel that the author should have given more information about fish, technology, and the fishing industry.)*

Thematic Focus

Facing Challenge Have students discuss how to influence fishing companies, government agencies, and consumers and thus do their part in preserving fish species.

ASSESSMENT

Quick Checks, p. 27

MEETING INDIVIDUAL NEEDS — ADVANCED LEARNERS

The Flip Side In this selection, the author presents one side of the overfishing problem. Some students might be interested in learning the concerns of those on the other side of the issue.

Activity Invite students to work in pairs to do further research on the topic of overfishing. Have them concentrate on the facts and opinions set forth by the fishermen, fishing companies, and fish supply companies. Ask them to write essays presenting their research and their conclusions. You might like to challenge students by asking them to present their own ideas for solving the problem. **L3**

FACING CHALLENGE 301

Responding to the Selection

PERSONAL RESPONSE

Students might suggest that the author's purpose is to make the public aware of the fish crisis. Others may feel the purpose is to try to move readers to take action.

Active Reading Response

For example, students might choose Review and find three paragraphs to rephrase in their own words.

Analyzing Literature

1. The fishing industry, equipped with sophisticated and huge equipment, is depleting the supply of many types of fish to the point of interfering with the reproduction and replenishment of these species. The continuous demand for fish fuels the industry's efforts.
2. Rebuilding a fishery may take generations, whereas ruining it takes only a few years.
3. Some of the technical advances in fishing are the use of computers, sonar, and huge nets that collect not only fish but also by-catch.
4. The UN and the U.S. Congress have produced a treaty to protect stocks of fish.
5. Some may see consumer demand as the cause. Others may blame the industry's greed.
6. If they want to make money, the fish distributors must supply the most popular fish.
7. The huge scale of fishing seems to be the fundamental cause. The industry could scale back its use of technical advances and use technology to help preserve the supply.
8. Some may feel that the industry will take action to save its own livelihood. Others may think that consumers or the government will take action once they learn about the problem.

Active Reading and Critical Thinking

Responding to Literature

PERSONAL RESPONSE

- Did you discover the author's purpose, as suggested in the **Reading Focus** on page 294? Were you convinced by the author's arguments about the "fish crisis"? Explain why or why not.

Active Reading Response

Look back at the strategies described in the **Active Reading Model** notes on pages 292–293. Choose one of the strategies and find three places in the article where you could apply it.

Analyzing Literature

RECALL

1. Summarize what has happened to the world's ocean fish supply in the 1990s.
2. Which takes longer, ruining a fishery or rebuilding one?
3. List the technical advances that have affected fishing.
4. What have the U.S. Congress and the United Nations done to solve the problem of overfishing?

Brackets connect questions that are paired to develop higher-level thinking skills.

INTERPRET

5. In your opinion, what is the leading cause of the depleted fish supply?
6. Why, do you think, do fishers converge at a fishery when a new fish becomes popular?
7. Which do you think has caused the most damage to the fish population, technical advances or the huge scale of the fishing industry? Explain your answer.
8. Do you think the fishing industry or consumers will ever take action on their own to prevent overfishing? Why or why not?

EVALUATE AND CONNECT

9. Do you think the writer presented both sides of the debate on overfishing? Use examples to support your answer.
10. How would your life be changed if the supply of ocean fish dwindled to almost nothing?

LITERARY ELEMENTS

Essay

An **essay** is a short piece of nonfiction writing on any topic. The purpose of an essay is to communicate an idea or opinion. In a **persuasive essay,** such as "The Fish Crisis," the author tries to convince the reader of an opinion. One persuasive technique essayists use is the addition of emotional words, as in this sentence from "The Fish Crisis": "[Overfishing is] a horrible thing to contemplate."

1. What is J. Madeleine Nash trying to persuade the reader to believe?
2. Give three examples in which the writer uses emotional words to persuade the reader.

● See **Literary Terms Handbook,** p. R4.

9. Some may say she did present both sides, describing first the problem and then the solutions. Others may feel she didn't give the industry a chance to tell its side of the story.
10. Students' answers will depend on their typical consumption of fish.

LITERARY ELEMENTS

1. The author is trying to get people to see that overfishing has damaging effects and should be controlled.
2. Some possibilities are the word *crisis* in the title; *a sobering report,* page 296; and *biological catastrophe,* page 298.

Additional Resources

Literary Elements Transparency 27

Literature and Writing

Writing About Literature

Looking at Sources A powerful persuasive essay or article like "The Fish Crisis" should contain facts and quotations from a number of trustworthy sources. Write a list of the major sources Nash uses in her article. Does the use of these sources help convince you that the author is right?

Creative Writing

Letter to the Editor On the editorial pages of newspapers, both professional journalists and local readers can express their opinions in print. Write a persuasive letter alerting the people in your community to the dangers of overfishing in the world's oceans. Read your letter aloud to your group or class.

Extending Your Response

Literature Groups

Persuade the Public! Your group has decided that everyone needs to know about the danger to the ocean fish supply. Brainstorm a slogan, and then design a poster that includes your warning and an illustration that calls attention to your cause.

Interdisciplinary Activity

Science/Math: Diagram Study the selection and take notes on the statistics listed in different parts of the essay. Then find a way to represent these facts in a graph or chart.

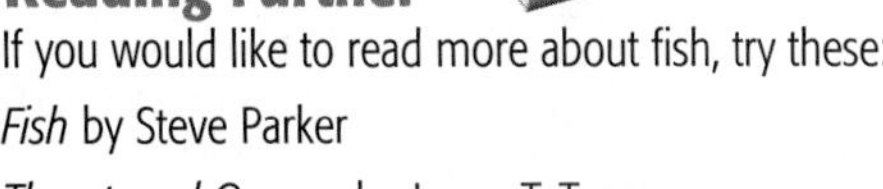

Reading Further

If you would like to read more about fish, try these:

Fish by Steve Parker

Threatened Oceans by Jenny T. Tesar

Save your work for your portfolio.

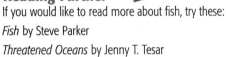

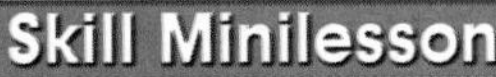

Skill Minilesson

Reteach • Review

VOCABULARY • SUFFIXES

If you *purify* something, you make it more *pure.* If you *electrify* a car, you make it *electric.* As you can see, the suffix *-fy* means "to make or cause to be." When the *-fy* suffix is added, an *e* or a *y* at the end of the original word will change to *i.* Sometimes an *i* is inserted to make the new word easier to pronounce.

PRACTICE Complete each sentence without using a form of the underlined word.

1. You might beautify a room by . . .
2. You could solidify water by . . .
3. You might simplify a statement by . . .
4. You could signify that you were happy by . . .
5. You could intensify your cheering by . . .

Literature and Writing

Writing About Literature

Students' responses should

- identify the specific sources
- explain whether the author's use of sources is effective

Creative Writing

Students' writing should

- reflect an awareness of the need to write with brevity and directness
- use techniques such as citing statistics and quoting authorities

Extending Your Response

Literature Groups Remind students that the posters should be eye-catching and get their message across in a few words.

Interdisciplinary Activity Remind students that using a chart is an effective way of conveying detailed factual information in a relatively small space. Suggest that students group facts of a common nature in the same chart.

Skill Minilesson

VOCABULARY • SUFFIXES

Some possibilities include

1. decorating it
2. freezing it
3. expressing the main idea without extra detail
4. smiling
5. shouting

Additional Resources

Vocabulary Practice, p. 18

ASSESSMENT

- ***Quick Checks,*** p. 27
- ***Selection and Theme Assessment,*** pp. 49–50
- ***Performance Assessment,*** p. 26
- ***Testmaker: ExamView Pro***
- ***Interactive Tutor: Self-Assessment***

MEDIA Connection

Objective

- To understand and apply strategies for reading a public opinion poll

Literature LINK

The Fish Crisis The Seaway public opinion poll report connects to "The Fish Crisis," the literature selection that immediately precedes this lesson. Point out the connection by telling students that both readings deal with humanity's relationship with nature.

Analyzing Media

1. Questions might include *Would you say that the oceans of the world are in poor condition, good condition, or excellent condition? Does the destruction of the ocean represent a serious threat, a very serious threat, or no threat to humans? Are commercial fishing and oil drilling taking too much out of the ocean? Are we allowing excessive waste, oil, and agricultural runoff to be dumped into the waters?*
2. Students may use a bar graph, chart, web, or Venn diagram.

Additional Resources

Media Connections, p. 6

inTIME ***inTIME*** **magazine**

MEDIA Connection

PUBLIC OPINION POLL

Polls are surveys done to get an idea of what a large body of people, like the American public, thinks about some topic, person, or product.

Americans Continue to Worry About the Decline of the Oceans

A Seaway Ocean Update, February 1998

As the International Year of the Ocean dawns, a new poll shows that more than half (59%) of Americans continue to view the health of the oceans today negatively, with 17% saying the oceans are in poor condition. Only one-fifth say the oceans are in good shape, while a mere 1% call the oceans' health "excellent."

The poll, conducted by the Washington, D.C.–based Mellman Group for SeaWeb, shows also that a majority (60%) believe the condition of the seas has become worse over the past few years, while only 11% say it has improved.

Nearly three-quarters (72%) agree that human beings are also in trouble as a result of the seas' problems, while 53% say that the destruction of the oceans represents a "very serious" threat to the quality of life today. Fifty percent believe we are currently taking too much out of the ocean in the form of commercial fishing and oil drilling, while 80% say we are dumping too much into the ocean in the form of waste, oil, and agricultural runoff.

"When a mere 1% call the condition of the ocean 'excellent,' it is obvious that Americans understand that we are doing more harm than good to our ocean," says Vikki Spruill, executive director of SeaWeb.

Analyzing Media

1. From the reported results, figure out what questions the people were asked. Then answer them yourself. Total the results for your class, and see how your class's opinions compare with those of the public.
2. Take your class's results and the statistics from the report, and put them into some graphic form—for example, a bar graph.

304

Teaching Support

interNET CONNECTION

Endangered Species To search for more information, have students enter such keywords in quotes as *endangered species, natural resource,* and *Sea Web.*

Reading Minilesson

Problem and Solution As students read this selection, they may feel that the poll focuses on problems that are caused by humans and that could be solved by changes in human behavior.

Activity Ask students to work in pairs or small groups to read the selection and keep a record of problems and solutions. Suggest that they use a two-column chart with the headings *Problems* and *Solutions.* **L2**

Additional Resources

 ***Reading Skills Practice Workbook***

Before You Read

Hurricanes

MEET PATRICIA LAUBER

A person who is setting out to tell a story offers a hand and says, 'Come with me and I will show you many wondrous things.'" So says award-winning writer Patricia Lauber, who has written more than ninety nonfiction books for young people. Her book, *Volcano: The Eruption and Healing of Mount St. Helens*, was named a Newbery Honor Book. Lauber was awarded the Washington Post/Children's Book Guild Award for her contribution to nonfiction for children.

Patricia Lauber was born in 1924. She lives in Connecticut, where she has experienced several hurricanes. "Hurricanes" comes from her 1996 book Hurricanes: Earth's Mightiest Storms.

READING FOCUS

Close your eyes and imagine this scene. You are at home, in the dark. The howling wind sounds like a rushing freight train hurtling toward the walls of your house. What are you thinking? How do you feel?

QuickWrite
Jot down at least three words that describe your thoughts and feelings as the storm heads your way.

Setting a Purpose
Read to find out about one of nature's most powerful storms.

BUILDING BACKGROUND

Did You Know? Hurricanes and typhoons are tropical cyclones that have steady winds of at least seventy-five miles per hour. Storms that occur in the Atlantic and Pacific oceans are called hurricanes. Storms that take place in the western Pacific are called typhoons. The main energy source for these kinds of storms is the heat released when water vapor condenses. Because only very moist air can supply the energy necessary for one of these storms, tropical cyclones can only form over oceans with water temperatures of at least 80 degrees Fahrenheit. After forming, these types of storms intensify as they pass over warmer water and weaken as they pass over colder water or land.

VOCABULARY PREVIEW

compact (kəm pakt′) *adj.* occupying a relatively small space or area; tightly packed; p. 306
evacuate (i vak′ ū āt′) *v.* to leave or clear an area; p. 307
ecology (ē kol′ ə jē) *n.* the relationship of living things to their environment and to each other; p. 309
unique (ū nēk′) *adj.* highly uncommon; rare; one-of-a-kind; p. 309

Before Reading

Objectives

- To read and analyze a selection about hurricanes
- To identify informational text
- To write a selection summary

Skills

Reading/Thinking: Summarizing; Evaluating; Distinguishing Fact and Opinion
Writing: Postcard
Vocabulary: Word Origins; Prefixes
Grammar/Language: Compound Predicates; Spelling Plurals
Listening/Speaking: News Broadcast
Collaboration: Literature Groups; Mural

Motivating STUDENTS

Literature Launchers: "In the Wake of a Storm"

Videodisc Side A, Segment 9 

Also available in VHS.

Selection Focus Transparency 28: Have students view and discuss the diagram showing a hurricane's ingredients.

Reading Focus: As an extension of the Reading Focus, have pairs of students use precise language and sensory imagery to share what their feelings would have been (or were) when severe weather hit.

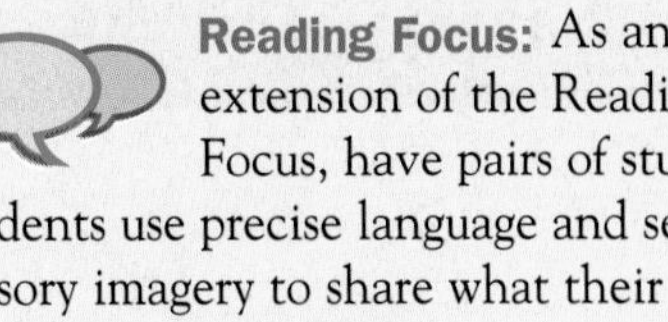

RESOURCE MANAGER

Teaching Tools and Resources
- Theme Three Planning Guide
- Literature Groups Sourcebook

Essential Lesson Support

Lesson-Specific Instruction
- Selection Focus Transparency 28
- Literary Elements Transparency 28
- Active Reading Guide,* p. 28
- Selection Vocabulary Practice, p. 19
- TIME *inTIME* magazine, pp. 12-13

Assessment
- Selection Quick Checks,* p. 28
- Sel. and Theme Assmt., pp. 51-52
- Testmaker: ExamView Pro
- Performance Assessment, p. 27

Systematic Language Instruction
- Gr. and Comp. Hbk., L. 6.5
- Vocabulary Power, Unit 3 Review/Test
- Spelling Power, Unit 3 Review/Proofreading

English Language Learners
- ELL Sourcebook, p. 51
- Spanish Summaries, p. 28
- Audio Library*
- English, Yes!

Spec. Needs/Strat. Interven.
- Interactive Rdg. Sbk., pp. T122-T125
- Interactive Rdg. Wkbk., pp. 52-53
- Inclusion Strat. Sbk., pp. 31-32, 37-38, 43-44, 77-78, 89-90
- Audio Library*

*Also available in Spanish

Reading the Selection

SUMMARY

Hurricane Andrew devastated southern Florida in August 1992. It came ashore south of Miami, carrying winds of almost 200 miles per hour that nearly destroyed Homestead and Florida City, killing 22 people and leaving 250,000 homeless. The storm also ripped through Everglades National Park, trashing mangrove swamps and other animal habitats. Nature has always healed itself after severe weather, but now human activities may prevent nature's healing.

Spanish Summaries, p. 28

A Active Reading Strategies

EVALUATE Ask students whether technology can protect people from devastating storms. *(Technology offers forecasts, giving people a chance to protect themselves, but it cannot keep storms from occurring.)*

VOCABULARY If you haven't previewed the selection vocabulary with students, stop and remind them to use context clues to unlock the meanings of new vocabulary words.

Additional Resources

Active Reading Guide, p. 28

Audio Library

Spanish Audio Library

Hurricanes: *Big Winds and Big Damage*

Patricia Lauber

In mid-August of 1992, satellite pictures showed a low-pressure area of wind and rain moving west across the Atlantic. Though the storm did not seem to amount to much, the National Hurricane Center in Miami, Florida, tracked it carefully.

By August 20 the storm was about 400 miles east of Puerto Rico. Here it weakened so much that it almost disappeared. The lower part of the storm was moving northwest, but the upper part was being blown northeast by strong high-altitude winds. For a time, it seemed the storm might be torn apart. Instead, the high-altitude winds began to flow around the storm. It charged ahead, with all its parts moving in the same direction.

A By then scientists at the Hurricane Center were working with computer models of storms. They were trying to predict the storm's behavior and decide whether people should be told to leave coastal areas. The scientists fed their computers all the data they had received from satellites, radar, and airplane flights into the storm.

By 4:00 A.M. of August 22, winds within the storm were blowing at more than 75 miles an hour. The storm had become a hurricane. First of the season, it was named Andrew.[1]

As its winds swirled ever faster, Andrew churned across the Bahamas. It was a furious and compact storm, with an eye[2] only eight miles wide and winds that reached out for 60 miles. It was heading for the east coast of Florida.

1. In North America, hurricanes tend to occur from June through November, with most striking in September. Each season's first storm is given a name beginning with an *A*. Male and female names are used alternately through the alphabet.
2. A hurricane's *eye,* or center, has very light winds and can be as much as several miles across. If you were caught in a hurricane as the eye passed over, you might well see clear, blue sky overhead.

Vocabulary

compact (kəm pakt′) *adj.* occupying a relatively small space or area; tightly packed

Teaching Support

CONNECTING TO OTHER SELECTIONS

The chart at the right shows three ways to connect "Hurricanes: Big Winds and Big Damage" to other selections in this book.

For specific teaching strategies, see the ***Theme Three Planning Guide.***

Connection	Title
Life Skills: Planning and Designing	→ "Almost Ready," p. 20
Thematic: Humans and Nature	→ "Miracles," p. 784
Literary: Nonfiction	→ "The Fish Crisis," p. 295

B The computer models could not predict exactly where Andrew would come ashore. For 250 miles, from Fort Lauderdale to Key West, people were ordered to evacuate all low-lying areas along the coast.

Sunday, August 23, dawned clear and fair in south Florida. The sky was blue with fleecy clouds. Temperatures rose into the 90s. The air was damp and salty. Herons and frigate birds drifted over blue waters. C

Vocabulary
evacuate (i vak′ ū āt′) *v.* to leave or clear an area

B Literary Elements

INFORMATIONAL TEXT Remind students to evaluate, as they read, the author's main purpose in this selection. Suggest that they take notes on the new facts they learn. *(The author's main purpose is to inform.)*

Historical Note

Hurricane Andrew was the most expensive natural disaster in U.S. history. Damage was estimated at $25 billion. Early-warning systems kept the death toll down to 58 people in Florida and Louisiana.

C Active Reading Strategies

EVALUATE Ask students how the author's description of the beautiful day contrasts with what one would expect of a hurricane. *(The sky is blue, clear, and calm. Describing the day like this will make the approaching hurricane more frightening.)*

FYI

Hurricanes From 1953 through 1978, all hurricanes were given women's names. They'd say, "Hurricane Agnes flirted with the coast" or "Camille threw a temper tantrum." Starting in 1979, the names given to the big winds are alternately male and female.

MEETING INDIVIDUAL NEEDS

ENGLISH LANGUAGE LEARNERS

The Importance of Weather Remind English language learners of the many ways that weather conditions affect our food, shelter, and way of life.

Activity Ask students to interview adults in their lives about the weather and other natural conditions in the countries they are from. Have them ask what types of natural disasters are likely to occur there and how they affect people's lives. Then have them report to the class, using illustrations if possible.

Additional Resources

English Language Learners Sourcebook, p. 51

J Literary Elements

SIMILE Point out that the author uses similes to help paint word pictures. Ask students to find the two similes on this page. *(They are* slash pines snapped like matchsticks, *paragraph 1, and* their seeds spread like wildfire, *paragraph 3.)*

K Active Reading Strategies

EVALUATE Ask students how the author's use of the word *fear* affects how they might feel about the scientists' statement of fact. *(By saying that the scientists "fear," the author makes the statement of fact seem more significant and makes the reader pay closer attention to what the scientists have to say.)*

L Critical Thinking

EVALUATING Ask students to stop to evaluate whether the author has done a good job of informing readers. Have them support their opinions with examples from the text. If you wish, share the following model to illustrate the thinking process involved in evaluating.

> **MODEL:** So far, I have learned a lot about Hurricane Andrew from this selection. The author has explained what a hurricane is and described clearly how Hurricane Andrew hit southern Florida. She has also described the aftermath of the storm. I think the author has written a very informative selection.

J in the park survived well. But in Andrew's winds, slash pines snapped like matchsticks. Gumbo-limbo, wild tamarind, and ancient mahogany trees were uprooted. The storm left behind a tangled mass of dead and dying plants, lying in torn-up ground.

The last hurricane that seriously damaged Everglades swept through in 1960. That time the park recovered well. Some fallen trees resprouted. Seeds from similar plants blew in on the winds or were carried in by animals.

Since then many changes have taken place in areas around the park. To the north, land has been drained and cleared for towns, ranches, and farms. The natural flow of water through the park has changed, and chemicals seep into the water. Housing developments have gone up right next to the park. And foreign plants have been brought in and planted just outside the park. Among these are Australian pines, Brazilian pepper shrubs, and melaleuca trees. All were brought in as ornamental plants. But they are a problem. Their seeds spread like wildfire, grow fast, and thrive in disturbed soil. Once they take hold, they are nearly impossible to get rid of.

Before Andrew, the park was under stress because of changes to the north. Now park scientists fear that foreign plants will invade the hurricane-damaged areas, take hold, and drive out native plants. This would change the park's plant life. It would also change the animal life, because animals depend on native plants for food and for places to nest and raise their young. K

No one knows how big a change will take place or how it will affect the songbirds and wading birds, the raccoons, bobcats, deer, alligators, snakes, and tree frogs. Park scientists can only wait and see.

Natural scientists are also concerned about damage to mangrove swamps along southern Biscayne Bay, where Andrew came ashore.

The storm surge spent itself on a string of small barrier islands.[4] But the hurricane's winds and waves battered the shore, which was lined with swamps of mangrove trees. The raging winds shredded the mangroves. When mangroves are lost, many food chains and food webs are affected. L

Mangroves are umbrella-shaped trees that can grow in salty water. There are

Mangrove trees have a system of exposed roots that help support the plant.

4. *Barrier islands* are long, narrow islands that lie in the shallow waters along a shore. They are made of sand and gravel piled up into ridges and dunes by waves and winds.

Teaching Support

Grammar and Language Minilesson

Compound Predicates Write the following sentence on the board: *Plant seeds blew in or were carried in.* Tell students that the underlined words are part of the compound predicate. A compound predicate has two or more simple predicates, or verbs, that have the same subject. The simple predicates are usually connected by *and, but,* or *or.*

Activity Write the following sentences on the board and have students determine the simple predicates in each:

1. The storm weakened, organized, and then charged ahead.
2. The hurricane beat and battered southern Florida.
3. The scientists observe and study the effects on Everglades National Park.
4. The armed forces had planned ahead and were ready to move. **L2**

Additional Resources

- ***Grammar and Language Transparency 27***
- ***Grammar and Language Workbook,*** pp. 53–54
- ***Grammar and Composition Handbook,*** Lesson 1.5
- ***Writer's Choice,*** Lesson 8.5

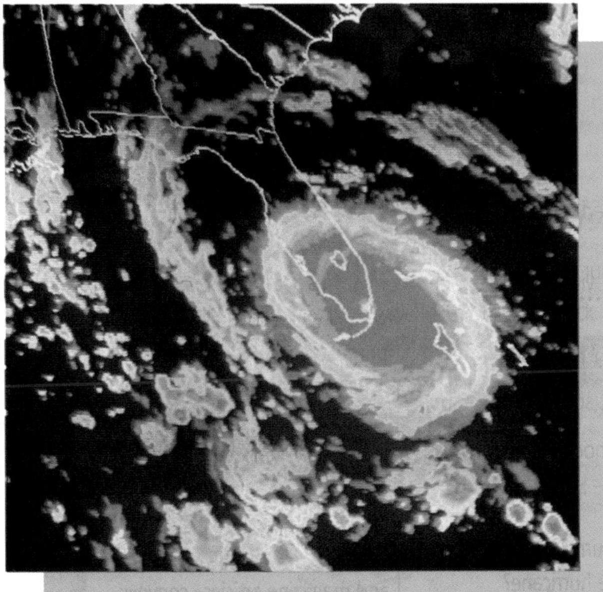

Satellite images help scientists track hurricanes. In this image of a hurricane over the state of Florida, the land areas are outlined by computer.

three kinds—the red, the black, and the white. The red is the kind most people are familiar with, because much of its root system is above ground. The roots arch out, like the legs of a crab, around the trunk. They protect the land against ocean storms.

M Mangroves are the start of many food chains. These trees shed leaves heavily. The leaves fall in the water, where they become food for bacteria and fungi. The bacteria and fungi are grazed, or fed on, by one-celled animals. All three are eaten by tiny crabs, shrimp, worms, insect young, and small fishes. These animals are in turn eaten by bigger ones—blue crabs, sardines, anchovies, eels, sunfish. They are also eaten by young tarpon, snook, gray snapper, spotted sea trout, and others, all of which grow up into big fishes that are at or near the head of food chains. These chains also include other fish eaters, among them alligators, herons, egrets, eagles, wood storks, white ibises, and humans.

N Because of the mangroves, the shores are rich in food for many animals. They are also a nursery for the young of many fishes and other sea creatures. They are important to the lives of animals and also to the lives of humans—to those who take their living from the sea and to those who eat food from the sea.

It will be years before anyone can tell how badly Andrew damaged the mangrove swamps and the food chains that begin in them. Florida has lost many miles of mangrove swamps in the past 30 years. They have been filled, cleared, and built on. The remaining ones are precious.

Hurricanes are part of nature. They are natural events. And they have been making landfalls for a very long time. In the past, nature always healed itself after a big blow—plant and animal life came back quickly to damaged areas. Today human activities may have changed the ways in which nature can heal itself. Scientists are concerned about these changes.

They are also concerned about another kind of change: the huge number of people who have moved to coastal areas. The years ahead, scientists say, may see more and more of earth's mightiest storms roaring in from the sea and putting these people at risk.

M Active Reading Strategies

VISUALIZE Guide students in visualizing the process of the food chain described here. Encourage them to picture all the details Lauber provides.

N Active Reading Strategies

QUESTION Ask students why they think the author included such specific information about mangroves. *(They are a very important part of the food chain and are therefore vital to the delicate balance of nature.)*

Thematic Focus

Facing Challenge Have students put themselves in the place of the people described on page 309. How would they meet the challenge of losing their possessions to a hurricane? How would they cope with camping out in rainy, mosquito-infested ruins without electricity? How do they think most young people would handle such a situation?

A&E HOME VIDEO.® *The following videotape program is available from Glencoe. Be sure to preview the video for appropriateness for your class.*

- Disasters in America, Hurricanes: Deadly Wind, Deadly Rain

ASSESSMENT

Quick Checks, p. 28

MEETING INDIVIDUAL NEEDS: SPECIAL NEEDS

Learning Disabled A large amount of detailed information about the food chain is presented on this page. Work with less-proficient readers to organize the steps visually.

Activity Have students work in pairs to illustrate the steps in the food chain. Ask students to draw six steps on a piece of paper, starting at the lower left side, and have them write *Mangroves* on the line to the right of the lowest step. As they read the information on this page, they can fill in the names of the animals that exist on each successively higher level of the food chain. **L2**

Additional Resources

Inclusion Strategies

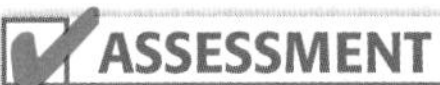

Skill Minilessons

GRAMMAR AND LANGUAGE
SPELLING: PLURALS

Sample paragraph:
Everglades National Park is home to reptiles and amphibians as well as to birds, fish, and mammals. Crabs, shrimp, worms, young insects, and small fishes feed on bacteria, fungi, and one-celled animals. At the top of the food chain, alligators, herons, egrets, eagles, wood storks, and white ibises eat many types of fish. So, of course, do humans.

READING AND THINKING
DISTINGUISHING FACT AND OPINION

Examples of facts:
- August 23 dawned clear and fair in south Florida.
- Housing developments have gone up right next to Everglades National Park.

Examples of opinions:
- A hurricane is the worst kind of natural disaster.
- Hurricanes love trailer parks.

VOCABULARY
PREFIXES THAT EXPRESS NUMBER

1. any shape (e.g., square, rectangle) with four sides
2. any animal with two feet
3. any one-syllable word
4. any animal with four feet
5. trisect it

Additional Resources

- ***Grammar and Language Workbook,*** pp. 297–300
- ***Grammar and Composition Handbook,*** Lesson 15.1
- ***Writer's Choice,*** Lesson 23.7
- ***Reading Skills Practice Workbook***
- ***Vocabulary Practice,*** p. 19

Skill Minilessons

Reteach · Review

GRAMMAR AND LANGUAGE • SPELLING PLURALS

The usual way to form plurals in English is to add *-s* or *-es.* However, there are some other general rules for forming plurals.

- If the noun ends in *s, sh, ch, x,* or *z,* then add *-es.* (bus/buses, tax/taxes, buzz/buzzes)
- If the noun ends in a consonant + *y,* then change *y* to *i* and add *-es.* (candy/candies)
- If the noun ends in *lf,* then change the *f* to *v* and add *-es.* (calf/calves)
- If the noun ends in *fe,* then change the *f* to *v* and add *-s.* (wife/wives)

PRACTICE Write a paragraph describing the different kinds of animals found at Everglades National Park. Underline each plural noun used in your paragraph. Check that each plural form is spelled correctly.

For more about forming plurals, see **Language Handbook,** pp. R46–R47.

READING AND THINKING • DISTINGUISHING FACT AND OPINION

A fact is something that can be proved to be true. An opinion, on the other hand, is someone's point of view about a topic.

Fact: Hurricane Andrew came ashore south of Miami, Florida, in the early hours of August 24, 1992.

Opinion: Hurricanes are scary.

When you include your opinion in a piece of writing, support it with facts and examples.

PRACTICE Reread "Hurricanes," and find two examples of facts. Then write two sentences of your own, expressing opinions about the topic of hurricanes. Share the facts and the opinions with your classmates. Write the sentences on the board, and ask classmates to tell whether each statement is a fact or an opinion.

For more about distinguishing fact and opinion, see **Reading Handbook,** pp. R93–R94.

VOCABULARY • PREFIXES THAT EXPRESS NUMBER

Unique comes from a Latin word that means "one." Something unique is one-of-a-kind. *Unity, unite,* and *unit* come from that same Latin word. Many other words use *uni-* as a prefix meaning "one." For example, the word *uniform* means "one form."

Here are some prefixes that express number:

one	*uni-, mono-*
two	*bi-, di-*
three	*tri-*
four	*quadri-, tetra-*

PRACTICE Use the list of prefixes that express number to answer the questions. A few hints are provided.

1. What common shape is a quadrilateral? (Hint: The word *lateral* means "side.")
2. Name an animal that is a biped. (Hint: *Ped* means "foot.")
3. Write down a word that is a monosyllable.
4. Name an animal that is a tetrapod. (Hint: *Pod* also means "foot.")
5. To divide something into two parts, you bisect it. What do you do if you divide it into three parts?

Subject-Verb Agreement

The **subject** of a sentence tells who or what is doing something. The **verb** tells what the subject is doing. These two parts of a sentence must match or "agree."

Singular: A **hurricane is** a big storm. **Plural:** **Hurricanes are** dangerous.

Problem 1 A subject is separated from the verb by an intervening phrase.
The hurricane, with its mighty winds, were terrifying.

Solution Ignore a prepositional phrase between a subject and a verb.
The hurricane, with its mighty winds, was terrifying.

Problem 2 A sentence begins with *here* or *there.*
Here is a writer's impressions of a hurricane's power.

Solution The subject is never *here* or *there.* In sentences beginning with *here* or *there,* the subject always comes after the verb.
Here are a writer's impressions of a hurricane's power.

Problem 3 A compound subject is joined by *or* or *nor.*
Neither mangrove swamps nor the food chain survive such a storm undamaged.

Solution If a compound subject is joined by *or* or *nor,* the verb agrees with the subject closest to it.
Neither mangrove swamps nor the food chain survives such a storm undamaged.

● For more about subject-verb agreement, see **Language Handbook,** pp. R14–R15.

EXERCISES

For each sentence, write the correct form of the verb in parentheses.

1. Mountain climbers on Mount Everest (faces, face) life-and-death challenges.
2. There (is, are) frequent storms late in the climbing season.
3. Years of planning (goes, go) into such a climb.
4. Neither careful planning nor the climbers' efforts (affects, affect) the force of nature.
5. There (is, are) no choice but to give up the climb.

Objective

- To recognize subject-verb agreement problems in sentences and use strategies for correcting them

Teaching Strategies

After students read the problems-and-solutions segment of the lesson, point out that another way to identify subject-verb agreement problems is to read a sentence aloud. Present the following examples and ask students if the sentence "sounds right" to them. Ask them to correct it orally.

- *There are the bag of groceries.*
- *The student, with all her classmates, were excited about the party.*
- *Neither the cat nor the hamsters likes the food.*

Exercises

1. face
2. are
3. go
4. affect
5. is

Additional Resources

- ***Grammar and Language Workbook,*** pp. 183–192
- ***Grammar and Composition Handbook,*** Lesson 10.1–10.5
- ***Writer's Choice,*** Lesson 16.1–16.5

Teaching Support

Writing Minilesson

Writing a Dramatic Account Ask students to share experiences they have had in which natural dangers, such as animals or weather, played a part. Explain that an experience doesn't need to be life-threatening to be dangerous or frightening.

Activity Have each student write a short account of the experience. Encourage students to include vivid details about the setting and how they felt before, during, and after the event. Ask students to pay special attention to subject-verb agreement in their work. Have them share what they have written with classmates. You may wish to assemble the accounts into an anthology of class adventures. **L2**

Additional Resources

- ***Writer's Choice,*** Lesson 3.3

Writing WORKSHOP

Objectives

- To create an editorial of approximately 500 to 700 words
- To plan, draft, revise, edit, and present a persuasive editorial
- To reflect on and assess one's editorial piece

GLENCOE TECHNOLOGY

WRITER'S ASSISTANT CD-ROM

Students can use Glencoe's templates and guidelines software for persuasive writing to aid them in working through the steps in the writing process in this lesson.

Teaching Strategies

PREWRITING

Gather Ideas You may wish to introduce the slogan: *Think Globally—Act Locally.* This might inspire students to recognize the wide range of topics about which they can write.

Focus Your Views In addition to the sentence completion activity in their books, have students think aloud about a few issues that concern people in their community.

Teaching Support

Writing WORKSHOP

Persuasive Writing: Editorial

You probably have strong opinions about many of the challenges that you face. When you write about your opinions, you clarify them for yourself. You may also convince others to share your opinions or spur your readers to take action.

Assignment: Follow the process explained in these pages to develop a persuasive editorial about an issue that matters to you.

- As you write your editorial, see the **Writing Handbook,** pp. R48–R53.

EVALUATION RUBRIC

By the time you complete this Writing Workshop, you will have

- written a persuasive editorial about an issue of interest to you
- developed an introduction that introduces your issue and includes a position statement
- presented at least three reasons in support of your position
- addressed potential objections to your position
- created a conclusion that motivates your readers to take action
- presented an editorial that is free of errors in grammar, usage, and mechanics

The Writing Process

PREWRITING

PREWRITING TIP

Try working in a group, brainstorming about different ways to complete each sentence.

Gather Ideas

Look through your reading journal for your views on issues raised in this unit. For example, you might wish for more concern for the environment and its inhabitants or more awareness of the struggles that young people or homeless people experience. To find other ideas, try completing the following sentences:

- I really think it's unfair that . . .
- One of the most helpful things that people today can do is . . .
- I don't think many people care enough about . . .

Focus Your Views

Filling in a pro/con chart can help you see both sides of an issue. As you look over your chart, ask yourself what underlying issue(s) your chart reveals. You might choose to explore your original issue or an underlying issue that you discover.

MEETING INDIVIDUAL NEEDS — ENGLISH LANGUAGE LEARNERS

Now Hear This You may wish to adapt the writing workshop for English language learners.

Activity Offer students a soapbox (a stool) on which to stand and express their opinions. You can do this as a class or in small groups. Discuss the ways in which people voice concerns throughout the world: demonstrations, newspaper columns, commercials, billboards, even bumper stickers. Have each English language learner create an object that expresses his or her opinion on an issue. This could include a collage, a picture or painting, a placard, a personally decorated T-shirt, or a poster.

Additional Resources

English Language Learners Sourcebook

Issue: Whether our town should set a 10:00 P.M. curfew for young people

Pros:
- May result in fewer troublemakers on the street
- May cut back on graffiti

Cons:
- Would not affect troublemakers
- Would be unfair to good kids and their parents
- Would be hard to enforce

Underlying Issue: Getting at the real causes of crime

Ask Yourself About Audience and Purpose

You might choose to write your persuasive editorial as a letter to a friend, as a newspaper or magazine editorial, or even as an op-ed piece for local TV. Because your purpose is to persuade, you must think carefully about your audience. Ask yourself the following questions:

- What are the ages, experience, and concerns of my audience?
- How can I best appeal to my audience?
- What facts should I give them?
- What objections might my audience raise, and how can I best respond?

Plan Your Strategy

Sum up your opinion in a sentence. This single-sentence position statement will guide your draft. Opinions need support, so plan several supporting points that can be backed up with reliable, convincing evidence (facts, examples, statistics).

Position Statement: Setting a curfew is a bad idea.

Point 1: A curfew would not affect troublemakers.

Evidence ⟶ Fact: Older teens and adults cause more crime than young people.

Point 2: There are few teenagers out on the streets after 10:00 P.M.

Evidence ⟶ Statistics (poll of my English class): None of us are allowed to stay out late.

Point 3: A curfew would be hard for the police to enforce.

Evidence ⟶ Example: The police would have to guess kids' ages.

Ask Yourself About Audience and Purpose Have students go through the selections to try to identify who the audience might have been in the minds of the writers. Prompt a discussion about the kinds of things that would appeal to various audiences. Encourage students to try to reach as broad an audience as possible with their editorials, using the techniques described in the Genre Focus on pages 290–291.

Plan Your Strategy In addition to writing single-sentence position statements, have students jot down all the points they wish to cover in their persuasive editorials. In cases in which students have strong feelings about the topic chosen, encourage them to plan where and how they will incorporate their arguments, their evidence, and their emotional appeals effectively in their work.

Additional Resources

- ***Writing and Proofreading Practice,*** pp. 1–7, 22–28
- ***Writing and Proofreading Transparencies 1–6, 11–14***
- ***Writer's Choice,*** Lessons 6.1–6.5

MEETING INDIVIDUAL NEEDS — MULTIPLE MODES OF EXPRESSION

Bodily/Kinesthetic Students who are inclined toward total physical response may appreciate an opportunity to act out their thoughts and opinions.

Activity Have students work in small groups with the goal of putting on a short play or skit that dramatizes a topic of concern for them, such as recycling or a local environmental issue. Encourage them to write a script, create costumes, and make a set. Let other students be audience members and write editorials on what they have seen. **L2**

DRAFTING

Start Your Draft Bring in a few opening sentences from newspaper or magazine editorials that you think are effective. Encourage students to start their drafts with a sentence that will grab the reader's interest.

Follow Through Remind students that while it is important to follow the organizational plans they have created, it is also important to let thoughts and images come freely to the page. This enables students to feel confident in their ability to write and think, even if the ability to organize is not one of their strengths.

REVISING

GLENCOE TECHNOLOGY

REVISING WITH STYLE CD-ROM

Invite students to use the *Revising with Style* CD-ROM, which offers instruction and exercises to help students improve their writing skills.

Plan Improvements Encourage students to read their editorials aloud to someone at home. Have them ask for feedback and then decide whether they agree with what has been said. You may wish to discuss ways of handling negative feedback on a controversial opinion during the revision process.

Teaching Support

Writing **WORKSHOP**

DRAFTING

DRAFTING TIP

Don't ignore valid objections that your audience might raise. Acknowledge them. Then offer reasonable responses.

Start Your Draft

Try opening with a question or a description that alerts your audience to your issue. For clarity, put a version of your position statement in this first paragraph.

Follow Through

With your prewriting notes for reference, write at least one paragraph about each supporting point. Include your evidence.

STUDENT MODEL · DRAFTING

I don't know anyone my age who is allowed to be out late at night. Our parents already set curfews for us. In fact, we took a poll in my English class about how late our parents let us stay out, and not one of the twenty-three students polled was allowed out alone after 9:30.

Complete Student Model on pp. R106–R107.

REVISING

REVISING TIP

To avoid generalizing, consider adding qualifiers—words such as *often, seldom, sometimes, few, many,* or *most.*

Plan Improvements

Take a break. After a few hours, reread your draft. Mark places where you could make improvements, such as clarifying a point or providing stronger evidence.

Use the **Rubric for Revising** as a guide for revising your draft. If you wish, read your editorial aloud to someone who disagrees with you. This will test its persuasive power.

RUBRIC FOR REVISING

Your revised persuasive editorial should have
- an introduction that clearly states the issue and your position on it
- a body that consists of at least three logical supporting points
- reliable evidence to support each point
- reasonable responses to objections that your readers might raise
- a motivating conclusion

Your revised persuasive editorial should be free of
- overgeneralizations
- errors in grammar, usage, and mechanics

Writing *Minilesson*

Power Words Students may find that they would like to use a powerful vocabulary for expressing strong thoughts and opinions. Point out that the reader will be jarred if a word seems too out of character for a piece, but adding colorful words and vivid phrases can go a long way in persuading an audience.

Activity Make sure students have access to a thesaurus and encourage them to use it during the writing process. Demonstrate the power of well-chosen words by distributing a persuasive piece of writing you admire, with a few key words left blank. Have students fill in the blanks with persuasive words. **L2**

Additional Resources

Writer's Choice, Lesson 16.1

EDITING/PROOFREADING

When you finish revising, go over your draft once more to correct errors in grammar, usage, and mechanics. Use the **Proofreading Checklist.**

Grammar Hint

One way to fix a run-on sentence is to use a semicolon between the two main clauses.

A curfew wouldn't stop troublemakers; they would just find a way around it.

PROOFREADING CHECKLIST

- ☑ There are no sentence fragments or run-on sentences.
- ☑ Verb forms are correct, and verb tenses are consistent.
- ☑ Verbs agree with their subjects.
- ☑ Comparative forms of modifiers are correct.
- ☑ Commas, semicolons, and end marks are used correctly.
- ☑ All words are spelled correctly.

STUDENT MODEL · EDITING/PROOFREADING

I would never say that graffiti isn't a problem; it is.

Complete Student Model on pp. R106–107.

Complete Student Model

For a complete version of the model developed in this Workshop, see **Writing Workshop Models**, pp. R106–R107.

PUBLISHING/PRESENTING

Consider submitting your editorial, letter to the editor, or op-ed piece to your school or local newspaper. As an alternative, you may wish to audiotape or videotape your persuasive editorial. Working with friends, prepare a taped "commentary session" that presents several opinion pieces and play it for your class.

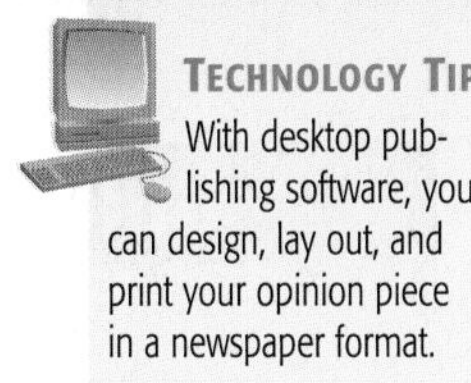

TECHNOLOGY TIP

With desktop publishing software, you can design, lay out, and print your opinion piece in a newspaper format.

Reflecting

- What grade would you give yourself on this piece of writing? Why does your work merit that grade?
- What other topic might you address in a persuasive piece? How might your writing process differ from the process you followed this time?

Save your work for your portfolio.

EDITING/PROOFREADING

Have students use the Proofreading Checklist as they review their work. Encourage them to check for each item on the list in a separate reading. Give them a few editorial symbols they can use for corrections.

Additional Resources

Grammar and Composition Handbook, Lesson 16.4

PUBLISHING/PRESENTING

Students may want to post their editorials on the Internet by locating Web sites dedicated to the topic they have chosen. If students have chosen to deliver their editorials orally on audiotape, on videotape, or "live," give them an opportunity to present their work to the class or to a group for feedback on the effectiveness of their arguments and the presentations.

Reflecting

Portfolio Have students ask themselves these questions as they review their persuasive editorials:

- Would I be persuaded if someone else had written this editorial?
- What parts of the writing process are most difficult for me? What parts do I look forward to?
- Have I done my best to make my opinion clear?

6+1 TRAITS™ OF WRITING

See the annotated **Writing Workshop Models** for additional help in evaluating student writing and in teaching the **6+1 Traits™ of effective writing.** Annotations and minilessons address and reinforce the **6+1 Traits™:** Ideas, Organization, Voice, Word Choice, Sentence Fluency, Conventions, and Presentation.

ASSESSMENT

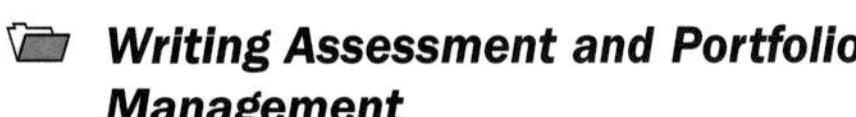

Writing Assessment and Portfolio Management

- Writing Assessment, pp. 1–12, 20–22
- Portfolio Management, pp. 38–45

Theme Assessment

Objectives

- To offer a personal response to the selections and activities in this theme
- To write a comparison of two pieces of nonfiction
- To complete a self-evaluation, set a goal, and devise a plan for achieving the goal

Responding to the Theme

1. Students should cite examples from the literature in their responses.
2. Have students express their current attitudes toward facing challenge. Accept all thoughtful observations.
3. Allow time for students to share their reports, persuasive memos, and news programs with classmates.

Analyzing Literature

Students' writing should

- include an introductory paragraph that identifies the two nonfiction selections.
- demonstrate an understanding of the elements of nonfiction writing.
- contain examples and quotes from each selection.

Evaluate and Set Goals

Evaluate

Have students list some of the activities they have completed for each task. Suggest that they add other tasks as well, such as working in pairs or small groups.

Have students use the class rubric they developed in the first theme's evaluation to assess their work.

Set Goals

Have students use pitchfork graphics to chart the steps they plan to take in achieving the goals they have set.

FACING CHALLENGE

Theme Assessment

Responding to the Theme

1. Which piece of fiction, nonfiction, or poetry in this theme most helped you think about how facing challenges can be a powerful experience? Explain your answer.
2. As a result of your reading in this unit, what new thoughts do you have about the following?
   - the kinds of challenges people face in their everyday lives
   - people's feelings and thoughts about facing those challenges
   - the importance of seeing challenge as a necessary part of life
3. Present your theme project to the class.

Analyzing Literature

COMPARE NONFICTION

Compare two pieces of nonfiction writing from this theme. Use examples and quotes from the selections to support your opinions.

Evaluate and Set Goals

1. Which of the following was most rewarding to you? Which was most difficult?
   - reading and thinking about the fiction, nonfiction, and poetry
   - doing independent writing
   - analyzing the selections in discussions
   - making presentations
   - doing research
2. Using the following scale, how would you assess your work in this theme? Give at least two reasons for your assessment.
   4 = outstanding 2 = fair
   3 = good 1 = weak
3. Based on what you found difficult in this theme, choose a goal to work toward in the next theme.
   - Write down your goal and three steps you will take to reach it.
   - Meet with your teacher to review your goal and your plan for achieving it.

Build Your Portfolio

SELECT

Select two pieces of work you did during this theme to include in your portfolio. Use the following questions to help you decide.

- Which work do you think is your best work?
- From which work did you learn the most?
- Which work "stretched" you the most?
- Which work did you enjoy the most?

REFLECT

Write some notes to accompany the work you selected. Use the following questions to guide you.

- What do you like best about the piece?
- What did you learn from creating it?
- What might you do differently if you were beginning this piece again?

ASSESSMENT

Writing Assessment and Portfolio Management

- Writing Assessment, pp. 1–12
- Portfolio Management, pp. 38–45

GLENCOE TECHNOLOGY

MINDJOGGER VIDEOQUIZZES VIDEODISC

Use *MindJogger* to review the Theme 3 content.

Theme 3
Side A

Also available in VHS.

Reading on Your Own

Have you liked reading the stories and poems in this theme? If you have, here are some other books you might enjoy.

Where the Red Fern Grows
by Wilson Rawls
This story of a young boy living in the Oklahoma Ozarks and the pair of hunting dogs he trains has become a favorite with young readers.

Hostage
by Edward Myers
Alyssa and Rob must use their wits and survival techniques after a fossil thief takes them hostage on a trek through the Utah desert.

Reach Higher
by Scottie Pippen Pippen tells about his life and the challenges he faced to become an NBA champion with the Chicago Bulls. The title describes his advice to his young readers.

The Outsiders
by S. E. Hinton Fourteen-year-old Ponyboy is proud to be a "greaser," until a friend kills a member of a rival gang and starts a chain of events that causes him to question his outsider status.

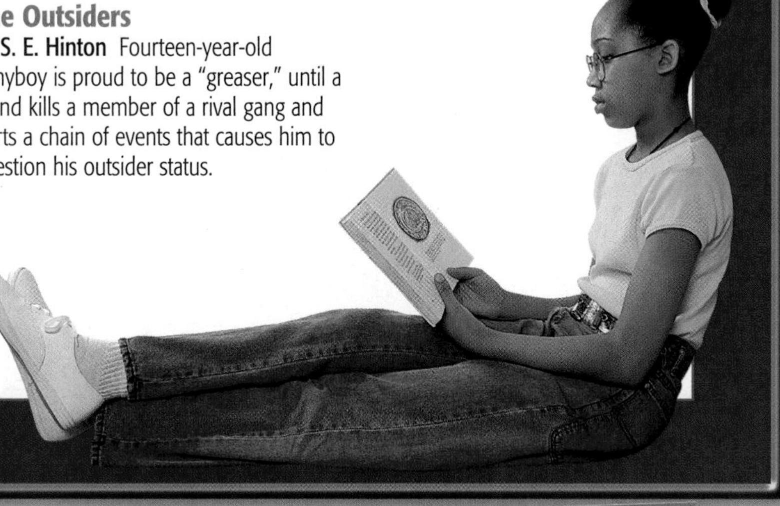

MEETING INDIVIDUAL NEEDS — SPECIAL NEEDS

You may wish to recommend *Reach Higher* by Scottie Pippen to your less-proficient readers. The many color photographs, large type, attractive layout, and inviting topic make this book appealing to reluctant readers. **L1**

The following books are rated for average students **(L2)** or for students who need more challenging reading material **(L3)**:

Where the Red Fern Grows by Wilson Rawls **(L2)**
Hostage by Edward P. Myers **(L2)**
The Outsiders by S. E. Hinton **(L3)**

Additional Resources
Inclusion Strategies

Reading on Your Own

Tips for Independent Reading

Stress the importance of each student's spending at least thirty minutes a day in independent reading and suggest books, such as those shown here, related to this theme.

Reading Fiction Review the basic elements of fiction—setting, characters, plot, point of view, and theme—and the five parts of a plot—exposition, rising action, climax, falling action, and resolution.

Practice Encourage students to identify each element and each stage of the plot in a novel or short story they are currently reading on their own. Suggest that students create a graphic that will help them keep track of the literary elements and stages of the plot as they read.

Glencoe Literature Library

Where the Red Fern Grows is available in the *Glencoe Literature Library*. For a complete listing of the titles, see the **Glencoe Resources for Independent Reading** in the front of this book.

The *Glencoe Literature Library Study Guide* provides instructional support and student activities for works in the *Glencoe Literature Library*.

At the MOVIES

Students who read ***Where the Red Fern Grows*** might enjoy seeing the movie version (1974, 97 minutes, G). Those who haven't read the book might be encouraged to do so by the movie.

Be sure to preview the video for appropriateness for your class.

Standardized Test Practice

TEST-TAKING TIP

A good way for students to figure out if a sentence is correct is for them to say it silently to themselves. If a sentence sounds awkward, it probably is not grammatically or structurally correct.

Answers and Analyses

1. B In this case *badly* is a modifier for *played the piano.* This means that it must come after the action it describes.
2. J The word *it* refers to the cereal that is being eaten. The pronoun must come after the noun it replaces. Students may notice that choice L also has problems in verb tense.
3. B This question may trick some students. Both B and C are grammatically correct, but choice C is not a good choice because it is a run-on sentence. Choice B is the best answer.
4. L Students should use the process of elimination to answer this question. Choice J contains two sentences, one of them clearly bad. Choice K has an error in tense. This leaves L as the best answer.
5. D Choices A, B, and C all have errors in word order. Students should carefully sound out each answer choice before choosing the best answer, D.
6. J Choices K and L have errors in sentence structure. Choice M seems to be correct, but when students take a closer look they may notice that a comma is needed after the introductory phrase *In the dark.* Thus J is the only possible answer.

Standardized Test Practice

Read the sentences in each numbered item. Choose the sentence that DOES NOT have a mistake in sentence structure.

1 **A** Badly I played the piano at the recital.
B I played the piano badly at the recital.
C At the recital, I badly played the piano.
D I badly played the piano at the recital.

2 **J** When you finish eating the cereal, put it away.
K Put it away, when the cereal is finished being eaten by you.
L When you finished putting away the cereal, it is eaten.
M When the cereal is finished being eaten by you, put it away.

3 **A** Liking to play fetch, the dog over there.
B The dog over there likes to play fetch.
C There is a dog over there, it likes to play fetch.
D The dog over there. It likes to play fetch.

4 **J** Herbert wants to go. Outside it is really nice out today.
K Herbert wants to go outside because it was really nice out today.
L Herbert wants to go outside. It is really nice out today.
M Herbert wants to go outside, it is really nice out today.

5 **A** In puddles I like to jump on rainy days.
B I like to jump on rainy days in puddles.
C On rainy days, in puddles I like to jump.
D I like to jump in puddles on rainy days.

6 **J** The flashlight helped Juan find his way in the dark.
K The flashlight in the dark helping Juan find his way.
L In the dark helping Juan find his way was the flashlight.
M In the dark the flashlight helped Juan find his way.

ENGLISH LANGUAGE LEARNERS

Sentence Structure
Students may benefit from a review of basic sentence types—simple, compound, and complex. Provide example sentences for each type, and point out the functions of nouns, pronouns, and verbs. Be sure to remind students that subjects and verbs must agree in number. A singular subject requires a singular verb, while a plural subject needs a plural verb.

Additional Resources

Grammar and Composition Handbook, pp. 64–141, 215–226

Standardized Test Practice

Read the sentences in each numbered item and look at the underlined words. The underlined words in each sentence may contain a mistake in word usage. Find the sentence in which the underlined words have CORRECT word usage.

7 A The flowers will soon lose her petals.
B The flowers will soon lose their petals.
C The flowers will soon lose his petals.
D The flowers will soon lose its petals.

8 J Sheila likes to mowing the grass.
K Sheila likes mow the grass.
L Sheila likes to mowed the grass.
M Sheila likes to mow the grass.

9 A The burning, hot coals cooked the meat.
B The burned, hot coals cooked the meat.
C The burning, hotting coals cooked the meat.
D The burn, hot coals cooked the meat.

10 J After we left the house, we are going to the dentist.
K After we left the house, we go to the dentist.
L After we left the house, we went to the dentist.
M After we left the house, we will go to the dentist.

11 A Brian spends a lot of time at their grandfather's house.
B Brian spends a lot of time at his grandfather's house.
C Brian spends a lot of time at its grandfather's house.
D Brian spends a lot of time at him grandfather's house.

12 J The movie I will see last night was great.
K The movie I seen last night was great.
L The movie I saw last night was great.
M The movie I see last night was great.

Answers and Analyses

7. B The correct pronoun to replace *flowers* is *their,* because *flowers* is neither singular nor a person.
8. M Infinitive use is indicated by the word *to* in front of the verb. This means that there should be no suffix, such as *-ed* or *-ing,* on the verb. That eliminates choices J and L. Choice K is missing the *to,* so the best answer is M.
9. A Ask students what is being described *(hot coals).* Remind them of the rules for using participles. *Hot* is not an action word, so it cannot end in *-ing. Burn* and *burned* are verbs. *Burnt* would be the descriptive term. That leaves choice A as the only possible answer.
10. L The first part of the sentence is in the past tense, so the second part must also be. The use of *went* (choice L) is the only correct answer.
11. B *Brian* is singular and masculine, so the pronoun that replaces the name must also be singular and masculine. Since the second part of the sentence requires a possessive pronoun, the word *his* (choice B) is the best answer.
12. L The words *last night* refer to the past, so the verb must be in the past tense. That eliminates choices J and M. The verb *seen* in choice K is a past participle that lacks the auxiliary verb, so it is an incomplete verb phrase. That leaves choice L as the best answer.

Tested Objectives

Item	Language Objective
1, 9	Proper use of modifiers
2	Passive vs. active voice
3–6	Sentence structure
7, 11	Pronoun-antecedent agreement
8, 10, 12	Proper use of verb forms

MORE PRACTICE

For additional practice, assign practice pages from one of the following standardized test resources available as part of Glencoe Literature.

Additional Resources
ITBS Preparation and Practice
SAT-9 Preparation and Practice
Terra Nova Preparation and Practice

Theme 4 At a Glance
Where the Heart Is

THEME OPENING

- **Introducing the Theme** (p. 325)
- **Exploring the Theme** (p. 326)
- **Theme Projects** (p. 327)

Theme 4: WHERE THE HEART IS

SELECTIONS

Bums in the Attic (p. 328)

In a Neighborhood in Los Angeles (p. 333)

The Courage That My Mother Had (p. 340)

Mother to Son (p. 340)

Media Connection: Kids from Chicago's Cabrini Green Learn Urban Farming in Arkansas (p. 345)

Antaeus (p. 346)

Home (p. 360)

the 1st (p. 360)

The Teacher Who Changed My Life (p. 367)

How I Learned English (p. 376)

Oh Broom, Get to Work (p. 382)

Anansi and His Visitor, Turtle (p. 382)

Active Reading Model: The Night the Bed Fell (p. 398)

Media Connection: Peanuts (p. 409)

The Dog Diaries (p. 410)

SKILL FEATURES

Interdisciplinary Connection (p. 332)

Technology Skills (pp. 338–339)

Reading and Thinking Skills (p. 366)

Grammar Link (p. 381)

Vocabulary Skills (p. 394)

Writing Skills (p. 395)

Genre Focus: Essay (p. 396)

Active Reading Strategies (p. 397)

WRITING WORKSHOP

Observation and Description: A Photo in Words (pp. 420–423)

THEME ASSESSMENT

- **Responding to the Theme, Analyzing Literature, Evaluate and Set Goals** (p. 424)
- **Build Your Portfolio** (p. 424)
- **Reading on Your Own** (p. 425)
  Dragonwings by Laurence Yep
  On the Way Home by Laura Ingalls Wilder and Rose Wilder Lane
  Homecoming by Cynthia Voigt
  Where Angels Glide at Dawn: New Stories from Latin America edited by Lori M. Carlson and Cynthia L. Ventura
- **Standardized Test Practice** (pp. 426–427)

KEYS TO LITERARY CONNECTIONS

Comparing Selections

The **Comparing Selections** feature in this theme provides opportunities for addressing diverse aspects of the reading and literature curriculum.

For example, in Comparing Selections—"The Teacher Who Changed My Life" and "How I Learned English"—on page 380, students look at similarities and differences in the experiences of immigrants trying to assimilate into a new culture. From this comparison, students can gain insight into the struggles and triumphs of the human spirit.

World Literature

The Student Edition contains a variety of literature that represents cultures from around the world. World literature selections are highlighted with the icon above.

TEACHING SUPPORT

The Teaching Support offers a wealth of interactive instructional support:

Meeting Individual Needs
- Special Needs
- English Language Learners
- Multiple Modes of Expression
- Advanced Learners

Internet Connection

Assessment

Portfolio Options

Minilessons
- Grammar and Language
- Reading
- Writing
- Listening and Speaking

Connecting to Other Selections

Real-World Connection

Interdisciplinary Connection

Life Skills Connection

Family and Community Activity

Key to Ability Levels

The activities throughout this theme have been coded for students of various abilities.

L1 BASIC activities for all students

L2 AVERAGE activities for average to above-average students

L3 ADVANCED LEARNERS activities for above-average students

Teaching Today

The Glencoe *Teaching Today* professional development Web site at www.teachingtoday.glencoe.com features daily teaching tips, free downloads, annotated Web resources, educational news, and a wealth of information on a wide range of topics.

Theme 4 At a Glance (continued)
Where the Heart Is

Reading Skills in this theme

Variety of Texts

In addition to autobiographical selections, this theme includes the following text types:

- short story
- poetry
- folk tale
- cartoon
- newspaper story
- comic strip

Comprehension Skills

The following instructional support for comprehension skills appears in this theme of the Student Edition:

- **Reading and Thinking Minilessons** (pp. 337, 344, 359, 393, 408, 419)
- **Making Connections** (p. 366)
- **Active Reading Strategies and Model** (pp. 397–408)

See also the **Reading Minilessons** in this book.

For strategies for reading longer works, such as novels and novellas, see "Tips for Independent Reading" on page 425.

Reading Resources

Active Reading Guide The ***Active Reading Guide*** provides graphic organizers and study guide questions to support students' reading of each selection. (***Active Reading Guide***, pp. 29–38)

Interactive Reading Sourcebook and **Interactive Reading Workbook** The ***Interactive Reading Sourcebook*** and ***Interactive Reading Workbook*** offer focused comprehension strategies and lessons on critical thinking skills as well as fluency practice and activities to teach and support phonics, decoding, spelling, and vocabulary development.

Vocabulary Power The ***Vocabulary Power*** workbook (Lessons 15–18) provides systematic teaching, practice, and assessment of vocabulary for better reading comprehension.

Audio Library Available on audiocassette and on CD, the ***Audio Library*** provides valuable comprehension support.

Glencoe Literature Library Each title in the ***Glencoe Literature Library*** includes a full-length work plus related readings. A separate Study Guide is available for each title.

Five–Star Stories These anthologies of familiar short stories adapted and abridged for a variety of reading levels include exercises to help increase students' vocabulary and improve their reading comprehension.

The Contemporary Readers ***The Contemporary Readers*** are nonfiction books linked to various themes and designed for developing readers from a wide range of backgrounds.

Literature Classics CD-ROM The selections on this CD-ROM can be searched by author, theme, or genre.

inTIME and Humanities Across TIME Coproductions of Glencoe and Time, Inc., these resources include a wealth of high-interest nonfiction related to the selections in this theme.

Assessment in this theme

Assessment in the Student Edition

This program offers a number of diverse ways to evaluate student understanding and skill proficiency. In the Student Edition, use the following:

- **Responding to Literature**
  Following each selection, students are asked to recall facts, interpret ideas, and evaluate concepts as they answer a variety of questions and complete activities to extend their understanding.
- **Theme Assessment (pp. 424–425)**
  Here students respond to the selections on personal and analytical levels. They also assume ownership of their learning by setting and evaluating goals and by selecting work for their portfolios.

See also the many **Assessment Resources** listed on the facing page.

Standardized Test Practice

The Princeton Review has developed the Standardized Test Practice pages found at the end of this thematic unit (pp. 426–427). For additional practice, direct students to the following resources:

- ITBS Preparation and Practice
- SAT-9 Preparation and Practice
- TerraNova Preparation and Practice

Writing Skills in this theme

Writing Skills

The Student Edition of Theme Four offers strong instructional support for writing skills:

In **Extending Your Response**, which follows each selection:

- **Writing About Literature**
- **Personal/Creative Writing**

See also the **Writing Minilessons** throughout the theme in this Teacher Wraparound Edition.

Writing Workshops

Theme Four concludes with a **Writing Workshop** that guides students through the process of writing a description (pp. 420–423).

Writing Resources

Writer's Assistant CD-ROM Each **Writing Workshop** is supplemented by an interactive writing guide on the ***Writer's Assistant*** CD-ROM. This easy- to-use writing guide provides prompts, templates, and other tools that lead students through the writing process.

Grammar and Composition Handbook The ***Grammar and Composition Handbook*** (Lessons 7.1–8.4) provides systematic instruction in English language conventions.

Spelling Power The ***Spelling Power*** workbook (Lessons 13–16) provides systematic teaching, practice, and assessment of spelling to help students become better spellers and thus enhance their writing.

Writing and Proofreading Practice Blackline masters present in-depth instruction and practice on a specific step in the writing process and proofreading (pp. 1–7, 29–34).

Writing and Proofreading Transparencies Transparencies provide graphic organizers and proofreading exercises for whole-class instruction (pp. 1–6, 15–16, 31–32).

Research and Report Writing Guide This resource provides extensive tips and activities to guide students in their writing projects in the literature classroom as well as in classes across the curriculum.

Style and Documentation Sourcebook for Writers This sourcebook is a combination reference and workbook, giving students the most up-to-date information and guidance regarding traditional as well as technological research strategies and documentation.

Revising with Style This resource offers instruction and exercises focusing on the revision process and covering topics from proofreading and correcting common grammatical errors to sentence combining and reordering.

Assessment Resources

Selection Quick Checks For each selection, a **Quick Check** of three to five short-answer questions measures students' literal comprehension.

Selection and Theme Assessment The ***Selection and Theme Assessment*** instrument tests students' abilities to recall, interpret, and evaluate what they've read. The tests consist of multiple-choice, short answer, and essay questions.

Performance Assessment Alternative assessment instruments and rubrics for Theme Four are found in the ***Performance Assessment*** ancillary.

Writing Assessment and Portfolio Management These notes and strategies, student models, and assessment tools assist with the task of measuring students' progress as writers and as monitors of their own writing.

Testmaker: ExamView Pro Teachers can customize selection and Theme Four tests by accessing the ***Testmaker*** database.

Interactive Tutor: Self-Assessment The ***Interactive Tutor: Self-Assessment*** software provides multiple-choice tests with immediate feedback to help students evaluate their knowledge and understanding of each literature selection.

MindJogger Videoquizzes Using a popular game show format, ***MindJogger Videoquizzes*** on videocassettes enable teachers to evaluate student understanding of Theme Four in a quick and fun manner.

Theme 4 RESOURCE MANAGER (continued)

Lessons	Essential Resources	English Language Learners
How I Learned English GREGORY DJANIKIAN PACING: 2 DAYS	**Lesson-Specific Instruction** Selection Focus Transp. 35 Active Reading Guide,* p. 35 Literary Elements Transp. 35 Quick Checks,* p. 35 Selection and Theme Assessment, pp. 61–62 Testmaker: ExamView Pro Performance Assessment, p. 33 **Systematic Language Instruction** Grammar and Comp. Hbk., L. 8.1	English Language Learners Sourcebook, p. 58 Spanish Summaries, p. 35 Spanish Translations, pp. 97–98 Audio Library* English, Yes!
Oh Broom, Get to Work YOSHIKO UCHIDA **Anansi and His Visitor, Turtle** EDNA MASON KAULA PACING: 3 DAYS	**Lesson-Specific Instruction** Selection Focus Transp. 36 Active Reading Guide,* p. 36 Literary Elements Transp. 36 Vocabulary Practice, p. 23 Quick Checks,* p. 36 Selection and Theme Assessment, pp. 63–64 Testmaker: ExamView Pro Performance Assessment, p. 34 **Systematic Language Instruction** Grammar and Comp. Hbk., L. 8.2	English Language Learners Sourcebook, pp. 59, 60, 61 Theme Four Planning Guide, p. 49 Spanish Summaries, p. 36 Spanish Translations, pp. 99–102 Audio Library* English, Yes!
The Night the Bed Fell JAMES THURBER PACING: 2 DAYS	**Lesson-Specific Instruction** Selection Focus Transp. 37 Active Reading Guide,* p. 37 Literary Elements Transp. 37 Vocabulary Practice, p. 24 Quick Checks,* p. 37 Selection and Theme Assessment, pp. 65–66 Testmaker: ExamView Pro Performance Assessment, p. 35 **Systematic Language Instruction** Grammar and Comp. Hbk., L. 8.3 Vocabulary Power, Lesson 18 Spelling Power, Lesson 16	English Language Learners Sourcebook, p. 62 Theme Four Planning Guide, p. 55 Spanish Summaries, p. 37 Spanish Translations, pp. 103–106 Audio Library* English, Yes!
The Dog Diaries MERRILL MARKOE PACING: 2 DAYS	**Lesson-Specific Instruction** Selection Focus Transp. 38 Active Reading Guide,* p. 38 Literary Elements Transp. 38 Vocabulary Practice, p. 25 Quick Checks,* p. 38 Selection and Theme Assessment, pp. 67–68 Testmaker: ExamView Pro Performance Assessment, p. 36 TIME *inTIME* magazine, p. 2 **Systematic Language Instruction** Grammar and Comp. Hbk., L. 8.4 Vocabulary Power, Unit 4 Review/Test Spelling Power, Unit 4 Review/ Proofreading	English Language Learners Sourcebook, p. 63 Theme Four Planning Guide, p. 63 Spanish Summaries, p. 38 Audio Library* English, Yes!
Writing **WORKSHOP** Descriptive Writing: A Photo in Words PACING: 2 DAYS	Writing Assessment and Portfolio Management, pp. 1–13, 23–25, 38–45	English Language Learners Sourcebook, p. 9 English, Yes!

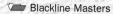

 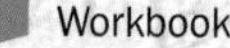 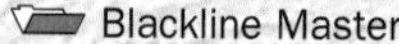    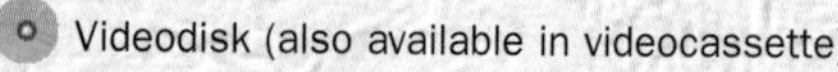

Key: Workbook, Blackline Masters, Textbook, Transparency, CD-ROM, Videodisk (also available in videocassette)

Special Needs/ Strategic Intervention	Reteaching and Enrichment
Interactive Reading Sourcebook, pp. T141–T143 Interactive Reading Workbook, p. 64 Theme Four Planning Guide, p. 44 Audio Library*	Reading Skills Practice Workbook, pp. 61–62 Interactive Tutor: Self-Assessment Vocabulary PuzzleMaker Web Site (lit.glencoe.com)
Interactive Reading Sourcebook, pp. T143–T146 Interactive Reading Workbook, pp. 65–66 Inclusion Strategies Sourcebook, pp. 79–80 Audio Library*	Reading Skills Practice Workbook, pp. 63–64 Grammar and Language Transparencies 32–33 Gr. and Lang. Wkbk., pp. 117–118, 127–128, 237–238, 291–292 Grammar and Comp. Hbk., L. 5.1, 6.1, 6.2, 12.2, 15.4 Interactive Tutor: Self-Assessment Vocabulary PuzzleMaker Web Site (lit.glencoe.com)
Interactive Reading Sourcebook, pp. T146–T148 Interactive Reading Workbook, pp. 67–68 Inclusion Strategies Sourcebook, pp. 47–48 Theme Four Planning Guide, p. 55 Audio Library*	Literature Launchers, Side A, Segment 12 Fine Art Transparency 2 Reading Skills Practice Workbook, pp. 65–66 Grammar and Language Transp. 35 Gr. and Lang. Wkbk., pp. 83–86, 275–276 Grammar and Comp. Hbk., L. 3.5, 13.8 TIME *Humanities Across TIME,* Cover 5 Interactive Tutor: Self-Assessment Vocabulary PuzzleMaker Web Site (lit.glencoe.com)
Interactive Reading Sourcebook, pp. T149–T151 Interactive Reading Workbook, pp. 69–70 Theme Four Planning Guide, p. 63 Audio Library*	Literature Launchers, Side A, Segment 10 Fine Art Transparency 27 Reading Skills Practice Workbook, pp. 67–68 Grammar and Language Transp. 36 Gr. and Lang. Wkbk., pp. 87–90, 183–184 Grammar and Comp. Hbk., L. 3.6, 10.1 Media Connection Activities, p. 8 TIME *inTIME* magazine, p. 32 TIME *Humanities Across TIME,* Cover 12 Interactive Tutor: Self-Assessment Vocabulary PuzzleMaker Web Site (lit.glencoe.com)
Inclusion Strategies Sourcebook, pp. 69–70	Writing and Proofreading Practice, pp. 1–7, 28–34 Writing and Proofreading Transparencies 1–6, 15–16, 31–32 Revising with Style Writer's Assistant

Web Audiocassette Diskette *Also available in Spanish

Theme RESOURCES

To explore the theme further, you may want to use these resources:

- Listening and Speaking Activities (pp. 10–12)
- Viewing and Representing Activities (pp. 1–6, 16–18)
- Critical Thinking Skills (pp. 9–11)
- Media Connection Activities (pp. 7–8)
- Interdisciplinary Activities (pp. 14–17)
- Family and Community Activities (p. 14)
- Selection and Theme Assessment (pp. 131–132)
- Performance Assessment, pp. 72, 97

TIME *Humanities Across TIME*

See also these additional theme planning resources:

- Theme Four Planning Guide
- Interactive Reading Sourcebook
- Literature Groups Sourcebook
- Interactive Lesson Planner
- Interactive Teacher Edition
- Glencoe Web Site <lit.glencoe.com>

Use Glencoe's ***Presentation Plus!*** This multimedia teaching tool lets you present dynamic lessons that will engage your students. Using Microsoft PowerPoint®, you can customize the presentation to create your own personalized lessons.

Where the Heart Is

Theme Objectives

- To enjoy reading about how and where people feel at home
- To analyze the literary elements in nonfiction, poetry, folktale, and short story selections
- To apply strategies for reading essays

Teaching Strategies

Have students read the quotation "Home is where one starts from" by T. S. Eliot in preparation for the discussion questions on page 325.

VIEWING THE PAINTING

Hands or stylized figures with oversized hands appear again and again in the art of Eduardo Kingman (1913–). The Ecuadorian artist has explored themes of sorrow and tenderness in paintings, murals, and book illustrations since the 1930s.

Responding to the Painting If necessary, tell students that the title of this painting translates to *Birthplace*. Ask:

- How does this painting reflect the theme? *(The hands seem to be cradling the small town, expressing loving care for the birthplace, or hometown.)*

Where the Heart Is

"Home is where one starts from."

–T. S. Eliot

Lugar Natal, 1989. Eduardo Kingman. Oil on canvas, 40 x 53 in. Inter-American Development Bank Art Collection, Washington, D.C. Reproduced by permission of the IDB.

324

TEACHER to TEACHER

BRINKLEY MIDDLE SCHOOL, MISSISSIPPI

When opening the theme "Where the Heart Is," I give my class the following writing prompt: "You are a passenger on the *Titanic* along with all of your friends and family. As the ship sinks, you are seated in a lifeboat. You must choose five of your friends or family members to be in the lifeboat too. Who will you choose and why? What factors will you consider in the decision?" Sometimes I assign vocabulary words to be used in their responses, such as nouns ending in *-ty—loyalty, responsibility, longevity,* and *honesty,* for example. This activity makes students reflect on the deeper meanings of life and, at the same time, sharpens their writing and vocabulary skills. After volunteers read their responses aloud, there is class discussion. As students challenge one another on the choices they have made or the reasons they present, the disagreements sharpen their critical thinking skills.

EMMA CLOWERS

THEME CONTENTS

GENRE FOCUS *ESSAY*

WHERE THE HEART IS 325

RESOURCE MANAGER

See the ***Theme Four Planning Guide*** for additional teaching notes, strategies, and resources for introducing the theme "Where the Heart Is."

Introducing the Theme

Direct your students' attention to the **Theme Contents.** Ask them to read through the list of selections. Discuss these questions:

- If you did not know the theme, what would you guess it is according to these titles? *(Students may guess family, childhood, school, or significant people in one's life.)*
- What genres are represented in the theme contents? *(Poems, personal narratives, short stories, folktales, and essays are included.)*
- Do any of these titles sound like something you could have written yourself? Which ones? Why? *(English language learners may choose "How I Learned English"; other students may identify titles that are relevant to their own experiences.)*

LITERATURE & HUMANITIES

Display the painting *The Family* from *U.S. History and Art*, Transparency 28. Have students discuss the family in the painting and compare it with their own ideas about what constitutes a family.

GLENCOE TECHNOLOGY

LITERATURE CLASSICS CD-ROM

Search for other selections related to the theme "Where the Heart Is."

Exploring the Theme

Where the Heart Is

Ask students to draw or paint pictures of the places they think of as home. Remind students that "home" does not have to be where they live; as the theme states, it is where the heart is.

Starting Points

Home Is Where the Heart Is

Introduce the word *nesting* and discuss its meaning. (Nesting *is the process of contributing to the building and maintenance of a nest, or home.)*

- Ask students if they are "nesters." Have them imagine they are birds. Would they prefer to sit in their nests or fly and explore what might be dangerous territory?
- After they create "top ten" lists, ask students to name things they do at home that contribute to the well-being of their households.

FINE ART TRANSPARENCY 27

You may wish to display ***Fine Art Transparency 27*** to enrich the concept.

Within Your Own Heart

Students may want to create postcards of the places they think of as home. Suggest that they write notes to family members and friends telling what they love most about them.

- Invite each student to refer to the notes to compose an "Ode to Home" and to think of the ode as a valentine—a poem or verse inspired by feelings about home—to send to a place he or she loves.

interNET CONNECTION

Quotations Suggest that students use *quotations, aphorisms,* or *proverbs* as keywords on a search engine to find other possible quotations. Once connected to a site, they can do a search using *home* as a keyword. Have them share their results with the class.

Exploring the Theme

Where the Heart Is

What would life be like without the love of your family and friends? How would you feel without the warmth and security of a place called home? In the stories, poems, and essays in this theme, you will meet characters who face these questions. To begin your own thinking about the theme, try one of the options below.

Starting Points

HOME IS WHERE THE HEART IS

Do you ever feel like the pair of birds in the cartoon–staying home with your family and doing something fun, like playing a game or baking something delicious?

- Brainstorm a list of things that you enjoy doing at home. Then, as a class, create a "top ten" list of favorite things to do at home.

WITHIN YOUR OWN HEART

Think about the people and places that are most important to you.

- What do you love most about your family members and friends? What makes your home special to you? Write a few notes about your feelings.

"I don't feel like going out. Why don't just the two of us stay in and open a can of worms?"

326 THEME 4

MEETING INDIVIDUAL NEEDS — ENGLISH LANGUAGE LEARNERS

Understanding the Theme's Title

Be sure students understand that "Where the Heart Is" is not a question but part of the familiar expression "Home is where the heart is." Also explain the rule for capitalizing titles: Capitalize the first word, last word, and all other words except for articles, coordinating conjunctions, and prepositions of four letters or fewer.

Activity After reading the introduction, have small groups create three new titles for this theme and write them on the board, capitalized correctly. Have the class identify, discuss, and correct any errors in capitalization.

Additional Resources

English Language Learners Sourcebook

Theme Projects

As you read the selections in this theme, try your hand at one of the projects below. Work on your own, with a partner, or with a group.

CRITICAL VIEWING
Families in Books and on Screen

1. Keep a journal about how families are portrayed in your favorite books and on your favorite television shows. How do the average fictional families look and act? What conclusions can you draw from your observations?
2. Organize your findings in a chart. Choose headings to represent the various categories of behavior you have found. You can use drawings or pictures from old magazines and newspapers to illustrate your chart.

interNET CONNECTION

To learn more about many of the authors in this and other themes, type an author's name into a search engine. For links relating to the selections, practice exercises, games, and more, visit the Glencoe Literature site at lit.glencoe.com.

LEARNING FOR LIFE
Writing a Policy Statement

Some of the characters in this unit are fortunate enough to speak two languages—the language of their parents' native country and English. In today's global economy, the ability to speak more than one language has great advantages.

1. Develop a policy statement for the establishment of a school-wide second-language program that would begin in kindergarten. Start with your own ideas about why knowing more than one language is important.
2. Draft a series of questions to obtain the information you want. Then gather information from teachers, bilingual students, librarians, and your family. Draft your policy statement and share it with the class.

MULTIMEDIA PROJECT
Homes Around the World

1. Gather data about the different kinds of homes people live in around the world. The **Interdisciplinary Connection** on page 332 shows some examples; see what others you can find. Look for information about architecture, life in other countries, and traditional cultures on the Web and in books and magazines.
2. Choose a kind of housing that interests you. Consider how it differs from the housing you are familiar with in such matters as size, architectural style, and building materials.
3. Build a model or draw pictures and diagrams of your chosen house. Present your finished project to the class.

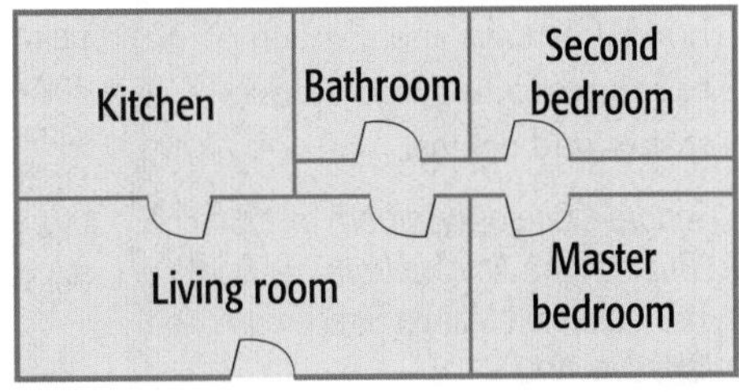

Family and Community Activity

Have student groups adopt a kindergarten or first-grade classroom. Ask students to think about their own earlier years and how important it is for young children to feel happy and secure. Encourage them to coordinate this effort with teachers from the younger grades. Have them visit the classrooms and talk to the children. Encourage your students to come up with a list of things they might do to create a home-away-from-home environment for these children at school. Ideas could include helping students hang pictures of their families on the walls, reading to students at recess one day a week, and greeting them individually each morning. **L2**

Additional Resources

Family and Community Activities, p. 14

Theme Projects

Teaching Strategies

The following suggestions may help your students plan and carry out their theme projects.

Critical Viewing

- Students can compare families like those on *The Brady Bunch* and *The Partridge Family* to current TV families.
- Use students' charts to discuss whether TV families represent real-life families.
- Ask students who choose fictional families from books to write what they like and don't like about these families in their journals.

Learning for Life

- Encourage students to poll classmates to find out how many languages are spoken in the class.
- Suggest that students find out what other local schools offer second-language programs.
- Recommend that students write their policy statements in English, translate them into the other languages spoken in your classroom, and create multilingual posters.

Multimedia Project

- Have students include a weather-related explanation for why homes are constructed this way.
- Encourage students to present overviews of the countries or regions in which the homes are found.

Additional Resources

- ***Interdisciplinary Activities,*** pp. 14–17
- ***Viewing and Representing Activities,*** pp. 16–18
- ***Listening and Speaking Activities,*** pp. 10–12
- ***Critical Thinking Skills,*** pp. 9–11
- ***Selection and Theme Assessment,*** pp. 131–132
- ***Performance Assessment,*** p. 72

Before Reading

Objectives

- To read and analyze a personal narrative about a young girl's feelings about home
- To identify first-person point of view in a narrative
- To write a paragraph analyzing the author's style

Skills

Writing: Journal Entry
Grammar/Language: Pronoun-Antecedent Agreement
Collaboration: Literature Groups; Art Activity

Motivating → STUDENTS

Selection Focus Transparency 29: Have students view and discuss the photograph of Chesterwood, the house in which sculptor Daniel Chester French lived. Compare the photograph to the houses the narrator describes.

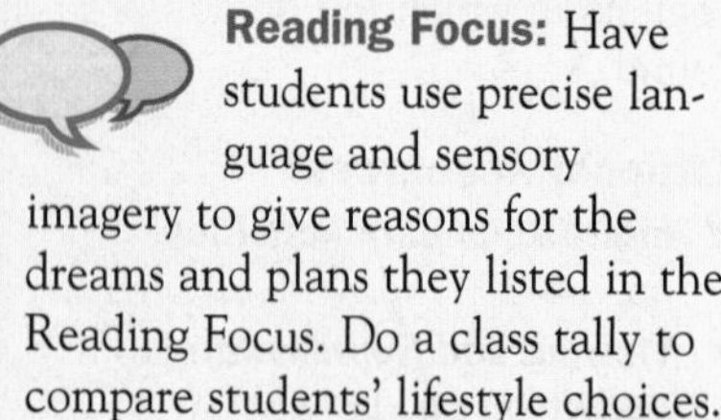

Reading Focus: Have students use precise language and sensory imagery to give reasons for the dreams and plans they listed in the Reading Focus. Do a class tally to compare students' lifestyle choices.

Before You Read

Bums in the Attic

MEET SANDRA CISNEROS

Sandra Cisneros (sis nā′ rōs′) was born in Chicago, the only daughter in a family with seven children. Her family frequently moved between the United States and Mexico because of her father's homesickness for Mexico. As a result, Cisneros often felt lonely and unsettled. "Because we moved so much," Cisneros said, ". . . I retreated inside myself." Throughout her childhood, Cisneros spent much of her time reading and writing stories and poems.

Sandra Cisneros was born in 1954. "Bums in the Attic" is from her book The House on Mango Street, *published in 1983.*

READING FOCUS

What are your dreams for the future? What will you do? Where will you live—in a house, in an apartment, on a farm?

QuickWrite
Describe in a few sentences how and where you imagine yourself living in the future.

Setting a Purpose
Read to find out what dream for the future is expressed in this selection.

BUILDING BACKGROUND

The Time and Place This selection is set in our time in Chicago, Illinois.

Did You Know? Organized in a series of vignettes, or brief scenes, *The House on Mango Street* tells the story of Esperanza Cordero, a young girl growing up in Chicago, who longs for a room of her own and a house of which she can be proud. When asked about her style of writing in *The House on Mango Street,* Sandra Cisneros commented, "I wanted to write stories that were a cross between poetry and fiction. . . . [I] wanted to write a collection which could be read at any random point without having any knowledge of what came before or after. Or, that could be read in a series to tell one big story."

RESOURCE MANAGER

Teaching Tools and Resources
- Theme Four Planning Guide
- Literature Groups Sourcebook
- Presentation Plus! CD-ROM

Essential Lesson Support

Lesson-Specific Instruction
- Selection Focus Transparency 29
- Literary Elements Transparency 29
- Active Reading Guide,* p. 29

Assessment
- Selection Quick Checks,* p. 29
- Sel. and Theme Assmt., p. 53
- Performance Assessment, p. 28
- Interactive Tutor: Self-Assessment

Systematic Language Instruction
- Gr. and Comp. Hbk., L. 7.1, 7.2
- Vocabulary Power, Lesson 15
- Spelling Power, Lesson 13

English Language Learners
- ELL Sourcebook, p. 52
- Spanish Summaries, p. 29
- Spanish Translations, p. 92
- Audio Library,*
- English, Yes!

Spec. Needs/Strat. Interven.
- Interactive Rdg. Sbk., pp. T126–T128
- Interactive Rdg. Wkbk., p. 54
- Inclusion Strat. Sbk., pp. 65–66
- Audio Library*

*Also available in Spanish

Bums in the Attic

Sandra Cisneros

I want a house on a hill like the ones with the gardens where Papa works. We go on Sundays, Papa's day off. I used to go. I don't anymore. You don't like to go out with us, Papa says. Getting too old? Getting too stuck-up, says Nenny. I don't tell them I am ashamed—all of us staring out the window like the hungry. I am tired of looking at what we can't have. When we win the lottery . . . Mama begins, and then I stop listening.

People who live on hills sleep so close to the stars they forget those of us who live too much on earth. They don't look down at all except to be content to live on hills. They have nothing to do with last week's garbage or fear of rats. Night comes. Nothing wakes them but the wind.

One day I'll own my own house, but I won't forget who I am or where I came from. Passing bums will ask, Can I come in? I'll offer them the attic, ask them to stay, because I know how it is to be without a house.

Some days after dinner, guests and I will sit in front of a fire. Floorboards will squeak upstairs. The attic grumble.

Rats? they'll ask.

Bums, I'll say, and I'll be happy.

Reading the Selection

SUMMARY

The narrator's family goes for a ride on Sundays to look at the big houses where her father works, but the girl, embarrassed by the family's staring at what they can't have, no longer joins them. She dreams of having a house of her own some day.

Spanish Summaries, p. 29

A Active Reading Strategies

PREDICT Have students use the title to predict what the selection will be about. Suggest that students revise their predictions as they read.

Additional Resources

Active Reading Guide, p. 29

Audio Library

Spanish Audio Library

B Literary Elements

FIRST-PERSON POINT OF VIEW Help students identify the first-person point of view in this story. Discuss how it affects readers' knowledge of the character's thoughts and feelings.

ASSESSMENT

Quick Checks, p. 29

Teaching Support

MEETING INDIVIDUAL NEEDS — ENGLISH LANGUAGE LEARNERS

Symbolism English language learners might find it difficult to understand the symbolism Cisneros uses in the selection. For example, a bird in flight often symbolizes freedom, and the color white often symbolizes purity. In "Bums in the Attic," the fact that rich people live on the hill symbolizes their position above the less fortunate in society.

Activity Pair English language learners with English-proficient students. Have them reread the story and list symbolic phrases and their meanings in a two-column chart.

Additional Resources

English Language Learners Sourcebook, p. 52

CONNECTING TO OTHER SELECTIONS

For a teaching strategy that connects "Bums in the Attic" to "Hollywood and the Pits," see the ***Theme Two Planning Guide.***

Responding to the Selection

PERSONAL RESPONSE

Some students may share the author's dream of being in a position to help the less fortunate. Some may dream of lives similar to their present lives, while others may dream of better, or simply different, lives.

Analyzing Literature

1. The narrator's family drives past the rich people's houses. She doesn't go because she is embarrassed.
2. She feels the people living high on the hill are too far removed from the people living down below to notice them.
3. She intends to own her own house.
4. Homeless people will ask if they can stay with her, and she will offer them space in her attic.
5. The narrator is embarrassed by her family because she knows they will never live in such houses.
6. She feels they live a privileged life and are unaware of or unconcerned about the poor people who live below them.
7. The narrator will remember when she was poor and will help those in the same situation. "I'll offer them the attic... I know how it is to be without a house."
8. The narrator will be happy and proud to tell her guests about the bums in the attic.
9. Students may suggest that the theme is knowing who you are, helping others, or having a dream.
10. Some students may think the narrator knows how it feels to be homeless. Because of her family's poor living conditions, she can understand how homeless people feel.

Active Reading and Critical Thinking

Responding to Literature

PERSONAL RESPONSE

- What do you think about the narrator's hopes and dreams for the future?
- Think back to your QuickWrite for the **Reading Focus** on page 328. How do your dreams for the future compare to the thoughts and feelings described in this selection? Write your response in your journal.

Analyzing Literature

RECALL

1. What does the narrator's family do on Sundays? Why doesn't the narrator go anymore?
2. According to the narrator, why do the people in the houses on the hill forget about other people?
3. What does the narrator intend to own when she grows up?
4. Describe how bums will end up in the narrator's attic.

Brackets connect questions that are paired to develop higher-level thinking skills.

INTERPRET

5. What is the narrator's attitude toward her family's Sunday activity? Why?
6. How does the narrator feel about the people who live on the hill? Explain.
7. What does the narrator mean when she says, "I won't forget who I am or where I came from"? Use quotations from the story to support your ideas.
8. How do you imagine the narrator will feel when she tells her guests that she has bums in the attic?

EVALUATE AND CONNECT

9. The **theme** of a piece of writing is the message that the writer hopes to communicate. What is the theme of this selection? Explain why you think so.
10. Do you think the narrator knows how it feels to be homeless, like the bums she mentions in her writing? Explain.

LITERARY ELEMENTS

First-Person Point of View

In a story, a book, or an essay, the **point of view** is the relationship of the narrator, or storyteller, to the story. In a story with **first-person point of view,** the story is always told by one of the characters, who refers to himself or herself as "I." All information about the story must come from this character. Readers can only know what this character knows and can only feel what this character feels. "Bums in the Attic" is an example of writing told from a first-person point of view.

1. Why do you think Cisneros wrote "Bums in the Attic" from a first-person point of view?
2. How would this piece be different if it were told from a third-person point of view? (See page 157.) Explain.

See **Literary Terms Handbook,** p. R8.

LITERATURE & HUMANITIES

Have students examine the painting *Why Not Use the "L"?* in *Art Talk*, page 284, and discuss how the characters react to homelessness. Have them compare Cisneros's and the artist's attitudes towards homeless people.

LITERARY ELEMENTS

1. Cisneros's use of first-person point of view allows the narrator to express feelings, thoughts, and ideas about real-life experiences.
2. If the piece were told from a third-person point of view, it would be less personal because the narrator would not be part of the experiences and feelings described.

Additional Resources

Literary Elements Transparency 29

Extending Your Response

Writing About Literature

Analyzing Style How would you describe the writer's style in this piece of writing? How does Cisneros create a response in her readers to the idea of bums in an attic? Does she use humor? Realism? Emotional situations? Write a paragraph explaining how Cisneros weaves together a style that makes her story effective. Support your conclusions with examples.

Creative Writing

Changing Point of View How would this selection be different if another character had narrated it? Choose a different character: Papa, Nenny, Mama, or one of the bums. Write a journal entry from the point of view of that person. Tell about the character's life and dreams for the future. Make up any details you wish.

Literature Groups

Home Is Where the Heart Is In a small group discussion, compare the details about the narrator's present life with her dreams for the future. How does the narrator hope her life will change? How does she intend to hang on to her identity? Do you think the narrator will one day live in a house on the hill? Why or why not? Support your ideas with details and quotations.

Art Activity

The House on the Hill Work with classmates to create a large floor plan of the house on the hill. Before drawing the house, make a list of all the necessary details, such as the fireplace, the garden, and the attic. Use your imagination for details the selection does not include. Display your plan.

Save your work for your portfolio.

Skill Minilesson

Reteach · Review

GRAMMAR AND LANGUAGE • PRONOUN-ANTECEDENT AGREEMENT

A **pronoun** is a word used in place of a noun or noun phrase. An **antecedent** is the word or words the pronoun refers to. A pronoun and its antecedent must agree in number and gender.

Mario brought his mother flowers. *She* was pleased with *them.*

She, a singular feminine pronoun, refers to *mother. Them,* a plural neuter (neither masculine nor feminine) pronoun, refers to *flowers.*

PRACTICE Write the appropriate pronoun for each numbered blank. After the pronoun, write its antecedent.

Sandra Cisneros wrote *The House on Mango Street* when (1) ______ was in her twenties. "Bums in the Attic" is from (2) ______ book. (3) ______ is one of a number of short pieces that make up the book. Each of these brief vignettes can stand on (4) ______ own, but together, Cisneros says, (5) ______ "tell one big story."

- For more about pronoun-antecedent agreement, see **Language Handbook,** p. R17.

Extending Your Response

Writing About Literature

Students' paragraphs should

- explain how Cisneros's unique style to make her story effective
- give examples of scenes that Cisneros describes humorously and those she relates realistically

Creative Writing

Students' journal entries should

- express the feelings of and include details about the character's life
- follow the style and tone of a journal entry

Literature Groups Encourage students to discuss the narrator's character to help them decide whether she will retain her identity and realize her dreams.

Art Activity Remind students that the narrator views the house on the hill as majestic and grand.

Skill Minilesson

GRAMMAR AND LANGUAGE

• PRONOUN-ANTECEDENT AGREEMENT

1. she, Sandra Cisneros
2. her, Sandra Cisneros
3. It, "Bums in the Attic"
4. its, each
5. they, vignettes

Additional Resources

- ***Grammar and Language Workbook,*** pp. 105–106
- ***Grammar and Composition Handbook,*** Lesson 4.3
- ***Writer's Choice,*** Lesson 11.2

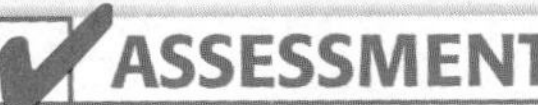

ASSESSMENT

- ***Quick Checks,*** p. 29
- ***Selection and Theme Assessment,*** p. 53
- ***Performance Assessment,*** p. 28
- ***Testmaker: ExamView Pro***
- ***Interactive Tutor: Self-Assessment***

Interdisciplinary Connection

Objectives

- To appreciate cultural differences in housing
- To understand and create a basic floor plan for a house

Teaching Strategies

It would be helpful if students could see a professionally drawn floor plan or blueprint of a house or room before they try to create their own. If you do not have a copy of a blueprint, you can find one in a home-design magazine. Bring in the sample and give students time to examine it. Explain that the blueprint contains instructions for the builders, plumbers, and electricians. Ask students to consider the floor plan they see in the blueprint and discuss whether they would change anything if they were building the house.

Activity

Floor plans may include students' homes, dream homes, or impressions of the houses from Zimbabwe, Mexico, Japan, or Mongolia described in the students' book.

Teaching Support

Interdisciplinary Connection

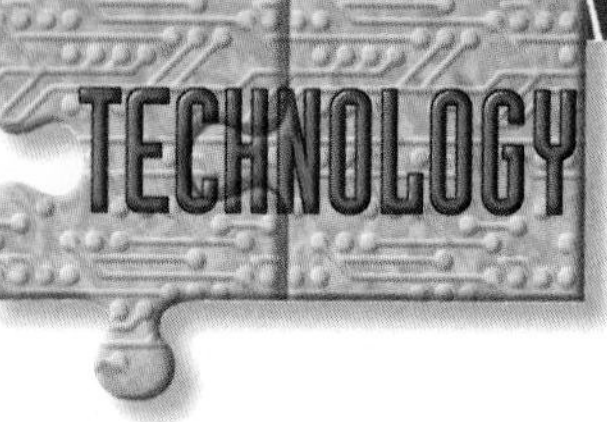

Architecture

No matter how similar the floor plans, no two homes are ever *exactly* the same. Throughout the world, the technology and design used in home construction varies greatly. However, all people build homes for the same reason: to feel comfortable and safe.

In Zimbabwe, villagers use wood, grass, or dried mud to construct a hut with circular walls. Inside, the hut remains cool and dry because of its thatched grass or corrugated metal roof. Zimbabweans build their huts close together to create a village.

Mexican villagers often build their own houses, too, shaping and drying clay into adobe bricks. The villagers typically whitewash their houses to deflect the hot sun. Sometimes colorful tiles add decoration to the roof or around windows and over the door frame.

Traditional Japanese houses use latticed paper walls to divide the living space into rooms. These sliding screens can be easily rearranged to add more space or to let summer breezes in. At night, the family unrolls futons onto woven grass mats *(tatami)* that cover the floor, and the rooms convert to bedrooms.

In Mongolia, nomadic families live in portable homes, similar to tents. This type of house, called a *yurt,* looks simple, but underneath its felt walls, a complex wooden frame keeps the structure from collapsing in desert winds. The family adds carpets and furniture to the single room to make it cozy.

ACTIVITY

With a partner or a group, research one of the home styles mentioned above or another style. Use both library and Internet sources. Put together an illustrated oral report on that style of housing.

MULTIPLE MODES OF EXPRESSION

Interpersonal Students who are community-oriented benefit from activities that allow them to exercise and develop such qualities as leadership, cooperation, and organization.

Activity Have students work in groups of five or six to design ideal towns for seventh-graders. Each group should decide what needs to be included, where the town will be located, and who will lead the project. They can decide what services, stores, restaurants, and recreational facilities should be part of the town they design. The towns may be drawn on butcher paper and presented to the class by group spokespersons. Have students determine in which town they would most like to live. **L3**

Before You Read

En un Barrio de Los Angeles / In a Neighborhood in Los Angeles

MEET FRANCISCO X. ALARCÓN

Francisco X. Alarcón (ä lär kōn´) arrived in this country from Mexico with only five dollars in his pocket. After working as a dishwasher and a migrant laborer, he began taking classes in an adult-education program in Los Angeles. By the time he had completed his education, Alarcón had received three college degrees. Today, as a poet, a professor, and a performer, Alarcón's mission is to bring his poetry to the widest possible audience.

Francisco X. Alarcón was born in 1954. This poem comes from his collection of poems Body in Flames, *published in 1990.*

READING FOCUS

Think of a family member you love. What is special about your relationship with this person?

Sharing Ideas

Jot down a list of things you love about this person. Share your list with your classmates.

Setting a Purpose

Read the poem to discover how the speaker feels about his grandmother and why he feels that way.

BUILDING BACKGROUND

The Language of the Poem "In a Neighborhood in Los Angeles" was originally written in Spanish. It was then translated into English. Both versions are presented here. If you or one of your classmates can read Spanish, read "En un Barrio de Los Angeles" aloud so that you can hear how it sounds in the original language.

Spanish-Speaking Californians Francisco X. Alarcón came to Los Angeles from Mexico. Spanish-speaking people, however, have been in California for a long time. Seven years before thirteen British colonies declared themselves the United States of America, Spanish missionaries founded the first of twenty-one missions they would build in California between 1769 and 1823. One of them was located in what is now Los Angeles. The Spanish also built a number of presidios—military posts—in California. When Mexico won its independence from Spain in 1821, California became part of Mexico. California didn't belong to the United States until the middle 1800s.

Before Reading

Objectives

- To read and analyze a poem about the author's grandmother
- To identify imagery in a poem
- To write a character sketch

Skills

Reading/Thinking: Inferring; Summarizing; Drawing Conclusions
Writing: Poem
Listening/Speaking: Performing a Tableau
Collaboration: Literature Groups

Motivating → STUDENTS

Selection Focus Transparency 30: Have students view and discuss the painting by Paul Klee.

Reading Focus: As an extension of the Reading Focus, have students work in pairs and use precise language and sensory imagery to discuss their family members. Encourage partners to ask each other for specific reasons why they consider a person special.

RESOURCE MANAGER

Teaching Tools and Resources
- Theme Four Planning Guide
- Literature Groups Sourcebook
- Presentation Plus! CD-ROM
- inTIME *inTIME* magazine, pp. 8–9

Essential Lesson Support

Lesson-Specific Instruction
- Selection Focus Transparency 30
- Literary Elements Transparency 30
- Active Reading Guide,* p. 30

Assessment
- Selection Quick Checks,* p. 30
- Sel. and Theme Assmt., p. 54
- Testmaker: ExamView Pro
- Performance Assessment, p. 29

Systematic Language Instruction
- Gr. and Comp. Hbk., L. 7.3

English Language Learners
- ELL Sourcebook, p. 53
- Spanish Summaries, p. 30
- Spanish Translations, pp. 93–94
- Audio Library,*
- English, Yes!

Spec. Needs/Strat. Interven.
- Interactive Rdg. Sbk., pp. T128–T130
- Interactive Rdg. Wkbk., p. 55
- Audio Library*

*Also available in Spanish

Reading the Selection

A Active Reading Strategies

CONNECT Ask students to think of something special they learned from a grandparent or another older person. Have volunteers share their answers with the class.

B Critical Thinking

INFERRING Explain to students that they can conclude something about the grandmother's character from the speaker's description of what she says and does. Ask them how they would describe her. *(She's affectionate, [soothing him] and fun-loving [singing to and dancing with chairs].)*

C Literary Elements

IMAGERY Explain that imagery is language that creates vivid sensory impressions. Ask students whether the language is creating a vivid picture of the grandmother. *(Students will probably say that they can see the grandma dancing and twirling around the kitchen.)*

Additional Resources

- ***Active Reading Guide,*** p. 30
- ***Audio Library***
- ***Spanish Audio Library***
- ***Spanish Summaries*** p. 30

En un Barrio de Los Angeles

In a Neighborhood in Los Angeles

Francisco X. Alarcón

Translated by Francisco Aragon

el español lo aprendí de mi abuela	I learned Spanish from my grandma
mijito no llores me decía	*mijito*° don't cry she'd tell me
en las mañanas cuando salían mis padres	on the mornings my parents would leave
a trabajar en las canerías de pescado	to work at the fish canneries
mi abuela platicaba con las sillas	my grandma would chat with chairs
les cantaba canciones antiguas	sing them old songs
les bailaba valses en la cocina	dance waltzes with them in the kitchen

4 *Mijito* (mē hē′ tō) means "my little child."

Teaching Support

CONNECTING TO OTHER SELECTIONS

For a teaching strategy that connects "In a Neighborhood in Los Angeles" to "The Scholarship Jacket," see the ***Theme Five Planning Guide.***

Meeting Individual Needs: ENGLISH LANGUAGE LEARNERS

Shades of Meaning Write these words on the board: *talk, chat, whisper, sing.* Point out that all these words have similar but not quite identical meanings. Ask students to think of words in their first languages that have slightly different meanings.

Activity Have small groups fill in the following chart for as many languages as they know.

English	Spanish	French
talk	hablar	parler
chat	platicar	causer
whisper	susurrar	chuchoter
sing	cantar	chanter

Additional Resources

- ***English Language Learners Sourcebook,*** p. 53

cuando decía
niño barrigón
se reía

con mi abuela
aprendí
a contar nubes

a reconocer
en las macetas
la yerbabuena

mi abuela
llevaba lunas
en el vestido

la montaña
el desierto
el mar de México

en sus ojos
yo las veía
en sus trenzas

yo los tocaba
con su voz
yo los olía

un día
me dijeron:
se fue muy lejos

pero yo aún
la siento
conmigo

diciéndome
quedito al oído
mijito

when she'd say
niño barrigón°
she'd laugh

with my grandma
I learned
to count clouds

to point out
in flowerpots
mint leaves

my grandma
wore moons
on her dress

Mexico's mountains
deserts
ocean

in her eyes
I'd see them
in her braids

I'd touch them
in her voice
smell them

one day
I was told:
she went far away

but still
I feel her
with me

whispering
in my ear
mijito

23 The grandmother was teasing the speaker by calling him *niño barrigón* (nēn′ yō bär′ rē gōn′), which means "big-bellied boy."

D Literary Elements

FREE VERSE Free verse has no fixed meter, rhyme scheme, line length, or stanza form. This poem is free verse except for which element? *(All stanzas have three lines.)*

E Literary Elements

IMAGERY How are the speaker's senses involved in the imagery in lines 34–42? *(In line 38, he sees Mexico's mountains, deserts, and ocean in his grandmother's braids. In lines 40–42, he touches and smells them, and he hears her.)*

F Active Reading Strategies

QUESTION Ask students what questions and answers they had when they read that "she went far away." *(Possibilities: Did the grandmother go back to Mexico? No, she would have said good-bye. She must have died.)*

Thematic Focus

Where the Heart Is The poet's grandmother lived in Los Angeles, but her heart was in Mexico. What should one do if one's heart is torn between two places?

ASSESSMENT

Quick Checks, p. 30

FINE ART TRANSPARENCY 10

You may wish to use ***Fine Art Transparency 10*** to help enrich the concept.

Reading Minilesson

Summarizing Explain to students that poems achieve much of their power through very careful word choice. Point out that putting a poem into one's own words is a good way to understand it better.

Activity Have students summarize four or five stanzas of the poem with one sentence. Point out that in paragraph form, the answers to the three following questions will summarize the events of the poem. **L2**

1. What did the grandmother do when the child's parents were at work? *(The child's grandmother taught him Spanish and entertained him by singing and dancing.)*
2. What sensory impressions did the speaker have of his grandmother? *(She wore moons on her dress and he could see, touch, and smell her memories of Mexico.)*
3. What happened to the grandmother? Where does the poet tell us she went? *(The poet tells us that she went away—probably died—but that he still feels her with him.)*

Additional Resources

Reading Skills Practice Workbook

Responding to the Selection

PERSONAL RESPONSE

Students may refer to one or more of the following images: the grandmother's singing and dancing with chairs; counting clouds; her dress with moons on it; or seeing Mexico's mountains, deserts, and ocean in her eyes and in her braids.

Analyzing Literature

1. She took care of him while his parents were at work.
2. She called him *mijito* or *niño barrigón*. She would chat and dance with chairs. She taught him to count clouds and recognize mint leaves. She shared her memories of Mexico.
3. Yes, because he has such happy memories of his time with her, and he describes her as a loving, entertaining person.
4. He says his grandmother died, but he still carries her with him.
5. Many students will say he manages to make her seem real by describing specific things she said and did.
6. The details of this poem may or may not remind students of an older relative.
7. The message is that love stays forever, even after the person who loved you dies ("but still/I feel her/with me").
8. She took care of him every day, almost like a parent. She made him feel secure and loved. She introduced him to his heritage.
9. Many students will say the translator captured both the sentiment and the rhythm of the poem.
10. Possible answer: My mother would like it because it would remind her of her mother, who also came here from another country or who also liked to sing and dance around the house.

Active Reading and Critical Thinking

Responding to Literature

PERSONAL RESPONSE

◆ What images from the poem linger in your mind?

Analyzing Literature

RECALL

1. Why did the speaker spend so much time with his grandmother as a child?
2. What are some special memories of his grandmother that the speaker shares with his readers?

Brackets connect questions that are paired to develop higher-level thinking skills.

INTERPRET

3. Do you think the speaker enjoyed being with his grandmother? Why or why not?
4. What does the speaker tell us in the last three stanzas of the poem?

EVALUATE AND CONNECT

5. How well does the poet succeed in making the grandmother in this poem seem real to you? Explain.
6. Do any of the details in this poem remind you of experiences you have had with a grandparent or another older relative? Explain.
7. What message about human relationships does this poem express? Use words from the poem to support your opinion.
8. Describe the special role the grandmother played in the speaker's life.
9. A good translator tries to put the style, meaning, and feeling of the original work into a different language. If you are bilingual in Spanish and English or can find someone who can translate each Spanish word of "En un Barrio de Los Angeles" for you, compare the two versions of the poem. Do both versions create the same feeling? Why or why not?
10. **Theme Connection** Think of someone you know who would enjoy reading this poem. Why would he or she enjoy it?

LITERARY ELEMENTS

Imagery

Imagery is language that creates vivid pictures and sensory impressions. Poets use words and phrases to create images that appeal to readers' senses. For example, in the poem "In a Neighborhood in Los Angeles," the poet uses several sensory images so that readers can visualize clearly the grandmother in the poem: "my grandma / would chat / with chairs / sing them / old / songs / dance / waltzes with them / in the kitchen." For readers, being able to "see" the grandmother talking, singing, and dancing with chairs leaves a wonderful sensory impression.

1. Pick out your favorite example of imagery in the poem and explain why you like it.
2. Select an especially effective image from another poem in this book and describe how details helped you to visualize the image.

● See **Literary Terms Handbook,** p. R5.

LITERARY ELEMENTS

1. Possible answer: I liked the final image of the grandmother whispering *mijito* in the poet's ear because it's comforting.
2. Possible answer: In "Slam, Dunk, & Hook" images like *bug-eyed, lanky, all hands & feet* and *our bodies spun on swivels of bone & faith* helped me visualize the players.

Additional Resources

 ***Literary Elements Transparency 30***

Extending Your Response

Writing About Literature

Character Sketch In this poem, the speaker describes his grandmother and the special relationship he shared with her. Write a paragraph describing how you picture the grandmother.

Creative Writing

Poem Write a short poem about a person who is, or was, important in your life. As a starting point, you may want to look back at the list you created in the **Reading Focus** on page 333. Use vivid images to describe the special nature of the relationship you and this person have shared together.

Performing

Tableau Select a dramatic moment from this poem. With a partner, create a tableau of that moment by getting into, freezing, and holding the exact pose of the characters in that scene. Choose a third person to tap each character one at a time. As each character is tapped, that person comes to life and speaks and acts just as that character would in the poem.

Literature Groups

Vivid Descriptions To the speaker of "In a Neighborhood in Los Angeles," time spent with his grandmother was an unforgettable part of his childhood. Pick out one or more descriptions that focus on the special nature of the speaker's relationship with his grandmother. Discuss how the descriptions explain the importance of the relationship. Then talk about the ways in which older people can be important in the lives of young people.

Reading Further

For more poetry, try these books:

Imaginary Gardens: American Poetry and Art for Young People edited by Charles Sullivan

Tortillitas Para Mamma: and Other Spanish Nursery Rhymes by Margot C. Griego

For biographies of some important Mexican Americans, try:

Famous Mexican Americans by Clarke Newlon

Cesar Chavez by Ruth Franchere

Save your work for your portfolio.

Skill Minilesson

Reteach · Review

READING AND THINKING • DRAWING CONCLUSIONS

As a skillful reader, you should always ask questions about what you read. Evaluate the characters, actions, and events. By using the details and the information in a piece of writing, you can draw conclusions that will help you understand the story or the poem.

- For more about drawing conclusions, see **Reading Handbook,** pp. R92–R93.

PRACTICE Reread "In a Neighborhood in Los Angeles." As you do, pay attention to the details and images that Alarcón includes about the speaker's special experiences with his grandmother. In a short paragraph, use the clues in the poem to draw your own conclusions about the speaker's feelings about his grandmother's death.

Extending Your Response

Writing About Literature

Students' character sketches should

- include sensory details
- create mental pictures for readers
- go beyond the information in the poem, containing new details that would go with this character

Creative Writing

Students' poems should

- make readers feel they know the person described
- give reasons why the writer loves the person

Performing Encourage students to spend time rehearsing their tableaux. If possible, videotape each group's performance and make tapes available for the class to view later.

Literature Groups Remind students to concentrate on the relationship between the speaker and his grandmother. COLLAB. LEARN.

Skill Minilesson

READING AND THINKING

- **DRAWING CONCLUSIONS**

Students' paragraphs should

- recognize that the speaker loved his grandmother and missed her when she died
- cite specifics in the poem that support their conclusions
- draw on their own experiences to support their conclusions

Additional Resources

Reading Skills Practice Workbook

ASSESSMENT

- ***Quick Checks,*** p. 30
- ***Selection and Theme Assessment,*** p. 54
- ***Performance Assessment,*** p. 29
- ***Testmaker: ExamView Pro***
- ***Interactive Tutor: Self-Assessment***

Technology Skills

Objectives

- To recognize reliable information posted on Internet sites
- To examine a site's credibility
- To separate fact from opinion when gathering information from Internet sites

Teaching Strategies

Walk students through the process of logging onto Web sites and model your thinking as you examine each site and form a judgment of it. For example: "This site looks interesting, but everyone on it belongs to the same organization. Their opinions may be interesting—but I'm only going to get one viewpoint." You may want to visit the sites of a news organization, a government agency, and a university. You can use such leading questions as *How reliable is the information the author of this site uses?* and *What makes you think so?* to prompt students' judgments.

Adapting to Available Technology

If the number of computers available is limited, have students work in small groups to perform the Practice. Each group member can select one site to visit, which all group members can then scrutinize for examples of fact and opinion.

Technology Skills

Internet: Judging Online Information

It's sometimes difficult to distinguish fact from opinion. A fact is a statement that can be supported by evidence. An opinion, on the other hand, represents a personal viewpoint, one that really can't be proved. When an opinion is stated strongly, it might be hard to recognize it for what it is: only one point of view.

Because the Internet is based on the free exchange of ideas, anyone can write and publish anything. It's up to you to decide whether a posting is fact or opinion. Remember: something isn't true just because you read about it on the Internet.

Fact or Opinion?

With a partner, decide which of the following statements are facts and which are opinions. How can you tell? Discuss your answers with the rest of the class.

1. Chickadee Net is a fun place for kids.
2. Owl Kids Online won the 1997 Internet Impact Award.
3. There will be 20.9 million kids online by the year 2002.
4. Kids go online to learn and have fun.
5. As the Internet becomes more user-friendly and accessible to the public at large, the number of schools and homes going online continues to grow.
6. SafeTeens.com is a site dedicated to keeping teens safe in cyberspace.
7. As of today, less than one percent of kids access the Internet from school.
8. The Internet can be viewed as one giant encyclopedia, but one important difference is obvious: the bulk of the Internet is written by unreliable sources.
9. The *Cool Site of the Day* crew selects an outstanding Web site each day of the year.
10. This slick Webzine with neon-bright, pop-art graphics dishes the best daily buzz about the alternative-music scene.

How Can You Tell?

One way to determine whether something you read on the Internet is true is to look for the name of the author. Is it someone whose name you recognize as an authority on the topic? An article about the movies written by a well-known movie reviewer, for example, is more believable than one written by someone you've never heard of. (Remember, however, that people you've never heard of may be experts in their fields.)

Another clue lies in the site's host. Information found at university or government sites can often be verified, whereas statements posted on Internet service providers may be difficult to confirm. You can tell a university sponsors a site

Teaching Support

Research on the Net Have students use search engines to locate Web sites for various types of organizations. URL extensions show whether organizations are commercial (.com), government (.gov), nonprofit (.org), network (.net), military (.mil), or educational (.edu). After the search, ask students which sites would be most useful for various types of research.

Meeting Individual Needs: SPECIAL NEEDS

Less-Proficient Readers Some students need help distinguishing fact from opinion.

Activity Before students begin reading material on Web sites, help less-proficient readers learn to distinguish between facts and opinions.

Fact or Opinion?

- Statements that begin "I think" or "I feel" are statements of opinion.
- Statements that include statistics or figures are usually statements of fact (although the facts may be incorrect).
- Descriptive words—*beautiful, terrible, wonderful, impressive*—usually indicate opinions. L1

Additional Resources

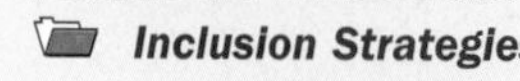

Inclusion Strategies

because the URL (Net address) ends with an *.edu* extension. Similarly, government sites end with *.gov.* Of course, just because something is posted from a college's Web site doesn't automatically make it true.

You can also determine the truthfulness of a posting if statements are backed up with sources. Sources may be noted directly in the text, in parentheses, or in hyperlinks. If the reference is hyperlinked, you can go to the original document to see for yourself whether the statement is a fact.

In many cases, time may be a factor in determining how accurate something is. An article about the current state of the Internet, for example, wouldn't be very reliable if it was posted three years ago. Look for information about when the document was published or last revised. (Such information, if it's given, usually comes at the beginning or the end of a site's home page.)

In many cases, you will have to rely on your own judgment. As you examine information on the Web, always ask yourself: Is this a fact or an opinion? Don't be misled because you agree totally with what an author says. Sharing an author's opinion doesn't make that opinion a fact.

On the other hand, don't think that a Web document is useless just because it contains someone's opinions. Very often, opinions are just what you want. You read editorials and essays for their authors' opinions. Reviews of books, movies, plays, and CDs can help you decide whether to spend your time and money on something. It's when opinions are based on faulty reasoning or prejudice that we need to mistrust them.

Technology Tip

A good way to avoid misinformation on the Internet is to keep the addresses of sites you've found trustworthy in your favorites (or bookmarks) folder. Here are a few sites you might find useful. For news, try *CNN* (www.cnn.com) and Yahooligans! News (www.yahooligans.com/content/news). For science topics, visit Discovery News Online (www.discovery. com/online). The National Geographic site (www.nationalgeographic.com) is useful for science and social studies topics. ESPN Sports Zone (espn.go.com) is excellent for sports news. Some of these sites also include fun activities or games.

Practice

1. Log on to the World Wide Web.
2. Browse through at least five sites that interest you. Look for examples of fact and opinion.
3. For each site, determine how believable the information offered is. Write down the name and URL of the site and the criteria you used to determine whether it is trustworthy.
4. Share your findings in a class-wide discussion.

ACTIVITIES

1. Start a class list of sites divided into *Mostly Fact* and *Mostly Opinion* categories. Add to the list as you discover new sites.
2. In your journal, keep a list of questionable "facts" you find on the Internet.
3. Write a letter to the editor of your school newspaper or to a Web site that accepts student contributions. In your letter, emphasize the importance of not believing everything you read. Include examples from your own research.

Activities

Suggest that students ask themselves these questions to recognize bias:

- Is the choice of words meant to influence my opinion?
- Is the material meant to be humorous or sarcastic?
- Is the writer trying to get me to take a particular action or buy something?

Students' letters should

- clearly state an opinion
- contain examples from Internet sites to support the opinion
- offer a strong conclusion

TechnoTalk

Playful Terms Do you like to *surf the Net,* explore *cyberspace,* or play *virtual reality* games? These terms describe new activities, but each has its origin in old terms. *Surfing the Net* comes from the phrase *channel surfing*—which in turn comes from the activity of *surfing,* riding a wave. The word *cyberspace* was first used by William Gibson in his 1984 science fiction novel *Neuromancer.* The term comes from the word part *cyber-,* which refers to computers. *Virtual* is an old term that refers to anything that does not physically exist. *Virtual reality,* however, is a new term, referring to a computer world that does not exist in the physical world.

Life Skills Connection

Favorite Sites To save the address (URL) of a reliable Web site:

1. Access the Internet.
2. Enter the URL in the address window; open the Web site.
3. Click on Favorites (Bookmarks) in the toolbar at the top of the screen.
4. Click on Add to Favorites in the pull-down menu.
5. The Web site's name appears in the Name box; click on OK. (Your browser may skip this stage.)

The Web site can then be accessed from Favorites (Bookmarks) on the menu bar.

Activity Write the steps on the board. Have students new to the procedure practice the steps in groups with experienced users.

Before Reading

Objectives

- To read and analyze two poems about mothers
- To identify figurative language in poetry
- To write an analysis of parents' roles

Skills

Reading/Thinking: Evaluating; Drawing Conclusions; Visualizing
Writing: Advice Column
Grammar/Language: Verb Tenses
Listening/Speaking: Reading Orally and Listening Effectively to Poetry
Collaboration: Literature Groups

Motivating STUDENTS

Selection Focus Transparency 31: Have students view and discuss the quote about poetry from Mark Strand.

Reading Focus: As an extension of the Reading Focus, have pairs of students use precise language and sensory imagery to share their ideas about the nonmaterial gifts parents give their children.

Before You Read

The Courage That My Mother Had and *Mother to Son*

MEET EDNA ST. VINCENT MILLAY

Edna St. Vincent Millay dreamed of becoming a pianist, but the Pulitzer Prize–winning poet focused her energies on writing. Millay wrote not only poetry, but also dramatic works, and even librettos for operas.

Edna St. Vincent Millay was born in Maine in 1892 and died in New York in 1950.

MEET LANGSTON HUGHES

During his career, Langston Hughes worked as a cook, busboy, seaman, reporter, and teacher. He produced poetry, novels, collections of short stories, works of nonfiction, plays, and nine children's books.

Langston Hughes was born in Joplin, Missouri, in 1902. He died in 1967 in New York City. "Mother to Son" appeared in his 1932 book The Dream Keeper and Other Poems.

READING FOCUS

What important kinds of nonmaterial "gifts," such as love and confidence, do parents try to give to their children?

Sharing Ideas
In small groups, talk about the many nonmaterial gifts that parents give to their children. Put together a list of these gifts. Why are they important?

Setting a Purpose
Reading these poems might help you to discover the kinds of gifts parents can give their children.

BUILDING BACKGROUND

Did You Know? Edna St. Vincent Millay and Langston Hughes shared some interesting similarities in their lives. Both came from single-parent homes. Both began writing poetry early. Millay saw her first verses published at age fourteen. Hughes had poems published in his high school's monthly magazine. Each later published one poem that made the critics take notice. Millay's breakthrough came with "Renascence," which she entered in a poetry contest at age twenty. Hughes began attracting attention after publishing "The Negro Speaks of Rivers" at age nineteen.

Each poet attended college, traveled a great deal overseas, lived for a time in Paris, and settled in New York City—Millay downtown in Greenwich Village, Hughes uptown in Harlem. Both were interested in the theater. Millay wrote a verse play and joined a theater company as an actress. Hughes wrote a play that had a successful run on Broadway. Both poets also wrote texts for operas.

In addition, the two poets worked all their adult lives for causes that were important to them—Millay for women's rights and Hughes for the rights of African Americans.

RESOURCE MANAGER

Teaching Tools and Resources
- Theme Four Planning Guide
- Literature Groups Sourcebook
- Presentation Plus! CD-ROM

Essential Lesson Support

Lesson-Specific Instruction
- Selection Focus Transparency 31
- Literary Elements Transparency 31
- Active Reading Guide,* p. 31

Assessment
- Selection Quick Checks,* p. 31
- Sel. and Theme Assmt., pp. 55–56
- Testmaker: ExamView Pro
- Performance Assessment, p. 30

Systematic Language Instruction
- Gr. and Comp. Hbk., L. 7.4

English Language Learners
- ELL Sourcebook, p. 54
- Spanish Summaries, p. 31
- Spanish Translations, pp. 95–96
- Audio Library*
- English, Yes!

Spec. Needs/Strat. Interven.
- Interactive Rdg. Sbk., pp. T130–T133
- Interactive Rdg. Wkbk., p. 56
- Audio Library*

*Also available in Spanish

The Courage That My Mother Had

Edna St. Vincent Millay

The courage that my mother had
Went with her, and is with her still:
Rock from New England quarried;°
Now granite in a granite hill.

The golden brooch° my mother wore
She left behind for me to wear;
I have no thing I treasure more:
Yet, it is something I could spare.

Oh, if instead she'd left to me
The thing she took into the grave!—
That courage like a rock, which she
Has no more need of, and I have.

3 **quarry:** to cut or blast rock from the earth for use in construction.

5 **brooch:** a piece of jewelry fastened by a clasp; an ornamental pin worn on clothing.

The Way It Is (detail). GG Kopilak. Private collection. Do you think the artist has captured in this woman's face the quality that Millay speaks of in her poem? Why or why not?

Reading the Selection

A Active Reading Strategies

PREDICT Have students use the title to predict what the poem will reveal about the main character. Have them verify or revise their predictions after reading the poem.

Viewing the Painting

Viewing Response *The woman's face is careworn. Her gaze, although somewhat sad, is direct, and she seems resolute.*

B Critical Thinking

EVALUATING Ask students whether they agree that the speaker hasn't inherited her mother's courage. *(Students may say that by observing her mother live courageously, she may have become brave herself.)*

Additional Resources

- ***Active Reading Guide,*** p. 31
- ***Audio Library***
- ***Spanish Audio Library***
- ***Spanish Summaries,*** p. 31

Teaching Support

Meeting Individual Needs — English Language Learners

Building Fluency Have English language learners discuss what the poem means to them. Does the speaker's mother remind them of their own mothers or grandmothers? Which kinds of courage are most valued in their native cultures? Give some examples: the courage to climb a mountain, to go through childbirth, or to be true to oneself.

Activity Pair students who need to build fluency in English with those who have strong oral language skills. Invite students to tape-record their thoughts about the poem and its relevance to their native cultures.

Additional Resources

- ***English Language Learners Sourcebook,*** p. 54

C Literary Elements

FIGURATIVE LANGUAGE: ***Metaphor*** This entire poem is a metaphor. The stairway is life. Ask students where that metaphor is spelled out. *(It is spelled out in lines 2 and 20:* Life for me ain't been no crystal stair.*)*

D Literary Elements

DIALECT Hughes gave this dialect to the speaker to show that she had little formal education, yet he clearly believed she had the eye and the soul of a poet.

E Critical Thinking

DRAWING CONCLUSIONS Is the mother's advice encouraging? *(It is encouraging because she's had a hard life but has prevailed.)*

Literature & Humanities

Show students the photograph *Ophelia, Nashville,* from the *National Music of Women in the Arts* CD and discuss how the hardships of life are expressed in it.

Thematic Focus

Where the Heart Is Ask students what they would think and feel as either woman's child.

ASSESSMENT

Quick Checks, p. 31

Mother to Son

Langston Hughes

Well, son, I'll tell you:
Life for me ain't been no crystal stair.
It's had tacks in it,
And splinters,
And boards torn up,
And places with no carpet on the floor—
Bare.
But all the time
I'se been a-climbin' on,
And reachin' landin's,
And turnin' corners,
And sometimes goin' in the dark
Where there ain't been no light.
So, boy, don't you turn back.
Don't you set down on the steps
'Cause you finds it kinder hard.
Don't you fall now—
For I'se still goin', honey,
I'se still climbin',
And life for me ain't been no crystal stair.

Survivor, 1978. Elizabeth Catlett. Linocut, 10⅞ x 9⅞ in. Armistad Research Center, Tulane University, New Orleans.

Teaching Support

Grammar and Language *Minilesson*

Verb Tenses Write on the board *to wear, wear, wore, will wear.* Explain that these are the infinitive (from Latin *infinitus* meaning "unlimited"—the form of a verb that expresses existence or action without indicating person or number) and the present, past, and future tenses of the verb *wear.*

Verb	Present	Past	Future
To have	have/has	had	will have

Activity Draw a four-column chart on the board and list the infinitives of several verbs in the first column. Then have students fill in the missing present, past, and future tenses of each verb. **L2**

Additional Resources

- ***Grammar and Language Transparency 28***
- ***Grammar and Language Workbook,*** pp. 83–86
- ***Grammar and Composition Handbook,*** Lesson 3.5
- ***Writer's Choice,*** Lesson 10.5

Responding to Literature

PERSONAL RESPONSE

- Which lines from each poem did you find most memorable? Why?

Analyzing Literature

RECALL

1. In "The Courage That My Mother Had," what did the mother leave the speaker of the poem when the mother died?
2. What does the speaker of "The Courage That My Mother Had" wish she had inherited? Why?
3. What advice does the speaker give her son in "Mother to Son"?

Brackets connect questions that are paired to develop higher-level thinking skills.

INTERPRET

4. What two unlike things are compared in "The Courage That My Mother Had"?
5. To what does the mother in "Mother to Son" compare her life?
6. What is the **theme** of "Mother to Son"?

EVALUATE AND CONNECT

7. How can parents leave their children gifts such as courage or confidence?
8. How are the mothers in the two poems alike?

LITERARY ELEMENTS

Figurative Language

Figurative language is imaginative language used by writers for descriptive effect. Instances of figurative language are called figures of speech. An **analogy** is a figure of speech in which two unlike things are compared on the basis of some characteristic they share. Similes and metaphors are types of analogies often used in literature. A **simile** uses the words *like* or *as* to compare two things. Have you ever heard someone described as being "pretty as a picture"? That's a simile. In a **metaphor,** one thing is described as if it *were* another. "This test is a breeze" is a metaphor.

1. Find an example of a simile in either poem. Explain what two things are being compared and why.
2. Find an example of a metaphor in either poem. What two things are being compared? How does the metaphor enrich the poem?

- See **Literary Terms Handbook,** pp. R1 and R4.

LITERARY ELEMENTS

1. Millay: *Courage like a rock* compares the intangible quality of courage to a tangible piece of granite to emphasize the mother's bravery.
2. Hughes: Throughout the poem, life is a stairway. The metaphor shows readers how hard the mother's life has been.

Additional Resources

Literary Elements Transparency 31

Responding to the Selection

PERSONAL RESPONSE

Example: From Millay, line 4, because the mother's courage is like granite. From Hughes, lines 18 and 19, because they show how this strong woman has never given up.

Analyzing Literature

1. She left her a golden brooch.
2. She wishes she had her mother's courage, because she needs it to get through life.
3. Don't turn back and don't fall. In other words, don't give up on life.
4. Courage (an intangible character trait) is compared to rock (very tangible, hard, unyielding granite).
5. She compares her life to a stairway that has splinters, tacks, and missing boards and is sometimes dark and uncarpeted.
6. The theme is that you have to keep trying, no matter how hard life is.
7. Parents can show their children by example how to live and thus reinforce good character traits in them.
8. Both mothers are strong, determined, and enduring.

Literary Elements

FIGURATIVE LANGUAGE Be sure students understand that *analogy* is the more general term and *simile* and *metaphor* are specific forms of analogies. Students may recall dealing with analogy items on standardized tests. Draw their attention to the Vocabulary Skills Minilesson on page 224 and review the format in which analogous relationships are shown on such test items. Ask if they can put figures from the poems into that format. For example, splintered steps : stairway :: difficulties : life, hard : granite :: courageous : speaker's mother

Extending Your Response

Literature Groups Remind students to discuss the reasons for any gender-specific differences.

Writing About Literature
Students' analyses should
- express a clear opinion about what parents give to children
- connect what children hope to learn with the concept of intangible gifts
- support their ideas with examples from the poems

Listening and Speaking
Encourage students to practice reading the poems out loud several times before they read them to their partners. Remind them to pause when punctuation indicates it (not at the end of every line) and not to overemphasize the rhythm.

Creative Writing
Students' advice columns should
- include realistic, age-appropriate questions
- give advice in a friendly, supportive tone that is not patronizing or judgmental

Skill Minilesson

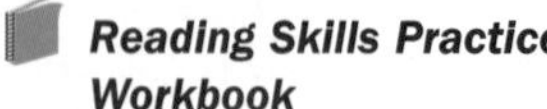

READING AND THINKING
- **VISUALIZING**

Students' sketches should
- either capture a scene the way a snapshot would or convey the scene impressionistically
- try to hint at the experience of the other senses

Additional Resources

Reading Skills Practice Workbook

Extending Your Response

Literature Groups
Dad's Turn Suppose these two poems had been called "The Courage That My Father Had" or "Father to Son." How would these poems be similar to or different from the poems you just read? Talk about the reasons for any similarities and differences you suggest.

Writing About Literature
Poetry and Ideas Mothers play an important role in both poems. These poets believe that parents give their children many things besides shelter, food, and clothing. Do you agree or disagree? What do children hope to learn from their parents? Review your list from the **Reading Focus** on page 340. Use examples from the poems to support your ideas.

Listening and Speaking
Appreciating Poetry Most poetry should be read aloud to be fully appreciated. As a poem is read, listeners may close their eyes, picture the images, and hear the natural rhythm of the lines. With a partner, take turns reading these poems to each other.

Creative Writing
An Advice Column Has a younger brother or sister or a good friend ever asked you for advice? Do you enjoy giving people words of wisdom? Write an advice column for a school newspaper. Make up some questions that students your age might ask, and then answer the questions with advice. Your tone may be serious, humorous, or both.

Reading Further
If you would like to read more by these poets, try these books:

The Block: Poems and *Black Misery* by Langston Hughes

Collected Sonnets of Edna St. Vincent Millay

Other books of poetry you might enjoy are:

Rainbows Are Made: Poems by Carl Sandburg

The Covered Bridge House and Other Poems by Kay Starbird

Save your work for your portfolio.

Skill Minilesson

Reteach · Review

READING AND THINKING • VISUALIZING

When you read or listen to a poem, remember to form pictures in your mind. Pay attention to the wide range of details in the poem, and make each detail a part of your sensory experience of the poem. Keep asking yourself:
- How does this (person, place, thing) look?
- What sounds does this poem make me think of?
- How does this detail feel, smell, or taste?

PRACTICE Reread each of the poems. As you do, try to visualize the different images in each poem. Draw a sketch that shows an important image in each poem. Then write a paragraph explaining why you chose those two images.

- For more about visualizing, see **Reading Handbook,** pp. R87–R88.

ASSESSMENT

- ***Quick Checks,*** p. 31
- ***Selection and Theme Assessment,*** pp. 55–56
- ***Performance Assessment,*** p. 30
- ***Testmaker: ExamView Pro***
- ***Interactive Tutor: Self-Assessment***

MEDIA Connection

NEWSPAPER STORY

What happens when you take a city person to the country? Sometimes, as you'll discover in this news story, the person will learn something that can be useful back in the city.

Kids from Chicago's Cabrini Green Learn Urban Farming in Arkansas

by Paisley Dodds—Associated Press, Tuesday, August 19, 1997

PERRYVILLE, Ark.—No overalls or straw hats in this crowd.

Fresh from Chicago's Cabrini Green housing complex and another development in Milwaukee, a dozen kids are visiting Arkansas to learn how to become inner-city farmers.

Growing cucumbers may keep 16-year-old Helen Marshbanks from joining a gang. Raising catfish under an apartment window sill may put more food on the table for the family of 14-year-old Darius Moore.

For 19-year-old Eric Brown, urban farming is a "cool" complement to playing basketball and watching television. "I want to be a writer when I grow up," Brown said. "But this thing, yeah, it's been real cool."

"For me, doing these kinds of projects has kept me out of trouble and out of gangs that are in my neighborhood," Marshbanks said Monday.

All are at a four-day, inner-city farming seminar at the Heifer International Project, an international grassroots organization.

The seminar, held on Heifer's 1,100-acre ranch in central Arkansas, provides some of the budding farmers their first time out of the city. They stay at the "Heifer Hilton"—a barn that sleeps about two dozen.

The seminar aims to show how to boost inner-city crops and expand into rooftop beekeeping, catfish harvesting, worm composting, goat-cheese making, and organic farming.

"We feel really good about doing this," Moore said. "There are a lot of people who can't afford things in our neighborhood. I think when people see what we're doing, they'll want to get involved too."

Learning professional techniques could help the gardening projects already running and encourage donors to keep them afloat, Marshbanks said.

"We can see what a difference it's made in our neighborhood," she said. "It makes people happy."

Analyzing Media

1. What kinds of skills will city kids learn from the Heifer International Project?
2. Suppose a similar project brought country kids to the city. What might they learn that would be helpful back on the farm?

MEDIA Connection

Objective

- To read and understand a newspaper story

Literature LINK

Antaeus This newspaper story connects to "Antaeus" (pp. 347–356). Point out to students that the urban children described in the newspaper story, who visit the Heifer ranch in Arkansas, learn surprising lessons about how to farm in the city. T. J., the main character in "Antaeus," moves from the country to the city and teaches his new friends how to farm on the rooftop of a building.

Analyzing Media

1. Responses might include growing cucumbers, raising catfish under a window sill, rooftop beekeeping, worm composting, goat-cheese making, and organic farming.
2. Some students may say they would learn about various foods, cultures, and languages, which is helpful no matter where a person lives; others may think of things that are fun or interesting to learn, like street games.

Additional Resources

Media Connections

inTIME magazine

Teaching Support

Reading Minilesson

Skimming Even before students read a story or text, they should be able to predict certain things about the story by observing its format.

Activity Have students look at the newspaper story in their books and practice finding information "at a glance." Ask them to list all the relevant information they find as they skim the story, looking for specific words or phrases that will give them an overview of the story. **L2**

Additional Resources

Reading Skills Practice Workbook

interNET CONNECTION

Urban Farming Have students use a search engine to find information on urban farming projects. Suggest they enter the keywords *organic farming* and *city farming.*

Before Reading

Objectives

- To read and analyze a short story about boys who create a roof garden
- To identify an allusion in a short story
- To write a character review

Skills

Reading/Thinking: Drawing Conclusions; Identifying Main Idea and Supporting Details; Synthesizing; Analyzing Arguments; Inferring; Stereotype
Writing: Character Description; Epilogue
Vocabulary: Analogies
Grammar/Language: Adjectives; Commas in Compound Sentences
Listening/Speaking: Readers Theater
Life Skills: Organizing; Proposal
Collaboration: Literature Groups; Interdisciplinary Activity

Motivating STUDENTS

Selection Focus Transparency 32: Have students view and discuss *Hercules Strangling Antaeus,* a sculpture by Antonio Pollaiuolo.

Reading Focus: As an extension of the Reading Focus, have pairs of students use precise language and sensory imagery to share memorable experiences they have had outdoors.

Before You Read

Antaeus

MEET BORDEN DEAL

The son of Mississippi farmers, Borden Deal explored the places of his childhood again and again in his writings. A prize-winning author, Deal wrote several novels and over one hundred short stories. The central themes running through much of Deal's work are the search for identity as well as the need for land of one's own. His story "Antaeus" focuses on both of these themes.

Borden Deal was born in 1922 in Mississippi. He died in Florida in 1985.

READING FOCUS

Do you feel a special bond to the world of nature? Do you enjoy hiking, gardening, or walking in the park?

Sharing Ideas

In small groups, talk about why many people need to feel connected in some way to nature. Make a list of ways that people of all ages enjoy the outdoors.

Setting a Purpose

Read to discover how some city boys learn about being connected to the land.

BUILDING BACKGROUND

The Time and Place The setting of this story is a northern city in the United States, sometime during World War II.

Did You Know? The title "Antaeus" refers to the name of a mighty wrestler from Greek mythology. Antaeus was a son of Gaia (jē′ ə), the goddess of the earth. His enormous strength came from contact with the earth, and he remained unbeatable as long as his feet touched the ground. The Greek hero Hercules learned of the source of Antaeus's strength and defeated him by lifting him off the ground.

VOCABULARY PREVIEW

robust (rō bust′) *adj.* strong and full of energy; p. 348
resolute (rez′ ə lo͞ot′) *adj.* determined; stubborn; p. 348
obscure (əb skyoor′) *adj.* difficult to understand; p. 350
awe (ô) *n.* wonder combined with respect; p. 351
inert (i nurt′) *adj.* without power to move or act; p. 352
bravado (brə vä′ dō) *n.* a false show of bravery; p. 353
principle (prin′ sə pəl) *n.* a basic law, truth, or belief; rule of personal conduct; p. 354
flourishing (flur′ ish ing) *adj.* growing or developing successfully; doing very well; p. 354
nurture (nur′ chər) *v.* to care for and help grow; p. 356

RESOURCE MANAGER

Teaching Tools and Resources
- Theme Four Planning Guide
- Literature Groups Sourcebook
- Presentation Plus! CD-ROM

Essential Lesson Support

Lesson-Specific Instruction
- Selection Focus Transparency 32
- Literary Elements Transparency 32
- Active Reading Guide,* p. 32
- Selection Vocabulary Practice, p. 20

Assessment
- Selection Quick Checks,* p. 32
- Sel. and Theme Assmt., pp. 57-58
- Testmaker: ExamView Pro
- Performance Assessment, p. 31

Systematic Language Instruction
- Gr. and Comp. Hbk., L. 7.5
- Vocabulary Power, Lesson 16
- Spelling Power, Lesson 14

English Language Learners
- ELL Sourcebook, p. 55
- Spanish Summaries, p. 32
- Audio Library*
- English, Yes!

Spec. Needs/Strat. Interven.
- Interactive Rdg. Sbk., pp. T133–T135
- Interactive Rdg. Wkbk., pp. 57-60
- Inclusion Strat. Sbk., pp. 13-14, 41-42, 67-68, 79-80
- Audio Library*

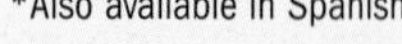

*Also available in Spanish

Antaeus

Borden Deal

This was during the wartime, when lots of people were coming North for jobs in factories and war industries,[1] when people moved around a lot more than they do now, and sometimes kids were thrown into new groups and new lives that were completely different from anything they had ever known before. I remember this one kid, T. J. his name was, from somewhere down South, whose family moved into our building during that time. They'd come North with everything they owned piled into the back seat of an old-model sedan that you wouldn't expect could make the trip, with T. J. and his three younger sisters riding shakily on top of the load of junk.

Our building was just like all the others there, with families crowded into a few rooms, and I guess there were twenty-five or thirty kids about my age in that one building. Of course, there were a few of us who formed a gang and ran together all the time after school, and I was the one who brought T. J. in and started the whole thing.

1. *[war industries]* During World War II (1939–1945), many U.S. industries switched from making consumer goods to producing weapons and equipment for the military.

Reading the Selection

SUMMARY

T. J., a boy from rural Alabama, moves to a northern city with his family. A boy he meets takes him to a factory roof where the boy and his friends can hang out unseen. T. J., who misses growing things, talks them into hauling dirt to the roof where they create a garden. When the factory owner finds it, he orders his men to get rid of it. Rather than let the men touch it, the boys shovel off the earth themselves. T. J. runs away and is found two weeks later, heading south.

Spanish Summaries, p. 32

A Active Reading Strategies

PREDICT Have students use the title and clues in the first paragraph to predict what the conflict in the story might be. Suggest that students revisit their predictions as they read to verify or revise them.

VOCABULARY If you haven't previewed the selection vocabulary with students, stop and remind them to use context clues to unlock the meanings of new vocabulary words.

Additional Resources

Active Reading Guide, p. 32

Audio Library

Spanish Audio Library

Teaching Support

CONNECTING TO OTHER SELECTIONS

The chart at the right shows three ways to connect "Antaeus" to other selections in this book.

For specific teaching strategies, see the ***Theme Four Planning Guide.***

Connection		Title
Life Skills: Planning and Designing	→	"Icarus and Daedalus," p. 737
Thematic: Rebellion	→	"I'll Walk the Tightrope," p. 231
Literary: Setting	→	"Rikki-tikki-tavi," p. 789

B Active Reading Strategies

VISUALIZE Ask students to visualize the factory building, the buildings around it, and the place where the boys meet. You might suggest that they use the author's details to draw sketches of the area.

C Active Reading Strategies

CONNECT Encourage students to remember a time they moved to a new town or school, met new friends, or simply found themselves in a new situation. Ask students whether they think T. J. feels awkward meeting the rest of the gang. *(T. J. feels confident and doesn't seem to be nervous about meeting this new bunch.)*

D Author's Craft

DIALECT Explain that dialect is a language variation spoken by a particular group, often within a particular region. Read aloud some examples of dialect from this selection, such as "Down yonder where I come from, we played out in the woods. Don't you-all have no woods around here?" Ask students why they think the author is using dialect to introduce T. J. *(The author presents dialect words and grammar to show how different T. J. is from the others and how his strength may come from his Alabama roots.)*

Did You Know?
A *parapet* is a low, protective wall along the edge of a roof or balcony.

B The building right next door to us was a factory where they made walking dolls. It was a low building with a flat, tarred roof that had a parapet all around it about head-high, and we'd found out a long time before that no one, not even the watchman, paid any attention to the roof because it was higher than any of the other buildings around. So my gang used the roof as a headquarters. We could get up there by crossing over to the fire escape from our own roof on a plank and then going on up. It was a secret place for us, where nobody else could go without our permission.

I remember the day I first took T. J. up there to meet the gang. He was a stocky, robust kid with a shock of white hair, nothing sissy about him except his voice; he talked in this slow, gentle voice like you never heard before. He talked different from any of us and you noticed it right away. But I liked him anyway, so I told him to come on up.

We climbed up over the parapet and dropped down on the roof. The rest of the gang were already there.

"Hi," I said. I jerked my thumb at T. J. "He just moved into the building yesterday."

He just stood there, not scared or anything, just looking, like the first time you see somebody you're not sure you're going to like.

"Hi," Blackie said. "Where are you from?"

"Marion County," T. J. said.

We laughed. "Marion County?" I said. "Where's that?"

He looked at me for a moment like I was a stranger, too. "It's in Alabama," he said, like I ought to know where it was. C

"What's your name?" Charley said.

"T. J.," he said, looking back at him. He had pale blue eyes that looked washed-out, but he looked directly at Charley, waiting for his reaction. He'll be all right, I thought. No sissy in him, except that voice. Who ever talked like that?

"T. J.," Blackie said. "That's just initials. What's your real name? Nobody in the world has just initials."

"I do," he said. "And they're T. J. That's all the name I got."

His voice was resolute with the knowledge of his rightness, and for a moment no one had anything to say. T. J. looked around at the rooftop and down at the black tar under his feet. "Down yonder where I come from," he said, "we played out in the woods. Don't you-all have no woods around here?" D

"Naw," Blackie said. "There's the park a few blocks over, but it's full of kids and cops and old women. You can't do a thing."

T. J. kept looking at the tar under his feet. "You mean you ain't got no fields to raise nothing in? . . . no watermelons or nothing?"

Vocabulary
robust (rō bust′) *adj.* strong and full of energy
resolute (rez′ ə lo͞ot′) *adj.* determined; stubborn

Teaching Support

MEETING INDIVIDUAL NEEDS — ENGLISH LANGUAGE LEARNERS

Dialogue That Mimics Speech
Write the following on the board: *"Naw," Blackie said. "There's the park a few blocks over, but it's full of kids and cops and old women. You can't do a thing."* Students may find it easier to understand dialogue that mimics speech if they hear it read aloud with expression and intonation.

Activity Pair English language learners with students proficient in English. Have partners read the dialogue aloud and substitute familiar language. Encourage students to record unfamiliar words and substitutions in their vocabulary notebooks.

Additional Resources
English Language Learners Sourcebook, p. 55

Early New York Evening, 1954. Jane Freilicher. Oil on canvas, 51½ x 31¾ in. Private collection. Courtesy Tibor de Nagy Gallery, New York.

Viewing the painting: How does putting a few flowers on a window sill compare with T. J.'s need for plant life?

349

FYI

Marion County Marion County is one of sixty-seven counties in Alabama. It is situated in the northwestern corner of the state. Some cities in Marion County include Hamilton, Hackleburg, and Winfield.

VIEWING THE PAINTING

Born in Brooklyn in 1924, Jane Freilicher grew up, studied art, and worked in New York, remaining a realist through an era when most of her contemporaries embraced abstract expressionism. Her landscapes and cityscapes use or adapt real scenes to express personal emotion or vision.

Viewing Response *Some students might say that it expresses a similar but less intense need than T. J.'s.*

Historical Note

When men left the workforce to join the military during World War II, women were called on to enter their jobs. The character Rosie the Riveter was a part of this effort. A poster, a popular song, and later a *Saturday Evening Post* cover illustration by Norman Rockwell made Rosie a symbol of the six million women who worked in factories and other jobs during the war years.

Writing Minilesson

Describing a Character Explain that a writer can describe a person by showing how the person looks and acts. Read aloud the physical descriptions of T. J. on page 348 and have students identify the details that help them "see" T. J. Ask students to note also phrases that describe T. J.'s actions and reactions.

Activity Invite each student to write a short description of a favorite celebrity (athlete, movie actor, or musical performer) and to use words and phrases that show how the person looks and how the person acts toward his or her fans. **L2**

Additional Resources

Writer's Choice, Lesson 3.5

E Literary Elements

ALLUSION Point out to students that this section reveals T. J.'s connection to the earth. Encourage students to begin asking themselves why they think the title of the story is "Antaeus." *(In Greek mythology, as long as Antaeus stayed connected to the earth, he could not be defeated.)*

F Literary Elements

PLOT Help students recognize that this paragraph gives important information about the story's plot. Here T. J. first proposes the idea of creating a rooftop garden.

G Active Reading Strategies

PREDICT Ask students to predict what will happen next. Do students think the boys will carry out the plan? How might they do it? What obstacles might they encounter?

Antaeus Have students search the Internet to learn more about the mythical Antaeus. Students might also search for information about Hercules (or Heracles), the hero who slew Antaeus.

Teaching Support

"Naw," I said scornfully. "What do you want to grow something for? The folks can buy everything they need at the store."

E He looked at me again with that strange, unknowing look. "In Marion County," he said, "I had my own acre of cotton and my own acre of corn. It was mine to plant and make ever' year."

He sounded like it was something to be proud of, and in some obscure way it made the rest of us angry. Blackie said, "Who'd want to have their own acre of cotton and corn? That's just work. What can you do with an acre of cotton and corn?"

T. J. looked at him. "Well, you get part of the bale offen[2] your acre," he said seriously. "And I fed my acre of corn to my calf."

We didn't really know what he was talking about, so we were more puzzled than angry; otherwise, I guess, we'd have chased him off the roof and wouldn't let him be part of our gang. But he was strange and different, and we were all attracted by his stolid[3] sense of rightness and belonging, maybe by the strange softness of his voice contrasting our own tones of speech into harshness.

F He moved his foot against the black tar. "We could make our own field right here," he said softly, thoughtfully. "Come spring we could raise us what we want to—watermelons and garden truck[4] and no telling what all."

"You'd have to be a good farmer to make these tar roofs grow any watermelons," I said. We all laughed.

But T. J. looked serious. "We could haul us some dirt up here," he said. "And spread it out even and water it, and before you know it, we'd have us a crop in here." He looked at us intently. "Wouldn't that be fun?"

"They wouldn't let us," Blackie said quickly.

"I thought you said this was you-all's roof," T. J. said to me. "That you-all could do anything you wanted to up here."

"They've never bothered us," I said. I felt the idea beginning to catch fire in me. It was a big idea, and it took a while for it to sink in; but the more I thought about it, the better I liked it. "Say," I said to the gang. "He might have something there. Just make us a regular roof garden, with flowers and grass and trees and everything. And all ours, too," I said. "We wouldn't let anybody up here except the ones we wanted to."

"It'd take a while to grow trees," T. J. said quickly, but we weren't paying any attention to him. They were all talking about it suddenly, all excited with the idea after I'd put it in a way they could catch hold of it. Only rich people had roof gardens, we knew, and the idea of our own private domain[5] excited them. G

"We could bring it up in sacks and boxes," Blackie said. "We'd have to do it while the folks weren't paying any attention to us, for we'd have to come up to the

2. *[offen]* This is an informal way of saying *off of.* T. J. is describing the situation of a sharecropper, who farms land owned by someone else and shares the crop or the profit from its sale with the landowner.
3. *Stolid* means "firm and unemotional."
4. Here, *truck* refers to vegetables, especially those driven by truck from farms to markets.
5. A *domain* is the area under the rule or control of a person or group.

Vocabulary
obscure (əb skyoor′) *adj.* difficult to understand

350

MEETING INDIVIDUAL NEEDS — MULTIPLE MODES OF EXPRESSION

Linguistic Students with strong auditory abilities might benefit from hearing the story read aloud, especially the parts with dialogue.

Activity Invite students to read the story aloud in small groups. Have group members read the parts of the narrator and the other characters. Encourage students to read with expression—varying the tone, volume, and pitch of their voices. Remind students to notice the author's descriptions of how characters speak: *scornfully, seriously, softly, thoughtfully,* and *quickly.* Students might like to try to mimic T. J.'s accent. You may wish to have students make an audiotape of the story. **L2**

roof of our building and then cross over with it."

"Where could we get the dirt?" somebody said worriedly.

"Out of those vacant lots over close to school," Blackie said. "Nobody'd notice if we scraped it up."

I slapped T. J. on the shoulder. "Man, you had a wonderful idea," I said, and everybody grinned at him, remembering that he had started it. "Our own private roof garden."

He grinned back. "It'll be ourn," he said. "All ourn." Then he looked thoughtful again. "Maybe I can lay my hands on some cotton seed, too. You think we could raise us some cotton?"

H We'd started big projects before at one time or another, like any gang of kids, but they'd always petered out for lack of organization and direction. But this one didn't; somehow or other T. J. kept it going all through the winter months. He kept talking about the watermelons and the cotton we'd raise, come spring, and when even that wouldn't work, he'd switch around to my idea of flowers and grass and trees, though he was always honest enough to add that it'd take a while to get any trees started. He always had it on his mind, and he'd mention it in school, getting them lined up to carry dirt that afternoon, saying in a casual way that he reckoned a few more weeks ought to see the job through.

Our little area of private earth grew slowly. T. J. was smart enough to start in one corner of the building, heaping up the carried earth two or three feet thick so that we had an immediate result to look at, to contemplate with awe. Some of the evenings T. J. alone was carrying earth up to the building, the rest of the gang distracted by other enterprises[6] or interests, but T. J. kept plugging along on his own, and eventually we'd all come back to him again, and then our own little acre would grow more rapidly.

I He was careful about the kind of dirt he'd let us carry up there, and more than once he dumped a sandy load over the parapet into the areaway below because it wasn't good enough. He found out the kinds of earth in all the vacant lots for blocks around. He'd pick it up and feel it and smell it, frozen though it was sometimes, and then he'd say it was good growing soil or it wasn't worth anything, and we'd have to go on somewhere else.

J Thinking about it now, I don't see how he kept us at it. It was hard work, lugging paper sacks and boxes of dirt all the way up the stairs of our own building, keeping out of the way of the grown-ups so they wouldn't catch on to what we were doing. They probably wouldn't have cared, for they didn't pay much attention to us, but we wanted to keep it secret anyway. Then we had to go through the trap door to our roof, teeter over a plank to the fire escape, then climb two or three stories to the parapet, and drop them down onto the roof. All that for a small pile of earth that sometimes didn't seem worth the effort.

6. Here, *enterprises* means "projects or activities."

Vocabulary

awe (ô) *n.* wonder combined with respect

H Literary Elements

ALLUSION Ask students in what ways T. J. reminds them of the mythical Antaeus. *(T. J. has become powerful—a leader—in the group of boys. Also, he is very focused on his task, always thinking of the earth from which he draws his strength.)*

I Critical Thinking

DRAWING CONCLUSIONS Guide students in drawing conclusions from what they already know about T. J.'s agricultural background, experience, and knowledge and what they learn about him in this paragraph. You may wish to use the following model to illustrate the thinking process involved in drawing conclusions.

Model: From what I've read so far, I know T. J. planted corn and cotton in Alabama. Now I learn that T. J. has gone to vacant lots and examined the earth. T. J. can determine whether soil is good for growing things just by feeling and smelling it. I think T. J. knows many specialized things about farming and growing things.

J Active Reading Strategies

RESPOND Encourage students to connect with what the boys are doing. If they were a member of this group, how would they respond to the task of hauling dirt? How do they feel about what the boys are doing?

Life Skills Connection

Organizing Explain to students that T. J. thinks about what needs to be done in order to create the roof garden. He has to organize the tasks and the people to perform them.

Activity Have groups of students organize an activity or event, such as a birthday party for a friend or family member, a classroom game-show contest, or a classroom art exhibit. Suggest that students organize the event by listing the tasks involved and who would do them. Tell students to number the tasks in the order in which they should be completed. Follow up with a discussion of how organizing helped make the event successful. **L2**

K Literary Elements

ALLUSION Point out to students that the author devotes this entire paragraph to describing the earth. Ask students how this reminds them of the mythical Antaeus. *(The life-giving features of the earth give T. J. the strength to continue living in the North.)*

L Active Reading Strategies

REVIEW Suggest that students pause at this point in the story to summarize what has happened so far. Ask students to tell the story in their own words.

VIEWING THE PAINTING

Antonio Berni (1905–1981) helped found a neorealist movement in his native Argentina. Much of his later work expresses a strong social awareness.

Responding to the painting *Many of the boys in the painting may be similar in age to those in "Antaeus," and they share the story's urban setting. However, they and their interest in soccer contrast with the story's gang, who appear to have had no driving interest until T. J. inspired them to create a roof garden.*

New Chicago Athletic Club, 1937. Antonio Berni. Oil on canvas, 184.3 x 300.3 cm. Museum of Modern Art, New York.

Viewing the painting: In what ways do these boys seem similar to those in the story?

But T. J. kept the vision bright within us, his words shrewd and calculated[7] toward the fulfillment of his dream; and he worked harder than any of us. He seemed driven toward a goal that we couldn't see, a particular point in time that would be definitely marked by signs and wonders that only he could see.

K The laborious[8] earth just lay there during the cold months, inert and lifeless, the clods lumpy and cold under our feet when we walked over it. But one day it rained, and afterward there was a softness in the air, and the earth was live and giving again with moisture and warmth.

L That evening T. J. smelled the air, his nostrils dilating with the odor of the earth under his feet. "It's spring," he said, and there was a gladness rising in his voice that filled us all with the same feeling. "It's mighty late for it, but it's spring. I'd just about decided it wasn't never gonna get here at all."

We were all sniffing at the air, too, trying to smell it the way that T. J. did, and I can still remember the sweet odor of the earth under our feet. It was the first time in my life that spring and spring earth had meant anything to me. I looked at T. J. then, knowing in a faint way the hunger within M

7. T. J.'s words are clever and practical *(shrewd)* and reasoned out beforehand *(calculated).*
8. The earth is *laborious* in that getting it to the roof required difficulty and hard labor.

Vocabulary
inert (i nurt′) *adj.* without power to move or act

Teaching Support

Reading Minilesson

Identifying Main Idea and Supporting Details Sometimes listing the supporting details of a story in chart form can help students better understand the main idea.

Activity Draw the following chart on the board and fill in the main idea. Have students reread pages 351–353 and jot down the supporting details: *T. J. alone carried the dirt to the roof. T. J. chose the dirt carefully, feeling it and smelling it. T. J. smelled spring in the air. T. J. was a new Antaeus, preparing his own bed of strength. T. J. wanted to grow something, even if it was grass. T. J. taught the boys how to prepare the earth and sow the seeds.* **L2**

Main Idea	Details
T.J. is connected to the earth.	

Additional Resources

Reading Skills Practice Workbook

M him through the toilsome[9] winter months, knowing the dream that lay behind his plan. He was a new Antaeus, preparing his own bed of strength.

"Planting time," he said. "We'll have to find us some seed."

"What do we do?" Blackie said. "How do we do it?"

"First we'll have to break up the clods," T. J. said. "That won't be hard to do. Then we plant the seed, and after a while they come up. Then you got you a crop." He frowned. "But you ain't got it raised yet. You got to tend it and hoe it and take care of it, and all the time it's growing and growing, while you're awake and while you're asleep. Then you lay it by when it's growed and let it ripen, and then you got you a crop."

"There's these wholesale seed houses over on Sixth," I said. "We could probably swipe some grass seed over there."

T. J. looked at the earth. "You-all seem mighty set on raising some grass," he said. "I ain't never put no effort into that. I spent all my life trying not to raise grass."

"But it's pretty," Blackie said. "We could play on it and take sunbaths on it. Like having our own lawn. Lots of people got lawns."

"Well," T. J. said. He looked at the rest of us, hesitant for the first time. He kept on looking at us for a moment. "I did have it in mind to raise some corn and vegetables. But we'll plant grass."

He was smart. He knew where to give in. And I don't suppose it made any difference to him, really. He just wanted to grow something, even if it was grass.

"Of course," he said. "I do think we ought to plant a row of watermelons. They'd be mighty nice to eat while we was a-laying on that grass."

We all laughed. "All right," I said. "We'll plant us a row of watermelons."

N Things went very quickly then. Perhaps half the roof was covered with the earth, the half that wasn't broken by ventilators, and we swiped pocketfuls of grass seed from the open bins in the wholesale seed house, mingling among the buyers on Saturdays and during the school lunch hour. T. J. showed us how to prepare the earth, breaking up the clods and smoothing it and sowing the grass seed. It looked rich and black now with moisture, receiving of the seed, and it seemed that the grass sprang up overnight, pale green in the early spring.

We couldn't keep from looking at it, unable to believe that we had created this delicate growth. We looked at T. J. with understanding now, knowing the fulfillment of the plan he had carried alone within his mind. We had worked without full understanding of the task, but he had known all the time.

We found that we couldn't walk or play on the delicate blades, as we had expected to, but we didn't mind. It was enough just to look at it, to realize that it was the work of our own hands, and each evening, the whole gang was there, trying to measure the growth that had been achieved that day.

O One time a foot was placed on the plot of ground, one time only, Blackie stepping onto it with sudden bravado. Then he

9. The months are *toilsome* (a synonym for *laborious*) in that they are difficult and tiresome.

Vocabulary
bravado (brə vä′ dō) *n.* a false show of bravery

M Literary Elements

ALLUSION Discuss with students why the author directly compares T. J. to Antaeus here. *(Antaeus got his physical strength from the earth, and T. J., too, feels connected to the earth through his love of growing things. At this point in the story, we know that T. J.'s connection gives him spiritual strength.)*

N Active Reading Strategies

VISUALIZE Encourage students to use the details the author gives them to visualize the roof garden. Suggest that they ask themselves *How does this scene look? What are the characters doing? What expressions might they have on their faces?*

O Critical Thinking

SYNTHESIZING Ask students whether they think the boys have changed. What does this paragraph reveal about them? *(The boys have grown to respect the earth, to understand the satisfaction of growing things, and to appreciate the work involved. This is revealed by the shame Blackie feels and the silence of the other boys.)*

Meeting Individual Needs: SPECIAL NEEDS

Learning Disabled Presenting a story visually often helps students comprehend what they read. Combine this strategy with partner reading by pairing learning-disabled students with proficient readers.

Activity Have partners read the paragraph in the first column on page 353 in which T. J. explains the steps for growing a crop. Ask students to draw simple pictures that illustrate these steps. **L1**

Additional Resources

Inclusion Strategies

Active Reading Strategies

CONNECT Ask students to think of a time when they sacrificed something to get something else they wanted.

Author's Craft

CONFLICT Point out to students that the author reveals the conflict of the story slowly, making readers wonder what the adults will do about the rooftop garden.

Active Reading Strategies

PREDICT Encourage students to stop at this point in the story and predict what will happen next. What do they think the men are going to do? What do they think the boys are going to do?

looked at the crushed blades and there was shame in his face. He did not do it again. This was his grass, too, and not to be desecrated.[10] No one said anything, for it was not necessary.

T. J. had reserved a small section for watermelons, and he was still trying to find some seed for it. The wholesale house didn't have any watermelon seed, and we didn't know where we could lay our hands on them. T. J. shaped the earth into mounds, ready to receive them, three mounds lying in a straight line along the edge of the grass plot.

We had just about decided that we'd have to buy the seed if we were to get them. It was a violation of our principles, but we were anxious to get the watermelons started. Somewhere or other, T. J. got his hands on a seed catalog and brought it one evening to our roof garden.

"We can order them now," he said, showing us the catalog. "Look!"

We all crowded around, looking at the fat, green watermelons pictured in full color on the pages. Some of them were split open, showing the red, tempting meat, making our mouths water.

"Now we got to scrape up some seed money," T. J. said, looking at us. "I got a quarter. How much you-all got?"

We made up a couple of dollars among us and T. J. nodded his head. "That'll be more than enough. Now we got to decide what kind to get. I think them Kleckley Sweets. What do you-all think?"

He was going into esoteric[11] matters beyond our reach. We hadn't even known there were different kinds of melons. So we just nodded our heads and agreed that yes, we thought the Kleckley Sweets too.

"I'll order them tonight," T. J. said. "We ought to have them in a few days."

"What are you boys doing up here?" an adult voice said behind us.

It startled us, for no one had ever come up here before, in all the time we had been using the roof of the factory. We jerked around and saw three men standing near the trap door at the other end of the roof. They weren't policemen, or night watchmen, but three men in plump business suits, looking at us. They walked toward us.

"What are you boys doing up here?" the one in the middle said again.

We stood still, guilt heavy among us, levied[12] by the tone of voice, and looked at the three strangers.

The men stared at the grass flourishing behind us. "What's this?" the man said. "How did this get up here?"

"Sure is growing good, ain't it?" T. J. said conversationally. "We planted it."

The men kept looking at the grass as if they didn't believe it. It was a thick carpet over the earth now, a patch of deep greenness startling in the sterile[13] industrial surroundings.

10. To treat something holy with disrespect is to *desecrate* (des′ ə krāt′) it.

11. *Esoteric* (es′ ə ter′ ik) matters are beyond the understanding or knowledge of most people. T. J.'s knowledge of melons and farming seems esoteric to the other boys.

12. Here, *levied* means "enforced."

13. Most often, *sterile* (ster′ əl) is used to mean free from bacteria—like a surgeon's instruments. Here, the meaning is "having little or no plant life."

Vocabulary

principle (prin′ sə pəl) *n.* a basic law, truth, or belief; rule of personal conduct
flourishing (flur′ ish ing) *adj.* growing or developing successfully; doing very well

354

Teaching Support

Listening and Speaking Minilesson

Readers Theater The purpose of readers theater is to suggest characters, action, and scenery so that listeners can interpret, imagine, and visualize a story. The narrator speaks to the audience and may read or explain what happens between sections of dialogue. All participants read with text in hand.

Activity Invite students to read "Antaeus" as readers theater. Assign roles for all characters and for one or more narrators. Ask students who are not performing to act as dialogue coaches to help partners practice reading expressively. Have students first perform for classmates. Later students may wish to perform for other students of the same age. **L2**

"Yes, sir," T. J. said proudly. "We toted that earth up here and planted that grass." He fluttered the seed catalog. "And we're just fixing to plant us some watermelon."

The man looked at him then, his eyes strange and faraway. "What do you mean, putting this on the roof of my building?" he said. "Do you want to go to jail?"

T. J. looked shaken. The rest of us were silent, frightened by the authority of his voice. We had grown up aware of adult authority, of policemen and night watchmen and teachers, and this man sounded like all the others. But it was a new thing to T. J.

"Well, you wasn't using the roof," T. J. said. He paused a moment and added shrewdly, "So we just thought to pretty it up a little bit."

"And sag it so I'd have to rebuild it," the man said sharply. He started turning away, saying to another man beside him, "See that all that junk is shoveled off by tomorrow."

"Yes, sir," the man said.

T. J. started forward. "You can't do that," he said. "We toted it up here, and it's our earth. We planted it and raised it and toted it up here."

The man stared at him coldly. "But it's my building," he said. "It's to be shoveled off tomorrow."

"It's our earth," T. J. said desperately. "You ain't got no right!"

The men walked on without listening and descended clumsily through the trap door. T. J. stood looking after them, his body tense with anger, until they had disappeared. They wouldn't even argue with him, wouldn't let him defend his earth rights.

He turned to us. "We won't let 'em do it," he said fiercely. "We'll stay up here all day tomorrow and the day after that, and we won't let 'em do it."

We just looked at him. We knew that there was no stopping it.

He saw it in our faces, and his face wavered for a moment before he gripped it into determination. "They ain't got no right," he said. "It's our earth. It's our land. Can't nobody touch a man's own land."

We kept looking at him, listening to the words but knowing that it was no use. The adult world had descended on us even in our richest dream, and we knew there was no calculating the adult world, no fighting it, no winning against it.

We started moving slowly toward the parapet and the fire escape, avoiding a last look at the green beauty of the earth that T. J. had planted for us, had planted deeply in our minds as well as in our experience. We filed slowly over the edge and down the steps to the plank, T. J. coming last, and all of us could feel the weight of his grief behind us.

"Wait a minute," he said suddenly, his voice harsh with the effort of calling.

We stopped and turned, held by the tone of his voice, and looked up at him standing above us on the fire escape.

"We can't stop them?" he said, looking down at us, his face strange in the dusky light. "There ain't no way to stop 'em?"

"No," Blackie said with finality.[14] "They own the building."

We stood still for a moment, looking up at T. J., caught into inaction by the decision working in his face. He stared back at us, and his face was pale and mean in the poor light, with a bald nakedness in his skin like cripples have sometimes.

14. Blackie speaks with decisiveness *(finality)*; the issue is settled.

S Literary Elements

ALLUSION Encourage students to compare T. J.'s confrontation with the man to Antaeus's battle with Hercules. *(The man attempts to take away T. J.'s source of strength. Hercules lifted Antaeus from his source of strength—the earth—to defeat him.)*

T Active Reading Strategies

CONNECT Ask students how they would react if they were in T. J.'s position. Encourage students to finish this sentence: *If I were T. J., I would...*

U Critical Thinking

ANALYZING ARGUMENTS Invite students to analyze T. J.'s argument from both sides. Ask students to explain why both the owner of the building and T. J. think they are right. *(The owner feels he is right to destroy the roof garden because the boys are trespassing and the weight of the earth and the water might bring down the roof. T. J. feels the owner cannot destroy the garden because he does not own it.)*

Real-World Connection

Enriching Enterprises Invite students to research one of the enterprises mentioned in the Media Connection article: rooftop beekeeping, catfish harvesting, worm composting, goat-cheese making, or organic farming. Encourage students to add other possibilities, such as creating an empty-lot nature park or vegetable garden.

Activity Ask each student to summarize the research in outline form and use the outline to make a chart. The chart should include headings such as *How to Farm* and *Why Farm?* Students might like to name the enterprise "The T. J. Project" after the boy who shared his knowledge of farming with city kids. **L2**

V Literary Elements

ALLUSION How does T. J.'s reaction allude to Antaeus? *(Like Antaeus, T. J. fights a powerful opponent.)*

W Active Reading Strategies

EVALUATE Is T. J.'s action here a realistic solution to the problem?

X Active Reading Strategies

RESPOND Discuss how the story ends. Was it a surprise? Were students anticipating another ending?

Y Critical Thinking

INFERRING Why is it the boys never again climb to the roof? *(Their leader is gone. The rooftop holds memories of a dream that was realized and then shattered.)*

Thematic Focus

Where the Heart Is T. J.'s heart was not in his new home. He missed the old one. What would students miss if they moved away?

FINE ART TRANSPARENCY 3

You may wish to use *Fine Art Transparency 3* to enrich the discussion.

ASSESSMENT

Quick Checks, p. 32

V "They ain't gonna touch my earth," he said fiercely. "They ain't gonna lay a hand on it! Come on."

He turned around and started up the fire escape again, almost running against the effort of climbing. We followed more slowly, not knowing what he intended to do. W By the time we reached him, he had seized a board and thrust it into the soil, scooping it up and flinging it over the parapet into the areaway below. He straightened and looked at us.

"They can't touch it," he said. "I won't let 'em lay a dirty hand on it!"

We saw it then. He stooped to his labor again, and we followed, the gusts of his anger moving in frenzied labor among us as we scattered along the edge of earth, scooping it and throwing it over the parapet, destroying with anger the growth we had nurtured with such tender care. The soil carried so laboriously upward to the light and the sun cascaded swiftly into the dark areaway, the green blades of grass crumpled and twisted in the falling.

It took less time than you would think; the task of destruction is infinitely easier than that of creation. We stopped at the end, leaving only a scattering of loose soil, and when it was finally over, a stillness stood among the group and over the factory building. We looked down at the bare sterility of black tar, felt the harsh texture of it under the soles of our shoes, and the anger had gone out of us, leaving only a sore aching in our minds, like overstretched muscles.

T. J. stood for a moment, his breathing slowing from anger and effort, caught into the same contemplation of destruction as all of us. He stooped slowly, finally, and picked up a lonely blade of grass left trampled under our feet and put it between his teeth, tasting it, sucking the greenness out of it into his mouth. Then he started walking toward the fire escape, moving before any of us were ready to move, and disappeared over the edge.

We followed him, but he was already halfway down to the ground, going on past the board where we crossed over, climbing down into the areaway. We saw the last section swing down with his weight, and then he stood on the concrete below us, looking at the small pile of anonymous[15] earth scattered by our throwing. X Then he walked across the place where we could see him and disappeared toward the street without glancing back, without looking up to see us watching him.

They did not find him for two weeks.

Then the Nashville police caught him just outside the Nashville freight yards. He was walking along the railroad track, still heading South, still heading home.

Y As for us, who had no remembered home to call us, none of us ever again climbed the escapeway to the roof.

15. The word *anonymous* has two main meanings: "of unknown authorship or origin" and "lacking personality or special features." Here, the scattered soil looks as though it could have come from anywhere. Without grass growing on it, it's just ordinary dirt.

Vocabulary
nurture (nur′ chər) *v.* to care for and help grow

Teaching Support

Grammar and Language *Minilesson*

Adjectives Write the following sentence on the board, without underlining the adjectives: *We looked down at the bare sterility of black tar, felt the harsh texture of it under the soles of our shoes, and the anger had gone out of us, leaving only a sore aching in our minds, like over-stretched muscles.* Remind students that most adjectives come before the nouns they modify. Ask volunteers to find and underline the adjectives.

Activity Write the following nouns without the underlined adjectives on the board. Ask students to find the adjectives on page 356 that describe each noun: *dirty* hand (par. 3) ; *frenzied* labor; *tender* care; *green* blades (par. 4); *loose* soil; *harsh* texture (par. 5). **L2**

Additional Resources

- ***Grammar and Language Transparency 29***
- ***Grammar and Language Workbook,*** pp. 117–118
- ***Grammar and Composition Handbook,*** Lesson 5.1
- ***Writer's Choice,*** Lesson 12.1

Responding to Literature

PERSONAL RESPONSE

- Were you surprised by the outcome of the story? Explain why or why not.
- Look back at your notes from the **Reading Focus** on page 346. Do any of the characters in the story connect to the world of nature in ways you discussed? Explain.

Analyzing Literature

RECALL

1. Where does the narrator take T. J. to meet his gang?
2. What does T. J. convince the gang to do?
3. Why does the narrator believe that the roof garden project did not fade away like other big projects the boys had started? Explain.
4. What happens after the roof garden is discovered? According to the narrator, where was T. J. going when he was found?

Brackets connect questions that are paired to develop higher-level thinking skills.

INTERPRET

5. At the beginning, how does the gang react to T. J.? What do readers learn about T. J. from his reaction to them?
6. Why do the boys become so excited by the thought of a roof garden? Explain.
7. What does the narrator mean when he says, "We were all sniffing at the air, too, trying to smell it the way that T. J. did"?
8. Why does T. J. react as he does to the discovery of the garden?

EVALUATE AND CONNECT

9. In your opinion, what was the most important thing T. J. taught the members of the gang? Explain.
10. Theme Connection State the theme, or main idea, of "Antaeus" in a single sentence. Then write a paragraph telling how the theme of this story relates to the general theme of this group of selections.

LITERARY ELEMENTS

Allusion

An **allusion** is a reference to a well-known character, place, or situation from another work of literature, music, art, history, politics, or science. When readers recognize an allusion, it enriches their understanding of the piece of writing by making a connection between two characters, places, or situations.

1. Explain the connection between T. J. and the mythical Antaeus. Is T. J. a modern-day hero? Why or why not? Support your ideas with examples from the story.
2. In your opinion, in what ways is the story strengthened by the allusion to Greek mythology? Explain.

● See **Literary Terms Handbook,** p. R1.

Responding to the Selection

PERSONAL RESPONSE

- Some students may be surprised by the outcome, because the boys had worked so hard to create the garden.
- Most students will choose T. J. Some students might relate to the boys because their love of nature slowly develops.

Analyzing Literature

1. The narrator takes T. J. to the roof of the factory next to the building where he lives.
2. T. J. convinces the gang to haul dirt to the roof and plant a garden.
3. The narrator believes the project did not fade away because T. J. kept it going. He talked about it all the time and organized all the tasks.
4. The boys scoop up the soil and throw it off the roof. T. J. then disappears for two weeks. When found, T. J. is heading south, probably to Alabama.
5. At first, the gang thinks T. J. is strange and different. Readers learn that T. J. is proud, self-confident, and determined.
6. The boys become excited by the thought of a roof garden because the narrator points out that it will be their own private place. They know a roof garden is usually something only rich people have.
7. The boys have come to appreciate T. J.'s farming expertise and want to experience what T. J. feels when he sniffs the air—an appreciation of spring and the earth.
8. T. J. feels he has rights to the earth and the men have no right to destroy the garden.
9. Some students may feel the most important thing T. J. teaches the gang members is an appreciation of the earth and growing things. Others may feel he teaches them determination.
10. The theme of the story is that a person needs land of his or her own. Students' paragraphs should explain that T. J.'s heart is in Marion County, Alabama.

LITERARY ELEMENTS

1. The earth is a source of strength for both T. J. and the mythical Antaeus. T. J. is a modern-day hero because he works hard to create and tries to prevent the men from destroying the garden.
2. The allusion to Antaeus lends mythic power to the character T. J.

Additional Resources

Literary Elements Transparency 32

Literature and Writing

Writing About Literature

Students' reviews should

- explain why they think the character does or does not seem true to life
- give examples of how the character changes over the course of the story
- give examples of obstacles the character has to overcome to reach his goals

Creative Writing

Students' epilogues should

- describe clearly what action T. J. takes
- tell when and where events take place
- follow the writing style of the story

Extending Your Response

Literature Groups After students talk about T. J. and before they debate, encourage them to discuss the narrator's way of life in the city.

Learning for Life Before students begin writing, encourage them to describe the lot and the neighborhood where it's located.

Interdisciplinary Activity Provide garden books and magazines as well as gardening articles from local newspapers for students' research.

Literature and Writing

Writing About Literature

Character Review Write a paragraph or two reviewing either T. J. or the narrator. In your opinion, does this person seem true to life? Why or why not? How does the character change over the course of the story? What obstacles does the character have to overcome to reach his goals? Support your opinions with examples and quotations from the story.

Creative Writing

Epilogue What do you think happens to T. J. after the final scene in the story? An **epilogue** is a brief concluding section to a novel, a story, or a poem. Write an epilogue to "Antaeus." Your epilogue might take place weeks, months, or many years after the end of the story.

Extending Your Response

Literature Groups

Home Is Where the Heart Is Talk about T. J.'s connection to nature. What does the earth represent to him? Why does he need to create a garden in the city? Do you think T. J. could ever be happy living in a city? Debate the question: Can country people and city people ever be happy living in the other's environment? Support your ideas with examples from the story and details from your own experience.

Learning for Life

Community Garden Proposal Is there a vacant lot near your school or somewhere in your town or city? Write a proposal to convince public officials to allow you to transform the vacant lot into a community garden. Describe how important a garden would be to the neighborhood. Outline a plan to complete the project, using students and other volunteers to do the work.

Interdisciplinary Activity

Art/Science Work with classmates to create a community garden in honor of T. J.'s vision. Find out which flowers or vegetables will thrive in your location and decide which ones to include in the garden. Decide on the size of the garden, the location of the plants within the garden, and additional items such as paths, benches, and lights. Make a mural of the garden to display on a classroom wall.

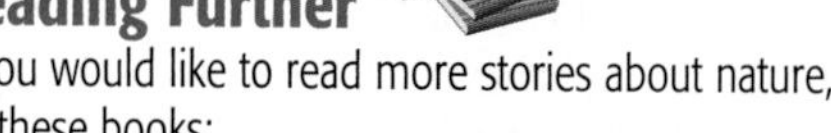

Reading Further

If you would like to read more stories about nature, try these books:

A Day No Pigs Would Die by Robert Newton Peck

The Island Keeper by Harry Mazer

Save your work for your portfolio.

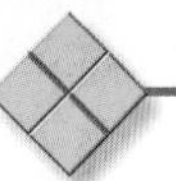

Skill Minilessons

Reteach · Review

GRAMMAR AND LANGUAGE • COMMAS IN COMPOUND SENTENCES

If the main clauses in a compound sentence are connected by a conjunction (*and, but,* or *or*), a comma should come before the conjunction.

Example: The soil was heavy, **but** the boys carried it up to the rooftop nevertheless.

PRACTICE Review "Antaeus" to find and copy two examples of compound sentences containing commas. Then write two compound sentences of your own, using commas and conjunctions correctly.

● For more about commas, see **Language Handbook**, pp. R37–R38.

READING AND THINKING • STEREOTYPE

A **stereotype** is an oversimplified or generalized opinion or prejudice about a particular group or issue. For example, someone who thinks that all Texans are either ranchers or oil drillers is using a stereotype. **Bias**—favoritism toward or against something—may lead people to use stereotypes. Stereotypes in writing can show a writer's bias. In fiction, they can show a character's bias.

PRACTICE Identify the following stereotypes from "Antaeus." Look back at the story if you need help.

1. In "Antaeus," the narrator says that there was "nothing sissy" about T. J. "except his voice." What stereotype does that comment demonstrate?
2. What stereotype do you think the man who ordered the boys off his roof had about teenagers?
3. What stereotype did the gang members probably have about grown-ups?

● For more about stereotypes, see **Literary Terms Handbook**, p. R10.

VOCABULARY • ANALOGIES: LEVELS OF INTENSITY

Analogies compare the relationships between things or ideas. One kind of analogy deals with levels of intensity. That is, the words in each pair have similar meanings, but one word is stronger, more intense than the other.

angry : furious :: happy : overjoyed

Angry and *furious* are similar in meaning, and so are *happy* and *overjoyed.* But in each pair, the second word describes a feeling that is more intense than the first word suggests. Someone who is extremely *angry* is *furious,* just as someone who is extremely *happy* is *overjoyed.*

To finish an analogy, think of the relationship between the first pair of words. Then find another pair of words that have the same relationship.

PRACTICE Complete each analogy.

1. surviving : flourishing ::
   a. thankful : grateful
   b. sad : lonely
   c. cautious : careless
   d. large : old
   e. damp : soaked
2. well : robust ::
   a. wrong : mistaken
   b. weak : small
   c. pretty : beautiful
   d. poetic : musical
   e. muscular : healthy

● For more about analogies, see **Communications Skills Handbook**, p. R67.

Skill Minilessons

GRAMMAR AND LANGUAGE
COMMAS IN COMPOUND SENTENCES

Examples of compound sentences:
- "His voice was resolute with the knowledge of his rightness, and for a moment no one had anything to say."
- "We had worked without full understanding of the task, but he had known all the time."

READING AND THINKING
STEREOTYPE

1. The narrator assumes that all boys should be tough and that a southern accent is not tough.
2. The man probably assumed that all teenagers are troublemakers.
3. The gang members probably believed that all grown-ups exercise their authority over younger people without real cause.

VOCABULARY
ANALOGIES: LEVELS OF INTENSITY

1. e
2. c

Additional Resources

- ***Grammar and Language Workbook,*** pp. 257–258
- ***Grammar and Composition Handbook,*** Lesson 13.3
- ***Writer's Choice,*** Lessons 20.3
- ***Reading Skills Practice Workbook***
- ***Vocabulary Practice,*** p. 20

ASSESSMENT

- ***Quick Checks,*** p. 32
- ***Selection and Theme Assessment,*** pp. 57–58
- ***Performance Assessment,*** p. 31
- ***Testmaker: ExamView Pro***
- ***Interactive Tutor: Self-Assessment***

Before Reading

Objectives

- To read and analyze a short story and a poem about home
- To identify the themes in a short story and a poem
- To write a paragraph or two explaining what the dialogue reveals about the characters

Skills

Reading/Thinking: Evaluating; Identifying Main Idea and Supporting Details; Inferring; Drawing Conclusions
Writing: One-Act Play
Vocabulary: Words Used in Unusual Ways
Grammar/Language: Possessive Nouns
Life Skills: Writing Persuasive Memos
Collaboration: Literature Groups

Motivating → STUDENTS

Selection Focus Transparency 33: Read aloud John Howard Payne's quotation about home and ask students to discuss what they think Payne means.

Reading Focus: As an extension of the Reading Focus, have students work with the same partners to create song lyrics about home.

Before You Read

Home and *the 1st*

MEET GWENDOLYN BROOKS

Gwendolyn Brooks's advice to young poets was "Tell your truth. Don't try to sugar it up." In 1950 Brooks became the first African American author to win the Pulitzer Prize for Poetry.

Gwendolyn Brooks was born in 1917 and died in 2000. Maud Martha, *the novel from which "Home" is taken, was published in 1953.*

MEET LUCILLE CLIFTON

Lucille Clifton now lives in Columbia, Maryland, where she is Distinguished Professor of Humanities at Saint Mary's College. Clifton is a former poet laureate of Maryland and has received numerous awards and prizes for her poetry.

Lucille Clifton was born in 1936. "the 1st" comes from Good Woman: Poems and a Memoir 1969–1980, *published in 1987.*

READING FOCUS

When you hear the word *home,* what do you think about? What are some things that make a home important to the people who live there?

Think/Pair/Share

Jot down your thoughts and feelings about the word *home.* Then share your ideas with a partner.

Setting a Purpose

As you read, look for what makes their home important to the characters in these selections.

Children Dancing, 1948. Robert Gwathmey (1903–1988). Oil on canvas, 32 x 40 in. The Butler Institute of American Art, Youngstown, OH.

VOCABULARY PREVIEW

obstinate (ob′ stə nit) *adj.* stubborn; difficult to overcome or control; p. 361

emphatic (em fat′ ik) *adj.* strongly expressive; forceful; p. 361

possessively (pə zes′ iv lē) *adv.* in a way that shows ownership or control; p. 361

staccato (stə kä′ tō) *adj.* made of short, sharp sounds or movements; p. 362

casually (kazh′ o͞o əl lē) *adv.* in a relaxed, informal way; p. 362

360 THEME 4

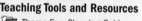

RESOURCE MANAGER

Teaching Tools and Resources
- Theme Four Planning Guide
- Literature Groups Sourcebook
- Presentation Plus! CD-ROM

Essential Lesson Support

Lesson-Specific Instruction
- Selection Focus Transparency 33
- Literary Elements Transparency 33
- Active Reading Guide,* p. 33
- Selection Vocabulary Practice, p. 21

Assessment
- Selection Quick Checks,* p. 33
- Sel. and Theme Assmt., pp. 59–60
- Testmaker: ExamView Pro
- Performance Assessment, p. 32

Systematic Language Instruction
- Gr. and Comp. Hbk., L. 7.6

English Language Learners
- ELL Sourcebook, p. 56
- Spanish Summaries, p. 33
- Audio Library*
- English, Yes!

Spec. Needs/Strat. Interven.
- Interactive Rdg. Sbk., pp. T136–T138
- Interactive Rdg. Wkbk., p. 61
- Inclusion Strat. Sbk., pp. 19–20, 37–38
- Audio Library*

* Also available in Spanish

Home

Gwendolyn Brooks

A What had been wanted was this always, this always to last, the talking softly on this porch, with the snake plant in the jardiniere[1] in the southwest corner, and the obstinate slip from Aunt Eppie's magnificent Michigan fern at the left side of the friendly door. Mama, Maud Martha and Helen rocked slowly in their rocking chairs, and looked at the late afternoon light on the lawn, and at the emphatic iron of the fence and at the poplar tree. These things might soon be theirs no longer. Those shafts and pools of light, the tree, the graceful iron, might soon be viewed possessively by different eyes.

Woman Holding a Jug, 1932–1933. James A. Porter. Oil on canvas. Carl Van Vechten Gallery of Fine Arts, Fisk University, Nashville, TN.

B Papa was to have gone that noon, during his lunch hour, to the office of the Home Owners' Loan. If he had not succeeded in getting another extension, they would be leaving this house in which they had lived for more than fourteen years. There was little hope. The Home Owners' Loan was hard. They sat, making their plans.

C "We'll be moving into a nice flat[2] somewhere," said Mama. "Somewhere on South Park, or Michigan, or in Washington Park Court." Those flats, as the girls and Mama knew well, were burdens on wages twice the size of Papa's. This was not mentioned now.

"They're much prettier than this old house," said Helen. "I have friends I'd just as soon not bring here. And I have other friends that wouldn't come down this far for anything, unless they were in a taxi."

Yesterday, Maud Martha would have attacked her. Tomorrow she might. Today she said nothing. She merely gazed at a little hopping robin in the tree, her tree, and tried to keep the fronts of her eyes dry.

"Well, I do know," said Mama, turning her hands over and over, "that I've been getting tireder and tireder of doing that

1. A *jardiniere* (järd′ ən ēr′) is an ornamental pot or plant stand.

2. Here, *flat* means "apartment."

Vocabulary
obstinate (ob′ stə nit) *adj.* stubborn; difficult to overcome or control
emphatic (em fat′ ik) *adj.* strongly expressive; forceful
possessively (pə zes′ iv lē) *adv.* in a way that shows ownership or control

Reading the Selection

A Active Reading Strategies

PREDICT Ask students to use the title and clues from the first paragraph to predict what this story might be about.

VOCABULARY If you haven't previewed the selection vocabulary with students, stop and remind them to use context clues to unlock the meanings of new vocabulary words.

B Literary Elements

THEME Remind students that the theme of a story is the primary message that is conveyed by the plot, setting, and characters. Encourage students to identify the theme as they read the story.

C Critical Thinking

EVALUATING Does Mama really believe they will move into a nice flat? Why does she say they will? *(She doesn't believe it. They are afraid they will have to move, so she is trying to make them feel better.)*

Additional Resources

- ***Active Reading Guide,*** p. 33
- ***Audio Library***
- ***Spanish Audio Library***
- ***Spanish Summaries,*** p. 33

Teaching Support

Reading *Minilesson*

Identifying Main Idea and Supporting Details Point out that in the second paragraph of "Home," the narrator explains the situation. The rest of the story is a series of conversations that show how each family member feels about what is taking place.

Activity Have students answer the following questions to identify the main idea and supporting details of this story:

- What is the main idea of the story?
- What does Mama say about moving?
- Does Helen agree or disagree?
- How does Maud Martha feel?
- What do they all really feel about the house? **L2**

Additional Resources

Reading Skills Practice Workbook

CONNECTING TO OTHER SELECTIONS
For a teaching strategy that connects "Home" to "Beware of the Dog," see the ***Theme Six Planning Guide.***

D **Literary Elements**

THEME What is the theme in Maud Martha's thoughts and feelings? *(Home is very important, and there is no other place like it.)*

E **Literary Elements**

THEME Ask students what other theme Mama expresses when she says, "And he'll have us...wherever"? *(Being together is the most important part of having a home.)*

F **Critical Thinking**

INFERRING Ask students to infer what Mama and the family are feeling when they see Papa coming home. You may wish to share the following model to illustrate the thinking process involved in inferring.

Model: At first the family talks about how those "flats" were much prettier than the house they live in. After reading that they want to jump over the fence to "shake the truth out of" Papa's collar, I know that they want to keep their house.

LITERATURE & HUMANITIES

Have students examine the quilt *Tar Beach* in *Introducing Art*, page 238, and discuss how the positive aspects of home are contrasted with a sense of dissatisfaction. Ask how this contrast relates to the story.

firing. From October to April, there's firing to be done."

"But lately we've been helping, Harry and I," said Maud Martha. "And sometimes in March and April and in October, and even in November, we could build a little fire in the fireplace. Sometimes the weather was just right for that."

She knew, from the way they looked at her, that this had been a mistake. They did not want to cry.

D But she felt that the little line of white, somewhat ridged with smoked purple, and all that cream-shot saffron,[3] would never drift across any western sky except that in back of this house. The rain would drum with as sweet a dullness nowhere but here. The birds on South Park were mechanical birds, no better than the poor caught canaries in those "rich" women's sun parlors.

"It's just going to kill Papa!" burst out Maud Martha. "He loves this house! He *lives* for this house!"

"He lives for us," said Helen. "It's us he loves. He wouldn't want the house, except for us."

E "And he'll have us," added Mama, "wherever."

"You know," Helen sighed, "if you want to know the truth, this is a relief. If this hadn't come up, we would have gone on, just dragged on, hanging out here forever."

3. The orange-yellow color *(saffron)* is streaked or mixed *(shot)* with a cream color.

"It might," allowed Mama, "be an act of God. God may just have reached down, and picked up the reins."

"Yes," Maud Martha cracked in, "that's what you always say—that God knows best."

Her mother looked at her quickly, decided the statement was not suspect, looked away.

Helen saw Papa coming. "There's Papa," said Helen.

They could not tell a thing from the way Papa was walking. It was that same dear little staccato walk, one shoulder down, then the other, then repeat, and repeat. They watched his progress. He passed the Kennedys', he passed the vacant lot, he passed Mrs. Blakemore's. They wanted to hurl themselves over the fence, into the street, and shake the truth out of his collar. He opened his gate—the gate—and still his stride and face told them nothing. F

"Hello," he said.

Mama got up and followed him through the front door. The girls knew better than to go in too.

Presently Mama's head emerged. Her eyes were lamps turned on.

"It's all right," she exclaimed. "He got it. It's all over. Everything is all right."

The door slammed shut. Mama's footsteps hurried away.

"I think," said Helen, rocking rapidly, "I think I'll give a party. I haven't given a party since I was eleven. I'd like some of my friends to just casually see that we're homeowners."

Vocabulary

staccato (stə kä′ tō) *adj.* made of short, sharp sounds or movements
casually (kazh′ o͞o əl lē) *adv.* in a relaxed, informal way

Teaching Support

Grammar and Language *Minilesson*

Possessive Nouns Remind students that a possessive noun names who or what owns or has something. Explain that possessive nouns can be common or proper nouns, singular or plural, and that they are formed in one of two ways. To form the possessive of most nouns, add an apostrophe and s *('s)*. To form the possessive of plural nouns already ending in s, add only an apostrophe *(')*. Direct students' attention to the possessive nouns on page 362 *(women's; Kennedys'; Mrs. Blakemore's).*

Activity Have students choose ten nouns from "Home" and write the possessive form of each. When students have written the possessive noun forms, ask them to write each one in a sentence. **L2**

Additional Resources

- ***Grammar and Language Transparency 30***
- ***Grammar and Language Workbook,*** pp. 65–66
- ***Grammar and Composition Handbook,*** Lesson 2.3
- ***Writer's Choice,*** Lesson 9.3

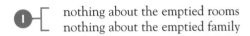

the 1st

Lucille Clifton

what i remember about that day
is boxes stacked across the walk
and couch springs curling through the air
and drawers and tables balanced on the curb
and us, hollering,
leaping up and around
happy to have a playground;

nothing about the emptied rooms
nothing about the emptied family

The Apartment, 1943. Jacob Lawrence. Gouache on paper, 21.25 x 29.25 in. The Hunter Museum of American Art, Chattanooga, TN.

G Author's Craft

AUTHOR'S PURPOSE Ask students why they think Lucille Clifton chose to call this poem "the 1st." *(The 1st refers to the first day of the month, which is the date on which many leases begin and end.)*

H Active Reading Strategies

QUESTION Ask students what playground is being referred to in the poem. *(The children are playing among the family's furniture and belongings, which are outside waiting to be moved.)*

I Critical Thinking

DRAWING CONCLUSIONS Ask students what they think the last two lines of the poem mean. *(The speaker only remembers playing, not the sadness of moving.)*

Thematic Focus

Where the Heart Is Invite students to talk about the relationship between home and family, focusing on the value of stability. At the same time, discuss how a family can provide an important home for the heart, even when people must move from place to place or be separated.

ASSESSMENT

Quick Checks, p. 33

MEETING INDIVIDUAL NEEDS — ENGLISH LANGUAGE LEARNERS

Understanding Poetry Explain to English language learners that the poem "the 1st" is essentially a single sentence, even though the first word is not capitalized and there is no end punctuation.

Activity Draw the following cluster diagram on the chalkboard and help students identify the important details. **COLLAB. LEARN.**

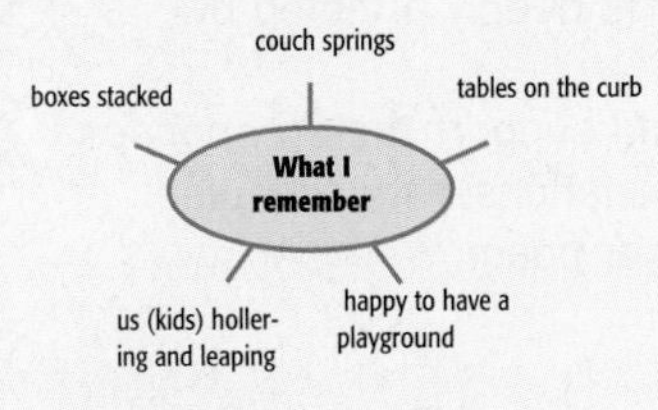
couch springs
boxes stacked
tables on the curb
What I remember
us (kids) hollering and leaping
happy to have a playground

Additional Resources

English Language Learners Sourcebook, p. 56

Responding to the Selection

PERSONAL RESPONSE

Students should offer clear explanations for their responses. Most students will probably agree with the importance of home expressed in both works. Some may realize that children can play even in the midst of a difficult situation.

Analyzing Literature

1. They are not able to pay their mortgage on time. Near the end of the story, Papa gets an extension of time to pay the mortgage.
2. The speaker is recalling a moving day. She remembers the happiness of playing but not the sadness of leaving.
3. The family loves their home and wants to keep it. For example: "It's just going to kill Papa!"; "He loves this house! He *lives* for this house!"
4. One emotion is light and playful; the other is dark and sad. The repetition of the last two lines emphasizes the finality of the move.
5. The short story form allows a writer to include dialogue and detailed description in order to explain more about what is going on. The poem form is more concise and allows a writer the chance to say a great deal with relatively few words and images.
6. The reader realizes that the speakers are not telling the truth when they act as if they want to move.
7. It is common for people who are afraid of something to act as if they aren't. Children often play with each other even when something is happening that is sad or difficult.
8. Most students will probably be able to relate to the hardships and fears that can accompany leaving a home.
9. In both cases, the home seems to be a strong focus for the entire family. Clifton refers to "the emptied family," implying that the family is deeply affected by moving.
10. Students should support their responses with clear explanations and examples from the story or poem.

Responding to Literature

PERSONAL RESPONSE

- What is your response to these selections? Explain.
- Review your notes from the **Reading Focus** on page 360. How do your thoughts and feelings about the word *home* compare with the thoughts and feelings of the characters in these selections?

Analyzing Literature

RECALL

1. What problem does the family in "Home" face? Near the end of the story, what news does Papa bring home?
2. In the poem "the 1st," what event is the speaker recalling from her childhood? What does she remember about her feelings? Explain.

Brackets connect questions that are paired to develop higher-level thinking skills.

INTERPRET

3. How does the family in "Home" feel about their home? Support your opinion with examples from the story.
4. What are the two conflicting images and emotions in the poem "the 1st"? Why, do you think, are the last two lines almost the same? Explain.

EVALUATE AND CONNECT

5. Both of these selections deal with the subject of moving and loss. How do the forms—a short story and a poem—allow the writers to deal differently with the same topic? Explain.
6. How does the dialogue between the characters in "Home" contribute to the story's suspense? Give examples.
7. In what ways do these selections seem true to life? Explain.
8. How do you feel about what happens to these families?
9. **Theme Connection** Why is a place to call home important to the characters in these selections? Explain.
10. Which of these selections do you prefer? Why? Use quotations from the selections to support your ideas.

LITERARY ELEMENTS

Theme

A **theme** is the message that is expressed in a work of literature. A story, a novel, a play, or a poem may have more than one theme, but one message will usually be the strongest. A theme may be stated directly, but more often it is revealed gradually, through the words, thoughts, and actions of the characters. Since readers usually need to *infer* the theme—that is, figure it out through reasoning—it is always open to interpretation. A strong piece of literature may mean different things to different people.

1. What is the theme of the story "Home"? Use examples from the story to support your ideas.
2. Summarize the central theme of the poem "the 1st."

● See **Literary Terms Handbook,** p. R11.

LITERARY ELEMENTS

1. Possible answer: Having a home is very special, and it is frightening to be forced to move. "It's all right.... He got it. It's all over. Everything is all right."
2. The speaker remembers moving day as a day of play. She has forgotten about the pain of leaving her home and the effect moving had on her family.

Additional Resources

Literary Elements Transparency 33

Extending Your Response

Writing About Literature

Dialogue Dialogue is conversation between characters. Readers learn a great deal of information through the dialogue in a story. Write a paragraph or two explaining what you learned from the dialogue in "Home" about the thoughts and feelings of the different characters.

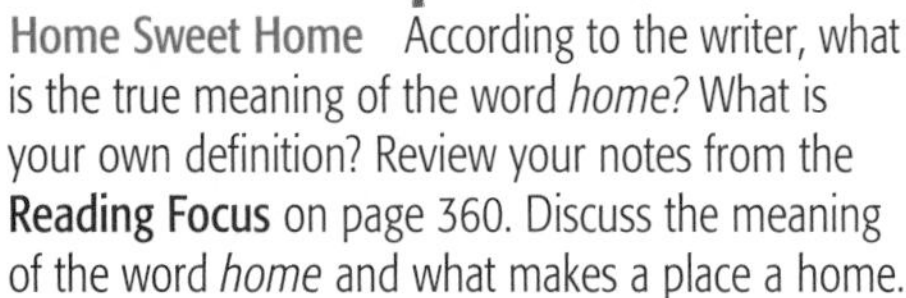

Creative Writing

One-Act Play With a partner, write a one-act play based on "the 1st." Think about the poem's central images and the different emotions they evoke. Make up any details you wish, including dialogue for the characters and stage directions that describe the setting and action. If you wish, perform your play. Use props to make the dramatization seem real.

Literature Groups

Home Sweet Home According to the writer, what is the true meaning of the word *home?* What is your own definition? Review your notes from the **Reading Focus** on page 360. Discuss the meaning of the word *home* and what makes a place a home.

Learning for Life

A Persuasive Memo Imagine you are Papa in the story "Home." The Home Owners' Loan Association has asked you to write them a memo explaining why you need another extension on your loan, how you intend to repay the loan, and what the house means to you and your family. Be persuasive!

Save your work for your portfolio.

Skill Minilesson

Reteach · Review

VOCABULARY • WORDS USED IN UNUSUAL WAYS

In "Home," Gwendolyn Brooks calls the iron of a fence *emphatic.* A fence can't really be emphatic. Brooks uses a figure of speech to suggest that the iron of the fence is strong and not flexible. This literary device, called **personification,** gives human qualities such as actions or feelings to an object, an idea, or an animal.

PRACTICE To complete each sentence, think about what is suggested by the underlined word.

1. A tired roof is probably
   a. sagging c. flat
   b. leaking
2. A bold flower probably has
   a. thorns c. bright colors
   b. a sweet smell
3. A heavy sky probably has many
   a. stars c. puffy clouds
   b. dark clouds
4. A forgiving rug doesn't
   a. look new c. show stains easily
   b. fit the room
5. An undecided path probably
   a. twists c. goes uphill
   b. is narrow

Extending Your Response

Writing About Literature

Students' paragraphs should
- explain what they learned from the dialogue in "Home"
- give examples to support their ideas

Creative Writing

Students' plays should
- be about the central images, emotions, and theme of the poem
- include made-up details and dialogue among the children

Literature Groups Most students will understand that the writer expresses her sense of *home* in these lines: *"He lives for us," said Helen. "It's us he loves. He wouldn't want the house, except for us."* It is the people in the family who really create a home.

Learning for Life As students write their memos, encourage them to focus on what the house means to them and their family. Stress that they should be both businesslike and persuasive.

Skill Minilesson

VOCABULARY
• **WORDS USED IN UNUSUAL WAYS**

1. a 2. c 3. b 4. c 5. a

Additional Resources

Vocabulary Practice, p. 21

ASSESSMENT

- ***Quick Checks,*** p. 33
- ***Selection and Theme Assessment,*** p. 59–60
- ***Performance Assessment,*** p. 32
- ***Testmaker: ExamView Pro***
- ***Interactive Tutor: Self-Assessment***

Objective

- To make connections with characters or situations in a story

Teaching Strategies

Ask students to talk about characters from fiction, television, movies, or real life with whom they identify. Discuss the kinds of characters students look for in the books they read or programs they watch. Encourage students to focus on what they can learn about themselves by connecting with a fictitious character.

Activity

1. Students may choose a character from a short story in the theme, such as T. J. in "Antaeus." This character may be familiar to students who have felt out of place at times.
2. Students may find similarities in the experiences or emotional aspects of the character and themselves but find differences in concrete circumstances, such as where and when the character lived.
3. Responses may include learning that people tend to react in similar ways to basic human experiences, such as kindness, cruelty, happiness, and sadness.

Additional Resources

Reading Skills Practice Workbook

Teaching Support

Making Connections

When you get involved in a story, you may identify with one or more of its characters. Skillful readers put themselves in a story by **making connections** between their own life experiences and the experiences of the characters. Thinking about these connections while you read makes a story more meaningful.

Read the following passage from "Home" by Gwendolyn Brooks. As you read, try to connect the situation in the story with a situation in your own life.

> "We'll be moving into a nice flat somewhere," said Mama. "Somewhere on South Park, or Michigan, or in Washington Park Court." Those flats, as the girls and Mama knew well, were burdens on wages twice the size of Papa's. This was not mentioned now.
>
> "They're much prettier than this old house," said Helen. "I have friends I'd just as soon not bring here. And I have other friends that wouldn't come down this far for anything, unless they were in a taxi."

Were you able to make a connection between your life and the characters and situation described in this excerpt? Perhaps you remembered a time when a relative or friend tried to comfort you after you did not make the team or the cast of the school play. Or, perhaps you recalled a time when you helped a friend see the brighter side of a difficult situation. Connecting your personal experiences with the actions, emotions, motivations, and situations of the characters in a story makes fiction come alive.

- For more about reading strategies, see **Reading Handbook,** pp. R73–R102.

ACTIVITY

Reread "Antaeus," by Borden Deal, or another short story of your choosing. Then answer the following questions.

1. Which character or event in the story reminded you of a person or situation in your own life?
2. How are the two characters or events alike? How are they different?
3. How did connecting the people and experiences in your own life to those in the story help you better understand the characters' emotions and motivations?

MEETING INDIVIDUAL NEEDS — SPECIAL NEEDS

Learning Disabled Students may find it easier to make connections with characters in the stories they read if the stories are read aloud first and difficult vocabulary is previewed.

Activity Read the passage from "Home" aloud to students. Have them fill in a chart to identify the characters, describe the scene, and explain the circumstances. Ask students to list words or phrases that describe how the characters feel. **L2**

Additional Resources

Inclusion Strategies

Before You Read

The Teacher Who Changed My Life

MEET NICHOLAS GAGE

When Nicholas Gage first came to America, he was nine years old and did not speak English. Thirty years later, when he left America for Greece, Gage was a top investigative reporter for *The New York Times*. He returned to Lia, the tiny remote village of his birth, to find his mother's murderers. The best-selling book he wrote about his search was named after his mother, *Eleni*. This autobiographical essay begins in 1953, when the author was a fourteen-year-old refugee from war-torn Greece.

Nicholas Gage was born in 1939. This story is part of his memoir, A Place for Us, *published in 1989.*

READING FOCUS

How can one person positively influence another's life? What people do you think of when it comes to making a difference?

Journal

Write a paragraph in your journal about a person who has been a big influence in your life.

Setting a Purpose

Read about one person who made a difference in a young person's life.

BUILDING BACKGROUND

Did You Know? Between 1940 and 1949, Greeks fought in two wars—World War II and a civil war. During this time, 600,000 Greeks were killed, including Nicholas Gage's mother. The civil war was mostly fought in the northern mountain villages, where Greek Communist guerrillas, who had fought the Germans in World War II, plotted to take over the Greek government. Their policy was to abduct over twenty-eight thousand Greek children and send them to Albania, Yugoslavia, and Bulgaria to grow up as Communists.

VOCABULARY PREVIEW

portly (pôrt′ lē) *adj.* having a stout but dignified appearance; p. 369
authoritarian (ə thôr′ ə tār′ ē ən) *adj.* having or expecting complete obedience to authority; p. 369
ultimately (ul′ tə mit lē) *adv.* in the end; finally; p. 369
perspective (pər spek′ tiv) *n.* point of view; p. 370
impoverished (im pov′ ər isht) *adj.* reduced to poverty; made very poor; p. 370
mortified (môr′ tə fīd′) *adj.* greatly embarrassed; p. 370
tact (takt) *n.* the ability to handle people or situations without causing displeasure or resentment; p. 370
ecstatic (ek stat′ ik) *adj.* overwhelmed with joy; p. 371
avidly (av′ id lē) *adv.* eagerly; enthusiastically; p. 372
consolation (kon′ sə lā′ shən) *n.* a comfort; p. 373

Before Reading

Objectives

- To read and analyze a personal narrative about a war refugee
- To identify the main idea of an essay
- To write an analysis of an author's strategies

Skills

Reading/Thinking: Inferring; Drawing Conclusions; Activating Prior Knowledge
Writing: Autobiographical Essay
Vocabulary: The Suffix *-arian*
Grammar/Language: Adverbs
Listening/Speaking: Storyteller
Collaboration: Literature Groups

Motivating STUDENTS

Literature Launchers: "Nicholas Gage and His Mentor"

Videodisc Side A, Segment 11 

Also available in VHS.

Selection Focus Transparency 34: Have students view and discuss the photograph of a village in Greece.

Reading Focus: As an extension of the Reading Focus, have pairs of students use precise language and sensory imagery to discuss how the people they wrote about made a difference in their lives.

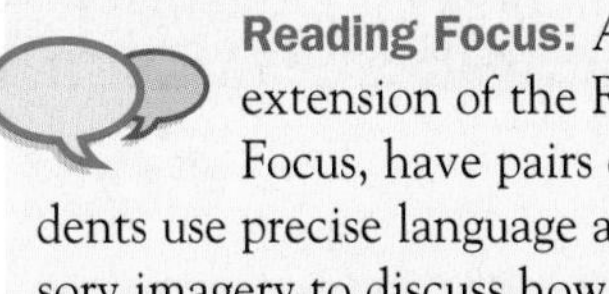

RESOURCE MANAGER

Teaching Tools and Resources
- Theme Four Planning Guide
- Literature Groups Sourcebook
- Presentation Plus! CD-ROM

Essential Lesson Support

Lesson-Specific Instruction
- Selection Focus Transparency 34
- Literary Elements Transparency 34
- Active Reading Guide,* p. 34
- Selection Vocabulary Practice, p. 22

Assessment
- Selection Quick Checks,* p. 34
- Sel. and Theme Assmt., pp. 61–62
- Testmaker: ExamView Pro
- Performance Assessment, p. 33

Systematic Language Instruction
- Gr. and Comp. Hbk., L. 7.7
- Vocabulary Power, Lesson 17
- Spelling Power, Lesson 15

English Language Learners
- ELL Sourcebook, p. 57
- Spanish Summaries, p. 34
- Audio Library*
- English, Yes!

Spec. Needs/Strat. Interven.
- Interactive Rdg. Sbk., pp. T138–T141
- Interactive Rdg. Wkbk., pp. 62–63
- Inclusion Strat. Sbk., pp. 39–40
- Audio Library*

* Also available in Spanish

Reading the Selection

SUMMARY

Nicholas Gage, a best-selling author, remembers the tough but caring teacher who introduced him to literature and the power of the written word. He describes coming to the United States as a young war refugee from Greece and meeting the teacher who instilled pride in his heritage and inspired him to write the story of his mother's tragic death in Greece.

Spanish Summaries, p. 34

A Active Reading Strategies

PREDICT Ask students if, by reading the title alone, they can predict what the author will learn from the teacher. Suggest that students revisit their predictions as they read to verify or to revise them.

VOCABULARY If you haven't previewed the selection vocabulary with students, stop and remind them to use context clues to unlock the meanings of new vocabulary words.

Additional Resources

- ***Active Reading Guide,*** p. 34
- ***Audio Library***
- ***Spanish Audio Library***

The Teacher Who Changed My Life

A

Nicholas Gage

The grown-up Nicholas and his former teacher, Marjorie Hurd Rabidou.

The person who set the course of my life in the new land I entered as a young war refugee—who, in fact, nearly dragged me onto the path that would bring all the blessings I've received in America—was a salty-tongued,[1] no-nonsense schoolteacher named Marjorie Hurd. When I entered her classroom in 1953, I had been to six schools in five years, starting in the Greek village where I was born in 1939.

When I stepped off a ship in New York Harbor on a gray March day in 1949, I was an undersized 9-year-old in short pants who had lost his mother and was coming to live with the father he didn't know. My mother, Eleni Gatzoyiannis, had been imprisoned, tortured, and shot B

1. A *salty-tongued* person speaks in a sharp, witty, and often sarcastic way.

Teaching Support

CONNECTING TO OTHER SELECTIONS

COMPARING selections

This selection is compared with "How I Learned English" on page 377. A lesson for teaching a comparison of the two selections appears on page 380.

The chart at the right shows three ways to connect "The Teacher Who Changed My Life" to other selections in this book.

For specific teaching strategies, see the ***Theme Four Planning Guide.***

Connection	Title
Life Skills: Teaching and Mentoring	→ "The Bird Like No Other," p. 473
Thematic: Growing Up	→ from *Barrio Boy,* p. 67
Literary: Memoir	→ from *Beyond the Limits,* p. 281

by Communist guerrillas[2] for sending me and three of my four sisters to freedom. She died so that her children could go to their father in the United States.

The portly, bald, well-dressed man who met me and my sisters seemed a foreign, authoritarian figure. I secretly resented him for not getting the whole family out of Greece early enough to save my mother. Ultimately, I would grow to love him and appreciate how he dealt with becoming a single parent at the age of 56, but at first our relationship was prickly,[3] full of hostility.

As Father drove us to our new home—a tenement in Worcester,[4] Mass.—and pointed out the huge brick building that would be our first school in America, I clutched my Greek notebooks from the refugee camp, hoping that my few years of schooling would impress my teachers in this cold, crowded country. They didn't. When my father led me and my 11-year-old sister to Greendale Elementary School, the grim-faced Yankee principal put the two of us in a class for the mentally retarded. There was no facility in those days for non-English-speaking children.

By the time I met Marjorie Hurd four years later, I had learned English, been placed in a normal, graded class and had even been chosen for the college preparatory track in the Worcester public school system. I was 13 years old when our father moved us yet again, and I entered Chandler Junior High shortly after the beginning of seventh grade. I found myself surrounded by richer, smarter and better-dressed classmates who looked askance[5] at my strange clothes and heavy accent. Shortly after I arrived, we were told to select a hobby to pursue during "club hour" on Fridays. The idea of hobbies and clubs made no sense to my immigrant ears, but I decided to follow the prettiest girl in my class—the blue-eyed daughter of the local Lutheran minister. She led me through the door marked "Newspaper Club" and into the presence of Miss Hurd, the newspaper adviser and English teacher who would become my mentor and my muse.[6]

A formidable, solidly built woman with salt-and-pepper hair, a steely eye and a flat Boston accent, Miss Hurd had no patience with layabouts. "What are all you goof-offs doing here?" she bellowed at the would-be journalists. "This is the Newspaper Club! We're going to put out a *newspaper*. So if there's anybody in this room who doesn't like work, I suggest you go across to the Glee Club now, because you're going to work your tails off here!"

I was soon under Miss Hurd's spell. She did indeed teach us to put out a newspaper, skills I honed during my next 25 years as a journalist. Soon I asked the principal

2. *Guerrillas* (gə ril′ əz) are members of small, organized forces, usually made up of volunteers who are not soldiers in a regular army.
3. Here, *prickly* means "difficult; troublesome."
4. *[Worcester]* This city's founders brought its oddly pronounced name with them from England. It's pronounced as if it were spelled *Wooster,* with an *o* sound as in *wood.*
5. The expression *looked askance* (ə skans′) means "viewed with suspicion or disapproval."
6. A *mentor* is a wise and trusted counselor, and a *muse* is a source of artistic inspiration.

Vocabulary

portly (pôrt′ lē) *adj.* having a stout but dignified appearance
authoritarian (ə thôr′ ə tār′ ē ən) *adj.* having or expecting complete obedience to authority
ultimately (ul′ tə mit lē) *adv.* in the end; finally

B Active Reading Strategies

RESPOND Encourage students to respond to the author's remembrance of his mother. What would students like to ask him? How do they feel when they read this somber paragraph? *(Students will probably want to ask the author what happened. They will probably say that they are saddened by such tragic circumstances.)*

C Active Reading Strategies

EVALUATE Ask students to evaluate the author's use of details and choice of words. Have students give examples of Gage's description of his father and his feelings toward him. *(Gage describes his father as portly, well-dressed, authoritarian, resented, loved, and appreciated.)*

D Author's Craft

CHARACTERIZATION: *Direct Characterization* Have students identify the direct statement about Miss Hurd. *(He describes her as a formidable woman who had no patience with lazy people.)* Ask how Gage reveals her personality with dialogue. *("What are all you goof-offs doing here?" she bellowed. "...you're going to work your tails off here!")*

MEETING INDIVIDUAL NEEDS — ENGLISH LANGUAGE LEARNERS

Connecting Ask English language learners whether they can relate to events in Nick's life. Have students make up conversations for the people in each scene. Students may choose
- Miss Hurd's talking with Nick about the writing assignment
- Nick's saying good-bye to his mother
- Classmates' telling Nick how they feel about his family's story

Activity Help students prepare by discussing the thoughts and feelings of each person in the scenes. Encourage students to talk about how they would feel if they were in the same position. **L2**

Additional Resources

English Language Learners Sourcebook, p. 57

to transfer me to her English class as well. There, she drilled us on grammar until I finally began to understand the logic and structure of the English language. She assigned stories for us to read and discuss; not tales of heroes, like the Greek myths I knew, but stories of underdogs—poor people, even immigrants, who seemed ordinary until a crisis drove them to do something extraordinary. She also introduced us to the literary wealth[7] of Greece—giving me a new perspective on my war-ravaged, impoverished homeland. I began to be proud of my origins.

E One day, after discussing how writers should write about what they know, she assigned us to compose an essay from our own experience. Fixing me with a stern look, she added, "Nick, I want you to write about what happened to your family in Greece." I had been trying to put those painful memories behind me and left the assignment until the last moment. Then, on a warm spring afternoon, I sat in my room with a yellow pad and pencil and stared out the window at the buds on the trees. I wrote that the coming of spring always reminded me of the last time I said goodbye to my mother on a green and gold day in 1948.

I kept writing, one line after another, telling how the Communist guerrillas occupied our village, took our home and food, how my mother started planning our escape when she learned that the children were to be sent to re-education camps behind the Iron Curtain[8] and how, at the last moment, she couldn't escape with us because the guerrillas sent her with a group of women to thresh wheat in a distant village. She promised she would try to get away on her own, she told me to be brave and hung a silver cross around my neck, and then she kissed me. I watched the line of women being led down into the ravine and up the other side, until they disappeared around the bend—my mother a tiny brown figure at the end who stopped for an instant to raise her hand in one last farewell. F

I wrote about our nighttime escape down the mountain, across the minefields, and into the lines of the Nationalist soldiers, who sent us to a refugee camp. It was there that we learned of our mother's execution. I felt very lucky to have come to America, I concluded, but every year, the coming of spring made me feel sad because it reminded me of the last time I saw my mother.

I handed in the essay, hoping never to see it again, but Miss Hurd had it published in the school paper. This mortified me at first, until I saw that my classmates reacted with sympathy and tact to my family's story. Without telling me, Miss

7. Greece's *literary wealth,* dating from about 750 to 300 B.C., includes plays, poems, and other texts that greatly influenced the development of European and American civilization.

8. During the years following World War II, the *Iron Curtain* was an imaginary barrier separating the former Soviet Union and its allies from the non-Communist world.

Vocabulary

perspective (pər spek′ tiv) *n.* point of view
impoverished (im pov′ ər isht) *adj.* reduced to poverty; made very poor
mortified (môr′ tə fīd′) *adj.* greatly embarrassed
tact (takt) *n.* the ability to handle people or situations without causing displeasure or resentment

E Critical Thinking

INFERRING Ask students to discuss why Miss Hurd asked Nick to write about what happened to his family in Greece. If you wish, share the following model to illustrate the thinking process involved in inferring.

Model: I think Miss Hurd knew that Nick had painful memories of leaving Greece. Because of the author's affection for her, I know that under her tough personality was a caring person. This makes me believe she thought writing about his painful experience would help Nick come to terms with his grief.

FYI

The Greek Civil War started in 1946. After three years of fighting, the democratically elected government, with aid from the United States, finally defeated the Communist rebels.

F Active Reading Strategies

REVIEW Have students summarize the story young Nick told in his essay. *(To escape from the Communist guerrillas, Nick's family left their village in Greece. They traveled in the mountains at night, crossed minefields, and reached a refugee camp. Nick's mother could not leave with them because the guerrillas had sent her to work in distant fields.)*

Teaching Support

Reading Minilesson

Activating Prior Knowledge Write the phrase *salt-and-pepper hair* on the board. Explore the phrase's meaning by using this think-aloud model: *I know salt is white and pepper is black, so I think salt-and-pepper hair must mean black hair that has white hair in it.* Some students may find it easier to understand the meanings of certain words, phrases, and expressions if they break them into parts.

Activity Have students work in small groups to reread the selection, looking for phrases or expressions whose meanings are unclear. Suggest that they list them as they read so that they can create glossaries of the terms. **L2**

Additional Resources

Reading Skills Practice Workbook

Hurd also submitted the essay to a contest sponsored by the Freedoms Foundation at Valley Forge, Pa., and it won a medal. The Worcester paper wrote about the award and quoted my essay at length. My father, by then a "five-and-dime-store chef," as the paper described him, was ecstatic with pride, and the Worcester Greek community celebrated the honor to one of its own.

For the first time I began to understand the power of the written word. A secret ambition took root in me. One day, I vowed, I would go back to Greece, find out the details of my mother's death and write about her life, so her grandchildren would know of her courage. Perhaps I would even track down the men who killed her and write of their crimes. Fulfilling that ambition would take me 30 years.

Meanwhile, I followed the literary path that Miss Hurd had so forcefully set me on. After junior high, I became the editor of my school paper at Classical High School and got a part-time job at the Worcester *Telegram and Gazette*. Although my father could only give me $50 and encouragement toward a college education, I managed to finance four years at Boston University with scholarships and part-time jobs in journalism. During my last year of college, an article I wrote about a friend who had died in the Philippines—the first person to lose his life working for the Peace Corps[9]—led to my winning the Hearst Award for College

9. A *scholarship* is money given to help a student continue his or her education. The *Peace Corps* is a U.S. program that sends volunteers to help people in poorer countries to improve their living conditions. It was begun by President Kennedy in 1961.

Vocabulary
ecstatic (ek stat′ ik) *adj.* overwhelmed with joy

Nicholas Gage's third-grade class. Nicholas is in the back row, second from the left.

Viewing the photograph: Compare this class photo with the one on page 69. How did students change between the early 1900s and the middle 1900s? How do today's students differ from both earlier groups?

G Literary Elements

MAIN IDEA Ask students to tell the main idea of the paragraph in their own words and give details that support it. *(The main idea is that Gage continued to write and went on to study journalism because of Miss Hurd's influence. Supporting details include the following: he was editor of his high school paper; he worked for the town's newspaper; he studied journalism at college; he won an award for his writing.)*

VIEWING THE PHOTOGRAPH

Viewing Response *Students should note that children's clothing styles changed between the early 1900s and mid-1900s and that the students in the later photo seem more at ease posing for a picture. They should also mention that Gage's schoolmates appear to be a more homogeneous group than the multi-ethnic Lincoln School class.*

MEETING INDIVIDUAL NEEDS — MULTIPLE MODES OF EXPRESSION

Linguistic To help students with strong writing abilities connect with the author and his experiences, encourage them to express their reactions to the selection in writing.

Activity Encourage students to read the memoir and determine what it is about the character or the author's use of language that affects them. Invite them to respond to their reading with a variety of writing forms, such as journal entries, poetry, character sketches, letters, or reviews. After reading these pages, for example, students might write character sketches of Nick's mother, journal entries about Nick's escape, or poems about a proud father. **L2**

Active Reading Strategies

RESPOND Encourage students to think about the author's description of his father here. How does it make them feel about Gage's relationship with his father? What does it tell them about his father? About Nicholas Gage?

Critical Thinking

INFERRING Ask students what they can infer about the author's view of his relationship with Miss Hurd, given this comparison to his mother. *(It seems that he views Miss Hurd as a mother figure—someone who shares the pride of his accomplishments with his father.)*

Literary Elements

MAIN IDEA Ask students what they learn about Mrs. Rabidou in this paragraph. What is the main idea? *(She continued to make a difference in the lives of many students.)*

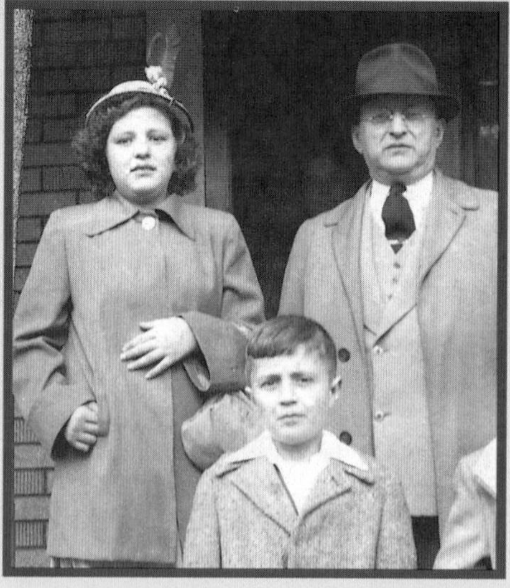
Young Nicholas with his sister and his father in 1950.

Journalism. And the plaque was given to me in the White House by President John F. Kennedy.

For a refugee who had never seen a motorized vehicle or indoor plumbing until he was 9, this was an unimaginable honor. When the Worcester paper ran a picture of me standing next to President Kennedy, my father rushed out to buy a new suit in order to be properly dressed to receive the congratulations of the Worcester Greeks. He clipped out the photograph, had it laminated in plastic and carried it in his breast pocket for the rest of his life to show everyone he met. I found the much-worn photo in his pocket on the day he died 20 years later.

In our isolated Greek village, my mother had bribed a cousin to teach her to read, for girls were not supposed to attend school beyond a certain age. She had always dreamed of her children receiving an education. She couldn't be there when I graduated from Boston University, but the person who came with my father and shared our joy was my former teacher, Marjorie Hurd. We celebrated not only my bachelor's degree but also the scholarships that paid my way to Columbia's Graduate School[10] of Journalism. There, I met the woman who would eventually become my wife. At our wedding and at the baptisms of our three children, Marjorie Hurd was always there, dancing alongside the Greeks.

By then, she was Mrs. Rabidou, for she had married a widower when she was in her early 40s. That didn't distract her from her vocation[11] of introducing young minds to English literature, however. She taught for a total of 41 years and continually would make a "project" of some balky student in whom she spied a spark of potential.[12] Often these were students from the most troubled homes, yet she would alternately bully and charm each one with her own special brand of tough love until the spark caught fire. She retired in 1981 at the age of 62 but still avidly follows the lives and careers of former students while overseeing her adult stepchildren and driving her husband on camping trips to New Hampshire.

10. Upon completing four years (usually) of study, college students receive an honor called a *bachelor's degree.* Some then go on to *graduate schools* for more advanced training.
11. Besides referring to an occupation, the word *vocation* can mean the particular work one feels called to do or is especially suited for.
12. A *balky* student is one who tends to stop short and refuse to go on. A student with *potential* has qualities or abilities capable of being developed.

Vocabulary
avidly (av′ id lē) *adv.* eagerly; enthusiastically

Teaching Support

Grammar and Language *Minilesson*

Adverbs Write this on the board, underlining the adverbs: *"I suggest you go across to the Glee Club now, because you're going to work your tails off here!"* Remind students that an adverb modifies a verb, an adjective, or another adverb. When it modifies a verb, it tells how, when, or where the action is done. Invite volunteers to identify the verb each adverb modifies *(across/go, now/go, off/work, here/work)* and what it tells about the action *(across/where, now/when, off/how, here/where).*

Activity Have students find a sentence in the selection with an adverb and identify the word it modifies. If it modifies a verb, ask them to identify whether the adverb tells how, when, or where the action was done. **L2**

Additional Resources

- ***Grammar and Language Transparency 31***
- ***Grammar and Language Workbook,*** pp. 127–128
- ***Grammar and Composition Handbook,*** Lessons 6.1, 6.2
- ***Writer's Choice,*** Lesson 12.6

Miss Hurd was one of the first to call me on Dec. 10, 1987, when President Reagan, in his television address after the summit meeting with Gorbachev, told the nation that Eleni Gatzoyiannis' dying cry, "My children!" had helped inspire him to seek an arms agreement[13] "for all the children of the world."

"I can't imagine a better monument for your mother," Miss Hurd said with an uncharacteristic catch in her voice.

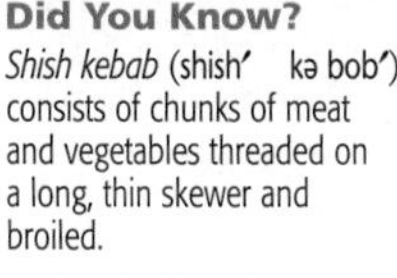

Did You Know?
Shish kebab (shish′ kə bob′) consists of chunks of meat and vegetables threaded on a long, thin skewer and broiled.

Although a bad hip makes it impossible for her to join in the Greek dancing, Marjorie Hurd Rabidou is still an honored and enthusiastic guest at all our family celebrations, including my 50th birthday picnic last summer, where the shish kebab was cooked on spits, clarinets and *bouzoukis* wailed, and costumed dancers led the guests in a serpentine[14] line around our colonial farmhouse, only 20 minutes from my first home in Worcester.

My sisters and I felt an aching void because my father was not there to lead the line, balancing a glass of wine on his head while he danced, the way he did at every celebration during his 92 years. But Miss Hurd was there, surveying the scene with quiet satisfaction. Although my parents are gone, her presence was a consolation, because I owe her so much.

This is truly the land of opportunity, and I would have enjoyed its bounty even if I hadn't walked into Miss Hurd's classroom in 1953. But she was the one who directed my grief and pain into writing, and if it weren't for her I wouldn't have become an investigative reporter and foreign correspondent, recorded the story of my mother's life and death in *Eleni* and now my father's story in *A Place for Us*, which is also a testament to the country that took us in. She was the catalyst[15] that sent me into journalism and indirectly caused all the good things that came after. But Miss Hurd would probably deny this emphatically. **K**

A few years ago, I answered the telephone and heard my former teacher's voice telling me, in that won't-take-no-for-an-answer tone of hers, that she had decided I was to write and deliver the eulogy[16] at her funeral. I agreed (she didn't leave me any choice), but that's one assignment I never want to do. I hope, Miss Hurd, that you'll accept this remembrance instead. **L**

13. In 1987 Mikhail *Gorbachev* was the leader of the Soviet Union. An *arms agreement* is a treaty in which nations agree to limits on certain kinds of weapons.
14. A *bouzouki* (boo zo͞o′ kē) is a stringed instrument similar to a mandolin; a *serpentine* (sur′ pən tēn′) line winds around, like a snake's body.
15. Here, the *testament* is a statement of gratitude and respect. A *catalyst* is one who stirs to action.
16. At a funeral, the *eulogy* (ū′ lə jē) is a speech praising the dead.

Vocabulary
consolation (kon′ sə lā′ shən) *n.* a comfort

K Literary Elements

MAIN IDEA Help students recognize the main idea of this paragraph by studying the details and determining how they relate to Miss Hurd. *(Miss Hurd was responsible for directing Gage to a career as a writer, which led to many of his achievements in life.)*

L Critical Thinking

DRAWING CONCLUSIONS Encourage students to share their feelings about the author and his relationship with Miss Hurd. Ask students how they feel about her request and Gage's response. *(Students will feel that they have mutual respect for each other. Gage had to accept the honor of delivering her eulogy but was saddened by the thought of having to do it at all.)*

Thematic Focus

Where the Heart Is Encourage students to discuss where the heart of young Nicholas Gage was. Have students talk about why his heart was in his homeland, in his father's house, and in school. Ask students for examples from the selection to support their responses.

ASSESSMENT

Quick Checks, p. 34

Real-World Connection

Refugees Provide students with magazine or newspaper articles about refugees who have come to the United States from a variety of countries.

Activity Arrange students in small groups and have each group discuss an article. Ask students to answer such questions as *From which country did the people come? Why did they leave their homelands? How are they adjusting to life in a new country? How are the children doing in school? What provisions have the schools made for non-English-speaking students?* Invite students to use the information and their own knowledge to generate a list of additional, unanswered questions for further research. **L2**

Responding to the Selection

PERSONAL RESPONSE

Some students may express thoughts about a teacher who has made a difference in their lives. Some students may react to the description of young Nicholas leaving his mother with feelings of sadness and horror.

Analyzing Literature

1. Non-English speakers were put into classes for the mentally retarded.
2. The author fell under Miss Hurd's spell of tough love and became a devoted, hardworking pupil.
3. The author was trying to forget what happened to his family during the Greek civil war.
4. Miss Hurd came to family events and supported him as a parent would.
5. The author's first school experience in America prompted him to learn English, move out of the class for the mentally retarded, and qualify for college preparatory classes.
6. Writing the essay inspired Nicholas Gage to become a professional writer and to return to Greece to research a book about his mother.
7. He earned undergraduate and graduate degrees. He won awards for his writing and met the president of the United States.
8. She was an understanding and caring person when he needed one the most. She remained in his life, expressing pride in his accomplishments.
9. A *mentor* is a trusted person who offers advice and direction. A *muse* is someone who inspires. Miss Hurd directed Gage toward a literary career and inspired him to write about his life.
10. Some students may think it is easier because schools provide for non-English speakers and communities offer outreach activities for refugees. Other students may think it is harder because not all refugees will meet a teacher like Miss Hurd.

Active Reading and Critical Thinking

Responding to Literature

PERSONAL RESPONSE

- What reactions and thoughts did you experience while reading this story?

Analyzing Literature

RECALL

1. According to the selection, how did the Worcester, Massachusetts, school system handle the education of non-English speakers in the 1950s?
2. Describe the "spell" that the author fell under as one of Miss Hurd's pupils.
3. What painful memories was the author trying to forget?
4. Give two examples of ways Miss Hurd became a part of the author's family.

Brackets connect questions that are paired to develop higher-level thinking skills.

INTERPRET

5. How did the author's first school experience in America shape him?
6. Miss Hurd assigned Nicholas Gage to write an essay about what happened to his family in Greece. What effect did that assignment have on the rest of his life?
7. In what ways did Gage live up to his mother's dreams for him?
8. In your opinion, why did Miss Hurd become such an important presence in Nicholas Gage's family life?

EVALUATE AND CONNECT

9. Theme Connection In Gage's **narrative,** he refers to his teacher as "my mentor and my muse." What do those words mean? Why do you think Gage chose those words?
10. There are children in this country today who are war refugees like Nicholas Gage. How do you imagine they are adjusting to life in America? Do you think it would be easier or harder than it was for Gage? Give reasons for your opinions.

LITERARY ELEMENTS

Main Idea

The most important idea expressed in a paragraph or an essay is called the **main idea.** The main idea in a paragraph may or may not be directly stated in a topic sentence. Sometimes the reader has to study all the details in the paragraph and make an educated guess about its main idea. The main idea of an essay might be stated in the title or in an introductory or concluding paragraph.

1. Does the title of this selection express the main idea? Support your opinion.
2. Imagine you wanted to tell someone about the essay "The Teacher Who Changed My Life." Write one or two sentences that express the main idea of the selection.

● See **Literary Terms Handbook,** p. R6.

LITERARY ELEMENTS

1. The title expresses the main idea. Gage states in the introductory paragraph, "The person who set the course of my life...was a salty-tongued, no-nonsense schoolteacher named Marjorie Hurd."
2. The writer Nicholas Gage credits one of his schoolteachers for his literary successes.

Additional Resources

 ***Literary Elements Transparency 34***

Extending Your Response

Writing About Literature

Author's Purpose In the midst of describing his teacher, Nicholas Gage summarizes a book he wrote about his mother's tragic death. Write a paragraph analyzing why the author chose to include this information. What emotional impact did he hope to create?

Creative Writing

Autobiographical Essay Develop your journal entry for the **Reading Focus** on page 367 into a personal narrative.

Listening and Speaking

Storyteller In ancient Greece, storytellers taught the Greek people their history and legends. Play the part of a modern storyteller and tell the story of someone who has had an influence on you or on society.

Literature Groups

Award Winner! Imagine that you and the other members of your group are among Miss Hurd's students. A national award is being presented to "The Teacher Who Changed My Life," and you have nominated Miss Hurd. With your group, develop a list of her qualities that would convince the judges to vote for Miss Hurd. Make your presentation to the class.

Reading Further

If you would like to read more about young people and their families caught in political turmoil, try these books:

The Endless Steppe by Esther Hautzig

My Brother Sam Is Dead by James Lincoln Collier

Farewell to Manzanar by Jeanne W. and James Houston

Save your work for your portfolio.

Skill Minilesson

Reteach • Review

VOCABULARY • THE SUFFIX *-arian*

Young Nicholas Gage's first impression of his father was of someone who seemed *authoritarian,* someone who believes in the use of *authority.* The suffix *-arian* means "one who or one that." It may mean "one who believes in," "one who supports," or "one who works in or with."

Understanding the suffix *-arian* may help you with some new words. For example, if you know that *utility* means "usefulness," you can figure out that a *utilitarian* kitchen contains things that are definitely useful.

PRACTICE Look carefully at the familiar part of each word on the left to match it to its meaning.

One who works with, believes in, or supports:

1. disciplinarian — a. people's right to be free
2. libertarian — b. system of rules and correction
3. grammarian — c. same treatment and rights for all
4. humanitarian — d. welfare of all people
5. equalitarian — e. rules for speaking and writing

Extending Your Response

Writing About Literature

Students' paragraphs should
- explain why they think Gage includes details about his mother's death
- give examples of emotional reactions to this information, including their own

Creative Writing

Students' personal narratives should
- characterize their subjects
- give examples of the person's influence
- follow the style of a personal narrative

Listening and Speaking

Encourage students to practice telling the story with expression, varying the volume and tone of voices and using gestures.

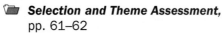

Literature Groups Suggest that students review the text for brainstorming ideas. Students might present a character sketch.

Skill Minilesson

VOCABULARY

• THE SUFFIX *-arian*

1. b **2.** a **3.** e **4.** d **5.** c

Additional Resources

Vocabulary Practice, p. 22

ASSESSMENT

- ***Quick Checks,*** p. 34
- ***Selection and Theme Assessment,*** pp. 61–62
- ***Performance Assessment,*** p. 33
- ***Testmaker: ExamView Pro***
- ***Interactive Tutor: Self-Assessment***

Before Reading

Objectives

- To read and analyze a poem about a young boy's introduction to English
- To identify setting in a poem
- To write a poem or a prose paragraph from another character's point of view

Skills

Reading/Thinking: Drawing Conclusions; Sequence of Events
Vocabulary: Context Clues
Collaboration: Literature Groups

Motivating → STUDENTS

Selection Focus Transparency 35: Explain to students as they view and discuss the photograph of a cricket game that even though cricket might seem unfamiliar to them, it remains popular in Great Britain and has become even more popular in India, which was formerly a British colony.

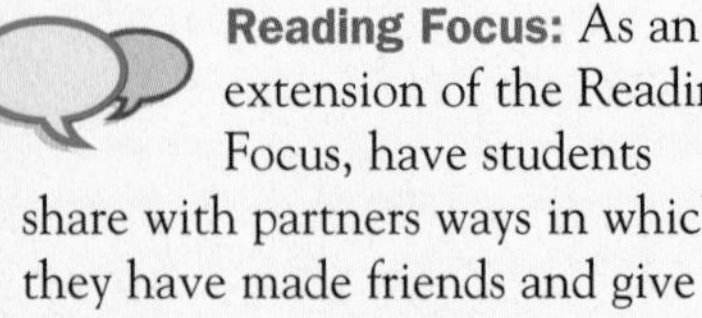

Reading Focus: As an extension of the Reading Focus, have students share with partners ways in which they have made friends and give details about their experiences.

Before You Read

How I Learned English

MEET GREGORY DJANIKIAN

Gregory Djanikian (jə nik′ ē ən) is an American who was born and raised in Egypt. Djanikian is an award-winning poet who has published several collections of his poems. He is currently the Director of Creative Writing at the University of Pennsylvania.

Gregory Djanikian was born in 1949. "How I Learned English" was published in 1987.

READING FOCUS

Imagine moving to a new school in a new country. How would you meet friends?

Chart It!

Work with your classmates to make a chart that shows the different ways you have made your current friends.

At School	In Sports or Clubs	At a Friend's House

Setting a Purpose

Read this poem to discover what bonds connect people.

BUILDING BACKGROUND

The Time and Place The poem is set sometime in the later half of the twentieth century in the town of Williamsport, Pennsylvania.

Did You Know? Baseball, or an English variation of the modern game called "rounders," has been around since the 1700s. In 1845 an amateur New York City player suggested a few changes in the game rules, including tagging the runner out. The new rules were adopted by many amateur New York City club teams, and the game's popularity grew. During the Civil War, soldiers from New York and New Jersey taught the game to other Americans.

Union Prisoners at Salisbury, N.C., 1863. Otto Boetticher. Colored stone lithograph with buff and blue tints, 21 x 37½ in. Lithographer: Sarony, Major and Knapp. The Stokes Collection. The New York Public Library.

376 THEME 4

RESOURCE MANAGER

Teaching Tools and Resources
- Theme Four Planning Guide
- Literature Groups Sourcebook
- Presentation Plus! CD-ROM

Essential Lesson Support

Lesson-Specific Instruction
- Selection Focus Transparency 35
- Literary Elements Transparency 35
- Active Reading Guide,* p. 35

Assessment
- Selection Quick Checks,* p. 35
- Sel. and Theme Assmt., pp. 61–62

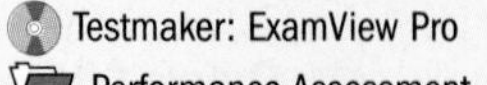

- Testmaker: ExamView Pro
- Performance Assessment, p. 33

Systematic Language Instruction
- Gr. and Comp. Hbk., L. 8.1

English Language Learners
- ELL Sourcebook, p. 58
- Spanish Summaries, p. 35
- Spanish Translations, p. 97–98
- Audio Library*
- English, Yes!

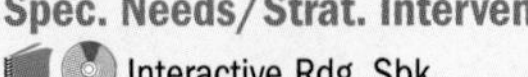

Spec. Needs/Strat. Interven.
- Interactive Rdg. Sbk., pp. T141–T143
- Interactive Rdg. Wkbk., p. 64

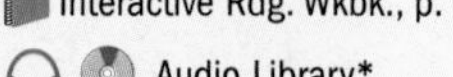

- Audio Library*

* Also available in Spanish

How I Learned English

A

Gregory Djanikian

It was in an empty lot
Ringed by elms and fir and honeysuckle.
Bill Corson was pitching in his buckskin jacket,
Chuck Keller, fat even as a boy, was on first,
His t-shirt riding up over his gut,
Ron O'Neill, Jim, Dennis, were talking it up
In the field, a blue sky above them
Tipped with cirrus.
And there I was,
Just off the plane and plopped in the middle
Of Williamsport, Pa. and a neighborhood game,
Unnatural and without any moves,
My notions of baseball and America
Growing fuzzier each time I whiffed.

B

Reading the Selection

A Active Reading Strategies

PREDICT Have students use the illustrations on these pages to predict how the poet learns English. Suggest they revisit their predictions as they read the poem to verify or to revise them.

B Literary Elements

SETTING Ask students to identify details about the setting that help them visualize the baseball game. *(The game is being played in an empty lot that has elm trees, firs, and honeysuckle shrubs around it. It is a beautiful day with just a few clouds in the sky.)*

Additional Resources

- ***Active Reading Guide,*** p. 35
- ***Audio Library***
- ***Spanish Audio Library***
- ***Spanish Summaries,*** p. 35

Vo•cab•u•lar•y Skills

Context Clues Encourage students to picture the setting as it's described, including the sky tipped with *cirrus*. Ask students what they think *cirrus* means considering its relationship with the sky. *(white, thin clouds)*

Teaching Support

Meeting Individual Needs: ENGLISH LANGUAGE LEARNERS

How Did You Learn English? Draw English language learners' attention to the story's title and the baseball on page 377. Ask them to make some predictions about what a baseball might have to do with learning English.

Activity As students read, make sure they understand the humor in the phrase *"Oh my shin."* Ask what part of the body *shin* refers to. Invite students to discuss why the poet thought it was important to join in the laughter rather than feel embarrassed. Afterward, invite students to share with the class some of their own funny stories about learning English.

Additional Resources

- ***English Language Learners Sourcebook,*** p. 58

COMPARING selections

This selection is compared with "The Teacher Who Changed My Life" on page 368. A lesson for teaching a comparison of the two selections appears on page 380.

Active Reading Strategies

CONNECT Have students recall a time when they were participating in a sport and saw a ball or another person coming toward them. Encourage students to share humorous stories about their experiences.

Active Reading Strategies

RESPOND Encourage students to express how they feel about the boys' laughing while the speaker is in pain. Remind them of the humorous nature of the incident. Ask students to describe how they would react if they were in the speaker's situation.

Critical Thinking

DRAWING CONCLUSIONS Have students think about the ending of the poem. Discuss whether they think it's a realistic conclusion. Do students feel that the writer's use of details and language enhances the ending? Have students give examples to support their opinions.

Thematic Focus

Where the Heart Is Have students discuss where they think the speaker's heart is. Point out that even though the speaker might daydream of another place, it is mentioned only once and is not identified.

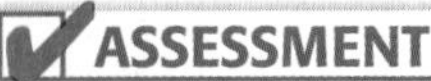

ASSESSMENT

Quick Checks, p. 35

So it was not impossible that I,
Banished° to the outfield and daydreaming
Of water, or a hotel in the mountains,
Would suddenly find myself in the path
Of a ball stung by Joe Barone.
I watched it closing in
Clean and untouched, transfixed°
By its easy arc before it hit
My forehead with a thud.
I fell back,
Dazed, clutching my brow,
Groaning, "Oh my shin, oh my shin,"
And everybody peeled away from me
And dropped from laughter, and there we were,
All of us writhing on the ground for one reason
Or another.
Someone said "shin" again,
There was a wild stamping of hands on the ground,
A kicking of feet, and the fit
Of laughter overtook me too,
And that was important, as important
As Joe Barone asking me how I was
Through his tears, picking me up
And dusting me off with hands like swatters,
And though my head felt heavy,
I played on till dusk
Missing flies and pop-ups and grounders
And calling out in desperation things like
"Yours" and "take it," but doing all right,
Tugging at my cap in just the right way,
Crouching low, my feet set,
"Hum baby" sweetly on my lips.

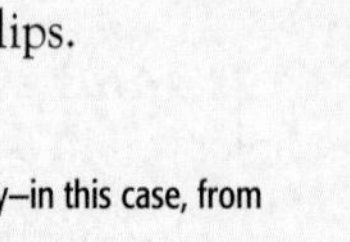

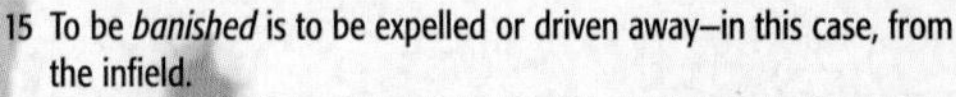

15 To be *banished* is to be expelled or driven away—in this case, from the infield.
20 To be *transfixed* is to be made motionless, as from wonder or fear.

Teaching Support

CONNECTING TO OTHER SELECTIONS
For a teaching strategy that connects "How I Learned English" to "Wait Till Next Year," see the ***Theme One Planning Guide.***

Reading *Minilesson*

Sequence of Events Explain to students that in poetry the sequence of events is not always clear. It is often helpful to pull the events from a story or a poem, paraphrase them, and then put them in the order in which they occurred. This can help readers keep straight not only the events but also the characters' involvement in those events.

Activity Reread the poem together and create a chart that tracks the sequence of events. Include the names of characters involved in each event. Then discuss how each event explains past action or leads to future action. **L2**

Additional Resources

Reading Skills Practice Workbook

Responding to Literature

PERSONAL RESPONSE

- Return to the **Reading Focus** on page 376. How does the speaker's experience connect with your ideas about making friends?

Analyzing Literature

RECALL AND INTERPRET

1. Why are the speaker's notions of America and baseball fuzzy?
2. Why do all the players end up on the ground when the speaker groans, "my shin, my shin"?
3. Why does the speaker mention the other players by name? Do you think they are still friends? Explain your answer.

EVALUATE AND CONNECT

4. At what point in the poem do you know that the boys have become friends? How does this experience connect with your own?
5. How does the poet bring to life the experience of playing a lighthearted baseball game?
6. Have you ever attempted to play a new game with strangers, or had a stranger join your own game? Describe your experience.

LITERARY ELEMENTS

Setting

The **setting** of a story, poem, or play is the time and place in which the events take place. The setting can include the geographic location, the time period, the season of the year, and even the time of day. Sometimes the writer describes all or part of the setting. For example, the poet tells the reader that the events in "How I Learned English" take place during a baseball game in the town of Williamsport, Pennsylvania.

1. How can you tell what time of day the baseball game started?
2. Why would a newly arrived immigrant find the setting of the poem meaningful?

- See **Literary Terms Handbook,** p. R10.

Extending Your Response

Literature Groups 

Changing Places Imagine that you are the speaker of "How I Learned English." Work with your group to write a series of letters about your new life in America to people in your old home town.

Writing About Literature 

Point of View "How I Learned English" is told from the point of view of a young boy who has recently immigrated to the United States. Write a brief poem or a prose paragraph from another character's point of view.

Responding to the Selection

PERSONAL RESPONSE

Students may describe experiences in which they have made friends through playing sports or humorous incidents.

Analyzing Literature

1. They are fuzzy because he has just moved to America. He seems unfamiliar with the game.
2. The other players laugh so hard they fall down because he uses the word *shin* instead of *forehead.*
3. He mentions names because they are new friends. Some students will note that the reference to "Chuck Keller, fat even as a boy," implies that the speaker knows him as an adult.
4. The friendship seems to begin when the boys laugh together and help the poet stand up. Students may relate experiences about new friends offering them help.
5. The poet uses vivid details, humor, informal language, and real-life images.
6. Students may describe experiences that were amusing, embarrassing, or enlightening.

Extending Your Response

Literature Groups Suggest that students include descriptions in the letters of the neighborhood, new activities, and new friends.

Writing About Literature

Students' writings should

- incorporate details from the poem
- include the feelings and observations of the character who is describing the action
- take the form of a poem or a short narrative

LITERARY ELEMENTS

1. It was most likely late afternoon, because there was a blue sky and the boys played until dusk.
2. Baseball is generally considered an American sport. Not only did the speaker learn a lesson in English from this game, he also made his first friends in America while playing.

Additional Resources

Literary Elements Transparency 35

ASSESSMENT

- ***Quick Checks,*** p. 35
- ***Selection and Theme Assessment,*** pp. 61–62
- ***Performance Assessment,*** p. 33
- ***Testmaker: ExamView Pro***
- ***Interactive Tutor: Self-Assessment***

Objective

- To compare a personal narrative and a poem, both about immigrants adjusting to life in the United States

COMPARE **RESPONSES**

1. Students should give reasons for their preferences.
2. Most students will agree that Gage includes more details about the immigrant experience. However, Djanikian offers a view of an immigrant's attempt to assimilate American culture as he makes friends.

COMPARE **CHARACTERS**

Students' conversations should

- describe each character's motivation to learn English
- explain how each character learned English
- share each character's feelings about learning English

Additional Resources

Literature Groups Sourcebook

COMPARE **EXPERIENCES**

Students should

- investigate the country's languages, customs, and activities
- use details from their research to visualize themselves in the country
- describe their way of communicating in a non-English-speaking country

Teaching Support

COMPARING SELECTIONS

The Teacher Who Changed My Life **and** How I Learned English

COMPARE **RESPONSES**

Both Nicholas Gage's personal narrative and Gregory Djanikian's poem focus on the experiences of a new immigrant.

1. Which selection did you prefer—the narrative or the poem? Give reasons for your answer.
2. From which selection did you learn more about the immigrant experience? What did you learn?

COMPARE **CHARACTERS**

In both selections, the narrator or speaker tells of his experience learning English. If Nicholas Gage and the speaker in "How I Learned English" could meet, what do you think they might tell each other? Write an imaginary conversation between the two characters as they compare their experiences of learning English.

COMPARE **EXPERIENCES**

The essay and the poem each give the reader a different sense of how it feels to be a new immigrant in this country.

- Think of a non-English-speaking country you would like to visit someday. Find pictures of the places that interest you. Try to find out a bit about the language and the customs.
- Close your eyes and imagine traveling to this country and meeting students your age. What would be a typical activity for them? Think about how you would communicate with your new friends.
- Share your ideas with a partner or a small group.

PORTFOLIO OPTIONS

Select and Reflect Encourage students to reflect on conversations they wrote for the activity above by asking themselves these questions:

- Is my dialogue believable?
- Did I include questions that these two characters might want to ask each other?

Activity Have students attach their reflections to their conversations and place them in their portfolios. At a later time, they might consider using the comments to revise their conversations as portfolio showcase pieces. **L2**

Additional Resources

Writing Assessment and Portfolio Management, pp. 38–45

Using Irregular Verbs Correctly

For **regular verbs,** the past form is made by adding *-ed* to the base. The past participle form is the same as the past form, but with a "helping" verb such as *has.*

Base form: I *like* poems. **Past form:** I *liked* the poem by Lucille Clifton.
Past participle form: I *have liked* most of the poems in this book.

Many **irregular verbs** use the same form for the past and the past participle.

Base form: *catch* **Past form:** *caught*
Past participle form: *has caught*

Some irregular verbs, however, have two different forms—one for use without a helping verb and another for use with a helping verb.

Base form: *grows* **Past form:** *grew*
Past participle form: *had grown*

Problem 1 an improperly formed irregular verb
The player ***standed*** *in the outfield.*

Solution *The player* ***stood*** *in the outfield.*

Problem 2 use of the past form when the past participle is needed
He ***seen*** *the ball before it hit him.*

Solution *He* ***had seen*** *the ball before it hit him.*

Here are the base form, past form, and past participle form of some irregular verbs.

begin, began, begun do, did, done know, knew, known
give, gave, given tell, told, told write, wrote, written

• For more about irregular verbs, see **Language Handbook,** p. R16.

EXERCISE

Write the correct form of each verb in parentheses.

1. Marjorie Hurd (give) Nicholas Gage an assignment.
2. He (write) the first essay he had ever (write).
3. He (tell) about how his journey had (begin) in a nighttime escape.
4. His classmates had not (knew) the difficulties Gage had (go) through.

Objective

- To recognize and use correctly past forms of regular and irregular verbs

Teaching Strategies

Ask students to draw a quick picture of one thing they did yesterday. Have them present their pictures and write a sentence on the board describing the activity. For example, *Yesterday, I baby-sat my sister; I rode my bike; I watched TV.* Go through the sentences on the board and ask students to determine which verbs are regular and which are irregular. List the verbs in two columns.

Exercise

1. gave
2. wrote/written
3. told/begun
4. known/gone

Additional Resources

- ***Grammar and Language Workbook,*** pp. 95–100
- ***Grammar and Composition Handbook,*** Lessons 3.11, 3.12
- ***Writer's Choice,*** Lesson 10.10

Teaching Support

Writing *Minilesson*

A Memoir Using "The Teacher Who Changed My Life" as an example, explain to students that a memoir is usually written in the past tense, since it focuses on the personal recollections of the writer. Ask students whether they think the poem "How I Learned English," by Gregory Djanikian, could be considered a memoir.

Activity Have each student choose a form in which to write: poem, essay, short story, article, or play. Then ask each to write a memoir about something or someone that changed his or her life. Have students read their memoirs aloud to the class or in small groups. **L2**

Additional Resources

- ***Writer's Choice,*** Lesson 1.4

0 Literary Elements

FOLKTALE Ask students what a folktale is and have them name various types of folktales. *(A folktale is a traditional story that has been passed along orally. Types of folktales include fairy tales, myths, legends, tall tales, trickster stories, and animal stories.)*

This story is an Ashanti tale. The Ashanti people live in the West African nation of Ghana. They are well known for their skills in making pottery and gold and silver ornaments. Beginning in medieval days, Ghana was an important gold trading center. The Ashanti people traded gold from the south for products (especially salt) from North Africa. Later they traded with Europeans.

Anansi and His Visitor, Turtle

A Story from the Ashanti People

Retold by Edna Mason Kaula

Teaching Support

CONNECTING TO OTHER SELECTIONS

For a teaching strategy that connects "Anansi and His Visitor, Turtle" to "The Force of Luck," see the ***Theme Six Planning Guide.***

Listening and Speaking Minilesson

Storytelling "Anansi and His Visitor, Turtle" is part of the oral tradition of the Ashanti culture. Invite interested students to try their hands at this ancient art.

Activity Have students choose folktales they enjoy that are relatively short and have an engaging plot. Some may want to memorize their tales, while others may just want to memorize key points or important dialogue. Have students practice using their voices to engage listeners. Let them practice using different voices for different characters and varying the pitch, tone, and loudness of their voices. Pausing while telling a story can also have a dramatic effect. When students are ready, have them perform their stories for a small group. **L2**

It was almost time for Sun to sink to his resting place when Turtle, tired and dusty from hours of wandering, came to Anansi's house in the middle of a clearing in the woods. Turtle was hungry and the appetizing aroma of freshly cooked fish and yams drew him to approach Anansi's door and to knock. Anansi jerked the door open. When he saw the tired stranger he was inwardly annoyed, but it was an unwritten law of his country that one must never, no never, refuse hospitality to a passer-by.

P

Anansi smiled grimly and said, "Come in, come in, and share my dinner, Mr. Turtle."

As Turtle stretched out one paw to help himself from the steaming platter Anansi almost choked on a mouthful of food. In a shocked voice he said, "Turtle, I must remind you that in my country it is ill-mannered to come to the table without first washing. Please go to the stream at the foot of the hill and wash your dusty paws."

Turtle waddled down the hill and waded in the water for a while. He even washed his face. By the time he had trudged back up the trail to Anansi's house, the platter of fish was half empty. Anansi was eating at a furious rate.

Turtle stretched out one paw to help himself to food, but again Anansi stopped him. "Turtle, your paws are still dusty. Please, go wash them."

Q

"It is the dust from the long trail up the hill," Turtle explained in a meek voice. Clearly, it was not Turtle's place to argue if he expected to share the delectable meal,

Viewing the painting: How does the artist combine animal and human characteristics in artwork here and on page 388? Why does he do so?

Vocabulary

meek (mēk) *adj.* patient and mild in manner; gentle

delectable (di lek′ tə bəl) *adj.* highly pleasing or delightful, especially to the taste; delicious

P Literary Elements

FIGURATIVE LANGUAGE: *Personification* Remind students that personification occurs when an animal or an object is given human characteristics. What human things do the characters do in the first few paragraphs of this tale? *(Sun rests at day's end. Turtle knocks on a door. Anansi cooks his food and invites Turtle in to be hospitable.)*

Q Literary Elements

CONFLICT Discuss the conflict of the story. *(The unwritten rule is that Anansi must invite Turtle in, but Anansi doesn't want to share his meal. To get around the rule, he tricks Turtle, who misses the meal.)*

VIEWING THE PAINTING

The illustrations on these two pages are by Andrew Glass, who has illustrated a number of books—his own as well as those of other authors—for young readers.

Viewing Response *The artist portrays animal features, such as the turtle's shell and the spider's eight legs, but he gives the animals human expressions and behaviors, shows them wearing human garments, and provides Anansi with a very human-looking table full of food. These details help make the characters accessible to readers and add to the story's humor.*

INTERDISCIPLINARY CONNECTION

Social Studies Meals play an important role in both "Oh Broom, Get to Work" and "Anansi and His Visitor, Turtle." Since one story is based on Japanese traditions and the other is an African folktale, the stories present an opportunity for learning about festive meals and customs in different cultures.

Activity Have small groups do research and plan short reports for the class on foods, festivals, or other interesting customs in cultures other than the one they now share with their classmates. Students who grew up in different cultures can draw on their own experience; others can do research, using personal interviews as well as books, magazines, and the Internet as sources. L2

Active Reading Strategies

PREDICT Ask students what might happen to Anansi. *(In trickster tales, like this one, characters usually get back at the one who played the trick. Therefore, Turtle will probably get even with Anansi.)*

Literary Elements

IRONY Verbal irony occurs when a character says one thing but means another. Turtle says, "Thank you for your wonderful hospitality, Anansi." Ask students why this statement is ironic. *(Turtle didn't get anything to eat, and he goes home "in a huff.")*

Literary Elements

REPETITION Turtle says, "I must remind you that in my country..." What does this sentence remind readers of? Have students explain what effect this repetition has. *(Anansi made an almost identical statement. Turtle's repetition makes it obvious that he is repaying Anansi for his earlier inhospitality.)*

Thematic Focus

Where the Heart Is Ask students to discuss how this story relates to the theme. Where is Anansi's heart when he goes through the motions of acting hospitable?

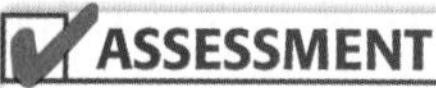

ASSESSMENT

Quick Checks, p. 36

so he crawled down the hill a second time and rewashed his paws. Turtle was careful to walk on the grass beside the dusty trail on the climb back to Anansi's house. He hurried, for by now he was ravenous.

But, oh dear! Anansi had scraped the platter bare of fish and yams. "My, that was a good dinner," he said, wiping the last drop of gravy from his chin.

"Thank you for your wonderful hospitality, Anansi. Some day you must visit me." And Turtle, in a huff, went on home.

Some months later Anansi visited Turtle. After creepy-crawling all day from one tall grass stem to the next, he found Turtle snoozing beside the river.

"Well, well," exclaimed Turtle. "So you have come to share my dinner. Make yourself comfortable, my dear Anansi, while I go below and prepare the food." He plunged into the river with a splash. Anansi was hungry. He paced the shore line and watched for Turtle's reappearance.

At last Turtle's head popped above the water. "Dinner is ready," he called as he bit into a huge clam. "Come on down." Then he disappeared from sight.

Anansi dived head first into the water, sank a few inches, then floated to the surface. His spindly legs and tiny body prevented him from sinking. He flipped and flapped his puny[1] arms, tried swallow dives and belly flops, but he could not reach the bed of the river.

Then that cunning spider schemed. He filled the pockets of his jacket with small round pebbles, dived into the river, and sank with a bump that landed him right at the dinner table. Before him was spread the most delicious meal he had ever seen. There were oysters and clams, mussels, slices of eel, and crabs. As a centerpiece, sprays of watercress rested against large pink shrimp. Anansi's eyes widened with pleasure, his stomach rumbled in anticipation.

Did You Know?
Watercress is a floating water plant bearing long clusters of small white flowers. Its leaves are eaten as salad greens.

Turtle, already seated at the table, swallowed a piece of eel, looked at Anansi and said, "Oh, Anansi, I must remind you that in my country it is ill-mannered to come to the table wearing a jacket. Please take it off."

Very slowly Anansi removed his jacket. Very slowly Anansi left the table. Without the weight of the pebbles to hold him down, he floated straight up through the green water and out of sight.

When you set out to outsmart another person to your own advantage, there is usually someone who can outsmart you.

1. *Puny* (pyōō′ nē) means "small and weak."

Vocabulary
ravenous (rav′ ə nəs) *adj.* extremely hungry
cunning (kun′ ing) *adj.* crafty; sly
anticipation (an tis′ ə pā′ shən) *n.* a feeling of excited expectation

Teaching Support

Grammar and Language Minilesson

Adjectives and Adverbs Remind students that an adjective is a word that modifies, or describes, a noun. An adverb, however, is a word that describes a verb, an adjective, or another adverb.

Activity Help students identify the adjectives and adverbs in the following sentences. Then point out the placement of the modifiers in the sentences.

1. His spindly legs and tiny body prevented him from sinking. *(adjectives)*
2. Very slowly Anansi removed his jacket. *(adverbs)*
3. Turtle bit into a huge clam. *(adjective)*

Ask students to write three sentences about the story, One should contain an adjective, one an adverb, and one both an adjective and an adverb. Remind them to pay attention to the proper placement of these modifiers. **L2**

Additional Resources

- ***Grammar and Language Transparency 33***
- ***Grammar and Language Workbook,*** pp. 117–118, 127–128
- ***Grammar and Composition Handbook,*** Lessons 5.1, 6.1, 6.2
- ***Writer's Choice,*** Lessons 12.1, 12.6

Responding to Literature

Oh Broom, Get to Work and *Anansi and His Visitor, Turtle*

PERSONAL RESPONSE

- Take another look at your list of ways to deal with guests from the **Reading Focus** on page 382. How do your ideas compare with the methods of the narrator in "Oh Broom, Get to Work" or Anansi in "Anansi and His Visitor, Turtle"?

Analyzing Literature

RECALL

1. What is Yo Chan's opinion about most of the visiting students?
2. What are the two meals served on holidays at Yo Chan's house?
3. What is the Japanese superstition about getting rid of guests who stay too long?
4. How does Anansi get rid of Turtle? What does Turtle do to Anansi to get even?

INTERPRET

5. Do you think Yo Chan appreciates her mother's hospitality to the young men? How can you tell?
6. From the description of cooking sukiyaki, what can you **infer** about Yo Chan's feelings toward her father and her heritage?
7. Does Yo Chan or Anansi feel guilty for sending the guests away? Support your opinion with evidence from the stories.
8. Why do you think the storyteller ends "Anansi and His Visitor, Turtle" with a moral?

EVALUATE AND CONNECT

9. The characters in "Anansi and His Visitor, Turtle" talk and act like people. How would your response to the story change if the characters were real human beings?
10. Do you think Yo Chan's reaction to her parents' guests is hospitable? How would you have behaved in her situation?

Brackets connect questions that are paired to develop higher-level thinking skills.

LITERARY ELEMENTS

Metaphors

Think about what you have learned about **figurative language.** A **metaphor** compares two seemingly different things by saying one thing is the other thing. A **simile** uses the words *like* or *as* to compare two things. In "Oh Broom, Get to Work," Yo Chan uses a metaphor when she calls the first uninvited guest "the gray-blob mushroom." He isn't actually a mushroom, but Yo Chan thinks he looks and acts like one.

1. Reread or skim "Oh Broom, Get to Work" to find another example of a metaphor and one of a simile. Write a sentence explaining what two things are being compared in each example.
2. Find and copy an example of a metaphor or a simile from any other selection in this theme. Tell what two things are being compared in it.

- See **Literary Terms Handbook**, p. R6.

Responding to the Selection

PERSONAL RESPONSE

Answers should compare students' ideas with the ideas of the characters in these two stories.

Analyzing Literature

1. Yo Chan thinks most of the visitors are boring.
2. Yo Chan's holiday meals are either a turkey dinner or a sukiyaki dinner.
3. The superstition is that if you stand a broom upside down and put a cloth over the bristles, the guest will leave.
4. Anansi has Turtle wash and rewash his hands until Anansi has eaten the entire meal. Turtle tells Anansi he can't wear a jacket to dinner. Without the jacket, Anansi can't eat at Turtle's underwater table because he lacks the rocks in the pockets that would keep him at the bottom of the river.
5. Yo Chan does not seem to appreciate her mother's hospitality because it means Yo Chan's mother has less time for her. Yo Chan stomps out without a word to the guest.
6. She admires her father's skill at making such mouthwatering food, and she is proud of her Japanese heritage.
7. No, Yo Chan says that she feels as if she has "evened the score a little." Anansi says, "My, that was a good dinner," as he finishes it. He shows no remorse.
8. The narrator wants readers to understand the point.
9. The story would seem farfetched because humans cannot breathe underwater, but listeners have already accepted Anansi's ability to talk and do other things real spiders can't do.
10. Some might say they think Yo Chan is rude, but they can understand why she is tired of all the guests.

LITERARY ELEMENTS

1. Metaphor: *another silent mushroom* compares a visitor with a mushroom. Simile: *its legs thrust in the air like two sticks* compares a dead bird's legs with sticks.
2. Examples should identify and explain a metaphor or a simile.

Additional Resources

Literary Elements Transparency 36

Literature and Writing

Writing About Literature

Students' paragraphs should

- describe similarities and differences in how the guests are treated in each of the stories
- compare these similarities and differences
- use smooth transitions to move from one example to the next

Creative Writing

Students' sequels should

- contain dialogue and behaviors in keeping with the characters' traits
- show reasonable motivation
- conclude logically

Extending Your Response

Literature Groups Encourage students on each side of this issue to list their main arguments. Then have them develop ways to counter what they imagine will be the other team's main arguments.

Interdisciplinary Activity Remind students that humor often arises when characters do the wrong thing with unexpected or surprising results. Encourage students to think of funny situations before they begin drawing their comic books. They may want to include a moral after each situation they show.

Learning for Life Letters should be written in proper letter format. They should introduce the student and explain why the student wants to stay with the Uchidas. Above all, the letters should be polite and respectful.

Literature and Writing

Writing About Literature

Comparing Characters Write a paragraph or two comparing the way the narrator in "Oh Broom, Get to Work" deals with uninvited guests with the way Anansi and Turtle treat each other in "Anansi and His Visitor, Turtle."

Creative Writing

The Next Meal What happened to the jacket that Anansi left at the bottom of the river with Turtle? Write a sequel to "Anansi and His Visitor, Turtle" in which Turtle returns the jacket and manages to drop in during another delicious meal at Anansi's house.

Extending Your Response

Literature Groups

Debating Indifference In the story, Yo Chan's mother says, "Don't ever be indifferent. That's the worst fault of all." Do you agree with this philosophy? Choose to be for or against this belief and hold a group debate.

Interdisciplinary Activity

Art The characters of Yo Chan and Anansi have been taught by their families and community that polite people (or animals) invite guests into their homes and treat them well. Yet both characters have trouble being kind hosts. Using the character of Yo Chan or Anansi as a narrator, create a comic book for younger children about the proper way to be a host. Include humorous drawings or cartoons to illustrate your rules.

Learning for Life

Letter of Introduction Imagine you are a Japanese student planning to study in Berkeley, California. You have heard from another student that the Uchidas are wonderful hosts who might let you stay at their home until you find a place of your own. Write a letter to the Uchidas introducing yourself and explaining your needs.

Reading Further

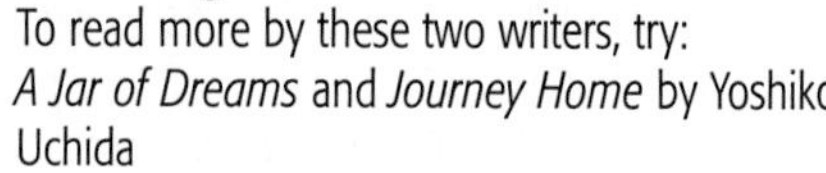

To read more by these two writers, try:
A Jar of Dreams and *Journey Home* by Yoshiko Uchida

African Village Folktales by Edna Mason Kaula

To learn more about Japanese Americans, try:

Japanese-American Journey: The Story of a People edited by Florence M. Hongo

Save your work for your portfolio.

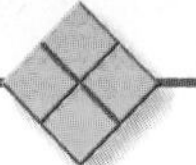

Skill Minilessons

Reteach · Review

GRAMMAR AND LANGUAGE • SUFFIXES AND THE SILENT *e*

For words ending with a silent *e,* remember to drop the final *e* when you add a suffix. For example, in the sentence: "The dead bird continued to *fascinate* Yo Chan," the word *fascinate* is a verb. The suffix *-ion* is added to *fascinate* to create the noun form in this sentence: "The dead sparrow filled me with dread and *fascination.*"

- For more about suffixes and spelling, see **Language Handbook,** pp. R44–R45.

PRACTICE Identify each word in the list as either the noun form or the verb form. Then use the other form of each word in a sentence.

1. confuse
2. invention
3. narrate
4. correction
5. protection

READING AND THINKING • PROBLEM/SOLUTION

The plots in most short stories contain one or more problems that the characters try to solve. In many stories, character development is revealed in the way characters respond to problems in their lives. In "Oh, Broom, Get to Work," the narrator tries to solve her major problem (too many guests) in a variety of ways until she comes upon the solution of the broom.

PRACTICE Reread "Anansi and His Visitor, Turtle," and find two problems that are solved by the end of the story.

- For more about helpful reading strategies, see **Reading Handbook,** p. R89.

VOCABULARY • SYNONYMS

Synonyms are words with similar meanings. That does not mean that they have the *same* meaning. For example, *neutral* and *indifferent* are synonyms. However, a judge, an umpire, or a referee should be neutral but not indifferent. *Neutral* suggests not taking sides, while *indifferent* suggests not caring.

PRACTICE Think about what the underlined word means in each sentence. Then choose the better synonym for that word *as it is used in the sentence.*

1. A friend who telephones during dinner might apologize for the <u>intrusion</u>.
   a. invasion   b. interruption
2. There's no excuse for being <u>pompous</u> about your school or family.
   a. proud   b. conceited
3. The pickup truck pulled into the parking lot, <u>laden</u> with gifts for the children.
   a. loaded   b. burdened

Skill Minilessons

GRAMMAR AND LANGUAGE
SUFFIXES AND THE SILENT *e*

Example sentences:

1. Verb; *Confusion ensued during the fire.*
2. Noun; *He will invent solutions for new problems.*
3. Verb; *The narration was long but exciting.*
4. Noun; *I correct my spelling mistakes when I proofread my work.*
5. Noun; *The dog will protect his owner.*

READING AND THINKING
PROBLEM/SOLUTION

1. Anansi solves the problem of how to get to the bottom of the river by putting stones in his jacket pocket.
2. Turtle solves the problem of how to get even by not allowing Anansi to wear his jacket at the dinner table.

VOCABULARY
SYNONYMS

1. b   2. b   3. a

Additional Resources

- ***Grammar and Language Workbook,*** pp. 291–292
- ***Grammar and Composition Handbook,*** Lesson 15.4
- ***Writer's Choice,*** Lesson 23.3
- ***Reading Skills Practice Workbook***
- ***Vocabulary Practice,*** p. 23

ASSESSMENT

- ***Quick Checks,*** p. 36
- ***Selection and Theme Assessment,*** pp. 63–64
- ***Performance Assessment,*** p. 34
- ***Testmaker: ExamView Pro***
- ***Interactive Tutor: Self-Assessment***

Objective

- To understand the elements of an essay

Teaching Strategies

Refer students to the idea expressed in their books that writing an essay is a way of "trying out" one's ideas.

Theme Explain to students that the theme of an essay is often the essential point of interest that motivates the writer to start writing about a topic in the first place.

Purpose Ask students to pay attention to the purpose of the essays they read in this theme and to think about what the writer's intentions are in each selection.

Style Ask students to try to imitate the style of a famous writer or a piece of writing they admire. Stress, however, the importance of developing one's own style.

Text Structure You may wish to have students review what they learned about text structures in Theme 3 (pages 290–291).

Tone Explain that a writer often uses different tones to express particular points and to explain how he or she views certain topics.

Teaching Support

ESSAY

The word *essay* comes from a French verb meaning "to try." The noun *essay* refers to a particular kind of writing. In an **essay,** an author "tries out" an idea in a short work of nonfiction focusing on a single subject. All essays contain the basic elements described on this page.

THEME refers to the main point or message of the essay. The theme of an essay may be stated directly in a thesis statement that appears in the introduction. The **thesis statement**–usually a single sentence–gives the main idea of the essay.

MODEL

"Bums in the Attic" begins with a clear, direct thesis statement: "I want a house on a hill like the ones with the gardens where Papa works."

PURPOSE refers to an author's reason for writing an essay. An essayist usually has one or more purposes in mind–to inform, to entertain, to persuade, or to tell about real people, places, and events.

The purpose of Nicholas Gage's "The Teacher Who Changed My Life" is to tell you about a remarkable person, ". . . a salty-tongued, no-nonsense school teacher named Marjorie Hurd."

TEXT STRUCTURE is the way a piece of writing is organized. A narrative essay such as Thurber's "The Night the Bed Fell" is meant to entertain. It is usually organized like a story, with a setting, characters, plot (in chronological order), and theme.

STYLE is an author's personal way of using language. You can see an essayist's style in his or her word choice, sentence patterns, and ways of moving from idea to idea.

In "The Night the Bed Fell," Thurber's style comes through in his lively, surprising language, ". . . it is almost necessary to throw furniture around, shake doors, and bark like a dog, to lend the proper atmosphere . . . to what is admittedly a somewhat incredible tale."

TONE is the author's attitude toward his or her subject. An essayist's tone may be witty or serious, sad or upbeat, scholarly or sarcastic, admiring or angry.

In "The Dog Diaries," Markoe describes her dogs with humor and honesty, "I pick dogs that remind me of myself–scrappy, mutt-faced, with a hint of mange."

396 THEME 4

MEETING INDIVIDUAL NEEDS — SPECIAL NEEDS

Learning Disabled Review with students the difference between fiction and nonfiction. Remind students that fiction is made-up, but nonfiction deals with real people and real experiences. Point out that historical fiction may read like a true story, but it contains characters and dialogue invented by the writer.

Activity Have students suggest at least one question relating to each of the elements of an essay; for example, *What is the main point of this selection?* Then show students how to use such questions to analyze a selection and determine what type of writing it is. **L2**

Additional Resources

Inclusion Strategies

Active Reading Strategies

Tips for Reading an Essay

When reading an essay, active readers use strategies like the ones below to build on their understanding of the essay and to evaluate what they have read.

- For more about these and other reading strategies, see **Reading Handbook,** pp. R85–R99.

PREDICT

While reading, ask yourself questions such as, "What does the title mean?" or "How will the author respond?" Combine clues in the text with what you already know to predict what will happen next.

QUESTION

Questioning helps you separate facts from opinions. Facts are statements that can be proved. Opinions express a person's beliefs and cannot be proved. Writers sometimes present strong opinions as if they were facts. Questioning will help you recognize the difference.

VISUALIZE

Use the details the essayist gives you to form pictures in your mind. As you read a descriptive passage in an essay, ask yourself, "What does this person look like?" or "Can I picture the scene the writer is describing?"

EVALUATE

After you finish reading an essay and reflecting on its ideas, think about what it means to you. Discuss it with your classmates. Listening to the observations of others will give you a deeper understanding of the essay.

APPLYING THE STRATEGIES

Read the following essay, "The Night the Bed Fell." Use the **Active Reading Model** notes in the margins as you read. Write your responses on a separate piece of paper or use self-stick notes.

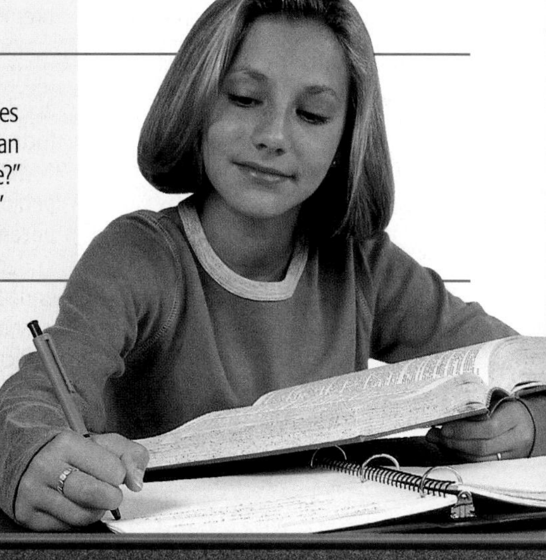

Active Reading Strategies

Objective

- To understand and apply strategies for reading essays

Teach the Strategies

Mention to students that an essay writer poses questions to himself or herself while writing. Readers should do the same as they read.

Predict

To help students keep track of their predictions, you may wish to have each of them make a learning chart with two headings:

- *What I know about the essay*
- *What I might learn by reading it*

Question

Point out to students that questioning the writer is just as important as questioning oneself during essay reading.

Visualize

The sensory details included in the essays in this theme will provide students with plenty of opportunity for visualization.

Evaluate

Ask students to use the chart described in the prediction process to evaluate what they have learned.

Teaching Support

Reading Journal

Surprising Behavior

In "The Night the Bed Fell," James Thurber presents an unusual story about a strange turn of events that occurred in his house one night. Invite students to discuss fears people have about the night.

Activity Encourage students to jot down notes as they read about each character's unusual behavior. After each description, have students tell whether the behavior seems funny to them. After reading, have students identify a part of the selection that would be especially good for reading aloud. Have students explain why it would be good for reading aloud and what sound effects, if any, they would add. L2

Before Reading

Objectives

- To read and analyze an essay about a family's hectic night
- To identify techniques of characterization in an essay
- To write an analysis of the story's climax

Skills

Reading/Thinking: Making Critical Judgments; Exaggeration; Cause and Effect
Writing: Characterizing; Different Point of View
Vocabulary: Antonyms; Root Words
Grammar/Language: Consistency in Verb Tense; Parentheses
Listening/Speaking: Oral Reading; Interviewing
Collaboration: Literature Groups

Motivating → STUDENTS

Literature Launchers: "James Thurber's World"

Videodisc Side A, Segment 12

Also available in VHS.

Selection Focus Transparency 37: Have students discuss the sense of humor of an artist who would draw a sketch like this.

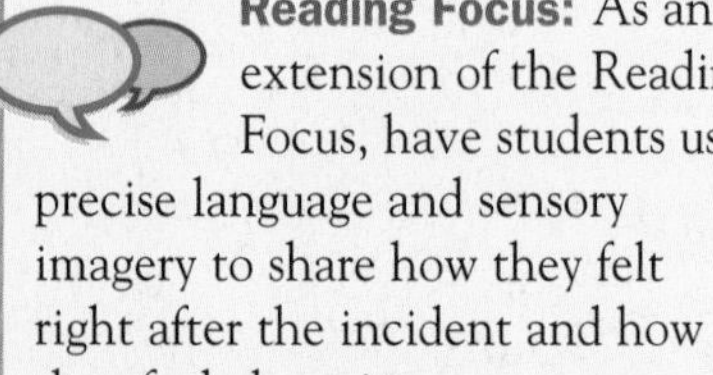

Reading Focus: As an extension of the Reading Focus, have students use precise language and sensory imagery to share how they felt right after the incident and how they feel about it now.

ACTIVE READING MODEL

Before You Read

The Night the Bed Fell

MEET JAMES THURBER

James Thurber is considered one of America's greatest humorists. He was born in Columbus, Ohio, the middle child in an eccentric family of three boys. He wrote hilarious-but-true stories about his unusual childhood home, but, as he explained, "all truths in that house were peculiar." He also used his wit and his artistic talent to create well-loved cartoons that were published in magazines and collected in books.

James Thurber was born in 1894 and died in 1961. This story was first published in 1933.

READING FOCUS

What stories about unusual relatives or humorous situations are retold again and again in your family?

QuickWrite
Write about a funny family incident—for example, a holiday meal that didn't turn out right, or a visit from a relative.

Setting a Purpose
Some titles tease your imagination. You might want to read this essay to find out what happened the night the bed fell.

BUILDING BACKGROUND

Did You Know? James Thurber was successful in nearly every category of writing. He was a newspaper reporter, magazine writer and editor, cartoonist, children's book writer, essayist, humorist, novelist, playwright, and screenwriter for movies and television!

VOCABULARY PREVIEW

premonition (prē′ mə nish′ ən) *n.* a feeling that something is about to happen; warning or sign; p. 400
destine (des′ tin) *v.* to determine beforehand; p. 400
avert (ə vurt′) *v.* to keep from happening; prevent; p. 401
fortitude (fôr tə to͞od′) *n.* firm courage or strength of mind in the face of pain or danger; p. 401
perilous (per′ə ləs) *adj.* dangerous; risky; p. 403
uncanny (un kan′ ē) *adj.* so strange as to cause fear or wonder; weird; p. 404
endeavor (en dev′ ər) *n.* a serious attempt to accomplish something; undertaking; p. 404
extricate (eks′ trə kāt′) *v.* to release from entanglement or difficulty; set free; p. 404
culprit (kul′ prit) *n.* one guilty of some offense; p. 405

398 THEME 4

RESOURCE MANAGER

Teaching Tools and Resources
- Theme Four Planning Guide
- Literature Groups Sourcebook
- Presentation Plus! CD-ROM

Essential Lesson Support

Lesson-Specific Instruction
- Selection Focus Transparency 37
- Literary Elements Transparency 37
- Active Reading Guide,* p. 37
- Selection Vocabulary Practice, p. 24

Assessment
- Selection Quick Checks,* p. 37
- Sel. and Theme Assmt., pp. 65–66
- Testmaker: ExamView Pro
- Performance Assessment, p. 35

Systematic Language Instruction
- Gr. and Comp. Hbk., L. 8.3
- Vocabulary Power, Lesson 18
- Spelling Power, Lesson 16

English Language Learners
- ELL Sourcebook, p. 62
- Spanish Summaries, p. 37
- Spanish Translations, p. 103–106
- Audio Library*
- English, Yes!

Spec. Needs/Strat. interven.
- Interactive Rdg. Sbk., pp. T146–T148
- Interactive Rdg. Wkbk., pp. 67–68
- Inclusion Strat. Sbk., pp. 47–48
- Audio Library*

* Also available in Spanish

The Night the Bed Fell

James Thurber

I suppose that the high-water mark of my youth in Columbus, Ohio, was the night the bed fell on my father. It makes a better recitation (unless, as some friends of mine have said, one has heard it five or six times) than it does a piece of writing, for it is almost necessary to throw furniture around, shake doors, and bark like a dog, to lend the proper atmosphere and verisimilitude[1] to what is admittedly a somewhat incredible tale. Still, it did take place.

ACTIVE READING MODEL

QUESTION

What details suggest that the tale might be humorous? **A**

1. If something has *verisimilitude* (ver′ ə si mil′ ə to͞od′), it has the appearance of being true.

Reading the Selection

SUMMARY

The narrator tells of an incident that occurs in his childhood home after he, his parents, two brothers, three aunts, dog, and visiting cousin—who have bizarre phobias and ways of dealing with them—have gone to sleep. The crash of the narrator's cot tipping over awakens the sleepers and their fears, creating incredible chaos in the night.

Spanish Summaries, p. 37

A Active Reading Strategies

QUESTION Have students look at Thurber's choice of words and the images they bring to mind. *(Students might focus on the picture of someone throwing furniture around, shaking doors, and barking like a dog while telling a story as an indicator that the story will be humorous.)*

VOCABULARY If you haven't previewed the selection vocabulary with students, stop and remind them to use context clues to unlock the meanings of new vocabulary words.

Additional Resources

Active Reading Guide, p. 37

Audio Library

Spanish Audio Library

Teaching Support

CONNECTING TO OTHER SELECTIONS

The chart at the right shows three ways to connect "The Night the Bed Fell" to other selections in this book.

For specific teaching strategies, see the ***Theme Four Planning Guide.***

Connection		Title
Life Skills: Problem Solving	→	"Icarus and Daedalus," p. 737
Thematic: Growing Pains	→	"A Crush," p. 149
Literary: Characterization	→	"Birthday Box," p. 175

B Active Reading Strategies

QUESTION *(Students should gather that Grandfather is not completely stable mentally.)*

C Literary Elements

CHARACTERIZATION Have students identify what the grandfather and cousin have in common. *(Both are somewhat strange in their behavior and thinking.)*

FYI

Breathing Unless there is illness or trauma, or a person purposely controls it, human breathing is automatic. The control center is located in the base of the human brain. Rate of breathing averages fourteen times per minute, and average lung capacity is three pints of air.

D Active Reading Strategies

PREDICT *(He's going to sniff the camphor.)* Help students see that since Thurber is announcing its place in the story, camphor will make an appearance later on.

E Author's Craft

CHARACTERIZATION Sometimes a narrator will make a direct comment about a character. What is the narrator saying here about his family members? *(The statement says that Briggs, as well as others, exhibits some peculiar behavior.)*

Teaching Support

The Night the Bed Fell

ACTIVE READING MODEL

B What do these details tell you about Grandfather's character?

It happened, then, that my father had decided to sleep in the attic one night, to be away where he could think. My mother opposed the notion strongly because, she said, the old wooden bed up there was unsafe: it was wobbly and the heavy headboard would crash down on father's head in case the bed fell, and kill him. There was no dissuading[2] him, however, and at a quarter past ten he closed the attic door behind him and went up the narrow twisting stairs. We later heard ominous creakings as he crawled into bed. Grandfather, who usually slept in the attic bed when he was with us, had disappeared some days before. (On these occasions he was usually gone six or eight days and returned growling and out of temper, with the news that the federal Union was run by a passel of blockheads and that the Army of the Potomac[3] didn't have a chance.) C

We had visiting us at this time a nervous first cousin of mine named Briggs Beall, who believed that he was likely to cease breathing when he was asleep. It was his feeling that if he were not awakened every hour during the night, he might die of suffocation. He had been accustomed to setting an alarm clock to ring at intervals until morning, but I persuaded him to abandon this. He slept in my room and I told him that I was such a light sleeper that if anybody quit breathing in the same room with me, I would wake instantly. He tested me the first night—which I had suspected he would—by holding his breath after my regular breathing had convinced him I was asleep. I was not asleep, however, and called to him. This seemed to allay his fears a little, but he took the precaution of putting a glass of spirits of camphor[4] on a little table at the head of his bed. In case I didn't arouse him until he was almost gone, he said, he would sniff the camphor, a powerful reviver. Briggs was not the only member of his family who had his crotchets.[5] E Old Aunt Melissa Beall (who could whistle like a man, with two fingers in her mouth) suffered under the premonition that she was destined to die on South High Street, because she had been born on South High Street and married on South High Street. Then there was Aunt Sarah

PREDICT

D What might happen to Briggs Beall later in the essay?

2. To *dissuade* is to argue or advise against an action or belief.
3. The *Army of the Potomac* was the eastern branch of the Union army during the Civil War.
4. To *allay* is to calm or relieve. *Spirits of camphor* is a strong-smelling, distilled mixture that is used to soothe aches.
5. The family members' *crotchets* are their peculiar ideas or beliefs.

Vocabulary

premonition (prē′ mə nish′ ən) *n.* a feeling that something is about to happen; warning or sign

destine (des′ tin) *v.* to determine beforehand

ENGLISH LANGUAGE LEARNERS

Idiomatic Expression Begin by making sure English language learners are aware that this is a humorous essay. Point out the clues on page 400 (paragraphs 1 and 2) where the author uses the idiomatic expression *in case*. The expression, in context, means "if," or "if something should happen."

Activity Have students use *in case* to replace the italicized words in these sentences:

1. I have an extra pen *if* this one runs dry.
2. Take the umbrella *in the event* it should rain.

Then have each student write a sentence or two using *in case*.

Additional Resources

English Language Learners Sourcebook, p. 62

Shoaf, who never went to bed at night without the fear that a burglar was going to get in and blow chloroform under her door through a tube. To avert this calamity—for she was in greater dread of anesthetics[6] than of losing her household goods—she always piled her money, silverware, and other valuables in a neat stack just outside her bedroom, with a note reading: "This is all I have. Please take it and do not use your chloroform, as this is all I have." Aunt Gracie Shoaf also had a burglar phobia,[7] but she met it with more fortitude. She was confident that burglars had been getting into her house every night for forty years. The fact that she never missed anything was to her no proof to the contrary. She always claimed that she scared them off before they could take anything, by throwing shoes down the hallway. When she went to bed she piled, where she could get at them handily, all the shoes there were about her house. Five minutes after she had turned off the light, she would sit up in bed and say "Hark!" Her husband, who had learned

CONNECT

How does the description of Aunt Gracie Shoaf's actions connect to the first paragraph, where the narrator says that to tell the story "it is almost necessary to throw furniture"?

6. The sweet-smelling fumes of *chloroform* used to be a common *anesthetic*–a substance used to put patients to sleep before surgery.
7. A *phobia* is a strong, continuing, and unreasonable fear.

Vocabulary

avert (ə vurt′) *v.* to keep from happening; prevent
fortitude (fôr′ tə to͞od′) *n.* firm courage or strength of mind in the face of pain or danger

F Critical Thinking

MAKING CRITICAL JUDGMENTS Fear of being burglarized is a serious matter. Ask students to judge what makes Aunt Sarah's and Aunt Gracie's fears funny. You may wish to share the following model to illustrate the thinking process involved in making critical judgments.

Model: While being concerned about burglars is natural, the peculiarities of Sarah's and Gracie's fears make them funny. Sarah ties up her valuables and leaves a note for the burglars; Gracie throws shoes down the hall and thinks this strategy has worked for forty years.

Vo•cab•u•lar•y Skills

Roots The word *fortitude* comes from the Latin *fortis*, meaning "strong." It can also mean "pluck," "grit," or "having backbone." Ask students to think of other words that share the same root.

G Active Reading Strategies

QUESTION Why does the author single out their crotchets dealing with nighttime behavior? *(This is the behavior that comes into play in this incident. The author does not want to divert the reader's attention from this incident.)*

H Active Reading Strategies

CONNECT *(The narrator's live reenactment of throwing shoes would be funny to see. It would enhance the drama of the retelling.)*

Writing Minilesson

Characterizing Students might enjoy taking the characters from this story and including them in their own writing.

Activity Ask students to create character traits these family members might have during the day. Encourage each student to write one paragraph to describe each character: Grandfather, Briggs, Aunt Melissa, Aunt Sarah, and Aunt Gracie.

Encourage students to think of normal behavior and then take it to an extreme; for example, Briggs may think it necessary to wear a snorkel in the shower. **L2**

Additional Resources

Writer's Choice, Lesson 3.5

On The Lighter Side

The family's bull terrier, Rex, is lucky to have a name. James Thurber owned more than forty dogs in his lifetime. In the short essay "How to Name a Dog," Thurber explains that most of those dogs were litters of puppies that he didn't keep long enough to name anything but Hey, You! and Cut That Out! and Let Go!

FYI

Strong Women
Thurber had little difficulty depicting strong women in his sketches and writing. In fact, much of his work shows women as being domineering in their relationships with men. "The Secret Life of Walter Mitty" is a good example of a Thurber story depicting that kind of woman.

At the MOVIES

• ***The Secret Life of Walter Mitty*** (1947, 110 minutes, not rated) James Thurber's famous short story was the source for this hilarious Danny Kaye movie. Preview it to decide whether it would be suitable for your students.

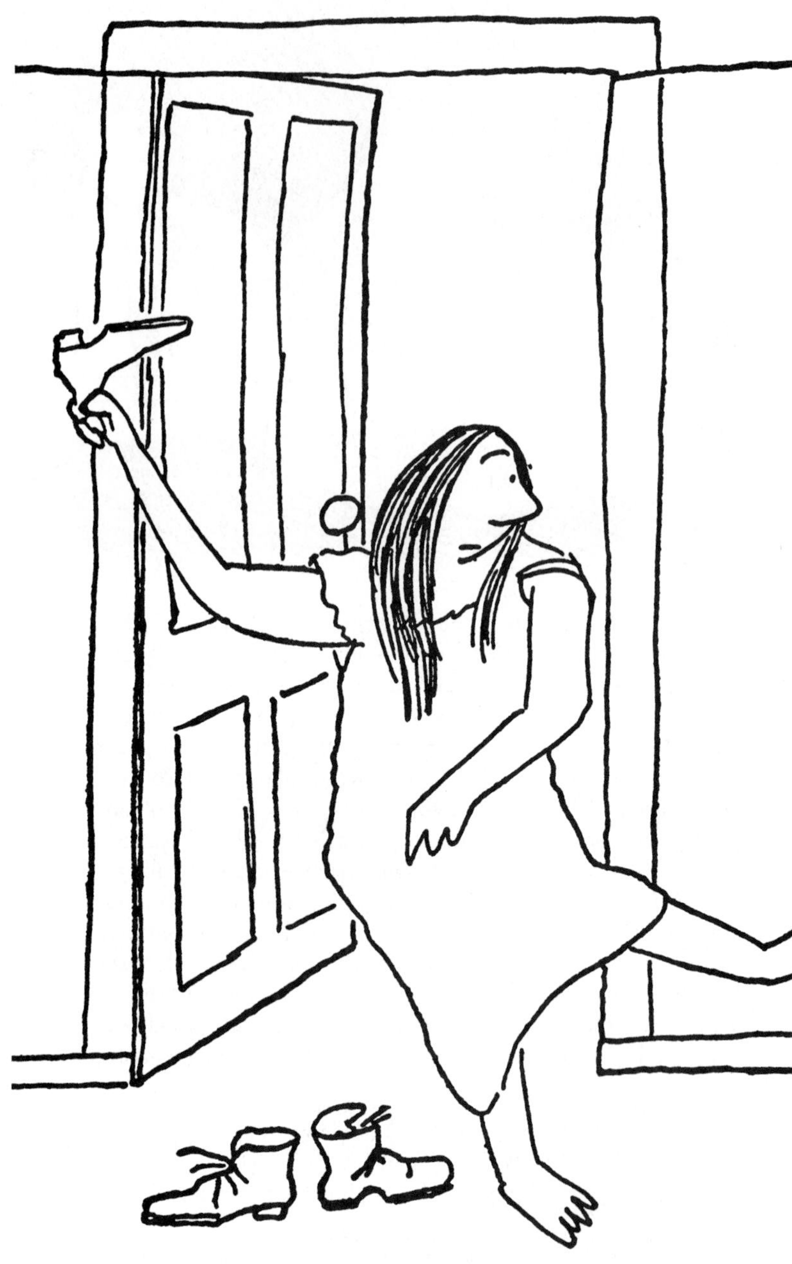

Teaching Support

Interdisciplinary Connection

Art Explain to students that drawings do not need to be literal renderings of reality to be effective. Many cartoons, comic strips, and other works use rather simple, even primitive, drawing. The key seems to be in capturing a particular physical or character trait, or capturing a moment in a person's behavior that viewers recognize and that prompts a response.

Activity Ask each student to create a simple pencil sketch of a person doing something unusual or atypical. Remind them not to worry about realistic accuracy but to strive more for capturing the moment. **L2**

to ignore the whole situation as long ago as 1903, would either be sound asleep or pretend to be sound asleep. In either case he would not respond to her tugging and pulling, so that presently she would arise, tiptoe to the door, open it slightly and heave a shoe down the hall in one direction, and its mate down the hall in the other direction. Some nights she threw them all, some nights only a couple of pair.

J But I am straying from the remarkable incidents that took place during the night that the bed fell on father. By midnight we were all in bed. The layout of the rooms and the disposition of their occupants is important to an understanding of what later occurred. In the front room upstairs (just under father's attic bedroom) were my mother and my brother Herman, who sometimes sang in his sleep, usually "Marching Through Georgia" or "Onward, Christian Soldiers." Briggs Beall and myself were in a room adjoining this one. My brother Roy was in a room across the hall from ours. Our bull terrier, Rex, slept in the hall.

My bed was an army cot, one of those affairs which are made wide enough to sleep on comfortably only by putting up, flat with the middle section, the two sides which ordinarily hang down like the sideboards of a drop-leaf table. When these sides are up, it is perilous to roll too far toward the edge, for then the cot is likely to tip completely over, bringing the whole bed down on top of one, with a tremendous banging crash. This, in fact, is precisely what happened, about two o'clock in the morning. (It was my mother who, in recalling the scene later, first referred to it as "the night the bed fell on your father.")

Did You Know?
A *canopy* is an overhanging covering, such as on a bed, throne, or building entrance.

Always a deep sleeper, slow to arouse (I had lied to Briggs), I was at first unconscious of what had happened when the iron cot rolled me onto the floor and toppled over on me. It left me still warmly bundled up and unhurt, for the bed rested above me like a canopy. Hence I did not wake up, only reached the edge of consciousness and went back. The racket, however, instantly awakened my mother, in the next room, who came to the immediate conclusion that her worst dread was realized: the big wooden bed upstairs had fallen on father. She therefore screamed, "Let's go to your poor father!" It was this shout, rather than the noise of my cot falling, that awakened Herman, in the same room with her. He thought that mother had become, for no apparent reason, hysterical.

Vocabulary
perilous (per′ ə ləs) *adj.* dangerous; risky

ACTIVE READING MODEL

REVIEW I
What does each of the narrator's relatives fear?

PREDICT K
Thurber is very precise about the layout of the rooms. Why do you think he wants you to know this information?

VISUALIZE L
How does Thurber help you visualize this kind of bed?

RESPOND M
Do you know anyone who sleeps this soundly? Is Thurber exaggerating? Why or why not?

I Active Reading Strategies

REVIEW *(Mother fears the bed will fall on father and kill him; Briggs fears suffocation; Aunt Melissa fears dying on South High Street; Aunt Sarah fears being killed by chloroform; Aunt Gracie fears burglars.)*

J Author's Craft

CHARACTERIZATION The narrator admits a weakness when he says he is "straying from" the story. Ask students what this says about him. *(He wants to make telling the story feel more personal.)*

K Active Reading Strategies

PREDICT *(Knowing this information will probably enable the reader to appreciate what follows.)* If students have a difficult time answering this question, revisit it again after they have finished reading page 405.

L Active Reading Strategies

VISUALIZE *(Thurber helps the reader visualize the bed by comparing it to a drop-leaf table, something readers may be more familiar with than a cot.)* If some students have a problem picturing this, have volunteers sketch both items on the board.

M Active Reading Strategies

RESPOND *(Some students may be sound sleepers or have experience with people who are. Some students may say that Thurber exaggerates to increase the drama.)*

Reading Minilesson

Cause and Effect This story, based on a series of quirky situations and comical outcomes, has two threads: the father and the bed and Briggs and James's sharing a room. Learning to analyze this story's cause-and-effect structure will also help students analyze expository writing.

Activity Use the diagram at the right. Have pairs of students select a thread, complete the diagram, and present it to a small group. These questions will help them identify causes and effects:

1. What happened?
2. Why did it happen?
3. What was the event's outcome? **L2**

Additional Resources

Reading Skills Practice Workbook

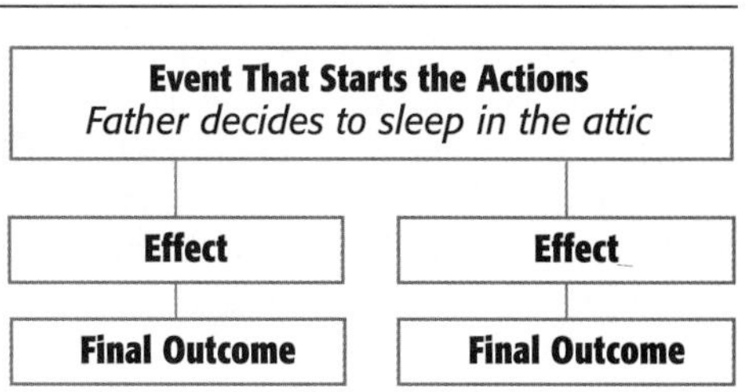

N Literary Elements

CHARACTERIZATION Ask students how Thurber prepared readers to believe the behavior being shown here. *(Earlier Thurber described the characters' crotchets, thus preparing readers to accept this bizarre behavior.)*

O Active Reading Strategies

PREDICT *(Briggs may knock over the camphor and add to the confusion.)* Remind students of Briggs' last concern before falling asleep.

P Active Reading Strategies

QUESTION *(Camphor is a strong-smelling liquid that can make people cough.)*

Q Literary Elements

DIALOGUE Ask students to read the direct speech aloud. Discuss why the author gives these exact quotes. *(This dialogue—for example,* Ugf, ahfg*—is funny. To have written "Briggs was choking" would not have been funny.)*

R Active Reading Strategies

CONNECT *(If students are reluctant to speak of personal situations, ask about movie or story plots revolving around misunderstandings.)*

S Active Reading Strategies

EVALUATE *(If the father were a sound sleeper and the battering were loud, it is quite possible he would react in this way.)*

ACTIVE READING MODEL

O PREDICT What do you think will happen to Briggs in all the confusion?

P QUESTION What do you learn about camphor from this description?

R CONNECT Have you ever been in a situation where simple misunderstandings caused comic complications?

S EVALUATE Take a minute to ask yourself if you think the father would really respond this way to the battering on the door.

"You're all right, Mamma!" he shouted, trying to calm her. They exchanged shout for shout for perhaps ten seconds: "Let's go to your poor father!" and "You're all right!" That woke up Briggs. By this time **N** I was conscious of what was going on, in a vague way, but did not yet realize that I was under my bed instead of on it. Briggs, awakening in the midst of loud shouts of fear and apprehension, came to the quick conclusion that he was suffocating and that we were all trying to "bring him out." With a low moan, he grasped the glass of camphor at the head of his bed and instead of sniffing it poured it over himself. The room reeked of camphor. "Ugf, ahfg," choked Briggs, like a drowning man, for he had almost succeeded in stopping his breath under the deluge of pungent[8] spirits. He leaped out of bed and groped toward the open window, but he came up against one that was closed. With his hand, he beat out the glass, and I could hear it crash and tinkle on the alleyway below. It was at this juncture that I, in trying to get up, had the uncanny sensation of feeling my bed above me! **Q** Foggy with sleep, I now suspected, in my turn, that the whole uproar was being made in a frantic endeavor to extricate me from what must be an unheard-of and perilous situation. "Get me out of this!" I bawled. "Get me out!" I think I had the nightmarish belief that I was entombed in a mine. "Gugh," gasped Briggs, floundering in his camphor.

By this time my mother, still shouting, pursued by Herman, still shouting, was trying to open the door to the attic, in order to go up and get my father's body out of the wreckage. The door was stuck, however, and wouldn't yield. Her frantic pulls on it only added to the general banging and confusion. Roy and the dog were now up, the one shouting questions, the other barking.

Father, farthest away and soundest sleeper of all, had by this time been awakened by the battering on the attic door. He decided that the house was on fire. "I'm coming, I'm coming!" he wailed in a slow, sleepy voice—it took him many minutes to regain full consciousness. My mother, still believing he was caught under the bed, detected in his "I'm coming!" the mournful, resigned note of one who is preparing to meet his Maker. "He's dying!" she shouted.

---

8. Briggs is overwhelmed by a flood *(deluge)* of strong-smelling, sharp-tasting *(pungent)* fumes.

Vocabulary

uncanny (un kan′ ē) *adj.* so strange as to cause fear or wonder; weird
endeavor (en dev′ ər) *n.* a serious attempt to accomplish something; undertaking
extricate (eks′ trə kāt′) *v.* to release from entanglement or difficulty; set free

Teaching Support

Grammar and Language Minilesson

Consistency in Verb Tense Point out that Thurber is consistent in his use of verb tenses. Explain to students that all of the verbs are in the past tense because all of the actions took place at the same time in the past: *yelled, believed, found, unlocked*, etc.

Activity Read the following passage and have students identify the inconsistencies in verb tense. Have them tell what form of the verbs should be used.

Last night people gathered for the rally. The candidate stands at the podium and waved to the crowd. Delegates danced on chairs and throw flowers. (*Stands* should be *stood;* *throw* should be *threw*) **L1**

Additional Resources

- ***Grammar and Language Transparency 35***
- ***Grammar and Language Workbook,*** pp. 83–86
- ***Grammar and Composition Handbook,*** Lesson 3.5
- ***Writer's Choice,*** Lesson 10.5

"I'm all right!" Briggs yelled to reassure her. "I'm all right!" He still believed that it was his own closeness to death that was worrying mother. I found at last the light switch in my room, unlocked the door, and Briggs and I joined the others at the attic door. The dog, who never did like Briggs, jumped for him—assuming that he was the culprit in whatever was going on—and Roy had to throw Rex and hold him. We could hear father crawling out of bed upstairs. Roy pulled the attic door open, with a mighty jerk, and father came down the stairs, sleepy and irritable but safe and sound. My mother began to weep when she saw him. Rex began to howl. "What in the name of God is going on here?" asked father.

U The situation was finally put together like a gigantic jigsaw puzzle. Father caught a cold from prowling around in his bare feet but there were no other bad results. "I'm glad," said mother, who always looked on the bright side of things, "that your grandfather wasn't here."

❖

ACTIVE READING MODEL

VISUALIZE

What would a videotape or photograph of this scene look like?

RESPOND

Do you agree with Thurber that this story would make "a better recitation than it does a piece of writing"? Why or why not?

Vocabulary
culprit (kul′ prit) *n.* one guilty of some offense

T Active Reading Strategies

VISUALIZE *(There would be a small hall crowded with people dressed for bed, rushing about and shouting. The dog is barking and jumping on Briggs.)*

U Literary Elements

FIGURATIVE LANGUAGE: *Simile* A simile compares two unlike things using *like* or *as.* Ask students to identify the things being compared in this sentence. *(The situation and a puzzle.)* What is common to both? *(Both begin scrambled and have many pieces to be put together.)*

V Active Reading Strategies

RESPOND *(Students may agree that the confusion and noise in the story make it suitable for a recitation.)*

Thematic Focus

Where the Heart Is What is Thurber's attitude toward his family? Is he mean-spirited or mocking in any way? Ask students to support their responses with details from the essay. *(The author is not mocking his relatives. He is never caustic or biting in talking about them.)*

FINE ART TRANSPARENCY 2

You may wish to use ***Fine Art Transparency 2*** to extend theme concepts.

ASSESSMENT

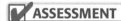

Quick Checks, p. 37

Listening and Speaking *Minilesson*

Interviewing Review the important aspects of interviewing:

- Prepare: Set a purpose. Develop a thorough list of questions to ask the interviewee.
- Interview: Listen carefully. Take notes. Get clarification on any important but unclear points. Ask for examples that support the person's statements.
- Conclude: Thank the person for taking the time to be interviewed.

Activity Have pairs of students role-play interviews with Thurber's family about the night the bed fell. Ask one student to identify his or her character while the partner prepares the interview accordingly. The class can take notes and discuss the strong points of the interviews, developing a list of effective interviewing techniques. **L2**

Responding to the Selection

PERSONAL RESPONSE

- Possibilities include humorous stories or stories about a similarly chaotic experience.
- If students choose the Visualize strategy, they might describe father's bed in the attic, Aunt Gracie's throwing shoes, and Rex's attacking Briggs.

Analyzing Literature

1. The night the bed fell on the narrator is what Thurber referred to as "the high-water mark of his youth."
2. Thurber describes his grandfather; cousin Briggs; aunts Melissa, Sarah, and Gracie; and brother Herman.
3. The narrator tips his cot over, causing a loud noise.
4. Mrs. Thurber thinks the bed in the attic fell on her husband.
5. Father thinks the house is on fire.
6. The first paragraph shows that Thurber's purpose is to entertain readers.
7. Because these people are somewhat strange, readers can believe that they would react as they do later in the story.
8. Her conclusion is consistent with her pessimistic personality.
9. The narrator admits at the beginning that the tale is "incredible," preparing us for what might seem like an exaggeration.
10. Students might choose a family situation that is already humorous or one that challenges them to create humor.

Active Reading and Critical Thinking

Responding to Literature

PERSONAL RESPONSE

- Take a look at your responses to the **Reading Focus** on page 398. Which of your family stories do you think Thurber would have most enjoyed hearing? Why?

Active Reading Response

Look back at the **Active Reading Strategies** described on page 397. Choose one of the strategies and find three places in the selection where you could apply it.

Analyzing Literature

RECALL

1. What did Thurber call "the high-water mark" of his youth?
2. Which relatives with "crotchets" or strange ideas does Thurber describe?
3. What starts the chain of events that Thurber narrates?
4. What does Mrs. Thurber think happened?
5. What does Father think is happening when he is awakened by all the noise?

Brackets connect questions that are paired to develop higher-level thinking skills.

INTERPRET

6. What can you tell from the first paragraph about Thurber's purpose for this essay?
7. How does the introduction of Thurber's strange relatives prepare you for the rest of the essay?
8. In what way is Mother's conclusion that Father is dying characteristic of her personality?

EVALUATE AND CONNECT

9. How does Thurber prepare readers that this essay, though based on fact, is going to be exaggerated and humorous?
10. Theme Connection How has this selection changed the way you think about your own family stories? What parts of your own family history might you use to write a humorous essay?

LITERARY ELEMENTS

Characterization

The methods a writer uses to develop the personality of a character are called **characterization.** In direct characterization, a writer makes direct statements about a character's personality, as in this description: "We had visiting us at this time a nervous first cousin of mine named Briggs Beall, who believed that he was likely to cease breathing when he was asleep." Characterization can also be indirect. Thurber does not directly state that his grandfather was eccentric. Rather, he describes the man's strange behavior to give readers that impression. Writers often characterize through a character's words, actions, and interactions with other characters.

1. Choose one of the characters in the essay. Then find and list all of the descriptions Thurber uses to characterize that person.
2. Write a sentence or two of your own describing that character's personality.

• See **Literary Terms Handbook,** p. R2.

LITERARY ELEMENTS

1. Students might choose Grandfather, who disappears for days at a time and returns with news of the Civil War.
2. Grandfather might be described as an interesting man who has lost touch with reality.

Additional Resources

Literary Elements Transparency 37

Literature and Writing

Writing About Literature

Recognizing Climax The **climax** is a story's point of highest interest, or turning point. Ask yourself, at what point is the conflict of the evening at Thurber's house resolved? When does the outcome of the essay become clear? Write a paragraph that describes the story's climax.

Creative Writing

Another Point of View Choose one of the characters in the essay. Retell the events from that character's point of view. Remember to begin this version from the moment in the evening where your character would have been aware of the strange happenings.

Extending Your Response

Literature Groups

Diagramming the Confusion The sequence of events in "The Night the Bed Fell" is quite elaborate. One way to help recall all the "remarkable incidents" is to make a chain-of-events diagram showing how each event caused the next event. Share your group's diagram with those of the other groups.

Interdisciplinary Activity

Art: A Cartoonist at Heart James Thurber is well known as a cartoonist. His cartoons were published for many years in magazines and books. Look at some examples of his cartoons. Then, in either his style or your own style, draw a series of cartoons about some of the events or characters in "The Night the Bed Fell."

Listening and Speaking

Oral Reading Take turns reading the essay aloud to the rest of the class. Pay attention to how your voice can reflect the selection's humorous events.

Reading Further

If you would like to read more humorous stories by James Thurber, try these books:

Fables for Our Time and Famous Poems

The 13 Clocks

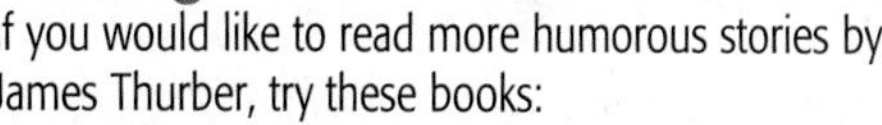

Save your work for your portfolio.

Literature and Writing

Writing About Literature

Students' explanations should

- identify the climax as the point at which Father exits the attic, safe and sound
- indicate that the outcome becomes clear in the last paragraph when the family members understand what's happened and that no one is hurt
- make specific references to the text

Creative Writing

Students' narratives should

- record events one after the other, as the original does
- keep with the personality of the character
- include the original narrator in the telling of the event

Extending Your Response

Literature Groups Suggest that students use boxes to encapsulate events and draw arrows from one to the other to indicate cause-and-effect relationships.

Interdisciplinary Activity Suggest that students choose characters and events not captured in the drawings in the selection.

Listening and Speaking Remind students that Thurber says the incident is ideal for being told aloud. Encourage students to have fun with different voices and sound effects.

Skill Minilessons

GRAMMAR AND LANGUAGE
PARENTHESES

Parentheses within sentences:
- p. 399: *(unless, as some friends...five or six times)*
- p. 403: *(just under father's attic bedroom)*
- p. 403: *(I had lied to Briggs)*

Complete sentences within parentheses:
- p. 400 *(On these occasions... didn't have a chance.)*
- p. 403: *(It was my mother..."the night the bed fell on your father.")*

READING AND THINKING
EXAGGERATION

Suggest that students exaggerate amounts, heights, and sounds as well as actions and reactions.

VOCABULARY
ANTONYMS

1. a
2. c
3. a
4. c
5. b

Additional Resources

- ***Grammar and Language Workbook,*** pp. 275–276
- ***Grammar and Composition Handbook,*** Lesson 13.8
- ***Writer's Choice,*** Lesson 20.8
- ***Reading Skills Practice Workbook***
- ***Vocabulary Practice,*** p. 24

Skill Minilessons

Reteach · Review

GRAMMAR AND LANGUAGE • PARENTHESES

Writers use parentheses to set off words that define, add information, or helpfully explain a word in the sentence. For example, in "The Night the Bed Fell," Thurber uses parentheses to set off a description: "Old Aunt Melissa Beall (who could whistle like a man, with two fingers in her mouth) suffered under the premonition that she was destined to die on South High Street." Parentheses can also be used around an entire sentence that adds extra information to a paragraph.

PRACTICE Skim "The Night the Bed Fell" to find three other examples of parentheses within sentences and two complete sentences that are enclosed in parentheses. Choose one of the examples and write about why you think Thurber chose to include the information within parentheses.

- For more about parentheses, see **Language Handbook,** pp. R41–R42.

READING AND THINKING • EXAGGERATION

Much of the humor in "The Night the Bed Fell" comes from Thurber's exaggeration of his characters' actions. He stretches the truth until his essay is much funnier than everyday life.

PRACTICE Think of something from your own life that you can tell as an **anecdote,** a short account of an interesting event or incident. First write your anecdote in a straightforward way, without humor. Then write it a second time, using exaggeration to make it humorous.

VOCABULARY • ANTONYMS

Finding synonyms is usually easier than finding **antonyms,** or opposites. You often have to think about what a word really means before you can figure out a good antonym for it. When you need to choose an antonym for a given word, don't give up just because the answer is not obvious right away. You might have to think about it.

PRACTICE Choose the word that is most closely opposite in meaning to the first word in each item.

1. **avert**
   a. cause b. discourage c. attempt
2. **uncanny**
   a. lovely b. pleasant c. normal
3. **perilous**
   a. safe b. boring c. fortunate
4. **fortitude**
   a. sadness b. playfulness c. weakness
5. **extricate**
   a. search b. trap c. irritate

ASSESSMENT

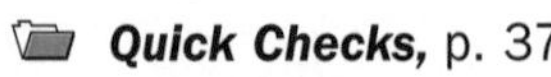

- ***Quick Checks,*** p. 37
- ***Selection and Theme Assessment,*** pp. 65–66
- ***Performance Assessment,*** p. 35
- ***Testmaker: ExamView Pro***
- ***Interactive Tutor: Self-Assessment***

MEDIA Connection

COMIC STRIP

Cartoon strips, or comic strips, are among the most popular newspaper features. Few comic strips have been as well liked or as long lasting as Charles Schulz's *Peanuts,* which began in 1950.

Analyzing Media

1. Why does the cartoonist have Snoopy respond with "Au revoir," the French words for "See you later"? How does that response contrast with what Charlie Brown has been saying to his dog?
2. Snoopy and many other animal characters used in cartoon strips speak and often do the same kinds of things humans do. How does this add to the humor of the strip?

Objective

- To understand and apply strategies for reading a cartoon strip

Literature LINK

The Dog Diaries This cartoon strip connects to "The Dog Diaries" (pp. 411–416). Highlight the connection by pointing out that Snoopy, the dog in the *Peanuts* cartoon, has a secret personality and sense of humor that escape the notice of his human friends. In "The Dog Diaries," Merrill Markoe seeks to understand the secret lives of her pets—by living as they do.

Analyzing Media

1. Some students may recognize the irony of the dog's speaking French to a boy who has just commented on the dog's lack of education; others may think Snoopy is just bored with Charlie Brown's chatter.
2. Students may say that it is the inappropriateness of having the animals say, think, and do things we attribute only to humans that creates humor.

Additional Resources

Media Connections, p. 8

inTIME ***inTIME* magazine**

Teaching Support

Reading Minilesson

Sequence of Events Point out to students the importance of the sequence of events in the *Peanuts* cartoon.

Activity Ask students to look through newspapers, magazines, or the Internet for comic strips that are organized in separate boxes, like the *Peanuts* cartoon on this page. Have students bring their cartoons to class and share them with partners. Then have students cut out each box of their cartoons and rearrange the boxes, jumbling the cartoon's sequence of events. Have partners reassemble the cartoons in the proper order. Discuss how important sequence of events is in making the humor clear. **L2**

Additional Resources

Reading Skills Practice Workbook

interNET CONNECTION

Comical Animals Have students use search engines to look for Web sites that focus on animals featured in cartoon strips.

Before Reading

Objectives

- To read and enjoy a humorous essay about the behavior of dogs
- To recognize the role of point of view in a work of nonfiction
- To write a humorous piece in the style of the selection's author

Skills

Reading/Thinking: Identifying Spatial Relationships; Evaluating; Drawing Conclusions; Identifying Author's Purpose; Inferring
Writing: Diary Entry
Vocabulary: Prefixes
Grammar/Language: Subject-Verb Agreement; Principal Parts of Verbs
Listening/Speaking: Performing Self-Written Script
Life Skills: Goal Setting
Collaboration: Literature Groups; Television Script

Motivating STUDENTS

Selection Launchers: "A Visit with Merrill Markoe"

Videodisc Side A, Segment 10

Also available in VHS.

Selection Focus Transparency 38: Have students view the transparency and encourage them to speculate about why the cartoonist decided on dogs to deliver the idea.

Reading Focus: Have small groups use precise language and sensory imagery to share ideas about why dogs are so popular all over the world.

Before You Read

The Dog Diaries

MEET MERRILL MARKOE

When Merrill Markoe's neighbors see her outside with Lewis and Beau, her two dogs, they must wonder if she is about to start barking. The Emmy-award-winning comedy writer has been known to imitate her dogs in an effort to understand them. Markoe has written humor for *Late Night with David Letterman*, a number of television specials, and popular magazines.

Merrill Markoe was born in 1949. This essay was first published in 1992.

READING FOCUS

Have you ever wondered why dogs chase their tails or why cats claw couches?

Think/Pair/Share

What is your personal theory about pet behavior? With a partner, discuss your thoughts on why pets do the strange things they do. Use examples from pets you know.

Setting a Purpose

Read this essay to find out what one dog owner discovers about the behavior of her dogs.

BUILDING BACKGROUND

Did You Know? The dog family includes wolves, foxes, jackals, and wild and domestic dogs. All members of the dog family have teeth adapted to kill their prey, chew meat, and gnaw bones. Whether they live in packs in the wild or alone in a home, they rely upon their alert ears and sensitive noses for survival.

VOCABULARY PREVIEW

infantile (in′ fən tīl′) *adj.* like an infant; childish; p. 413
comprehend (kom′ pri hend′) *v.* to grasp mentally; understand fully; p. 413
ascertain (as′ ər tān′) *v.* to find out with certainty; determine; p. 413
obsession (əb sesh′ ən) *n.* a single emotion or idea that occupies or troubles the mind; p. 414
murky (mur′ kē) *adj.* dark; not clear; p. 414
etiquette (et′ i kit) *n.* the rules of good manners and polite behavior; p. 414
collaborator (kə lab′ ə rā′ tər) *n.* one who works or cooperates with another; p. 415
confront (kən frunt′) *v.* to come face to face with; stand facing; p. 416

410 THEME 4

RESOURCE MANAGER

Teaching Tools and Resources
- Theme Four Planning Guide
- Literature Groups Sourcebook
- Presentation Plus! CD-ROM

Essential Lesson Support

Lesson-Specific Instruction
- Selection Focus Transparency 38
- Literary Elements Transparency 38
- Active Reading Guide,* p. 38
- Selection Vocabulary Practice, p. 25
- inTIME *inTIME* magazine, p. 32

Assessment
- Selection Quick Checks,* p. 38
- Sel. and Theme Assmt., pp. 67–68
- Testmaker: ExamView Pro
- Performance Assessment, p. 36

Systematic Language Instruction
- Gr. and Comp. Hbk., L. 8.4
- Vocabulary Power, Unit 4 Review/Test
- Spelling Power, Unit 4 Review/Proofreading

English Language Learners
- ELL Sourcebook, p. 63

- Spanish Summaries, p. 38
- Audio Library*
- English, Yes!

Spec. Needs/Strat. Interven.
- Interactive Reading Sourcebook, pp. T149–T151
- Interactive Rdg. Wkbk., pp. 69–70
- Audio Library*

* Also available in Spanish

Merrill Markoe

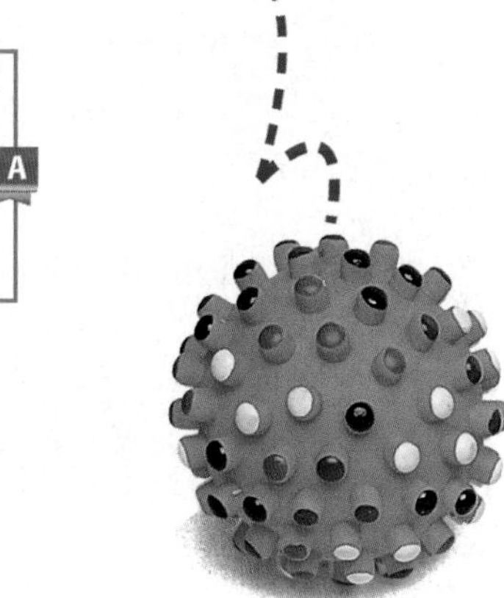

I pick dogs that remind me of myself—scrappy, mutt-faced, with a hint of mange.[1] People look for a reflection of their own personalities or the person they dream of being in the eyes of an animal companion. That is the reason I sometimes look into the face of my dog Stan and see wistful sadness and existential angst,[2] when all he is actually doing is slowly scanning the ceiling for flies.

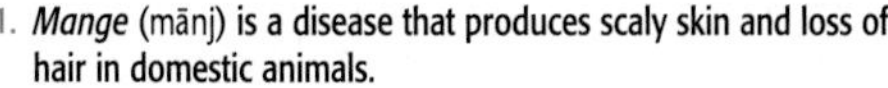

1. *Mange* (mānj) is a disease that produces scaly skin and loss of hair in domestic animals.
2. *Existential angst* (eg′ zis ten′ shəl ängst) involves feelings of depression or worry over the value and meaning of one's life.

Reading the Selection

SUMMARY

In an attempt to understand her two dogs better, their owner decides to live as one of them for a day and record their adventures in a diary. She writes from a dog's point of view but inserts some human comments on their activities. At dinnertime the man of the house says harsh things about the mess the dogs made in the house, so the narrator—in a final person-as-dog gesture—waits until his back is turned and uses her teeth to steal his sandwich from his plate.

Spanish Summaries, p. 38

A Active Reading Strategies

CONNECT Encourage students to think about dogs they know and their owners. Have them discuss whether the author's generalization is valid.

VOCABULARY If you haven't previewed the selection vocabulary with students, stop and remind them to use context clues to unlock the meanings of new vocabulary words.

Additional Resources

Active Reading Guide, p. 38

Audio Library

Spanish Audio Library

Teaching Support

CONNECTING TO OTHER SELECTIONS

The chart at the right shows three ways to connect "The Dog Diaries" to other selections in this book.

For specific teaching strategies, see the ***Theme Four Planning Guide.***

Connection		Title
Life Skills: Implementing and Performing	→	"Fish Cheeks," p.77
Thematic: Facing Challenge	→	"A Boy and His Dog," p. 243
Literary: Point of View	→	"Almost Ready," p. 20

VIEWING THE PAINTING

George Rodrigue, born in 1944 in New Iberia, Louisiana, is best known for his Cajun landscapes, his portraits, and his blue dog paintings. The dog's name is Tiffany.

Viewing Response *There are many possible answers. In fact, Rodrigue's first blue dog was a loup-garou, or Cajun ghost dog, that looked blue in the moonlight.*

Historical Note

Wild canines learned to follow early hunters for meat scraps left at campsites. Humans may have begun keeping them around because they warned of threatening animals. Gradually, an interdependent relationship developed.

On The Lighter Side

"The probable view of the fox terrier or dachshund which lies upon our hearthrug is that he is one of a pack, the other members of which are the human inhabitants of the house… From the dog's point of view, his master is an elongated and abnormally cunning dog."

—Louise Robinson

My Favorite Part of Town, 1990. George Rodrigue. Oil on canvas, 30 x 24 in. Private collection.

Viewing the painting: Why do you think the artist painted the dog blue?

Teaching Support

MEETING INDIVIDUAL NEEDS — ENGLISH LANGUAGE LEARNERS

Pets Across Cultures People in almost every culture have pets. Pets are enjoyed by city-dwellers, suburbanites, and those who live in rural areas. In different countries and different types of locations, however, people may have different kinds of pets. Ask students to discuss pets in various cultures or in different locations.

Activity Have students plan and conduct a survey on pets in different cultures. Help students develop a set of questions to use for the survey. Then have students interview people from a variety of cultures or locations and compare their results.

Additional Resources

English Language Learners Sourcebook, p. 63

We pet owners demand a great deal from our pets. When we give them the job, it's a career position. Pets are required to listen to us blithely,[3] even if we talk to them in infantile and goofy tones of voice that we'd never dare use around another human being for fear of being forced into psychiatric observation. On top of that, we make them wear little sweaters or jackets, and not just the cool kind with the push-up sleeves, either, but weird little felt ones that say, *It's raining cats and dogs*.

We are pretty sure that we and our pets share the same reality, until one day we come home to find that our wistful, intelligent friend who reminds us of our better self has decided a good way to spend the day is to open a box of Brillo pads, unravel a few, distribute some throughout the house, and eat or wear all the rest. And we shake our heads in an inability to comprehend what went wrong here.

Is he bored or is he just out for revenge? He certainly can't be as stupid as this would indicate. In order to answer these questions more fully, I felt I needed some kind of new perspective, a perspective that comes from really knowing both sides of the story.

Thus, I made up my mind to live with my pets as one of them: to share their hopes, their fears, their squeaking vinyl lamb chops, their drinking space at the toilet.

What follows is the revealing, sometimes shocking, sometimes terrifying, sometimes really stupid diary that resulted.

8:45 A.M. We have been lying on our sides in the kitchen for almost an hour now. We started out in the bedroom with just our heads under the bed. But then one of us heard something, and we all ran to the back door. I think our quick response was rather effective because, although I never ascertained exactly what we heard to begin with, I also can't say I recall ever hearing it again.

9:00 A.M. We carefully inspected the molding in the hallway, which led us straight to the heating duct by the bedroom. Just a coincidence? None of us was really sure. So we watched it suspiciously for a while. Then we watched it for a little while longer.

Then, never letting it out of our sight, we all took a nap.

10:00 A.M. I don't really know whose idea it was to yank back the edge of the carpet and pull apart the carpet pad, but talk about a rousing good time! How strange that I could have lived in this house for all these years, and never before felt the fur of a carpet between my teeth. Or actually bit into a moist, chewy chunk of carpet padding. I will never again think of the carpet as simply a covering for the floor.

11:15 A.M. When we all wound up in the kitchen, the other two began to stare at me eagerly. Their meaning was clear. The pressure was on for me to produce snacks. They remembered the old me—the one with the prehensile[4] thumb, the one who could

3. To listen *blithely* is to do so in a lighthearted and carefree way.

4. A thumb that can grasp something by folding around it is *prehensile* (prē hen′ sil). Some monkeys have prehensile fingers and tails.

Vocabulary

infantile (in′ fən tīl′) *adj.* like an infant; childish
comprehend (kom′ pri hend′) *v.* to grasp mentally; understand fully
ascertain (as′ ər tān′) *v.* to find out with certainty; determine

B Literary Elements

POINT OF VIEW The author is poking fun at pet owners. Ask students how her point of view makes "poking fun" acceptable. *(The author includes herself in the group and sees some of her group's behaviors and attitudes as humorous.)*

C Author's Craft

TONE: *Humor* One way of achieving humor is through contrast. Ask students to identify the contrast in this passage and explain why it is funny. *(The author puts in the same list the human qualities of "hopes" and "fears" along with the very animal-like "vinyl lamb chops" and "drinking space at the toilet.")*

D Literary Elements

POINT OF VIEW Still speaking in the first person, the narrator switches to the plural. Ask students who else is included in "we." *(Her two dogs are included.)* What does this change in point of view accomplish? *(It shows us that the narrator is now in the dogs' "group" mentality.)*

E Literary Elements

ABSTRACT VS. CONCRETE LANGUAGE To make the experiment humorous yet factual, the author includes concrete details of dog behavior. Ask students to list dog behaviors in this sequence and comment on the accuracy of the details. *(Actions include inspecting the molding, following it, staring at the heating duct, and losing interest in it. The details accurately capture a dog's behavior.)*

Reading Minilesson

Identifying Spatial Relationships

This strategy helps readers use distance, shape, and location descriptors to understand setting, plot events, character's actions, or causality. Some spatial signal words that answer the "where" question include *between, below, left, near, in,* and *beside.* Encourage students to look for signal words as they read the story.

Activity Have students work in groups. Have each group choose one scene from the story and create a diagram or sketch of the scene. Ask each group to create a customized title for it that includes a spatial signal word. **L2**

Additional Resources

Reading Skills Practice Workbook

DRAFTING

Catch Your Reader's Eye Remind students that the first sentence written is not necessarily the best first sentence for a passage. Encourage them to look over their first paragraphs to find favorite sentences or images that may be used as effective opening sentences.

Work with Details In addition to following their prewriting plans, students may wish to use the pages of random details and images they created during the prewriting process.

REVISING

Take Another Look If students exchange papers with partners, they can have the partners read their passages aloud. Hearing their work read by someone else can be a valuable part of the revising process. If the partner stumbles over certain words or phrases, the writer might want to go back and make sure the syntax is clear. In addition, the writer may form new impressions while listening to the work and can revise it accordingly.

GLENCOE TECHNOLOGY

REVISING WITH STYLE
CD-ROM
Invite students to use the *Revising with Style* CD-ROM, which offers instruction and exercises to help students improve their writing skills.

Teaching Support

DRAFTING

DRAFTING TIP
If you get a new idea while drafting, go ahead and try it. If it leads you off track, your prewriting notes can bring you back.

TECHNOLOGY TIP
On a computer, copy your draft before you revise. By saving the original, you are free to experiment. If an experiment doesn't turn out well, you can return to your original draft and try again.

Catch Your Reader's Eye

Try beginning with a single vivid image. Show the person in a characteristic pose. Show the place at one specific time. You might go on to state your main impression near the end of this first paragraph.

STUDENT MODEL • DRAFTING

From the window of the bus, I can see the golden meadow, the big white house with the red roof, and the trees that circle the hidden pond. Behind them are the mountains that tower over everything like giants.

Complete Student Model on p. R108.

Work with Details

Follow your prewriting plan, using sensory details to illustrate your statements. Include details that show your feelings so that readers can tell what the place or person means to you. To conclude, you might refer again to your main impression and reflect on the role that this place or person plays in your life.

REVISING

REVISING TIP
If you reword your main impression to make it more precise, adjust your paragraphs to illustrate the revised version.

Take Another Look

Read over your description. Did your main impression change as you drafted? If so, reword it now to reflect your new insights. Use the **Rubric for Revising** to plan other changes, or trade papers with a partner and go over the rubric with each other. Keep revising until your description is as good as you can make it.

RUBRIC FOR REVISING

Your revised descriptive essay should have
- a vivid introduction that captures readers' attention and that states your main impression
- a consistent pattern of organization
- details that appeal to the senses
- a conclusion that restates and reflects on your main impression

Your revised essay should be free of
- irrelevant details
- errors in grammar, usage, and mechanics

Writing Minilesson

Descriptive Images In revising and refining their passages, students may benefit from hearing which of their descriptions and images classmates enjoyed most.

Activity Set up small writing workshop groups around the classroom. Give students time to read their passages aloud to their groups. Ask listeners to jot down notes on the descriptions, images, or impressions they liked best. When a student has finished reading, the other writers in the workshop group can let him or her know which details left an impression on them. **L2**

Additional Resources

Writer's Choice, Lesson 3.2

EDITING/PROOFREADING

Before you make a final copy of your description, use the **Proofreading Checklist** to spot errors. Correct any that you find.

Grammar Hint

In a compound sentence, you can use *however* to join two clauses. Put a semicolon before *however* and a comma after it.

I liked winters there; however, I think summer was my favorite season.

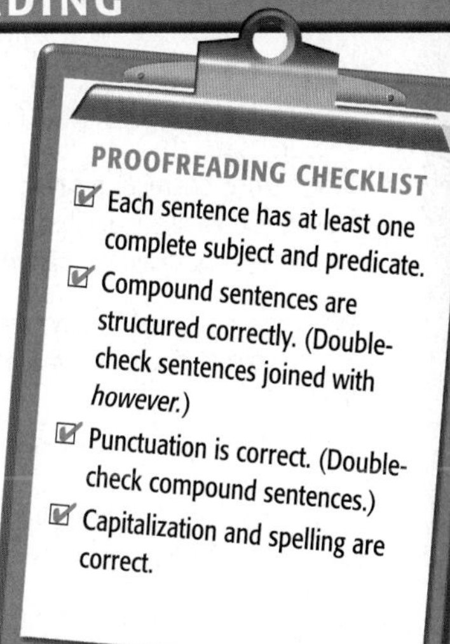

PROOFREADING CHECKLIST

- Each sentence has at least one complete subject and predicate.
- Compound sentences are structured correctly. (Double-check sentences joined with *however.*)
- Punctuation is correct. (Double-check compound sentences.)
- Capitalization and spelling are correct.

STUDENT MODEL • EDITING/PROOFREADING

I no longer live near the Pond; however, I often visited it in my mind.

Complete Student Model on p. R108.

Complete Student Model

For a complete version of the model developed in this Workshop, see **Writing Workshop Models**, p. R108.

PUBLISHING/PRESENTING

Consider submitting your description to a magazine that publishes young people's writing. Your teacher or a librarian can suggest magazines, show you how to find their addresses, and help you prepare your manuscript for submission.

PRESENTING TIP

Some magazines have Web sites that tell you how to submit manuscripts.

Reflecting

Take time to think about the following questions; then write your responses.

- Did your view of your subject change as you worked on this description? If so, explain how. If not, offer some ideas about why it did not.
- Which aspects of your subject come through best in your description? Which aspects come through only faintly or are left out?

Save your work for your portfolio.

EDITING/PROOFREADING

Have students use the Proofreading Checklist to review their work. Encourage them to check for each item on the list in separate readings, paying special attention to compound sentences.

Additional Resources

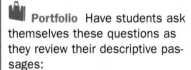

Grammar and Composition Handbook, Lesson 16.4

PUBLISHING/PRESENTING

Have students read through a few magazines that publish writing for young readers to determine which publication might be most receptive to the passage they have written.

Reflecting

Portfolio Have students ask themselves these questions as they review their descriptive passages:

- Would the person I have written about recognize himself or herself?
- If someone were to draw a picture of the place I have described, what would it look like?
- What parts of descriptive writing are most difficult for me? What parts do I like best?

6+1 TRAITS™ OF WRITING

See the annotated **Writing Workshop Models** on pp. R103–R115 for additional help in evaluating student writing and in teaching the **6+1 Traits™ of effective writing.** Annotations and minilessons address and reinforce the **6+1 Traits™:** Ideas, Organization, Voice, Word Choice, Sentence Fluency, Conventions, and Presentation.

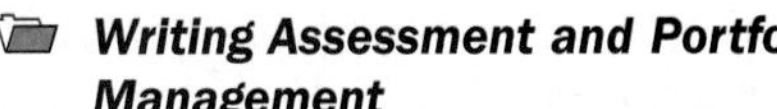

ASSESSMENT

Writing Assessment and Portfolio Management

- Writing Assessment, pp. 1–12, 23–25
- Portfolio Management, pp. 39–45

Theme Assessment

Objectives

- To offer a personal response to the selections and activities in this theme
- To write a comparison of two essays
- To complete a self-evaluation, set a goal, and devise a plan for achieving the goal

Responding to the Theme

1. Students should cite examples from selections in their responses.
2. Have students explain what they learned by relating the selections to their own experiences with home and family.
3. Allow time for students to share their charts, policy statements, and home projects with the class.

Analyzing Literature

Students' writing should

- include an introductory paragraph that identifies the two essays and the element being compared
- contain examples and quotes taken directly from the essays

Evaluate and Set Goals

Evaluate

Have students review the work they have done in Theme 4 and compile a list of activities they have completed for each task. Suggest that they add other tasks as well, such as viewing and discussing artwork.

Set Goals

Have students create goal pyramids. The goal should be written at the top of the pyramid and the three steps needed to achieve it in three tiers beneath the goal. Suggest that students also make detailed notes to use for each step. Discuss students' plans in individual conferences.

Theme Assessment

Responding to the Theme

1. Which story, poem, or essay in this theme most helped you think about what home and family mean to you? Explain your answer.
2. What new ideas do you have about the following as a result of reading the literature in this theme?
   - How the people and places you love affect your life
   - The importance of seeing warmth and humor in family situations
3. Present your theme project to the class.

Analyzing Literature

COMPARE ESSAYS

Compare two essays from this theme. You may compare them in terms of point of view, use of humor, vividness of characters, or the author's purpose. Remember to support your opinions with quotations from the essays.

Evaluate and Set Goals

1. Which of the following tasks was most rewarding to you? Which was most difficult?
   - reading and thinking about the stories, poems, and essays
   - doing independent writing
   - analyzing the stories, poems, and essays in discussions
   - performing dramatizations
   - doing research
2. Using the following scale, how would you assess your work in this theme? Give at least two reasons for your assessment.

   4 = outstanding   2 = fair
   3 = good   1 = weak
3. Based on what you found difficult in this theme, choose a goal to work toward in the next theme.
   - Write down your goal and three steps you will need to take to help you reach it.
   - Meet with your teacher to review your goal and your plan for achieving it.

Build Your Portfolio

SELECT

Select two pieces of work you did during this theme to include in your portfolio. Use the following questions to help you decide.

- Which work do you consider your best?
- From which work did you learn the most?
- Which work did you enjoy the most?

REFLECT

Write some notes to accompany the work you selected. Use these questions to guide you.

- What do you like best about the piece?
- What did you learn from creating it?
- What might you do differently if you were beginning this piece again?

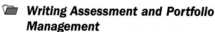

ASSESSMENT

Writing Assessment and Portfolio Management

- Writing Assessment, pp. 1–12
- Portfolio Management, pp. 39–45

GLENCOE TECHNOLOGY

MINDJOGGER VIDEOQUIZZES VIDEODISC

Use ***MindJogger*** to review the Theme Four content.

Theme 4
Side A

Also available in VHS.

Reading on Your Own

Have you enjoyed reading the essays, stories, and poems in this theme? Here are some other books you might like.

Dragonwings

by Laurence Yep A Chinese immigrant father and son build a flying machine in the era of the Wright brothers and the San Francisco earthquake.

Homecoming

by Cynthia Voigt This poignant story focuses on the four Tillerman kids, left parentless when they are abandoned by their mother. They must struggle to stay together and to find someone to shelter them and love them.

Where Angels Glide at Dawn: New Stories from Latin America

edited by Lori M. Carlson and Cynthia L. Ventura Homes and families provide a background in several of these ten stories from Latin America. The stories display a variety of cultures and writing styles.

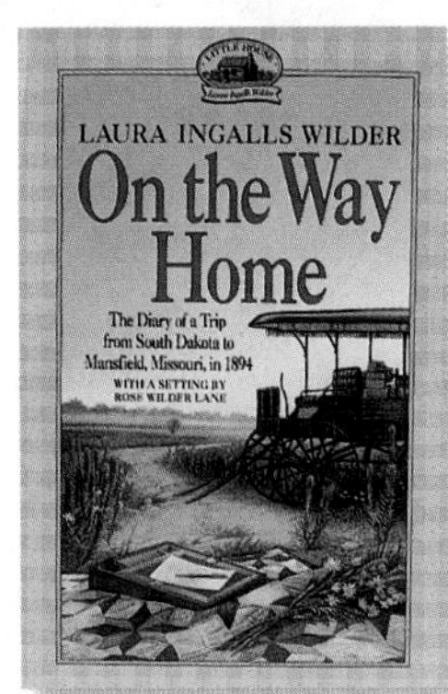

On the Way Home

by Laura Ingalls Wilder and Rose Wilder Lane The diary of the author of *Little House on the Prairie* describes her family's exciting 1894 journey from South Dakota to a new home in the Missouri Ozarks. Her daughter adds her own memories of the trip.

Reading on Your Own

Tips for Independent Reading

Stress the importance of each student's spending at least thirty minutes a day in independent reading and suggest books, such as those shown here, related to this theme.

Writer's Craft The books described here can be read primarily for entertainment. Remind students that besides reading at a normal rate to enjoy the stories, they will find it interesting at times to read more slowly to appreciate the writers' craft—word choice, use of imagery, sentence patterns—and to discover models for their own writing.

Practice Have students take notes as they read so that later they can share with the class or a group particularly apt descriptions; appealing analogies, similes, and metaphors; effective transitions; interesting new words or phrases; and familiar words used a new way.

Glencoe Literature Library

Dragonwings is available in the *Glencoe Literature Library*. For a complete listing of the titles, see the **Glencoe Resources for Independent Reading** in the front of this book.

The *Glencoe Literature Library Study Guide* provides instructional support and student activities for works in the *Glencoe Literature Library*.

MEETING INDIVIDUAL NEEDS — SPECIAL NEEDS

You may wish to recommend *Dragonwings*, by Laurence Yep, to your less-proficient readers and English language learners. Language is a challenge faced by one of the characters in this exciting story. **L1**

The following books are rated for average readers (L2) or for students who need more challenging reading (L3):

- *Homecoming* by Cynthia Voigt **L2**
- *On the Way Home* by Laura Ingalls Wilder and Rose Wilder Lane **L2**
- *Where Angels Glide at Dawn: New Stories from Latin America* edited by Lori M. Carlson and Cynthia L. Ventura **L3**

Additional Resources

Inclusion Strategies

Standardized Test Practice

TEST-TAKING TIP

Review the idea of "best possible answer" with the students. Let them know that sometimes more than one answer will seem correct and other times none of the answers will seem correct. When this happens, they should use the process of elimination to eliminate as many answers as possible and then choose the answer that is the "least bad" out of the remaining answers.

TEST-TAKING TIP

Remind students not to leave any answers blank. There are no penalties for wrong answers, so students should fill in every answer on the test. When students really do not know the answer, the best method is to eliminate as many choices as possible, take their best guess, and move on to the next question. They can always come back to the item if they have time left.

Answers and Analyses

1. B This is an example of figurative language, which writers use to create an image in the reader's mind. "Fluttering" and "orange" describe the actual flag, while the reference to "tongue" draws an analogy between the look and movement of the flag in the wind and the look and movement of a tongue.

Standardized Test Practice

Read the passage. Then read each question on page 427. Decide which is the best answer to each question. Mark the letter for that answer on your paper.

Learning the Game

Rita stared ahead at the green grass curving out before her. She could make out the fluttering orange tongue of the flag 250 yards away. She was on the shortest hole at the Shady Views Golf Course, but Rita knew that she was no expert at the first swing off the tee.

Her father sensed her apprehension and gave her a little smile. "It's OK," he said. "I've got a feeling this one is going to work out for you just fine."

"I just can't use this driver," Rita complained, holding up the club in question as if it were a poisonous snake. "I can hit pretty well with the shorter clubs, but I need more practice with the drivers."

"Nothing to it," her father shrugged. "You've got the basics down. Take a wide stance, relax your shoulders, and breathe through the swing. I've seen you do it before. Stop worrying about it and just try it."

"All right," Rita sighed, planting her feet. She limbered her knees and loosely shook her head back and forth. "Talk me through it, okay?"

Her father moved around her and studied her form with a practiced eye. He remembered the first time he had taken Rita golfing after she had expressed interest in the sport—she had been ten years old, but she hadn't been all that bad! True, she needed more work with the bigger clubs, especially the drivers. But he was certain that once she crossed that hurdle, she could be a great player.

"Take a few practice swings . . . very nice. A little wider in your stance . . ."

Rita adjusted her feet accordingly.

"Good!" her father said. "No, no. Straighten the left elbow."

Rita made the correction.

"Yes! Now remember to keep your head tucked. Don't look up until after you've swung through."

"OK. You've helped," Rita mumbled. "Now let me swing."

There was silence for a moment while Rita and her golf ball held quiet commerce with each other. Rita's father knew that golf might not be a game for folks who thought too much, but it surely was a game for those who could concentrate. He knew that Rita could focus with amazing intensity.

Rita took in a sharp breath and slowly released it. Her arms drew back the golf club like a ballet dancer moving through heavy water, graceful and poised. The head of the club rose like a new moon until it crested over her ear. Then the swing came down, rocketing the club around like a whipcord, slicing through the air with a sizzling *huwuuuff!* The ball exploded forward

ENGLISH LANGUAGE LEARNERS

Sports Imagery Ask the class to think about a specific sporting event they have been to. Ask them to write a short poem including images they recall from that particular day. Poems should be written in complete sentences and need not rhyme. Example: "At the basketball game, the ball bounced into the fence. / Red uniforms spun around on the court. / An orange basketball flew." If writing a poem is inappropriate, have students record as many clear images as possible. Go over these images as a class.

like a rifle shot, bolting through the air. Rita and her father watched it fly straight as an arrow toward the flag pin so many yards away.

"That's a keeper—" Rita's father started to say, but then he cut himself off. Suddenly he spun on his heel and dove for his golf bag, digging through a pocket until he found his field glasses. Holding the binoculars up to his eyes for a brief moment, he held his breath before letting out a huge shout.

"What? What is it?" Rita demanded.

"See for yourself," her father laughed, pressing the glasses into her hand.

Rita held the binoculars up to her own eyes and scanned the distant putting green for a sign of her ball. She couldn't find it anywhere. "Did I sink it in the water trap?" she asked. "Why can't I see it?"

Her father's grin was so huge it nearly fell off his face. "Because it's in the cup, Rita," he laughed. "Congratulations! That's your first hole-in-one!"

1 The author refers to the flag as a "fluttering orange tongue" because —
  A the flag was very far away.
  B the flag looked and moved like a tongue.
  C Rita wasn't exactly sure what the flag was.
  D that's what flags are called on golf courses.

2 The main purpose of the story is to show that —
  J sometimes it's better to ask for advice rather than feel discouraged.
  K golf can be a great sport for fathers and daughters to play together.
  L a hole-in-one is one of the rarest events in all sports.
  M hitting with a driver in golf is a difficult skill to master.

3 How does the way Rita feels at the beginning of the story differ from the way her father feels?
  A Rita feels nervous. Her father feels uncertain.
  B Rita feels excited. Her father feels confident.
  C Rita feels uncertain. Her father feels confident.
  D Rita feels confident. Her father feels nervous.

4 Rita wanted her father to talk her through the swing with the driver because —
  J she knew that she was good.
  K she had been playing since she was ten.
  L she was uncertain of her own ability to swing the driver.
  M she wanted to hit a hole-in-one.

5 What literary device does the author use to show Rita and her father's interactions?
  A Flashback
  B Humor
  C Repetition
  D Dialogue

Answers and Analyses

2. J Because all four choices have something to do with the story, this question may be difficult to answer. The main clue to the answer is the father's saying, "Golf is not a game for people who think too much." Choice J is best because it is supported by evidence in the passage. Remind students that correct answers are *always* supported by information in the passage.

3. C To answer this type of question, students must rely upon specific clues from actions taken by the characters of the story. Rita is described as "apprehensive." This, together with her difficulty in swinging a large club, indicates that she is nervous. Rita's father acts calm, and his thoughts show that he has confidence in his daughter. The question states that the way Rita feels *differs* from the way her father feels, ruling out choice A. Using context and general descriptions, students can determine that choice C is best.

4. L The passage states that Rita is nervous about swinging the club. This helps eliminate choices K and M. Choice J can also be eliminated because the father mentions that Rita is a good golfer who just needs work with the large clubs. This leaves L as the best choice.

5. D Students need to understand each of these terms. However, even if students are not familiar with every device, they can still use the process of elimination. A brief flashback is used in the story, but it has nothing to do with the interaction, which rules out choice A. Choice B, *humor,* is not relevant, since the story is not humorous. Choice C can be eliminated because nothing is repeated in the passage. However, the two characters do talk to each other; this is *dialogue.* Therefore, choice D is best.

Tested Objectives

Item	Reading Objective
1	Vocabulary: identify figures of speech
2	Narrative analysis: identify theme
3	Narrative analysis: contrast points of view
4	Narrative analysis: analyze characterization
5	Narrative analysis: analyze literary elements

Theme 5 At a Glance

At the Crossroads

THEME OPENING

Theme 5: AT THE CROSSROADS

SELECTIONS

SKILL FEATURES

WRITING WORKSHOP

THEME ASSESSMENT

- **Responding to the Theme, Analyzing Literature, Evaluate and Set Goals** (p. 534)
- **Build Your Portfolio** (p. 534)
- **Reading on Your Own** (p. 535)
  The Slave Dancer by Paula Fox
  Sounder by William Armstrong
  Father Figure by Richard Peck
  Running Out of Time by Margaret Peterson Haddix
- **Standardized Test Practice** (pp. 536–537)

KEYS TO LITERARY CONNECTIONS

Comparing Selections

The **Comparing Selections** feature in this theme provides opportunities for addressing diverse aspects of the reading and literature curriculum.

For example, in Comparing Selections on page 447, students look closely at the messages and life choices of the young men in "Amigo Brothers" by Piri Thomas and the speaker in "Your World" by Georgia Douglas Johnson.

World Literature

The Student Edition contains a variety of literature that represents cultures from around the world. World literature selections are highlighted with the icon above.

TEACHING SUPPORT

The Teaching Support offers a wealth of interactive instructional support:

Meeting Individual Needs
- Special Needs
- English Language Learners
- Multiple Modes of Expression
- Advanced Learners

Internet Connection

Assessment

Portfolio Options

Minilessons
- Grammar and Language
- Reading
- Writing
- Listening and Speaking

Connecting to Other Selections

Real-World Connection

Interdisciplinary Connection

Life Skills Connection

Family and Community Activity

Key to Ability Levels

The activities throughout this theme have been coded for students of various abilities.

L1 **BASIC** activities for all students

L2 **AVERAGE** activities for average to above-average students

L3 **ADVANCED LEARNERS** activities for above-average students

Teaching Today

The Glencoe *Teaching Today* professional development Web site at www.teachingtoday.glencoe.com features daily teaching tips, free downloads, annotated Web resources, educational news, and a wealth of information on a wide range of topics.

Theme 5 At a Glance
At the Crossroads

Reading Skills in this theme

Variety of Texts

In addition to a full-length drama, this theme includes the following text types:

- short story
- poem
- cartoon
- folktale
- Web site

Comprehension Skills

The following instructional support for comprehension skills appears in this theme of the Student Edition:

- **Reading and Thinking Minilessons** (pp. 458, 469, 498, 527)
- **Drawing Conclusions** (p. 470)
- **Active Reading Strategies and Model** (pp. 502–527)

See also the **Reading Minilessons** throughout the theme in this Teacher Wraparound Edition.

For strategies for reading longer works, such as novels and novellas, see "Tips for Independent Reading" on page 535.

Reading Resources

Active Reading Guide The ***Active Reading Guide*** provides graphic organizers and study guide questions to support students' reading of each selection. (***Active Reading Guide***, pp. 39–45)

Interactive Reading Sourcebook and **Interactive Reading Workbook** The ***Interactive Reading Sourcebook*** and ***Interactive Reading Workbook*** offer focused comprehension strategies and lessons on critical thinking skills as well as fluency practice and activities to teach and support phonics, decoding, spelling, and vocabulary development.

Vocabulary Power The ***Vocabulary Power*** workbook (Lessons 19–23) provides systematic teaching, practice, and assessment of vocabulary for better reading comprehension.

Audio Library Available on audiocassette and on CD, the ***Audio Library*** provides valuable comprehension support.

Glencoe Literature Library Each title in the ***Glencoe Literature Library*** includes a full-length work plus related readings. A separate Study Guide is available for each title.

Five–Star Stories These anthologies of familiar short stories adapted and abridged for a variety of reading levels include exercises to help increase students' vocabulary and improve their reading comprehension.

The Contemporary Readers ***The Contemporary Readers*** are nonfiction books linked to various themes and designed for developing readers from a wide range of backgrounds.

Literature Classics CD-ROM The selections on this CD-ROM can be searched by author, theme, or genre.

inTIME and Humanities Across TIME Coproductions of Glencoe and Time, Inc., these resources include a wealth of high-interest nonfiction related to the selections in this theme.

Assessment in this theme

Assessment in the Student Edition

This program offers a number of diverse ways to evaluate student understanding and skill proficiency. In the Student Edition, use the following:

- **Responding to Literature**
  Following each selection, students are asked to recall facts, interpret ideas, and evaluate concepts as they answer a variety of questions and complete activities to extend their understanding.
- **Theme Assessment (pp. 534–535)**
  Here students respond to the selections on personal and analytical levels. They also assume ownership of their learning by setting and evaluating goals and by selecting work for their portfolios.

See also the many **Assessment Resources** listed on the facing page.

Standardized Test Practice

The Princeton Review has developed the Standardized Test Practice pages found at the end of this thematic unit (pp. 536–537). For additional practice, direct students to the following resources:

- ITBS Preparation and Practice
- SAT-9 Preparation and Practice
- TerraNova Preparation and Practice

Writing Skills in this theme

Writing Skills

The Student Edition of Theme Five offers strong instructional support for writing skills:

In **Extending Your Response**, which follows each selection:
- **Writing About Literature**
- **Personal/Creative Writing**

See also the **Writing Minilessons** throughout the theme in this Teacher Wraparound Edition.

Writing Workshops

Theme Five concludes with a **Writing Workshop** that guides students through the process of writing a definition essay (pp. 530–533).

Writing Resources

Writer's Assistant CD-ROM Each **Writing Workshop** is supplemented by an interactive writing guide on the ***Writer's Assistant*** CD-ROM. This easy- to-use writing guide provides prompts, templates, and other tools that lead students through the writing process.

Grammar and Composition Handbook The ***Grammar and Composition Handbook*** (Lessons 8.5–10.3) provides systematic instruction in English language conventions.

Spelling Power The ***Spelling Power*** workbook (Lessons 17–20) provides systematic teaching, practice, and assessment of spelling to help students become better spellers and thus enhance their writing.

Writing and Proofreading Practice Blackline masters present in-depth instruction and practice on a specific step in the writing process and proofreading (pp. 1–7, 35–42).

Writing and Proofreading Transparencies Transparencies provide graphic organizers and proofreading exercises for whole-class instruction (pp. 1–6, 17–18, 33–34).

Research and Report Writing Guide This resource provides extensive tips and activities to guide students in their writing projects in the literature classroom as well as in classes across the curriculum.

Style and Documentation Sourcebook for Writers This sourcebook is a combination reference and workbook, giving students the most up-to-date information and guidance regarding traditional as well as technological research strategies and documentation.

Revising with Style This resource offers instruction and exercises focusing on the revision process and covering topics from proofreading and correcting common grammatical errors to sentence combining and reordering.

Assessment Resources

Selection Quick Checks For each selection, a **Quick Check** of three to five short-answer questions measures students' literal comprehension.

Selection and Theme Assessment The ***Selection and Theme Assessment*** instrument tests students' abilities to recall, interpret, and evaluate what they've read. The tests consist of multiple-choice, short answer, and essay questions.

Performance Assessment Alternative assessment instruments and rubrics for Theme Five are found in the ***Performance Assessment*** ancillary.

Writing Assessment and Portfolio Management These notes and strategies, student models, and assessment tools assist with the task of measuring students' progress as writers and as monitors of their own writing.

Testmaker: ExamView Pro Teachers can customize selection and Theme Five tests by accessing the ***Testmaker*** database.

Interactive Tutor: Self-Assessment The ***Interactive Tutor: Self-Assessment*** software provides multiple-choice tests with immediate feedback to help students evaluate their knowledge and understanding of each literature selection.

MindJogger Videoquizzes Using a popular game show format, ***MindJogger Videoquizzes*** on videocassettes enable teachers to evaluate student understanding of Theme Five in a quick and fun manner.

Theme 5 Skills Scope and Sequence

Lessons	Literary Elements	Reading and Thinking	Writing
Amigo Brothers Piri Thomas DRP:54 Lexile:760	Internal/External Conflict, SE p. 442; *TWE pp. 434, 437, 438, 440* *Setting, TWE p. 434* *Imagery, TWE p. 440* *Character, TWE p. 441* *Plot, TWE p. 441*	*Evaluating, TWE pp. 434, 436* *Comparing/Contrasting, TWE p. 435* *Logical Reasoning, TWE p. 436* *Drawing Conclusions, TWE p. 439*	Analyzing an Ending, SE p. 443 Newspaper Article, SE p. 443 *Using Realistic Language, TWE p. 437*
Your World Georgia Douglas Johnson	Symbol, SE p. 446 *Symbol, TWE p. 445*	Comparing Selections, SE p. 447	Analyze Theme, SE p. 446
The Scholarship Jacket Marta Salinas DRP:54 Lexile:690	Resolution, SE p. 456; *TWE p. 455* *Character, TWE p. 452*	Questioning/Clarifying, SE p. 458 *Inferring, TWE pp. 452, 454* *Drawing Conclusions, TWE pp. 452, 453, 455* *Sequence of Events, TWE p. 453*	Critical Review of Story, SE p. 457 Journal Entry, SE p. 457
All Summer in a Day Ray Bradbury DRP:52 Lexile:670	Science Fiction, SE p. 467 *Figures of Speech, TWE p. 462* *Science Fiction, TWE pp. 462, 464, 465, 466* *Character, TWE p. 463*	Web site, SE p. 459 Inference, SE p. 469 Drawing Conclusions, SE p. 470 *Activating Prior Knowledge, TWE p. 459* *Inferring, TWE pp. 462, 463* *Monitor Comp., TWE p. 463* *Draw Conclusions, TWE p. 464, 466* *Crit. Judg., TWE p. 466*	Paragraph (Setting), SE p. 468 Sequel to Science Fiction, SE p. 468
Primer Lesson Carl Sandburg **The Bird Like No Other** Dorothy West DRP:58 Lexile:880	Descriptive Details, SE p. 478 *Personification, TWE p. 472* *Repetition, TWE p. 472* *Details, TWE pp. 473, 476, 477* *Character, TWE p. 473* *Literary Language, TWE p. 474*	*Inferring, TWE p. 473* *Synthesizing, TWE p. 473* *Sequencing, TWE p. 473* *Drawing Conclusions, TWE p. 476*	Paragraph (Poem's Theme), SE p. 479 Personal Letter (Different Point of View), SE p. 479
The Old Demon Pearl S. Buck DRP:52 Lexile:630 **The Boy and His Grandfather** Rudolfo A. Anaya DRP:50 Lexile:750	Theme, SE p. 496 *Simile, TWE p. 484* *Implied Theme, TWE pp. 484, 485, 488, 489, 491* *Narrator, TWE p. 485* *Characterization, TWE p. 492* *Plot, TWE pp. 493, 494* *Allegory, TWE p. 495*	Summarizing, SE p. 498 *Drawing Conclusions, TWE pp. 484, 487, 489, 493* *Cause and Effect, TWE p. 484* *Inferring, TWE p. 486* *Evaluating, TWE pp. 487, 490* *Synthesizing, TWE p. 489* *Logical Reasoning, TWE p. 491*	Paragraph (Analyzing Descriptions), SE p. 497 Essay (Personal Courage), SE p. 497 ELL *Describing a Setting, TWE p. 483* *Narrating Action, TWE p. 487*
The Monsters Are Due On Maple Street Rod Serling	Drama, SE p. 500 Teleplay, SE p. 525; *TWE pp. 506, 508, 509, 510, 512, 513, 523* *Mood, TWE p. 506* *Characterization, TWE pp. 508, 509, 510, 513* *Foreshadowing, TWE p. 511* *Irony, TWE p. 517* *Symbol, TWE p. 519*	Drama, SE p. 502 Visualizing, SE p. 527 Web site, SE p. 528 *Classifying, TWE p. 507; Evaluating, TWE pp. 510, 512, 515, 518; Source Credibility, TWE p. 511; Purpose for Rdg., TWE pp. 511, 528; Compare/Contrast, TWE p. 516; Synthesizing, TWE p. 521 Generalizing, TWE p. 522*	Paragraph (Conflict), SE p. 526 Description from Another Point of View, SE p. 526 *Narrative, TWE p. 514* *Narrating Action with Verbs, TWE p. 522* *Analytical Writing, TWE p. 524*
Writing Workshop Expository Writing: Definition Essay			*Paragraph Development, TWE p. 532*

Key: Student material is in roman. Teacher material is in italic. Technology ELL English Language Learners

Vocabulary and Spelling	Grammar and Language	Listening, Speaking, and Viewing	Life Skills; Study and Research; Technology
Unlocking Meaning, SE 443 *Context Clues,* TWE p. 434 ELL *Spanish Words,* TWE p. 434 *Etymology,* TWE pp. 437, 440	*Action Verbs,* TWE p. 440	Literature Groups, SE p. 443 Radio Script, SE p. 443 SN *Sports Training,* TWE p. 436 *Describing a Match,* TWE p. 438	*Internet Connection,* TWE p. 441 *Tournament,* TWE p. 441
	Comparative and Superlative Adjectives, TWE p. 445	Literature Groups, SE p. 446 Small Group Discussions, SE p. 449 ELL *Group Discussion Tips,* TWE p. 449	Health, SE p. 448
The Prefix: *-dis,* SE p. 458 *Word Meanings,* TWE p. 453	Using Adverbs and Adjectives, SE p. 458 *Subject-Verb Agreement,* TWE p. 454	Literature Groups, SE p. 457 ELL *Visualizing Words,* TWE p. 452	Learning For Life: Graduation Speech, SE p. 457 *Real-World Connection: Awards,* TWE p. 455
Latin Roots: *vit* and *viv,* SE p. 469	Avoiding Double Negatives, SE p. 469 *Commas to Set Off Interrupters,* TWE p. 466	Literature Groups, SE p. 468 ELL *Sunny Day and Rainy Day Activities,* TWE p. 462 SN *Less-Proficient Readers,* TWE p. 470	Creating a Travel Brochure, SE p. 468 *Job Search,* TWE p. 465
Analogies, SE p. 479 *Word Mappings,* TWE p. 472 ELL *Forms of Address,* TWE p. 472 *Multiple Suffixes,* TWE p. 474	*Using Troublesome Words:* Its *and* It's, TWE p. 476	Literature Groups, SE p. 479 SN *Less-Proficient Readers,* TWE p. 474	Becoming an Active Viewer, SE p. 480 *Extraordinary People,* TWE p. 477
The Prefix *mal-,* SE p. 498 *Etymology,* TWE p. 486 *Suffixes,* TWE p. 488	Participles and Participial Phrases, SE p. 498 *Verbs in the Past Tense,* TWE p. 488	Literature Groups, SE p. 497 Prepare and Present a Story Orally, SE p. 497 SN *Less-Proficient Readers,* TWE p. 490 *Video,* TWE p. 493 *Film,* TWE p. 494 *Create and Enact a Dialogue,* TWE p. 486	*Methods of Flood Control,* TWE p. 485 *Political Conflict,* TWE p. 491 *Decision Making,* TWE p. 492
Base Words, SE p. 527 Idioms, SE p. 529 SN *Less-Proficient Readers,* TWE p. 503 SN *Idioms,* TWE p. 506 *Idioms,* TWE p. 512 *Roots,* TWE p. 515 *Synonyms,* TWE p. 518 ELL *Idioms,* TWE p. 529	Apostrophes, SE p. 527 *Using End Marks,* TWE p. 509 *Complete Sentences,* TWE p. 520	Literature Groups, SE p. 526 ELL *Understanding Drama,* TWE p. 500 *Film,* TWE p. 506 *Less-Proficient Readers,* TWE pp. 510, 519 ELL *Symbolism in Names,* TWE p. 512 *Music,* TWE p. 515 *Oral Reading: Teleplay,* TWE p. 518	News Broadcast, SE p. 526 Internet Connection, SE p. 526 *Lifelong Learning,* TWE p. 513 *Crowd Behavior,* TWE p. 517 ELL *Nonverbal Language,* TWE p. 521 *Screenwriters,* TWE p. 523 *Real-World Connection: Riots,* TWE p. 523
		ELL *Preparing for Definition Essays,* TWE p. 530	

SN Special Needs/Strategic Intervention

Theme 5 RESOURCE MANAGER

Lessons	Essential Resources	English Language Learners
Amigo Brothers Piri Thomas Pacing: 2 Days	**Lesson-Specific Instruction** Selection Focus Transp. 39 Active Reading Guide,* p. 39 Literary Elements Transp. 39 Vocabulary Practice, p. 26 Quick Checks,* p. 39 Selection and Theme Assessment, pp. 69–70 Testmaker: ExamView Pro Performance Assessment, p. 37 **Systematic Language Instruction** Grammar and Comp. Hbk., L. 8.5 Vocabulary Power, Lesson 19 Spelling Power, Lesson 17	English Language Learners Sourcebook, p. 64 Theme Five Planning Guide, p. 6 Spanish Summaries, p. 39 Spanish Translations, pp. 107–114 Audio Library* English, Yes!
Your World Georgia Douglas Johnson Pacing: 1 Day	**Lesson-Specific Instruction** Selection Focus Transp. 40 Active Reading Guide,* p. 40 Literary Elements Transp. 40 Quick Checks,* p. 40 Selection and Theme Assessment, pp. 69–70 Testmaker: ExamView Pro Performance Assessment, p. 37 **Systematic Language Instruction** Grammar and Comp. Hbk., L. 8.6 Vocabulary Power, Lesson 20	English Language Learners Sourcebook, p. 65 Theme Five Planning Guide, p. 14 Spanish Summaries, p. 40 Audio Library* English, Yes!
The Scholarship Jacket Marta Salinas Pacing: 2 Days	**Lesson-Specific Instruction** Selection Focus Transp. 41 Active Reading Guide,* p. 41 Literary Elements Transp. 41 Vocabulary Practice, p. 27 Quick Checks,* p. 41 Selection and Theme Assessment, pp. 71–72 Testmaker: ExamView Pro Performance Assessment, p. 38 **Systematic Language Instruction** Grammar and Comp. Hbk., L. 9.2 Vocabulary Power, Lesson 21 Spelling Power, Lesson 18	English Language Learners Sourcebook, p. 66 Theme Five Planning Guide, p. 19 Spanish Summaries, p. 41 Spanish Translations, pp. 115–118 Audio Library* English, Yes!
All Summer in a Day Ray Bradbury Pacing: 2 Days	**Lesson-Specific Instruction** Selection Focus Transp. 42 Active Reading Guide,* p. 42 Literary Elements Transp. 42 Vocabulary Practice, p. 28 Quick Checks,* p. 42 Selection and Theme Assessment, pp. 73–74 Testmaker: ExamView Pro Performance Assessment, p. 39 TIME *inTIME* magazine, pp. 24–25 **Systematic Language Instruction** Grammar and Comp. Hbk., L. 9.3 Vocabulary Power, Lesson 22 Spelling Power, Lesson 19	English Language Learners Sourcebook, p. 67 Spanish Summaries, p. 42 Spanish Translations, pp. 119–122 Audio Library* English, Yes!
Primer Lesson Gwendolyn Brooks **The Bird Like No Other** Lucille Clifton Pacing: 2 Days	**Lesson-Specific Instruction** Selection Focus Transp. 43 Active Reading Guide,* p. 43 Literary Elements Transp. 43 Vocabulary Practice, p. 29 Quick Checks,* p. 43 Selection and Theme Assessment, pp. 75–76 Testmaker: ExamView Pro Performance Assessment, p. 40 **Systematic Language Instruction** Grammar and Comp. Hbk., L. 10.1	English Language Learners Sourcebook, p. 68 Spanish Summaries, p. 43 Audio Library* English, Yes!

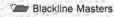

Key:  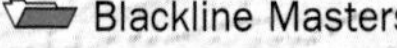 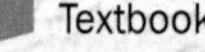 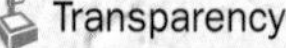  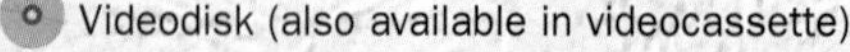
Workbook · Blackline Masters · Textbook · Transparency · CD-ROM · Videodisk (also available in videocassette)

Special Needs/ Strategic Intervention	Reteaching and Enrichment
Interactive Reading Sourcebook, pp. T152–T155 Interactive Reading Workbook, pp. 71–74 Inclusion Strategies Sourcebook, pp. 53–54 Theme Five Planning Guide, p. 6 Audio Library*	Literature Launchers, Side B, Segment 14 Reading Skills Practice Workbook, pp. 69–70 Grammar and Language Transp. 37 Gr. and Lang. Wkbk., pp. 73–74 Grammar and Comp. Hbk., L.3.1 Interactive Tutor: Self-Assessment Vocabulary PuzzleMaker Web Site (lit.glencoe.com)
Interactive Reading Sourcebook, pp. T155–T156 Interactive Reading Workbook, p. 75 Inclusion Strategies Sourcebook, pp. 73–74 Theme Five Planning Guide, p. 14 Audio Library*	Grammar and Language Transp. 38 Gr. and Lang. Wkbk., pp. 121–124 Grammar and Comp. Hbk., L.5.3, 5.4 TIME *Humanities Across TIME,* Cover 7 Interactive Tutor: Self-Assessment Vocabulary PuzzleMaker Web Site (lit.glencoe.com)
Interactive Reading Sourcebook, pp. T157–T159 Interactive Reading Workbook, pp. 76–77 Inclusion Strategies Sourcebook, pp. 35–36, 43–44 Theme Five Planning Guide, p. 19 Audio Library*	Fine Art Transparency 5 Reading Skills Practice Workbook, pp. 71–72 Grammar and Language Transp. 39 Gr. and Lang. Wkbk., pp. 117–118, 127–128, 183–184 Grammar and Comp. Hbk., L.5.1, 6.1, 6.2, 10.1 Interactive Tutor: Self-Assessment Vocabulary PuzzleMaker Web Site (lit.glencoe.com)
Interactive Reading Sourcebook, pp. T159–T162 Interactive Reading Workbook, pp. 78–79 Theme Five Planning Guide, p. 27 Audio Library*	Literature Launchers, Side B, Segment 13 Reading Skills Practice Workbook, pp. 73–74 Grammar and Language Transp. 40 Gr. and Lang. Wkbk., pp. 135–136, 255–256 Grammar and Comp. Hbk., L.6.5, 13.2 Media Connection Activities, p. 9 Interactive Tutor: Self-Assessment Vocabulary PuzzleMaker Web Site (lit.glencoe.com)
Interactive Reading Sourcebook, pp. T163–T165 Interactive Reading Workbook, p. 80 Theme Five Planning Guide, p. 35 Audio Library*	Reading Skills Practice Workbook, pp. 75–76 Grammar and Language Transp. 41 Gr. and Lang. Wkbk., pp. 223–224 Interactive Tutor: Self-Assessment Vocabulary PuzzleMaker Web Site (lit.glencoe.com)

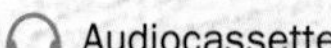

Web   Audiocassette   Diskette   *Also available in Spanish

Independent Reading

Encourage students to spend thirty minutes each day in independent reading. The following Glencoe components and outside resources provide opportunities for reading related to this theme.

The Glencoe Literature Library

You may want to assign one or more of these titles for independent reading. For a complete listing of titles available in the Glencoe Literature Library, see page T96 of this book.

- *The Slave Dancer* by Paula Fox
- *Sounder* by William H. Armstrong
- *Anne Frank Remembered: The Story of the Woman Who Helped to Hide the Frank Family* by Miep Gies and Alison Leslie Gold
- *Number the Stars* by Lois Lowry
- *Cezanne Pinto* by Mary Stolz

inTIME News stories, feature articles, reviews, profiles, and essays in the magazine connect to an author, work, or theme in the Student Edition. See the ***inTIME* Teacher's Guide** for specific connections to this theme.

Resources for Less-Proficient Readers

For reading especially created for less-proficient readers, suggest

- *Five-Star Stories*
- *The Contemporary Readers*

Additional Resources for Independent Reading

The following titles are listed with specific reading selections throughout this theme. You may want to suggest that students look for these in your local or school library.

- *On the Way Home* by Laura Ingalls Wilder and Rose Wilder
- *Shadow Boxer* by Chris Lynch
- *Muhammad Ali* by Norman Macht
- *The Anaya Reader* by Rudolfo Anaya
- *A Summer Life* by Gary Soto
- *The Martian Chronicles* by Ray Bradbury
- *The Complete Poems of Carl Sandburg* by Carl Sandburg
- *The Richer, the Poorer* by Dorothy West
- *The Remarkable Journey of Prince Jen* by Alexander Lloyd
- *Homesick: My Own Story* by Jean Fritz
- *Father Figure* by Richard Peck
- *Running Out of Time* by Margaret Peterson

RESOURCE MANAGER (continued)

Lessons	Essential Resources		English Language Learners
The Old Demon PEARL S. BUCK **The Boy and His Grandfather** RUDOLFO A. ANAYA PACING: 2 DAYS	**Lesson-Specific Instruction** Selection Focus Transp. 44 Active Reading Guide,* p. 44 Literary Elements Transp. 44 Vocabulary Practice, p. 30 Quick Checks,* p. 44 Selection and Theme Assessment, pp. 77–78	Testmaker: ExamView Pro Performance Assessment, p. 41 **Systematic Language Instruction** Grammar and Comp. Hbk., L. 10.2 Vocabulary Power, Lesson 23 Spelling Power, Lesson 20	English Language Learners Sourcebook, p. 69 Theme Five Planning Guide, p. 41 Spanish Summaries, p. 44 Spanish Translations, p. 123 Audio Library* English, Yes!
The Monsters Are Due On Maple Street ROD SERLING PACING: 4 DAYS	**Lesson-Specific Instruction** Selection Focus Transp. 45 Active Reading Guide,* p. 45 Literary Elements Transp. 45 Vocabulary Practice, p. 31 Quick Checks,* p. 45 Selection and Theme Assessment, pp. 79–80 Testmaker: ExamView Pro	Performance Assessment, p. 42 TIME *inTIME* magazine, pp. 24–25 **Systematic Language Instruction** Grammar and Comp. Hbk., L. 10.3 Vocabulary Power, Unit 5 Review/Test Spelling Power, Unit 5 Review/ Proofreading	English Language Learners Sourcebook, pp. 70, 71, 72, 73 Spanish Summaries, p. 45 Spanish Translations, pp. 124–138 Audio Library* English, Yes!
Writing WORKSHOP Expository Writing: Definition Essay PACING: 2 DAYS	Writing Assessment and Portfolio Management, pp. 1–13, 26–28, 38–45		English Language Learners Sourcebook, p. 9 English, Yes!

Key: 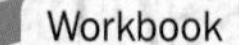 Workbook 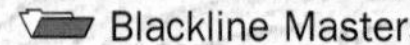 Blackline Masters 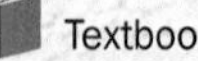 Textbook  Transparency  CD-ROM 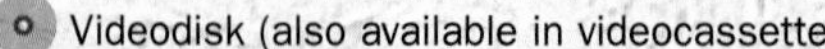 Videodisk (also available in videocassette)

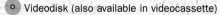

Special Needs/ Strategic Intervention	Reteaching and Enrichment
Interactive Reading Sourcebook, pp. T165–T168 Interactive Reading Workbook, pp. 81–84 Inclusion Strategies Sourcebook, pp. 21–22 Theme Five Planning Guide, p. 41	Literature Launchers, Side B, Segment 15 Reading Skills Practice Workbook, pp. 77–78 Grammar and Language Transp. 42 Gr. and Lang. Wkbk., pp. 83–86, 167–170 Grammar and Comp. Hbk., L. 3.5, 9.1 Interactive Tutor: Self-Assessment Vocabulary PuzzleMaker Web Site (lit.glencoe.com) Audio Library*
Interactive Reading Sourcebook, pp. T169–T171 Interactive Reading Workbook, pp. 85–88 Inclusion Strategies Sourcebook, pp. 75–76 Theme Five Planning Guide, p. 47 Audio Library*	Reading Skills Practice Workbook, pp. 79–80 Grammar and Language Transp. 43, 44 Gr. and Lang. Wkbk., pp. 55–56, 253–254, 273–274 Grammar and Comp. Hbk., L. 1.2, 13.1, 13.7 Media Connection Activities, p. 10 TIME *Humanities Across TIME,* Cover 6 Interactive Tutor: Self-Assessment Vocabulary PuzzleMaker Web Site (lit.glencoe.com)
	Writing and Proofreading Practice, pp. 1–7, 35–42 Writing and Proofreading Transparencies 1–6, 17–18, 19–20, 33–34 Revising with Style Writer's Assistant

Theme RESOURCES

To explore the theme further you may want to use these resources:

- Listening and Speaking Activities (pp. 13–15)
- Viewing and Representing Activities (pp. 1–6, 19–21)
- Critical Thinking Skills (pp. 12–14)
- Media Connection Activities (pp. 9–10)
- Interdisciplinary Activities (pp. 18–21)
- Family and Community Activities (p. 15)
- Selection and Theme Assessment (pp. 133–134)
- Performance Assessment (pp. 73, 98)

TIME Humanities Across TIME

See also these additional theme planning resources:

- Theme Five Planning Guide
- Interactive Reading Sourcebook
- Literature Groups Sourcebook
- Interactive Lesson Planner
- Interactive Teacher Edition
- Glencoe Web Site <lit.glencoe.com>

Use Glencoe's ***Presentation Plus!*** This multimedia teaching tool lets you present dynamic lessons that will engage your students. Using Microsoft PowerPoint®, you can customize the presentation to create your own personalized lessons.

 Web 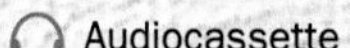 Audiocassette Diskette *Also available in Spanish

At the Crossroads

At the Crossroads

Theme Objectives

- To enjoy reading about people who confront tough decisions with courage and ingenuity
- To analyze the literary elements in poetry, folktale, short story, and drama selections
- To apply strategies for reading drama

Teaching Strategies

Have students read the quotation from "The Road Not Taken" by Robert Frost in preparation for the discussion questions below.

VIEWING THE PHOTOGRAPH

Responding to the Photograph

- What might the roads in the quote represent? *(They could represent life's journey.)*
- What difference might taking the less-traveled road make? *(It could provide experiences most other travelers would never have and great satisfaction in having accomplished something special.)*

TEACHER *to* TEACHER

HARWOOD MIDDLE SCHOOL • EVANSVILLE, IN.

When opening the theme "At The Crossroads," I have students write "Live and Learn" sentences. I say, "From birth to death, our entire lives are journeys on which we live and learn. Along the way we encounter many crossroads. What have you lived and learned?" I give a few examples: "I've learned that going out with pretty girls is not all that it's cracked up to be. I've learned that two heads are better than one, provided one of those heads isn't two-faced. I've learned the best way to shut out trouble is to have an open mind, open heart, and open arms." First, each student writes ten sentences, and then in groups they decide on the ten best sentences and refine them. We pick the best thirty or forty as a class and display them in the hall.

DAVE BARCLAY

> “Two roads diverged in a wood, and I—
> I took the one less traveled by,
> And that has made all the difference.”
>
> —Robert Frost
> "The Road Not Taken"

THEME CONTENTS

GENRE FOCUS DRAMA

Introducing the Theme

Direct your students' attention to the **Theme Contents.** Ask them to read through the list of selections. Present these questions for discussion:

- Another word for *crossroads* is *intersection.* Which titles in the Contents indicate stories about intersections where the natural and supernatural worlds meet? *(Students may say "All Summer in a Day," "The Old Demon," and "The Monsters Are Due on Maple Street.")*
- What might the characters in these diverse genres (stories, poems, folktales, and a teleplay) have in common? *(Students may speculate that the characters are confronted with challenging decisions to make or problems to solve.)*
- Do any of the titles give you a clue as to what the crossroads in the story might be? *(Students may think that family decisions are being considered in selections such as "Amigo Brothers" and "The Boy and his Grandfather.")*

FINE ART TRANSPARENCY 20

You may wish to use ***Fine Art Transparency 20*** to enrich students' thinking about the theme.

GLENCOE TECHNOLOGY

LITERATURE CLASSICS CD-ROM

Search for other selections related to the theme "At the Crossroads."

RESOURCE MANAGER

See the ***Theme Five Planning Guide*** for additional teaching notes, strategies, and resources for introducing the theme "At the Crossroads."

Exploring the Theme

At the Crossroads

Students may offer situations such as how to handle moving to a new school, getting caught up in arguments between friends, and deciding on the appropriate strategy in an ambiguous situation.

Have students draw portraits of themselves standing at a crossroads in their lives. Ask them to give the viewer a sense of the dilemma by including street names for each road they could choose or by labeling the elements of the conflict in some other way. For example, students might draw themselves looking confused by two choices marked: *Join in gossip* and *Be loyal to my friend.*

Starting Points

A Tough Decision

Have students think of a time they or someone they know used humor to extricate themselves from a sticky situation, as Charlie Brown does in the comic strip.

- Introduce the word *diplomat.* Explain that a *diplomat* is a government representative who is skilled in dealing with people tactfully. Ask students if they think Charlie Brown offered a *diplomatic* answer to Peppermint Pattie's question. Have them try to include at least one other diplomatic response in their dialogues.
- Invite students to write and dramatize their dialogues, using other well-known characters from the *Peanuts* cartoon in addition to the three pictured here.

Exploring the Theme

At the Crossroads

Have you ever been at a point in your life where you had a difficult problem to solve or a decision to make? In this theme's stories, poems, and play, you will meet characters who confront their problems by making courageous or difficult decisions. Begin thinking about the theme by trying one of the activities below.

Starting Points

A TOUGH DECISION

Can you identify with Charlie Brown's difficult situation?

- What other decisions could Charlie Brown have made? With a partner or in a small group, write and then dramatize a dialogue between Charlie Brown and his friends, discussing the different decisions he might have made.

WHICH WAY TO TURN

You have to make choices and decisions every day of your life. Sometimes the decision is easy. Which movie should you see next Saturday? Other times the decision is more difficult. Should you stand up for an unpopular cause in which you believe strongly?

- Write a list of some decisions you have made today. Explain which decisions were more difficult for you to make and why.

PEANUTS

by Charles M. Schulz

WELL, CHUCK, HAVE YOU DECIDED? WHO DO YOU LIKE BEST, MARCIE OR ME?
IF IT'S A TIE, DO WE GO INTO OVERTIME?

Which Way to Turn

Have students rate themselves as decision makers using these questions: *Do I make decisions quickly? Do I worry over every little decision I make? Do I think things through? Do I often look back and regret my decisions—or, when I make a bad decision, do I chalk it up to experience and move on?* After students have made up their lists of decisions, ask them to draw a star next to the decisions they are happy with.

Interviewing Tools Students can use a search engine to find out more about technical tools they can use to interview people. They might use such keywords as *audio, video,* or *photos.*

Theme Projects

As you read the selections in this theme, complete one of the projects below. Work on your own, with a partner, or with a group.

LEARNING FOR LIFE

Interview Questions

People make personal decisions every day about many small and large problems. Some people make decisions that affect many other people. Think about doctors, school principals, mayors, presidents of corporations, and the president of the United States.

1. Develop a list of questions to ask a local decision maker about how she or he solves problems.
2. Interview the person—on the phone, by e-mail, by regular mail, or in person.
3. Write a memo to summarize the results of your interview for your class.

interNET CONNECTION

As you think about your project, visit the Glencoe Web site at lit.glencoe.com. While you are there, you can find out more about the authors and selections in this theme.

MULTIMEDIA PROJECT

A Decision Maker

Select a person who has come to a crossroads in life and has made a difficult or important decision.

1. Find people through biographies, magazine articles, other library research, or personal contact.
2. Using a tape recorder or video camera, interview the person you have chosen to report on or other people who can comment on that person's decision.
3. Gather information from a variety of sources to add to your presentation—for example, photos, newspaper clippings, or objects that are connected to the person's decision. Use these objects along with your audio or video interviews to create a multimedia presentation for the class.

CRITICAL THINKING

Personal Problem-Solving Techniques

1. Think about a problem you have had and about how you tried to solve it.
2. Create a flowchart that illustrates your problem-solving process. On the chart, indicate the steps you took to solve the problem, the point where you had to make an important decision, and the end solution.

Family and Community Activity

Decision Making Have each student investigate a decision made at the community level within the last year by reading past issues of the local newspaper and talking to parents and other members of the community. Then each can create a visual representation of how this decision was made, such as steps in a staircase or a journey from one point to another. Suggest that they include information on

- what the issue was
- why it was brought to the forefront
- who made the decision and why
- what the outcome was

Additional Resources

Family and Community Activities, p. 15

Theme Projects

Teaching Strategies

These suggestions may help students carry out their theme projects.

Learning For Life

- Help students start a list of topics entitled *What I want to know.* Help them change each topic into a question or series of questions.
- Students can compile their findings in a booklet.

Multimedia Project

- Suggest that students conduct initial interviews to gather background information and explain the project to the people being interviewed. Questions for follow-up interviews can then be written, using information gathered in the initial interviews.
- Before preparing the final presentation, each student should decide his or her purpose by asking: Do I hope to inform, persuade, or entertain my audience?

Critical Thinking

- Students may want to talk about the problems, how they solved them, and who helped them before creating the flowcharts.
- Allow time for students to share their completed flowcharts with partners and to note any comments or feedback partners offer.

Additional Resources

- ***Interdisciplinary Activities,*** pp. 18–21
- ***Viewing and Representing Activities,*** pp. 19–21
- ***Listening and Speaking Activities,*** pp. 13–15
- ***Critical Thinking Skills,*** pp. 12–14
- ***Selection and Theme Assessment,*** pp. 133–134
- ***Performance Assessment,*** p. 73

Before Reading

Objectives

- To read and analyze a short story
- To recognize and describe external and internal conflict in a story
- To write an analysis of an ending

Skills

Reading/Thinking: Evaluating; Logical Reasoning; Drawing Conclusions; Comparing and Contrasting
Writing: Using Realistic Language; Newspaper Article
Vocabulary: Etymology; Context Clues; Unlocking Meaning
Grammar/Language: Action Verbs
Listening/Speaking: Broadcast
Collaboration: Literature Groups

Motivating → STUDENTS

Literature Launchers: "Golden Gloves"

Videodisc Side B, Segment 14

Also available in VHS.

Selection Focus Transparency 39: Have students discuss the quotation.

Reading Focus: Have groups compare charts to see how often each trait was listed.

Before You Read

Amigo Brothers

MEET PIRI THOMAS

Piri Thomas first began writing while serving a prison term for attempted armed robbery. For Thomas, creative writing was a way to escape his prison surroundings, break down stereotypes used to judge people of African American and Puerto Rican descent, and change his life. After his release from prison, Thomas began working in drug rehabilitation centers. His autobiography and novels are known for their use of the Spanish Harlem dialect and for the tough reality they portray.

Piri Thomas was born in 1928. This story was first published in 1978 in the collection Stories from El Barrio.

READING FOCUS

Think about your closest friend. What qualities make that person such a good friend?

Chart It!
Create a chart that shows the character traits that you feel make a good friend.

Setting a Purpose
Read to find out how two friends respond to a test of their friendship.

BUILDING BACKGROUND

In the ancient Greek Olympic games, boxers were not classified in different weight divisions. The strongest and largest boxers held the greatest advantage in competition. Today, professional boxers compete in eight different weight divisions, so that they are evenly matched in size. The divisions range from flyweight, 112 pounds or less, to heavyweight, 195 pounds and over.

VOCABULARY PREVIEW

devastating (dev′ əs tāt′ ing) *adj.* causing great pain, damage, or destruction; overwhelming; p. 434
wary (wār′ ē) *adj.* cautious; on the alert; p. 437
perpetual (pər pech′ o͞o əl) *adj.* constant; unceasing; p. 437
improvise (im′ prə vīz′) *v.* to invent, compose, or do without much preparation; p. 438
nimble (nim′ bəl) *adj.* light and quick in movement; p. 439
flail (flāl) *v.* to wave or swing, especially swiftly or violently; p. 440
evading (i vād′ ing) *adj.* escaping or avoiding; p. 440
surge (surj) *v.* to rise or increase suddenly; move with a violent swelling motion, as waves; p. 441

RESOURCE MANAGER

Teaching Tools and Resources
- Theme Five Planning Guide
- Literature Groups Sourcebook

Essential Lesson Support

Lesson-Specific Instruction
- Selection Focus Transparency 39
- Literary Elements Transparency 39
- Active Reading Guide,* p. 39
- Selection Vocabulary Practice, p. 26

Assessment
- Selection Quick Checks,* p. 39
- Sel. and Theme Assmt., pp. 69–70
- Testmaker: ExamView Pro
- Performance Assessment, p. 37

Systematic Language Instruction
- Gr. and Comp. Hbk., L. 8.5
- Vocabulary Power, Lesson 19
- Spelling Power, Lesson 17

English Language Learners
- ELL Sourcebook, p. 64
- Spanish Summaries, p. 39
- Spanish Translations, pp. 107–114
- Audio Library*
- English, Yes!

Spec. Needs/Strat. Interven.
- Interactive Rdg. Sbk., pp. T152–T155
- Interactive Rdg. Wkbk., pp. 71–74
- Inclusion Strat. Sbk., pp. 53–54
- Audio Library*

* Also available in Spanish

Amigo Brothers

Piri Thomas

Antonio Cruz and Felix Varga were both seventeen years old. They were so together in friendship that they felt themselves to be brothers. They had known each other since childhood, growing up on the lower east side of Manhattan in the same tenement building on Fifth Street between Avenue A and Avenue B.

Antonio was fair, lean, and lanky, while Felix was dark, short, and husky. Antonio's hair was always falling over his eyes, while Felix wore his black hair in a natural Afro style.

Each youngster had a dream of someday becoming lightweight[1] champion of the world. Every chance they had the boys worked out, sometimes at the Boys Club on 10th Street and Avenue A and sometimes at the pro's gym on 14th Street. Early morning sunrises would find them running along the East River Drive, wrapped in sweat shirts, short towels around their necks, and handkerchiefs Apache style around their foreheads.

While some youngsters were into street negatives, Antonio and Felix slept, ate, rapped, and dreamt positive. Between them, they had a collection of *Fight* magazines second to none, plus a scrapbook filled with torn tickets to every boxing match they had ever attended, and some clippings of their own. If asked a question about any given fighter, they would immediately zip out from their memory banks divisions, weights, records of fights, knock-outs, technical knock-outs,[2] and draws or losses.

Each had fought many bouts representing their community and had won two gold-plated medals plus a silver and bronze medallion. The difference was in their style. Antonio's lean form and long reach made him the better boxer, while Felix's short and muscular frame made him the better slugger. Whenever they had met in the ring for sparring sessions,[3] it had always been hot and heavy.

1. Boxers compete in classes, or divisions, based on their weight. In professional boxing, the *lightweight* division is 131–135 pounds.

2. In a *technical knock-out,* the boxer is judged to be physically unable to go on fighting. A TKO can be called by an official, the fighter, or the fighter's coach.

3. *Sparring sessions* are practice fights.

SUMMARY

Antonio and Felix are great friends and amateur boxers. They each dream of one day being lightweight champion of the world. But there is a problem. The two best buddies must fight each other in the division finals and the winner will represent the Boys Club in the Golden Gloves Championship Tournament. Can their friendship survive this test?

Spanish Summaries, p. 39

A Active Reading Strategies

PREDICT Have students look at the title of this story and the picture. Then let a volunteer read the first paragraph aloud. Who do students think the Amigo Brothers are? What do they think the Amigo Brothers like to do? What do they imagine the conflict will be? Have students revisit their predictions as they read to verify or revise them.

VOCABULARY If you haven't previewed the selection vocabulary with students, stop and remind them to use context clues to unlock the meanings of new vocabulary words.

Additional Resources

Active Reading Guide, p. 39

Audio Library

Spanish Audio Library

Teaching Support

CONNECTING TO OTHER SELECTIONS

This selection is paired with "Your World" on page 445. A lesson for teaching a comparison of the two selections appears on page 447.

The chart at the right shows three ways to connect "Amigo Brothers" to other selections in this book.

For specific teaching strategies, see the ***Theme Five Planning Guide***.

Connection	Title
Life Skills: Problem Solving	→ "Too Soon a Woman," p. 235
Thematic: Challenge	→ "Strong Men Weep," p. 26
Literary: Short Story	→ "Lob's Girl," p. 659

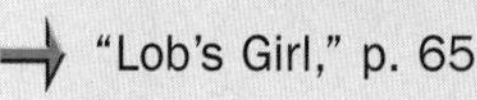

B Literary Elements

PLOT: *External Conflict* Have students explain the conflict between Antonio and Felix. How does it affect the boys' relationship? *(They must fight each other in the division finals. The winner will represent the Boys Club in the Golden Gloves championship. It causes a wall to rise between them.)*

C Literary Elements

SETTING Encourage students to think about the story's setting. Ask them to list clues from the story and explain their importance. *(The story takes place in New York City. Descriptions of the city include: dirty East River's edge and shores of Brooklyn. The names make the story seem authentic, as if the author were familiar with the area.)*

D Critical Thinking

EVALUATING Have students list examples of English and Spanish slang and explain the effect the slang has on the story. *(The narrator uses words like* ace-boon buddies, bro, panin, *and* cheverote. *The use of these slang words makes the boys' dialogue seem real.)*

Vo•cab•u•lar•y Skills

Context Clues A welterweight boxer is a fairly lightweight boxer. Therefore, a welterweight tugboat is a boat that is small in comparison to what it is pulling.

Amigo Brothers

B Now, after a series of elimination bouts,[4] they had been informed that they were to meet each other in the division finals that were scheduled for the seventh of August, two weeks away—the winner to represent the Boys Club in the Golden Gloves Championship Tournament.

The two boys continued to run together along the East River Drive. But even when joking with each other, they both sensed a wall rising between them.

C One morning less than a week before their bout, they met as usual for their daily work-out. They fooled around with a few jabs at the air, slapped skin, and then took off, running lightly along the dirty East River's edge.

Antonio glanced at Felix who kept his eyes purposely straight ahead, pausing from time to time to do some fancy leg work while throwing one-twos followed by upper cuts to an imaginary jaw. Antonio then beat the air with a barrage of body blows and short devastating lefts with an over-hand jaw-breaking right.

D After a mile or so, Felix puffed and said, "Let's stop a while, bro. I think we both got something to say to each other."

Antonio nodded. It was not natural to be acting as though nothing unusual was happening when two ace-boon buddies[5] were going to be blasting each other within a few short days.

They rested their elbows on the railing separating them from the river. Antonio wiped his face with his short towel. The sunrise was now creating day.

Felix leaned heavily on the river's railing and stared across to the shores of Brooklyn. Finally, he broke the silence.

"Man, I don't know how to come out with it."

Antonio helped. "It's about our fight, right?"

"Yeah, right." Felix's eyes squinted at the rising orange sun.

"I've been thinking about it too, *panin*. In fact, since we found out it was going to be me and you, I've been awake at night, pulling punches[6] on you, trying not to hurt you."

"Same here. It ain't natural not to think about the fight. I mean, we both are *cheverote*[7] fighters and we both want to win. But only one of us can win. There ain't no draws in the eliminations."

Felix tapped Antonio gently on the shoulder. "I don't mean to sound like I'm bragging, bro. But I wanna win, fair and square."

Antonio nodded quietly. "Yeah. We both know that in the ring the better man wins. Friend or no friend, brother or no . . ."

Felix finished it for him. "Brother. Tony, let's promise something right here. Okay?"

"If it's fair, *hermano*, I'm for it." Antonio admired the courage of a tug boat pulling a barge five times its welterweight[8] size.

4. *[elimination bouts]* These are fights in a tournament; the winners advance to fight again, but the losers are eliminated from competition.
5. Here, *ace* means "best" and *boon* means "merry," so *ace-boon buddies* are best friends who share fun and good times.
6. In American Spanish slang, *panin* (pä′ nēn) means "pal; buddy." *Pulling punches* is holding back from delivering full-strength blows.
7. *Cheverote* (che ve rō′ tā) is American Spanish slang for "really cool; fine."
8. *Hermano* (ār män′ ō) means "brother." A professional *welterweight* boxer weighs between 141 and 147 pounds.

Vocabulary
devastating (dev′ əs tāt′ ing) *adj.* causing great pain, damage, or destruction; overwhelming

Teaching Support

MEETING INDIVIDUAL NEEDS — ENGLISH LANGUAGE LEARNERS

Spanish Words Have English language learners look at the words on page 434 in italic type. Let students explain what these words have in common. *(They are Spanish words.)*

Activity Have students begin a chart listing the Spanish words used in this story in the first column. In a second column, have students write an English definition for each word. If students speak Spanish, have them explain to other students several ways in which these words might be used.

Spanish Word	English Meaning
panin	buddy
cheverote	very fine

Additional Resources

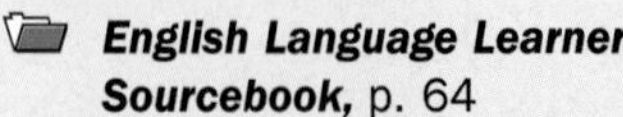

English Language Learners Sourcebook, p. 64

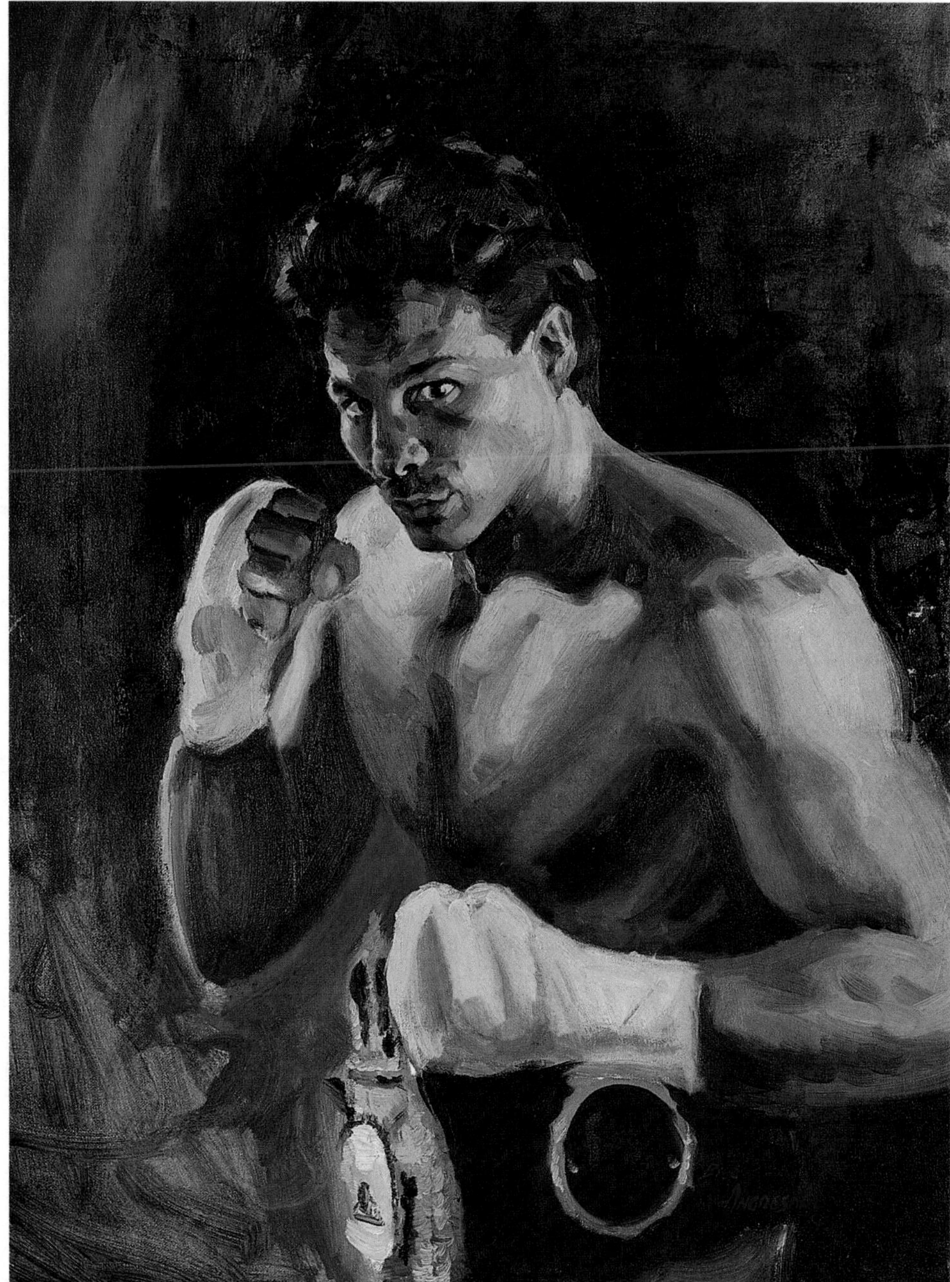

Vinny Pazienza, 1996. Bill Angresano. Oil on canvas, 24 x 20 in. Big Fights Boxing Memorabilia, New York.

Viewing the painting: Does this fighter seem to have the same determination as the *amigo* brothers? Explain your opinion.

VIEWING THE PAINTING

Artist Bill Angresano was himself a New Jersey Golden Gloves semi-finalist in the 1970s. This painting is probably of Rhode Islander Vinnie Pazienza at a match fought against Dana Rosenblatt in 1996. Rosenblatt led the entire fight until Pazienza landed a punch that knocked Rosenblatt out. Said Pazienza of the match, "The war is over only when you quit, and I don't quit." Pazienza said about boxing, "It's not just the fight that counts; it's everything. It's what happens between the rounds, and it's the intensity."

Viewing Response *Pazienza looks determined and focused. He seems to be fighting with the intensity of the amigo brothers.*

Historical Note

Boxing In ancient Greece, boxing was a popular sport and an Olympic event. Roman boxers wore metal-studded gloves that could kill their opponents. In the 1700s, boxing became popular in London. Fighters did not wear gloves and were allowed to pull hair or hit opponents who were down. By the late 1800s, boxers began wearing gloves, and the sport began emphasizing skill and strength.

Reading Minilesson

Comparing and Contrasting Antonio Cruz and Felix Varga share a dream. Yet the two boxers are different from each other in many ways. On the board, draw a Venn diagram.

Activity Encourage students to list ways that Antonio and Felix are alike and ways they are different. **L2**

Differences *Antonio*	Likenesses	Differences *Felix*
fair lean lanky	• want to be world lightweight champ • work out every chance	dark husky short

Additional Resources

Reading Skills Practice Workbook

E Active Reading Strategies

PREDICT Have students predict how the two boys will treat each other when they meet in the ring. The following model illustrates the thinking process involved in predicting.

Model: I know the boys are serious boxers with big dreams. Although they are friends and do not want to hurt each other, I think they will fight as hard as they can. Only then will the fight be fair and show who is the better boxer.

F Critical Thinking

EVALUATING Have students explain why the boys decide to separate before the fight. *(They think they can prepare better mentally if they don't see each other before the fight.)*

G Critical Thinking

LOGICAL REASONING Ask students if they think the boys could get together again "like nothing ever happened" after the fight? *(The boys may not feel as if they are equals anymore, and it could affect their relationship. They might see a new side of each other in the ring—one they don't like.)*

H Active Reading Strategies

CONNECT Have students explain why Antonio thinks knocking Felix out early will spare him. How would they feel? *(A first-round knockout is less painful than being pummeled for the complete match. However, a quick knockout might be humiliating.)*

Teaching Support

E "It's fair, Tony. When we get into the ring, it's gotta be like we never met. We gotta be like two heavy strangers that want the same thing and only one can have it. You understand, don'tcha?"

"*Si*, I know." Tony smiled. "No pulling punches. We go all the way."

F "Yeah, that's right. Listen, Tony. Don't you think it's a good idea if we don't see each other until the day of the fight? I'm going to stay with my Aunt Lucy in the Bronx. I can use Gleason's Gym for working out. My manager says he got some sparring partners with more or less your style."

Tony scratched his nose pensively.[9] "Yeah, it would be better for our heads." He held out his hand, palm upward. "Deal?"

"Deal." Felix lightly slapped open skin.

"Ready for some more running?" Tony asked lamely.

"Naw, bro. Let's cut it here. You go on. I kinda like to get things together in my head."

"You ain't worried, are you?" Tony asked.

G "No way, man." Felix laughed out loud. "I got too much smarts for that. I just think it's cooler if we split right here. After the fight, we can get it together again like nothing ever happened."

The amigo brothers were not ashamed to hug each other tightly.

"Guess you're right. Watch yourself, Felix. I hear there's some pretty heavy dudes up in the Bronx. *Sauvecito*,[10] okay?"

"Okay. You watch yourself too, *sabe?*"[11]

Tony jogged away. Felix watched his friend disappear from view, throwing rights and lefts. Both fighters had a lot of psyching[12] up to do before the big fight.

The days in training passed much too slowly. Although they kept out of each other's way, they were aware of each other's progress via the ghetto grapevine.

The evening before the big fight, Tony made his way to the roof of his tenement. In the quiet early dark, he peered over the ledge. Six stories below the lights of the city blinked and the sounds of cars mingled with the curses and the laughter of children in the street. He tried not to think of Felix, feeling he had succeeded in psyching his mind. But only in the ring would he really know. To spare Felix hurt, he would have to knock him out, early and quick. H

Up in the South Bronx, Felix decided to take in a movie in an effort to keep Antonio's face away from his fists. The flick was *The Champion* with Kirk Douglas, the third time Felix was seeing it.

The champion was getting the daylights beat out of him. He was saved only by the sound of the bell.

Felix became the champ and Tony the challenger.

The movie audience was going out of its head. The champ hunched his shoulders grunting and sniffing red blood back into his broken nose. The challenger, confident that he had the championship in the bag, threw a left. The champ countered with a dynamite right.

Felix's right arm felt the shock. Antonio's face, superimposed on the screen, was hit by the awesome force of the blow. Felix saw himself in the ring, blasting

9. Doing a thing *pensively* is doing it in a deeply thoughtful and, perhaps, sad way.
10. This American Spanish slang expression translates as "Take it easy" or "Be cool." Pronunciation: *sauvecito* (sä′ vā sē′ tō)
11. *Sabe?* (sä′ bā) means "You know?"
12. *Psyching* (sī′ king) *up* is getting into the right mental or emotional state.

Meeting Individual Needs — SPECIAL NEEDS

Emotional Help students realize that while boxing is a dangerous sport, the emphasis in modern boxing is on athletic skill and strength, rather than on brawling and maiming. In Golden Gloves boxing, the contestants wear helmets and thickly padded gloves to minimize injury.

Activity Have students work in pairs to create a chart comparing how Felix and Antonio train with the way athletes in another sport prepare. Ask students to share their comparisons with the class. What do they find appealing or unappealing about these types of training? **L1**

Additional Resources

Inclusion Strategies

Antonio against the ropes. The champ had to be forcibly restrained. The challenger fell slowly to the canvas.

When Felix finally left the theatre, he had figured out how to psyche himself for tomorrow's fight. It was Felix the Champion vs. Antonio the Challenger.

I

He walked up some dark streets, deserted except for small pockets of wary-looking kids wearing gang colors. Despite the fact that he was Puerto Rican like them, they eyed him as a stranger to their turf. Felix did a fast shuffle, bobbing and weaving, while letting loose a torrent of blows that would demolish whatever got in its way. It seemed to impress the brothers, who went about their own business.

Finding no takers, Felix decided to split to his aunt's. Walking the streets had not relaxed him, neither had the fight flick. All it had done was to stir him up. He let himself quietly into his Aunt Lucy's apartment and went straight to bed, falling into a fitful sleep with sounds of the gong for Round One.

J

Antonio was passing some heavy time on his rooftop. How would the fight tomorrow affect his relationship with Felix? After all, fighting was like any other profession. Friendship had nothing to do with it. A gnawing doubt crept in. He cut negative thinking real quick by doing some speedy fancy dance steps, bobbing and weaving like mercury.[13] The night air was blurred with perpetual motions of left hooks and right crosses. Felix, his *amigo* brother, was not going to be Felix at all in the ring. Just an opponent with another face. Antonio went to sleep, hearing the opening bell for the first round. Like his friend in the South Bronx, he prayed for victory, via a quick clean knock-out in the first round.

Large posters plastered all over the walls of local shops announced the fight between Antonio Cruz and Felix Vargas as the main bout.

The fight had created great interest in the neighborhood. Antonio and Felix were well liked and respected. Each had his own loyal following.

Antonio's fans had unbridled[14] faith in his boxing skills. On the other side, Felix's admirers trusted in his dynamite-packed fists.

Felix had returned to his apartment early in the morning of August 7th and stayed there, hoping to avoid seeing Antonio. He turned the radio on to *salsa*[15] music sounds and then tried to read while waiting for word from his manager.

The fight was scheduled to take place in Tompkins Square Park. It had been decided that the gymnasium of the Boys Club was not large enough to hold all the people who were sure to attend. In Tompkins Square Park, everyone who wanted could view the fight, whether from ringside or window fire escapes or tenement rooftops.

The morning of the fight Tompkins Square was a beehive of activity with

13. *Mercury* is a metal that is liquid at room temperature and moves about as if it were alive.

14. Here, *unbridled* means "uncontrolled."

15. *Salsa* is lively Latin American dance music that uses elements of rhythm and blues, jazz, and rock.

Vocabulary

wary (wār′ ē) *adj.* cautious; on the alert

perpetual (pər pech′ o͞o əl) *adj.* constant; unceasing

I Literary Elements

PLOT: *External Conflict* Ask students to describe the external conflict Felix faces after leaving the theater. Have students explain how Felix defuses the situation. *(Felix encounters gang members who distrust him. To defuse the situation, he shows off his boxing moves. The group leaves him alone.)*

J Literary Elements

PLOT: *Internal Conflict* Have students identify the internal conflict Antonio struggles with on his rooftop. *(Antonio worries about how the fight will affect his relationship with Felix.)*

Vo•cab•u•lar•y Skills

Etymology In ancient Greece, each city had a gymnasium where young men exercised, played sports, and studied philosophy, music, and literature. Because it is hot in Greece, the men exercised in the nude. The word *gymnasium* means "school for naked exercise." In English, *gymnasium* has come to mean "a place for physical activity." In Germany, a gymnasium is a high school.

Writing Minilesson

Using Realistic Language Write on the board:

1. *Felix decided to split.*
2. *The fight flick had not relaxed him.*
3. *It had stirred him up.*

Explain to students that the underlined language is informal and makes the story seem authentic. Have students restate the sentences without slang. *(Felix decided to leave. The fight movie had not relaxed him. It had upset him.)*

Activity Have students write a paragraph or story about an activity they engage in. Encourage students to use realistic, informal speech patterns to lend an air of authenticity to their work. **L2**

Additional Resources

Writer's Choice, Lesson 4.4

K Literary Elements

INTERNAL CONFLICT Have students describe the kind of person Antonio is. Why do students think Antonio waves back at Felix? *(He is serious about boxing and a good friend. He does not want to hurt Felix by not waving.)*

L Active Reading Strategies

VISUALIZE Encourage students to visualize each fighter in his fighting gear. Encourage them to remember what each fighter looks like as they read the later descriptions of the match.

M Active Reading Strategies

CONNECT Have students explain why the boys turn away from each other and face their corners. *(They want to get mentally composed for the fight.)* Ask students how they would handle this kind of situation.

Literature & Humanities

Have students examine the painting *Both Members of the Club* from the book *American Art History and Culture*, page 433. Ask small groups to discuss where they might place it in an illustrated version of this story.

Teaching Support

numerous workers setting up the ring, the seats, and the guest speakers' stand. The scheduled bouts began shortly after noon and the park had begun filling up even earlier.

The local junior high school across from Tompkins Square Park served as the dressing room for all the fighters. Each was given a separate classroom with desk tops, covered with mats, serving as resting tables. Antonio thought he caught a glimpse of Felix waving to him from a room at the far end of the corridor. He waved back just in case it had been him. K

The fighters changed from their street clothes into fighting gear. Antonio wore white trunks, black socks, and black shoes. Felix wore sky blue trunks, red socks, and white boxing shoes. Each had dressing gowns to match their fighting trunks with their names neatly stitched on the back. L

The loudspeakers blared into the open windows of the school. There were speeches by dignitaries, community leaders, and great boxers of yesteryear. Some were well prepared, some improvised on the spot. They all carried the same message of great pleasure and honor at being part of such a historic event. This great day was in the tradition of champions emerging from the streets of the lower east side.

Interwoven with the speeches were the sounds of the other boxing events. After the sixth bout, Felix was much relieved when his trainer Charlie said, "Time change. Quick knock-out. This is it. We're on."

Waiting time was over. Felix was escorted from the classroom by a dozen fans in white T-shirts with the word FELIX across their fronts.

Antonio was escorted down a different stairwell and guided through a roped-off path.

As the two climbed into the ring, the crowd exploded with a roar. Antonio and Felix both bowed gracefully and then raised their arms in acknowledgment.

Antonio tried to be cool, but even as the roar was in its first birth, he turned slowly to meet Felix's eyes looking directly into his. Felix nodded his head and Antonio responded. And both as one, just as quickly, turned away to face his own corner. M

Bong—bong—bong. The roar turned to stillness.

"Ladies and Gentlemen, *Señores y Señoras.*"[16]

The announcer spoke slowly, pleased at his bilingual[17] efforts.

"Now the moment we have all been waiting for—the main event between two fine young Puerto Rican fighters, products of our lower east side.

"In this corner, weighing 134 pounds, Felix Vargas. And in this corner, weighing 133 pounds, Antonio Cruz. The winner will represent the Boys Club in the tournament of champions, the Golden Gloves. There will be no draw. May the best man win."

The cheering of the crowd shook the window panes of the old buildings surrounding Tompkins Square Park. At the center of the ring, the referee was giving instructions to the youngsters.

"Keep your punches up. No low blows. No punching on the back of the head. Keep your heads up. Understand. Let's

16. Pronunciation: *Señores y Señoras* (sen yôr′ ās ē sen yôr′ əs)
17. A *bilingual* person can use two languages.

Vocabulary
improvise (im′ prə vīz′) *v.* to invent, compose, or do without much preparation

Listening and Speaking *Minilesson*

Describing a Match Explain to students that real boxers use fighting strategies much like those of Felix and Antonio.

Activity Have interested students watch a boxing match on TV. Encourage them to take notes to keep track of who is leading each round and what strategies each boxer uses. Then have students describe the highlights of the match to the class. Have students try to re-create the suspense and excitement of the fight by varying the pitch, tone, and loudness of their voices. Remind students that pausing while speaking can have a dramatic effect, too. **L2**

Boxing. G. Cominetti. 75.3 x 92 cm. Private collection.

Viewing the painting: Is the artist's style of painting appropriate to the subject? Why or why not?

have a clean fight. Now shake hands and come out fighting."

Both youngsters touched gloves and nodded. They turned and danced quickly to their corners. Their head towels and dressing gowns were lifted neatly from their shoulders by their trainers' nimble fingers. Antonio crossed himself. Felix did the same.

BONG! BONG! ROUND ONE. Felix and Antonio turned and faced each other squarely in a fighting pose. Felix wasted no time. He came in fast, head low, half hunched toward his right shoulder, and lashed out with a straight left. He missed a right cross as Antonio slipped the punch and countered with one-two-three lefts that snapped Felix's head back, sending a mild shock coursing through him. If Felix had any small doubt about their friendship affecting their fight, it was being neatly dispelled.[18]

Antonio danced, a joy to behold. His left hand was like a piston pumping jabs one right after another with seeming ease. Felix bobbed and weaved and never stopped boring in. He knew that at long range he was at a disadvantage. Antonio had too much reach on him. Only by coming in close could Felix hope to achieve the dreamed-of knockout. N

Antonio knew the dynamite that was stored in his *amigo* brother's fist. He ducked a short right and missed a left hook. Felix trapped him against the ropes just long enough to pour some punishing rights and lefts to Antonio's hard midsection. Antonio slipped away from Felix, crashing two lefts to his head, which set Felix's right ear to ringing.

Bong! Both *amigos* froze a punch well on its way, sending up a roar of approval for good sportsmanship. O

Felix walked briskly back to his corner. His right ear had not stopped ringing. Antonio gracefully danced his way toward his stool none the worse, except for glowing glove burns, showing angry red against the whiteness of his midribs.

"Watch that right, Tony." His trainer talked into his ear. "Remember Felix

18. To *dispel* something is to make it go away or disappear.

Vocabulary

nimble (nim′ bəl) *adj.* light and quick in movement

VIEWING THE PAINTING

Viewing Response *Cominetti's style is appropriate to the subject because he shows movement by capturing people in the middle of an action rather than while they are still.*

N Active Reading Strategies

REVIEW Have students describe Felix's boxing strategy. *(His strategy is to come in close and knock Antonio out with his powerful punches.)* What is Antonio's strategy? *(Antonio's strategy is to keep his distance and use his longer reach to knock out Felix.)*

O Critical Thinking

DRAWING CONCLUSIONS The two boys end round one by halting their punches in midair. Do your students think the two will keep this composure throughout the fight? The following model illustrates the thinking process involved in drawing conclusions.

Model: I know that both boys want badly to win. As the fight progresses, I think one or both of the boys will become more desperate. I think they will fight with less composure and caution.

MEETING INDIVIDUAL NEEDS: MULTIPLE MODES OF EXPRESSION

Bodily/Kinesthetic Some students may gain a better understanding of the concepts in this story if they use their kinesthetic skills. Encourage them to find out more about boxing moves and strategies.

Activity Have students visit a gym, talk to a coach, or conduct research to find out more about the boxing moves and stances mentioned in this story, such as a fighting pose, right jabs, left hooks, right crosses, overhand left, looping right to the body, bobbing, shuffling, weaving, feinting, short rights, haymakers, and ducking. Then have students demonstrate these moves and stances for the class, explaining when each move might be necessary. L2

P **Active Reading Strategies**

EVALUATE Have students explain how the advice of Antonio's trainer differs from that of Felix's trainer. *(Antonio's trainer warns Antonio not to drop his hands to block body punches or Felix will hit Antonio in the head. Felix's trainer tells Felix to get in close or Antonio will punch from outside Felix's range.)*

Q **Literary Elements**

IMAGERY Have students describe what Felix does when hurt. *(He plays possum: he pretends to be hurt badly, which draws an opponent in to finish him off.)*

R **Literary Elements**

PLOT: *External Conflict* Ask students to describe what happens in the last paragraph on this page and what the conflict is now. *(Both Felix and Antonio get knocked to the canvas. Both fighters are fighting for survival.)*

Vo•cab•u•lar•y Skills

Etymology St. Mary of Bethlehem Hospital opened in England in 1330 to care for the mentally ill. People referred to the hospital as *Bedlam*, short for *Bethlehem*. Since medications to treat the mentally ill did not exist then, such a hospital was often a place of uproar and confusion, which is what *bedlam* now connotes.

always goes to the body. He'll want you to drop your hands for his overhand left or right. Got it?"

Antonio nodded, spraying water out between his teeth. He felt better as his sore midsection was being firmly rubbed.

Felix's corner was also busy.

"You gotta get in there, fella." Felix's trainer poured water over his curly Afro locks. "Get in there or he's gonna chop you up from way back."

Bong! Bong! Round two. Felix was off his stool and rushed Antonio like a bull, sending a hard right to his head. Beads of water exploded from Antonio's long hair.

Antonio, hurt, sent back a blurring barrage of lefts and rights that only meant pain to Felix, who returned with a short left to the head followed by a looping right to the body. Antonio countered with his own flurry, forcing Felix to give ground. But not for long.

Felix bobbed and weaved, bobbed and weaved, occasionally punching his two gloves together.

Antonio waited for the rush that was sure to come. Felix closed in and feinted[19] with his left shoulder and threw his right instead. Lights suddenly exploded inside Felix's head as Antonio slipped the blow and hit him with a pistonlike left, catching him flush on the point of his chin.

Bedlam[20] broke loose as Felix's legs momentarily buckled. He fought off a series of rights and lefts and came back with a strong right that taught Antonio respect.

Antonio danced in carefully. He knew Felix had the habit of playing possum when hurt, to sucker an opponent within reach of the powerful bombs he carried in each fist.

A right to the head slowed Antonio's pretty dancing. He answered with his own left at Felix's right eye that began puffing up within three seconds.

Antonio, a bit too eager, moved in too close and Felix had him entangled into a rip-roaring, punching toe-to-toe slugfest that brought the whole Tompkins Square Park screaming to its feet.

Rights to the body. Lefts to the head. Neither fighter was giving an inch. Suddenly a short right caught Antonio squarely on the chin. His long legs turned to jelly and his arms flailed out desperately. Felix, grunting like a bull, threw wild punches from every direction. Antonio, groggy, bobbed and weaved, evading most of the blows. Suddenly his head cleared. His left flashed out hard and straight catching Felix on the bridge of his nose.

Felix lashed back with a haymaker, right off the ghetto streets. At the same instant, his eye caught another left hook from Antonio. Felix swung out trying to clear the pain. Only the frenzied screaming of those along ringside let him know that he had dropped Antonio. Fighting off the growing haze, Antonio struggled to his feet, got up, ducked, and threw a smashing right that dropped Felix flat on his back.

19. To *feint* is to make a movement intended to fool an opponent.
20. Noisy uproar and confusion is *bedlam*.

Vocabulary

flail (flāl) *v.* to wave or swing, especially swiftly or violently
evading (i vād′ ing) *adj.* escaping or avoiding

Teaching Support

Grammar and Language *Minilesson*

Action Verbs Write the following on the board: *Felix tapped his gloves. What did Felix do? He tapped.* Remind students that action verbs describe mental actions *(think, prefer, regard)* as well as physical actions. Students can tell if a word is an action word by changing a sentence into a "do" question. The answer, *tapped*, indicates an action. Explain that since sporting events are games of fast action, writers often use vivid action words to make events come alive for readers.

Activity Have students write sentences using each of the following action verbs: *block, tackle, catch, charge*, and *attack*. **L2**

Additional Resources

- ***Grammar and Language Transparency 37***
- ***Grammar and Language Workbook***, pp. 73–74
- ***Grammar and Composition Handbook***, Lesson 3.1
- ***Writer's Choice***, Lesson 10.1

Felix got up as fast as he could in his own corner, groggy but still game. He didn't even hear the count. In a fog, he heard the roaring of the crowd, who seemed to have gone insane. His head cleared to hear the bell sound at the end of the round. He was very glad. His trainer sat him down on the stool.

In his corner, Antonio was doing what all fighters do when they are hurt. They sit and smile at everyone.

The referee signaled the ring doctor to check the fighters out. He did so and then gave his okay. The cold water sponges brought clarity to both *amigo* brothers. They were rubbed until their circulation ran free.

Bong! Round three—the final round. Up to now it had been tic-tac-toe, pretty much even. But everyone knew there could be no draw and that this round would decide the winner.

This time, to Felix's surprise, it was Antonio who came out fast, charging across the ring. Felix braced himself but couldn't ward off the barrage of punches. Antonio drove Felix hard against the ropes.

The crowd ate it up. Thus far the two had fought with *mucho corazón*.[21] Felix tapped his gloves and commenced his attack anew. Antonio, throwing boxer's caution to the winds, jumped in to meet him.

Both pounded away. Neither gave an inch and neither fell to the canvas. Felix's left eye was tightly closed. Claret[22] red blood poured from Antonio's nose. They fought toe-to-toe.

The sounds of their blows were loud in contrast to the silence of a crowd gone completely mute.

Bong! Bong! Bong! The bell sounded over and over again. Felix and Antonio were past hearing. Their blows continued to pound on each other like hailstones.

Finally the referee and the two trainers pried Felix and Antonio apart. Cold water was poured over them to bring them back to their senses.

They looked around and then rushed toward each other. A cry of alarm surged through Tompkins Square Park. Was this a fight to the death instead of a boxing match?

The fear soon gave way to wave upon wave of cheering as the two *amigos* embraced.

No matter what the decision, they knew they would always be champions to each other.

BONG! BONG! BONG! "Ladies and Gentlemen. *Señores* and *Señoras*. The winner and representative to the Golden Gloves Tournament of Champions is . . ."

The announcer turned to point to the winner and found himself alone. Arm in arm the champions had already left the ring.

21. They fought with "great heart." Pronunciation: *mucho corazón* (mōō′ chō kō′ rə zōn′)

22. *Claret* (klar′ it) is a dark, purplish-red color.

Vocabulary

surge (surj) *v.* to rise or increase suddenly; move with a violent swelling motion, as waves

S Literary Elements

CHARACTER Ask students how the author reveals Antonio's personality by having him smile when he is actually in pain. *(The author reveals how much self-pride Antonio has by not showing the pain he feels.)*

T Literary Elements

PLOT: *Rising Action* Have students describe how the author increases reader interest when Round three begins. *(Readers know that the fight is even and that this round will decide the outcome. Antonio changes strategy and charges Felix.)*

U Active Reading Strategies

REVIEW Have students review how Round three ends. How does this compare with the end of Round one? *(After Round three, the two don't stop punching when the bell rings. They don't even hear the bell. In Round one, they both stopped their punches in midair.)*

Thematic Focus

At the Crossroads Ask students to explain how this story relates to the theme "At the Crossroads." At what crossroads are Felix and Antonio? *(Throughout the story, their friendship is threatened.)*

ASSESSMENT

Quick Checks, p. 39

Boxing Students can use a search engine to find out more about boxing. They might use such keywords as *champions, rounds,* and *heavyweight.*

Real-World Connection

In This Corner Invite students to use research from the Internet, the school library, or the U.S. Olympic Committee to create posters announcing a tournament.

Activity Have students work in small groups. Ask each group to review the information they have gathered and to decide which part they will use to illustrate their poster. **L2**

Before Reading

Objectives

- To read and appreciate a poem about a speaker at a turning point
- To recognize symbolism in poetry
- To write a paragraph that analyzes how imagery supports the theme of a poem

Skills

Writing: Imagery and Theme
Grammar/Language: Comparative and Superlative Adjectives
Collaboration: Literature Groups

Motivating STUDENTS

Selection Focus Transparency 40: Have students view and discuss the quote from Tom Bradley. Invite them to explain why they agree or disagree with the quotation.

Reading Focus: As an extension of the Reading Focus, have pairs of students share and compare their dreams. Encourage students to list things they can do to ensure that they reach their goals.

Before You Read

Your World

MEET GEORGIA DOUGLAS JOHNSON

Georgia Douglas Johnson inspired younger African American writers in the early 1900s. From her home in Washington, D.C., she hosted weekly meetings with Harlem Renaissance writers such as Countee Cullen and Langston Hughes. Johnson was one of the first African American female poets to gain wide recognition. Born in Georgia, she studied at Atlanta University and Oberlin Conservatory in Ohio. Johnson's works often advocated greater rights for women and minorities.

Georgia Douglas Johnson was born in 1877 and died in 1966.

READING FOCUS

Think of a challenge you face now or will face in the near future. Does it seem a bit scary, or even overwhelming?

Journal

Describe the challenge and what makes it seem frightening or overwhelming.

Setting a Purpose

Read to discover what one poet has to say about meeting new challenges.

BUILDING BACKGROUND

Did You Know? From 1920 to 1930, in Harlem, a mostly African American part of New York City, a group of writers, artists, and composers took part in a cultural movement that came to be known as the Harlem Renaissance. In their poems, novels, plays, and music, these men and women expressed a renewed pride in their heritage and their community.

The Ascent of Ethiopia, 1932. Loïs Mailou Jones. Oil on canvas, 23½ x 17¼ in. Milwaukee Art Museum, Purchase, African-American Acquisition Fund, matching funds from Suzanne and Richard Pieper, with additional funds from Arthur and Dorothy Nelle Sanders.

RESOURCE MANAGER

Teaching Tools and Resources
- Theme Five Planning Guide
- Literature Groups Sourcebook

Essential Lesson Support

Lesson-Specific Instruction
- Selection Focus Transparency 40
- Literary Elements Transparency 40
- Active Reading Guide,* p. 40

Assessment
- Selection Quick Checks,* p. 40
- Sel. and Theme Assmt., pp. 69–70
- Testmaker: ExamView Pro
- Performance Assessment, p. 37

Systematic Language Instruction
- Gr. and Comp. Hbk., L. 8.6
- Vocabulary Power, Lesson 20

English Language Learners
- ELL Sourcebook, p. 65
- Spanish Summaries, p. 40
- Audio Library*

Spec. Needs/Strat. Interven.
- Interactive Rdg. Sbk., pp. T155–T156
- Interactive Rdg. Wkbk., p. 75
- Inclusion Strat. Sbk., pp. 73–74
-  Audio Library*

* Also available in Spanish

Your World

Georgia Douglas Johnson

Your world is as big as you make it.
I know, for I used to abide
In the narrowest nest in a corner,
My wings pressing close to my side.

But I sighted the distant horizon
Where the sky line encircled the sea
And I throbbed with a burning desire
To travel this immensity.

I battered the cordons around me
And cradled my wings on the breeze
Then soared to the uttermost reaches
With rapture, with power, with ease!

2 Here, *abide* may mean either "dwell" or "remain."
8 Anything of great size or extent is an *immensity.*
9 *Cordons* are barriers.
12 *Rapture* is the condition of being carried away by strong emotion, such as joy or love.

Reading the Selection

A Active Reading Strategies

PREDICT Ask students to read only the first line of the poem and predict what the poet might mean by it. *(Students might say that they have the power to take advantage of the many opportunities they might discover.)*

B Literary Elements

SYMBOL Explain to students that a symbol is something that means more than just what it is. Ask students what the nest and wings might symbolize in lines 3–4. *(The nest symbolizes her small world. The wings symbolize a willingness to try new things in spite of her fear of the unknown.)*

C Literary Elements

SYMBOL Ask students to explain what the soaring bird in the last stanza symbolizes. *(It symbolizes a person who has set a lofty goal and achieved it.)*

Additional Resources

- ***Active Reading Guide,*** p. 40
- ***Audio Library***
- ***Spanish Audio Library***
- ***Spanish Summaries,*** p. 40

Teaching Support

Grammar and Language Minilesson

Comparative and Superlative Adjectives Comparative adjectives compare two items. Superlative adjectives compare more than two and add emphasis.

Activity Ask students to identify the adjectives in these sentences.

1. It's the chef's best dish. *(superlative)*
2. He was taller than she. *(comparative)*

L2

Additional Resources

- ***Grammar and Language Transparency 38***
- ***Grammar and Language Workbook,*** pp. 121–124
- ***Grammar and Composition Handbook,*** Lessons 5.3, 5.4
- ***Writer's Choice,*** Lessons 12.3, 12.4

Comparing Selections

This selection is compared with "Amigo Brothers" on page 433. A lesson for teaching a comparison of the two selections appears on page 447.

Responding to the Selection

PERSONAL RESPONSE

Students might feel more motivated to face their challenges after reading this poem.

Analyzing Literature

1. The speaker is compared to a bird. The metaphor works because the speaker overcomes a challenge and soars to new heights, much like a bird.
2. *Narrowest nest* uses alliteration. The repeated beginning consonant sound gives emphasis to the image.
3. The speaker sees the horizon and wants to travel there.
4. Yes. People can overcome obstacles on the path to success.
5. In the beginning, the speaker is afraid to try. By the end, the speaker is not afraid to try, and soars.
6. The rhythm emphasizes the words *rapture, power,* and *ease*. It instills in the reader a sense that anything is possible.

Extending Your Response

Literature Groups Before students begin writing the poem, encourage them to think of a symbol that works for their group. They may want to ask how they see themselves: as birds, as fish, as automobiles, as jets, and so on.

Writing About Literature

Students' paragraphs should
- clearly state a theme found in "My World"
- use images from the poem to support their ideas
- contain a concluding or summarizing sentence

Responding to Literature

PERSONAL RESPONSE

- How might this poem inspire you to face the challenge you described for the **Reading Focus** on page 444?

Analyzing Literature

RECALL AND INTERPRET

1. To what creature does the speaker compare himself or herself? Do you think the **metaphor** works in the poem? Why or why not?
2. **Alliteration** is the repetition of the consonant sounds at the beginnings of words. Find an example of alliteration in the first stanza of "Your World." How does it contribute to the poem's effect?
3. What does the speaker see in the second stanza? How does this change the direction of his or her life?

EVALUATE AND CONNECT

4. Do you agree with the speaker's belief that "Your world is as big as you make it"? Explain your answer.
5. How does the speaker change during the poem? Summarize the differences in the speaker at the beginning and end of the poem.
6. Read the last two lines of the poem aloud. How does the rhythm contribute to the poem's emotional effect?

LITERARY ELEMENTS

Symbol

In literature, when a person, a place, an object, or an action stands for something else, it becomes a **symbol.** For example, a dove is a symbol for peace. Writers use symbols in stories and poems to add meaning and to emphasize the theme. In "Your World," the poet uses a bird's nest as a symbol of a life with no room to grow.

1. What do the speaker's wings symbolize in the first and third stanzas?
2. What does "battered the cordons" mean? How does the poet use this image as a symbol?

- See **Literary Terms Handbook,** p. R11.

Extending Your Response

Literature Groups

Classroom Changes Discuss "Your World" with your group. How does the poet's use of symbol add emphasis to her ideas? Then, using the poem as a model, work together to compose a new short poem, "Our World."

Writing About Literature

Imagery and Theme What is the **theme**—the poet's main idea or message—of "Your World"? Write a paragraph analyzing how the poet's use of imagery supports the poem's theme.

ASSESSMENT

- ***Quick Checks,*** p. 40
- ***Selection and Theme Assessment,*** pp. 69-70
- ***Performance Assessment,*** p. 37
- ***Testmaker: ExamView Pro***
- ***Interactive Tutor: Self-Assessment***

LITERARY ELEMENTS

1. The wings symbolize the speaker's willingness to try. In the first stanza the speaker didn't try—wings pressed close to the side. In the third, the speaker did try—and soared.
2. It means "smashed the barriers." This is a symbol for overcoming obstacles.

Additional Resources

Literary Elements Transparency 40

COMPARING SELECTIONS

Amigo Brothers and *Your World*

COMPARE THEMES

In "Amigo Brothers" and "Your World," people arrive at crossroads in their lives. Think about the decisions or changes they make to open up new directions and possibilities.

1. At what crossroads do Antonio and Felix find themselves? What decisions do they each make?
2. What advice does the speaker of "Your World" have for others who stand at the crossroads?
3. The speaker in "Your World" was inspired to leave "the narrowest nest" and soar "to the uttermost reaches." What dreams are calling Antonio and Felix away from their current lives toward a larger world?

COMPARE RESPONSES

"Amigo Brothers" and "Your World" offer inspiring messages in different forms–one a short story, the other a poem.

1. Which selection do you find more inspiring? Why?
2. What life lesson is reinforced in "Amigo Brothers"?
3. The speaker in "Your World" believes that people must break through certain barriers in order to change. What barriers do the characters in "Amigo Brothers" break through?

COMPARE ACTIONS

The poem "Your World" is a call to action. The speaker breaks the bonds of a narrow life and finds opportunities in the larger world. It is a poem that could inspire young people to think differently about their own lives.

- What do you think would happen to Antonio or Felix if they read "Your World" and took it to heart?
- Write a letter from one *amigo* brother to the other about what the poem meant to him, and how he thinks the philosophy in the poem could benefit each of their lives.

COMPARING *selections*

Objective

- To compare a short story and a poem, both of which relate to the theme "At the Crossroads"

COMPARE THEMES

1. Antonio and Felix have to decide if a boxing match is more important than their friendship. They preserve their friendship by fighting their best fight.
2. The speaker's advice is to try.
3. Each dreams of being lightweight boxing champion of the world.

COMPARE RESPONSES

1. Answers should explain why students feel the way they do.
2. Friendships are important. A good one can weather adversity.
3. The friends in "Amigo Brothers" must break through the barrier created by their having to fight each other.

COMPARE ACTIONS

- They would be inspired by the poem to work toward their goal.
- Students' letters should be written in proper format from the point of view of either Antonio or Felix.

Additional Resources

Literature Groups Sourcebook

Teaching Support

PORTFOLIO OPTIONS

Select and Reflect Have students reflect on the letters they wrote by asking themselves these questions:

- Does my letter explain what the poem means to the character in his life?
- Do I use examples from the story or events that could have happened in the character's life to support my ideas?
- Do I clearly explain how the message of the poem can help the two friends?

Students should clip their reflections to their letters and place them in their portfolios. **L2**

Additional Resources

Writing Assessment and Portfolio Management, pp. 39–45

Interdisciplinary Connection

Objectives

- To understand and express the benefits of physical fitness

Teaching Strategies

Ask students to pantomime a household chore they are required to do, such as sweeping the floor, making a bed, washing dishes, emptying trash, or hanging laundry. Encourage classmates to pantomime the same activity in a way that transforms it into an exercise, creating a series of "household aerobic exercises." Remind students that the muscles and endurance they build pushing a vacuum cleaner can help them train for a marathon.

Activity

Point out to students that health and exercise magazines and newsletters, as well as a health textbook if they have access to one, would be possible sources of materials to summarize. Stress the importance of putting their summaries into their own words (unless they feel a need to quote a phrase or sentence from the original source).

Stress that students' summaries should demonstrate their understanding of the material they are summarizing. Have students present their summaries orally in small groups.

Teaching Support

Interdisciplinary Connection

Physical Fitness

In the short story "Amigo Brothers," Antonio and Felix keep themselves physically fit by working out at the gym and by running. However, you don't need to be a sports pro or have special training to enjoy being physically active and fit. In fact, you don't even need to be particularly athletic to have fun that's good for your body.

One family, the Kuntzelmans, planned a unique "walk across America" to see how far they could travel as a team. They totaled the miles they walked near home, then marked those distances across a United States map each week. After walking enough miles to reach Mexico, the whole family celebrated by eating at a local Mexican restaurant.

At a middle school in Naperville, Illinois, students discovered a way everyone could track his or her personal best. Rather than competing against each other, each student individually decided how far to run, then recorded the distance, using a heart monitor to watch for an improved heart rate.

Changing everyday habits can get your body moving and increase your fitness, too. Here are a few tips:

- Ride your bike or walk when you visit a friend or go on an errand.
- Whenever possible, take the stairs instead of an elevator or escalator.
- Dance to your favorite CD, jump rope, swim, build a snow fort, or just stretch your muscles after sitting through a movie or TV show–or an English class.
- Go outside for a game of kickball, baseball, basketball, soccer, or even a short walk.

ACTIVITY

Find an article or chapter on exercise or physical fitness that you consider interesting. Search on the Internet, in magazines, or in books. Write a summary of the article to read to the class. Remember, a summary should be in your own words and should include only the most important ideas and details. It should demonstrate your understanding of the material summarized.

Meeting Individual Needs: MULTIPLE MODES OF EXPRESSION

Musical/Bodily/Kinesthetic
Encourage musically inclined students to team up with kinesthetic learners to develop a dance routine promoting physical fitness among middle school students.

Activity In small groups, students can work together to come up with a dance or exercise routine simple enough for anyone, including students with disabilities. Musical students should find or make up a song or rap/jazz chant to accompany the short exercise routine developed by kinesthetic learners. Have students teach the routine to the class. You may wish to videotape the exercise routine and song to show other classes. **L2**

LISTENING, SPEAKING, and VIEWING

Small-Group Discussions

In "Amigo Brothers," Antonio and Felix need to talk before their bout, but it's difficult. They make the discussion work by helping each other. They listen carefully, suggest phrases, and check to make sure they have understood each other. When you join a small-group discussion, you can use the same strategies to help make the discussion work. Try these tips.

Group Discussion Tips

- Take turns talking. Help everyone get a chance to be heard. If there is a group leader, follow his or her directions.
- Listen carefully. Try repeating others' points in your own words to be sure you understand them.
- To keep the discussion on track, make only comments that deal directly with the topic.
- Avoid interrupting or raising your voice. If you are interrupted, resume in an even tone after the interruption ends.
- Disagree with ideas, not with people. Avoid personal comments or put-downs.
- When someone criticizes your ideas, listen quietly. Give the criticism careful thought before you respond.

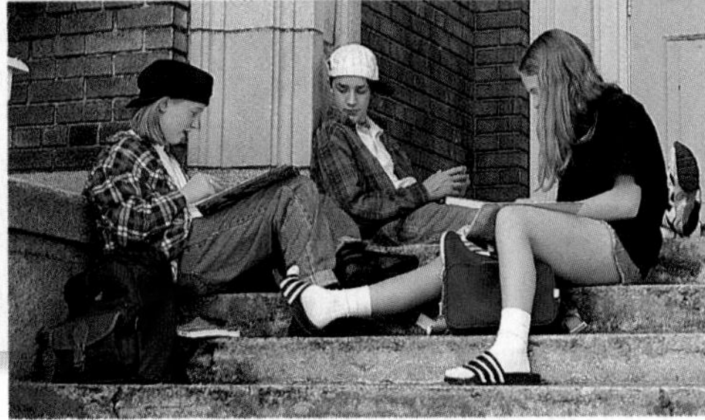

ACTIVITIES

1. Watch a group discussion on television, in a film or video, or in real life. Note how group members follow (or ignore) the tips listed above. Then share your observations with classmates.
2. Join a small-group discussion of ideas that group members have written about. Afterwards, rate your own performance on each tip listed above.

LISTENING, SPEAKING, and VIEWING

Objective

- To recognize and practice strategies for participating in small group discussions

Teaching Strategies

Ask students to describe how it feels when someone interrupts them, raises his or her voice, or doesn't listen. Go through the tips in the student edition and discuss with students why and how communication suffers when people don't respect these basic guidelines. Students might create humorous role-plays to dramatize each of the tips.

Activities

1. Students can keep a list of discussion participants' names and a list in numerical order of the Group Discussion Tips. They may chart their observations using these lists.
2. Students may wish to rate their performance of the Group Discussion Tips on a scale of 1 to 10. If so, they can create graphs that represent their strengths and weaknesses as discussion participants.

Teaching Support

MEETING INDIVIDUAL NEEDS: ENGLISH LANGUAGE LEARNERS

Group Discussion Tips Have English language learners as well as students who are proficient in English work in small groups to create posters that describe and illustrate the Group Discussion Tips.

Activity Assign each group one of the tips. Have them copy it onto posterboard or butcher paper and think of an imaginative way to illustrate it. They can use collage, paintings, drawings, magazine or newspaper pictures, cartoons, or photographs. Finally, have them hang their posters in class and encourage English language learners to ask questions about any tips they still don't understand.

Additional Resources

English Language Learners Sourcebook, p. 65

Before Reading

Objectives

- To read and analyze a short story about a girl and a prize
- To state the final outcome, or resolution, of a story
- To write a critical review of a short story

Skills

Reading/Thinking: Inferring; Drawing Conclusions; Sequence of Events; Questioning/Clarifying
Writing: Critical Review; Journal Entry
Vocabulary: Word Meanings; Negative Prefixes
Grammar/Language: Subject-Verb Agreement; Adverbs and Adjectives
Life Skills: Graduation Speech
Collaboration: Literature Groups

Motivating STUDENTS

Selection Focus Transparency 41: Encourage students to discuss how allowing a small injustice or unfairness can lead to allowing greater injustices.

Reading Focus: As an extension of the Reading Focus, have students in small groups describe awards they have received. Ask each student how he or she would have felt if the award had gone to someone else.

Before You Read

The Scholarship Jacket

MEET MARTA SALINAS

Marta Salinas is the author of many short stories. Her short story "The Scholarship Jacket" was first published in *Cuentos Chicanos: A Short Story Anthology*. Her work has also appeared in the *Los Angeles Herald Examiner* and in *California Living* magazine.

READING FOCUS

Think about an award you have earned or would like to earn.

Think/Pair/Share
For what did you receive an award? What did you do to prepare for it? Or, what award would you be pleased to get? What would you have to do to earn it? Describe what receiving it was like (or would be like) for you.

Setting a Purpose
Read the story to find out what a school award means to a young girl.

BUILDING BACKGROUND

The Time and Place This story takes place in recent time in a small town in Texas.

Did You Know? Have you ever heard of the word *valedictorian?* The word comes from the Latin word *valedicere,* which means "to say farewell." A valedictorian is the student who has achieved the highest grades in a graduating class during all his or her years at school. This person is usually given the honor of giving the farewell address at the graduation ceremony.

VOCABULARY PREVIEW

coincidence (kō in′ si dəns) *n.* an accidental occurrence of events, ideas, or circumstances at the same time, without one causing the other; p. 452
dismay (dis mā′) *n.* a feeling of alarm or uneasiness; p. 453
muster (mus′ tər) *v.* to find and gather together; collect; p. 453
withdrawn (with drôn′) *adj.* shy, reserved, or unsociable; p. 454
vile (vīl) *adj.* very bad; unpleasant; foul; p. 455

RESOURCE MANAGER

Teaching Tools and Resources
- Theme Five Planning Guide
- Literature Groups Sourcebook

Essential Lesson Support

Lesson-Specific Instruction
- Selection Focus Transparency 41
- Literary Elements Transparency 41
- Active Reading Guide,* p. 41
- Selection Vocabulary Practice, p. 27

Assessment
- Selection Quick Checks,* p. 41
- Sel. and Theme Assmt., pp. 71–72
- Testmaker: ExamView Pro
- Performance Assessment, p. 38

Systematic Language Instruction
- Gr. and Comp. Hbk., L. 9.2
- Vocabulary Power, Lesson 21
- Spelling Power, Lesson 18

English Language Learners
- ELL Sourcebook, p. 66
- Spanish Summaries, p. 41
- Spanish Translations, pp. 115–118
-  Audio Library*
- English, Yes!

Spec. Needs/Strat. Interven.
- Interactive Rdg. Sbk., pp. T157–T159
- Interactive Rdg. Wkbk., pp. 76–77
- Inclusion Strat. Sbk., pp. 35–36, 43–44
- Audio Library*

* Also available in Spanish

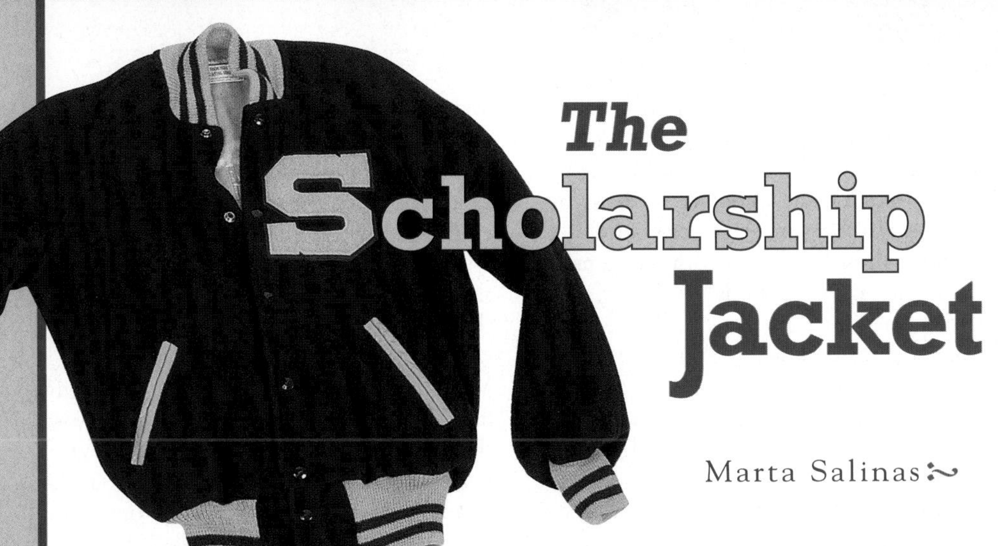

The Scholarship Jacket

Marta Salinas

The small Texas school that I attended carried out a tradition every year during the eighth grade graduation; a beautiful gold and green jacket, the school colors, was awarded to the class valedictorian, the student who had maintained the highest grades for eight years. The scholarship jacket had a big gold S on the left front side and the winner's name was written in gold letters on the pocket.

My oldest sister Rosie had won the jacket a few years back and I fully expected to win also. I was fourteen and in the eighth grade. I had been a straight A student since the first grade, and the last year I had looked forward to owning that jacket. My father was a farm laborer who couldn't earn enough money to feed eight children, so when I was six I was given to my grandparents to raise. We couldn't participate in sports at school because there were registration fees, uniform costs, and trips out of town; so even though we were quite agile and athletic, there would never be a sports school jacket for us. This one, the scholarship jacket, was our only chance.

In May, close to graduation, spring fever struck, and no one paid any attention in class; instead we stared out the windows and at each other, wanting to speed up the last few weeks of school. I despaired every time I looked in the mirror. Pencil thin, not a curve anywhere, I was called "Beanpole" and "String Bean" and I knew that's what I looked like.

Reading the Selection

SUMMARY

Marta has the highest grade point average in her school. In years past, the school has awarded a scholarship jacket to the valedictorian. This year, however, the jacket may go to a student with an influential father rather than to the real winner.

Spanish Summaries, p. 41

A Active Reading Strategies

PREDICT Invite students to read the title "The Scholarship Jacket" and the first two paragraphs of the story aloud. Have students predict whether the narrator will win the scholarship jacket like her oldest sister. Suggest that students revisit their predictions as they read to verify or to revise them.

VOCABULARY If you haven't previewed the selection vocabulary with students, stop and remind them to use context clues to unlock the meanings of new vocabulary words.

Additional Resources

- ***Active Reading Guide,*** p. 41
- ***Audio Library***
- ***Spanish Audio Library***

Teaching Support

CONNECTING TO OTHER SELECTIONS

The chart at the right shows three ways to connect "The Scholarship Jacket" to other selections in this book.

For specific teaching strategies, see the ***Theme Five Planning Guide.***

Connection		Title
Life Skills: Setting Goals	→	"The Smallest Dragonboy," p. 683
Thematic: Family	→	"In a Neighborhood in Los Angeles," p. 334
Literary: Conflict	→	"The Old Demon," p. 483

B Literary Elements

CHARACTER Ask students what we learn about Marta's personality from this description. *(Marta is unhappy with the way she looks, but she knows she is smart.)*

C Critical Thinking

INFERRING Ask students what the conflict is between Mr. Boone and Mr. Schmidt. *(Mr. Boone wants Mr. Schmidt to lie so that another student will get Marta's scholarship jacket.)*

D Active Reading Strategies

REVIEW Have students tell what they have learned so far about Joann and her father. *(Joann's grades are not as good as Marta's; Joann's father is on the school board and owns the only store in town.)*

E Critical Thinking

DRAWING CONCLUSIONS Ask students why they think the school board changed its policy. Use the following model to illustrate the thinking process involved in drawing conclusions.

Model: Joann's father owns the only store in town, meaning he is probably wealthy and influential. I think he used his position on the board to influence the others.

Teaching Support

The Scholarship Jacket

A flat chest, no hips, and a brain, that's what I had. That really isn't much for a fourteen-year-old to work with, I thought, as I absentmindedly wandered from my history class to the gym. Another hour of sweating in basketball and displaying my toothpick legs was coming up. Then I remembered my P.E. shorts were still in a bag under my desk where I'd forgotten them. I had to walk all the way back and get them. Coach Thompson was a real bear if anyone wasn't dressed for P.E. She had said I was a good forward and once she even tried to talk Grandma into letting me join the team. Grandma, of course, said no.

I was almost back at my classroom's door when I heard angry voices and arguing. I stopped. I didn't mean to eavesdrop; I just hesitated, not knowing what to do. I needed those shorts and I was going to be late, but I didn't want to interrupt an argument between my teachers. I recognized the voices: Mr. Schmidt, my history teacher, and Mr. Boone, my math teacher. They seemed to be arguing about me. I couldn't believe it. I still remember the shock that rooted me flat against the wall as if I were trying to blend in with the graffiti written there.

"I refuse to do it! I don't care who her father is, her grades don't even begin to compare to Martha's. I won't lie or falsify records. Martha[1] has a straight A plus average and you know it." That was Mr. Schmidt and he sounded very angry. Mr. Boone's voice sounded calm and quiet.

"Look, Joann's father is not only on the Board, he owns the only store in town; we could say it was a close tie and—"

The pounding in my ears drowned out the rest of the words, only a word here and there filtered through. ". . . Martha is Mexican. . . . resign. . . . won't do it. . . ." Mr. Schmidt came rushing out, and luckily for me went down the opposite way toward the auditorium, so he didn't see me. Shaking, I waited a few minutes and then went in and grabbed my bag and fled from the room. Mr. Boone looked up when I came in but didn't say anything. To this day I don't remember if I got in trouble in P.E. for being late or how I made it through the rest of the afternoon. I went home very sad and cried into my pillow that night so grandmother wouldn't hear me. It seemed a cruel coincidence that I had overheard that conversation.

The next day when the principal called me into his office, I knew what it would be about. He looked uncomfortable and unhappy. I decided I wasn't going to make it any easier for him so I looked him straight in the eye. He looked away and fidgeted with the papers on his desk.

"Martha," he said, "there's been a change in policy this year regarding the scholarship jacket. As you know, it has always been free." He cleared his throat and continued. "This year the Board decided to charge fifteen dollars—which still won't cover the complete cost of the jacket."

1. The main character is called "Martha" at school and "Marta" at home. Martha is an English version of the main character's Spanish name.

Vocabulary

coincidence (kō in′ si dəns) *n.* an accidental occurrence of events, ideas, or circumstances at the same time, without one causing the other

ENGLISH LANGUAGE LEARNERS

Visualizing Words Explain that writers often choose words to create images in readers' minds. For example, *toothpick legs* helps us visualize legs as skinny as toothpicks.

Activity Have pairs or small groups of students examine these sentences:

Coach Thompson was a real bear.
The music drowned what he said.
Only a word or two filtered through.

Have each student draw a picture of an image created by one of the underlined words in these sentences.

Additional Resources

English Language Learners Sourcebook, p. 66

I stared at him in shock and a small sound of dismay escaped my throat. I hadn't expected this. He still avoided looking in my eyes.

"So if you are unable to pay the fifteen dollars for the jacket, it will be given to the next one in line."

Standing with all the dignity I could muster, I said, "I'll speak to my grandfather about it, sir, and let you know tomorrow." I cried on the walk home from the bus stop. The dirt road was a quarter of a mile from the highway, so by the time I got home, my eyes were red and puffy.

"Where's Grandpa?" I asked Grandma, looking down at the floor so she wouldn't ask me why I'd been crying. She was sewing on a quilt and didn't look up.

"I think he's out back working in the bean field."

I went outside and looked out at the fields. There he was. I could see him walking between the rows, his body bent over the little plants, hoe in hand. I walked slowly out to him, trying to think how I could best ask him for the money. There was a cool breeze blowing and a sweet smell of mesquite in the air, but I didn't appreciate it. I kicked at a dirt clod. I wanted that jacket so much. It was more than just being a valedictorian and giving a little thank you speech for the jacket on graduation night. It represented eight years of hard work and expectation. I knew I had to be honest with Grandpa; it was my only chance. He saw me and looked up.

Did You Know?
Mesquite (mes kēt′) is a small thorny tree. Its pleasant-smelling wood is a favored barbecue fuel in the Southwest.

He waited for me to speak. I cleared my throat nervously and clasped my hands behind my back so he wouldn't see them shaking. "Grandpa, I have a big favor to ask you," I said in Spanish, the only language he knew. He still waited silently. I tried again. "Grandpa, this year the principal said the scholarship jacket is not going to be free. It's going to cost fifteen dollars and I have to take the money in tomorrow, otherwise it'll be given to someone else." The last words came out in an eager rush. Grandpa straightened up tiredly and leaned his chin on the hoe handle. He looked out over the field that was filled with the tiny green bean plants. I waited, desperately hoping he'd say I could have the money.

He turned to me and asked quietly, "What does a scholarship jacket mean?"

I answered quickly; maybe there was a chance. "It means you've earned it by having the highest grades for eight years and that's why they're giving it to you." Too late I realized the significance of my words. Grandpa knew that I understood it was not a matter of money. It wasn't that. He went back to hoeing the weeds that sprang up between the delicate little bean plants. It was a time consuming job; sometimes the small shoots were right

Vocabulary
dismay (dis mā′) *n.* a feeling of alarm or uneasiness
muster (mus′ tər) *v.* to find and gather together; collect

F Active Reading Strategies

CONNECT Have students explain what it means when another person won't look them in the eye when talking. What do they think it means when the principal won't look Marta in the eye? *(Not looking someone in the eye can mean you are intimidated or shy or uneasy. The principal is uncomfortable with what he is doing.)*

Vo•cab•u•lar•y Skills

Word Meanings People often confuse *principal* and *principle*. Explain to students that one way to keep the words straight is to remember that *principal* always means "chief." For example, the *principal* of a school is the chief of the school and the *principal* reason is the chief reason. *Principle* always means "rule or law," as in a fundamental *principle* of human nature.

G Active Reading Strategies

EVALUATE Have students think about this scene. What impression do they get of Marta's grandfather? *(He is a hardworking farmer who cares about his land.)*

H Critical Thinking

DRAWING CONCLUSIONS Have students explain what having to pay for the jacket means. *(Paying for the jacket means that the jacket is no longer about achievement; it is only about who is most willing or able to pay for it.)*

Reading Minilesson

Sequence of Events One thing that makes a story engaging to readers is the way its characters change over time.

Activity Invite students to create a chart, illustrating how Marta, the principal, and the grandfather change as they respond to events in the story. When the chart is complete, have students discuss the changes. **L2**

Character	Event	What Happens
Principal	School board changes rules	Tells Marta she must buy jacket
Marta	Learns jacket cost $15	Asks grandfather for the money
Grandfather	Learns Marta needs $15	Tells her if she pays it won't be a scholarship jacket

Additional Resources

Reading Skills Practice Workbook

VIEWING THE PAINTING

Ernest L. Blumenschein, born in Pittsburgh, Pennsylvania, in 1874, studied art in Cincinnati, New York, and Paris, France. He settled permanently in Taos, New Mexico, in 1919, where he was a founding member of the Taos Society of Artists.

Viewing Response *The laborer in the painting is reminiscent of Marta's grandfather, who was a farmer in Texas.*

I Active Reading Strategies

CONNECT Have students ever been mad at a parent even though they knew the parent was right? Have students explain what they would feel and do if they were in Marta's position.

J Critical Thinking

INFERRING Have students explain how the principal's behavior is different during this second meeting. *(He looks Marta in the eyes.)* What do students think this means? *(The principal has changed and he feels good about himself.)*

K Active Reading Strategies

PREDICT Have students explain what they think will happen next. *(They may think that he is going to make a fair decision and not be pushed around by Joann's father.)*

New Mexico Peon, 1942. Ernest L. Blumenschein. Oil on canvas, 40 x 25 in. Gerald Peters Gallery, Sante Fe.

Viewing the painting: Does the person in the painting remind you of any character in the story? Explain.

next to each other. Finally he spoke again.

"Then if you pay for it, Marta, it's not a scholarship jacket, is it? Tell your principal I will not pay the fifteen dollars."

I walked back to the house and locked myself in the bathroom for a long time. I was angry with grandfather even though I knew he was right, and I was angry with the Board, whoever they were. Why did they have to change the rules just when it was my turn to win the jacket? I

It was a very sad and withdrawn girl who dragged into the principal's office the next day. This time he did look me in the eyes. J

"What did your grandfather say?"

I sat very straight in my chair.

"He said to tell you he won't pay the fifteen dollars."

The principal muttered something I couldn't understand under his breath, and walked over to the window. He stood looking out at something outside. He looked bigger than usual when he stood up; he was a tall gaunt[2] K

2. A *gaunt* person is thin and bony.

Vocabulary
withdrawn (with drôn′) *adj.* shy, reserved, or unsociable

Teaching Support

Grammar and Language *Minilesson*

Subject-Verb Agreement Explain to students that writers must be careful to make subjects and verbs agree. For example, in this story the author writes:

I waited for him to speak.
Your grandfather has the money.
He looked at me.
I'll tell the board.
I spoke in a rush.
Your grandmother needs help.

Activity Have pairs of students decide whether the verb in each of these sentences tells about something that has happened, is happening now, or will happen. Then have students take turns changing the tense of the verbs or making the subjects plural in these sentences. Students should make sure subjects and verbs agree. **L2**

Additional Resources

- ***Grammar and Language Transparency 39***
- ***Grammar and Language Workbook,*** pp. 183–184
- ***Grammar and Composition Handbook,*** Lesson 10.1
- ***Writer's Choice,*** Lesson 16.1

man with gray hair, and I watched the back of his head while I waited for him to speak.

L "Why?" he finally asked. "Your grandfather has the money. Doesn't he own a small bean farm?"

I looked at him, forcing my eyes to stay dry. "He said if I had to pay for it, then it wouldn't be a scholarship jacket," I said and stood up to leave. "I guess you'll just have to give it to Joann." I hadn't meant to say that; it had just slipped out. I was almost to the door when he stopped me.

"Martha—wait."

I turned and looked at him, waiting. What did he want now? I could feel my heart pounding. Something bitter and vile tasting was coming up in my mouth; I was afraid I was going to be sick. I didn't need any sympathy speeches. He sighed loudly M and went back to his big desk. He looked at me, biting his lip, as if thinking.

"Okay. We'll make an exception in your case. I'll tell the Board, you'll get your jacket."

I could hardly believe it. I spoke in a trembling rush. "Oh, thank you sir!" Suddenly I felt great. I didn't know about adrenalin[3] in those days, but I knew something was pumping through me, making me feel as tall as the sky. I wanted to yell, jump, run the mile, do something. I ran out so I could cry in the hall where there was no one to see me. At the end of the day, Mr. Schmidt winked at me and said, "I hear you're getting a scholarship jacket this year."

His face looked as happy and innocent as a baby's, but I knew better. Without answering I gave him a quick hug and ran to the bus. I cried on the walk home again, but this time because I was so happy. I couldn't wait to tell Grandpa and ran straight to the field. I joined him in the row where he was working and without saying anything I crouched down and started pulling up the weeds with my hands. Grandpa worked alongside me for a few minutes, but he didn't ask what had happened. After I had a little pile of weeds between the rows, I stood up and faced him.

"The principal said he's making an exception for me, Grandpa, and I'm getting the jacket after all. That's after I told him what you said."

Grandpa didn't say anything, he just gave me a pat on the shoulder and a smile. He pulled out the crumpled red handkerchief that he always carried in his back pocket and wiped the sweat off his forehead. N

"Better go see if your grandmother needs any help with supper."

I gave him a big grin. He didn't fool me. I skipped and ran back to the house whistling some silly tune.

3. A chemical released into the blood in times of stress or excitement, *adrenalin* (ə dren′ əl in) increases the body's energy.

Vocabulary
vile (vīl) *adj.* very bad; unpleasant; foul

L Literary Elements

RESOLUTION What do students think the grandfather's refusal to pay for the jacket says about him? *(He is a man of principle. He thinks paying for the jacket would diminish its worth.)*

M Literary Elements

RESOLUTION Ask students what this tells about the principal. *(His body language indicates that the decision was difficult.)*

N Critical Thinking

DRAWING CONCLUSIONS Invite students to explain how the grandfather feels when Marta tells him she is getting the jacket after all. *(The grandfather is happy. This may not be apparent because the grandfather doesn't say it, but Marta knows.)*

You may wish to use ***Fine Art Transparency 5*** to discuss why some objects hold special meaning.

Thematic Focus

At the Crossroads Have students discuss how this story relates to the theme "At the Crossroads." At what crossroads do Marta and the principal find themselves?

ASSESSMENT

 ***Quick Checks,*** p. 41

REAL-WORLD CONNECTION

Awards Invite students to use research from the Internet, the school library, or the local board of education to find out more about awards granted in their district or state. On the Internet students can use a search engine to find information about specific awards and how to achieve them. They can enter such keywords as *scholarships, awards, merit,* or *state.*

Activity Have students use information they have gathered to create an "information bulletin" that can be posted in the classroom listing all the different awards they can apply for. Suggest that they use the information they gathered and their own knowledge to generate a list of additional, unanswered questions for further research. **L3**

Responding to the Selection

PERSONAL RESPONSE

Encourage students to describe an emotion they would feel and what they would do.

Analyzing Literature

1. It's a jacket given to the student who has earned the highest grades for eight years.
2. She learns that she might not receive the scholarship jacket even though she has the highest grades.
3. He tells her that the jacket will cost fifteen dollars this year.
4. Grandpa says he will not pay the fifteen dollars.
5. Marta expects to receive the jacket because she has the highest grades in the school. The jacket is important because Marta has worked hard for it.
6. Mr. Schmidt and Mr. Boone are arguing about who should receive the scholarship jacket. Mr. Schmidt is angry because Mr. Boone wants him to lie or falsify records.
7. Joann's father wants his daughter to receive it. He is a powerful man on the school board. The other members of the school board do not want to make him angry, so they go along with his proposal.
8. Grandpa decides not to pay the fifteen dollars. Grandpa means that if the jacket must be bought, it is not an award.
9. The principal is at first influenced by Joann's father. Then he learns that Marta's grandfather believes that paying for the jacket compromises its meaning. The principal agrees.
10. The jacket should be important to Marta because she has worked hard for it for eight years.

Active Reading and Critical Thinking

Responding to Literature

PERSONAL RESPONSE

- Think back to the notes you wrote in the **Reading Focus** on page 450. How would you feel if someone who didn't work for an award received it? What would you do?

Analyzing Literature

RECALL

1. What is the scholarship jacket?
2. What does Marta learn when she accidentally overhears two teachers arguing?
3. What does the principal tell Marta when she is called into his office the next day?
4. What is Grandpa's reaction when Marta asks him for the money?

Brackets connect questions that are paired to develop higher-level thinking skills.

INTERPRET

5. As the story begins, why does Marta expect to receive the jacket? Why is the jacket so important to her?
6. Why are Mr. Schmidt and Mr. Boone arguing? Why might Mr. Schmidt have sounded so angry?
7. In your opinion, why was the policy regarding the scholarship jacket changed? Explain.
8. Theme Connection What was Grandpa's decision concerning the jacket? What does Grandpa mean when he says, "If you pay for it, Marta, it's not a scholarship jacket, is it?"

EVALUATE AND CONNECT

9. A conclusion based on known information is called an **inference.** What can you infer about the character of the principal in this story? How does his attitude about the jacket change? Explain.
10. Should the jacket be so important to Marta? Why or why not?

LITERARY ELEMENTS

Resolution

In a story, novel, or play, the **resolution** is the part of the plot that presents the final outcome of the story. At that time, the plot's conflicts are resolved and the story ends. For example, in "Amigo Brothers" the resolution occurs once the final bell sounds and the two champions leave the ring, arm in arm.

1. What happens at the resolution of "The Scholarship Jacket"? What problem is solved? How do the main characters feel?
2. Think about one of your favorite stories from this book. What happens at the resolution of the story?

- See **Literary Terms Handbook,** p. R9.

LITERARY ELEMENTS

1. Marta gets the scholarship jacket. The principal stands up to the school board to make sure Marta gets the jacket. All the main characters feel pleased and happy.
2. Answers should describe what happens at the end to solve the problem in the story.

Additional Resources

Literary Elements Transparency 41

Literature and Writing

Writing About Literature

Critical Review A **critical review** of a story evaluates it. Is the story good, bad, or somewhere in between? The review supports its opinions with examples or quotations from the work. Write a critical review of "The Scholarship Jacket," concentrating on its plot, characters, and theme.

Creative Writing

Journal Imagine you are Marta. You have just learned that you will be given the scholarship jacket after all. At this moment, how do you, as Marta, feel? In your journal, describe the events of the last few days and your feelings about those events.

Extending Your Response

Literature Groups

Keeping Promises Discuss what it means to keep a promise. What promise in the story is broken? What message does a student, such as Marta, receive when a promise is broken? Which characters in the story understand what it means to keep a promise? Together, write a statement explaining why it is important to keep a promise. Share your statement with the other literature groups.

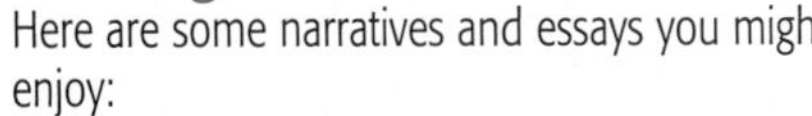

Learning for Life

Graduation Speech As the valedictorian of her graduating class, Marta will probably give a speech at the graduation ceremony. Write a speech for Marta that expresses her feelings about her award and what it represents to her and to her family. Perform your speech before a small group and ask them to comment on its effectiveness.

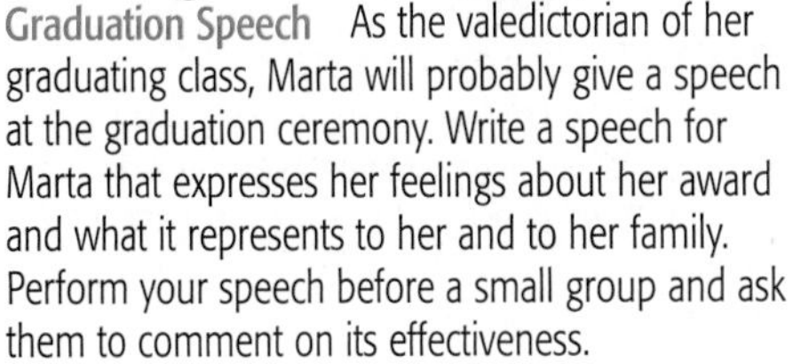

Interdisciplinary Activity

Art Design and create an award for someone special in your life. Choose a person to honor. You might pick a friend, a relative, or a teacher. Make the award out of any available materials. Be sure the award includes a descriptive title, such as Best Listener or Our Family's Finest Pizza Maker.

Reading Further

Here are some narratives and essays you might enjoy:

A Summer Life by Gary Soto

The Anaya Reader by Rudolfo Anaya

Save your work for your portfolio.

Literature and Writing

Writing About Literature

Students' reviews should

- briefly summarize the story
- clearly explain why they would or would not recommend the story to others
- contain examples from the story to support their ideas

Creative Writing

Students' journal entries should

- be written from Marta's point of view
- describe how Marta feels about the events of the last few days
- describe how Marta feels at the moment she learns that she will receive the jacket after all

Extending Your Response

Literature Groups Before students meet as groups, encourage them to answer the listed questions briefly. Then, in groups, have students share their ideas. The groups can then discuss why it is important to keep a promise.

Learning for Life Invite volunteers to present their speeches to the class. Encourage class members to listen attentively.

Interdisciplinary Activity Encourage each student to first make a miniature sketch of the award, so he or she can see what it will look like. Students may want to use a computer graphics program to design the awards.

Skill Minilessons

GRAMMAR AND LANGUAGE
USING ADVERBS AND ADJECTIVES

Students' paragraphs should
- use *good* and *bad* as adjectives
- use *well* and *badly* as adverbs
- use *well* to describe someone's health

READING AND THINKING
QUESTIONING/CLARIFYING

Students' questions should
- investigate confusing parts of the story
- help them clear up the meaning of confusing parts of the story
- help to enhance understanding of the story's characters and events

VOCABULARY
MORE NEGATIVE PREFIXES

1. miscommunicate
2. misquote
3. disillusion
4. unknown
5. misfocus
6. mistrust
7. disqualify
8. unselfish

This lesson complements the one on page 181 on the Latin negative prefixes *in-, im-,ir-,* and *il-*. Ask students to name another prefix that turns a word into its opposite. *(non-)* To further extend, list the following prefixes on the board. Ask students to discuss their meanings and suggest words that include them. (Meanings and word examples are shown.)

de- (away, reversal) *depart, decode*
pre- (before) *preview, preteen*
post- (after) *postpone, postgame*
sub- (under, lower) *subzero, submarine*

Be sure students note that an added prefix does not change the spelling of the base word.

Additional Resources

- ***Grammar and Language Workbook,*** pp. 117–118, 127–128
- ***Grammar and Composition Handbook,*** Lessons 5.1, 6.1, 6.2
- ***Writer's Choice,*** Lessons 12.1, 12.6
- ***Reading Skills Practice Workbook***
- ***Vocabulary Practice,*** p. 27

Skill Minilessons

Reteach • Review

GRAMMAR AND LANGUAGE • USING ADVERBS AND ADJECTIVES

Good and *bad* are adjectives. Use them after linking verbs. *Well* and *badly* are adverbs. Use them to describe action verbs. *Well* may also be used as an adjective when describing someone's health. In this case it will follow a linking verb. Here are some examples.

The Sanchez sisters were **good** dancers. (adjective)
The rainy weather was **bad** for a picnic. (predicate adjective)
Rain **badly** damaged the crops. (adverb)
My grandmother sings **well.** (adverb)
After a long illness, Grandpa is finally **well.** (adjective)

PRACTICE Write a paragraph reviewing one of the stories you have read in this book. In the paragraph, include the words *good, bad, badly,* and *well.* Trade paragraphs with a partner and edit each other's work.

- For more about adverbs and adjectives, see **Language Handbook,** pp. R18 and R27.

READING AND THINKING • QUESTIONING/CLARIFYING

Questioning what you are reading helps you understand more clearly the characters and events in a short story or a novel. As you read, ask yourself questions such as these:
- What's really going on here?
- Why did she or he say that?
- Why is the writer describing this?

PRACTICE Reread "The Scholarship Jacket." Write two or three questions about the story that help clarify what is happening. Trade questions with a partner and answer each other's questions.

- For more about these and other reading strategies, see **Reading Handbook,** p. R87.

VOCABULARY • MORE NEGATIVE PREFIXES

A negative prefix, such as the Latin prefix *dis-* and the Anglo-Saxon prefixes *un-* and *mis-,* can change some words into their antonyms. *Disapproval* is the opposite of *approval. Undo* is the opposite of *do.* To *misbehave* is to behave badly.

Sometimes a base word can take either of two of these prefixes. For example, *mistrust* and *distrust* are both proper forms of words with the base word *trust.* Often, however, only one negative prefix can be used correctly with a particular base word. For example, you can *misbehave,* but you can't *unbehave* or *disbehave.*

PRACTICE Add one of the prefixes *un-, dis-,* or *mis-* to each underlined word to create a word that reflects the meaning of each phrase. Use a dictionary to check whether you have used the correct prefix.

1. to communicate badly
2. to quote wrongly
3. to take away someone's illusion
4. not known
5. to focus badly
6. to not trust someone
7. to make someone not qualify
8. not selfish

ASSESSMENT

- ***Quick Checks,*** p. 41
- ***Selection and Theme Assessment,*** pp. 71–72
- ***Performance Assessment,*** p. 38
- ***Testmaker: ExamView Pro***
- ***Interactive Tutor: Self-Assessment***

MEDIA Connection

WEB SITE

Sites on the World Wide Web can keep you informed about the latest developments in space exploration. Spacecraft images have shown a Venus far different from what early writers of science fiction described.

The Face of Venus

Address: www.hawastsoc.org/solar/eng/homepage.htm

Astronomers refer to Venus as Earth's sister planet. Both are similar in size, mass, density and volume. Both formed about the same time and condensed out of the same nebula. However, during the last few years scientists have found that the kinship ends here. Venus is very different from the Earth. It has no oceans and is surrounded by a heavy atmosphere composed mainly of carbon dioxide with virtually no water vapor. Its clouds are composed of sulfuric acid droplets. At the surface, the atmospheric pressure is 92 times that of Earth at sea level.

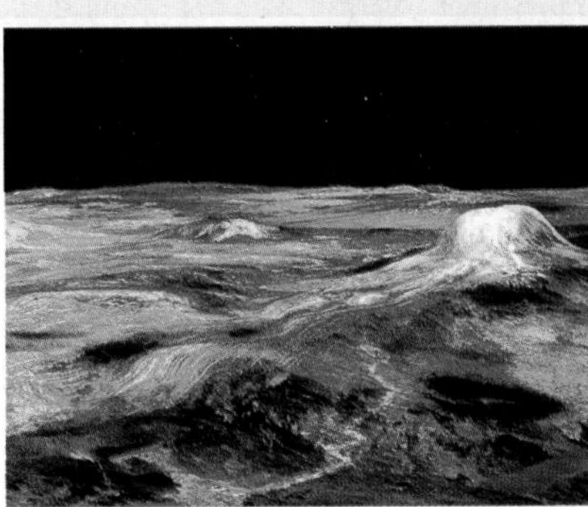

Venus is scorched with a surface temperature of about 482°C (900°F). This high temperature is primarily due to a runaway greenhouse effect caused by the heavy atmosphere of carbon dioxide. Sunlight passes through the atmosphere to heat the surface of the planet. Heat is radiated out, but is trapped by the dense atmosphere and not allowed to escape into space. This makes Venus hotter than Mercury.

A Venusian day is 243 Earth days and is longer than its year of 225 days. Oddly, Venus rotates from east to west. To an observer on Venus, the Sun would rise in the west and set in the east.

Until just recently, Venus's dense cloud cover has prevented scientists from uncovering the geological nature of the surface. Developments in radar telescopes and radar imaging systems orbiting the planet have made it possible to see through the cloud deck to the surface below. As spacecraft began mapping the planet, a new picture of Venus emerged.

Analyzing Media

1. What conditions would make it difficult for us to live on Venus? Do you think it will ever happen? Explain your answer.
2. How does the writing on this Web page differ from other nonfiction writing in this book?

MEDIA Connection

Objective

- To read and understand a Web site

Literature LINK

All Summer in a Day This Web site connects to "All Summer in a Day" (pp. 461–466). Point out to students that the site gives scientific information about the cloud-covered planet. "All Summer in a Day" is a science fiction story about a group of children who live on Venus and spend their lives waiting for the sun.

Analyzing Media

1. Students may cite the heavy sulfuric cloud cover of Venus, extreme heat and lack of water, and the inability to grow food in these conditions. Some students may believe that life on Venus will be possible in the future with advanced technology.
2. The writing is informational text. Its purpose is to convey information—facts about Venus. Ask students where else they might find such writing. Point out that textbooks, manuals, and most newspaper and magazine articles are similar in intent.

Additional Resources

Media Connections, p. 9

*in*TIME **Magazine**

Teaching Support

Reading Minilesson

Activating Prior Knowledge Students can create a time capsule of information about the planets in our solar system today.

Activity Divide the class into nine groups. Have each group choose one planet. List questions such as *What is the weather like on this planet? What is it made of? How many moons does it have? What color is it?* Encourage each group to write everything they can about their planet, including myths, lore, or folk stories, and draw a picture of it. Groups can then share their reports and discuss where to bury them in hopes of having them discovered in 100 years. **L2**

Additional Resources

 ***Reading Skills Practice Workbook***

interNET CONNECTION

Web Site Have students locate other Web sites to research missions sent to Venus. Keywords could be *NASA, space program, Venus missions, Venera,* and *Magellan.*

Before Reading

Objectives

- To read and analyze a science-fiction story
- To identify elements common to science-fiction literature
- To write a paragraph that explains the importance of setting

Skills

Reading/Thinking: Inferring; Drawing Conclusions; Making Critical Judgments; Monitoring Comprehension; Inference from Setting
Writing: Sequel
Vocabulary: Latin Roots: *vit* and *viv*
Grammar/Language: Commas; Avoiding Double Negatives
Collaboration: Literature Groups

Motivating → STUDENTS

Literature Launchers: "All About Ray Bradbury"

Videodisc
Side B, Segment 13

Also available in VHS.

Selection Focus Transparency 42: Share the quote and discuss the questions that follow.

Reading Focus: Have students discuss how the weather can affect one's mood. Ask students how they think people respond to living in very cold and dark climates.

Before You Read

All Summer in a Day

MEET
RAY BRADBURY

Ray Bradbury has been writing since he was a boy. "My parents had given me a toy typewriter for Christmas," Bradbury wrote, "and I stormed it with words. Anytime I liked I could turn a faucet on each finger and let the miracles out, yes, into machines and onto paper where I might freeze and control them forever. I haven't stopped writing since." Besides his novels and short stories, Bradbury has written poetry and plays for stage, screen, and television.

Ray Bradbury was born in Waukegan, Illinois, in 1920. This story was first published in 1954.

READING FOCUS

Imagine living where it rains continuously and the sun shines only once every seven years.

Think/Pair/Share
Take a moment to jot down how life would be different. How would nonstop rain make you feel? Share your thoughts and feelings with a partner.

Setting a Purpose
Read the story to discover one version of life on another planet.

BUILDING BACKGROUND

The Time and Place The story takes place at a school on the planet Venus, sometime in the future.

Did You Know? Some science-fiction writers try to be as scientifically correct as they can. Ray Bradbury is not one of those writers. Character, style, and theme are far more important to him than scientific accuracy. Today, we know much more about Venus than anyone knew when Bradbury wrote this story. Still, the story remains fascinating in spite of its outdated science.

VOCABULARY PREVIEW

frail (frāl) *adj.* lacking in strength; weak; p. 463
vital (vīt′ əl) *adj.* of primary importance; essential; p. 464
consequence (kon′ sə kwens′) *n.* importance; significance; p. 464
apparatus (ap′ ə rat′ əs) *n.* something created or invented for a particular purpose; p. 465
tumultuously (too mul′ cho͞o əs lē) *adv.* in a wildly excited, confused, or disturbed way; p. 465
resilient (ri zil′ yənt) *adj.* capable of springing back into shape or position after being bent, stretched, or compressed; p. 465

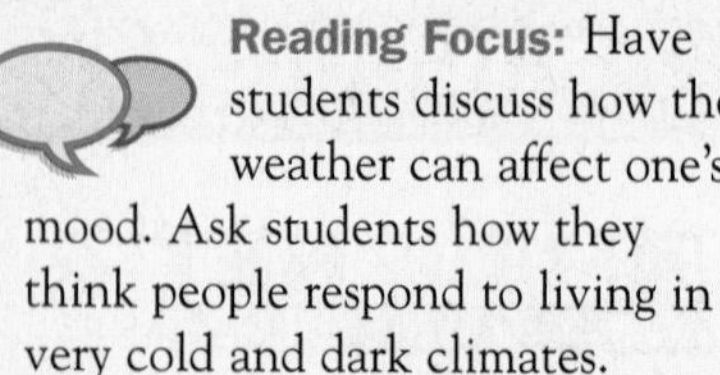

RESOURCE MANAGER

Teaching Tools and Resources
- Theme Five Planning Guide
- Literature Groups Sourcebook

Essential Lesson Support
Lesson-Specific Instruction
- Selection Focus Transparency 42
- Literary Elements Transparency 42
- Active Reading Guide,* p. 42
- Selection Vocabulary Practice, p. 28
- TIME *inTIME* magazine, pp. 24–25

Assessment
- Selection Quick Checks,* p. 42
- Sel. and Theme Assmt., pp. 73–74
- Testmaker: ExamView Pro
- Performance Assessment, p. 39

Systematic Language Instruction
- Gr. and Comp. Hbk., L. 9.3
- Vocabulary Power, Lesson 22
- Spelling Power, Lesson 19

English Language Learners
- ELL Sourcebook, p. 67
- Spanish Summaries, p. 42
- Spanish Translations, pp. 119–122
- Audio Library*
- English, Yes!

Spec. Needs/Strat. Interven.
- Interactive Rdg. Sbk., pp. T159–T162
- Interactive Rdg. Wkbk., pp. 78–79
- Audio Library*

* Also available in Spanish

All Summer in a Day

Ray Bradbury

"READY?"

"Ready."

"Now?"

"Soon."

"Do the scientists really know? Will it happen today, will it?"

"Look, look; see for yourself!"

The children pressed to each other like so many roses, so many weeds, intermixed, peering out for a look at the hidden sun.

It rained.

It had been raining for seven years; thousand upon thousands of days compounded and filled from one end to the other with rain, with the drum and gush of water, with the sweet crystal fall of showers and the concussion[1] of storms so heavy they were tidal waves come over the islands. A thousand forests had been crushed under the rain and grown up a thousand times to be crushed again. And this was the way life was forever on the planet Venus, and this was the schoolroom of the children of the rocket men and women who had come to a raining world to set up civilization and live out their lives.

1. Here, *concussion* refers to a violent shaking or pounding.

Reading the Selection

SUMMARY

Margot goes to school underground on the planet Venus, where outside, lightning flashes, the wind howls, and the rain pours all the time. Once every seven years, the sun briefly shines. Margot alone among her peers has seen the sun, for she arrived from Earth five years earlier. Margot longs for the sun, but her peers do not understand, and this makes Margot an outcast. The day the sun comes out, Margot's classmates lock her in a closet.

Spanish Summaries, p. 42

A Active Reading Strategies

PREDICT Ask students what the title "All Summer in a Day" might mean. Read the first nine lines and ask them if they can predict what the conflict in the story may be. Suggest that students revisit their predictions as they read to verify or revise them.

VOCABULARY If you haven't previewed the selection vocabulary with students, stop and remind them to use context clues to unlock the meanings of new vocabulary words.

Additional Resources

Active Reading Guide, p. 42

Audio Library

Spanish Audio Library

Teaching Support

CONNECTING TO OTHER SELECTIONS

The chart at the right shows three ways to connect "All Summer in a Day" to other selections in this book.

For specific teaching strategies, see the ***Theme Five Planning Guide.***

Connection		Title
Life Skills: Assimilating	→	from *Barrio Boy,* p. 67
Thematic: The Different	→	"Antaeus," p. 347
Literary: Science Fiction	→	"Key Item," p. 675

B Critical Thinking

INFERRING Ask students why they think Margot stands apart from the group. The following model illustrates the thinking process involved in inferring.

Model: Margot must not feel connected to the group since she is the only one who remembers the warmth of the sun on Earth. She must feel like a stranger.

C Literary Elements

FIGURES OF SPEECH: *Simile* Remind students that a simile uses *like* or *as* to compare seemingly unlike things. What similes are used here to describe the sun? *(It is like a blushing in the face and a lemon.)*

D Literary Elements

SCIENCE FICTION: *Mood* Ask students what they feel when reading Margot's poem and the description of her "quiet voice." *(Students might say that they feel her sadness and her longing for the sun.)*

E Active Reading Strategies

QUESTION Invite students to explain why William is critical of Margot. *(William doesn't understand Margot. He doesn't seem to like her because she keeps to herself.)*

"It's stopping, it's stopping!"

"Yes, yes!"

B Margot stood apart from them, from these children who could never remember a time when there wasn't rain and rain and rain. They were all nine years old, and if there had been a day, seven years ago, when the sun came out for an hour and showed its face to the stunned world, they could not recall. Sometimes, at night, she heard them stir, in remembrance, and she knew they were dreaming and remembering gold or a yellow crayon or a coin large enough to buy the world with. C She knew they thought they remembered a warmness, like a blushing in the face, in the body, in the arms and legs and trembling hands. But then they always awoke to the tatting drum, the endless shaking down of clear bead necklaces upon the roof, the walk, the gardens, the forests, and their dreams were gone.

All day yesterday they had read in class about the sun. About how like a lemon it was, and how hot. And they had written small stories or essays or poems about it:

D

I think the sun is a flower,
That blooms for just one hour.

That was Margot's poem, read in a quiet voice in the still classroom while the rain was falling outside.

E "Aw, you didn't write that!" protested one of the boys.

"I did," said Margot. "I *did*."

"William!" said the teacher.

But that was yesterday. Now the rain was slackening, and the children were crushed in the great thick windows.

"Where's teacher?"

"She'll be back."

"She'd better hurry, we'll miss it!"

They turned on themselves, like a feverish wheel, all tumbling spokes.

Teaching Support

MEETING INDIVIDUAL NEEDS

ENGLISH LANGUAGE LEARNERS

Sunny Day and Rainy Day Activities This story presents a good opportunity for exploring activities related to the weather.

Activity Have students work in small groups. On one half of a piece of poster board, students can list and draw activities related to sunny weather. On the other half, they can do the same for rainy weather. Encourage volunteers to explain the activities.

Sunny Weather Activities	Rainy Weather Activities
Swim outdoors	Play indoors
Play baseball	Walk in the rain

Additional Resources

English Language Learners Sourcebook, p. 67

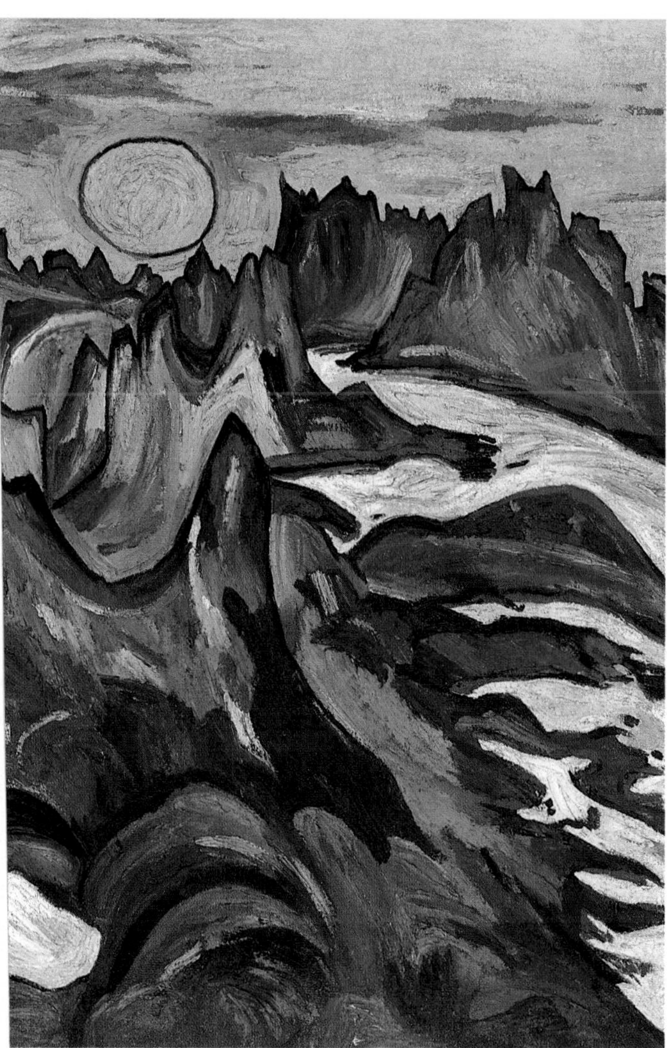

Midnight Sun, Lofoten, 1937 (detail). William H. Johnson. Oil on burlap, 41½ x 59⅛ in. National Museum of American Art, Washington, DC.

Viewing the painting: In what way does this painting reflect the emotions in this story?

Margot stood alone. She was a very frail girl who looked as if she had been lost in the rain for years and the rain had washed out the blue from her eyes and the red from her mouth and the yellow from her hair. She was an old photograph dusted from an album, whitened away, and if she spoke at all her voice would be a ghost. Now she stood, separate, staring at the rain and the loud wet world beyond the huge glass. F

"What're *you* looking at?" said William.

Margot said nothing.

"Speak when you're spoken to." He gave her a shove. But she did not move; rather she let herself be moved only by him and nothing else.

They edged away from her, they would not look at her. She felt them go away. And this was because she would play no games with them in the echoing tunnels of the underground city. If they tagged her and ran, she stood blinking after them and did not follow. When the class sang songs about happiness and life and games her lips barely moved. Only when they sang about the sun and the summer did her lips move as she watched the drenched windows. G H

And then, of course, the biggest crime of all was that she had come here only five

Vocabulary
frail (frāl) *adj.* lacking in strength; weak

Viewing the Painting

Encourage students to locate Norway on a map and to find Lofoten. *(An island group off the northwest coast.)* In the summer, in far northern regions like Lofoten, the sun never drops below the horizon, so it is daylight all night long.

Viewing Response *The painting is appropriate because the sun in Lofoten doesn't set in the summer. This is exactly the opposite of what happens in the story, where the sun rarely shines. Both conditions create an unusual landscape.*

F Literary Elements

CHARACTER Have students describe what Margot looks like and what her appearance says about her. *(Margot looks pale. This is a reflection of how she truly feels about the rain... washed out and lifeless.)*

G Active Reading Strategies

CONNECT Have students explain how they would feel about someone who would not participate in their games or activities. *(Students will probably say that they would avoid that student.)*

H Critical Thinking

INFERRING Have students describe the one thing that seems to make Margot happy. *(The sun or singing about the sun makes Margot happy.)*

Reading Minilesson

Monitoring Comprehension Bradbury uses many sensory images to describe story events. Write the following on the board:

1. They always awoke to the tatting drum, the endless shaking down of clear bead necklaces upon the roof.
2. She would play no games with them in the echoing tunnels of the underground city.

Activity Have students work in small groups to prepare charts that list the images in the sentences and what senses they appeal to. **L2**

Sight	Touch	Hearing
photograph	*bead necklaces*	*tatting drum*

Additional Resources

 ***Reading Skills Practice Workbook***

P Critical Thinking

DRAWING CONCLUSIONS Have students explain why one of the girls wails and begins to cry. *(She feels a raindrop, which means the storms are returning and the sun will be gone. It makes her unhappy.)*

Q Literary Elements

SCIENCE FICTION: *Setting* Invite students to describe elements of this world that indicate it is a science-fiction world. *(The children live in an underground house; the sky is dark as midnight most of the time; and rain falls in avalanches.)*

R Critical Thinking

MAKING CRITICAL JUDGMENTS How do students think the children feel about what they did to Margot? What gestures indicate how the children feel? *(They are ashamed. They now know Margot was right about the sun and feel bad that they made her miss it. They look at their hands and feet; they won't look one another in the eyes; and their faces are solemn.)*

Thematic Focus

At the Crossroads Have students discuss how this story relates to the theme "At the Crossroads." What crossroads have Margot and her classmates reached?

ASSESSMENT

Quick Checks, p. 42

and listened and listened to the silence which suspended them in a blessed sea of no sound and no motion. They looked at everything and savored everything. Then, wildly, like animals escaped from their caves, they ran and ran in shouting circles. They ran for an hour and did not stop running.

And then—

P In the midst of their running one of the girls wailed.

Everyone stopped.

The girl, standing in the open, held out her hand.

"Oh, look, look," she said, trembling.

They came slowly to look at her opened palm.

In the center of it, cupped and huge, was a single raindrop.

She began to cry, looking at it.

They glanced quietly at the sky.

"Oh. Oh."

Q A few cold drops fell on their noses and their cheeks and their mouths. The sun faded behind a stir of mist. A wind blew cool around them. They turned and started to walk back toward the underground house, their hands at their sides, their smiles vanishing away.

A boom of thunder startled them and like leaves before a new hurricane, they tumbled upon each other and ran. Lightning struck ten miles away, five miles away, a mile, a half mile. The sky darkened into midnight in a flash.

They stood in the doorway of the underground for a moment until it was raining hard. Then they closed the door and heard the gigantic sound of the rain falling in tons and avalanches, everywhere and forever.

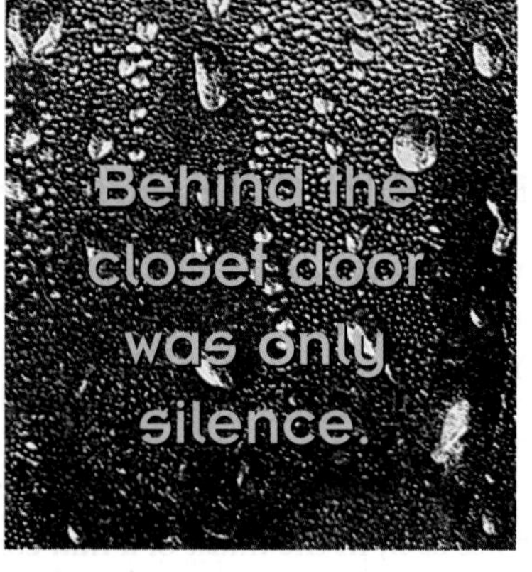
Behind the
closet door
was only
silence.

"Will it be seven more years?"

"Yes. Seven."

Then one of them gave a little cry.

"Margot!"

"What?"

"She's still in the closet where we locked her."

"Margot."

R They stood as if someone had driven them, like so many stakes, into the floor. They looked at each other and then looked away. They glanced out at the world that was raining now and raining and raining steadily. They could not meet each other's glances. Their faces were solemn and pale. They looked at their hands and feet, their faces down.

"Margot."

One of the girls said, "Well . . . ?"

No one moved.

"Go on," whispered the girl.

They walked slowly down the hall in the sound of cold rain. They turned through the doorway to the room in the sound of the storm and thunder, lightning on their faces, blue and terrible. They walked over to the closet door slowly and stood by it.

Behind the closet door was only silence.

They unlocked the door, even more slowly, and let Margot out.

❖

Teaching Support

Grammar and Language Minilesson

Commas to Set Off Interrupters Write the following on the board:

The girl held out her hand.

Invite students to suggest ways one could add the phrase *standing in the open* to this sentence. One solution is to write *The girl, standing in the open, held out her hand.* Since *standing in the open* interrupts the flow of the sentence, it is set off by commas.

Activity Have students work in pairs to find five other examples of interrupters set off by commas on this page. Have students rewrite each of these sentences without the interrupters to prove that the sentences can indeed stand alone without the interrupters. Finally, have students write five sentences of their own that use interrupters set off by commas. **L2**

Additional Resources

- ***Grammar and Language Transparency 40***
- ***Grammar and Language Workbook,*** pp. 255–256
- ***Grammar and Composition Handbook,*** Lesson 13.2
- ***Writer's Choice,*** Lesson 20.2

Responding to Literature

PERSONAL RESPONSE

- If you were Margot, how would you feel about missing the sun? What would you say to those who put you in the closet?
- What should be done to the students who locked Margot in the closet?

Analyzing Literature

RECALL

1. As the story begins, where are the children and what are they doing?
2. Why is the day a special one? How long has it rained?
3. Who is Margot, and why do the other children dislike her?
4. What do the children do when the rain stops? Why doesn't Margot go with them?

Brackets connect questions that are paired to develop higher-level thinking skills.

INTERPRET

5. How do you think the children felt as the special time approached? Support your opinion with details from the story.
6. What effect has the rain had on the planet?
7. Why is Margot different from the other children? Do you think her parents will take her back to Earth? Why or why not?
8. According to the author, when the children are playing outside, they act "like animals escaped from their caves." Why?

EVALUATE AND CONNECT

9. What do you think the title of the story means?
10. Theme Connection Do you know of situations in which children acted as cruelly as Margot's classmates do? How *should* young people behave with someone who is new to their school or neighborhood or who is in some way different from them?

LITERARY ELEMENTS

Science Fiction

Science fiction is a form of literature that explores imaginary worlds of the past, the present, and the future. Science fiction often has characters living in the future or shows people using technology that is not available today. Nevertheless, these characters deal with current issues and problems, such as prejudice, fear, and isolation.

1. What is the current problem faced by the main character in "All Summer in a Day"?
2. Describe a setting for a science-fiction story you might write someday.

- See **Literary Terms Handbook,** p. R9.

Responding to the Selection

PERSONAL RESPONSE

Students should describe their reactions, positive or negative, their feelings about how Margot was treated, and what should be done about it.

Analyzing Literature

1. The children on the planet Venus are crowded at a window waiting for the sun.
2. It has rained for seven years. The day is special because the sun is supposed to appear.
3. Margot is a girl who misses the sun. The other children dislike her because she won't play games with them or participate in any other activities except singing songs about the sun.
4. The children go outside to play in the sun. Margot doesn't go because the children have locked her in a closet.
5. The children are excited, which is demonstrated by the way they crowd at the window waiting for the sun.
6. The rain has crushed thousands of forests. The landscape is gray, black, and white because the clouds block the sun.
7. Margot is different because she is the only child who remembers what the sun is like and she constantly longs for it. Her parents will probably take her back to Earth because she is miserable on Venus.
8. They have escaped from a world of underground tunnels and homes to play outdoors, which is rare. Usually they are cooped up indoors because of the rain.
9. It means that the sun (and summer) only last one day on Venus. It also means that things we associate with the sun—light, warmth, happiness—only last one day there.
10. Answers should include logical reasons to support ideas.

LITERARY ELEMENTS

1. The modern problem is Margot's not being liked by her peers because she is different from them.
2. Answers should describe a world that is different in some ways from our contemporary world.

Additional Resources

Literary Elements Transparency 42

Literature and Writing

Writing About Literature

Students' paragraphs should

- explain how the setting of the story affects characters' actions and story events
- contain examples from the story to support their ideas
- have a clear topic sentence and conclusion

Creative Writing

Students' sequels should

- use "All Summer in a Day" as a model for writing their science-fiction sequels
- describe where Margot is, how she feels, and how others feel about her
- use writing processes, such as prewriting, drafting, revising, editing, and proofreading, to create the stories

Extending Your Response

Literature Groups Before students meet as groups, encourage them to answer each of these questions themselves. Then in groups, have students share their ideas. The groups can then discuss and further explore each question.

Learning for Life Before they start, encourage students to jot down ideas, sketch, doodle, and write snippets of snappy prose that could appear in the brochures.

Art Activity Have students plan the important features they want to include (terrain, roads and paths, buildings, plants and trees, rivers, and so on). Also, have them include a legend and a scale.

Literature and Writing

Writing About Literature

Setting How does the setting of "All Summer in a Day" play an important part in the story? Review your notes from the **Reading Focus** on page 460 and think about the effect such a setting would have on your own actions and moods. Then consider what effect the setting has on the story's events and on the actions of the characters. Write a paragraph explaining why the setting of "All Summer in a Day" is so important to the story.

Creative Writing

A Sequel What will the children say to Margot after they let her out? What will happen to Margot in the days, months, or years ahead? Write a sequel to the story, starting with the unlocking of the door. Set the scene carefully, and use dialogue as well as narrative text. Be sure to describe the characters' facial expressions and gestures to help your readers understand what they are feeling.

Until very recently, this is all people could see of cloud-covered Venus. New radar imaging has allowed us to see through this cloud cover.

Extending Your Response

Literature Groups

A Question of Innocence In small groups, discuss how Bradbury uses vivid details and memorable characterizations to build suspense in this story and to deal with the question of the children's innocence. As readers, when do you know that something will happen to Margot? Are you surprised by the children's cruelty? Why do the children treat Margot as an outsider? What do you think Bradbury is saying about children?

Learning for Life

A Brochure Imagine that you work for a travel agency that plans trips to Venus. Create a brochure describing the trip and what life is like on Venus. Use details from the story as a starting point, but make up any added details you need.

Art Activity

Make a Map Think about the setting of "All Summer in a Day." What do you think the school looks like? As the children look through the classroom window, what do they see? Draw a map of the schoolyard setting of this story. Use the story details and descriptions to help you, but feel free to use your imagination to add new details.

Reading Further

If you would like to read more by Ray Bradbury, try these books:

The Martian Chronicles
Twice Twenty-Two

Save your work for your portfolio.

Skill Minilessons

Reteach · Review

GRAMMAR AND LANGUAGE • AVOIDING DOUBLE NEGATIVES

Negative words express the idea of "no." *Not* is a negative word. *Not* often appears in a shortened form as part of a contraction, such as *isn't* ("is not"). Other words–for example, *never, none, nobody, nowhere,* and *nothing*–may be used to express the negative. Two negatives used together in the same sentence create a **double negative.** Avoid using double negatives in your writing.

Nonstandard: You **shouldn't never** swim alone.

You can correct a sentence with a double negative in two ways:

1. Remove one of the negative words:
   Improved: You shouldn't swim alone.
2. Replace one of the negative words with a positive word:
   Improved: You shouldn't ever swim alone.

PRACTICE Revise the following paragraph by correcting each double negative you find.

The rain didn't never stop. It rained and rained until nobody could not remember the color of the sky. Plants couldn't never grow because they didn't never receive the warmth of the sun. Neither humans nor animals nor plants could never thrive in this rain-swept place.

For more about negative adverbs, see **Language Handbook,** p. R27.

READING AND THINKING • INFERENCE FROM SETTING

You can use what you know about the setting to help you infer other details about life for the characters in this story. For example, since you know from the setting that it rains all the time, you can infer that most aspects of life take place indoors.

PRACTICE Reread "All Summer in a Day" and think about what you can infer about the kinds of activities and games the children in this story enjoy. Write a paragraph explaining your conclusions and how you arrived at them.

For more about making inferences, see **Reading Handbook,** pp. R92–R93.

VOCABULARY • THE LATIN ROOTS *vit* AND *viv*

The root of *vital* is *vit,* which comes from a Latin word meaning "life." People must meet their *vital* needs, such as their needs for air, food, and water. *Vitamins* have that name because they are necessary for life. Over time, *vit* has come to have the somewhat broader meaning of "extremely important; absolutely necessary." Something of *vital* concern should receive immediate attention. The root *viv* is similar to *vit;* it means "live."

PRACTICE Use what you know about the roots *vit* and *viv* to answer each question.

1. Would someone show *vivacity* by leaping, coughing, or stumbling?
2. Does a *vivid* description of something make it seem frightening, boring, or real?
3. If there is a *revival* of an old-fashioned style, does it die out or become popular again?
4. What is the best synonym for *vitality–energy, hunger,* or *luck?*
5. Do people tend to feel *revitalized* after doing hard work, hearing a lullaby, or getting a good night's sleep?

Skill Minilessons

GRAMMAR AND LANGUAGE
AVOIDING DOUBLE NEGATIVES

Sample corrected paragraph:
The rain didn't stop. It rained and rained until nobody could remember the color of the sky. Plants couldn't grow because they didn't receive the warmth of the sun. No humans or animals or plants could thrive in this rain-swept place.

READING AND THINKING
INFERENCE FROM SETTING

Students' paragraphs should
- make logical inferences based on information in the story
- use details from the story to support their inferences
- contain a clear topic sentence and conclusion

VOCABULARY
LATIN ROOTS: *vit* AND *viv*

1. leaping
2. real
3. become popular again
4. energy
5. getting a good night's sleep

Additional Resources

- ***Grammar and Language Workbook,*** pp. 135–136
- ***Grammar and Composition Handbook,*** Lesson 6.5
- ***Writer's Choice,*** Lesson 12.10
- ***Reading Skills Practice Workbook***
- ***Vocabulary Practice,*** p. 28

ASSESSMENT

- ***Quick Checks,*** p. 42
- ***Selection and Theme Assessment,*** pp. 73–74
- ***Performance Assessment,*** p. 39
- ***Testmaker: ExamView Pro***
- ***Interactive Tutor: Self-Assessment***

Reading and Thinking Skills

Objective

- To recognize and use strategies for drawing conclusions

Teaching Strategies

After students read and discuss the passage in their books from "The Scholarship Jacket," ask them to think about Margot, the character who was locked in a closet by her classmates in "All Summer in a Day." The story ends without giving us a chance to hear how Margot felt or what her classmates said to her. Have students suggest a final paragraph to the story based on their own conclusions.

Exercise

1. Clues might include the fact that the boys worked out every chance they got and went running every morning.
2. Students might mention experiences in which a strict regimen, commitment to training, or daily discipline helped them achieve a dream.

Additional Resources

Reading Skills Practice Workbook

Drawing Conclusions

As a skillful reader, you are always **drawing conclusions,** or figuring out much more than an author states directly. To do this, you often must combine clues about characters and events in the text with your own knowledge and experience. For example, read the following passage from "The Scholarship Jacket."

> The next day when the principal called me into his office, I knew what it would be about. He looked uncomfortable and unhappy. I decided I wasn't going to make it any easier for him so I looked him straight in the eye. He looked away and fidgeted with the papers on his desk.

Details in this passage help you draw some conclusions about the feelings of the principal and the narrator. From the description of the principal looking "uncomfortable and unhappy" and fidgeting with his papers, you can draw the conclusion that he is nervous. From the description of the narrator, who "looked him straight in the eye," you can draw the conclusion that she is unwilling to be treated unfairly.

- For more about drawing conclusions, see **Reading Handbook,** p. R93.

EXERCISE

Read the following passage from "Amigo Brothers." Then answer the questions.

> Every chance they had, the boys worked out, sometimes at the Boys Club on 10th Street and Avenue A and sometimes at the pro's gym on 14th Street. Early morning sunrises would find them running along the East River Drive, wrapped in sweat shirts, short towels around their necks, and handkerchiefs Apache style around their foreheads.

1. What clues help you draw conclusions about how seriously the boys take their dreams?
2. How does your own experience, as well as the details in the passage, help you draw that conclusion?

Teaching Support

MEETING INDIVIDUAL NEEDS — SPECIAL NEEDS

Less-Proficient Readers Write the last paragraph on page 465 on the board.

Activity Begin by erasing one or two keywords from each sentence. (You may wish to indicate missing words by drawing dots or dashes where words belong.) Then, ask a volunteer to read a sentence and fill in the missing words orally. Continue the process, with the remaining sentences. Make the complete paragraph reappear by having students write the words back in the blanks and read the sentences aloud. **L1**

Additional Resources

Inclusion Strategies

Before You Read

Primer Lesson and *The Bird Like No Other*

MEET CARL SANDBURG

Carl Sandburg first saw Chicago when he was eighteen. Those images of city life would later appear in his *Chicago Poems*. Most of his poems echo the poet's Midwestern values.

Carl Sandburg was born in 1878 in Galesburg, Illinois. He died in 1967.

MEET DOROTHY WEST

Just nineteen years old when she arrived in New York City, Dorothy West was known as "the Kid" by the other Harlem Renaissance writers. Her writing career has spanned eight decades. Her second novel, *The Wedding*, was published in 1995, when she was eighty-seven years old.

Dorothy West was born in 1907 in Boston, Massachusetts. She died in 1998.

READING FOCUS

Have you ever said something in anger or frustration that you later regretted? What advice might you give to someone who is feeling angry or frustrated?

Journal
Take a moment to write your responses to these questions in your journal.

Setting a Purpose
Read these selections to discover what the writers have to say about the power of words.

BUILDING BACKGROUND

Did You Know? A great surge of artistic activity took place in Harlem during the 1920s. This area in New York City became a magnet, attracting African American writers, artists, actors, musicians, and dancers. This artistic movement became known as the Harlem Renaissance.

VOCABULARY PREVIEW

obligation (ob′ lə gā′ shən) *n.* a sense of duty; a responsibility; p. 474
uncommitted (un′ kə mit′ id) *adj.* not having or showing a particular opinion, view, or course of action; p. 474
woe (wō) *n.* great sadness or suffering; great trouble or misfortune; p. 474
initiative (i nish′ ə tiv) *n.* the action of taking the first step; p. 476
soberly (sō′ bər lē) *adv.* very seriously; p. 476

Before Reading

Objectives

- To read and analyze a poem and a short story
- To identify details that authors use to create memorable portraits
- To write an evaluation

Skills

Reading/Thinking: Inferring; Synthesizing; Sequencing; Drawing Conclusions
Writing: Letter
Vocabulary: Word Mapping; Multiple Suffixes; Analogies
Grammar/Language: Troublesome Words: *Its* and *It's*
Listening/Speaking: Discussion
Collaboration: Literature Groups

Motivating STUDENTS

Selection Focus Transparency 43: Have students read and discuss the quote by Thomas Jefferson.

Reading Focus: As an extension of the Reading Focus, have students write song lyrics about the power of words and the need to use caution when speaking.

RESOURCE MANAGER

Teaching Tools and Resources
- Theme Five Planning Guide
- Literature Groups Sourcebook

Essential Lesson Support

Lesson-Specific Instruction
- Selection Focus Transparency 43
- Literary Elements Transparency 43
- Active Reading Guide,* p. 43
- Selection Vocabulary Practice, p. 29

Assessment
- Selection Quick Checks,* p. 43
- Sel. and Theme Assmt., pp. 75–76
- Testmaker: ExamView Pro
- Performance Assessment, p. 40

Systematic Language Instruction
- Gr. and Comp. Hbk., L. 10.1

English Language Learners
- ELL Sourcebook, p. 68
- Spanish Summaries, p. 43
- Audio Library*
- English, Yes!

Spec. Needs/Strat. Interven.
- Interactive Rdg. Sbk., pp. T163–T165
- Interactive Rdg. Wkbk., p. 80
- Audio Library*

* Also available in Spanish

Reading the Selection

A Active Reading Strategies

PREDICT To predict what the title of the poem might mean, ask students to think of words similar to *primer*. *(Prime and primary are similar, so a primer lesson might be one upon which other lessons are based.)*

B Literary Elements

PERSONIFICATION Have students look at the details in lines 4–6. What traits does Sandburg give to proud words? *(He gives them human traits.)*

C Literary Elements

REPETITION Ask students to discuss why they think Sandburg repeats the first line at the end of the poem. *(This is the central message of the poem—to be careful about what you say because words are very powerful.)*

Vo•cab•u•lar•y Skills

Word Mappings Have students map the word *proud* as it is used in this poem. *(The word map should contain words that show scorn, disdain, and contempt.)*

- ***Active Reading Guide,*** p. 43
- ***Audio Library***
- ***Spanish Audio Library***
- ***Spanish Summaries,*** p. 43

[A] Primer Lesson

Carl Sandburg

Look out how you use proud words.
When you let proud words go, it is
   not easy to call them back.
[B] They wear long boots, hard boots; they
   walk off proud; they can't hear you
   calling—
[C] Look out how you use proud words.

Teaching Support

CONNECTING TO OTHER SELECTIONS
For a teaching strategy that connects "Primer Lesson" to "After Twenty Years," see the *Theme Six Planning Guide.*

ENGLISH LANGUAGE LEARNERS

Forms of Address In "The Bird Like No Other," Aunt Emily is not actually Colby's aunt. Explain to English language learners that the words *aunt* and *uncle* are sometimes used as terms of endearment for close friends of a family.

Activity Invite students to talk about how they address family members and family friends in their own cultures. Encourage them to compare them with those that are common in the United States. You might also point out that different regions and cultural groups in the United States also have different practices.

Additional Resources

- ***English Language Learners Sourcebook,*** p. 68

The Bird Like No Other

Dorothy West

D Colby ran through the woods. He ran hard, as if he were putting his house and family behind him forever.

E The woods were not a dark forest of towering trees. They were just scrub oak and stunted pine with plenty of room for the sun to dapple[1] the road. The road, really a footpath worn by time, was so much a part of Colby's summers that at any point he knew how many trees to count before he reached the one with the hollow that caught the rain and gave the birds a drinking cup.

Haunted House, Aspen, 1996 (detail). Debby West. Acrylic on canvas, 24 x 18 in. Gallery Contemporanea, Jacksonville, FL.

As the clearing came in sight with its cluster of cottages, Colby began to call Aunt Emily, the stridency[2] in his voice commanding her to shut out the sweeter sounds of summer.

F Whatever Aunt Emily was doing, Colby knew, she would stop what she was doing. Wherever she was, she would start for the porch, so that by the time Colby pounded up the stairs, she would be sitting on her old porch glider, waiting for him to fling himself down beside her and cool his hot anger in her calm.

G Aunt Emily was a courtesy aunt, a family friend of many years. When Colby's mother was a little girl, she played with Aunt Emily's little boy when they came on holiday from their separate cities. Then Aunt Emily lost her little boy in a winter accident on an icy street. When vacation time came again, it took all her courage to reopen her cottage. But she knew she must do it this saddest summer of all if she was ever to learn to live in a world that could not bend its tempo to the slow cadence[3] of grief.

1. The sun would *dapple* the road by casting spots of light into the shadows.
2. *Stridency* is a quality of being loud and harsh.
3. *Tempo* means "pace" or "speed," and *cadence* means "rhythm" or "beat."

D Critical Thinking

INFERRING Have students explain what feelings or emotions Colby seems to have in this scene. *(He is upset about something to do with his family.)*

E Literary Elements

DETAILS Have students revisit the details of this scene to describe the atmosphere of the woods. *(It is familiar and reassuring. Details include* not a dark forest, sun to dapple, so much a part of Colby's summers, *and* gave the birds a drinking cup.*)*

F Literary Elements

CHARACTER Ask students what they learn about Aunt Emily through these details. *(Aunt Emily is in tune with Colby's moods and feelings. He can depend on her ability to calm him down.)*

G Critical Thinking

SYNTHESIZING Have students think about the information West provides in this last paragraph. Ask them to synthesize the details. *(Aunt Emily is an old and trusted family friend whose young son died in an accident. She knows that life goes on despite grief, and she forces herself to open up her summer cottage.)*

Reading Minilesson

Sequencing Explain to students that an author often begins a story with action taking place in the present, then interrupts the story to give readers important background information.

Activity Suggest that groups each complete a chart to help distinguish background information from present action. **L2**

Present Action	Background
Colby runs through the woods and calls for Aunt Emily as he approaches.	*Aunt Emily's son and Colby's mother played together as children.*

Additional Resources

 ***Reading Skills Practice Workbook***

CONNECTING TO OTHER SELECTIONS
For a teaching strategy that connects "A Bird Like No Other" to "Strawberries," see the ***Theme Seven Planning Guide.***

H Active Reading Strategies

QUESTION Ask students why they think Aunt Emily feels that a little girl is no substitute for a little boy. *(She misses her son deeply; girls play differently.)*

I Literary Elements

LITERARY LANGUAGE Ask students to picture being "at the bottom of a heap of scrapping sisters." Ask students to describe Colby's feelings in more matter-of-fact terms. *(Look for descriptions to convey a sense of being ignored or trapped.)*

J Active Reading Strategies

VISUALIZE Ask students to picture this scene. Ask them to describe it in their own words or sketch it.

Vo•cab•u•lar•y Skills

Multiple Suffixes Review the concept that the suffix *-less* added to a noun signals "without." So *sound* + *less* means "without sound." Have students supply other examples of nouns that take *-less* *(care, window, noise, effort)*. Remind students that the suffix *-ly* forms a word that answers the question *How? Soundlessly* means "silently, without a sound."

Colby's sister made frequent visits with her dolls. She brought the dolls that didn't cry or didn't wet because they were always rewarded with a tea party for their good behavior. She eased the summer's sorrow for Aunt Emily, who felt an obligation to show this trusting child a cheerful face and to take an interest in her eager talk.

All the same, though Aunt Emily felt a bit ungrateful thinking it, a little girl dressing her dolls for a tea party is no substitute for a little boy playing cowboys and Indians at the top of his lungs.

Colby's family would have agreed with her. His mother adored him because he was her long-awaited son, five years younger than the youngest of his three sisters. His father was pleased and proud to have another male aboard.

But Colby couldn't see where he came first with anybody. As far as he was concerned he was always at the bottom of a heap of scrapping sisters. No matter how good he tried to be, his day most generally depended on how good his sisters decided to be. His rights were never mightier than their wrongs.

Aunt Emily had been Colby's sounding board[4] ever since the summer he was four. One day that summer, his mother postponed a promised boat ride because his sisters had fought with each other all morning over whose turn it was to use the paint box that somebody had given them together. When they began to make each other cry, they were sent upstairs as punishment, and the outing was postponed.

Colby felt he was being punished for blows he hadn't struck and tears he hadn't caused. He had to tell somebody before he burst. Since he knew the way to Aunt Emily's, he went to tell her.

She took a look at his clouded-over face, plumped him down on her old porch glider, then went inside to telephone his mother that Colby wasn't lost, just decamped. His mother told her what had happened, and Aunt Emily listened with uncommitted little clucks. She wasn't any Solomon[5] to decide if it was more important to punish the bad than to keep a promise to the good.

She could hear him banging back and forth on the glider, waiting in hot impatience to tell his tale of woe. The old glider screeched and groaned at his assault on its unoiled joints.

Standing inside her screen door, wincing in sympathy, Aunt Emily knew that neither she nor any nearby neighbor could take that tortured sound much longer. She tried to think of something to distract Colby's mind until he calmed down. A blue jay flew across her line of vision, a bird familiar to the landscape, but the unexciting sight bloomed into an idea.

Shutting the screen door soundlessly, approaching Colby on whispering feet, she put her finger to her lips and sat down beside him.

4. A *sounding board* can be a person to whom one expresses opinions or ideas as a way of testing, or sounding them out.

5. Here, *decamped* refers to having run away, quickly and secretly. Famous for his great wisdom, *Solomon* was a king of Israel in the tenth century B.C.

Vocabulary

obligation (ob′ lə gā′ shən) *n.* a sense of duty; a responsibility

uncommitted (un′ kə mit′ id) *adj.* not having or showing a particular opinion, view, or course of action

woe (wō) *n.* great sadness or suffering; great trouble or misfortune

Teaching Support

MEETING INDIVIDUAL NEEDS — SPECIAL NEEDS

Less-Proficient Readers Students who are having difficulties reading the selection may benefit from hearing you read passages aloud, then reading them aloud with you.

Activity Ask students to work in pairs to practice reading the first two paragraphs on this page aloud. Encourage them to make their reading sound as natural as possible, using appropriate tone, pronunciation, and pauses. Students can select parts of the story and provide a dramatic reading for the class. **L2**

Additional Resources

Inclusion Strategies

Full Moon Gossip, 1997. Gustavo Novoa. Acrylic on canvas, 36 x 36 in. Wally Findlay Galleries, New York.

Viewing the painting: Which aspects of this painting are realistic? Which are imaginative? Could any of these birds be "the bird like no other"? Explain your answer.

Historical Note

Solomon (973–933 B.C.) was an ancient Hebrew king, famous for his wisdom and his ability to make and maintain peace among his people and with neighboring countries.

VIEWING THE PAINTING

Gustavo Novoa studied art in both France and his native country, Chile. Influenced by impressionism, surrealism, and ecology, Novoa's paintings bring together wild creatures from a variety of habitats, who often appear in unlikely urban settings. Another of his paintings can be seen on page 768.

Viewing Response *Given their vivid colors and unusual shapes, many of these birds could appear to be "the bird like no other" in most areas of the United States.*

On The Lighter Side

Do birds gossip? Some birds have a great capacity for learning language—particularly parrots. Some species of these brightly colored birds can learn to speak many words, including family member's names and names of common household objects.

MEETING INDIVIDUAL NEEDS: MULTIPLE MODES OF EXPRESSION

Spatial Students who have strong visual or spatial abilities may enjoy creating a bird mural. In creating the mural, students will better understand how Colby and Aunt Emily might have imagined "The Bird Like No Other."

Activity Using encyclopedias, Internet sites, or field guides, have students find out how different types of birds look. Ask them to choose one image and sketch it in pencil. Point out that they should not be concerned with depicting the bird with great accuracy. Invite them, rather, to give the impressions of the bird's shape, colors, and movement. Finally, have students color or paint their birds on the mural, creating a fantasy landscape in which a "bird like no other" might appear. **L2**

K Active Reading Strategies

QUESTION Ask students why they think Aunt Emily claims that she has seen this unique bird. You may wish to model the thinking process involved in questioning.

Model: I know Aunt Emily just spoke with Colby's mother, so she knows he is upset. She is trying to think of something to distract Colby's attention until he calms down. I think this is why she tells him to look for the bird like no other.

L Literary Elements

DETAILS Have students identify the details that show that Colby is very upset and angry. *(He flings himself up the stairs and flings himself down on the poor old glider.)*

M Critical Thinking

DRAWING CONCLUSIONS Discuss with students why they think Aunt Emily has finally told Colby the truth about the bird. *(Some students might say that since Colby is eight, Aunt Emily thinks he is old enough to deal effectively with his angry feelings.)*

K As he stared at her round-eyed, his swinging suspended, she said softly, "Colby, before you came the most beautiful bird I ever saw was sitting on my hydrangea bush. He almost took my breath. I never saw a bird of so many colors. When you came running, he flew away. But if we don't talk or make any noise, he may come back."

After a moment of reflection,[6] Colby's curiosity pulled out the plug in his sea of troubles, and he settled back.

That was the way this gentle fiction began. When Aunt Emily decided that the beautiful bird was gone for the day, Colby was wearing an agreeable face of a normal color. Taking the initiative, a shameless triumph over a small boy, Aunt Emily plunged into a story before Colby could get his mouth open to begin his own.

For the rest of that summer, and in the summers that followed, when Colby came glad or when Colby came only a little bit mad, the right to speak first was his automatically. But when Colby came breathing fire, by uncanny coincidence,[7] the bird like no other had just left the yard.

It was soon routine for Colby to seal his lips and settle down to wait.

L Now he was eight, and on this angry morning when he flung himself up Aunt Emily's stairs, and flung himself down beside her on the poor old glider that responded as expected to a sudden shock, it was plainly a morning to search the sky for the bird like no other.

Before Aunt Emily could comb a fresh story out of her memory, Colby got a speech in ahead of her. He said in an excited whisper, "I see it, I see it. I see the bird you said was so beautiful. I guess he's every color in the world."

Jerking upright in stunned surprise, making the glider wearily protest, Aunt Emily asked in a shaken voice, "Where?"

"On that tree over there, see, over there."

By a confluence[8] of golden sunlight and blue sky and green leaves and shimmering summer air, a bird on a swinging bough took on an astonishing beauty.

For a moment Aunt Emily couldn't believe her eyes. But in another moment her eyes stopped playing tricks. And suddenly she wanted to stop playing tricks, too.

"Colby, look again. That's a jay. There never was a bird like the one I told you about. I made him up." 

As if to give credence[9] to her confession, the bird on the bough released itself from its brief enchantment and flew away in the dress of a blue jay.

Colby spoke slowly. "Why did you make up a bird to tell me about?"

Aunt Emily started to answer, but asked instead, "Don't you know why, Colby?"

"I think so," he said soberly.

"Will you tell me?"

6. *Reflection* is serious and careful thinking.

7. An *uncanny coincidence* is a really strange occurrence of two things happening at the same time.

8. A *confluence* is a flowing together, or meeting, of two or more things.

9. Although *credence* (krēd′ əns) usually means "belief," here, the author is using the very old meaning of "believability" or "deserving trust."

Vocabulary

initiative (i nish′ ə tiv) *n.* the action of taking the first step

soberly (sō′ bər lē) *adv.* very seriously

Teaching Support

Grammar and Language Minilesson

Using Troublesome Words: Its and It's Review the concept that one form indicates possession; the other is a shortened form of *it is.* Ask a volunteer to identify the word that is short for *it is.* Have a student explain what a contraction is. *(It is a word made by replacing some letters with an apostrophe to combine two words into one.)* Invite volunteers to indicate which form of the word completes each sentence below.

The dog wagged ____ tail as I approached.

____ time for my favorite show.

Activity Have students write one or two paragraphs about Colby and his Aunt Emily. Students should use at least three examples of *its* and three examples of *it's* in their writing. **L2**

Additional Resources

Grammar and Language Transparency 41

Grammar and Language Workbook, pp. 223–224

Writer's Choice, Lesson 17.2

When I Was a Child, 1996. Dr. Samella Lewis. Oil on canvas, 39¾ x 30 in. Stella Jones Gallery, New Orleans, LA.

Viewing the painting: How is the boy in the painting like or unlike Colby?

"To make me sit still so I wouldn't say bad things about my family when I was mad. But you didn't want to make me sit still like a punishment. So you made me sit still like we were waiting to see something wonderful."

"I see the wonderful thing I've been waiting for. I see a little boy who's learned about family loyalty. It's as beautiful to look at as that bird."

Colby got up. He scuffed his sneakers. "Well, I guess I'll go home now. See you, Aunt Emily."

N He bounded down the stairs and began to run home, running faster and faster. Aunt Emily's eyes filled with sentimental tears. He was trying to catch up with the kind of man he was going to be. He was rushing toward understanding.

VIEWING THE PAINTING

Painter, graphic artist, sculptor, art historian, and educator Samella Lewis was born in New Orleans in 1924. She earned a Ph.D. in fine arts and art history from Ohio State University, and is regarded as the foremost authority on twentieth century African American art and artists.

Viewing Response *The boy in the painting looks solitary and lonely, as if he could use a friend like Aunt Emily.*

N Literary Elements

DETAILS Ask students to discuss the details on this page that describe how Colby has grown emotionally. *(Details include Colby's description of why Aunt Emily made up the bird, Aunt Emily's description of Colby, and the last two sentences of the story.)*

Thematic Focus

At the Crossroads Ask students to discuss times when they have had to go through difficult transitions or changes, or have had to make important decisions in their lives. Encourage them to think of older people who might have helped them during these times.

ASSESSMENT

Quick Checks, p. 43

REAL-WORLD CONNECTION

Extraordinary People Students might enjoy learning about real people who have inspired and affected others.

Activity Invite students to use the Internet or the school library to research a person who has made a strong impression on them, such as a poet, a writer, or a political leader. Some possible examples are Dr. Martin Luther King Jr., Robert Frost, Maya Angelou, Nelson Mandela, and John F. Kennedy. Ask students to describe the character traits they most admire in the person they choose. Suggest they find one inspiring quotation from that person to share with the class. **L2**

Responding to the Selection

PERSONAL RESPONSE

Some students might agree that it is best to avoid saying things in anger or out of pride. Others might suggest practical ways to calm down when angry.

Analyzing Literature

1. The speaker warns the reader of proud words.
2. He comes there to talk to her, often when he is angry or upset.
3. Aunt Emily tells Colby to sit quietly and look for a very beautiful and unusual bird.
4. The speaker might use "proud words" to describe words spoken in anger or arrogance.
5. Once proud words are spoken, they come to life. The person who spoke them no longer has control over them.
6. The central image is one of uncontrolled anger or arrogant words stomping away to do damage.
7. Aunt Emily is a mentor and a kind of substitute mother for Colby when he is feeling upset. She has lost her son, and Colby is searching for an understanding adult.
8. She thinks he is old enough to understand why she told the lie. She also feels that he has learned how to deal with his anger effectively.
9. Most students will agree that once words are spoken, other people remember them. Words are very powerful.
10. Colby learns the value of using positive rather than negative teaching and the importance of family loyalty. This helps him become a thoughtful, understanding, and caring person.

Responding to Literature

PERSONAL RESPONSE

- Think back to the **Reading Focus** on page 471. How does your advice compare or contrast with the advice suggested in "Primer Lesson" or "The Bird Like No Other"? Add your latest thoughts to your journal.

Brackets connect questions that are paired to develop higher-level thinking skills.

Bird in Flight–Bird Series II, 1981. Freshman Brown. Prisma colors on bfk rives. Private collection.

Analyzing Literature

RECALL

1. About what kind of words does the speaker of "Primer Lesson" warn the reader?
2. What usually causes Colby to run to Aunt Emily's cottage?
3. What does Aunt Emily tell Colby whenever he arrives angry?

INTERPRET

4. What does the speaker in "Primer Lesson" mean by "proud words"?
5. According to "Primer Lesson," why is it not easy to call back proud words?
6. What is the central image of "Primer Lesson"? What does this image suggest?
7. How would you describe the relationship between Aunt Emily and Colby? Why do they share this relationship?
8. Why does Aunt Emily admit to Colby that she made up the story about the bird?

EVALUATE AND CONNECT

9. Do you agree that it isn't easy to call back proud words? Why or why not?
10. **Theme Connection** In your opinion, what valuable lessons does Colby learn from Aunt Emily? Explain why those lessons are important.

LITERARY ELEMENTS

Descriptive Details

Writers use **descriptive details** to create memorable portraits of characters, places, objects, and events. Good writers help readers imagine what they describe by choosing details carefully and expressing them in vivid language. Dorothy West, for example, tells us that Colby "pounded up the stairs," and that Aunt Emily waited "for him to fling himself down beside her and cool his hot anger in her calm."

1. Describe two details in "The Bird Like No Other" that create a picture of the road leading to Aunt Emily's cottage.
2. Pick out a detail describing Colby that helps you imagine him more clearly.

● See **Literary Terms Handbook,** p. R3.

LITERARY ELEMENTS

1. The woods were not a dark forest, just scrub oak and stunted pine. Also, the road was just a footpath worn by time.
2. One possible response: "After a moment of reflection, Colby's curiosity pulled out the plug in his sea of troubles, and he settled back."

Additional Resources

Literary Elements Transparency 43

Extending Your Response

Writing About Literature

The Poet's Theme Do you think that Sandburg was effective in getting across his **theme,** or central idea, in "Primer Lesson"? Write a paragraph or two explaining your opinion. Use details from the poem to support your assessment.

Literature Groups

Proud Words Discuss with your group what Sandburg means by "proud words." What kind of person might use proud words? What kind of situation might cause someone to use them? Is the use of proud words ever warranted or justified? Share your group's thoughts with the rest of the class.

Art Activity

The Bird Like No Other How do you see Aunt Emily's fictional bird? Create your own drawing or painting of the bird.

Creative Writing

Letter to Aunt Emily Imagine that you are Colby as a teenager. Write a letter to Aunt Emily from Colby's point of view, describing some of the problems you now face. Express to Aunt Emily what her relationship has come to mean to you over the years and what advice you wish she could offer you now. Then trade letters with a partner. Next, imagine yourself as Aunt Emily, and answer your partner's letter.

Reading Further

Here are some other works by Carl Sandburg and Dorothy West you might enjoy:
The Complete Poems of Carl Sandburg
The Richer, the Poorer by Dorothy West

Save your work for your portfolio.

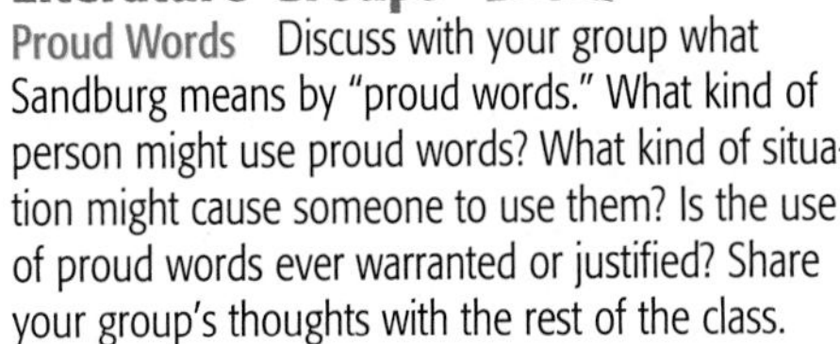

Skill Minilesson

Reteach • Review

VOCABULARY • ANALOGIES: DEFINING CHARACTERISTICS

One kind of **analogy** deals with "defining characteristics," that is, characteristics that are a necessary part of what makes the person or thing what it is.

fur : rabbit :: wool : sheep

Fur is a characteristic of a *rabbit* just as *wool* is a characteristic of a *sheep.* Every analogy contains two pairs of words. Decide what the relationship is between the first pair of words. Then find the word that will complete the second pair and show the same relationship.

PRACTICE Choose the word that best completes each analogy.

1. wings : fly :: feet :
   a. legs b. walk c. person
2. dishonesty : thief :: initiative :
   a. leader b. judge c. coward
3. wall : house :: page :
   a. turn b. book c. read
4. displeasure : fury :: gloominess :
   a. delight b. anger c. woe
5. gift : present :: obligation :
   a. duty b. decision c. fault

Extending Your Response

Writing About Literature

Students' paragraphs should

- explain whether they think Sandburg was effective in communicating his message
- include details from the poem to support their opinions

Creative Writing

Students' reviews should

- describe some of the problems that Colby faces as a teenager
- express to Aunt Emily what her relationship has come to mean and ask her for advice
- respond to Colby's letter from Aunt Emily's point of view

Literature Groups Be sure that students explore the several definitions of the word *proud.* Help them distinguish between the kind of pride that is negative and that which is a positive and essential component of living.

Art Activity Provide students with bright colors for their drawings or paintings of the bird.

Skill Minilesson

VOCABULARY • ANALOGIES

1. b 2. a 3. b 4. c 5. a

Additional Resources

Vocabulary Practice, p. 29

ASSESSMENT

- ***Quick Checks,*** p. 43
- ***Selection and Theme Assessment,*** pp. 75–76
- ***Performance Assessment,*** p. 40
- ***Testmaker: ExamView Pro***
- ***Interactive Tutor: Self-Assessment***

Technology Skills

Objectives

- To use and understand active viewing techniques
- To use the Internet to find screenwriting tips
- To rewrite a scene as a screenplay

Teaching Strategies

Use a video students might enjoy to model active viewing techniques. Help students observe the kinds of things that active viewers notice. For example, "They've just started playing scary music. I think that means something suspenseful is going to happen." Draw students' attention to various aspects of filmmaking:

- camera movements and angles
- how music can affect a viewer's experience
- transitions that move viewers from one setting to another, such as fades, dissolves, or cuts

Adapting to Available Technology

Encourage students to view particular scenes more closely by using features available on VCR and DVD players: freeze frame, advancing in slow motion, and advancing frame by frame. If your school's equipment has none of these features, have students use the rewind function and the counter to view a particular scene over and over again so that they can analyze it.

Teaching Support

Technology Skills

Becoming an Active Viewer

Did you know that directors of movies and television shows use many of the same storytelling elements that writers of novels and short stories do? Movies and television dramas are set in a particular time and place, or **setting.** They generally have a story line, or **plot,** that probably includes a **conflict** that leads to a **climax.** The actors help give the **characters** they play certain traits, which become part of their **characterization.** Camera work and lighting help establish the **mood** of the story, which may also include **suspense.** Even such literary elements as **symbolism, theme,** and **imagery** may be part of a movie or teleplay. (If any of the boldfaced terms above puzzle you, look for them in your **Literary Terms Handbook,** starting on page R1.)

Technology Tip

To discuss film, you need to know some of the vocabulary of filmmaking. A movie is made up of many—probably hundreds of—shots. A **shot** is a single sequence in which the camera films without interruption. The switch from one shot to another is called a **cut.** Cutting is the responsibility of the film editor. A **scene** in a movie is all the consecutive shots in a single setting. Movie cameras can **pan** (swing from one side to another), **zoom** (use a special lens to move toward or away from a subject), or move in a number of other ways, either carried by hand or on various mechanisms. As you learn more about filmmaking, your appreciation of the art will grow.

Practice Active Viewing Strategies

As you begin to recognize the techniques filmmakers use, you will need to practice active viewing strategies. For example, look at this still photo of a shot from the classic film *Citizen Kane.* In this shot, young Charles Foster Kane (the boy) is being introduced to the man who is about to become his guardian. Study the scene to answer the following questions.

Connect

- What emotion is the boy expressing? How can you tell? Have you ever felt this way?

Question

- Why is the guardian positioned between the boy and his father?
- Why do you think the boy is being sent away? What do you see in the scene that might suggest a reason?

Meeting Individual Needs: Multiple Modes of Expression

Musical Students with strong musical abilities may respond to movies more readily through sound than through visuals or words. These students can use active listening techniques to help them understand movie and television dramas.

Activity As students watch a movie, suggest they focus on the background music and sounds as well as on the images and dialogue. Have them create a two-column chart, noting each sound element in the left column and each emotion, mood, or idea created by that element in the right column. After their viewing is over, invite students to discuss how sound effects and music affect the viewing of a film. **L2**

Predict

- How might this scene relate to what will happen later in the movie?

Evaluate

- Why is this scene set outdoors on a cold winter day? Is there some connection between the setting and the action?
- What is your impression of the guardian? What gives you that impression?
- What do you think of the mother? Why?

Respond

- Can you identify with any of these characters? Why or why not?

The Art of Film

When you view a movie or TV drama, you should be aware of the filmmaker's art. Notice how a scene is framed, and how the actors are arranged. Looking at a single picture from a movie can start you thinking, but you need to remember that movies are *motion* pictures. How actors move may tell you something about their character. How they move in relation to one another can reveal relationships.

The camera can also move. It may pan from one character to another or from one place to another. It can follow a character as he or she moves. It can zoom in on something, drawing your attention to it, or zoom out to show you where something is taking place.

Look at camera angles. The camera can make a character seem smaller or weaker by looking down. Looking upward, it can make a person seem stronger or domineering. Tilted at an angle, it gives the viewer a sense of unease.

Watch for how a scene is edited. For example, cutting quickly from shot to shot can create excitement. A long scene with few or no cuts can create a sense of calm.

Listen to the background music. Does it add to or detract from the mood of what you're seeing? How?

All this doesn't mean that you need to strain to find meaning in everything you see. Viewing a situation comedy on TV doesn't require much care. But when you view a serious movie made by a good filmmaker, you'll find it a much richer experience if you view actively.

Technology Tip

When you see a movie on a television screen, you may not be seeing the movie as it was meant it to be seen. Most movies today are made in a wide-screen format. To fit the shape of a TV screen, the sides of the movie are cut off. Sometimes the movie may cut or pan back and forth between two characters who were originally shown on opposite sides of the wide screen. This adds cuts or pans that were not intended by the director, the film editor, or the director of photography. Until wide-screen digital TV becomes widely available, or unless you watch a wide-screen VHS or DVD version, keep in mind that you're not seeing exactly what the filmmakers intended.

ACTIVITIES

1. Practice active viewing strategies when you watch television or a movie. What methods do directors and actors use to get their messages across? Write your conclusions in your journal.
2. Do an Internet search to find tips on screenwriting.
3. Rewrite a scene from one of the stories in this book as a screenplay. Describe how the scene should look, where actors should be, how they will move, and what sound effects or music should accompany the scene.

Activities

You may wish to have the class generate a list on the board that students can copy into their notebooks for easy reference. Suggest that students pause in their viewing every fifteen or twenty minutes to think about the following:

- How does the filmmaker want me to feel?
- What is the camera doing?
- How does the filmmaker feel about the characters on screen right now? How can I tell?
- What kind of sounds and music am I hearing? How is that affecting me?

Students' rewritten scenes should

- describe what the scene looks like, where the actors are, and how they move
- include sound effects or music to enhance the scene
- describe unusual camera angles or camera movements

TechnoTalk

Filmmaking Jargon Like any other profession, filmmaking has its own special vocabulary:

LS (long shot), in which the camera shows the entire setting, or shows the full figure of a person

MS (medium shot), in which one or more people are shown from the waist up

CU (closeup), in which only one person's face is shown, or in which a single body part or object is shown at close range

VO (voice-over), in which the audience hears the narrator but does not see the person speaking.

Interdisciplinary Connection

Art Invite students interested in filmmaking to make a short film or video—a narrative, a music video, or a short documentary.

Activity Help students work in small groups to begin by planning their films. They may want to make a series of sketches (called a *storyboard*) that show what to shoot, where the actors will stand, how the shot will be framed, and how the camera will move. If your filmmakers are planning to use dialogue, they should also prepare a shooting script, which tells what each character says and does. Have students share their creations with the whole class. **L3**

Before Reading

Objectives

- To read and analyze two short stories about facing challenges
- To uncover the implied themes
- To write a paragraph expressing an opinion on descriptive writing

Skills

Reading/Thinking: Drawing Conclusions; Inferring; Logical Reasoning; Synthesizing; Evaluating; Cause and Effect; Summarizing; Identifying Main Idea and Supporting Detail
Writing: Narrating Action
Vocabulary: Etymology; Suffixes; Prefixes: *mal-* and *mis-*
Grammar/Language: Verbs in the Past Tense; Participles and Participial Phrases
Listening/Speaking: Enacting a Dialogue; Oral Storytelling; Debate
Life Skills: Decision Making
Collaboration: Literature Groups

Motivating → STUDENTS

Literature Launchers: "Pearl Buck and Her World"

Videodisc Side B, Segment 15

Also available in VHS.

Selection Focus Transparency 44: Use the quotation to generate a discussion on old age.

Reading Focus: Have pairs of students tell how they would react in the face of danger.

Before You Read

The Old Demon and *The Boy and His Grandfather*

MEET PEARL S. BUCK

Pearl S. Buck was the first American woman to win the Nobel Prize for Literature. Many of her novels, stories, plays, and essays reflect her experience of growing up, living, and working in China for nearly forty years.

Pearl S. Buck was born in 1892 and died in 1973.

MEET RUDOLFO A. ANAYA

One of the founding fathers of modern Hispanic American literature, Rudolfo Anaya (ro͞o dôl′ fō ä nä′ yä) has written fiction, plays, and essays, mostly set in his native New Mexico. Anaya often weaves Hispanic legends and folktales into his work.

Rudolfo A. Anaya was born in 1937.

READING FOCUS

Do you ever wonder how you would react in a time of danger or need? Could you be as courageous as you had to be?

Discuss
With a small group, discuss how you and people you know might respond to the needs of the sick or neglected.

Setting a Purpose
Read these stories to discover how others respond to danger or the needs of others.

BUILDING BACKGROUND

The Time and Place "The Old Demon" takes place in China in the late 1930s, after Japan invaded China.

Did You Know? The Yellow River (Huang Ho in Chinese) got its name from the yellow silt that is carried with the current and gives the river a yellowish color. Once every twenty-five years or so, the river overflows its banks, and a massive flood destroys villages, livestock, and people. For this reason, the Yellow River is often referred to as "China's Sorrow."

VOCABULARY PREVIEW

malicious (mə lish′ əs) *adj.* having or showing a desire to harm another; p. 484
quavering (kwā′ vər ing) *adj.* trembling or shaking; p. 484
somberly (som′ bər lē) *adv.* in a gloomy manner; p. 490
tentatively (ten′ tə tiv lē) *adv.* hesitantly; uncertainly; p. 492
discern (di surn′) *v.* to detect or recognize; p. 492
acutely (ə kūt′ lē) *adv.* sharply and with intensity; p. 493
impetuous (im pech′ o͞o əs) *adj.* marked by force or violent action; p. 494

482 THEME 5

RESOURCE MANAGER

Teaching Tools and Resources
- Theme Five Planning Guide
- Literature Groups Sourcebook

Essential Lesson Support
Lesson-Specific Instruction
- Selection Focus Transparency 44
- Literary Elements Transparency 44
- Active Reading Guide,* p. 44
- Selection Vocabulary Practice, p. 30

Assessment
- Selection Quick Checks,* p. 44
- Sel. and Theme Assmt., pp. 77–78
- Testmaker: ExamView Pro
- Performance Assessment, p. 41

Systematic Language Instruction
- Gr. and Comp. Hbk., L. 10.2
- Vocabulary Power, Lesson 23
- Spelling Power, Lesson 20

English Language Learners
- ELL Sourcebook, p. 69
- Spanish Summaries, p. 44
- Spanish Translations, p. 123
- Theme Five Planning Guide
- Audio Library*
- English, Yes!

Spec. Needs/Strat. Interven.
- Interactive Rdg. Sbk., pp. T165–T168
- Interactive Rdg. Wkbk., pp. 81–84
- Inclusion Strat. Sbk., pp. 21–22
- Audio Library*

* Also available in Spanish

The Old Demon

Pearl S. Buck

A

Old Mrs. Wang knew, of course, that there was a war. Everybody had known for a long time that there was war going on and that Japanese were killing Chinese. But still it was not real and no more than hearsay since none of the Wangs had been killed. The Village of Three Mile Wangs on the flat banks of the Yellow River, which was old Mrs. Wang's clan village, had never seen a Japanese. This was how they came to be talking about Japanese at all.

Emperor Kuang Wu, of the Western Han Dynasty, Fording a River. Ch'iu Ying (active 1510–1551). Hanging scroll, ink and color on silk, height: 67¼ in. National Gallery of Canada, Ottawa.

Reading the Selection

SUMMARY

The Old Demon Mrs. Wang is the elderly leader of her village on the Yellow River during China's war with Japan. When Mrs. Wang sees the Japanese army coming across the plain, she opens the floodgates of the river, engulfing the Japanese army and saving the villagers.

The Boy and His Grandfather An old man is neglected by his son. The old man's grandson, through an act of kindness, reminds his father to treat the old man with care and dignity.

Spanish Summaries, p. 44

A Active Reading Strategies

PREDICT Ask students to predict what "The Old Demon" might be.

VOCABULARY If you haven't previewed the selection vocabulary with students, stop and remind them to use context clues to unlock the meanings of new vocabulary words.

Additional Resources

Active Reading Guide, p. 44
Audio Library
Spanish Audio Library

Teaching Support

MEETING INDIVIDUAL NEEDS — ENGLISH LANGUAGE LEARNERS

Describing a Setting Explain that the setting of a story often helps create an atmosphere or mood.

Activity Have students work in small groups. Ask them to read the first paragraph carefully and write down the details that describe the setting. Then suggest that they rewrite the paragraph in their own words. *(Old Mrs. Wang lives in the village of Three Mile Wangs along the banks of the Yellow River. Even though there is a war going on between China and Japan, the villagers have not yet experienced it.)*

Additional Resources

Literary Elements Transparency 44

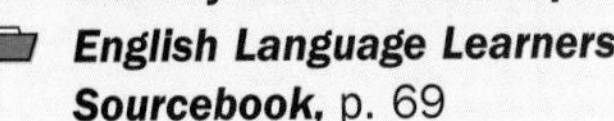

English Language Learners Sourcebook, p. 69

CONNECTING TO OTHER SELECTIONS

For a teaching strategy that connects "The Old Demon" to "Rip Van Winkle," turn to page 49 in the ***Theme Two Planning Guide.***

H Critical Thinking

INFERRING Ask students what is revealed about how the other villagers feel toward Mrs. Wang. *(They seem to have the utmost respect for her.)*

Vo•cab•u•lar•y Skills

Etymology The word *wheedle* means "to persuade by flattery or smooth words; to coax." The word comes from an Old English word meaning "to beg."

I Active Reading Strategies

REVIEW Ask students to put in their own words what Mrs. Wang is thinking. *(At first, she says only coarse people want to fight and assumes the Japanese are not that way. Then she plans to be kind to them, thereby changing their minds about fighting. At the end, however, she is puzzled by their motives.)*

VIEWING THE PAINTING

Viewing Response *The painting shows a group of people who look stressed and exhausted. They appear to have left their homes on short notice because they are carrying very little. Perhaps they have been displaced by disaster, such as a war or a flood like the one in the story.*

"The moon is coming up!" he cried. "That's not good. Airplanes come out on moonlight nights."

"Where do you learn all this about airplanes?" old Mrs. Wang exclaimed. "It is tiresome to me," she said, so severely that no one spoke. In this silence, leaning upon the arm of Little Pig's wife she descended slowly the earthen steps which led down into the village, using her long pipe in the other hand as a walking stick. Behind her the villagers came down, one by one, to bed. No one moved before she did, but none stayed long after her.

And in her own bed at last, behind the blue cotton mosquito curtains which Little Pig's wife fastened securely, she fell peacefully asleep. She had lain awake a little while thinking about the Japanese and wondering why they wanted to fight. Only very coarse persons wanted wars. In her mind she saw large coarse persons. If they came one must wheedle them, she thought, invite them to drink tea, and explain to

Exiles, 1939. Chen Baoyi. Oil. Courtesy Dr. Michael Sullivan, St. Catherine's College, Oxford, England.

Viewing the painting: What story does the painting tell? What connection could you make between the painting and "The Old Demon"?

Teaching Support

Listening and Speaking *Minilesson*

Enacting a Dialogue Remind students that in the culture of the story, elders allowed little dissent. In our culture, while respect for authority is still called for, disagreements are often permitted if they are raised in a respectful manner.

Activity Have students work in pairs to create a dialogue between Mrs. Wang and Little Pig that is set in our culture today. Have Little Pig be more persistent in explaining the airplanes, while showing no disrespect. Have Mrs. Wang be as closed-minded as in the story. Have one student "play" Mrs. Wang and the other, Little Pig; then have them reverse the roles. **L2**

them, reasonably—only why should they come to a peaceful farming village . . . ?

So she was not in the least prepared for Little Pig's wife screaming at her that the Japanese had come. She sat up in bed muttering, "The tea bowls—the tea—"

"Grandmother, there's no time!" Little Pig's wife screamed. "They're here—they're here!"

"Where?" old Mrs. Wang cried, now awake.

"In the sky!" Little Pig's wife wailed.

They had all run out at that, into the clear early dawn, and gazed up. There, like wild geese flying in autumn, were great bird-like shapes.

"But what are they?" old Mrs. Wang cried.

And then, like a silver egg dropping, something drifted straight down and fell at the far end of the village in a field. A fountain of earth flew up, and they all ran to see it. There was a hole thirty feet across, as big as a pond. They were so astonished they could not speak, and then, before anyone could say anything, another and another egg began to fall and everybody was running, running . . .

Everybody, that is, but Mrs. Wang. When Little Pig's wife seized her hand to drag her along, old Mrs. Wang pulled away and sat down against the bank of the dike.

J "I can't run," she remarked. "I haven't run in seventy years, since before my feet were bound.[4] You go on. Where's Little Pig?" She looked around. Little Pig was already gone. "Like his grandfather," she remarked, "always the first to run."

But Little Pig's wife would not leave her, not, that is, until old Mrs. Wang reminded her that it was her duty.

K "If Little Pig is dead," she said, "then it is necessary that his son be born alive." And when the girl still hesitated, she struck at her gently with her pipe. "Go on—go on," she exclaimed.

So unwillingly, because now they could scarcely hear each other speak for the roar of the dipping planes, Little Pig's wife went on with the others.

By now, although only a few minutes had passed, the village was in ruins and the straw roofs and wooden beams were blazing. Everybody was gone. As they passed they had shrieked at old Mrs. Wang to come on, and she had called back pleasantly:

"I'm coming—I'm coming!"

But she did not go. She sat quite alone watching now what was an extraordinary spectacle. For soon other planes came, from where she did not know, but they attacked the first ones. The sun came up over the fields of ripening wheat, and in the clear summery air the planes wheeled and darted and spat at each other. L When this was over, she thought, she would go back into the village and see if anything was left. Here and there a wall stood, supporting a roof. She could not see her own house from here. But she was not unused to war. M Once bandits had looted their village, and houses had been burned then, too. Well, now it had happened again. Burning houses one could see often, but not this darting silvery shining battle in the air. She understood none of it—not what those things were, nor how they

4. *[feet were bound]* The Chinese once believed that tiny feet added to a woman's beauty, so the feet of many Chinese girls were tightly wrapped to limit their growth. This painful process resulted in small but badly deformed feet. The practice was ended in the early 1900s.

J Critical Thinking

DRAWING CONCLUSIONS Ask students why Mrs. Wang says she can't run. *(Her feet were small and deformed as a result of being bound when she was a young girl. Running on them was not possible.)*

K Critical Thinking

EVALUATING Ask students this question: Is Mrs. Wang's sending Little Pig's wife away consistent with what we know of Mrs. Wang? *(Yes. Here Mrs. Wang shows her leadership ability, as she has before. She concerns herself with the safety of others, as she did daily by checking the dikes.)*

L Literary Elements

PERSONIFICATION Point out that the description of the planes spitting on each other is an example of personification: objects (the planes) are given human characteristics.

M Active Reading Strategies

RESPOND Ask students to imagine how Mrs. Wang perceives the burning of the village by bandits and its bombing by Japanese airplanes. *(She can probably understand the bandits better because they come as men, visible. The Japanese are represented by airplanes, which she has never seen before and does not understand.)*

Writing Minilesson

Narrating Action The bombing of the village creates chaos. To convey that chaos, the author crowds many different actions into a short space, as in the paragraph in column 1 beginning, "And then." Note that the sentences contain a number of events described rapidly without much detail.

Activity Write a paragraph narrating an action scene, such as the end-of-the-day dismissal from school, a storm, or a celebration after a championship game. Focus on the action, inserting many different actions in the paragraph to give the sense of uncontrolled activity. **L2**

Additional Resources

Writer's Choice, Lesson 4.3

VIEWING THE PAINTING

Viewing Response *The details in the painting look rather wild and ferocious, but the result of their stormy behavior, the rain, will be beneficial. The river in the story is beneficent when it stays within its banks and evil when it breaks through to cause disastrous floods.*

N Literary Elements

IMPLIED THEME: *Plot* Ask students what they think the complication to the story will be with the crash of a Japanese plane in Mrs. Wang's field. *(It raises the action to a new level and adds to the conflict.)*

Vo•cab•u•lar•y Skills

Suffixes The meaning of the word *doubtless* is "without doubt." Adding the suffix *-less* reverses the meaning of many words: *clueless, fearless.* Sometimes the spelling of the root word changes when the suffix is added: *mercy (merciless).*

O Active Reading Strategies

PREDICT Ask students who they think the pilot of the plane is. *(More than likely it is a Japanese pilot.)*

Beneficent Rain DETAIL #5 and #6. Chang Yu-ts'ai (1295–1316). Handscroll. Ink on silk. 10⅝ x 106¾ in. The Metropolitan Museum of Art, New York.

Viewing the painting: *Beneficent* means "doing or resulting in good." Do you find the details in the painting beneficent? Is the river in the story beneficent? Why or why not?

stayed up in the sky. She simply sat, growing hungry, and watching.

"I'd like to see one close," she said aloud. And at that moment, as though in answer, one of them pointed suddenly downward, and, wheeling and twisting as though it were wounded, it fell head down in a field which Little Pig had ploughed only yesterday for soybeans. And in an instant the sky was empty again, and there was only this wounded thing on the ground and herself.

N She hoisted herself carefully from the earth. At her age she need be afraid of nothing. She could, she decided, go and see what it was. So, leaning on her bamboo pipe, she made her way slowly across the fields. Behind her in the sudden stillness two or three village dogs appeared and followed, creeping close to her in their terror. When they drew near to the fallen plane, they barked furiously. Then she hit them with her pipe.

"Be quiet," she scolded, "there's already been noise enough to split my ears!"

She tapped the airplane.

"Metal," she told the dogs. "Silver, doubtless," she added. Melted up, it would make them all rich.

She walked around it, examining it closely. What made it fly? It seemed dead. Nothing moved or made a sound within it. Then, coming to the side to which it tipped, she saw a young man in it, slumped into a heap in a little seat. The dogs growled, but she struck at them again and they fell back.

"Are you dead?" she inquired politely.

O The young man moved a little at her voice, but did not speak. She drew nearer and peered into the hole in which he sat. His side was bleeding.

"Wounded!" she exclaimed. She took his wrist. It was warm, but inert, and when she let it go, it dropped against the side of the hole. She stared at him. He had black hair and a dark skin like a Chinese and still he did not look like a Chinese.

Teaching Support

Grammar and Language *Minilesson*

Verbs in the Past Tense The past tense of a verb names an action that has already happened. The past tense of most verbs is formed by adding *-ed* to the base form of the verb: *talk, talk-ed.* Irregular verbs, however, do not form their past tenses by adding *-ed.* These verbs change internally: *drink, drank; seek, sought.* A few verbs, such as *cut,* keep the same form for present and past: I *cut* the paper now; I *cut* the paper yesterday.

Activity Have students complete the table below, filling in the present or past tense verbs. **L2**

Present	Past
roar	roared
see	saw
know	knew
fight	fought
wrench	wrenched

Additional Resources

- ***Grammar and Language Transparency 42***
- ***Grammar and Language Workbook,*** pp. 83–86
- ***Grammar and Composition Handbook,*** Lesson 3.5
- ***Writer's Choice,*** Lesson 10.5

"He must be a Southerner," she thought. Well, the chief thing was, he was alive.

"You had better come out," she remarked. "I'll put some herb plaster on your side."

The young man muttered something dully.

"What did you say?" she asked. But he did not say it again.

"I am still quite strong," she decided after a moment. So she reached in and seized him about the waist and pulled him out slowly, panting a good deal. Fortunately he was rather a little fellow and very light. When she had him on the ground, he seemed to find his feet; and he stood shakily and clung to her, and she held him up.

P

"Now if you can walk to my house," she said, "I'll see if it is there."

Then he said something, quite clearly. She listened and could not understand a word of it. She pulled away from him and stared.

"What's that?" she asked.

He pointed at the dogs. They were standing growling, their ruffs up. Then he spoke again, and as he spoke he crumpled to the ground. The dogs fell on him, so that she had to beat them off with her hands.

Q

"Get away!" she shouted. "Who told *you* to kill him?"

And then, when they had slunk back, she heaved him somehow onto her back; and, trembling, half carrying, half pulling him, she dragged him to the ruined village and laid him in the street while she went to find her house, taking the dogs with her.

R

Her house was quite gone. She found the place easily enough. This was where it should be, opposite the water gate into the dike. She had always watched that gate herself. Miraculously it was not injured now, nor was the dike broken. It would be easy enough to rebuild the house. Only, for the present, it was gone.

So she went back to the young man. He was lying as she had left him, propped

P Critical Thinking

SYNTHESIZING Ask students why, based on what they learned of Mrs. Wang earlier, she does not think the pilot is Japanese. *(She had thought earlier of the Japanese as being big and coarse. Apparently this pilot is not. And he looks somewhat Chinese, she says.)*

Q Critical Thinking

DRAWING CONCLUSIONS Ask students why the dogs are so intent on growling at and even attacking the pilot. *(Perhaps they are hostile because he is a stranger; or perhaps the bombing has terrified them.)*

R Literary Elements

IMPLIED THEME Ask students what this description of Mrs. Wang's heaving the pilot "somehow on her back" tells them about her personality. *(The description tells us that Mrs. Wang is a determined, caring, and principled woman.)*

MEETING INDIVIDUAL NEEDS — MULTIPLE MODES OF EXPRESSION

Interpersonal Mrs. Wang and the downed pilot do not speak the same language. Have students work in pairs to try to deal with the problem of communicating without words.

Activity Have one student "play" Mrs. Wang and the other the pilot. Have them try to communicate without words.

For example:

"Are you hurt?"
"My rib seems to be broken."
"I will help you out of the plane."

Students can create other messages that would be conveyed in this situation. Then have different pairs enact their "conversations" before the class with the observers trying to determine what is being "said." **L2**

Active Reading Strategies

CONNECT Ask students what they think the pilot is trying to say to Mrs. Wang. *(He might be trying to explain where he is hurt, thanking her for helping him, or warning her about another attack.)*

Active Reading Strategies

VISUALIZE Ask students to visualize the destroyed bakery. Suggest that they recall some of the details without looking at the text.

Critical Thinking

EVALUATING Ask students to identify an admirable trait of Mrs. Wang's character. You may use the following model to illustrate the thinking process in evaluating character.

Model: Mrs. Wang's village has been bombed, her home destroyed, and her family sent running. For food, she has to fumble through a bombed-out bakery. She has lost just about everything, yet I see her resiliency, her ability to shrug off the devastation and joke about herself, "It's hard to kill an old thing like me." I think this is a strong person.

Teaching Support

against the dike, panting and very pale. He had opened his coat and he had a little bag from which he was taking out strips of cloth and a bottle of something. And again he spoke, and again she understood nothing. Then he made signs and she saw it was water he wanted, so she took up a broken pot from one of many blown about the street, and, going up the dike, she filled it with river water and brought it down again and washed his wound, and she tore off the strips he made from the rolls of bandaging. He knew how to put the cloth over the gaping wound and he made signs to her, and she followed these signs. All the time he was trying to tell her something, but she could understand nothing.

"You must be from the South, sir," she said. It was easy to see that he had education. He looked very clever. "I have heard your language is different from ours." She laughed a little to put him at his ease, but he only stared at her somberly with dull eyes. So she said brightly, "Now if I could find something for us to eat, it would be nice."

He did not answer. Indeed he lay back, panting still more heavily, and stared into space as though she had not spoken.

"You would be better with food," she went on. "And so would I," she added. She was beginning to feel unbearably hungry.

"It's hard to kill an old thing like me," she remarked cheerfully.

It occurred to her that in the baker's shop there might be some bread. Even if it were dusty with fallen mortar, it would still be bread. She would go and see. But before she went she moved the soldier a little so that he lay in the edge of shadow cast by a willow tree that grew in the bank of the dike. Then she went to the baker's shop. The dogs were gone.

The baker's shop was, like everything else, in ruins. No one was there. At first she saw nothing but the mass of crumpled earthen walls. But then she remembered that the oven was just inside the door, and the door frame still stood erect, supporting one end of the roof. She stood in this frame, and, running her hand in underneath the fallen roof inside, she felt the wooden cover of the iron caldron.[5] Under this there might be steamed bread. She worked her arm delicately and carefully in. It took quite a long time, but, even so, clouds of lime and dust almost choked her. Nevertheless she was right. She squeezed her hand under the cover and felt the firm smooth skin of the big steamed bread rolls, and one by one she drew out four.

"It's hard to kill an old thing like me," she remarked cheerfully to no one, and she began to eat one of the rolls as she walked

5. A *caldron* is a large kettle.

Vocabulary

somberly (som′ bər lē) *adv.* in a gloomy manner

MEETING INDIVIDUAL NEEDS — SPECIAL NEEDS

Less-Proficient Readers Suggest that students make use of callouts to help them grasp key ideas in a story or article before they actually read the text.

Activity Using the quote in the callout, have students explain what they expect to happen in the story. Does it foreshadow more difficulties for Mrs. Wang, or does it predict a happy ending? **L1**

Additional Resources

Inclusion Strategies

back. If she had a bit of garlic and a bowl of tea—but one couldn't have everything in these times.

It was at this moment that she heard voices. When she came in sight of the soldier, she saw surrounding him a crowd of other soldiers, who had apparently come from nowhere. They were staring down at the wounded soldier, whose eyes were now closed.

"Where did you get this Japanese, Old Mother?" they shouted at her.

"What Japanese?" she asked, coming to them.

"This one!" they shouted.

"Is he a Japanese?" she cried in the greatest astonishment. "But he looks like us—his eyes are black, his skin—"

"Japanese!" one of them shouted at her.

"Well," she said quietly, "he dropped out of the sky."

"Give me that bread!" another shouted.

"Take it," she said, "all except this one for him."

"A Japanese monkey eat good bread?" the soldier shouted.

"I suppose he is hungry also," old Mrs. Wang replied. She began to dislike these men. But then, she had always disliked soldiers.

"I wish you would go away," she said. "What are you doing here? Our village has always been peaceful."

"It certainly looks very peaceful now," one of the men said, grinning, "as peaceful as a grave. Do you know who did that, Old Mother? The Japanese!"

"I suppose so," she agreed. Then she asked, "Why? That's what I don't understand."

"Why? Because they want our land, that's why!"

"Our land!" she repeated. "Why, they can't have our land!"

"Never!" they shouted.

But all this time while they were talking and chewing the bread they had divided among themselves, they were watching the eastern horizon.

"Why do you keep looking east?" old Mrs. Wang now asked.

"The Japanese are coming from there," the man replied who had taken the bread.

"Are you running away from them?" she asked, surprised.

"There are only a handful of us," he said apologetically. "We were left to guard a village—Pao An, in the county of—"

"I know that village," old Mrs. Wang interrupted. "You needn't tell me. I was a girl there. How is the old Pao who keeps the tea shop in the main street? He's my brother."

"Everybody is dead there," the man replied. "The Japanese have taken it—a great army of men came with their foreign guns and tanks, so what could we do?"

"Of course, only run," she agreed. Nevertheless she felt dazed and sick. So he was dead, that one brother she had left! She was now the last of her father's family.

But the soldiers were straggling away again leaving her alone.

"They'll be coming, those little black dwarfs," they were saying. "We'd best go on."

Nevertheless, one lingered a moment, the one who had taken the bread, to stare down at the young wounded man, who lay with his eyes shut, not having moved at all.

"Is he dead?" he inquired. Then, before Mrs. Wang could answer, he pulled a short knife out of his belt. "Dead or not, I'll give him a punch or two with this—"

V Active Reading Strategies

RESPOND Ask students if they are surprised that Mrs. Wang still wants to feed the pilot even after she finds out he is Japanese. *(Some may be surprised, because she must realize he destroyed her home. Others might think that seeing this wounded Japanese face-to-face, she views him as a human being.)*

W Critical Thinking

LOGICAL REASONING Ask students if knowing that the Japanese want the land will change Mrs. Wang's attitude toward the pilot. *(Some may think it will, while others may see Mrs. Wang as too gentle to inflict harm on this wounded man.)*

X Literary Elements

IMPLIED THEME: *Conflict* Ask students what they think the news of Mrs. Wang's brother being killed will do to her conflicting feelings toward the pilot. *(Mrs. Wang is truly upset by the news but doesn't seem to connect this one human being with the invading Japanese.)*

Interdisciplinary Connection

Social Studies Mention that many conflicts between nations have been caused by the desire for land. People, of course, need land to live on and grow food on, so land is vital to survival.

Activity Have students research conflicts between sets of states, nations or ethnic groups and determine whether land was a major cause of the conflict. If so, have them identify the specific issues involved. Conflicts that students might look into are ones between mainland China and Taiwan or China and Tibet. Have students report on their findings orally or in a written paper. **L2**

VIEWING THE PAINTING

With the founding of the People's Republic of China in 1949, much of the country's art was infused with political content. In recent years, however, Chinese art has been less political.

Viewing Response *Carte blanche means "the freedom to use one's own judgment," and the painting shows freedom in nature.*

FYI

The Noble Eightfold Path is a dominant theme in Buddhism. Following this path consists of: right views, right intentions, right speech, right action, right livelihood, right effort, right-mindedness, and right contemplation.

Y Author's Craft

CHARACTERIZATION Ask students for a word that identifies Mrs. Wang's thoughts on and actions toward this Japanese pilot. *(Motherly, caring, and kind describe Mrs. Wang's actions and her desire to make him better.)*

Carte Blanche, 1990. Bonnie Kwan Huo. Watercolor, 23.5 x 36.5 cm. Private collection.

Viewing the painting: Look up the meaning of this painting's title and discuss whether you think it is appropriate. How does this landscape differ from the one in the story?

But old Mrs. Wang pushed his arm away.

"No, you won't," she said with authority. "If he is dead, then there is no use in sending him into purgatory all in pieces. I am a good Buddhist myself."

The man laughed. "Oh well, he is dead," he answered; and then, seeing his comrades already at a distance, he ran after them.

A Japanese, was he? Old Mrs. Wang, left alone with this inert figure, looked at him tentatively. He was very young, she could see, now that his eyes were closed. His hand, limp in unconsciousness, looked like a boy's hand, unformed and still growing. She felt his wrist but could discern no pulse. She leaned over him and held to his lips the half of her roll which she had not eaten.

"Eat," she said very loudly and distinctly. "Bread!"

Vocabulary

tentatively (ten′ tə tiv lē) *adv.* hesitantly; uncertainly

discern (di surn′) *v.* to detect or recognize

Teaching Support

LITERATURE & HUMANITIES

To help focus students' thinking on the themes and conflicts in this story, have them examine the painting *Both Members of This Club* on page 433 of *American Art History and Culture* and discuss its placement in an illustrated version of this story.

LIFE SKILLS CONNECTION

Decision Making Mrs. Wang is strong and consistent in protecting the young pilot. She never wavers in her decision.

Activity Have students work in groups to discuss how people make decisions when under pressure. Suggest that students consider ideas on the topic that they have heard and read about as well as those from their own experiences. Encourage each group to make a list of character traits that may be helpful in difficult situations and a list of those that may be detrimental in the same situation. Let groups share their examples with the class as a whole. **L2**

But there was no answer. Evidently he was dead. He must have died while she was getting the bread out of the oven.

There was nothing to do then but to finish the bread herself. And when that was done, she wondered if she ought not to follow after Little Pig and his wife and all the villagers. The sun was mounting and it was growing hot. If she were going, she had better go. But first she would climb the dike and see what the direction was. They had gone straight west, and as far as the eye could look westward was a great plain. She might even see a good-sized crowd miles away. Anyway, she could see the next village, and they might all be there.

So she climbed the dike slowly, getting very hot. There was a slight breeze on top of the dike and it felt good. She was shocked to see the river very near the top of the dike. Why, it had risen in the last hour!

Z "You old demon!" she said severely. Let the river god hear it if he liked. He was evil, that he was—to threaten flood when there had been all this other trouble.

She stooped and bathed her cheeks and her wrists. The water was quite cold, as though with fresh rains somewhere. Then she stood up and gazed around her. To the west there was nothing except in the far distance the soldiers still half-running, and beyond them the blur of the next village, which stood on a long rise of ground. She had better set out for that village. Doubtless Little Pig and his wife were there waiting for her.

Just as she was about to climb down and start out, she saw something on the eastern horizon. It was at first only an immense cloud of dust. But, as she stared at it, very quickly it became a lot of black dots and shining spots. Then she saw what it was. It was a lot of men—an army. Instantly she knew what army.

"That's the Japanese," she thought. Yes, above them were the buzzing silver planes. They circled about, seeming to search for someone.

"I don't know who you're looking for," she muttered, "unless it's me and Little Pig and his wife. We're the only ones left. You've already killed my brother Pao."

She had almost forgotten that Pao was dead. Now she remembered it acutely. He had such a nice shop—always clean, and the tea good and the best meat dumplings to be had and the price always the same. Pao was a good man. Besides, what about his wife and his seven children? Doubtless they were all killed, too. Now these Japanese were looking for her. It occurred to her that on the dike she could easily be seen. So she clambered hastily down. AA

It was when she was about halfway down that she thought of the water gate. This old river—it had been a curse to them since time began. Why should it not make up a little now for all the wickedness it had done? It was plotting wickedness again, trying to steal over its banks. Well, why not? She wavered a moment. It was a pity, of course, that the young dead Japanese would be swept into the flood. He was a nice-looking boy, and she had saved him from being stabbed. It was not quite the same as saving his life, of course, but still it was a little the same. If he had been BB

Vocabulary
acutely (ə kūt′ lē) *adv.* sharply and with intensity

Z Active Reading Strategies

REVIEW Have students recall the predictions they made earlier about who or what the "old demon" would be. Now that they know the demon is the river, ask them to predict the role the river will play in the story's climax. *(Some may see that the river will somehow play a role in the conflict between the Japanese and the Chinese.)*

AA Literary Elements

CLIMAX Ask students why this moment is the turning point of the story. *(This is where the resolution of the conflict becomes clear to Mrs. Wang.)*

BB Critical Thinking

DRAWING CONCLUSIONS Ask students what Mrs. Wang has in mind when she thinks this is the river's chance to make up for all its past wickedness. *(She is thinking that the river will have the opportunity to protect her people from the Japanese.)*

A&E HOME VIDEO.® For a graphic look at a flood closer to home, try the following videotape program, available from Glencoe. Be sure to preview the video for appropriateness for your class.

- *Underwater: The Great Flood of '93**

*Also available in the *Glencoe Literature Video Library*.

Real-World Connection

Stereotyping Groups of People To understand Mrs. Wang's kindness toward her enemy, ask students to think about their feelings when they meet people from different backgrounds, countries, and religions. Do they react the same way to all?

Activity Have students discuss in small groups the way a person's attitude toward a group of people affects his or her personal contact with that individual or group. Suggest that students share some of their personal experiences. Ask what lesson such experiences teach about stereotyping entire groups of people. **L2**

CC Literary Elements

RESOLUTION Ask students how they feel about the falling action and what it suggests about the possible outcome of the story. *(Mrs. Wang's bravery and kindness to the very end will probably make them admire her character.)*

DD Active Reading Strategies

RESPOND Ask students how they feel about the story's ending. *(Some may feel sad and disappointed that Mrs. Wang dies. Others may feel she dies a hero's death; because her attitude was good, they do not feel bad.)*

At the MOVIES

The following video will tell students more about the author of this story. Be sure to preview the video for appropriateness for your class.

- ***Pearl Buck: The Woman, the World, and Two Good Earths****

*Also available in the *Glencoe Literature Video Library*.

Teaching Support

Did You Know?
A *sluice* is a gate or valve used to control the flow of water through an artificial channel, which is also called a sluice.

alive, he would have been saved. She went over to him and tugged at him until he lay well under the top of the bank. Then she went down again.

She knew perfectly how to open the water gate. Any child knew how to open the sluice for crops. But she knew also how to swing open the whole gate. The question was, could she open it quickly enough to get out of the way?

"I'm only one old woman," she muttered. She hesitated a second more. Well, it would be a pity not to see what sort of a baby Little Pig's wife would have, but one could not see everything. She had seen a great deal in this life. There was an end to what one could see, anyway.

CC She glanced again to the east. There were the Japanese coming across the plain. They were a long clear line of black, dotted with thousands of glittering points. If she opened this gate, the impetuous water would roar toward them, rushing into the plains, rolling into a wide lake, drowning them, maybe. Certainly they could not keep on marching nearer and nearer to her, and to Little Pig and his wife who were waiting for her. Well, Little Pig and his wife—they would wonder about her—but they would never dream of this. It would make a good story—she would have enjoyed telling it.

She turned resolutely to the gate. Well, some people fought with airplanes and some with guns, but you could fight with a river, too, if it were a wicked one like this one. She wrenched out a huge wooden pin. It was slippery with silvery green moss. The rill[6] of water burst into a strong jet. When she wrenched one more pin, the rest would give way themselves. She began pulling at it, and felt it slip a little from its hole.

"I might be able to get myself out of purgatory with this," she thought, "and maybe they'll let me have that old man of mine, too. What's a hand of his to all this? Then we'll—"

The pin slipped away suddenly, and the gate burst flat against her and knocked her breath away. She had only time to gasp, to the river:

"Come on, you old demon!"

Then she felt it seize her and lift her up to the sky. It was beneath her and around her. It rolled her joyfully hither and thither, and then, holding her close and enfolded, it went rushing against the enemy. DD

6. A *rill* is a small stream.

Vocabulary
impetuous (im pech′ o͞o əs) *adj.* marked by force or violent action

MEETING INDIVIDUAL NEEDS — ADVANCED LEARNERS

Handscroll Painting Students might be interested in learning more about Chinese and Japanese cultures. Have students research handscroll painting in Chinese and Japanese art. Possible sources of information include encyclopedias, art histories, and Internet Web sites.

Activity Have students work in teams or individually, either to prepare a presentation on handscroll art, providing samples of this form, or to create their own handscroll painting or drawing. Students can share their information or artwork with the class. **L2**

The Boy and His Grandfather

Rudolfo A. Anaya

In the old days it was not unusual to find several generations living together in one home. Usually, everyone lived in peace and harmony, but this situation caused problems for one man whose household included, besides his wife and small son, his elderly father.

It so happened that the daughter-in-law took a dislike to the old man. He was always in the way, she said, and she insisted he be removed to a small room apart from the house.

Because the old man was out of sight, he was often neglected. Sometimes he even went hungry. They took poor care of him, and in winter the old man often suffered from the cold. One day the little grandson visited his grandfather.

"My little one," the grandfather said, "go and find a blanket and cover me. It is cold and I am freezing."

The small boy ran to the barn to look for a blanket, and there he found a rug.

"Father, please cut this rug in half," he asked his father.

"Why? What are you going to do with it?"

"I'm going to take it to my grandfather because he is cold."

"Well, take the entire rug," replied his father.

"No," his son answered, "I cannot take it all. I want you to cut it in half so I can save the other half for you when you are as old as my grandfather. Then I will have it for you so you will not be cold."

His son's response was enough to make the man realize how poorly he had treated his own father. The man then brought his father back into his home and ordered that a warm room be prepared. From that time on he took care of his father's needs and visited him frequently every day.

❖

Active Reading Strategies

PREDICT In many stories a young person learns something from an older person. After reading the title, have students predict what this story is about.

FYI

The Aging of America
In 1996, 69 million Americans were under 18 years of age while almost 34 million were 65 or older. Over the next 50 years, those groups will become about equal in number: 95 million will be 18 and under; 96 million will be 65 and over.

Literary Elements

ALLEGORY This story is an allegory, a narrative in which characters and events stand for abstract ideas or forces, so that the literal sense has a parallel symbolic sense. Ask students who the grandfather and the father might represent. *(The grandfather might represent all old people; the father, the next generation.)*

Thematic Focus

At the Crossroads Have students discuss what type of crossroads face Mrs. Wang in "The Old Demon" and the father in "The Boy and His Grandfather"?

ASSESSMENT

Quick Checks, p. 44

Reading Minilesson

Identifying Main Idea and Supporting Details A change of attitude is a significant human accomplishment and a common occurrence in fiction. Suggest that events leading to a major change in a character often point to the main idea.

Activity Have students use the questions below to identify the details that lead to the main idea of the story. **L2**

- Which character changes? *(The boy's father.)*
- In what way does the character change? *(He treats his own father with dignity.)*
- What is the story's main idea? *(Be kind to your elders.)*

Additional Resources

Reading Skills Practice Workbook

CONNECTING TO OTHER SELECTIONS
For a teaching strategy that connects "The Boy and His Grandfather" to "A Crush," see the ***Theme Two Planning Guide.***

Responding to the Selection

PERSONAL RESPONSE

Some students may feel Mrs. Wang should have tried to save herself. Others may feel she was right to make sacrifices to save others.
It would be hard to say the boy did not do the right thing. He was trying to be kind to his grandfather and to prepare to be kind years later to his father.

Analyzing Literature

1. The two forces endangering the village are the river and the Japanese army.
2. All the villagers except Mrs. Wang run.
3. Mrs. Wang's final action is to open the floodgates to keep the Japanese army from catching her family.
4. When the boy says he will keep half the rug for when his father becomes old, the father realizes how unkind he has been to his own father.
5. She fears the river more because she has seen its evil powers. She has never seen the Japanese army do anything.
6. Perhaps, as the leader of the village, she feels the need to patrol the area and see if anyone else remains. Perhaps she just doesn't want to run from her home.
7. She makes the decision because it is the only way she can preserve the next generation.
8. Be kind to old people because some day you will be old and will look for kindness.
9. The title reflects the story in that the demon, which had caused so much havoc for the villagers, now becomes their ally.
10. Remind students that the enemy need not be as threatening as a raging river or a hostile army.

Active Reading and Critical Thinking

Responding to Literature

PERSONAL RESPONSE

- Do you think Mrs. Wang took the correct action at the end of the story? Why or why not?
- Do you think the grandson in "The Boy and His Grandfather" did the right thing? Why or why not?

Analyzing Literature

RECALL

1. What two forces endanger the village in "The Old Demon"?
2. What do all the villagers do when the bombs begin to fall?
3. What is Mrs. Wang's final action?
4. What makes the father in "The Boy and His Grandfather" change his attitude about the grandfather?

Brackets connect questions that are paired to develop higher-level thinking skills.

INTERPRET

5. What does Mrs. Wang fear more—the river or the Japanese? Explain your answer.
6. In your opinion, why does Mrs. Wang choose to stay after the village is bombed?
7. In your opinion, why does Mrs. Wang make the decision she makes at the end of the story?
8. "The Boy and His Grandfather" is a story that teaches a lesson. Write that lesson in one sentence.

EVALUATE AND CONNECT

9. Why is the title "The Old Demon" appropriate for the story?
10. **Theme Connection** Do you think that decisions you have had to make in your life have prepared you to face an enemy with courage, as Mrs. Wang does in "The Old Demon"? Explain.

LITERARY ELEMENTS

Theme

Some stories, poems, or novels have a stated **theme** in which the main idea is expressed as a general statement. More frequently, however, literary works have an **implied theme,** which is revealed through such elements as plot, character, setting, and point of view. In "The Old Demon," the implied theme is revealed through the character of Mrs. Wang.

1. How do Mrs. Wang's actions throughout the story show that she feels it is her duty to protect her family and village?
2. What do you think is the implied theme of "The Old Demon"? What is the implied theme of "The Boy and His Grandfather"?

- See **Literary Terms Handbook,** p. R11.

LITERARY ELEMENTS

1. She looks after the dike and sends Little Pig's wife away to protect her.
2. The theme of "The Old Demon" is that some people live by their principles, regardless of the consequences. The theme of "The Boy and His Grandfather" is that we should care for the elderly because we too will be old some day.

Additional Resources

 ***Literary Elements Transparency 44***

Literature and Writing

Writing About Literature

Analyzing Descriptions Pearl S. Buck knew the force of the Yellow River. She wanted to portray its power in her story. Write a paragraph that expresses your opinion about the effectiveness of her descriptions. Use examples from the story.

Personal Writing

Reflection on Personal Courage Recall the discussion you had in the **Reading Focus** on page 482. Then write a brief essay reflecting upon how you imagine you would respond to a needy person.

Chinese cities as well as the countryside were affected by this flood in the 1930s.

Extending Your Response

Literature Groups

Debating a Plan of Action Did Mrs. Wang make the right decision? Work with your group to decide whether you are for or against her action. Find another group that has chosen the opposite stand and hold a debate.

Interdisciplinary Activity

Social Studies Find out all you can about China's major rivers—their names, locations, tributaries (smaller rivers that flow into them), and how they are used by the Chinese. Use both library resources and the Internet for your research. Then draw a map of the river systems for the class. Include the names of the rivers and any major cities along them.

Listening and Speaking

The Art of Storytelling "The Boy and His Grandfather" is the kind of story that one generation passes on to the next orally. Prepare your own telling of the story. Practice telling it until you no longer need notes. Then invite family, friends, or young children to hear your version.

Reading Further

To read more about China, try these books:

Homesick: My Own Story by Jean Fritz

The Remarkable Journey of Prince Jen by Lloyd Alexander

Save your work for your portfolio.

Literature and Writing

Writing About Literature

Students' paragraphs should

- state their opinions of the effectiveness of the description
- quote passages and tell why each is effective or not

Personal Writing

Students' essays should

- be clear in telling how they would respond
- illustrate with specific situations or circumstances

Extending Your Response

Literature Groups Students might focus on Mrs. Wang's independence in making the decision alone and on her history of caring for others.

Interdisciplinary Activity

Encyclopedias, the Internet, and atlases are some of the sources to which students can go for information. Treatments of China's agriculture and industry should cover the country's use of the rivers.

Listening and Speaking

Suggest that students may modify and modernize the story to suit their own situations.

Skill Minilessons

GRAMMAR AND LANGUAGE
PARTICIPLES AND PARTICIPIAL PHRASES

Some possibilities
p. 484: "The evening was beautiful, the sky so clear and still that the willows overhanging the dike were reflected even in the muddy water." Modifies *willows.*
p. 485: "and she had come, blushing and twisting her hands together, to hide among the women." Modifies *she.*

READING AND THINKING
SUMMARIZING

Key events: daughter-in-law dislikes old man; he is made to live apart from others; old man's request for a blanket; the boy's request of his father; the father's reaction.

Have students read their summaries aloud in small groups. Suggest that they critique one another's summaries in relation to both content and delivery.

VOCABULARY
THE PREFIXES *mal-* and *mis-*

1. b	6. j
2. a	7. i
3. e	8. d
4. g	9. f
5. h	10. f

Additional Resources

- ***Grammar and Language Workbook,*** pp. 167–170
- ***Grammar and Composition Handbook,*** Lesson 9.1
- ***Writer's Choice,*** Lesson 15.1
- ***Reading Skills Practice Workbook***
- ***Vocabulary Practice,*** p. 30

Skill Minilesson

Reteach • Review

GRAMMAR AND LANGUAGE • PARTICIPLES AND PARTICIPIAL PHRASES

A **present participle** is formed by adding *-ing* to a verb. A **past participle** is formed by adding *-ed* to a verb.

A participle often functions as an adjective to modify nouns or pronouns.

the ruined village
burning houses

A **participial phrase** is a group of words that includes a participle and other words that complete its meaning. For example:

So, *leaning on her bamboo pipe,* she made her way slowly across the fields.

The participial phrase *leaning on her bamboo pipe* modifies the pronoun *she.*

PRACTICE Review "The Old Demon" to find two sentences having participial phrases. Copy each sentence, underline the participial phrase, and tell what word or words it modifies.

- For more about participles, see **Language Handbook,** pp. R29–R30.

READING AND THINKING • SUMMARIZING

When you summarize a piece of writing, you state the main ideas of the selection in your own words. You omit unimportant details so that the summary is much briefer than the original piece. For example, in a summary of "The Old Demon," you would be sure to include that the pilot was a wounded Japanese soldier. You would not need to mention that he pointed to the dogs before he fell on the ground.

PRACTICE Write a summary of "The Boy and His Grandfather." Be sure to include all the key events in chronological order. When you edit your writing, check that you have written everything in your own words and that you have deleted any unimportant details.

- For more about summarizing, see **Reading Handbook,** p. R92.

VOCABULARY • THE PREFIXES *mal-* AND *mis-*

Something *malicious* always involves an effort to cause harm. The Latin prefix *mal-,* which means "evil" or "bad," gives this word its meaning. It is similar to the Anglo-Saxon prefix *mis-,* which means "bad" or "wrong."

PRACTICE Use what you know about the prefixes *mal-* and *mis-* and familiar base words to match each word on the left with its meaning.

1. malnutrition	a. dissatisfied
2. malcontent	b. poor nourishment
3. misdeed	c. bad luck
4. malodorous	d. broken; not working
5. misshapen	e. bad act
6. maltreatment	f. say incorrectly
7. misguided	g. bad-smelling
8. malfunctioning	h. badly shaped
9. misfortune	i. led astray
10. mispronounce	j. abuse; injury

ASSESSMENT

- ***Quick Checks,*** p. 44
- ***Selection and Theme Assessment,*** pp. 77–78
- ***Performance Assessment,*** p. 41
- ***Testmaker: ExamView Pro***
- ***Interactive Tutor: Self-Assessment***

Using Pronouns

Every pronoun gets its meaning from a noun, or another pronoun, called its antecedent. It must be clear exactly *which* antecedent a pronoun refers to. In addition, personal pronouns have different forms depending on whether they are used in a sentence as its subject or as the object of a verb or a preposition.

Subjective form:	I	he	she	we	they
Objective form:	me	him	her	us	them

Problem 1 A pronoun that can refer to more than one antecedent

Before Felix's fight with Antonio, he goes to stay with his aunt.

[Who goes to stay with Aunt Lucy? *He* could refer to *Felix* or *Antonio.*]

Solution A Use a noun in place of the pronoun.

Before his fight with Antonio, Felix goes to stay with his aunt.

Solution B Rewrite the sentence so that any pronoun reference is clear.

Felix goes to stay with his aunt before his fight with Antonio.

Problem 2 Confusion between subject pronouns and object pronouns

Him and Antonio know they must forget their friendship during the fight. After the bell, the trainers must pull Antonio and he apart.

Solution In the first sentence, use the subject pronoun *he* in the subject of the sentence. In the second sentence, "Antonio and he" is the object of the verb *pull.* Use the object pronoun *him.*

He and Antonio know they must forget their friendship during the fight. After the bell, the trainers must pull Antonio and him apart.

• For more about pronouns, see **Language Handbook**, p. R17.

EXERCISE

Rewrite each sentence as needed. If a sentence has no pronoun problems, write *C.*

1. The children saw raindrops as they fell from the sky.
2. The teacher assumed that Margot and them had gone outside.
3. As the children lay down on the jungle plants, they sighed and squeaked.
4. "All Summer in a Day" caused a disagreement between my friend Lucy and I.

Objective

- To recognize and use subjective and objective pronouns correctly

Teaching Strategies

After students read the problems and solutions, point out that another way to determine correct pronoun usage is to isolate the pronouns. For example: *She and I both love that song.* *(She loves that song; I love that song.)* They called him and me into the office. *(They called him into the office; They called me into the office.)*

Exercise

1. The children saw raindrops falling from the sky.
2. The teacher assumed that Margot and they had gone outside.
3. The children sighed and squeaked as they lay down on the jungle plants.
4. "All Summer in a Day" caused a disagreement between my friend Lucy and me.

Additional Resources

- ***Grammar and Language Workbook,*** pp. 107–108
- ***Grammar and Composition Handbook,*** Lesson 4.2
- ***Writer's Choice,*** Lesson 11.3

Teaching Support

Writing Minilesson

Plot Treatment Explain to students that a plot treatment is a short summary or outline of the main events in a story, a film, or a play.

Activity Ask students to imagine they are screenwriters and have them write brief plot treatments for the selections they have liked best so far in Theme Five. Have them work in pairs to discuss the plot of the selection they have chosen and to write a summary of its main events in ten complete sentences. To extend the activity, ask the partners to write a brief character description for each character in the story they choose. **L2**

Additional Resources

- ***Writer's Choice,*** Lesson 4.1

Objective

- To understand the elements of drama

Teaching Strategies

Help students make a list of all the places in their communities where drama can be seen. Have them use available resources to create a class guidebook of all the theaters, playhouses, and dramatic arts organizations that operate locally. Suggest they use a spreadsheet or database program to store the information on a computer or local network. Encourage students to take advantage of performances that might be free to the public or to students.

Dialogue Deliver the following line of dialogue: "May the force be with you." (The line is used in almost all of the *Star Wars* movies.) You can substitute other well-known lines from recent popular movies or television shows with which your students are likely to be familiar. Explain that bits of dialogue from plays and films often enter popular culture and become part of the way we speak. Play a game in which one student says a line of dialogue he or she likes and classmates guess which popular film, TV program, or play it comes from.

Teaching Support

DRAMA

If you've ever seen a live **drama,** you know that it can "grab" you. Drama, whether a stage play, a movie, or a TV show, brings literature to life. When you *read* a drama, you need to recognize its special features, and you must use your imagination to make up for the lack of a stage, scenery, and the actions of actors.

FEATURES OF DRAMA

From ancient times through the eighteenth century, most plays were written, partly or wholly, as verse. Most modern plays, including those written for movies or television, are written in prose, the language of ordinary conversation.

On the printed page, drama looks different from other literature. A drama appears as a **script**—a set of words and instructions to be used by actors. Longer scripts are divided into sections called **acts,** and each act may be divided into smaller sections called **scenes.** Each act or scene usually includes the following features:

DIALOGUE–lines spoken by characters. Each line of dialogue is preceded by the name of the character who speaks it. The names are printed in all capital letters, bold type, italic type, or some combination of those features. Each name may be followed by a period, a colon, or no punctuation.

MODEL: "The Monsters Are Due on Maple Street"

STEVE. What do you mean? What are you talking about?

TOMMY. They don't want us to leave. That's why they shut everything off.

ENGLISH LANGUAGE LEARNERS

Understanding Drama The elements and features of drama can be culture-bound and therefore difficult for English language learners to grasp.

Activity You may wish to conduct an International Drama Festival in your class and have students work in groups to report on traditional theater from around the world. Examples might include shadow puppets in Indonesia, Bunraku and Kabuki theater in Japan, Chinese opera, Cambodian ballet, and folkloric dancing in Mexico. Encourage students to create the elements of this theater in a live production of their own.

Additional Resources

English Language Learners Sourcebook

ELEMENTS OF DRAMA

Dramatic Conflicts in *Star Wars*		
Internal		
Luke Skywalker's obligation to stay home and help his uncle	vs.	his need to "try his wings"
Luke's desire to master the Force	vs.	his inexperience and lack of confidence
External		
Rebel Alliance	vs.	the Galactic Empire
Obi Wan Kenobe	vs.	Darth Vader
Han Solo's Millennium Falcon	vs.	the Storm Troopers' tie-fighters

The elements of drama, like the elements of fiction, include character, setting, theme, and plot. (For more about these elements, see **Literary Terms Handbook,** pages R1–R11.) In a dramatic plot, look especially for **conflicts,** or problems that characters must deal with. Some conflicts are **external**—clashes between two characters, or between a character and an outside force. Other conflicts are **internal**—clashes between opposing feelings within a character. The chart shows some external and internal conflicts from a movie that you probably know.

STAGE DIRECTIONS–words–often in italics and enclosed within brackets–describing characters and telling actors how to move or speak; indicating settings, props, sound effects, and lighting; and, for films and teleplays, giving camera directions. Some playwrights give very brief stage directions; others write extremely long ones, specifying, for example, every aspect of a character's appearance, actions, and even his or her thoughts

> STEVE. [*Raising his voice and looking toward porch.*] Guess it was a meteor, honey. Came awful close, didn't it?
>
> MRS. BRAND. Too close for my money! Much too close.
>
> [*The camera pans across the various porches to people who stand there watching and talking in low tones.*]

CAST OF CHARACTERS–a list at the beginning of a play naming, and sometimes giving brief descriptions of, the characters. The cast of characters may also give readers information about how characters are related, for example:

John, Sarah's husband
Timmy, their son

> CHARACTERS
> NARRATOR
> STEVE BRAND
> MRS. BRAND
> DON MARTIN
> TOMMY

Elements of Drama You may wish to prepare English language learners for the table on page 501 of their books by showing all or part of *Star Wars*. Write the names of the main characters on the board and familiarize students with the basic story line before they view the movie.

Stage Directions Enact a short scene and ask students to write what happened, using stage directions like the ones in their books. For example, you could enter the classroom, look at the class, exclaim that you are in the wrong room, and run out. Students might write: Teacher: [looking at the students with a shocked expression] "I'm in the wrong room!"

Cast of Characters Have students draw up a cast of characters for one of the selections they have read in Theme Five. Explain that this would be necessary if they were to rewrite the selection as a play, teleplay, or film script.

Grammar and Language *Minilesson*

Style in Printed Plays Point out to students that typography and punctuation are used to make stage directions and the names of speakers in a printed play easy to identify and distinguish from the dialogue. Stage directions—which indicate characters' actions and movements, the sounds or sights in a scene, and camera movements in a screenplay or teleplay—are usually set in italics and enclosed in brackets. [*Shakes his head.*] Speakers' names are usually set in capital letters and followed by a colon or a period.

Activity Have students look at the stage directions on page 506 of the teleplay to see what other characteristics are true of them. *(They may come between lines of dialogue or within them. They range from a single word to many lines. Even one-word stage directions begin with a capital letter and end with a period.)*

Active Reading Strategies

Objective

- To understand and apply strategies for reading drama

Teach the Strategies

Ask students to list the plays they have seen. Find out if they have ever read a play. Discuss the difference between watching and reading a play.

Predict

Have students watch the first half of a sitcom. Ask them to predict the outcome and write down the clues they used to predict what would happen. Then have them watch the second half of the sitcom. Discuss the accuracy of their predictions.

Visualize

Suggest that students imagine they are camera operators shooting the play. As they read, their imaginations "pan" the scene, action, and characters of the drama.

Question

Have students jot down questions that occur to them as they read.

Respond

Discuss how people respond to what they see, hear, and feel when they are watching a drama. Remind them that reading a drama can evoke the same responses.

Teaching Support

ACTIVE READING MODEL

Active Reading Strategies

Tips for Reading a Drama

When reading a drama, skillful readers use strategies that help them follow the action of the play. These strategies also help readers by prompting them to question and evaluate what they read.

- For more about these and other reading strategies, see **Reading Handbook,** pp. R82–R96.

PREDICT

Combine clues in the play with what you already know to make educated guesses about what will happen next.

Ask Yourself . . .

- What action will this character take?
- What will happen next?

VISUALIZE

Reading the stage directions carefully will help you visualize the action of the play.

Ask Yourself . . .

- How does this scene look?

QUESTION

Keep asking yourself questions to help you clarify what is happening. Ask questions about the motivations of the characters.

Ask Yourself . . .

- What is really happening in this scene?
- What causes that character to act this way?

RESPOND

Don't wait until the play is over to respond to it. Think about what the play means to you while you are still reading it.

Say to Yourself . . .

- If I were this character, I would ___________ .
- I'd like to ask the playwright why ___________ .

Reading Journal

Who Are the Monsters?

Rod Serling's teleplay "The Monsters Are Due on Maple Street" provides readers with a glimpse of a small community unraveled by fears and prejudices. Invite students to discuss whether people should be more frightened by aliens and the world outside our universe or by the human race.

Activity As they read "The Monsters Are Due on Maple Street," invite students to create a chart in their reading journals that lists their predictions. After each prediction, have students jot down how each event actually turned out. After reading, invite students to tell what they think the major characters should have done. L2

REVIEW

Pause every page or two to think about what you have read. Summarize what is happening so you are sure you understand what has happened so far in the drama.

Ask Yourself . . .

- What happened in this scene?
- Do I understand what the playwright has written here?

EVALUATE

To evaluate means to make judgments. You can evaluate what the playwright has done during your reading as well as after you have finished the play.

Ask Yourself . . .

- Are these characters believable?
- Why did the playwright decide to have the plot take this turn?
- Would I enjoy seeing this play?

THE STRATEGIES

Read the following teleplay, "The Monsters Are Due on Maple Street." Use the **Active Reading Model** notes in the margins as you read. Write your responses on a separate piece of paper or use stick-on notes.

Review

One way to help students review the drama "The Monsters Are Due on Maple Street" is to have them identify the scenes within each act. They can use stick-on notes to indicate where a new scene begins. Have them ask themselves the review questions in their books and other questions they come up with at the end of each scene. Encourage students to practice their review skills by reading a scene and summarizing it for a classmate who hasn't read the scene yet.

Evaluate

One way to help students evaluate the drama is to have them think about what they've learned about the characters' personality traits; what the sequence of events was before the plot took a certain turn; and whether the plot had a narrative hook to catch their attention.

MEETING INDIVIDUAL NEEDS — SPECIAL NEEDS

Less-Proficient Readers Less-proficient readers may have trouble with some of the vocabulary in "The Monsters Are Due on Maple Street." To help them, you might want to suggest that students preview the teleplay to identify unfamiliar words. Encourage them to sound out each word using sound-letter cues, and look up its meaning in this textbook's glossary or in a dictionary.

Activity Have student volunteers take roles and read the speeches of specific characters in the teleplay. Allow time beforehand for students to review their parts and familiarize themselves with new vocabulary words. **L2**

AT THE CROSSROADS 503

Before Reading

Objectives

- To read and enjoy a television play
- To identify and understand the elements of a teleplay
- To write about conflict in the play

Skills

Reading/Thinking: Drawing Conclusions; Inferring; Making Critical Judgments; Classifying; Comparing and Contrasting; Visualizing; Evaluating; Judging the Credibility of a Source; Setting a Purpose for Reading; Synthesizing; Generalizing

Writing: Narrating; Different Point of View; Narrative; Analytical Writing

Vocabulary: Root Meanings; Synonyms; Idioms; Base Words

Grammar/Language: Using End Marks; Apostrophes; Complete Sentences

Listening/Speaking: Oral Reading; News Broadcast

Life Skills: Understanding Crowd Behavior

Collaboration: Literature Groups

Motivating STUDENTS

Selection Focus Transparency 45: Have students think about and discuss the concept of "monsters."

Reading Focus: Have students use precise language and sensory imagery to describe the personalities, hobbies, and oddities of people living in their neighborhoods.

ACTIVE READING MODEL

Before You Read

The Monsters Are Due on Maple Street

MEET ROD SERLING

Although Rod Serling became best known as the creator and host of *The Twilight Zone*, a popular fantasy and science-fiction television series, he was first and foremost a writer. Between 1951 and 1955, he wrote more than seventy TV dramas. Three of Serling's six Emmy Awards were for pre-*Twilight Zone* plays. In the five seasons *The Twilight Zone* was on the air from 1959 to 1964, Serling wrote nearly two out of every three of the show's 156 plays. The following selection was one of those plays.

Rod Serling was born in New York in 1924 and died in 1975.

READING FOCUS

Lights flicker on and off. Cars start and stop. Telephones ring and go dead. Imagine these things happening in your town.

Journal

Describe how you think your neighbors would react to a series of strange occurrences on your street.

Setting a Purpose

Read to find out what happens on Maple Street.

BUILDING BACKGROUND

Did You Know? "The Monsters Are Due on Maple Street" is a play written especially for television. The stage notes, written specifically for the television camera, include

- *pan* to turn the camera to follow a moving person or object
- *cut* to switch from one scene to another
- *close-up* to move the camera close to the subject, such as a person's face
- *long shot* to film a subject from a long distance away

VOCABULARY PREVIEW

reflective (ri flek′ tiv) *adj.* showing serious and careful thinking; thoughtful; p. 507

intimidated (in tim′ ə dāt′ əd) *adj.* made timid or fearful; bullied; p. 510

instill (in stil′) *v.* to put in gradually, little by little; p. 510

validity (və lid′ ə tē) *n.* state of being supported by facts; truth; p. 511

defiant (di fī′ ənt) *adj.* showing bold resistance to authority or an opponent; p. 511

antagonism (an tag′ ə niz′ əm) *n.* hostility; p. 511

incriminate (in krim′ ə nāt′) *v.* to show the guilt of; p. 515

legitimate (li jit′ ə mit) *adj.* that which follows the rules; lawful; p. 517

explicit (eks plis′ it) *adj.* clearly expressed; p. 524

prejudice (prej′ ə dis) *n.* an unfavorable opinion or judgment formed unfairly; p. 524

RESOURCE MANAGER

Teaching Tools and Resources
- Theme Five Planning Guide
- Literature Groups Sourcebook

Essential Lesson Support

Lesson-Specific Instruction
- Selection Focus Transparency 45
- Literary Elements Transparency 45
- Active Reading Guide,* p. 45
- Selection Vocabulary Practice, p. 31

Assessment
- Selection Quick Checks,* p. 45
- Sel. and Theme Assmt., pp. 79–80
- Testmaker: ExamView Pro
- Performance Assessment, p. 42

Systematic Language Instruction
- Gr. and Comp. Hbk., L. 10.3
- Vocabulary Power, Unit 5 Review/Test
- Spelling Power, Unit 5 Review/Proofreading

English Language Learners
- ELL Sourcebook, pp. 70–73
- Spanish Summaries, p. 45
- Spanish Translations, pp. 124–138
- Audio Library*
- English, Yes!

Spec. Needs/Strat. Interven.
- Interactive Rdg. Sbk., pp. T169–T171
- Interactive Rdg. Wkbk., pp. 85–88
- Inclusion Strat. Sbk., pp. 75–76
- Audio Library*

* Also available in Spanish

ACTIVE READING MODEL

THE MONSTERS ARE DUE ON MAPLE STREET

Rod Serling

CHARACTERS

NARRATOR	FIGURE ONE	FIGURE TWO
Residents of Maple Street:		
STEVE BRAND	CHARLIE'S WIFE	MRS. GOODMAN
MRS. BRAND	TOMMY	WOMAN
DON MARTIN	SALLY, TOMMY'S MOTHER	MAN ONE
PETE VAN HORN	LES GOODMAN	MAN TWO
CHARLIE		

ACT I

[Fade in on a shot of the night sky. The various nebulae[1] *and planet bodies stand out in sharp, sparkling relief, and the camera begins a slow pan across the Heavens.]*

NARRATOR'S VOICE. There is a fifth dimension beyond that which is known to man. It is a dimension as vast as space, and as timeless as infinity. It is the middle ground between light and shadow—between science and superstition. And it lies between the pit of man's fears and the summit of his knowledge. This is the dimension of imagination. It is an area which we call The Twilight Zone.

QUESTION

Why does the play begin with a shot of the night sky? What do the narrator's words tell you about the play that is about to begin?

1. The word *nebulae* (neb′ yə lē′) refers to bright, cloudlike masses of dust and gases that are visible in the night sky.

Reading the Selection

SUMMARY

One night after a mysterious roar and a flash of light, all the homes on a suburban street lose power. Batteries in cars and radios go dead. People come out to discuss the situation. A boy says that in a similar situation he read about, space monsters were responsible. When one neighbor's car starts, people accuse him of being responsible for the blackout or being in league with those who are. They begin blaming one another, and the accusations lead to violence. Figures observing the scene from far above explain that the best way to destroy a group of people is to plant a seed of dissension among them.

Spanish Summaries, p. 45

A Active Reading Strategies

QUESTION *(The shot of the night sky indicates that the play is about outer space or the unknown. The narrator's words suggest it will be eerie.)*

VOCABULARY Remind students to use context clues to unlock the meanings of new vocabulary words.

Additional Resources

- ***Active Reading Guide,*** p. 45
- ***Audio Library***
- ***Spanish Audio Library***

Teaching Support

CONNECTING TO OTHER SELECTIONS

The chart at the right shows three ways to connect "The Monsters Are Due on Maple Street" to other selections in this book.

For specific teaching strategies, see the ***Theme Five Planning Guide.***

Connection	Title
Life Skills: Problem Solving	"Racing the Great Bear," p. 268
Thematic: A Delicate Balance	"We Are All One," p. 773
Literary: Dialogue	"Oh Broom, Get to Work," p. 383

B Active Reading Strategies

VISUALIZE *(Ask students to visualize the street and then fill in the people: the man polishing his car; the neighbor watching; the Good Humor man.)*

C Literary Elements

MOOD Ask students to describe the mood created by the narrator's exposition of the details in this setting. *(It creates the calm, pleasant mood of a friendly neighborhood in a small town.)*

D Literary Elements

NARRATOR Ask students what they think about the narrator's use of the future tense. *(The narrator, unlike other characters, knows the future.)*

E Literary Elements

TELEPLAY: *Stage Directions* Point out to students the detailed stage directions. Ask students what the purpose of these directions might be. *(These directions indicate how characters move and act, and what sights and sounds are included in the scene.)*

F Active Reading Strategies

PREDICT *(It could have been a meteor, an unidentified object, or a missile.)*

At the MOVIES

"The Monsters Are Due on Maple Street" and another episode written by Rod Serling are available on the following video. Be sure to preview it for appropriateness for your class.

- ***Twilight Zone: Volume 2***

Teaching Support

The Monsters Are Due On Maple Street

ACTIVE READING MODEL

VISUALIZE

B Try to visualize the setting the playwright is describing. Can you see it?

[The camera has begun to pan down until it passes the horizon and is on a sign which reads "Maple Street." Pan down until we are shooting down at an angle toward the street below. It's a tree-lined, quiet residential American street, very typical of the small town. The houses have front porches on which people sit and swing on gliders, conversing across from house to house. STEVE BRAND *polishes his car parked in front of his house. His neighbor,* DON MARTIN, *leans against the fender watching him. A Good Humor man rides a bicycle and is just in the process of stopping to sell some ice cream to a couple of kids. Two women gossip on the front lawn. Another man waters his lawn.]*

C **NARRATOR'S VOICE.** Maple Street, U.S.A., late summer. A tree-lined little world of front porch gliders, hop scotch, the laughter of children, and the bell of an ice cream vendor.

[There is a pause and the camera moves over to a shot of the Good Humor man and two small boys who are standing alongside, just buying ice cream.]

D **NARRATOR'S VOICE.** At the sound of the roar and the flash of light it will be precisely 6:43 P.M. on Maple Street.

E *[At this moment one of the little boys,* TOMMY, *looks up to listen to a sound of a tremendous screeching roar from overhead. A flash of light plays on both their faces and then it moves down the street past lawns and porches and rooftops and then disappears.*

Various people leave their porches and stop what they're doing to stare up at the sky. STEVE BRAND, *the man who's been polishing his car, now stands there transfixed,*[2] *staring upwards. He looks at* DON MARTIN, *his neighbor from across the street.]*

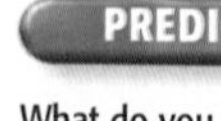

PREDICT

F What do you think that flash of light was?

STEVE. What was that? A meteor?

DON. *[Nods.]* That's what it looked like. I didn't hear any crash though, did you?

STEVE. *[Shakes his head.]* Nope. I didn't hear anything except a roar.

MRS. BRAND. *[From her porch.]* Steve? What was that?

STEVE. *[Raising his voice and looking toward porch.]* Guess it was a meteor, honey. Came awful close, didn't it?

MRS. BRAND. Too close for my money! Much too close.

[The camera pans across the various porches to people who stand there watching and talking in low tones.]

2. To be *transfixed* is to be made motionless, as from wonder or fear.

MEETING INDIVIDUAL NEEDS — ENGLISH LANGUAGE LEARNERS

Idioms Explain to English language learners that idioms are expressions that should not be taken literally. For example "too close for my money" does not actually involve any money. It is an idiom, a way of saying "in my opinion."

Activity As students read the selection, have them look for additional examples of idioms. Other examples in the selection include *run a check on* (p. 512); *for laughs* (p. 516); *set a foot on* and *keep an eye on* (both on p. 517). Have students work in small groups to compare the idioms they found and discuss what they mean.

Additional Resources

English Language Learners Sourcebook, p. 70

Portrait of Orleans, 1950. Edward Hopper. Oil on canvas, 26 x 40 in. Fine Arts Museum of San Francisco.

Viewing the painting: In what ways is this street like the street in the teleplay?

NARRATOR'S VOICE. Maple Street. Six-forty-four P.M. on a late September evening. [*A pause.*] Maple Street in the last calm and reflective moment . . . before the monsters came!

[*The camera slowly pans across the porches again. We see a man screwing a light bulb on a front porch, then getting down off the stool to flick the switch and finding that nothing happens.*

Another man is working on an electric power mower. He plugs in the plug, flicks on the switch of the power mower, off and on, with nothing happening. Through the window of a front porch, we see a woman pushing her finger back and forth on the dial hook. Her voice is indistinct and distant, but intelligible and repetitive.]

WOMAN. Operator, operator, something's wrong on the phone, operator!

[*MRS. BRAND comes out on the porch and calls to STEVE.*]

MRS. BRAND. [*Calling.*] Steve, the power's off. I had the soup on the stove and the stove just stopped working.

WOMAN. Same thing over here. I can't get anybody on the phone either. The phone seems to be dead.

QUESTION

What do these wordless actions suggest to you? What do you think is happening on Maple Street?

Vocabulary

reflective (ri flek′ tiv) *adj.* showing serious and careful thinking; thoughtful

G Critical Thinking

MAKING CRITICAL JUDGMENTS Ask students why they think the author, through the narrator, tells us that the monsters came, eliminating any uncertainty and suspense about their coming. You may wish to share the following model to illustrate the thinking process in making critical judgments.

Model: The author tells us right away that the monsters came. So I have to conclude that the fact that they came was not the most important thing. Who they were, what they did, and why they came may be more important.

H Active Reading Strategies

QUESTION *(It seems that something has gone wrong in the neighborhood. Students may suggest that the monsters are planning to attack the people on Maple Street.)*

Viewing the Painting

Edward Hopper (1882–1967) worked for a time as a commercial illustrator, but he later gained fame as a central figure in the American Scene movement, expressing the emptiness and loneliness of town life.

Viewing Response *Like the street in the teleplay, Hopper's street looks normal and conventional on the surface.*

Reading Minilesson

Classifying Viewers of a teleplay often have to classify events based only on what they see. To help students do this, draw the diagram at the right on the board.

Activity Ask students to identify the actions that take place at each house. Then have them tell what all these happenings have in common. **L2**

Happening at 1st House	Happening at 2nd House	Happening at 3rd House

Additional Resources

Reading Skills Practice Workbook

I Literary Elements

TELEPLAY: *Stage Directions* Call attention to the word *VOICES*. Ask students what this word refers to. *(Various people on the street utter the short statements that follow. Because we do not see the people clearly, no names are associated with any of the utterances.)*

J Active Reading Strategies

PREDICT *(It couldn't be a power failure if the transistor radio is not working. Maybe more strange things will happen.)*

K Literary Elements

CHARACTERIZATION Ask students to give their impressions of the four characters, based on these comments. *(Steve seems inquisitive and thoughtful, trying to analyze the problem. Don seems more apt to come to a quick, simple conclusion. Charlie seems analytical, yet at the same time sounds a bit argumentative. The woman seems a bit of an alarmist—she is just restating the problem as everyone already knows it.)*

ACTIVE READING MODEL

PREDICT

J Do you think it's just a power failure? What will happen next?

[*We look down on the street as we hear the voices creep up from below, small, mildly disturbed voices highlighting these kinds of phrases:*]

I

VOICES.
Electricity's off.
Phone won't work.
Can't get a thing on the radio.
My power mower won't move, won't work at all.
Radio's gone dead!

[*PETE VAN HORN, a tall, thin man, is seen standing in front of his house.*]

VAN HORN. I'll cut through the back yard . . . See if the power's still on on Floral Street. I'll be right back!

[*He walks past the side of his house and disappears into the back yard. The camera pans down slowly until we're looking at ten or eleven people standing around the street and overflowing to the curb and sidewalk. In the background is STEVE BRAND's car.*]

K

STEVE. Doesn't make sense. Why should the power go off all of a sudden, and the phone line?

DON. Maybe some sort of an electrical storm or something.

CHARLIE. That don't seem likely. Sky's just as blue as anything. Not a cloud. No lightning. No thunder. No nothing. How could it be a storm?

WOMAN. I can't get a thing on the radio. Not even the portable.

[*The people again murmur softly in wonderment and question.*]

CHARLIE. Well, why don't you go downtown and check with the police, though they'll probably think we're crazy or something. A little power failure and right away we get all flustered[3] and everything.

3. To be *flustered* is to be embarrassed, nervous, or confused.

Teaching Support

MEETING INDIVIDUAL NEEDS

MULTIPLE MODES OF EXPRESSION

Spatial Mention that elements of setting and costumes can indicate the time of a story. Students can recognize television shows that were produced a number of years ago by the clothes people are wearing, hairstyles, furniture, cars, and so on.

Activity Draw a car that might replace the one on the page if the play were being staged today, or draw a costume that would indicate the present time or a much earlier time. **L2**

ACTIVE READING MODEL

L

STEVE. It isn't just the power failure, Charlie. If it was, we'd still be able to get a broadcast on the portable.

[*There's a murmur of reaction to this.* STEVE *looks from face to face and then over to his car.*]

STEVE. I'll run downtown. We'll get this all straightened out.

[*He walks over to the car, gets in it, turns the key. Looking through the open car door, we see the crowd watching him from the other side.* STEVE *starts the engine. It turns over sluggishly and then just stops dead. He tries it again and this time he can't get it to turn over. Then, very slowly and reflectively, he turns the key back to "off" and slowly gets out of the car. The people stare at* STEVE. *He stands for a moment by the car, then walks toward the group.*]

M

STEVE. I don't understand it. It was working fine before . . .

DON. Out of gas?

STEVE. [*Shakes his head.*] I just had it filled up.

WOMAN. What's it mean?

CHARLIE. It's just as if . . . as if everything had stopped. [*Then he turns toward* STEVE.] We'd better walk downtown. [*Another murmur of assent*[4] *at this.*]

STEVE. The two of us can go, Charlie. [*He turns to look back at the car.*] It couldn't be the meteor. A meteor couldn't do *this.*

RESPOND

N

Would you walk downtown if you were Steve or Charlie?

[*He and* CHARLIE *exchange a look, then they start to walk away from the group.*

O

We see TOMMY, *a serious-faced fourteen-year-old in spectacles who stands a few feet away from the group. He is halfway between them and the two men, who start to walk down the sidewalk.*]

TOMMY. Mr. Brand . . . you better not!

STEVE. Why not?

TOMMY. They don't want you to.

[STEVE *and* CHARLIE *exchange a grin, and* STEVE *looks back toward the boy.*]

STEVE. *Who* doesn't want us to?

TOMMY. [*Jerks his head in the general direction of the distant horizon.*] Them!

STEVE. Them?

CHARLIE. Who are them?

QUESTION

P

Who is the "them" Tommy refers to? What makes you think so?

4. An expression of agreement is *assent.*

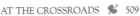

L Critical Thinking

INFERRING Ask students why they think the reactions of the crowd are twice noted in the stage direction. *(Their faces show their concern or their dependence on Steve. Perhaps the author wants the audience to see the crowd as it grows.)*

M Literary Elements

DIALOGUE The playwright has limited space. Characters must say what has to be said to move the plot and reveal their personalities.

N Active Reading Strategies

RESPOND *(Students may say they would if they wanted to find answers. A person frozen by fear of the unknown would be unable to go anywhere.)*

O Literary Elements

CHARACTERIZATION What do the details of Tommy's appearance suggest about him? *(His serious face might suggest he is not a practical joker. Perhaps the author is implying he knows what he is talking about.)*

P Active Reading Strategies

QUESTION *("Them" might be referring to the monsters because Tommy looks off to the horizon.)*

Grammar and Language *Minilesson*

Using End Marks Explain to students that the period, the question mark, and the exclamation point all signal the end of a sentence. The end punctuation also helps readers identify the type of sentence being read. A period indicates a statement; a question mark indicates an interrogative sentence; and an exclamation point indicates a command or a sentence that expresses strong emotion.

Activity Write the following sentences on the board. Have students identify what type of sentence each is, based on the end punctuation.

1. Mr. Brand... you better not! *(strong emotion)*
2. Why not? *(interrogative)*
3. They don't want you to. *(statement)*
4. Who doesn't want us to? *(interrogative)*
5. Them! *(strong emotion)* **L2**

Additional Resources

- ***Grammar and Language Transparency 43***
- ***Grammar and Language Workbook,*** pp. 253–254
- ***Grammar and Composition Handbook,*** Lesson 13.1
- ***Writer's Choice,*** Lesson 20.1

Q Literary Elements

TELEPLAY: *Stage Directions* Call attention to the directions indicating the way Steve talks to the boy. Ask students why these directions are important. In what other way might the very same words be said? *(The directions are important because they ensure that Steve speaks to Tommy gently. The same words could be barked out, creating a totally different tone and relationship with the boy.)*

R Active Reading Strategies

QUESTION *(Maybe Tommy, frightened by his reading, believes it to be true and not just science fiction.)*

S Literary Elements

CHARACTERIZATION Ask students what they think of Sally, based on this one line. *(She is being protective of her son.)*

T Critical Thinking

EVALUATING Ask students to identify the roles played by Steve, the Woman, and Tommy. *(Steve may be the hero; the Woman may be the antagonist, troublemaker, or "voice of the people"; and Tommy may be an instrument of either wisdom or fear.)*

Teaching Support

The Monsters Are Due On Maple Street

ACTIVE READING MODEL

TOMMY. [*Very intently.*] Whoever was in that thing that came by overhead.

[*STEVE knits his brows for a moment, cocking his head questioningly. His voice is intense.*]

STEVE. What?

TOMMY. Whoever was in that thing that came over. I don't think they want us to leave here.

[*STEVE leaves CHARLIE and walks over to the boy. He kneels down in front of him. He forces his voice to remain gentle. He reaches out and holds the boy.*]

STEVE. What do you mean? What are you talking about?

TOMMY. They don't want us to leave. That's why they shut everything off.

STEVE. What makes you say that? Whatever gave you that idea?

WOMAN. [*From the crowd.*] Now isn't that the craziest thing you ever heard?

QUESTION Why do you think Tommy is being so persistent?

TOMMY. [*Persistently but a little intimidated by the crowd.*] It's always that way, in every story I ever read about a ship landing from outer space.

WOMAN. [*To the boy's mother, SALLY, who stands on the fringe of the crowd.*] From outer space, yet! Sally, you better get that boy of yours up to bed. He's been reading too many comic books or seeing too many movies or something.

SALLY. Tommy, come over here and stop that kind of talk.

STEVE. Go ahead, Tommy. We'll be right back. And you'll see. That wasn't any ship or anything like it. That was just a . . . a meteor or something. Likely as not— [*He turns to the group, now trying to weight his words with an optimism*[5] *he obviously doesn't feel but is desperately trying to instill in himself as well as the others.*] No doubt it did have something to do with all this power failure and the rest of it. Meteors can do some crazy things. Like sunspots.

DON. [*Picking up the cue.*] Sure. That's the kind of thing—like sunspots. They raise Cain[6] with radio reception all over the world. And this thing being so close—why, there's no telling the sort of stuff

5. *Optimism* means "a hopeful or cheerful view of things."
6. *[raise Cain]* This expression means "cause trouble."

Vocabulary

intimidated (in tim′ ə dāt′ əd) *adj.* made timid or fearful; bullied
instill (in stil′) *v.* to put in gradually, little by little

MEETING INDIVIDUAL NEEDS: SPECIAL NEEDS

Less-Proficient Readers Remind students that in the 1950s, people knew less about space and science than we do today. It is possible that someone who sounded knowledgeable might be believed.

Activity Divide students into small groups containing both less-proficient readers and better readers. Ask each group to determine its area of expertise, such as sports, TV shows, music, or computer games. Have each group prepare a presentation for the rest of the class to convince them of their expertise. **L1**

Additional Resources

Inclusion Strategies

ACTIVE READING MODEL

it can do. [*He wets his lips, smiles nervously.*] Go ahead, Charlie. You and Steve go into town and see if that isn't what's causing it all.

U

[*STEVE and CHARLIE again walk away from the group down the sidewalk. The people watch silently.*

TOMMY stares at them, biting his lips, and finally calling out again.]

TOMMY. Mr. Brand!

[*The two men stop again. TOMMY takes a step toward them.*]

TOMMY. Mr. Brand . . . please don't leave here.

[*STEVE and CHARLIE stop once again and turn toward the boy. There's a murmur in the crowd, a murmur of irritation and concern as if the boy were bringing up fears that shouldn't be brought up; words which carried with them a strange kind of validity that came without logic but nonetheless registered and had meaning and effect. Again we hear a murmur of reaction from the crowd.*

TOMMY is partly frightened and partly defiant as well.]

EVALUATE

Does this make sense to you?

V

TOMMY. You might not even be able to get to town. It was that way in the story. Nobody could leave. Nobody except—

STEVE. Except who?

W

TOMMY. Except the people they'd sent down ahead of them. They looked just like humans. And it wasn't until the ship landed that—

[*The boy suddenly stops again, conscious of the parents staring at them and of the sudden hush of the crowd.*]

SALLY. [*In a whisper, sensing the antagonism of the crowd.*] Tommy, please son . . . honey, don't talk that way—

MAN ONE. That kid shouldn't talk that way . . . and we shouldn't stand here listening to him. Why this is the craziest thing I ever heard of. The kid tells us a comic book plot and here we stand listening—

PREDICT

Will the person called "Man One" be an important character in the play? On what do you base your opinion?

X

[*STEVE walks toward the camera, stops by the boy.*]

STEVE. Go ahead, Tommy. What kind of story was this? What about the people that they sent out ahead?

TOMMY. That was the way they prepared things for the landing. They sent four people. A mother and a father and two kids who looked just like humans . . . but they weren't.

Vocabulary

validity (və lid′ ə tē) *n.* state of being supported by facts; truth

defiant (di fī′ ənt) *adj.* showing bold resistance to authority or an opponent

antagonism (an tag′ ə niz′ əm) *n.* unfriendliness; hostility

U Literary Elements

FORESHADOWING Stories and plays often heighten suspense by foreshadowing, or conveying, a mood of impending doom. Could Tommy's statement be seen as a foreshadowing clue? *(Yes, Tommy's hesitancy and his use of the word "please" convey a fear of what can happen.)*

V Active Reading Strategies

EVALUATE *(It makes sense because the crowd is influenced by the strange events. Maybe the two adults should not have been swayed by the fears of a young boy and should have gone for help anyway.)*

W Critical Thinking

JUDGING THE CREDIBILITY OF A SOURCE Ask students if they notice how Tommy is presenting the scenario in bits and pieces, giving more detail as he speaks. Ask students what kind of information makes a source credible. *(Someone is credible who gives detail, follows a logical pattern, and presents facts or solid sources for the information.)*

X Active Reading Strategies

PREDICT *(The man will probably not be an important character in the play. He would probably have a name if he were.)*

Reading Minilesson

Setting a Purpose for Reading Explain that readers should begin to study the characters and weigh their impact.

Activity You may wish to have each student develop a table like the one at the right to take notes throughout the reading of the teleplay. **L2**

Additional Resources

Reading Skills Practice Workbook

Character	What Character Thinks, Says, Does	What the Character Is Like
Tommy	*Concerned about his neighbors' safety; tells about sci-fi story*	*Serious, bookish, persistent in the face of opposition*
Steve	*Allows Tommy to talk.*	*Strong; a leader, takes charge*

Y Literary Elements

TELEPLAY: *Stage Directions* Ask students why Steve is looking at the crowd. Why is the crowd repeatedly caught on camera? *(Steve wants to see the crowd's reaction to Tommy's comments. He's concerned about their behavior; conveying that concern to the audience may be why the director keeps putting the crowd on camera.)*

Z Critical Thinking

EVALUATING Note that there is no answer to Charlie's question about Pete's getting back. Ask students why the author has a character raise the question but then interrupts with something else before there is an answer. *(Perhaps the author merely wants to remind the audience that Pete left and has not yet returned. Pete will more than likely play a critical role later in the play.)*

Vo•cab•u•lar•y Skills

Idioms Because a play's dialogue is written to sound much like ordinary speech, idioms will appear frequently. Recall that an idiom is an expression that means something other than its literal meaning. Here *no dice* is an idiom meaning "no" or "it didn't work."

AA Active Reading Strategies

PREDICT *(Because of the tension, the group might react with fear to the car's starting by itself.)*

The Monsters Are Due On Maple Street

ACTIVE READING MODEL

Y

[There's another silence as STEVE *looks toward the crowd and then toward* TOMMY. *He wears a tight grin.]*

STEVE. Well, I guess what we'd better do then is to run a check on the neighborhood and see which ones of us are really human.

[There's laughter at this, but it's a laughter that comes from a desperate attempt to lighten the atmosphere. It's a release kind of laugh. The people look at one another in the middle of their laughter.]

Z

CHARLIE. There must be somethin' better to do than stand around makin' bum jokes about it. *[Rubs his jaw nervously.]* I wonder if Floral Street's got the same deal we got. *[He looks past the houses.]* Where is Pete Van Horn anyway? Didn't he get back yet?

[Suddenly there's the sound of a car's engine starting to turn over. We look across the street toward the driveway of LES GOODMAN*'s house. He's at the wheel trying to start the car.]*

SALLY. Can you get it started, Les?

[He gets out of the car, shaking his head.]

GOODMAN. No dice.

[He walks toward the group. He stops suddenly as behind him, inexplicably[7] *and with a noise that inserts itself into the silence, the car engine starts up all by itself.* GOODMAN *whirls around to stare toward it.*
The car idles roughly, smoke coming from the exhaust, the frame shaking gently.
GOODMAN*'s eyes go wide, and he runs over to his car.*
The people stare toward the car.]

AA PREDICT

How will the group react to the car's starting by itself?

MAN ONE. He got the car started somehow. He got his car started!

[The camera pans along the faces of the people as they stare, somehow caught up by this revelation and somehow, illogically, wildly, frightened.]

WOMAN. How come his car just up and started like that?

SALLY. All by itself. He wasn't anywheres near it. It started all by itself.

*[*DON *approaches the group, stops a few feet away to look toward* GOODMAN*'s car and then back toward the group.]*

DON. And he never did come out to look at that thing that flew overhead. He wasn't even interested. *[He turns to the faces in the group, his face taut and serious.]* Why? Why didn't he come out with the rest of us to look?

---

7. Something that happens *inexplicably* (in′ iks plik′ ə blē) is impossible to understand or explain.

Teaching Support

MEETING INDIVIDUAL NEEDS

ENGLISH LANGUAGE LEARNERS

Symbolism in Names Mention that the names of characters often suggest the types of people or roles they are to play.

Activity Divide the class into small groups that contain both English language learners and English-proficient students. Have them work together to create new, more descriptive names for characters in the teleplay. For example, Pete Van Horn could be renamed Pete Messenger, as he is to return with news for the neighbors. Have groups share their new names with each other.

Additional Resources

English Language Learners Sourcebook, p. 71

Did You Know?
A *metamorphosis* is a complete change, as when a caterpillar becomes a butterfly.

CHARLIE. He always was an oddball. Him and his whole family. Real oddball.

DON. What do you say we ask him?

[The group suddenly starts toward the house. In this brief fraction of a moment they take the first step toward performing a metamorphosis that changes people from a group into a mob. They begin to head purposefully across the street toward the house at the end. STEVE *stands in front of them. For a moment their fear almost turns their walk into a wild stampede, but* STEVE*'s voice, loud, incisive,*[8] *and commanding, makes them stop.]*

STEVE. Wait a minute . . . wait a minute! Let's not be a mob!

[The people stop as a group, seem to pause for a moment, and then much more quietly and slowly start to walk across the street. GOODMAN *stands alone facing the people.]*

GOODMAN. I just don't understand it. I tried to start it and it wouldn't start. You saw me. All of you saw me.

[And now, just as suddenly as the engine started, it stops and there's a long silence that is gradually intruded upon by the frightened murmuring of the people.]

GOODMAN. I don't understand. I swear . . . I don't understand. What's happening?

DON. Maybe you better tell us. Nothing's working on this street. Nothing. No lights, no power, no radio. *[And then meaningfully]* Nothing except one car—yours!

[The people pick this up and now their murmuring becomes a loud chant filling the air with accusations and demands for action. Two of the men pass DON *and head toward* GOODMAN*, who backs away, backing into his car and now at bay.]*[9]

GOODMAN. Wait a minute now. You keep your distance—all of you. So I've got a car that starts by itself—well, that's a freak thing, I admit it. But does that make me some kind of a criminal or something? I don't know why the car works—it just does!

ACTIVE READING MODEL

VISUALIZE
Take a minute to picture this scene as if you were on the street but apart from the group.

REVIEW
What has happened up to this point? How have the characters reacted to these events? Can you tell yet who the main characters are?

8. Steve's *incisive* voice is sharp and forceful.
9. *[at bay]* This describes the position of a cornered animal that is forced to turn and face its pursuers.

BB Active Reading Strategies

TELEPLAY: *Stage Directions* Ask students how they would act if they were actors in this crowd. What kind of body language would they use to convey that, unbeknown to themselves, they were turning from a crowd into a mob. *(They would perhaps raise their arms, make angry faces, shout, surge forward, or shake their fists.)*

CC Active Reading Strategies

VISUALIZE *(Visualize the group, and then identify the different characters, such as Steve, commanding them to stop.)*

DD Literary Elements

CHARACTERIZATION In this one line Steve demonstrates his leadership qualities. Ask students what in particular shows his leadership. *(He's not afraid to oppose the group. A leader is a good communicator, and he uses the right word,* mob, *that his neighbors should react to.)*

EE Active Reading Strategies

REVIEW *(There was a loud noise in this peaceful neighborhood. Since then, the phone lines, electricity, and machines won't work. The characters are uneasy because of a science-fiction story a young boy told, and they begin to suspect each other of wrongdoing. The main characters so far are Steve, Don, Charlie, Les, Tommy, Sally, and the Woman.)*

LIFE SKILLS CONNECTION

Lifelong Learning One of the most difficult things to do is to stand firm in one's beliefs when everyone else is thinking and acting in another way. Resisting the temptation to run with the herd is a major challenge. For example:

- staying at home to study or baby-sit when everyone else is going to a concert
- not allowing someone to be bullied

Activity Have small groups of students discuss incidents they know about in which an individual (perhaps themselves) had to fight the impulse to follow the crowd and do something opposed to their beliefs, principles, or wishes. Encourage each group to share their experiences with the class. **L2**

VIEWING THE PAINTING

Hopper often used light to isolate people or objects, lending his paintings a feeling of loneliness.

Viewing Response *The artist combines light (the well-lit house front and lighted windows) with darkness (the shadowy background and dark awnings and bushes) to create a mysterious mood. A playwright might create a similar effect by combining "normal" settings and characters with hints of the strange and supernatural.*

FF Active Reading Strategies

QUESTION *(A "monster kick" means that the group is focused on the idea that monsters are responsible for these problems. Steve is trying to explain to Les why the group is behaving this way and might say "monster kick" to lighten the situation.)*

GG Active Reading Strategies

REVIEW Here Steve says "the general impression holds..." Ask what Steve's reaction to the notion of an alien family on the street had been before. *(Previously Steve didn't even acknowledge that as an option.)*

Room for Tourists, 1945. Edward Hopper. Oil on canvas, 30¼ x 42⅛ in. Yale University Art Gallery, New Haven, CT.

Viewing the painting: What mood does the artist create in this painting? How might a playwright create a similar mood?

[This stops the crowd momentarily and now GOODMAN, *still backing away, goes toward his front porch. He goes up the steps and then stops to stand facing the mob.*

We see a long shot of STEVE *as he comes through the crowd.]*

FF **QUESTION** What's a "monster kick"? Why does Steve say that?

STEVE. [*Quietly.*] We're all on a monster kick, Les. Seems that the general impression holds that maybe one family isn't what we think they GG

Teaching Support

Writing Minilesson

Narrative A narrative is a story that usually answers the question "what happened." In a teleplay, the writer narrates in the present tense, using stage directions to tell what actors are doing and what is happening.

Activity Write the following short set of directions and ask students to add to them: *The door opens. The teacher comes in. Students rush to their desks.* Explain that the scene takes place in a classroom. Suggest that students describe what certain actors are doing and what sounds can be heard. Have them use verbs in the present tense in writing the directions. **L2**

Additional Resources

Writer's Choice, Lessons 4.1–4.7

are. Monsters from outer space or something. Different than us. Fifth columnists[10] from the vast beyond. [*He chuckles.*] You know anybody that might fit that description around here on Maple Street?

GOODMAN. What is this, a gag or something? This a practical joke or something?

[*We see a close-up of the porch light as it suddenly goes out. There's a murmur from the group.*]

GOODMAN. Now I suppose that's supposed to incriminate me! The light goes on and off. That really does it, doesn't it?

[*He looks around the faces of the people.*] I just don't understand this— [*He wets his lips, looking from face to face.*] Look, you all know me. We've lived here five years. Right in this house. We're no different from any of the rest of you! We're no different at all. Really . . . this whole thing is just . . . just weird—

WOMAN. Well, if that's the case, Les Goodman, explain why— [*She stops suddenly, clamping her mouth shut.*]

GOODMAN. [*Softly.*] Explain what?

STEVE. [*Interjecting.*] Look, let's forget this—

CHARLIE. [*Overlapping him.*] Go ahead, let her talk. What about it? Explain what?

WOMAN. [*A little reluctantly.*] Well . . . sometimes I go to bed late at night. A couple of times . . . a couple of times I'd come out on the porch and I'd see Mr. Goodman here in the wee hours of the morning standing out in front of his house . . . looking up at the sky. [*She looks around the circle of*

10. *Fifth columnists* are traitors.

Vocabulary
incriminate (in krim′ ə nāt′) *v.* to show the guilt of

ACTIVE READING MODEL

RESPOND
How would you feel at this point if you were Goodman?

Active Reading Strategies

RESPOND *(Goodman probably feels betrayed and frightened because all the people he's known as neighbors for five years are lining up against him.)*

Critical Thinking

EVALUATING Ask students to compare Steve's comment here with what he says at the top of the page. How has he changed? *(At the top of the page Steve was raising the issue most people were thinking, and he seemed to believe in it somewhat. Here, however, he seems to be rejecting it as a possibility.)*

Vocabulary Skills

Roots The stage directions have Steve "interjecting" a comment. *Interject* literally means "to throw" (*ject*) "between" (*inter*). Other words are built on the same roots: *eject* (throw out from within), *reject* (throw away as useless, or refuse to take), and *object* (to give a reason to oppose).

Interdisciplinary Connection

Music Music can be a critical supporting force in a television play or series. It is another way of communicating. Music can create suspense or a sense of foreboding or indicate what will be happening next. Music used in a television series can also become a familiar part of our everyday lives.

Activity Ask students how many of them know the musical theme from *The Twilight Zone*. If possible, play a tape of the theme music for the class. Ask students to suggest other TV series whose theme music has become part of American culture. **L2**

Active Reading Strategies

EVALUATE *(Sometimes fear makes people want to blame someone for things that go wrong, even if that someone is a neighbor.)*

Active Reading Strategies

REVIEW *(So far, the lights have gone out, cars do not start, and there are no radio transmissions. A young boy has made them believe that they are the victims of aliens. The neighbors begin to suspect each other—especially Les.)*

Active Reading Strategies

QUESTION *(A few hours have passed since act 1. In act 1 we learned that it was 6:43 P.M. in late summer. In line 1 of act 2, it says that it is night and that Mrs. Goodman lights a candle, indicating that it is dark.)*

ACTIVE READING MODEL

EVALUATE

JJ Would a person really say something like this about a neighbor?

REVIEW

KK So far, what has actually happened?

QUESTION

LL How much time has passed since the end of act 1? How can you tell?

faces.] That's right, looking up at the sky as if . . . as if he were waiting for something. [*A pause.*] As if he were looking for something.

[*There's a murmur of reaction from the crowd again.*
We cut suddenly to a group shot. As GOODMAN *starts toward them, they back away frightened.*]

GOODMAN. You know really . . . this is for laughs. You know what I'm guilty of? [*He laughs.*] I'm guilty of insomnia.[11] Now what's the penalty for insomnia? [*At this point the laugh, the humor, leaves his voice.*] Did you hear what I said? I said it was insomnia. [*A pause as he looks around, then shouts.*] I said it was insomnia! You fools. You scared, frightened rabbits, you. You're sick people, do you know that? You're sick people—all of you! And you don't even know what you're starting because let me tell you . . . let me tell you—this thing you're starting—that should frighten you. As God is my witness . . . you're letting something begin here that's a nightmare!

ACT II

[*We see a medium shot of the Goodman entry hall at night. On the side table rests an unlit candle.* MRS. GOODMAN *walks into the scene, a glass of milk in hand. She sets the milk down on the table, lights the candle with a match from a box on the table, picks up the glass of milk, and starts out of scene.*

MRS. GOODMAN *comes through her porch door, glass of milk in hand. The entry hall, with table and lit candle, can be seen behind her.*

Outside, the camera slowly pans down the sidewalk, taking in little knots of people who stand around talking in low voices. At the end of each conversation they look toward LES GOODMAN'S *house. From the various houses we can see candlelight but no electricity, and there's an all-pervading quiet that blankets the whole area, disturbed only by the almost whispered voices of the people as they stand around. The camera pans over to one group where* CHARLIE *stands. He stares across at* GOODMAN'S *house.*

We see a long shot of the house. Two men stand across the street in almost sentry-like poses. Then we see a medium shot of a group of people.]

SALLY. [*A little timorously.*][12] It just doesn't seem right, though, keeping watch on them. Why . . . he was right when he said he was one of our neighbors. Why, I've known Ethel Goodman ever since they moved in. We've been good friends—

11. *Insomnia* is restless sleep or the inability to fall asleep.
12. *Timorously* (tim′ ər əs lē) means "lacking courage or self-confidence; timidly."

Teaching Support

Reading Minilesson

Comparing and Contrasting The close of act 1 and the beginning of act 2 are very different, creating totally different moods. The mood at the close of act 1 is tense and charged with anger, as Goodman rants wildly at his neighbors in fearful defiance.

Activity Have students read the details from the opening of act 2 and describe the mood those details create. *(Act 2 opens in a more subdued manner. Mrs. Goodman is carrying a glass of milk and a candle. People are standing and talking in quiet voices. The tension is still there, but the open hostility and anger have, for the moment, diminished.)* **L2**

Additional Resources

Reading Skills Practice Workbook

CHARLIE. That don't prove a thing. Any guy who'd spend his time lookin' up at the sky early in the morning—well, there's something wrong with that kind of person. There's something that ain't legitimate. Maybe under normal circumstances we could let it go by, but these aren't normal circumstances. Why, look at this street! Nothin' but candles. Why, it's like goin' back into the dark ages or somethin'! MM

[STEVE walks down the steps of his porch, walks down the street over to LES GOODMAN's house, and then stops at the foot of the steps. GOODMAN stands there, his wife behind him, very frightened.]

GOODMAN. Just stay right where you are, Steve. We don't want any trouble, but this time if anybody sets foot on my porch, that's what they're going to get—trouble!

STEVE. Look, Les—

GOODMAN. I've already explained to you people. I don't sleep very well at night sometimes. I get up and I take a walk and I look up at the sky. I look at the stars!

MRS. GOODMAN. That's exactly what he does. Why this whole thing, it's . . . it's some kind of madness or something.

STEVE. *[Nods grimly.]* That's exactly what it is—some kind of madness.

CHARLIE'S VOICE. *[Shrill, from across the street.]* You best watch who you're seen with, Steve! Until we get this all straightened out, you ain't exactly above suspicion yourself.

NN **STEVE.** *[Whirling around toward him.]* Or you, Charlie. Or any of us, it seems. From age eight on up.

WOMAN. What I'd like to know is—what are we gonna do? Just stand around here all night?

CHARLIE. There's nothin' else we can do! *[He turns back looking toward STEVE and GOODMAN again.]* One of 'em'll tip their hand. They got to.

STEVE. *[Raising his voice.]* There's something you can do, Charlie. You could go home and keep your mouth shut. You could quit strutting around like a self-appointed hanging judge and just climb into bed and forget it.

CHARLIE. You sound real anxious to have that happen, Steve. I think we better keep our eye on you too!

PREDICT OO
Toward what do events appear to be moving? What is going to happen next?

RESPOND PP
If you were Steve, how would you be feeling now?

Vocabulary
legitimate (li jit′ ə mit) *adj.* that which follows the rules; lawful

MM Literary Elements

IRONY Mention that a useful element in writing is *irony,* defined as a method of expression in which the conveyed meaning of the words is the opposite of what is in the speaker's mind. Ask students if they see anything ironic in Charlie's last sentence here. *(Students may see that, while Charlie is referring to the darkness as the absence of light, readers may see a different meaning in "dark ages," a meaning suggesting that these people may be behaving like primitives.)*

NN Critical Thinking

EVALUATING Ask students what is happening to these people. *(Students may see that, in their fear, the neighbors distrust one another: no one is above suspicion.)*

OO Active Reading Strategies

PREDICT *(It seems that the characters are so agitated that they might begin to act on their fear and distrust of one another. Something unfortunate will probably happen.)*

PP Active Reading Strategies

RESPOND *(Students would probably be feeling surprised that their long-time neighbor and friend would turn on them.)*

Life Skills Connection

Understanding Crowd Behavior Explain to students that "crowd control" has always been an issue around the world. Some organizations, such as the police, actually take classes in this skill.

Activity Ask students for their comments on crowd behavior and crowd control. Have them discuss incidents in which they feared or actually saw a crowd getting out of control; for example, during a fire drill in school or a game in a large stadium. Have them explain what measures can be taken to protect oneself in such situations. **L2**

Literary Elements

PLOT Ask students why the author introduces new elements at different points in the play. *(The new elements add new twists and keep the audience attentive, trying to figure out where they will lead.)*

Active Reading Strategies

RESPOND *(Students may say they would feel angry and defiant.)*

Critical Thinking

EVALUATING Steve verbalizes the fear of monsters that many of his neighbors have been harboring. Is this statement going to help him or hurt him? You may wish to share the following model to illustrate the thinking process in evaluating.

Model: Steve is trying to help by bringing everyone's fears out into the open. He is trying to make people realize how silly the idea sounds. However, he could be hurting himself, as people may not see the sarcasm in his speech and take his words literally.

Vo•cab•u•lar•y Skills

Synonyms The use of the verb *whirls* in the stage direction is much more specific than the similar action verb *turns*. All good writers try to use the most specific verb to identify an action. Have students check a thesaurus or a synonym finder for alternates for *look*, *walk*, and *speak*.

Teaching Support

The Monsters Are Due On Maple Street

ACTIVE READING MODEL

DON. [*As if he were taking the bit in his teeth, takes a hesitant step to the front.*] I think everything might as well come out now. [*He turns toward* STEVE.] Your wife's done plenty of talking, Steve, about how odd you are!

CHARLIE. [*Picking this up, his eyes widening.*] Go ahead, tell us what she's said.

[*We see a long shot of* STEVE *as he walks toward them from across the street.*]

STEVE. Go ahead, what's my wife said? Let's get it all out. Let's pick out every idiosyncrasy of every single man, woman, and child on the street. And then we might as well set up some kind of kangaroo court.[13] How about a firing squad at dawn, Charlie, so we can get rid of all the suspects? Narrow them down. Make it easier for you.

DON. There's no need gettin' so upset, Steve. It's just that . . . well . . . Myra's talked about how there's been plenty of nights you spent hours down in your basement workin' on some kind of radio or something. Well, none of us have ever seen that radio—

[*By this time* STEVE *has reached the group. He stands there defiantly close to them.*]

RESPOND
How would you react at this point if you were Steve?

CHARLIE. Go ahead, Steve. What kind of "radio set" you workin' on? I never seen it. Neither has anyone else. Who you talk to on that radio set? And who talks to you?

STEVE. I'm surprised at you, Charlie. How come you're so dense all of a sudden? [*A pause.*] Who do I talk to? I talk to monsters from outer space. I talk to three-headed green men who fly over here in what look like meteors.

[STEVE's *wife steps down from the porch, bites her lip, calls out.*]

MRS. BRAND. Steve! Steve, please. [*Then looking around, frightened, she walks toward the group.*] It's just a ham radio[14] set, that's all. I bought him a book on it myself. It's just a ham radio set. A lot of people have them. I can show it to you. It's right down in the basement.

STEVE. [*Whirls around toward her.*] Show them nothing! If they want to look inside our house—let them get a search warrant.

CHARLIE. Look, buddy, you can't afford to—

13. An *idiosyncrasy* (id′ ē ə sing′ krə sē) is a personal way of acting; an odd mannerism. A *kangaroo court* is an unofficial, irregular trial in which the verdict is often decided beforehand and fair legal procedures are ignored.
14. *Ham radio* is a hobby in which a person operates his or her own radio station, sending messages by voice or Morse code.

Listening and Speaking Minilesson

Oral Reading The author writes the dialogue, and the actors, with the help of the director, determine how to deliver the lines depending on the mood and action of the passage.

Activity Have students work with one or two classmates to rehearse and recite some of the dialogue on this page. Suggest that they try different ways of speaking, such as quickly, slowly, sharply, angrily, or calmly. Have each pair or team decide which is the best delivery to convey the meaning of each line. Have them keep in mind the character's personality as described by the author. After doing the recitation once, have them rotate the parts and do it again. **L2**

ACTIVE READING MODEL

STEVE. [*Interrupting.*] Charlie, don't tell me what I can afford! And stop telling me who's dangerous and who isn't and who's safe and who's a menace. [*He turns to the group and shouts.*] And you're with him, too—all of you! You're standing here all set to crucify—all set to find a scapegoat[15]—all desperate to point some kind of a finger at a neighbor! Well now look, friends, the only thing that's gonna happen is that we'll eat each other up alive—

[*He stops abruptly as* CHARLIE *suddenly grabs his arm.*]

CHARLIE. [*In a hushed voice.*] That's not the only thing that can happen to us.

[*Cut to a long shot looking down the street. A figure has suddenly materialized in the gloom and in the silence we can hear the clickety-clack of slow, measured footsteps on concrete as the figure walks slowly toward them. One of the women lets out a stifled cry. The young mother grabs her boy as do a couple of others.*]

PREDICT

Who do you think the dark figure down the street is?

TOMMY. [*Shouting, frightened.*] It's the monster! It's the monster!

[*Another woman lets out a wail and the people fall back in a group, staring toward the darkness and the approaching figure.*

We see a medium group shot of the people as they stand in the shadows watching. DON MARTIN *joins them, carrying a shotgun. He holds it up.*]

DON. We may need this.

UU

STEVE. A shotgun? [*He pulls it out of* DON'*s hand.*] Good Lord—will anybody think a thought around here? Will you people wise up? What good would a shotgun do against—

[*Now* CHARLIE *pulls the gun from* STEVE'*s hand.*]

CHARLIE. No more talk, Steve. You're going to talk us into a grave! You'd let whatever's out there walk right over us, wouldn't yuh? Well, some of us won't!

[*He swings the gun around to point it toward the sidewalk.*

The dark figure continues to walk toward them.

The group stands there, fearful, apprehensive, mothers clutching children, men standing in front of wives. CHARLIE *slowly raises the gun. As the figure gets closer and closer he suddenly pulls the trigger. The sound of it explodes in the stillness. There is a long angle shot looking down at the figure, who suddenly lets out a small cry, stumbles forward onto his knees and then falls forward on his face.* DON, CHARLIE, *and* STEVE *race*

EVALUATE

Take a minute to ask yourself if you think Charlie would really do this.

15. A *scapegoat* is someone who is made to take the blame and suffer for the mistakes or misfortunes of another person or a group.

TT Active Reading Strategies

PREDICT *(The figure could be the monster or anyone from the neighborhood. Because of the darkness and the tenseness of the situation, anyone could look threatening.)*

UU Literary Elements

SYMBOL Until now, Steve has been the leader by virtue of his ability to control the group with his words. But when the gun appears, he seems to have lost that power to Charlie. Ask students what the gun might symbolize. *(The gun might symbolize a shift from a group governed by thought and discussion [Steve] to one governed by force [Charlie and the gun].)*

VV Active Reading Strategies

EVALUATE *(Students might say that this action is in character for Charlie because he's been consistently temperamental and quick to judge.)*

MEETING INDIVIDUAL NEEDS — SPECIAL NEEDS

Less-Proficient Readers To help students better understand the story, point out that no one in the group calls out, "Who's there?"

Activity Have students work in small groups to think of at least three reasons why no one calls out to the figure. Ask the groups to share their observations. Students may suggest the following:

- People are too frightened to speak.
- If the figure hasn't seen them, a call might give away their position.
- In fiction, things are often allowed to happen for the sake of the story.
- In real life, people sometimes behave in inexplicable ways.

L2

Additional Resources

Inclusion Strategies

VIEWING THE PAINTING

Viewing Response *The darkening, glowering sky is like the growing darkness in the teleplay. Small human figures might be shown staring in awe at the sky, suggesting the power and mystery of darkness.*

FYI

War of the Worlds In 1938, Orson Welles created a panic with a radio adaptation of H. G. Wells's "War of the Worlds." The radio transmission, closely imitating the broadcasts of that time, described the invasion of New Jersey by Martian aliens so realistically that it caused thousands of people to leave their homes and try to escape.

Rod Serling, the host of *The Twilight Zone*, was cocreator of another weekly series named *Night Gallery*. Its setting was a museum where Rod Serling would introduce tales of fantasy, horror, and science fiction.

Stormy Midnight, 1995. Jane Wilson. Oil on linen, 18 x 18 in. Courtesy Fischbach Gallery, New York.

Viewing the painting: If you were to add people to this scene, what would they be doing? Why? How does the mood of the painting compare with the mood of the play?

Teaching Support

Grammar and Language *Minilesson*

Complete Sentences Write the following sentence fragment on the board: *With few variations.* Note that in dialogue, characters often speak in sentence fragments. That is, the group of words may look like a sentence, but it lacks a subject or predicate to make it stand as an independent, complete thought. Written as a complete sentence, the fragment above could be *The pattern is always the same, with few variations.*

Activity Have students find other sentence fragments in the text and write them as complete sentences (For example, Figure One's exchange: *"By no means." should be, "This place is by no means unique.")* **L2**

Additional Resources

- ***Grammar and Language Transparency 44***
- ***Grammar and Language Workbook,*** pp. 55–56
- ***Grammar and Composition Handbook,*** Lesson 1.2
- ***Writer's Choice,*** Lesson 8.2

ACTIVE READING MODEL

forward over to him. STEVE *is there first and turns the man over. Now the crowd gathers around them.*]

STEVE. [*Slowly looks up.*] It's Pete Van Horn.

DON. [*In a hushed voice.*] Pete Van Horn! He was just gonna go over to the next block to see if the power was on—

WOMAN. You killed him, Charlie. You shot him dead!

WW **CHARLIE.** [*Looks around at the circle of faces, his eyes frightened, his face contorted.*] But . . . but I didn't know who he was. I certainly didn't know who he was. He comes walkin' out of the darkness—how am I supposed to know who he was? [*He grabs* STEVE.] Steve—you know why I shot! How was I supposed to know he wasn't a monster or something? [*He grabs* DON *now.*] We're all scared of the same thing, I was just tryin' to . . . tryin' to protect my home, that's all! Look, all of you, that's all I was tryin' to do. [*He looks down wildly at the body.*] I didn't know it was somebody we knew! I didn't know—

Can you picture this scene?

[*There's a sudden hush and then an intake of breath. We see a medium shot of the living room window of* CHARLIE'*s house. The window is not lit, but suddenly the house lights come on behind it.*]

WOMAN. [*In a very hushed voice.*] Charlie . . . Charlie . . . the lights just went on in your house. Why did the lights just go on?

DON. What about it, Charlie? How come you're the only one with lights now?

GOODMAN. That's what I'd like to know.

[*A pause as they all stare toward* CHARLIE.]

YY **GOODMAN.** You were so quick to kill, Charlie and you were so quick to tell us who we had to be careful of. Well, maybe you had to kill. Maybe Peter there was trying to tell us something. Maybe he'd found out something and came back to tell us who there was amongst us we should watch out for—

REVIEW ZZ

How would you summarize what has happened so far?

[CHARLIE *backs away from the group, his eyes wide with fright.*]

CHARLIE. No . . . no . . . it's nothing of the sort! I don't know why the lights are on, I swear I don't. Somebody's pulling a gag or something.

[*He bumps against* STEVE, *who grabs him and whirls him around.*]

STEVE. A gag? A gag? Charlie, there's a dead man on the sidewalk and you killed him. Does this thing look like a gag to you?

[CHARLIE *breaks away and screams as he runs toward his house.*]

CHARLIE. No! No! Please!

Critical Thinking

SYNTHESIZING Ask students to synthesize the role of The Woman by adding what she says here to what she has said earlier. *(The Woman seems to be an instigator who sees the worst in every situation and highlights it, as she does here. She doesn't take sides but just stirs up trouble.)*

XX Active Reading Strategies

VISUALIZE *(Students can visualize the body of Pete Van Horn on the ground with all the neighbors around him. Then they can see the frightened face of Charlie when he realizes what he has done.)*

YY Critical Thinking

DRAWING CONCLUSIONS Ask students why Les Goodman feels no compassion for Charlie now that the crowd has turned against him. *(Probably because Charlie was encouraging the crowd to suspect Les of being a monster and did not support his own best friend, Steve.)*

ZZ Active Reading Strategies

REVIEW *(The crowd is still looking for the monster among them. Charlie in his wild fear takes a gun and shoots Pete Van Horn, a neighbor, and then the crowd turns on him.)*

MEETING INDIVIDUAL NEEDS

ENGLISH LANGUAGE LEARNERS

Nonverbal Language Facial expressions, body movements, and sounds are all part of nonverbal language that crosses language barriers. Remind English language learners that they are already "reading" nonverbal language, whether or not they are aware of it.

Activity Divide the class into small groups that include both English language learners and English-proficient students. Ask them to identify some nonverbal language and to put it into words. Then have students demonstrate their examples. Later, discuss any cultural differences that students have noted.

Additional Resources

English Language Learners Sourcebook, p. 72

AAA Critical Thinking

GENERALIZING Until now, except for Charlie's shooting the unidentified figure, all the aggression has been nonphysical. Now it is becoming physical and ugly. Ask students what is happening to these people. *(The people are so wrapped up in their fear they are not thinking clearly or thinking at all. They are acting like people from the "dark ages," when brute force determined every outcome.)*

BBB Active Reading Strategies

VISUALIZE *(Students might want to shoot this scene from Charlie's house or from above to show the crowd scene and Charlie and his wife.)*

CCC Active Reading Strategies

QUESTION *(No, Charlie doesn't really believe it. In his fear he is grasping at straws to save himself. He stammers and his speech is halting as he searches desperately for an answer that will shift the crowd's attention from him.)*

Teaching Support

The Monsters Are Due On Maple Street

ACTIVE READING MODEL

AAA [*A man breaks away from the crowd to chase* CHARLIE. *We see a long angle shot looking down as the man tackles* CHARLIE *and lands on top of him. The other people start to run toward them.* CHARLIE *is up on his feet, breaks away from the other man's grasp, lands a couple of desperate punches that push the man aside. Then he forces his way, fighting, through the crowd to once again break free, jumps up on his front porch. A rock thrown from the group smashes a window alongside of him, the broken glass flying past him. A couple of pieces cut him. He stands there perspiring, rumpled, blood running down from a cut on the cheek. His wife breaks away from the group to throw herself into his arms. He buries his face against her. We can see the crowd converging on the porch now.*]

VISUALIZE

BBB If you were the director, how would you have the camera operator shoot this scene?

VOICES.

It must have been him.
He's the one.
We got to get Charlie.

[*Another rock lands on the porch. Now* CHARLIE *pushes his wife behind him, facing the group.*]

CHARLIE. Look, look I swear to you . . . it isn't me . . . but I do know who it is . . . I swear to you, I do know who it is. I know who the monster is here. I know who it is that doesn't belong. I swear to you I know.

GOODMAN. [*Shouting.*] What are you waiting for?

WOMAN. [*Shouting.*] Come on, Charlie, come on.

MAN ONE. [*Shouting.*] Who is it, Charlie, tell us!

DON. [*Pushing his way to the front of the crowd*] All right, Charlie, let's hear it!

[CHARLIE*'s eyes dart around wildly.*]

CHARLIE. It's . . . it's . . .

MAN TWO. [*Screaming.*] Go ahead, Charlie, tell us.

CHARLIE. It's . . . it's the kid. It's Tommy. He's the one.

QUESTION

CCC Does Charlie really believe what he is saying? What makes you think so?

[*There's a gasp from the crowd as we cut to a shot of* SALLY *holding her son* TOMMY. *The boy at first doesn't understand and then, realizing the eyes are all on him, buries his face against his mother.*]

SALLY. [*Backs away.*] That's crazy! That's crazy! He's a little boy.

WOMAN. But he knew! He was the only one who knew! He told us all about it. Well, how did he know? How *could* he have known?

[*The various people take this up and repeat the question aloud.*]

VOICES.

How could he know?

Writing *Minilesson*

Narrating Action with Verbs In the stage directions at the top of the page, the sentences are relatively short and without much descriptive detail. But there are many action verbs: *tackles, breaks away, lands,* and *forces.*

Activity Narrate a scene with many people in it, such as in a cafeteria, at a game, or at a mall. Write short sentences that narrate the action through the use of strong, specific action verbs. Keep descriptive details to a minimum. **L2**

Additional Resources

Writer's Choice, Lesson 4.5

Who told him?
Make the kid answer.

DON. It was Charlie who killed old man Van Horn.

WOMAN. But it was the kid here who knew what was going to happen all the time. He was the one who knew!

[*We see a close-up of* STEVE.]

STEVE. Are you all gone crazy? [*Pause as he looks about.*] Stop.

DDD

[*A fist crashes at* STEVE*'s face, staggering him back out of the frame of the picture.*

There are several close camera shots suggesting the coming of violence. A hand fires a rifle. A fist clenches. A hand grabs the hammer from VAN HORN*'s body, etc. Meanwhile, we hear the following lines.*]

DON. Charlie has to be the one—Where's my rifle—

WOMAN. Les Goodman's the one. His car started! Let's wreck it.

MRS. GOODMAN. What about Steve's radio—He's the one that called them—

MR. GOODMAN. Smash the radio. Get me a hammer. Get me something.

STEVE. Stop—Stop—

CHARLIE. Where's that kid—Let's get him.

MAN ONE. Get Steve—Get Charlie—They're working together.

[*The crowd starts to converge around the mother, who grabs the child and starts to run with him. The crowd starts to follow, at first walking fast, and then running after him.*

We see a full shot of the street as suddenly CHARLIE*'s lights go off and the lights in another house go on. They stay on for a moment, then from across the street other lights go on and then off again.*]

MAN ONE. [*Shouting.*] It isn't the kid . . . it's Bob Weaver's house.

WOMAN. It isn't Bob Weaver's house, it's Don Martin's place.

CHARLIE. I tell you it's the kid.

DON. It's Charlie. He's the one.

[*We move into a series of close-ups of various people as they shout, accuse, scream, interspersing these shots with shots of houses as the lights go on and off, and then slowly in the middle of this nightmarish morass*[16] *of sight and sound the camera starts to pull away, until once again we've*

16. ***Interspersing*** means "scattering or mixing in over brief periods." A ***morass*** (mə ras′) is any difficult, confused, or entangling condition or situation.

ACTIVE READING MODEL

EVALUATE EEE

Has the playwright kept the character of Steve consistent throughout the story? How would you describe Steve?

EVALUATE FFF

What mood does the playwright create with this scene? How does he create that mood?

DDD Literary Elements

TELEPLAY: *Stage Directions* Ask students what these close shots add to the story and the emotion. *(These close shots show individuals ready for physical violence, and they raise the tension level for the audience.)*

EEE Active Reading Strategies

EVALUATE *(The playwright has always kept the character of Steve as the voice of reason throughout the story. Steve is presented as brave, reasonable, compassionate, and not easily swayed by the crowd or by fear.)*

FFF Active Reading Strategies

EVALUATE *(The playwright creates an unsettling mood through chaos and confusion, with each character shouting and accusing and the lights going on and off.)*

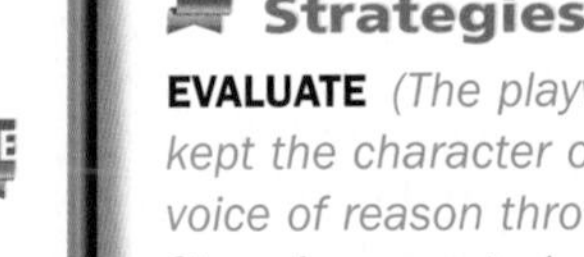

LITERATURE & HUMANITIES

Have students examine the painting *Catastrophe No. 2* in *Art Talk*, page 94. Ask them what will probably happen to the people and their houses. How does their reaction compare to the reactions of the characters in Serling's play?

REAL-WORLD CONNECTION

Riots Students may better understand the story by studying the dynamics of riots.

Activity Have students research riots in newspapers, in magazines, or on the Internet. Students may work in small groups to discuss their findings. Ask them to categorize the types of incidents that sparked the riots, and have them compare their findings. **L2**

interNET CONNECTION

Screenwriters Students can use a search engine to find out more about screenwriters. In addition to the word *screenwriting*, they might use such keywords as *play, film, TV, colleges,* or *guild*.

Active Reading Strategies

QUESTION *(It seems that the figures are creatures from outer space. They are trying to destroy humans by tricking them into destroying each other.)*

Active Reading Strategies

RESPOND *(Students might recognize that the play is trying to get a message across—that humans are too quick to judge and suspect each other of wrongdoing. Students might feel uncomfortable about the Narrator's observations.)*

Thematic Focus

At the Crossroads Ask students what they they think about the irrationality of the mob and how it relates to the theme. *(There are many opportunities for the characters in the story to make the right decision, control their fears, and work together for a solution to their dilemma. Instead, they allow themselves to become a mob and resort to violence.)*

ASSESSMENT

Quick Checks, p. 45

ACTIVE READING MODEL

reached the opening shot looking at the Maple Street sign from high above. The camera continues to move away until we dissolve to a shot looking toward the metal side of a space craft, which sits shrouded in darkness. An open door throws out a beam of light from the illuminated interior. Two figures silhouetted against the bright lights appear. We get only a vague feeling of form, but nothing more explicit than that.]

QUESTION Who are these figures? Where are they from? What are they doing?

FIGURE ONE. Understand the procedure now? Just stop a few of their machines and radios and telephones and lawn mowers . . . Throw them into darkness for a few hours, and then you just sit back and watch the pattern.

FIGURE TWO. And this pattern is always the same?

FIGURE ONE. With few variations. They pick the most dangerous enemy they can find . . . and it's themselves. And all we need do is sit back . . . and watch.

FIGURE TWO. Then I take it this place . . . this Maple Street . . . is not unique.

FIGURE ONE. [*Shaking his head.*] By no means. Their world is full of Maple Streets. And we'll go from one to the other and let them destroy themselves. One to the other . . . one to the other . . . one to the other—

[*Now the camera pans up for a shot of the starry sky and over this we hear the* NARRATOR'S VOICE.]

NARRATOR'S VOICE. The tools of conquest do not necessarily come with bombs and explosions and fallout.[17] There are weapons that are simply thoughts, attitudes, prejudices—to be found only in the minds of men. For the record, prejudices can kill and suspicion can destroy and a thoughtless frightened search for a scapegoat has a fallout all its own for the children . . . and the children yet unborn. [*A pause.*] And the pity of it is . . . that these things cannot be confined to . . . The Twilight Zone!

RESPOND What is your reaction to the ending of this play?

17. *Fallout* is the radioactive dust particles that result from a nuclear explosion and fall to earth from the atmosphere.

Vocabulary
explicit (eks plis′ it) *adj.* clearly expressed
prejudice (prej′ ə dis) *n.* an unfavorable opinion or judgment formed unfairly

Teaching Support

Writing Minilesson

Analytical Writing Many mysteries and horror stories take place at night. Is the nighttime more suited for such stories than daytime?

Activity Write a paragraph answering this question, giving reasons and examples to support your position. Complete the diagram to prepare for writing. **L2**

Your position on the subject: ________
Reason/Example: ________
Reason/Example: ________
Conclusion: ________

Additional Resources

Writer's Choice, Lesson 6.1–6.5

Responding to Literature

PERSONAL RESPONSE

- What is your reaction to this play? Recall the **Reading Focus** on page 504. How do the reactions of the neighbors in the teleplay compare or contrast with how you imagined your own neighbors reacting to strange occurrences?

Active Reading Response

Review the strategies described in the **Active Reading Model** on pages 502–503. Choose one of the strategies and find three additional places in the teleplay where you could apply it.

Analyzing Literature

RECALL

1. What is the first sign of trouble on Maple Street?
2. Who is Tommy? Describe him and explain what he tells Steve.
3. Who is the first person the neighbors begin to suspect?
4. What events lead to the shooting?

Brackets connect questions that are paired to develop higher-level thinking skills.

INTERPRET

5. At the beginning of the play, what is the **mood** on Maple Street? What causes the mood to change?
6. What role do you think Tommy plays in this drama?
7. Why do the people on Maple Street begin to turn on each other?
8. At what point do the neighbors become a "mob"? Why does this happen? Use quotations from the play to support your ideas.

EVALUATE AND CONNECT

9. How do the aliens use their understanding of human nature to accomplish their goal? Explain.
10. The narrator says, "The tools of conquest do not necessarily come with bombs." How does the play portray that idea?

LITERARY ELEMENTS

Teleplay

"The Monsters Are Due on Maple Street" is a **teleplay,** or a play written especially for television. Its format is similar to that of a stage play. Like a play, the teleplay is divided into **scenes** and **acts.** Stage directions, meant for the actors and the studio crew, are in italic type and are enclosed in brackets. The main difference between the format of a play and a teleplay is the addition of camera directions.

1. Identify a stage direction that describes the setting of the teleplay.
2. Find where Act II begins. Tell why you think Serling divided the play at that particular point.

- See **Literary Terms Handbook,** p. R11.

Responding to the Selection

PERSONAL RESPONSE

Some students may say that maybe their neighbors would react as the people in the play do. Others may feel that their neighbors would be more unified and rational.

Analyzing Literature

1. The first sign of trouble is the apparent power failure.
2. Tommy is a fourteen-year-old boy who reads a lot. He tells Steve he read a story in which the power failure was caused by aliens from space.
3. The neighbors first suspect Les Goodman.
4. Don Martin joins the group in the street, carrying a shotgun. When a figure comes walking toward them from the end of the street, the crowd cannot make out who it is in the dark. Charlie takes the gun and shoots the figure.
5. The mood is pleasant and calm. The mysterious power outage causes the mood to change.
6. Tommy triggers a line of thinking that eventually undoes the whole group. His mention of aliens gradually becomes a real possibility for some people, and then they act on it.
7. In their fear, they cannot accept the fact that they don't know the cause of this outage. They turn on each other because they want to find a culprit.
8. They become a mob when they accuse Les Goodman and follow him to his house. *"Now I suppose that's supposed to incriminate me! The light goes on and off."* There is no logical reason for accusing him, but they do.
9. The aliens know that the best way to destroy a human community is to set it against itself. The aliens plant the seed for disagreement, and people's fears grow into hostility toward one another.
10. By exciting hostility among people, the aliens split the community, making it ripe for conquest without bombs or any other type of weapon.

LITERARY ELEMENTS

1. One example is page 505, act I.
2. Act I ends just as the crowd has decided Goodman is the villain. He says they are "sick" and letting a "nightmare" begin. Ending act I here enables the audience to reflect on what is happening. The audience can contemplate what Goodman means by this "nightmare."

Additional Resources

Literary Elements Transparency 45

Literature and Writing

Writing About Literature

Students' explanations should

- identify the two forces in the main conflict
- identify other conflicts in the play
- support their ideas with specific references and tell why these forces are in conflict

Creative Writing

Students' messages should

- state what the aliens are trying to accomplish
- explain their strategy for accomplishing it
- summarize the effects of their strategy

Extending Your Response

Learning for Life Students might gather information on the story by answering the *where, when, who, why,* and *how* questions of good reporting as they plan their presentation. Encourage the groups to carefully plot their story and make sure that the anchor and reporters convey the necessary background information to their viewers. Group members portraying characters from the play should try to capture the appropriate character traits and emotions.

Literature Groups Students might focus on the "evidence" people used to accuse one another and on the issue of what constitutes being a "monster."

Literature and Writing

Writing About Literature

Thinking About Conflict **Conflict** is the struggle between two opposing forces at the center of a plot in a story or drama. What do you think is the main conflict in this teleplay? What other conflicts are portrayed? Write one or two paragraphs describing your ideas. Support your ideas with examples from the teleplay.

Creative Writing

From an Alien's Point of View Imagine that you are one of the aliens on the spacecraft. You are sending home a message about the events on Maple Street. Describe what you and your fellow aliens did and what happened as a result. Explain how you were able to get the "Earthlings" to accomplish your goals.

Extending Your Response

Learning for Life

News Broadcast Work with a group to prepare a television news report about the events on Maple Street. Decide at which point in the play your "live" report will take place. Divide the group into a TV anchor person, on-the-spot reporters, and characters from the play who will be interviewed. After rehearsing it, present your newscast to the class.

interNET CONNECTION

You can find out more about "The Twilight Zone," Rod Serling, and science fiction in general at many sites on the World Wide Web. Just type "twilight zone," "rod serling," or "science fiction" in the subject window of your search engine.

Literature Groups

Who Are the *Real* Monsters? "The Monsters Are Due on Maple Street" describes a neighborhood changed by fear. Do you agree with the author that human beings can be turned into "monsters"? Talk about the central question raised in this play: Who are the real monsters on Maple Street? How does fear change people? Support your ideas with examples from the play.

Reading Further

If you would like to read more by Rod Serling, try this book:

Stories from The Twilight Zone

Save your work for your portfolio.

Skill Minilesson

Reteach · Review

GRAMMAR AND LANGUAGE • APOSTROPHES

Do you know the difference between *its* and *it's?* The pronoun *its* shows possession. The word *it's* is a contraction of *it is.* The apostrophe (') in *it's* is used to indicate where the letter *i* has been left out.

Its setting is a typical American town. [possessive pronoun]

It's a drama about how fear destroys people's lives. [contraction of *it is*]

PRACTICE Write a paragraph describing "The Monsters Are Due on Maple Street" for someone who hasn't read it. Use the possessive pronoun *its* as well as the contraction *it's* in your paragraph.

- For more about using apostrophes, see **Language Handbook,** p. R19.

READING AND THINKING • VISUALIZING

A teleplay is meant to be seen on a screen. Therefore, when you read a teleplay, imagine that you are seeing the drama in your mind. Use the details to help you picture the different scenes as you read. Keep asking yourself:

How does this scene look? What is going on here? What is each character doing?

PRACTICE Work with a partner. Pick out one scene to read to your partner. As you read, your partner should draw a sketch showing what is going on in the scene. Then trade roles and draw a sketch as you listen to your partner read a different scene.

- For more about visualizing, see **Reading Handbook,** pp. R87–R88.

VOCABULARY • BASE WORDS

Base words are whole words that form the "base" of new words when prefixes or suffixes (or both) are attached to them. For example, *drama* is the base word in *dramatic* and *dramatize. Sure* is the base word in *unsure* and *surely.* Familiar base words can help you unlock the meanings of unfamiliar words. For example, *construct* is a good clue to the meaning of *unreconstructed,* and knowing the meaning of *specific* can help you understand *specification.*
Spelling tip: When a silent e comes at the end of a base word, the e is sometimes dropped when a suffix is added. For example: *judge → judging*

PRACTICE Use what you know about base words and familiar prefixes and suffixes to match each word on the left to its meaning.

1. undesirable	a. cannot be avoided
2. inescapable	b. not wanted
3. illogical	c. unable to be foretold
4. nonexistent	d. determining worth again
5. revaluation	e. that which surrounds
6. presuppose	f. senseless
7. encirclement	g. found nowhere
8. unpredictable	h. assume beforehand

Skill Minilessons

GRAMMAR AND LANGUAGE
MECHANICS: APOSTROPHES

Students' paragraphs should contain the use of *its* and *it's*.

READING AND THINKING
VISUALIZING

The quality of the sketches is less critical than the details they captured.

VOCABULARY
BASE WORDS

1. b 2. a 3. e 4. c 5. d

Additional Resources

- ***Grammar and Language Workbook,*** pp. 273–274
- ***Grammar and Composition Handbook,*** Lesson 13.7
- ***Writer's Choice,*** Lesson 20.7
- ***Reading Skills Practice Workbook***
- ***Vocabulary Practice,*** p. 21

ASSESSMENT

- ***Quick Checks,*** p. 45
- ***Selection and Theme Assessment,*** pp. 79–80
- ***Performance Assessment,*** p. 42
- ***Testmaker: ExamView Pro***
- ***Interactive Tutor: Self-Assessment***

MEDIA Connection

Objective

- To read and understand a Web site

Literature LINK

The Monsters Are Due on Maple Street This Web site connects to "The Monsters Are Due on Maple Street" (pp. 505–524). Explain to students that the Web site is a summary of Episode 42 of the television series *The Twilight Zone*, while the selection they have just read is a teleplay of an episode from the same series. In both episodes, characters' actions are dictated by a fear of the unusual and the unknown.

Analyzing Media

Explain, if necessary, the expression "Beauty is in the eye of the beholder," and ask students to discuss the appropriateness of the title.

1. Students may say that keeping the characters' faces hidden allows viewers to assume Janet Tyler is the disfigured one.
2. Students' summaries should be as brief and easy to follow as the *Twilight Zone* summary, which can serve as a model.

Additional Resources

Media Connections, p. 10

in TIME ***magazine***

MEDIA Connection

WEB SITE

"The Monsters Are Due on Maple Street" was written for the TV series *The Twilight Zone*. On some Web sites devoted to the series, you can find plot summaries of all the episodes. Here's an example.

The Eye of the Beholder

Address: http://www.the5thdimension.com/shows/

TWILIGHT ZONE

Episode 42 •
November 11, 1960

Janet Tyler is having her eleventh state-sponsored operation, the maximum allowed. The surgery is necessary because she is an outcast with a hideous face. The nurses commiserate with her, and her doctor is quite sympathetic. Janet believes the situation is hopeless and takes comfort in the bandages covering her face.

While talking with her doctor, Janet breaks down and starts crying because she just wants to look like everybody else and therefore enjoy the same privileges. However, if the surgery fails she will be forced to live in a village with other "freaks" away from normal society, which doesn't sit well with Janet, who calls it a "ghetto." She starts crying out against the state and pleads for her doctor to take off the bandages to see if the last experiment worked. He agrees to do so.

Slowly, the doctor starts to take off the bandages, layer by layer. The last layer is removed, the nurses cover their faces in horror, and the doctor drops his scissors: there has been no change. Janet Tyler raises her head, and appears to us to be quite beautiful. She tries to run and is pinned against the wall by her doctor and nurse, who turns on the light. The faces of the others are revealed: pig-like nose, protruding lips, bone outlines, they are the ones that are "normal." Janet escapes their grasps and runs down many hallways, eventually stopping in front of Walter Smith, a similar outcast who has come to take her to the village. He tries to remind her to always remember that beauty is in the eye of the beholder.

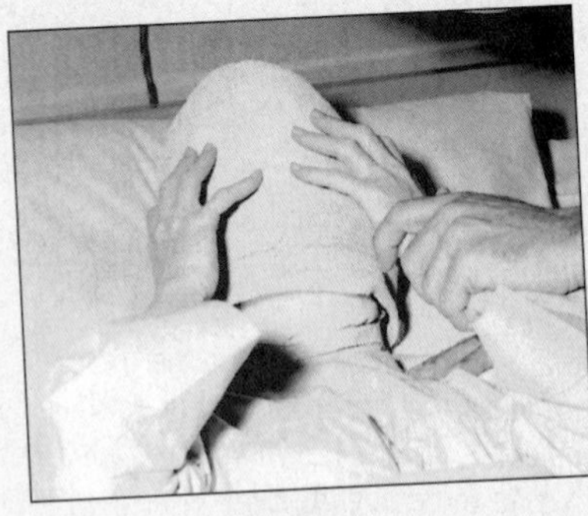

Analyzing Media

1. In your opinion, why did the scriptwriter keep all the characters' faces hidden from viewers until the end of the teleplay?
2. Write a summary of a TV drama or movie you have recently seen.

Teaching Support

The Twilight Zone Have students enter this title in the search engines to locate other Web sites devoted to this series.

Reading Minilesson

Setting a Purpose for Reading Have students discuss the difference between reading the teleplay "The Monsters Are Due on Maple Street" and reading Episode 42 of *The Twilight Zone*.

Activity Divide students into small groups. Have each group take one paragraph of Episode 42, "The Eye of the Beholder." Suggest that students read the paragraph carefully, mining it for details. Then ask them to list the details in a chart under *Dialogue, Cast of Characters,* and *Stage Directions.* **L2**

Additional Resources

Reading Skills Practice Workbook

Vo•cab•u•lar•y Skills

Idioms

When you step off a ladder, you put your foot down. When you firmly refuse to allow something, you put your foot down. In the first sentence, the words *put your foot down* have their ordinary, literal meaning. In the second, they do not. To "put one's foot down" is often used as an **idiom**—a word or phrase that has a special meaning different from the ordinary meaning of the word or words.

The English language contains many idioms. "He's on the ball." "She's really steamed." "They jumped the gun." "I'm all tied up." Many of them are so familiar they cause no problems. Unfamiliar idioms, however, can cause confusion.

There are two useful ways to figure out the meaning of an unfamiliar idiom. One is to think about what the ordinary meanings of the words suggest.

- If the father in "The Boy and His Grandfather" tried to defend his bad treatment of his own father, he wouldn't have a leg to stand on.

Even if you had never seen the underlined idiom, you could understand that it means not having any support. The father would have no basis for such a defense.

A second way to approach idioms is to use context clues.

- Mrs. Wang had never worked out a plan for using the river's power against the enemy; her action resulted from a spur of the moment decision.

Context clues in the sentence suggest that "spur of the moment" means the opposite of "planned in advance."

EXERCISE

Write a short definition of each underlined idiom.

1. The villagers know that their only hope for survival is to flee, so they get out while the getting is good.
2. It is useless to argue with the hard-nosed Mrs. Wang.
3. Once Mrs. Wang has decided to open the sluice, she lets no grass grow under her feet.
4. It isn't easy for Mrs. Wang to rescue the injured pilot, but she sees it through.
5. Who would expect a sudden flood across dry land? When the enemy soldiers see the mighty river boiling toward them, the sight will throw them for a loop.

Vo•cab•u•lar•y Skills

Objective

- To recognize and use idiomatic expressions correctly

Teaching Strategies

Have students list some of the idiomatic expressions they use or hear everyday. Encourage them to spend a day listening for the expressions they, their classmates, their teachers, and their family members use. Ask students to keep a few notecards and jot down the expressions as they hear them. Create a class dictionary of all the idiomatic expressions heard in one day.

Exercise

1. They get out while they can.
2. Mrs. Wang is stubborn.
3. She moves quickly.
4. She finishes the task.
5. The sight will shock them.

Additional Resources

Vocabulary Power

Teaching Support

MEETING INDIVIDUAL NEEDS — ENGLISH LANGUAGE LEARNERS

Idioms Students who are not yet proficient in English may find idioms particularly challenging.

Activity Have students work in mixed groups. Ask them to create flip books for the idioms by folding a piece of paper in half lengthwise and making three cuts in one half. Students should select four idioms from any selection and write them, and their own definitions, one on each of the four flaps. Encourage students to add humorous illustrations as well. Beneath each flap, students can copy the sentence from the selection in which the idiom appears, or write a new sentence using the idiom.

Additional Resources

English Language Learners Sourcebook, p. 73

Writing WORKSHOP

Objectives

- To create a definition essay of approximately 500–700 words
- To plan, draft, revise, edit, and present a definition essay
- To reflect on and assess the essay

GLENCOE TECHNOLOGY

WRITER'S ASSISTANT CD-ROM

Students can use Glencoe's templates and guidelines software for expository writing to aid them in working through the steps in the writing process in this lesson.

Teaching Strategies

PREWRITING

Choose a Character and a Quality Have students team up with partners to discuss the character traits and qualities that interest them most. Encourage them to talk to their partners about people from their own lives who possess these qualities. Suggest that they draw comparisons between a person they know and a character from one of the selections. Ask them to tell their partners something this person did or said that reveals an interesting personal quality.

Teaching Support

Writing WORKSHOP

Expository Writing: Definition Essay

What does loyalty mean to you? How would you define courage or cowardice, cruelty or compassion? To define a concept, you explain what it is and why it's important. You use examples to show your audience exactly what you mean.

Assignment: Follow the process explained in these pages to write an essay in which you define a personal quality. Use one or more of the characters from selections you've read in this book as examples to support your definition.

- As you write your expository essay, refer to the **Writing Handbook,** pp. R48–R61.

EVALUATION RUBRIC

By the time you complete this Writing Workshop, you will have

- written an essay that defines a personal quality
- captured readers' attention and stated your thesis in your introduction
- used real-life or fictional examples to explain the quality
- linked ideas with clear transitions
- restated your thesis in your conclusion
- written an essay free of errors in grammar, usage, and mechanics

The Writing Process

PREWRITING

PREWRITING TIP

To narrow down your selection of a quality to write about, look at the titles of the selections in the table of contents. As you glance at each title, try to recall the character or characters involved in the selection. Which ones can you remember most vividly? Which stand out as having a character trait you find appealing or especially interesting?

Choose a Character and a Quality

To find a topic for your essay, you can look through your journal or brainstorm with classmates. You can also ask yourself questions such as the following:

- What quality in a friend means the most to me? Which character shows that quality most or least?
- Which character do I remember best?
- Why has he or she stayed in my mind?
- What are his or her main qualities?

Choose one quality that you understand, admire, or consider important.

Rosa Parks

MEETING INDIVIDUAL NEEDS — ENGLISH LANGUAGE LEARNERS

Preparing for Definition Essays Help English language learners choose characters for their definition essays by creating a matching game.

Activity Have students work in small groups that include students at various levels of English proficiency. Ask each group to come up with a list of ten characters from the selections in this theme and write their names in a column numbered 1 to 10. Ask students to write one personal quality of each character in a second column, arranged A to J. Have students exchange papers and match each character with the appropriate trait.

Additional Resources

English Language Learners Sourcebook

Explore Your Ideas

You might start with a dictionary. Look up the quality you have chosen and copy the dictionary definition into your journal. Then, in a focused freewriting, move beyond that definition, using your own words. Explore what the quality means to you and how you've seen it demonstrated. Write about people or characters who show that quality.

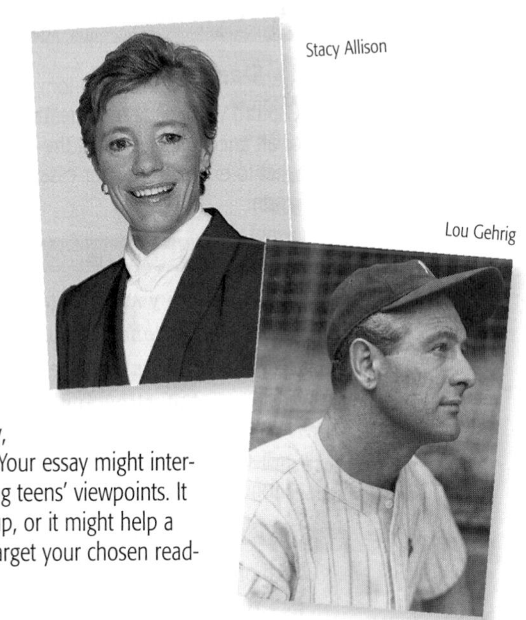

Stacy Allison

Lou Gehrig

Think About Audience and Purpose

Your teacher and classmates will read your essay, and you might aim at a wider audience as well. Your essay might interest a newspaper or magazine columnist exploring teens' viewpoints. It might inspire members of a special-interest group, or it might help a younger person learn about behavior choices. Target your chosen readers with writing that will appeal to them. Your purpose is to communicate to your audience what a certain personal quality means to you.

Plan Your Approach

Look over your prewriting notes and then create a sentence or two summing up your definition. This **thesis statement** will guide you as you plan and draft. Rough out the main points that will support your thesis statement. You might discuss what the quality is and isn't, how it affects people's lives, and what it means to you. To illustrate each point, write notes on examples of actions by a character in this theme and by people in real life.

Stacy Allison—Courageously climbed to top of Mount Everest on second attempt in spite of disappointing defeat on first try

Lou Gehrig—Showed courage in facing a life-threatening disease. Gave "lucky man" speech in Yankee Stadium when forced to quit baseball while still a young man

Rosa Parks—African American woman who showed courage in fighting against segregation in the early days of the Civil Rights movement

Explore Your Ideas In addition to the focused freewriting suggested on this page, students may wish to build on their ideas by creating an acrostic, using the quality they have chosen to explore. Suggest that they write the word (*honesty,* for example) vertically and use each letter as part of a new word, phrase, or character name they wish to include in their essays.

Think About Audience and Purpose Remind students that if they are interested in publishing their essays in a newspaper or magazine, they may want to consider using well-known figures from public life as examples of their qualities. They will need to provide background information if they draw entirely from reading selections, since many readers will be unfamiliar with the characters.

Plan Your Approach If students are having difficulty planning their essays, suggest that they make a list of questions to answer when they write. For example:

- What quality will I define?
- Why have I chosen this quality?
- What does the quality mean to me?
- How does it affect my life?
- Have I ever met or read about a person who possesses this quality?

Additional Resources

Writing and Proofreading Practice, pp. 1–7, 35–42

Writing and Proofreading Transparencies 1–6, 17–18, 33–34

Writer's Choice, Lesson 5.4

MEETING INDIVIDUAL NEEDS — MULTIPLE MODES OF EXPRESSION

Logical/Mathematical Students who enjoy applying logical structure to their work may wish to plan and organize their definition essays on a three-pronged pitchfork graphic.

Activity Draw a three-pronged horizontal pitchfork on the board to model the use of this graphic. On the handle of the pitchfork, write the name of a personal quality, such as *loyalty*. On each of the three prongs, write a word or phrase about the topic, such as *Something I Admire; Mrs. Wang; Actions That Show Loyalty.* These serve as themes for students to develop in the main paragraphs of their essays. Encourage students to continue creating prongs until they have included all the information they plan to cover in their definition essays. **L2**

Theme Assessment

Objectives

- To offer a personal response to the selections, discussions, and activities in this theme
- To write a comparison of two characters
- To complete a self-evaluation, set a goal, and devise a plan for achieving the goal

Responding to the Theme

1. Students should be able to support their choices.
2. Accept all reasonable answers.
3. Allow time for students to share their interviews, presentations, and flowcharts with the class.

Analyzing Literature

Students' writing should include

- an introductory paragraph that identifies the two characters and the selection(s) the characters come from
- a comparison of the characters' problems and their ways of responding to them
- examples and quotations from the text

Evaluate and Set Goals

Evaluate

Have each student compile a list of activities completed for each task. Suggest that they add other tasks as well, such as accessing a Web site.

Set Goals

Have each student create a web to record their goals and the steps for achieving them. Discuss students' goals and plans in individual conferences.

AT THE CROSSROADS

Theme Assessment

Responding to the Theme

1. Which story, poem, or play in this theme most helped you think about the kinds of crossroads people face at certain times in their lives? Explain your answer.
2. What new ideas do you have about the following as a result of reading the literature in this theme?
   - the points in people's lives when they must make difficult choices
   - how people go about making decisions when faced with a problem
3. Present your theme project to the class.

Analyzing Literature

COMPARE CHARACTERS

Compare two characters from this theme. You may compare the problems they encounter and how they respond to those problems. Remember to support your opinions with examples and quotations from the selections.

Evaluate and Set Goals

1. Which of the following tasks was most rewarding to you? Which was most difficult?
   - reading and thinking about selections
   - doing independent writing
   - analyzing the stories, poems, and teleplay in discussions
   - performing dramatizations
   - making presentations
   - doing research
2. Using the following scale, how would you assess your work in this unit? Give at least two reasons for your assessment.

   4 = outstanding — 2 = fair
   3 = good — 1 = weak
3. Based on what you found difficult in this theme, choose a goal to work toward in the next theme.
   - Write down your goal and three steps you will take to help you reach it.
   - Meet with your teacher to review your goal and your plan for achieving it.

Build Your Portfolio

SELECT

Select two pieces of work you did during this theme to include in your portfolio. Use the following questions to help you decide.

- ✦ Which work do you consider your best?
- ✦ From which work did you learn the most?
- ✦ Which work did you enjoy the most?

REFLECT

Write some notes to accompany the work you selected. Use these questions as guides.

- ✦ What do you like best about the piece?
- ✦ What did you learn from creating it?
- ✦ What might you do differently if you were beginning this piece again?

ASSESSMENT

Writing Assessment and Portfolio Management

- Writing Assessment, pp. 1–12
- Portfolio Management, pp. 39–45

GLENCOE TECHNOLOGY

MINDJOGGER VIDEOQUIZZES VIDEODISC

Use *MindJogger* to review the Theme 5 content.

Theme 5
Side B

Also available in VHS.

Reading on Your Own

Have you enjoyed reading the literature in this theme?
If so, here are some other books you might like.

The Slave Dancer

by Paula Fox Jesse is kidnapped and forced to serve on a slave ship. He witnesses the horrors of slavery while providing music as the slaves are forced to exercise to keep themselves strong so they will remain "profitable investments."

Sounder

by William Armstrong This award-winning novel deals with the hard lives of African American sharecroppers in the rural South a century ago and with a young boy's growth in understanding with the help of the family's devoted dog.

Father Figure

by Richard Peck Jim's role as a substitute father for his younger brother is threatened when, after their mother's death, the boys are sent to spend the summer with their long-absent father.

Running Out of Time

by Margaret Peterson Haddix This exciting thriller tells the story of a thirteen-year-old girl who makes a decision to escape from her community in order to save her family and friends.

Reading on Your Own

Tips for Independent Reading
Stress the importance of each student's spending at least thirty minutes a day in independent reading and suggest books, such as those shown here, related to this theme.

Visualizing The novels on this page would lend themselves well to dramatization, so they make for exciting reading when students visualize the stories. Visualizing requires

- paying close attention to imagery and details
- picturing a scene's sights, smells, feelings, sounds, and tastes
- imagining a character's voice, appearance, expressions, and actions

Practice Ask students to select a favorite passage from one of the stories or narrative poems in this theme and look for imagery and details that helped in visualizing a character or a setting.

Glencoe Literature Library

The Slave Dancer and ***Sounder*** are available in the *Glencoe Literature Library*. For a complete list of titles, see the *Glencoe Resources for Independent Reading* in the front of this book.

The *Glencoe Literature Library Study Guide* provides instructional support and activities for works in the *Glencoe Literature Library*.

At the MOVIES

Be sure to preview the following video for appropriateness for your class.

- ***Sounder*** (1972, 105 minutes, G)

SPECIAL NEEDS

You may wish to recommend *Sounder* by William Armstrong to students who are less-proficient readers. The simple, eloquent writing style makes this book appropriate for these students. **L1**

The following books are rated for average readers (**L2**) or for students who need more challenging reading material (**L3**):

- *The Slave Dancer* by Paula Fox **L2**
- *Father Figure* by Richard Peck **L2**
- *Running Out of Time* by Margaret Peterson Haddix **L3**

Additional Resources
Inclusion Strategies

Standardized Test Practice

Test-Taking Tip

Students are often prone to misspelling words with affixes. By isolating the base and affix in each word, students can more easily recognize exactly which affix and base are being combined. If students break a word down into its base and affix, they'll be less likely to feel that these words are spelled arbitrarily and more likely to see the reason for the correct spelling.

Answers and Analyses

Students should recognize that

1. C The correct spelling is *microphone.* Students should be able to recognize that the base word, *phone,* is misspelled.
2. L The correct spelling is *unnatural.* Students should recognize the prefix *un-* and the base word *natural.* The complete spelling of the word *natural* must remain intact. Ask students to take note that the *n* is not dropped.
3. A The correct spelling is *unbelievable.* Remind students that a silent e is dropped when a suffix beginning with a vowel is added.
4. J The correct spelling is *illegal.* The prefix *il-* is being combined with the base word *legal.*
5. D The correct spelling is *decimal.*
6. L The correct spelling is *peacefully.* Although *peaceful* has only one l, the suffix *-ly* is being added to it. Therefore, both the suffix and base word should remain intact.

Standardized Test Practice

Read the phrase in each numbered item. Choose the phrase in which the italicized word is NOT spelled correctly.

1 A the *librarian's* desk
B to wait *patiently*
C a broken *microphon*
D pieces of *unlined* paper

2 J *boyish* charm
K *inscribed* her name
L an *unatural* color
M *rebuild* the shed

3 A told an *unbelieveable* story
B good *insulation* in the attic
C known for his *kindness*
D ate only *nonfat* desserts

4 J made an *ilegal* play
K to *repay* completely
L a *valuable* painting
M *reappearing* in an instant

5 A *superhuman* efforts
B a *terrific* sport
C *semisweet* chocolate
D the *deccimal* system

6 J on a *tripod*
K riding a *unicycle*
L to sleep *peacefuly*
M a talented *violinist*

7 A *prettyest* time of year
B *exchange* this blouse
C a *childhood* friend
D passed the *examination*

8 J making *inconsiderate* remarks
K *tropical* plants in the garden
L to *missdial* a number
M *unforgivable* behavior

Meeting Individual Needs — ENGLISH LANGUAGE LEARNERS

Spelling and Pronunciation Spelling and pronunciation go hand in hand. As a class, read through each test question. Ask volunteers to identify which word is spelled incorrectly. Once the misspelled word has been identified, ask a volunteer to spell the word correctly on the board and then pronounce it.

9 A a *mercyless* judge
B end of the *decade*
C *rewrite* this paragraph
D *antibacterial* soap

10 J *leadership* training
K *accidently* broke the vase
L musical *conductor*
M an *inactive* account

11 A *biweekly* meetings
B *global* warming
C near the Bermuda *Triangle*
D *preveiws* of coming attractions

12 J going on *vacasion*
K watch *television*
L good *nutrition*
M on a *mission*

13 A a *sensible* shoe
B an unfortunate *dissagreement*
C *darkness* descended
D *returning* at noon

14 J a bowl of *indigestible* noodles
K drawn with a *superfine* point
L out of *alinement*
M *copiloting* the plane

15 A an *extrordinary* idea
B *biography* of a hero
C to a painless *dentist*
D in a yellow *submarine*

16 J *flexible* rules
K through a powerful *telescope*
L a *pleasureable* afternoon
M *postponing* the race again

Answers and Analyses

7. A The correct spelling is *prettiest.* Have students take note that many words ending in y are altered when a suffix is added. Consider reviewing these rules with them.

8. L The correct spelling is *misdial.* The prefix *mis-* is being combined with the base word *dial.*

9. B The correct spelling is *merciless.* As with question 7, the spelling of this word follows the rules for base words that end in *y.*

10. K The correct spelling is *accidentally.* The suffix *-ly* is being added to the word *accidental.*

11. D The correct spelling is *previews.* The word *views* is misspelled.

12. J The correct spelling is *vacation.* This question illustrates how the suffixes *-tion* and *-sion* can sound similar at the end of a word.

13. B The correct spelling is *disagreement.* The prefix *dis-* and the suffix *-ment* are added to the base word *agree.*

14. L The correct spelling is *alignment.* The base word *align* is misspelled.

15. A The correct spelling is *extraordinary.* This is a compound word. In this case, both base words, *extra* and *ordinary,* keep their spellings.

16. L The correct spelling is *pleasurable.* The silent *-e* at the end of *pleasure* is dropped when the suffix -able is added.

The Princeton Review — Test-Taking Tip

Remind students that the best way to improve their spelling is to read and observe the spellings of words. Tell students to look up difficult words in the dictionary and to keep a list of these difficult words so they can practice them.

Tested Objectives

Item	Language Objective
1 - 6	Spelling: spell derivatives correctly by applying the spellings of bases and affixes

MORE PRACTICE

For additional practice, assign practice pages from one of the following standardized test resources available as part of Glencoe Literature.

Additional Resources
ITBS Preparation and Practice
SAT-9 Preparation and Practice
Terra Nova Preparation and Practice

Theme 6 At a Glance

Twists and Turns

THEME OPENING

- **Introducing the Theme** (p. 539)
- **Exploring the Theme** (p. 540)
- **Theme Projects** (p. 541)

Theme 6: TWISTS AND TURNS

SELECTIONS

Media Connection: Calvin and Hobbes (p. 542)

Charles (p. 543)

No News (p. 543)

Who's On First (p. 554)

After Twenty Years (p. 564)

The Million-Pound Bank Note (p. 572)

The Force of Luck (p. 590)

Beware of the Dog (p. 602)

Active Reading Model: The Highwayman (p. 620)

Annabel Lee (p. 628)

Media Connection: ***from*** **My Ninety Years** (p. 634)

The Cremation of Sam McGee (p. 635)

SKILL FEATURES

Grammar Link (p. 553)

Technology Skills (pp. 562–563)

Listening, Speaking, and Viewing (p. 571)

Interdisciplinary Connection (p. 601)

Genre Focus: Poetry (pp. 616–617)

Active Reading Strategies (pp. 618–619)

Vocabulary Skills (p. 633)

Reading and Thinking Skills (p. 643)

WRITING WORKSHOP

Narrative Writing: Short Story (pp. 644–647)

THEME ASSESSMENT

- **Responding to the Theme, Analyzing Literature, Evaluate and Set Goals** (p. 648)
- **Build Your Portfolio** (p. 648)
- **Reading on Your Own** (p. 649)
  - *The Adventures of Tom Sawyer* by Mark Twain
  - *The Oxford Book of Story Poems* edited by Michael Harrison and Christopher Stuart-Clark
  - *The One Who Came Back* by Joan Mazzio
  - *Talking to the Sun* selected by Kenneth Koch and Kate Farrell
- **Standardized Test Practice** (pp. 650–651)

KEYS TO LITERARY CONNECTIONS

Comparing Selections

The **Comparing Selections** feature in this theme provides opportunities for addressing diverse aspects of the reading and literature curriculum.

For example, in Comparing Selections on page 600, students take a closer look at the characters and plots of "The Million-Pound Bank Note" by Mark Twain and "The Force of Luck" by Rudolfo A. Anaya. Through this comparison, students can gain insight into human instinct and motivation.

World Literature

The Student Edition contains a variety of literature that represents cultures from around the world. World literature selections are highlighted with the icon above.

TEACHING SUPPORT

The Teaching Support offers a wealth of interactive instructional support:

Meeting Individual Needs
- Special Needs
- English Language Learners
- Multiple Modes of Expression
- Advanced Learners

Internet Connection

Assessment

Portfolio Options

Minilessons
- Grammar and Language
- Reading
- Writing
- Listening and Speaking

Connecting to Other Selections

Real-World Connection

Interdisciplinary Connection

Life Skills Connection

Family and Community Activity

Key to Ability Levels

The activities throughout this theme have been coded for students of various abilities.

L1 BASIC activities for all students

L2 AVERAGE activities for average to above-average students

L3 ADVANCED LEARNERS activities for above-average students

Teaching Today

The Glencoe *Teaching Today* professional development Web site at www.teachingtoday.glencoe.com features daily teaching tips, free downloads, annotated Web resources, educational news, and a wealth of information on a wide range of topics.

Reading Skills in this theme

Variety of Texts

In addition to poetry, this theme includes the following text types:

- short story
- folktale
- comedy script
- drama
- cartoon strip
- oral history

Comprehension Skills

The following instructional support for comprehension skills appears in this theme of the Student Edition:

- **Reading and Thinking Minilessons** (pp. 552, 615, 642)
- **Active Reading Strategies and Model** (pp. 618–627)
- **Identifying Cause-and-Effect Relationships** (p. 643)

See also the **Reading Minilessons** throughout the theme in this Teacher Wraparound Edition.

For strategies for reading longer works, such as novels and novellas, see "Tips for Independent Reading" on page 649.

Reading Resources

Active Reading Guide The ***Active Reading Guide*** provides graphic organizers and study guide questions to support students' reading of each selection. (***Active Reading Guide***, pp. 46–54)

Interactive Reading Sourcebook and **Interactive Reading Workbook** The ***Interactive Reading Sourcebook*** and ***Interactive Reading Workbook*** offer focused comprehension strategies and lessons on critical thinking skills as well as fluency practice and activities to teach and support phonics, decoding, spelling, and vocabulary development.

Vocabulary Power The ***Vocabulary Power*** workbook (Lessons 24-28) provides systematic teaching, practice, and assessment of vocabulary for better reading comprehension.

Audio Library Available on audiocassette and on CD, the ***Audio Library*** provides valuable comprehension support.

Glencoe Literature Library Each title in the ***Glencoe Literature Library*** includes a full-length work plus related readings. A separate Study Guide is available for each title.

Five–Star Stories These anthologies of familiar short stories adapted and abridged for a variety of reading levels include exercises to help increase students' vocabulary and improve their reading comprehension.

The Contemporary Readers ***The Contemporary Readers*** are nonfiction books linked to various themes and designed for developing readers from a wide range of backgrounds.

Literature Classics CD-ROM The selections on this CD-ROM can be searched by author, theme, or genre.

inTIME and Humanities Across TIME Coproductions of Glencoe and Time, Inc., these resources include a wealth of high-interest nonfiction related to the selections in this theme.

Assessment in this theme

Assessment in the Student Edition

This program offers a number of diverse ways to evaluate student understanding and skill proficiency. In the Student Edition, use the following:

- **Responding to Literature**
  Following each selection, students are asked to recall facts, interpret ideas, and evaluate concepts as they answer a variety of questions and complete activities to extend their understanding.
- **Theme Assessment (pp. 648–649)**
  Here students respond to the selections on personal and analytical levels. They also assume ownership of their learning by setting and evaluating goals and by selecting work for their portfolios.

See also the many **Assessment Resources** listed on the facing page.

Standardized Test Practice

The Princeton Review has developed the Standardized Test Practice pages found at the end of this thematic unit (pp. 650–651). For additional practice, direct students to the following resources:

- ITBS Preparation and Practice
- SAT-9 Preparation and Practice
- TerraNova Preparation and Practice

Writing Skills in this theme

Writing Skills

The Student Edition of Theme Six offers strong instructional support for writing skills:

In **Extending Your Response**, which follows each selection:

- **Writing About Literature**
- **Personal/Creative Writing**

See also the **Writing Minilessons** throughout the theme in this Teacher Wraparound Edition.

Writing Workshops

Theme Six concludes with a **Writing Workshop** that guides students through the process of writing an autobiographical anecdote (pp. 644–647).

Writing Resources

Writer's Assistant CD-ROM Each **Writing Workshop** is supplemented by an interactive writing guide on the ***Writer's Assistant*** CD-ROM. This easy- to-use writing guide provides prompts, templates, and other tools that lead students through the writing process.

Grammar and Composition Handbook The ***Grammar and Composition Handbook*** (Lessons 10.4-11.7) provides systematic instruction in English language conventions.

Spelling Power The ***Spelling Power*** workbook (Lessons 21-24) provides systematic teaching, practice, and assessment of spelling to help students become better spellers and thus enhance their writing.

Writing and Proofreading Practice Blackline masters present in-depth instruction and practice on a specific step in the writing process and proofreading (pp. 1–7, 43–49).

Writing and Proofreading Transparencies Transparencies provide graphic organizers and proofreading exercises for whole-class instruction (pp. 1–6, 21–22, 35–36).

Research and Report Writing Guide This resource provides extensive tips and activities to guide students in their writing projects in the literature classroom as well as in classes across the curriculum.

Style and Documentation Sourcebook for Writers This sourcebook is a combination reference and workbook, giving students the most up-to-date information and guidance regarding traditional as well as technological research strategies and documentation.

Revising with Style This resource offers instruction and exercises focusing on the revision process and covering topics from proofreading and correcting common grammatical errors to sentence combining and reordering.

Assessment Resources

Selection Quick Checks For each selection, a **Quick Check** of three to five short-answer questions measures students' literal comprehension.

Selection and Theme Assessment The ***Selection and Theme Assessment*** instrument tests students' abilities to recall, interpret, and evaluate what they've read. The tests consist of multiple-choice, short answer, and essay questions.

Performance Assessment Alternative assessment instruments and rubrics for Theme Six are found in the ***Performance Assessment*** ancillary.

Writing Assessment and Portfolio Management These notes and strategies, student models, and assessment tools assist with the task of measuring students' progress as writers and as monitors of their own writing.

Testmaker: ExamView Pro Teachers can customize selection and Theme Six tests by accessing the ***Testmaker*** database.

Interactive Tutor: Self-Assessment The ***Interactive Tutor: Self-Assessment*** software provides multiple-choice tests with immediate feedback to help students evaluate their knowledge and understanding of each literature selection.

MindJogger Videoquizzes Using a popular game show format, ***MindJogger Videoquizzes*** on videocassettes enable teachers to evaluate student understanding of Theme Six in a quick and fun manner.

Theme 6 RESOURCE MANAGER

Lessons	Essential Resources		English Language Learners
Charles SHIRLEY JACKSON **No News** CONNIE REGAN-BLAKE AND BARBARA FREEMAN PACING: 2 DAYS	**Lesson-Specific Instruction** Selection Focus Transp. 46 Active Reading Guide,* p. 46 Literary Elements Transp. 46 Vocabulary Practice, p. 32 Quick Checks,* p. 46 Selection and Theme Assessment, pp. 81–82 Testmaker: ExamView Pro Performance Assessment, p. 43	**Systematic Language Instruction** Grammar and Comp. Hbk., L.10.4 Vocabulary Power, Lesson 24 Spelling Power, Lesson 21	English Language Learners Sourcebook, p. 74 Spanish Summaries, p. 46 Audio Library* English, Yes!
Who's on First? BUD ABBOTT AND LOU COSTELLO PACING: 2 DAYS	**Lesson-Specific Instruction** Selection Focus Transp. 47 Active Reading Guide,* p. 47 Literary Elements Transp. 47 Quick Checks,* p. 47 Selection and Theme Assessment, p. 83 Testmaker: ExamView Pro Performance Assessment, p. 44	**Systematic Language Instruction** Grammar and Comp. Hbk., L.10.5	English Language Learners Sourcebook, p. 75 Spanish Summaries, p. 47 Audio Library* English, Yes!
After Twenty Years O. HENRY PACING: 1 DAY	**Lesson-Specific Instruction** Selection Focus Transp. 48 Active Reading Guide,* p. 48 Literary Elements Transp. 48 Vocabulary Practice, p. 33 Quick Checks,* p. 48 Selection and Theme Assessment, p. 84	Testmaker: ExamView Pro Performance Assessment, p. 48 **Systematic Language Instruction** Grammar and Comp. Hbk., L.11.1 Vocabulary Power, Lesson 25 Spelling Power, Lesson 22	English Language Learners Sourcebook, pp. 76, 77 Theme Six Planning Guide, p. 20 Spanish Summaries, p. 48 Spanish Translations, pp. 139–141 Audio Library* English, Yes!
The Million-Pound Bank Note MARK TWAIN PACING: 3 DAYS	**Lesson-Specific Instruction** Selection Focus Transp. 49 Active Reading Guide,* p. 49 Literary Elements Transp. 49 Vocabulary Practice, p. 34 Quick Checks,* p. 49 Selection and Theme Assessment, pp. 85–86	Testmaker: ExamView Pro Performance Assessment, p. 46 **Systematic Language Instruction** Grammar and Comp. Hbk., L.11.2	English Language Learners Sourcebook, p. 78 Spanish Summaries, p. 49 Spanish Translations, pp. 142–157 Audio Library* English, Yes!
The Force of Luck RUDOLFO A. ANAYA PACING: 2 DAYS	**Lesson-Specific Instruction** Selection Focus Transp. 50 Active Reading Guide,* p. 50 Literary Elements Transp. 50 Vocabulary Practice, p. 35 Quick Checks,* p. 50 Selection and Theme Assessment, pp. 87–88	Testmaker: ExamView Pro Performance Assessment, p. 47 **Systematic Language Instruction** Grammar and Comp. Hbk., L.11.3 Vocabulary Power, Lesson 26 Spelling Power, Lesson 23	English Language Learners Sourcebook, p. 79 Spanish Summaries, p. 50 Audio Library* English, Yes!

Key: Workbook Blackline Masters Textbook Transparency CD-ROM Videodisk (also available in videocassette)

Special Needs/ Strategic Intervention	Reteaching and Enrichment
Interactive Reading Sourcebook, pp. T172–T174 Interactive Reading Workbook, pp. 89–90 Inclusion Strategies Sourcebook, pp. 71–72 Theme Six Planning Guide, p. 6 Audio Library*	Fine Art Transparency 23 Reading Skills Practice Workbook, pp. 81–82 Grammar and Language Transp. 45 Gr. and Lang. Wkbk., pp. 107–108, 255–256, 259–260, 273–274 Grammar and Comp. Hbk., L.4.2, 13.2–13.4, 13.7 Media Connection Activities, p. 11 Interactive Tutor: Self-Assessment Vocabulary PuzzleMaker Web Site (lit.glencoe.com)
Interactive Reading Sourcebook, pp. T175–T177 Interactive Reading Workbook, pp. 91–92 Inclusion Strategies Sourcebook, pp. 43–44 Theme Six Planning Guide, p. 12 Audio Library*	Literature Launchers, Side B, Segment 16 Reading Skills Practice Workbook, pp. 83–84 Grammar and Language Transp. 46 Gr. and Lang. Wkbk., pp. 227–228, 295–296 Grammar and Comp. Hbk., L.15.1 TIME *Humanities Across TIME*, Cover 1 Interactive Tutor: Self-Assessment Vocabulary PuzzleMaker Web Site (lit.glencoe.com)
Interactive Reading Sourcebook, pp. T177–T179 Interactive Reading Workbook, pp. 93–94 Inclusion Strategies Sourcebook, pp. 51–52, 95–96 Theme Six Planning Guide, p. 20 Audio Library*	Fine Art Transparency 11 Reading Skills Practice Workbook, pp. 85–86 Grammar and Language Transp. 47 Gr. and Lang. Wkbk., pp. 157–158 Grammar and Comp. Hbk., L.8.3 Interactive Tutor: Self-Assessment Vocabulary PuzzleMaker Web Site (lit.glencoe.com)
Interactive Reading Sourcebook, pp. T180–T183 Interactive Reading Workbook, pp. 95–98 Inclusion Strategies Sourcebook, pp. 83–84 Theme Six Planning Guide, p. 28 Audio Library*	Literature Launchers, Side B, Segment 17 Reading Skills Practice Workbook, pp. 87–88 Grammar and Language Transp. 48 Gr. and Lang. Wkbk., pp. 257–258 Grammar and Comp. Hbk., L.13.3 Interactive Tutor: Self-Assessment Vocabulary PuzzleMaker Web Site (lit.glencoe.com)
Interactive Reading Sourcebook, pp. T183–T185 Interactive Reading Workbook, pp. 99–100 Inclusion Strategies Sourcebook, pp. 85–86 Audio Library*	Fine Art Transparency 26 Reading Skills Practice Workbook, pp. 89–90 Grammar and Language Transp. 49 Gr. and Lang. Wkbk., pp. 51–52 Grammar and Comp. Hbk., L. 1.3 Interactive Tutor: Self-Assessment Vocabulary PuzzleMaker Web Site (lit.glencoe.com)

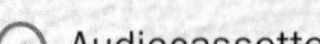

Web   Audiocassette   Diskette   *Also available in Spanish

Independent Reading

Encourage students to spend thirty minutes each day in independent reading. The following Glencoe components and outside resources provide opportunities for reading related to this theme.

The Glencoe Literature Library

You may want to assign one or more of these titles for independent reading. For a complete listing of titles available in the Glencoe Literature Library, see page T96 of this book.

- *The Adventures of Tom Sawyer* by Mark Twain
- *A Christmas Carol* by Charles Dickens
- *The House of Dies Drear* by Virginia Hamilton
- *Tuck Everlasting* by Natalie Babbitt
- *The True Confessions of Charlotte Doyle* by Avi

inTIME News stories, feature articles, reviews, profiles, and essays in the magazine connect to an author, work, or theme in the Student Edition. See the **inTIME Teacher's Guide** for specific connections to this theme.

Resources for Less-Proficient Readers

For reading especially created for less-proficient readers, suggest

- *Five-Star Stories*
- *The Contemporary Readers*

Additional Resources for Independent Reading

The following titles are listed with specific reading selections throughout this theme. You may want to suggest that students look for these in your local or school library.

- *The Laugh Book* compiled by Joanna Cole and Stephanie Calmenson
- *Incognito Mosquito* by E. A. Hass
- *The Best Short Stories of O. Henry*
- *The Prince and the Pauper* by Mark Twain
- *A Connecticut Yankee in King Arthur's Court* by Mark Twain
- *Baseball in April and Other Stories* by Gary Soto
- *Over to You: Ten Stories of Flyers and Flying* by Roald Dahl
- *Great Tales and Poems of Edgar Allan Poe*
- *The Best of Robert Service*
- *The Oxford Book of Story Poems* edited by Michael Harrison and Christopher Stuart-Clark
- *Talking to the Sun* selected by Kenneth Koch and Kate Farrell
- *The One Who Came Back* by Joann Mazzio

Theme 6 RESOURCE MANAGER (continued)

Lessons	Essential Resources	English Language Learners
BEWARE OF THE DOG Roald Dahl Pacing: 2 Days	**Lesson-Specific Instruction** Selection Focus Transp. 51 Active Reading Guide,* p. 51 Literary Elements Transp. 51 Vocabulary Practice, p. 36 Quick Checks,* p. 51 Selection and Theme Assessment, pp. 89–90 Testmaker: ExamView Pro Performance Assessment, p. 48 **Systematic Language Instruction** Grammar and Comp. Hbk., L.11.4 Vocabulary Power, Lesson 27 Spelling Power, Lesson 24	English Language Learners Sourcebook, p. 80 Spanish Summaries, p. 51 Spanish Translations, pp. 158–165 Audio Library* English, Yes!
The Highwayman Alfred Noyes Pacing: 2 Days	**Lesson-Specific Instruction** Selection Focus Transp. 52 Active Reading Guide,* p. 52 Literary Elements Transp. 52 Quick Checks,* p. 52 Selection and Theme Assessment, pp. 91–92 Testmaker: ExamView Pro Performance Assessment, p. 49 **Systematic Language Instruction** Grammar and Comp. Hbk., L.11.5 Vocabulary Power, Lesson 28	English Language Learners Sourcebook, p. 81 Spanish Summaries, p. 52 Audio Library* English, Yes!
ANNABEL LEE Edgar Allan Poe Pacing: 2 Days	**Lesson-Specific Instruction** Selection Focus Transp. 53 Active Reading Guide,* p. 53 Literary Elements Transp. 53 Quick Checks,* p. 53 Selection and Theme Assessment, p. 93 Testmaker: ExamView Pro Performance Assessment, p. 50 **Systematic Language Instruction** Grammar and Comp. Hbk., L.11.6	English Language Learners Sourcebook, p. 82 Theme Six Planning Guide, p. 60 Spanish Summaries, p. 53 Audio Library* English, Yes!
THE CREMATION OF SAM MCGEE Robert W. Service Pacing: 2 Days	**Lesson-Specific Instruction** Selection Focus Transp. 54 Active Reading Guide,* p. 54 Literary Elements Transp. 54 Quick Checks,* p. 54 Selection and Theme Assessment, p. 94 Testmaker: ExamView Pro Performance Assessment, p. 51 **Systematic Language Instruction** Grammar and Comp. Hbk., L.11.7 Vocabulary Power, Unit 6 Review/Test Spelling Power, Unit 6 Review/Proofreading	English Language Learners Sourcebook, p. 83 Spanish Summaries, p. 54 Spanish Translations, pp. 166–170 Audio Library* English, Yes!
Writing WORKSHOP Narrative Writing: Short Story Pacing: 2 Days	**Lesson-Specific Instruction** Writing Assessment and Portfolio Management, pp. 1–13, 29–31, 38–45	English Language Learners Sourcebook, p. 9 English, Yes!

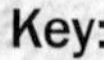

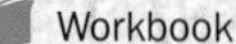

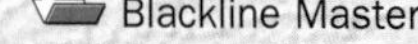

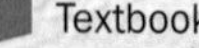

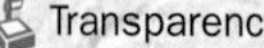

Special Needs/ Strategic Intervention	Reteaching and Enrichment
Interactive Reading Sourcebook, pp. T186–T188 Interactive Reading Workbook, pp. 101–102 Inclusion Strategies Sourcebook, pp. 87–88 Theme Six Planning Guide, p. 44 Audio Library*	Literature Launchers, Side B, Segment 18 Fine Art Transparency 13 Reading Skills Practice Workbook, pp. 91–92 Grammar and Language Transp. 50 Gr. and Lang. Wkbk., pp. 155–156, 223–224 Grammar and Comp. Hbk., L.3.11, 3.12, 8.2 Interactive Tutor: Self-Assessment Vocabulary PuzzleMaker Web Site (lit.glencoe.com)
Interactive Reading Sourcebook, pp. T188–T190 Interactive Reading Workbook, pp. 103–104 Inclusion Strategies Sourcebook, pp. 43–44, 45–46 Theme Six Planning Guide, p. 52 Audio Library*	Reading Skills Practice Workbook, pp. 93–94 Grammar and Language Transp. 51 Gr. and Lang. Wkbk., pp. 117–118, 153–154 Grammar and Comp. Hbk., L.5.1, 14.1 Interactive Tutor: Self-Assessment Vocabulary PuzzleMaker Web Site (lit.glencoe.com)
Interactive Reading Sourcebook, pp. T191–T193 Interactive Reading Workbook, pp. 105–106 Theme Six Planning Guide, p. 60 Audio Library*	Gr. and Lang. Wkbk., pp. 253–254 Grammar and Comp. Hbk., L.13.1 Interactive Tutor: Self-Assessment Vocabulary PuzzleMaker Web Site (lit.glencoe.com)
Interactive Reading Sourcebook, pp. T193–T196 Interactive Reading Workbook, pp. 107–108 Inclusion Strategies Sourcebook, pp. 25–26, 67–68 Theme Six Planning Guide, p. 65 Audio Library*	Reading Skills Practice Workbook, pp. 95–96 Grammar and Language Transp. 52 Gr. and Lang. Wkbk., pp. 265–266 Grammar and Comp. Hbk., L.13.5 Media Connection Activities, p. 12 Interactive Tutor: Self-Assessment Vocabulary PuzzleMaker Web Site (lit.glencoe.com)
Inclusion Strategies Sourcebook, pp. 73–74	Writing and Proofreading Practice, pp. 1–7, 43–49 Writing and Proofreading Transparencies 1–6, 21–22, 35–36 Revising with Style Writer's Assistant

Theme RESOURCES

To explore the theme further, you may want to use these resources:

- Listening and Speaking Activities (pp. 16–18)
- Viewing and Representing Activities (pp. 1–6, 22–24)
- Critical Thinking Skills (pp. 15–17)
- Media Connection Activities (pp. 11–12)
- Interdisciplinary Activities (pp. 22–25)
- Family and Community Activities (p. 16)
- Selection and Theme Assessment (pp. 135–136)
- Performance Assessment, pp. 74, 98

TIME Humanities Across TIME

See also these additional theme planning resources:

- Theme Six Planning Guide
- Interactive Reading Sourcebook
- Literature Groups Sourcebook
- Interactive Lesson Planner
- Interactive Teacher Edition
- Glencoe Web Site <lit.glencoe.com>

Use Glencoe's ***Presentation Plus!*** This multimedia teaching tool lets you present dynamic lessons that will engage your students. Using Microsoft PowerPoint®, you can customize the presentation to create your own personalized lessons.

 Web  Audiocassette Diskette *Also available in Spanish

Twists and Turns

Theme Objectives

- To enjoy reading about the tricks of fate that influence people's lives
- To analyze the literary elements in poetry, folktale, short story, and comedy selections
- To apply strategies for reading poetry

Teaching Strategies

Have students read the quote from "Nobody Knows My Name" by James Baldwin in preparation for the discussion questions on page 539.

VIEWING THE ART

Responding to the Art After discussing the Baldwin quotation, direct students to the photo of the maze. Ask:

- Have you ever seen or been in a maze like this one?
- James Baldwin says that life is like a water wheel. In what way can life also be like a maze? *(Life is full of twists and turns. As in a maze, you must make choices, and you never know what might be around the next curve.)*

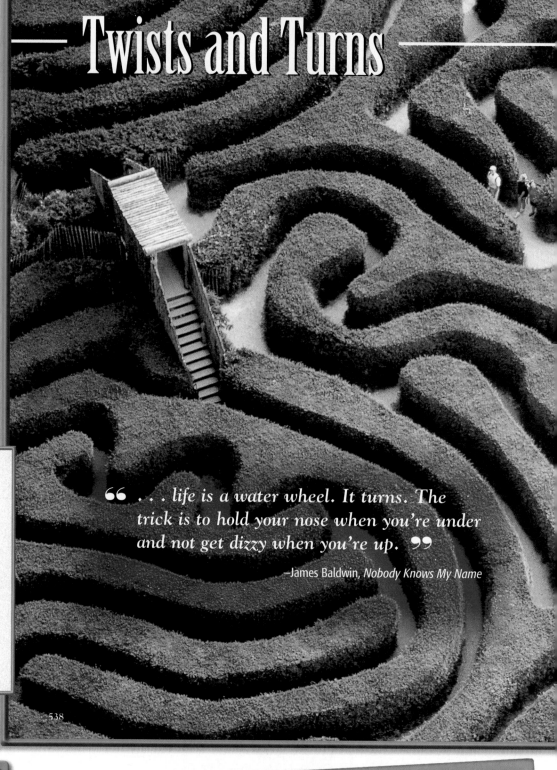

Twists and Turns

". . . life is a water wheel. It turns. The trick is to hold your nose when you're under and not get dizzy when you're up."

—James Baldwin, *Nobody Knows My Name*

538

TEACHER to TEACHER

J.P. ELDER MIDDLE SCHOOL • FORTH WORTH, TEXAS

My students can be very one-sided in their observations. So, when introducing the theme "Twists and Turns," I have all the students stand on their chairs, and I ask, "How does the room look to you?" Next, I'll have a few students sit on the floor in a corner and ask, "How does the room look to you now?" We discuss how the classroom—a place where they sit every day and largely take for granted—can offer a different perspective. To reinforce the idea, I read the children's picture book *True Story of the Three Little Pigs,* which is told from the point of view of the Big Bad Wolf. We discuss how the book illustrates the fact that, when we change our perspective, the story changes. Then I talk about the twists and turns of life that they'll see if they keep their eyes open.

LEE A. FELTS

THEME CONTENTS

RESOURCE MANAGER

See the ***Theme Six Planning Guide*** for additional teaching notes, strategies, and resources for introducing the theme "Twists and Turns."

GLENCOE TECHNOLOGY

LITERATURE CLASSICS CD-ROM

Search for other selections related to the theme "Twists and Turns."

Introducing the Theme

Direct your students' attention to the **Theme Contents.** Ask them to read through the list of selections. Present these questions for discussion:

- Do any of the short story titles seem to suggest that the story might have a surprise ending? *(Students may mention that the stories by O. Henry, Mark Twain, and Rudolfo A. Anaya have mysterious titles and therefore could result in a surprise ending.)*
- Look at the list of authors in Theme 6. Have you read anything by these writers before? What kind of writing do you expect from Mark Twain? Edgar Allan Poe? Roald Dahl? *(Students might expect Mark Twain's writing to be comical, Edgar Allan Poe's writing to be dark and serious, and Roald Dahl's writing to be directed at children.)*
- As you read the titles, which selection interests you most? Why?

Additional Resources

- ***Interdisciplinary Activities,*** pp. 22–25
- ***Viewing and Representing Activities,*** pp. 22–24
- ***Listening and Speaking Activities,*** pp. 16–18
- ***Critical Thinking Skills,*** pp. 15–17
- ***Selection and Theme Assessment,*** pp. 135–136
- ***Performance Assessment,*** p. 74
- ***Fine Art Transparency 12***

LITERATURE & HUMANITIES

Have students examine *The Jungle* from the CD *National Museum of Women in the Arts*, and discuss why the artist might have chosen to show most of the figure but kept the face hidden. Is this twist meant to evoke curiosity or self-reflection?

Exploring the Theme

Twists and Turns

Introduce the phrase *sleight-of-hand* to students and discuss its meaning. *(*Sleight-of-hand *is a skill in using the hands to confuse, deceive, or perform tricks. It is also known as* legerdemain, *from the Old French for "light of hand.")* Ask students to work in groups or pairs to prepare card or "magic" tricks that employ sleight-of-hand to show the class.

Starting Points

A View with a Twist
Students may think the character in *Modern Times* appears to be taking it calmly. Students might respond that they would feel shocked, afraid, and angry.

Appreciating Life's Bumps
In some cultures, the saying *"May all your dreams come true"* is a blessing. In other cultures, it's a curse. Ask each student to choose a personal dream and ask what would happen if it unexpectedly came true.

Point out that a single event can impact the various people involved in it very differently. Ask students who know a "blessing in disguise" story to tell it from two viewpoints: their own and another person's.

After students draw their pictures, allow time for them to share their experiences in small groups.

FINE ART TRANSPARENCY 12

You may wish to use ***Fine Art Transparency 12*** to enrich thinking.

Exploring the Theme

Twists and Turns

What makes literature interesting? The same twists and turns that make life interesting. In this theme, you will discover the surprising actions that characters take in order to deal with life's unexpected events. To begin your own thinking about the theme, choose one of the options below.

Starting Points

A VIEW WITH A TWIST
How often do you try looking at, reading, or thinking about something from a different point of view? Sometimes, by simply trying another viewpoint, your impression of reality can change dramatically.

- In Charlie Chaplin's classic comedy film *Modern Times,* his character gets pulled into the gears of a huge machine. How do you think he felt about this plot twist? How would you feel?

APPRECIATING LIFE'S BUMPS
Life doesn't always go smoothly. Sometimes, however, difficulties turn out to be surprise blessings. At other times, events you look forward to can turn out to be disasters. These all become the life experiences that make good stories.

- Think about an entertaining or dramatic event in your life that you have described more than once to your family and friends. Draw a picture of this moment when, out of the blue, life surprised you in a positive or negative way.

Charlie Chaplin in the movie *Modern Times.*

Family and Community Activity

Have students create situations through which they can observe what happens when positive, unexpected events occur in people's lives. Ask each student to secretly choose a person for whom he or she would like to do something kind. Have students list ten things to do for this person and compile a schedule for when to do them. As they read the selections in Theme 6, students should do their secret acts of kindness, and each should keep a short journal of the experience. Journal entries could include what the act was, when and how it was done, what the person's reaction was, and how long it was possible to remain anonymous.

Additional Resources
Family and Community Activities, p. 16

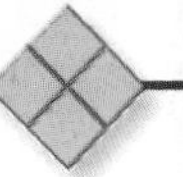

Theme Projects

As you read the selections in this theme, complete one of the projects below. Work on your own, with a partner, or with a group.

LEARNING FOR LIFE

Writing an Incident Report

Events in real life are often the inspiration for events in fiction. Take notes about an actual news event that you have read or heard about.

1. Write a report as if you were an official investigating the incident. Describe the people involved, the series of events that led to the incident, the incident itself, and the outcome.
2. Share your report with the class. Ask classmates to help you check for any missing information.

PERFORMING

Storytelling

1. Choose a story with an unusual twist in the plot.
2. To learn the story, read it more than once. Then make an outline using your own words.
3. Practice telling the story in front of a mirror. Remember that facial expressions and gestures are important parts of the storyteller's art.
4. Perform your story in front of an audience. Make sure to use your voice to emphasize any surprises in the plot.

CRITICAL READING

Discovering the Unexpected

1. Review the plots of the stories and poems you have read recently.
2. Choose a plot with a turn of events that surprised you.
3. Rewrite the climax of the plot so that the outcome changes. Share your new story with your classmates.

interNET CONNECTION

Look for other literature selections on the theme "Twists and Turns." For example, try short stories by O. Henry or H. H. Munro (Saki). Search by author on the On-Line Books Page: http://digital.library.upenn.edu/books.

MULTIMEDIA PROJECT

Dramatizing

1. Working with a large group or the whole class, choose a story with a plot twist. It can be a story from this theme, from another theme, or from a source other than your literature book.
2. Discuss the story. Then work together to turn it into a script for a radio or television play.
3. Assign tasks to group members. You will need actors, a director, people to provide sound effects (for a radio play), scenery and perhaps costumes (for television), and background music. If you want to present your dramatization on audiotape or videotape, you will also need a technical crew to run the equipment.
4. Rehearse your script carefully. Then perform your story in front of an audience, or record it for presentation on audiotape or videotape.

interNET CONNECTION

Twists and Turns Students can use a search engine to find out more about unexpected turns of events. They might use such keywords as *exploration, invention, history, updated fairy tales,* or any other point of interest.

Theme Projects

Teaching Strategies

The following suggestions may help your students plan and carry out their theme projects.

Learning for Life

- Bring in newspapers and magazines for students to look through to find events that interest them. Suggest that they use the Internet and other library resources to gather as much information as they can about the stories.
- Encourage students to report on historical events if current events do not interest them.
- Invite each student to write a rough draft of a fictionalized story based on the selected real-life incident. The draft could include who the main characters are, where the story takes place, what the main event is, and how the story ends.

Multimedia Project

- If students have difficulty thinking of a story with an unusual plot twist, recommend other stories written by this theme's authors, such as O. Henry, Edgar Allan Poe, and Shirley Jackson.
- Students may wish to videotape their storytelling performances individually or in a group and show them to the class.

Critical Reading

- Allow time for students to review the stories and poems in Themes 1–5.
- Students' papers should include the climax of the story as it appears in the book, with the new version beneath it.
- When students share their new stories with the class, have each one give a short synopsis of the original story to refresh classmates' memories.

MEDIA Connection

Objective

- To compare a comic strip with a written anecdote.

Literature LINK

Charles In this comic strip, which connects to "Charles," by Shirley Jackson (pp. 544–548), Calvin has created a portrait of himself that communicates to his parents something about how he's feeling in school. Laurie, the kindergartner in "Charles," is equally amusing when he creates an entire persona for himself as a way of letting his parents know what is happening at school.

Analyzing Media

1. Possible answers include that Calvin is a creative child, that his behavior is a bit wild, or that he sees himself as different from the other students.
2. Students will probably say that their versions require many more words to describe the characters' actions and expressions, which the cartoonist can show with a few simply drawn lines.

Additional Resources

Media Connections, p. 11

***inTIME* magazine**

Teaching Support

MEDIA Connection

COMIC STRIP

This comic strip comes from one of Bill Watterson's *Calvin and Hobbes* collections. As in most humorous comic strips, the humor arises from an unexpected twist.

Analyzing Media

1. What does Calvin's self-portrait suggest about his behavior at school?
2. Rewrite the cartoon strip as a words-only anecdote. Then discuss the differences between your version and the cartoon strip.

Self-portraits Have students use a search engine to look for self-portraits by artists of their choice. Suggest that they try entering the name of the artist, such as: *Van Gogh, Monet, Warhol, Chagall;* or keywords such as *impressionism, painters, self-portraits.*

Reading Minilesson

Identifying Author's Purpose The twists and turns of everyday life are the raw material from which comic strip writers get their ideas.

Activity Ask students to do a comic strip treasure hunt over the next few days. Have students write a description of each comic strip they see, where they see it, and who the writer is. After students have collected a few days' worth of comic strips, ask them to share their findings with the class. Encourage them to try to identify the writer's purpose in writing the comic strip. **L2**

Additional Resources

 ***Reading Skills Practice Workbook***

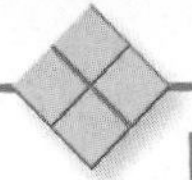

Before You Read

Charles and *No News*

MEET SHIRLEY JACKSON

Shirley Jackson's fiction is filled with strange twists and turns. In most of her novels and short stories, she explores the darker side of human life. However, Jackson also wrote humorously about family life, as she does in "Charles."

Shirley Jackson was born in 1919 and died in 1965.

MEET CONNIE REGAN-BLAKE AND BARBARA FREEMAN

Regan-Blake and Freeman are cousins who started telling stories as children. They have traveled around the country collecting and telling stories for more than twenty years. Many of their stories, like "No News," are set in the rural South.

Connie Regan-Blake was born in 1947; Barbara Freeman was born in 1944.

READING FOCUS

Have you ever heard the expression *read between the lines?*

Sharing Ideas

In a small group, talk about the meaning of the expression and give examples of moments when the expression might be used in conversation.

Setting a Purpose

Try to read between the lines to discover the twists and turns in these two selections.

BUILDING BACKGROUND

Did You Know? Children entering school must learn to get along with each other, follow directions, and help with classroom routines. In kindergarten, children become accustomed to a school setting and learn to play together.

VOCABULARY PREVIEW

raucous (rô′ kəs) *adj.* loud and rough-sounding; p. 544
insolently (in′ sə lənt lē) *adv.* in a boldly rude manner; p. 544
simultaneously (sī′ məl tā′ nē əs lē) *adv.* at the same time; p. 546
solemnly (sol′ əm lē) *adv.* seriously; p. 546
reformation (ref′ ər mā′ shən) *n.* a change for the better; improvement; p. 547
cynically (sin′ ə kəl lē) *adv.* in a way that shows doubt or disbelief; doubtfully; p. 547
primly (prim′ lē) *adv.* in a stiffly formal manner; p. 548
lapse (laps) *n.* a slipping or falling away; p. 548

Before Reading

Objectives

- To read and analyze two stories about dealing with bad news
- To identify plot elements in two stories
- To write a paragraph describing foreshadowing

Skills

Reading/Thinking: Comparing and Contrasting; Inferring; Drawing Conclusions
Writing: Narrative
Vocabulary: The Prefix *re-*
Grammar/Language: Apostrophes; Correct Pronoun Use
Listening/Speaking: Dramatization; Interview
Collaboration: Performance; Literature Groups

Motivating STUDENTS

Selection Focus Transparency 46: Have students read and discuss the quotation from William Shakespeare's *Antony and Cleopatra*.

Reading Focus: As an extension of the Reading Focus, have students work in small groups to create one or more cartoons that express the idea of reading between the lines.

RESOURCE MANAGER

Teaching Tools and Resources
- Theme Six Planning Guide
- Literature Groups Sourcebook

Essential Lesson Support

Lesson-Specific Instruction
- Selection Focus Transparency 46
- Literary Elements Transparency 46
- Active Reading Guide,* p. 46
- Selection Vocabulary Practice, p. 32

Assessment
- Selection Quick Checks,* p. 46
- Sel. and Theme Assmt., pp. 81–82
- Testmaker: ExamView Pro
- Performance Assessment, p. 43

Systematic Language Instruction
- Gr. and Comp. Hbk., L. 10.4
- Vocabulary Power, Lesson 24
- Spelling Power, Lesson 21

English Language Learners
- ELL Sourcebook, p. 74
- Spanish Summaries, p. 46
- Audio Library*
- English, Yes!

Spec. Needs/Strat. Interven.
- Interactive Rdg. Sbk., pp. T172–T174
- Interactive Rdg. Wkbk., pp. 89–90
- Inclusion Strat. Sbk., pp. 71–72
- Audio Library*

* Also available in Spanish

Reading the Selection

SUMMARY

In these two humorous stories, the main characters must face new and unexpected situations. Laurie can only describe his difficult kindergarten experiences by attributing them to the fictional bad boy, "Charles." In "No News," Georgeanne explains to her friend in a very convoluted manner the many tragedies that have taken place in her absence.

 ***Spanish Summaries,*** p. 46

A Active Reading Strategies

PREDICT Ask students to use the title of the selection and details from the first paragraph to predict what they think the story is about. *(The crayons around the title "Charles" might help students predict that the story is about a young child.)*

VOCABULARY If you haven't previewed the selection vocabulary with students, stop and remind them to use context clues to unlock the meanings of new vocabulary words.

Additional Resources

Active Reading Guide, p. 46

Audio Library
Spanish Audio Library

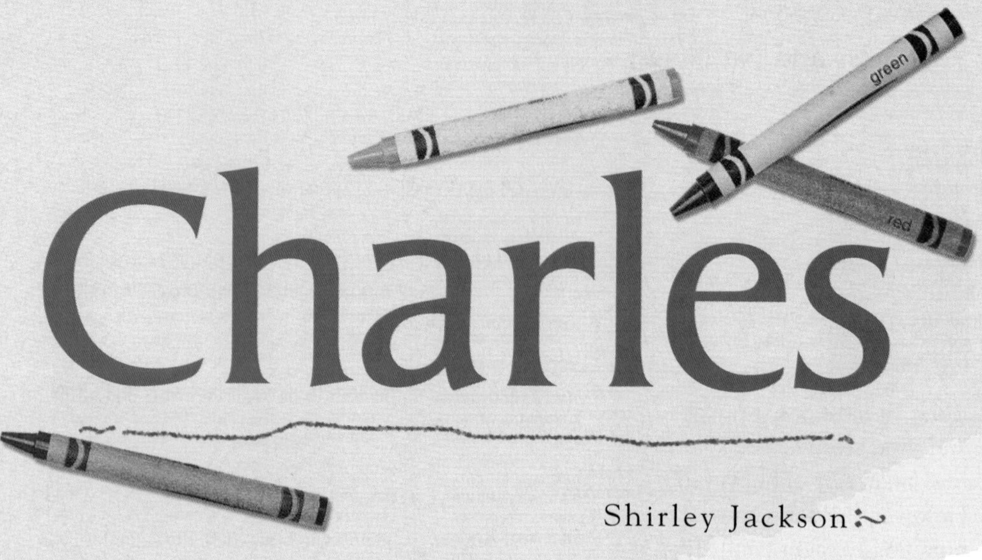

Charles

Shirley Jackson

A The day my son Laurie started kindergarten he renounced corduroy overalls with bibs and began wearing blue jeans with a belt; I watched him go off the first morning with the older girl next door, seeing clearly that an era of my life was ended, my sweet-voiced nursery-school tot replaced by a long-trousered, swaggering character who forgot to stop at the corner and wave good-bye to me.

He came home the same way, the front door slamming open, his cap on the floor, and the voice suddenly become raucous shouting, "Isn't anybody *here?*"

At lunch he spoke insolently to his father, spilled his baby sister's milk, and remarked that his teacher said we were not to take the name of the Lord in vain.

"How *was* school today?" I asked, elaborately casual.

"All right," he said.

"Did you learn anything?" his father asked.

Laurie regarded his father coldly. "I didn't learn nothing," he said.

"Anything," I said. "Didn't learn anything."

"The teacher spanked a boy, though," Laurie said, addressing his bread and butter. "For being fresh," he added, with his mouth full.

Vocabulary

raucous (rô′ kəs) *adj.* loud and rough-sounding
insolently (in′ sə lənt lē) *adv.* in a boldly rude manner

Teaching Support

CONNECTING TO OTHER SELECTIONS
For a teaching strategy that connects "Charles" to "A Crush," see the ***Theme Two Planning Guide***.

MEETING INDIVIDUAL NEEDS — ENGLISH LANGUAGE LEARNERS

Cultural Differences Some English language learners may be surprised by the way Laurie and Charles speak and act toward adults. You may wish to use the exchanges on these pages to discuss how adults and young children in various cultures relate to each other.

Activity Have students in small groups discuss what might have happened in their own cultures if they had behaved the way Laurie or Charles do in the story. Point out that there are many different standards of behavior, and that they can depend greatly upon individual cultural and family backgrounds.

Additional Resources

English Language Learners Sourcebook, p. 74

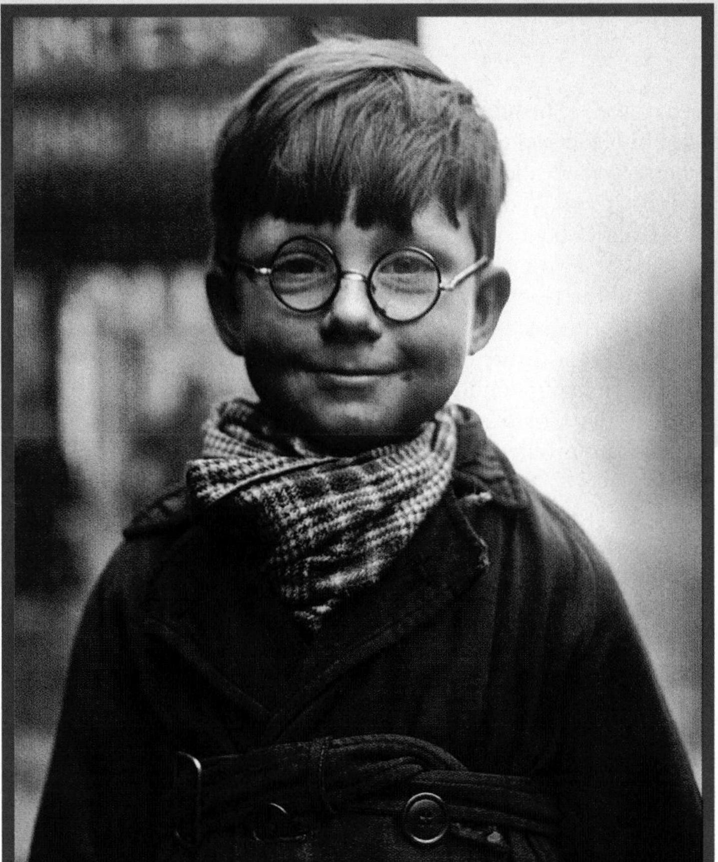

Viewing the photograph: What words would you use to describe this boy's personality? Would you use similar words to describe anyone in the story?

"What did he do?" I asked. "Who was it?"

Laurie thought. "It was Charles," he said. "He was fresh. The teacher spanked him and made him stand in a corner. He B was awfully fresh."

"What did he do?" I asked again, but Laurie slid off his chair, took a cookie, and left, while his father was still saying, "See here, young man."

The next day Laurie remarked at lunch, as soon as he sat down, "Well, Charles was C bad again today." He grinned enormously and said, "Today Charles hit the teacher."

"Good heavens," I said, mindful of the Lord's name, "I suppose he got spanked again?"

"He sure did," Laurie said. "Look up," he said to his father.

"What?" his father said, looking up.

"Look down," Laurie said. "Look at my thumb. Gee, you're dumb." He began to laugh insanely.

"Why did Charles hit the teacher?" D I asked quickly.

"Because she tried to make him color with red crayons," Laurie said. "Charles wanted to

B Literary Elements

PLOT: *Exposition* Ask a volunteer to summarize the story's action thus far. *(Laurie has begun kindergarten and has immediately changed from a sweet boy into a rude child.)*

C Active Reading Strategies

QUESTION Ask students why they think Laurie "grins enormously" when he describes what Charles has done. *(Most students will think that Laurie is fascinated by the misbehaving Charles and seems to be entertained by the trouble he causes.)*

D Literary Elements

CHARACTER Discuss with students their reaction to Laurie's accounts of Charles's hitting the teacher. What do they think is driving him to enjoy this kind of unruly behavior? *(Laurie seems to be acting out some of Charles's unruliness and venting his own frustration about the new rules in school.)*

VIEWING THE PHOTOGRAPH

Viewing Response *Some possible words are* mischievous, naughty, sly, confident, *and* bold*—words that might describe Charles.*

LIFE SKILLS CONNECTION

Interpersonal Skills Ask students how they feel when they are introduced to a new group of people for the first time.

Activity Ask students to work in pairs or small groups to discuss the best experiences and the worst experiences they have had when meeting new people, such as in a new school, a sports team, a club, or a family gathering. Were they angry, uncomfortable, hopeful? Have them list their reactions on a *Good Feelings/Bad Feelings* chart. You may wish to have groups share their finds with one another. **L1**

E Literary Elements

PLOT: *Conflict* Ask students to discuss the central conflict that is described in this paragraph. *(Charles is having a difficult time adjusting to school; he doesn't get along with his teacher or the other students.)*

F Active Reading Strategies

RESPOND Ask students if they agree with Laurie's father that Laurie may as well meet people like Charles now as later. *(Some students may agree. Others will say that Charles may be a very bad role model for Laurie, who is still very young.)*

G Active Reading Strategies

CONNECT Ask students if they would be allowed to speak to their parents or guardians as Laurie speaks to his.

color with green crayons so he hit the teacher and she spanked him and said nobody play with Charles but everybody did."

E The third day—it was Wednesday of the first week—Charles bounced a see-saw on to the head of a little girl and made her bleed, and the teacher made him stay inside all during recess. Thursday Charles had to stand in a corner during story-time because he kept pounding his feet on the floor. Friday Charles was deprived of blackboard privileges because he threw chalk.

On Saturday I remarked to my husband, "Do you think kindergarten is too unsettling for Laurie? All this toughness, and bad grammar, and this Charles boy sounds like such a bad influence."

F "It'll be all right," my husband said reassuringly. "Bound to be people like Charles in the world. Might as well meet them now as later."

On Monday Laurie came home late, full of news. "Charles," he shouted as he came up the hill; I was waiting anxiously on the front steps. "Charles," Laurie yelled all the way up the hill, "Charles was bad again."

"Come right in," I said, as soon as he came close enough. "Lunch is waiting."

"You know what Charles did?" he demanded, following me through the door. "Charles yelled so in school they sent a boy in from first grade to tell the teacher she had to make Charles keep quiet, and so Charles had to stay after school. And so all the children stayed to watch him."

G "What did he do?" I asked.

"He just sat there," Laurie said, climbing into his chair at the table. "Hi, Pop, y'old dust mop."

"Charles had to stay after school today," I told my husband. "Everyone stayed with him."

"What does this Charles look like?" my husband asked Laurie. "What's his other name?"

"He's bigger than me," Laurie said. "And he doesn't have any galoshes and he doesn't ever wear a jacket."

Monday night was the first Parent-Teachers meeting, and only the fact that the baby had a cold kept me from going; I wanted passionately to meet Charles's mother. On Tuesday Laurie remarked suddenly, "Our teacher had a friend come to see her in school today."

"Charles's mother?" my husband and I asked simultaneously.

"Naaah," Laurie said scornfully. "It was a man who came and made us do exercises, we had to touch our toes. Look." He climbed down from his chair and squatted down and touched his toes. "Like this," he said. He got solemnly back into his chair and said, picking up his fork, "Charles didn't even *do* exercises."

"That's fine," I said heartily. "Didn't Charles want to do exercises?"

"Naaah," Laurie said. "Charles was so fresh to the teacher's friend he wasn't *let* do exercises."

"Fresh again?" I said.

"He kicked the teacher's friend," Laurie said. "The teacher's friend told Charles to

Vocabulary

simultaneously (sī′ məl tā′ nē əs lē) *adv.* at the same time

solemnly (sol′ əm lē) *adv.* seriously

Teaching Support

Reading Minilesson

Comparing and Contrasting Review the processes of comparing and contrasting that help us analyze how things, ideas, facts, persons, or events are alike and how they are different. Students might benefit from comparing and contrasting Laurie and Charles.

Activity Have students work in small groups and revisit the story to look for details describing each boy's behavior. Ask them to create a Venn diagram to compare the boys. Then lead the class in a discussion about the similarities and differences between Laurie and Charles. **L2**

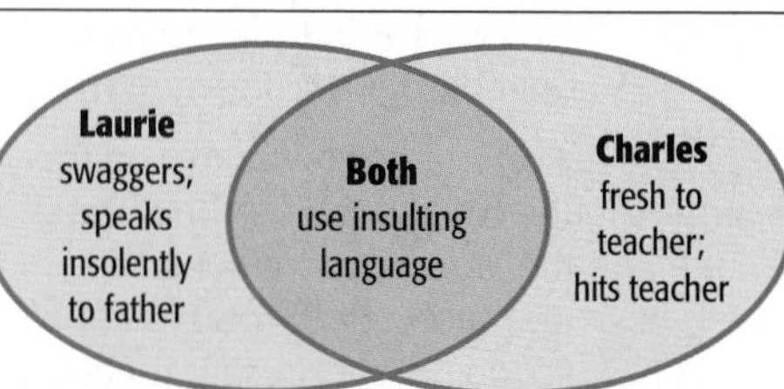

Additional Resources

Reading Skills Practice Workbook

touch his toes like I just did and Charles kicked him."

"What are they going to do about Charles, do you suppose?" Laurie's father asked him.

Laurie shrugged elaborately. "Throw him out of school, I guess," he said.

Wednesday and Thursday were routine; Charles yelled during story hour and hit a boy in the stomach and made him cry. On Friday Charles stayed after school again and so did all the other children.

With the third week of kindergarten Charles was an institution[1] in our family; the baby was being a Charles when she cried all afternoon; Laurie did a Charles when he filled his wagon full of mud and pulled it through the kitchen; even my husband, when he caught his elbow in the telephone cord and pulled telephone, ashtray, and a bowl of flowers off the table, said, after the first minute, "Looks like Charles."

H During the third and fourth weeks it looked like a reformation in Charles; Laurie reported grimly at lunch on Thursday of the third week, "Charles was so good today the teacher gave him an apple."

"What?" I said, and my husband added warily, "You mean Charles?"

"Charles," Laurie said. "He gave the crayons around and he picked up the books afterward and the teacher said he was her helper."

"What happened?" I asked incredulously.

"He was her helper, that's all," Laurie said, and shrugged.

"Can this be true, about Charles?" I asked my husband that night. "Can something like this happen?"

I "Wait and see," my husband said cynically. "When you've got a Charles to deal with, this may mean he's only plotting."

J He seemed to be wrong. For over a week Charles was the teacher's helper; each day he handed things out and he picked things up; no one had to stay after school.

"The P.T.A. meeting's next week again," I told my husband one evening. "I'm going to find Charles's mother there."

"Ask her what happened to Charles," my husband said. "I'd like to know."

"I'd like to know myself," I said.

On Friday of that week things were back to normal. "You know what Charles did today?" Laurie demanded at the lunch table, in a voice slightly awed. "He told a little girl to say a word and she said it and the teacher washed her mouth out with soap and Charles laughed."

K "What word?" his father asked unwisely, and Laurie said, "I'll have to whisper it to you, it's so bad." He got down off his chair and went around to his father. His father bent his head down and Laurie whispered joyfully. His father's eyes widened.

"Did Charles tell the little girl to say *that?*" he asked respectfully.

"She said it *twice*," Laurie said. "Charles told her to say it *twice*."

1. Here, *institution* means "a regular feature or tradition."

Vocabulary

reformation (ref′ ər mā′ shən) *n.* a change for the better; improvement

cynically (sin′ ə kəl lē) *adv.* in a way that shows doubt or disbelief; doubtfully

H Literary Elements

PLOT: *Foreshadowing* Laurie reports Charles's good behavior "grimly." Ask students how this contrasts with the way he reports Charles's bad behavior. *(Laurie reported Charles's bad behavior with an enormous grin.)*

I Active Reading Strategies

QUESTION Ask students what Laurie's father means by the word *plotting.* *(Charles may be pretending to cooperate in order to lull the teacher into a false sense of security while he plans his next move.)*

J Active Reading Strategies

EVALUATE Ask students to describe how Charles's behavior has changed. *(Charles begins to behave himself and is very helpful in class.)*

K Critical Thinking

INFERRING Ask students to infer why Laurie takes so much joy in whispering the "bad word" to his father. *(Perhaps Laurie finds the opportunity exciting because it allows him to do something that is forbidden.)*

MEETING INDIVIDUAL NEEDS — MULTIPLE MODES OF EXPRESSION

Musical Students with strong musical abilities may better understand Charles by writing a song about him. All students may find that the song-writing activity gives them a deeper insight into Charles's character.

Activity Have students work in small groups to create a song about Charles. Have them discuss his character, and then have them write lyrics. Ask them to describe what he has done, what has happened to him, how it has affected the class, and how the teacher might feel about him. Some students may want to use a melody from a song they already know well. When students have finished their songs, ask volunteers to perform them for the class. **L2**

L Literary Elements

PLOT: *Climax* Ask students how they think the P.T.A. meeting fits into the sequence of events. Could this be the turning point of the story? *(It could be the story's climax, since Laurie's mother will probably meet Charles's mother.)*

M Author's Craft

POINT OF VIEW Ask students to discuss why the author might have written the story from the mother's point of view. *(Telling the story from the mother's point of view keeps the mystery of the story going.)*

N Literary Elements

PLOT: *Resolution* Ask students to explain in their own words how the mystery of Charles is finally resolved. *(Guide students in understanding that all of Laurie's stories about Charles's bad behavior were really about Laurie's behavior. The mother that Laurie's mother is so anxious to meet is herself.)*

"What happened to Charles?" my husband asked.

"Nothing," Laurie said. "He was passing out the crayons."

Monday morning Charles abandoned the little girl and said the evil word himself three or four times, getting his mouth washed out with soap each time. He also threw chalk.

L My husband came to the door with me that evening as I set out for the P.T.A. meeting. "Invite her over for a cup of tea after the meeting," he said. "I want to get a look at her."

"If only she's there," I said prayerfully.

"She'll be there," my husband said. "I don't see how they could hold a P.T.A. meeting without Charles's mother."

M At the meeting I sat restlessly, scanning each comfortable matronly[2] face, trying to determine which one hid the secret of Charles. None of them looked to me haggard[3] enough. No one stood up in the meeting and apologized for the way her son had been acting. No one mentioned Charles.

After the meeting I identified and sought out Laurie's kindergarten teacher. She had a plate with a cup of tea and a piece of chocolate cake; I had a plate with a cup of tea and a piece of marshmallow cake. We maneuvered up to one another cautiously, and smiled.

"I've been so anxious to meet you," I said. "I'm Laurie's mother."

N "We're all so interested in Laurie," she said.

"Well, he certainly likes kindergarten," I said. "He talks about it all the time."

"We had a little trouble adjusting, the first week or so," she said primly, "but now he's a fine little helper. With occasional lapses, of course."

"Laurie usually adjusts very quickly," I said. "I suppose this time it's Charles's influence."

"Charles?"

"Yes," I said, laughing, "you must have your hands full in that kindergarten, with Charles."

"Charles?" she said. "We don't have any Charles in the kindergarten."

2. Another word for *matronly* would be "motherly." It refers to a mature woman, especially one who is married and has children.
3. A *haggard* person looks worn out as a result of grief, worry, illness—or dealing with a boy like Charles.

Vocabulary
primly (prim′ lē) *adv.* in a stiffly formal manner
lapse (laps) *n.* a slipping or falling away

Teaching Support

Grammar and Language Minilesson

Apostrophes Write the following sentences from the story on the board:

> *If only she's there. She'll be there. I don't see how they could hold a P.T.A. meeting without Charles's mother.*

Review the use of an apostrophe to show possession and to substitute for a missing letter in a contraction.

Activity Have students make a list of words that use apostrophes in contractions and to show possession. Then tell them to write paragraphs that describe Laurie's mother telling his father about the P.T.A. meeting. Direct them to include in the paragraphs examples of apostrophes used in contractions and to show possession. **L2**

Additional Resources

- ***Grammar and Language Transparency 45***
- ***Grammar and Language Workbook,*** pp. 273–274
- ***Grammar and Composition Handbook,*** Lesson 13.7
- ***Writer's Choice,*** Lesson 20.7

No News

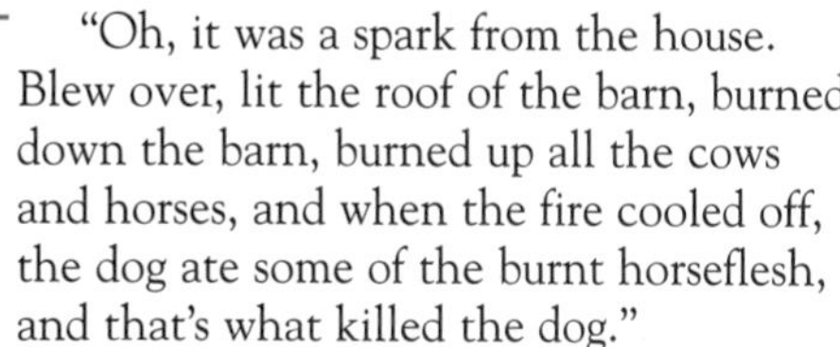

Retold by Connie Regan-Blake and Barbara Freeman

A certain Southern lady was returning home after recuperating[1] in the mountains for three months. Her friend Georgeanne met her at the railway station.

"Georgeanne, has there been any news while I've been away?"

"Oh, no, there's no news."

"No news? Surely something has occurred in my absence. Why, I've been gone for nearly three months, and I'm anxious for any little bit of news you may have."

"Oh, now, since you mentioned it—'course it don't amount to much—but since you've been away, your dog died."

"My dog died? How did my dog die?"

"He ate some of the burnt horseflesh, and that's what killed the dog."

"Burnt horseflesh?"

"Well, after the fire cooled off, the dog ate some of the burnt horseflesh, and that's what killed the dog."

"Fire cooled off?"

"Well, the barn burned down, burned up all of the cows and horses, and when the fire cooled down, the dog ate some of the burnt horseflesh, and that's what killed the dog."

"My barn burned down? How did my barn burn down?"

"Oh, it was a spark from the house. Blew over, lit the roof of the barn, burned down the barn, burned up all the cows and horses, and when the fire cooled off, the dog ate some of the burnt horseflesh, and that's what killed the dog."

P

"A spark from the house?"

"Oh, yes, now that's completely burned down."

"But how did my house burn down?"

"It was the candle flame that lit the curtains, shot up the side of the wall, and burned down the house; a spark flew over on the roof of the barn, burned down the barn, burned up all of the cows and horses, and when the fire cooled off, the dog ate some of the burnt horseflesh, and that's what killed the dog."

"Candles? I don't even allow candles in my house. How did the candles get into my house?"

"Oh, they were around the coffin."

O

"Coffin? Who died?"

"Oh, now you needn't worry about that. Since you've been away, your mother-in-law died."

"Oh, my mother-in-law. What a pity. How did she die?"

"Well, some folks say that it was the shock of hearing that your husband had

Q

run away with the choir leader. But other than that, there ain't been no news."

1. To *recuperate* (ri kōō′ pə rāt′) is to regain health or strength.

O Literary Elements

PLOT: *Rising Action* Explain to students that this tale has an unusual plot structure. The events are exposed in reverse order—each effect in a chain of events is revealed before the cause.

P Active Reading Strategies

QUESTION Ask students to think about why Georgeanne is telling her friend the news in this way. *(Students may suggest that she does not want to tell all the terrible news at once.)*

Q Author's Craft

IRONY Have students discuss why Georgeanne's statement at the end of the story is ironic. *(She says that other than that, there's no news, but "that" turns out to be a series of terrible tragedies.)*

Thematic Focus

Twists and Turns Have students discuss how both of these selections illustrate the comic presentation of serious issues—a child's misbehaving in school and a woman's devastating loss. Invite students to share their responses to twists and turns of the plots.

FINE ART TRANSPARENCY 23

You may wish to use ***Fine Art Transparency 23*** to extend the discussion.

REAL-WORLD CONNECTION

Humor Students might enjoy adding humor to a story about a real person who must accept unpleasant news. They can choose a news article or a story of someone they know.

Activity Ask students to create a cartoon that illustrates what happened in the article and how the person coped with what took place. Encourage students to create humorous, eye-catching titles for their cartoons. Then work with the class to create a "funny page" by pasting each cartoon on posterboard or butcher paper. **L2**

ASSESSMENT

Quick Checks, p. 46

Responding to the Selection

PERSONAL RESPONSE

Encourage students to explain what first made them think that something unusual might be happening in these stories.

Analyzing Literature

1. He becomes raucous and insolent.
2. Laurie acts out at home to some extent, mostly with rude language, but is basically obedient. Charles is out of control, using rude language, hitting the teacher, and teasing other children.
3. They stay after school with Charles to watch him.
4. The woman's dog died, all her cows and horses were killed after the barn burned, her house burned down, her mother-in-law died, and her husband ran off with the choir leader.
5. Laurie probably feels that in order to defend himself against an unknown situation, he has to act bigger and stronger than he actually is.
6. Most likely Laurie wants to tell his parents what has been taking place at school but is afraid to admit that he is misbehaving.
7. At first because Laurie talks about him constantly. Later, Charles becomes a symbol for anything that goes wrong.
8. Georgeanne casually relates the tragedies of her friend's life in a series of drawn-out cause-and-effect relationships.
9. Both plots contain characters who are faced with new situations or unexpected events and end with a surprise twist.
10. Be sure that students support their opinions with concrete examples from the selections.

Active Reading and Critical Thinking

Responding to Literature

PERSONAL RESPONSE

- Recall the **Reading Focus** on page 543. In each story, when did you first decide that you needed to read between the lines?

Analyzing Literature

RECALL

1. How does Laurie change when he starts kindergarten?
2. Compare Laurie's behavior at home with Charles's actions at school. How are their behaviors similar? How are they different?
3. According to Laurie, why do he and all the other children stay after school with Charles?
4. What does the Southern lady find out after her friend assures her that "there's no news"?

Brackets connect questions that are paired to develop higher-level thinking skills.

INTERPRET

5. Why do you think Laurie turns into a "swaggering character" when he begins kindergarten? Explain.
6. In your opinion, why does Laurie tell stories about Charles at home?
7. Why is Charles such a fascination in Laurie's household?
8. An *understatement* is a statement that plays down the importance of something. How does "No News" illustrate the word *understatement?*

EVALUATE AND CONNECT

9. Theme Connection How do the **plots** of both selections reflect the theme of this unit? (For more about plot, see page R8.)
10. Which story do you prefer? Why?

LITERARY ELEMENTS

Plot Twist

The sequence of events in a story is called the **plot.** Usually the plot is built around a central **conflict** in which opposing sides are involved in a struggle or a problem that must be resolved. The turning point of the plot is called the **climax,** the point of highest interest. This is the point where the outcome of the conflict is determined. In some plots, the climax includes an unexpected turn of events, called a **plot twist.** "Charles" is an example of a story with a plot twist.

1. What is the plot twist in "Charles"?
2. In one or two sentences, describe the plot twist in "No News."
3. What does the plot twist at the end add to the story "No News"?

- See **Literary Terms Handbook,** p. R8.

LITERARY ELEMENTS

1. Laurie's mother learns that the mischievous Charles is really Laurie.
2. Georgeanne says that nothing has happened while her friend has been away, but then relates a chain of tragedies in her friend's life.
3. The last line adds a humorous touch to the end of the story.

Additional Resources

Literary Elements Transparency 46

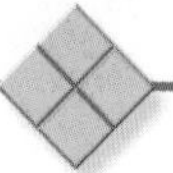

Literature and Writing

Writing About Literature

Foreshadowing When writers give clues or hints about something that will occur later, they are **foreshadowing** the later event or development. Reread "Charles" carefully. Identify the details that foreshadow the plot twist at the end. Write a paragraph describing how Jackson foreshadows the ending of her story.

Personal Writing

Time Travel Think about yourself in your kindergarten or preschool days. Did you ever tell an exaggerated story—to your parents, your friends, or a teacher? Did you ever have a problem in school? How was it resolved? Write a narrative describing an early school experience.

Extending Your Response

Performing

Dramatization With a partner or in a small group, choose either story to dramatize. If you choose "Charles," pick out one or two scenes to perform. Think about what Laurie says and does as well as how his body looks and moves.

Listening and Speaking

Interview Interview a kindergarten student, a teacher, or someone else who works with young children. Find out what kindergarteners are like. Before the interview, make a list of questions that will help you find out about the thoughts, interests, and daily activities of a five- or six-year-old child.

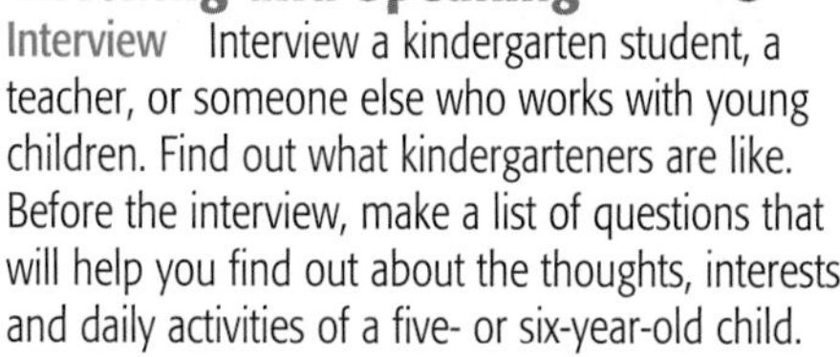

Literature Groups

Turning Real Life into Fiction How do you think authors turn real life into stories? In small groups, make a list of real-life events at your school. Work together to turn one or more of these events into a work of fiction. Share your story with your classmates.

Save your work for your portfolio.

Literature and Writing

Writing About Literature

Students' paragraphs should

- describe how Jackson foreshadows the ending of her story
- identify the details that foreshadow the plot twist at the end

Personal Writing

Students' narratives should

- describe a problem or other early school experience
- explain whether the problem was resolved and how

Extending Your Response

Performing Encourage students to spend time preparing their dramatization by writing a script and rehearsing their parts.

Listening and Speaking As students prepare to conduct their interviews, encourage them to think of questions that will inspire another person to talk about his or her experience.

Literature Groups Encourage each group of students to work cooperatively in creating its own story, one that reflects the experiences of one or more members of the group.

Skill Minilessons

GRAMMAR AND LANGUAGE
CORRECT PRONOUN USE

Practice

1. I
2. me
3. I
4. her
5. me

READING AND THINKING
DRAWING CONCLUSIONS

Example: Laurie was unable to cope with the new school situation and was equally unable to ask his parents directly for help. Making up Charles was one way for Laurie to let his parents know that things were not entirely smooth at school. It was almost as if Laurie had two sides, one "good" and one "bad."

VOCABULARY
THE PREFIX *re-*

1. d
2. e
3. a
4. b
5. c

Additional Resources

- ***Grammar and Language Workbook,*** pp. 107–108
- ***Grammar and Composition Handbook,*** Lesson 4.2
- ***Writer's Choice,*** Lesson 11.3
- ***Reading Skills Practice Workbook***
- ***Vocabulary Practice,*** p. 32

Skill Minilessons

Reteach · Review

GRAMMAR AND LANGUAGE • CORRECT PRONOUN USE

A **subject pronoun** is used as the subject of a sentence. An **object pronoun** is used as the object of a verb or a preposition. If you are unsure of which form of the pronoun to use, say the sentence aloud with only the pronoun as the subject or the object. Your ear should tell you which form is right.

He and his mother walked home. *(subject)*
Tell Laurie and **me** about school. *(object of verb)*
Mother read a story to **him.** *(object of preposition)*

Be especially careful when a sentence has two subjects or two objects.

Laurie and **I** played together. *(subject)*
Those games were fun for **Laurie** and **me.** *(object of preposition)*

PRACTICE Choose the correct form of the pronoun.

1. Laurie and (I, me) were in the same class.
2. Laurie told my husband and (I, me) story after story about Charles.
3. She and (I, me) were amazed at Charles's behavior.
4. The teacher asked for the crayon, but Charles refused to give it to (she, her).
5. Just between you and (I, me), I don't think Charles really existed.

- For more about pronouns, see **Language Handbook,** p. R17.

READING AND THINKING • DRAWING CONCLUSIONS

Stories include details about characters and events. By combining these details with your own knowledge and experience, you can draw conclusions that will help you understand a story.

- For more on drawing conclusions, see **Reading Handbook,** pp. R92–R104.

PRACTICE The author doesn't reveal why Laurie told stories about a boy that didn't exist. You have to draw conclusions to figure it out for yourself. Write a paragraph giving your conclusions about Laurie's tales about Charles.

VOCABULARY • THE PREFIX *re-*

Some prefixes have more than one meaning. The prefix *re-* can mean either "again" or "back."

When Charles's behavior improved, it looked like a *reformation.* It seemed that Charles had been "formed again." However, if you *recall* something, you don't call it again, you call it back. A ball that *rebounds* bounces back. When *re-* is attached to a word, think about the meaning of the word without the prefix and then add either "again" or "back."

PRACTICE Use what you know about the prefix *re-* to match each word to its definition.

1. repress	a. to say again
2. recoil	b. to copy or make again
3. restate	c. a coming back inside
4. reproduce	d. to push or hold back
5. reentry	e. to spring back when let go

ASSESSMENT

- ***Quick Checks,*** p. 46
- ***Selection and Theme Assessment,*** pp. 81–82
- ***Performance Assessment,*** p. 43
- ***Testmaker: ExamView Pro***
- ***Interactive Tutor: Self-Assessment***

Using Commas Correctly

Speakers use their voices to make their meanings clear. In writing, commas separate words or parts of sentences to make the meaning clear.

Problem 1 Missing commas in a series

Georgeanne met her friend answered questions and provided news.

Solution Use commas to separate three or more items in a series.

Georgeanne met her friend, answered questions, and provided news.

Problem 2 Missing commas with direct quotations

"If the story weren't so funny" I said "it would be sad."

Solution Use commas before and after words that interrupt a quotation.

"If the story weren't so funny," I said, "it would be sad."

Problem 3 Missing commas with nonessential appositives

The barn a wooden structure burned down.

Solution Use commas to set off the nonessential appositive.

The barn, a wooden structure, burned down.

The **appositive,** *a wooden structure,* gives more information about the noun *barn.* Since it doesn't change the meaning of the sentence, it is a **nonessential appositive** and should be set off by commas.

• For more about commas, see **Language Handbook,** p. R19.

EXERCISE

Rewrite the sentences, adding commas wherever they are needed.

1. Laurie a kindergarten student told stories about Charles.
2. Charles sassed the teacher yelled pounded his feet and threw chalk.
3. "Charles" said Laurie "didn't do exercises hit a child and had to stay after school."
4. The narrator of the story Laurie's mother was eager to meet Charles's mother.
5. "When I got a chance to speak with his teacher" Laurie's mother said to her husband "I asked her about Charles."

Objective

- To recognize and correctly use commas

Teaching Strategies

After reviewing the three rules of comma usage on page 553, you may wish to read aloud a few sentences from "Charles" and ask students to supply commas where they would be appropriate.

Exercise

1. Laurie, a kindergarten student, told stories about Charles.
2. Charles sassed the teacher, yelled, pounded his feet, and threw chalk.
3. "Charles," said Laurie, "didn't do exercises, hit a child, and had to stay after school."
4. The narrator of the story, Laurie's mother, was eager to meet Charles's mother.
5. "When I got a chance to speak with his teacher," Laurie's mother said to her husband, "I asked her about Charles."

Additional Resources

- ***Grammar and Language Workbook,*** pp. 255–256, 259–260
- ***Grammar and Composition Handbook,*** Lessons 13.2–13.4
- ***Writer's Choice,*** Lessons 20.2–20.4

Teaching Support

Writing Minilesson

Punctuating Quotations Choose three sentences of dialogue from "Charles" to read aloud. Have the class write the sentences in their notebooks exactly as they hear them, placing the proper punctuation.

Activity Ask students to write three quotations they like on index cards. Quotes can come from a famous person, a book of quotations, friends, or family members. Have students write their quotations without punctuation and exchange cards with a partner. Partners can rewrite the quotes on the other side of the index card with the correct punctuation. Encourage pairs to check each other's work. **L2**

Additional Resources

- ***Writer's Choice,*** Lesson 20.6

Before Reading

Objectives

- To read and analyze a comedy sketch
- To explain how dialogue reveals characters' personalities
- To write a paragraph that explains how puns create humor

Skills

Reading/Thinking: Drawing Conclusions; Monitoring Comprehension
Writing: Comedy Routine
Vocabulary: Homonyms; Dialect
Grammar/Language: Using *Who's* and *Whose*
Listening/Speaking: Comedy Routine
Collaboration: Literature Groups; Performing

Motivating STUDENTS

Literature Launchers: "Abbot and Costello: Echoes of Laughter"

Videodisc Side B, Segment 16

Also available in VHS.

Selection Focus Transparency 47: Have students read the cartoon and respond to the questions. Help them connect the image with their own experience.

Reading Focus: As an extension of the Reading Focus, invite students to give examples of their favorite kinds of humor.

Before You Read

Who's on First?

MEET ABBOTT AND COSTELLO

Bud Abbott and Lou Costello were a slapstick comedy team who became two of the most popular film and television entertainers of the 1940s and 1950s. Their comedy routines featured Abbott as the witty straight man and Costello as the bumbling innocent. Their comedy skits were based on old vaudeville routines, but the comics freshened the material by ad-libbing, making up lines on the spot. Some say that they never performed a scene the same way twice.

Bud Abbott was born in 1895 and died in 1974. Lou Costello was born in 1906 and died in 1959.

READING FOCUS

What makes you laugh? Do you like jokes, slapstick, plays on words?

Ask It!

Create a questionnaire about humor. Ask questions such as

- What different kinds of humor can you name?
- Which type of humor do you prefer? Why?
- What good examples of humor have you read or seen recently?
- Why is humor important to humans?

Make copies of your questionnaire, and have friends and family members fill it out. Compile your results, and share the information with others in your class.

Setting a Purpose

Read this comedy sketch for enjoyment. Then read it again to discover why it's funny.

BUILDING BACKGROUND

Did You Know? "Who's on First?" is a comedy sketch created, performed, and made famous by the comedy team of Abbott and Costello. The team first performed this hilarious baseball skit on the Kate Smith Show, a radio program of the early 1940s. They performed it many, many times after that, including in a movie and on their television series *The Abbott and Costello Show.* The routine is memorialized on a plaque in the Baseball Hall of Fame in Cooperstown, New York.

Abbott and Costello with the Andrews Sisters, a popular singing trio, in the 1941 film *Buck Privates.*

RESOURCE MANAGER

Teaching Tools and Resources
- Theme Six Planning Guide
- Literature Groups Sourcebook

Essential Lesson Support

Lesson-Specific Instruction
- Selection Focus Transparency 47
- Literary Elements Transparency 47
- Active Reading Guide,* p. 47

Assessment
- Selection Quick Checks,* p. 47
- Sel. and Theme Assmt., p. 83
- Testmaker: ExamView Pro
- Performance Assessment, p. 44

Systematic Language Instruction
- Gr. and Comp. Hbk., L. 10.5

English Language Learners
- ELL Sourcebook, p. 75
- Spanish Summaries, p. 47
- Audio Library*
- English, Yes!

Spec. Needs/Strat. Interven.
- Interactive Rdg. Sbk., pp. T175–T177
- Interactive Rdg. Wkbk., pp. 91–92
- Inclusion Strat. Sbk., pp. 43-44
- Audio Library*

* Also available in Spanish

Reading the Selection

SUMMARY

Sebastian asks Dexter to tell him the names of the baseball players on the St. Louis team. Dexter tells him that the first, second, and third basemen are named *Who, What,* and *I Don't Know.* Sebastian doesn't understand that these are actually the players' names, and a confused and hilarious dialogue begins when he innocently asks, "Who's playin' first?"

Spanish Summaries, p. 47

Who's on First?

Bud Abbott and Lou Costello

SEBASTIAN. Peanuts!

DEXTER. Peanuts!

SEBASTIAN. Popcorn!

DEXTER. Popcorn!

SEBASTIAN. Crackerjack!

DEXTER. Crackerjack!

SEBASTIAN. Get your packages of Crackerjack here!

DEXTER. —Crackerjack—will you keep quiet? Sebastian! Sebastian, please! Don't interrupt my act!

SEBASTIAN. Ladies and gentlemen and also the children—will you excuse me for a minute, please? Thank you.

DEXTER. What do you want to do?

SEBASTIAN. Look, Mr. Broadhurst—

DEXTER. What are you doing?

A Active Reading Strategies

PREDICT Have students use the title, author credit, and photograph to predict what the story will be about. Suggest that they revisit their predictions at the end of the sketch.

Additional Resources

Active Reading Guide, p. 47
Audio Library
Spanish Audio Library

Teaching Support

CONNECTING TO OTHER SELECTIONS

The chart at the right shows three ways to connect "Who's on First" to other selections in this book.

For specific teaching strategies, see the ***Theme Six Planning Guide.***

Connection	Title
Life Skills: Interpersonal	→ "How I Learned English," p. 377
Thematic: For Laughs	→ "The Night the Bed Fell," p. 399
Literary: Drama	→ "The Monsters Are Due on Maple Street," p. 505

B **Literary Elements**

DIALOGUE "Who's on First?" consists entirely of dialogue. Engage students in a discussion about the differences between writing dialogue only and writing a piece that consists of narrative and dialogue. *(Guide students in understanding that when a piece consists of only dialogue, all details and other information must be revealed through the characters' words. Narratives can provide details and insights apart from what the characters say.)*

C **Active Reading Strategies**

QUESTION Ask students what Sebastian thinks Dexter is telling him when he uses the words *Who, What,* and *I Don't Know.* What is Dexter actually saying? *(Sebastian thinks that Dexter doesn't know the players' names. Dexter is saying the real names of the players.)*

D **Literary Elements**

CONFLICT Have students explain the conflict that is developing. What is the conflict and why is it happening? *(Sebastian and Dexter cannot understand each other because they are having a basic misunderstanding about the word* who's, *a misunderstanding that neither of them can clear up.)*

Who's on First?

SEBASTIAN. I love baseball!

DEXTER. Well, we all love baseball.

SEBASTIAN. When we get to St. Louis, will you tell me the guys' names on the team so when I go to see them in that St. Louis ballpark I'll be able to know those fellows? **B**

DEXTER. Then you'll go and peddle your popcorn and won't interrupt the act anymore?

SEBASTIAN. Yes, sir.

DEXTER. All right. But you know, strange as it may seem, they give ballplayers nowadays very peculiar names.

SEBASTIAN. Funny names?

DEXTER. Nicknames. Nicknames.

SEBASTIAN. Not—not as funny as my name—Sebastian Dinwiddie.

DEXTER. Oh, yes, yes, yes!

SEBASTIAN. Funnier than that?

DEXTER. Oh, absolutely. Yes. Now on the St. Louis team we have Who's on first, What's on second, I Don't Know is on third— **C**

SEBASTIAN. That's what I want to find out. I want you to tell me the names of the fellows on the St. Louis team.

DEXTER. I'm telling you. Who's on first, What's on second, I Don't Know is on third—

SEBASTIAN. You know the fellows' names?

DEXTER. Yes.

SEBASTIAN. Well, then, who's playin' first?

DEXTER. Yes!

SEBASTIAN. I mean the fellow's name on first base.

DEXTER. Who.

SEBASTIAN. The fellow playin' first base for St. Louis.

DEXTER. Who.

SEBASTIAN. The guy on first base.

DEXTER. Who is on first.

SEBASTIAN. Well, what are you askin' me for?

DEXTER. I'm not asking you—I'm telling you. *Who is on first.* **D**

SEBASTIAN. I'm asking you—who's on first?

DEXTER. That's the man's name!

SEBASTIAN. That's whose name?

DEXTER. Yes.

SEBASTIAN. Well, go ahead and tell me!

DEXTER. Who.

SEBASTIAN. The guy on first.

DEXTER. Who.

SEBASTIAN. The first baseman.

DEXTER. Who is on first.

SEBASTIAN. Have you got a first baseman on first?

DEXTER. Certainly.

SEBASTIAN. Then who's playing first?

DEXTER. Absolutely.

SEBASTIAN. When you pay off the first baseman every month, who gets the money?

DEXTER. Every dollar of it. And why not, the man's entitled to it.

Teaching Support

MEETING INDIVIDUAL NEEDS **ENGLISH LANGUAGE LEARNERS**

Understanding Humor To help English language learners better understand "Who's on First?" you may wish to show the layout of a baseball field. Label the bases and the infield and outfield positions.

Activity Discuss the positions and other baseball terms that may be confusing, such as *shortstop, pitcher, catcher,* and *triple play*. If you have students who know the game well, you might wish to have them take turns explaining the game and key terms to their classmates. Encourage students to listen to the audiotape as many times as they wish.

Additional Resources

English Language Learners Sourcebook, p. 75

E

SEBASTIAN. Who is?

DEXTER. Yes.

SEBASTIAN. So who gets it?

DEXTER. Why shouldn't he? Sometimes his wife comes down and collects it.

SEBASTIAN. Whose wife?

DEXTER. Yes. After all, the man earns it.

SEBASTIAN. Who does?

DEXTER. Absolutely.

SEBASTIAN. Well, all I'm trying to find out is what's the guy's name on first base.

DEXTER. Oh, no, no. What is on second base.

SEBASTIAN. I'm not asking you who's on second.

DEXTER. Who's on first.

SEBASTIAN. That's what I'm trying to find out.

DEXTER. Well, don't change the players around.

SEBASTIAN. I'm not changing nobody.

DEXTER. Now, take it easy.

F

SEBASTIAN. What's the guy's name on first base?

DEXTER. What's the guy's name on second base.

SEBASTIAN. I'm not askin' ya who is on second.

DEXTER. Who's on first.

SEBASTIAN. I don't know.

DEXTER. He's on third. We're not talking about him.

SEBASTIAN. How could I get on third base?

DEXTER. You mentioned his name.

SEBASTIAN. If I mentioned the third baseman's name, who did I say is playing third?

DEXTER. No, Who's playing first.

SEBASTIAN. Stay offa first, will ya?

DEXTER. Well, what do you want me to do?

G

SEBASTIAN. Now what's the guy's name on first base?

DEXTER. What's on second.

SEBASTIAN. I'm not asking ya who's on second.

DEXTER. Who's on first.

SEBASTIAN. I don't know.

DEXTER. He's on third.

SEBASTIAN. There I go back on third again.

DEXTER. Well, I can't change their names.

SEBASTIAN. Say, will you please stay on third base, Mr. Broadhurst.

DEXTER. Please. Now, what is it you want to know?

SEBASTIAN. What is the fellow's name on third base?

DEXTER. What is the fellow's name on second base.

SEBASTIAN. I'm not askin' ya who's on second.

DEXTER. Who's on first.

SEBASTIAN. I don't know.

DEXTER AND SEBASTIAN. *Third base!*

SEBASTIAN. You got a pitcher on the team?

E Author's Craft

DIALOGUE Abbott and Costello use short sentences and responses. Ask students why the sketch might be written this way. *(Short sentences quicken the pace and accurately represent real conversation.)*

Vo•cab•u•lar•y Skills

Dialect The comedy routine shows how people really speak. For example, Sebastian uses the word *offa* for *off of* and *ya* for *you*. *(Other examples of dialect include* askin', gotta, *and* playin'.*)*

F Active Reading Strategies

VISUALIZE Visualizing the infield bases may help students keep track of what is taking place.

G Literary Elements

COMEDY: *Repetition* Discuss why the skit gets funnier each time Sebastian and Dexter repeat the same misunderstandings. *(Repetition enables the reader to anticipate what's coming.)*

At the MOVIES

Be sure to preview the following video for appropriateness for your class.

- ***The Naughty Nineties*** (1945, 72 minutes, NR), includes the "Who's on First" routine. Seeing the actors perform it will help students appreciate its humor.

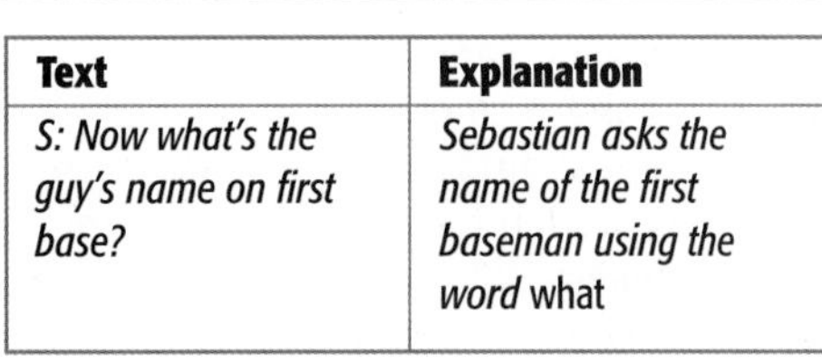

Reading Minilesson

Monitoring Comprehension The routine in "Who's on First?" is funny, but it is also complex. Confusing passages can become clearer when students restate or explain the material in their own words.

Activity Have pairs of students choose dialogue that could cause confusion and jot it in the left column of a chart. In the right column, have them explain what is happening. **L2**

Text	Explanation
S: Now what's the guy's name on first base?	*Sebastian asks the name of the first baseman using the word* what

Additional Resources

Reading Skills Practice Workbook

H Literary Elements

INDIRECT CHARACTERIZATION Ask students what they learn about the characters from the dialogue. *(Most students will say that Sebastian is very literal-minded and not too smart, while Dexter is not very helpful and may be having fun at Sebastian's expense.)*

I Literary Elements

PLOT: *Rising Action* Remind students that the rising action in a plot adds to the conflict or problems in a story. Point out that Sebastian says "Third base" with Dexter. How does this action build excitement? *(This builds excitement because the audience thinks Sebastian might be catching on.)*

J Critical Thinking

DRAWING CONCLUSIONS Have students draw conclusions about what Sebastian can understand and how he has responded to Dexter. The following model illustrates the thinking process involved in drawing conclusions.

Model: Sebastian does not seem to be very smart. He's confused and doesn't understand that *Who* and *What* are names. However, when he and Dexter both say "Third base," he seems to understand something. But then he says, "I don't even know what I'm talking about." I'd say he still doesn't understand.

Teaching Support

DEXTER. Wouldn't this be a fine team without a pitcher?

SEBASTIAN. I don't know. Tell me the pitcher's name.

DEXTER. Tomorrow.

SEBASTIAN. You don't want to tell me today?

DEXTER. I'm telling you, man.

SEBASTIAN. Then go ahead.

DEXTER. Tomorrow.

SEBASTIAN. What time?

DEXTER. What time what?

SEBASTIAN. What time tomorrow are you gonna tell me who's pitching?

DEXTER. Now listen, Who is not pitching. Who is on—

SEBASTIAN. I'll break your arm if you say who's on first.

DEXTER. Then why come up here and ask?

SEBASTIAN. I want to know what's the pitcher's name.

DEXTER. What's on second.

SEBASTIAN. I don't know.

SEBASTIAN AND DEXTER. *Third base!*

SEBASTIAN. Gotta catcher?

DEXTER. Yes.

SEBASTIAN. I'm a good catcher, too, you know.

DEXTER. I know that.

SEBASTIAN. I would like to play for the St. Louis team.

DEXTER. Well, I might arrange that.

SEBASTIAN. I would like to catch. Now, I'm being a good catcher, Tomorrow's pitching on the team, and I'm catching.

DEXTER. Yes.

SEBASTIAN. Tomorrow throws the ball and the guy up bunts the ball.

DEXTER. Yes.

SEBASTIAN. Now, when he bunts the ball—me being a good catcher—I want to throw the guy out at first base, so I pick up the ball and throw it to who?

DEXTER. Now that's the first thing you've said right.

SEBASTIAN. I DON'T EVEN KNOW WHAT I'M TALKING ABOUT.

DEXTER. Well, that's all you have to do.

SEBASTIAN. Is to throw it to first base.

DEXTER. Yes.

SEBASTIAN. Now who's got it?

DEXTER. Naturally.

SEBASTIAN. Who has it?

DEXTER. Naturally.

SEBASTIAN. Naturally.

DEXTER. Naturally.

SEBASTIAN. O.K.

DEXTER. Now you've got it.

SEBASTIAN. I pick up the ball and I throw it to Naturally.

DEXTER. No you don't, you throw the ball to first base.

SEBASTIAN. Then who gets it?

DEXTER. Naturally.

SEBASTIAN. O.K.

DEXTER. All right.

Grammar and Language *Minilesson*

Using Troublesome Words: Homophones Write the words *who's* and *whose* on the board. Remind students that homophones are words that sound the same but are spelled differently. They are entirely different words with different meanings. *Who's* is a contraction of the words *who is*. *Whose* is the possessive form of *who*.

Activity Read the following sentences aloud and ask students to write them down, using the correct form of the homophones. Remind students to consider how the word is used in the sentence to determine its spelling. **L2**

- *Who's* going to the game today?
- *Whose* ticket is this?
- *Who's* the first baseman for the team?
- *Whose* baseball glove is this?

Additional Resources

- ***Grammar and Language Transparency 46***
- ***Grammar and Language Workbook,*** pp. 227–228, 295–296
- ***Grammar and Composition Handbook,*** Lesson 15.1
- ***Writer's Choice,*** Lessons 17.2, 23.5

SEBASTIAN. I throw the ball to Naturally.

DEXTER. You don't. You throw it to Who.

SEBASTIAN. Naturally.

DEXTER. Well, naturally. Say it that way.

SEBASTIAN. That's what I said.

DEXTER. You did not.

SEBASTIAN. I said I'd throw the ball to Naturally.

K

DEXTER. You don't. You throw it to Who.

SEBASTIAN. Naturally.

DEXTER. Yes.

SEBASTIAN. So I throw the ball to first base and Naturally gets it.

DEXTER. No. You throw the ball to first base—

SEBASTIAN. Then who gets it?

DEXTER. Naturally.

SEBASTIAN. That's what I'm saying.

DEXTER. You're not saying that.

SEBASTIAN. Excuse me, folks.

DEXTER. Now, don't get excited. Now, don't get excited.

SEBASTIAN. I throw the ball to first base.

DEXTER. Then Who gets it.

SEBASTIAN. He better get it.

DEXTER. That's it. All right now, don't get excited. Take it easy.

SEBASTIAN. Now I throw the ball to first base, whoever it is grabs the ball, so the guy runs to second.

DEXTER. Uh-huh.

SEBASTIAN. Who picks up the ball and throws it to What. What throws it to I Don't Know. I Don't Know throws it back to Tomorrow—a triple play.

DEXTER. Yeah. It could be.

SEBASTIAN. And I don't care.

L

DEXTER. What was that?

SEBASTIAN. I said, *I don't care*.

DEXTER. Oh, that's our shortstop!

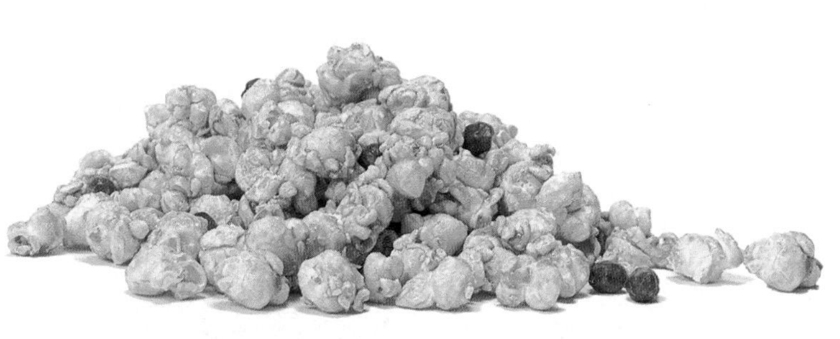

K Literary Elements

DIALOGUE: *Comedy* Ask a pair of volunteers to read this fast-paced dialogue to get the flavor of a comedy skit that has its roots in vaudeville. Encourage students to reread aloud all or part of the skit, concentrating on their timing.

FYI

Triple Play A triple play takes place when the team in the field gets three players out in one play. Though this is always possible, it is a rare event in baseball.

L Literary Elements

DIALOGUE: *Comedy* Ask students if they were surprised by the "punch line" delivered at the end by Sebastian. *(The line, "I don't care," adds a new name to the confusion. It keeps the skit funny to the end.)*

Thematic Focus

Twists and Turns Simple twists and turns in communication between people are quite common. Have students describe a funny experience that was brought about by misunderstanding someone's directions or statements.

ASSESSMENT

Quick Checks, p. 47

Real-World Connection

Mixed-up communication is a common cause of laughter. Have students use comic strips to discuss some other elements of humor in communication.

Activity Have students find a comic strip, such as *Calvin and Hobbes* or *Garfield,* about confused communication. When they have found examples, have students share their comic strips with the class and discuss what makes them funny. As an extension, students might enjoy creating their own comic strips or stories about mixed-up communication. **L2**

Responding to the Selection

PERSONAL RESPONSE

- Students' responses should exhibit their own tastes and those of the people they have interviewed.
- Have students compare and contrast their favorite kind of humor with that of Abbott and Costello.

Analyzing Literature

1. Dexter is playing to the audience and already presenting himself as being in control of Sebastian's role.
2. He wants to be able to identify the players when he goes to the game.
3. He is confused, frustrated, and angry. By the end he says he doesn't care.
4. Sebastian associates "I don't know" with "Third base," but not as a name.
5. Sebastian seems to defer to Dexter. Dexter is calm and in control. Sebastian is easily excited.
6. They should understand the positions and simple terms of baseball.
7. The humor depends on a play on words. For example, *who* and *what* are used as pronouns and as people's names.
8. Most students will answer positively, since the play on words is still valid.
9. Most students will answer positively, because the play on words is well written and baseball is one of America's favorite sports.
10. Most students should be able to remember a situation in which communication was very difficult.

Active Reading and Critical Thinking

Responding to Literature

PERSONAL RESPONSE

- Take a look at your questionnaire results from the **Reading Focus** on page 554. Does "Who's on First?" fit into any of the categories you listed? Which ones?
- Who's your favorite comic or comedy team? How do Abbott and Costello compare with your favorite?

Analyzing Literature

RECALL

1. To what is Dexter referring when he says, "Don't interrupt my act"?
2. Why does Sebastian want to know the names of the players on the St. Louis team?
3. What is Sebastian's reaction to Dexter's information about the players? Does his reaction change by the end of the skit?
4. Does Sebastian ever understand any of the player's names? Give an example.

Brackets connect questions that are paired to develop higher-level thinking skills.

INTERPRET

5. What do you learn about Sebastian's personality from the opening of the skit? What do you learn about Dexter's personality?
6. What knowledge about baseball does the audience need in order to fully appreciate the skit?
7. On what does the humor of "Who's on First?" depend? Explain.

EVALUATE AND CONNECT

8. Do you think the skit is as funny today as it was in the 1940s? Why or why not?
9. "Who's on First?" has been included in a number of anthologies of great American humor. If you were an editor of such a book, would you include it? Why or why not?
10. Have you ever tried to explain something but had no luck in communicating your information? Describe the situation.

LITERARY ELEMENTS

Dialogue

In a play, the plot and the characters' personalities are revealed through the conversations between characters. These conversations are called **dialogue.** In the written form of a play, the dialogue appears following the characters' names. Quotation marks are not used around the characters' words.

Dialogue is not limited to drama. In fiction, writers move a plot along through the characters' own words and interactions. Dialogue also gives readers a break from writing in which a narrator tells everything.

1. What can you tell about Sebastian and Dexter from the dialogue?
2. Would "Who's on First?" be as funny if it were written as a story without dialogue? Why or why not?

- See **Literary Terms Handbook,** p. R3.

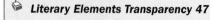

® Be sure to preview the following video for appropriateness for your class.

- ***Abbott & Costello Meet Biography***

LITERARY ELEMENTS

1. Dexter is in control; Sebastian is innocent, literal, and slow to catch on. Dexter doesn't try to clear up the confusion; he may be making fun of Sebastian.
2. No. Though it is possible to describe what takes place, the humor lies in the way the two characters speak quickly back and forth.

Additional Resources

Literary Elements Transparency 47

Extending Your Response

Writing About Literature

Puns Most of the humor in "Who's on First?" is based on puns. A **pun** is a play on words based on two different meanings of the same word or two different words with the same pronunciation. For example, *who* is used both as a pronoun that asks a question and as a player's name. Choose one section of the routine and write a paragraph explaining how the puns create humor.

Literature Groups

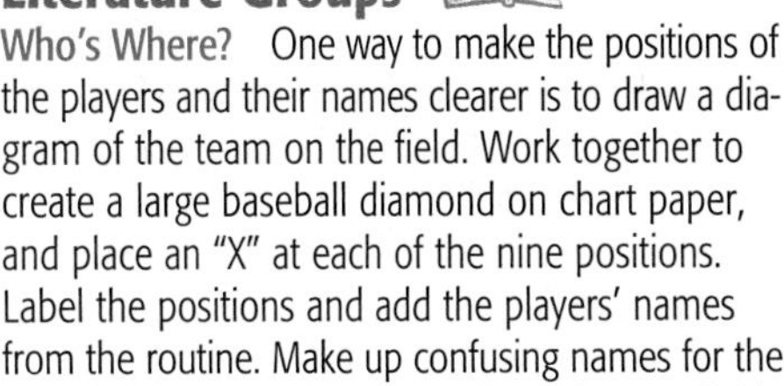

Who's Where? One way to make the positions of the players and their names clearer is to draw a diagram of the team on the field. Work together to create a large baseball diamond on chart paper, and place an "X" at each of the nine positions. Label the positions and add the players' names from the routine. Make up confusing names for the three outfield positions–left, right, and center field–not mentioned in the script. Share your chart with the class.

Creative Writing

Further Confusion Choose a team sport other than baseball. Write a comedy routine using the same names as "Who's on First?" but with positions and action to match the new sport.

Performing

Vaudeville Timing Read "Who's on First?" with a partner, each of you taking one of the parts. You will soon find out that to make the skit truly funny, the dialogue must be spoken with split-second timing. Practice with the script until you feel you can make people laugh at every funny line. Then perform your routine for your classmates or another class.

Reading Further

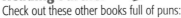

Check out these other books full of puns:

The Laugh Book compiled by Joanna Cole and Stephanie Calmenson

Incognito Mosquito by E. A. Hass

Save your work for your portfolio.

Skill Minilesson

Reteach · Review

VOCABULARY • HOMONYMS

The puns in "Who's on First?" are **homonyms,** words that sound or look alike. Here's another pun.

How do you get down off an elephant?
You don't. You get down off a duck.

To appreciate the pun, you must recognize that *down* can mean "from a higher to a lower place" or "the soft feathers of a duck." Puns have been used in literature dating back at least as far as biblical times. Some of the greatest writers have used them.

Puns are also used in jokes, everyday conversation, newspaper headlines, and advertising.

PRACTICE Work alone or with a partner to practice punning.

1. Make a list of at least five pairs of homonyms. (Remember, many homonyms are spelled differently–for example *peace* and *piece.*)
2. Choose at least one pair of homonyms on your list to make a humorous pun. Share your pun with the class.

Extending Your Response

Writing About Literature

Students' paragraphs should

- focus on one section of the routine
- explain how Abbott and Costello use puns to create the humor

Creative Writing

Students' routines should

- use the same names as "Who's on First?" but apply them to positions in a different sport
- match the action to the new sport

Literature Groups Have students who fully understand baseball help explain the positions to those who do not. Encourage groups to work together, sharing equally the tasks of setting up the paper, making up names, and creating the drawing.

Performing Have students spend an adequate amount of time rehearsing the piece. Encourage students to memorize part or all of the piece.

Skill Minilesson

VOCABULARY • HOMONYMS

1. *Examples:* ball/ball; tear/tear; pair/pear; meet/meat; deer/dear
2. *Example answer:* Where do golfers go to dance? To the golf ball.

ASSESSMENT

- ***Quick Checks,*** p. 47
- ***Selection and Theme Assessment,*** p. 83
- ***Performance Assessment,*** p. 44
- ***Testmaker: ExamView Pro***
- ***Interactive Tutor: Self-Assessment***

Technology Skills

Objectives

- To understand and use hypertext software
- To use hypertext software to complete a writing assignment
- To post a hypertext stack to a school Web site or Intranet site

Teaching Strategies

Help students see how hypertext can help readers follow a train of thought by demonstrating with a site on the Web that includes hypertext and clicking from link to link. You may want to include some or all of the following tasks in your demonstration of hypertext software:

- creating a new hypertext card
- linking cards to create a stack
- adding hyperlinks to graphics, sounds, and animation
- saving and printing a hypertext stack

Adapting to Available Technology

Hypertext software is available for both PCs and Macs. If your school computers do not have large amounts of memory, you may want to suggest that students create hypertext links only to additional text (rather than to videos, animation, or complicated graphics, which use large amounts of memory).

Technology Skills

Multimedia: Using Hypertext

When you learned to read, you trained your eyes to focus on letters that form words and words that form sentences. As you read, your eyes move from left to right and top to bottom on a page. But your mind may not always want to go along with your eyes. That's because the mind is capable of processing a lot of information at once. Suppose you're reading an article about cats. You may run across the line, "Cats, considered sacred by the ancient Egyptians, were often featured in Egyptian art." Before reading the next sentence, you may wonder briefly what such art looked like. But if the article doesn't have pictures, you have to put the thought out of your mind and continue reading.

Hypertext is a computer feature that allows you to follow such trains of thought by linking keywords with related data. You can click on words or phrases that will take you to more information. These clickable words are known as **hyperlinks,** or hotlinks, and they are usually differentiated from regular text through color, bold type, or underlining. If the story about cats were written on a computer in hypertext, it might look something like this:

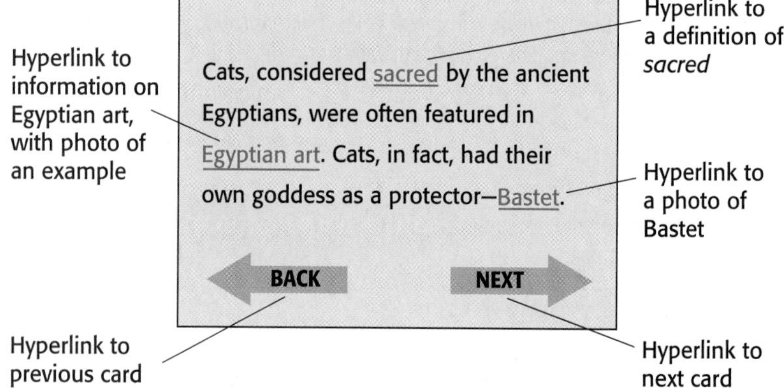
Hyperlink to information on Egyptian art, with photo of an example
Cats, considered sacred by the ancient Egyptians, were often featured in Egyptian art. Cats, in fact, had their own goddess as a protector—Bastet.
Hyperlink to a definition of *sacred*
Hyperlink to a photo of Bastet
BACK
NEXT
Hyperlink to previous card
Hyperlink to next card

Hypertext Software

Hypertext software programs and presentation software allow *you* to write stories, reports, or essays that contain many pages of linked text, graphics, sounds, and even animation! Each page is known as a card, and a group of cards is known as a stack.

Teaching Support

MEETING INDIVIDUAL NEEDS: MULTIPLE MODES OF EXPRESSION

Customized Learning Methods
Hypertext software can allow students with different learning styles to make use of their particular approach.

Activity Invite students to create a hypertext stack in a format that suits their individual learning styles. For example, a logical/mathematical learner might create a timeline or flow chart with links that expand on key dates or important concepts. A spatial learner might create a map, with each site name linked to additional information about that site. A musical learner could create a report on music with links to songs or types of music. Linguistic learners could create stories or essays with links to important concepts. **L2**

To familiarize yourself with your hypertext software, open the program and click on its tutorial. The computer will lead you through the steps of creating a simple stack. (If your software lacks a tutorial, its manufacturer may offer one at its Web site on the Net. Otherwise, find the program's manual, ask your teacher or lab instructor for help, or use the topics in the Help index to learn how to use the program.)

Practice

Hypertext programs are fairly "intuitive." That means that you can figure out the items on their menus and toolbars from their names or by trying them out yourself. Many items and procedures are similar to those you will be familiar with from other software you use–word processing programs, for example.

The following chart may be useful. It tells you how to do some basic operations. The steps are separated by slash marks. For example, *File/New* means pull down the File menu and select New from the options on the menu.

To change a font size or style	Options/Text Style
To include a button that moves the reader to another card	Objects/Add a Button/Actions/Places to Go
To add graphics	File/Add Clip Art [or Photo, Movie]
To add sounds	Objects/Add a Button/Actions/Things to Do/ Play a Sound

1. To create your own hypertext stack, click on **File/New** and follow the prompts.
2. Explore the program by creating a stack that contains at least four linked cards. The stack can be about whatever you like: a short story, an autobiographical sketch, a review, essay, or article about literature, music, television, movies, or any other topic you wish.
3. If you have access to files of clip art, photos, or sounds (including music), add hyperlinks to appropriate graphics or sounds to your stack.
4. Save the stack when you have finished. (Your teacher or lab instructor will tell you where to save it.) Also, print out a copy to put in your portfolio.

ACTIVITIES

1. Complete one of the writing assignments from this unit using hypertext software. Present your work to your classmates.
2. Post your stack to your school's Web site or Intranet.
3. Volunteer to create stacks that describe your school's extracurricular activities. These stacks can be kept in the library and accessed by students who want to learn more about clubs and sports.

Activities

Before beginning, encourage students to suggest organizational strategies for different types of writing using hypertext. For example, some students might suggest creating a new card for each new concept. Others may suggest creating links for important vocabulary words or tangential information. And some may suggest links for visuals, sounds, or photos that augment or help explain the text.

Students' writing assignments should

- demonstrate an ability to use hypertext software to link several cards on one topic
- include links to clip art, photographs, or sounds if these are available
- be correctly posted to the school's Web site or Intranet site

TechnoTalk

New Terms The word *hypertext* was first coined in 1965. It refers to text that is not linear and that contains links to additional text. The links are usually presented in a color and are sometimes underlined or in a different font. When a user clicks or double clicks on a link, they move to a new page or card. *Hypermedia* originally meant hypertext that included links to music, videos, animation, or other media in addition to text links. However, over time, the term *hypertext* has come to be virtually interchangeable with *hypermedia.*

INTERDISCIPLINARY CONNECTION

Science/Social Studies Invite small groups of students to create a hypertext dictionary of important concepts they are learning in science class or a hypertext map to explore a key idea in history or geography.

Activity Have students work in small groups to gather words or concepts to be defined in their dictionary, or to draw a map showing an important historical or geographical concept. Have students divide up the task of creating definitions or explaining places on the map. Finally, have each group create links to the information that group members have compiled. **L2**

Before Reading

Objectives

- To read and analyze a short story about two friends who meet after twenty years
- To recognize how the elements of a short story create its overall impact
- To identify two examples of irony and explain what is ironic about each

Skills

Reading/Thinking: Drawing Conclusions; Comparing and Contrasting
Writing: Paragraph Analyzing Loyalty
Vocabulary: The Suffix *-ity*
Grammar/Language: Adjective Clauses
Life Skills: Newspaper Crime Report
Collaboration: Literature Groups

Motivating STUDENTS

Selection Focus Transparency 48: Have students read the quote from O. Henry. Encourage them to think of times when a story has altered their views about a person, a place, or an event.

Reading Focus: As an extension of the Reading Focus, encourage students to work in small groups to debate the issue of loyalty and friendship.

Before You Read

After Twenty Years

MEET O. HENRY

William Sydney Porter, who used the pen name O. Henry, led a varied but difficult life. Many of his life experiences became material for his stories. He first worked in his uncle's drugstore in North Carolina, then as a sheepherder on a ranch in Texas. He was also a bank teller, a fugitive in Honduras, a prisoner, a magazine editor, and a newspaper writer before he began writing the stories that made him famous. Many of his stories contain a surprise ending or an ironic twist.

William Sydney Porter was born in 1862 and died in 1910.

READING FOCUS

How do you feel about loyalty between friends?

QuickWrite

Write about whether you think a person should always expect loyalty from a friend, no matter what the situation.

Setting a Purpose

Read this story to find out what tests the loyalty of two old friends.

BUILDING BACKGROUND

The Time and Place This story takes place in New York City in the late 1800s.

Did You Know? William Sydney Porter, writing under the name O. Henry, became one of America's most loved writers. Porter's first published stories were written in prison. He spent three years in prison for stealing money from the bank where he worked. He claimed he was innocent, but by using a pseudonym, he made sure his readers would not know about his past.

VOCABULARY PREVIEW

habitual (hə bich′ o͞o əl) *adj.* done by habit; p. 565
intricate (in′ tri kit) *adj.* full of complicated detail; p. 565
artful (ärt′ fəl) *adj.* done with skill or cleverness; p. 565
correspond (kôr′ ə spond′) *v.* to communicate by exchanging letters; p. 567
dismally (diz′ məl lē) *adv.* in a gloomy, cheerless way; p. 567
absurdity (ab sur′ də tē) *n.* the state of being ridiculous, senseless, or irrational; p. 567
moderately (mod′ ər it lē) *adv.* neither too great nor too small; within limits; p. 568

RESOURCE MANAGER

Teaching Tools and Resources
- Theme Six Planning Guide
- Literature Groups Sourcebook

Essential Lesson Support

Lesson-Specific Instruction
- Selection Focus Transparency 48
- Literary Elements Transparency 48
- Active Reading Guide,* p. 48
- Selection Vocabulary Practice, p. 33

Assessment
- Selection Quick Checks,* p. 48
- Sel. and Theme Assmt., p. 84
- Testmaker: ExamView Pro
- Performance Assessment, p. 45

Systematic Language Instruction
- Gr. and Comp. Hbk., L. 11.1
- Vocabulary Power, Lesson 25
- Spelling Power, Lesson 22

English Language Learners
- ELL Sourcebook, pp. 76–77
- Spanish Summaries, p. 48
- Spanish Translations, pp. 139–141
- Audio Library*
- English, Yes!

Spec. Needs/Strat. Interven.
- Interactive Rdg. Sbk., pp. T177–T179
- Interactive Rdg. Wkbk., pp. 93–94
- Inclusion Strat. Sbk., pp. 51–52, 95–96
- Audio Library*

* Also available in Spanish

After Twenty Years

O. Henry

The policeman on the beat moved up the avenue impressively. The impressiveness was habitual and not for show, for spectators were few. The time was barely 10 o'clock at night, but chilly gusts of wind with a taste of rain in them had well nigh depeopled the streets.

A Trying doors as he went, twirling his club with many intricate and artful movements, turning now and then to cast his watchful eye adown the pacific thoroughfare, the officer, with his stalwart[1] form and slight swagger, made a fine picture of a guardian of the peace. The vicinity was one that kept early hours. Now and then you might see the lights of a cigar store or of an all-night lunch counter; but the majority of the doors belonged to business places that had long since been closed.

When about midway of a certain block the policeman suddenly slowed his walk. In the doorway of a darkened hardware store a man leaned, with an unlighted cigar in his mouth. As the policeman walked up to him the man spoke up quickly.

"It's all right, officer," he said, reassuringly. "I'm just waiting for a friend. It's an appointment made twenty years ago. Sounds a little funny to you, doesn't it? Well, I'll explain if you'd like to make certain it's all straight. About that long ago there used to be a restaurant where this store stands—'Big Joe' Brady's restaurant."

"Until five years ago," said the policeman. "It was torn down then."

1. *Pacific* means "calm; peaceful," and *stalwart* means "physically strong."

Vocabulary

habitual (hə bich′ o͞o əl) *adj.* done by habit
intricate (in′ tri kit) *adj.* full of complicated detail
artful (ärt′ fəl) *adj.* done with skill or cleverness

Reading the Selection

SUMMARY

A policeman, patrolling a deserted New York City street on a rainy night, encounters a man in a doorway. The man says he is waiting for his old friend, Jimmy, whom he had agreed to meet at this time and place twenty years ago. After the policeman leaves, "Jimmy" arrives, arrests the man, and hands him a note. The note is from the policeman explaining that he is the real Jimmy, and that he had recognized his old friend as a wanted criminal but could not arrest him face-to-face.

Spanish Summaries, p. 48

A Active Reading Strategies

PREDICT Have students read the title and the first four paragraphs, consider the setting and mood, and predict whether the meeting will be a happy one.

VOCABULARY If you haven't previewed the selection vocabulary with students, stop and remind them to use context clues to unlock the meanings of new vocabulary words.

Additional Resources

Active Reading Guide, p. 48
Audio Library
Spanish Audio Library

Teaching Support

CONNECTING TO OTHER SELECTIONS

The chart at the right shows three ways to connect "After Twenty Years" to other selections in this book.

For specific teaching strategies, see the ***Theme Six Planning Guide.***

Connection	Title
Life Skills: Lifelong Learning	"To James," p. 253
Thematic: Humility	"Primer Lesson," p. 472
Literary: Character	"The Bird Like No Other," p. 473

VIEWING THE PAINTING

Charles Burchfield (1893–1967) was an artist who focused on urban scenes, such as docks, bridges, and industrial areas, in the poorer parts of small cities.

Viewing Response *The wet, empty night streets create a dark and foreboding mood. O. Henry also describes a bleak and lonely setting.*

FYI

O. Henry named his 1906 book of stories about New York City *The Four Million*. A society leader said that there were only 400 people worth knowing in New York—the wealthiest citizens. O. Henry's title declared that all four million New Yorkers had stories worth telling.

B Author's Craft

CHARACTERIZATION Ask students to explain how O. Henry describes this man. *(He portrays the character as well-off in a showy way, but somehow shady because of the scar near his right eyebrow.)*

C Literary Elements

SHORT STORY: *Plot* Have students discuss why the man's explanation is important to the story. *(It introduces the story's characters, setting, and situation.)*

Rainy Night, 1939. Charles Burchfield. Watercolor over pencil, 30 x 42 in. San Diego Museum of Art.

Viewing the painting: What mood does the painting create? What details help create that mood? What details does O. Henry use to create a mood in the story?

B The man in the doorway struck a match and lit his cigar. The light showed a pale, square-jawed face with keen eyes, and a little white scar near his right eyebrow. His scarfpin was a large diamond, oddly set.

"Twenty years ago tonight," said the man, "I dined here at 'Big Joe' Brady's with Jimmy Wells, my best chum, and the finest chap in the world. He and I were raised here in New York, just like two brothers, together. I was eighteen and Jimmy was twenty. The next morning I was to start for the West to make my fortune. You couldn't have dragged Jimmy out of New York; he thought it was the only place on earth. Well, we agreed that night that we would C

Teaching Support

MEETING INDIVIDUAL NEEDS — ENGLISH LANGUAGE LEARNERS

Language from Another Era Explain to English language learners that some of the words and phrases found in this story are not common today.

Activity Write the following in the left column of a chart: *chum, chap, straight, scarfpin, meets, a big proposition, get my pile,* and *gets in a groove.* Have English language learners work with English proficient students to fill in definitions and pronunciations of the terms in the right column. Encourage students to use context clues and to consider the placement of the words in the sentence as they work. Students can use a dictionary as necessary to help develop or confirm their explanations.

Additional Resources

English Language Learners Sourcebook, p. 76

meet here again exactly twenty years from that date and time, no matter what our conditions might be or from what distance we might have to come. We figured that in twenty years each of us ought to have our destiny worked out and our fortunes made, whatever they were going to be."

"It sounds pretty interesting," said the policeman. "Rather a long time between meets, though, it seems to me. Haven't you heard from your friend since you left?"

"Well, yes, for a time we corresponded," said the other. "But after a year or two we lost track of each other. You see, the West is a pretty big proposition, and I kept hustling around over it pretty lively. But I know Jimmy will meet me here if he's alive, for he always was the truest, staunchest[2] old chap in the world. He'll never forget. I came a thousand miles to stand in this door tonight, and it's worth it if my old partner turns up."

The waiting man pulled out a handsome watch, the lids of it set with small diamonds.

"Three minutes to ten," he announced. "It was exactly ten o'clock when we parted here at the restaurant door."

"Did pretty well out West, didn't you?" asked the policeman.

"You bet! I hope Jimmy has done half as well. He was a kind of plodder,[3] though, good fellow as he was. I've had to compete with some of the sharpest wits going to get my pile. A man gets in a groove in New York. It takes the West to put a razor-edge on him."

The policeman twirled his club and took a step or two.

"I'll be on my way. Hope your friend comes around all right. Going to call time on him sharp?"

"I should say not!" said the other. "I'll give him half an hour at least. If Jimmy is alive on earth he'll be here by that time. So long, officer."

"Good-night, sir," said the policeman, passing on along his beat, trying doors as he went.

There was now a fine, cold drizzle falling, and the wind had risen from its uncertain puffs into a steady blow. The few foot passengers astir in that quarter hurried dismally and silently along with coat collars turned high and pocketed hands. And in the door of the hardware store the man who had come a thousand miles to fill an appointment, uncertain almost to absurdity, with the friend of his youth, smoked his cigar and waited.

2. Here, *proposition* means "a challenging opportunity" and *staunchest* means "most loyal and dependable."

3. A *plodder* is someone who moves slowly, but the man means that Jimmy was not a quick thinker.

Vocabulary
correspond (kôr′ ə spond′) *v.* to communicate by exchanging letters
dismally (diz′ məl lē) *adv.* in a gloomy, cheerless way
absurdity (ab sur′ də tē) *n.* the state of being ridiculous, senseless, or irrational

D Literary Elements

DIALOGUE: *Short Story* Ask students what the dialogue reveals about the man in the doorway. *(The man feels that Jimmy Wells is still his best friend. He values loyalty and he trusts his friend.)*

E Literary Elements

FORESHADOWING Ask students what they think O. Henry is preparing readers to expect. *(He lets the reader know that the man in the doorway has become rich ("to get my pile"), and is sure his friend probably has not, foreshadowing a conflict.)*

F Critical Thinking

DRAWING CONCLUSIONS Encourage students to think about the policeman's question. Do they find it strange? *(Even though it sounds like a friendly chat, the policeman seems to have something in mind.)*

G Literary Elements

SHORT STORY: *Setting* Invite students to explain how they think this description affects the mood of the story. *(Details seem to build up tension in the story: the storm has increased in intensity; there are only a few people outdoors, and they are described as hurrying "dismally.")*

You may wish to use ***Fine Art Transparency 11*** to extend theme-related concepts.

Reading Minilesson

Comparing and Contrasting "After Twenty Years" focuses on two very different characters. Though they are old friends, their personalities are almost opposite, and their lives have gone in very different directions.

Activity Have students create a Venn diagram showing how Bob and Jimmy are different and similar. **L2**

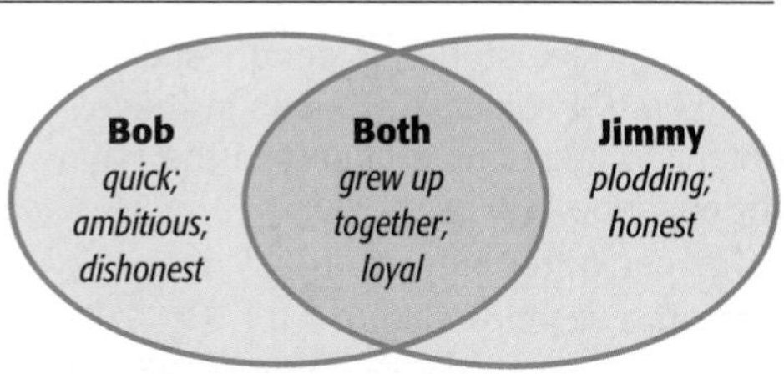

Additional Resources

Reading Skills Practice Workbook

H Literary Elements

SHORT STORY: *Rising Action* Ask students to describe the rising action and its purpose in this story. *(After the long wait and all the discussion, Jimmy has finally arrived. The tension increases and readers will at last learn what is really happening.)*

I Literary Elements

FORESHADOWING It would be strange for Bob not to remember that his friend is so tall. Have students explain what O. Henry might be hinting. *(When the man thinks twice about this man being Jimmy, so should the reader.)*

J Literary Elements

SHORT STORY: *Climax* The climax of a story is the point of greatest emotional intensity or suspense. Have students explain where they think the climax of this story is. *(The climax occurs when Bob realizes the man is not Jimmy.)*

Thematic Focus

Twists and Turns Have students discuss the unexpected events that take place in this story and how they relate to the theme.

ASSESSMENT

Quick Checks, p. 48

About twenty minutes he waited, and then a tall man in a long overcoat, with collar turned up to his ears, hurried across from the opposite side of the street. He went directly to the waiting man.

"Is that you, Bob?" he asked, doubtfully.

"Is that you, Jimmy Wells?" cried the man in the door.

"Bless my heart!" exclaimed the new arrival, grasping both the other's hands with his own. "It's Bob, sure as fate. I was certain I'd find you here if you were still in existence. Well, well, well!—twenty years is a long time. The old restaurant's gone, Bob; I wish it had lasted, so we could have had another dinner there. How has the West treated you, old man?"

"Bully;[4] it has given me everything I asked it for. You've changed lots, Jimmy. I never thought you were so tall by two or three inches."

"Oh, I grew a bit after I was twenty."

"Doing well in New York, Jimmy?"

"Moderately. I have a position in one of the city departments. Come on, Bob; we'll go around to a place I know of, and have a good long talk about old times."

The two men started up the street, arm in arm. The man from the West, his egotism[5] enlarged by success, was beginning to outline the history of his career. The other, submerged in his overcoat, listened with interest.

At the corner stood a drug store, brilliant with electric lights. When they came into this glare each of them turned simultaneously to gaze upon the other's face.

The man from the West stopped suddenly and released his arm.

"You're not Jimmy Wells," he snapped. "Twenty years is a long time, but not long enough to change a man's nose from a Roman to a pug."[6]

"It sometimes changes a good man into a bad one," said the tall man. "You've been under arrest for ten minutes, 'Silky' Bob. Chicago thinks you may have dropped over our way and wires us she wants to have a chat with you. Going quietly, are you? That's sensible. Now, before we go on to the station here's a note I was asked to hand you. You may read it here at the window. It's from Patrolman Wells."

The man from the West unfolded the little piece of paper handed him. His hand was steady when he began to read, but it trembled a little by the time he had finished. The note was rather short.

> BOB: I was at the appointed place on time. When you struck the match to light your cigar I saw it was the face of the man wanted in Chicago. Somehow I couldn't do it myself, so I went around and got a plain clothes[7] man to do the job.
>
> JIMMY.

4. *Bully* is slang for "excellent; first-rate."
5. Here, *egotism* refers to an exaggerated sense of self-importance.
6. A *Roman nose* is long and bold, while a *pug* is short, thick, and turned-up.
7. *Plain clothes* refers to a police officer who does not wear a uniform while on duty.

Vocabulary
moderately (mod′ ər it lē) *adv.* neither too great nor too small; within limits

Teaching Support

Grammar and Language *Minilesson*

Adjective Clauses Write the following example on the board:

- *Then a man who wore a long overcoat hurried across the street.*

Point out that *"who wore a long overcoat"* tells something about the noun *man.* An adjective clause adds information about a noun or a pronoun in the main clause and is usually introduced by a relative pronoun *(that, which, who, what, etc.).*

Activity Have students identify and underline the adjective clauses in these sentences and double underline the nouns they describe. **L2**

1. The cabin that sits on the hill is our favorite vacation spot.
2. Susan is a person who excels at many different sports.
3. The chess game, which was very challenging, lasted seven hours.

Additional Resources

Grammar and Language Transparency 47

Grammar and Language Workbook, pp. 157–158

Grammar and Composition Handbook, Lesson 8.3

Writer's Choice, Lesson 14.3

Responding to Literature

PERSONAL RESPONSE

- What surprised you most about the ending of the story?
- Can you think of an alternative ending for the story?

Analyzing Literature

RECALL

1. For whom is the man from the West waiting? What promise did he make twenty years ago?
2. What does the Westerner tell the police officer about Jimmy's character?
3. After the police officer leaves, who approaches the Westerner?
4. What does Jimmy reveal in his note?

Brackets connect questions that are paired to develop higher-level thinking skills.

INTERPRET

5. Why does the man from the West try so hard to reassure the police officer?
6. What is Jimmy Wells's internal conflict in the story?
7. What does the Westerner's physical reaction to the note tell you about his emotional state?
8. What do you think motivated Jimmy to do what he did to his old friend at the end?

EVALUATE AND CONNECT

9. In your opinion, what is the author saying about measuring success in a person's life? How has Jimmy been both more successful and less successful than Bob?
10. Theme Connection Did O. Henry surprise you? Why or why not?

LITERARY ELEMENTS

Short Story

A **short story** is a brief work of fiction that usually can be read in one sitting. Short stories have the usual elements of fiction—plot, character, setting, and theme. These are the events, people, places, and ideas that make a short story complete. The combination of these elements determines the story's overall impact on the reader.

1. What surprising facts do you learn about each character at the end of O. Henry's story?
2. What theme does the story communicate about the twists and turns of life and the way people can change?

- See **Literary Terms Handbook,** p. R10.

Night Shadows. Edward Hopper (1882–1967). Etching, sheet: 12 3/16 x 15 15/16 in., plate: 7 x 8 1/4 in. Whitney Museum of American Art, New York. Josephine N. Hopper bequest.

Responding to the Selection

PERSONAL RESPONSE

- Students will probably say that the policeman was Jimmy Wells or that Bob was a wanted man.
- Students may say that Bob could have recognized Jimmy and escaped.

Analyzing Literature

1. The man is waiting for his old friend. He promised twenty years ago to meet him at this spot.
2. He tells the policeman that Jimmy is a good fellow but a bit plodding.
3. Another man, who says he is Jimmy, approaches the Westerner.
4. Jimmy reveals that he had to do his duty as a policeman, but that he could not personally arrest his old friend.
5. He does not want the policeman to question him.
6. Jimmy Wells cannot bring himself to arrest his old friend even though he recognizes him as a wanted criminal.
7. The Westerner's hands begin to tremble when he realizes that his friend has turned him in. It tells that he is extremely shaken by the revelation.
8. Jimmy is motivated by his sense of duty as a policeman.
9. The author is saying that success can't be measured by wealth alone, since Bob, with all his money, has had to live in hiding. Most students will probably say that Jimmy has been more successful in leading an honest life, even though he has been less successful at making money.
10. Most students will say they were surprised by some aspect of the story. Encourage them to explain their answers with details from the story.

LITERARY ELEMENTS

1. The man claiming to be Jimmy is not. The policeman is Bob's old friend who recognizes him as a wanted criminal.
2. Even people who begin their lives the same way can become very different, based on their personalities and the circumstances of their lives.

Additional Resources

Literary Elements Transparency 48

Extending Your Response

Personal Writing

Students' responses should

- describe how they feel about Jimmy's choice to do his duty and turn in a friend
- draw examples from the story and from their own experience

Literature Groups Before students complete the chart, have them discuss how they think each character might change in the future due to his life circumstances.

Learning for Life To give students a sense of newspaper reporting style, show them examples of crime reports. Have them read their own reports aloud in small groups.

Writing About Literature

Students' paragraphs should

- identify two specific examples of irony in the story
- explain what is ironic about each example

Skill Minilesson

VOCABULARY • THE SUFFIX *-ity*

1. c
2. a
3. e
4. b
5. d

Additional Resources

Vocabulary Practice, p. 33

Extending Your Response

Personal Writing

Judging Loyalty Look back at what you wrote about loyalty in the **Reading Focus** on page 564. Then write a response to Jimmy's choice in choosing between personal loyalty to a friend and loyalty to his duty as a police officer.

Literature Groups

Friend or Foe? Use examples from the story to create a chart that compares and contrasts Jimmy and Bob. Consider their physical and emotional characteristics and their past and future lives.

Characteristics	Jimmy	Bob
Physical		
Emotional		
Career		

Learning for Life

Crime Column Write a report for the crime section of the newspaper to inform the public of the arrest of "Silky" Bob. Include a description of the suspect and a tribute to the quick thinking of Officer Jimmy Wells.

Writing About Literature

Irony **Irony** is a difference between appearance and reality. A story is ironic when it focuses on the differences between the way things seem to be and the way they actually are. In a paragraph, identify two specific examples of irony in "After Twenty Years" and explain what is ironic about each.

Reading Further

If you would like to read other stories by O. Henry, try these books:

The Best Short Stories of O. Henry

The Gift of the Magi and Other Stories

Save your work for your portfolio.

Skill Minilesson

Reteach · Review

VOCABULARY • THE SUFFIX *-ity*

When *-ity* is added to the end of a word, it adds the meaning "state or condition." *Absurd* means "ridiculous," and *absurdity* means "the state of being ridiculous." Adding the suffix *-ity* usually changes the way the base word sounds. For example, the first syllable is stressed in *rapid,* but the second syllable is stressed in *rapidity.* Remember that when a suffix is added to most words ending with a silent *e,* the *e* is dropped: *antique* + *-ity* = *antiquity.*

PRACTICE Use what you know about familiar words and the suffix *-ity* to match each word with a word that has a similar meaning.

1. solidity
2. illegality
3. abnormality
4. antiquity
5. circularity

a. lawlessness
b. oldness
c. hardness
d. roundness
e. oddness

ASSESSMENT

Quick Checks, p. 48

Selection and Theme Assessment, p. 84

Performance Assessment, p. 45

Testmaker: ExamView Pro

Interactive Tutor: Self-Assessment

LISTENING, SPEAKING, and VIEWING

Storytelling

Is there a trick to telling a story aloud to an audience? Not really. All you have to do is practice. Learn your story well enough so that, even if you use notes, you don't have to read them word-for-word. Above all, practice. Practice in front of a mirror to be comfortable with yourself. Practice in front of a friend, and ask for feedback. Practice with a tape recorder or video camera to experiment with your voice and body language.

Whether you're spinning a tale you know by heart or telling a story you've written yourself, the following guidelines can help.

Storytelling Guidelines

- Stand or sit with good posture; it helps your voice to carry.
- Look at your listeners. When they return your gaze, you have their attention. Maintain eye contact as you speak.
- Change positions from time to time so that you don't tense up.
- Vary your volume and pacing to fit the story.
- Keep checking your listeners' responses. If they fidget, ask yourself why.
- Feel free to "talk with your hands." If you wish, take on characters' roles by changing your posture, gestures, and tone of voice.

ACTIVITIES

1. With a classmate, practice and take turns telling a story you both know well. Follow the above guidelines.
2. Tell classmates a story you have written. Score yourself afterward on how well you followed the **Storytelling Guidelines.**

LISTENING, SPEAKING, and VIEWING

Objective

- To recognize and apply strategies for storytelling

Teaching Strategies

After reading the storytelling guidelines on page 571, you may ask students to demonstrate the techniques with partners. They can use a typical opening line, such as, *Once upon a time, there lived a lonely prince...* over and over as they demonstrate standing and sitting with good/bad posture, looking/not looking at listeners, varying volume/speaking in a monotone. Encourage students to exaggerate the techniques as a way of becoming comfortable and having fun with the guidelines. Have each speaker's partner offer helpful suggestions for improving the speaker's delivery.

Activities

1. Students may decide to tell the same story or choose different stories both are familiar with.
2. Some students may wish to make a written checklist of the guidelines in order to score themselves in each category. Others may prefer to score themselves with an overall rating.

Teaching Support

MEETING INDIVIDUAL NEEDS

ENGLISH LANGUAGE LEARNERS

Group Storytelling Encourage English language learners to share a group story with the class, either orally or in written form.

Activity To encourage collaboration, have students form a circle, and explain that everyone will contribute one sentence to a class story. Begin with a simple story opener, such as, *Once, there was a girl who lived on a mountain.* Ask the next student to add a line. The story is always repeated from the beginning as it builds, giving English language learners plenty of opportunity to listen, understand, and contribute to creating the group story.

Additional Resources

English Language Learners Sourcebook, p. 77

Before Reading

Objectives

- To read and analyze a radio drama
- To explain the effects of various kinds of stage directions
- To compare and contrast dialogues and monologues in a radio drama

Skills

Reading/Thinking: Inferring; Synthesizing; Drawing Conclusions; Making Critical Judgments; Verifying Predictions; Cause and Effect; Comparing and Contrasting
Writing: Rewriting a Play as a Short Story; Writing Newspaper Article
Vocabulary: Etymology
Grammar/Language: Using Commas to Join Main Clauses
Listening/Speaking: Reading a Scene
Life Skills: Creating and Producing
Collaboration: Creating a Radio Play; Literature Groups

Motivating → STUDENTS

Literature Launchers: "An American Icon: Mark Twain"

Videodisc Side B, Segment 17

Also available in VHS.

Selection Focus Transparency 49: Have students view the transparency and discuss the questions.

Reading Focus: Invite students to discuss the needs and desires that many people have in common.

Before You Read

The Million-Pound Bank Note

MEET MARK TWAIN

Mark Twain found inspiration for his writing in childhood experiences along the Mississippi River, as well as from being a riverboat pilot, a gold panner, and a journalist. Generations of readers worldwide have enjoyed his work as a novelist, short-story writer, essayist, humorist, journalist, and literary critic. He is one of the great figures of American literature.

Samuel Langhorne Clemens, better known as Mark Twain, was born in 1835 and died in 1910.

READING FOCUS

What would you do with a million dollars?

Graph It!
Gather suggestions from your classmates and work together to graph the class's responses.

Setting a Purpose
Read this play to find out how one man is affected by having a banknote worth a million British pounds.

BUILDING BACKGROUND

The Time and Place The story takes place in the late 1800s.

This scene is from the 1954 film version of Twain's story, titled *Man with a Million.*

VOCABULARY PREVIEW

proposition (prop′ ə zish′ ən) *n.* something offered for consideration; proposal; p. 573
conceive (kən sēv′) *v.* to form an image or idea of; p. 577
competent (kom′ pət ənt) *adj.* having enough ability for the purpose; capable; p. 577
rebuke (ri būk′) *n.* an expression of sharp criticism or disapproval; p. 578
eccentric (ik sen′ trik) *adj.* not usual or normal in behavior; peculiar; p. 578
benefactor (ben′ ə fak′ tər) *n.* one who gives financial assistance; p. 584
shrewd (shro͞od) *adj.* sharp, clever, and practical; p. 584

RESOURCE MANAGER

Teaching Tools and Resources
- Theme Six Planning Guide
- Literature Groups Sourcebook

Essential Lesson Support

Lesson-Specific Instruction
- Selection Focus Transparency 49
- Literary Elements Transparency 49
- Active Reading Guide,* p. 49
- Selection Vocabulary Practice, p. 34

Assessment
- Selection Quick Checks,* p. 49
- Sel. and Theme Assmt., pp. 85-86
- Testmaker: ExamView Pro
- Performance Assessment, p. 46

Systematic Language Instruction
- Gr. and Comp. Hbk., L. 11.2

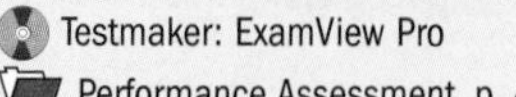

English Language Learners
- ELL Sourcebook, p. 78
- Spanish Summaries, p. 49
- Spanish Translations, pp. 142-157
- Audio Library*
- English, Yes!

Spec. Needs/Strat. Interven.
- Interactive Rdg. Sbk., pp. T180-T183
- Interactive Rdg. Wkbk., pp. 95-98
- Inclusion Strat. Sbk., pp. 83-84
- Audio Library*

* Also available in Spanish

The Million-Pound Bank Note

Mark Twain

Dramatized for radio by Walter Hackett

CAST OF CHARACTERS

HENRY ADAMS	SERVANT	SECOND MAN
LLOYD HASTINGS	TOD	WOMAN
FIRST COCKNEY	MR. SMEDLEY	THIRD MAN
GORDON FEATHERSTONE	HOTEL MANAGER	BUTLER
ABEL FEATHERSTONE	SECOND COCKNEY	PORTIA LANGHAM
ALBERT HAWKINS	FIRST MAN	SIR ALFRED

HENRY. When I was twenty-seven years old, I was a mining broker's clerk in San Francisco. I was alone in the world, and had nothing to depend upon but my wits and a clean reputation. These were setting my feet in the road to eventual fortune, and I was content with the prospect. During my spare time, I did outside work. One of my part-time employers was Lloyd Hastings, a mining broker. During this period I was helping Hastings to verify[1] the Gould and Curry Extension papers, covering what seemed to be a highly valuable gold mine. One morning at two, after six hard hours of work on these papers, Lloyd Hastings and I went to the What Cheer restaurant in Frisco. As we lingered over our coffee, he offered me a proposition.

HASTINGS. Henry, how would you like to go to London?

HENRY. Thank you, no.

HASTINGS. Listen to me. I'm thinking of taking a month's option[2] on the Gould and Curry Extension for the locators.

HENRY. And—?

HASTINGS. They want one million dollars for it.

HENRY. Not too much—if the claim works out the way it appears it may.

HASTINGS. I'm going to try to sell it to London interests, which means a trip there, and I want you to go with me, because you know more about these papers than I.

1. Here, *prospect* means "possibility of future success." To *verify* the papers is to check the accuracy of their information.

2. In financial terms, an *option* is a right to buy or sell something for a certain price and within a certain time.

Vocabulary

proposition (prop′ ə zish′ ən) *n.* something offered for consideration; proposal

Reading the Selection

SUMMARY

Henry is an American alone in London with no money. Two wealthy brothers give Henry a million-pound bank note for one month. They have made a bet about what Henry will do with the money. Henry knows that he cannot cash a million-pound note at a bank. No one will believe the money is his, and he will be arrested. How will Henry survive?

Spanish Summaries, p. 49

A Active Reading Strategies

PREDICT Invite students to look at the title and the cast of characters. Then have volunteers read the first page aloud. Encourage students to predict what the central conflict will be, whether Henry will go to London, and whether Hastings will sell the mine option for a million dollars.

VOCABULARY If you haven't previewed the selection vocabulary with students, stop and remind them to use context clues to unlock the meanings of new vocabulary words.

Additional Resources

- ***Active Reading Guide,*** p. 49
- ***Audio Library***
- ***Spanish Audio Library***

Teaching Support

CONNECTING TO OTHER SELECTIONS

COMPARING selections

This selection is compared with "Force of Luck" on pages 591–598. A lesson for teaching a comparison of the two selections appears on page 600.

The chart at the right shows three other ways to connect "The Million-Pound Bank Note" to other selections in this book.

For specific teaching strategies, see the ***Theme Six Planning Guide.***

Connection	Title
Life Skills: Interpersonal Skills	→ "The Teacher Who Changed My Life," p. 368
Thematic: Decisions	→ "Amigo Brothers," p. 433
Literary: Dialogue	→ "All Summer in a Day," p. 461

Viewing the Painting

Joseph Pennell was an American artist born in 1857. Like Henry in this drama, Pennell moved to London. Pennell created more than 1,500 works showing buildings and landscapes. His subjects ranged from English factories to Greek temples.

Viewing Response *Some students might choose to go on a shopping spree in the local shops. Others might opt for a meal at the best restaurant in London, a suite at a luxury hotel, a sightseeing tour, or any combination of these and other options.*

N Critical Thinking

DRAWING CONCLUSIONS Invite students to explain what Henry has learned from his experience in the restaurant that he may be remembering here. *(Henry has learned that stores cannot make change for his bank note and may, therefore, give him the goods he wants on credit.)*

O Literary Elements

STAGE DIRECTIONS Invite students to explain how these stage directions help the actors say their lines. *(Explanations like "he stutters and fumbles" and "raising voice" indicate that Tod should sound flustered and nervous. Until now he has seemed self-assured and condescending toward Henry.)*

West Front of St. Paul's from Ludgate Hill. Joseph Pennell (1857–1926). Gouache en grisaille on paper laid down on board, 20 x 13¾ in. Private collection.

Viewing the painting: What would you want to see or do if you were in this scene with a million-pound bank note?

TOD. Hah!

N HENRY. I simply don't wish to put you to the trouble of changing a large note.

TOD. As long as rebukes are going around, I might say that it wasn't quite your affair to infer[16] that we couldn't change any note that you might happen to be carrying around. On the contrary, we *can*.

HENRY. Oh, very well. I apologize. Here you are.

TOD. Thank you. [*A complete change. He stutters and fumbles.*] Ah—it's—ah—that is—we—ah—you see—It's— [*Quickly.*] take it back, please. [*Raising voice.*] Mr. Smedley! Mr. Smedley! Help! Oh, Mr. Smedley. O

SMEDLEY. [*Coming in. A fussy man.*] What is it, Tod, what is it? Stop shouting!

TOD. Oh, but Mr. Smedley, I can't control myself.

SMEDLEY. What's up? What's the trouble? What's wanting? Who's this?

HENRY. I am a customer and I am waiting for my change.

SMEDLEY. Change, change! Tod, give him his change. Get it for him.

TOD. Get him his change! It's easy for you to say that, Mr. Smedley, but look at the bill yourself.

SMEDLEY. Bill, bill! Let me see it! [*Pause.*] Tod, you ass, selling an eccentric millionaire

16. Here, *infer* means "to come to a conclusion based on something assumed."

Vocabulary

rebuke (ri būk′) *n.* an expression of sharp criticism or disapproval

eccentric (ik sen′ trik) *adj.* not usual or normal in behavior; peculiar

Teaching Support

Listening and Speaking *Minilesson*

Reading a Scene Aloud Work with students to list some guidelines on the board to help students read aloud a scene, such as the one between Tod and Henry. *(Practice. Read some parts slower or faster, louder or softer. Make eye contact. Don't rush. Read with feeling.)*

Activity Encourage pairs of students to examine the stage directions in the scene for ideas about how to say the lines. Then have pairs practice reading aloud the scene beginning with "No chores to be done here..." and ending with "Oh, Mr. Smedley." When pairs are ready, invite them to present their scenes to the class. Encourage audience members to listen attentively to help the performers feel confident. **L2**

such an unspeakable suit as that. Tod, you're a fool—a born fool! Drives every millionaire away from this place, because he can't tell a millionaire from a tramp. Here, sir, are some suits more in keeping with your position.

HENRY. Thank you, but this one will do.

SMEDLEY. Of course it won't do! I shall burn it. Tod, burn this suit at once.

TOD. Yes, Mr. Smedley.

P **SMEDLEY.** We shall be honored to outfit you completely, sir . . . morning clothes, evening dress, sack suits, tweeds, shetlands—everything you need. Come, Tod, book and pen. Now—length of leg, 32 inches; sleeve—

HENRY. But look here, I can't give you an order for suits, unless you can wait indefinitely,[17] or change this bill.

SMEDLEY. Indefinitely, sir. It's a weak word, a weak word. *Eternally, that's* the word, sir. Tod, rush these things through. Let the minor customers wait. Set down the gentleman's address and—

Q **HENRY.** I'm changing my quarters. I'll drop in and leave the new address.

SMEDLEY. Quite right, sir, quite right. One moment—allow me to show you out, sir. And don't worry about paying us. [*Fading.*] Your credit is the highest. Good day, sir, good day. You honor us greatly, sir.

R **HENRY.** [*As though sighing.*] Well, don't you see what was bound to happen? I drifted naturally into whatever I wanted. Take my hotel, for example. I merely showed the resident manager my million-pound note, and he said:

MANAGER. We are honored to have you as a guest, sir. Now, I have just the suite for you. It consists of a bedroom, sitting room, a dressing room, a dining room, two baths and—

HENRY. I'll pay you a month in advance with this.

MANAGER. [*Laughing.*] You honor our simple hotel, sir. Pray, don't worry about the bill.

HENRY. But it may be several months before I can pay you.

MANAGER. We're not worried, Mr.—er—

HENRY. Henry Adams.

MANAGER. Mr. Adams, you are a most distinguished guest. [*Fading.*] Anything you desire, please name it and we shall procure it for you immediately. Thank you, sir.

HENRY. And there I was, sumptuously housed in an expensive hotel in Hanover Square. I took my dinners there, but for breakfast I stuck by Hawkins' humble feeding-house, where I had got my first meal on my million-pound bank note. I was the making of Hawkins. S

[SOUND. *Rattle of dishes and silver, customers' voices ad-libbing*[18] *in background.*]

HAWKINS. Business is brisk, sir, very brisk, indeed, and has been ever since you and your million-pound bank note became patrons of my humble establishment. I've had to hire extra help, put in additional tables. Look for yourself, sir. There's a long line waiting to get in. Why, I'm famous and fair on my way to becoming wealthy.

17. To wait *indefinitely* would be for an unlimited length of time.

18. *Ad libbing* is saying things that are not written in a script.

P Active Reading Strategies

EVALUATE Encourage students to explain why shop owners treat Henry so differently once they see the bank note. *(They think Henry is rich and powerful, even though he dresses like a beggar.)*

Q Active Reading Strategies

QUESTION Have students explain why Henry says he is changing his quarters. *(Henry doesn't yet have a place to live, so he can't give an address.)*

R Literary Elements

NARRATOR Encourage students to offer an explanation of this monologue's purpose. Why does Henry speak directly to the radio audience? *(To help listeners realize that the action is moving from the tailor shop to a hotel.)*

S Critical Thinking

DRAWING CONCLUSIONS Have students explain how Henry is the "making of Hawkins." *(As word spreads that Henry, who people think is a millionaire, eats at Hawkins' eating-house, it becomes very popular.)*

Writing Minilesson

Rewriting a Play as a Short Story Mark Twain's original version, written as a short story, described important elements through narration. This radio drama, on the other hand, has to depend exclusively on what the characters say.

Activity Have students rewrite one of the scenes as it might appear in a short story. They should include a description of the setting to help readers picture the scene and descriptions of the characters' behavior and thoughts. After the scenes have been written, discuss what students have learned about the characteristics of drama and prose fiction. **L2**

Additional Resources

Writer's Choice, Lessons 4.1–4.4

Critical Thinking

MAKING CRITICAL JUDGMENTS Have students discuss whether Henry is being honest. *(Henry allows others to believe he is rich, even though the money isn't his.)*

Active Reading Strategies

PREDICT Now that Henry is famous and people recognize him on the street, do students think his problems are over? Or will his notoriety lead to new problems? Have them explain their predictions. *(Some may feel his financial problems are over. Others may feel he will have new problems, such as having destitute people ask him for money or thieves try to steal his money.)*

Critical Thinking

VERIFYING PREDICTIONS Have students check the predictions they made on p. 574. Now that Henry is reconnected with Hastings, have them reevaluate their earlier predictions. *(Some may still think Henry will help Hastings sell the mine. Others may think that Henry will work for Hastings, since Henry needs money.)*

COCKNEY 2. Pardon me, Guv'ner,[19] but aren't you the gentleman what owns the million-pound bank note?

HAWKINS. Look here, you, go away and stop bothering Mr.— Mr.—

HENRY. Adams.

HAWKINS. Mr. Adams.

COCKNEY 2. I was just anxious to get a look at him.

HAWKINS. Who? Mr. Adams?

COCKNEY 2. No. The bank note.

HENRY. Glad to oblige. There you are.

COCKNEY 2. By George, it *is* real. [*Fading.*] Now I can go home and tell me old lady I've seen it with me own eyes. I hopes she believes me, but she won't.

HAWKINS. Mr. Adams, I wonder if I couldn't force upon you a small loan—even a large one.

HENRY. Oh, no.

HAWKINS. Please allow me, sir.

HENRY. [*Relenting.*][20] Well, as a matter of fact, I haven't gotten around to changing this note.

HAWKINS. Fifty pounds might help tide you over. You know, a little spending money?

HENRY. It would help, a bit.

HAWKINS. I consider it a great honor. [*Fading.*] Indeed, a very great honor. Here you are, Mr. Adams, fifty pounds it is. [*Fading.*] And don't worry about repaying me.

HENRY. I was in, now, and must sink or swim. I walked on air. And it was natural, for I had become one of the notorieties[21] of London. It turned my head, not just a little, but a great deal. The newspapers referred to me as the "Vest-Pocket Millionaire." Then came the climaxing stroke: "Punch" caricatured[22] me! Wherever I went, people cried:

MAN 1. There he goes!

MAN 2. That's him!

WOMAN 1. Morning, Guv'ner.

MAN 3. He's a bit of all right, he is.

HENRY. Why, I just swam in glory all day long. About the tenth day of my fame I fulfilled my duty to my country by calling upon the American Ambassador. He received me with enthusiasm, and insisted that I attend a dinner party he was giving the following night. Two important things happened at that dinner. I met two people who were to play important roles in the little drama I was living. Among the guests was a lovely English girl, named Portia Langham, whom I fell in love with in two minutes, and she with me; I could see it without glasses. And just before dinner, the butler announced:

[BIZ. *Guests ad-libbing in background, very politely.*]

BUTLER. [*Calling out.*] Mr. Lloyd Hastings.

HENRY. I stared at Hastings and he at me, his mouth open in surprise.

HASTINGS. I, er—pardon me, but are you? No, of course you can't be.

HENRY. [*Chuckling.*] But I am, Lloyd.

HASTINGS. Henry, I'm speechless. [*Suddenly.*] Don't tell me that you're also the Vest-Pocket Millionaire?

19. *Guv'ner* ("Governor") is Cockney dialect for addressing a man in authority or of a higher social class.
20. Here, *relenting* means "giving in."
21. A *notoriety* is someone who has become a celebrity.
22. *Punch* is a British humor magazine. It *caricatured* Henry in a cartoon that ridiculously exaggerated his features.

Teaching Support

INTERDISCIPLINARY CONNECTION

Social Studies/Economics When this drama was written, one British pound equaled approximately five U.S. dollars.

Activity Students may work in pairs or small groups to examine exchange rates around the world today. Exchange rates are listed in many newspapers. They can also be found on the Internet. Have students first research how much one British pound is worth in U.S. dollars today. Then have students determine what unit of currency is used in Canada, Mexico, or any other country that interests them. Students can then find the worth of one unit of that currency in U.S. dollars. Encourage students to create a chart with their findings and share them with the rest of the class. **L2**

HENRY. Correct!

HASTINGS. I've seen your own name coupled with the nickname, but it never occurred to me you were *the* Henry Adams. Why, it isn't six months since you were clerking in Frisco, and sitting up nights helping me verify the Gould and Curry Extension papers. The idea of your being in London, and a vast millionaire, and a colossal celebrity! It's out of the Arabian Nights!

HENRY. I can't realize it myself.

W **HASTINGS.** It was just three months ago that we were eating together, and I tried to persuade you to come to London with me. You turned me down and now here you are. How did you happen to come, and what gave you this incredible start?

HENRY. I'll tell you all about it, but not now.

HASTINGS. When?

HENRY. The end of this month.

HASTINGS. Make it a week.

HENRY. I can't. How's your business venture coming along?

HASTINGS. [*Sighing.*] You were a true prophet, Henry. I wish I hadn't come.

HENRY. Stop with me, when we leave here, and tell me all about it. I want to hear the whole story.

X **HASTINGS.** You'll hear it, every last dismal word. [*Fading a bit.*] I'm so grateful to find a willing and sympathetic ear.[23]

[BIZ. *Background ad-libbing out. A pause, then:*]

[PIANO. *Playing semi-classical tune in background.*]

HENRY. After dinner there was coffee and an informal piano recital and dear Miss Langham—lovely Portia Langham, the English girl. I eased her away from the music and the guests, to the library, where we talked.

[PIANO. *Out.*]

PORTIA. I'm really quite excited, Mr. Adams, meeting you like this. A millionaire!

HENRY. But I'm not one.

PORTIA. B-but of course you are.

HENRY. You're wrong.

PORTIA. I don't understand.

HENRY. You will! You will, that is, if you allow me to see you tomorrow.

PORTIA. [*As though smiling.*] Well, Mr. Adams—

HENRY. Henry.

PORTIA. Henry, then. I will give the invitation serious thought.

HENRY. Tomorrow is going to be a sunny day, just right for a picnic in the country. Yes?

PORTIA. Yes.

HENRY. I'll tell you the whole story then.

PORTIA. Do you think you should?

HENRY. Certainly! After all, we're going to be married. Y

PORTIA. [*Amazed.*] We—we're—going to—marry!

HENRY. Absolutely! I'll call for you at noon. Where?

PORTIA. Meet me here.

HENRY. You're a guest here?

23. One who listens in a caring way is said to have a *sympathetic ear*.

Cultural Note

The Arabian Nights, or the *Thousand and One Nights*, is a series of ancient stories thought to be from Persia. Some of the most famous tales involve Aladdin and Ali Baba, who become wealthy with the help of a magic lamp, a magic ring, or the magic words *Open Sesame*.

W Active Reading Strategies

QUESTION Since Hastings and Henry last saw each other, three months earlier, have students figure out how long Henry must have spent on the ship coming to London. *(Since Henry has been in London for only eleven days, he must have been on the ship for more than two months.)* Using a wall map of the world, demonstrate—or have a student volunteer do so—the sea route from San Francisco to London before the Panama Canal existed.

X Literary Elements

STAGE DIRECTIONS Have students explain what the sounds of conversation, a pause, and then piano playing indicate to the radio audience. *(Dinner is over, and an after-dinner piano recital has begun.)*

Y Active Reading Strategies

EVALUATE Ask students if they think Henry is serious about marrying Portia. *(Students might note that Henry is in love with Portia and is boldly expressing his wishes.)*

Reading Minilesson

Cause and Effect Many events in this story cause other events to happen. For example, by not eating the pear, Henry causes two rich brothers to think he is a good candidate for their bet.

Activity Have students number a sheet of paper from 1 to 5. Beside each number have them list one cause from the story and its effect or effects. If students have trouble separating causes from effects, have them use this sentence to help: "Because of [something], [something else] happens." Encourage students to add to their lists as they read the rest of this play. **L2**

Additional Resources

Reading Skills Practice Workbook

Z Literary Elements

STAGE DIRECTIONS Have students think about how Portia's speech probably sounds after the stage directions say "fading." *(Her voice gets quieter and quieter as she is leaving the scene.)*

AA Literary Elements

NARRATOR Ask students to discuss the purpose of this monologue. *(It lets listeners know that the setting has changed, and that Henry is now home. Also, it lets readers know Henry's state of mind: he is deep in thought, infatuated with Portia.)*

BB Literary Elements

CONFLICT Have students identify the conflict Hastings faces. *(The option on the mine expires at the end of the month, which is fast approaching, and the buyers have backed away from the deal.)*

CC Active Reading Strategies

QUESTION Have students explain why Henry doesn't take Hastings up on the deal. *(The money does not belong to him, so Henry does not want to take the risk of losing it.)*

Teaching Support

PORTIA. N—no, but it will be more convenient.

HENRY. Do you like me?

PORTIA. Yes, Henry. [*Fading.*] You're a very unusual young man, even if you are a millionaire, and even if you claim you aren't.

HENRY. All the way home I was in the clouds, Hastings talking, and I not hearing a word. When we reached my suite, he said to me:

HASTINGS. This luxury makes me realize how poor, how defeated I am. Even the drippings of your daily income would seem like a tremendous fortune to me.

HENRY. Unreel your story, Lloyd.

HASTINGS. I told you the whole story on the way over here.

HENRY. You did?

HASTINGS. Yes.

HENRY. I'll be hanged if I heard a word of it.

HASTINGS. Are you well?

HENRY. Yes. I'm in love.

HASTINGS. That English girl you were speaking to?

HENRY. Yes. I'm going to marry her.

HASTINGS. Small wonder you didn't hear a word I said.

HENRY. Now I'm all attention.

HASTINGS. I came here with what I thought was a grand opportunity. I have an option to sell the Gould and Curry Mine and keep all I can get over a million dollars.

HENRY. Sounds like a good proposition.

HASTINGS. Yes, it's a fine claim.

HENRY. Well?

HASTINGS. The parties here whom I tried to interest have backed down. And so here I am trying to peddle a gold mine, but with nary a buyer in sight. In addition, I am almost penniless.

HENRY. Surely you'll find a buyer.

HASTINGS. My option on the mine expires in a matter of days; in fact, at the end of this month.

HENRY. You *are* in a fix.

HASTINGS. Henry, you can save me. Will you do it?

HENRY. I? How?

HASTINGS. Give me a million dollars and my passage home for my option.

HENRY. I can't.

HASTINGS. But you're wealthy.

HENRY. I—I—not really.

HASTINGS. You have a million pounds—five millions of dollars. Buy the mine and you'll double, maybe triple your investment.

HENRY. I'd like to help, but I can't.

HASTINGS. You know the value of this mine, as well as I do.

HENRY. [*Tired.*] Oh, Lloyd, I wish I could explain, but I can't. What you ask is impossible.

HASTINGS. That's quite all right. I'm sorry to have bothered you, Henry. [*Fading.*] You must have a good reason in turning me down, I'm sure.

HENRY. It hurt me to have to refuse Lloyd, but it made me comprehend my delicate and precarious[24] position. Here I was, deep in debt, not a cent in the world, in love

24. *Precarious* means "exposed to risk or danger."

MEETING INDIVIDUAL NEEDS — MULTIPLE MODES OF EXPRESSION

Musical Students with strong musical abilities may respond to this drama more readily through music. These students can use music to help them understand the mood, tone, and feelings generated by different parts of the dramatization.

Activity As students read the story, have them stop whenever the story reminds them of a song, a piece of music, or a sound. Have them jot down the title of the song or a description of the sound along with the emotion or mood it evokes. Students may select suspenseful music in places and romantic music in other places. Some students may want to tape-record music or sound effects to accompany the drama. **L2**

with a lovely girl, and nothing in front of me but a promise of a position, if, *if* I won the bet for the nameless brother. Nothing could save me. The next day, Portia and I went on our picnic in the country. I told her the whole story, down to the last detail. Her reaction wasn't exactly what I thought it would be.

[SOUND. *Bird singing in background. Weave in and out of this scene.*]

DD

PORTIA. [*Laughs.*] Oh, Henry, that's priceless.

HENRY. [*A bit stiffly.*] I fail to see the humor.

PORTIA. But I do, more than you can imagine.

HENRY. Here I am mixed up in a bet between two eccentric old men, and for all they care I might well be in jail.

PORTIA. [*Still laughing.*] Wonderful, the funniest thing I've ever heard.

HENRY. Pardon me if I don't laugh.

PORTIA. [*Stops laughing.*] Sorry, but it is both funny and pathetic.[25] But you say that one of the men is going to offer you a position?

HENRY. If I win the bet.

PORTIA. Which one is he?

HENRY. I don't know. But I have one solution. If I win, I get the position. Now, I've kept a very careful track of every cent I either owe or have borrowed, and I'm going to pay it back from my salary. If the position pays me six hundred pounds a year, I'll—I'll—

PORTIA. You'll what?

HENRY. I'll— [*He whistles.*] To date I owe exactly six hundred pounds, my whole year's salary.

PORTIA. And the month isn't ended.

HENRY. If I'm careful, my second year's salary may carry me through. Oh, dear, that *is* going to make it difficult for us to get married immediately, isn't it?

PORTIA. [*Dreamily.*] Yes, it is. [*Suddenly.*] Henry, what are you talking about? Marriage! You don't know me.

EE

HENRY. I know your name, your nationality, your age, and, most important, I know that I love you. I also know that you love me.

PORTIA. Please be sensible.

HENRY. I can't. I'm in love.

PORTIA. All this sounds like a play.

HENRY. It is—a wonderful one. I'll admit my owing my first two years' pay is going to pose a problem insofar as our getting married is concerned. [*Suddenly.*] I have it! The day I confront those two old gentlemen, I'll take you with me.

PORTIA. Oh, no. It wouldn't be proper.

HENRY. But so much depends upon that meeting. With you there, I can get the old boys to raise my salary—say, to a thousand pounds a year. Perhaps fifteen hundred. Say you'll go with me.

PORTIA. I'll go.

FF

HENRY. In that case, I'll demand two thousand a year, so we can get married immediately.

PORTIA. Henry.

HENRY. Yes?

PORTIA. Keep your expenses down for the balance of the month. Don't dip into your third year's salary.

25. Something that's *pathetic* inspires pity or sadness.

DD Critical Thinking

DRAWING CONCLUSIONS Portia thinks Henry's story is funny, but Twain doesn't have her explain why. Have students explain what this may indicate about Portia. *(Portia seems to know more than she is letting on. Perhaps she thinks the situation is funny because she knows something that Henry doesn't.)*

EE Active Reading Strategies

PREDICT Ask students whether they think Henry and Portia will get married. *(Portia doesn't care that Henry is not a millionaire, so perhaps they really will get married. Or Portia knows something she isn't telling; whatever it is might interfere with their marriage plans.)*

FF Literary Elements

CHARACTER Have students explain how Portia feels. *(Portia is happy that Henry wants to marry her. She is amused by his financial situation but not alarmed, even though Henry is in debt.)*

Life Skills Connection

Creating and Producing Invite students to use this play as a model to create their own brief scene for a radio play. Students can create a scene in which Henry shows the bank note to a local merchant to obtain something he needs, such as a haircut, shoes, or a taxi ride.

Activity Have small groups of students work together to think of a situation involving Henry Adams and a merchant. Have them establish a setting for the theme. Then have the group write dialogue and stage directions appropriate for a radio play. Next, have students think about sound effects or music and gather any props needed to make the sounds. Encourage students to practice their scenes and then to tape-record them. Have them play their audiotapes for the class. **L2**

Literary Elements

CONFLICT Have students explain in their own words Henry's problems now. *(Henry is heavily in debt. He doesn't know whether he will win the bet and be able to pay off his debts.)*

Active Reading Strategies

PREDICT Henry allows Hastings to use his name freely. Do students think this will help Hastings sell his option? You may wish to use the following model to illustrate the thinking process involved in predicting.

Model: Since Henry is now famous and people think he is rich, I think the use of Henry's name will help Hastings sell the mine. Most people will believe Henry's financial advice because they think he must be financially savvy to have become so rich.

Vocabulary Skills

Etymology *Fortnight* comes from the Middle English word *fourtenight,* which meant "fourteen nights." Today a fortnight still means fourteen days and nights, or two weeks.

HENRY. And that is how matters stood at that point. Thoughts raced through my mind. What if I lost the bet for my nameless benefactor? What if he failed to give me a position? Then the answer came to me, like a flash of lightning. I roused Lloyd Hastings from bed. He was a bit bewildered.

HASTINGS. I don't understand you. What are you getting at?

HENRY. Lloyd, I'm going to save you. Save you—understand!

HASTINGS. No.

HENRY. I'll save you, but not in the way you ask, for that wouldn't be fair, after your hard work and the risks you've run. Now, I don't need to buy a mine. I can keep my capital moving without that; it's what I'm doing all the time. I know all about your mine; I know its immense value and can swear to it if anybody wishes it. You shall sell it inside of the fortnight[26] for three million cash.

HASTINGS. Three million!

HENRY. Right!

HASTINGS. But how?

HENRY. By using my name freely—and right now my name is on the tip of everybody's tongue. We'll divide the profits, share and share alike.

HASTINGS. [*Overjoyed.*] I may use your name! Your name—think of it! Man, they'll flock in droves, these rich English. They'll fight for that stock. I'm a made man,[27] a made man forever. [*Fading.*] I'll never forget you as long as I live . . . never, never . . .

HENRY. In less than twenty-four hours London was abuzz! I hadn't anything to do, day after day, but sit home, and wait for calls.

SIR ALFRED. Then I may assume, Mr. Adams, that you consider this mining property a sound investment?

HENRY. A very sound investment, Sir Alfred.

SIR ALFRED. And what of this American chap, Hastings?

HENRY. I know him very well, and he is as sound as the mine.

SIR ALFRED. Then I think I shall invest in this property. Your recommendation does it.

[SOUND. *Telephone bell.*]

HENRY. Excuse me, Sir Alfred.

[SOUND. *Receiver lifted from hook.*]

HENRY. [*Into phone.*] Yes, this is Henry Adams. Who? Sir John Hardcastle. Yes, Sir John. The Gould and Curry Extension? Yes, I know a great deal about it. I certainly would recommend it as a shrewd investment. The mine is worth far more than the asking price. Yes, Mr. Hastings is very well known in the States. Honest as the day is long, as they say. Yes, I suggest you contact Mr. Hastings. Thank you. Not at all. Good day, Sir John.

26. In financial terms, *capital* is wealth that is used to produce more wealth. A *fortnight* is two weeks.

27. A *made man* is one who is assured of success.

Vocabulary

benefactor (ben′ ə fak′ tər) *n.* one who gives financial assistance

shrewd (shrōōd) *adj.* sharp, clever, and practical

Teaching Support

Reading Minilesson

Comparing and Contrasting The interaction between Henry and Hastings on this page shows the ways in which the two men are alike and different. Draw a Venn diagram, like the one at the right, on the board. Label the left circle *HENRY* and the right circle *HASTINGS*.

Activity Have students complete the diagram and add their own ideas to it. Encourage students to think creatively as they compare the two men. Invite volunteers to share their best ideas with the rest of the class. **L2**

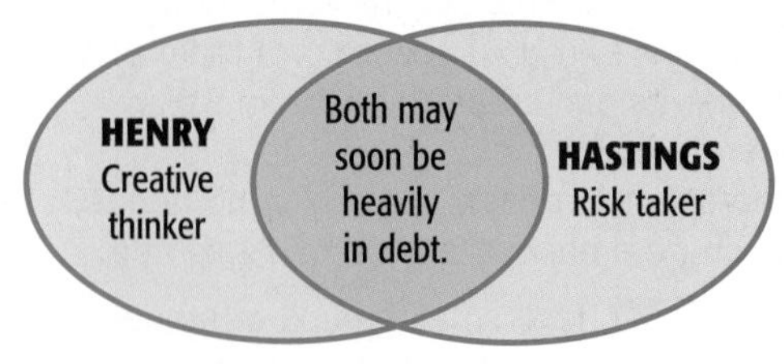

Additional Resources

Reading Skills Practice Workbook

Indeed! Edward C. Clifford (1858–1910). Christopher Wood Gallery, London.

Viewing the painting: Compare this picture with the scene from the movie on page 572. Which do you think is truer to the story? Why?

[SOUND. *Receiver replaced onto hook.*]

II

SIR ALFRED. That clinches it. If Sir John is in, so am I. Do you suppose that your Mr. Hastings would mind if I brought in a few discreet friends on this venture?

HENRY. Er, no, in fact I'm sure he wouldn't. Mr. Hastings is a very democratic chap.

SIR ALFRED. Directly I shall go and call upon Mr. Hastings. By the way, exactly where is this mine?

HENRY. California.

SIR ALFRED. Is that near Washington, D.C.?

HENRY. Not exactly.

SIR ALFRED. A pity, for I had thought of asking the British Ambassador to look at it. [*Fading.*] Well, I'm off. Thank you for your advice. Good day, Mr. Adams.

JJ

HENRY. And that's the way it went—a steady stream of wealthy Londoners asking my advice, which, of course, I gave freely. Meanwhile I said not a word to Portia about the possible sale of the mine. I wanted to save it as a surprise; and then there always was the possibility the sale might fall through. The day the month was up, she and I, dressed in our best, went to the house on Portland Place. As we waited for the two old gentlemen to enter, we talked excitedly.

PORTIA. You're certain you have the bank note with you?

VIEWING THE PAINTING

Viewing Response *Some students might say that the movie is truer because it was based on the story. Others might say that the painting is truer to the story because it was probably painted closer to the time of the story, and the clothing, hairstyles, and behavior of the couple would be more accurate.*

II Active Reading Strategies

EVALUATE Have students explain what makes this scene funny. *(Sir Alfred is going to invest in the mine; in fact, he is even going to recommend the deal to friends. Yet, he doesn't know where the mine is. He wonders if the mine in California is near Washington, D.C.)*

JJ Literary Elements

NARRATOR Have students explain the purpose of this monologue. *(It is to let listeners know that Henry hasn't told Portia about the deal, that time has passed and the month is up, and that Henry and Portia are on their way to see the two wealthy brothers.)*

MEETING INDIVIDUAL NEEDS — ADVANCED LEARNERS

Mark Twain Students who are interested in Mark Twain might enjoy conducting research to learn more about him. The are many Twain resources available, including biographical information; *The New York Times* articles from the 1800s by and about Twain; the complete text of many short stories and books; information about Twain's influence on popular culture today; as well as photos, cartoons, and illustrations of Twain.

Activity Encourage students to use the school library, the public library, or the Internet to find more information on Twain. If students use the Internet, encourage them to use a variety of keywords, such as *Samuel Clemens, Huckleberry Finn,* and *The New York Times,* in addition to Twain's name. **L3**

KK Literary Elements

CHARACTER Encourage students to suggest words or phrases that describe what Gordon and Abel are like. *(The brothers are wealthy and competitive, but Abel is also a good loser.)*

LL Active Reading Strategies

QUESTION Have students explain why the brothers would not have given Henry the money if he had boldly eaten the pear. *(The brothers wanted someone with a sense of pride. If Henry had picked up the pear without hesitation, the brothers would have thought Henry reacted without thinking of the consequences.)*

MM Active Reading Strategies

REVIEW Tell students that 200,000 pounds equaled about one million U.S. dollars at the time. Based on this information, encourage students to figure out how much the mine sold for. *(Since Henry and Hastings split any money left over after the $1 million, the mine must have sold for $3 million.)*

HENRY. Right here. Portia, dearest, the way you look it's a crime to ask for a salary a single penny under three thousand a year.

PORTIA. You'll ruin us.

HENRY. Just trust in me. It'll come out all right.

PORTIA. [*Worried.*] Please remember if we ask for too much we may get no salary at all; and then what will become of us, with no way in the world to earn our living? [*Fading.*] Please handle this delicately, Henry.

HENRY. When the two old gentlemen entered, of course they were surprised to see Portia with me. I asked them to introduce themselves, which they did.

GORDON. I am Gordon Featherstone.

ABEL. And I am Abel Featherstone.

HENRY. Gentlemen, I am ready to report, but first may I ask which of you bet on me?

GORDON. It was I. Have you the million-pound note?

KK

HENRY. Here it is, sir.

GORDON. Ah! I've won. *Now* what do you say, Abel?

ABEL. I say he did survive, and I've lost twenty thousand pounds. I never would have believed it.

HENRY. Perhaps you might enlighten[28] me as to the terms of the bet.

GORDON. Gladly! The Bank of England once issued two notes of a million pounds each. Only one of these had been used and cancelled; the other lay in the vaults. Well, Abel and I got to wondering what would happen to a perfectly honest and intelligent stranger turned adrift in London without a friend and with no money in the world but the million-pound bank note. Abel said he would starve to death, and I claimed he wouldn't. My brother said he would be arrested if he offered the note at a bank. Well, we went on arguing until I bet him twenty thousand pounds that the man would live thirty days, *anyway,* on that million, and keep out of jail, too.

ABEL. And I took him up.

HENRY. How did you know I was the right choice?

ABEL. After talking with you, we decided you had all the qualifications.

GORDON. And that pear incident, if you had picked it up very boldly, it would have proved to us you were nothing but a tramp. LL

HENRY. You don't know how tempted I was to do just that.

GORDON. And so you shall receive your reward—a choice of any position you can fill.

HENRY. First I ask that you look at this scrap of paper, all of you. You, too, Portia.

GORDON. A certificate of deposit in the London and County Bank—

ABEL. In the sum of—

GORDON. Two hundred thousand pounds.

PORTIA. Henry, is it yours?

HENRY. It is. It represents my share of the sale of a mining property in California, sold by my friend Lloyd Hastings; a sort of commission, as it were. It all came about by thirty days' judicious[29] use of that little loan you gentlemen let me have. And the only use I made of it was to buy trifles and offer the bill in change. MM

28. To *enlighten* is to give or reveal knowledge or wisdom.

29. *Judicious* means "showing good judgment."

Teaching Support

Grammar and Language *Minilesson*

Using Commas to Join Main Clauses Write the following complete sentence on the board: *Abel said he would starve to death, and I claimed he wouldn't.* Explain that there is a comma before *and* in the sentence because it separates main clauses. *(Abel said he would starve to death. I claimed he wouldn't.)* Commas are used to separate main clauses connected by *and, but,* or *or.*

Activity Have students, individually or in pairs, skim pages 574, 575, and 582 for other examples that use commas before *and, but,* or *or.* Ask them to rewrite each of these sentences as two separate sentences. Finally, have students write five sentences of their own that use commas to join two main clauses. **L2**

Additional Resources

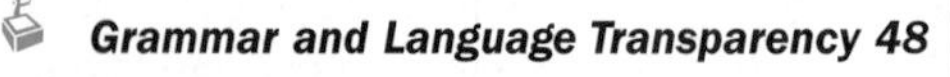

Grammar and Language Transparency 48

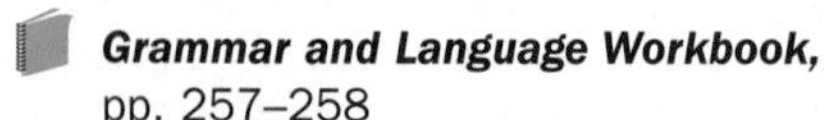

Grammar and Language Workbook, pp. 257–258

Grammar and Composition Handbook, Lesson 13.3

Writer's Choice, Lesson 20.3

ABEL. Come, this is astonishing.

GORDON. It's incredible.

HENRY. [*Laughing.*] I can prove it.

PORTIA. Henry, is that really your money? Have you been fibbing to me?

HENRY. I have, indeed. But you'll forgive me, I know.

PORTIA. [*Half-smiling.*] Don't you be so sure.

HENRY. Oh, you'll get over it. Come, let's be going.

GORDON. Wait! I promised to give you a situation, you know.

HENRY. Thank you, but I really don't want one.

PORTIA. Henry, I'm ashamed of you. You don't even thank the good gentleman. May I do it for you?

HENRY. If you can improve upon it.

PORTIA. I shall. Uncle Abel, first, thank you for making this possible. And, dear Father—

HENRY. Hold on. You're her uncle?

ABEL. I am.

HENRY. And you—

GORDON. Yes, I'm her step-father.

PORTIA. And the dearest one that ever was. You understand now, don't you, Henry, why I was able to laugh when you told me the story of the bet with the two nameless gentlemen. Of course I couldn't miss knowing that it was this house and that the two men were Father and Uncle Abel.

HENRY. Sir, you *have* got a situation open that I want.

GORDON. Name it.

HENRY. Son-in-law.

GORDON. Well, well, well! But if you haven't ever served in that capacity, you of course can't furnish satisfactory recommendations to satisfy the conditions of the contract.

HENRY. Only just try me for thirty or forty years.

GORDON. What do you think, Abel?

ABEL. Well, he does look to be a satisfactory sort.

GORDON. And you, Portia?

PORTIA. I agree—heartily.

GORDON. Very well. Take her along. If you hurry, you can reach the license bureau before it closes. [*Fading.*] Hop to it now.

HENRY. Happy, we two? Indeed, yes! And when London got the whole history of my adventure for a month, how it did talk. My Portia's father took the million-pound bank note to the Bank of England, cashed it, had it cancelled, and he gave it to us at our wedding. Framed, it now hangs in our home. It gave me my Portia, but for it I could not have remained in London, would not have appeared at the American Ambassador's, never should have met her. And so I always say: Yes, it's a million-pounder; but it made but one purchase in its life, and then got the article for only about a tenth part of its value.

THE END

Author's Craft

CHARACTERS Have students consider why Twain portrayed Gordon Featherstone as Portia's stepfather rather than her father. *(If Gordon were Portia's father, he would have the same last name as Portia. Readers might suspect that Portia and Gordon are related, which would spoil the surprise at the end.)*

Active Reading Strategies

REVIEW Encourage students to explain what they think the last sentence of this drama means. *(The only item the bank note ever bought Henry was Portia, and Portia is worth much more to Henry than the bank note was worth.)*

Thematic Focus

Twists and Turns Ask students how they feel about the twists and turns in this drama. How do students think the moral of this play relates to those of other stories in this theme?

ASSESSMENT

Quick Checks, p. 49

HOME VIDEO.® The following videotape program is available from Glencoe. Be sure to preview it for appropriateness for your class.

- ***Mark Twain: His Amazing Adventure****

*Also available in the *Glencoe Literature Video Library*.

REAL-WORLD CONNECTION

Romance Throughout history, romance has been an engaging topic for artists to explore, for falling in love is an experience shared by many people throughout the world.

Activity Have students analyze a humorous treatment of a romance in a modern comic strip, a short story, or a movie or TV comedy. Encourage students to compare any humorous incidents they find with the humorous incidents in "The Million-Pound Bank Note." In what ways are Henry and Portia portrayed like the other characters students find? In what ways are the characters different? Ask students to discuss what characteristics of romance seem universal, and have them share their ideas with the class. **L2**

Responding to the Selection

PERSONAL RESPONSE

Students might find that their ideas are similar to Henry's since people the world over share the same basic wants and needs.

Analyzing Literature

1. Hastings wants Henry to go to London to help sell the mine claim because Henry knows the mine papers better than Hastings does.
2. The two wealthy men offer Henry money and bet on what he will do with it. Henry thinks they have made a mistake when he sees the note's value.
3. The shop people give Henry goods on credit when they see the note's value. The shop owners spread the word that Henry is a millionaire, and Henry becomes the talk of the town.
4. Henry lets Hastings use his name to sell the mine. Henry and Hastings divide the profits from the mine sale.
5. It is ironic because Henry has refused Hastings's expense-paid trip to London.
6. Gordon and Abel are trying to test both honesty and intelligence.
7. Henry doesn't look or act like a millionaire, but he has a million pounds in his vest pocket.
8. Henry's success shows that he is a creative problem solver and an astute businessman.
9. The ending is surprising, but Twain has given clues about the outcome. Twain portrays the brothers as good judges of character, and therefore believable when they bet on Henry's honesty. Portia's connection to the two gentlemen is made believable by her introduction to and relationship with Henry.

Active Reading and Critical Thinking

Responding to Literature

PERSONAL RESPONSE

- Take a look at the graph you created in the **Reading Focus** on page 572. How do your ideas of what to do with a million dollars compare with how Henry uses the million-pound note?

Analyzing Literature

RECALL

1. Why did Hastings want Henry to travel to London, England?
2. What do the two wealthy gentlemen offer Henry? What is his response when he realizes the value of the bill?
3. How do the shop people respond to the million-pound note? How do they contribute to Henry's fame?
4. How does Henry manage to earn his own fortune?

INTERPRET

5. Why is it ironic that Henry finds himself on a freighter bound for London?
6. What do you think Gordon and Abel are trying to test?
7. Why does Henry achieve fame as the "Vest-Pocket Millionaire"?
8. What does Henry's success with the uncashed million-pound note tell you about his personality and business skills?

Brackets connect questions that are paired to develop higher-level thinking skills.

EVALUATE AND CONNECT

9. Were you surprised by the climax of the story? Do you think Twain gave enough clues to make the gentlemen's bet and Portia's connection to the two men believable? Explain.
10. Theme Connection How does having a million-pound bank note affect Henry? How would it affect you?

LITERARY ELEMENTS

Stage Directions

Mark Twain originally wrote "The Million-Pound Bank Note" as a short story. Many years later, Walter Hackett adapted the story as a radio play. Like a traditional play, a radio play includes **stage directions** written in italic type and set in brackets. However, directions about scenery, movement, lighting, or props are unnecessary. In a radio play, the audience must use its imagination to visualize the characters and the setting. The only stage directions deal with sound effects and how the actors should say their lines.

1. Compare Henry's first meal at Hawkins's restaurant on pages 575–576 with the stage directions on page 579 when he returns there. What difference would the addition of sound effects make to the listener?
2. A number of times in the play the word *fading* appears within a character's speech. What effect do you think the dramatist is trying to achieve in these places? What would the speech sound like?

- See **Literary Terms Handbook,** p. R10.

10. Having a million pounds doesn't affect Henry's integrity, but it does give him the confidence to achieve his goals. Students might say that it would enable them to afford many material things or allow them to achieve their own personal goals.

LITERARY ELEMENTS

1. The addition of sound effects makes listeners realize that the eating house is now packed with customers.
2. The word *fading* lets listeners know that the scene is ending and a new scene will soon begin. The speech would gradually become softer.

Additional Resources

Literary Elements Transparency 49

Extending Your Response

Writing About Literature

Dialogue and Monologue This dramatization contains **dialogue**—conversations between characters—and **monologues**—speeches Henry directs to the audience. From which of these do you learn more about Henry? From which do you learn more about the action in the play? Support your ideas with quotations from the play.

Creative Writing

Henry's Headlines Write a series of brief newspaper articles from the point of view of a London journalist hot on the trail to describe Henry's wealth, adventures, and romance.

Literature Groups

Making Judgments Discuss the assumptions people make about Henry when they see his shabby clothes and how those assumptions change when they see his million-pound note. What conclusions can be drawn about how the appearance of wealth affects our judgment of people?

interNET CONNECTION

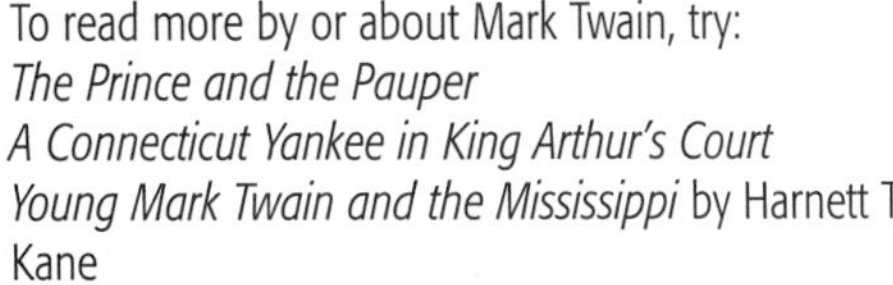

You can find out more about Mark Twain and his writings on the Internet. Just type *Mark Twain* or *Samuel Clemens* in the subject window of a search engine. You can even find the entire text of some of his novels and short stories if you'd like to read them.

Reading Further

To read more by or about Mark Twain, try:

The Prince and the Pauper
A Connecticut Yankee in King Arthur's Court
Young Mark Twain and the Mississippi by Harnett T. Kane

Save your work for your portfolio.

Skill Minilesson

Reteach · Review

VOCABULARY • ETYMOLOGY

Words have histories. Knowing where a word comes from can help you understand what it means now and why it means that. For example, *eccentric* comes from the Greek words *ek,* meaning "out of," and *kentron,* meaning "center." So an *eccentric* millionaire is one who is sort of "off center," or odd.

The history of a word is called its **etymology.** Here are the etymologies of some other words from "The Million-Pound Bank Note."

proposition: from the Latin *pro-* ("forward") and *positio* ("to place")
benefactor: from the Latin *bene-* ("well") and *facere* ("to do").
rebuke: from the Latin *re-* ("back") and the Old French *buchier* ("to beat")

PRACTICE Choose one of the words from the above list and briefly explain how the etymology of that word is connected to its present-day meaning.

Extending Your Response

Writing About Literature

Students' analyses should

- indicate that monologues tell most about Henry; dialogues tell most about the action
- use quotations from the story
- indicate that monologues also help listeners make the transition from one setting to another

Creative Writing

Students' newspaper articles should

- describe Henry's adventures in London
- contain opening paragraphs that stir interest in the story
- be written from the point of view of a newspaper reporter in the late 1800s

Literature Groups Before students meet, encourage them to review the story to see what assumptions people make about Henry in his shabby clothes and how those assumptions change.

Skill Minilesson

VOCABULARY • ETYMOLOGY

Students should clearly explain how the meanings of the words in the etymologies provided relate to the words' modern definitions.

Additional Resources

Vocabulary Practice, p. 34

interNET CONNECTION

Word Derivations Invite students to go online and use a search engine to locate the *Web of On-line Dictionaries.* Students can search the site's etymology dictionaries for information about the derivations of new or unfamiliar words in this section.

ASSESSMENT

- ***Quick Checks,*** p. 49
- ***Selection and Theme Assessment,*** pp. 85–86
- ***Performance Assessment,*** p. 46
- ***Testmaker: ExamView Pro***
- ***Interactive Tutor: Self-Assessment***

Before Reading

Objectives

- To read and analyze a folktale about a miller's changing fortune
- To recognize and discuss elements common to folktales
- To write two monologues comparing stages in a person's life

Skills

Reading/Thinking: Using Text Structures; Logical Reasoning; Drawing Conclusions; Synthesizing; Analyzing Arguments
Writing: Write a Different Ending
Vocabulary: Etymology
Grammar/Language: Identifying the Subject of a Sentence
Listening/Speaking: Storytelling
Collaboration: Literature Groups

Motivating → STUDENTS

Selection Focus Transparency 50: Have students think about and discuss whether they have any control over their luck.

Reading Focus: As an extension of the Reading Focus, have students in small groups compare their ideas about good fortune, hard work, and honesty.

Before You Read

The Force of Luck

MEET RUDOLFO A. ANAYA

The land and culture of his native New Mexico has inspired Rudolfo A. Anaya (ro͞o dôl′ fō ä nā′ yä) since he was a child. Anaya was born in Pastura, a village on a vast plain covered with small farming communities. He has written that "the most important elements of my childhood are the people of those villages and the wide open plains." In his short stories, novels, and plays, Anaya draws upon Mexican legends, myths, and symbolism to create an insight into the Mexican American community.

Rudolfo A. Anaya was born in 1937. This story is part of a collection called Cuentos: Tales from the Hispanic Southwest.

READING FOCUS

Do you believe good fortune comes to those who are hard-working and honest or to those who are simply lucky?

Journal

In your journal, write your own ideas about good fortune.

Setting a Purpose

Read this story to find out what roles hard work and luck play in the life of one character.

BUILDING BACKGROUND

Time and Place This story, like many folktales, takes place in a small village sometime in the past.

Did You Know? "The Force of Luck" is part of the oral tradition of the Hispanic people who lived in the American Southwest. The *cuentistas,* or oral storytellers, played an important role in the life of writer Rudolfo A. Anaya. Anaya comments, "[Storytelling] is a tradition one often loses when one moves into print, but its elements are strong and as valuable today as they have been historically."

VOCABULARY PREVIEW

prosperous (pros′ pər əs) *adj.* having wealth or good fortune; successful; p. 592
squander (skwon′ dər) *v.* to spend or use in a reckless or wasteful manner; p. 593
spendthrift (spend′ thrift′) *n.* one who spends money generously or wastefully; p. 594
novelty (nov′ əl tē) *n.* anything new and unusual; p. 595
jest (jest) *v.* to speak or act in a playful manner; joke; p. 596
intact (in takt′) *adj.* undamaged and whole; p. 598

RESOURCE MANAGER

Teaching Tools and Resources
- Theme Six Planning Guide
- Literature Groups Sourcebook

Essential Lesson Support

Lesson-Specific Instruction
- Selection Focus Transparency 50
- Literary Elements Transparency 50
- Active Reading Guide,* p. 50
- Selection Vocabulary Practice, p. 35

Assessment
- Selection Quick Checks,* p. 50
- Sel. and Theme Assmt., pp. 87–88
- Testmaker: ExamView Pro
- Performance Assessment, p. 47

Systematic Language Instruction
- Gr. and Comp. Hbk., L. 11.3
- Vocabulary Power, Lesson 26
- Spelling Power, Lesson 23

English Language Learners
- ELL Sourcebook, p. 79
- Spanish Summaries, p. 50
- Audio Library*
- English, Yes!

Spec. Needs/Strat. Interven.
- Interactive Rdg. Sbk., pp. T183–T185
- Interactive Rdg. Wkbk., pp. 99–100
- Inclusion Strat. Sbk., pp. 85–86
- Audio Library*

* Also available in Spanish

The Force of Luck

Retold by Rudolfo A. Anaya

Farmers (Agricultores), 1935. Antonio Gattorno. Gouache and ink on paper laid down on board, 17½ x 19½ in. Private collection.

Reading the Selection

SUMMARY

Two wealthy men give an honest but poor miller $200 to see whether it is luck or money that makes a man prosper. The miller loses the money. The men give him another $200. He loses that, too. Then the men give the miller a worthless piece of lead. It leads him to a valuable diamond that allows him to start his own business and become wealthy. Is it luck or money that is responsible for the miller's prosperity?

Spanish Summaries, p. 50

A Active Reading Strategies

PREDICT Have students use the title of the story, what they know about folktales, and clues from the art to predict what the problem in the story may be. Suggest that students revisit their predictions as they read to verify or revise them.

VOCABULARY If you haven't previewed the selection vocabulary with students, stop and remind them to use context clues to unlock the meanings of new vocabulary words.

Additional Resources

Active Reading Guide, p. 50
Audio Library
Spanish Audio Library

Teaching Support

CONNECTING TO OTHER SELECTIONS

COMPARING *selections*

This selection is compared with "The Million-Pound Bank Note" on page 573. A lesson for teaching a comparison of the two selections appears on page 600.

The chart at the right shows three other ways to connect "The Force of Luck" to other selections in this book. For specific teaching strategies, see the ***Theme Six Planning Guide.***

Connection	Title
Life Skills: Supporting and Contributing	→ "The Scholarship Jacket," p. 451
Thematic: Changes	→ "Rip Van Winkle," p. 185
Literary: Folktale	→ "Anansi and His Visitor, Turtle," p. 388

Active Reading Strategies

RESPOND Have students discuss other stories in which people try to settle a bet or a disagreement. Have them explain what happens in this type of story. *(In this type of story, usually two people disagree about an issue and find a third party to settle the dispute.)*

FYI

A *bit* is an amount equal to 1/8 of a dollar (or 12 1/2 cents). Since the United States does not have 1/2 cent coins, *bit* is almost always used in plural form: 2 bits (or 25 cents), 4 bits (or 50 cents), 6 bits (or 75 cents).

Active Reading Strategies

PREDICT Have students predict whether the money will change the miller's life.

Active Reading Strategies

REVIEW Ask students to name the developments up to this point in the story. *(We have been introduced to the characters, the setting, and the conflict.)*

Teaching Support

The Force of Luck

Once two wealthy friends got into a heated argument. One said that it was money which made a man prosperous, and the other maintained that it wasn't money, but luck, which made the man. They argued for some time and finally decided that if only they could find an honorable man then perhaps they could prove their respective points of view.[1]

One day while they were passing through a small village they came upon a miller who was grinding corn and wheat. They paused to ask the man how he ran his business. The miller replied that he worked for a master and that he earned only four bits a day, and with that he had to support a family of five.

The friends were surprised. "Do you mean to tell us you can maintain a family of five on only fifteen dollars a month?" one asked.

"I live modestly to make ends meet," the humble miller replied.

The two friends privately agreed that if they put this man to a test perhaps they could resolve their argument.

"I am going to make you an offer," one of them said to the miller. "I will give you two hundred dollars and you may do whatever you want with the money."

"But why would you give me this money when you've just met me?" the miller asked.

"Well, my good man, my friend and I have a long standing argument. He contends that it is luck which elevates a man to high position, and I say it is money. By giving you this money perhaps we can settle our argument. Here, take it, and do with it what you want!"

So the poor miller took the money and spent the rest of the day thinking about the strange meeting which had presented him with more money than he had ever seen. What could he possibly do with all this money? Be that as it may, he had the money in his pocket and he could do with it whatever he wanted.

When the day's work was done, the miller decided the first thing he would do would be to buy food for his family. He took out ten dollars and wrapped the rest of the money in a cloth and put the bundle in his bag. Then he went to the market and bought supplies and a good piece of meat to take home.

On the way home he was attacked by a hawk that had smelled the meat which the miller carried. The miller fought off the bird but in the struggle he lost the bundle of money. Before the miller knew what was happening the hawk grabbed the bag and flew away with it. When he realized what had happened he fell into deep thought.

"Ah," he moaned, "wouldn't it have been better to let that hungry bird have the meat! I could have bought a lot more meat with the money he took. Alas, now I'm in the same poverty as before! And worse, because now those two men will say I am a thief! I should have thought carefully and bought nothing. Yes, I should have gone straight home and this wouldn't have happened!"

1. *Prove their respective points of view* means that each man was interested in proving his opinion the correct one.

Vocabulary

prosperous (pros′ pər əs) *adj.* having wealth or good fortune; successful

Meeting Individual Needs: ENGLISH LANGUAGE LEARNERS

Folktales Explain to English language learners that folktales are handed down from generation to generation and that they exist in almost every culture.

Activity Have students work in mixed groups to share stories about hard work, honesty, or luck leading to good fortune. Ask each group to select one story, establish a setting and a point of view for it, describe the characters, and explain what happens to them. Invite groups to present their tales orally to the class. Encourage the class to look for common features, themes, or values in the stories.

Additional Resources

English Language Learners Sourcebook, p. 79

So he gathered what was left of his provisions[2] and continued home, and when he arrived he told his family the entire story.

When he was finished telling his story his wife said, "It has been our lot[3] to be poor, but have faith in God and maybe someday our luck will change."

The next day the miller got up and went to work as usual. He wondered what the two men would say about his story. But since he had never been a man of money he soon forgot the entire matter.

Three months after he had lost the money to the hawk, it happened that the two wealthy men returned to the village. As soon as they saw the miller they approached him to ask if his luck had changed. When the miller saw them he felt ashamed and afraid that they would think that he had squandered the money on worthless things. But he decided to tell them the truth and as soon as they had greeted each other he told his story. The men believed him. In fact, the one who insisted that it was money and not luck which made a man prosper took out another two hundred dollars and gave it to the miller.

"Let's try again," he said, "and let's see what happens this time."

The miller didn't know what to think. "Kind sir, maybe it would be better if you put this money in the hands of another man," he said.

"No," the man insisted, "I want to give it to you because you are an honest man, and if we are going to settle our argument you have to take the money!"

The miller thanked them and promised to do his best. Then as soon as the two men left he began to think what to do with the money so that it wouldn't disappear as it had the first time. The thing to do was to take the money straight home. He took out ten dollars, wrapped the rest in a cloth, and headed home.

When he arrived his wife wasn't at home. At first he didn't know what to do with the money. He went to the pantry where he had stored a large earthenware jar filled with bran. That was as safe a place as any to hide the money, he thought, so he emptied out the grain and put the bundle of money at the bottom of the jar, then covered it up with the grain. Satisfied that the money was safe he returned to work.

That afternoon when he arrived home from work he was greeted by his wife.

"Look, my husband, today I bought some good clay with which to whitewash the entire house."

"And how did you buy the clay if we don't have any money?" he asked.

"Well, the man who was selling the clay was willing to trade for jewelry, money, or anything of value," she said. "The only thing we had of value was the jar full of bran, so I traded it for the clay. Isn't it wonderful, I think we have enough clay to whitewash these two rooms!"

The man groaned and pulled his hair.

"Oh, you crazy woman! What have you done? We're ruined again!"

2. The miller's *provisions* are his food supplies.
3. Here, *lot* means "fate; final outcome."

Vocabulary
squander (skwon′ dər) *v.* to spend or use in a reckless or wasteful manner

E Literary Elements

CHARACTER Ask students to describe the miller and his wife. *(They are poor. The man regrets losing the money, but the wife is not upset. She accepts their position in life and has faith that their luck will change someday.)*

F Active Reading Strategies

PREDICT Encourage students to predict what might happen when the miller receives the second $200. *(Students may suggest that the miller will lose the money again. Others may think he will use the money wisely.)*

G Literary Elements

PLOT: *Foreshadowing* Have students explain why the storyteller sets it up so that the wife is not at home when the miller arrives with the second $200. How might this lack of communication affect what happens next? *(The wife is not home when the miller hides the money; it might foreshadow a situation in which the wife mistakenly moves, misplaces, or loses the money.)*

Reading Minilesson

Using Text Structures Folktales often have a repetitive structure that makes the events in them predictable. Students may benefit from recording and discussing these events.

Activity Ask students to fill in the following story chart as they read. Ask them to include each important event as the plot unfolds. Encourage students to notice the repetition that occurs and to predict what may happen next. **L2**

Setting:	
Characters:	
Problem:	
Event 1:	
Event 2:	

Additional Resources

Reading Skills Practice Workbook

VIEWING THE PAINTING

Diego Rivera is one of Mexico's most famous artists. His subject matter often deals with life in Mexico, Mexican history, or social problems. Because Rivera believed that art should not be hidden away, he often painted large murals on the walls of public buildings.

Viewing Response *Most students will think the woman is similar to the miller's wife.*

H Active Reading Strategies

QUESTION Have students recall what happened the first time the miller told the two men he lost the money. Do students think the two men will believe him again? *(The men believe him the first time because he seems honest. They will probably believe he had bad luck again.)*

I Literary Elements

FOLKTALE Have students explain how the repetition in this story could help an oral storyteller tell this tale. *(It is easier to remember the events of a story if they happen in a predictable manner. The pattern allows the storyteller to stretch the story and keep his listeners interested.)*

La Molendera I, 1924. Diego Rivera. *Encaustica sobre tela,* 90 x 117 cm. Museo de Arte Moderno, Bosque de Chapultepec, Mexico.

Viewing the painting: Which character in the story does this woman come closest to illustrating?

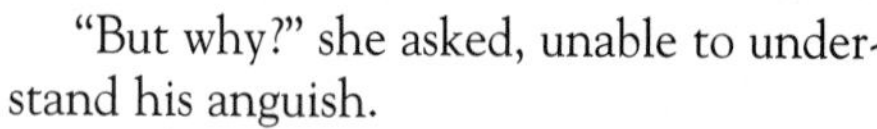

"But why?" she asked, unable to understand his anguish.

"Today I met the same two friends who gave me the two hundred dollars three months ago," he explained. "And after I told them how I lost the money they gave me another two hundred. And I, to make sure the money was safe, came home and hid it inside the jar of bran—the same jar you have traded for dirt! Now we're as poor as we were before! And what am I going to tell the two men? They'll think I'm a liar and a thief for sure!"

"Let them think what they want," his wife said calmly. "We will only have in our lives what the good Lord wants us to have. It is our lot to be poor until God wills it otherwise."

So the miller was consoled and the next day he went to work as usual. Time came and went, and one day the two wealthy friends returned to ask the miller how he had done with the second two hundred dollars. When the poor miller saw them he was afraid they would accuse him of being a liar and a spendthrift. But he

Vocabulary

spendthrift (spend′ thrift′) *n.* one who spends money generously or wastefully

Teaching Support

MEETING INDIVIDUAL NEEDS SPECIAL NEEDS

Less-Proficient Readers Some students may not understand what type of work the miller does. Explain that a miller grinds (or mills) grain into flour. A place where this is done is called a mill.

Activity Have students work in small groups to list what they think a miller's job entails. You may want to prompt them with questions like these:

- What does a miller have to do?
- What does the miller do with the ground grain?
- Why is ground grain important to people? **L1**

Additional Resources

Inclusion Strategies

decided to be truthful and as soon as they had greeted each other he told them what had happened to the money.

"That is why poor men remain honest," the man who had given him the money said. "Because they don't have money they can't get into trouble. But I find your stories hard to believe. I think you gambled and lost the money. That's why you're telling us these wild stories."

"Either way," he continued, "I still believe that it is money and not luck which makes a man prosper."

"Well, you certainly didn't prove your point by giving the money to this poor miller," his friend reminded him. "Good evening, you luckless man," he said to the miller.

"Thank you, friends," the miller said.

"Oh, by the way, here is a worthless piece of lead I've been carrying around. Maybe you can use it for something," said the man who believed in luck. Then the two men left, still debating their points of view on life.

Since the lead was practically worthless, the miller thought nothing of it and put it in his jacket pocket. He forgot all about it until he arrived home. When he threw his jacket on a chair he heard a thump and he remembered the piece of lead. He took it out of the pocket and threw it under the table. Later that night after the family had eaten and gone to bed, they heard a knock at the door.

"Who is it? What do you want?" the miller asked.

"It's me, your neighbor," a voice answered. The miller recognized the fisherman's wife. "My husband sent me to ask you if you have any lead you can spare. He is going fishing tomorrow and he needs the lead to weight down the nets."

The miller remembered the lead he had thrown under the table. He got up, found it, and gave it to the woman.

"Thank you very much, neighbor," the woman said. "I promise you the first fish my husband catches will be yours."

"Think nothing of it," the miller said and returned to bed. The next day he got up and went to work without thinking any more of the incident. But in the afternoon when he returned home he found his wife cooking a big fish for dinner.

"Since when are we so well off we can afford fish for supper?" he asked his wife.

"Don't you remember that our neighbor promised us the first fish her husband caught?" his wife reminded him. "Well this was the fish he caught the first time he threw his net. So it's ours, and it's a beauty. But you should have been here when I gutted him! I found a large piece of glass in his stomach!"

"And what did you do with it?"

"Oh, I gave it to the children to play with," she shrugged.

When the miller saw the piece of glass he noticed it shone so brightly it appeared to illuminate the room, but because he knew nothing about jewels he didn't realize its value and left it to the children. But the bright glass was such a novelty that the children were soon fighting over it and raising a terrible fuss.

Now it so happened that the miller and his wife had other neighbors who were

Vocabulary
novelty (nov′ əl tē) *n.* anything new and unusual

J Active Reading Strategies

RESPOND Ask students whether they agree with the man who says that people without money cannot get into trouble. *(Most students will think the statement is not true because people without money do get into trouble.)*

K Critical Thinking

LOGICAL REASONING Ask students to bring to mind what they know about folktales and apply it to the characters and events in this story. How do students think the story might develop after the miller meets the two men for the third time? *(The man who believes in luck gives the miller a piece of lead instead of $200. Perhaps luck will play a role this time.)*

L Active Reading Strategies

QUESTION Have students explain what usually happens to people who help others in stories. Do students think the miller will be rewarded for helping his neighbor? *(In folktales people are rewarded for helping others. Because this is a traditional tale, the miller will probably be rewarded.)*

M Literary Elements

FORESHADOWING Have students explain how this paragraph suggests that the piece of glass may be valuable. *(The glass shines so brilliantly it lights up the room, which indicates that it is special. The paragraph also says the miller knows nothing about jewels, which hints that the glass might be a jewel.)*

Listening and Speaking Minilesson

Storytelling Write on the board these guidelines for selecting a story to tell orally:

1. The story should have a good opening.
2. It shouldn't be very complicated.
3. It should be relatively short.
4. It should be interesting to listen to (i.e., funny, scary, suspenseful).

Activity Encourage each student to select a tale from this book or another source to tell out loud to a small group. Students should practice telling their stories several times. They may want to experiment with speaking loud, soft, fast, slow, high, or low to indicate the different characters they are portraying. Encourage listeners to listen carefully and try to visualize story events as they hear them. **L2**

Active Reading Strategies

QUESTION Have students explain why the doctor tells the pilot that his buddies are not allowed to visit him. *(The doctor wants to provide a logical reason for the lack of visitors.)*

Literary Elements

PLOT: *Rising Action* Ask students what the information about the Junkers 88 German bomber adds to the sequence of events. *(This description introduces a conflict and contributes to the rising action of the story.)*

Active Reading Strategies

PREDICT What do your students think the answer is to the pilot's question: Why aren't there sirens and guns? *(Perhaps the pilot is still disoriented. Maybe Germany has captured Brighton.)*

Historical Note

The Junkers 88 (pronounced YOONG-kers 88) was an important bomber in the German air force, or *Luftwaffe*, in World War II (1939-1945). In the early years of the war, strong air support contributed to the German army's ability to invade Poland, France, Belgium, Holland, Norway, Denmark, Austria, and Czechoslovakia.

would take off and buzz around viciously in small circles. It always landed back in the same place on the ceiling and started running and stopping all over again. He watched it for so long that after a while it was no longer a fly, but only a black speck upon a sea of gray, and he was still watching it when the nurse opened the door, and stood aside while the doctor came in. He was an Army doctor, a major, and he had some last war ribbons on his chest. He was bald and small, but he had a cheerful face and kind eyes.

"Well, well," he said. "So you've decided to wake up at last. How are you feeling?"

"I feel all right."

"That's the stuff. You'll be up and about in no time."

The doctor took his wrist to feel his pulse.

"By the way," he said, "some of the lads from your squadron[6] were ringing up and asking about you. They wanted to come along and see you, but I said that they'd better wait a day or two. Told them you were all right and that they could come and see you a little later on. Just lie quiet and take it easy for a bit. Got something to read?" He glanced at the table with the roses. "No. Well, nurse will look after you. She'll get you anything you want." With that he waved his hand and went out, followed by the large clean nurse.

When they had gone, he lay back and looked at the ceiling again. The fly was still there and as he lay watching it, he heard the noise of an airplane in the distance. He lay listening to the sound of its engines. It was a long way away. I wonder what it is, he thought. Let me see if I can place it. Suddenly he jerked his head sharply to one side. Anyone who has been bombed can tell the noise of a Junkers 88. They can tell most other German bombers for that matter, but especially a Junkers 88. The engines seem to sing a duet. There is a deep vibrating bass voice and with it there is a high pitched tenor. It is the singing of the tenor which makes the sound of a JU-88 something which one cannot mistake.

He lay listening to the noise and he felt quite certain about what it was. But where were the sirens and where were the guns? That German pilot certainly had a nerve coming near Brighton alone in daylight.

The aircraft was always far away and soon the noise faded away into the distance. Later on there was another. This one, too, was far away, but there was the same deep undulating bass and the high singing tenor and there was no mistaking it. He had heard that noise every day during the Battle.[7]

He was puzzled. There was a bell on the table by the bed. He reached out his hand and rang it. He heard the noise of footsteps down the corridor. The nurse came in.

"Nurse, what were those airplanes?"

"I'm sure I don't know. I didn't hear them. Probably fighters or bombers. I expect they were returning from France. Why, what's the matter?"

"They were JU-88's. I'm sure they were JU-88's. I know the sound of the engines. There were two of them. What were they doing over here?"

The nurse came up to the side of his bed and began to straighten out the sheets and tuck them in under the mattress.

6. An air force *squadron* is a group of planes that fly into combat together.

7. The *Battle* refers to the Battle of Britain, a series of air battles over Great Britain from June 1940 to April 1941.

Teaching Support

Literature & Humanities

To provide background about the music of the times, play "Boogie Woogie Bugle Boy" from *American Music: Cultural Traditions, Volume 2, Track 12,* which features some songs popular during World War II.

SPECIAL NEEDS

Less-Proficient Readers This story provides students with an opportunity to study words systematically across a content area.

Activity Have students work in pairs to sketch a Spitfire (using the image on the first page as a model). Then give them a list of words with which to label their drawings. Finally, have them add any other labels for airplanes that they already know. **L1**

Additional Resources

Inclusion Strategies

Bundles of Lictors Are Flying over England: Italian and German Bomber Wing in Operation, 1940. Hans Liska. Gouache. Berlin.

Viewing the painting: Imagine yourself as a pilot who had to fight against squadrons of enemy planes like these day after day. How would you feel?

Once toward evening he heard the noise of another aircraft. It was far away, but even so he knew that it was a single-engined machine. It was going fast; he could tell that. He could not place it. It wasn't a Spit, and it wasn't a Hurricane. It did not sound like an American engine either. They make more noise. He did not know what it was, and it worried him greatly. Perhaps I am very ill, he thought. Perhaps I am imagining things. Perhaps I am a little delirious.[9] I simply do not know what to think.

That evening the nurse came in with a basin of hot water and began to wash him.

"Well," she said, "I hope you don't still think that we're being bombed."

She had taken off his pajama top and was soaping his right arm with a flannel. He did not answer.

She rinsed the flannel in the water, rubbed more soap on it, and began to wash his chest.

"You're looking fine this evening," she said. "They operated on you as soon as you came in. They did a marvelous job. You'll be all right. I've got a brother in the R.A.F.,"[10] she added. "Flying bombers."

"Gracious me, what things you imagine. You mustn't worry about a thing like that. Would you like me to get you something to read?"

"No, thank you."

She patted his pillow and brushed back the hair from his forehead with her hand.

"They never come over in daylight any longer. You know that. They were probably Lancasters or Flying Fortresses."[8]

8. *Lancasters* were British bomber planes. American B-17 bombers were called *Flying Fortresses* because of their heavy armor and many guns.

9. The *Hurricane* was another type of British fighter plane. The pilot thinks he may be in a temporary state of confusion *(delirious),* which can result from a high fever.

10. *R.A.F.* stands for Royal Air Force.

VIEWING THE PAINTING

Viewing Response *Students may indicate that they would feel a rush of adrenaline, fear, excitement, or dread. Day after day, the experience might become routine and numb a pilot's feelings.*

M Active Reading Strategies

EVALUATE Have students explain how the nurse's response makes the pilot feel. *(The nurse's dismissal of what he says probably makes the pilot more confused and distrustful of the nurse.)*

N Literary Elements

SUSPENSE The pilot hears a plane he cannot identify. Invite your students to explain how this creates suspense in the story. *(It is unclear whether the pilot is just feverish and confused or if something else very strange is going on. This uncertainty creates suspense.)*

MEETING INDIVIDUAL NEEDS — ADVANCED LEARNERS

Some students may be interested in conducting research to find out more about England's role in World War II. To give the activity a more modern twist, challenge students to use only information gathered from electronic sources.

Activity Have students conduct Internet research or use other computer resources to create a multimedia presentation or timeline dealing with the Battle of Britain or Britain's role in World War II. Have students write their own text but borrow graphics, photos, or audio clips as needed to enhance their presentations. Remind students to cite their sources properly. **L3**

O Author's Craft

FLASHBACK Invite students to explain how the author uses this flashback to introduce more contradictions in the pilot's mind. *(The flashback allows the pilot to recall that the water in Brighton is soft, not hard, as the nurse complains.)*

P Critical Thinking

INFERRING What can readers begin to infer when the pilot stops in mid-sentence here? *(The pilot is beginning to realize that things are not as they seem to be.)*

Q Literary Elements

PLOT: ***Suspense*** What clues in this paragraph increase the level of suspense? *(The clues about the Junkers 88s and the hard water contradict the pilot's experience.)*

Historical Note

To prepare for the invasion of Britain, Germany staged daylight air raids against British ports and Royal Air Force (RAF) installations. After suffering major losses, the Germans switched to nighttime air raids on London and other cities. London was attacked for 57 consecutive nights beginning September 7, 1940. The bombing, called "the Blitz" from the German word *blitzkrieg* ("lightning war"), continued for eight months. Greatly outnumbered, the RAF held on, ruining the invasion plan.

Teaching Support

He said, "I went to school in Brighton."

She looked up quickly. "Well, that's fine," she said. "I expect you'll know some people in the town."

"Yes," he said, "I know quite a few."

She had finished washing his chest and arms. Now she turned back the bedclothes so that his left leg was uncovered. She did it in such a way that his bandaged stump remained under the sheets. She began to wash his left leg and the rest of his body. This was the first time he had had a bed-bath and he was embarrassed. She laid a towel under his leg and began washing his foot with the flannel. She said, "This wretched soap won't lather at all. It's the water. It's as hard as nails."[11]

He said, "None of the soap is very good now and, of course, with hard water it's hopeless." As he said it he remembered something. He remembered the baths which he used to take at school in Brighton, in the long stone-floored bathroom which had four baths in a room. He remembered how the water was so soft that you had to take a shower afterwards to get all the soap off your body, and he remembered how the foam used to float on the surface of the water, so that you could not see your legs underneath. He remembered that sometimes they were given calcium tablets because the school doctor used to say that soft water was bad for the teeth.

"In Brighton," he said, "the water isn't . . ."

He did not finish the sentence. Something had occurred to him; something so fantastic and absurd that for a moment he felt like telling the nurse about it and having a good laugh.

She looked up. "The water isn't what?" she said.

"Nothing," he answered. "I was dreaming."

She rinsed the flannel in the basin, wiped the soap off his leg and dried him with a towel.

"It's nice to be washed," he said. "I feel better." He was feeling his face with his hand. "I need a shave."

"We'll do that tomorrow," she said. "Perhaps you can do it yourself then."

That night he could not sleep. He lay awake thinking of the Junkers 88's and of the hardness of the water. He could think of nothing else. They *were* JU-88's, he said to himself. I know they were. And yet it is not possible, because they would not be flying around so low over here in broad daylight. I know that it is true and yet I know that it is impossible. Perhaps I am ill. Perhaps I am behaving like a fool and do not know what I am doing or saying. Perhaps I am delirious. For a long time he lay awake thinking these things, and once he sat up in bed and said aloud, "I will prove that I am not crazy. I will make a little speech about something complicated and intellectual. I will talk about what to do with Germany after the war." But before he had time to begin, he was asleep.

He woke just as the first light of day was showing through the slit in the curtains over the window. The room was still

11. *Hard as nails* refers to hard water, which contains minerals that prevent soap from dissolving easily.

Vocabulary

intellectual (int′ əl ek′ cho͞o əl) *adj.* appealing to or involving mental ability

Writing Minilesson

Writing a Descriptive Scene This story begins after the pilot has been wounded in battle. Encourage the class to discuss what might have happened to the pilot before the story begins. Let students use what they know about World War II, airplanes, and the story so far to present some possible scenarios.

Activity Have interested students create air battle scenes that describe what happened to the pilot before he got shot. Encourage students to use this story as a writing model for creating descriptive and realistic paragraphs. Have students write their scenes, as Dahl does, from the pilot's point of view. **L2**

Additional Resources

 ***Writer's Choice,*** Lesson 3.3

German Junker 88

dark, but he could tell that it was already beginning to get light outside. He lay looking at the gray light which was showing through the slit in the curtain and as he lay there he remembered the day before. He remembered the Junkers 88's and the hardness of the water; he remembered the large pleasant nurse and the kind doctor, and now a small grain of doubt took root in his mind and it began to grow.

R He looked around the room. The nurse had taken the roses out the night before. There was nothing except the table. The room was bare. It was no longer warm or friendly. It was not even comfortable. It was cold and empty and very quiet.

S Slowly the grain of doubt grew, and with it came fear, a light, dancing fear that warned but did not frighten; the kind of fear that one gets not because one is afraid, but because one feels that there is something wrong. Quickly the doubt and the fear grew so that he became restless and angry, and when he touched his forehead with his hand, he found that it was damp with sweat. He knew then that he must do something; that he must find some way of proving to himself that he was either right or wrong, and he looked up and saw again the window and the green curtains. From where he lay, that window was right in front of him, but it was fully ten yards away. Somehow he must reach it and look out. The idea became an obsession with him and soon he could think of nothing except the window. But what about his leg? He put his hand underneath the bedclothes and felt the thick bandaged stump which was all that was left on the right hand side. It seemed all right. It didn't hurt. But it would not be easy.

He sat up. Then he pushed the bedclothes aside and put his left leg on the floor. Slowly, carefully, he swung his body over until he had both hands on the floor as well; then he was out of bed, kneeling on the carpet. He looked at the stump. It was very short and thick, covered with bandages. It was beginning to hurt and he could feel it throbbing. He wanted to collapse, lie down on the carpet and do nothing but he knew that he must go on.

T With two arms and one leg, he crawled over toward the window. He would reach forward as far as he could with his arms, then he would give a little jump and slide his left leg along after them. Each time he did it, it jarred his wound so that he gave a soft grunt of pain, but he continued to crawl across the floor on two hands and one knee. When he got to the window he reached up, and one at a time he placed both hands on the sill. Slowly he raised himself up until he was standing on his left leg. Then quickly he pushed aside the curtains and looked out.

He saw a small house with a gray tiled roof standing alone beside a narrow lane, and immediately behind it there was a plowed field. In front of the house there was

R Critical Thinking

LOGICAL REASONING The hospital room has not changed much. Have students explain why the pilot is no longer at ease there. *(The pilot's attitude has changed. The room no longer feels warm and friendly to him because he is beginning to doubt the doctor and nurse.)*

S Active Reading Strategies

RESPOND Encourage students to discuss the pilot's view of his situation. *(He has become worried that something is wrong, but he doesn't know what it is.)* Have students explain what they would do if they were the pilot. *(Students may say that they would ask the doctor or nurse questions about Brighton that anyone living there would know, ask why there are no other patients in the hospital, insist on personally contacting family, and insist that buddies be allowed to visit.)*

T Active Reading Strategies

PREDICT Have students predict what the pilot will see when he looks out the window. *(The pilot may see that the town is occupied by German soldiers, that Brighton has been destroyed, or that he is not in Brighton.)*

Meeting Individual Needs: Multiple Modes of Expression

Logical/Mathematical Students with strong logical/mathematical abilities may respond to this story in an analytical and conceptual way. They can use coded messages to help them understand the frustration and danger inherent in the pilot's situation.

Activity Encourage students to work in small groups to analyze how the pilot might get a coded message to people in the outside world. Students can create codes or ciphers and exchange coded messages with partners. Students can explain to the class how they coded their messages and the problems they encountered in the process. **L2**

U Critical Thinking

LOGICAL REASONING Encourage students to explain the importance of the *garde au chien* sign. *(The sign helps the pilot resolve his confusion: He is in France; that's why the water is hard and he hears Junkers 88s.)*

When this story takes place, Germany controlled France and the Atlantic Coast. If the pilot is in France, he is in territory controlled by England's enemy, Germany.

V Active Reading Strategies

QUESTION Discuss with students why the nurse tells the pilot he was in Brighton when he is in France. *(The nurse wants him to feel at home and let his guard down.)*

W Active Reading Strategies

CONNECT Have students describe situations in which they get nervous. Then have them explain why the nurse might be nervous. *(The nurse may be nervous because she is hiding something from the pilot.)*

Teaching Support

an untidy garden, and there was a green hedge separating the garden from the lane. He was looking at the hedge when he saw the sign. It was just a piece of board nailed to the top of a short pole, and because the hedge had not been trimmed for a long time, the branches had grown out around the sign so that it seemed almost as though it had been placed in the middle of the hedge. There was something written on the board with white paint. He pressed his head against the glass of the window, trying to read what it said. The first letter was a G, he could see that. The second was an A, and the third was an R. One after another he managed to see what the letters were. There were three words, and slowly he spelled the letters out aloud to himself as he managed to read them. G–A–R–D–E A–U C–H–I–E–N. *Garde au chien*. That is what it said.

Did You Know?
Along a hedge near a house in France, the words *garde au chien* (gard ō shyen) would warn visitors to "beware of the dog."

He stood there balancing on one leg and holding tightly to the edges of the window sill with his hands, staring at the sign and at the white-washed lettering of the words. For a moment he could think of nothing at all. He stood there looking at the sign, repeating the words over and over to himself. Slowly he began to realize the full meaning of the thing. He looked up at the cottage and at the plowed field. He looked at the small orchard on the left of the cottage and he looked at the green countryside beyond. "So this is France," he said. "I am in France."

Now the throbbing in his right thigh was very great. It felt as though someone was pounding the end of his stump with a hammer and suddenly the pain became so intense that it affected his head. For a moment he thought he was going to fall. Quickly he knelt down again, crawled back to the bed and hoisted himself in. He pulled the bedclothes over himself and lay back on the pillow, exhausted. He could still think of nothing at all except the small sign by the hedge and the plowed field and the orchard. It was the words on the sign that he could not forget.

It was some time before the nurse came in. She came carrying a basin of hot water and she said, "Good morning, how are you today?"

He said, "Good morning, nurse."

The pain was still great under the bandages, but he did not wish to tell this woman anything. He looked at her as she busied herself with getting the washing things ready. He looked at her more carefully now. Her hair was very fair. She was tall and big-boned and her face seemed pleasant. But there was something a little uneasy about her eyes. They were never still. They never looked at anything for more than a moment and they moved too quickly from one place to another in the room. There was something about her movements also. They were too sharp and nervous to go well with the casual manner in which she spoke.

Vocabulary
intense (in tens′) *adj.* of a very high degree; very strong

MEETING INDIVIDUAL NEEDS — SPECIAL NEEDS

Learning Disabled Some students may not fully comprehend why being in France is dangerous for this pilot. They may better understand this concept by looking at a map of Europe.

Activity Give students a blank map and have them label the following countries: England, France, and Germany. Explain that in World War II, England and France both fought against Germany. Then Germany overran France and took control of it. Ask students to discuss why it is dangerous for the pilot to be in France. *(If the pilot is in France, he is in the hands of the enemy.)* **L2**

Additional Resources

Inclusion Strategies

She set down the basin, took off his pajama top and began to wash him.

X "Did you sleep well?"

"Yes."

"Good," she said. She was washing his arms and his chest.

Y "I believe there's someone coming down to see you from the Air Ministry after breakfast," she went on. "They want a report or something. I expect you know all about it. How you got shot down and all that. I won't let him stay long, so don't worry."

He did not answer. She finished washing him and gave him a toothbrush and some toothpowder. He brushed his teeth, rinsed his mouth and spat the water out into the basin.

Later she brought him his breakfast on a tray, but he did not want to eat. He was still feeling weak and sick and he wished only to lie still and think about what had happened. And there was a sentence running through his head. It was a sentence which Johnny, the Intelligence Officer of his squadron, always repeated to the pilots every day before they went out. He could see Johnny now, leaning against the wall of the dispersal hut[12] with his pipe in his hand, saying,

12. An *Intelligence Officer* gathers and studies information about the enemy. He informs the R.A.F. pilots of enemy activities that would affect their missions and trains them to safeguard information from the enemy. The pilots get their flight instructions in the *dispersal hut.*

Trees Near Douarnenez. Jules Eugene Pages (1867–1946). Oil on canvas, 21¼ x 25¾ in. Private collection.

Viewing the painting: This could be the scene the British pilot saw from his window. Why do you suppose he was sent to a place like this?

X Active Reading Strategies

QUESTION Have students recall whether the pilot has really slept well that night. Ask students why the pilot might lie to the nurse about how he slept. *(The pilot has not slept well and does not share the information with the nurse because he no longer trusts her.)*

Y Active Reading Strategies

EVALUATE Have students explain why someone from the British Air Ministry would want to talk to the pilot about getting shot down. Have students explain whether this information would also be valuable to the enemy. *(All pilots are debriefed after a mission. The intelligence is also very important to the enemy because it would provide information about the other side's strength, tactics, and methods of operation.)*

VIEWING THE PAINTING

Douarnenez, the town this scene is near, is along the Atlantic coast in Brittany, at the far western part of France.

Viewing Response *Students might suggest that the location is quiet, not heavily populated, and presumably away from any military action that might arouse suspicion in the British airman.*

Listening and Speaking *Minilesson*

Reading Aloud Have students develop some guidelines for reading a scene aloud. Record them on the board. *(Read some parts slower or faster, louder or softer. Don't rush. Read with feeling. Make sure you understand the text you are reading, and read it with confidence to reflect that understanding.)*

Activity Assign pairs of students one of the scenes to read aloud to the rest of the class. Have students think about how the pilot would feel in each situation and then read aloud to show those emotions. The class should listen for the way the pilot's emotions and attitudes change as the scenes progress. **L2**

VIEWING THE PAINTING

Belgian painter René Magritte (1898–1967) was a well-known Surrealist who delighted in symbols and illogical images. *La Grande Famille* includes three of his favorite motifs: sky, clouds, and sea.

Viewing Response *Students may say the dove is a symbol of peace and might suggest that its flight could symbolize the British airman's desire for freedom.*

Z Literary Elements

FLASHBACK Encourage your students to explain how remembering the Intelligence Officer prepares the pilot for the resolution of the story. *(The pilot realizes he has been captured by the enemy; the flashback reminds him to give only his name, rank, and number.)*

Thematic Focus

Twists and Turns Review with students the different twists and turns this story takes and how it relates to the theme.

FINE ART TRANSPARENCY 13

You may wish to use ***Fine Art Transparency 13*** to enrich the discussion.

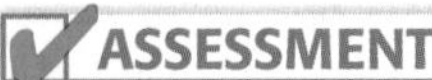

ASSESSMENT

Quick Checks, p. 51

La Grande Famille, 1947. René Magritte. Oil on canvas, 100 x 81 cm. Copyright ARS, New York. Private collection.

Viewing the painting: What does this painting say to you? How would you connect it with the story?

Z "And if they get you, don't forget, just your name, rank, and number. Nothing else. For God's sake, say nothing else."

"There you are," she said as she put the tray on his lap. "I've got you an egg. Can you manage all right?"

"Yes."

She stood beside the bed. "Are you feeling all right?"

"Yes."

"Good. If you want another egg I might be able to get you one."

"This is all right."

"Well, just ring the bell if you want any more." And she went out.

He had just finished eating, when the nurse came in again.

She said, "Wing Commander Roberts is here. I've told him that he can only stay for a few minutes."

She beckoned with her hand and the Wing Commander came in.

"Sorry to bother you like this," he said.

He was an ordinary R.A.F. officer, dressed in a uniform which was a little shabby. He wore wings and a D.F.C.[13] He was fairly tall and thin with plenty of black hair. His teeth, which were irregular and widely spaced, stuck out a little even when he closed his mouth. As he spoke he took a printed form and pencil from his pocket and he pulled up a chair and sat down.

"How are you feeling?"

There was no answer.

"Tough luck about your leg. I know how you feel. I hear you put up a fine show before they got you."

The man in the bed was lying quite still, watching the man in the chair.

The man in the chair said, "Well, let's get this stuff over. I'm afraid you'll have to answer a few questions so that I can fill in this combat report. Let me see now, first of all, what was your squadron?"

The man in the bed did not move. He looked straight at the Wing Commander and he said, "My name is Peter Williamson. My rank is Squadron Leader, and my number is nine seven two four five seven."

13. An R.A.F. pilot would wear a small badge shaped like flying *wings.* The *D.F.C.,* or *Distinguished Flying Cross,* was a medal awarded for heroism.

Teaching Support

Grammar and Language *Minilesson*

***Troublesome Words:* Lie** Write these sentences on the board to illustrate how to use *lie* in the past, present, and future tenses:

1. Yesterday the pilot lay listening to the Junkers 88s.
2. Today he lies in bed.
3. Tomorrow he will still lie in bed.

Have volunteers explain why Dahl sometimes used *lie* and other times *lay* to mean "reclining" in bed. *(Lay is the past tense. Lie is the present tense.)*

Activity Have students write five sentences using lie in the present, past, and future tenses. Have them include the words *yesterday, today,* or *tomorrow* in each sentence to show that they understand when the action occurs. **L2**

Additional Resources

- ***Grammar and Language Transparency 50***
- ***Grammar and Language Workbook,*** pp. 223–224
- ***Grammar and Composition Handbook,*** Lessons 3.11, 3.12
- ***Writer's Choice,*** Lesson 17.2

Responding to Literature

PERSONAL RESPONSE

- What was your reaction to this story? Did you find this story suspenseful, mysterious, both? How does the story relate to your response to the **Reading Focus** on page 602? Describe your impressions in your journal.

Analyzing Literature

RECALL

1. Briefly describe the main character in the story. Who is he and what is he doing as the story opens?
2. Where does the pilot end up? What are his injuries?
3. Describe the things that make the pilot become suspicious about his location. What does he decide to do to test his suspicions?

Brackets connect questions that are paired to develop higher-level thinking skills.

INTERPRET

4. What is the importance of the French phrase *garde au chien?*
5. What sort of person is the pilot? How does he come to realize what has happened to him? Support your ideas with examples from the story.
6. How does the author inform you about the pilot's misfortune?
7. In describing the **setting** of the story, Dahl uses details that intensify the mood of suspense. Pick out details that help create this mood. (See **Literary Terms Handbook,** page R10.)
8. Why do you think Dahl named the story "Beware of the Dog"?

EVALUATE AND CONNECT

9. In the last paragraph of the story, why does the pilot respond the way he does to the wing commander? If you were the pilot, what would you have done?
10. At what point in the story did you begin to suspect that the pilot was not where the nurse said he was? How does Dahl build toward that suspicion?

LITERARY ELEMENTS

Flashback

A **flashback** is an interruption in the sequence of a piece of writing to describe a scene that happened at an earlier time. Skillful writers sometimes use flashbacks to give background information to readers so they can better understand what is happening at the present time.

For example, a character in a story may meet someone he or she knew years earlier. A flashback to that earlier time could tell the reader about the relationship between the two characters.

1. How is a flashback used in "Beware of the Dog"? Describe the scene that is presented in the flashback.
2. Sometimes a flashback can appear in the form of a dream. Why do you think Roald Dahl chose to begin the story the way he did?

- See **Literary Terms Handbook,** p. R4.

LITERARY ELEMENTS

1. Flashback is used to describe how the pilot is forced to bail out and to hook readers' interest.
2. It creates interest and intrigue. It also tells the reader how the main character got into this situation.

Additional Resources

Literary Elements Transparency 51

Responding to the Selection

PERSONAL RESPONSE

Students should describe their reactions to the story as well as how the story relates to their ideas about waking up in an unfamiliar place.

Analyzing Literature

1. The main character is a Spitfire pilot for the RAF. He is piloting his plane back to England after having been wounded in battle.
2. The pilot has been shot in a leg, which has been amputated. At first he thinks he is in a hospital in Brighton, England.
3. He hears Junkers 88s flying overhead and he remembers Brighton had soft water. He decides he must look out the window to see where he is.
4. The fact that this "Beware of the Dog" sign is in French makes the pilot realize that he is in France.
5. The pilot is perceptive and wary. He hears the Junkers 88 and remembers that Brighton has soft water. He looks out the window and realizes that he is in enemy territory in France.
6. The pilot daydreams and imagines landing, injured, in England and surprising his buddies.
7. After the pilot's doubts begin to grow, Dahl describes his room as "cold and empty and very quiet." It is no longer warm and friendly.
8. The French sign helps the pilot figure out where he is. The sign might also mean "Beware of the Enemy."
9. He realizes that the enemy has captured him, and he doesn't want to give them any information.
10. Suspicion might begin when the pilot discovers that the water is hard. Dahl adds to the suspicion by having Junkers 88s fly overhead in daylight.

Literature and Writing

Writing About Literature
Students' analyses should
- describe specific techniques Dahl uses to build suspense in this story
- use examples from the story to support ideas
- describe general techniques Dahl uses that students could incorporate into their own writing

Personal Writing
Students' epilogues should
- describe what happens to the pilot after this story ends
- use what they already know about the pilot to accurately describe his responses
- incorporate descriptions of the setting and the war into a plausible scenario

Extending Your Response

Interdisciplinary Activity
Encourage students to color-code their map so it is easy for others to understand. In addition, have them include a legend and a compass rose.

Learning for Life Remind students to develop questions that require more than a yes-or-no answer. When they answer questions, encourage them to base their answers on what they know about World War II and the pilot in this story.

Literature Groups Before students meet, encourage them to jot down some initial impressions about the options available to the pilot.

Literature and Writing

Writing About Literature
Suspense **Suspense,** a state of uncertainty or fear about how something will turn out, is an essential element of this story. How does the writer build suspense? How does he raise questions in your mind about what will happen next? Write a brief analysis of how suspense is created in this story. Use examples from the story.

Personal Writing
An Epilogue An **epilogue** is a passage added to the end of a written work. What do you think will happen to the pilot after the end of this story? Write a brief epilogue describing what happens to the pilot and why.

Extending Your Response

Interdisciplinary Activity
Social Studies: Map It! With a partner or in a small group, research the role of British fighter pilots in World War II. Using your research and the information in the story, create a map that shows the possible route of the ill-fated flight, a possible point of origin, and where the pilot might have ended up in France.

Learning for Life
Interview a Vet Imagine you are a journalist sent to interview the pilot after the end of the war. Write a list of the questions you would ask the pilot. Then work with a partner, taking turns as pilot and interviewer as you answer each other's questions.

Literature Groups
A Difficult Decision The main character in this story faces a difficult decision. Once he realizes that he is in enemy hands, what should he do? What are his options? In small groups, discuss the pilot's situation, his options, and his decision. Support your ideas with examples and quotations from the story.

Reading Further
If you would like to read more Roald Dahl stories like this one, try:

Over to You: Ten Stories of Flyers and Flying

Another book set at the time of World War II is:

Good Night, Mr. Tom by Michelle Magorian

Save your work for your portfolio.

Skill Minilessons

Reteach • Review

GRAMMAR AND LANGUAGE • COMPLEX SENTENCES

A **complex sentence** is a sentence with one main clause and one or more subordinate clauses. In the following examples, the main clauses are in regular type, and the subordinate clauses are in *italic* type.

When he woke up, the pilot looked around.
The room had one light, *which was very dim.*
The pilot knew *that his options were limited.*

PRACTICE Write a paragraph describing the main character in "Beware of the Dog." Use at least three complex sentences in your description. Then trade paragraphs with a partner and read his or her paragraph. As you read, find the complex sentences and underline each main clause once and each subordinate clause twice.

- For more about complex sentences, see **Language Handbook,** p. R32.

READING AND THINKING • MONITORING COMPREHENSION

As a skillful reader, you should always ask questions about what you read and also evaluate the characters, actions, and events to make sure you understand what is happening. Remember to question and evaluate while you are reading—not just after you have finished. As you read, ask yourself questions such as these:

- Does this event make sense?
- What's really going on here?
- Would this character really say or do this?
- What is the writer describing? Why?

PRACTICE Review "Beware of the Dog." Write at least five questions about the characters, events, and setting of the story. Make them questions that require more than a simple yes or no for answers. Next, trade your questions with a partner. Answer each other's questions and then discuss your answers.

- For more about monitoring comprehension, see **Reading Handbook,** pp. R85–R97.

VOCABULARY • USING CONTEXT CLUES FOR MULTIPLE-MEANING WORDS

Some words have multiple meanings that are similar. In "Beware of the Dog," *giddy* means "dizzy or lightheaded." It describes the kind of whirling feeling a person gets after spinning around or from being very sick. *Giddy* can also mean "causing dizziness." It can also mean "not serious or steady; silly."

To know which definition of a multiple-meaning word is correct, look for context clues in the sentence or paragraph the word is in.

PRACTICE Use context clues to decide which meaning of *giddy* is the right one in each sentence.

a. dizzy or lightheaded
b. causing dizziness
c. not serious, silly

1. Lisa looked down from her *giddy* perch near the top of the tree.
2. I must have sounded foolish, giggling in such a *giddy* way.
3. Harry complained of feeling *giddy,* and then he fell backwards in a faint.
4. How can figure skaters spin as they do without becoming *giddy*?
5. The children could not calm down and listen; they were too *giddy* with excitement.

Skill Minilessons

GRAMMAR AND LANGUAGE
COMPLEX SENTENCES

If students have difficulty distinguishing main from subordinate clauses in their partner's paragraphs, have them read the clauses out loud to hear which can stand alone as sentences. These are main clauses.

READING AND THINKING
MONITORING COMPREHENSION

Students questions should

- help clarify the significance of story events
- require the one who responds to form opinions or make judgments
- provide insight into the author's purpose or the pilot's motivation

VOCABULARY
USING CONTEXT CLUES FOR MULTIPLE-MEANING WORDS

1. b
2. c
3. a
4. a
5. c

Additional Resources

- ***Grammar and Language Workbook,*** pp. 155–156
- ***Grammar and Composition Handbook,*** Lesson 8.2
- ***Writer's Choice,*** Lesson 14.2
- ***Reading Skills Practice Workbook,*** pp. 91–92
- ***Vocabulary Practice,*** p. 36

ASSESSMENT

- ***Quick Checks,*** p. 51
- ***Selection and Theme Assessment,*** pp. 89–90
- ***Performance Assessment,*** p. 48
- ***Testmaker: ExamView Pro***
- ***Interactive Tutor: Self-Assessment***

Objective

- To understand the elements of poetry

Teaching Strategies

Ask students if they can remember any poetry from their childhood, such as nursery rhymes, prayers, jump rope chants, or clapping games. Ask students if any of these elements helped them remember those poems and chants even after many years: rhythm, rhyme, images, colorful language, the sound of the words.

Form Explain that the form of a poem can make the poem visually interesting on the page. Students may wish to experiment with form by writing a poem that has an unusual shape.

Imagery An image in poetry can be thought of as a picture painted with words. Ask students to describe the image that comes to mind when they read the stanza of "The Highwayman" on the bottom of the page. Which senses does this stanza appeal to? Ask them to do quick sketches of the picture brought to mind by the words.

Teaching Support

POETRY

Poetry is a form of writing that uses not only words, but also form, patterns of sound, imagery, and figurative language to convey its message. Any poem will include some or all of the elements described on these two pages.

- For more about the various elements of poetry, see **Literary Terms Handbook,** p. R8.

The Arch of Nero, 1846. Thomas Cole. Oil on canvas, 60 x 48 in. The Newark Museum, Newark, NJ.

ELEMENTS OF POETRY

FORM A poem's form is its appearance. Poems are divided into lines. Many poems, especially longer ones, may also be divided into groups of lines called **stanzas.** Stanzas function like paragraphs in a story. Each one contains a single idea or takes the idea one step further. The opening stanza of "The Highwayman," for example, sets the scene for the narrative poem.

MODEL

The wind was a torrent of darkness
among the gusty trees.
The moon was a ghostly galleon
tossed upon cloudy seas.
The road was a ribbon of moonlight
over the purple moor,
And the highwayman came riding—
Riding—riding—
The highwayman came riding, up to
the old inn door.

IMAGERY Poets use words and phrases that appeal to the reader's senses of sight, sound, touch, taste, and smell. Notice in the model from "The Highwayman" how the poet uses words to help you "see" an angry man on horseback.

Back, he spurred like a madman,
shouting curses to the sky,
With the white road smoking behind
him and his rapier brandished high.

MEETING INDIVIDUAL NEEDS — ENGLISH LANGUAGE LEARNERS

World Poetry Some English language learners will find it challenging to understand the elements of poetry and identify them in English-language poems. Images, metaphors, and similes often require advanced-level vocabulary skills. The spirit of poetry, however, is something that is universal.

Activity Ask each student to bring in a favorite poem that is written either in English or in their native language. Have the students work in groups. Ask them to read each poem aloud, translating if necessary. Have each student choose one image from the poem and draw a picture that represents the image.

Additional Resources

English Language Learners Sourcebook

SOUND Some poems use techniques of sound such as the following.

- **Rhythm** is the pattern of beats or stresses in a poem. Poets use patterns of stressed and unstressed syllables to create a regular rhythm. In the model, the stressed syllables are printed in **bold** type. Try beating out the rhythm with a finger as you read these lines.
- **Rhyme** is the repetition of the same or similar sounds, usually in stressed syllables at the ends of lines, but sometimes within a line as well, as in this model.
- **Alliteration** is the repetition of consonant sounds at the beginnings of words. Read aloud the model example to hear its alliteration.

> • **She** was a **child** and **I** was a **child,**
> In this **king**dom **by** the **sea:**
> But we **loved** with a **love** that was
> **more** than **love**–
> **I** and my **Ann**abel **Lee;**
>
> • There are strange things **done** in the
> midnight **sun**
> By the men who moil for gold;
>
> • Over the **c**obbles he **c**lattered and
> **c**lashed . . .

FIGURES OF SPEECH Figures of speech are a special kind of imagery. They create pictures by making comparisons.

- A **simile** is a comparison using *like* or *as.*
- A **metaphor** describes one thing as if it *were* another.
- **Personification** gives human characteristics to something nonhuman.

> • Talk of your cold! through the parka's
> fold it stabbed like a driven nail.
>
> • The moon was a ghostly galleon
> tossed upon cloudy seas.
>
> • . . . and the stars o'erhead
> were dancing heel and toe . . .

In "The Highwayman," images create a picture of Tim. Which figures are used to describe his eyes and his hair?

His eyes were hollows of madness, his hair like
mouldy hay,

THEME The **theme** of a poem is its central or main idea. To identify a poem's theme, ask yourself what ideas or insights about life or human nature you have found in the poem.

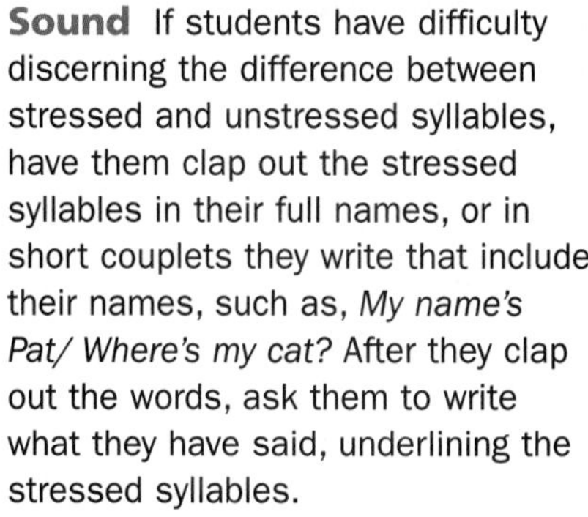

Sound If students have difficulty discerning the difference between stressed and unstressed syllables, have them clap out the stressed syllables in their full names, or in short couplets they write that include their names, such as, *My name's Pat/ Where's my cat?* After they clap out the words, ask them to write what they have said, underlining the stressed syllables.

Figures of Speech Write the following sentences on the board:

- My love is like a rose.
- Our love bloomed in the garden.
- The rose tipped its head as we passed by.

After students have read about figures of speech on page 617, ask them to identify which of the above is an example of a simile, metaphor, and personification. Encourage students to write their own examples of each.

Theme Explain that the theme of a poem is often hard to find on first reading. The reader may have a general sense of what the poem is about, but additional readings of the poem often help clarify thoughts and feelings about it.

Technology

Poetry Table

Students can use a word processing program to create a table of poetry elements as they read the poems in this unit.

Activity Ask each student to open a new document and insert a six-column table as shown. For each poem, a new row can be added to the table and information can be keyed in about each of the five elements of that poem. Encourage the use of quotation marks when including direct examples of imagery and figures of speech from the poems. **L2**

Title	Form	Sound	Imagery	Figures of Speech	Theme

Active Reading Strategies

Objective

- To understand and apply strategies for reading and comprehending poetry

Teach the Strategies

Remind students that poetry is all around them, not only in a literature class, but also in song lyrics, raps, jazz chants, and childhood rhymes. Poems come in all lengths, forms, and levels of language.

Preview

Tell students that previewing will make a poem seem familiar to them before they actually read it.

Listen

Suggest that students take turns reading the poems to each other. Listeners should just listen to enjoy the spoken language rather than read along.

Visualize

Suggest that students make a habit of visualizing favorite images as they read through a poem. Visualizing will help them remember the image.

Question

Point out to students that they may have many questions when they first read a poem since the language and images are often more compressed and intense in poetry than in prose.

Teaching Support

ACTIVE READING MODEL

Active Reading Strategies

Tips for Reading Poetry

Poetry is a kind of imaginative writing in which thoughts and feelings are expressed in rhythmic, compressed language. Skillful readers use strategies that help them understand the meaning of a poem.

- For more about reading strategies, see **Reading Handbook,** pp. R73–R102.

PREVIEW

Before reading the poem, just stop to look at it. Think about its form.

Ask Yourself . . .

- How long is the poem? Is it broken into stanzas?
- Are the individual lines short or long?
- How does the poet use punctuation?

LISTEN

Read the poem aloud. Listen for patterns of rhythm and rhyme.

Ask Yourself . . .

- Does the poet use rhyme? What rhythm and rhyming patterns can I discover?

VISUALIZE

Look for the poet's use of imagery and figures of speech.

Ask Yourself . . .

- What images does the poem contain? Can I imagine what the poet describes?

QUESTION

Since poetry is such a compact form of literature, poets think very carefully about each word they use. As a skillful reader, you, too, should think about each word.

Ask Yourself . . .

- Why did the poet choose this particular word or phrase?
- Why does the poet use this image or comparison?

618 THEME 6

Reading Journal

Does Love Conquer All?

The poet Alfred Noyes presents in "The Highwayman" a tale about a robber and the woman he loves. Invite students to discuss whether people have any control over the person with whom they fall in love.

Activity As they read "The Highwayman," invite students to copy into their reading journals the rhymes and images they especially like. After reading, have students give their opinions of the choices made by Bess and the highwayman. L1

CONNECT

As you read, think about the theme of the poem. Discuss the poem with your classmates. There is no "right answer" when you read a poem.

Ask Yourself . . .

- How do the events and images in the poem connect to my own experience?
- What message is the poet trying to get across?

RESPOND

Think about whether feelings, events, or images from the poem remind you of something in your own life. Think about what the poem means to you.

Ask Yourself . . .

- Do I like the sound of the rhyme pattern?
- Is the poet's imagery appropriate for the poem's theme?

EVALUATE

Read the poem several times. As you read, think about your reactions to the poem. Evaluate what the poem has to say.

Ask Yourself . . .

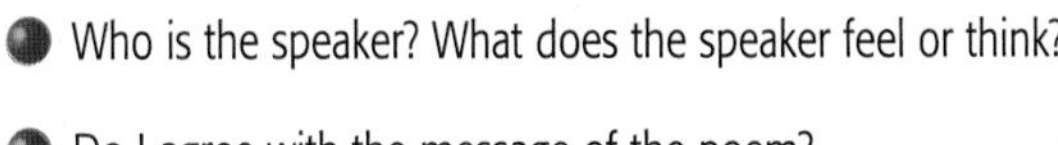

- Who is the speaker? What does the speaker feel or think?
- Do I agree with the message of the poem?

APPLYING THE STRATEGIES

Read the following poem, "The Highwayman." Use the **Active Reading** notes in the margins as you read. Write your responses on a separate piece of paper or use stick-on notes.

Connect

Encourage students to share their impressions of the poem with each other. Ask them to focus on images, scenes, and characters in the poem with which they feel a connection, and to explain why.

Respond

Have students imagine that the poet has sent the poem to each of them in the mail. As they read the poem, they may wonder what the events and images have to do with them and their lives. If they read the poem as if it has been written specifically for them, their experience as readers may be sharpened.

Evaluate

Some students may need to read the poem several times before they can evaluate its meaning. Suggest that they jot down impressions as they read to help their comprehension.

Grammar and Language *Minilesson*

Capitalization in Poetry As students begin reading the poems in this theme, point out again a convention that is usually observed in the writing of poetry—capitalizing the first word of each line even though it is not the beginning of a sentence. In free verse—poetry that lacks a regular metrical pattern or rhyme scheme—the convention is observed less often.

Activity Ask students to look back through the book at poetry selections that they have already read to find one poem they like in which the first word of each line is capitalized and one in which this convention is not observed. Ask them to explain what effect the capitalization or lack of it has on their reading of the poems. **L2**

Before Reading

Objectives

- To read and appreciate the twists and turns in a narrative poem
- To recognize and understand the purpose of onomatopoeia
- To write about narrative elements in a poem

Skills

Reading/Thinking: Evaluating; Monitoring Comprehension; Drawing Conclusions
Writing: Interview Questions
Vocabulary: Multiple-Meaning Words
Grammar/Language: Compound Sentences; Colorful Adjectives
Listening/Speaking: Choral Reading
Collaboration: Literature Groups

Motivating STUDENTS

Selection Focus Transparency 52: Have students view the quote and discuss its figurative meaning.

Reading Focus: As an extension of the Reading Focus, have students in small groups discuss what made their favorite adventure books or movies exciting.

ACTIVE READING MODEL

Before You Read

The Highwayman

MEET ALFRED NOYES

Alfred Noyes was one of the most popular British poets of the early twentieth century. Because he became a successful poet while still in his twenties, Noyes was able to continue a career as a full-time poet. While many other British poets writing at that time were thoroughly modern in their writing styles, Noyes chose to write traditional poetry in the manner of the great nineteenth-century Romantic poets.

Alfred Noyes was born in England in 1880 and died in 1958.

READING FOCUS

Do you enjoy dramatic adventure stories?

Sharing Ideas
Think about adventure stories you have enjoyed reading or seeing as movies. Jot down the titles of a few favorites to share with your classmates.

Setting a Purpose
Read this poem to enjoy its story.

BUILDING BACKGROUND

By the eighteenth century, horse-drawn coaches traveled regularly on English roads. They were preyed upon by armed thieves on horseback called highwaymen, who would stop coaches at gunpoint and demand that the passengers surrender their money and other valuables. A few highwaymen, such as Dick Turpin, became legends in their time, inspiring songs, poems, and stories in the popular newspapers of the time—at least until they were caught and hanged for their crimes.

RESOURCE MANAGER

Teaching Tools and Resources
- Theme Six Planning Guide
- Literature Groups Sourcebook

Essential Lesson Support

Lesson-Specific Instruction
- Selection Focus Transparency 52
- Literary Elements Transparency 52
- Active Reading Guide,* p. 52

Assessment
- Selection Quick Checks,* p. 52
- Sel. and Theme Assmt., pp. 91–92
- Testmaker: ExamView Pro
- Performance Assessment, p. 49

Systematic Language Instruction
- Gr. and Comp. Hbk., L. 11.5
- Vocabulary Power, Lesson 28

English Language Learners
- ELL Sourcebook, p. 81
- Spanish Summaries, p. 52
- Audio Library*
- English, Yes!

Spec. Needs/Strat. Interven.
- Interactive Rdg. Sbk., pp. T188–T190
- Interactive Rdg. Wkbk., pp. 103–104
- Inclusion Strat. Sbk., pp. 43–46
- Audio Library*

* Also available in Spanish

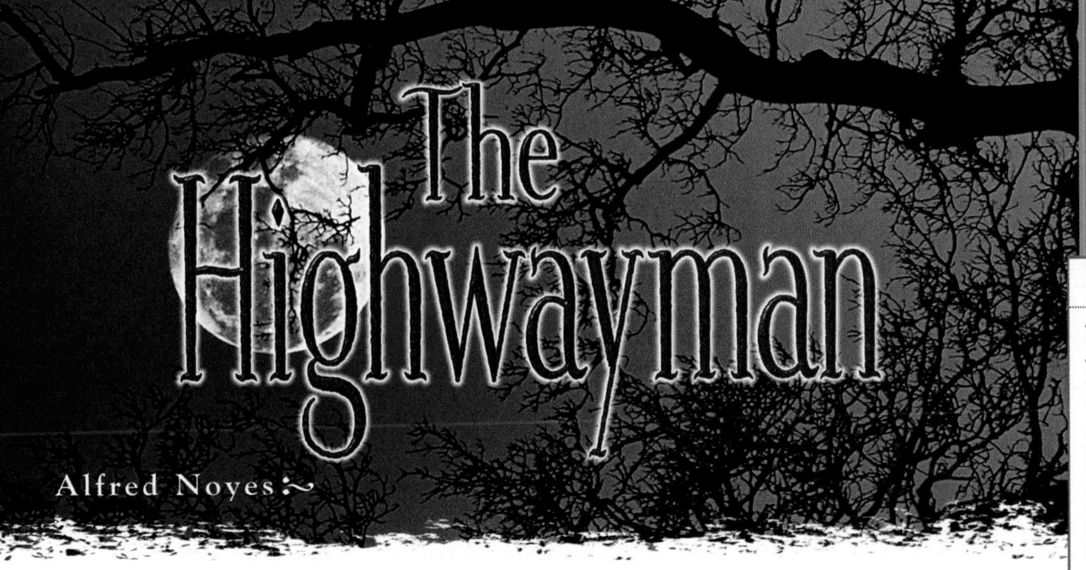

ACTIVE READING MODEL

PART 1

The wind was a torrent of darkness among the gusty trees.
The moon was a ghostly galleon° tossed upon cloudy seas.
The road was a ribbon of moonlight over the purple moor,°
And the highwayman came riding—
Riding—riding—
The highwayman came riding, up to the old inn door.

He'd a French cocked hat on his forehead, a bunch of lace at his chin,
A coat of the claret velvet, and breeches of brown doeskin.
They fitted with never a wrinkle. His boots were up to the thigh.
And he rode with a jewelled twinkle,
His pistol butts a-twinkle,
His rapier° hilt° a-twinkle, under the jewelled sky.

PREVIEW Take a minute to think about the shape of this poem. How are the lines of the poem grouped? How many parts does it have? **A**

VISUALIZE How does this description help you "see" the highwayman? **B**

2 A *galleon* (gal' yən) is a large sailing ship of the 1400s–1600s.
3 A *moor* is an area of open, rolling, wild land, usually a grassy wetland.
12 A *rapier* is a long, lightweight sword, and the *hilt* is its handle.

Reading the Selection

SUMMARY

The highwayman is a thief in eighteenth-century England. He promises to return to his love, Bess, by moonlight. King George's redcoats learn of his planned return. They capture Bess and lie in wait for the highwayman. When Bess hears the highwayman returning, she shoots herself to warn the highwayman away. The highwayman retreats, but soon finds out Bess is dead. Enraged, he rides back to avenge her death and is killed himself.

Spanish Summaries, p. 52

A Active Reading Strategies

PREVIEW *(The lines are grouped in paragraphs called stanzas. Each stanza has six lines. The poem has two parts.)*

B Active Reading Strategies

VISUALIZE *(The details give a clear image of the highwayman. Details include his hat, his suede boots, his pistol, and his sword.)*

Additional Resources

Active Reading Guide, pp. 52
Audio Library
Spanish Audio Library

Teaching Support

CONNECTING TO OTHER SELECTIONS

The chart at the right shows three ways to connect "The Highwayman" to other selections in this book.

For specific teaching strategies, see the ***Theme Six Planning Guide.***

Connection		Title
Life Skills: Making Decisions	→	"The Wreck of the Hesperus," p. 227
Thematic: Outcasts	→	"Antaeus," p. 347
Literary: Repetition	→	"Growing Pains," p. 133

C Literary Elements

ONOMATOPOEIA Have students list examples of onomatopoeia in this stanza, and explain what effect these words have on the poem. *(The words* clattered, clashed, *and* tapped *help the reader "hear" the action of the poem.)*

D Active Reading Strategies

QUESTION *(The images describe a lovelorn, pale, and jealous man. They set a mood of dread.)*

E Author's Craft

FORESHADOWING Ask students why they think the poet describes Tim by saying that "His eyes were hollows of madness." *(Tim loves Bess and is crazed because she loves the highwayman. The poet is foreshadowing something dark.)*

F Literary Elements

PLOT: *Rising Action* Have students read lines 25–30 and discuss how these lines add to the tension in the poem. *(The reader knows that Tim is listening as the highwayman explains his plans to steal gold and return before morning.)*

G Active Reading Strategies

QUESTION *(These lines illustrate the love the highwayman and Bess feel for each other.)*

ACTIVE READING MODEL

C

Over the cobbles he clattered and clashed in the dark inn yard.
He tapped with his whip on the shutters, but all was locked and
barred.
He whistled a tune to the window, and who should be waiting
there
But the landlord's black-eyed daughter,
Bess, the landlord's daughter,
Plaiting° a dark red love-knot into her long black hair.

D **QUESTION** What do these images tell us about Tim?

E

And dark in the dark old inn yard a stable wicket° creaked
Where Tim the ostler° listened. His face was white and peaked.°
His eyes were hollows of madness, his hair like mouldy hay,
But he loved the landlord's daughter,
The landlord's red-lipped daughter.
Dumb as a dog he listened, and he heard the robber say—

F

"One kiss, my bonny° sweetheart, I'm after a prize tonight,
But I shall be back with the yellow gold before the morning
light;
Yet, if they press me sharply, and harry° me through the day,
Then look for me by moonlight,
Watch for me by moonlight,
I'll come to thee by moonlight, though hell should bar the way."

G **QUESTION** What is happening here?

He rose upright in the stirrups. He scarce could reach her hand,
But she loosened her hair in the casement.° His face burnt like a
brand°
As the black cascade of perfume came tumbling over his breast;
And he kissed its waves in the moonlight,
(O, sweet black waves in the moonlight!)
Then he tugged at his rein in the moonlight, and galloped away
to the west.

18 Bess is braiding *(plaiting)* a red ribbon into her hair.
19 A *wicket* is a small door or gate; this one leads into the stable.
20 As the *ostler* (a shorter form of *hostler*), it's Tim's job to take care of the horses at the inn. A *peaked* face looks pale and sickly.
25 *Bonny* (a Scottish word) means "good-looking, fine, or admirable."
27 To *harry* is to trouble, bother, or worry.
32 The *casement* is the window frame, and the *brand* is a burning torch.

Teaching Support

MEETING INDIVIDUAL NEEDS — ENGLISH LANGUAGE LEARNERS

Picture the Highwayman English language learners might find it easier to understand this poem if they can visualize the highwayman. Begin by having students look up the word *highwayman* in the dictionary.

Activity Have students work in small groups to create illustrations of the highwayman. Ask each group to look up unfamiliar words or phrases in the poem that describe the highwayman's appearance and include these details in their drawings. Encourage them to label the drawings and display them so others can refer to them as they read the poem.

Additional Resources

English Language Learners Sourcebook, p. 81

Moon Landing, 1977. Jamie Wyeth. Oil on canvas, 29 x 43 in. Private collection.
Viewing the painting: What lines of the poem might this painting illustrate?

PART 2

He did not come in the dawning. He did not come at noon;
And out of the tawny° sunset, before the rise of the moon,
When the road was a gypsy's ribbon, looping the purple moor,
A red coat troop° came marching—
Marching—marching—
King George's men came marching, up to the old inn door.

They said no word to the landlord. They drank his ale instead,
But they gagged his daughter, and bound her, to the foot of her
narrow bed.
Two of them knelt at her casement, with muskets at their side!
There was death at every window;
And hell at one dark window;
For Bess could see, through her casement, the road that *he*
would ride.

38 *Tawny* is a brownish-gold color.
40 The *red coat troop* is a group of soldiers wearing bright red coats.

QUESTION [H]
Why have the redcoats appeared?

LISTEN [I]
Why does the poet repeat the word *marching?* Where else does he use repetition?

VIEWING THE PAINTING

Born in 1946, Jamie Wyeth is the third generation of a painting dynasty that began with his grandfather N. C. Wyeth (whose illustrations for "Rip Van Winkle" may be seen elsewhere in this book), and continued with his father, Andrew Wyeth.

Viewing Response *Students might suggest that the painting could illustrate any of the lines describing a moonlit night.*

H Active Reading Strategies

QUESTION *(The redcoats go straight to the inn and wait. It seems that Tim has told them of the highwayman's planned return.)*

I Active Reading Strategies

LISTEN *(The poet repeats the word* marching *to emphasize the danger the soldiers represent. In each stanza, the fifth line repeats words from the previous line. This is part of the poem's form.)*

J Critical Thinking

EVALUATING Have students explain why the redcoats tie up Bess and kneel at the windows with their guns. *(They have learned that the highwayman is returning to Bess and want to ambush him.)*

Reading Minilesson

Monitoring Comprehension To help students comprehend the poem, you may wish to have them work with the following questions while reading the selection: *What is the conflict? What is happening?* and *What can I predict?*

Activity Have students use a three-column chart to write their responses to the questions as they read the poem. They can use their charts to answer the questions that follow the selection. **L2**

What is the conflict?	What is happening?	What can I predict?

Additional Resources

Reading Skills Practice Workbook

TWISTS AND TURNS 623

D Active Reading Strategies

EVALUATE Ask students to discuss the speaker's statement that the angels' envy was the reason for Annabel's death. *(Some students may feel the speaker must find a reason—someone to blame for the tragedy.)*

E Critical Thinking

ELABORATING Ask students to read lines 32 and 33 and explain their meaning. *(Though death has separated the two lovers physically, they will always be together in spirit.)*

LITERATURE & HUMANITIES

To help students understand mood, show them the painting *Will-o-the-Wisp* from the CD *National Museum of Women in the Arts* and discuss what features remind them of the mood in "Annabel Lee."

Thematic Focus

Twists and Turns Have students discuss how this poem relates to the theme.

Teaching Support

And this was the reason that, long ago,
In this kingdom by the sea,
A wind blew out of a cloud by night
Chilling my Annabel Lee;
So that her high-born kinsmen came
And bore her away from me,
To shut her up in a sepulcher°
In this kingdom by the sea.

D
The angels, not half so happy in Heaven,
Went envying her and me;
Yes! that was the reason (as all men know,
In this kingdom by the sea)
That the wind came out of the cloud, chilling
And killing my Annabel Lee.

But our love it was stronger by far than the love
Of those who were older than we—
Of many far wiser than we—
And neither the angels in Heaven above
Nor the demons down under the sea
E
Can ever dissever° my soul from the soul
Of the beautiful Annabel Lee:—

For the moon never beams without bringing me dreams
Of the beautiful Annabel Lee;
And the stars never rise but I see the bright eyes
Of the beautiful Annabel Lee;
And so, all the night-tide, I lie down by the side
Of my darling, my darling, my life and my bride
In her sepulcher there by the sea—
In her tomb by the side of the sea.

19 A *sepulcher* (sep′ əl kər) is a tomb or burial place.
32 To *dissever* is to separate or split apart.

Reading Minilesson

Paraphrasing Readers can strengthen their comprehension skills by paraphrasing, or restating, the meaning of a passage in their own words. For example: "Four score and seven years ago our fathers brought forth, upon this continent, a new nation..." Paraphrase: *Eighty-seven years ago, our ancestors formed a new nation.*

Activity Have students paraphrase the last stanza of "Annabel Lee." *(Every night I dream of the beautiful Annabel Lee, and I see her eyes in the bright stars. All night I lie down beside the woman who was my wife and my life in her seaside tomb.)* **L2**

Additional Resources

Reading Skills Practice Workbook

630 THEME 6

Responding to Literature

PERSONAL RESPONSE

- What are your thoughts about the relationship between the speaker and Annabel Lee?

Analyzing Literature

RECALL

1. What is the relationship between the poem's speaker and Annabel Lee?
2. Where is the speaker at the end of the poem?

INTERPRET

3. To be *idealized* means "to be made a model of perfection." Do you think the speaker of the poem has idealized Annabel Lee? Why or why not?
4. From whose point of view is this poem told? How does this point of view affect what the poem tells?
5. What are the basic themes of this poem?

Storm Light, 1995. Jane Wilson. Oil on linen, 80 x 74 in. Courtesy Fischbach Gallery, New York.

EVALUATE AND CONNECT

6. How does Poe use rhyme and repetition in the poem, and to what effect?
7. Give an example of **alliteration** in "Annabel Lee" and tell why you think Poe uses it in this poem. (See **Literary Terms Handbook**, page R1.)
8. Does this poem seem true to life? Why or why not?
9. Theme Connection What unexpected event do the lovers in the poem face? How does the poem's speaker deal with it?
10. Think of a time when you lost something or someone you felt very strongly about. How did the experience affect you?

Brackets connect questions that are paired to develop higher-level thinking skills.

LITERARY ELEMENTS

Rhythm and Meter

Like a song, a poem has rhythm. In poetry, **rhythm** is the pattern of beats made by stressed and unstressed syllables. Some poems have a predictable rhythm, called **meter.** To find the meter of a poem, try scanning, or reading the poem to find the pattern of stressed (´) and unstressed (˘) syllables. For example:

Ĭt wăs mány ănd mány ă
yéar ăgó,
Ĭn ă kíngdŏm bý thĕ séa,

When you read a poem, pay attention to the rhythm, but don't stress the beats so much that the poem sounds sing-song.

1. With a partner, practice reading aloud a stanza of "Annabel Lee." Then work together to copy the stanza and mark its pattern of stressed and unstressed syllables.
2. Choose another poem from this book and mark the rhythm pattern of a stanza or several lines.

- See **Literary Terms Handbook,** pp. R9 and R6.

Responding to the Selection

PERSONAL RESPONSE

Some students may be moved by such a close, loving relationship. Others may think the speaker idealizes the relationship.

Analyzing Literature

1. The two were married and loved each other.
2. The speaker says he is lying in the tomb with her.
3. Some may say he has not idealized her because he truly loves her. Others may say he does idealize her, as being so perfect that the angels took her life out of jealousy.
4. The poem is told from the point of view of Annabel's lover. He has been so emotionally shaken by her death that he cannot be objective.
5. One theme is that even death cannot separate the spirits of two lovers.
6. Poe rhymes the last words of every other line of each stanza, but varies the pattern for emphasis. He uses internal rhyme in some lines, such as line 32 *(ever dissever),* line 34 (*beams* and *dreams*), and line 36 (*rise* and *eyes*). He repeats "Annabel Lee" and "the kingdom by the sea," which give a musical quality to the poem.
7. An example is "kinsmen came" (line 17). The *k* sound has a harshness that reinforces the harshness of the action being described.
8. Some may say it is because Poe accurately expresses the pain of loss. Others may say it isn't, because the poet's idealization of the woman and their love is excessive.
9. The unexpected event is Annabel Lee's death. The speaker blames the angels and sleeps in her tomb at night.
10. Answers will depend on the experiences of the student.

LITERARY ELEMENTS

1. Suggest that students exaggerate the stressed syllables to determine the meter, and then reduce the stress, reading the lines with natural emphasis.
2. Suggest that students choose a poem with a different rhythm and meter from "Annabel Lee."

Additional Resources

Literary Elements Transparency 53

® The following videotape program is available from Glencoe. Be sure to preview the video for appropriateness for your class.

- ***Biography: Edgar Allan Poe****

*Also available in the *Glencoe Literature Video Library*

Extendi

Writing Al

Students' exp

- refer to the and the cl Annabel
- quote pass each affec
- not overlo as the wor

Literature may have dif validity of th speaker, mo agree with it

Personal students inc event as wel

Listening Students mi with costum or another.

Sk

GRAMMA LANGUAG

- ACTIVE AN

1. The cri Lee."
2. The de have in
3. Tubercu his fost

You may w although t ly preferre the passive example, t not to stre the action *written by*

Additiona

Gram Work

Gram Hand

K Literary Elements

IMAGERY Ask students how the imagery in this stanza reflects the internal struggle of the speaker. *(The speaker's distaste for the cremation is reflected in the images of the fire, the wind blowing, and the black smoke streaking the sky.)*

L Author's Craft

POINT OF VIEW Ask students if the poet's use of the first-person point of view makes this story more exciting to the reader. *(Some students will say it does, because they feel the speaker's struggle and discomfort with the promise he made to a dying man.)*

M Literary Elements

MOOD Ask students how the mood in the tale has changed from one of anguish to one of joy. *(The speaker describes Sam McGee as looking "cool and calm" instead of raving and ghostly, creating an uplifting mood.)*

Thematic Focus

Twists and Turns Have students discuss other strange twists and turns they have experienced or heard about, whether in real life or in stories.

ASSESSMENT

Quick Checks, p. 54

The flames just soared, and the furnace roared—
such a blaze you seldom see;
And I burrowed a hole in the glowing coal,
and I stuffed in Sam McGee.

Then I made a hike, for I didn't like
to hear him sizzle so;
And the heavens scowled, and the huskies howled,
and the wind began to blow.
It was icy cold, but the hot sweat rolled down my cheeks,
and I don't know why;
And the greasy smoke in an inky cloak
went streaking down the sky.

I do not know how long in the snow
I wrestled with grisly fear;
But the stars came out and they danced about
ere° again I ventured near;
I was sick with dread, but I bravely said:
"I'll just take a peep inside.
I guess he's cooked, and it's time I looked,"
. . . then the door I opened wide.

And there sat Sam, looking cool and calm,
in the heart of the furnace roar;
And he wore a smile you could see a mile, and he said:
"Please close that door.
It's fine in here, but I greatly fear
you'll let in the cold and storm—
Since I left Plumtree, down in Tennessee,
it's the first time I've been warm."

There are strange things done in the midnight sun
By the men who moil for gold;
The Arctic trails have their secret tales
That would make your blood run cold;
The Northern Lights have seen queer sights,
But the queerest they ever did see
Was that night on the marge of Lake Lebarge
I cremated Sam McGee.

54 *Ere* (âr) is an old word for *before.*

Teaching Support

Grammar and Language *Minilesson*

Semicolons Point out the author's frequent use of the semicolon. The semicolon is generally used to join parts of a compound sentence or two independent clauses closely related in thought. Explain the thought relationship of the clauses joined by the semicolon in lines 51–52. *(These lines describe the cold and smoke—images of the setting.)*

Activity Have students work with partners to determine the thought relationships in the following lines:

1. lines 15–16 *(describe responses to the bitter cold)*
2. lines 19–20 *(Sam knows he is about to die and asks the narrator to honor his last request.)*
3. lines 45–46 *(describe how the narrator builds a fire)* **L2**

Additional Resources

Grammar and Language Transparency 52

Grammar and Language Workbook, pp. 265–266

Grammar and Composition Handbook, Lesson 13.5

Writer's Choice, Lesson 20.5

Responding to Literature

PERSONAL RESPONSE

- Were you surprised by the ending of the poem? Why or why not?

Analyzing Literature

RECALL

1. Where did Sam McGee come from?
2. Why did Sam request that he be cremated?
3. Describe the twist at the end of the poem.

INTERPRET

4. What phrases in the opening stanza (lines 1–8) of "The Cremation of Sam McGee" **foreshadow** the strange plot twist in the poem? (See **Literary Terms Handbook,** page R5.)
5. How does Service use **humor** in the narration of this strange tale? Give examples to support your opinion.
6. What is the central conflict in the plot of the poem? How is the conflict resolved?

EVALUATE AND CONNECT

7. Describe the relationship between the speaker and Sam McGee. What attitude toward friendship is expressed in the poem?
8. Imagery plays an important part in this poem. Pick out your favorite image from the poem and explain why you like it.
9. Personal Connection Does reading this poem make you want to visit the Yukon? Why or why not?
10. Theme Connection How does the speaker of the poem deal with the unexpected event that occurs during the trip?

Brackets connect questions that are paired to develop higher-level thinking skills.

LITERARY ELEMENTS

Rhyme

The most common type of rhyme in poetry is **end rhyme,** rhyme that occurs at the ends of lines. An example is the words *gold* and *cold* at the ends of lines 2 and 4. **Internal rhyme,** on the other hand, occurs within a single line of poetry—for example, the words *done* and *sun* in line 1.

1. Find and quote at least two other examples of internal and end rhymes in the poem.
2. Write a short poem about cold (or hot) weather. Then mark the rhyme pattern of your poem.

- See **Literary Terms Handbook,** p. R9.

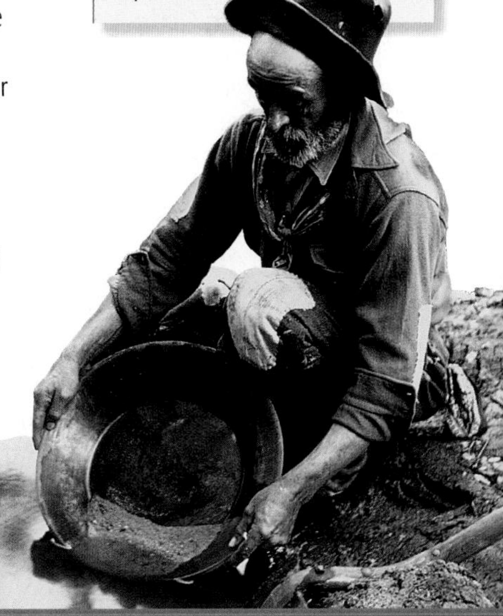

Responding to the Selection

PERSONAL RESPONSE

If they were surprised, encourage students to discuss how they thought the poem might end.

Analyzing Literature

1. Sam came from Tennessee.
2. Sam wanted to be cremated because he hated the cold and dreaded the thought of being buried in an icy grave.
3. At the end of the poem, after building a fire and throwing Sam's body into it, the speaker returns to find Sam sitting up and talking.
4. The strange plot twist at the end may be foreshadowed by phrases such as: "strange things done," "queer sights," and "queerest."
5. Part of Service's humor comes from the situation and the speaker's manner of telling about it. For example: in lines 43–44, he rhymes "frozen chum" with "cre-ma-tor-eum."
6. The central conflict is in the speaker's distaste for the act of cremating his friend and his obligation to do it.
7. The men do not seem to be close, and the speaker even seems annoyed by Sam's "whimpering," but there is a bond and a loyalty formed by their being together for so long in a challenging environment.
8. Favorite imagery may include: line 14, the cold "stabbed like a driven nail"; line 15, "lashes froze"; lines 35–36, huskies "howled"; lines 49–50, "to hear him sizzle" and "the heavens howled."
9. Some may want to visit the Yukon because they are attracted by nature; others may not fancy the idea of experiencing such cold temperatures.
10. The speaker agonizes over his promise, but he fulfills it.

LITERARY ELEMENTS

1. *End rhyme* includes: "blows/knows"; "spell/hell"; and "trail/nail." *Internal rhyme* includes: "fed/o'erhead"; "me/he"; and "dead/dread."
2. Suggest that students try to use both end and internal rhyme.

Additional Resources

Literary Elements Transparency 54

Extending Your Response

Literature Groups Students might have different opinions about the poem's being a tall tale. Have students use specifics in making a case for or against the poem's being a tall tale.

Performing Some students may do the reading and others the sound effects, then reverse roles.

Writing About Literature

Students' paragraphs should

- begin with a topic sentence expressing the writer's attitude in general terms
- refer to the imagery of the wind and cold, including images of sound and touch as well as sight
- explain how each image affects them

Creative Writing

Students' reports should

- include quotations from eye-witnesses
- give background information about the members of the Yukon dog-sled teams
- provide background information about the towns or territory
- contain effective transitions to make smooth connections between ideas

Skill Minilesson

READING AND THINKING

• SEQUENCE OF EVENTS

Suggest that students focus on the major elements of each event, not on the minor details.

Additional Resources

Reading Skills Practice Workbook

Extending Your Response

Literature Groups

Tall Tales A **tall tale** is a kind of folktale in which the characters, their physical traits, and their deeds are often greatly exaggerated in a humorous fashion. Paul Bunyan and John Henry are examples of tall tale heroes. In small groups, talk about whether or not "The Cremation of Sam McGee" is a tall tale. Use examples from the poem to support your opinion.

His Hammer in His Hand. Palmer C. Hayden (1870–1973). From the John Henry Series, Museum of African American Art, Los Angeles. Palmer C. Hayden Collection. Gift of Miriam A. Hayden. Photo by Armando Solis.

Performing

Audio Only As a class activity, divide the poem into sections and work in small groups to prepare the different sections for a performance of the poem for radio. On radio, you can't depend on an actor's gestures—everything must be done with the voice. However, you can add sound effects, such as blowing wind or the sound of a dogsled. To give the illusion of a radio show, have each group present its segment *behind* the rest of the class.

Writing About Literature

Setting Pick out examples of vivid adjectives or figurative language that describe either the bitter cold setting or the Yukon landscape. Then review your notes from the **Reading Focus** on page 635. In a short paragraph, explain how the writer's vivid language helps you to "feel" the icy temperatures of the setting as if you were there.

Creative Writing

Wilderness Report Turn the plot of "The Cremation of Sam McGee" into a television news report. Add any details you need to create the report, including eyewitness interviews with members of other Yukon dogsled trips as well as local weather reports.

Reading Further

If you would like to read more by Robert Service, try any of the following:

The Best of Robert Service

Best Tales of the Yukon

The Shooting of Dan McGrew and Other Poems

Save your work for your portfolio.

Skill Minilesson

Reteach · Review

READING AND THINKING • SEQUENCE OF EVENTS

The events in a story should take place in a logical order. That is, the reader should be able to see how each event leads to the next one. Most stories follow chronological order, the time order in which the events naturally happen.

PRACTICE Reread the poem. As you do, make a list of the events in the poem in the order in which they occur.

- For more on sequence, see **Reading Handbook**, p. R91.

ASSESSMENT

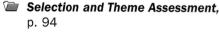

- ***Quick Checks,*** p. 54
- ***Selection and Theme Assessment,*** p. 94
- ***Performance Assessment,*** p. 51
- ***Testmaker: ExamView Pro***
- ***Interactive Tutor: Self-Assessment***

Identifying Cause-and-Effect Relationships

In a **cause-and-effect relationship,** one event or action causes other things to happen. For example, a character does something wrong (cause) and then feels guilty about what he or she did (effect). The character may then try to correct the wrong that was done (a new effect caused by the character's feelings of guilt).

For example, consider this passage from "After Twenty Years."

> The policeman on the beat moved up the avenue impressively. . . . The time was barely 10 o'clock at night, but chilly gusts of wind with a taste of rain in them had well-nigh depeopled the streets.

This passage contains a cause and its effect. The effect, or result, is the almost empty streets. The cause, or reason, is that chilly winds and the possibility of rain have kept people indoors.

As you try to identify cause-and-effect relationships in the literature you read, always look for clue words like *because, since, as a result,* and *so.* However, the causes of narrative events are not always stated directly. When the cause is not obvious to you, look back over the selection to identify it.

- For more on cause and effect, see **Reading Handbook,** p. R89.

ACTIVITY

Read the following passage from "The Force of Luck." Then answer the questions.

> On the way home he [the miller] was attacked by a hawk that had smelled the meat which the miller carried. The miller fought off the bird but in the struggle he lost the bundle of money. Before the miller knew what was happening the hawk grabbed the bag and flew away with it.

1. What caused the hawk to attack the miller?
2. What effect did the hawk's actions have on the miller?

Objective

- To recognize and use strategies for identifying cause-and-effect relationships

Teaching Strategies

Ask students to identify one cause-and-effect relationship for each of the selections in this theme. For example:

Charles
Cause: Laurie's behavior at school
Effect: Laurie invented Charles

No News
Cause: The candle flame lit the curtains
Effect: The house burned down

Who's on First
Cause: A baseball player named "Who"
Effect: Confusion about players' names

The Million-Pound Bank Note
Cause: A bet between two brothers
Effect: A man becomes rich

Activity

1. The hawk smelled the meat that the miller was carrying.
2. The miller fought off the bird, but in the struggle he lost the money he had been given.

Additional Resources

Reading Skills Practice Workbook, pp. 95–96

Teaching Support

MEETING INDIVIDUAL NEEDS — SPECIAL NEEDS

Less-Proficient Readers may find it challenging to identify cause-and-effect relationships in what they read, especially in long selections.

Activity Have students complete the chart as shown. Give them additional incomplete charts, supplying either a cause or an effect, and have them work in groups to complete charts. **L1**

Cause	Effect
The hawk smelled the meat.	*The hawk attacked the miller.*

Additional Resources

 ***Inclusion Strategies***

Objectives

- To create a short story of approximately 500 to 700 words
- To plan, draft, revise, edit, and present a short story based on a poem
- To reflect on and assess one's short story

GLENCOE TECHNOLOGY

WRITER'S ASSISTANT CD-ROM

Students can use Glencoe's templates and guidelines software for narrative writing to aid them in working through the steps in the writing process in the lesson.

Teaching Strategies

PREWRITING

Search for story ideas In addition to answering the questions in their books, students should consider the mysterious elements contained in each poem. Exploring a mysterious character or situation can be an intriguing task for a short story writer.

Teaching Support

Writing WORKSHOP

Narrative Writing: Short Story

As you've learned from the narrative poems in this theme, a poem can tell a story—and it can hint at stories left untold. Whose stories do the three narrative poems in this theme leave untold?

Assignment: Follow the process explained in this Workshop to write a short story based on a poem.

- As you write your short story, refer to the **Writing Handbook,** pp. R48–R54.

EVALUATION RUBRIC

By the time you complete this Writing Workshop, you will have

- written a short story based on a poem
- created an opening that captures readers' interest
- generated a plot line with exposition, conflict, rising action, climax, and resolution
- established a setting
- developed complex major and minor characters
- presented a short story free of errors in grammar, usage, and mechanics

The Writing Process

PREWRITING

PREWRITING TIP

Imagine a meeting between characters from two poems. What if the speaker in "Annabel Lee" met Bess, of "The Highwayman"? What story might unfold then?

TECHNOLOGY TIP

Use your computer to create separate files for several story ideas. If one doesn't work out, you can switch to another.

Search for Story Ideas

Look again at "The Highwayman," "Annabel Lee," and "The Cremation of Sam McGee." Notice that each poem tells the stories of at least two characters. Use questions like the following to find story ideas to explore:

- With which character do I most identify?
- Which character do I find the most interesting?
- What might have happened before the events in the poems?
- What might happen after the events in the poems?
- What new endings might I give the poems?
- What might a character from one poem do in the setting of another poem?

MEETING INDIVIDUAL NEEDS — ENGLISH LANGUAGE LEARNERS

Elements of Poems Expand the prewriting activity on page 644 to help English language learners recall aspects of the poems they have read.

Activity Have students work in small groups to complete information sheets on each of the three poems in Theme Six. Write the following questions on the board:

1. What is the title of the poem?
2. Who is the poet?
3. Who are the main characters?
4. What words does the poet use to describe the setting?
5. What happens in the poem?

Additional Resources

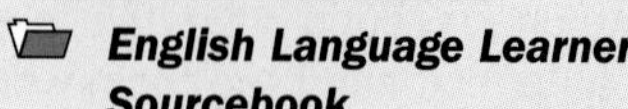

English Language Learners Sourcebook

Make a Plan

Choose a story idea that intrigues you. Then explore it by filling in a story map like the following one. You can borrow details of setting, characters, point of view, and plot from one or more of the poems in this theme, or you can create your own variations.

Characters:	The speaker in "Annabel Lee" and Annabel's brother Randolf
Setting:	a tomb by the sea
Point of view:	first person: The speaker from the poem will be the narrator.
Plot:	The narrator begs Randolf to take him to Annabel's tomb. Randolf reluctantly leads him there and then leaves. The narrator discovers that Randolf has locked him in the tomb.

Make sure that your plot includes exposition, conflict, rising action, climax, and resolution. To review the parts of a standard plot line and other literary elements, refer to the Genre Focus on pages 144–145.

Choose Your Audience and Purpose

Will your story entertain, amuse, or perhaps provide some chills? Will it be a children's story, a tale for your classmates to enjoy, or a story for a mixed audience, such as the readers of a popular magazine? Knowing your audience will help you plan your writing. Children may need vivid action and simple language. A mixed audience might not understand the same literary terms or references that your classmates would.

Put Events in Order

The events in a story may or may not be given in chronological order. Filling in a sequence chart like the one below can help you organize the events in the best way for your story.

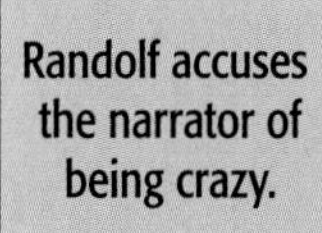
Randolf accuses the narrator of being crazy.

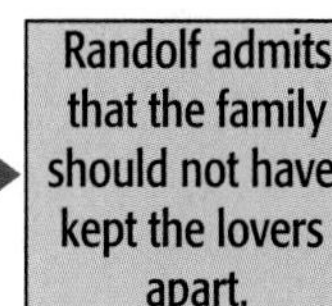
Randolf admits that the family should not have kept the lovers apart.

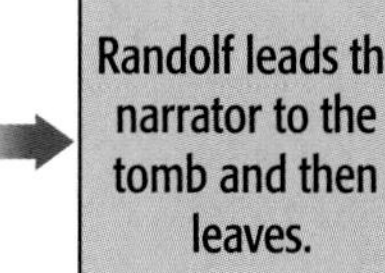
Randolf leads the narrator to the tomb and then leaves.

The narrator realizes that he is trapped in the tomb.

Make a plan Suggest that students work in pairs to bounce their story ideas around. Point out that the planning phase of the writing process is the one that many writers love most—the possibilities are endless. A story starts with an idea but has a way of taking on a life of its own once the writer begins writing. A good plan helps the writer stay focused on the story yet remain open to colorful details and plot twists as they arise.

Choose your audience and purpose Remind students to consider their audience as they write their stories. The poems in Theme Six have elements in them that might frighten young children, but these same elements could provide chilling excitement for older readers.

Put events in order Encourage students to fill in sequence charts like the one in their book. They may wish to expand the charts to include supporting details for each event as the story's plot unwinds.

Additional Resources

- ***Writing and Proofreading Practice,*** pp. 1–7, 43–49
- ***Writing and Proofreading Transparencies 1–6, 21–22, 35–36***
- ***Writer's Choice,*** Lesson 4.3

MEETING INDIVIDUAL NEEDS: MULTIPLE MODES OF EXPRESSION

Intrapersonal While certain steps in the writing process can be enhanced by group or pair activities, the act of writing itself is often a quiet, personal pursuit. Students who display strong intrapersonal learning capabilities may find it necessary to create a nonclassroom environment conducive to creative writing.

Activity Give students time to list places they like to go when they are alone. Have each student imagine or draw the ideal writing place: a place to be alone with one's thoughts. Help students explore the options available at school, such as the library, an office, or an outdoor space. Encourage each of them to find or make a special place in which to write a story. **L2**

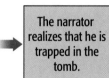

DRAFTING

Create an opening Write a few opening lines from stories you like on the board and tell students why you like them. You may wish to have an anthology of short stories in the classroom for students to look through to see how other writers started their stories.

Draft your story Remind students of the standard pattern that a short story usually follows. The plot begins with exposition that establishes the setting and characters and introduces a conflict. The conflict triggers a rising action that culminates in a climax. Finally, the denouement tells the result of the story's action and often summarizes what happens to the characters in the end.

REVISING

Map out changes Encourage students to work with partners to discuss the changes they want to make in their stories. Partners can help each other find "holes" in the plots—where an event seems out of sequence or is missing altogether. Have students read their stories aloud to a partner.

GLENCOE TECHNOLOGY

REVISING WITH STYLE CD-ROM

Students can use the exercises in the *Revising with Style* CD-ROM to improve their writing skills.

Teaching Support

DRAFTING

DRAFTING TIP
Don't try to explain too much about your characters. Instead, reveal details about them through their actions, thoughts, and words.

Create an Opening

You can pull readers into your story with any of several types of openers:

- an intriguing line of dialogue
- an image of a character in action (even a small action, such as a sigh)
- a mysterious comment about the story to come

Then move right into your chain of events and get your story down on paper.

Draft Your Story

Be sure to include transitions, such as *at first, next, soon, before that, afterwards, later,* or *meanwhile* to keep the order of events clear for your readers.

STUDENT MODEL • DRAFTING

Her brother put his hand on my shoulder and pointed. At first I could not make out what he wanted me to see. Then I knew.

Complete Student Model on pp. R111–112.

REVISING

REVISING TIP
One way to give your story a "finished" feel is to refer again to something from the opening, perhaps showing it in a new light.

Map Out Changes

Take a short break before you revise. Then take a new look at your story. Is it on its way toward creating the effects you had hoped for? Using the **Rubric for Revising,** map out improvements. A peer reader can offer useful feedback and ideas.

RUBRIC FOR REVISING
Your revised short story should have
- an opening that uses intriguing dialogue, a significant action, or another compelling device
- a well-defined setting
- a strong, well-developed plot line
- characters revealed through actions, thoughts, and words
- transitions to show the order of events
- no irrelevant characters, events, or details
- no errors in grammar, usage, and mechanics

Writing Minilesson

Character Development Introduce techniques that writers use to develop their characters by asking students to list ways in which they get to know people. An opinion of someone, for example, may be based on what the person says, how old the person is, what the person looks like, or where the person is from. Explain that a good way to develop a character in fiction is to let the character speak.

Activity Ask students to read aloud the dialogue they have written in their short stories. If their stories do not contain dialogue, encourage students to experiment with putting a few lines of dialogue in. Have students work in pairs to read the dialogue to a partner. Encourage the partner to give his or her impression of the character. Suggest that the writer evaluate this impression and check whether it matches the way he or she meant the character to be. If not, they should revise their dialogue accordingly. **L2**

Additional Resources

Writer's Choice, Lesson 4.4

EDITING/PROOFREADING

Use the **Proofreading Checklist** to help you spot and correct errors in grammar, usage, and mechanics. Pay special attention to comma usage, as shown in the **Grammar Link** on page 553.

Grammar Hint

The words *someone*, *anyone*, and *everyone* are singular. With these words, use singular possessive pronouns such as *his* or *her* instead of the plural possessive pronoun *their*.

Everyone has **his** or **her** own opinion about the poem.

PROOFREADING CHECKLIST

- All pronouns agree with their antecedents. (Double-check agreement with the word *everyone.*)
- There are no sentence fragments or run-ons.
- All verbs agree with their subjects.
- Punctuation is correct.
- Spelling and capitalization are correct.

STUDENT MODEL • EDITING/PROOFREADING

When someone loses ~~their~~ his or her true love, life seems unfair.

Complete Student Model on pp. R111–R112.

Complete Student Model

For a complete version of the model developed in this Workshop, see **Writing Workshop Models**, pp. R111–R112.

PUBLISHING/PRESENTING

Read your story aloud to your class, using the guidelines and suggestions on Speaking Effectively in the **Communications Skills Handbook,** page R69.

Reflecting

Take time to think over the following questions before writing your responses.

- What was the trickiest part of writing your story? How might you do it differently next time?
- Do you prefer writing fictional stories, like this one, or nonfiction narratives? Explain your preference.

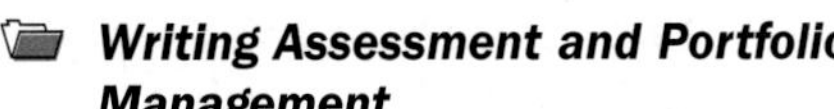

Save your work for your portfolio.

EDITING/PROOFREADING

Explain to students that it is often difficult for writers to proofread and edit their own work. Writers often ask a friend to read their writing and circle spelling, grammar, or usage errors. Suggest that students work in pairs or small groups to help one another proofread their stories.

Additional Resources

Grammar and Composition Handbook, Lesson 16.4

PUBLISHING/PRESENTING

Students may wish to do readings of their work, the way many writers conduct readings in bookstores, schools, and libraries. You may wish to set up a literary night, when students simulate the experience of "giving a reading." Short stories could also be compiled into a class literary anthology.

Reflecting

Portfolio Have students ask themselves these questions as they review their writing:

- Is my story based on one of the poems we have read in class?
- Does it have a clear sequence of events?
- Does my story include setting, characters, and plot?

6+1 TRAITS™ OF WRITING

See the annotated **Writing Workshop Models** on pp. R13–R36 for additional help in evaluating student writing and in teaching the **6+1 Traits™ of effective writing.** Annotations and minilessons address and reinforce the **6+1 Traits™:** Ideas, Organization, Voice, Word Choice, Sentence Fluency, Conventions, and Presentation.

ASSESSMENT

Writing Assessment and Portfolio Management

- Writing Assessment, pp. 1–12, 29–31
- Portfolio Management, pp. 38–45

Theme Assessment

Objectives

- To offer a personal response to the writers' craft in this theme
- To write a comparison of two narrative poems
- To complete a self-evaluation, set a goal, and devise a plan for achieving the goal

Responding to the Theme

1. Students should be able to support their choices with specific examples.
2. Accept all thoughtful answers and observations.
3. Allow time for students to share their incident reports, storytelling performances, and rewritten stories with classmates.

Analyzing Literature

Students' writing should include

- an introductory paragraph that identifies the two poems and the elements they plan to compare
- examples and details from the poems to support their conclusions

Evaluate and Set Goals

Evaluate

Have students list the activities they have completed for each task on this page. Suggest that they add other tasks as well, such as interviewing people.

Set Goals

Have each student create a chart on which to record their goals and the steps for achieving them. Discuss students' goals and plans in individual conferences.

TWISTS AND TURNS

Theme Assessment

Responding to the Theme

1. Which selection helped you notice how writers add a spark of the unexpected to their work? Explain your answer.
2. What new ideas do you have about the following as a result of reading the literature in this theme?
   - the role of luck in people's lives
   - how life's ups and downs are part of the normal course of human events
3. Present your theme project to the class.

Analyzing Literature

COMPARE NARRATIVE POEMS

Write an essay of at least one page comparing two of the narrative poems from this theme. You may compare such elements as setting, plot, characters, and point of view; examine the use of rhyme and meter; or concentrate on the poems' twists and turns. Include quotations to illustrate your comparisons or back up your conclusions.

Evaluate and Set Goals

1. Which of the following tasks was most rewarding to you? Which was most difficult?
   - reading and thinking about the stories, poems, and plays
   - doing independent writing
   - analyzing the selections in discussions
   - performing dramatizations
2. Using the following scale, how would you assess your work in this theme? Give at least two reasons for your assessment.
   4 = outstanding 2 = fair
   3 = good 1 = weak
3. Based on what you found difficult in this theme, choose a goal to work toward in the next theme.
   - Write down your goal and three steps you will take to reach it.
   - Meet with your teacher to review your goal and your plan for achieving it.

Build Your Portfolio

SELECT

Select two pieces of work you did during this theme to include in your portfolio. Use the following questions to help you decide.

- Which do you consider your best work?
- From which did you learn the most?
- Which work challenged you the most?
- Which work did you enjoy the most?

REFLECT

Write some notes to accompany the work you selected. Use the following questions to guide you.

- What do you like best about the piece?
- What did you learn from creating it?
- What might you do differently if you were beginning this piece again?

ASSESSMENT

Writing Assessment and Portfolio Management

- Writing Assessment, pp. 1–12
- Portfolio Management, pp. 38–45

GLENCOE TECHNOLOGY

MINDJOGGER VIDEOQUIZZES VIDEODISC

Use *MindJogger* to review the Theme 6 content.

Theme 6
Side B

Also available in VHS.

Reading on Your Own

Have you enjoyed reading the literature in this theme? If so, you might be interested in reading the following books.

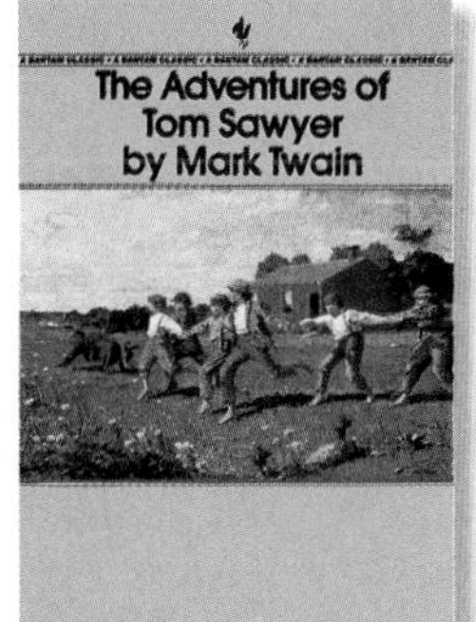

The Adventures of Tom Sawyer

by Mark Twain Twain's classic story has plenty of comic trickery, twists, and turns, including Tom's attending his own funeral.

The Oxford Book of Story Poems

edited by Michael Harrison and Christopher Stuart-Clark This collection of narrative poetry includes classic and modern poems that will make you laugh, poems that will amaze you, and poems that will thrill and chill you.

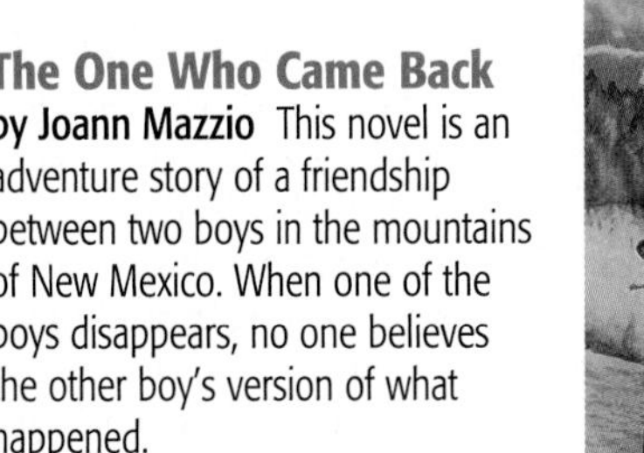

The One Who Came Back

by Joann Mazzio This novel is an adventure story of a friendship between two boys in the mountains of New Mexico. When one of the boys disappears, no one believes the other boy's version of what happened.

Talking to the Sun

selected by Kenneth Koch and Kate Farrell This anthology of poetry from ancient times to the present is illustrated with reproductions of artworks from the Metropolitan Museum of Art in New York.

Reading on Your Own

Tips for Independent Reading

Stress the importance of each student's spending at least thirty minutes a day in independent reading and suggest books, such as those shown here, related to this theme.

Reading Poetry Poetry usually requires more careful reading than narrative prose because of its compact form, compressed language, imagery, and figures of speech. To fully understand and enjoy a poem, skillful readers

- look at its form—the size and shape of the stanzas, length of the lines, and punctuation
- read it aloud and listen for patterns of rhythm and rhyme
- consider each carefully chosen word and why the poet chose it
- look for imagery and figures of speech and visualize what the poet describes
- try to connect its feelings with their own lives
- evaluate its message and the way it is presented
- determine their reactions to it

Practice Ask each student to select a poem and respond to it by

- creating an image the poem suggests using a medium other than writing
- composing a piece or a lyric that expresses the poem's ideas, feelings, or rhythms
- crafting a poem that uses the rhythm, rhyme scheme, or theme of the selected poem

Glencoe Literature Library

The Adventures of Tom Sawyer is available in the *Glencoe Literature Library*. For a complete listing of the titles, see the **Glencoe Resources for Independent Reading** in the front of this book.

The *Glencoe Literature Library: Study Guide* provides instructional support and student activities for works in the *Glencoe Library*.

Meeting Individual Needs — SPECIAL NEEDS

You may wish to recommend to your less-proficient readers *The Oxford Book of Story Poems* edited by Michael Harrison and Christopher Stuart-Clark.

The following books are rated for average readers (**L2**) or for students who need more challenging reading (**L3**):

- *The Adventures of Tom Sawyer* by Mark Twain **L2**
- *The One Who Came Back* by Joann Mazzio **L2**
- *Talking to the Sun* selected by Kenneth Koch and Kate Farrell **L3**

Additional Resources

Inclusion Strategies

Standardized Test Practice

TEST-TAKING TIP

Remind students that they should always look back to the passage when answering questions. The passage will *always* provide facts, information, or clues that support the best answer. If an answer cannot be supported by information or clues in the passage, it is not the best answer.

TEST-TAKING TIP

While reading the passage, students should look for clues to the author's purpose. Is the author making an argument? Raising a question? Describing a historical event?

Students should also look for clues about the author's attitude or tone toward the subject matter. Is the author's tone objective and scientific, or impassioned and argumentative?

Remind students not to memorize passages. There is no need to do so since they can go back and refer to the passage whenever they need to.

TEST-TAKING TIP

Questions that ask about the author's opinions or ask students to predict what will happen next must be supported by information from the passage.

Answers and Analyses

1. A Students should refer back to the story for clues in the character's actions and dialogue. Blakely's triumphant cheer in the last sentence of the passage indicates that he is happy. Even if the definition of *elated* is not known, the other three choices should be eliminated fairly easily.

Standardized Test Practice

Read the following passage. Then read each question on page 651. Decide which is the best answer to each question. Mark the letter for that answer on your paper.

Captain Thomas's Last Flight?

When the first explosion hit the hull of his starship, Captain Hunter Thomas grabbed for the shipwide microphone and began yelling. "Damage report! Blakely! What's happening?"

There was a moment of static on the line before Blakely's voice crackled into Thomas's cabin. "You'd better get to the bridge, Captain. We've got company."

Thomas was already off his bunk, jamming his feet into his flight boots and groping for his tunic. He was halfway out the door when Blakely's voice crackled over the intercom again.

"Pirates, Captain. It looks like the Derellians."

Thomas's voice came out in a growl. "How many?"

Another static-filled pause, until Thomas heard, "Five."

Then the ship rocked horribly to starboard, another explosion tearing like a claw into the vital flight and life support mechanisms. With another few blasts like that one, the hull might crack like an eggshell.

Thomas tucked his head and sprinted for the bridge. He arrived to find Blakely whirling about, careening from one control panel to the next, trying to keep the ship's many automated systems running. The look on the first mate's face told Thomas all he needed to know. They were in very deep trouble.

"What does the damage look like, Blakely?"

Blakely didn't look up. His eyes were glued to a computer screen. His fingers punched furiously at buttons and switches. "Third engine gone. Navigation computer damaged. Pulsar guns disabled."

"Life support status?"

Blakely sighed. "Holding."

Blakely punched the emergency distress signal on the communications console. A red light began to flash, signifying that an all-purpose emergency broadcast was being sent out to any ships in the vicinity. Blakely didn't have much hope that anyone would come, though. Few ships could tangle with a fleet of Derellian pirates.

Thomas gripped the steering controls and aimed straight for the first of the five ships he saw. "Signal all hands to abandon ship, Blakely. Get the crew to safety. See to it personally. I'm going to hold out as long as I can."

Blakely looked at his captain and friend, but said nothing. Thomas was already veering through the inky space between two more ships, dodg-

ENGLISH LANGUAGE LEARNERS

Place, Time, and Mood Ask students to use clues in the story to identify the elements of place, time, and mood. For example, what clues indicate where the story takes place? During what time period do students guess this story may have taken place—past, present, or future? Ask students to support their ideas with evidence from the story.

ing their fire. The two men had flown together for two years.

"Move it, Blakely! Now!"

When Blakely spoke, his voice was little more than a whisper. "Yes, Captain Thomas." He forced his legs to carry him toward the gangway to the escape pods.

The ship rocked once again under the weight of a crushing explosion. Warning lights began to flash, sirens screamed, smoke hissed from the computer consoles of the bridge like steam escaping a cooking pot. Blakely stood straight to salute his good friend Captain Thomas once more before he turned and ran down the gangway, screaming for his crew to board the escape pods and fly away to safety.

A few minutes later, from several miles distance, Blakely stared through the portal of his escape pod and watched distant explosions flower in the infinite night of space. *Goodbye, Captain,* he thought.

Then the loudspeaker squawked and a familiar voice echoed through the cabin of the pod. "Don't give up on me now, Blake. They've given up! We're free and clear!"

The Captain!

"Hang tight, Blakely. I'll be back on my next pass to pick you all up!"

Blakely cheered triumphantly and ran to tell the crew.

---

1 How did Blakely feel at the end of the story?
A Elated
B Amused
C Embarrassed
D Confused

2 In this story, the word careening means —
J walking slowly.
K wandering.
L lurching.
M fainting.

3 What will probably happen next?
A Blakely will help Captain Thomas fight off the Derellians.
B Captain Thomas will go down with his ship.
C Captain Thomas will fly to where the crew's pods are.
D The crew members will rebel against Captain Thomas for making them leave the ship.

4 Why didn't Blakely look at Thomas when he arrived at the bridge?
J Blakely couldn't open his eyes after the explosion.
K Blakely was worried that Thomas would be angry about the ship.
L Blakely was trying to survey the damage done to the ship.
M Blakely knew it would be the last time he'd see Thomas.

5 The author would probably describe Captain Thomas as —
A bossy and intolerant
B nervous and inhibited
C happy and charming
D brave and selfless

STOP

Answers and Analyses

2. L Using *careening* as the key word, students should go back and reread what is taking place when that word is used. They will see that Blakely is involved in a great deal of physical motion. He is neither *walking slowly* nor *fainting,* so choices J and M can be eliminated. *Wandering* also indicates movement, but usually over a large space and in a slow fashion. The process of elimination leaves only *lurching* as a possible answer.

3. C Clues to what will happen after the story ends are usually found near the conclusion of a story. In this case, the captain says "I'll be back on my next pass to pick you all up!" This is a good clue that he will do exactly that. None of the other answers is supported by the story.

4. L Students should find the context of this action to answer the question. The passage states that Blakely's "eyes were glued to a computer screen." His actions indicate he is trying to find the information he needs to answer the captain's question. He is clearly able to see, so choice J is incorrect. There is nothing to indicate he is worried that the captain will be angry. And his fear that he will not see the captain again is not mentioned until much later in the story. By elimination, students will be able to recognize that choice L is best.

5. D Choice D is the best answer because it is supported by the captain's actions. The captain tells Blakely "get the crew to safety . . . I'm going to hold out as long as I can." He is doing what he can to save the crew. Even if students do not know the meaning of *selfless,* they can see that the captain is *brave.* The correct answer is always supported by information from the passage. Therefore, choice D is the best answer.

Tested Objective

Item	Reading Objective
1	Analyze characterization through thoughts, words, speech, actions, and descriptions
2	Vocabulary development
3	Narrative analysis: identify events that advance the plot and how each event explains or foreshadows actions
4	Analyze text which uses cause and effect patterns
5	Expository critique: assess the adequacy and accuracy of author's evidence to support claims and assertions

MORE PRACTICE

For additional practice, assign practice pages from one of the following standardized test resources available as part of Glencoe Literature.

Additional Resources
ITBS Preparation and Practice
SAT-9 Preparation and Practice
Terra Nova Preparation and Practice

Theme 7 At a Glance
A Different Dimension

THEME OPENING

- **Introducing the Theme** (p. 653)
- **Exploring the Theme** (p. 654)
- **Theme Projects** (p. 655)

Theme 7: A DIFFERENT DIMENSION

SELECTIONS

Media Connection: Seizure-Alert Dog Is Girl's Lifeline (pp. 656–657)

Lob's Girl (p. 658)

Key Item (p. 674)

The Smallest Dragonboy (p. 682)

Active Reading Model: Aunty Misery (p. 700)

Strawberries (p. 706)

Atalanta's Race (p. 713)

Atalanta (p. 713)

Cat and Rat: The Legend of the Chinese Zodiac (p. 725)

Icarus and Daedalus (p. 736)

Prometheus (p. 742)

Media Connection: First Ballad Interlude from Benjamin Britten's *Paul Bunyan* (p. 748)

The Bunyans (p. 749)

Brer Rabbit and Brer Lion (p. 749)

SKILL FEATURES

Reading and Thinking Skills (p. 672)

Writing Skills (p. 673)

Interdisciplinary Connection (p. 681)

Genre Focus: Legends, Myths, and Folklore (p. 698)

Active Reading Strategies (p. 699)

Grammar Link (p. 712)

Vocabulary Skills (p. 735)

WRITING WORKSHOP

Expository Writing: Book Review (pp. 760–763)

THEME ASSESSMENT

- **Responding to the Theme, Analyzing Literature, Evaluate and Set Goals** (p. 764)
- **Build Your Portfolio** (p. 764)
- **Reading on Your Own** (p. 765)
  A Wrinkle in Time by Madeleine L'Engle
  Maniac Magee by Jerry Spinelli
  Big Men, Big Country: A Collection of American Tall Tales by Paul Robert Walker
  Cut from the Same Cloth: American Women of Myth, Legend, and Tall Tale by Robert D. San Souci
- **Standardized Test Practice** (pp. 766–767)

KEYS TO LITERARY CONNECTIONS

Comparing Selections

The **Comparing Selections** feature in this theme provides opportunities for addressing diverse aspects of the reading and literature curriculum.

For example, in Comparing Selections on page 747, students take a closer look at the ideas in "Icarus and Daedalus" by Josephine Preston Peabody and "Prometheus" retold by Bernard Evslin. Through this comparison students can develop insights about the importance of myths in certain cultures.

World Literature

The Student Edition contains a variety of literature that represents cultures from around the world. World literature selections are highlighted with the icon above.

TEACHING SUPPORT

The Teaching Support offers a wealth of interactive instructional support:

Meeting Individual Needs
- Special Needs
- English Language Learners
- Multiple Modes of Expression
- Advanced Learners

Internet Connection

Assessment

Portfolio Options

Minilessons
- Grammar and Language
- Reading
- Writing
- Listening and Speaking

Connecting to Other Selections

Real-World Connection

Interdisciplinary Connection

Life Skills Connection

Family and Community Activity

Key to Ability Levels

The activities throughout this theme have been coded for students of various abilities.

L1 BASIC activities for all students

L2 AVERAGE activities for average to above-average students

L3 ADVANCED LEARNERS activities for above-average students

Teaching Today

The Glencoe *Teaching Today* professional development Web site at www.teachingtoday.glencoe.com features daily teaching tips, free downloads, annotated Web resources, educational news, and a wealth of information on a wide range of topics.

Theme 7 At a Glance
A Different Dimension

Reading Skills in this theme

Variety of Texts

In addition to legend, myth, and folklore, this theme includes the following text types:

- short story
- cartoon
- magazine article
- opera libretto

Comprehension Skills

The following support appears in the Student Edition:

- **Reading and Thinking Minilessons** (pp. 671, 697, 705, 724, 734, 759)
- **Monitoring Comprehension** (p. 672)
- **Active Reading Strategies and Model** (pp. 699–705)

See also the **Reading Minilessons** throughout the theme in this Teacher Wraparound Edition.

For strategies for reading longer works, such as novels and novellas, see "Tips for Independent Reading" on page 765.

Reading Resources

Active Reading Guide The ***Active Reading Guide*** provides graphic organizers and study guide questions to support students' reading of each selection. (***Active Reading Guide***, pp. 55–64)

Interactive Reading Sourcebook and **Interactive Reading Workbook** The ***Interactive Reading Sourcebook*** and ***Interactive Reading Workbook*** offer focused comprehension strategies and lessons on critical thinking skills as well as fluency practice and activities to teach and support phonics, decoding, spelling, and vocabulary development.

Vocabulary Power The ***Vocabulary Power*** workbook (Lessons 29–32) provides systematic teaching, practice, and assessment of vocabulary for better reading comprehension.

Audio Library Available on audiocassette and on CD, the ***Audio Library*** provides valuable comprehension support.

Glencoe Literature Library Each title in the ***Glencoe Literature Library*** includes a full-length work plus related readings. A separate Study Guide is available for each title.

Five-Star Stories These anthologies of familiar short stories adapted and abridged for a variety of reading levels include exercises to help increase students' vocabulary and improve their reading comprehension.

The Contemporary Readers ***The Contemporary Readers*** are nonfiction books linked to various themes and designed for developing readers from a wide range of backgrounds.

Literature Classics CD-ROM The selections on this CD-ROM can be searched by author, theme, or genre.

inTIME and Humanities Across TIME Coproductions of Glencoe and Time, Inc., these resources include a wealth of high-interest nonfiction related to the selections in this theme.

Assessment in this theme

Assessment in the Student Edition

This program offers a number of diverse ways to evaluate student understanding and skill proficiency. In the Student Edition, use the following:

- **Responding to Literature**
  Following each selection, students are asked to recall facts, interpret ideas, and evaluate concepts as they answer a variety of questions and complete activities to extend their understanding.
- **Theme Assessment (pp. 764–765)**
  Here students respond to the selections on personal and analytical levels. They also assume ownership of their learning by setting and evaluating goals and by selecting work for their portfolios.

See also the many **Assessment Resources** listed on the facing page.

Standardized Test Practice

The Princeton Review has developed the Standardized Test Practice pages found at the end of this thematic unit (pp. 766–767). For additional practice, direct students to the following resources:

- ITBS Preparation and Practice
- SAT-9 Preparation and Practice
- TerraNova Preparation and Practice

Writing Skills in this theme

Writing Skills

The Student Edition of Theme Seven offers strong instructional support for writing skills:

In **Extending Your Response**, which follows each selection:

- **Writing About Literature**
- **Personal/Creative Writing**

See also the **Writing Minilessons** throughout the theme in this Teacher Wraparound Edition.

Writing Workshops

Theme Seven concludes with a **Writing Workshop** that guides students through the process of writing an autobiographical anecdote (pp. 760–763).

Writing Resources

Writer's Assistant CD-ROM Each **Writing Workshop** is supplemented by an interactive writing guide on the ***Writer's Assistant*** CD-ROM. This easy- to-use writing guide provides prompts, templates, and other tools that lead students through the writing process.

Grammar and Composition Handbook The ***Grammar and Composition Handbook*** (Lessons 11.8–13.4) provides systematic instruction in English language conventions.

Spelling Power The ***Spelling Power*** workbook (Lessons 25–28) provides systematic teaching, practice, and assessment of spelling to help students become better spellers and thus enhance their writing.

Writing and Proofreading Practice Blackline masters present in-depth instruction and practice on a specific step in the writing process and proofreading (pp. 1–7, 50–56).

Writing and Proofreading Transparencies Transparencies provide graphic organizers and proofreading exercises for whole-class instruction (pp. 1–6, 37–38).

Research and Report Writing Guide This resource provides extensive tips and activities to guide students in their writing projects in the literature classroom as well as in classes across the curriculum.

Style and Documentation Sourcebook for Writers This sourcebook is a combination reference and workbook, giving students the most up-to-date information and guidance regarding traditional as well as technological research strategies and documentation.

Revising with Style This resource offers instruction and exercises focusing on the revision process and covering topics from proofreading and correcting common grammatical errors to sentence combining and reordering.

Assessment Resources

Selection Quick Checks For each selection, a **Quick Check** of three to five short-answer questions measures students' literal comprehension.

Selection and Theme Assessment The ***Selection and Theme Assessment*** instrument tests students' abilities to recall, interpret, and evaluate what they've read. The tests consist of multiple-choice, short answer, and essay questions.

Performance Assessment Alternative assessment instruments and rubrics for Theme Seven are found in the ***Performance Assessment*** ancillary.

Writing Assessment and Portfolio Management These notes and strategies, student models, and assessment tools assist with the task of measuring students' progress as writers and as monitors of their own writing.

Testmaker: ExamView Pro Teachers can customize selection and Theme Seven tests by accessing the ***Testmaker*** database.

Interactive Tutor: Self-Assessment The ***Interactive Tutor: Self-Assessment*** software provides multiple-choice tests with immediate feedback to help students evaluate their knowledge and understanding of each literature selection.

MindJogger Videoquizzes Using a popular game show format, ***MindJogger Videoquizzes*** on videocassettes enable teachers to evaluate student understanding of Theme Seven in a quick and fun manner.

Theme 7 Skills Scope and Sequence

Lessons	Literary Elements	Reading and Thinking	Writing
Lob's Girl Joan Aiken DRP:56 Lexile:780	Suspense, SE p. 669; *TWE pp. 664, 666, 667* *Foreshadowing, TWE p. 660* *Hyperbole, TWE p. 662; Repetition, TWE p. 664; Mood, TWE p. 663*	Magazine Article, SE p. 656; Scanning, SE p. 671; Monitoring Comp., SE p. 672 *Logical Reasoning, TWE pp. 661, 663* *Graphic Aids, TWE p. 661; Inferring, TWE p. 666; Evaluating, TWE p. 668*	Resolution, SE p. 670 Journal Entry, SE p. 670 Using Sentence Variety, SE p. 673 SN *Physically Disabled, TWE p. 657* *Creating Suspense, TWE p. 664*
Key Item Isaac Asimov DRP:54 Lexile:560	Irony, SE p. 679 *Irony, TWE p. 677*	*Inferring, TWE p. 676* *Comparing and Contrasting, TWE p. 677* *Synthesizing, TWE p. 678*	Main Characters, SE p. 680 Description: Personal View of the Future, SE p. 680
The Smallest Dragonboy Anne McCaffrey DRP:62 Lexile:860	Legends, Myths, and Folklore, SE p. 698 Fantasy, SE p. 695; *TWE pp. 684, 687, 692, 694* *Character, TWE p. 685*	Legends, Myths, and Folklore, SE p. 699 *Graphic Aids, TWE p. 685* *Draw. Conclu., TWE pp. 686, 689, 690, 691, 694* *Analyze Arguments, TWE p. 688*	Setting, SE p. 696 Sequel, SE p. 696 *Another Point of View, TWE p. 689*
Aunty Misery Judith Ortiz Cofer DRP:57 Lexile:880	Fable, SE p. 703	Generalizing, SE p. 705 *Comparing and Contrasting, TWE p. 702*	Story Elements, SE p. 704 Write a Fable, SE p. 704
Strawberries Gayle Ross DRP:53 Lexile:790	Tone, SE p. 710 *Tone, TWE pp. 708, 709*	*Cause and Effect, TWE p. 709*	Conflict, Write a Myth, SE p. 711 *Write an Exercise, TWE p. 712*
Atalanta's Race Rex Warner DRP:54 **Atalanta** Betty Miles DRP:51 Lexile:820	Description, SE p. 722; *TWE pp. 716, 717, 719, 721* *Characterization, TWE pp. 717, 719* *Simile, TWE p. 720*	Chronological Order, SE p. 724 *Draw. Conclu., TWE p. 715* *Inferring, TWE pp. 716, 717* *Sequencing, TWE p. 716* *Synthesizing, TWE p. 719* *Verifying Predict., TWE p. 721*	Characterization, SE p. 723 Journal Entry, SE p. 723 *Description of the Setting, TWE p. 715* *Describing a Festive Scene, TWE p. 719*
Cat and Rat Ed Young DRP:49 Lexile:620	Legend, SE p. 732 *Imagery, TWE p. 728* *Legend, TWE p. 729*	Using Graphic Aids, SE p. 734 *Analyze Argumts., Purpose for Rdg., TWE p. 727; Critical Judgments, TWE p. 730; Elaborating, TWE p. 731*	Diagram Plot, SE p. 733 Write and Illustrate Legend, SE p. 733
Icarus and Daedalus Josephine Preston Peabody DRP:57 Lexile:950	Myth, SE p. 740 *Myth, TWE p. 738*	*Identifying Spatial Relationships, TWE p. 738*	Characterization, SE p. 741 News Report, SE p. 741
Prometheus Bernard Evslin DRP:54 Lexile:750	Theme, SE p. 746 *Theme, TWE pp. 744, 745*	Comparing Selections, SE p. 747	Myth, SE p. 746
The Bunyans Audrey Wood DRP:56 Lexile:930 **Brer Rabbit and Brer Lion** Julius Lester DRP:44 Lexile:440	Folktales and Tall Tales, SE p. 757; *TWE pp. 751–754* *Mood, TWE p. 751* *Trickster Tale, TWE p. 755*	Opera Libretto, SE p. 748 Paraphrasing, SE p. 759 *Cause and Effect, TWE p. 748* *Problem and Solution, TWE p. 750* *Drawing Conclusions, TWE p. 753* *Synthesizing, TWE p. 756*	Dialogue, SE p. 758 Sequel, SE p. 758 *Tall Tale, TWE p. 751* *Telling Tales, TWE p. 753*
Writing Workshop Expository Writing: Book Review			ELL *Creating Book Jackets, TWE p. 760*

Key: Student material is in roman. *Teacher material is in italic.*  ELL English Language Learners

Vocabulary and Spelling	Grammar and Language	Listening, Speaking, and Viewing	Life Skills; Study and Research; Technology
Unlocking Meaning, SE p. 671 *Multiple-Meaning Words,* *TWE pp. 661, 662* SN *Less Proficient Readers,* *TWE p. 662*	Apostrophes in Possessives, SE p. 671 *Using Troublesome Words, TWE p. 668* *Identifying Lively Sentence Patterns, TWE p. 673*	Literature Groups, SE p. 670 ELL *Life in a Fishing Village, TWE p. 660* *Creating a Radio Drama, TWE p. 663* *Film, TWE p. 667*	Service Plan, SE p. 670 Research Dogs, SE p. 670 *Leading and Organizing, TWE p. 665* SN *Less-Proficient Readers, TWE p. 672*
Etymology, SE p. 680 ELL *Computer Terminology, TWE p. 676*	*Compound Predicates, TWE p. 678*	Literature Groups, SE p. 680	User's Manual, SE p. 680 Communication, SE p. 681 Etymology of English Phrases, *TWE p. 680*
Synonyms: Shades of Meaning, SE p. 697 SN *Less-Proficient Readers, TWE p. 686*	Writing Numbers, SE p. 697 *Infinitives, TWE p. 694*	Literature Groups, SE p. 696 News Story, SE p. 696 ELL *Dragon Stories, TWE p. 684* *Debate, TWE p. 688*	*Creating and Producing, TWE p. 690* *Interdisciplinary Connection: Research Planets, TWE p. 691* *Dragon Love, TWE p. 692*
Analogies, SE p. 705	Frequently Misspelled Words, SE p. 705	Literature Groups, SE p. 704	Interdisciplinary Activity: Research Puerto Rico, SE p. 704
Synonyms: Thesaurus, SE p. 711	Capitalization, SE p. 712	Lit. Groups, Role-Play, SE p. 711 ELL *Folktales, TWE p. 708*	
Analogies, SE p. 724 *Prefix* twi-, *TWE p. 720*	Spelling Compound Words, SE p. 724 *Irregular Verbs, TWE p. 720*	Lit. Grp., Role-Play SE p. 723 ELL *Women in Society, TWE p. 714* *Narration, TWE p. 717* SN *Less-Proficient Readers, TWE p. 718* *Survey, TWE p. 721*	Interdisciplinary Activity: Research Fitness, SE p. 723
The Suffix *-ful*, SE p. 734 ELL *Beastly English, TWE p. 728* *Analyzing Word Parts, TWE p. 735* *Word Families, TWE p. 735*	Apostrophes in Contractions, SE p. 734 *Commas in a Series, TWE p. 730*	Literature Groups, SE p. 733 Story Dramatization, SE p. 733	Research Calendars, SE p. 733 *Decision Making, TWE p. 729* *Research Legends, TWE p. 731*
Definitions, SE p. 741 ELL *Prefixes, TWE p. 739*		Literature Groups, SE p. 741	Definitions, *TWE p. 741*
ELL *Multiple-Meaning Words, TWE p. 745*	*Dashes, TWE p. 744*	Literature Groups, SE p. 746	
Etymology, SE p. 759 ELL *Dialect, TWE p. 755*	Quotation Marks, SE p. 759 *Apostrophes, TWE p. 756*	Literature Groups, SE p. 758 Dramatization, SE p. 758 *Telling Tales, TWE p. 753*	Research Natural Wonders, SE p. 758 SN *Less-Proficient Readers, TWE p. 752* *Real-World Connection: Research Fairy Tales, TWE p. 754*
		SN *Learning Disabled, TWE p. 762*	

SN Special Needs/Strategic Intervention

Theme 7 RESOURCE MANAGER

Lessons	Essential Resources		English Language Learners
Lob's Girl Joan Aiken Pacing: 3 Days	**Lesson-Specific Instruction** Selection Focus Transp. 55 Active Reading Guide,* p. 55 Literary Elements Transp. 55 Vocabulary Practice, p. 37 Quick Checks,* p. 55 Selection and Theme Assessment, pp. 95–96 Testmaker: ExamView Pro Performance Assessment, p. 52	**Systematic Language Instruction** Grammar and Comp. Hbk., L. 11.8	English Language Learners Sourcebook, p. 84 Theme Seven Planning Guide, p. 6 Spanish Summaries, p. 55 Audio Library* English, Yes!
KEY ITEM Isaac Asimov Pacing: 2 Days	**Lesson-Specific Instruction** Selection Focus Transp. 56 Active Reading Guide,* p. 56 Literary Elements Transp. 56 Vocabulary Practice, p. 38 Quick Checks,* p. 56 Selection and Theme Assessment, pp. 97–98 Testmaker: ExamView Pro Performance Assessment, p. 44 TIME *inTIME* magazine, pp. 18–20	**Systematic Language Instruction** Grammar and Comp. Hbk., L. 11.9 Vocabulary Power, Lesson 29 Spelling Power, Lesson 25	English Language Learners Sourcebook, p. 85 Spanish Summaries, p. 56 Audio Library* English, Yes!
The Smallest Dragonboy Anne McCaffrey Pacing: 3 Days	**Lesson-Specific Instruction** Selection Focus Transp. 57 Active Reading Guide,* p. 57 Literary Elements Transp. 57 Vocabulary Practice, p. 39 Quick Checks,* p. 57 Selection and Theme Assessment, pp. 99–100	Testmaker: ExamView Pro Performance Assessment, p. 54 **Systematic Language Instruction** Grammar and Comp. Hbk., L. 11.10	English Language Learners Sourcebook, p. 86 Spanish Summaries, p. 57 Spanish Translations, pp. 171–182 Audio Library* English, Yes!
Aunty Misery Judith Ortiz Cofer Pacing: 2 Days	**Lesson-Specific Instruction** Selection Focus Transp. 58 Active Reading Guide,* p. 58 Literary Elements Transp. 58 Vocabulary Practice, p. 40 Quick Checks,* p. 58 Selection and Theme Assessment, p. 101	Testmaker: ExamView Pro Performance Assessment, p. 55 **Systematic Language Instruction** Grammar and Comp. Hbk., L.12.1 Vocabulary Power, Lesson 30	Theme Seven Planning Guide, p. 30 Spanish Summaries, p. 58 Spanish Translations, pp. 183–184 Audio Library* English, Yes!
Strawberries Gayle Ross Pacing: 2 Days	**Lesson-Specific Instruction** Selection Focus Transp. 59 Active Reading Guide,* p. 59 Literary Elements Transp. 59 Vocabulary Practice, p. 41 Quick Checks,* p. 59 Selection and Theme Assessment, p. 102	Testmaker: ExamView Pro Performance Assessment, p. 56 **Systematic Language Instruction** Grammar and Comp. Hbk., L.12	English Language Learners Sourcebook, p. 87 Spanish Summaries, p. 59 Spanish Translations, pp. 185–186 Audio Library* English, Yes!

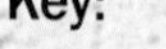

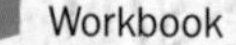

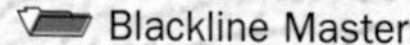

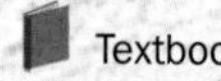

Special Needs/ Strategic Intervention	Reteaching and Enrichment
Interactive Reading Sourcebook, pp. T197–T199 Interactive Reading Workbook, pp. 109–110 Inclusion Strategies Sourcebook, pp. 91–92 Theme Seven Planning Guide, p. 6 Audio Library*	Literature Launchers, Side B, Segment 21 Reading Skills Practice Workbook, pp. 97–98 Grammar and Language Transp. 53 Gr. and Lang. Wkbk., pp. 223–224, 227–228, 273–274 Grammar and Comp. Hbk., L.13.7 Media Connection Activities, p. 13 TIME *inTIME* magazine, p. 2 Interactive Tutor: Self-Assessment Vocabulary PuzzleMaker Web Site (lit.glencoe.com)
Interactive Reading Sourcebook, pp. T199–T202 Interactive Reading Workbook, pp. 111–112 Inclusion Strategies Sourcebook, pp. 93–94 Theme Seven Planning Guide, p. 14 Audio Library*	Literature Launchers, Side B, Segment 19 Reading Skills Practice Workbook, pp. 99–100 Grammar and Language Transp. 55 Gr. and Lang. Wkbk., pp. 53–54 Grammar and Comp. Hbk., L.1.5 TIME *Humanities Across TIME*, Cover 19 Interactive Tutor: Self-Assessment Vocabulary PuzzleMaker Web Site (lit.glencoe.com)
Interactive Reading Sourcebook, pp. T202–T204 Interactive Reading Workbook, pp. 113–116 Inclusion Strategies Sourcebook, pp. 97–98 Theme Seven Planning Guide, p. 22 Audio Library*	Reading Skills Practice Workbook, pp. 101–102 Grammar and Language Transp. 56 Gr. and Lang. Wkbk., pp. 175–178, 279–280 Grammar and Comp. Hbk., L. 9.3, 13.10 Interactive Tutor: Self-Assessment Vocabulary PuzzleMaker Web Site (lit.glencoe.com)
Interactive Reading Sourcebook, pp. T205–T207 Interactive Reading Workbook, pp. 117–118 Theme Seven Planning Guide, p. 30 Audio Library*	Reading Skills Practice Workbook, pp. 103–104 Gr. and Lang. Wkbk., pp. 297–300 Grammar and Comp. Hbk., L.15.1, 15.2 Interactive Tutor: Self-Assessment Vocabulary PuzzleMaker Web Site (lit.glencoe.com)
Interactive Reading Sourcebook, pp. T208–T210 Interactive Reading Workbook, pp. 119–120 Theme Seven Planning Guide, p. 35 Audio Library*	Literature Launchers, Side B, Segment 20 Fine Art Transparency 28 Reading Skills Practice Workbook, pp. 105–106 Interactive Tutor: Self-Assessment Vocabulary PuzzleMaker Web Site (lit.glencoe.com)

Web   Audiocassette   Diskette   *Also available in Spanish

INDEPENDENT READING

Encourage students to spend thirty minutes each day in independent reading. The following Glencoe components and outside resources provide opportunities for reading related to this theme.

The Glencoe Literature Library

You may want to assign one or more of these titles for independent reading. For a complete listing of titles available in the Glencoe Literature Library, see page T96 of this book.

- *A Wrinkle in Time* by Madeleine L'Engle
- *Bridge to Terabitha* by Katherine Paterson
- *Dandelion Wine* by Ray Bradbury
- *Mrs. Frisby and the Rats NIHM* by Robert O'Brien
- *Treasure Island* by Robert Louis Stevenson

inTIME News stories, feature articles, reviews, profiles, and essays in the magazine connect to an author, work, or theme in the Student Edition. See the ***inTIME* Teacher's Guide** for specific connections to this theme.

Resources for Less-Proficient Readers

For reading especially created for less-proficient readers, suggest

- *Five-Star Stories*
- *The Contemporary Readers*

Additional Resources for Independent Reading

The following titles are listed with specific reading selections throughout this theme. You may want to suggest that students look for these in your local or school library.

- *The Wolves of Willoughby Chase* by Joan Aiken
- *Robot Dreams* by Isaac Asimov
- *Dragonseye* by Anne McCaffrey
- *Perez and Martina: A Puerto Rican Folktale* by Pura Belpre
- *The Terrible EEK: A Japanese Tale* by Patricia A. Compton
- *How Rabbit Tricked Otter and Other Cherokee Trickster Stories* by Gayle Ross
- *A Treasury of Stories from Around the World* by Linda Jennings
- *Island of the Mighty: Stories of Old Britain* by Haydn Middleton
- *Min-Yo and the Moon Dragon* by Elizabeth Hillman
- *How the Ox Star Fell from Heaven* by Lily Toy Hong
- *The Napping House* by Audrey Wood
- *Maniac Magee* by Jerry Spinelli

Theme 7 RESOURCE MANAGER (continued)

Lessons	Essential Resources		English Language Learners
Atalanta's Race Rex Warner **Atalanta** Betty Miles Pacing: 2 Days	**Lesson-Specific Instruction** Selection Focus Transp. 60 Active Reading Guide,* p. 60 Literary Elements Transp. 60 Vocabulary Practice, p. 42 Quick Checks,* p. 60 Selection and Theme Assessment, pp. 103–104	Testmaker: ExamView Pro Performance Assessment, p. 57 TIME *inTIME* magazine, p. 27 **Systematic Language Instruction** Grammar and Comp. Hbk., L. 12.3 Vocabulary Power, Lesson 26	English Language Learners Sourcebook, p. 88 Theme Seven Planning Guide, p. 43 Spanish Summaries, p. 60 Audio Library* English, Yes!
Cat and Rat Ed Young Pacing: 2 Days	**Lesson-Specific Instruction** Selection Focus Transp. 61 Active Reading Guide,* p. 61 Literary Elements Transp. 61 Vocabulary Practice, p. 43 Quick Checks,* p. 61 Selection and Theme Assessment, pp. 105–106	Testmaker: ExamView Pro Performance Assessment, p. 58 **Systematic Language Instruction** Grammar and Comp. Hbk., L. 12.4 Vocabulary Power, Lesson 31	English Language Learners Sourcebook, pp. 89, 90 Spanish Summaries, p. 61 Spanish Translations, pp. 187–189 Audio Library* English, Yes!
Icarus and Daedalus Josephine Preston Peabody Pacing: 1 Day	**Lesson-Specific Instruction** Selection Focus Transp. 62 Active Reading Guide,* p. 62 Literary Elements Transp. 62 Vocabulary Practice, p. 44 Quick Checks,* p. 62 Selection and Theme Assessment, pp. 107–108	Testmaker: ExamView Pro Performance Assessment, p. 59 **Systematic Language Instruction** Grammar and Comp. Hbk., L. 13.1 Spelling Power, Lesson 27	English Language Learners Sourcebook, p. 91 Spanish Summaries, p. 62 Spanish Translations, pp. 190–191 Audio Library* English, Yes!
PROMETHEUS Bernard Evslin Pacing: 2 Days	**Lesson-Specific Instruction** Selection Focus Transp. 63 Active Reading Guide,* p. 63 Literary Elements Transp. 63 Vocabulary Practice, p. 45 Quick Checks,* p. 63 Selection and Theme Assessment, pp. 107–108	Testmaker: ExamView Pro Performance Assessment, p. 59 **Systematic Language Instruction** Grammar and Comp. Hbk., L. 13.2 Vocabulary Power, Lesson 32 Spelling Power, Lesson 28	English Language Learners Sourcebook, p. 92 Spanish Summaries, p. 63 Spanish Translations, pp. 192–194 Audio Library* English, Yes!
The Bunyans Audrey Wood **Brer Rabbit and Brer Lion** Julius Lester Pacing: 2 Days	**Lesson-Specific Instruction** Selection Focus Transp. 64 Active Reading Guide,* p. 64 Literary Elements Transp. 64 Vocabulary Practice, p. 46 Quick Checks,* p. 64 Selection and Theme Assessment, pp. 109–110	Testmaker: ExamView Pro Performance Assessment, p. 60 **Systematic Language Instruction** Grammar and Comp. Hbk., L. 13.3–13.4 Vocabulary Power, Unit 7 Review/Test Spelling Power, Unit 7 Review/ Proofreading	English Language Learners Sourcebook, p. 93 Spanish Summaries, p. 75 Spanish Translations, p. 64 Audio Library* English, Yes!
Writing WORKSHOP Expository Writing: Book Review Pacing: 2 Days	Writing Assessment and Portfolio Management, pp. 1-13, 32-34, 38-45		English Language Learners Sourcebook, p. 9 English, Yes!

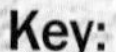
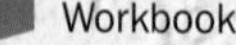
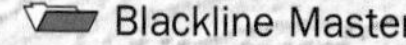
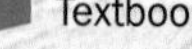
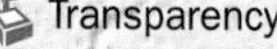

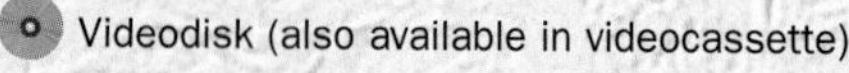

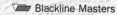

Key: Workbook | Blackline Masters | Textbook | Transparency | CD-ROM | Videodisk (also available in videocassette)

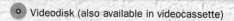

Special Needs/ Strategic Intervention	Reteaching and Enrichment
Interactive Reading Sourcebook, pp. T210–T213 Interactive Reading Workbook, pp. 121–122 Inclusion Strategies Sourcebook, pp. 81–82, 89–90 Theme Seven Planning Guide, p. 43 Audio Library*	Reading Skills Practice Workbook, pp. 107–108 Grammar and Language Transp. 57 Gr. and Lang. Wkbk., pp. 95–100, 297–300 Grammar and Comp. Hbk., L.3.11, 3.12, 15.1 Interactive Tutor: Self-Assessment Vocabulary PuzzleMaker Web Site (lit.glencoe.com)
Interactive Reading Sourcebook, pp. T213–T215 Interactive Reading Workbook, pp. 123–124 Inclusion Strategies Sourcebook, pp. 99–100 Theme Seven Planning Guide, p. 49 Audio Library*	Reading Skills Practice Workbook, pp. 109–110 Grammar and Language Transp. 58 Gr. and Lang. Wkbk., pp. 255–256, 273–274 Grammar and Comp. Hbk., L.13.2, 13.7 Interactive Tutor: Self-Assessment Vocabulary PuzzleMaker Web Site (lit.glencoe.com)
Interactive Reading Sourcebook, pp. T216–T218 Interactive Reading Workbook, pp. 125–126 Inclusion Strategies Sourcebook, pp. 25–26 Theme Seven Planning Guide, p. 57 Audio Library*	Fine Art Transparency 25 Reading Skills Practice Workbook, pp. 111–112 Interactive Tutor: Self-Assessment Vocabulary PuzzleMaker Web Site (lit.glencoe.com)
Interactive Reading Sourcebook, pp. T218–T221 Interactive Reading Workbook, pp. 127–128 Theme Seven Planning Guide, p. 65 Audio Library*	Reading Skills Practice Workbook, pp. 113–114 Grammar and Language Transp. 59 Gr. and Lang. Wkbk., pp. 275–276 Grammar and Comp. Hbk., L.13.8 Interactive Tutor: Self-Assessment Vocabulary PuzzleMaker Web Site (lit.glencoe.com)
Interactive Reading Sourcebook, pp. T221–T224 Interactive Reading Workbook, pp. 129–131 Inclusion Strategies Sourcebook, pp. 77–78 Theme Seven Planning Guide, p. 73 Audio Library*	Reading Skills Practice Workbook, pp. 115–116 Grammar and Language Transp. 60 Gr. and Lang. Wkbk., pp. 267–270 Grammar and Comp. Hbk., L.13.6, 13.7 Media Connection Activities, p. 14 Interactive Tutor: Self-Assessment Vocabulary PuzzleMaker Web Site (lit.glencoe.com)
Inclusion Strategies Sourcebook, pp. 67–68	Writing and Proofreading Practice, pp. 1–7, 50–56 Writing and Proofreading Transparencies 1–6, 37–38 Revising with Style Writer's Assistant

Web 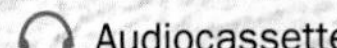 Audiocassette Diskette *Also available in Spanish

Theme RESOURCES

To explore the theme further you may want to use these resources:

- Listening and Speaking Activities (pp. 19–21)
- Viewing and Representing Activities (pp. 1–6, 25–27)
- Critical Thinking Skills (pp. 18–19)
- Media Connection Activities (pp. 13–14)
- Interdisciplinary Activities (pp. 26–29)
- Family and Community Activities (p. 17)
- Selection and Theme Assessment (pp. 137–138)
- Performance Assessment (pp. 75, 99)

TIME Humanities Across TIME

See also these additional theme planning resources:

- Theme Seven Planning Guide
- Interactive Reading Sourcebook
- Literature Groups Sourcebook
- Interactive Lesson Planner
- Interactive Teacher Edition
- Glencoe Web Site <lit.glencoe.com>

Use Glencoe's *Presentation Plus!* This multimedia teaching tool lets you present dynamic lessons that will engage your students. Using Microsoft PowerPoint®, you can customize the presentation to create your own personalized lessons.

A Different Dimension

Theme Objectives

- To enjoy reading about magical and mythical events
- To analyze the literary elements in folktale, myth, legend, and short story selections
- To apply strategies for reading legends, myths, and folklore

Teaching Strategies

Have students read the quotation from *"Magic Words"* in preparation for the questions below.

VIEWING THE PAINTING

The title of the painting by Maria Angelica Ruiz-Tagle means "Yesterday, I had a dream."

Responding to the Painting
Discussion Questions:

- Why would this painting be chosen to represent the theme? What mythical horses do you know of? *(Students may mention Pegasus, the winged horse in Greek mythology.)*
- How might the images in the painting relate to the quote "That was the time when ... the human mind had mysterious powers"?

A Different Dimension

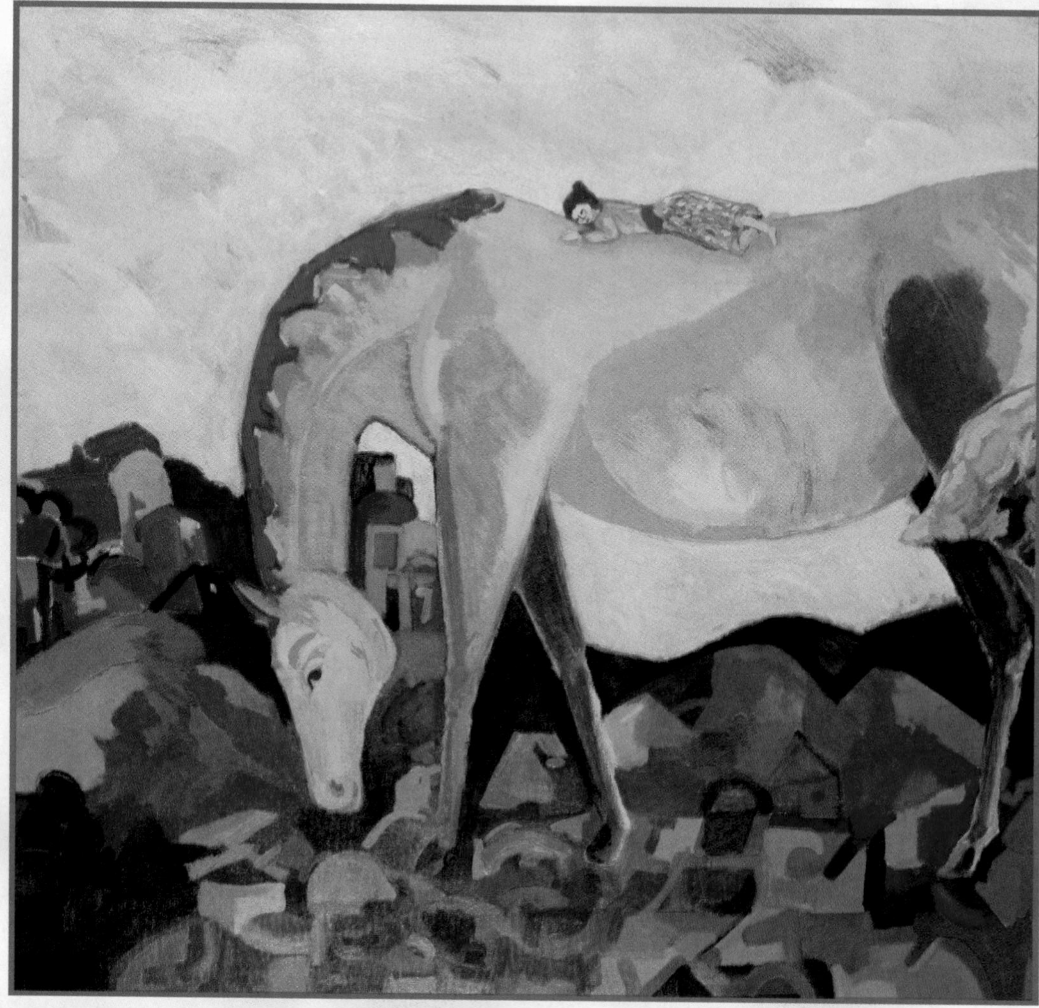

Ayer Tuve un Sueño, 1990. Maria Angelica Ruiz-Tagle. Oil on canvas, 100 x 120 cm. Kactus Foto, Santiago, Chile.

652

TEACHER *to* TEACHER

NAUTILUS MIDDLE SCHOOL • MIAMI, FLORIDA

I introduce the theme "A Different Dimension" with a short lesson on Greek mythology that focuses on the different qualities possessed by the Greek pantheon of deities. In Greek mythology, gods and goddesses had certain characteristics that defined them. For example, Athena, the goddess of wisdom, was represented by an owl, the symbol for wisdom. Following class discussion, students choose various teachers and staff people to be "school gods and goddesses" by designating a special quality to each along with a representative symbol. For example, a student may designate a teacher the "god of detention" with a watch and chain as his symbol. Each student then draws a picture of the chosen god or goddess and his or her symbol and writes an essay that supports the illustration.

CYNTHIA CASTILLO

"That was the time when words were like magic. The human mind had mysterious powers. A word spoken by chance might have strange consequences."

–"Magic Words," Songs and Stories of the Netsilik Eskimos

THEME CONTENTS

GENRE FOCUS *LEGENDS, MYTHS, AND FOLKLORE*

RESOURCE MANAGER

See the ***Theme Seven Planning Guide*** for additional teaching notes, strategies, and resources for introducing the theme "A Different Dimension."

Introducing the Theme

Direct your students' attention to the **Theme Contents.** Ask them to read through the list of selections. Present these questions for discussion:

- What do several of the selections have in common? *(Students may say that many are familiar myths and legends passed down through storytelling.)*
- As you read the table of contents, can you tell where some of the stories in this theme originated? *(Students may mention Greece, China, and the United States.)*
- Do you know what special powers or attributes any of these mythical figures possess? *(Students may know of Paul Bunyan and his extraordinary size or of Prometheus stealing fire from the gods.)*

LITERATURE & HUMANITIES

Have students examine the painting *Plate 69...* on the CD *National Museum of Women in the Arts* and create their own myths using these two characters.

GLENCOE TECHNOLOGY

LITERATURE CLASSICS CD-ROM

Search for other selections related to the theme "A Different Dimension."

Exploring the Theme

A Different Dimension

In addition to the power of words to transport and transform us, children in many parts of the world use "magic words" that are supposed to make wonderful or startling things happen. *Abracadabra* is a magic word common in the United States.

Starting Points

When the Moon Is Full

After students describe what is happening in the cartoon, ask them what they think Maynard's wife usually means when she asks him to come out and look at the moon.

- Prompt a discussion about the romantic relationship people have with the moon. Find out whether students think the moon is romantic, and why.
- Have students talk about things that are known or believed to happen at the time of the full moon. *(Students may say that animals howl, people act strangely, tides are affected, and creatures like werewolves and vampires come out.)*
- You may wish to post students' cartoons around the classroom and refer to the various fates of Maynard and his wife as students read the selections in this theme.

Traveling to Another Dimension

Suggest that students turn to their dreams for ideas about magical places. They may want to talk to partners about dreams they have had that took place in strange or wonderful realms and regions.

- Invite students to draw or paint pictures of the settings for their fantasies.
- Remind students that many parts of our earthly landscape have taken on mythical characteristics in poems and stories through the years. You may wish to use Fine Art Transparency 22 to enrich students' thinking about the theme.

Exploring the Theme

A Different Dimension

The magical power of words has always been able to transport listeners and readers to other worlds. In this theme, you will discover how the magic of words can carry you to places such as ancient Greece and China, the imaginary planet of Pern, and the legendary American frontier. Begin thinking about the theme by selecting one of the activities below.

Starting Points

WHEN THE MOON IS FULL

Writers and artists like to imagine life in different dimensions. The couple in this cartoon are certainly about to enter a new dimension!

- What do you think is happening? Draw a cartoon strip with two or three more panels showing what might happen next to Maynard and his wife.

TRAVELING TO ANOTHER DIMENSION

Have you ever used your imagination to travel to another dimension?

- Describe a setting for a fantasy you might write. It can take place in the past, in the future, on another planet, or even on an Earth that never really existed. The place can be as strange or as magical as you can imagine.

"Maynard, I do think that just this once you should come out and see the moon!"

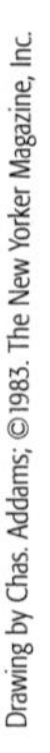

Family and Community Activity

Mapping the Stars Ask students to make star maps at least three times a week throughout the course of Theme 7. They will need construction paper, colored pencils, markers or small stick-on stars, and a flashlight. Students should select a patch of sky that is visible from home and stand in exactly the same place each time they observe and record the stars. Have them mark the positions of the brightest stars on a sheet of construction paper and write the date and time of each observation. Observing at the same time each night is the best way to detect how the star map changes. Encourage students to compare maps and compile booklets of their own star maps at the end of the theme.

Additional Resources

Family and Community Activities, p. 17

Theme Projects

As you read the selections in this theme, complete one of the projects below. Work on your own, with a partner, or with a group.

CRITICAL READING

Different Dimensions in Literature

1. Alone or with a partner, brainstorm a list of fantasy or science-fiction novels, short stories, TV episodes, or movies you have read or seen. Then choose at least four of them that you think are especially good.
2. Plan a chart to prepare a detailed comparison of your choices. Use headings such as Title, Author(s), Setting (time and place), Plot Summary, Characters, Theme(s), and Evaluation.
3. Use your completed chart to write an essay telling what elements good science-fiction or fantasy stories have in common. Use examples from the stories to back up your opinions.
4. Decorate your chart with drawings or pictures clipped from old magazines or downloaded from the Internet and display it for the class along with your essay.

For more project ideas, check out some fantasy, science-fiction, myth, legend, or folklore sites on the Web. You can also try the Glencoe Literature site at lit.glencoe.com.

LEARNING FOR LIFE

Travel Itinerary

1. Plan an itinerary, or traveler's guide, for a trip to a different dimension.
2. Decide how you will travel: in a time machine, a spacecraft, or even on the back of a dragon. Decide what sights you will see and what people or creatures you will meet there.
3. Make a map of your journey. Use it for a presentation in which you describe your visit.

MULTIMEDIA PROJECT

Creating an Imaginary World

1. Working in a small group, collect pictures of places that would make good settings for a story set in a different dimension.
2. Create a diorama using or adapting the scenery you found. Use modeling clay or cutouts to add to your display the kinds of people or creatures who might live in your "different dimension."
3. Share your world with your classmates. If you wish, use the scene you have created as an inspiration for writing or dramatizing a story.

Greek Mythology Students may wish to use a search engine to find more information about Ancient Greece. They may use keywords such as *Greek Gods, Mount Olympus,* or *Troy.*

Theme Assessment

Teaching Strategies

The following suggestions may help students with their theme projects.

Critical Reading

- Students may wish to compare and contrast print and film versions of the same story.
- In step 2, have students add a heading for notes on the stories' social implications.
- Suggest that students create book and movie lists based on the selections they have chosen.

Learning for Life

- Have students create names for the dimension, the creatures that inhabit it, and the language they speak.
- Ask students to translate a few "useful phrases" for travelers who visit this dimension.
- Invite students to make travel posters advertising future trips to this dimension.

Multimedia Project

Help students develop a list of worlds they would like to create, such as a recycled world, or a world where everything is reversed.

- Ask groups to write brief histories of the worlds they create.
- Have students read or perform their stories.

Additional Resources

- ***Interdisciplinary Activities,*** pp. 26–29
- ***Viewing and Representing Activities,*** pp. 25–27
- ***Listening and Speaking Activities,*** pp. 19–21
- ***Critical Thinking Skills,*** pp. 18–19
- ***Selection and Theme Assessment,*** pp. 137–138
- ***Performance Assessment,*** p. 75

MEDIA Connection

Objective

- To understand and apply strategies for reading a magazine article

Literature LINK

Lob's Girl "Seizure-Alert Dog Is Girl's Lifeline" connects to the literature selection "Lob's Girl" (pp. 658–668). In each story, a young girl inspires love, devotion, and lifelong companionship in her dog.

Service-Dog Training Have students use a search engine to find out how dogs are trained to help humans. Suggest that students enter keywords such as *dog training, guide dogs,* and *Canine Partners for Life.*

MEDIA Connection

MAGAZINE ARTICLE

This article comes from a magazine for dog lovers. Why do you think it appeared in a section called "Dogs That Make a Difference"?

Seizure-Alert Dog Is Girl's Lifeline

by Sarah Christie—*Dog Fancy,* June 1997

Emily Ramsey's world just grew a little bigger. For the first time in her life, the 13-year-old middle school student from Racine, Wis., is now able to cruise the mall, ride the school bus, and participate in after-school sports without constant supervision. That's standard operating procedure for most teenagers, but for one with epilepsy, the world is a perilous place.

Seizures strike without warning, making simple acts such as walking down stairs, crossing the street, or going for a swim potentially life-threatening. These days Emily can do all that and more, thanks to her constant companion, Watson.

Watson is a seizure-alert dog, able to warn his owner of epileptic attacks before they strike.

The skill goes beyond regular service-dog training. It can't be taught or bred for. Nobody knows how Watson is able to predict these spells—one theory is that dogs sense chemical changes preceding the attacks—but the details don't matter to Emily. She knows only that her dog's intuition is a lifeline she almost didn't dare hope for.

Watson was an improbable candidate for service dog school. He had been left at a veterinarian's office to be put to sleep for a broken foot at 6 months of age. A clinic employee saved him. The sympathetic veterinary technician, who also worked as a volunteer at CPL [Canine Partners for Life], saw promise in the lame pup.

Thus began the education of Watson. During his year at CPL, he mastered the arts of pushing wheelchairs, opening refrigerator and sliding glass doors, paying cashiers, and retrieving coins off cement floors. But the only way to know if Watson could predict Emily's seizures was to pair the two and wait and see.

Teaching Support

Reading Minilesson

Problem and Solution Many of the problems Emily used to face can now be solved, thanks to Watson.

Activity Draw the following chart on the board and ask students to help complete the steps from problem to solution. Ask students to identify a problem and outline the steps they could take to solve the problem, with or without the help of another. **L2**

Problem: Emily couldn't go to the mall because of her seizures.
Step 1
Step 2
Step 3
Solution:

Additional Resources

Reading Skills Practice Workbook

When dog met girl, there was no turning back. "It was love at first sight for both of them," [Emily's mother, Mary] Ramsey said. "He knew this was his person. They bonded very strongly, very quickly."

A month later, Emily returned to the CPL kennel for three weeks' training. Watson was put to the test right away.

"It was the middle of the night in the motel when Emily started seizuring," Ramsey said. "And Watson woke me up barking. I turned on the light and he was straddling her on the bed, looking straight down at her."

Eventually Watson learned that Emily's spells, frightening as they are, were only temporary. His concern turned to vigilance as he realized the importance of remaining with her at all times. After only three or four episodes, he began signaling coming attacks by whining and licking Emily's face. This has been refined into a deep, throaty whine, alerting Emily that she has about 45 minutes to prepare herself for a seizure.

But Watson's protectiveness goes beyond his special early-warning system. If Emily has had a particularly bad night, Watson won't allow her to exert herself the next day. He will forgo his morning walk and refuse to let her off the property. Nor will he allow her to go into the pool for a swim. "The uncanny thing is, he makes these decisions all by himself," Ramsey said. "He's decided that he knows what's best for Emily, and nobody would think about questioning his judgment."

Emily's mother credits Watson for improving her daughter's quality of life in ways nothing else has. Emily has her own reasons for loving Watson. "He's always there for me," she said without hesitation. "He's my best friend."

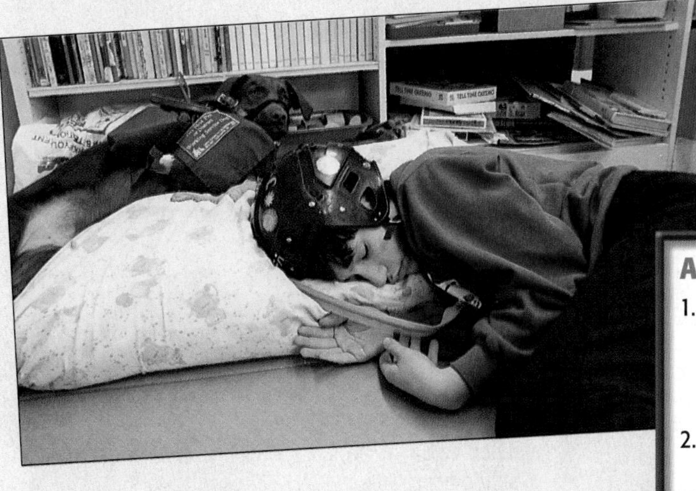

Analyzing Media

1. How did this article affect your understanding of the relationship between dogs and humans?
2. What characteristics tell you that this article is an example of informative nonfiction?

FYI

The German shepherd, the Labrador retriever, the St. Bernard, and the Siberian husky are a few examples of dog breeds most often used as police dogs, guide dogs, and rescue dogs. These dogs are valued for their intelligence, obedience, and loyalty.

Analyzing Media

1. Students may mention the "nonverbal" relationship that is evident between Watson and Emily, the strong connection dogs form with their owners, or the way dogs are willing to use their instincts to help humans.
2. The article tells a true story and, although many readers will say that it also entertains, its primary purpose is to inform. Its reader-friendly style is typical of magazine nonfiction.

Informational Text

For more examples of informational text, direct students to the articles in *inTIME* magazine.

Additional Resources

Media Connections, p. 13

Meeting Individual Needs: SPECIAL NEEDS

Classroom Challenges These students may benefit from working with other students to discuss the physical and mental challenges they face in the classroom.

Activity Have special needs students and their classmates work together in groups. Ask each group to discuss the challenges special needs students face and to create a list of suggestions about how to resolve them. Then, have students write a magazine article explaining the issues and possible solutions.

Additional Resources

Inclusion Strategies

Before Reading

Objectives

- To read and analyze a short story
- To recognize and understand the purpose of suspense in a story
- To analyze a story's resolution

Skills

Reading/Thinking: Graphic Aids; Reasoning; Inferring; Drawing Conclusions; Evaluating; Scanning
Writing: Suspense; Journal Entry
Vocabulary: Multiple-Meaning Words; Unlocking Meaning
Grammar/Language: Troublesome Words; Apostrophes
Listening/Speaking: Radio Drama
Life Skills: Leading and Organizing; Community Service Plan
Collaboration: Literature Groups

Motivating STUDENTS

Literature Launchers: "Getting to Know Joan Aiken"

Videodisc Side B, Segment 21

Also available in VHS.

Selection Focus Transparency 55: Have students view the transparency and then discuss the questions provided.

Reading Focus: Have groups use precise language and sensory imagery to share stories about devoted animals.

Before You Read

Lob's Girl

MEET JOAN AIKEN

British author Joan Aiken says that she writes "the sort of thing I should have liked to read myself." She began creating poems and stories when she was five years old. Aiken's first work was published when she was seventeen, and she has since written more than eighty books and short-story collections. She is best known for historic fiction with mysterious or enchanted characters and settings.

Joan Aiken was born in 1924. This story was published in 1982.

READING FOCUS

Do you think the bond between an animal and a human can be as strong as the bond between two humans?

QuickWrite
Write about what it is like, or would be like, to have an animal as a devoted friend.

Setting a Purpose
Read this story to find out about the powerful bond between a young girl and her dog.

BUILDING BACKGROUND

The Time and Place The story takes place over the course of nine years in a fishing village in southwestern England.

Did You Know? Dogs have been known to travel great distances to find their owners or to return to their original homes. Scientists are unsure of how dogs manage to find their way, but they know that a dog's sense of smell is a powerful tool. Their scent memory is probably stronger than their sight memory. For example, dogs remember the arrangement of objects in a room by their different scents rather than by how they look.

VOCABULARY PREVIEW

secretive (sē′ kri tiv) *adj.* keeping one's thoughts and feelings to oneself; p. 663
hurtle (hurt′ əl) *v.* to move rapidly, especially with much force; p. 664
aggrieved (ə grēvd′) *adj.* feeling wronged, as by an insult or unfair treatment; p. 666
succeed (sək sēd′) *v.* to come or happen after in time, place, or order; p. 666
haggard (hag′ ərd) *adj.* looking worn as a result of grief, worry, or illness; p. 666
agitated (aj′ ə tāt′ əd) *adj.* excited, nervous, or disturbed; stirred up; p. 667

RESOURCE MANAGER

Teaching Tools and Resources
- Theme Seven Planning Guide
- Literature Groups Sourcebook

Essential Lesson Support
Lesson-Specific Instruction
- Selection Focus Transparency 55
- Literary Elements Transparency 55
- Active Reading Guide,* p. 55
- Selection Vocabulary Practice, p. 37
- *inTIME* magazine, p. 2

Assessment
- Selection Quick Checks,* p. 55
- Sel. and Theme Assmt., pp. 95–96
- Testmaker: ExamView Pro
- Performance Assessment, p. 52

Systematic Language Instruction
- Gr. & Comp. Hdbk., L. 11.8

English Language Learners
- ELL Sourcebook, p. 84
- Spanish Summaries, p. 55
- Audio Library*
- English, Yes!

Spec. Needs/Strat. Interven.
- Interactive Rdg. Sbk., pp. T197–T199
- Interactive Rdg. Wkbk., pp. 109–110
- Inclusion Strat. Sbk., pp. 91–92
- Audio Library*

*Also available in Spanish

Lob's Girl

Joan Aiken

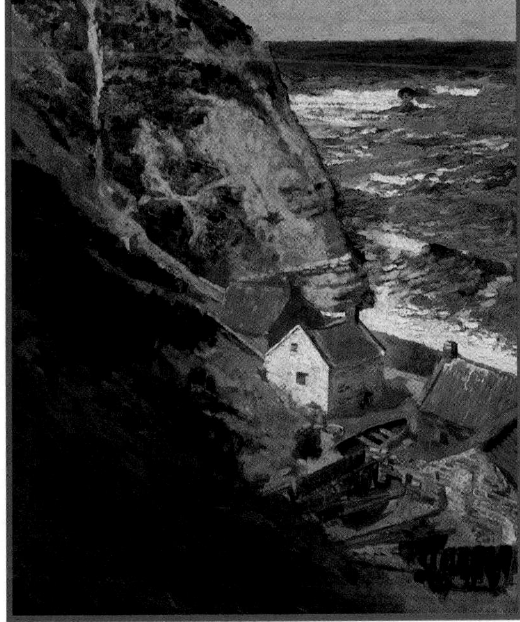

Staithes, Yorkshire. Dame Laura Knight, 1877–1970. Oil on canvas, 29½ x 24½ in. Private collection. How does the artist show the isolation of this home and yard?

A Some people choose their dogs, and some dogs choose their people. The Pengelly family had no say in the choosing of Lob; he came to them in the second way, and very decisively.

It began on the beach, the summer when Sandy was five, Don, her older brother, twelve, and the twins were three. Sandy was really Alexandra, because her grandmother had a beautiful picture of a queen in a diamond tiara[1] and high collar of pearls. It hung by Granny Pearce's kitchen sink and was as familiar as the doormat. When Sandy was born everyone agreed that she was the living spit[2] of the picture, and so she was called Alexandra and Sandy for short.

On this summer day she was lying peacefully reading a comic and not keeping an eye on the twins, who didn't need it because they were occupied in seeing which of them could wrap the most seaweed around the other one's legs. Father—Bert Pengelly—and Don were up on the

1. A *tiara* (tē ar′ ə) is a woman's crownlike headdress, often made with jewels and precious metals.

2. *Living spit* is British slang for "exact likeness," which Americans would call "spitting image."

Reading the Selection

SUMMARY

Lob, a German shepherd, twice walks four hundred miles to reach Sandy, a girl he loves. One stormy evening, Sandy is hit by a truck and falls into a coma. Lob gets into the hospital where his whining rouses Sandy. Then he runs off. Later, it is learned that Lob was killed by the same truck that hit Sandy.

Spanish Summaries, p. 55

A Active Reading Strategies

PREDICT Have students read the first five lines to predict who Lob is, how he chooses the Pengellys, and what the conflict in the story could be.

VOCABULARY If you haven't previewed the selection vocabulary with students, stop and remind them to use context clues to unlock the meanings of new vocabulary words.

Additional Resources

Active Reading Guide, p. 55
Audio Library
Spanish Audio Library

Teaching Support

CONNECTING TO OTHER SELECTIONS

The chart at the right shows three ways to connect "Lob's Girl" to other selections in this book.

For specific teaching strategies, see the ***Theme Seven Planning Guide.***

Connection	Title
Life Skills: Lifelong Learning	→ "The Dog Diaries," p. 411
Thematic: Loyalty	→ "Rikki-tikki-tavi," p. 789
Literary: Resolution	→ "Aunty Misery," p. 701

VIEWING THE PAINTING

Viewing Response *Her viewpoint is high above it, and there is no apparent way to reach it, except by sea.*

B Active Reading Strategies

CONNECT Have students describe how this family is like and different from the family or families they know. *(Sandy is like many other big sisters who are supposed to keep an eye on younger siblings but don't watch too closely. The father works as a fisherman. The mother is a homemaker.)*

FYI

German Shepherds

The word *shepherd* comes from the words *sheep* and *herder*. Originally German shepherds were used to herd and protect flocks of sheep. German shepherds are intelligent, loyal, and courageous. For these reasons, they are often used as guide dogs.

C Literary Elements

FORESHADOWING Ask students what they think the author means when she says that Lob gave himself, as well as the stick, to Sandy. *(Lob is somehow going to become Sandy's dog.)*

D Active Reading Strategies

VISUALIZE Have students visualize the setting and explain how the narrow, steep, twisting road contrasts with the fishing village. *(The village seems peaceful and safe, but the access road is treacherous.)*

Teaching Support

Hard[3] painting the bottom boards of the boat in which Father went fishing for pilchards. And Mother—Jean Pengelly—was getting ahead with making the Christmas puddings[4] because she never felt easy in her mind if they weren't made and safely put away by the end of August. As usual, each member of the family was happily getting on with his or her own affairs. Little did they guess how soon this state of things would be changed by the large new member who was going to erupt into their midst.

Sandy rolled onto her back to make sure that the twins were not climbing on slippery rocks or getting cut off by the tide. At the same moment a large body struck her forcibly in the midriff and she was covered by flying sand. Instinctively she shut her eyes and felt the sand being wiped off her face by something that seemed like a warm, rough, damp flannel. She opened her eyes and looked. It was a tongue. Its owner was a large and bouncy young Alsatian, or German shepherd, with topaz[5] eyes, black-tipped prick ears, a thick, soft coat, and a bushy black-tipped tail.

Did You Know?
Alsatians, also called German shepherds, were originally bred in Germany. They are noted for their intelligence and loyalty.

"Lob!" shouted a man farther up the beach. "Lob, come here!"

But Lob, as if trying to atone for the surprise he had given her, went on licking the sand off Sandy's face, wagging his tail so hard while he kept on knocking up more clouds of sand. His owner, a gray-haired man with a limp, walked over as quickly as he could and seized him by the collar.

"I hope he didn't give you a fright?" the man said to Sandy. "He meant it in play—he's only young."

"Oh, no, I think he's *beautiful,*" said Sandy truly. She picked up a bit of driftwood and threw it. Lob, whisking easily out of his master's grip, was after it like a sand-colored bullet. He came back with the stick, beaming, and gave it to Sandy. At the same time he gave himself, though no one else was aware of this at the time. But with Sandy, too, it was love at first sight, and when, after a lot more stick-throwing, she and the twins joined Father and Don to go home for tea, they cast many a backward glance at Lob being led firmly away by his master.

"I wish we could play with him every day," Tess sighed.

"Why can't we?" said Tim.

Sandy explained, "Because Mr. Dodsworth, who owns him, is from Liverpool, and he is only staying at the Fisherman's Arms till Saturday."

"Is Liverpool a long way off?"

"Right at the other end of England from Cornwall, I'm afraid."

It was a Cornish fishing village where the Pengelly family lived, with rocks and cliffs and a strip of beach and a little round harbor, and palm trees growing in the gardens of the little whitewashed stone houses. The village was approached by a narrow, steep, twisting hill-road, and

3. The *Hard* is a place for landing and launching boats. *Pilchards* are small herring-like fish.
4. *Christmas puddings* are a traditional British dessert similar to a fruitcake.
5. *Topaz* eyes are a bright, clear yellow-gold.

MEETING INDIVIDUAL NEEDS — ENGLISH LANGUAGE LEARNERS

Life in a Fishing Village For some English language learners from other parts of the world, or for their families, fishing may have been, or may still be, an important part of life.

Activity Have small groups of students work together to share stories about fishing in other parts of the world and locally: where people fish, what they fish for, when they fish, what tools they use (nets, boats, line, bait), and how they prepare the fish once they catch them. Some students may want to make illustrations of certain fish or how they are caught. Invite groups to share their findings.

Additional Resources

English Language Learners Sourcebook, p. 84

guarded by a notice that said LOW GEAR FOR 1 1/2 MILES, DANGEROUS TO CYCLISTS.

The Pengelly children went home to scones[6] with Cornish cream and jam, thinking they had seen the last of Lob. But they were much mistaken. The whole family was playing cards by the fire in the front room after supper when there was a loud thump and a crash of china in the kitchen.

"My Christmas puddings!" exclaimed Jean, and ran out.

"Did you put TNT in them, then?" her husband said.

But it was Lob, who, finding the front door shut, had gone around to the back and bounced in through the open kitchen window, where the puddings were cooling on the sill. Luckily only the smallest was knocked down and broken.

Lob stood on his hind legs and plastered Sandy's face with licks. Then he did the same for the twins, who shrieked with joy.

"Where does this friend of yours come from?" inquired Mr. Pengelly.

"He's staying at the Fisherman's Arms—I mean his owner is."

"Then he must go back there. Find a bit of string, Sandy, to tie to his collar."

"I wonder how he found his way here," Mrs. Pengelly said when the reluctant Lob had been led whining away and Sandy had explained about their afternoon's game on the beach. "Fisherman's Arms is right round the other side of the harbor."

Lob's owner scolded him and thanked Mr. Pengelly for bringing him back. Jean Pengelly warned the children that they had better not encourage Lob any more if they met him on the beach, or it would only lead to more trouble. So they dutifully took no notice of him the next day until he spoiled their good resolutions by dashing up to them with joyful barks, wagging his tail so hard that he winded Tess and knocked Tim's legs from under him.

They had a happy day, playing on the sand.

The next day was Saturday. Sandy had found out that Mr. Dodsworth was to catch the half-past-nine train. She went out secretly, down to the station, nodded to Mr. Hoskins, the stationmaster, who wouldn't dream of charging any local for a platform ticket, and climbed up on the footbridge that led over the tracks. She didn't want to be seen, but she did want to see. She saw Mr. Dodsworth get on the train, accompanied by an unhappy-looking Lob with drooping ears and tail. Then she saw the train slide away out of sight around the next headland, with a melancholy wail that sounded like Lob's last good-bye.

Sandy wished she hadn't had the idea of coming to the station. She walked home miserably, with her shoulders hunched and her hands in her pockets. For the rest of the day she was so cross and unlike herself that Tess and Tim were quite surprised, and her mother gave her a dose of senna.[7]

A week passed. Then, one evening, Mrs. Pengelly and the younger children were in the front room playing snakes and ladders. Mr. Pengelly and Don had gone fishing on the evening tide. If your father is a fisherman, he will never be home at the same time from one week to the next.

Suddenly, history repeating itself, there was a crash from the kitchen. Jean Pengelly leaped up, crying, "My blackberry jelly!"

6. *Scones* are sweet biscuits.

7. *Senna* is a medicine made from senna plants and used as a laxative.

E Active Reading Strategies

QUESTION Have students explain why the author describes this sign on the road. *(This shows how dangerous the road is, and it prepares readers for a critical event.)*

F Active Reading Strategies

EVALUATE Have students explain why they think Lob has returned. *(He has decided he wants to be with Sandy. Earlier, the author revealed that Lob gave his loyalty to Sandy.)*

Vocabulary Skills

Multiple-Meaning Words Although *plaster* has one entry in the dictionary, one spelling, and one pronunciation, it has more than one meaning: *n.* "a wall coating," "a paste applied to the body for healing," and *v.* "to cover, smear." Have students volunteer definitions of the word and ask them to identify which one fits.

G Critical Thinking

LOGICAL REASONING Based on what has happened in the past, what do students think is happening here? *(Lob has returned by climbing through the kitchen window again, where he has knocked over blackberry jelly.)*

Reading Minilesson

Using Graphic Aids It may be easier for some students to understand events in this story if they look at a map of England to help them visualize Cornwall's location and to see how far Lob travels.

Activity Have students create a map of England that shows Liverpool, Cornwall, Plymouth, the English Channel, and the Atlantic Ocean. Encourage students to draw the maps to scale and to include a key so others can tell the distance between Cornwall and Liverpool or Cornwall and Plymouth. Invite students to refer to their maps as they read the story. **L2**

Additional Resources

Reading Skills Practice Workbook

H Literary Elements

FIGURES OF SPEECH: *Hyperbole*
Explain to students that hyperbole is a figure of speech in which exaggeration is used to express strong emotion, make a point, or evoke humor. What effect is exaggeration supposed to have here? *(Lob's tongue cannot be a yard long. It adds humor and emphasizes how happy Lob is.)*

I Author's Craft

CHARACTERIZATION Have students describe Lob's personality. *(Lob is determined and persistent; he loves Sandy and will not be separated from her.)*

Vocabulary Skills

Multiple-Meaning Words *Draft* has at least fourteen different meanings. Have students volunteer definitions, then select the one that fits here. *("Planning, doing a rough sketch of a written piece" fits here.)*

J Active Reading Strategies

CONNECT Have students explain how they would feel if they had to say goodbye forever to someone they loved. How do the children show their feelings? *(Don, an adolescent, walks out of the house. The young twins cry. Sandy feels bruised.)*

She and the children had spent the morning picking and the afternoon boiling fruit.

But Sandy was ahead of her mother. With flushed cheeks and eyes like stars she had darted into the kitchen, where she and Lob were hugging one another in a frenzy of joy. About a yard of his tongue was out, and he was licking every part of her that he could reach.

"Good heavens!" exclaimed Jean. "How in the world did *he* get here?"

"He must have walked," said Sandy. "Look at his feet."

They were worn, dusty, and tarry. One had a cut on the pad.

"They ought to be bathed," said Jean Pengelly. "Sandy, run a bowl of warm water while I get the disinfectant."

"What'll we do about him, Mother?" said Sandy anxiously.

Mrs. Pengelly looked at her daughter's pleading eyes and sighed.

"He must go back to his owner, of course," she said, making her voice firm. "Your dad can get the address from the Fisherman's tomorrow, and phone him or send a telegram. In the meantime he'd better have a long drink and a good meal."

Lob was very grateful for the drink and the meal, and made no objection to having his feet washed. Then he flopped down on the hearthrug and slept in front of the fire they had lit because it was a cold, wet evening, with his head on Sandy's feet. He was a very tired dog. He had walked all the way from Liverpool to Cornwall, which is more than four hundred miles.

The next day Mr. Pengelly phoned Lob's owner, and the following morning Mr. Dodsworth arrived off the night train, decidedly put out, to take his pet home. That parting was worse than the first. Lob whined, Don walked out of the house, the twins burst out crying, and Sandy crept up to her bedroom afterward and lay with her face pressed into the quilt, feeling as if she were bruised all over.

Jean Pengelly took them all into Plymouth to see the circus on the next day and the twins cheered up a little, but even the hour's ride in the train each way and the Liberty horses and performing seals could not cure Sandy's sore heart.

She need not have bothered, though. In ten days' time Lob was back—limping this time, with a torn ear and a patch missing out of his furry coat, as if he had met and tangled with an enemy or two in the course of his four-hundred-mile walk.

Bert Pengelly rang up Liverpool again. Mr. Dodsworth, when he answered, sounded weary. He said, "That dog has already cost me two days that I can't spare away from my work—plus endless time in police stations and drafting newspaper advertisements. I'm too old for these ups and downs. I think we'd better face the fact, Mr. Pengelly, that it's your family he wants to stay with—that is, if you want to have him."

Bert Pengelly gulped. He was not a rich man; and Lob was a pedigreed[8] dog. He said cautiously, "How much would you be asking for him?"

"Good heavens, man, I'm not suggesting I'd sell him to you. You must have him as a gift. Think of the train fares I'll be saving. You'll be doing me a good turn."

"Is he a big eater?" Bert asked doubtfully.

By this time the children, breathless in the background listening to one side of this conversation, had realized what was in

8. A *pedigreed* dog has papers showing that its ancestors were the same breed.

Teaching Support

MEETING INDIVIDUAL NEEDS: SPECIAL NEEDS

Less-Proficient Readers Less-proficient readers might need help interpreting some of the British expressions in the story. Write these sentences on the board:

- *For the rest of the day she was so cross and unlike herself...*
- *Bert Pengelly rang up Liverpool again.*
- *You'll be doing me a good turn.*

Activity Encourage pairs of students to use context clues to write brief definitions for the underlined phrases. **L1**

Additional Resources
Inclusion Strategies

the wind and were dancing up and down with their hands clasped beseechingly.[9]

"Oh, not for his size," Lob's owner assured Bert. "Two or three pounds of meat a day and some vegetables and gravy and biscuits—he does very well on that."

Alexandra's father looked over the telephone at his daughter's swimming eyes and trembling lips. He reached a decision. "Well, then, Mr. Dodsworth," he said briskly, "we'll accept your offer and thank you very much. The children will be overjoyed and you can be sure Lob has come to a good home. They'll look after him and see he gets enough exercise. But I can tell you," he ended firmly, "if he wants to settle in with us he'll have to learn to eat a lot of fish."

So that was how Lob came to live with the Pengelly family. Everybody loved him and he loved them all. But there was never any question who came first with him. He was Sandy's dog. He slept by her bed and followed her everywhere he was allowed.

K Nine years went by, and each summer Mr. Dodsworth came back to stay at the Fisherman's Arms and call on his erstwhile dog. Lob always met him with recognition and dignified pleasure, accompanied him for a walk or two—but showed no signs of wishing to return to Liverpool. His place, he intimated,[10] was definitely with the Pengellys.

In the course of nine years Lob changed less than Sandy. As she went into her teens he became a little slower, a little stiffer, there was a touch of gray on his nose, but he was still a handsome dog. He and Sandy still loved one another devotedly.

L One evening in October all the summer visitors had left, and the little fishing town looked empty and secretive. It was a wet, windy dusk. When the children came home from school—even the twins were at high school[11] now, and Don was a full-fledged fisherman—Jean Pengelly said, "Sandy, your Aunt Rebecca says she's lonesome because Uncle Will Hoskins has gone out trawling,[12] and she wants one of you to go and spend the evening with her. You go, dear; you can take your homework with you."

Sandy looked far from enthusiastic.

"Can I take Lob with me?"

"You know Aunt Becky doesn't really like dogs— Oh, very well." Mrs. Pengelly sighed. "I suppose she'll have to put up with him as well as you."

Reluctantly Sandy tidied herself, took her schoolbag, put on the damp raincoat she had just taken off, fastened Lob's lead to his collar, and set off to walk through the dusk to Aunt Becky's cottage, which was five minutes' climb up the steep hill.

M The wind was howling through the shrouds of boats drawn up on the Hard.

Did You Know?
A boat's *shrouds* are ropes that help support the masts.

9. *Beseechingly* means "in a begging or pleading manner."
10. Lob belonged to Mr. Dodsworth in earlier times *(erstwhile)*. To *intimate* is to hint at something without stating it directly.
11. An English *high school* starts with what would be the sixth or seventh grade in the United States.
12. *Trawling* is fishing with large nets that are dragged across the water's bottom.

Vocabulary
secretive (sē′ kri tiv) *adj.* keeping one's thoughts and feelings to oneself

On The Lighter Side

Dog Biscuit The Romans *circa* 100 B.C. are credited with producing the first dedicated pet food—a hard dark bran biscuit called an *autopyron*. Because it was thought to help digestion, the biscuit was given to both dogs and enslaved people..

K Active Reading Strategies

PREDICT Invite students to predict what may be about to happen. *(Since nine years is a long time for a dog, students may predict that the aging Lob will die soon. Others may predict that something will happen on the steep hill.)*

L Critical Thinking

LOGICAL REASONING Have students explain why the story now focuses on one day in October nine years after Lob comes to live with the Pengellys. *(Something important is going to happen.)*

M Literary Elements

MOOD Invite your students to describe the story's mood at this point. *(It is dark; the wind howls; the mood is ominous.)*

Listening and Speaking Minilesson

Creating a Radio Drama As you name a sound, have students suggest feelings that it can evoke in listeners. For example, if you say *laughter*, students might say *happiness*. If you say *howling wind*, students might say *fear* or *suspense*.

Activity Have small groups of students select one scene from the story to read as a radio drama. Encourage them to create sound effects to accompany their drama. The sound effects should capture the mood or atmosphere of the passage. Encourage groups to practice their dramas and then perform them for the class. Have class members close their eyes as they listen. After each performance, have listeners describe the feelings and images each scene created in their minds. **L2**

N Literary Elements

SUSPENSE Invite students to explain how suspense builds in this paragraph. *(On a dark and rainy night, a truck has just hurtled down the hill Sandy and Lob climbed; but they aren't mentioned.)*

O Literary Elements

REPETITION Have students explain why they think the author again mentions the steep hill. *(Perhaps it is to remind readers how dangerous it is or to build suspense over Sandy and Lob.)*

P Literary Elements

SUSPENSE Encourage students to explain why the author describes the object by the wall as a pile of clothes or maybe the body of a child. *(The author doesn't spell out what has happened and builds suspense by withholding details.)*

Q Active Reading Strategies

PREDICT Invite students to predict what has happened to Lob. *(Perhaps Lob was killed by the truck; perhaps he ran away to get help; or maybe he is injured.)*

"Put some cheerful music on, do," said Jean Pengelly to the nearest twin. "Anything to drown that wretched sound while I make your dad's supper." So Don, who had just come in, put on some rock music, loud. Which was why the Pengellys did not hear the truck hurtle down the hill and crash against the post office wall a few minutes later.

Dr. Travers was driving through Cornwall with his wife, taking a late holiday before patients began coming down with winter colds and flu. He saw the sign that said STEEP HILL. LOW GEAR FOR 1 1/2 MILES. Dutifully he changed into second gear.

"We must be nearly there," said his wife, looking out her window. "I noticed a sign on the coast road that said the Fisherman's Arms was two miles. What a narrow, dangerous hill! But the cottages are very pretty— Oh, Frank, stop, *stop!* There's a child, I'm sure it's a child—by the wall over there!"

Dr. Travers jammed on his brakes and brought the car to a stop. A little stream ran down by the road in a shallow stone culvert,[13] and half in the water lay something that looked, in the dusk, like a pile of clothes—or was it the body of a child? Mrs. Travers was out of the car in a flash, but her husband was quicker.

"Don't touch her, Emily!" he said sharply. "She's been hit. Can't be more than a few minutes. Remember that truck that overtook us half a mile back, speeding like the devil? Here, quick, go into that cottage and phone for an ambulance. The girl's in a bad way. I'll stay here and do what I can to stop the bleeding. Don't waste a minute."

Doctors are expert at stopping dangerous bleeding, for they know the right places to press. This Dr. Travers was able to do, but he didn't dare do more; the girl was lying in a queerly crumpled heap, and he guessed she had a number of bones broken and that it would be highly dangerous to move her. He watched her with great concentration, wondering where the truck had got to and what other damage it had done.

Mrs. Travers was very quick. She had seen plenty of accident cases and knew the importance of speed. The first cottage she tried had a phone; in four minutes she was back, and in six an ambulance was wailing down the hill.

Its attendants lifted the child onto a stretcher as carefully as if she were made of fine thistledown. The ambulance sped off to Plymouth—for the local cottage hospital[14] did not take serious accident cases—and Dr. Travers went down to the police station to report what he had done.

He found that the police already knew about the speeding truck—which had suffered from loss of brakes and ended up with its radiator halfway through the post office wall. The driver was concussed and shocked, but the police thought he was the only person injured— until Dr. Travers told his tale.

13. A *culvert* is a drainage ditch.

14. *Cottage hospital* is a British term for a small hospital with a staff of local doctors.

Vocabulary
hurtle (hurt′ əl) *v.* to move rapidly, especially with much force

Teaching Support

Writing Minilesson

Creating Suspense Encourage students to help you list ways the author creates suspense in this story:

- *by not telling readers what is happening and making them guess*
- *by creating a setting that seems spooky and dangerous*
- *by having characters perform an action that seems dangerous*

Activity Have students write suspenseful stories. They may want to plan their tales by thinking about an event involving a dog or other pet, a scary event, or a setting that creates a mood of fear or worry.

Encourage students to use "Lob's Girl" as a writing model for creating suspense and mood. **L2**

Additional Resources

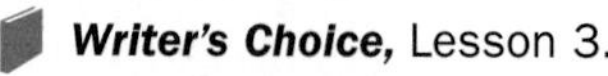
Writer's Choice, Lesson 3.3

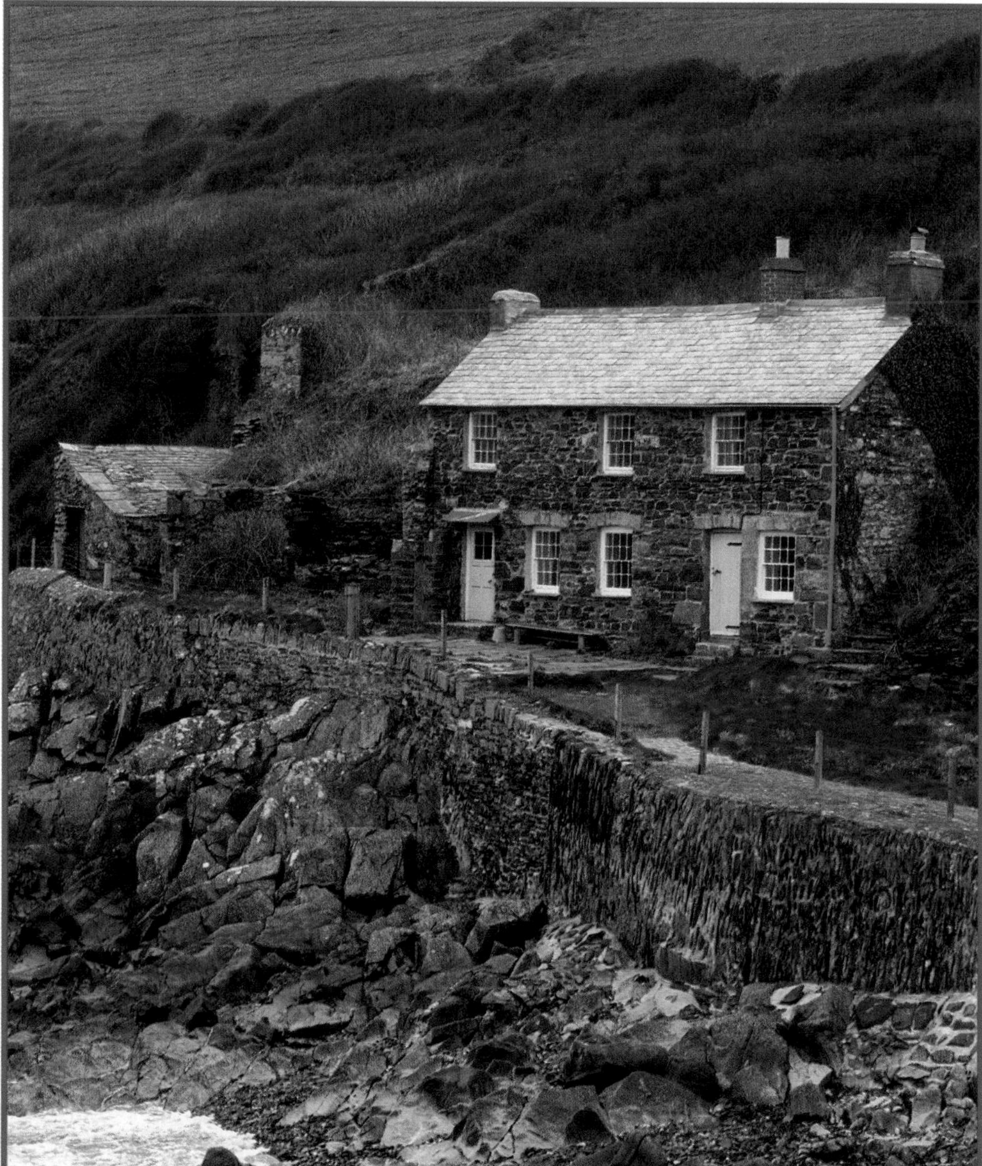

Viewing the photograph: Compare the home shown here with the painting *Straithes, Yorkshire,* on page 659. Which of the two pictures is closer to your image of the story's setting? Why?

VIEWING THE PAINTING

The photograph shows a stately home close to the sea. It looks quite large and is accessible from the road.

Viewing Response *Both homes are near the sea, but the home in Yorkshire is in a more rugged setting. The home on this page looks peaceful and calm. Many students will think the home in Yorkshire seems more like the one in the story because it is surrounded by a steep hill.*

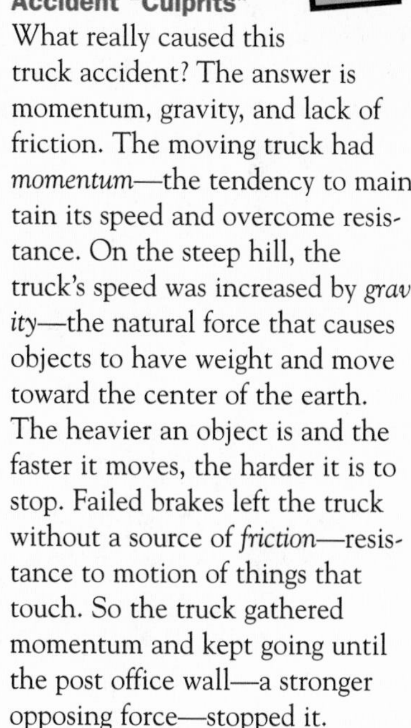

FYI

Accident "Culprits"
What really caused this truck accident? The answer is momentum, gravity, and lack of friction. The moving truck had *momentum*—the tendency to maintain its speed and overcome resistance. On the steep hill, the truck's speed was increased by *gravity*—the natural force that causes objects to have weight and move toward the center of the earth. The heavier an object is and the faster it moves, the harder it is to stop. Failed brakes left the truck without a source of *friction*—resistance to motion of things that touch. So the truck gathered momentum and kept going until the post office wall—a stronger opposing force—stopped it.

LIFE SKILLS CONNECTION

Leading and Organizing Invite a group of students to think about a dangerous place in their community, such as an intersection in need of a stop sign, a residential street that drivers speed through, a place that needs a streetlight, or a bridge with a missing railing.

Activity Have students analyze the problem and decide what they think should be done about it (such as installing speed bumps or lights). Then have students attend a neighborhood association meeting or set up an appointment with the mayor to discuss the problem and its solution. The mayor or association members may have ideas about the next step students can take to help solve the problem. **L2**

R Critical Thinking

INFERRING Have students explain why Aunt Rebecca's attitude changes. *(Aunt Rebecca learns that Sandy has been hit by a truck and may die.)*

S Literary Elements

SUSPENSE Have students explain why the author has not mentioned Lob until now. *(She builds suspense by not revealing where Lob is.)*

T Critical Thinking

DRAWING CONCLUSIONS Ask students to explain why it is bad that Sandy has shown no signs of regaining consciousness. *(The doctor told Bert and Jean that Sandy had a chance if she showed signs of coming out of the coma.)*

At half-past nine that night Aunt Rebecca Hoskins was sitting by her fire thinking aggrieved thoughts about the inconsiderateness of nieces who were asked to supper and never turned up when she was startled by a neighbor, who burst in exclaiming, "Have you heard about Sandy Pengelly, then, Mrs. Hoskins? Terrible thing, poor little soul, and they don't know if she's likely to live. Police have got the truck driver that hit her—ah, it didn't ought to be allowed, speeding through the place like that at umpty miles an hour, they ought to jail him for life—not that that'd be any comfort to poor Bert and Jean."

Horrified, Aunt Rebecca put on a coat and went down to her brother's house. She found the family with white shocked faces; Bert and Jean were about to drive off to the hospital where Sandy had been taken, and the twins were crying bitterly. Lob was nowhere to be seen. But Aunt Rebecca was not interested in dogs; she did not inquire about him.

"Thank the lord you've come, Beck," said her brother. "Will you stay the night with Don and the twins? Don's out looking for Lob and heaven knows when we'll be back; we may get a bed with Jean's mother in Plymouth."

"Oh, if only I'd never invited the poor child," wailed Mrs. Hoskins. But Bert and Jean hardly heard her.

That night seemed to last forever. The twins cried themselves to sleep. Don came home very late and grim-faced. Bert and Jean sat in a waiting room of the Western Counties Hospital, but Sandy was unconscious, they were told, and she remained so. All that could be done for her was done. She was given transfusions to replace all the blood she had lost. The broken bones were set and put in slings and cradles.[15]

"Is she a healthy girl? Has she a good constitution?"[16] the emergency doctor asked.

"Aye, doctor, she is that," Bert said hoarsely. The lump in Jean's throat prevented her from answering: she merely nodded.

"Then she ought to have a chance. But I won't conceal from you that her condition is very serious, unless she shows signs of coming out from this coma."

But as hour succeeded hour, Sandy showed no signs of recovering consciousness. Her parents sat in the waiting room with haggard faces; sometimes one of them would go to telephone the family at home, or try to get a little sleep at the home of Granny Pearce, not far away.

At noon next day Dr. and Mrs. Travers went to the Pengelly cottage to inquire how Sandy was doing, but the report was gloomy: "Still in a very serious condition." The twins were miserably unhappy. They forgot that they had sometimes called their elder sister bossy and only remembered how often she had shared her pocket money with them, how she read to them and took them for picnics and helped with their homework.

15. Here, the *cradles* are frames that keep Sandy's bedclothes from touching her injuries.
16. Here, *constitution* refers to a person's physical condition.

Vocabulary

aggrieved (ə grēvd′) *adj.* feeling wronged, as by an insult or unfair treatment
succeed (sək sēd′) *v.* to come or happen after in time, place, or order
haggard (hag′ ərd) *adj.* looking worn as a result of grief, worry, or illness

Teaching Support

MEETING INDIVIDUAL NEEDS — MULTIPLE MODES OF EXPRESSION

Linguistic Students with linguistic skills may enjoy interviewing in order to learn more about careers in which people care for dogs, such as dog training or dog grooming.

Activity Have students work in pairs or small groups to set up an interview with a veterinarian, a dog trainer, or a dog groomer. Have the class help the interviewer brainstorm a list of questions for the interview. Encourage students to ask their interviewee questions such as how to examine a dog's teeth, how to teach a dog one command (such as *heel*), or how to groom a dog. Then have students prepare a demonstration to illustrate what they've learned to the class. **L2**

Now there was no Sandy, no Mother and Dad, Don went around with a gray, shuttered face, and worse still, there was no Lob.

The Western Counties Hospital is a large one, with dozens of different departments and five or six connected buildings, each with three or four entrances. By that afternoon it became noticeable that a dog seemed to have taken up position outside the hospital, with the fixed intention of getting in. Patiently he would try first one entrance and then another, all the way around, and then begin again. Sometimes he would get a little way inside, following a visitor, but animals were, of course, forbidden, and he was always kindly but firmly turned out again. Sometimes the guard at the main entrance gave him a pat or offered him a bit of sandwich—he looked so wet and beseeching and desperate. But he never ate the sandwich. No one seemed to own him or to know where he came from: Plymouth is a large city and he might have belonged to anybody.

At tea time Granny Pearce came through the pouring rain to bring a flask of hot tea with brandy in it to her daughter and son-in-law. Just as she reached the main entrance the guard was gently but forcibly shoving out a large, agitated, soaking-wet Alsatian dog.

"No, old fellow, you can *not* come in. Hospitals are for people, not for dogs."

"Why, bless me," exclaimed old Mrs. Pearce. "That's Lob! Here, Lob. Lobby boy!"

Lob ran to her, whining. Mrs. Pearce walked up to the desk.

"I'm sorry, madam, you can't bring that dog in here," the guard said.

Mrs. Pearce was a very determined old lady. She looked the porter in the eye.

"Now, see here, young man. That dog has walked twenty miles from St. Killan to get to my granddaughter. Heaven knows how he knew she was here, but it's plain he knows. And he ought to have his rights! He ought to get to see her! Do you know," she went on, bristling, "that dog has walked the length of England—*twice*—to be with that girl? And you think you can keep him out with your fiddling rules and regulations?"

"I'll have to ask the medical officer," the guard said weakly.

"You do that, young man." Granny Pearce sat down in a determined manner, shutting her umbrella, and Lob sat patiently dripping at her feet. Every now and then he shook his head, as if to dislodge something heavy that was tied around his neck.

Presently a tired, thin, intelligent-looking man in a white coat came downstairs, with an impressive, silver-haired man in a dark suit, and there was a low-voiced discussion. Granny Pearce eyed them, biding her time.

"Frankly . . . not much to lose," said the older man. The man in the white coat approached Granny Pearce.

"It's strictly against every rule, but as it's such a serious case we are making an exception," he said to her quietly. "But only *outside* her bedroom door—and only for a moment or two."

Without a word, Granny Pearce rose and stumped upstairs. Lob followed close to her skirts, as if he knew his hope lay with her.

Vocabulary
agitated (aj′ ə tāt′ əd) *adj.* excited, nervous, or disturbed; stirred up

U Active Reading Strategies

EVALUATE Have students explain who they think this dog is and what it wants. *(The dog is Lob. It wants to get inside the hospital to see Sandy.)*

V Literary Elements

SUSPENSE Encourage students to explain how the author creates suspense in this paragraph. *(The author sets up details to make readers wonder whether the dog will ever get in, and, if so, how.)*

W Active Reading Strategies

QUESTION Have students explain why they think Lob shakes his head "as if to dislodge something heavy that was tied around his neck." *(Maybe the dog hurt his neck in the accident.)* Suggest students revisit this interpretation of Lob's behavior after they finish reading the story.

At the MOVIES

Be sure to preview the following video for appropriateness for your class:

- ***Lassie Come Home*** (1943, 88 minutes, G) After more than half a century, this remains *the* classic faithful dog movie.

Real-World Connection

Amazing Canines Invite students to read magazine articles about German shepherds or other dogs that have performed amazing feats, such as walking many miles to get home or saving someone's life.

Activity Encourage students to find articles about dogs that have performed amazing feats. Some students may want to visit Internet sites with additional information about German shepherds. Encourage students to take notes on the articles they especially enjoy. Then have them use their notes to describe the dogs' amazing feats to the rest of the class. Encourage students to use this information and their own knowledge to raise additional, unanswered questions about dogs for further research. **L2**

Active Reading Strategies

EVALUATE Ask students to explain why Bert and Jean are "white-faced and shocked" when they see Lob. *(The hospital is far from their home; they thought Lob was lost; or they thought Lob was killed.)*

Critical Thinking

EVALUATING Have students explain whether or not they think the dog in the hospital was Lob. You may wish to share the following model.

Model: Now I know Lob was killed, but Lob has a history of overcoming obstacles to be with Sandy. The dog in the hospital shook his head as if to dislodge something heavy around his neck. I now know that Don tied concrete to Lob's collar and buried him at sea. Perhaps Lob has made his most difficult journey of all.

Thematic Focus

A Different Dimension Have students explain how this story relates to the theme. *(Lob seems to have returned from a different dimension to help Sandy.)*

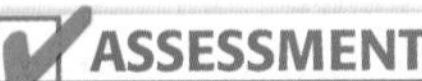
ASSESSMENT

Quick Checks, p. 55

They waited in the green-floored corridor outside Sandy's room. The door was half shut. Bert and Jean were inside. Everything was terribly quiet. A nurse came out. The white-coated man asked her something and she shook her head. She had left the door ajar, and through it could now be seen a high, narrow bed with a lot of gadgets around it. Sandy lay there, very flat under the covers, very still. Her head was turned away. All Lob's attention was riveted on the bed. He strained toward it, but Granny Pearce clasped his collar firmly.

"I've done a lot for you, my boy, now you behave yourself," she whispered grimly. Lob let out a faint whine, anxious and pleading.

At the sound of that whine Sandy stirred just a little. She sighed and moved her head the least fraction. Lob whined again. And then Sandy turned her head right over. Her eyes opened, looking at the door.

"Lob?" she murmured—no more than a breath of sound. "Lobby, boy?"

The doctor by Granny Pearce drew a quick, sharp breath. Sandy moved her left arm—the one that was not broken—from below the covers and let her hand dangle down, feeling, as she always did in the mornings, for Lob's furry head. The doctor nodded slowly.

"All right," he whispered. "Let him go to the bedside. But keep ahold of him."

Granny Pearce and Lob moved to the bedside. Now she could see Bert and Jean, white-faced and shocked, on the far side of the bed. But she didn't look at them. She looked at the smile on her granddaughter's face as the groping fingers found Lob's wet ears and gently pulled them. "Good boy," whispered Sandy, and fell asleep again.

Granny Pearce led Lob out into the passage again. There she let go of him and he ran off swiftly down the stairs. She would have followed him, but Bert and Jean had come out into the passage, and she spoke to Bert fiercely.

"*I* don't know why you were so foolish as not to bring the dog before! Leaving him to find the way here himself—"

"But, Mother!" said Jean Pengelly. "That can't have been Lob. What a chance to take! Suppose Sandy hadn't—" She stopped, with her handkerchief pressed to her mouth.

"Not Lob? I've known that dog nine years! I suppose I ought to know my own granddaughter's dog?"

"Listen, Mother," said Bert. "Lob was killed by the same truck that hit Sandy. Don found him—when he went to look for Sandy's schoolbag. He was—he was dead. Ribs all smashed. No question of that. Don told me on the phone—he and Will Hoskins rowed a half mile out to sea and sank the dog with a lump of concrete tied to his collar. Poor old boy. Still—he was getting on. Couldn't have lasted forever."

"*Sank him at sea?* Then what—?"

Slowly old Mrs. Pearce, and then the other two, turned to look at the trail of dripping-wet footprints that led down the hospital stairs.

In the Pengellys' garden they have a stone, under the palm tree. It says: "Lob. Sandy's dog. Buried at sea."

❖

Teaching Support

Grammar and Language *Minilesson*

Using Troublesome Words Put the following chart on the board and discuss each word's meaning:

Word	Meaning	Example
its	the possessive form of it	The dog wags its tail.
it's	the contraction of it is	It's raining cats and dogs.
their	the possessive form of they	Their raincoats are completely soaked.
they're	the contraction of they are	See if they're dry yet.

Activity Have students choose the correct form to complete each of the following sentences.

- Some people choose *(they're, their)* dogs.
- *(It's, Its)* tongue was a yard long.
- Sandy helped them with *(they're, their)* homework.
- *(It's, Its)* against the rules. **L2**

Additional Resources

Grammar and Language Transparency 53

Grammar and Language Workbook, pp. 223–224, 227–228

Grammar and Composition Handbook, Lesson 4.4

Writer's Choice, Lesson 17.2

Responding to Literature

PERSONAL RESPONSE

- What do you think really happened in the hospital room?

Analyzing Literature

RECALL

1. How far does Lob travel to reach the Pengelly family after his owner returns to Liverpool?
2. Why does Lob's owner give the dog away?
3. What happens to Sandy nine years after she meets Lob?
4. What visitor does Granny Pearce see outside the hospital? How does Sandy respond to the visitor?

Brackets connect questions that are paired to develop higher-level thinking skills.

INTERPRET

5. What do you think would motivate a dog like Lob to travel great distances to return to a place he had once visited?
6. Describe the difference between the former owner's and Sandy's attachment to Lob.
7. The author includes a detailed description of the accident scene. In your opinion, why doesn't the author reveal at that point that the victim is Sandy?
8. Why are Sandy's parents especially shocked at Sandy's response to the dog?

EVALUATE AND CONNECT

9. Do you believe a pet could actually cause a medical change in a patient? Explain.
10. Theme Connection What does the story's ending suggest about the power of Sandy's and Lob's feelings for each other?

LITERARY ELEMENTS

Suspense

Have you ever been so anxious while reading a story that you've held your breath or bitten your nails? That feeling of uncertainty about what will happen next in a story is caused by the **suspense** a writer creates. Writers can build suspense by raising questions in a reader's mind about characters and their motivations, by describing a mood that is threatening or mysterious, or by including hints about possible developments.

1. How does the author build suspense about whether Lob will get to Sandy's hospital room?
2. Describe briefly how suspense was created in another story you have read.

- See **Literary Terms Handbook,** p. R11.

Responding to the Selection

PERSONAL RESPONSE

Students' ideas about what happened in the hospital room should be supported by evidence from the story.

Analyzing Literature

1. Lob travels four hundred miles.
2. Lob's owner gives the dog to the Pengellys because Lob keeps returning to them.
3. Sandy is hit by a truck nine years after she meets Lob.
4. Granny Pearce sees Lob outside the hospital. Sandy responds to Lob in the hospital by recovering from her coma.
5. Lob is motivated by a strong bond with Sandy.
6. The former owner was nice to Lob, but Sandy deeply loves Lob.
7. The author doesn't reveal that the accident victim is Sandy because she wants to build suspense.
8. Sandy's parents are shocked because they know that Lob was killed by the truck.
9. Sample: A pet could cause a medical change in a patient if the patient loves the animal.
10. The ending suggests that Sandy's and Lob's love was so strong that Lob returned from a different dimension to help Sandy.

LITERARY ELEMENTS

1. The author describes Lob's persistent but unsuccessful attempts to get into the hospital.
2. Students should use examples from the selected stories to support their ideas about how the authors create suspense.

Additional Resources

Literary Elements Transparency 55

Literature and Writing

Writing About Literature

Students' paragraphs should

- explain what occurs during the story's resolution
- analyze the effectiveness of the resolution
- describe the effect other methods of resolving the story would have on readers

Personal Writing

Students' journal entries should

- describe their reactions to Lob
- use examples from the story to explain whether Lob was believable
- explain whether they could be as close to an animal as Sandy was to Lob

Extending Your Response

Literature Groups Before students meet, encourage them to think about what may happen next in the story. Have them each create a brief illustration showing one idea to share with the group.

Learning for Life Encourage students to develop plans that could really be put into action. When they are finished, encourage pairs to work together with the animals to implement their plans.

Interdisciplinary Activity

Students will find many sites on the Internet devoted to specific dog breeds and their special talents. Students may want to define their search terms with breed names, such as *Labrador Retriever, Beagle,* or *Golden Retriever.*

Literature and Writing

Writing About Literature

Resolution Do you think Joan Aiken wrote a satisfying conclusion to the story? Write a paragraph that analyzes the effectiveness of the story's **resolution.**

Personal Writing

Special Connections Look back at what you wrote about animals and people in the **Reading Focus** on page 658. Then write about your reaction to the character of Lob in a journal entry. Do you think he was believable? Can you imagine being as close to an animal as Sandy was to Lob?

Extending Your Response

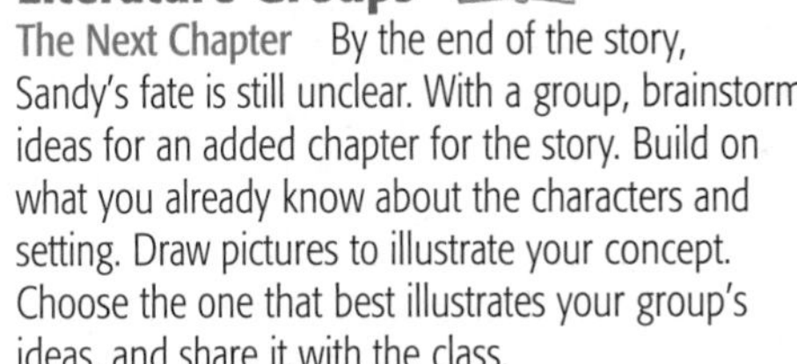

Literature Groups

The Next Chapter By the end of the story, Sandy's fate is still unclear. With a group, brainstorm ideas for an added chapter for the story. Build on what you already know about the characters and setting. Draw pictures to illustrate your concept. Choose the one that best illustrates your group's ideas, and share it with the class.

Learning for Life

Community Service Plan Visits from animals can have a beneficial effect on the sick and elderly. Work with a partner to write a plan for your own community that involves students, their pets, and people who could be cheered by visits.

Interdisciplinary Activity

Science Alsatians are used frequently as guide dogs for the sight-impaired. Research ways in which another dog breed has been used to help humans. Consider such skills as hunting, herding, rescuing, guarding, and assisting the disabled. Present your findings as a television reporter.

Reading Further

If you would like to read other mysterious stories by Joan Aiken, try these:

The Wolves of Willoughby Chase

Night Fall

Save your work for your portfolio.

Skill Minilessons

Reteach · Review

GRAMMAR AND LANGUAGE • APOSTROPHES IN POSSESSIVES

An **apostrophe** can be used to show possession. Follow these rules for forming possessives:

- Use an apostrophe and an *s* to form the possessive of a singular noun.
  Lob + **'s** = Lob**'s**
- Use an apostrophe and an *s* to form the possessive of a plural noun that does not end in *s*.
  children + **'s** = children**'s**
- Use an apostrophe alone to form the possessive of a plural noun that ends in *s*.
  dogs + **'** = dogs**'**

PRACTICE Write the possessive form of each word below.

1. Sandy
2. ambulances
3. ears
4. people
5. houses
6. train
7. women
8. telegram

For more about apostrophes, see **Language Handbook,** p. R40.

READING AND THINKING • SCANNING

Scanning is a method of rapid reading in which you search quickly through a piece of writing for a particular piece of information. You can scan to look for the answer to a specific question. When scanning, run your eyes across each page of the story until they fall on the word or words you need.

For more about scanning and related reading strategies, see **Reading Handbook,** pp. R76–R80.

PRACTICE Scan "Lob's Girl" to find the following information:

1. whose picture hangs by Granny Pearce's kitchen sink
2. a physical description of Lob
3. the names of two people who stayed at the Fisherman's Arms
4. the number of years Lob is a member of the family

VOCABULARY • UNLOCKING MEANING

Within *secretive,* you can see the word *secret.* These two words are related words. Using what you know about one can help you understand the other. Use what you know about each italicized word to complete each statement correctly.

PRACTICE Use what you know about each italicized word to complete the item.

1. *agitated* If an agitator spoke to a crowd of people, he or she would
   a. stir them up
   b. make them laugh
   c. calm them down
2. *succeed* The successor to the president of the United States is the
   a. Congress
   b. Supreme Court
   c. next president
3. *resolution* A resolute person could be described as
   a. worried
   b. determined
   c. confused
4. *aggrieved* If you write down your grievances, you make a list of
   a. possessions
   b. complaints
   c. assignments

Skill Minilessons

GRAMMAR AND LANGUAGE
APOSTROPHES IN POSSESSIVES

1. Sandy's
2. ambulances'
3. ears'
4. people's
5. houses'
6. train's
7. women's
8. telegram's

READING AND THINKING
SCANNING

1. a queen in a diamond tiara and pearls
2. topaz eyes; black-tipped ears; a thick, soft coat; bushy black-tipped tail
3. Mr. Dodsworth; Dr. Travers and his wife
4. nine years

VOCABULARY
UNLOCKING MEANING

1. a 2. c 3. b 4. b

Additional Resources

- ***Grammar and Language Workbook,*** pp. 273–274
- ***Grammar and Composition Handbook,*** Lesson 13.7
- ***Writer's Choice,*** Lesson 20.7
- ***Reading Skills Practice Workbook,*** pp. 97–98
- ***Vocabulary Practice,*** p. 37

ASSESSMENT

- ***Quick Checks,*** p. 55
- ***Selection and Theme Assessment,*** pp. 95–96
- ***Performance Assessment,*** p. 52
- ***Testmaker: ExamView Pro***
- ***Interactive Tutor: Self-Assessment***

Objective

- To recognize and use strategies for monitoring comprehension

Teaching Strategies

Dramatize the question-asking strategies suggested on page 672 by having students practice asking their questions aloud. Use the sample paragraph, or any paragraph from the previous story. Have students read silently, but ask the questions they have out loud, as if they were speaking directly to the writer. Questions don't have to be formed completely. For example, if students practice using the sample paragraph they may ask: *How do they know that? Why didn't he do more?*

Exercise

1. Answers may include: What does the hospital look like? Who is the dog? What happened to the dog after the accident? Why is the dog hanging around the hospital?
2. Students may say that the dog doesn't give up easily. He is determined to get into the hospital even if he has to wait patiently or try unsuccessfully many times.

Additional Resources

Reading Skills Practice Workbook

Teaching Support

Monitoring Comprehension

To get the most out of their reading, active readers ask questions as they read. By asking questions, they monitor their comprehension of a piece of writing. Ask yourself questions as you read the following passage from "Lob's Girl."

> Doctors are experts at stopping dangerous bleeding, for they know the right places to press. This Dr. Travers was able to do, but he didn't dare do more; the girl was lying in a queerly crumpled heap, and he guessed she had a number of bones broken and that it would be highly dangerous to move her. He watched her with great concentration, wondering where the truck had got to and what other damage it had done.

What does the doctor do for the injured girl? What does the writer mean by a "crumpled heap"? Why does the doctor wonder about the truck? If you can answer these kinds of questions about the scene, then you understand exactly what is happening. If not, stop and reread the passage until you can figure out what is going on.

- For more about monitoring comprehension, see **Reading Handbook,** pp. R85–R87.

EXERCISE

Read the following excerpt from "Lob's Girl." Then answer the questions.

> By that afternoon it became noticeable that a dog seemed to have taken up position outside the hospital, with the fixed intention of getting in. Patiently he would try first one entrance and then another, all the way around, and then begin again. Sometimes he would get a little way inside, following a visitor, but animals were, of course, forbidden, and he was always kindly but firmly turned out again.

1. Write at least two questions you might ask yourself as you monitor your comprehension of the passage.
2. From reading this description, what do you learn about the determination of the dog?

MEETING INDIVIDUAL NEEDS — SPECIAL NEEDS

Less-Proficient Readers Write this sentence from "Lob's Girl" on the board: *Some people choose their dogs, and some dogs choose their people.*

Activity Ask each student to choose an opening sentence from a paragraph in "Lob's Girl" and write it on an index card, along with as many questions that relate to it as possible. Have students exchange cards and hunt for the answers to one another's questions in the story. **L1**

Additional Resources

Inclusion Strategies

Writing Skills

Using Sentence Variety

What do these sentences from "Lob's Girl" have in common?

He must have walked.

He was a very tired dog.

Bert Pengelly rang up Liverpool again.

If you guessed that they are all fairly short sentences, you're right. There's nothing wrong with short sentences, but good writers like to vary their sentence patterns to avoid monotony. Notice the varied lengths in the following sentences from "Lob's Girl." You can add variety to your sentences by using techniques like these.

Alternate shorter sentences and longer sentences:

A week passed. Then, one evening, Mrs. Pengelly and the younger children were in the front room playing snakes and ladders.

Combine short sentences into long ones:

Lob's owner scolded him. He thanked Mrs. Pengelly for bringing him back.

Lob's owner scolded him and thanked Mrs. Pengelly for bringing him back.

Start with an adjective or adverb:

Horrified, Aunt Rebecca put on a coat and went down to her brother's house.

Start with an adverb phrase:

Without a word, Granny Pearce rose and stumped upstairs.

Start with a subordinate clause:

Just as she reached the main entrance, the guard was gently but forcibly shoving out a large, agitated, soaking-wet Alsatian dog.

EXERCISES

1. Look over something you have written. Revise it to increase the variety of your sentence patterns. Use the techniques shown above.
2. Write a paragraph describing a scene from your favorite animal story, television show, or movie. Vary your sentence patterns, using the techniques shown above.

Writing Skills

Objective

- To recognize and use sentence variety in writing

Teaching Strategies

Remind students that it is acceptable to use short sentences, but that it is important not to use *only* short sentences. You may wish to have students practice their sentence-combining skills with the following sentences: *The man was tired. The man swung hard. The man swung fast. The man had a rope. The man reached the summit.*

Exercises

1. Students should be able to identify which of the techniques they used to vary sentence patterns.
2. Some students may be able to write paragraphs with varied sentence patterns in a first draft. Others may wish to rewrite their paragraphs focusing specifically on this task after a first draft has been written.

Additional Resources

- ***Writer's Choice,*** Lesson 2.8

Teaching Support

Grammar and Language Minilesson

Identifying Lively Sentence Patterns Writers use a mix of simple, compound, and complex sentences when they write, just as we do when we speak.

Activity Have students work in small groups. Ask each group to find and read aloud a paragraph or poem that demonstrates lively sentence patterning, tell why they chose it, and explain how sentence variety affects its impact. **L2**

Additional Resources

- ***Grammar and Language Transparency 54***
- ***Grammar and Language Workbook,*** pp. 323–324
- ***Grammar and Composition Handbook,*** Lesson 1.6
- ***Writer's Choice,*** Lesson 2.8

Before Reading

Objectives

- To read and analyze a short story about a computer
- To recognize and understand the purpose of irony
- To write a paragraph about a computer as a main character

Skills

Reading/Thinking: Inferring; Drawing Conclusions; Synthesizing; Comparing and Contrasting
Writing: Vision of the Future
Vocabulary: Etymology
Grammar/Language: Compound Predicates
Life Skills: User's Manual
Collaboration: Literature Groups

Motivating STUDENTS

Literature Launchers: "The Many Worlds of Isaac Asimov"

Videodisc Side B, Segment 19

Also available in VHS.

Selection Focus Transparency 56: Have students discuss whether scientists of the future will be able to alter people's personalities.

Reading Focus: As an extension of the Reading Focus, have students work in small groups to discuss whether computers could become as smart as people one day.

Before You Read

Key Item

MEET ISAAC ASIMOV

Isaac Asimov (ī′ zək a′ zi môf) described his talent for explaining scientific principles as the ability to "read a dozen dull books and make one interesting book out of them." Asimov wrote or edited more than 500 books in his lifetime—far more than millions of Americans will read in a lifetime. Born in Russia, Asimov was raised in Brooklyn, New York. In addition to writing, he worked as a biochemist and taught biochemistry at Boston University.

Isaac Asimov was born in 1920 and died in 1992. "Key Item" was first published in 1968.

READING FOCUS

Are computers becoming more and more human-like?

Graph It!

Ask ten people whether computers will ever be as smart as humans, and if so, how soon. Compile your results in a graph and share it with the class.

Setting a Purpose

Read this story to find out what the "key item" is.

BUILDING BACKGROUND

The modern digital computer was first imagined by British mathematician Alan Turing in 1936. It looked like an automatic typewriter with math symbols instead of letters. Today, computers can turn appliances on and off, direct satellites, and create three-dimensional models of machines that do not exist. Chess-playing supercomputers can compute more than 100 million chess positions per second and have won games against world chess champions.

VOCABULARY PREVIEW

therapy (ther′ ə pē) *n.* treatment of an injury, disease, or mental disorder; p. 676
efficient (i fish′ ənt) *adj.* producing a desired effect with a minimum of effort or waste; p. 677
sufficient (sə fish′ ənt) *adj.* adequate; enough; p. 677
accede (ək sēd′) *v.* to give in; go along with; p. 677
collective (kə lek′ tiv) *adj.* having to do with a group of persons or things; common; shared; p. 677

674 THEME 7

RESOURCE MANAGER

Teaching Tools and Resources
- Theme Seven Planning Guide
- Literature Groups Sourcebook

Essential Lesson Support

Lesson-Specific Instruction
- Selection Focus Transparency 56
- Literary Elements Transparency 56
- Active Reading Guide,* p. 56
- Selection Vocabulary Practice, p. 38
- inTIME *inTIME* magazine, p. 18–20

Assessment
- Selection Quick Checks,* p. 56
- Sel. and Theme Assmt., pp. 97–98
- Testmaker: ExamView Pro
- Performance Assessment, p. 53

Systematic Language Instruction
- Gr. & Comp. Hdbk., L. 11.9
- Vocabulary Power, Lesson 29
- Spelling Power, Lesson 25

English Language Learners
- ELL Sourcebook, p. 85
- Spanish Summaries, p. 56
- Audio Library*
- English, Yes!

Spec. Needs/Strat. Interven.
- Interactive Rdg. Sbk., pp. T199–T202
- Interactive Rdg. Wkbk., pp. 111–112
- Inclusion Strat. Sbk., pp. 93–94
- Audio Library*

*Also available in Spanish

KEY ITEM

Isaac Asimov

Jack Weaver came out of the vitals[1] of Multivac looking utterly worn and disgusted.

From the stool, where the other maintained his own stolid[2] watch, Todd Nemerson said, "Nothing?"

"Nothing," said Weaver. "Nothing, nothing, nothing. No one can find anything wrong with it."

"Except that it won't work, you mean."

"You're no help sitting there!"

"I'm thinking."

"Thinking!" Weaver showed a canine[3] at one side of his mouth.

Nemerson stirred impatiently on his stool. "Why not? There are six teams of computer technologists roaming around in the corridors of Multivac. They haven't come up with anything in three days. Can't you spare one person to think?"

"It's not a matter of thinking. We've got to look. Somewhere a relay is stuck."

"It's not that simple, Jack!"

"Who says it's simple. You know how many million relays we have there?"

1. *Vitals* are parts that are necessary to keep a body alive or a machine operating. Here, the word refers to small chambers containing such parts inside Multivac.
2. A *stolid* (stol′ id) person is behaving unemotionally, without excitement.
3. Weaver shows his disgust by curling his upper lip, revealing a tooth. The two pointed teeth on each side of the top front teeth are called *canine* (kā′ nīn) teeth.

Reading the Selection

SUMMARY

The world's economy depends on Multivac, a huge computer. One day, it refuses to answer a question. Computer scientists spend three days looking for the problem without success. Todd Nemerson thinks Multivac is almost human and that to solve the problem, they must figure out why a human wouldn't answer the question.

Spanish Summaries, p. 56

A Active Reading Strategies

PREDICT Invite students to look at the title and have volunteers read the first page aloud. Ask students to describe the problem and use what they already know about computers to predict how the problem may be solved. Suggest that they revisit their predictions as they read to verify or revise them.

VOCABULARY If you haven't previewed the selection vocabulary with students, stop and remind them to use context clues to unlock the meanings of new vocabulary words.

Additional Resources

- ***Active Reading Guide,*** p. 56
- ***Audio Library***
- ***Spanish Audio Library***

Teaching Support

CONNECTING TO OTHER SELECTIONS

The chart at the right shows three ways to connect "Key Item" to other selections in this book.

For specific teaching strategies, see the ***Theme Seven Planning Guide.***

Connection		Title
Life Skills: Problem Solving	→	"The Million-Pound Bank Note," p. 573
Thematic: Surprises	→	"Beware of the Dog," p. 603
Literary: Science Fiction	→	"All Summer in a Day," p. 461

B Active Reading Strategies

EVALUATE If Nemerson had finished this sentence, he might have said *"...Multivac becomes human?"* You may wish to use the following model.

Model: I know Multivac is just a machine. It doesn't have nerves and other biological features that contribute to human emotions. On the other hand, Multivac has become as complex as a human brain, so perhaps it can have some complex human feelings, too.

C Critical Thinking

INFERRING Have students explain why the world's economy depends on knowing the price of wheat next summer. *(Nations can plan better. For example, if the price will be high, governments that need wheat can raise the cash needed. If the price will be low, governments can spend their money on other things.)*

D Active Reading Strategies

EVALUATE Encourage students to explain what the key item is. *(The key item is whatever is causing the computer to fail—whatever is preventing it from functioning the way people want it to.)*

"That doesn't matter. If it were just a relay, Multivac would have alternate circuits, devices for locating the flaw, and facilities to repair or replace the ailing part. The trouble is, Multivac won't only not answer the original question, it won't tell us what's wrong with it. —And meanwhile, there'll be panic in every city if we don't do something. The world's economy depends on Multivac, and everyone knows that."

"I know it, too. But what's there to do?"

"I told you, *think*. There must be something we're missing completely. Look, Jack, there isn't a computer bigwig in a hundred years who hasn't devoted himself to making Multivac more complicated. It can do so much now—hell, it can even talk and listen. It's practically as complex as the human brain. We can't understand the human brain, so why should we understand Multivac?"

"Aw, come on. Next you'll be saying Multivac is human."

"Why not?" Nemerson grew absorbed and seemed to sink into himself. "Now that you mention it, why not? Could we tell if Multivac passed the thin dividing line where it stopped being a machine and started being human? *Is* there a dividing line, for that matter? If the brain is just more complex than Multivac, and we keep making Multivac more complex, isn't there a point where . . ." He mumbled down into silence.

Weaver said impatiently, "What are you driving at? Suppose Multivac were human. How would that help us find out why it isn't working?"

"For a human reason, maybe. Suppose *you* were asked the most probable price of wheat next summer and didn't answer. Why wouldn't you answer?"

"Because I wouldn't know. But Multivac would know! We've given it all the factors. It can analyze futures in weather, politics, and economics. We know it can. It's done it before."

"All right. Suppose I asked the question and you knew the answer but didn't tell me. Why not?"

Weaver snarled, "Because I had a brain tumor. Because I had been knocked out. Doggone it, because my machinery was out of order. That's just what we're trying to find out about Multivac. We're looking for the place where its machinery is out of order, for the key item."

"Only you haven't found it." Nemerson got off his stool. "Listen, ask me the question Multivac stalled on."

"How? Shall I run the tape through you?"

"Come on, Jack. Give me the talk that goes along with it. You do talk to Multivac, don't you?"

"I've got to. Therapy."

Nemerson nodded. "Yes, that's the story. Therapy. That's the official story. We talk to it in order to pretend it's a human being so that we don't get neurotic[4] over having a machine know so much more than we do. We turn a frightening metal monster into a protective father image."

"If you want to put it that way."

"Well, it's wrong and you know it. A computer as complex as Multivac *must* talk

4. *Neurotic* (noo rot′ ik) having symptoms of an emotional disorder.

Vocabulary
therapy (ther′ ə pē) *n.* treatment of an injury, disease, or mental disorder

Teaching Support

MEETING INDIVIDUAL NEEDS — ENGLISH LANGUAGE LEARNERS

Computer Terminology This story provides an opportunity for English language learners to become familiar with words related to computers.

Activity Encourage small groups of students to complete sketches of the inside of the Multivac computer and the control wall with its dials and lights. Then have students reread the selection to find words with which to label their drawings. *(relay, program, tape with coded dots, control wall, dials, lights, valves)* Encourage students to add computer terms they already know. They can refer to their drawings as they complete the Responding to Literature pages.

Additional Resources

English Language Learners Sourcebook, p. 85

and listen to be efficient. Just putting in and taking out coded dots isn't sufficient. At a certain level of complexity, Multivac must be made to seem human because, by God, it *is* human. Come on, Jack, ask me the question. I want to see my reaction to it."

Jack Weaver flushed. "This is silly."

"Come on, will you?"

It was a measure of Weaver's depression and desperation that he acceded. Half sullenly, he pretended to be feeding the program into Multivac, speaking as he did so in his usual manner. He commented on the latest information concerning farm unrest, talked about the new equations describing jet-stream contortions, lectured on the solar constant.

He began stiffly enough, but warmed to this task out of long habit, and when the last of the program was slammed home, he almost closed contact with a physical snap at Todd Nemerson's waist.

He ended briskly, "All right, now. Work that out and give us the answer pronto."

For a moment, having done, Jack Weaver stood there, nostrils flaring, as though he was feeling once more the excitement of throwing into action the most gigantic and glorious machine ever put together by the mind and hands of humans.

Then he remembered and muttered, "All right. That's it."

E Nemerson said, "At least I know now why *I* wouldn't answer, so let's try that on Multivac. Look, clear Multivac; make sure the investigators have their paws off it. Then run the program into it and let me do the talking. Just once."

Weaver shrugged and turned to Multivac's control wall, filled with its somber, unwinking dials and lights. Slowly he cleared it. One by one he ordered the teams away.

Then, with a deep breath, he began once more feeding the program into Multivac. It was the twelfth time all told, the dozenth time. Somewhere a distant news commentator would spread the word that they were trying again. All over the world a Multivac-dependent people would be holding its collective breath.

Nemerson talked as Weaver fed the data silently. He talked diffidently,[5] trying to remember what it was that Weaver had said, but waiting for the moment when the key item might be added.

F Weaver was done and now a note of tension was in Nemerson's voice. He said, "All right, now, Multivac. Work that out and give us the answer." He paused and added the key item. He said, "*Please!*"

G And all over Multivac, the valves and relays went joyously to work. After all, a machine has feelings—when it isn't a machine anymore.

5. *Diffidently* means "in a way that shows a lack of confidence; shyly."

Vocabulary

efficient (i fish′ ənt) *adj.* producing a desired effect with a minimum of effort or waste
sufficient (sə fish′ ənt) *adj.* adequate; enough
accede (ək sēd′) *v.* to give in; go along with
collective (kə lek′ tiv) *adj.* having to do with a group of persons or things; common; shared

FYI

Jet stream is a high-speed air current, usually found between seven and nine miles above the Earth's surface, that moves generally west to east at speeds reaching over 200 miles per hour. **Solar constant** is the amount of radiation coming from the sun, measured at the outside of the atmosphere.

E Active Reading Strategies

PREDICT Encourage students to explain why they think Nemerson would not answer the question if he were asked to do so. *(He thinks Weaver is not asking politely.)*

F Critical Thinking

DRAWING CONCLUSIONS Have students explain what the key item is. *(The word please is the key item.)* Why do students think it is needed now and never before? *(The computer thinks more like a human and expects common courtesy.)*

G Literary Elements

IRONY Have students explain why the ending to this story is ironic. *(Six teams of computer technologists spent three days looking for a way to fix the computer, when all that was needed was one little word: please.)*

Reading Minilesson

Comparing and Contrasting Explain that the name Multivac suggests that the computer, like other early computers, uses vacuum tubes instead of chips. So many vacuum tubes were needed in early computers that they filled entire rooms.

Activity Have students work in small groups to list other ways Multivac is similar to and different from computers today. Then have them create a Venn diagram that compares Multivac to a modern computer. **L2**

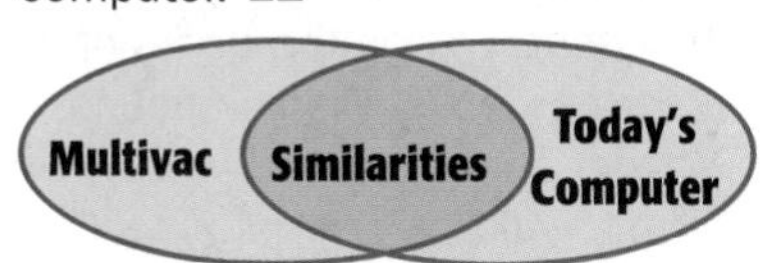

Additional Resources

Reading Skills Practice Workbook

VIEWING THE CARTOON

Dan Piraro, born in Oklahoma and raised in Texas, is a nationally syndicated cartoonist whose work appears in newspapers and in several books of cartoons. His humor is based on improbable combinations of the real and the unreal.

Viewing Response *Similar: The computer has humanlike feelings. It talks. Different: The computer is small. It doesn't have a control wall or dials.*

H Active Reading Strategies

RESPOND Have students discuss whether they think computers will ever have human emotions.

I Critical Thinking

SYNTHESIZING Have students explain the humor in this cartoon. *(The cartoon uses a play on words. "The computer is down" usually means that the computer is broken. But* down *also means "sad.")*

Thematic Focus

A Different Dimension Have students explain how this story relates to the theme. *(The story is about a computer that crosses the line dividing computers and humans.)*

ASSESSMENT

Quick Checks, p. 56

Bizzaro

I don't feel very good about myself right now. I don't know what it is, I just feel sort of..... oh, I don't know. Could I just be alone for a little while?
THE COMPUTER IS DOWN AGAIN.
PIRARO.
Dan Piraro/Universal Press Syndicate.

Viewing the cartoon: In what ways is the theme of this cartoon similar to and different from Asimov's story?

Teaching Support

Grammar and Language Minilesson

Compound Predicates A compound predicate has two or more simple predicates, or verbs, that have the same subject. Write this sentence on the board and ask a volunteer to identify the compound predicate: *Weaver shrugged and turned to Multivac's control wall.*

Activity Have students work independently to write five sentences with compound predicates about this story. **L2**

Additional Resources

- ***Grammar and Language Transparency 55***
- ***Grammar and Language Workbook,*** pp. 53–54
- ***Grammar and Composition Handbook,*** Lesson 1.5
- ***Writer's Choice,*** Lesson 8.5

Responding to Literature

PERSONAL RESPONSE

- Did the story end the way you expected it would? Why or why not?

Analyzing Literature

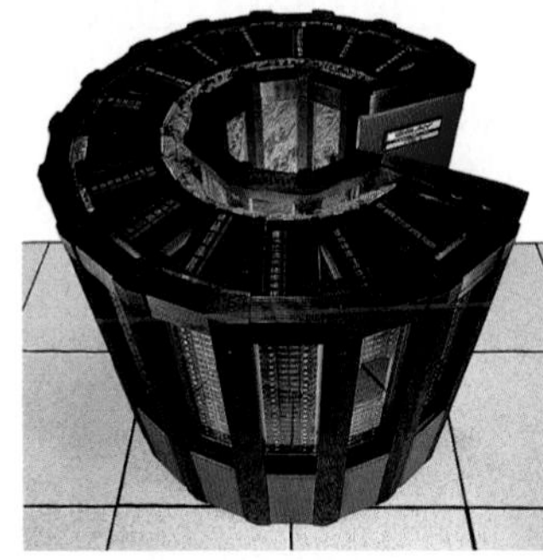

RECALL

1. What is Multivac and what does it do?
2. Why is the breakdown causing panic in every city?
3. What does Nemerson ask Weaver to do to help solve the problem of finding the key item?
4. What does the key item turn out to be?

Brackets connect questions that are paired to develop higher-level thinking skills.

INTERPRET

5. Why does Nemerson think Multivac could be human?
6. How is the future world of this story different from our world?
7. How does Weaver's attitude toward Multivac differ from Nemerson's?
8. In your opinion, how did Nemerson figure out what the key item was?

EVALUATE AND CONNECT

9. Theme Connection Some of the technologies in Asimov's stories have been invented or were discovered years after he wrote about them. In your opinion, could the events in "Key Item" ever really happen? Explain why or why not.
10. How would your life be affected if you lived in a world where computers were nearly human?

LITERARY ELEMENTS

Irony

Irony is the difference between the way things seem to be and the way they actually are. Irony can also contrast what is expected with what actually happens. Authors use irony to create humor or strong emotion. Surprise endings often involve irony. In "Key Item," for example, the answer to why the computer isn't responding is ironic.

1. Why is the title of this story an example of irony? Explain fully.
2. Think about some of the other selections you have read in this book. Explain how irony is used in one of them.

- See **Literary Terms Handbook,** p. R6.

Responding to the Selection

PERSONAL RESPONSE

Students should use examples from the story to fully explain their ideas.

Analyzing Literature

1. Multivac is a huge computer that the world depends on for important information.
2. Every city in the world depends on Multivac's calculations.
3. Nemerson wants Weaver to ask him the question that Multivac stalled on.
4. The key item turns out to be the word *please.*
5. Nemerson thinks Multivac could be human because scientists have been making it more and more complex, just like a human brain.
6. The world in the story is different because our entire world does not rely on one huge computer.
7. Weaver thinks of Multivac as an inanimate tool. Nemerson thinks Multivac may have human emotions.
8. Nemerson realizes that he doesn't like the way Weaver talked to him.
9. Sample: The events in "Key Item" could not happen because humans are smarter than computers. Or: The events could happen. It is only a matter of time before scientists build computers that have humanlike emotions.
10. Computers would be doing more complex tasks in every area of human endeavor.

LITERARY ELEMENTS

1. The "key item" seems to be some complicated technical fix. Instead, it's the word *please*.
2. Examples should show a difference between the way things seem to be and the way they actually are.

Additional Resources

 ***Literary Elements Transparency 56***

Extending Your Response

Writing About Literature

Students' paragraphs should

- describe important qualities of main characters
- explain why Multivac has the qualities of a main character
- include examples from the story to show Multivac's qualities

Personal Writing

Students' visions should

- incorporate results they graphed based on the question in the Reading Focus
- describe a world of the future
- show the future world as exciting, frightening, or something else

Learning for Life If possible, have available for students' use several examples of various kinds of user manuals and instruction sheets. Some students may be ready for the challenge of writing a set of instructions of their own (e.g., how to set the timer on a VCR).

Literature Groups Students might extend this activity by using the dictionary to find definitions for the terms.

Skill Minilesson

VOCABULARY • ETYMOLOGY

Encourage students to use the glossary in this textbook to check their answers.

1. umbrella 2. give up land
3. one that is operated by a group

Additional Resources

Vocabulary Practice, p. 38

Extending Your Response

Writing About Literature

Main Characters Although Jack Weaver and Todd Nemerson are the first two characters readers meet in "Key Item," there is also a third character in the story. Write a paragraph explaining why Multivac should be viewed as an important character.

Learning for Life

User's Manual Get a copy of the user's manual or instruction sheet for using a simple mechanical device–for example, a stapler, a can opener, a mechanical pencil or pencil sharpener. Read it carefully. Then explain the use of the device to a partner and see if he or she understands your instructions.

Literature Groups

The Science in Science Fiction All science-fiction stories are based on scientific information. Make a list of scientific facts or jargon that Asimov includes in "Key Item." Share your list with other groups.

Personal Writing

Life in a Technological Future Some people are excited to imagine a life in which humans depend on smarter and smarter machines. Others are fearful about what a super-technological world might be like. Drawing upon the results of your question in the **Reading Focus** on page 674, create a vision of how you believe people may use computers many years from now. Write a description of your vision.

Reading Further

Try these other robot stories by Isaac Asimov:

I, Robot

Robot Dreams

If you like science fiction, try one or all of these three connected novels by John Christopher: *The White Mountains*, *The City of Gold and Lead*, and *The Pool of Fire*

Save your work for your portfolio.

Skill Minilesson

Reteach · Review

VOCABULARY • ETYMOLOGY

The etymology, or history, of the word *collective* shows that it comes from the Latin *com,* meaning "together," and *legere,* "to gather." To gather things together is to *collect* them.

When Weaver *acceded* to Nemerson, he gave in. *Accede* comes from the Latin *ad,* meaning "to," and *cedere,* "to yield," which combine to mean "to yield to."

The dials and lights of the unworking Multivac are described as *somber,* which comes from the Latin *sub,* meaning "under," and *umbra,* "shade."

PRACTICE Use the information about etymologies to answer the questions.

1. What word comes from the Latin *umbra* and names something that can block the sun or the rain?
2. When a nation *cedes* land, does that nation buy land, give up land, or use land wisely?
3. Is a *collective* farm one that is successful, one that is operated by a group, or one that specializes in multiple crops?

ASSESSMENT

- ***Quick Checks,*** p. 56
- ***Selection and Theme Assessment,*** pp. 97–98
- ***Performance Assessment,*** p. 53
- ***Testmaker: ExamView Pro***
- ***Interactive Tutor: Self-Assessment***

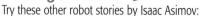

interNET CONNECTION

Etymology of English Phrases English Language Learners may enjoy exploring the *Web of On-line Dictionaries*, especially the section on the etymology of 6,000 English phrases, such as "batteries not included" and "the third degree." Students may search for a particular phrase or browse a list of phrases and read about their meanings and origins.

Interdisciplinary Connection

Communicating on the Net

Netiquette

"Netiquette" is a set of rules for behavior on the Internet. Many of these rules are not much different from the rules of etiquette for any other behavior. Put simply, you should behave toward others on the Net as you'd like them to behave toward you.

Other rules are unique to the Net. For example, DON'T SHOUT! Using all capital letters is considered shouting. It's also considered impolite and the sign of a "newbie," or newcomer. To emphasize a word or phrase, put *asterisks* before and after it.

Speaking of newbies, if you visit a new newsgroup or chat room, don't start out by asking too many questions. First read the FAQs (pronounced "faks"). FAQs stands for Frequently Asked Questions, and you'll nearly always find a set of them (with answers) at a newsgroup or chat site.

Acronyms

FAQ is an **acronym**. An acronym uses initials to stand for a phrase. Here are some examples often used on the Net.

ASAP	as soon as possible
B4N	[good]bye for now
BRB	be right back
BTW	by the way
CUL	see you later
F2F	face to face
IMHO	in my humble opinion
KWIM	know what I mean?
TIA	thanks in advance

Smileys and Emoticons

In face-to-face communication, you can read people's expressions or body language to tell if they are happy, sad, or joking. But how do you know whether people are joking or serious online? Two popular tools that help relay such information on the computer screen are *smileys* and *emoticons.*

Smileys

:-)	= happy
:-(	= sad
:'-(	= crying
'-)	= a wink
:-x	= my lips are sealed

Smileys are images made with the characters found on a keyboard. Viewed sideways, they make pictures. Examples: a happy face :) a happy face with a nose :-)

Emoticons (a word made by putting together *emotion* and *icons*) tell your online penpal how you feel. For instance, instead of writing *I'm sad that I have to miss art class on Thursday,* you could write: *I have to miss art class on Thursday* <*sad*>. You create emoticons by putting < > symbols around a word that tells a reader what you're doing or feeling. Here are a few more examples:

<blush> <angry> <giggle> <wink> <silly grin>

ACTIVITIES

1. Make up at least two emoticons and two acronyms. Use your made-up emoticons and acronyms, and some from the lists on this page, to compose an e-mail to a real or an imaginary friend.
2. Explain to a younger person how to make and use emoticons.

Interdisciplinary Connection

Objective

- To understand and apply strategies for communicating on the Net

Teaching Strategies

Work with students to list some differences between Netiquette and face-to-face (F2F) etiquette. Discuss the advantages and disadvantages of communicating with a friend using e-mail. In addition to the activities on the student page, ask students to create a "smiley" or facial expression using keyboard icons and punctuation marks. You may wish to draw the icons on the board if students do not have access to computers in the classroom.

Activities

1. Students might create emotions such as <confused> or <shrug>. Sample acronyms could include such items as BBI (better believe it) or PR (please respond). An e-mail message based on the activity might read *Maria: I'm not sure I want to go to the party. <confused> Do you know who* <u>*will*</u> *be going? PR, okay?*
2. Students should use the knowledge they acquired in this Interdisciplinary Connection to teach a younger person to make and use emoticons.

Teaching Support

MEETING INDIVIDUAL NEEDS: MULTIPLE MODES OF EXPRESSION

Linguistic Students who think linguistically will find that the focus on words, wordplay, and creative use of language in computer communication offers them new opportunities for self-expression.

Activity Have students work in pairs to describe memorable experiences they have had. Encourage students to prepare e-mails about their experiences. Their e-mails should include as many emotions, invented words, acronyms, and expressions as possible. Have students exchange e-mails with their partners. **L2**

B Active Reading Strategies

EVALUATE Have students explain what Keevan's goal is and how that goal is achieved. *(Keevan wants to become a dragonrider. When the dragons hatch, each chooses a boy to be its lifetime companion, or dragonrider.)*

C Literary Elements

FANTASY Have students explain what elements of this story indicate that it is a fantasy. Encourage students to explain what in the story could exist in real life. *(In real life dragons, dragon eggs, and dragonriders falling from the skies do not exist, but conflict between a small boy and larger boys who tease him could happen.)*

D Active Reading Strategies

RESPOND Have students explain Keevan's disadvantages and advantages in being chosen as a dragonrider. *(Keevan is smaller, younger, and weaker than the other candidates. But Keevan works twice as hard as they do and can run faster, too.)*

E Active Reading Strategies

QUESTION Invite students to think about what qualities might be important to a dragon. *(Some qualities include loyalty, courage, intelligence, and patience.)*

Dragonriders, even if they were still only hopeful candidates for the glowing eggs which were hardening on the hot sands of the Hatching Ground cavern, were expected to be punctual and prepared. Sloth was not tolerated by the weyrleader of Benden Weyr. A good record was especially important now. It was very near hatching time, when the baby dragons would crack their mottled shells and stagger forth to choose their lifetime companions. The very thought of that glorious moment made Keevan's breath catch in his throat. To be chosen—to be a dragonrider! To sit astride the neck of the winged beast with the jeweled eyes: to be his friend in telepathic communion[1] with him for life; to be his companion in good times and fighting extremes; to fly effortlessly over the lands of Pern! Or, thrillingly, *between* to any point anywhere on the world! Flying *between* was done on dragonback or not at all, and it was dangerous.

Keevan glanced upward, past the black mouths of the weyr caves in which grown dragons and their chosen riders lived, toward the Star Stones that crowned the ridge of the old volcano that was Benden Weyr. On the height, the blue watch dragon, his rider mounted on his neck, stretched the great transparent pinions[2] that carried him on the winds of Pern to fight the evil Thread that fell at certain times from the sky. The many-faceted rainbow jewels of his eyes glistened momentarily in the greeny sun. He folded his great wings to his back, and the watchpair resumed their statuesque pose of alertness.

Then the enticing view was obscured as Keevan passed into the Hatching Ground cavern. The sands underfoot were hot, even through heavy wher-hide boots. How the bootmaker had protested having to sew so small! Keevan was forced to wonder again why being small was reprehensible.[3] People were always calling him "babe" and shooing him away as being "too small" or "too young" for this or that. Keevan was constantly working, twice as hard as any other boy his age, to prove himself capable. What if his muscles weren't as big as Beterli's? They were just as hard. And if he couldn't overpower anyone in a wrestling match, he could outdistance everyone in a footrace.

"Maybe if you run fast enough," Beterli had jeered on the occasion when Keevan had been goaded[4] to boast of his swiftness, "you could catch a dragon. That's the only way you'll make a dragonrider!"

"You just wait and see, Beterli, you just wait," Keevan had replied. He would have liked to wipe the contemptuous[5] smile from Beterli's face, but the guy didn't fight fair even when the wingsecond was watching. "No one knows what Impresses a dragon!"

"They've got to be able to *find* you first, babe!"

1. In *telepathic communion,* thoughts are shared directly between two minds.
2. A bird's *pinions* are its wings or wing feathers.
3. Something that's *reprehensible* is deserving of sharp criticism.
4. To *goad* means "to pressure someone to do something; urge on."
5. *Contemptuous* means "proud and scornful."

Vocabulary

enticing (en tīs′ ing) *adj.* offering pleasure or reward
jeer (jēr) *v.* to make fun of (someone or something) rudely and openly

Teaching Support

Meeting Individual Needs: ENGLISH LANGUAGE LEARNERS

Dragon Stories Dragons are found in stories from many cultures around the world. In some stories, dragons breathe fire and are evil. In others, dragons are friendly and good. Invite English language learners to think of stories they know from their cultures about dragons or other fantastic creatures.

Activity Ask small groups of students to work together to share and discuss dragon stories. Have each group work together to create a comic strip that tells a story about one dragon. Have students display their dragon comics for the rest of the class to read.

Additional Resources

English Language Learners Sourcebook, p. 86

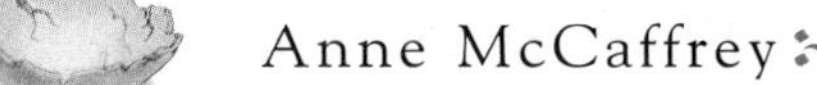

F Yes, being the smallest candidate was not an enviable position. It was therefore imperative[6] that Keevan Impress a dragon in his first hatching. That would wipe the smile off every face in the cavern, and accord him the respect due any dragonrider, even the smallest one.

Besides, no one knew exactly what Impressed the baby dragons as they struggled from their shells in search of their lifetime partners.

G "I like to believe that dragons see into a man's heart," Keevan's foster mother, Mende, told him. "If they find goodness, honesty, a flexible mind, patience, courage—and you've that in quantity, dear Keevan—that's what dragons look for. I've seen many a well-grown lad left standing on the sands, Hatching Day, in favor of someone not so strong or tall or handsome. And if my memory serves me" (which it usually did—Mende knew every word of every Harper's tale worth telling, although Keevan did not interrupt her to say so), "I don't believe that F'lar, our weyrleader, was all that tall when bronze Mnementh chose him. And Mnementh was the only bronze dragon of that hatching."

Dreams of Impressing a bronze were beyond Keevan's boldest reflections, although that goal dominated[7] the thoughts of every other hopeful candidate. Green dragons were small and fast and more numerous. There was more prestige[8] in Impressing a blue or a brown than a green. Being practical, Keevan seldom dreamed as high as a big fighting brown, like Canth, F'nor's fine fellow, the biggest brown on all Pern. But to fly a bronze? H Bronzes were almost as big as the queen, and only they took the air when a queen flew at mating time. A bronze rider could aspire to become weyrleader! Well, Keevan would console himself, brown riders could aspire to become wingseconds, and that wasn't bad. He'd even settle for a green dragon: they were small, but so was he. No matter! He simply had to Impress a dragon his first time in the Hatching Ground. Then no one in the weyr would taunt[9] him anymore for being so small.

"Shells," thought Keevan now, "but the sands are hot!"

"Impression time is imminent, candidates," the wingsecond was saying as everyone crowded respectfully close to him. "See the extent of the striations[10] on this promising egg." The stretch marks *were* larger than yesterday.

I Everyone leaned forward and nodded thoughtfully. That particular egg was the one Beterli had marked as his own, and no other candidate dared, on pain of being beaten by Beterli on the first opportunity, to approach it. The egg was marked by a large yellowish splotch in the shape of a dragon backwinging to land, talons outstretched to grasp rock. Everyone knew that bronze eggs bore distinctive markings. And naturally, Beterli, who'd been presented at eight Impressions already and

6. If something is *imperative,* it is absolutely necessary.
7. To *dominate* is to control.
8. Someone with *prestige* is admired and respected by others.
9. To *taunt* is to make fun of in a scornful, insulting way.
10. Something *imminent* is likely to happen soon. The *striations* are grooves or marks—as used here, they are probably cracks that appear as the eggs begin to hatch.

Vocabulary
enviable (en′ vē ə bəl) *adj.* good enough to be highly desired

F Active Reading Strategies

CONNECT Have students think about how they feel when others tease or belittle them. Then have students explain how Keevan probably feels and why being a dragonrider is important to him. *(Keevan probably feels unhappy and frustrated. He wants to be chosen a dragonrider so the other boys will treat him with respect.)*

G Critical Thinking

JUDGING THE CREDIBILITY OF A SOURCE Have students explain why Mende's ideas about what dragons look for may be more credible than the other boys' ideas. *(Mende has seen many hatchings and knows from experience that the strongest boys are not always picked. She knows dragons look for courage, goodness, honesty, and patience.)*

H Literary Elements

CHARACTER Using what they know about Keevan so far, invite students to describe his character. *(Keevan tries hard. According to Mende, he is courageous; he is humble and practical; and he wants the other boys to respect him.)*

I Active Reading Strategies

EVALUATE Have students explain whether Beterli's efforts to keep the other boys away from "his" egg will have an effect on who the hatchling chooses. *(If the hatchling doesn't like Beterli, it will not choose him even if he guards the egg.)*

Reading Minilesson

Using Graphic Aids Students might better understand the relationship between Keevan and Beterli if they create a chart to summarize and keep track of encounters between them.

Activity Have students answer these questions to help them begin the chart.

- Why does Beterli walk fast?
- What does Beterli say to Keevan about his swiftness?
- What does Beterli do in the Hatching Ground? L2

Keevan and Beterli's Relationship	
1. Why does Beterli walk fast?	Beterli walks fast so Keevan will have trouble keeping up.

Additional Resources

Reading Skills Practice Workbook

J Critical Thinking

DRAWING CONCLUSIONS Have students explain why Beterli treats Keevan poorly. *(Beterli is probably ashamed that he has been passed over eight times. It makes him feel tough to tease Keevan.)*

K Active Reading Strategies

PREDICT Have students predict whether they think Keevan and Beterli will be chosen by a dragon and why. *(Students may say that Keevan seems to have all of the qualities that a dragon looks for in a companion. Also, Beterli has been passed over before.)*

VIEWING THE PAINTING

Viewing Response *Yes, these dragons are intentionally frightening. They look mean and ready to fight. They are not like the dragons in the story, who are friendly to humans and presumably to each other.*

L Active Reading Strategies

RESPOND Ask students if they think Keevan's stroking of Beterli's egg will have an effect on the dragon inside. *(Some may think the dragon will establish a bond with Keevan and choose him.)*

was the biggest of the candidates, had chosen it.

"I'd say that the great opening day is almost upon us," the wingsecond went on, and then his face assumed a grave expression. "As we well know, there are only forty eggs and seventy-two candidates. Some of you may be disappointed on the great day. That doesn't necessarily mean you aren't dragonrider material, just that *the* dragon for you hasn't been shelled. You'll have other hatchings, and it's no disgrace to be left behind an Impression or two. Or more."

Keevan was positive that the wingsecond's eyes rested on Beterli, who'd been stood off at so many Impressions already. Keevan tried to squinch down so the wingsecond wouldn't notice him. Keevan had been reminded too often that he was eligible to be a candidate by one day only. He, of all the hopefuls, was most likely to be left standing on the great day. One more reason why he simply had to Impress at his first hatching.

"Now move about among the eggs," the wingsecond said. "Touch them. We don't know that it does any good, but it certainly doesn't do any harm."

Some of the boys laughed nervously, but everyone immediately began to circulate among the eggs. Beterli stepped up officiously to "his" egg, daring anyone to come near it. Keevan smiled, because he had already touched it . . . every inspection day . . . as the others were leaving the Hatching Ground, when no one could see him crouch and stroke it.

Keevan had an egg he concentrated on, too, one drawn slightly to the far side of the others. The shell bore a soft greenish blue tinge with a faint creamy swirl design. The consensus[11] was that this egg contained a mere green, so Keevan was rarely bothered by rivals. He was somewhat perturbed then to see Beterli wandering over to him.

"I don't know why you're allowed in this Impression, Keevan. There are enough of us without a babe," Beterli said, shaking his head.

"I'm of age." Keevan kept his voice level, telling himself not to be bothered by mere words.

"Yah!" Beterli made a show of standing on his

The Two Mythical Dragons. Sir Roy Calne, F. R. S. Private collection.

Viewing the painting: Are these mythical dragons intended to be frightening? Do they fit with your image of dragons in the story? Give reasons for your answer.

11. A *consensus* is an opinion shared by most members of a group.

Teaching Support

MEETING INDIVIDUAL NEEDS — SPECIAL NEEDS

Less-Proficient Readers Some students may find the language that the inhabitants of Pern speak confusing. They may need practice using context clues to understand words. Write the following sentence from the story on the board: *Any boy who is over twelve turns has the right to stand in the Hatching Ground.* *(years)*

Activity Have students use context clues to write a brief definition for each of these words: *wher, shelled, tuff,* and *babes.* **L2**

Additional Resources

Inclusion Strategies

toe tips. "You can't even see over an egg; Hatching Day, you better get in front or the dragons won't see you at all. 'Course, you could get run down that way in the mad scramble. Oh, I forget, you can run fast, can't you?"

"You'd better make sure a dragon sees *you,* this time, Beterli," Keevan replied. "You're almost overage, aren't you?"

Beterli flushed and took a step forward, hand half-raised. Keevan stood his ground, but if Beterli advanced one more step, he would call the wingsecond. No one fought on the Hatching Ground. Surely Beterli knew that much.

Fortunately, at that moment the wingsecond called the boys together and led them from the Hatching Ground to start on evening chores.

There were "glows" to be replenished in the main kitchen caverns and sleeping cubicles, the major hallways, and the queen's apartment. Firestone sacks had to be filled against Thread attack, and black rock brought to the kitchen hearths. The boys fell to their chores, tantalized[12] by the odors of roasting meat. The population of the weyr began to assemble for the evening meal, and the dragonriders came in from the Feeding Ground or their sweep checks.

It was the time of day Keevan liked best: once the chores were done, before dinner was served, a fellow could often get close to the dragonriders and listen to their talk. Tonight Keevan's father, K'last, was at the main dragonrider table. It puzzled Keevan how his father, a brown rider and a tall man, could *be* his father—because he, Keevan, was so small. It obviously never puzzled K'last when he deigned to notice his small son: "In a few more turns, you'll be as tall as I am—or taller!"

K'last was pouring Benden drink all around the table. The dragonriders were relaxing. There'd be no Thread attack for three more days, and they'd be in the mood to tell tall tales, better than Harper yarns, about impossible maneuvers they'd done a-dragonback. When Thread attack was closer, their talk would change to a discussion of tactics of evasion, of going *between,* how long to suspend there until the burning but fragile Thread would freeze and crack and fall harmlessly off dragon and man. They would dispute the exact moment to feed firestone to the dragon so he'd have the best flame ready to sear Thread midair and render[13] it harmless to ground—and man—below. There was such a lot to know and understand about being a dragonrider that sometimes Keevan was overwhelmed. How would he ever be able to remember everything he ought to know at the right moment? He couldn't dare ask such a question; this would only have given additional weight to the notion that he was too young yet to be a dragonrider.

"Having older candidates makes good sense," L'vel was saying, as Keevan settled down near the table. "Why waste four to five years of a dragon's fighting prime until his rider grows up enough to stand the rigors?" L'vel had Impressed a blue of Ramoth's

12. To *tantalize* is to tempt or tease someone with something that person cannot have.

13. *Sear* means "scorch or burn," and *render,* as used here, means "make."

Vocabulary
replenish (ri plen′ ish) *v.* to provide a new supply

M Active Reading Strategies

VISUALIZE Have students think about how this scene looks. *(Pern has caverns and underground tunnels. Coal-like rock is used for cooking fuel, and there are no cars, appliances, or radios.)*

N Active Reading Strategies

QUESTION Encourage your students to describe how family life on Pern is different from life on Earth. *(Children do not live with parents but with foster mothers. Keevan knows who his father is and admires him, but his father is not involved in his life.)*

O Literary Elements

FANTASY Encourage students to explain which of these events could occur only in a fantasy story. *(When the Thread attack is near, dragonriders talk about tactics for fighting Thread and getting the best fire from a dragon.)*

P Active Reading Strategies

REVIEW Have students restate L'vel's argument against young candidates in their own words. *(L'vel thinks it takes too long for a young candidate to grow up enough to fight Thread and that this wastes a dragon's prime fighting years.)*

MULTIPLE MODES OF EXPRESSION

Spatial Students with special spatial abilities might benefit from creating maps or models of Pern. Encourage these students to visualize the layout of Pern and decide on a form to represent this layout.

Activity Have interested students create maps or three-dimensional models of Pern that show the places mentioned in this story. Some students may want to create cut-away drawings to show underground caverns, the Hatching Ground, and aboveground sites. Others may want to create bird's eye maps of Pern. Display student maps and models in a prominent place, so other students can refer to them as they read this story. **L2**

Critical Thinking

DRAWING CONCLUSIONS Have students explain where the words in italic type are coming from and why. *(They are coming from the dragon. Early in the story, the author mentioned that dragons can communicate telepathically with their riders.)*

Active Reading Strategies

RESPOND Invite students to explain how Impressing a bronze dragon may change Keevan's life. *(Bronze dragons are the highest-ranking dragons. To ride a bronze dragon means that Keevan will be respected and admired by others. In addition, it means Keevan may one day become a leader of Pern.)*

Literary Elements

FANTASY Have students explain what makes this paragraph a fantasy. *(Not only is the paragraph about a dragon, it is about a dragon that communicates telepathically with people.)*

Thematic Focus

A Different Dimension Have students explain how this story relates to the theme. *(Dragons, dragonriders, and the other fantasy elements of this story are from another dimension.)*

Quick Checks, p. 57

the entrance after all. Oh, what have we there, in the shadows?"

Keevan heard with dismay the sound of voices nearing him. He tried to burrow into the sand. The mere thought of how he would be teased and taunted now was unbearable.

Don't worry! Please don't worry! The thought was urgent, but not his own.

Someone kicked sand over Keevan and butted roughly against him.

"Go away. Leave me alone!" he cried.

Why? was the injured-sounding question inserted into his mind. There was no voice, no tone, but the question was there, perfectly clear, in his head.

Incredulous, Keevan lifted his head and stared into the glowing jeweled eyes of a small bronze dragon. His wings were wet; the tips hung drooping to the sand. And he sagged in the middle on his unsteady legs, although he was making a great effort to keep erect.

Keevan dragged himself to his knees, oblivious to the pain of his leg. He wasn't even aware that he was ringed by the boys passed over, while thirty-one pairs of resentful eyes watched him Impress the dragon. The weyrleaders looked on, amused and surprised at the draconic[26] choice, which could not be forced. Could not be questioned. Could not be changed.

Why? asked the dragon again. *Don't you like me?* His eyes whirled with anxiety, and his tone was so piteous that Keevan staggered forward and threw his arms around the dragon's neck, stroking his eye ridges, patting the damp, soft hide, opening the fragile-looking wings to dry them, and assuring the hatchling wordlessly over and over again that he was the most perfect, most beautiful, most beloved dragon in the entire weyr, in all the weyrs of Pern.

"What's his name, K'van?" asked Lessa, smiling warmly at the new dragonrider. K'van stared up at her for a long moment. Lessa would know as soon as he did. Lessa was the only person who could "receive" from all dragons, not only her own Ramoth. Then he gave her a radiant smile, recognizing the traditional shortening of his name that raised him forever to the rank of dragonrider.

My name is Heath, thought the dragon mildly and hiccuped in sudden urgency: *I'm hungry.*

"Dragons are born hungry," said Lessa, laughing. "F'lar, give the boy a hand. He can barely manage his own legs, much less a dragon's."

K'van remembered his stick and drew himself up. "We'll be just fine, thank you."

"You may be the smallest dragonrider ever, young K'van, but you're the bravest," said F'lar.

And Heath agreed! Pride and joy so leaped in both chests that K'van wondered if his heart would burst right out of his body. He looped an arm around Heath's neck and the pair—the smallest dragonboy, and the hatchling who wouldn't choose anybody else—walked out of the Hatching Ground together forever.

26. Keevan either doesn't notice or doesn't pay attention to (is *oblivious* to) the pain. *Draconic* means "having to do with a dragon."

Teaching Support

Grammar and Language Minilesson

Infinitives An infinitive is a verb form (verbal) most commonly used as a noun in a sentence, but it is also used as an adjective or an adverb. Knowing how to use infinitives gives writers tools to vary their sentences and keep their readers interested.

Activity Have students work in pairs to identify the infinitive in each sentence below and tell how it is used.

1. Keevan didn't have the strength to fight Beterli. *(adjective)*
2. Keevan bent to hear the hatching sounds better. *(adverb)*
3. Heath was born hungry and wanted to eat. *(noun)*

Ask each student to write three story-related sentences using infinitives. **L3**

Additional Resources

Grammar and Language Transparency 56

Grammar and Language Workbook, pp. 175–178

Grammar and Composition Handbook, Lesson 9.3

Writer's Choice, Lesson 15.3

Responding to Literature

PERSONAL RESPONSE

- What was your reaction to this story? Record your responses in your journal. Describe your thoughts and feelings as you followed Keevan through his experience.

Analyzing Literature

RECALL

1. What is a dragonrider, and how does someone become one?
2. Why is Keevan teased by the other dragonboys?
3. What are the different colors of dragons? Which ones were the most desirable?
4. According to Keevan's foster mother, what do dragons look for in their lifetime partners?

Brackets connect questions that are paired to develop higher-level thinking skills.

INTERPRET

5. Why are the dragons and their riders so important to the people of Pern?
6. Why does Keevan's "breath catch in his throat" at the thought of the moment of hatching time? Explain.
7. Why does Keevan hope to ride a brown dragon?
8. In your opinion, why does Heath choose Keevan? Explain.

EVALUATE AND CONNECT

9. How would most people cope with the cruel teasing Keevan faced daily? How would you?
10. Theme Connection
    Would you like to live on Pern? Why or why not?

Paisaje con Volcano en Primer Plano. Dr. Atl (aka Gerard Murillo) (1875–1964). Atl colors on Masonite, 15¾ x 15¾ in. Galeria de Arte Misrachi, Mexico City.

LITERARY ELEMENTS

Fantasy

Anne McCaffrey's Pern stories combine science fiction (the setting on another planet in the future) with fantasy (fire-breathing dragons). Much like science fiction, **fantasy** explores unreal worlds or the real world with unreal elements, like dragons, ghosts, magic, or characters with superhuman qualities. As in much of the best science fiction, however, the emotions and conflicts of characters in a fantasy are often those of ordinary people. Readers can recognize themselves in the personal struggles and adventures of the characters.

1. Which elements in "The Smallest Dragonboy" are fantastic rather than realistic?
2. What is the realistic problem faced by Keevan?

● See **Literary Terms Handbook,** p. R4.

Responding to the Selection

PERSONAL RESPONSE

Students should describe the thoughts and feelings they had as they read about Keevan's experiences.

Analyzing Literature

1. A dragonrider is a person who rides a flying dragon to protect the people of Pern from dangerous Thread. A rider is chosen by a dragon when it hatches.
2. Keevan is teased because he is smaller than the other boys.
3. Dragons can be green, blue, brown, or bronze. It is good to Impress a blue or brown dragon, but bronze dragons are the most desirable.
4. Dragons look for boys who are good, honest, patient, courageous, and have flexible minds.
5. Dragons and their riders fly above Pern to destroy deadly Thread before it falls on the people of Pern.
6. Keevan very much wants to be chosen by a dragon. The thought of being picked is very emotional for him.
7. Brown dragons are respected, high-ranking dragons—not the highest, though. Riders of brown dragons could become wingseconds, which was respectable.
8. Heath chooses Keevan because he is brave, determined, and caring. Bravery and determination would be important in the dangerous job of fighting Thread.
9. Students may say that they'd ignore the teaser, try to avoid him, or do something nice for him in the hope that he would stop teasing.
10. Samples: Yes, because it seems an exciting life. No, because it seems like a primitive world without modern conveniences or equal rights for males and females.

LITERARY ELEMENTS

1. ***Fantastic elements:*** flying, fire-breathing dragons, dragonriders, and telepathic communication.
2. ***Realistic problem:*** Keevan is teased because he is smaller than the other boys.

Additional Resources

Literary Elements Transparency 57

Literature and Writing

Writing About Literature

Students' paragraphs should

- describe the setting of the story
- explain how the setting affects the story's events
- analyze why the setting is so important to the story

Creative Writing

Students' sequels should

- use what they already know about Pern, Keevan, and Heath
- have a beginning, a middle, and an end
- contain elements of fantasy

Extending Your Response

Literature Groups Before students meet, encourage them to review their notes about peer-pressure experiences. Have each group member describe one peer-pressure experience Keevan had and compare it to an experience a person in real life might have.

Performing Have each student prepare a script that describes what occurs. Students may want to interview Keevan or another eyewitness for their stories.

Interdisciplinary Activity

Invite students to try methods of drawing or mapping that they have never tried before, such as using chalk or creating a geologic map.

Literature and Writing

Writing About Literature

Setting What is the setting of "The Smallest Dragonboy"? Think about how the setting affects events in the plot. Then write a paragraph explaining why setting is so important to the story.

Creative Writing

A Sequel What might happen to Keevan and his dragon sometime in the future? Will they be called upon to defend Pern against the evil Thread? Write a summary of a sequel telling of a later adventure.

Extending Your Response

Literature Groups

Hopes and Dreams Think about Keevan's hopes and dreams. Think about his relationship with his family and his interactions with the other dragonboys. Review your notes from the **Reading Focus** on page 682. Then work together to create a chart comparing and contrasting Keevan's experiences with his peers with the experiences you and your classmates discussed.

Performing

Eyewitness News: Hatching Day! Imagine that you are a TV news reporter sent to cover this year's Hatching Day. What do you see? Whom do you interview? Write a TV news story based on the events in "The Smallest Dragonboy." Feel free to make up any details you wish. Perform your news story for your classmates in an oral presentation.

Interdisciplinary Activity

Art Imagine what the setting of "The Smallest Dragonboy" looks like. Make a list of the places mentioned in the story, and then draw a picture or map of the setting. Use the story details and descriptions to help you, but feel free to use your imagination to add new details.

Reading Further

If you would like to read more by Anne McCaffrey, try these:

The Dolphins of Pern

Dragonseye

Save your work for your portfolio.

Dragon's Handiwork. Gregory Blake Larson (b. 1961). Pencil and watercolor, 16 x 13 in. Private collection.

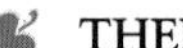

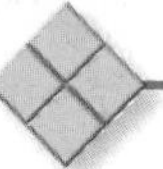

Skill Minilessons

Reteach · Review

GRAMMAR AND LANGUAGE • WRITING NUMBERS

In writing, you either spell out numbers, or you write them as numerals. Follow these rules.

- Spell out numbers you can write in one or two words.
  The city is **twenty-five** miles from here.
- Spell out any number that begins a sentence.
  One hundred and thirty-four children came to school in spite of the snowstorm.
- Use numerals for numbers of more than two words not at the beginning of a sentence.
  The city is **465** miles away.
- Write a very large number as a numeral followed by the word *million* or *billion.*
  The planet is **3 billion** miles away.
- If related numbers appear in the same sentence and one of them should be written as a numeral, use all numerals.
  She wrote **10** novels and more than **150** short stories.

PRACTICE Write a sentence of your own to demonstrate each one of the previous rules.

For more about similar usage problems, see **Language Handbook,** p. R43.

READING AND THINKING • CLASSIFYING

Skillful readers organize information by classifying things into categories. When you **classify,** you think about how things are alike and then put similar things into groups. In "The Smallest Dragonboy," for example, Keevan and the other boys could be classified as dragonboys.

PRACTICE Skim "The Smallest Dragonboy" and find two other groups of things that can be put into categories.

For more about organizing information, see **Reading Handbook,** pp. R88–R89.

VOCABULARY • SYNONYMS: SHADES OF MEANING

Synonyms differ in their meanings–sometimes in important ways. For example, you could be pleasant and gentle while you *urge* someone to do something, but not while you *goad* someone. A *goaded* person feels forced or driven to do something he or she most likely doesn't want to do.

PRACTICE Think about what the underlined word means in each sentence. Then choose the better synonym for that word *that makes sense in the sentence.*

1. The neighborhood bully ridiculed Billy when he came outside holding his sister's hand.
   a. teased b. mocked
2. The enticing sign said "Everything half price."
   a. inviting b. charming
3. As the phone interrupted her for the fifth time, Mrs. Frye groaned in exasperation.
   a. annoyance b. rage
4. After the tornado, their desolated town needed to be almost totally rebuilt.
   a. ruined b. gloomy

Skill Minilessons

GRAMMAR AND LANGUAGE
WRITING NUMBERS

Samples:

1. I live ten minutes from school.
2. Eight hundred and fifty-three students go to my school.
3. We drove 1132 miles on our vacation.
4. Approximately 7 million people live in New York City.
5. I have 6 quarters and 133 pennies.

READING AND THINKING
CLASSIFYING

Sample categories:

- Dragons: green, blue, brown, and bronze
- Dragonriders: green riders, blue riders, brown riders, and bronze riders

VOCABULARY
SYNONYMS: SHADES OF MEANING

1. b
2. a
3. a
4. a

Additional Resources

- ***Grammar and Language Workbook,*** pp. 279–280
- ***Grammar and Composition Handbook,*** Lesson 13.10
- ***Writer's Choice,*** Lesson 20.10
- ***Reading Skills Practice Workbook,*** pp. 101–102
- ***Vocabulary Practice,*** p. 39

ASSESSMENT

- ***Quick Checks,*** p. 57
- ***Selection and Theme Assessment,*** pp. 99–100
- ***Performance Assessment,*** p. 54
- ***Testmaker: ExamView Pro***
- ***Interactive Tutor: Self-Assessment***

Objective

- To understand the elements of legends, myths, and folklore

Teaching Strategies

Ask students to share stories they have heard that fit the descriptions in their books. Have them list legendary figures or mythical heroes they have heard about. Encourage students to explore their own cultural heritage for folkloric tales they could bring in and share with classmates.

Legends Have students talk about modern-day legends and describe what they consider "legendary behavior" to be. Encourage them to find pictures in magazines of people they think of as the living legends of their generation.

Myths Point out to students that the word *myth* has come to mean something that isn't true. People might say, "That's just a myth," meaning "That's just a falsehood."

Folklore Point out to students that *folklore* can be thought of as the collection of stories, songs, tales, and jokes that helps members of a culture stay connected to one another. Folkloric expression is a way of preserving the shared past of a people or nation.

Teaching Support

LEGENDS, MYTHS, AND FOLKLORE

Long before there was written language, there was folklore. One storyteller calls myths, legends, and folk stories "stories that aren't true on the outside, but are true on the inside." Some of these stories are humorous; some are serious, even tragic, and filled with the power of ancient cultures and the spoken word.

Most of these stories were passed down orally from one teller to the next over hundreds of years. They are still evolving today. They may change a little each time the speaker or writer adds his or her own touches. In this way, the oldest stories in the world stay new.

LEGENDS, which relate amazing events or accomplishments, are stories known throughout a cultural group. Their heroes may be humans, animals, or even plants, enchanted objects, or forces of nature. Some legendary human heroes actually lived, but over the years their reputations grew larger than life. In this theme, you'll read the Chinese legend "Cat and Rat" and learn about the Chinese calendar.

MYTHS are traditional stories about gods and goddesses or how things came to be. These stories usually reflect a culture's religious or other deeply held beliefs. In the myth "Icarus and Daedalus," two mortals try to fly like the god Apollo. They learn that, unlike their gods, humans have limits.

FOLKLORE is a general term covering folktales, proverbs, ritual speeches, folk songs, fables, and many other forms of literature handed down by word of mouth. "The Bunyans," a story about Paul Bunyan and his family, is an example of a type of folktale called the tall tale. Some scholars classify legends and myths as forms of folklore.

The Two Mythical Dragons (detail).

Some Common Types of Folklore

jokes	fables
riddles	fairy tales
proverbs	folktales
anecdotes	legends
animal tales	myths

Technology

Folklore Table

Students can use word processing software to create tables of folkloric elements as they read the stories in this unit. Have each student create a table like the one below.

Title	Type of Story	Cultural Origin	Hero(es)	Fantastic Elements	Main Event	Outcome

Activity For each myth, legend, or folktale, students can add a new row to the table and type in information about each of the six elements of that story. Students can use their completed tables as tools for study and review. **L2**

ACTIVE READING MODEL

Active Reading Strategies

Legends, myths, and folklore are part of the earliest and longest-lasting literature—the ancient stories that tell about the beliefs, histories, joys, and sorrows of people from every corner of the world. When reading legends, myths, and folktales, skillful readers use strategies that help them understand how the characters—human and imaginary—respond to their settings and situations.

- For more about reading strategies and reading across cultures, see **Reading Handbook,** pp. R73–R80.

PREVIEW

Before reading a legend, myth, or folktale, look at the title and the illustrations. Previewing helps you get an overall look at, or sense of, the text before you begin reading it.

VISUALIZE

As you read, use the author's descriptions to try to imagine the setting and characters.

CONNECT

Even a legend, myth, or folktale from another place or time can have great meaning to a modern reader. Connect the story to experiences in your own life.

QUESTION

As you read the story, ask yourself questions about the characters, the events, and the ideas.

PREDICT

Even while reading a story with magical events, you should try to predict what might happen next or how the tale might end.

APPLYING THE STRATEGIES

Read the following folktale, "Aunty Misery." Use the Active Reading Model notes in the margins as you read. Write your responses on a separate piece of paper or use stick-on notes.

Active Reading Strategies

Objective

- To understand and apply strategies for reading and comprehending myths, legends, and folklore

Teach the Strategies

Remind students that most myths, legends, and folktales come to us through the oral tradition. Readers, like listeners, remain actively engaged in these stories by practicing the following techniques.

Preview Ask students to approach the story as they would listen to a storyteller. What do they think the title means? Can they tell where the story comes from?

Visualize The supernatural world is often a natural part of myths, legends, and folk stories. Students may wish to visualize and draw pictures of the spirits they read about.

Connect Although the external settings and circumstances of many myths and legends may be unfamiliar to students, the internal truths they reveal are often universal. Encourage students to relate these truths to beliefs they have formed.

Question Point out to students that they may wish to practice questioning the capabilities of the characters within the "fantastic" context of the story rather than questioning the possibility of their existence.

Teaching Support

Reading Journal

Universal Notions

The author Judith Ortiz Cofer presents in "Aunty Misery" a Puerto Rican folktale about misery and death. Invite students to discuss how death is portrayed in this country. (Frequently as the grim reaper, a person dressed in black with a scythe.) Invite students to share any sayings they know about death. *(Sample: two things are certain in life: death and taxes.)*

Activity As they read, ask students to draw a flowchart in which they show the order of the story events. After reading, have students list the pros and cons of Aunty Misery's decision to keep Death stuck in the pear tree. **L2**

Before Reading

Objectives

- To read a fable about two things in life that everyone experiences
- To recognize the characteristics of a fable
- To write about the story elements found in a fable

Skills

Reading/Thinking: Comparing and Contrasting; Generalizing
Writing: Fable
Vocabulary: Analogies
Grammar/Language: Frequently Misspelled Words
Listening/Speaking: Group Presentation
Collaboration: Literature Groups

Motivating STUDENTS

Selection Focus Transparency 58: Have students discuss the quotation and list things in life that happen to everyone whether they are prepared or not *(such as birth, death, fortune, misfortune)*.

Reading Focus: As an extension of the Reading Focus, have students in small groups list two good things that happen in everyone's life.

ACTIVE READING MODEL

Before You Read

Aunty Misery

MEET JUDITH ORTIZ COFER

English was not Judith Ortiz Cofer's first language. Born in Puerto Rico, she learned English only after her family moved to the United States. "It was a challenge," she said, "not only to learn English, but to master it enough to teach it and—the ultimate goal—to write poetry in it." Cofer's writing reflects the split between her two childhood homes: the island of Puerto Rico and the United States. She has written, "My family is one of the main topics of my poetry. In tracing their lives, I discover more about mine."

Judith Ortiz Cofer was born in Puerto Rico in 1952.

READING FOCUS

What do you imagine would happen if human beings could live forever?

Sharing Ideas
In a small group, talk about how the world would change if people lived forever. Discuss the positive and negative results of such a change in the human life cycle.

Setting a Purpose
Read to enjoy this Puerto Rican tale.

BUILDING BACKGROUND

The Time and Place "Aunty Misery" is set in a Spanish-speaking country sometime in the distant past.

Did You Know? The Commonwealth of Puerto Rico is made up of one large and several smaller islands located about 1,000 miles southeast of Florida. It has been a part of the United States since 1898. The island's culture is a blend of the people who have lived there–the Native Americans, the Spanish who conquered the island in 1509, and the Africans who were first brought there as slaves to work on the sugar plantations. The majority of today's Puerto Rican population is of Hispanic background.

VOCABULARY PREVIEW

sorcerer (sor′ sər ər) *n.* a person who practices magic with the aid of evil spirits; p. 701
taunt (tônt) *v.* to make fun of in a scornful, insulting way; p. 701
gnarled (närld) *adj.* rough, twisted, and knotty, as a tree trunk or branches; p. 702
potion (pō′ shən) *n.* a drink, especially of a liquid that is supposed to have magical powers; p. 702

RESOURCE MANAGER

Teaching Tools and Resources
- Theme Seven Planning Guide
- Literature Groups Sourcebook

Essential Lesson Support

Lesson-Specific Instruction
- Selection Focus Transparency 58
- Literary Elements Transparency 58
- Active Reading Guide,* p. 58
- Selection Vocabulary Practice, p. 40

Assessment
- Selection Quick Checks,* p. 58
- Sel. and Theme Assmt., p. 101
- Testmaker: ExamView Pro
- Performance Assessment, p. 55

Systematic Language Instruction
- Gr. & Comp. Hdbk., L. 12.1
- Vocabulary Power, Lesson 30

English Language Learners
- Spanish Summaries, p. 58
- Spanish Translations, pp. 183–184
- Audio Library*
- English, Yes!

Spec. Needs/Strat. Interven.
- Interactive Rdg. Sbk., pp. T205–T207
- Interactive Rdg. Wkbk., pp. 117–118
- Audio Library*

*Also available in Spanish

Aunty Misery

A Folktale from Puerto Rico

Judith Ortiz Cofer

ACTIVE READING MODEL

This is a story about an old, a very old woman who lived alone in her little hut with no other company than a beautiful pear tree that grew at her door. She spent all her time taking care of this tree. The neighborhood children drove the old woman crazy by stealing her fruit. They would climb her tree, shake its delicate limbs, and run away with armloads of golden pears, yelling insults at *la Tia Miseria,*[1] Aunty Misery, as they called her.

One day, a traveler stopped at the old woman's hut and asked her for permission to spend the night under her roof. Aunty Misery saw that he had an honest face and bid the pilgrim come in. She fed him and made a bed for him in front of her hearth. In the morning the stranger told her that he would show his gratitude for her hospitality by granting her one wish.

"There is only one thing that I desire," said Aunty Misery.

"Ask, and it shall be yours," replied the stranger, who was a sorcerer in disguise.

"I wish that anyone who climbs up my pear tree should not be able to come back down until I permit it."

"Your wish is granted," said the stranger, touching the pear tree as he left Aunty Misery's house.

And so it happened that when the children came back to taunt the old woman and to steal her fruit, she stood at her window watching them. Several of them shimmied[2] up the trunk of the pear tree and

PREVIEW [A]

What is the origin of this folktale?

VISUALIZE [B]

Can you picture Aunty Misery? What words does the author use to help you see the character?

QUESTION [C]

What does the fact that the traveler can grant wishes tell you about the tale?

CONNECT [D]

Have you ever known someone like Aunty Misery?

1. *La Tia Miseria* (lä tē′ ə mē′ ze rē′ ə)
2. *Shimmied* means "shook or vibrated," which is what the tree might have done as the children shinnied up it. To *shinny* is to climb by using the hands, arms, feet, and legs to pull and push oneself up.

Vocabulary

sorcerer (sor′ sər ər) *n.* a person who practices magic with the aid of evil spirits

taunt (tônt) *v.* to make fun of in a scornful, insulting way

Reading the Selection

SUMMARY

Children steal the fruit from Aunty Misery's pear tree. A sorcerer grants her a wish, and then tree climbers can't get down without her permission. Even Death gets stuck in the tree until he promises never to come for Aunty again.

Spanish Summaries, p. 58

[A] Active Reading Strategies

PREVIEW *(It is from Puerto Rico.)*

VOCABULARY Remind students to use context clues to unlock the meanings of new vocabulary words.

[B] Active Reading Strategies

VISUALIZE Have students draw Aunty Misery and her house.

[C] Active Reading Strategies

QUESTION *(It will probably be about extraordinary events.)*

[D] Active Reading Strategies

CONNECT *(Students should compare Aunty Misery with someone they know.)*

Additional Resources

Active Reading Guide, p. 58

Audio Library

Spanish Audio Library

Teaching Support

CONNECTING TO OTHER SELECTIONS

For a teaching strategy that connects "Aunty Misery" to "Lob's Girl," see the ***Theme Seven Planning Guide.***

LITERATURE & HUMANITIES

To introduce students to another woman who personifies a painful human emotion, play the song "La Llorona" (track 26) from the second CD of *The World of Music.* This song is about the Latino myth of a woman who represents grief.

Literature and Writing

Writing About Literature

Students' writing should

- accurately identify the characters, plot, setting, and lesson of "Aunty Misery"
- explain how these elements work together in a fable
- explain how a fable is different from other kinds of stories

Creative Writing

Students' fables should

- contain elements of a short story: characters, plot, and setting
- contain elements of a fable, such as a moral
- use this fable as a writing model to create characters, such as Death and Misery, who represent aspects of the human experience

Extending Your Response

Literature Groups Before students meet, encourage them to jot down a few ideas or to review the Venn diagrams they created for the Reading Minilesson on page 702. Then, in groups, have each member briefly contribute and summarize a comparison or a contrasting idea.

Art Activity Encourage students to try drawing tools they haven't used before, such as charcoal or pastels. Then have them focus on the feeling their scenes create in their minds.

Interdisciplinary Activity Encourage students to share what they already know about Puerto Rico. Remind students that an interview with someone who is part of the Puerto Rican culture is valuable research.

Literature and Writing

Writing About Literature

Story Elements Although fables are brief, they usually contain all the elements of a short story. Briefly identify the characters, plot, setting, and theme (or lesson) of "Aunty Misery."

Creative Writing

Folktale Write your own fable about two things "you can always count on running into in this world." Choose two things other than misery and death that you believe are always part of the human experience.

Extending Your Response

Literature Groups

Spiritual Effects Aunty Misery isn't the only human character in the story whose life is changed by supernatural characters. Using examples from the text, compare and contrast the roles of the two supernatural characters. How do these spiritual strangers affect the lives of the human characters?

Art Activity

Scene Illustration Create an illustration of a descriptive scene from the story. Choose a scene that is especially vivid–such as the children stuck in the pear tree or Aunty Misery, as bent and gnarled as her pear tree.

Interdisciplinary Activity

Social Studies Working with a small group, study the culture of Puerto Rico. Have each group member research one of the following: the history of the people, the geography of their homeland, their religious beliefs, art and music, their relationship to the government of the United States. To combine what you have learned, plan a group presentation that includes pictures, maps, and music.

Reading Further

If you would like to read more folktales, try these:

Perez and Martina: A Puerto Rican Folktale by Pura Belpré

The Terrible EEK: A Japanese Tale retold by Patricia A. Compton

Save your work for your portfolio.

Dona Rosita Morillo, 1944. Frida Kahlo. Oil on canvas mounted on Masonite, 30½ x 28½ in. Fundacion Dolores Olmedo, Mexico City, D.F., Mexico.

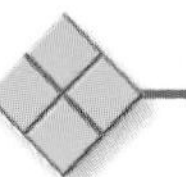

Skill Minilessons

Reteach · Review

GRAMMAR AND LANGUAGE • FREQUENTLY MISSPELLED WORDS

Simple words may be misspelled because a word is mistaken for a similar one–for example, confusing *they're* (a contraction for *they are*) for *their* or *there.* Some other often-confused words are *whose* and *who's; its* and *it's;* and *your* and *you're.* If you are confused about which to use, use a dictionary for help.

PRACTICE Write the word that should be used in each sentence.

1. There once was a woman (whose, who's) pear tree attracted all the children in the neighborhood.
2. "Those children over (their, there, they're) are stealing my pears," she complained.
3. "(Your, You're) pears will remain untouched," the stranger promised.
4. "(Its, It's) branches will remain unbroken," he added.
5. "(Your, You're) very kind," Aunty Misery replied.

● For more about frequently misspelled words, see **Language Handbook,** p. R44.

READING AND THINKING • GENERALIZING

Generalizing is forming a general rule or conclusion based on particular facts or examples. For example, based on "Aunty Misery" and similar stories, you might generalize that many folktales try to explain why some condition exists in the real world.

● For more about generalizing, see **Reading Handbook,** p. R92.

PRACTICE Based on your own experience and reading, make a generalization about each of the following.

1. why people enjoy fantasy or science fiction
2. the main difference between folklore and modern fiction

VOCABULARY • ANALOGIES

An **analogy** is a comparison based on the relationships between things or ideas. Each of the two pairs of words in an analogy illustrates the same relationship.

eyes : vision :: ears : hearing

The relationship between the words can be expressed in a sentence. "*Eyes* are used for *vision* as *ears* are used for *hearing.*" The phrase "are used for" describes the relationship, which is the same in each half, or word pair, of the analogy.

PRACTICE Choose the word that best completes each analogy.

1. puppy : dog :: child :
   a. baby b. adult c. person
2. taunt : scorn :: praise :
   a. approval b. complaint c. gratitude
3. man : woman :: rooster :
   a. egg b. crow c. hen
4. potion : drink :: song :
   a. notes b. music c. sing

● For more about analogies, see **Communications Skills Handbook,** p. R67.

Skill Minilessons

GRAMMAR AND LANGUAGE
FREQUENTLY MISSPELLED WORDS

1. whose
2. there
3. Your
4. Its
5. You're

READING AND THINKING
GENERALIZING

1. Students should make generalizations based on their own experiences.
2. Students should cite examples from folklore and modern fiction to support their ideas.

VOCABULARY
ANALOGIES

1. b
2. a
3. c
4. b

Additional Resources

- ***Grammar and Language Workbook,*** pp. 297–300
- ***Grammar and Composition Handbook,*** Lessons 15.1, 15.2
- ***Writer's Choice,*** Lesson 23.8
- ***Reading Skills Practice Workbook,*** pp. 103–104
- ***Vocabulary Practice,*** p. 40

ASSESSMENT

- ***Quick Checks,*** p. 58
- ***Selection and Theme Assessment,*** pp. 101
- ***Performance Assessment,*** p. 55
- ***Testmaker: ExamView Pro***
- ***Interactive Tutor: Self-Assessment***

B Literary Elements

TONE Ask students to think about what the lean detail and absence of any emotional words other than *pity* might imply about the author's attitude toward the characters and events. *(She's serious and generally matter-of-fact, impartial.)*

C Active Reading Strategies

VISUALIZE Ask students to describe how the couple looks. *(She walks angrily, gazing straight ahead. The man may look sad as he follows her, his shoulders drooping.)*

D Active Reading Strategies

PREDICT Ask students to predict what the woman will do when she sees the new fruit. The following model illustrates the thinking process involved in predicting.

Model: I think the spirit will be successful this time; the woman will be curious about this new fruit. When she stops to look, her husband may catch up to her.

FYI

Strong emotions, such as anger, cause the brain to secrete adrenaline, a strong hormone that stimulates the body to produce extra glucose quickly. This natural sugar helps supply additional energy to respond to stress, allowing a person to walk for a long time.

Teaching Support

The man sat alone in his house. But as time went by, he grew lonelier and lonelier. The anger left him, and all that remained was a terrible grief and despair, and he began to cry.

A spirit heard the man crying and took pity on him. The spirit said, "Man, why do you cry?"

The man said, "My wife has left me."

The spirit said, "Why did your woman leave?"

The man just hung his head and said nothing.

The spirit asked, "You quarreled with her?"

And the man nodded.

"Would you quarrel with her again?" asked the spirit.

The man said, "No." He wanted only to live with his wife as they had lived before—in peace, in happiness, and in love.

"I have seen your woman," the spirit said. "She is walking to the east toward the rising sun."

The man followed his wife, but he could not overtake her. Everyone knows an angry woman walks fast.

Finally, the spirit said, "I'll go ahead and see if I can make her slow her steps." So the spirit found the woman walking, her footsteps fast and angry and her gaze fixed straight ahead. There was pain in her heart.

The spirit saw some huckleberry bushes growing along the trail, so with a wave of his hand, he made the bushes burst into bloom and ripen into fruit. But the woman's gaze remained fixed. She looked neither to the right nor to the left, and she didn't see the berries. Her footsteps didn't slow.

Again, the spirit waved his hand, and one by one, all of the berries growing along the trail burst into bloom and ripened into fruit. But still, the woman's gaze remained fixed. She saw nothing but her anger and pain, and her footsteps didn't slow.

And again, the spirit waved his hand, and, one by one, the trees of the forest—the peach, the pear, the apple, the wild cherry—burst into bloom and ripened into fruit. But still, the woman's eyes remained fixed, and even still, she saw nothing but her anger and pain. And her footsteps didn't slow.

Then finally, the spirit thought, "I will create an entirely new fruit—one that grows very, very close to the ground so the woman must forget her anger and bend her head for a moment." So the spirit waved his hand, and a thick green carpet began to grow along the trail. Then the carpet became starred with tiny white flowers, and each flower gradually ripened into a berry that was the color and shape of the human heart.

As the woman walked, she crushed the tiny berries, and the delicious aroma came up through her nose. She stopped and

Vocabulary

despair (di spār′) *n.* complete loss of hope; desperation

overtake (ō′ vər tāk′) *v.* to catch up with or to reach and then pass

fixed (fikst) *adj.* steadily directed and unchanging

aroma (ə rō′ mə) *n.* a pleasant smell; odor

MEETING INDIVIDUAL NEEDS: ENGLISH LANGUAGE LEARNERS

Folktales Almost every culture has stories that have been passed down orally from generation to generation. Some of these stories are about love or about how things first came to be.

Activity Have students break into small groups to share stories from their cultures about love or about how something came to be. Then have each group select one story and act it out for the rest of the class. Allow students ample time to practice. Students may want to make some visuals to enhance the stories. Encourage the class to notice which values are important in each story.

Additional Resources

English Language Learners Sourcebook, p. 87

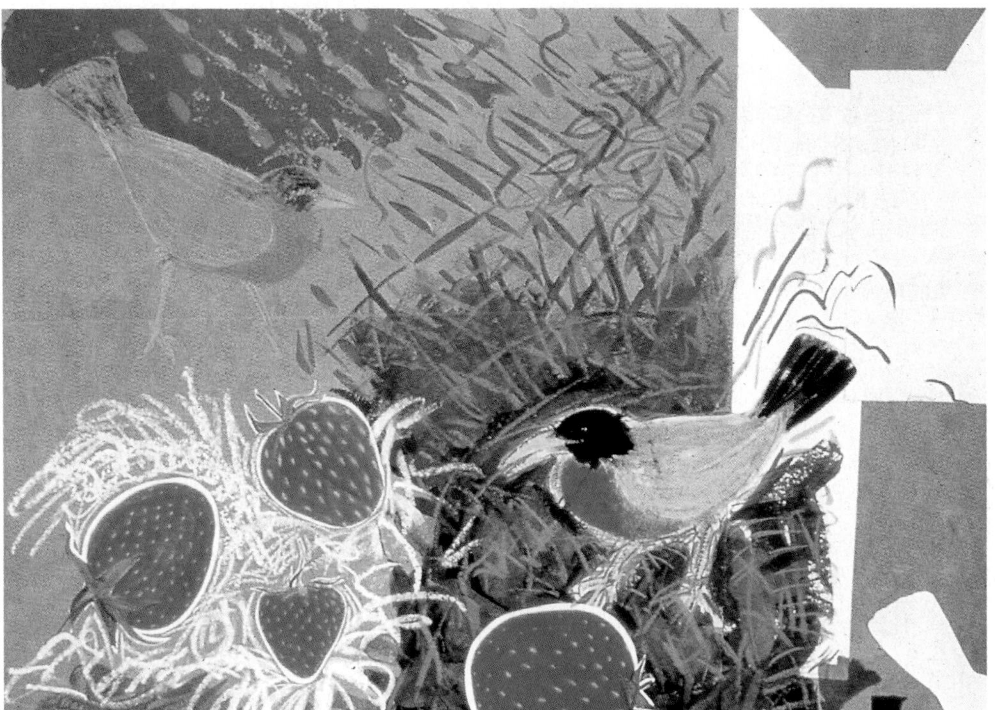

Strawberry Dance, 1983. G. Peter Jemison. Mixed media on handmade paper, 22 x 30 in. Private collection, by permission of the artist.

Viewing the painting: How does the mood of this artwork reflect the mood of the story's ending?

E looked down, and she saw the berries. She picked one and ate it, and she discovered its taste was as sweet as love itself. So she began walking slowly, picking berries as she went, and as she leaned down to pick a berry, she saw her husband coming behind her.

F The anger had gone from her heart, and all that remained was the love she had always known. So she stopped for him, and together, they picked and ate the berries. Finally, they returned to their home, where they lived out their days in peace, happiness, and love.

And that's how the world's very first strawberries brought peace between men and women in the world and why to this day they are called the berries of love.

Viewing the Painting

Viewing Response *The colors and style of the art, with the subjects nesting and "dancing" among the strawberries, convey the same bright, peaceful mood found at the end of the story.*

E Literary Elements

TONE Have a volunteer read this passage aloud as a newswriter might deliver it. Ask students to discuss what would make this passage more matter-of-fact. *(Take out the simile and say that the strawberry tasted sweet.)*

F Active Reading Strategies

RESPOND Ask students which human values are portrayed in this story. *(forgiveness, love, the letting go of anger, and the wisdom to appreciate the importance of another person)*

Thematic Focus

A Different Dimension Have students explain what this story has to do with the theme. *(A spirit from a different dimension helps resolve the conflict.)*

Fine Art Transparency 28

You may wish to use ***Fine Art Transparency 28*** to explore reasons people have for being angry with loved ones and how to calm that anger.

Assessment

Quick Checks, p. 59

Reading Minilesson

Cause and Effect Draw the following chart on the board and invite students to help fill in the first causes and effects from the story.

Activity Have students reread the story to identify and to list cause and effect transitions on the chart. Have the class discuss any disagreements and reach a consensus on the major causes and effects in this story. **L2**

Cause	Effect
1. *A man and wife fight.*	*The woman leaves in anger.*
2. *The man misses his wife.*	*He hurries after her.*

Additional Resources

Reading Skills Practice Workbook

Responding to the Selection

PERSONAL RESPONSE

Students should explain how their thoughts have changed or expanded.

Analyzing Literature

1. The woman leaves her husband because a quarrel makes her angry.
2. A spirit tries to slow the woman down so her husband can catch up to her.
3. The berries and trees in bloom have no effect on the woman.
4. Strawberries finally slow her down.
5. The man cannot overtake his wife because her anger causes her to walk very fast.
6. The woman cannot see the blossoming bushes and trees because her gaze is fixed straight ahead.
7. The spirit decides to create a new fruit that grows close to the ground so the woman will bend her head for a moment and forget her anger.
8. The woman crushes the strawberries under her feet as she walks, releasing a pleasant scent. She stops to look at the berries she has never seen before.
9. "Strawberries" teaches the reader that by holding onto anger you prevent yourself from seeing the beautiful things in life. In this story, the woman missed the beautiful huckleberries and fruit trees.
10. "Strawberries" indicates that the Cherokee may have believed that without love, life is lonely and unhappy. It also indicates that letting go of anger helps you enjoy life, and that the ability to forget quarrels is an important human value.

Active Reading and Critical Thinking

Responding to Literature

PERSONAL RESPONSE

- How did this tale change or add to your thoughts about love?

Analyzing Literature

RECALL

1. What causes the woman to leave her husband?
2. Why does the spirit want to slow the angry woman's steps?
3. What effect do the blooming huckleberries and trees of the forest have upon the woman?
4. What finally slows the woman down?

Brackets connect questions that are paired to develop higher-level thinking skills.

INTERPRET

5. Why is the man unable to overtake his wife?
6. Why isn't the woman able to see the blossoming bushes and trees?
7. Why does the spirit decide to create a new fruit?
8. Why do the strawberries make the woman slow down?

EVALUATE AND CONNECT

9. What does "Strawberries" teach the reader about letting go of anger?
10. Theme Connection "Strawberries" is a Cherokee myth. What does it tell you about what the Cherokee people believe about love?

LITERARY ELEMENTS

Tone

The **tone** of a piece of writing expresses to readers the author's feelings and attitude toward his or her subject, ideas, theme, or characters. A written piece may express seriousness, humor, nostalgia, or any number of other feelings. Formal writing, for example, usually creates a serious tone; colloquial writing can create a light, humorous tone. Factors that contribute to tone are the writer's sentence construction and choice of words, the kinds of details used, and the images created. In poetry, the rhythm may help to create a tone. A rhythm can encourage readers to skip lightly along the poet's words or mournfully drag them out.

1. Reread the first paragraphs of "Aunty Misery" and "Strawberries." What tone does each author create? How?
2. Choose a poem you read earlier in this book. How does the poet create its tone?

- See **Literary Terms Handbook**, p. R11.

LITERARY ELEMENTS

1. The authors create a serious tone by presenting a problem that needs to be solved.
2. Students should be able to support their answers with examples.

Additional Resources

 ***Literary Elements Transparency 59***

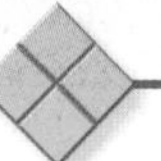

Literature and Writing

Writing About Literature

Conflict **Conflict** refers to the struggle between two opposing forces. Write briefly about the conflict that is central to "Strawberries." Explain what caused the conflict and how it was resolved.

Creative Writing

The First . . . "Strawberries" is a Cherokee myth about how strawberries came to be. Write a myth to explain the origin of the fruit, flower, or plant you illustrated for the **Reading Focus** on page 706.

Extending Your Response

Literature Groups

Anger Management In addition to telling about the origin of strawberries, the myth also presents the idea that anger can ruin love. Do you agree? How could the man and woman in the myth have prevented their quarrel or dealt with their anger? Share your group's opinions with the class.

Performing

Role-Playing What do the husband and wife in "Strawberries" argue about? What do they say to each other as they walk back home? With a partner, consider these questions. Then role-play one of these two dialogues from the story.

Reading Further

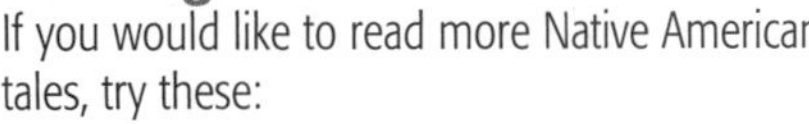

If you would like to read more Native American tales, try these:

How Rabbit Tricked Otter and Other Cherokee Trickster Stories, told by Gayle Ross

Mai'ii and Cousin Horned Toad: A Traditional Navajo Story by Shonto Begay

Save your work for your portfolio.

Skill Minilesson

Reteach • Review

VOCABULARY • SYNONYMS: THESAURUS

The angry woman in "Strawberries" would not have tasted berries that had a *stink.* What made her stop was the berries' *aroma. Smell, stink, aroma,* and *scent* are synonyms, but each word has its own distinctive meaning. A **thesaurus** is a dictionary of synonyms. It can help you find differences among synonyms so that you can use the one best suited to your purpose.

PRACTICE For each sentence, decide whether *smell, scent, stink,* or *aroma* is the best choice.

1. The kitchen filled with the ___ of apple pie.
2. Even blindfolded, I would know I was in the barn by the familiar ___ .
3. The ___ in my room was a mixture of wet dog and dirty socks.
4. The ___ of her favorite perfume told me that my mother had been in my room.

Literature and Writing

Writing About Literature

Students' writing should

- explain that the conflict is about a husband trying to reconcile with his wife after a fight
- indicate that a quarrel causes the conflict and that help from a spirit resolves it
- use examples from the story to support their ideas

Creative Writing

Students' myths should

- indicate how a fruit, a flower, or a plant came to be
- show an important human value, such as forgiveness or love
- teach a lesson about human behavior

Extending Your Response

Literature Groups Have each group create a chart showing the most effective ways to deal with anger. Have groups share their charts and explain their ideas.

Performing Partners may want to improvise the scene a few times to figure out what the characters are likely to say. Then they can memorize and rehearse their lines.

Skill Minilesson

VOCABULARY

• **SYNONYMS: THESAURUS**

1. aroma
2. smell
3. stink
4. scent

Additional Resources

Vocabulary Practice, p. 41

ASSESSMENT

- ***Quick Checks,*** p. 59
- ***Selection and Theme Assessment,*** p. 102
- ***Performance Assessment,*** p. 56
- ***Testmaker: ExamView Pro***
- ***Interactive Tutor: Self-Assessment***

Objective

- To recognize and apply strategies for using capitalization correctly

Teaching Strategies

Point out to students that sometimes people mistakenly capitalize words in order to emphasize their importance. Remind students that there are other ways to emphasize importance, such as underlining the word, and that capitalization should not be used in this case.

Exercise

1. correct
2. call Aunt Millie
3. speak Spanish
4. the Empire State Building
5. tell Mom and Dad
6. a German composer
7. correct
8. correct
9. the Puerto Rican flag
10. correct

Additional Resources

- ***Grammar and Language Workbook,*** pp. 235–246
- ***Grammar and Composition Handbook,*** Lessons 12.1–12.4
- ***Writer's Choice,*** Lessons 19.1–19.4

Teaching Support

Capitalization

A proper noun names a particular person, place, or thing. A proper adjective is formed from a proper noun. Proper nouns and proper adjectives are capitalized.

Problem 1 Words referring to ethnic groups, nationalities, and languages
Some french folk songs are sung in english in the United States.

Solution Capitalize names of ethnic groups, nationalities, and languages and the adjectives formed from them.
Some French folk songs are sung in English in the United States.

Problem 2 Words that name family relationships
I told mom, aunt Martha, and my grandfather about "Aunty Misery."

Solution Capitalize the word that names a family relationship only if it is part of the person's name or used in place of the person's name.
I told Mom, Aunt Martha, and my grandfather about "Aunty Misery."

Problem 3 Names of organizations and structures
The American folklore society seeks to study and preserve folklore.
There are songs about the Brooklyn bridge but not the sears tower.

Solution Capitalize the names of organizations and structures.
The American Folklore Society seeks to study and preserve folklore.
There are songs about the Brooklyn Bridge but not the Sears Tower.

• For more about capitalization, see **Language Handbook,** p. R20.

EXERCISE

Write *Correct* if the phrase is capitalized correctly. If it is capitalized incorrectly, rewrite the phrase to correct it.

1. my sister, Sue
2. call aunt Millie
3. speak spanish
4. the empire state building
5. tell mom and dad
6. a german composer
7. my favorite uncle
8. the U.S. Congress
9. the puerto rican flag
10. a mother's worries

Writing Minilesson

Writing an Exercise Work with students to create a list of word categories that are routinely capitalized in English. Some categories are days of the week, months of the year, planets, countries, languages, and song titles.

Activity Have students work in groups of three to five "teachers." Explain that each group will prepare a short capitalization lesson and writing exercise for another group. Exercises can include sentences, stories, poems, "test questions," or any other writing activities students feel will help their peers learn and practice capitalization. **L2**

Additional Resources

- ***Writer's Choice,*** Lessons 19.1–19.4

Before You Read

Atalanta's Race and *Atalanta*

MEET REX WARNER

A novelist, Greek scholar, poet, translator, and critic, Rex Warner spent the early days of his career as a schoolteacher in England and Egypt. He later served as director of the British Institute in Athens, Greece. In 1961 Warner moved to the United States. His novels, often written as allegories, focus on the power of government.

Rex Warner was born in England in 1905 and died in 1986.

MEET BETTY MILES

Betty Miles's first full-time job, as an assistant kindergarten teacher, inspired her to write children's books. When asked about her writing, Miles replied, "I put my own feelings into my characters, and say things through them that I might be too shy to say in person. . . . For me, the greatest reward of writing is being told that 'you know just how I feel.'"

Betty Miles was born in Chicago in 1928.

READING FOCUS

The ancient Greeks believed that fate was an all-powerful force in everyday life. More people today believe that their fate depends on their own actions and decisions. How do you feel about what influences people's futures?

Think/Pair/Share

Take a moment to jot down your thoughts and feelings about the question. Then share your ideas with a partner, and discuss how we can influence our future lives.

Setting a Purpose

Read two versions of the same myth to see how they differ.

BUILDING BACKGROUND

Did You Know? Greek myths have had a long-lasting influence on literature, including classic Greek and Roman dramas based on these myths. The borrowing of these themes continues today, not only in drama, poetry, and fiction but in motion pictures and television features. Even many of the comic book or TV superheroes can be traced back to such ancient Greek models as Hercules and Achilles.

VOCABULARY PREVIEW

condemn (kən dem′) *v.* to criticize sharply; p. 715
envious (en′ vē əs) *adj.* having resentment over, and a wish to possess for oneself, something possessed by another; p. 715
parched (pärcht) *adj.* severely in need of moisture; p. 717
hallowed (hal′ ōd) *adj.* regarded as sacred or holy; p. 717
fleetest (flēt′ əst) *adj.* swiftest; fastest; p. 719
jubilant (jo͞o′ bə lənt) *adj.* filled with great joy; p. 721
claim (klām) *v.* to ask for or demand possession of one's right to something; p. 721

Before Reading

Objectives

- To read and understand two versions of a myth
- To see how details are used to describe people, places, things, and events
- To write a paragraph describing a character

Skills

Reading/Thinking: Sequencing; Drawing Conclusions; Inferring; Synthesizing; Verifying Predictions; Chronological Order
Writing: Description of the Setting; Journal Entry
Vocabulary: The Prefix *twi-;* Analogies
Grammar/Language: Irregular Verbs; Spelling Compound Words
Listening/Speaking: Radio Narration
Collaboration: Literature Groups

Motivating STUDENTS

Selection Focus Transparency 60: Have students interpret and discuss the cartoon in the Selection Focus Transparency.

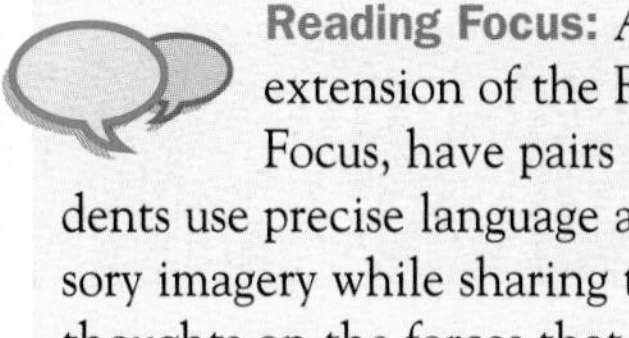

Reading Focus: As an extension of the Reading Focus, have pairs of students use precise language and sensory imagery while sharing their thoughts on the forces that shape their lives and on what part the roles of free will and self-determination play in them.

RESOURCE MANAGER

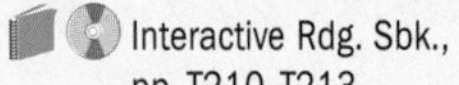

Teaching Tools and Resources
- Theme Seven Planning Guide
- Literature Groups Sourcebook

Essential Lesson Support

Lesson-Specific Instruction
- Selection Focus Transparency 60
- Literary Elements Transparency 60
- Active Reading Guide,* p. 60
- Selection Vocabulary Practice, p. 42

Assessment
- Selection Quick Checks,* p. 60
- Sel. and Theme Assmt., pp. 103–104
- Testmaker: ExamView Pro
- Performance Assessment, p. 57

Systematic Language Instruction
- Gr. & Comp. Hdbk., L. 12.3
- Vocabulary Power, Lesson 26

English Language Learners
- ELL Sourcebook, p. 88
- Spanish Summaries, p. 60
- Audio Library*
- English, Yes!

Spec. Needs/Strat. Interven.
- Interactive Rdg. Sbk., pp. T210–T213
- Interactive Rdg. Wkbk., pp. 121–122
- Inclusion Strat. Sbk., pp. 81–82, 89–90
- Audio Library*

*Also available in Spanish

Reading the Selection

SUMMARY

In "Atalanta's Race," the oracle warns Atalanta that marrying will bring her disaster. Terrified, she says that she will marry the man who beats her in a foot race, but all the losers must die. Venus helps Hippomenes win, but he forgets to thank her. Venus punishes him and Atalanta by luring them into spending the night at the forbidden temple of Cybele. Angry, Cybele transforms them into lions.
"Atalanta" is a modern spin on the same myth. The race between Atalanta and a young admirer named John is a tie. The king offers her in marriage to John, who leaves the decision to Atalanta. In the end, they become friends.

Spanish Summaries, p. 60

Active Reading Strategies

PREDICT Ask students to use the title and the first two paragraphs to predict whom and what they think the "race" will involve.

Additional Resources

Active Reading Guide, p. 60
Audio Library
Spanish Audio Library

Atalanta's Race

Rex Warner

The huntress Atalanta,[1] whom Meleager,[2] before he died, had loved, could run faster even than the fastest runners among men. Nor was her beauty inferior to her swiftness of foot; both were beyond praise.

When Atalanta asked the oracle[3] about whom she ought to marry, the god replied: "Do not take a husband, Atalanta. If you do, it will bring disaster on you. Yet you will not escape, and though you will continue to live, you will not be yourself."

1. According to Greek myths, the Greek heroine *Atalanta* was abandoned at birth and rescued by a bear. Later found by hunters who raised her, Atalanta grew into a daring child who excelled at all physical activities.
2. In Greek mythology, *Meleager* (mel′ ē ā′ gər) was the son of a king whose country was ravaged by a wild boar. Meleager put together a band of heroes to drive the boar away, and he himself killed it.
3. In ancient Greece, an *oracle* was a priest through whom the gods sometimes answered the questions of worshipers.

Teaching Support

CONNECTING TO OTHER SELECTIONS
For a teaching strategy that connects "Atalanta's Race" to the selection from *Rosa Parks: My Story,* see the ***Theme One Planning Guide.***

MEETING INDIVIDUAL NEEDS — ENGLISH LANGUAGE LEARNERS

Women in Society The story raises many cultural issues. Depending on their backgrounds, English language learners may find issues that are either familiar or puzzling to them.

Activity Separate the class into small groups. Have students think about and discuss male attitudes toward females who are able to run faster than men.

Encourage students to share their experiences in and knowledge of different cultures. Discussions can be expanded to include other competitive situations, such as earning better grades and making larger salaries.

Additional Resources

English Language Learners Sourcebook, p. 88

Terrified by these words, Atalanta lived in the dark woods unmarried. There were many men who wished to marry her, but to them, in their eagerness, she said: "No one can have me for his wife unless first he beats me in a race. If you will, you may run with me. If any of you wins, he shall have me as a prize. But those who are defeated will have death for their reward. These are the conditions for the race."

Cruel indeed she was, but her beauty had such power that numbers of young men were impatient to race with her on these terms.

There was a young man called Hippomenes,[4] who had come to watch the contest. At first he had said to himself: "What man in his senses would run such a risk to get a wife?" and he had condemned the young men for being too madly in love. But when he saw her face and her body all stripped for the race—a face and a body like Venus's[5] own—he was lost in astonishment and, stretching out his hands, he said: "I had no right to blame the young men. I did not know what the prize was for which they were running."

As he spoke his own heart caught on fire with love for her and, in jealous fear, he hoped that none of the young men would be able to beat her in the race. Then he said to himself: "But why should not I try my fortune? When one takes a risk, the gods help one."

By now the race had started, and the girl sped past him on feet that seemed to have wings. Though she went fast as an arrow, he admired her beauty still more. Indeed she looked particularly beautiful when running. In the breeze her hair streamed back over her ivory shoulders; the ribbons with their bright borders fluttered at her knees; the white of her young body flushed rose-red, as when a purple awning is drawn over white marble and makes the stone glow with its own color. While Hippomenes fixed his eyes on her, she reached the winning post and was crowned with the victor's garland. The young men, with groans, suffered the penalty of death according to the agreement which they had made.

Did You Know?
The victor's *garland* was a small wreath of flowers, leaves, or vines worn about the head as a symbol of honor.

Their fate, however, had no effect on Hippomenes. He came forward and, fixing his eyes on Atalanta, said: "Why do you win an easy glory by conquering these slow movers? Now run with me. If I win, it will be no disgrace to you. I am a king's son and Neptune[6] is my great-grandfather. And, if you defeat me, it will be an honor to be able to say that you defeated Hippomenes."

As he spoke, Atalanta looked at him with a softer expression in her eyes. She wondered whether she really wanted to conquer or to be conquered. She thought to herself: "What god, envious of beautiful

4. *Hippomenes* (hi pom′ ə nēz′)
5. *Venus* was the goddess of beauty and love.
6. *Neptune* was the god of the sea.

Vocabulary
condemn (kən dem′) *v.* to criticize sharply
envious (en′ vē əs) *adj.* having resentment over, and a wish to possess for oneself, something possessed by another

VOCABULARY If you haven't previewed the selection vocabulary with students, stop and remind them to use context clues to unlock the meanings of new vocabulary words.

B Critical Thinking

DRAWING CONCLUSIONS Ask students why Atalanta sets such drastic conditions for the runners. The following model illustrates the thinking process involved in drawing conclusions.

Model: Atalanta is terrified by the oracle's warning, so she tries to avoid marriage. She probably thinks that by threatening the losers with death, they won't want to race her.

C Active Reading Strategies

EVALUATE Invite students to share their opinions on the wisdom of risking one's life to acquire something based exclusively on its outward appearance. *(Some students may think it is all right to take such a risk, but others may point to examples in history where such a risk proved fatal.)*

D Author's Craft

DESCRIPTION The author chooses specific details to convey personalities and atmosphere in this story. How is Atalanta "beautiful while running"? *(Atalanta's hair "streamed back over her ivory shoulders," bright ribbons "fluttered at her knees," and her body glowed.)*

Writing Minilesson

Description of the Setting Writers usually include details about the settings of their stories. Have students skim page 715 (col. 2) to the very top of page 717 and note details of the setting. *(The race course is sandy and the people shout.)*

Activity Have students work in small groups. Encourage them to visualize the setting of the race and brainstorm to fill in the details. Ask each group to work together to write a brief description of the setting of the race. Encourage them to use their imaginations to create vivid details. **L2**

Additional Resources

 ***Writer's Choice,*** Lesson 3.2

VIEWING THE PHOTOGRAPH

Viewing Response *The photo-collage suggests various stages of a race and gives an impression of movement that a single shot of a runner could not convey. Like Atalanta, this present-day runner is probably the goal-oriented product of self-discipline and intense training.*

E Critical Thinking

INFERRING Atalanta does not show the same compassion for the other men who race her as she does for Hippomenes. Ask students what that might imply. *(It implies that she feels something special for this young man.)*

Cultural Note

Love Goddess Venus (called Aphrodite by the Greeks) was worshipped in ancient Greece and Rome as the goddess of love.

F Literary Elements

DESCRIPTION Ask students how this long description of the golden apple tree might increase a reader's interest in the story. *(Students may say that readers will be curious to see what role it plays in the story.)*

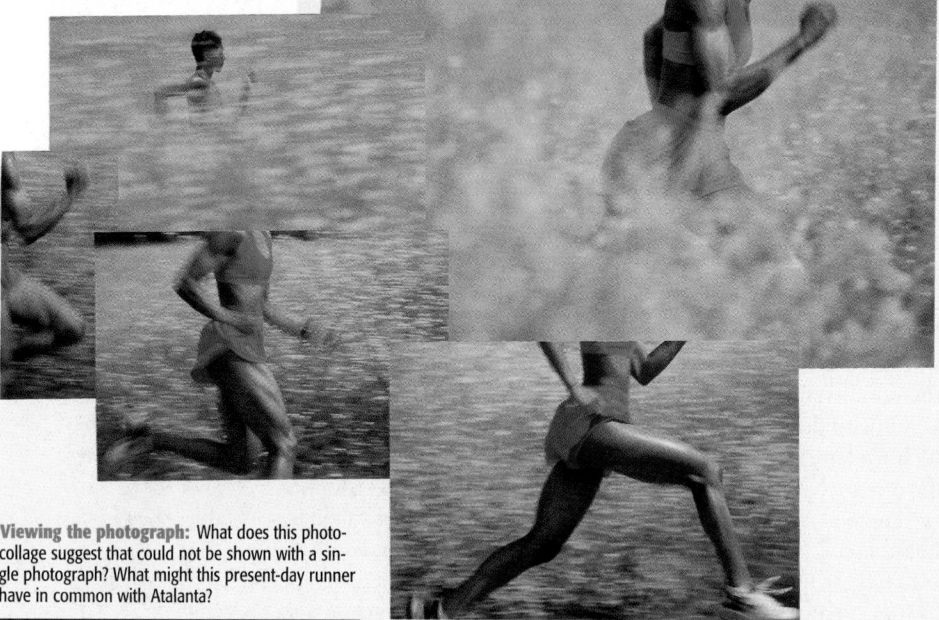

Viewing the photograph: What does this photo-collage suggest that could not be shown with a single photograph? What might this present-day runner have in common with Atalanta?

E young men, wants to destroy this one and makes him seek marriage with me at the risk of his dear life? In my opinion, I am not worth it. It is not his beauty that touches me (though I might easily be touched by that); it is because he is still only a boy. And then there is his courage, and the fact that he is willing to risk so much for me. Why should he die, simply because he wants to live with me? I wish he would go, while he still may, and realize that it is fatal to want to marry me. Indeed he deserves to live. If only I were happier, if only the fates[7] had not forbidden me to marry, he would be the man that I would choose."

Meanwhile Atalanta's father and the whole people demanded that the race should take place. Hippomenes prayed to Venus and said: "O goddess, you put this love into my heart. Now be near me in my trial and aid me!"

A gentle breeze carried his prayer to the goddess and she was moved by it. Little time, however, remained in which she could help him. But it happened that she had just returned from her sacred island of Cyprus,[8] where in one of her temple gardens grows a golden apple tree. The leaves are gold; the branches and the fruit rattle with metal as the wind stirs them. Venus had in her hand three golden apples which she had just picked from this tree. Now she came down to earth, making herself visible only to Hippomenes, and showed him how to use the apples. F

Then the trumpets sounded and the two runners darted forward from the starting post, skimming over the sandy course with feet so light that it would seem they might have run over the sea or over the waving heads of standing corn. The crowd shouted their applause.[9] "Now, Hippomenes," they

7. The *fates* were three goddesses who controlled human lives and fortunes.

8. *Cyprus* is an island in the Mediterranean Sea, south of Turkey.

9. Here, *applause* means simply "praise."

Teaching Support

Reading *Minilesson*

Sequencing Explain that a myth, like other traditional stories, has a plot. Readers can better understand the plot of a story by analyzing the story's sequence of events.

Activity Have each student develop a graphic organizer to keep track of the sequence of events in the story. When the graphic organizers are complete, ask students whether there are events or details that still confuse them. Have them discuss whether the sequence of events led to a logical conclusion. Students can use their charts to answer the questions that follow the selection. **L2**

Additional Resources

Reading Skills Practice Workbook

Atalanta's Race

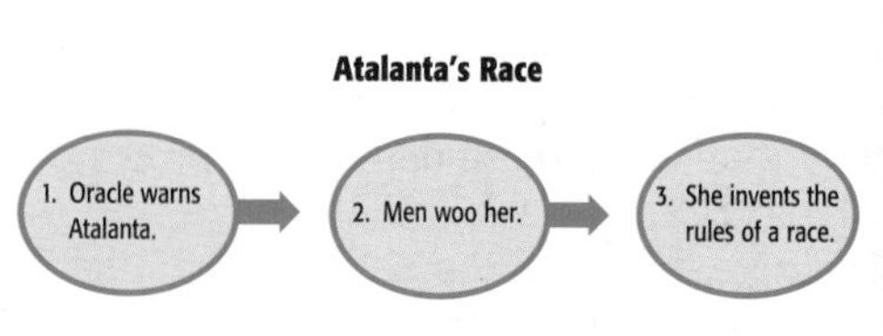
1. Oracle warns Atalanta.
2. Men woo her.
3. She invents the rules of a race.

cried, "run as you have never run before! You are winning." It would be difficult to say whether Hippomenes or Atalanta herself was most pleased with this encouragement. For some time Atalanta, though she might have passed the young man, did not do so. She ran by his side, looking into his face. Then, half unwillingly, she left him behind. He, with parched throat and straining lungs, followed after; still the winning post was far in the distance; and now he took one of the golden apples which Venus had given him and threw it in her way. The girl looked with wonder at the shining fruit and, longing to have it, stopped running so that she could pick it up. Hippomenes passed her and again the spectators shouted out their applause. Soon, however, Atalanta made up the ground that she had lost and again left Hippomenes behind. He threw the second apple, once more took the lead and once more was overtaken. Now they were in sight of the winning post, and Hippomenes, with a prayer to Venus, threw the last apple rather sideways, so that it went some distance from the course. Atalanta seemed to hesitate whether she should go after it or not, but Venus made her go, and, when she had picked up the apple, she made it heavier, handicapping the girl not only by the time she had lost but by the weight of what she was carrying. This time she could not catch up Hippomenes. He passed the winning post first and claimed her as his bride.

Then, indeed, Hippomenes should have offered thanks to Venus, but he forgot entirely the goddess who had helped him, neither giving thanks nor making sacrifice.

Venus was angry and determined to make an example of them both. On their way to the home of Hippomenes they came to a holy temple, sacred to the mother of the gods, great Cybele. No mortal[10] was allowed to pass the night in this temple, so hallowed was the spot; but Venus put it into the hearts of Hippomenes and Atalanta, who were tired from their journey, to rest there all night and treat the temple of the goddess as though it were a common inn. So in the most holy of the temple's shrines, where wooden images of the ancient gods turned away their eyes in horror at the profanation,[11] they rested together. But the terrible goddess, her head crowned with a crown of towers, appeared to them. She covered their necks, which had been so smooth, with tawny manes of hair; their fingers became sharp claws, and their arms turned to legs. Most of their weight went to their chests, and behind them they swept the sandy ground with long tails. Instead of the palace they had hoped for, they lived in the savage woods, a lion and a lioness, terrible to others but, when Cybele needed them, tame enough to draw her chariot, champing the iron bits between their gnashing jaws.

10. *Cybele* (sib′ ə lē) and the other gods were *immortals*—beings who would never die. A *mortal* is a human being.

11. *Profanation* is an act of disrespect or scorn for sacred beings or objects, such as this holy shrine.

Vocabulary

parched (pärcht) *adj.* severely in need of moisture

hallowed (hal′ ōd) *adj.* regarded as sacred or holy

G Literary Elements

CHARACTERIZATION Ask students what Atalanta's actions here reveal about her. *(She seems to have good intentions, but is torn by her love for Hippomenes and fear of the oracle's warning.)*

Cultural Note

Cybele is the Phrygian name for the mother of the gods. (Phrygia was across the Aegean Sea from Greece, in Asia Minor.) The Greeks also called her Rhea, and to the Romans, she was Magna Mater ("Great Mother").

H Critical Thinking

INFERRING Ask students to what degree Venus is involved in the outcome of the race. *(Venus tells Hippomenes where and when to throw the apples and makes Atalanta pick them up. She even makes the third apple heavier.)*

I Author's Craft

FORESHADOWING What development could this negative description of Hippomenes' action possibly foreshadow? *(It foreshadows doom for Hippomenes for being ungrateful to Venus.)*

J Literary Elements

DESCRIPTION: *Plot Resolution* Ask what the description of Venus's anger and her choice of punishment reveals. *(The harshness of the punishment conveys the importance of gratitude, respect, and obedience to rules.)*

Listening and Speaking Minilesson

Radio Narration of the Race This race, with its exciting action, competitive spirit, and cheering crowd, is very similar to the athletic events witnessed today. In fact, the scene of the race lends itself nicely to oral narration.

Activity Have students work in pairs or small groups to prepare radio scripts of the race between Atalanta and Hippomenes. Encourage students to use descriptions that help listeners "see" the action in their minds and enjoy listening to the tale being told aloud. Then they may tape their scripts, reading aloud the text in the voice of a radio announcer or a pair of announcers. Remind them to vary the quality, tone, and pace of their voices to convey excitement and suspense. **L2**

A DIFFERENT DIMENSION 717

Active Reading Strategies

PREDICT Knowing that this selection is a variation of the first, ask students how they think the two may differ. Have them consider the "fairy tale-like" opening. *(Students may predict that the fairy tale opening sentence forecasts a happier ending to this story than the first.)*

Author's Craft

INDIRECT CHARACTERIZATION Ask students how the author reveals Atalanta's personality through the dialogue between her and her father, the king. *(When the powerful king expresses his inability to make a choice in regard to a marriage partner for her, Atalanta tells him that she will make the choice herself or perhaps choose not to marry at all. This makes her more like a modern woman than one living in ancient Greece.)*

Atalanta

Betty Miles

Once upon a time, not long ago, there lived a princess named Atalanta, who could run as fast as the wind.

She was so bright, and so clever, and could build things and fix things so wonderfully, that many young men wished to marry her.

"What shall I do?" said Atalanta's father, who was a powerful king. "So many young men want to marry you, and I don't know how to choose."

"You don't have to choose, Father," Atalanta said. "I will choose. And I'm not sure that I will choose to marry anyone at all."

"Of course you will," said the king. "Everybody gets married. It is what people do."

Teaching Support

CONNECTING TO OTHER SELECTIONS
For a teaching strategy that connects "Atalanta" to "Racing the Great Bear," see the *Theme Three Planning Guide.*

MEETING INDIVIDUAL NEEDS: SPECIAL NEEDS

Less-Proficient Readers Remind students that a story's plot begins with the exposition, which introduces the story's characters, setting, and situation.

Activity Have students work in pairs to gather the information revealed in the exposition, using the following questions to start:

1. Who are the key characters?
2. What do the opening details tell about Atalanta?
3. What may the conflict of the story be?

L2

Additional Resources

Inclusion Strategies

M "But," Atalanta told him, with a toss of her head, "I intend to go out and see the world. When I come home, perhaps I will marry and perhaps I will not."

The king did not like this at all. He was a very ordinary king; that is, he was powerful and used to having his own way. So he did not answer Atalanta, but simply N told her, "I have decided how to choose the young man you will marry. I will hold a great race, and the winner—the swiftest, fleetest young man of all—will win the right to marry you."

Now Atalanta was a clever girl as well as a swift runner. She saw that she might win both the argument and the race—provided that she herself could run in the race, too. "Very well," she said. "But you must let me race along with the others. If I am not the winner, I will accept the wishes of the young man who is."

The king agreed to this. He was pleased; he would have his way, marry off his daughter, and enjoy a fine day of racing as well. So he directed his messengers to travel throughout the kingdom announcing the race with its wonderful prize: the chance to marry the bright Atalanta.

As the day of the race drew near, flags were raised in the streets of the town, and banners were hung near the grassy field where the race would be run. Baskets of ripe plums and peaches, wheels of cheese, ropes of sausages and onions, and loaves of crusty bread were gathered for the crowds.

Meanwhile, Atalanta herself was preparing for the race. Each day at dawn, dressed in soft green trousers and a shirt of yellow silk, she went to the field in secret and ran across it—slowly at first, then fast and faster, until she could run the course more quickly than anyone had ever run it before.

As the day of the race grew nearer, young men began to crowd into the town. Each was sure he could win the prize, except for one; that was Young John, who lived in the town. He saw Atalanta day by day as she bought nails and wood to make a pigeon house, or chose parts for her telescope, or laughed with her friends. Young John saw the princess only from a distance, but near enough to know how bright and clever she was. He wished very much to race with her, to win, and to earn the right to talk with her and become her friend. O

"For surely," he said to himself, "it is not right for Atalanta's father to give her away to the winner of the race. Atalanta herself must choose the person she wants to marry, or whether she wishes to marry at all. Still, if I could only win the race, I would be free to speak to her, and to ask for her friendship."

Each evening, after his studies of the stars and the seas, Young John went to the field in secret and practiced running across

Vocabulary
fleetest (flēt′ əst) *adj.* swiftest; fastest

M Literary Elements

DESCRIPTION Ask students what the author conveys about the princess through the detail "with a toss of her head." *(The detail conveys an independence of spirit. She has her own mind and plans.)*

N Critical Thinking

SYNTHESIZING Have students contrast the reason for the race in "Atalanta's Race" and this selection. *(In "Atalanta's Race," Atalanta decides upon the race as a way of discouraging any suitors. In this selection, the king decides upon the race as a way to find a suitor for his daughter and force her to marry.)*

O Literary Elements

CHARACTERIZATION Ask students to give their impressions of Young John. *(Young John is kind and well-intentioned. He admires the princess for her mind and is only interested in becoming her friend.)*

® The following videotape program, suitable for use with the Greek mythology selections in this theme, is available from Glencoe. Be sure to preview the video for appropriateness for your class.

- Ancient Mysteries: Powerful Gods of Mt. Olympus*

*Also available in the *Glencoe Literature Video Library*.

ADVANCED LEARNERS

Describing a Festive Scene Review the description of the streets on race day. Point out the itemization of the various things—flags, banners, different kinds of food—that make the scene festive. Many things are mentioned, but no one item in any great detail.

Activity Have students work individually or in pairs to write descriptions of festive scenes they have experienced, such as a birthday party, a carnival, or a street festival. Remind them to include many sensory details, such as sounds, smells, textures, and tastes, as well as sights. **L2**

Vocabulary Skills

Prefix *twi-* The prefix *twi-* means two, as in *twice* and *twin*. The word *twilight* is built on the word *light* coupled with *twi*. *Twilight* is formed by the light of day and nightfall. The word *twilight* as used here means "the soft, diffused light from the sky when the sun is below the horizon, either from daybreak to sunrise, or, more commonly, from sunset to nightfall."

it. Night after night, he ran fast as the wind across the twilight field, until he could cross it more quickly than anyone had ever crossed it before.

At last, the day of the race arrived.

Trumpets sounded in the early morning, and the young men gathered at the edge of the field, along with Atalanta herself, the prize they sought. The king and his friends sat in soft chairs, and the townspeople stood along the course.

The king rose to address them all. "Good day," he said to the crowds. "Good luck," he said to the young men. To Atalanta he said, "Good-bye. I must tell you farewell, for tomorrow you will be married."

P "I am not so sure of that, Father," Atalanta answered. She was dressed for the race in trousers of crimson and a shirt of silk as blue as the sky, and she laughed Q as she looked up and down the line of young men.

"Not one of them," she said to herself, "can win the race, for I will run fast as the wind and leave them all behind."

And now a bugle sounded, a flag was dropped, and the runners were off!

The crowds cheered as the young men and Atalanta began to race across the field. At first they ran as a group, but Atalanta soon pulled ahead, with three of the young men close after her. As they neared the halfway point, one young man put on a great burst of speed and seemed to pull ahead for an instant, but then he gasped and fell back. Atalanta shot on.

Soon another young man, tense with the effort, drew near to Atalanta. He

P Active Reading Strategies

VISUALIZE Ask students to visualize the starting line of the race with all the young men and Atalanta, dressed in red pants and a blue shirt, looking them over with disdain.

Q Literary Elements

FIGURES OF SPEECH: *Simile* Point out the author's use of a simile to describe the color of Atalanta's shirt. Ask students to find another simile in this passage. *("I will run as fast as the wind.")*

Viewing the Painting

In the opening ceremonies of the Olympic Games, participating athletes bear the Olympic flag into the stadium, where it flies while the games go on.

Viewing Response *Given what we know about her ability, Atalanta would probably win medals in one or more of the running events.*

Viewing the photograph: Today, a runner as fast as Atalanta would probably run in the Olympic Games. How do you think she would do against today's competitors?

Teaching Support

Grammar and Language *Minilesson*

Irregular Verbs Explain to students that many verbs form their past tense by adding *-ed* to the present form of the verb, but some do not. The past tense of irregular verbs is formed by changing the spelling of the word itself.

Activity Ask students to reread this page and list examples of irregular verbs in the past tense and then write the present tense of those verbs. Students may use a dictionary to find each verb's present tense. **L2**

Past	Present
ran	run
sat	sit
stood	stand
rose	rise
said	say
began	begin
shot	shoot
fell	fall

Additional Resources

- ***Grammar and Language Transparency 56***
- ***Grammar and Language Workbook,*** pp. 95–100
- ***Grammar and Composition Handbook,*** Lessons 3.11, 3.12
- ***Writer's Choice,*** Lesson 10.9

reached out as though to touch her sleeve, stumbled for an instant, and lost speed. Atalanta smiled as she ran on. I have almost won, she thought.

But then another young man came near. This was Young John, running like the wind, as steadily and as swiftly as Atalanta herself. Atalanta felt his closeness, and in a sudden burst she dashed ahead.

R Young John might have given up at this, but he never stopped running. Nothing at all, thought he, will keep me from winning the chance to speak with Atalanta. And on he ran, swift as the wind, until he ran as her equal, side by side with her, toward the golden ribbon that marked the race's end. Atalanta raced even faster to pull ahead, but Young John was a strong match for her. Smiling with the pleasure of the race, Atalanta and Young John reached the finish line together, and together they broke through the golden ribbon.

Trumpets blew. The crowd shouted and leaped about. The king rose. "Who is that young man?" he asked.

"It is Young John from the town," the people told him.

"Very well. Young John," said the king, as John and Atalanta stood before him, exhausted and jubilant from their efforts. "You have not won the race, but you have come closer to winning than any man here. And so I give you the prize that was promised—the right to marry my daughter."

Young John smiled at Atalanta, and she smiled back. "Thank you, sir," said John to the king, "but I could not possibly marry your daughter unless she wished to marry me. I have run this race for the chance to talk with Atalanta, and, if she is willing, I am ready to claim my prize."

Atalanta laughed with pleasure. "And I," she said to John, "could not possibly marry before I have seen the world. But I would like nothing better than to spend the afternoon with you."

Then the two of them sat and talked on the grassy field, as the crowds went away. They ate bread and cheese and purple plums. Atalanta told John about her telescopes and her pigeons, and John told Atalanta about his globes and his studies of geography. At the end of the day, they were friends.

S On the next day, John sailed off to discover new lands. And Atalanta set off to visit the great cities.

By this time, each of them has had wonderful adventures, and seen marvelous sights. Perhaps some day they will be married, and perhaps they will not. In any case, they are friends. And it is certain that they are both living happily ever after.

Vocabulary

jubilant (jo͞o′ bə lənt) *adj.* filled with great joy

claim (klām) *v.* to ask for or demand possession of one's right to something

R Literary Elements

DESCRIPTION: *Symbolism* Ask students what the fact that Atalanta and John are running side by side "as equals" symbolizes. *(The fact that Atalanta and John run side by side symbolizes that they view each other as equals in all things.)*

S Critical Thinking

VERIFYING PREDICTIONS Ask students whether the ending of the story matches their predictions. How does the story's closing line coincide with what its opening lines foreshadowed? *(Some students will say that their predictions were correct, but that it is not the happy ending they imagined.)*

Thematic Focus

A Different Dimension Discuss with students how these two versions of this myth illustrate the theme of this section. *("Atalanta's Race" includes the involvement of the gods and similar mythological occurrences that are quite "magical" and removed from modern life. "Atalanta" offers a different dimension by putting a modern twist on the myth.)*

ASSESSMENT

Quick Checks, p. 60

Real-World Connection

Attitudes Have students discuss which attitudes toward women exhibited in these selections still relate to attitudes toward women in the world today.

Activity Have students work in small groups to create short questionnaires that can be used to survey the opinions of their classmates on the attitudes discussed. Students may wish to pool their efforts and produce only two different questionnaires. Then half the class can answer one and the other half can answer the other. It may be interesting for students to compare the results of the two questionnaires. **L2**

Responding to the Selection

PERSONAL RESPONSE

Encourage students to discuss human dependence or independence, particularly in relation to authority figures.

Analyzing Literature

1. The warning was that she would bring disaster on herself if she married.
2. Her strategy was to race her suitors and win. Whoever lost the race died. They took that risk because of her great beauty.
3. In the first version, she is less assertive and self-sufficient than in the second.
4. Betty Miles's version leaves out the oracle's warning, Venus's assistance to Hippomenes, and the disastrous ending.
5. Her attempt to avoid marriage simply because of the oracle's warning shows her respect for the power of the gods.
6. It meant that she would continue to live, but in a different form.
7. In both, she showed her determination and courage by working hard to avoid something she did not want. In the first version, Atalanta used her running ability to "escape" marriage. In the second, she relied more on her intelligence and her assertiveness.
8. Perhaps because Miles is writing for a modern audience, she wants to convey a message about the equality of women. Her message would not be as effective if the gods have the power to override a person's will no matter what that person does.
9. Some readers may prefer the first for its magical quality and suspense. Others may like the second version for its modern messages.

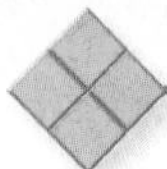

Active Reading and Critical Thinking

Responding to Literature

PERSONAL RESPONSE

- What was your reaction to these stories? How do these tales relate to your response for the **Reading Focus** on page 713? Describe your impressions in your journal.

Analyzing Literature

RECALL

1. In "Atalanta's Race," what warning did the oracle give Atalanta?
2. In "Atalanta's Race," what strategy did Atalanta use to avoid marriage? Why were young men willing to risk their lives for her?
3. How does the character of Atalanta differ in the two versions of the myth?
4. What parts of the myth included in Rex Warner's version are left out of Betty Miles's version?

Brackets connect questions that are paired to develop higher-level thinking skills.

INTERPRET

5. How did Atalanta's actions in "Atalanta's Race" show her respect for the oracle and the decrees of fate? Explain.
6. Explain what the oracle's warning that "though you will continue to live, you will not be yourself" meant.
7. In either version, what does the reader discover about Atalanta's sense of determination and courage in dealing with her life? Identify details to support your ideas.
8. Why do you think Betty Miles left out parts of the Atalanta myth that are included in Rex Warner's version?

EVALUATE AND CONNECT

9. Which version of the myth did you enjoy more? Why?
10. Think of someone who would enjoy reading these myths. What about these stories would appeal to that person?

LITERARY ELEMENTS

Description

A **description** is a carefully detailed portrayal of a person, place, thing, or event. Strong description is an important element in both fiction and nonfiction writing. Skillful writers select details carefully so that their readers can see, hear, smell, taste, and feel what is being described. Both of these myths come alive through the vivid descriptions of the main characters and their worlds.

1. Skim the myths and pick out a description that helps you imagine a particular character or scene. Explain which details help you imagine the character or scene clearly.
2. Choose your favorite description in either myth and explain why it appeals to you.

- See **Literary Terms Handbook,** p. R3.

10. This person would probably also enjoy learning about other cultures, especially ancient Greece and the power of the gods.

LITERARY ELEMENTS

1. On page 715, Warner describes Atalanta's hair in the breeze, touching her shoulders while she runs.
2. Students should use specific examples from the text to support their choices.

Additional Resources

Literary Elements Transparency 60

Literature and Writing

Writing About Literature

Characterization In both myths, the two main characters are revealed through their actions as well as their words. Write a paragraph describing either Atalanta or Hippomenes/John as you picture that person.

Creative Writing

Journal Entry Imagine you are either Atalanta or Hippomenes/John right before the race. What are you thinking and feeling? Write a journal entry describing your thoughts and feelings. Use the myth as a jumping-off point, but feel free to make up details of your own.

Extending Your Response

Literature Groups

Discussing Conflict You know that conflict, the struggle between two or more forces, makes stories interesting. There are four common types of conflict in literature: with nature; with fate; with other people or society; and with oneself. Working in small groups, discuss the kinds of conflicts present in both versions of the Atalanta myth, and talk about which conflict is the most difficult. Support your thoughts and ideas with examples from the myths.

Performing

Live from Ancient Greece! Imagine you are a reporter sent to cover the race by the Hellenic News Network. Interview either Atalanta or Hippomenes after the race. With a partner, create a script that describes the race and the two competitors to use as an introduction before the interview begins. Plan a series of questions to ask, but be ready to ask follow-up questions as the interview proceeds. Share your interview with the class by presenting it as a "live" news report.

Interdisciplinary Activity

Health Physical fitness is good for anyone, not just professional athletes or competitive runners like Atalanta. What are some ways in which people your age can keep fit? Work with a small group to plan a fitness program for average teenagers who don't wish to be competitive athletes. Present your plan to the class.

Reading Further

If you would like to read other myths or folktales, try these books:

Island of the Mighty: Stories of Old Britain by Haydn Middleton

A Treasury of Stories from Around the World chosen by Linda Jennings

 **Save your work for your portfolio.**

Literature and Writing

Writing About Literature

Students' paragraphs should

- use their own words in giving their impressions of the characters
- not be limited to physical features but should also include character traits

Creative Writing

Students' journal entries should

- explain the student's thoughts and feelings clearly, not the character's
- be personal and imaginative in handling this topic

Extending Your Response

Literature Groups Students may focus on Atalanta's conflict with the gods, on her competition with the men pursuing her, on her difference of opinion with her father, or on her contradictory inner feelings about Hippomenes/John.

Interdisciplinary Activity Internet sources, health magazines, and physical education instructors are some sources of information. In presenting a fitness plan to the class, perhaps one student can demonstrate an exercise while another explains it.

Performing Suggest that students may modify the story to suit their own situations. Remind them that a script is important, even if the interview is supposed to look spontaneous.

Skill Minilessons

GRAMMAR AND LANGUAGE
SPELLING COMPOUND WORDS

Students may use additional words such as:
god + mother = godmother
hind + sight = hindsight
hitch + hike = hitchhike

READING AND THINKING
CHRONOLOGICAL ORDER

"Atalanta's Race "

1. Atalanta receives a warning from the oracle.
2. To discourage her suitors, she sets up the conditions of the race.
3. Hippomenes wins with the help of Venus.
4. Venus punishes the couple.

VOCABULARY
ANALOGIES

1. a 3. a 5. b
2. c 4. b

Additional Resources

- ***Grammar and Language Workbook,*** pp. 297–300
- ***Grammar and Composition Handbook,*** Lesson 15.1
- ***Writer's Choice,*** Lesson 23.7
- ***Reading Skills Practice Workbook,*** pp. 107–108
- ***Vocabulary Practice,*** p. 42

Skill Minilessons

Reteach · Review

GRAMMAR AND LANGUAGE • SPELLING COMPOUND WORDS

The word *grandfather* is a compound word made up of the words *grand* and *father.* The rule for spelling compound words is simple. Keep the original spelling of both words, no matter how the words begin or end.

night + time = nighttime
easy + going = easygoing

PRACTICE Write a paragraph describing the race held to find a worthy husband for Atalanta. Make up any details you wish to describe the race. Use at least three compound words in your description. Then trade paragraphs with a partner and read each other's paragraphs. As you read, underline each compound word you find, and check that it is spelled correctly.

- For more about compound words, see **Language Handbook,** Spelling, p. R47.

READING AND THINKING • CHRONOLOGICAL ORDER

The events in both myths are told in chronological order, or the order in which they occur. As a skillful reader, you should always ask questions so you are sure you understand what is going on. As you read, ask yourself questions such as the following.

- What happened first?
- What happened next?
- Do the steps, or the events, occur in an order that makes sense?

PRACTICE Review either myth. Outline the steps taken to find a suitable mate for Atalanta. Write the steps in the order in which they happened in the myth.

- For more about sequencing and chronological order, see **Reading Handbook,** p. R91.

VOCABULARY • ANALOGIES

An analogy is a type of comparison that is based on the relationships between things or ideas. To complete analogies, you must figure out what relationships exist between words. For example, choose an answer for this incomplete analogy:

toe : foot :: finger : ?

Is the answer *nail, thumb,* or *hand?* All three of these words "go with" *finger,* but only one is related in the same way that *foot* goes with *toe.* A *finger* is part of a *hand,* just as a *toe* is part of a *foot.*

- For more about analogies, see **Communications Skills Handbook,** p. R67.

PRACTICE Choose the word that best completes each analogy.

1. lift : drop :: condemn :
   a. praise b. scold c. ban
2. starving : hunger :: parched :
   a. throat b. rain c. thirst
3. cheetah : fleetest :: giraffe :
   a. tallest b. biggest c. rarest
4. terrified : fearful :: jubilant :
   a. relieved b. joyful c. sorry
5. irritable : grouchy :: envious :
   a. sad b. jealous c. suspicious

ASSESSMENT

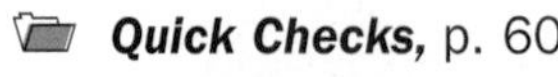

- ***Quick Checks,*** p. 60
- ***Selection and Theme Assessment,*** pp. 103–104
- ***Performance Assessment,*** p. 57
- ***Testmaker: ExamView Pro***
- ***Interactive Tutor: Self-Assessment***

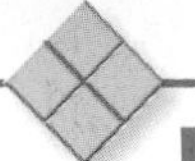

Before You Read

Cat and Rat: The Legend of the Chinese Zodiac

MEET
ED YOUNG

Ed Young, who provides both the words and the pictures for "Cat and Rat," says, "There are things that words do that pictures never can, and likewise, there are images that words can never describe." Young was born in China and lived there until he attended college in the United States. He often uses the traditional Chinese technique of brushing ink on rice paper for his artwork. Young was encouraged to become a children's book illustrator after years of sketching animals at New York City's Central Park Zoo.

Ed Young was born in 1931 in Tientsin, China. This story was published in 1995.

READING FOCUS

Why do you think cats are so good at catching rats?

Think/Pair/Share
Think about a quick explanation for a cat's talents. Share your ideas with a partner.

Setting a Purpose
Read this story to find out about the legendary origins of the relationship between cats and rats.

BUILDING BACKGROUND

The Time and Place This legend is set in China more than 5,000 years ago.

Did You Know? The traditional Chinese calendar is arranged in twelve-year cycles. Each year in the zodiac (the twelve constellations seen in the sky around the earth's orbit) is named after an animal. The zodiac was first introduced to the Chinese people nearly 5,000 years ago by the Emperor Huang Di. According to Chinese astrology, people's personalities share characteristics with the animal that rules their birth year.

VOCABULARY PREVIEW

resourceful (ri sôrs′ fəl) *adj.* capable or skillful in dealing with new or difficult situations; p. 727

podium (pō′ dē əm) *n.* a small, raised platform or stand with a slanted shelf for holding a speaker's papers; p. 728

pounce (pouns) *v.* to swoop down, spring, or leap suddenly in attack; p. 729

Before Reading

Objectives

- To read and understand a legend about another place and time
- To read and identify elements of the legend
- To write an animal tale

Skills

Reading/Thinking: Analyzing Arguments; Drawing Conclusions; Inferring; Making Critical Judgments; Elaborating; Using Graphic Aids; Setting a Purpose for Reading
Writing: Legend
Vocabulary: Using Graphic Aids
Grammar/Language: Commas in a Series; Apostrophes
Listening/Speaking: Dramatization
Life Skills: Decision Making
Collaboration: Literature Groups

Motivating STUDENTS

Selection Focus Transparency 61: Show students the transparency of the Aztec calendar stone. Discuss the skill and perseverance, as well as the knowledge, that were needed to create such an instrument in 400 B.C.

Reading Focus: As an extension of the Reading Focus, have pairs of students use precise language and sensory imagery to express their thoughts on the personalities and traits of cats.

RESOURCE MANAGER

Teaching Tools and Resources
- Theme Seven Planning Guide
- Literature Groups Sourcebook

Essential Lesson Support

Lesson-Specific Instruction
- Selection Focus Transparency 61
- Literary Elements Transparency 61
- Active Reading Guide,* p. 61
- Selection Vocabulary Practice, p. 43

Assessment
- Selection Quick Checks,* p. 61
- Sel. and Theme Assmt., pp. 105–106
- Testmaker: ExamView Pro
- Performance Assessment, p. 58

Systematic Language Instruction
- Gr. & Comp. Hdbk., L. 12.4
- Vocabulary Power, Lesson 31

English Language Learners
- ELL Sourcebook, pp. 89–90
- Spanish Summaries, p. 61
- Spanish Translations, pp. 187–189
- Audio Library*
- English, Yes!

Spec. Needs/Strat. Interven.
- Interactive Rdg. Sbk., pp. T213–T215
- Interactive Rdg. Wkbk., pp. 123–124
- Inclusion Strat. Sbk., pp. 99–100
- Audio Library*

*Also available in Spanish

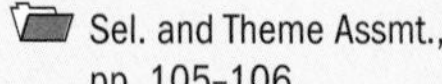
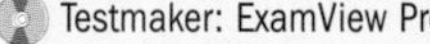

Reading the Selection

SUMMARY

In ancient China, Cat and Rat were good friends. Then the Emperor announced a race. He would name a year of the calendar for each of the first twelve animals to cross the finish line. Cat and Rat, two of the smallest in the race, got a head start by riding on the back of the early rising water buffalo. As they were crossing the river, selfish Rat pushed Cat into the water. She swam as fast as she could but did not finish in time. So to this day, Cat and Rat are enemies.

Spanish Summaries, p. 61

A Active Reading Strategies

PREDICT Ask what students know about the zodiac and how a cat and a rat may be linked to it. *(Students may know that animals are an element in the Chinese zodiac and predict that this story tells why.)*

VOCABULARY If you haven't previewed the selection vocabulary with students, stop and remind them to use context clues to unlock the meanings of new vocabulary words.

Additional Resources

- ***Active Reading Guide,*** p. 61
- ***Audio Library***
- ***Spanish Audio Library***

Teaching Support

A

CONNECTING TO OTHER SELECTIONS

The chart at the right shows three ways to connect "Cat and Rat: The Legend of the Chinese Zodiac" to other selections in this book.

For specific teaching strategies, see the ***Theme Seven Planning Guide.***

Connection		Title
Life Skills: Supporting and Contributing	→	from *Beyond the Limits*, p. 281
Thematic: Twists and Turns	→	"The Cremation of Sam McGee," p. 636
Literary: Legend	→	"Rip Van Winkle," p. 185

726 THEME 7

Cat and Rat: The Legend of the Chinese Zodiac

Ed Young

In China, a long, long time ago, there lived a cat and a rat. They were best friends. They ate together. They played together. They slept together.

One day, the Emperor decided to hold a race among all the animals in the land. The first twelve animals to cross the finish line would have a year in the Chinese calendar named after them. This would be quite an honor.

"But winning the race will not be easy," warned the Emperor. "You must run through the thickest part of the forest and then swim across the river at its widest point."

Cat and Rat each wanted to be the first to cross the finish line. But they knew that they would be two of the smallest animals in the race. B

"We will never make it," Rat complained to Cat.

"Oh, I think we will," replied the resourceful cat.

"We'll ask the water buffalo to help us," said the cat. "He could give us a head start. He always wakes

Vocabulary

resourceful (ri sôrs′ fəl) *adj.* capable or skillful in dealing with new or difficult situations

Historical Note

Astrology, developed as early as 3000 B.C., is the study of how events on earth correspond to the movements of astronomical objects. Astrologers map the positions of these objects on charts called horoscopes. A circle represents the plane on which the earth orbits the sun. The circle is divided into twelve sections—the signs of the zodiac.

FYI

Calendars Not all calendars are the same. New Year's Day, for example, is celebrated January 1 in the Gregorian calendar, which was introduced in 1582. Prior to that, most European countries observed New Year's Day on March 25. The Jewish New Year is celebrated between mid-September and early October. The Chinese New Year is celebrated between January 10 and February 19.

B Critical Thinking

ANALYZING ARGUMENTS Ask students why Rat and Cat, being the smallest animals in the race, are at a disadvantage. *(Their short legs put them at a disadvantage because the race involves crossing a forest and a river.)*

Reading Minilesson

Setting a Purpose for Reading The initial purpose for reading may change depending on what new questions arise. Explain to students that some good questions to ask when they begin reading are *Who are the characters? Where does the story take place? What is the situation?*

Activity Invite volunteers to model processes for setting and revising purposes for reading fiction. The process should include these steps: 1. Identify the material as fiction or nonfiction. 2. When setting a purpose, skim the illustrations and the first page or two to find out what the selection is about. 3. Decide what information is important to find out. **L2**

Additional Resources

Reading Skills Practice Workbook

C Critical Thinking

DRAWING CONCLUSIONS Ask students to describe Buffalo's personality and use story details to support their conclusions. *(Buffalo seems to have an easy-going, generous personality. Even though they are in a competition, Buffalo is willing to help his friends.)*

D Active Reading Strategies

QUESTION Encourage students to raise questions about Rat's treatment of his friend Cat. *(It is unrealistic to suggest that a friend would do such a thing, although that sometimes happens to friends when a prize is involved.)*

E Literary Elements

IMAGERY Through a careful choice of verbs, the author gives a clear picture of each animal at the finish line. Each picture is accurate for that animal, and each is different from the others. For example, "Tiger came roaring." Ask students to identify verbs describing other animals' crossing of the line. *(Rabbit darted, Snake slithered, and Horse thundered. All of these verbs indicate the way these animals actually move.)*

up before sunrise. Maybe we could even ride on his back."

So Cat and Rat convinced Buffalo to wake them up early on the day of the race. The next morning, Buffalo was up long before dawn. "Wake up, lazybones," he said to the sleeping cat and rat. "We had better get started."

Cat and Rat climbed on the buffalo's back. But they were so sleepy that by the time they had fully awakened, they were half way across the river.

Rat woke up first. He saw the Emperor standing at the finish line far, far away. Why should I share the glory of first place with Cat and Buffalo? thought the rat selfishly.

"Wake up, my friend," he cried to Cat. "Look at all the tasty fish swimming in the water."

Cat licked her lips. She leaned over for a closer look, and Rat gave her a little push. SPLASH! She tumbled into the water.

Buffalo turned his head to see what had made the splash. He didn't see the cat, though. What he saw instead were the other animals in the race—and they were close behind him. Without giving Cat or Rat another thought, he sped toward the Emperor.

Just as Buffalo neared the riverbank, the clever rat leaped from behind his ear and crossed the finish line in first place.

"How did such a small animal win the race?" asked the Emperor in surprise.

"I may be small but I am also smart," replied the rat. He scampered up onto the winner's podium. Buffalo knew he had been tricked into second place, but he could only grunt in dismay.

Back in the river, Cat tried to swim along with the other animals. She hated water. But if she had to swim in it to win the race, she would do so.

Far ahead of her, Tiger came roaring across the finish line. "Am I first?" he growled.

"No," said the rat smugly. "You'd have to be awfully clever to beat me."

"And you'd have to get up extra early to beat me," added the buffalo.

Cat scrambled onto a log. She paused to shake herself off and to catch her breath.

By then the sky was dark and a great storm was blowing. A dragon appeared in the clouds above. He was much, much too big to run through woods or swim across a river, so the Emperor had told him he could race through the sky, braving the rains and the wind.

But no sooner had he begun his descent to the earth, than the rabbit darted across the finish line in front of him, taking fourth place. The dragon had to be content with fifth.

In the river, the cat heaved a great sigh, then plunged into the water again. "I can still make it," she told herself. But Snake slithered across the finish line next and hissed a silvery greeting to the five animals who had arrived before him. Snake was number six.

Cat swam as fast as she could. A few moments later, she heard the sound of galloping hooves in the distance. Horse thundered across the finish line in seventh place.

Vocabulary
podium (pō′ dē əm) *n.* a small, raised platform or stand with a slanted shelf for holding a speaker's papers

Teaching Support

MEETING INDIVIDUAL NEEDS — ENGLISH LANGUAGE LEARNERS

Beastly English Explain to English language learners that the English language is full of words and phrases inspired by animals. In fact, certain animal words are used to describe human behavior or character traits that resemble the animal's characteristics.

Activity Have a mixed group of students find out what human behavior or traits each of the following animal words describes: *ape, badger, bug, chicken, duck, parrot, rat,* and *worm.* Students can then use three or four of these terms in sentences. **L2**

Additional Resources

English Language Learners Sourcebook, p. 89

Goat and Monkey weren't far behind. They jumped onto the log on which Cat had rested and paddled across the finish line almost at the same time. But Goat beat Monkey by a hair.

While the nine winners waited patiently with the Emperor, Cat watched Rooster struggle toward the finish line. F Dog could easily have swum ahead of Rooster, but she couldn't resist playing in the water for just a few minutes longer.

From CAT AND RAT: THE LEGEND OF THE CHINESE ZODIAC by Ed Young, ©1995 by Ed Young. Reprinted by permission of Henry Holt and Company, Inc.

Viewing the painting: What event in the legend does this painting show? Does the mood of the painting match the mood of the story? Explain.

"Number ten!" called the Emperor as Rooster staggered in. "Number eleven!" he cried when Dog arrived.

G "Who will be number twelve?" asked the Emperor. "I need just one more animal."

"Me! I will!" called Cat, and she swam even faster.

Unfortunately for Cat, Pig rushed across the finish line in front of her.

"Number twelve!" cried the Emperor, but Cat was still too far away.

"Congratulations to all the winners!" said the Emperor. "One of the twelve years will be named after each of you."

Suddenly, up rushed Cat. She was tired and wet and more than a little unhappy about swimming across the river on her own. "How did I do?" she asked anxiously. "Am I one of the winners?"

"Sorry, dear Cat," replied the Emperor. "All twelve places have been filled."

Upon hearing this news, Cat let out a yowl and tried to pounce on Rat. Her claws scratched the tip of his tail, but Rat squeezed under the Emperor's chair just in time.

And that is why, to this very day, Cat and Rat are enemies.

Vocabulary

pounce (pouns) *v.* to swoop down, spring, or leap suddenly in attack

VIEWING THE PAINTING

Born in Tientsin, China, and brought up in Shanghai, Ed Young cites Chinese painting as a major influence on his work. The Caldecott medalist has illustrated children's books—his own and those of other writers—for more than two decades.

Viewing Response *The painting shows Rat pushing Cat into the water. The painting conveys a mood of surprise, like that in the story, in which a small rat's ruthless cleverness wins out over superior size and strength.*

F Critical Thinking

INFERRING Ask students what the cause of Dog's finishing eleventh instead of tenth tells about dogs in general. You may wish to model the thinking process involved in inferring.

Model: Dog couldn't resist the temptation to play in the water a few minutes longer, even with the finish line in sight. This shows that dogs are, above all, playful animals.

G Literary Elements

LEGEND Ask students what they think the purpose of this legend is, and have them support their reasoning. *(While entertainment is an important objective of the story, the legend's prime purpose is to give people a way of learning about and remembering the Chinese calendar.)*

LIFE SKILLS CONNECTION

Decision Making Mention that Rat's selfish action destroys a friendship which is never restored. He won glory, but lost a friend.

Activity Have students in small groups identify situations in which people have to choose between things and friends. Have them write decision-making guidelines that lie somewhere between these two extremes. **L2**

Extreme	Middle	Extreme
Never do anything to upset a friend	Talk to the friend about conflicting interests and decide together	Do whatever feels good at the time

Ⓗ Critical Thinking

MAKING CRITICAL JUDGMENTS Have students read the description of the Buffalo (Ox) in the graphic and explain how the description does or does not match Buffalo's personality in the story. *(In the story, Buffalo is patient and dependable, waking the Cat and Rat and carrying them across the river. Buffalo shows perseverance in completing the race.)*

Ⓘ Active Reading Strategies

CONNECT Have students read the personality descriptions in the graphics and then have each create a composite of an ideal friend, choosing the most appealing characteristics of each animal.

Rat

1996, 1984, 1972, 1960, 1948, 1936, 1924, 1912, 1900

Rats are innovative and know how to use opportunities to their advantage. They love to collect and organize and tend to be most active while others are at rest. Rats need to be careful not to lose their tempers or to become greedy. Rats get along best with Dragons and Monkeys and least with Horses.

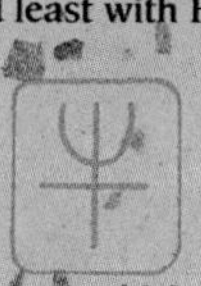

Ox (Buffalo)

1997, 1985, 1973, 1961, 1949, 1937, 1925, 1913, 1901

Ⓗ Ox are honest, conservative, and patient by nature. They are happy when alone. Since friends and family find them dependable, they will make good mothers or fathers. Ox can be stubborn when pushed. They may be slow in starting things, but always complete what they begin. Ox are better friends with Snakes and Roosters and can get into trouble with Goats.

Tiger

1998, 1986, 1974, 1962, 1950, 1938, 1926, 1914, 1902

Ⓘ Tigers are powerful, courageous, and like to take chances—qualities that make them natural leaders. Because of this, they must weigh matters before taking action on them. Tigers need to be careful not to let their brashness offend others. Dogs and Horses are friends with Tigers, but Monkeys are not.

Rabbit

1999, 1987, 1975, 1963, 1951, 1939, 1927, 1915, 1903

This is the luckiest sign of all. Rabbits are gentle, talented, gracious, and friendly. Because of these qualities, they are popular wherever they go as mediators of conflicts. Sometimes Rabbits are overly shy and sentimental, but they almost always succeed at what they do. Their best friends are Goats or Pigs. Roosters may be enemies.

Dragon

2000, 1988, 1976, 1964, 1952, 1940, 1928, 1916, 1904

Dragons have a superimagination and are unique, energetic, and dramatic. Dragons are also moody and can be too perfectionistic. They make good friends with Monkeys and Rats but should beware of Dogs.

Snake

2001, 1989, 1977, 1965, 1953, 1941, 1929, 1917, 1905

Snakes are talented and graceful, intuitive and wise. They are subtle in their ways and care about their looks. Snakes can be stingy at times, but if they use their good qualities to help others, many people will benefit. Snakes' best friends are Roosters and Ox, while their enemies are Pigs.

Teaching Support

Grammar and Language *Minilesson*

Commas in a Series Remind students to use commas to separate three or more items in a series. Write these sentences on the board:

1. An ox is honest conservative and patient by nature.
2. Their energy high spirits and optimism make horses popular among friends.
3. Snakes are talented graceful and wise.

Ask for volunteers to come up to the board to insert commas where they belong.

Activity Then, have students select five animals from the story and write a descriptive sentence about each. Every sentence must include at least three items in a series, i.e., three adjectives, three verbs, or three nouns. **L2**

Additional Resources

- ***Grammar and Language Transparency 58***
- ***Grammar and Language Workbook,*** pp. 255–256
- ***Grammar and Composition Handbook,*** Lesson 13.2
- ***Writer's Choice,*** Lesson 20.2

Horse

2002, 1990, 1978, 1966, 1954, 1942, 1930, 1918, 1906

Horses' energy, high spirits, and optimism make them popular among friends. They have a very independent streak and like to travel alone. Horses must learn patience and learn to finish what they start. They should marry Tigers or Dogs but not Rats.

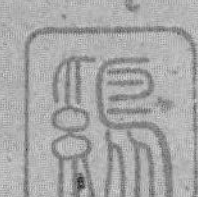

Rooster

2005, 1993, 1981, 1969, 1957, 1945, 1933, 1921, 1909

Roosters are punctual, reliable, independent, and enjoy being on center stage. They are careful and unique but sometimes conceited. Snakes and Ox are friends but Rabbits are trouble.

Goat

2003, 1991, 1979, 1967, 1955, 1943, 1931, 1919, 1907

Although Goats are sometimes shy, they are always loving, gentle, elegant, and creative. They must learn to be direct and to venture out of comfortable situations. Goats get along well with Pigs and Rabbits but are not as friendly with Ox.

Dog

2006, 1994, 1982, 1970, 1958, 1946, 1934, 1922, 1910

Dogs are gregarious, loyal, honest, fun-loving team players. They are also helpful and optimistic but may spend too much time worrying about things. For friendship, Dogs should look to Horses or Tigers. Watch out for Dragons.

Monkey

2004, 1992, 1980, 1968, 1956, 1944, 1932, 1920, 1908

People pay attention to Monkeys because they are very smart. They are confident, energetic, happy, and curious. However, Monkeys can become overly confident, getting ahead of themselves and becoming confused. Monkeys should stay away from Tigers and look for Dragons or Rats as friends.

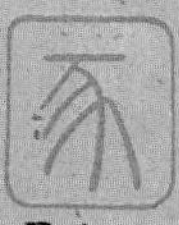

Pig

2007, 1995, 1983, 1971, 1959, 1947, 1935, 1923, 1911

Pigs are noble and physically strong and will sacrifice anything for the welfare of their family. Their friendships are long-lasting, even though they may not always be easy. Pigs can sometimes be reckless. They should stay away from other Pigs and make friends with Rabbits or Goats.

J Critical Thinking

ELABORATING Have students explain why they think "Roosters may be enemies" of Rabbits, and "Snakes and Ox are friends" of Roosters. *(Perhaps because rabbits are shy, whereas roosters enjoy being center stage. Roosters are reliable and snakes can be helpful to others. The Ox is also dependable.)*

Thematic Focus

A Different Dimension Ask students how this selection relates to the theme. *(It provides a different dimension of understanding of the Chinese zodiac.)*

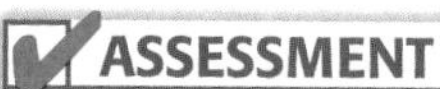

ASSESSMENT

Quick Checks, p. 61

Real-World Connection

Legends Students may learn about legends by listening to people tell them, by researching them on the Internet, or by reading about them in history books or other reliably documented resources. Legends serve to teach and to instill in people the important values of their culture.

Activity Have students research legends, such as George Washington and the cherry tree, Abraham Lincoln reading by firelight, or Paul Revere and his midnight ride. Have each group report to the class on the legend, telling what it is about and what cultural or national values the legend fosters among people. **L2**

Responding to the Selection

PERSONAL RESPONSE

Some students may have expected a more realistic explanation of the relationship between the cat and rat.

Analyzing Literature

1. The emperor will name a year of the calendar after each of the first twelve animals that finish the race.
2. Cat's plan is for Rat and Cat to ride on the back of Buffalo.
3. Rat tricks Cat into looking at the fish and then pushes her into the water. When Buffalo brings Rat close to shore, Rat jumps off his back and scampers ahead of him to finish first.
4. Twelve animals finish before Cat. She lets out a yowl and chases Rat.
5. Rat says, "We will never make it," which shows his pessimism. Cat is more positive and resourceful, thinking up a plan.
6. The legend teaches us that rats are selfish, sneaky creatures.
7. Cats and rats are enemies because Rat tricked Cat out of a great honor.
8. Rat in the story is innovative, opportunistic, and active while others rest. Rat shows a tendency toward greediness.
9. Some students may feel this kind of story may help children remember at least some of the animals because the story puts the abstract concept into concrete form.
10. Students will probably say that their choices are based on more than the generalizations given in the zodiac.

Active Reading and Critical Thinking

Responding to Literature

PERSONAL RESPONSE

- How does the ancient Chinese explanation about cats and rats compare with the ideas you shared in the **Reading Focus** on page 725?

Analyzing Literature

RECALL

1. How does the emperor plan to use the results of the race?
2. What is Cat's plan for succeeding in the race?
3. How does Rat manage to finish the race?
4. How many animals cross the finish line before Cat? How does she react to the results of the race?

Brackets connect questions that are paired to develop higher-level thinking skills.

INTERPRET

5. What do you learn about the personalities of Cat and Rat when they first hear about the race?
6. What does the legend teach about rats in general?
7. According to this tale, why are cats and rats enemies?

EVALUATE AND CONNECT

8. Read the description of people born under the sign of the Rat in the zodiac chart. Which characteristics does Rat in the story share with this description?
9. In your opinion, would this kind of imaginative explanation for the Chinese calendar help children remember the animals associated with each year? Why or why not?
10. Personal Connection Would you use the Chinese Zodiac or something similar to it as a guide for choosing your friends? Why or why not?

LITERARY ELEMENTS

Legend

Legends, folktales, and myths are part of folk literature—the collected beliefs and traditions of a people. A **legend** is a story, handed down from generation to generation, about a specific person or thing. Legends share some characteristics of folktales and myths. For example, they may include explanations of how things in nature came about. However, legends are usually associated with a particular person or place and often deal someone or something that exists or existed historically. For example, the twelve-month zodiac in "Cat and Rat" has been the center of Chinese astrology for thousands of years.

1. How does the "Cat and Rat" legend explain why cats are great rat catchers?
2. Do you think the twelve zodiac animals were really chosen as a result of a race? Why or why not?

- See **Literary Terms Handbook,** p. R6.

LITERARY ELEMENTS

1. Rat tricked Cat out of having a year in the Chinese calendar named after her. Ever since, Cat has sought revenge.
2. The legend of the race was probably written to promote knowledge of the already-existing calendar.

Additional Resources

 ***Literary Elements Transparency 61***

Literature and Writing

Writing About Literature

Plot The plot of "Cat and Rat" begins with Cat and Rat as friends and ends when they become enemies. Using the diagram on pages 144–145 as a model, draw and label a diagram identifying the five stages of the legend's plot.

Creative Writing

Why Do . . . ? Think of your favorite animal. Then choose one of the animal's more interesting traits or physical characteristics to explain in a legend. Illustrate your tale with pictures that call attention to the characteristic you explained.

Extending Your Response

Literature Groups

Reality and Fantasy Myths, legends, and folktales combine reality and fantasy. For example, an emperor inventing a new calendar could be a realistic event. However, a cat and a rat having a conversation is fantasy. List other examples of reality and fantasy in "Cat and Rat." Compare your findings with those of the rest of the class.

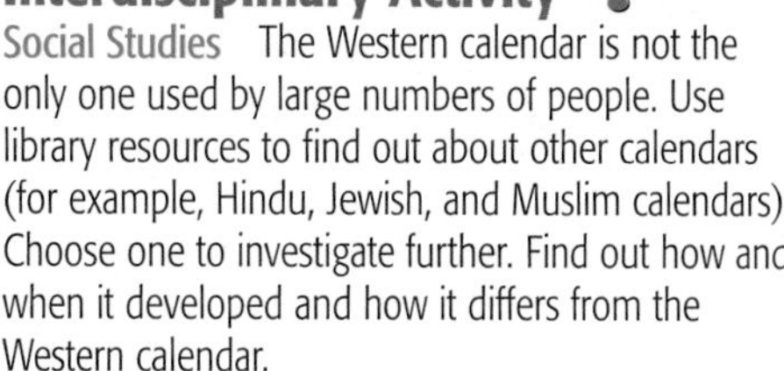

Performing

Dramatize Form an acting troupe to perform "Cat and Rat." Adapt the story so that it takes place in a present-day setting. Write a script, and then choose students to take the parts of the emperor, the various animals, and a narrator. You may want to design and build simple scenery and make costumes that suggest the various characters as well. Perform the legend for another class.

Interdisciplinary Activity

Social Studies The Western calendar is not the only one used by large numbers of people. Use library resources to find out about other calendars (for example, Hindu, Jewish, and Muslim calendars). Choose one to investigate further. Find out how and when it developed and how it differs from the Western calendar.

Reading Further

If you would like to read other Chinese legends, try:

How the Ox Star Fell from Heaven by Lily Toy Hong

Min-Yo and the Moon Dragon by Elizabeth Hillman

Save your work for your portfolio.

Literature and Writing

Writing About Literature

Students' diagrams should

- identify and label the five stages of the legend's plot
- identify the events at each stage

Creative Writing

Students' tales should

- portray the animals' general characteristics as accurately as possible
- use illustrations that convey an idea without being attempts at great artistic creation

Extending Your Response

Literature Groups Students may view the animosity between the cat and the rat as realism, but their competing in a race as fantasy.

Performing Suggest that students use their imaginations in adapting the story. For example, because it is not possible to use a river in their performance, students may create another type of obstacle the "animals" must overcome.

Interdisciplinary Activity Internet sources and encyclopedias can provide the information needed. Suggest that in starting their research students prepare lists of questions that they can use, but not be limited to, as they work.

Skill Minilessons

GRAMMAR AND LANGUAGE
APOSTROPHES IN CONTRACTIONS

1. They'd
2. We'll
3. We'd
4. They'd
5. I'm

READING AND THINKING
USING GRAPHIC AIDS

Students may find some points of agreement and disagreement when matching their personalities to the one described in the graphic. They can include both in their paragraphs. Encourage them to give explanations or examples of how their personalities do or do not match the zodiac profile.

VOCABULARY
THE SUFFIX *-ful*

1. having much skill
2. brilliant, well-worked
3. policy that leads to waste
4. response accompanied by tears
5. number of coins that would fit in one hand

Additional Resources

- ***Grammar and Language Workbook,*** pp. 273–274
- ***Grammar and Composition Handbook,*** Lesson 13.7
- ***Writer's Choice,*** Lesson 20.7
- ***Reading Skills Practice Workbook,*** p. 109–110
- ***Vocabulary Practice,*** p. 43

Skill Minilessons

Reteach • Review

GRAMMAR AND LANGUAGE • APOSTROPHES IN CONTRACTIONS

A **contraction** is a word made by putting two words together and replacing one or more letters with an apostrophe.

it + is = it's	we + are = we're
I + will = I'll	she + would = she'd

PRACTICE Copy each sentence from the story. Then find and underline two words that could be combined into a contraction. Write the contraction above the words.

1. They would be two of the smallest.
2. We will never make it.
3. We had better get started.
4. They had fully awakened.
5. But I am also smart.

• For more about apostrophe usage, see **Language Handbook,** pp. R40–R41.

READING AND THINKING • USING GRAPHIC AIDS

Stories and novels are most often illustrated by drawings or paintings, but sometimes a story includes a graphic aid. A **graphic aid** is a chart, graph, map, or other illustration that organizes information for the reader. The graphic aid in "Cat and Rat" is the chart of the zodiac. Without this chart, the purpose of the legend would be difficult to understand. The zodiac chart shows the order of the twelve year names, the Chinese symbol for each year, the birth years for anyone born between 1900 and 2007, as well as the personality traits for people born in each of the twelve years.

PRACTICE In what year were you born? Look up your birth year on the zodiac chart on pages 730–731. Then write a paragraph explaining how your personality does or does not match the one described in the graphic. Find out the birth years of members of your family, and compare their personality traits with those described under the matching animals.

• For more about interpreting graphic aids, see **Reading Handbook,** pp. 101–102.

VOCABULARY • THE SUFFIX *-FUL*

A *hopeful* person is full of hope; a *cheerful* one is full of cheer; a *fearful* one is full of fear. In each of these cases, you could define the word by simply adding "full of" to the base word. However, you can't always define a word this way. For example, a *dreadful* sight is not a sight that is full of dread; it's a sight that fills the viewer with dread. An area with many natural resources, such as oil, is "rich in resources" or "resource rich," but not *resourceful.*

PRACTICE Briefly explain what each underlined word means.

1. a skillful athlete
2. a masterful plan
3. a wasteful policy
4. a tearful response
5. a handful of coins

• For more about adding suffixes, see **Language Handbook,** Spelling, pp. R44–R45.

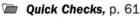

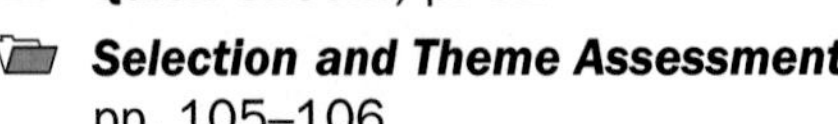

- ***Quick Checks,*** p. 61
- ***Selection and Theme Assessment,*** pp. 105–106
- ***Performance Assessment,*** p. 58
- ***Testmaker: ExamView Pro***
- ***Interactive Tutor: Self-Assessment***

Vo•cab•u•lar•y *Skills*

Analyzing Word Parts

The best source of information for the meaning of an unfamiliar word is a dictionary, but a dictionary is not always handy. Context clues are often useful, but in many cases, there are not enough context clues to provide adequate help. Many words themselves contain clues to their meanings. Familiar base words, roots, or other word parts can provide information about the meaning of the word.

"The Smallest Dragonboy" says, "Being the youngest candidate was not an enviable position." The sentence provides little help for the meaning of *enviable.* It could mean "lucky" or "common" or many other things. However, the word itself is helpful because it is made up of the base word *envy* and the suffix *-able.* Putting these clues together provides an idea very close to the actual meaning of "able to be envied."

A word may have a familiar root. For example, look at *spectacle* in this sentence:

> "The Bunyan family must have been quite a spectacle."

If you are familiar with words like *spectator* or *inspect,* you can figure out that a *spectacle* is something that is seen. The Latin root *spec* (or *spect*) means "to look at."

Analyzing words is not a substitute for looking them up in a good dictionary. A word part may look like a familiar root, but it might not be one. Also, the meaning of the word may have changed over time. Still, analyzing words can sometimes provide real help when you need to guess at a meaning.

EXERCISE

Analyze the underlined words, using whatever clues they contain to help you. Then match each word to its meaning on the right.

1. a new modification	a. to abuse
2. to dislocate a knee	b. harmful or damaging
3. a migratory way of life	c. one who is not thankful
4. to be a noncombatant	d. a slight change in form
5. to identify a precondition	e. characterized by moving from place to place
6. behave like an ingrate	f. a small piece or fragment
7. an injurious act	g. to put out of the proper position
8. to use some leverage	h. increased means of accomplishing a purpose
9. to maltreat someone	i. one whose duties do not include actual fighting
10. a snippet of information	j. something required before something else can occur

Vo•cab•u•lar•y *Skills*

Objective

- To recognize and use strategies for analyzing words

Teaching Strategies

Ask students to conduct a vocabulary hunt through the stories in this theme to find a word they don't know the meaning of. Have them write the word down and try to figure out its meaning by analyzing the base, root, prefix, and/or suffix of the word. Encourage students to use one another as resources in analyzing their words. They may also use hard-bound or electronic dictionaries to clarify the meanings and usage of words.

Exercise

1. d
2. g
3. e
4. i
5. j
6. c
7. b
8. h
9. a
10. f

Additional Resources

Vocabulary Power

Teaching Support

MEETING INDIVIDUAL NEEDS

ENGLISH LANGUAGE LEARNERS

Word Families Exposure to word families can help English language learners analyze new words and expand their vocabularies. Write these roots and their meanings on the board: *geo* (earth), *luna* (moon), *therme* (heat), and *bios* (life).

Activity Have students work in mixed groups. Ask them to choose one of the root words listed on the board and write six words that contain that root, one per card, on index cards and to illustrate the words on the other sides of the cards.

Additional Resources

English Language Learners Sourcebook, p. 90

Before Reading

Objectives

- To read and analyze a myth about a boy who ignores his father's advice
- To learn and identify the important elements of myths
- To describe one of the characters on the basis of the author's characterization

Skills

Reading/Thinking: Identifying Spatial Relationships
Writing: News Report
Vocabulary: Dictionary Skills: Definitions
Collaboration: Literature Groups

Motivating STUDENTS

Selection Focus Transparency 62: Have students view the transparency and discuss the questions provided.

Reading Focus: As an extension of the Reading Focus, have small groups discuss how they distinguish good advice from poor advice and identify which factors influence their decisions.

Before You Read

Icarus and Daedalus

MEET JOSEPHINE PRESTON PEABODY

Josephine Preston Peabody's parents introduced her to literature and the theater at a young age. As a result, Peabody grew up reading and writing constantly. She published her first poem when she was fourteen years old. Six years later, the publication of her poems in magazines helped her to attend Radcliffe College. One of her verse dramas, "The Piper," was based on the Pied Piper legend and was produced at theaters in New York City and London.

Josephine Preston Peabody was born in Brooklyn, New York, in 1874 and died in Cambridge, Massachusetts, in 1922.

READING FOCUS

Have you ever known someone who ignored caution and did something dangerous?

Journal
Write your thoughts and feelings about failing to heed good advice. Then share your ideas in a small-group discussion.

Setting a Purpose
Read this story to find out what happens to Icarus and Daedalus.

BUILDING BACKGROUND

The Time and Place This story takes place on the Greek island of Crete in the legendary time when both mortals and gods inhabited ancient Greece.

Did You Know? The word *myth* comes from *mythos,* a Greek word meaning "story." A myth is a special kind of story, usually involving gods and goddesses. The origins of the Greek myths are unknown, but they likely developed over many hundreds of years of oral retellings before the Greeks developed writing. They were already very old by around 850 B.C., when the Greek writer Homer referred to them in his poems. The Greek myths tell the stories of the gods and goddesses, their lives on Mount Olympus, and their interactions with the mortals on earth.

VOCABULARY PREVIEW

veer (vēr) *v.* to shift or change direction; p. 737
waver (wā′ vər) *v.* to become unsteady; p. 738
rash (rash) *adj.* done without thought or preparation; reckless; p. 738
reel (rēl) *v.* to turn or seem to turn round and round; whirl; p. 739
quench (kwench) *v.* to satisfy or put an end to a need or desire; p. 739
vainly (vān′ lē) *adv.* without success; uselessly; p. 739

736 THEME 7

RESOURCE MANAGER

Teaching Tools and Resources
- Theme Seven Planning Guide
- Literature Groups Sourcebook

Essential Lesson Support

Lesson-Specific Instruction
- Selection Focus Transparency 62
- Literary Elements Transparency 62
- Active Reading Guide,* p. 62
- Selection Vocabulary Practice, p. 44

Assessment
- Selection Quick Checks,* p. 62
- Sel. and Theme Assmt., pp. 107–108
- Testmaker: ExamView Pro
- Performance Assessment, p. 59

Systematic Language Instruction
- Gr. & Comp. Hdbk., L. 13.1
- Spelling Power, Lesson 27

English Language Learners
- ELL Sourcebook, p. 91
- Spanish Summaries, p. 62
- Spanish Translations, pp. 190–191
- Audio Library*
- English, Yes!

Spec. Needs/Strat. Interven.
- Interactive Rdg. Sbk., pp. T216–T218
- Interactive Rdg. Wkbk., pp. 125–126
- Inclusion Strat. Sbk., pp. 25–26
- Audio Library*

*Also available in Spanish

Icarus and Daedalus

Josephine Preston Peabody

Among all those mortals who grew so wise that they learned the secrets of the gods, none was more cunning than Daedalus.[1]

He once built, for King Minos of Crete, a wonderful Labyrinth of winding ways so cunningly tangled up and twisted around that, once inside, you could never find your way out again without a magic clue. But the king's favor veered with the wind, and one day he had his master architect imprisoned in a tower. Daedalus managed to escape from his cell; but it seemed impossible to leave the island, since every ship that came or went was well guarded by order of the king.

At length, watching the sea gulls in the air—the only creatures that were sure of liberty—he thought of a plan for himself and his young son Icarus,[2] who was captive with him.

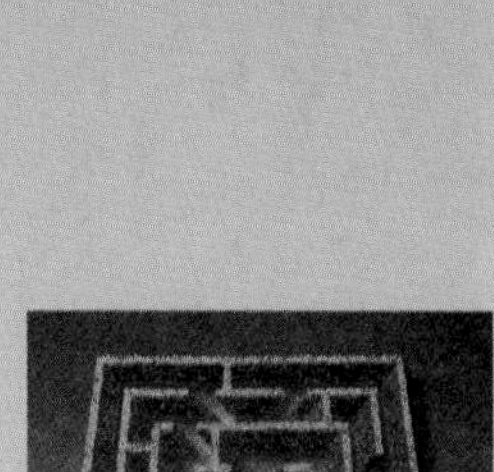

Did You Know?
The *Labyrinth* (lab′ ə rinth′) was a huge maze in which a complicated, twisted path enclosed by high walls made it impossible for people to find the way out once they had entered it.

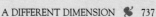

1. *Daedalus* (ded′ əl əs)
2. *Icarus* (ik′ ər əs)

Vocabulary
veer (vēr) *v.* to shift or change direction

Reading the Selection

SUMMARY

King Minos has imprisoned the master architect Daedalus and his son, Icarus, on an island. Daedalus builds wings they can use to escape. He warns the boy not to fly too high or too low, but in the joy of flying, Icarus forgets the warning. When he flies too close to the sun, his wings melt, and in terror he falls to his death. Filled with grief, Daedalus vows never to attempt to fly again.

Spanish Summaries, p. 62

A Active Reading Strategies

PREDICT Have students read this page and then predict what will happen to Daedalus and Icarus. *(Context clues tell them that Daedalus is an ingenious inventor, so students may predict he will find a way to escape from the island.)*

VOCABULARY If you haven't previewed the selection vocabulary with students, stop and remind them to use context clues to unlock the meanings of new vocabulary words.

Additional Resources

- ***Active Reading Guide,*** p. 62
- ***Audio Library***
- ***Spanish Audio Library***

Teaching Support

CONNECTING TO OTHER SELECTIONS

COMPARING selections

This selection is compared with "Prometheus" on page 742. A lesson for teaching a comparison of the two selections appears on page 747.

The chart at the right shows three ways to connect "Icarus and Daedalus" to other selections in this book.

For specific teaching strategies, see the ***Theme Seven Planning Guide.***

Connection		Title
Life Skills: Teaching and Mentoring	→	"Racing the Great Bear," p. 268
Thematic: Facing Challenge	→	"Dreams," p. 261
Literary: Narrator	→	"The Wreck of the Hesperus," p. 227

VIEWING THE PAINTING

This painting was done during Matisse's late life when, due to ill health, he could not paint at an easel. He worked in bed and produced a series of works on paper that he painted, cut out, and pasted in place.

Viewing Response *The dancing Icarus painted by Matisse seems to throw caution to the wind, just as Icarus did in the myth.*

B Literary Elements

MYTH: *Character* Ask students what this passage reveals about Daedalus' relationship with his son. *(He is a careful and caring father.)*

C Literary Elements

MYTH: *Point of View* Ask students who is telling the story and what he reveals about the characters. *(There is a nameless narrator who lets readers in on the characters' thoughts and conversations.)*

LITERATURE & HUMANITIES

Have students examine the portrayal of Icarus in *Introducing Art*, page 76. Discuss why Matisse might have chosen to portray Icarus in this way and how the artist creates a sense of movement.

Icarus, 1947. Henri Matisse. From the *Jazz* series. Gouache on paper, 42 x 32.5 cm. COPYRIGHT ARS, New York, Ecole des Beaux Arts, Paris.

Viewing the painting: How is the flight of Icarus, as described in the myth, like the Icarus painted by Matisse? What important differences do you see?

Little by little, he gathered a store of feathers great and small. He fastened these together with thread, molded them in with wax, and so fashioned two great wings like those of a bird. When they were done, Daedalus fitted them to his own shoulders, and after one or two efforts, he found that by waving his arms he could winnow the air and cleave[3] it, as a swimmer does the sea. He held himself aloft, wavered this way and that with the wind, and at last, like a great fledgling,[4] he learned to fly.

Without delay, he fell to work on a pair of wings for the boy Icarus, and taught him carefully how to use them, bidding him beware of rash adventures among **B** the stars. "Remember," said the father, "never to fly very low or very high, for the fogs about the earth **C**

3. Here, *winnow* and *cleave* both mean "to separate or divide."
4. A *fledgling* is a young bird that hasn't yet grown the feathers it needs to fly.

Vocabulary
waver (wā′ vər) *v.* to become unsteady
rash (rash) *adj.* done without thought or preparation; reckless

Teaching Support

Reading Minilesson

Identifying Spatial Relationships Words that refer to location or distance help readers visualize the setting, plot events, and characters' actions in a story. Some words that are clues to location or distance include *between, below, about, left, alongside, here, outside, around, close to, far, right, over, near, in, into, beside, middle, next to, beyond, north, east, on, opposite, there, inside, in front of, under, out, behind, across, above, toward, by,* and *away from.* These words help answer the question "Where?"

Activity Have students work in small groups and have each group choose a scene from the story. Ask each group to develop stage directions and write details for scenery and the location of characters for a play based on the scene they choose from the story. When they have completed their work, engage them in a discussion about how understanding spatial relationships in a selection can help readers understand that selection better. **L3**

Additional Resources

 ***Reading Skills Practice Workbook***

would weigh you down, but the blaze of the sun will surely melt your feathers apart if you go too near."

For Icarus, these cautions went in at one ear and out by the other. Who could remember to be careful when he was to fly for the first time? Are birds careful? Not they! And not an idea remained in the boy's head but the one joy of escape.

The day came, and the fair wind that was to set them free. The father bird put on his wings, and, while the light urged them to be gone, he waited to see that all was well with Icarus, for the two could not fly hand in hand. Up they rose, the boy after his father. The hateful ground of Crete sank beneath them; and the country folk, who caught a glimpse of them when they were high above the treetops, took it for a vision of the gods—Apollo, perhaps, with Cupid[5] after him.

At first there was a terror in the joy. The wide vacancy of the air dazed them—a glance downward made their brains reel. But when a great wind filled their wings, and Icarus felt himself sustained, like a halcyon-bird[6] in the hollow of a wave, like a child uplifted by his mother, he forgot everything in the world but joy. He forgot Crete and the other islands that he had passed over: he saw but vaguely that winged thing in the distance before him that was his father Daedalus. He longed for one draft[7] of flight to quench the thirst of his captivity: he stretched out his arms to the sky and made toward the highest heavens.

Alas for him! Warmer and warmer grew the air. Those arms, that had seemed to uphold him, relaxed. His wings wavered, drooped. He fluttered his young hands vainly—he was falling—and in that terror he remembered. The heat of the sun had melted the wax from his wings; the feathers were falling, one by one, like snowflakes; and there was none to help.

He fell like a leaf tossed down the wind, down, down, with one cry that overtook Daedalus far away. When he returned, and sought high and low for the poor boy, he saw nothing but the bird-like feathers afloat on the water, and he knew that Icarus was drowned.

The nearest island he named Icaria, in memory of the child; but he, in heavy grief, went to the temple of Apollo in Sicily, and there hung up his wings as an offering. Never again did he attempt to fly.

5. In mythology, *Apollo* is the god of the sun, and *Cupid* is the god of love.
6. Here, *sustained* means to be kept from sinking or falling. The *halcyon-bird* (hal′ sē ən), or kingfisher, glides slowly and smoothly near the water's surface as it hunts for fish.
7. Here, *draft* means "taste."

Vocabulary

reel (rēl) *v.* to turn or seem to turn round and round; whirl
quench (kwench) *v.* to satisfy or put an end to a need or desire
vainly (vān′ lē) *adv.* without success; uselessly

D Active Reading Strategies

CONNECT Ask students if they can relate this passage to instances in their own lives when they have not listened to the advice of an older person. Encourage students to share their experiences.

E Author's Craft

MYTH: *Figurative Language* Discuss the way the author uses figurative language to hint at ideas behind the action in this passage. *(Flying gave Icarus a sense of happiness he had not felt since his mother lifted him in her arms. He longed to be free of captivity.)*

Thematic Focus

A Different Dimension Myths often include elements that are impossible or unrealistic and seem to be from another dimension. Explain that by evoking an unreal world, myths speak to universal truths, letting the reader know that the tale is more than a simple story and has much to teach.

FINE ART TRANSPARENCY 25

You may wish to use ***Fine Art Transparency 25*** to enrich the discussion.

ASSESSMENT

Quick Checks, p. 62

MEETING INDIVIDUAL NEEDS: ENGLISH LANGUAGE LEARNERS

Prefixes The prefix *re-* means "again," "once more," or "back," as in *remember* (to be mindful of again); *remain* (to stay back); and *return* (to turn back). Explain that knowing the meaning of *re-* will help English language learners understand the meanings of other words that contain this prefix.

Activity Have students write the definitions of the following words that use the prefix *re-*. If necessary, help students look up meanings in the dictionary.

relearn *(to learn again)*
relight *(to light again)*
recapture *(to capture again)*

Additional Resources

English Language Learners Sourcebook, p. 91

Responding to the Selection

PERSONAL RESPONSE

Students might explain that Icarus was young and did not know how to listen; he also became overwhelmed with joy when he began to fly.

Analyzing Literature

1. King Minos locks them in a tower on the island and guards all the ships.
2. Daedalus loves his son Icarus.
3. Icarus flies too close to the sun, melting his wings. He drowns in the sea.
4. Daedalus goes to the temple of Apollo in Sicily, hangs up his wings, and never flies again.
5. Since Crete is an island, there are only two ways for Daedalus and his son to escape: by sea or by air. King Minos guards all the ships, so the only way left for them to escape is to fly.
6. Yes. Daedalus makes wings for Icarus and warns him about the dangers he is to avoid. He is heartbroken when he loses his son and never flies again.
7. Because Icarus gets carried away with his sense of freedom, he forgets his father's words of warning.
8. Some students may think that Daedalus feels responsible. Perhaps he should not have flown so far ahead of his son.
9. Students will probably say yes, they would listen to the father's advice. He is known to be a genius and he would not warn about the risk of flying if it were not a real danger.
10. Students will probably feel sad about the tragic ending of this story. It is a tragedy that Daedalus escapes imprisonment but loses his son.

Active Reading and Critical Thinking

Responding to Literature

PERSONAL RESPONSE

- Why didn't Icarus listen to his father's words of wisdom? Describe your impressions in your journal.

Analyzing Literature

RECALL

1. What does King Minos do to keep Daedalus and Icarus from escaping Crete?
2. Describe the relationship between Daedalus and Icarus.
3. What happens to Icarus?
4. What does Daedalus do once he reaches safety?

Brackets connect questions that are paired to develop higher-level thinking skills.

INTERPRET

5. How does the setting of the story influence the plot? Support your ideas with details from the story.
6. Do you think that Daedalus is a concerned father? Why or why not? Support your opinion with examples.
7. Why does Icarus disobey his father's words of caution?
8. Do you think Daedalus feels responsible for what happens to his son? Why or why not?

EVALUATE AND CONNECT

9. Imagine that you are Icarus. Would you listen to your father's advice? Why or why not?
10. How do you feel about what happens to the main characters in this myth? Explain.

LITERARY ELEMENTS

Myth

People in every culture throughout the world have created myths. A **myth** is an ancient story of unknown origins, often involving gods and heroes. Myths originally helped people try to explain how natural events and human actions happened. There are myths about every facet of human life, from the creation of the world to an understanding of why things grow. In fact, collections of myths, called mythologies, generally account for everything in the experience of a particular culture.

1. What elements in "Icarus and Daedalus" fit the definition of a myth?
2. What can you learn about ancient Greek culture from reading this myth?

- See **Literary Terms Handbook,** p. R7.

LITERARY ELEMENTS

1. The story refers to the Greek gods and describes how humans can fly with bird feathers.
2. In ancient Greece they believed in the gods Apollo and Cupid; King Minos ruled the island of Crete; and Daedalus built the famous Labyrinth.

Additional Resources

 ***Literary Elements Transparency 62***

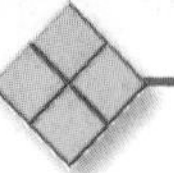

Literature and Writing

Writing About Literature

Characterization **Characterization** refers to the ways in which an author informs readers about the characters in a story. You learn about characters through their thoughts, words, actions, and interactions with other characters, and from what other characters say about them. Describe one of the characters as you picture him from the author's characterization.

Creative Writing

The Greek Gazette Imagine that you have been assigned to write a news story about Daedalus and his flight to freedom. Interview a partner who plays the role of Daedalus just as he and Icarus are preparing for their journey. Then write a news report based on the interview and the results of the flight. Share your news story with your classmates in an oral presentation.

Extending Your Response

Literature Groups

Thinking About Theme Discuss the theme of "Icarus and Daedalus." Focus on the questions: What did Daedalus fear would happen to his son? Why did Icarus choose to ignore his father's words of caution? Review your notes from the **Reading Focus** on page 736, and talk about the meaning of this myth as it relates to life today.

Art Activity

Modeling Create a model or draw a diagram of Daedalus's flying machine as you picture it.

Save your work for your portfolio.

Skill Minilesson

Reteach • Review

VOCABULARY • DICTIONARY SKILLS: DEFINITIONS

vain (vān) *adj.* **1.** too interested in, or proud of, one's own abilities, appearance, or accomplishments: *a vain man.* **2.** not successful or effective: *a vain attempt.* **3.** of no real value or meaning; empty: *a vain promise. adv.* vainly

PRACTICE Study the dictionary definitions above. Decide which meaning of *vain* (or *vainly*) is used in each sentence and write the number of that meaning.

1. One might expect *vain* satisfaction in a man who had accomplished what no other had ever done.
2. After all, Daedalus triumphed over King Minos's *vain* efforts to confine him.
3. Instead of *vainly* showing off his ability, however, Daedalus never flew again.
4. Liberty itself seemed *vain* to him when achieved at the cost of his son.
5. Could he have known how *vain* his warnings would be?

Literature and Writing

Writing About Literature

Students' descriptions should
- tell how they picture one of the characters
- use the author's characterization as a basis for the description

Creative Writing

Students' news reports should
- include an interview with Daedalus as he and Icarus are preparing for their escape
- describe what took place during and after the flight

Extending Your Response

Literature Groups As students discuss the myth, be sure they see its universal aspect: everyone has opportunities to heed or ignore the advice of others. Have students share examples from their own experience.

Art Activity Provide students with time and materials to complete their models or diagrams. When they have finished, have them share their work with the class.

Skill Minilesson

VOCABULARY • DICTIONARY SKILLS: DEFINITIONS

1. 1
2. 2
3. 1
4. 3
5. 2

Additional Resources

Vocabulary Practice, p. 44

interNET CONNECTION

Definitions Invite students to go online and use a search engine to locate the *Web of Online Dictionaries*. Students can search the site's many dictionaries for information about the meanings of new or unfamiliar words and example sentences using the words.

ASSESSMENT

- ***Quick Checks,*** p. 62
- ***Selection and Theme Assessment,*** pp. 107–108
- ***Performance Assessment,*** p. 59
- ***Testmaker: ExamView Pro***
- ***Interactive Tutor: Self-Assessment***

Before Reading

Objectives

- To read and analyze a Greek myth about how fire was given to humans
- To identify the theme of a Greek myth
- To explain how "Prometheus" might have been an ancient Greek explanation for the origins of civilization

Skills

Reading/Thinking: Drawing Conclusions
Writing: Journal Writing
Grammar/Language: Dashes
Collaboration: Literature Groups

Motivating → STUDENTS

Selection Focus Transparency 63: Have students read and discuss the quote by Joseph Campbell. Invite them to think of examples of both heroes and celebrities.

Reading Focus: As an extension of the Reading Focus, invite students to create a poster with the caption "Knowledge is power." After students have discussed the expression, encourage them to develop images that fit their ideas.

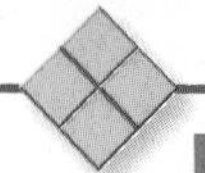

Before You Read

Prometheus

MEET BERNARD EVSLIN

Having written plays for the stage and screen and published a novel for adults, Bernard Evslin (əv′ slin) decided on a career shift. In the mid-1960s, he began retelling myths and other ancient stories for an audience of young readers. His gift was his ability to retell ancient tales, whether from Greek mythology or the Bible, with such colorful details and contemporary language that some of the oldest stories in the world captured the interests of young readers.

Bernard Evslin was born in Pennsylvania in 1916 and died in Hawaii in 1993. This story was published in 1966.

READING FOCUS

Think about the expression "Knowledge is power." What does it mean? Do you agree or disagree with it? Why?

Sharing Ideas
Jot down your ideas about the meaning of the expression, and then share them in a small-group discussion.

Setting a Purpose
Read this myth to find out what a giant thinks about knowledge.

BUILDING BACKGROUND

The Time and Place This story takes place in Greece in the days when the gods and goddesses of Greek mythology were thought to rule the lives of mortals.

Did You Know? In Greek art, Prometheus is often pictured chained to a rock, his body attacked by vultures.

Coppa laconica con punizione di Atlante e Prometeo, 630–100 B.C. Pottery. Museo Gregoriano Etrusco, Vaticano.

VOCABULARY PREVIEW

decree (di krē′) *n.* an official rule, order, or decision; p. 743
aptitude (ap′ tə to͞od′) *n.* a natural ability; talent; p. 743
humility (hū mil′ ə tē) *n.* the quality of being humble or modest; p. 744
spite (spīt) *n.* a desire to hurt or annoy another person; p. 744
agony (ag′ ə nē) *n.* great pain and suffering of the mind or body; p. 745
hover (huv′ ər) *v.* to remain as if suspended in the air over a particular spot; p. 745

RESOURCE MANAGER

Teaching Tools and Resources
- Theme Seven Planning Guide
- Literature Groups Sourcebook

Essential Lesson Support

Lesson-Specific Instruction
- Selection Focus Transparency 63
- Literary Elements Transparency 63
- Active Reading Guide,* p. 63
- Selection Vocabulary Practice, p. 45

Assessment
- Selection Quick Checks,* p. 63
- Sel. and Theme Assmt., pp. 107–108
- Testmaker: ExamView Pro
- Performance Assessment, p. 59

Systematic Language Instruction
- Gr. & Comp. Hdbk., L. 13.2
- Vocabulary Power, Lesson 32
- Spelling Power, Lesson 28

English Language Learners
- ELL Sourcebook, p. 92
- Spanish Summaries, p. 63
- Spanish Translations, pp. 192–194
- Audio Library*
- English, Yes!

Spec. Needs/Strat. Interven.
- Interactive Rdg. Sbk., pp. T218–T221
- Interactive Rdg. Wkbk., pp. 127–128
- Audio Library*

*Also available in Spanish

PROMETHEUS

Retold by Bernard Evslin

Prometheus was a young Titan, no great admirer of Zeus.[1] Although he knew the great lord of the sky hated explicit questions, he did not hesitate to beard[2] him when there was something he wanted to know.

One morning he came to Zeus and said, "O Thunderer, I do not understand your design. You have caused the race of man to appear on earth, but you keep him in ignorance and darkness."

"Perhaps you had better leave the race of man to me," said Zeus. "What you call ignorance is innocence. What you call darkness is the shadow of my decree. Man is happy now. And he is so framed that he will remain happy unless someone persuades him that he is unhappy. Let us not speak of this again."

But Prometheus said, "Look at him. Look below. He crouches in caves. He is at the mercy of beast and weather. He eats his meat raw. If you mean something by this, enlighten me with your wisdom. Tell me why you refuse to give man the gift of fire."

Zeus answered, "Do you not know, Prometheus, that every gift brings a penalty? This is the way the Fates weave destiny—by which gods also must abide.[3] Man does not have fire, true, nor the crafts which fire teaches. On the other hand, he does not know disease, warfare, old age, or that inward pest called worry. He is happy, I say, happy without fire. And so he shall remain."

"Happy as beasts are happy," said Prometheus. "Of what use to make a separate race called man and endow[4] him with little fur, some wit, and a curious charm of unpredictability? If he must live like this, why separate him from the beasts at all?"

"He has another quality," said Zeus, "the capacity for worship. An aptitude for admiring our power, being puzzled by our riddles and amazed by our caprice.[5] That is why he was made."

"Would not fire, and the graces he can put on with fire, make him more interesting?"

"More interesting, perhaps, but infinitely more dangerous. For there is this in man

1. According to Greek myths, *Prometheus* (prə mē′ thē əs) and the other *Titans* (tīt′ ənz) belonged to a race of giants who once ruled the world. They were overthrown by *Zeus* (zo͞os) and other gods.
2. To *beard* Zeus was to meet him boldly, face-to-face.
3. The ancient Greeks believed that three goddesses, sisters called the *Fates,* controlled human lives and fortunes. Even the gods had to go along with, or *abide,* the sisters' decisions.
4. To *endow* is to give a quality, ability, or talent to someone.
5. The gods' *caprice* was their tendency to change their minds suddenly and for little or no reason.

Vocabulary
decree (di krē′) *n.* an official rule, order, or decision
aptitude (ap′ tə to͞od′) *n.* a natural ability; talent

Reading the Selection

SUMMARY

Prometheus asks Zeus why he did not give humans the gift of fire. Zeus explains that humans would misuse fire and have many troubles, including disease, war, old age, and worry. Prometheus disobeys Zeus and introduces fire to humans. When Zeus finds out, he has Prometheus captured and chained to a rock, with two vultures to guard and torture Prometheus forever. Centuries later, Prometheus is finally rescued by Heracles.

Spanish Summaries, p. 63

A Active Reading Strategies

PREDICT Ask students to read the first three lines and predict what the conflict may be in this myth. *(Prometheus will probably challenge Zeus's authority.)*

VOCABULARY If you haven't previewed the selection vocabulary with students, stop and remind them to use context clues to unlock the meanings of new vocabulary words.

Additional Resources

Active Reading Guide, p. 63
Audio Library
Spanish Audio Library

Teaching Support

CONNECTING TO OTHER SELECTIONS

This selection is compared with "Icarus and Daedalus" on pages 736–741. A lesson for teaching a comparison of the two selections appears on page 747.

The chart at the right shows three ways to connect "Prometheus" to other selections in this book.

For specific teaching strategies, see the ***Theme Seven Planning Guide.***

Connection	Title
Life Skills: Decision Making	→ "After Twenty Years," p. 565
Thematic: Decisions	→ "The Monsters Are Due on Maple Street," p. 505
Literary: Myth	→ "The Highwayman," p. 621

VIEWING THE MOSAIC

This image is made of thousands of individually cut colored tiles inlaid in mortar. Many ancient cultures, including Greek, Islamic, and Roman cultures, used mosaics to represent a great variety of images.

Viewing Response *Students will probably cite examples from medicine, science, and technology.*

B Literary Elements

THEME Use Zeus's words to begin a discussion about the myth theme. *(Zeus, a god, does not want his creations to think they are his equals.)*

C Active Reading Strategies

PREDICT What might happen next in the relationship between Zeus and Prometheus?

Model: I think Zeus is very powerful and wants complete authority and respect. Prometheus will push him too far.

Cultural Note

The Titans There were seven pairs of Titans led by King Cronus. They ruled the world until Zeus led a revolt and overthrew them, except for Prometheus, who fought on Zeus's side.

Prometheus Giving Fire to Man. 1st century A.D. Mosaic tile. Museo delle Terme, Rome.

Viewing the mosaic: The ancient Greeks considered the gift of fire an important event. They celebrated the Prometheus myth in their literature and their art. Can you think of any modern "gift" that has had such an influence?

too: a vaunting pride that needs little sustenance to make it swell to giant size. Improve his lot,[6] and he will forget that which makes him pleasing—his sense of worship, his humility. He will grow big and poisoned with pride and fancy himself a god, and before we know it, we shall see him storming Olympus. Enough, Prometheus! I have been patient with you, but do not try me too far. Go now and trouble me no more with your speculations."

Prometheus was not satisfied. All that night he lay awake making plans. Then he left his couch at dawn and, standing tiptoe on Olympus, stretched his arm to the eastern horizon where the first faint flames of the sun were flickering. In his hand he held a reed filled with a dry fiber; he thrust it into the sunrise until a spark smoldered. Then he put the reed in his tunic and came down from the mountain.

At first men were frightened by the gift. It was so hot, so quick; it bit sharply when you touched it and for pure spite made the shadows dance. They thanked Prometheus and asked him to take it away. But he took the haunch of a newly killed deer and held it over the fire. And when the meat began to sear and sputter, filling the cave with its rich smells, the people felt themselves

6. *Vaunting* pride is boastful. *Sustenance* means "support or assistance." Here, *lot* refers to humans' situations in life or the conditions in which they live.

Vocabulary

humility (hū mil′ ə tē) *n.* the quality of being humble or modest

spite (spīt) *n.* a desire to hurt or annoy another person

Teaching Support

Grammar and Language Minilesson

Dashes Write these sentences on the board:

- Then you must stop, or it will eat everything in sight—and you too.
- Prometheus was a Titan—a brash youth—who suffered a terrible fate.

Explain that the dash shows a sudden break or change in thought or speech. If the sentence continues, a second dash marks the end of the interruption.

Activity Write these sentences—without the dashes—on the board. Have students add dashes where needed.

1. This is the way the Fates weave destiny—the gods' destinies, too.
2. Zeus refused Prometheus's request—a thoughtful one.
3. Men suspected—no, they knew—a terrible thing happened on the mountain.

L2

Additional Resources

- ***Grammar and Language Transparency 59***
- ***Grammar and Language Workbook,*** pp. 275–276
- ***Grammar and Composition Handbook,*** Lesson 13.8
- ***Writer's Choice,*** Lesson 20.8

melting with hunger and flung themselves on the meat and devoured it greedily, burning their tongues.

"This that I have brought you is called 'fire,'" Prometheus said. "It is an ill-natured spirit, a little brother of the sun, but if you handle it carefully, it can change your whole life. It is very greedy; you must feed it twigs, but only until it becomes a proper size. Then you must stop, or it will eat everything in sight—and you too. If it escapes, use this magic: water. It fears the water spirit, and if you touch it with water, it will fly away until you need it again."

He left the fire burning in the first cave, with children staring at it wide-eyed, and then went to every cave in the land.

Then one day Zeus looked down from the mountain and was amazed. Everything had changed. Man had come out of his cave. Zeus saw woodmen's huts, farmhouses, villages, walled towns, even a castle or two. He saw men cooking their food, carrying torches to light their way at night. He saw forges blazing, men beating out ploughs, keels,[7] swords, spears. They were making ships and raising white wings of sails and daring to use the fury of the winds for their journeys. They were wearing helmets, riding out in chariots to do battle, like the gods themselves.

Zeus was full of rage. He seized his largest thunderbolt. "So they want fire," he said to himself. "I'll give them fire—more than they can use. I'll turn their miserable little ball of earth into a cinder." But then another thought came to him, and he lowered his arm. "No," he said to himself, "I shall have vengeance—and entertainment too. Let them destroy themselves with their new skills. This will make a long, twisted game, interesting to watch. I'll attend to them later. My first business is with Prometheus."

He called his giant guards and had them seize Prometheus, drag him off to the Caucasus, and there bind him to a mountain peak with great chains specially forged by Hephaestus[8]—chains which even a Titan in agony could not break. And when the friend of man was bound to the mountain, Zeus sent two vultures to hover about him forever, tearing at his belly and eating his liver.

Men knew a terrible thing was happening on the mountain, but they did not know what. But the wind shrieked like a giant in torment and sometimes like fierce birds.

Many centuries he lay there—until another hero was born brave enough to defy the gods. He climbed to the peak in the Caucasus and struck the shackles from Prometheus and killed the vultures. His name was Heracles.[9]

7. A blacksmith uses a *forge* to heat and soften metal so that it can be hammered into desired shapes. A shipbuilder makes a *keel,* the main timber that runs the length of a boat's bottom.

8. The *Caucasus* Mountains, in southeastern Russia between the Black and Caspian Seas, separate Europe and Asia. *Hephaestus* (hi fes′ təs) was the god of fire and metalworking.

9. *Heracles* (her′ ə klēz′) is the Greek name for Hercules, who was the son of Zeus and a human woman.

Vocabulary

agony (ag′ ə nē) *n.* great pain and suffering of the mind or body
hover (huv′ ər) *v.* to remain as if suspended in the air over a particular spot

D Author's Craft

PERSONIFICATION Ask students why they think the author gives fire human traits. *(It helps Prometheus explain fire in terms that simple humans understand.)*

E Literary Elements

THEME Ask students what message they think this method of punishment delivers. *(Authority figures have good reasons for forbidding certain activities. Punishment for disobeying warns others.)*

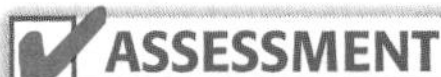

Heracles was the greatest Greek hero. Because Heracles' mother was a mortal, Zeus's wife Hera hated him. Hera caused Heracles to kill his wife and children. He purified himself by completing twelve labors and was made immortal.

Thematic Focus

A Different Dimension Invite students to suggest ways that "Prometheus" evokes the theme. *(The story includes gods and giants from a different era and dimension.)*

ASSESSMENT

Quick Checks, p. 63

MEETING INDIVIDUAL NEEDS: ENGLISH LANGUAGE LEARNERS

Multiple-Meaning Words Explain to English language learners that many words in the English language have more than one meaning, often depending on how they are used.

Activity Have students create a chart with the terms *saw, handle, fly, fire, watch,* and *break.* When students encounter each word in their reading, help them determine the definition that applies.

New Definition	Word	New Definition
tool for cutting	saw	past tense of see

Additional Resources

English Language Learners Sourcebook, p. 92

Responding to the Selection

PERSONAL RESPONSE

Students will probably mention man's first encounter with fire or Prometheus and the vultures.

Analyzing Literature

1. Prometheus requests fire. He feels sorry for humans.
2. Zeus's refusal is not justified. Fire's benefits would outweigh its disadvantages.
3. Prometheus asks Zeus to give fire to humans; Zeus refuses, but Prometheus gives it to them; humans change a great deal; Zeus chains Prometheus to a mountain where vultures attack him. The fire symbolizes knowledge which can also be dangerous if misused.
4. Fire enables people to stay warm, make tools, cook food, and frighten away animals.
5. He was a hero. He helped humans even though he was afraid.
6. Students' responses should name, and give reasons for naming, someone in the modern world who can be said to be creative and daring or original. Important scientists and artists are likely candidates.

Extending Your Response

Literature Groups

Have students state whether they agree with Prometheus and then relate to the expression theme.

Writing About Literature

Students' paragraphs should

- describe how the myth was an ancient explanation for the origins of the civilized world
- include things students think are essential to civilization

Responding to Literature

PERSONAL RESPONSE

- What images from the myth linger in your mind? Record them in your journal.

Analyzing Literature

RECALL AND INTERPRET

1. What gift for human beings does Prometheus request from Zeus? Why do you think he makes such a request?
2. What is Zeus's response to the request? Do you think this response was justified? Explain your answer.
3. What series of events make up the plot of this myth? Why do you think this myth was created?

EVALUATE AND CONNECT

4. Why was fire so important to the development of human civilization?
5. Do you think Prometheus was a hero or a fool? Use examples to support your opinion.
6. The English adjective *Promethean,* which means "daringly creative or original," is derived from the mythical Titan's name. Think of someone in the modern world who could be described as Promethean. Give reasons for your answer.

LITERARY ELEMENTS

Theme

A **theme** is the message, or general truth about life, expressed in a work of literature. A piece of writing may have a **stated theme,** which is expressed directly, or an **implied theme,** which is revealed gradually through the thoughts and actions of the characters. There may be one theme or several in a single piece of writing.

1. What is the theme of "Prometheus"? Support your ideas with examples and quotations from the myth.
2. In a paragraph, discuss the theme of another selection you have read.

● See **Literary Terms Handbook,** p. R11.

Extending Your Response

Literature Groups

Is Knowledge Power? In this myth, Prometheus argues that human beings need the gift of fire to bring them out of ignorance and darkness. Do you agree with him? Review your notes from the **Reading Focus** on page 742. Then discuss how the expression "Knowledge is power" relates to the theme of this myth.

Writing About Literature

Myth Brainstorm a list of things you think are essential to civilization. Then write one or two paragraphs describing how this myth might have been the ancient Greeks' explanation for the origins of the civilized world.

ASSESSMENT

- ***Quick Checks,*** p. 63
- ***Selection and Theme Assessment*** pp. 107–108
- ***Performance Assessment,*** p. 59
- ***Testmaker: ExamView Pro***
- ***Interactive Tutor: Self-Assessment***

LITERARY ELEMENTS

1. Knowledge can be both a useful and a dangerous tool. The givers of knowledge must take responsibility for their actions.
2. Answers will depend upon students' choice of selection.

Additional Resources

Literary Elements Transparency 63

Critical Thinking

COMPARING SELECTIONS

Icarus and Daedalus **and** PROMETHEUS

COMPARE **MYTHS**

"Icarus and Daedalus" and "Prometheus" are Greek myths that portray characters attempting to use intelligence to outwit their fates. The themes of knowledge and freedom play an important role in both these myths.

1. How does Daedalus use his intelligence? Does he succeed in reaching his goal? Why or why not?
2. How does Prometheus use his intelligence? Does he succeed in reaching his goal? Why or why not?
3. How are these myths alike? How are they different?
4. Which myth do you prefer? Why?

Icarus, 1947 (detail).

COMPARE **IDEAS**

What is the meaning of the word *hero?* Are any of the characters in these two myths heroes?

- In small groups, talk about the kinds of personal characteristics, qualities, and actions that define a hero. Make a list of the characteristics of a hero. List some fictional as well as real-life examples.
- Look at each of the main characters in the two myths, and talk about whether or not each character's actions and personal qualities were heroic.
- Share your ideas and definitions in a discussion with your classmates.

COMPARE **ENDINGS**

Compare the endings of these myths. How are they alike? How are they different? How else might each of these selections have ended?

- What else might have happened to Icarus and Daedalus? Perhaps they stayed on the island of Crete or they escaped by boat. What about Prometheus? What else might have happened to him?
- Use your imagination to write an alternate ending to either myth. Feel free to use Zeus or any other Greek god or goddess in your ending, and make up any new details you wish.

COMPARING selections

Objective

- To compare myths that deal with how knowledge and power can be both beneficial and dangerous

COMPARE **MYTHS**

1. He makes wings with which he can fly. He escapes from the island with Icarus, but in the end he loses his son.
2. He steals fire and gives it to human beings. He reaches his goal but is punished terribly.
3. Because ignorant Icarus and defiant Prometheus ignore advice, they suffer terrible consequences.
4. Students should support their opinions with examples.

COMPARE **IDEAS**

Students' definitions should

- include characteristics, qualities, and actions that define a hero
- state whether the main characters in the two myths were heroes
- support ideas with examples from each myth

Additional Resources

 ***Literature Groups Sourcebook***

COMPARE **ENDINGS**

Students' alternate endings should

- be based on the plot and characters in one of these myths
- be consistent with what they know about gods and goddesses

Teaching Support

PORTFOLIO OPTIONS

Select and Reflect Have students reflect on the endings they wrote for the activity above by answering these questions:

- Is my ending based on the characters and plot of the myth?
- Have I included new elements that create a logical and very different conclusion to the story?

Students should place their alternate endings in their portfolios along with their reflections. You may wish at a later time to have them revise their work and present the endings as portfolio showcase pieces. **L2**

Additional Resources

Writing Assessment and Portfolio Management, pp. 38–45

Objective

- To read and understand an opera libretto

Literature LINK

The Bunyans This libretto connects to "The Bunyans," pages 750–754. While the opera text describes the magical beginning of Paul Bunyan's life and his legendary size, "The Bunyans" recounts, in tall-tale fashion, the fantastic feats of the whole Bunyan family. Explain that the text of an opera is contained in the libretto.

Analyzing Media

Possible answers include:

1. Paul Bunyan grew 6 inches every day, gained 346 pounds a week, was as tall as the Empire State Building, had a 3.7-mile stride, and scratched his shin with a pine tree.
2. Some students may say that since *Paul Bunyan* is a folk story, a folksinger is an appropriate choice. Others may say the composer wanted to make the song sound informal and down-to-earth, so he chose a folksinger.

Additional Resources

Media Connections, p. 14

***in TIME* magazine**

MEDIA Connection

OPERA LIBRETTO

The poet W. H. Auden wrote the libretto, or text, for Benjamin Britten's opera about the American folk hero Paul Bunyan. This ballad is sung by a folksinger in the opera.

First Ballad Interlude from Benjamin Britten's *Paul Bunyan*

by W. H. Auden

The cold wind blew through the crooked thorn,
Up in the North a boy was born.

His hair was black, and his eyes were blue,
His mouth turned up at the corners too.

A fairy stood beside his bed;
"You shall never, never grow old," she said,

"Paul Bunyan is to be your name";
Then she departed whence she came.

You must believe me when I say,
He grew six inches every day.

You must believe me when I speak,
He gained 346 pounds every week.

He grew so fast, by the time he was eight,
He was as tall as the Empire State.

The length of his stride's a historical fact;
3.7 miles to be exact.

When he ordered a jacket, the New England mills
For months had no more unemployment ills.

When he wanted a snapshot to send to his friends,
They found they had to use a telephoto lens.

But let me tell you in advance,
His dreams were of greater significance.

His favorite dream was of felling trees,
A fancy which grew by swift degrees.

One night he dreamt he was to be
The greatest logger in history.

He woke to feel something stroking his brow,
And found it was the tongue of an enormous cow.

From horn to horn or from lug to lug,
Was forty-seven axe-heads and a baccy plug.

But what would have most bewildered you
Was the color of her hide, which was bright bright blue.

But Bunyan wasn't surprised at all;
Said, "I'll call you Babe, you call me Paul."

He pointed to a meadow, said, "Take a bite:
For you're leaving with me for the South tonight."

Over the mountains, across the streams
They went to find Paul Bunyan's dreams.

The bear and the beaver waved a paw,
The magpie chattered, the squirrel swore.

The trappers ran out from their lonely huts
Scratching their heads with their rifle-butts.

For a year and a day they traveled fast.
"This is the place," Paul said at last.

The forest stretched for miles around,
The sound of their breathing was the only sound.

Paul picked a pine-tree and scratched his shins,
Said, "This is the place where our work begins."

Analyzing Media

1. Paul Bunyan is a tall-tale hero, and tall tales exaggerate, or go beyond the truth. What details in the ballad are clearly exaggerations?
2. In the opera, the ballad is performed by a folk singer rather than an opera singer. Why do you think the composer might prefer that kind of voice?

748 THEME 7

Teaching Support

Opera Have students use a search engine to find out more about Benjamin Britten's opera *Paul Bunyan*. Suggest they try entering keywords like *Britten, Bunyan, opera,* and *American opera.*

Reading Minilesson

Cause and Effect Much of the humor in the Paul Bunyan stories is drawn from silly cause-and-effect relationships, as shown in the chart to the right.

Cause	Teeny spills a silo of syrup in her hair.
Effect	Bears burrow into her sticky hair.
Cause	The Bunyans cannot get the bears out of Teeny's curls.
Effect	Paul creates Niagara Falls to wash them out.

Activity Have students work in small groups to create cause-and-effect "towers" for the fabled causes of Mammoth Cave, Big Sur, Bryce Canyon, the Great Sand Dunes of Colorado, the Rocky Mountains, and Old Faithful. **L2**

Additional Resources

Reading Skills Practice Workbook

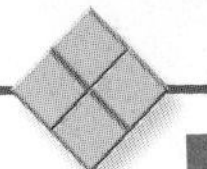

Before You Read

The Bunyans and *Brer Rabbit and Brer Lion*

MEET AUDREY WOOD

An artist and a children's book writer, Audrey Wood created this new Paul Bunyan story to add to the wonderful tradition of the American tall tale. Wood has written and illustrated many other books in collaboration with her husband, Don Wood.

Audrey Wood lives in Santa Barbara, California.

MEET JULIUS LESTER

Julius Lester's fiction and nonfiction focuses on preserving the history and heritage of African Americans. Lester has been a professional musician and singer, a host of radio and television programs, a university professor, and a writer of both adult and children's books.

Julius Lester was born in 1939. He lives in Amherst, Massachusetts.

READING FOCUS

Think about your favorite fictional characters. Are they realistic characters, or are they fantasy creatures or clever animals that inhabit the world of folktales and myths?

Think/Pair/Share

List some of your favorite fictional characters, and explain why you like them. Then share your ideas with a partner.

Setting a Purpose

Read to enjoy these two folktales.

BUILDING BACKGROUND

Did You Know? Stories about the legendary giant Paul Bunyan were first published in Minnesota in 1910, but they were told years earlier in lumber camps around the country. As the stories were passed on, Paul's deeds grew more and more incredible until the stories developed into the type of folklore called tall tales.

The character of the trickster has appeared in the folktales of many cultures throughout the world. In Theme 4 you read a story about Anansi, a trickster in African folktales. Brer Rabbit is a version of Anansi that developed in America. (*Brer,* also spelled *br'er,* is a shortened form of *brother.*) The Brer Rabbit stories were passed on orally by African Americans for generations before anyone put them into writing.

VOCABULARY PREVIEW

cordially (kôr′ jəl lē) *adv.* in a genuinely warm and friendly way; p. 752

barren (bar′ ən) *adj.* having little or no plant life; bare; empty; p. 753

fanciful (fan′ si fəl) *adj.* showing imagination in design or construction; imaginative; p. 753

sensation (sen sā′ shən) *n.* a cause of excitement or great interest; a wonder; p. 754

colossal (kə los′ əl) *adj.* extraordinarily or awesomely large; p. 754

Before Reading

Objectives

- To read and analyze a tall tale and a folktale
- To identify important elements in tall tales and folktales
- To explain what is revealed through dialogue about a story's main characters

Skills

Reading/Thinking: Problem and Solution; Drawing Conclusions; Synthesizing; Paraphrasing
Writing: Tall Tale; Sequel
Vocabulary: Etymology
Grammar/Language: Apostrophes; Quotation Marks
Listening/Speaking: Trickster Tale Dramatization
Collaboration: Literature Groups

Motivating STUDENTS

Selection Focus Transparency 64: Have students view the transparency and then discuss the questions provided.

Reading Focus: As an extension of the Reading Focus, have students use precise language and sensory imagery in writing new stories that combine two or more of their favorite characters from different sources.

RESOURCE MANAGER

Teaching Tools and Resources
- Theme Seven Planning Guide
- Literature Groups Sourcebook

Essential Lesson Support

Lesson-Specific Instruction
- Selection Focus Transparency 64
- Literary Elements Transparency 64
- Active Reading Guide,* p. 64
- Selection Vocabulary Practice, p. 46

Assessment
- Selection Quick Checks,* p. 64
- Sel. and Theme Assmt., pp. 109–110
- Testmaker: ExamView Pro
- Performance Assessment, p. 60

Systematic Language Instruction
- Gr. & Comp. Hdbk., L. 13.3, 13.4
- Vocabulary Power
- Spelling Power

English Language Learners
- ELL Sourcebook, p. 93
- Spanish Summaries, p. 64
- Audio Library*
- English, Yes!

Spec. Needs/Strat. Interven.
- Interactive Rdg. Sbk., pp. T221–T224
- Interactive Rdg. Wkbk., pp. 129–131
- Inclusion Strat. Sbk., pp. 77–78
- Audio Library*

*Also available in Spanish

Reading the Selection

SUMMARY

"The Bunyans" is a modern retelling of the tall tale about how the famous giant woodsman, Paul Bunyan, and his family create some of the natural wonders of North America.

"Brer Rabbit and Brer Lion" is a folktale about how a puny rabbit outwits a lion by convincing him that a hurricane is coming and that he must let the rabbit tie him to a tree for safety. This feat creates a reputation for the rabbit as a cunning and worthy adversary.

Spanish Summaries, p. 64

A Active Reading Strategies

CONNECT Have students tell what they know about some of the deeds that have been attributed to Paul Bunyan. Then explain that this story is a modern version that adds new elements to the traditional tale.

VOCABULARY If you haven't previewed the selection vocabulary with students, stop and remind them to use context clues to unlock the meanings of new vocabulary words.

Additional Resources

- ***Active Reading Guide,*** p. 64
- ***Audio Library***
- ***Spanish Audio Library***

The Bunyans

Audrey Wood

The Bunyans, Illustration by David Shannon from THE BUNYANS by Audrey Wood. Published by the BLUE SKY PRESS.

Teaching Support

Reading Minilesson

Problem and Solution "The Bunyans" is a tall tale that focuses on how a family of giants solves a series of challenging problems. The result of some of their actions is the creation of some very famous American landmarks. Draw the following chart on the board.

Activity As students read the story, have them fill in the chart with the four different "problems" encountered by the Bunyans, the solutions found by the Bunyans, and the end results of their actions. L2

Additional Resources

Reading Skills Practice Workbook

Problem	Solution	Result
Carrie loses her lucky wishbone.	She digs in the ground to find it.	Mammoth Cave is created.

Storyteller's Note
Now I suppose that you have heard about the mighty logger Paul Bunyan and his great blue ox named Babe. In the early days of our country, Paul and Babe cleared the land for the settlers, so farms and cities could spring up. And you probably know that Paul was taller than a redwood tree, stronger than fifty grizzly bears, and smarter than a library full of books. But you may not know that Paul was married and had two fine children.
A DIFFERENT DIMENSION 751

B Active Reading Strategies

VISUALIZE Have students look carefully at the illustrations of Paul Bunyan and Babe. Encourage students to visualize how Paul and Babe would fit in a hallway of their school. Would Paul's boots fit in the average school locker?

C Author's Craft

MOOD Ask students who is speaking and to whom they are speaking. What atmosphere is created in the story? *(The storyteller is addressing the reader directly. The informal and relaxed atmosphere helps to draw the reader in.)*

D Literary Elements

TALL TALE: *Character* As students read this page, ask them to identify the details that make this story a tall tale. *(Paul was taller than a redwood tree, stronger than fifty grizzly bears, and smarter than a library full of books.)*

Writing Minilesson

Tall Tale Explain to students that a tall tale needs to have a beginning, a middle, and an end peppered with humor and exaggeration. Readers have to be able to visualize the setting, the character(s), and the plot.

Activity Have each student write an episode in which one or more of the Bunyans produce another natural wonder, preferably a North American natural wonder that they have seen or know something about. Encourage them to make the new adventures consistent with what they know about the character traits of the Bunyan family. **L2**

Additional Resources

Writer's Choice, Lesson 4.5

E Literary Elements

AUTHOR'S PURPOSE Have students discuss what the author's purpose is in rewriting an old American tall tale. *(Students might say that the author's primary purpose is to humorously relate the deeds to familiar landmarks to entertain readers.)*

FYI

Mammoth Cave, located in Kentucky, is one of the largest caves in the world. It contains more than 191 miles of passageways on five levels and is thought to be over 300 million years old. The limestone from which it is formed was once the bottom of a sea.

F Active Reading Strategies

VISUALIZE Have students take a moment to visualize the humorous scene of Teeny wrestling with a big purple puma and accidentally pouring a silo of syrup on her head.

G Literary Elements

TALL TALE Ask students to list the exaggerated details in the story up to this point. *(They include Paul digging up an acre of cane; Carrie digging the cavern; the wedding invitations; Teeny wrestling a puma; the silo of syrup; bears burrowing in Teeny's curls; and Paul digging a hole in the riverbed to create Niagara Falls.)*

Teaching Support

E One day when Paul Bunyan was out clearing a road through the forests of Kentucky, a great pounding began to shake the earth. Looking around, Paul discovered an enormous hole in the side of a hill. The lumberjack pulled up an acre of dry cane and fashioned a torch to light his way.

Paul climbed inside the hole and followed the sound underground for miles, until he came to a large cavern glistening with crystals. By the flickering light of his torch, he saw a gigantic woman banging a behemoth[1] pickax against a wall.

It was love at first sight.

"I'm Carrie McIntie," the gigantic woman said. "I was sitting on the hill when my lucky wishbone fell down a crack into the earth. I've been digging all day trying to find it."

With a grin on his face as wide as the Missouri River, Paul reached into his shirt pocket. "I've got one too," he said, pulling out *his* lucky wishbone. "Marry me, Carrie, and we'll share mine."

Carrie agreed, and their wedding invitations were mailed out right away.

The invitations were so large, only one needed to be sent to each state. Everyone could read them for miles!

The invitations said: *You are cordially invited to the mammoth wedding of Paul Bunyan and Carrie McIntie.* The couple were married in the enormous crystal chamber that Carrie had carved, and after the ceremony, folks began to call it "Mammoth Cave." The giantess had dug more than two hundred miles, making it the longest cave in the world, so the name fit perfectly.

Paul and Carrie settled down on a farm in Maine, and soon there were two new Bunyans. While Pa Bunyan traveled with his logging crew, Ma Bunyan worked the farm and cared for their jumbo boy, named Little Jean, and their gigantic girl, named Teeny.

One morning when Pa Bunyan was home between jobs, Ma Bunyan cooked up a hearty breakfast of pancakes and syrup. F Teeny was wrestling with her big purple puma[2] named Slink and accidentally dumped a silo of syrup on her head. Teeny's hair was so sweet, bears crawled into it and burrowed deep in her curls. Try as they might, Pa and Ma Bunyan couldn't wash them out.

"We'll need a forceful shower of water to get rid of those varmints!"[3] Ma Bunyan declared.

Pa Bunyan had an idea. He placed his daughter on Babe, and he led them to the Niagara River in Canada. G The gargantuan[4] father scooped out a huge hole in the middle of the riverbed. As the great river roared down into the deep hole, Teeny cried out in delight, "Niagara falls!" Teeny showered in the waterfall, and the pesky bears were washed downstream.

When Little Jean was five, he wanted to work too, so he followed his pa out to his logging camp in Montana. Thinking his son was too young to do much of

1. A *behemoth* (bi hē′ məth) object is monstrously large.
2. The *puma* (pū′ mə) is a mountain lion.
3. Here, *varmint* means "a pesky animal."
4. From the name of a fictional giant, *gargantuan* means "enormous; huge."

Vocabulary
cordially (kôr′ jəl lē) *adv.* in a genuinely warm and friendly way

MEETING INDIVIDUAL NEEDS — SPECIAL NEEDS

Less-Proficient Readers To help students monitor their comprehension while reading the story, you may wish to provide them with some clues to connect the play on words with actual landmarks in the United States.

Activity As students read this story, have them fill in a chart with the other stories of landmark creations.

Additional Resources
Inclusion Strategies

Bunyan Action	Landmark Connection
Carrie McIntie was looking for her wishbone and dug an enormous crystal chamber in the side of a hill.	Mammoth Cave

anything, Paul set Little Jean down in a barren canyon in Utah to play for the day. When the lumberjack went to fetch him, he couldn't believe his eyes. Little Jean had carved the canyon into a wonderland of fanciful shapes.

Pa Bunyan got tongue-tied and said, "That's a mighty *brice* nanyon, coy, I mean, a mighty nice canyon, boy!" Somehow part of the mix-up stuck.

To this day the canyon is known as Bryce Canyon.

After all that sculpting, Little Jean's shoes were full of sand. Pa knew Ma Bunyan wouldn't want her clean floors dirtied up, so he told Little Jean to sit down and empty out his shoes.

H The sand from Little Jean's shoes blew away on the eastern wind and settled down a state away. It covered a valley ten miles long, making sand dunes eight hundred feet high. Everyone knows that's how the Great Sand Dunes of Colorado came to be.

The Bunyans. Illustration by David Shannon from THE BUNYANS by Audrey Wood. Published by the BLUE SKY PRESS. Illustrations ©1996 by David Shannon. Reprinted by permission of Scholastic, Inc. The BLUE SKY PRESS is a registered trademark of Scholastic, Inc.

Viewing the painting: This illustration was created for Audrey Wood's story. How does it add to the reader's appreciation of the tale?

I One summer, Little Jean and Teeny wanted to go to the beach. Ma Bunyan told them to follow a river to the ocean. But all the rivers flowed west back then, so they missed the Atlantic Ocean and ended up on the other side of the country instead.

J Ma Bunyan tracked them out to the Pacific Ocean, where she found Teeny riding on the backs of two blue whales and Little Jean carving out fifty zigzag miles of the California coast.

When Ma Bunyan saw what her son had done, she exclaimed, "What's the big

Vocabulary

barren (bar′ ən) *adj.* having little or no plant life; bare; empty

fanciful (fan′ si fəl) *adj.* showing imagination in design or construction; imaginative

H Literary Elements

HYPERBOLE Have students identify a hyperbole in the events that take place in Utah. *(Little Jean creates sand dunes 800 feet high by dumping out his shoes.)*

VIEWING THE PAINTING

In 1998, writer and illustrator David Shannon won the prestigious Caldecott Medal for *No, David,* a book based on one he wrote and illustrated when he was only five years old.

Viewing Response *The illustration helps readers appreciate Ma Bunyan's energy and her size in relation to the trees and mountains around her.*

I Literary Elements

TALL TALE: *Setting* Encourage students to identify story elements that make this tall tale American. *(The story takes place entirely in the United States and describes the formation of a few famous American natural landmarks.)*

J Critical Thinking

DRAWING CONCLUSIONS Ask students to discuss how tall the Bunyans might be. *(Students might guess that the Bunyans are hundreds of feet tall based on their adventures and accomplishments.)*

MEETING INDIVIDUAL NEEDS: ADVANCED LEARNERS

Telling Tales "The Bunyans" is a wildly imaginative story about the fantastic adventures of the Bunyan family. This American tall tale has been passed down orally, each generation adding a little more to it, as happens in this selection.

Activity Have students work alone or in pairs to create oral presentations of tall tales. They can be about any subject or personality they choose, but the narrators must speak directly to the listeners. Encourage students to have the characters use authentic dialect or idioms to make the presentations more interesting. When their creations are ready, the students may present them orally to the whole class. **L3**

Ⓝ Critical Thinking

SYNTHESIZING Have students discuss what they think the message of this story is. *(The message is that if you are clever enough, you can outsmart others who are more powerful.)*

VIEWING THE PAINTING

Christian Pierre, now working in Jacksonville, Florida, has had her work reproduced as book covers, on brochures, and as editorial illustrations. Another of her paintings can be seen on page 223.

Viewing Response *Lions are thought of as strong and fierce. In the tale, the unhappy Brer Lion is fearful and bumbling. The lion in the painting looks pleasant and friendly.*

Thematic Focus

A Different Dimension Have students review both stories and identify elements that take the reader into another dimension. Then invite them to discuss how the characters and events in "Brer Rabbit and Brer Lion" relate to aspects of modern life.

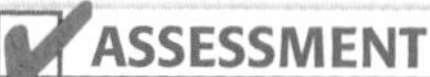

ASSESSMENT

Quick Checks, p. 64

He was trucking through the woods when he ran smack into Brer Lion. Now, don't come telling me ain't no lions in the United States. Ain't none here now. But back in yonder times, all the animals lived everywhere. The lions and tigers and elephants and foxes and what 'nall run around with each other like they was family. So that's how come wasn't unusual for Brer Rabbit to run up on Brer Lion like he done that day.

"What's your hurry, Brer Rabbit?"

"Run, Brer Lion! There's a hurricane coming."

Brer Lion got scared. "I'm too heavy to run, Brer Rabbit. What am I going to do?"

"Lay down, Brer Lion. Lay down! Get close to the ground!"

Brer Lion shook his head. "The wind might pick me up and blow me away."

"Hug a tree, Brer Lion! Hug a tree!"

"But what if the wind blows all day and into the night?"

"Let me tie you to the tree, Brer Lion. Let me tie you to the tree."

Brer Lion liked that idea. Brer Rabbit tied him to the tree and sat down next to it. After a while, Brer Lion got tired of hugging the tree.

"Brer Rabbit? I don't hear no hurricane."

Brer Rabbit listened. "Neither do I."

"Brer Rabbit? I don't hear no wind."

Brer Rabbit listened. "Neither do I."

"Brer Rabbit? Ain't a leaf moving in the trees."

Brer Rabbit looked up. "Sho' ain't."

"So untie me."

"I'm afraid to, Brer Lion."

Brer Lion began to roar. He roared so loud and so long, the foundations of the Earth started shaking. Least that's what it seemed like, and the other animals came from all over to see what was going on.

When they got close, Brer Rabbit jumped up and began strutting around the tied-up Brer Lion. When the animals saw what Brer Rabbit had done to Brer Lion, you'd better believe it was the forty-eleventh of Octorerarry before they messed with him again. Ⓝ

Emma's Lion, 1994. Christian Pierre. Acrylic on Masonite, 16 x 20 in. Private collection.

Viewing the painting: What qualities do you usually attribute to lions? Which of these qualities does the lion in the folktale show? Which qualities do you see in the painting?

Teaching Support

Grammar and Language *Minilesson*

Apostrophes Point out Lester's frequent use of contractions in this story. Write these examples on the board:

Now, don't come telling me ain't no lions in the United States. Sho' ain't.

Discuss each contraction with students, pointing out that *ain't* is a common word in several American dialects, though it is not accepted as correct in formal English. Explain that *sho'* is short for "sure."

Activity Have students form a contraction for each word in parentheses. **L2**

1. "(I am) too heavy to run, Brer Rabbit." *(I'm)*
2. "I (do not) hear no hurricane." *(don't)*
3. "Marry me, Carrie, and (we will) share mine." *(we'll)*
4. "(What is) the big idea, sir!?" *(What's)*

L2

Additional Resources

- ***Grammar and Language Transparency 60***
- ***Grammar and Language Workbook,*** pp. 273–274
- ***Grammar and Composition Handbook,*** Lesson 13.7
- ***Writer's Choice,*** Lesson 20.7

Responding to Literature

PERSONAL RESPONSE

- What was your reaction to these tales? Record your responses in your journal.

Analyzing Literature

RECALL

1. Describe the Bunyan family.
2. What are some of the natural features of North America that the Bunyans built?
3. What lesson does Brer Lion learn?

Brackets connect questions that are paired to develop higher-level thinking skills.

INTERPRET

4. Compare and contrast the ordinary actions of the Bunyans and the extraordinary results of their actions.
5. What personality traits does Brer Rabbit have that help him get the better of a much larger animal?
6. What does the final sentence in "Brer Rabbit and Brer Lion" mean? When exactly is the "forty-eleventh of Octorerarry"? Explain.
7. How do you think Brer Rabbit feels at the end of this tale? Compare his feelings with those of Brer Lion.
8. If you could add a moral, or lesson, to the end of "Brer Rabbit and Brer Lion," what would it be?

EVALUATE AND CONNECT

9. What role does humor play in these tales? Explain.
10. Which tale did you prefer? Why?

LITERARY ELEMENTS

Folktales and Tall Tales

Folktales are stories that have been passed down from generation to generation. In many folktales, the characters are animals or ordinary people who have unusual experiences. **Tall tales** are a specific kind of American folktale that often describes one aspect of frontier life, such as logging (Paul Bunyan) or cattle ranching (Pecos Bill). Some tall tales are based on the deeds of people who actually lived—for example, Annie Oakley and Davy Crockett. In tall tales, the characters, their physical attributes, and their deeds are greatly exaggerated for humorous effect.

1. Give at least two reasons why "The Bunyans" would be considered a tall tale.
2. What message about life is illustrated in "Brer Rabbit and Brer Lion"?

• See **Literary Terms Handbook**, pp. R4–R5 and R11.

Responding to the Selection

PERSONAL RESPONSE

Students may find these tales entertaining and see that they also offer insights into how people think and live.

Analyzing Literature

1. Paul and Carrie are two giants who have two giant children, Teeny and Little Jean.
2. They are Mammoth Cave, Niagara Falls, Bryce Canyon, the Great Sand Dunes of Colorado, Big Sur, the Rocky Mountains, and Old Faithful.
3. He learns not to believe everything he hears, especially from Brer Rabbit.
4. Carrie digs in the ground and creates a huge cavern; Paul washes Teeny's hair and makes Niagara Falls; Little Jean empties sand out of his shoes and makes 800-foot-high dunes.
5. He is innocent-looking but clever.
6. It means that the other animals will never bother Brer Rabbit. The date is one that doesn't exist.
7. He is very proud and full of himself, whereas Brer Lion is humiliated and angry.
8. Most students will say something like "Be very careful what you believe."
9. "The Bunyans" is funny because everything is so exaggerated, which is entertaining. The humor in Brer Rabbit helps the reader enjoy the story and get its message.
10. Students should explain their choices with examples from one or both of the stories.

LITERARY ELEMENTS

1. The main characters are enormous giants, and they created many huge natural features.
2. Cunning can win out over brute strength.

Additional Resources

Literary Elements Transparency 64

Literature and Writing

Writing About Literature

Students' paragraphs should
- explain what they learned from dialogue about the main characters in one of the tales
- use examples from the tale to illustrate their ideas

Creative Writing

Students' sequels should
- describe events that may have happened after the end of one of the stories
- include new details that are consistent with the characters in the story as it is

Extending Your Response

Literature Groups Before students compare characters, have them list important traits for each of the main characters in "The Bunyans" and "Brer Rabbit and Brer Lion."

Performing Allow students plenty of time to research and prepare their dramatizations. You might want to have students create masks for the main characters in the story.

Interdisciplinary Activity Help students locate sources of information on wind and water erosion, rivers, geothermal activity, the formation of mountain ranges, and relevant natural forces.

Literature and Writing

Writing About Literature

Dialogue Readers learn a great deal through the dialogue in a story. Write a paragraph explaining what you learned about the main characters from the dialogue in one of these folktales.

Creative Writing

Writing a Sequel Choose one of the stories and write a sequel, or continuation, of that tale. What else might happen to the Bunyans or Brer Rabbit? Feel free to make up any details you wish.

Extending Your Response

Literature Groups

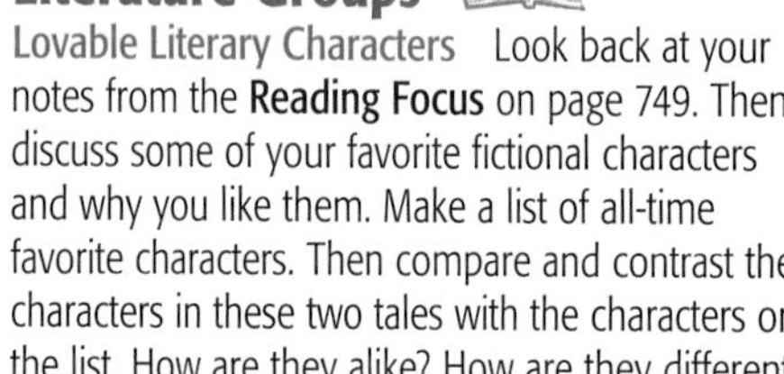

Lovable Literary Characters Look back at your notes from the **Reading Focus** on page 749. Then discuss some of your favorite fictional characters and why you like them. Make a list of all-time favorite characters. Then compare and contrast the characters in these two tales with the characters on the list. How are they alike? How are they different?

Performing

Trickster Tale Dramatization The trickster is a familiar figure in folktales of many cultures. The sly coyote is as well-known a trickster in Native American folklore as Brer Rabbit is in African American folktales. Working in small groups, find a trickster tale, and dramatize the tale for another class.

Interdisciplinary Activity

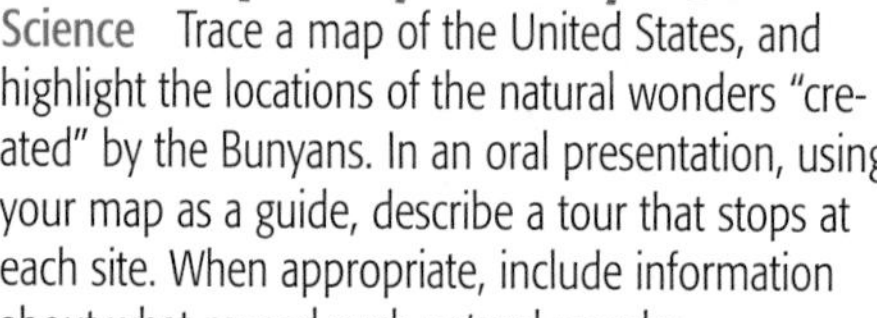

Science Trace a map of the United States, and highlight the locations of the natural wonders "created" by the Bunyans. In an oral presentation, using your map as a guide, describe a tour that stops at each site. When appropriate, include information about what caused each natural wonder.

Reading Further

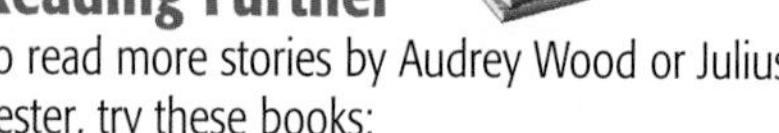

To read more stories by Audrey Wood or Julius Lester, try these books:

The Napping House by Audrey Wood

More Tales of Uncle Remus by Julius Lester

Save your work for your portfolio.

Skill Minilessons

Reteach · Review

GRAMMAR AND LANGUAGE • QUOTATION MARKS

Remember these rules when using quotation marks in your writing.

- Use quotation marks before and after the exact words in a direct quotation.

  "I'm Carrie McIntie," the gigantic woman said.

- Use quotation marks with both parts of a divided quotation.

  "Brer Rabbit," said Brer Lion, "I don't hear no hurricane."

- Use commas to separate phrases such as *he said* from the quotation (as in the example above).
- Always place commas and periods inside closing quotation marks (as in the examples). Place a question mark or an exclamation point inside the quotation marks only if it is part of the quotation.

  "Hug a tree!!" Brer Rabbit exclaimed. Why do you think he told Brer Lion to "Hug a tree"?

PRACTICE In pairs, create a dialogue between two characters from either selection. Once you have written your dialogue, proofread it to check for correct punctuation. Dramatize it for the class.

For more about the use of quotation marks, see **Language Handbook,** pp. R39–R40.

READING AND THINKING • PARAPHRASING

When you paraphrase, you use your own words to briefly restate the content of a piece of writing. Paraphrasing a written work, or a portion of it, can help you understand the writer's meaning.

PRACTICE Reread "Brer Rabbit and Brer Lion" or "The Bunyans." Then write a paragraph paraphrasing what happens in the story.

For more about paraphrasing, see **Reading Handbook,** p. R91.

VOCABULARY • ETYMOLOGY

The word *fanciful* is related to *fancy* and *fantasy,* all of which come from the Latin word *phantasia. Phantasia,* in turn, came from the Greek word *phantasie,* which means something like "a making visible." The Greeks used the word to describe the mind's ability to "picture" something that is just an idea or isn't really there.

PRACTICE Use the etymology given above to answer the questions.

1. Which would a *fanciful* person be able to do—see long distances, see through a phony smile, or see animals in the shapes made by clouds?
2. What do you need in order to *fantasize*—a pencil, an imagination, or a camera?
3. Which word do you think comes from the same root as *fanciful*—*phantom* or *fan?*
4. Which word does not come from the same root as *fanciful*—*fantastic* or *fanatic?*

ASSESSMENT

- ***Quick Checks,*** p. 64
- ***Selection and Theme Assessment,*** pp. 109–110
- ***Performance Assessment,*** p. 60
- ***Testmaker: ExamView Pro***
- ***Interactive Tutor: Self-Assessment***

Skill Minilessons

GRAMMAR AND LANGUAGE
QUOTATION MARKS

Possible answer: "Dad, could you make a lake for me tomorrow?" asked Teeny. "I could, but I think you could do it yourself," replied Paul. "You're right," said Teeny, "but it would take me all day."

READING AND THINKING
PARAPHRASING

Brer Rabbit runs from high winds straight into Brer Lion. To save himself, he convinces Brer Lion that a hurricane is coming and that the only way to save himself is to let Rabbit tie him to a tree. After Lion is tied up, he notices that there is no storm. He asks Brer Rabbit to untie him, and when Brer Rabbit refuses, he roars with anger. This attracts all the animals, who arrive and think that Brer Rabbit is someone to be reckoned with since he has overpowered Brer Lion.

VOCABULARY
ETYMOLOGY

1. see animals in the shapes made by clouds
2. an imagination
3. phantom
4. fanatic

Additional Resources

- ***Grammar and Language Workbook,*** pp. 267–270
- ***Grammar and Composition Handbook,*** Lesson 13.6
- ***Writer's Choice,*** Lesson 20.6
- ***Reading Skills Practice Workbook,*** pp. 115–116
- ***Vocabulary Practice,*** p. 46

Writing WORKSHOP

Objectives

- To create a book review of approximately 500 to 700 words
- To plan, draft, revise, edit, and present a book review
- To reflect on and assess one's book review

GLENCOE TECHNOLOGY

WRITER'S ASSISTANT CD-ROM

Students can use Glencoe's templates and guidelines software for expository writing to aid them in working through the steps in the writing process in the lesson.

Teaching Strategies

PREWRITING

Pick a Book Point out to students that if they choose a book they feel strongly about, it will make the reviewing process easier and more interesting. A review is based in large part on the opinion of the reviewer. Therefore, the more passionately a reviewer feels about a book, the more dynamic his or her review might be.

Teaching Support

Writing WORKSHOP

Expository Writing: Book Review

Some books grab you from the beginning, while others leave you cold. After reading a book, you probably form your own opinion of it. In a book review, you express your opinion and back it up to help your audience decide whether to read the book.

Assignment: Follow the process explained in these pages to develop your own book review.

- As you write your book review, refer to the **Writing Handbook,** pp. R48–R59.

EVALUATION RUBRIC

By the time you complete this Writing Workshop, you will have

- written a book review
- developed an attention-getting introduction
- summarized the book's main ideas and significant details
- analyzed the book's main literary elements
- supported each point with evidence
- created a conclusion that states your opinion
- presented a book review free of errors in grammar, usage, and mechanics

The Writing Process

PREWRITING

PREWRITING TIP

Choose a book that you respond to strongly, either positively or negatively. Strong feelings will help give your review a clear focus.

Pick a Book

To choose a book to review, try searching the library catalog for books by authors in this theme. The books listed under Reading Further will give you a good start. As an alternative, brainstorm to make a list of books that you've already read. List them under categories such as Funniest, Most Confusing, Most Predictable, Most Thought Provoking, Most True to Life, or even Most Disappointing. Then look over your list to choose a book you feel strongly about.

Look at the Elements

After you have read or reread the book, sum up your opinion of it. To support your opinion, examine the book's literary elements. Consider its theme or themes—the insights or lessons about life that the book provides. The chart on the next page shows other elements that you might evaluate.

MEETING INDIVIDUAL NEEDS — ENGLISH LANGUAGE LEARNERS

Creating Book Jackets Depending on his or her level of proficiency, an English language learner can follow the steps in the writing process to create a book jacket for one of the selections in the theme, rather than write a book review.

Activity Review the selections students have read in this theme. Have each English language learner choose one story and create a book jacket that includes the title, the author, an illustration, a short synopsis, and the opinion of at least one reader. Students can follow the same steps as their English-proficient peers as they proceed through the Writing Workshop.

Evaluating Literary Elements		
For Fiction	**For Nonfiction**	**For Poetry**
• Plot and Conflict: fast-moving? suspenseful? complex? • Characters: lifelike? well developed? developed by words or actions? • Setting: realistic? imaginative? • Narrative Point of View: first person? third person? effect of point of view?	• Point of View: biased? consistent? understandable? • Style: formal? personal? humorous? • Content: clear? detailed? • Structure: effectively organized? why or why not?	• Language: sensory? emotional? creative? • Form: narrative or lyric? short or long? unusual? • Sound: rhyme? meter? • Figures of Speech: similes? metaphors? symbols?

Know Your Purpose and Audience

If you review a young-adult book, your audience will probably be your classmates. For other books, your audience may be younger children, older people, or a mixed group. Because your purpose is to inform your audience, you'll need to support your opinions about the book. Include examples or quotations to back up each point you make. Choose examples with your readers in mind. Consider their interests, their age, and their concerns. Remember to give readers a brief summary of the book, including only the main ideas and most significant details.

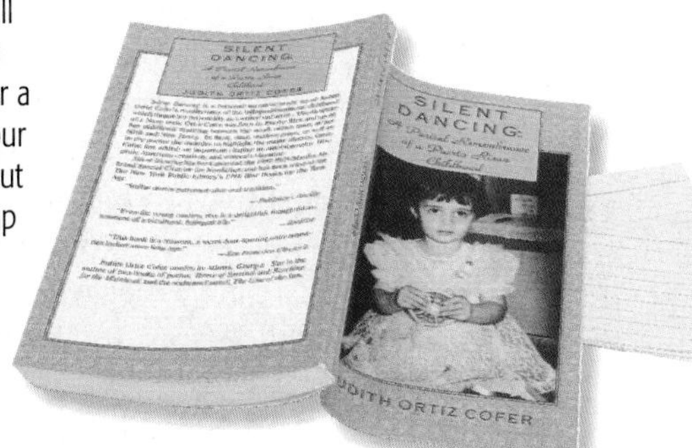

Organize

Get ready to draft by filling in a form like the one below.

About the Book

Title: *My Side of the Mountain*
Author: *Jean Craighead George*
Summary: *Sam Gribley learns survival skills when he lives on his own in the Catskill Mountains.*
My Opinion: *I liked this book. It tells an interesting story and teaches facts about plants and animals.*

Elements and Evaluation

Point of View: *First person, from Sam's point of view, which makes the story seem more personal.*
Style: *Easy to read and realistic*
Characters: *Sam's ability to survive shows that he is smart. His dialogue with other characters shows that he is also sometimes lonely.*

Look at the Elements Suggest that students make notes for their reviews as they read or reread the book. The chart on page 761 can serve as a guide to elements students should keep in mind as they prepare to write. Students may also wish to create logs of quotes, images, or supporting details with page numbers for easy reference.

Know Your Purpose and Audience Point out that most people who read book reviews are readers who want to know whether to read or avoid reading the book being reviewed. They will be interested in the opinion of the reviewer as well as in a concise summary of the book.

Organize Have students use the form to keep track of all the information they want to include in their reviews. Point out that many book reviews present a balanced view of the book first and the opinion of the reviewer afterward. Others start off with the reviewer's opinion and remarks. Either way, organizing information in an efficient manner beforehand can help the reviewer write with confidence and conviction.

Additional Resources

- ***Writing and Proofreading Practice,*** pp. 1–7, 50–56
- ***Writing and Proofreading Transparencies 1–6, 37–38***
- ***Writer's Choice,*** Lesson 5.9

MULTIPLE MODES OF EXPRESSION

Interpersonal Students who learn best in cooperative groups may wish to work together during the organizational phase of the writing process. Establishing a book club will offer students a chance to socialize, give advice, and state opinions.

Activity Have students form small groups and pass their books around for other book club members to see and discuss. Book club members may wish to decide how to organize their reviews orally, bouncing ideas off each other. Students can take notes, create graphic organizers, or listen and organize their ideas mentally before writing. After the reviews have been written, students may wish to discuss what they learned by writing them. **L2**

DRAFTING

Start with the Book Point out to students that a book reviewer can use wordplay in a review by creating a pun out of the title of the book, such as "Readers will want to join *The Joy Luck Club* (by Amy Tan)." This is a way of mentioning the book in the beginning of the review while also hinting at the reviewer's opinion.

Summarizing Remind students that the summary of the book should
- be in the student's own words (except for quotations)
- include only main ideas and the most important details
- reflect the book's underlying meaning

Support Your Opinion Remind students that it is important for a reviewer to balance information about the book with opinions regarding it. Readers will feel frustrated if a reviewer focuses too sharply on one area and neglects another. A good reviewer is able to state an opinion clearly and support it with examples from the book.

REVISING

Take a Second Look Students may wish to use stick-on notes during the revision process. This can be particularly helpful if they want to insert quotes from the books or opinions they have forgotten. Students who benefit from reading their work aloud might read to partners and ask their partners' opinions, using the "Rubric for Revising" guidelines.

Teaching Support

DRAFTING

DRAFTING TIP

Your book review should have four basic parts: an **introduction** that gives the basic information about the book and its author, a **summary** of the book (in your own words), an **analysis** of the book's literary elements (with well-chosen examples or quotations), and your **conclusion** about the book's worth.

Start with the Book

Catch your readers' attention with a surprising quotation from the book or with an interesting statement about it. Then provide the basic information: the book's title and author and your summary. You can also state your opinion directly at this point—or you can save it for the end.

Support Your Opinion

Evaluate each of the elements in your prewriting plan. Comment on strong points as well as weak points, choosing words that make your opinions clear. Back up your statements with examples or quotations. Close with a recommendation to readers.

STUDENT MODEL • DRAFTING

There is a conflict in Sam's mind. Part of him wants to stay in the woods forever, away from the city. "People live too close together," he tells one of the boys who come to visit. But Sam also enjoys company.

Complete Student Model on p. R113.

REVISING

REVISING TIP

Your analysis should focus on the book's meaning. Avoid unimportant details.

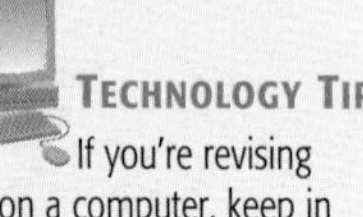

TECHNOLOGY TIP

If you're revising on a computer, keep in mind that your word processor's spelling checker can't distinguish between correctly spelled homonyms. If you mean *their* but type *there*, the spelling checker will not detect the error.

Take a Second Look

Take a break. Then return to your draft, looking for parts that need improvement. Use the **Rubric for Revising** as a guideline. On your own or with a partner, experiment with changes until your draft satisfies you.

RUBRIC FOR REVISING

Your revised book review should have
- an attention-getting introduction that provides basic facts about the book
- a body that summarizes the book's main ideas and details and that analyzes its main literary elements
- a conclusion that states and supports your opinion of the book

Your revised book review should be free of
- unsupported opinions
- errors in grammar, usage, and mechanics

MEETING INDIVIDUAL NEEDS — SPECIAL NEEDS

Special Needs Any student who is visually impaired or who has a learning disability that prevents full participation in the Writing Workshop may wish to complete an adapted version of the book review assignment.

Activity Encourage the student to listen to an audiotaped version of a book of interest. Then have him or her prepare an oral book review. The final version of the book review can be taped on a cassette and "aired" for the class during the Publishing/Presenting phase of the workshop. **L1**

Additional Resources

Inclusion Strategies

GLENCOE TECHNOLOGY

REVISING WITH STYLE CD-ROM

Invite students to use the *Revising with Style* CD-ROM, which offers instruction and exercises to help students improve their writing skills.

EDITING/PROOFREADING

Use the **Proofreading Checklist** to go over your revision once more, correcting errors in grammar and mechanics. Pay special attention to capitalization, as shown in the **Grammar Link** on page 712.

PROOFREADING CHECKLIST

- ☑ Subjects and verbs agree
- ☑ Sentences are complete; there are no fragments or run-ons.
- ☑ Verbs are in the active voice wherever possible
- ☑ Pronouns agree with their antecedents.
- ☑ Modifiers are used correctly.
- ☑ Spelling, punctuation, and capitalization are correct.

Grammar Hint

As you know, a verb must agree with its subject. Don't be tricked by phrases that come between subject and verb:

One of the main characters is a falcon.

STUDENT MODEL • EDITING/PROOFREADING

The main purpose of the drawings ~~are~~ is to show what the plants look like.

Complete Student Model on p. R113.

Complete Student Model

For a complete version of the model developed in this Workshop, see **Writing Workshop Models**, p. R113.

PUBLISHING/PRESENTING

Present your book review to the class as a radio broadcast. Since a radio audience can't see you, you will need to use vocal techniques to get your ideas across.

PRESENTING TIP

As an alternative, you might publish your book review on the Internet. Some large online booksellers invite readers to review books.

Reflecting

Think about the following questions and then write responses.

- Which part of your review do you consider the strongest? Why?
- How has writing your review changed your understanding of the book you chose? Explain.

Save your work for your portfolio.

EDITING/PROOFREADING

Point out that many writers give their work to friends for editing and proofreading. It is sometimes difficult to see one's own errors. The "Proofreading Checklist" on the student page can help students edit their own work and can serve as a guide when they proofread their peers' reviews.

PUBLISHING/PRESENTING

Encourage students to present their book reviews to the class. Classmates can create a personal reading list based on books that were reviewed. Encourage students who created audio book reviews to play them for classmates at this time.

Oral Review Have students present their book reviews orally within groups. Remind them that their reviews should include an effective summary of the book in their own words, their opinion of the book, the evidence and/or quotations from the book to support their opinion.

Reflecting

Portfolio Suggest that students ask themselves the following questions as they review their writing:

Does my book review
- provide a clear, concise summary of the book?
- present my opinion in an interesting, well-supported manner?
- persuade readers to read the book?

OR
- discourage readers from reading the book?

6+1 TRAITS™ OF WRITING

See the annotated **Writing Workshop Models** on pp. R13–R36 for additional help in evaluating student writing and in teaching the **6+1 Traits™ of effective writing.** Annotations and minilessons address and reinforce the **6+1 Traits™:** Ideas, Organization, Voice, Word Choice, Sentence Fluency, Conventions, and Presentation.

ASSESSMENT

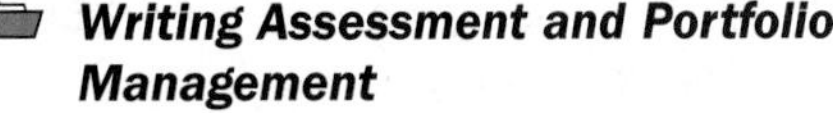

Writing Assessment and Portfolio Management
- Writing Assessment, pp. 1–12, 32–34
- Portfolio Management, pp. 38–45

Theme Assessment

Objectives

- To offer a personal response to the stories, myths, and folklore in this theme
- To write a comparison of two stories
- To complete a self-evaluation, set a goal, and devise a plan for achieving the goal

Responding to the Theme

1. Students should provide insight into the reasons for their choices.
2. Accept all thoughtful answers and observations.
3. Allow time for students to share their charts, travel itineraries, and dioramas with classmates.

Analyzing Literature

Students' writing should include

- an introductory paragraph identifying the characters and stories to be compared
- an analysis of the characters' differences and similarities
- examples and details from the stories

Evaluate and Set Goals

Evaluate

Have students list activities they have completed for each task on this page. Suggest that they add other tasks as well, such as creating a graphic.

Have students use the class rubric they developed in the first theme's evaluation to assess their work.

Set Goals

Have students record their goals and plot steps for achieving them on a timeline. Discuss students' goals and plans in individual conferences.

A DIFFERENT DIMENSION

Theme Assessment

Responding to the Theme

1. Which myth, legend, folktale, or story in this theme did you most enjoy reading? What was it about the story that you particularly liked?
2. What new ideas do you have about the following as a result of reading the literature in this theme?
   - the use of supernatural characters to further the plot of a story
   - the way imaginative settings or situations add interest to a story
3. Present your theme project to the class.

Analyzing Literature

COMPARE TALES

Compare the characters from any two stories in this theme. How are they alike? How do they differ? How do they cope with any problems or difficulties they encounter? Support your analysis with quotations from the selections.

Evaluate and Set Goals

1. Which of the following tasks did you find most rewarding? Which was most difficult?
   - reading and thinking about the stories
   - doing independent writing
   - analyzing the stories in discussions
   - performing dramatizations
   - doing research
2. Using the following scale, how would you assess your work in this theme? Give at least two reasons for your assessment.

   4 = outstanding   2 = fair
   3 = good   1 = weak
3. Based on what you found difficult in this theme, choose a goal to work toward in the next theme.
   - Write your goal and three steps you will take to help you reach it.
   - Meet with your teacher to review your goal and your plan for achieving it.

Build Your Portfolio

SELECT

Select two pieces of work you did during this theme to include in your portfolio. Use the following questions to help you decide.

- ✦ Which work do you consider your best work?
- ✦ From which work did you learn the most?
- ✦ Which work "stretched" you the most?
- ✦ Which work did you enjoy the most?

REFLECT

Write some notes to accompany the work you selected. Use the following questions to guide you.

- ✦ What do you like best about the piece?
- ✦ What did you learn from creating it?
- ✦ What might you do differently if you were beginning this piece again?

ASSESSMENT

Writing Assessment and Portfolio Management

- Writing Assessment, pp. 1–12
- Portfolio Management, pp. 38–45

GLENCOE TECHNOLOGY

MINDJOGGER VIDEOQUIZZES VIDEODISC

Use *MindJogger* to review the Theme 7 content.

Theme 7
Side B

Also available in VHS.

Reading on Your Own

Have you enjoyed reading the literature in this theme? If so, you might be interested in the following books.

A Wrinkle in Time

by Madeleine L'Engle In this award-winning novel, Meg and Charles, along with their friend Calvin, search through time and space for their missing father.

Maniac Magee

by Jerry Spinelli A modern-day folktale about a twelve-year-old boy who appears in a town, amazes everyone with his deeds, and becomes a legend.

Big Men, Big Country: A Collection of American Tall Tales

by Paul Robert Walker Stories portray nine American tall-tale heroes, including Paul Bunyan, Pecos Bill, Sluefoot Sue, and Davy Crockett.

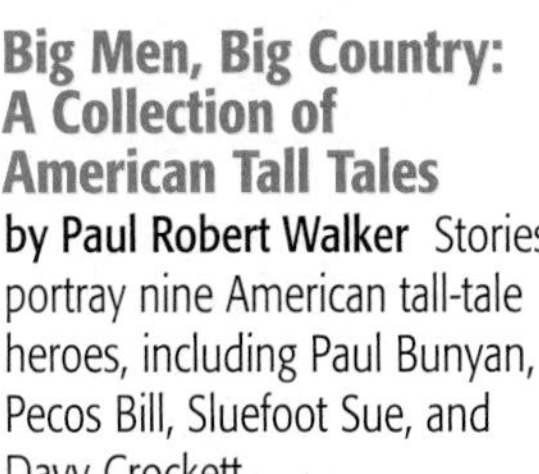

Cut from the Same Cloth: American Women of Myth, Legend, and Tall Tale

by Robert D. San Souci The author retells stories about legendary, larger-than-life women from various American cultures.

Reading on Your Own

Tips for Independent Reading

Stress the importance of each student's spending at least thirty minutes a day in independent reading and suggest books, such as those shown here, related to this theme.

Fantastic Fiction As students read the books recommended here or similar books, remind them that legends, myths, folktales, fantasy, and science fiction often differ in many ways from realistic fiction. Settings may be exotic or fantastic and characters more (or less) than human. Plots may follow a logic of their own. Help students understand the need to accept the conventions of such fiction.

Practice Have small groups each compare the basic elements of one type of fantastic fiction with those of realistic fiction. (For example, compare setting, plot, characters, and theme in realistic stories with the same elements in a myth, folktale, tall tale, fantasy, or science fiction story.) As each group presents its results to the class for discussion, combine the information into a master chart.

Glencoe Literature Library

A Wrinkle in Time by Madeline L'Engle is available in the *Glencoe Literature Library*. For a complete listing of the titles, see the **Glencoe Resources for Independent Reading** in the front of this book.

The *Glencoe Literature Library Study Guide* provides instructional support and student activities for works in the *Glencoe Literature Library*.

Meeting Individual Needs: SPECIAL NEEDS

You may wish to recommend Madeleine L'Engle's *A Wrinkle in Time* to your less-proficient readers. The storyline is easy to follow, and the narrative writing and dialogue are quite manageable. **L1**

Activity The following books are rated for average readers **(L2)** or for students who need more challenging material **(L3)**.

- *Big Men, Big Country: A Collection of American Tall Tales* by Paul Robert Walker **L2**
- *Cut from the Same Cloth: American Women of Myth, Legend, and Tall Tale* by Robert D. San Souci **L2**
- *Maniac Magee* by Jerry Spinelli **L3**

Additional Resources

Inclusion Strategies

Standardized Test Practice

Answers and Analyses

1. **C** Remind students that *Uncle Lester* is capitalized because it refers to a specific person.
2. **L** The term *the chef* indicates who Mrs. Anderson is. Such a title must be separated by commas from the rest of the sentence.
3. **A** A semicolon joins two related independent clauses.
4. **K** In this example, *French* is a proper noun and must be capitalized; *scientists* is a common noun and should not be capitalized.
5. **C** Choice A uses a comma unnecessarily, and choice B uses a semicolon unnecessarily, so they can both be eliminated. Choice C is correct because it uses a hyphen to join two words as a hyphenated compound that acts as an adjective modifying *gas station.*
6. **M** A quotation must be set off from the rest of the sentence by a comma, have quotation marks at the beginning and end, and have the first word of a new sentence begin with a capital letter. Only choice M meets all of these criteria.
7. **A** All words in a proper noun, such as a store or brand name, must be capitalized.
8. **K** A book title is capitalized and written in italics or underlined. Articles and short conjunctions and prepositions should remain lowercase unless they are the first word of the title.

TEST-TAKING TIP

After students have read a question, considered the answer choices, and picked an answer, they should put that question behind them. If there is time, students can always go back to review their answers, but they should not let troublesome questions they've already attempted to answer distract them while working on a new question.

Standardized Test Practice

Read the sentences in each numbered item. Look at the underlined words. Choose the sentence in which the underlined words have CORRECT capitalization and punctuation.

1
- A My uncle lester is a great friend.
- B My Uncle lester is a great friend.
- C My Uncle Lester is a great friend.
- D My uncle Lester is a great friend.

2
- J After we ate dinner, Mrs. Anderson the chef, served us dessert.
- K After we ate dinner, Mrs. Anderson the chef served us dessert.
- L After we ate dinner, Mrs. Anderson, the chef, served us dessert.
- M After we ate dinner, Mrs. Anderson, the chef served us dessert.

3
- A I don't want waffles; I want toast.
- B I don't want waffles: I want toast.
- C I don't want waffles I want toast.
- D I don't want waffles, I want toast.

4
- J The French Scientists described the experiment.
- K The French scientists described the experiment.
- L The french Scientists described the experiment.
- M The french scientists described the experiment.

5
- A My mom pulled the car into a self, service gas station.
- B My mom pulled the car into a self; service gas station.
- C My mom pulled the car into a self-service gas station.
- D My mom pulled the car into a self service gas station.

6
- J As I raced out the door, my father yelled "Be careful!"
- K As I raced out the door, my father yelled, "be careful!"
- L As I raced out the door, my father yelled, be careful!"
- M As I raced out the door, my father yelled, "Be careful!"

7
- A Jared went to Lundeen Drug Store to buy toothpaste.
- B Jared went to Lundeen drug store to buy toothpaste.
- C Jared went to lundeen drug store to buy toothpaste.
- D Jared went to Lundeen Drug store to buy toothpaste.

MEETING INDIVIDUAL NEEDS

ENGLISH LANGUAGE LEARNERS

Using Grammar Ask students to imagine that they are writing a letter to a pen pal describing their neighborhood. Have students write down all the parts of the letter that have some form of capitalization. Some examples they may use are the salutation, names of persons, streets, cities, or months in the heading or inside address, the closing, and other proper nouns within the body of the letter. This will give students a good sense of which words should be capitalized in the sentences above.

8 J My favorite book is *The Wind In The Willows*.
K My favorite book is *The Wind in the Willows*.
L My favorite book is *The Wind In the Willows*.
M My favorite book is *The Wind in The Willows*.

9 A The park is closed, let's go to my house.
B The park is closed let's go to my house.
C The park is closed: let's go to my house.
D The park is closed; let's go to my house.

10 J Both dogs tails were wagging.
K Both dogs' tails were wagging.
L Both dogs tail's were wagging.
M Both dog's tails were wagging.

11 A My doctor's name is Doctor Colgan.
B My doctor's name is doctor colgan.
C My doctor's name is Doctor colgan.
D My doctor's name is doctor Colgan.

12 J Mr. Ramirez my soccer coach, is also my neighbor.
K Mr. Ramirez, my soccer coach, is also my neighbor.
L Mr. Ramirez, my soccer coach; is also my neighbor.
M Mr. Ramirez, my soccer coach is also my neighbor.

13 A "The play is at 6,30," said Mrs. Hatcher.
B "The play is at 6:30, said Mrs. Hatcher.
C "The play is at 6:30," said Mrs. Hatcher.
D "The play is at 6:30" said Mrs. Hatcher.

14 J Manuela speaks english and spanish.
K Manuela speaks english and Spanish.
L Manuela speaks English and spanish.
M Manuela speaks English and Spanish.

15 A Mr. dominic's cat is meowing.
B Mr. Dominics' cat is meowing.
C Mr. Dominic's cat is meowing.
D Mr. Dominics cat is meowing.

16 J I hope to visit the Empire State Building some day.
K I hope to visit the Empire state Building some day.
L I hope to visit the Empire State building some day.
M I hope to visit the Empire state building some day.

Answers and Analyses

9. D A semicolon connects two independent clauses that are connected in meaning. In this case, they are going to the house because the park is closed. The semicolon connects these two thoughts in a single sentence.
10. K The apostrophe is used in this example to indicate possession. The tails belong to the dogs. The apostrophe comes after the s because dogs' is plural possessive. This is indicated by the word both.
11. A All parts of a proper noun must be capitalized. In this case *Doctor* is a title, and that makes it part of the person's name.
12. K In this example, the phrase *my soccer coach* describes who Mr. Ramirez is. Commas are used to separate an appositive from the rest of the sentence.
13. C Choice C is the only answer that uses the colon, comma, and quotation marks correctly. Choice A uses a comma instead of a colon for the notation of time; choice B is missing the closing set of quotation marks; and choice D does not have a comma at the end of the quote to separate it from the rest of the sentence. This is a good opportunity for students to use the process of elimination.
14. M Languages and nationalities are considered proper nouns and must be capitalized. Students should be able to eliminate choices K and L immediately.
15. C *Mr. Dominic* is singular, so the possessive of his name would add an *apostrophe* before the *s*. Choice A is incorrect because the name is not capitalized.
16. J The *Empire State Building* is the name of a building, so it is a proper noun. All the words must be capitalized.

Tested Objectives

Item	Reading Objective
1, 4, 7, 8, 11, 14, 16	Use correct capitalization
2, 3, 5, 6, 9, 10, 12, 13, 15	Identify and use hyphen, dash, brackets, and semicolon between two clauses of a compound sentence that are not joined by a conjunction

Theme 8 At a Glance
A Delicate Balance

THEME OPENING

- **Introducing the Theme** (p. 769)
- **Exploring the Theme** (p. 770)
- **Theme Projects** (p. 771)

Theme 8: A DELICATE BALANCE

SELECTIONS

We Are All One (p. 772) 

Media Connection: ***from*** **"See Bobby Run"** (p. 780)

Birdfoot's Grampa (p. 782)

Miracles (p. 782)

Media Connection: The Jungle Book (p. 787)

Rikki-tikki-tavi (p. 788)

Uncle Tony's Goat (p. 806)

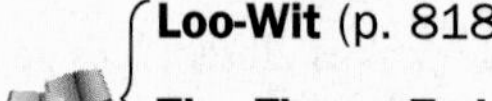

Loo-Wit (p. 818)

The Flower-Fed Buffaloes (p. 822)

Turkeys (p. 826)

The Pasture (p. 834)

Short Poems (p. 840)

SKILL FEATURES

Vocabulary Skills (p. 781)

Interdisciplinary Connection (p. 805)

Grammar Link (p. 816)

Listening, Speaking, and Viewing (p. 817)

Making Inferences (p. 833)

Genre Focus: Short Forms of Poetry (pp. 838–839)

WRITING WORKSHOP

Expository Writing: Cause-and-Effect Essay (pp. 846–849)

THEME ASSESSMENT

- **Responding to the Theme, Analyzing Literature, Evaluate and Set Goals** (p. 850)
- **Build Your Portfolio** (p. 850)
- **Reading on Your Own** (p. 851)
  The Call of the Wild by Jack London
  Cricket Never Does: A Collection of Haiku and Tanka by Myra Cohn Livingston
  Hatchet by Gary Paulsen
  My Life with the Chimpanzees by Jane Goodall
- **Standardized Test Practice** (pp. 852–853)

KEYS TO LITERARY CONNECTIONS

Comparing Selections

The **Comparing Selections** feature in this theme provides opportunities for addressing diverse aspects of the reading and literature curriculum.

For example, in Comparing Selections on page 825, students compare the themes and poetic language of "Loo-Wit" and "The Flower-Fed Buffaloes." Students are asked to consider the relationship human beings have with nature.

World Literature

The Student Edition contains a variety of literature that represents cultures from around the world. World literature selections are highlighted with the icon above.

TEACHING SUPPORT

The Teaching Support offers a wealth of interactive instructional support:

Meeting Individual Needs
- Special Needs
- English Language Learners
- Multiple Modes of Expression
- Advanced Learners

Internet Connection

Assessment

Portfolio Options

Minilessons
- Grammar and Language
- Reading
- Writing
- Listening and Speaking

Connecting to Other Selections

Real-World Connection

Interdisciplinary Connection

Life Skills Connection

Family and Community Activity

Key to Ability Levels

The activities throughout this theme have been coded for students of various abilities.

L1 BASIC activities for all students

L2 AVERAGE activities for average to above-average students

L3 ADVANCED LEARNERS activities for above-average students

Teaching Today

The Glencoe *Teaching Today* professional development Web site at www.teachingtoday.glencoe.com features daily teaching tips, free downloads, annotated Web resources, educational news, and a wealth of information on a wide range of topics.

Theme 8 At a Glance
A Delicate Balance

Reading Skills in this theme

Variety of Texts

In addition to autobiographical selections, this theme includes the following text types:

- folktale
- short story
- humorous essay
- cartoon
- journal entry
- movie review

Comprehension Skills

The following instructional support for comprehension skills appears in this theme of the Student Edition:

- **Reading and Thinking Minilessons** (pp. 804, 815, 821, 832, 845)
- **Making Inferences** (p. 833)

See also the **Reading Minilessons** throughout the theme in this Teacher Wraparound Edition.

For strategies for reading longer works, such as novels and novellas, see "Tips for Independent Reading" on page 851.

Reading Resources

Active Reading Guide The ***Active Reading Guide*** provides graphic organizers and study guide questions to support students' reading of each selection. (***Active Reading Guide***, pp. 65–73)

Interactive Reading Sourcebook and **Interactive Reading Workbook** The ***Interactive Reading Sourcebook*** and ***Interactive Reading Workbook*** offer focused comprehension strategies and lessons on critical thinking skills as well as fluency practice and activities to teach and support phonics, decoding, spelling, and vocabulary development.

Vocabulary Power The ***Vocabulary Power*** workbook (Lessons 33–36) provides systematic teaching, practice, and assessment of vocabulary for better reading comprehension.

Audio Library Available on audiocassette and on CD, the ***Audio Library*** provides valuable comprehension support.

Glencoe Literature Library Each title in the ***Glencoe Literature Library*** includes a full-length work plus related readings. A separate Study Guide is available for each title.

Five–Star Stories These anthologies of familiar short stories adapted and abridged for a variety of reading levels include exercises to help increase students' vocabulary and improve their reading comprehension.

The Contemporary Readers ***The Contemporary Readers*** are nonfiction books linked to various themes and designed for developing readers from a wide range of backgrounds.

Literature Classics CD-ROM The selections on this CD-ROM can be searched by author, theme, or genre.

***in*TIME and Humanities Across TIME** Coproductions of Glencoe and Time, Inc., these resources include a wealth of high-interest nonfiction related to the selections in this theme.

Assessment in this theme

Assessment in the Student Edition

This program offers a number of diverse ways to evaluate student understanding and skill proficiency. In the Student Edition, use the following:

- **Responding to Literature**
  Following each selection, students are asked to recall facts, interpret ideas, and evaluate concepts as they answer a variety of questions and complete activities to extend their understanding.
- **Theme Assessment (pp. 850–851)**
  Here students respond to the selections on personal and analytical levels. They also assume ownership of their learning by setting and evaluating goals and by selecting work for their portfolios.

See also the many **Assessment Resources** listed on the facing page.

Standardized Test Practice

The Princeton Review has developed the Standardized Test Practice pages found at the end of this thematic unit (pp. 852–853). For additional practice, direct students to the following resources:

- ITBS Preparation and Practice
- SAT-9 Preparation and Practice
- TerraNova Preparation and Practice

Writing Skills in this theme

Writing Skills

The Student Edition of Theme Eight offers strong instructional support for writing skills:

In **Extending Your Response**, which follows each selection:

- **Writing About Literature**
- **Personal/Creative Writing**

See also the **Writing Minilessons** throughout the theme in this Teacher Wraparound Edition.

Writing Workshops

Theme Eight concludes with a **Writing Workshop** that guides students through the process of writing a cause-and-effect essay (pp. 846–849).

Writing Resources

Writer's Assistant CD-ROM Each **Writing Workshop** is supplemented by an interactive writing guide on the ***Writer's Assistant*** CD-ROM. This easy- to-use writing guide provides prompts, templates, and other tools that lead students through the writing process.

Grammar and Composition Handbook The ***Grammar and Composition Handbook*** (Lessons 13.5–14.5) provides systematic instruction in English language conventions.

Spelling Power The ***Spelling Power*** workbook (Lessons 29–32) provides systematic teaching, practice, and assessment of spelling to help students become better spellers and thus enhance their writing.

Writing and Proofreading Practice Blackline masters present in-depth instruction and practice on a specific step in the writing process and proofreading (pp. 1–7, 57–63).

Writing and Proofreading Transparencies Transparencies provide graphic organizers and proofreading exercises for whole-class instruction (pp. 1–6, 23–24, 39–40).

Research and Report Writing Guide This resource provides extensive tips and activities to guide students in their writing projects in the literature classroom as well as in classes across the curriculum.

Style and Documentation Sourcebook for Writers This sourcebook is a combination reference and workbook, giving students the most up-to-date information and guidance regarding traditional as well as technological research strategies and documentation.

Revising with Style This resource offers instruction and exercises focusing on the revision process and covering topics from proofreading and correcting common grammatical errors to sentence combining and reordering.

Assessment Resources

Selection Quick Checks For each selection, a **Quick Check** of three to five short-answer questions measures students' literal comprehension.

Selection and Theme Assessment The ***Selection and Theme Assessment*** instrument tests students' abilities to recall, interpret, and evaluate what they've read. The tests consist of multiple-choice, short answer, and essay questions.

Performance Assessment Alternative assessment instruments and rubrics for Theme Eight are found in the ***Performance Assessment*** ancillary.

Writing Assessment and Portfolio Management These notes and strategies, student models, and assessment tools assist with the task of measuring students' progress as writers and as monitors of their own writing.

Testmaker: ExamView Pro Teachers can customize selection and Theme Eight tests by accessing the ***Testmaker*** database.

Interactive Tutor: Self-Assessment The ***Interactive Tutor: Self-Assessment*** software provides multiple-choice tests with immediate feedback to help students evaluate their knowledge and understanding of each literature selection.

MindJogger Videoquizzes Using a popular game show format, ***MindJogger Videoquizzes*** on videocassettes enable teachers to evaluate student understanding of Theme Eight in a quick and fun manner.

Theme 8 Skills Scope and Sequence

Lessons	Literary Elements	Reading and Thinking	Writing
We Are All One Laurence Yep DRP:51 Lexile:680	Plot, SE p. 778 *Character, TWE p. 774* *Plot: Sequence of Events, TWE pp. 774, 775* *Repetition, TWE p. 775* *Theme, TWE p. 777* *Folktale, TWE p. 777*	*Drawing Conclusions, TWE p. 774* *Inferring, TWE p. 775* *Monitoring Comprehension, TWE p. 775*	Paragraph (Imagery), SE p. 779 Journal Entry, SE p. 779
Birdfoot's Grampa Joseph Bruchac **Miracles** Walt Whitman	Theme, SE p. 785 *Characterization, TWE p. 783*	Journal, SE p. 780 *Setting a Purpose for Reading, TWE p. 780* *Using Graphic Aids, TWE p. 784*	Describing a Character, SE p. 786 Short Poem, SE p. 786
Rikki-tikki-tavi Rudyard Kipling DRP:57 Lexile:970	Anthropomorphism, SE p. 802; *TWE pp. 790, 791, 796, 797, 798, 799, 801* *Narrator, TWE p. 790* *Characterization, TWE p. 793* *Humor, TWE p. 796* *Mood, TWE p. 797* *Onomatopoeia, TWE p. 799*	Movie Review, SE p. 787 Evaluating, SE p. 804 *Identifying Author's Purpose, TWE p. 787* *Inferring, TWE pp. 791, 794* *Using Graphic Aids, TWE p. 791* *Drawing Conclusions, TWE p. 792* *Identifying Bias, TWE p. 795* *Evaluating, TWE p. 798*	Explanation (Setting), SE p. 803 News Article, SE p. 803 *Writing from Another Point of View, TWE p. 797*
Uncle Tony's Goat Leslie Marmon Silko DRP:55 Lexile:850	Narrator, SE p. 813; *TWE pp. 808, 811* *Foreshadowing, TWE p. 809*	Problem/Solution, SE p. 815 *Logical Reasoning, TWE p. 808* *Graphic Aids, TWE p. 809* *Drawing Conclusions, TWE pp. 811, 812*	Paragraph (Setting), SE p. 814 Rewrite Story, SE p. 814
Loo-Wit Wendy Rose	Extended Metaphor, SE p. 820 *Extended Metaphor, TWE p. 819*	Elaborating, SE p. 821	Describing a Poem's Impact, SE p. 821 Metaphor, SE p. 821
The Flower-Fed Buffaloes Vachel Lindsay	Alliteration, SE p. 824 *Alliteration, TWE p. 823*	*Comparing Selections, TWE p. 825* *Identifying Assumptions, TWE p. 823*	
Turkeys Bailey White DRP:58 Lexile:850	Author's Purpose, SE p. 830 *Author's Purpose, TWE pp. 828, 829*	Cause and Effect, SE p. 832 Making Inferences, SE p. 833 *Evaluating, TWE p. 829* *Problem and Solution, TWE p. 829* SN *Less-Proficient Readers, TWE p. 833*	Another Point of View, SE p. 831 Journal Entry, SE p. 831
The Pasture Robert Frost	Rhythm: End-Stopped Lines, SE p. 836; *TWE p. 835* *Assonance, TWE p. 835*		Paragraph (Mood), SE p. 837 Poem, SE p. 837
Short Poems Matsuo Bashō, Myra Cohn Livingston, Raymond R. Patterson, Ann Atwood	Short Forms of Poetry, SE p. 838 Personification, SE p. 843; *TWE pp. 841, 842* *Symbol, TWE p. 841* *Haiku, TWE p. 841*	Spatial Rel./Spatial Order, SE p. 845 *Comparing and Contrasting, TWE p. 842*	Imagery/Mood, SE p. 844 Cinquain or Limerick, SE p. 844 ELL *Translation, TWE p. 838* *Haiku, TWE p. 841*
Writing Workshop Expository Writing: Research Report			*Developing Paragraphs, TWE p. 848*

Key: Student material is in roman. *Teacher material is in italic.* 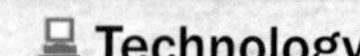 Technology ELL English Language Learners

Vocabulary and Spelling	Grammar and Language	Listening, Speaking, and Viewing	Life Skills; Study and Research; Technology
Synonyms, SE p. 779 *Etymology,* TWE p. 776	*Past Perfect Tense,* TWE p. 776	Literature Groups, SE p. 779 Storytelling, SE p. 779 ELL *Folktales,* TWE p. 774	Interdisciplinary Activity: Research Buddhism, SE p. 779 *Nature,* TWE p. 777
Dictionary Skills: Prounounciation, SE p. 781 ELL Sound Symbol Correlation, TWE p. 781	Sensory Language, SE p. 786	Literature Groups, SE p. 786 Appreciating Poetry, SE p. 786 ELL *Indirect Quotations,* TWE p. 783	
Dictionary Skills: Definitions, SE p. 804 SN *Visually Impaired,* TWE p. 792 *Word Origins,* TWE p. 792 *Etymology,* TWE p. 795	Personal Pronouns, SE p. 804 *Using Semicolons,* TWE p. 800 ELL *Understanding Long Sentences,* TWE p. 790	Literature Groups, SE p. 803 Performing: Readers Theater, SE p. 803 *Analyzing a Video,* TWE p. 796 ELL *Predators,* TWE p. 798 *Interviewing,* TWE p. 799	Interdisciplinary Activity: Research Snakes, SE p. 803 Interdisciplinary Connection: Science, SE p. 805 *Cobra vs. Mongoose,* TWE p. 794 *Research Animals,* TWE p. 795 *Interviewing,* TWE p. 799
Unlocking Meaning, SE p. 815	Consistent Verb Tenses, SE p. 815 ELL *Possessives,* TWE p. 808 *Apostrophes in Contractions,* TWE p. 812	Literature Groups, SE p. 814 Critical Viewing, SE p. 817	Learning for Life: Police Report, SE p. 814 Internet Connection, SE p. 814 *Interview,* TWE p. 811 ELL *Focus Groups,* TWE p. 817
		Literature Groups, SE p. 821 Role-Play, SE p. 821	
	Using Hyphens, TWE p. 823	Literature Groups, SE p. 824 Poetry Reading, SE p. 824	
The Prefix *de–*, SE p. 832	Run-On Sentences, SE p. 832	Literature Groups, SE p. 831	Interdisciplinary Activity: Research Birds, SE p. 831 Internet Connection, SE p. 831 SN *Learning Disabled,* TWE p. 828
Mechanics: Semicolon, Colon, SE p. 837		Literature Groups, SE p. 837 Read Poems Aloud, SE p. 837 *Choral Speaking,* TWE p. 835 *Less-Proficient Readers,* TWE p. 833	
Compound Words, SE p. 845	Prepositional Phrases, SE p. 845	Readers' Theater, SE p. 844 Literature Groups, SE p. 844	
		ELL *Discussing the Issue,* TWE p. 846	

SN **Special Needs/Strategic Intervention**

Theme 8 RESOURCE MANAGER

Lessons	Essential Resources	English Language Learners
We Are All One Laurence Yep Pacing: 1 Day	**Lesson-Specific Instruction** Selection Focus Transp. 65 Active Reading Guide,* p. 65 Literary Elements Transp. 65 Vocabulary Practice, p. 47 Quick Checks,* p. 65 Selection and Theme Assessment, pp. 111–112 Testmaker: ExamView Pro Performance Assessment, p. 61 **Systematic Language Instruction** Grammar and Comp. Hbk., L.13.5 Vocabulary Power, Lesson 33 Spelling Power, Lesson 29	English Language Learners Sourcebook, p. 94 Spanish Summaries, p. 65 Spanish Translations, pp. 195–198 Audio Library* English, Yes!
Birdfoot's Grampa Joseph Bruchac **Miracles** Walt Whitman Pacing: 2 Days	**Lesson-Specific Instruction** Selection Focus Transp. 66 Active Reading Guide,* p. 66 Literary Elements Transp. 66 Quick Checks,* p. 66 Selection and Theme Assessment, pp. 113–114 Testmaker: ExamView Pro Performance Assessment, p. 62 TIME *inTIME* magazine, pp. 8–9 **Systematic Language Instruction** Grammar and Comp. Hbk., L.13.6	English Language Learners Sourcebook, pp. 95, 96 Spanish Summaries, p. 66 Audio Library* English, Yes!
Rikki-tikki-tavi Rudyard Kipling Pacing: 3 Days	**Lesson-Specific Instruction** Selection Focus Transp. 67 Active Reading Guide,* p. 67 Literary Elements Transp. 67 Vocabulary Practice, p. 48 Quick Checks,* p. 67 Selection and Theme Assessment, pp. 115–116 Testmaker: ExamView Pro Performance Assessment, p. 63 **Systematic Language Instruction** Grammar and Comp. Hbk., L.13.7 Vocabulary Power, Lesson 30	English Language Learners Sourcebook, pp. 97, 98 Theme Eight Planning Guide, p. 19 Spanish Summaries, p. 67 Spanish Translations, pp. 199–211 Audio Library* English, Yes!
Uncle Tony's Goat Leslie Marmon Silko Pacing: 3 Days	**Lesson-Specific Instruction** Selection Focus Transp. 68 Active Reading Guide,* p. 68 Literary Elements Transp. 68 Vocabulary Practice, p. 49 Quick Checks,* p. 68 Selection and Theme Assessment, pp. 117–118 Testmaker: ExamView Pro Performance Assessment, p. 64 **Systematic Language Instruction** Grammar and Comp. Hbk., L.13.8 Vocabulary Power, Lesson 34	English Language Learners Sourcebook, pp. 99, 100 Theme Eight Planning Guide, p. 27 Spanish Summaries, p. 68 Audio Library* English, Yes!
Loo-Wit Wendy Rose Pacing: 1 Day	**Lesson-Specific Instruction** Selection Focus Transp. 69 Active Reading Guide,* p. 69 Literary Elements Transp. 69 Quick Checks,* p. 69 Selection and Theme Assessment, pp. 119–120 Testmaker: ExamView Pro Performance Assessment, p. 65 TIME *inTIME* magazine, pp. 12–13 **Systematic Language Instruction** Grammar and Comp. Hbk., L.13.9	English Language Learners Sourcebook, p. 101 Spanish Summaries, p. 69 Audio Library* English, Yes!

Key: Workbook · Blackline Masters · Textbook · Transparency · CD-ROM · Videodisk (also available in videocassette)

Special Needs/ Strategic Intervention	Reteaching and Enrichment
Interactive Reading Sourcebook, pp. T225–T227 Interactive Reading Workbook, pp. 132–133 Audio Library* Theme Eight Planning Guide, p. 6	Reading Skills Practice Workbook, pp. 117–118 Grammar and Language Transp. 61 Gr. and Lang. Wkbk., pp. 93–94 Grammar and Comp. Hbk., L.3.8 TIME *Humanities Across TIME*, Cover 17 Interactive Tutor: Self-Assessment Vocabulary PuzzleMaker Web Site (lit.glencoe.com)
Interactive Reading Sourcebook, pp. T228–T230 Interactive Reading Workbook, p. 134 Theme Eight Planning Guide, p. 14 Audio Library*	Literature Launchers, Side B, Segment 24 Fine Art Transparency 19 Gr. and Lang. Wkbk., pp. 117–118 Grammar and Comp. Hbk., L.5.1 Media Connection Activities, p. 15 Interactive Tutor: Self-Assessment Vocabulary PuzzleMaker Web Site (lit.glencoe.com)
Interactive Reading Sourcebook, pp. T230–T233 Interactive Reading Workbook, pp. 135–138 Theme Eight Planning Guide, p. 19 Audio Library*	Literature Launchers, Side B, Segment 22 Reading Skills Practice Workbook, pp. 119–120 Grammar and Language Transp. 62 Gr. and Lang. Wkbk., pp. 103–104, 265–266 Grammar and Comp. Hbk., L.4.1, 13.5 Media Connection Activities, p. 16 Interactive Tutor: Self-Assessment
Interactive Reading Sourcebook, pp. T234–T237 Interactive Reading Workbook, pp. 139–140 Theme Eight Planning Guide, p. 27 Audio Library*	Literature Launchers, Side B, Segment 23 Reading Skills Practice Workbook, pp. 121–122 Grammar and Language Transp. 63 Gr. and Lang. Wkbk., pp. 83–84, 273–274 Grammar and Comp. Hbk., L.3.5, 13.7 Interactive Tutor: Self-Assessment Vocabulary PuzzleMaker Web Site (lit.glencoe.com)
Interactive Reading Sourcebook, pp. T237–T239 Interactive Reading Workbook, p. 141 Theme Eight Planning Guide, p. 35 Audio Library*	Interactive Tutor: Self-Assessment Web Site (lit.glencoe.com)

Web Audiocassette Diskette *Also available in Spanish

INDEPENDENT READING

Encourage students to spend thirty minutes each day in independent reading. The following Glencoe components and outside resources provide opportunities for reading related to this theme.

The Glencoe Literature Library

You may want to assign one or more of these titles for independent reading. For a complete listing of titles available in the Glencoe Literature Library, see page T96 of this book.

- *Hatchet* by Gary Paulsen
- *The Call of the Wild* by Jack London
- *Julie of the Wolves* by Jean Craighead George
- *High Elk' s Treasure* by Virginia Driving Hawk Sneve
- *The Glory Field* by Walter Dean Myers

***in*TIME** News stories, feature articles, reviews, profiles, and essays in the magazine connect to an author, work, or theme in the Student Edition. See the ***inTIME* Teacher's Guide** for specific connections to this theme.

Resources for Less-Proficient Readers

For reading especially created for less-proficient readers, suggest

- *Five-Star Stories*
- *The Contemporary Readers*

Additional Resources for Independent Reading

The following titles are listed with specific reading selections throughout this theme. You may want to suggest that students look for these in your local or school library.

- *Tongues of Jade* by Laurence Yep
- *Child of the Owl* by Laurence Yep
- *The Girl Who Married the Moon* by Joseph Bruchac
- *Walt Whitman: Poetry for Young People* by Walt Whitman
- *The Jungle Book* by Rudyard Kipling
- *Desert Dwellers: Native People of the American Southwest* by Warren S. Scott
- *Growing Up* by Russell Baker
- *My Life and Hard Times* by James Thurber
- *You Come, Too* by Robert Frost
- *My Life with the Chimpanzees* by Jane Goodall
- *Cricket Never Does: A Collection of Haiku and Tanka* by Myra Cohn Livingston

Theme 8 RESOURCE MANAGER (continued)

Lessons	Essential Resources		English Language Learners
	Lesson-Specific Instruction	**Systematic Language Instruction**	
The Flower-Fed Buffaloes Vachel Lindsay Pacing: 1 Day	Selection Focus Transp. 70 Active Reading Guide,* p. 70 Literary Elements Transp. 70 Quick Checks,* p. 70 Selection and Theme Assessment, pp. 119–120 Testmaker: ExamView Pro Performance Assessment, p. 65 TIME *inTIME* magazine, pp. 10–11, 16–17	Grammar and Comp. Hbk., L.13.10 Vocabulary Power, Lesson 35 Spelling Power, Lesson 31	Theme Eight Planning Guide, p. 42 Spanish Summaries, p. 70 Spanish Translations, p. 212 Audio Library* English, Yes!
Turkeys Bailey White Pacing: 2 Days	Selection Focus Transp. 71 Active Reading Guide,* p. 71 Literary Elements Transp. 71 Vocabulary Practice, p. 50 Quick Checks,* p. 71 Selection and Theme Assessment, pp. 121–122 Testmaker: ExamView Pro Performance Assessment, p. 66 TIME *inTIME* magazine, pp. 16–17	Grammar and Comp. Hbk., L.14.1–14.2 Vocabulary Power, Lesson 36 Spelling Power, Lesson 32	Theme Eight Planning Guide, p. 47 Spanish Summaries, p. 71 Spanish Translations, pp. 213–214 Audio Library* English, Yes!
The Pasture Robert Frost Pacing: 1 Day	Selection Focus Transp. 72 Active Reading Guide,* p. 72 Literary Elements Transp. 72 Quick Checks,* p. 72 Selection and Theme Assessment, p. 123 Testmaker: ExamView Pro Performance Assessment, p. 67	Grammar and Comp. Hbk., L.14.3	Theme Eight Planning Guide, p. 54 Spanish Summaries, p. 72 Spanish Translations, p. 215 Audio Library* English, Yes!
Short Poems Matsuo Bashō, Myra Cohn Livingston, Raymond R. Patterson, Ann Atwood Pacing: 2 Days	Selection Focus Transp. 73 Active Reading Guide,* p. 73 Literary Elements Transp. 73 Quick Checks,* p. 73 Selection and Theme Assessment, p. 124 Testmaker: ExamView Pro Performance Assessment, p. 68	Grammar and Comp. Hbk., L.14.4–14.5 Vocabulary Power, Unit 8 Review/Test Spelling Power, Unit 8 Review/ Proofreading	Spanish Summaries, p. 73 Spanish Translations, p. 216 Audio Library* English, Yes!
Writing Workshop Expository Writing: Research Report Pacing: 2 Days	Writing Assessment and Portfolio Management, pp. 1–13, 35–37, 38–45		English Language Learners Sourcebook, p. 9 English, Yes!

Key: Workbook, Blackline Masters, Textbook, Transparency, CD-ROM, Videodisk (also available in videocassette)

Special Needs/ Strategic Intervention	Reteaching and Enrichment
Interactive Reading Sourcebook, pp. T240-T241 Interactive Reading Workbook, p. 142 Audio Library*	Gr. and Lang. Wkbk., pp. 275-276 Grammar and Comp. Hbk., L. 13.8 Interactive Tutor: Self-Assessment Vocabulary PuzzleMaker Web Site (lit.glencoe.com)
Interactive Reading Sourcebook, pp. T242-T244 Interactive Reading Workbook, pp. 143-144 Audio Library*	Reading Skills Practice Workbook, pp. 123-124 Gr. and Lang. Wkbk., pp. 26-27, 57-58 Grammar and Comp. Hbk., L. 1.6 Interactive Tutor: Self-Assessment
Interactive Reading Sourcebook, pp. T244-T247 Interactive Reading Workbook, p. 145 Theme Eight Planning Guide, p. 52 Audio Library*	Gr. and Lang. Wkbk., pp. 265-266 Grammar and Comp. Hbk., L. 13.5 Interactive Tutor: Self-Assessment Vocabulary PuzzleMaker Web Site (lit.glencoe.com)
Interactive Reading Sourcebook, pp. T247-T249 Interactive Reading Workbook, p. 146 Theme Eight Planning Guide, p. 57 Audio Library*	Fine Art Transparency 6 Gr. and Lang. Wkbk., pp. 142-143 Grammar and Comp. Hbk., L. 7.1 Interactive Tutor: Self-Assessment Vocabulary PuzzleMaker Web Site (lit.glencoe.com)
Inclusion Strategies Sourcebook, pp. 75-76	Writing and Proofreading Practice, pp. 1-7, 57-63 Writing and Proofreading Transparencies 1-6, 23-24, 39-40 Revising with Style Writer's Assistant

 Web 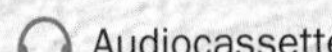 Audiocassette Diskette *Also available in Spanish

Theme RESOURCES

To explore the theme further you may want to use these resources:

- Listening and Speaking Activities (pp. 22-24)
- Viewing and Representing Activities (pp. 1-6, 28-30)
- Critical Thinking Skills (pp. 20-22)
- Media Connection Activities (pp. 15-16)
- Interdisciplinary Activities (pp. 30-33)
- Family and Community Activities (pp.18-19)
- Selection and Theme Assessment (pp. 139-140)
- Performance Assessment (pp. 76, 99)

TIME Humanities Across TIME

See also these additional theme planning resources:

- Theme Eight Planning Guide
- Interactive Reading Sourcebook
- Literature Groups Sourcebook
- Interactive Lesson Planner
- Interactive Teacher Edition
- Glencoe Web Site <lit.glencoe.com>

Use Glencoe's ***Presentation Plus!*** This multimedia teaching tool lets you present dynamic lessons that will engage your students. Using Microsoft PowerPoint®, you can customize the presentation to create your own personalized lessons.

A Delicate Balance

Theme Objectives

- To enjoy reading about the natural world and people's place within it
- To analyze the literary elements in nonfiction, poetry, folktale, and short story selections
- To apply strategies for reading short forms of poetry

Teaching Strategies

Have students read the quotation from Woody Guthrie's song in preparation for the questions below.

VIEWING THE PAINTING

In Chilean-born Gustavo Novoa's dreamlike paintings, predators and their prey coexist peacefully in the wild, and even in modern urban settings.

Responding to the Art Discussion Questions:

- What animals do you see in this painting? *(lion, ostrich, flamingos, zebras)*
- Where are they? *(in Central Park)*
- How would you relate the painting to the theme? *(Wild animals appear to be at home in a city park—in balance with each other and with an urban setting.)*

A Delicate Balance

Central Park. Gustavo Novoa (b. 1941). 24 x 18 in. Wally Findlay Galleries, New York.

768

TEACHER *to* TEACHER

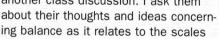

DRIPPING SPRINGS MIDDLE SCHOOL • AUSTIN, TX

To impress upon students the importance of balance, I have them all stand with their left foot and left shoulder touching a wall. On command they are to lift their right foot off the floor. In this off-balanced position, anyone managing to lift his or her foot would fall, but most students don't even try because the brain realizes the body is unbalanced and automatically communicates that to the foot. Then, we brainstorm to come up with all the activities and catch phrases in which balance plays a part and discuss how prevalent the idea of balance is in our lives. I use the idea of the scales of justice as a jumping off point for another class discussion. I ask them about their thoughts and ideas concerning balance as it relates to the scales of justice.

KAREN D. THOMPSON

"This land is your land, this land is my land . . . This land was made for you and me."

–Woody Guthrie

THEME CONTENTS

GENRE FOCUS **SHORT FORMS OF POETRY**

Introducing the Theme

Direct your students' attention to the **Theme Contents.** Ask them to read through the list of selections. Present these questions for discussion:

- Does the tone of the theme seem friendly or unfriendly toward the natural world? Explain your response. *(Students may say that titles such as "We Are All One," "Miracles," "Turkeys," "The Pasture," and "Flower-Fed Buffaloes" seem to be friendly toward nature.)*
- Are there any words in these titles that sound nonsensical to you? *(possibly "Rikki-tikki-tavi" and "Loo-Wit")* What might they mean?
- Do you recognize the name of the man who wrote "Birdfoot's Grampa"? Where have you read the words of Joseph Bruchac before? *(Students may recall discussing Joseph Bruchac's words from* Flying with the Eagle, Racing the Great Bear *in Theme 3, page 216 and reading his legend "Racing the Great Bear" on pages 268–275.)*

FINE ART TRANSPARENCY 16

You may wish to use ***Fine Arts Transparency 16*** to explore what *delicate balance* connotes.

LITERATURE & HUMANITIES

Have students examine the painting *Summer and Winter* from the CD *National Museum of Women in the Arts* and use these two mythical characters as a starting point for writing a short myth of their own.

RESOURCE MANAGER

See the ***Theme Eight Planning Guide*** for additional teaching notes, strategies, and resources for introducing the theme "A Delicate Balance."

GLENCOE TECHNOLOGY

LITERATURE CLASSICS CD-ROM

Search for other selections related to the theme "A Delicate Balance."

Exploring the Theme

A Delicate Balance

- Some students may think that we interact responsibly and compassionately with the natural world, while others may disagree, citing a history of environmentally dangerous practices.
- Students may say that the world as seen through the eyes of other creatures would differ from the way it looks to us. Animals who are hunted or killed for food and skins are probably afraid of humans and find the world a treacherous place; our pets, on the other hand, probably see the world as a safe and comfortable environment.

Starting Points

Escape to Nature

Some students may say that animals are happy to be free, while others may worry that the animals will not know how to fend for themselves in their natural habitats. They have been given their freedom because the pet shop is going out of business.

- Allow time for students to share their captions with each other and their ideas about people's relationships with animals.

Through the Lens

Talk with students about anthropomorphism—the attribution of human form or characteristics to animals or objects. Prepare them to see role reversal when, in "The Dog Diaries," a human takes on the behavior and characteristics of an animal. Have students be aware of anthropomorphism when they write about their experiences from an animal's perspective.

Exploring the Theme

A Delicate Balance

We share the planet Earth with a great number and variety of other creatures. How do we interact with the natural world? How might the world look through the eyes of the other creatures who share this planet with us? In the stories, poems, and essays in this theme, you will find a variety of possible responses to these questions. Try one of the options below to start your own thinking about the theme.

ESCAPE TO NATURE

Human beings today often feel removed from the natural world. We spend many more hours indoors than outside. In this cartoon, assorted animals who have also been separated from nature are released into a new life outdoors.

- What might happen to the creatures in this picture? Why have they been given their freedom? Write a caption for the cartoon that expresses some of your ideas about people's relationships with animals.
- Put yourself in the animal's place and write a few notes about how the experience may have seemed from the animal's point of view. (For an example of writing from an animal's point of view, you might want to reread "The Dog Diaries," pages 411–416.)

THROUGH THE LENS OF EXPERIENCE

Think about an experience you've had with an animal—a pet, a farm animal, an animal in a zoo, or one in the wild. If you haven't had an interesting animal experience, use your imagination to make one up.

Students can use a search engine to find out more about endangered species and their habitats. Suggest that they use such keywords as *rain forest, endangered species,* and *conservation.*

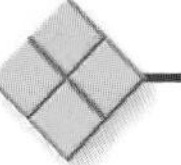

Theme Projects

As you read the selections in this theme, try your hand at one of the projects below. Work on your own, with a partner, or with a group.

LEARNING FOR LIFE

Policy Statement

1. Develop a policy for the ethical treatment of animals as pets or in zoos. Start by listing your own ideas.
2. Gather input from teachers, other students, pet owners, zookeepers, the local humane society, or books and magazines. Draft your policy statement. Share it with the class.

CRITICAL VIEWING

Animals in Nature

1. Collect ten or more photos and other illustrations of animals in their natural habitats. Look through magazines, catalogs, and old calendars for a variety of animals and environments.
2. Study the images. What kind of connection do you make between each animal and its habitat? Write an introduction to your collection that describes the connection between animals and their environments.

interNET CONNECTION

Check out the Web for more project ideas. On the Web you can also find out about the selections and authors included in this theme. Try the Glencoe Web site at lit.glencoe.com.

MULTIMEDIA PROJECT

Author Presentation

1. Gather data about an author from this theme. Record each source of information or graphics so that you can prepare a bibliography at the end of your report. (See pages R55–R59 for information on preparing a bibliography.)
2. Use hypertext software to create a multimedia presentation about the author you choose.
3. Present interesting facts about the author's life, using a visual format such as a timeline. If possible, include a picture of the author.
4. Organize and present your work to the class.

Family and Community Activity

Volunteer Work Ask students to spend two hours volunteering at the local chapter of the Humane Society, an animal shelter, a veterinary clinic, a sanctuary, a zoo, or an organization that deals with the care of animals. Have students prepare posters based on their experiences. Each poster should include a picture of the student in a volunteer capacity, pictures or descriptions of the animals the student worked with, and a brief summary of what the student did as a volunteer. A list of tasks volunteers could do at this organization and the name of a volunteering coordinator would also be of interest.

Additional Resources

- ***Family and Community Activities,*** pp. 18–19

Theme Projects

Teaching Strategies

The following suggestions may help your students plan and carry out their theme projects.

Learning for Life

- To help students identify ethical issues involved in animal treatment and to focus their ideas, suggest that they brainstorm a list of questions, such as: Is it right to keep pets on leashes? Are neutering and declawing unethical? Are zoos simply animal prisons? Are some zoos more humane than others? If so, how?
- Encourage students to gather policy statements from local organizations that deal with animals.

Critical Viewing

- Students may wish to do this project in pairs or small groups.
- Students can alter the activity by choosing a habitat, such as a jungle, plain, desert, or forest, and finding pictures of ten animals that share the habitat.
- Suggest that students include insects, amphibians, fish, and birds in their studies.

Multimedia Project

As students gather material, suggest that they read other works by the author and try to get a sense of what his or her major themes are.

Additional Resources

- ***Interdisciplinary Activities,*** pp. 30–33
- ***Viewing and Representing Activities,*** pp. 1–6, 28–30
- ***Listening and Speaking Activities,*** pp. 22–24
- ***Critical Thinking Skills,*** pp. 20–22
- ***Selection and Theme Assessment,*** pp. 139–140
- ***Performance Assessment,*** p. 76

B Author's Craft

CHARACTER Ask students how the author presents the peddler's character and possible future actions in this passage. *(The author shows him to be a kind person who cares about what is happening around him, even to the ants he encounters along the way in his quest for the magical herb.)*

C Literary Elements

PLOT: *Sequence of Events* Have students summarize the most important events of the story so far. *(A peddler hears of a rich man's eye disease. He goes into the forest to find a magic herb to cure the man. He interrupts his search to help some ants in trouble.)*

D Critical Thinking

DRAWING CONCLUSIONS Have volunteers explain who the queen and soldiers are in the peddler's dream. *(They represent the ant queen and the soldier ants.)*

When the old peddler heard the announcement, he remembered something his mother had said. She had once told him about a magical herb that was good for the eyes. So he packed up his baskets and went back to the single tiny room in which his family lived.

When he told his plan to his wife, she scolded him, "If you go off on this crazy hunt, how are we supposed to eat?"

Usually the peddler gave in to his wife, but this time he was stubborn. "There are two baskets of candy," he said. "I'll be back before they're gone."

The next morning, as soon as the soldiers opened the gates, he was the first one to leave the city. He did not stop until he was deep inside the woods. As a boy, he had often wandered there. He had liked to pretend that the shadowy forest was a green sea and he was a fish slipping through the cool waters.

As he examined the ground, he noticed ants scurrying about. On their backs were larvae[2] like white grains of rice. A rock had fallen into a stream, so the water now spilled into the ant's nest.

"We're all one," the kind-hearted peddler said. So he waded into the shallow stream and put the rock on the bank. Then with a sharp stick, he dug a shallow ditch that sent the rest of the water back into the stream.

Without another thought about his good deed, he began to search through the forest. He looked everywhere; but as the day went on, he grew sleepy. "Ho-hum. I got up too early. I'll take just a short nap," he decided, and lay down in the shade of an old tree, where he fell right asleep.

In his dreams, the old peddler found himself standing in the middle of a great city. Tall buildings rose high overhead. He couldn't see the sky even when he tilted back his head. An escort of soldiers marched up to him with a loud clatter of their black lacquer armor. "Our queen wishes to see you," the captain said.

The frightened peddler could only obey and let the fierce soldiers lead him into a shining palace. There, a woman with a high crown sat upon a tall throne. Trembling, the old peddler fell to his knees and touched his forehead against the floor.

But the queen ordered him to stand. "Like the great Emperor Yü of long ago, you tamed the great flood. We are all one now. You have only to ask, and I or any of my people will come to your aid."

The old peddler cleared his throat. "I am looking for a certain herb. It will cure any disease of the eyes."

The queen shook her head regretfully. "I have never heard of that herb. But you will surely find it if you keep looking for it."

And then the old peddler woke. Sitting up, he saw that in his wanderings he had come back to the ants' nest. It was there he had taken his nap. His dream city had been the ants' nest itself.

"This is a good omen," he said to himself, and he began searching even harder. He was so determined to find the herb that

2. *Larvae* (lär′ vē) is the plural of *larva,* which is the early, worm-like form of an insect; a caterpillar is the larva of a butterfly or moth.

Vocabulary

scurry (skur′ ē) *v.* to run or move briskly or in an agitated way
regretfully (ri gret′ fəl lē) *adv.* in a way that shows sorrow, distress, or disappointment
omen (ō′ mən) *n.* a sign or event thought to foretell good or bad fortune

Teaching Support

Literature & Humanities

Have students examine *The Peaceable Kingdom,* in the book *Introducing Art,* page 140, portraying different kinds of people and animals living in harmony. Ask students what similarities exist between the messages of the story and the painting.

Meeting Individual Needs: English Language Learners

Folktales Every culture has stories that have been passed down from generation to generation. Some of these stories tell about respecting nature or being kind to people and animals.

Activity Ask small groups of students to share stories from their cultures about kindness to people or animals or about respecting nature. Then have each group select one story and draw a comic strip showing major story events. Invite groups to display their comic strips for the rest of the class and explain who the people in the story are and what happens to them.

Additional Resources

English Language Learners Sourcebook, p. 94

he did not notice how time had passed. He was surprised when he saw how the light was fading. He looked all around then. There was no sight of his city—only strange hills. He realized then that he had searched so far he had gotten lost.

Night was coming fast and with it the cold. He rubbed his arms and hunted for shelter. In the twilight, he thought he could see the green tiles of a roof.

He stumbled through the growing darkness until he reached a ruined temple. Weeds grew through cracks in the stones and most of the roof itself had fallen in. Still, the ruins would provide some protection.

Did You Know?
A *centipede* is a long, flat insect with many pairs of legs. The prefix *centi-* means either "hundred" or "hundredth part of," and *pede* comes from the Latin word for "foot."

As he started inside, he saw a centipede with bright orange skin and red tufts of fur along its back. Yellow dots covered its sides like a dozen tiny eyes. It was also rushing into the temple as fast as it could, but there was a bird swooping down toward it.

The old peddler waved his arms and shouted, scaring the bird away. Then he put down his palm in front of the insect. "We are all one, you and I." The many feet tickled his skin as the centipede climbed onto his hand.

Inside the temple, he gathered dried leaves and found old sticks of wood and soon he had a fire going. The peddler even picked some fresh leaves for the centipede from a bush near the temple doorway.

"I may have to go hungry, but you don't have to, friend."

Stretching out beside the fire, the old peddler pillowed his head on his arms. He was so tired that he soon fell asleep, but even in his sleep he dreamed he was still searching in the woods. Suddenly he thought he heard footsteps near his head. He woke instantly and looked about, but he only saw the brightly colored centipede.

"Was it you, friend?" The old peddler chuckled and, lying down, he closed his eyes again. "I must be getting nervous."

"We are one, you and I," a voice said faintly—as if from a long distance. "If you go south, you will find a pine tree with two trunks. By its roots, you will find a magic bead. A cousin of mine spat on it years ago. Dissolve that bead in wine and tell the rich man to drink it if he wants to heal his eyes."

The old peddler trembled when he heard the voice, because he realized that the centipede was magical. He wanted to run from the temple, but he couldn't even get up. It was as if he were glued to the floor.

But then the old peddler reasoned with himself: If the centipede had wanted to hurt me, it could have long ago. Instead, it seems to want to help me.

So the old peddler stayed where he was, but he did not dare open his eyes. When the first sunlight fell through the roof, he raised one eyelid cautiously. There was no sign of the centipede. He sat up and looked around, but the magical centipede was gone.

He followed the centipede's instructions when he left the temple. Traveling south, he kept a sharp eye out for the pine tree with two trunks. He walked until late in the afternoon, but all he saw were normal pine trees.

E Literary Elements

PLOT: *Sequence of Events* Have students describe what important event occurs after the peddler finds the ruined temple. *(The peddler saves a centipede and feeds it, even though he has no food himself.)*

F Author's Craft

REPETITION Have students think about how the author uses repetition to develop the story. *(He presents a pattern of behavior for the peddler that gives the reader insight into what might happen in the story.)*

G Critical Thinking

INFERRING Have students explain whether they think the peddler will find the pine tree with two trunks. You may wish to share the following model to illustrate the process of making inferences.

Model: I think the peddler will find the pine tree eventually because good people in folktales are usually rewarded. But the peddler still has not been helped by the ants. I think the ants will have to help him before the story can be resolved. Perhaps the ants will help the peddler find the pine tree with two trunks.

Reading Minilesson

Monitoring Comprehension Review with students the process of detecting when something doesn't make sense. Then, go over the steps that can be taken to remedy the situation. Jot important points on the board: *Identify the problem or question; Adjust reading rate; Reread; Self-question; Paraphrase; Visualize.*

Activity Have students work in small groups. They can use "We Are All One" as the basis to develop think-aloud models explaining how to detect and remedy comprehension breakdowns. Each group should model the process for the class. L2

Additional Resources

Reading Skills Practice Workbook

VIEWING THE PAINTING

The painting should help students picture the setting of the folktale. The old peddler and his wife may have lived in a village similar to the one in the painting. They might have worn clothes like those seen in the painting.

Vo•cab•u•lar•y Skills

Etymology The Middle English word *bede* comes from the Old English word *gebed*, which meant "a prayer." To keep track of prayers, people used a string of small round balls (today called a rosary). Since each round ball stood for one *bede* (or prayer), the word eventually came to mean the round balls themselves. Today *bead* means a small object that can be threaded on a string.

River Scene. 18th century, China. Free Library, Philadelphia, PA.

Viewing the painting: How does this painting add to your understanding of the setting of "We Are All One"?

Teaching Support

Grammar and Language *Minilesson*

Past Perfect Tense Write this sentence from the story on the board to illustrate the concept of past perfect tense: *He remembered something his mother had said.* The past perfect tense of a verb names an action that happened before another action or event in the past. What the peddler's mother said happened before the peddler remembered. Invite students to identify what happened before the weeds grew through the cracks in this example: *Weeds grew through the cracks and most of the roof had fallen in.* *(The roof fell in.)*

Activity Have students look for other examples of the past perfect tense in this story. (There are many examples on pages 774 and 775.) Then have students list which event happened first and which event happened second. **L2**

Additional Resources

- ***Grammar and Language Transparency 61***
- ***Grammar and Language Workbook,*** pp. 93–94
- ***Grammar and Composition Handbook,*** Lesson 3.8
- ***Writer's Choice,*** Lesson 10.8

Wearily he sat down and sighed. Even if he found the pine tree, he couldn't be sure that he would find the bead. Someone else might even have discovered it a long time ago.

But something made him look a little longer. Just when he was thinking about turning back, he saw the odd tree. Somehow his tired legs managed to carry him over to the tree, and he got down on his knees. But the ground was covered with pine needles and his old eyes were too weak. The old peddler could have wept with frustration, and then he remembered the ants.

He began to call, "Ants, ants, we are all one."

Almost immediately, thousands of ants came boiling out of nowhere. Delighted, the old man held up his fingers. "I'm looking for a bead. It might be very tiny."

Then, careful not to crush any of his little helpers, the old man sat down to wait. In no time, the ants reappeared with a tiny bead. With trembling fingers, the old man took the bead from them and examined it. It was colored orange and looked as if it had yellow eyes on the sides.

There was nothing very special about the bead, but the old peddler treated it like a fine jewel. Putting the bead into his pouch, the old peddler bowed his head. "I thank you and I thank your queen," the old man said. After the ants disappeared among the pine needles, he made his way out of the woods.

The next day, he reached the house of the rich man. However, he was so poor and ragged that the gatekeeper only laughed at him. "How could an old beggar like you help my master?"

The old peddler tried to argue. "Beggar or rich man, we are all one."

But it so happened that the rich man was passing by the gates. He went over to the old peddler. "I said anyone could see me. But it'll mean a stick across your back if you're wasting my time."

The old peddler took out the pouch. "Dissolve this bead in some wine and drink it down." Then, turning the pouch upside down, he shook the tiny bead onto his palm and handed it to the rich man.

The rich man immediately called for a cup of wine. Dropping the bead into the wine, he waited a moment and then drank it down. Instantly the pain vanished. Shortly after that, his eyes healed.

The rich man was so happy and grateful that he doubled the reward. And the kindly old peddler and his family lived comfortably for the rest of their lives.

Vocabulary

frustration (frus trā′ shən) *n.* disappointment or irritation at being kept from doing or achieving something

H Literary Elements

THEME Have students explain what they think the theme of this story is. *(The theme is the story's title—we are all one. Humans and animals are all a vital part of the world, and we should all help each other whenever we get a chance.)*

I Active Reading Strategies

VISUALIZE Have students describe what the colors of the bead remind them of. *(The bead is orange with yellow spots, the same colors and pattern as on the centipede.)*

J Author's Craft

FOLKTALE Based on other folktales students have read, have them explain how the ending the author uses is typical. *(Goodness and kindness are rewarded. The rich man rewards the peddler with a comfortable lifestyle. The peddler and his family live happily ever after.)*

Thematic Focus

A Delicate Balance Have students explain how this selection relates to the theme "A Delicate Balance." *(The delicate balance of nature includes life and death. In this story, the peddler interferes with death by helping the ants keep water out of their nest and preventing a bird from eating the centipede.)*

ASSESSMENT

 ***Quick Checks,*** p. 65

Real-World Connection

Journals Journals can tell a story, record personal change, or simply keep track of observations from day to day.

Activity Encourage students to look closely at the natural world around them. They do not need to go into a forest to see the natural world. They can find insects in a schoolyard, birds in a parking lot, or people in a mall. Invite students to choose one spot to observe nature (human or animal). Have students take notes in a journal. Encourage students to visit the same spot several times and to record how nature changes at different times of day or different days of the week. Finally, have students draw some conclusions about what they see and share their observations with the rest of the class. **L2**

Responding to the Selection

PERSONAL RESPONSE

Some students may have enjoyed the magical aspects of this story; others may have felt that the magic made the story too farfetched.

Analyzing Literature

1. The peddler thinks he can cure the rich man because he remembers something his mother told him. His wife does not believe he will find the herb. She calls the hunt "crazy."
2. The peddler first saves an ants' nest.
3. The centipede tells the peddler where to find a magic bead.
4. The peddler says, "We are all one."
5. The peddler is kindhearted; he gives away as much candy as he sells, so he is always poor. The peddler wants to win the reward because the money will help his family.
6. The dream had a queen and soldiers, who are the ants. The queen tells the peddler that because he saved them from a flood, he only has to ask and the queen or her helpers will come to his aid.
7. The ants help the peddler find the bead. This was foreshadowed by the peddler's dream.
8. Sample: No, wealth will not change the peddler. He is so kindhearted he will probably use his money to help those less fortunate than he is.
9. Sample: This story's moral, we are all one, can help people recognize that although there are differences, whether someone is rich or poor, Chinese-speaking or English-speaking, we all deserve respect.
10. Sample: Wars would end. Different opinions would be tolerated. Wealthier people would share with poorer people.

Active Reading and Critical Thinking

Responding to Literature

PERSONAL RESPONSE

- What were your thoughts about the magical aspects of this folktale?

Analyzing Literature

RECALL

1. Why does the peddler believe he can win the reward? Does his wife believe in his idea?
2. What is the peddler's first gesture of kindness toward another creature?
3. What is the centipede's advice to the peddler?
4. How does the peddler sum up his belief about the difference between the rich and the poor?

Brackets connect questions that are paired to develop higher-level thinking skills.

INTERPRET

5. What details does the author reveal to explain why the peddler wanted to win the reward?
6. How was the peddler's dream connected to his rescuing the ant's nest?
7. Who helped the peddler follow the centipede's advice? How was this event foreshadowed earlier in the tale?
8. By the end of the tale, the peddler has plenty of money. Do you believe his behavior will change now that he is rich? Explain how the author's description of the character led you to your opinion.

EVALUATE AND CONNECT

9. In your opinion, why did Chinese immigrants continue to tell this ancient tale after they arrived in America? How might the folktale have been a "strategy" for living among strangers in a different country?
10. Theme Connection The title of the tale summarizes the philosophy of the peddler. How do you imagine the world would change if most people shared this belief?

LITERARY ELEMENTS

Plot

A **plot** is the series of events in a story that shows the characters in action, trying to resolve one or more conflicts or problems. One way to determine a story's plot is first to identify the problems. In "We Are All One," for example, the rich man's problem with his eyes sets the story's events in motion. Next, ask yourself: What characters are involved? What will happen next? What is the solution to the problem?

1. Why does the peddler become involved in the rich man's problem? What other problems does the peddler face?
2. Briefly list the series of events that make up the plot of "We Are All One."

See **Literary Terms Handbook,** p. R8.

Landscape, early 18th century. Yao Song. Private collection.

LITERARY ELEMENTS

1. The peddler gets involved to help the rich man. The peddler is poor and ragged.
2. While hunting for a magic healing herb, a peddler saves an ant colony and a centipede. They help him find a magic bead that cures a rich man, who rewards the peddler by making him well-off for life.

Additional Resources

Literary Elements Transparency 65

Extending Your Response

Writing About Literature

Imagery One of the points of the story is that all of nature is interconnected. Scan the story, looking for images of the landscape and the animals. Write a paragraph using the imagery you found to show the storyteller's love and respect for the natural world.

Personal Writing

Life's Connections How does the candy peddler's treatment of all living things compare with your own response in the **Reading Focus** on page 772? Did the story make you look at this issue in a different way? Answer these questions in a journal entry.

Performing

Storyteller's Circle "We Are All One" began as an oral tale. Working in a small group, divide the story into sections, one section for each group member. Perform the story for another class.

Literature Groups

Literary Quests The **quest,** a search or pursuit to find some object or achieve some goal, is a theme found in literature and popular media ranging from the Greek myths to *The Lord of the Rings* and the *Star Wars* movies. What is the quest in "We Are All One"? With your group, share ideas about stories you know that are based on a quest. What do these stories have in common?

Interdisciplinary Activity

Social Studies The belief that animal life is as sacred as human life is important in many religions, including Buddhism. Research Buddhism. Discover how it is practiced in China and in America. Then present your findings in an oral report.

Reading Further

If you would like to read other books by Laurence Yep, try *Tongues of Jade* and *Child of the Owl*

Save your work for your portfolio.

Skill Minilesson

Reteach · Review

VOCABULARY • SYNONYMS

Just because two words are synonyms does not mean that one can be substituted for the other in every situation. Thinking carefully about words will help you use them accurately.

PRACTICE In each question, the italicized words are synonyms. For each, choose the more accurate word.

1. Does a rocket *scurry* or *zoom* into the sky?
2. If you can't go to a party you want to go to, do you stay home *regretfully* or *apologetically?*
3. If a friend told you you would be lucky today and you believed it, would you regard your friend's comment as an *omen* or a *fore-warning?*
4. If you receive a radio as a gift instead of the camera you had hoped for, do you feel *frustration* or *disappointment?*

Extending Your Response

Writing About Literature

Students' paragraphs should

- describe how imagery shows the author's love and respect for the natural world
- contain a clear topic sentence and concise closing

Personal Writing

Students' journal entries should

- compare the peddler's treatment of living things with their ideas
- explain how this story alters their ideas about the treatment of living things
- contain their thoughts about the interconnectedness of all living things

Performing Before students perform, have them experiment with varying the volume, rate, pitch, and rhythm of their voices for dramatic effect.

Literature Groups

Encourage students to recall other quest stories. Then, in groups, have each member briefly describe one quest story.

Interdisciplinary Activity

Encourage students to visit a library and use a card or computer catalog to find books on Buddhism.

Skill Minilesson

VOCABULARY • SYNONYMS

1. zoom
2. regretfully
3. omen
4. disappointment

Additional Resources

Vocabulary Practice, p. 47

ASSESSMENT

- ***Quick Checks,*** p. 65
- ***Selection and Theme Assessment,*** pp. 111–112
- ***Performance Assessment,*** p. 61
- ***Testmaker: ExamView Pro***
- ***Interactive Tutor: Self-Assessment***

MEDIA Connection

Objective

- To read and understand journal excerpts

Literature LINK

Birdfoot's Grampa and **Miracles** Edie Scher's journal "See Robby Run" connects to Joseph Bruchac's poem "Birdfoot's Grampa" and Walt Whitman's "Miracles." In each encounter Scher describes, she recognizes a connectedness to the world, the sense of being a part of a greater experience.

Analyzing Media

Possible answers include being better than others, doing something to the best of one's ability, gaining material rewards, and feeling good about an achievement.

Additional Resources

Media Connections, p. 15

inTIME **magazine**

Down's Syndrome Have students use a search engine to find out more about Down's syndrome. They might use such keywords as *Down's syndrome, adapted sports for kids,* or *children with disabilities.*

MEDIA Connection

JOURNAL

A personal journal can tell about people other than the writer. In these journal excerpts, Edie Scher records her observations on a young runner's progress during a summer.

from "See Robby Run"

by Edie Scher—*Runner's World,* March 1998

May 30: Heading toward my driveway at the end of a run, I hear the rhythm of sneakered foot-falls behind me and turn to see a father and his young son engaged in a coaching session.

"Come on, Robby, that's good. Keep up those arms!" Words of encouragement for a beginning runner, I figure. . . .

"Great morning for a run!" I say.

The boy stops in his tracks and grins. His father smiles at me and gently places a hand on his son's shoulder. "C'mon Robby. Let's keep going." Robby waves happily, and they continue down the block, a tall, handsome father and his 10-year-old Down's syndrome son, whose spanking-clean running shoes and freshly ironed T-shirt announce his newness to the sport.

June 28: Robby has a different partner this morning. His mother does not jog, but instead walks purposefully beside him. When Robby sees me and becomes distracted, she encourages him as her husband would. "His father's on a business trip, and I don't want to stop the momentum," she tells me.

July 5: Robby's father is back, and it looks as if Mom will continue to join them. She walks a few steps behind while her husband talks Robby through his workout. In the middle of the block, Robby stops and turns to ask his mother to run, too. His father cheerfully urges him to continue.

August 11: I look forward to my daily encounter with Robby and his parents. His athletic improvement, while minimal, inspires me by the lesson it teaches. We each run our race and push forward for our own reasons; winning means something different for each runner.

August 22: Robby's two sisters have returned from summer camp and now join his team. Robby's running style has not changed much, but his stride seems to have more bounce. He points to his sisters with obvious pride, stopping to tell me their names. . . . Robby's feet will never leave the pavement with the grace and speed of theirs, but he is not aware of that; his spirit is not competitive, only joyful, as he pushes himself to catch up with them.

September 10: School has resumed, and Robby's sisters and mother no longer run with him. I look at Robby carefully today. He seems a little taller, a little slimmer. Is it my imagination that his stride is a little smoother?

I wait to wave to them before I head up my driveway. They both wave back, but this time Robby does not stop running, and his father lovingly cheers him on for this new personal best.

Analyzing Media

The writer says, "We each run our race and push forward for our own reasons; winning means something different for each runner." What does winning mean to you?

Teaching Support

Reading Minilesson

Setting a Purpose for Reading

Readers who enjoy reading journals and diaries are often interested in the viewpoint of the writer as well as in the writer's experience.

Activity Suggest that students go to the library and find a book or magazine article written in journal/diary form. Have students read several entries and write a journal entry of their own in which they describe what they have read. Encourage them to make candid observations about the writer's perspective as well as the topic. **L2**

Additional Resources

Reading Skills Practice Workbook

Vo•cab•u•lar•y *Skills*

Dictionary Skills: Pronunciation

One of the most important kinds of information you can find in a dictionary is how to pronounce words.

Any vowel letter can be pronounced in different ways. In a dictionary pronunciation, a vowel without any symbol has its normal "short" sound, like the vowels in *pat, pet, pit, hot,* and *hut.* Other vowel sounds are shown by symbols, such as a straight line above the vowel to show that it is "long." (Long vowels "say their own name.")

Following are some additional pronunciation symbols:

ä	an **ah** sound, as in **father**
ô	an **aw** sound, as in **coffee** and **law**
oo	the vowel sound in **wood**
o͞o	the vowel sound in **fool**
oi	the vowel sound in **toy**
ou	an **ow** sound, as in **cow** and **out**
ə	the unaccented vowel sound at the end of **pencil, lemon, taken**
th	**th** as in **thin**
t̲h̲	**th** as in **this**
zh	the sound in the middle of **treasure** or the end of **garage**

An accent mark (′) follows the syllable you should stress. Emphasizing the correct syllable is important in pronunciation.

EXERCISES

1. Use the pronunciation given for each word to answer the question.
   a. Does *brood* (bro͞od) rhyme with *rude, road,* or *rod?*
   b. Does the first syllable of *scuttle* (skut′ əl) rhyme with *cute* or *cut?*
   c. Does *cower* (kou′ ər) rhyme with *lower* or *power?*
   d. Does the *g* in *lunge* (lunj) sound like the *g* in *rage* or in *rag?*
   e. Does the first syllable of *valiant* (val′ yənt) rhyme with *sale, pal,* or *call?*
2. Decide which word is represented by each dictionary pronunciation.
   a. lo͞os — Is this word *lose* or *loose?*
   b. i rās′ — Is this word *erase* or *earache?*
   c. kwī′ it — Is this word *quite, quiet,* or *quit?*
   d. hal′ lōd — Is this word *hollowed, halo,* or *hallowed?*
   e. kon′ stənt — Is this word *consonant, constant,* or *consent?*

Vo•cab•u•lar•y *Skills*

Objective

- To recognize and use strategies for pronouncing words correctly

Teaching Strategies

Have students locate a pronunciation key at the beginning of their dictionaries. Then, ask them to locate the International Phonetic Alphabet (IPA), which often appears alongside the pronunciation key.

Have students familiarize themselves with the IPA and write their names in phonetic transcription. Point out that anyone who can read and use the IPA could pronounce these names correctly. Knowledge of pronunciation symbols and phonetic transcription can help, not only in English pronunciation, but also in learning how to pronounce words in other languages.

Exercises

1. a. rude b. cut c. power d. rage e. pal
2. a. loose b. erase c. quiet d. hallowed e. constant

Additional Resources

Vocabulary Power

Teaching Support

MEETING INDIVIDUAL NEEDS

ENGLISH LANGUAGE LEARNERS

Sound/Symbol Correlation

Pronunciation keys and phonetic symbols can be especially difficult for English language learners. Students whose first language is not based on a Roman alphabet face even more difficulty.

Activity Have mixed groups of students open their dictionaries to any page, close their eyes, and point to a word. Ask them to copy the pronunciation for the word selected on the front of an index card and the word itself on the back of the card. Have students exchange cards and use the Pronunciation Key in the dictionary, as well as their own knowledge of sound-letter relationships, to figure out how the word should be pronounced.

Additional Resources

English Language Learners Sourcebook, p. 95

Before Reading

Objectives

- To read and enjoy two poems about the natural world
- To state the theme of two poems
- To write a description of a character

Skills

Reading/Thinking: Using Graphic Aids
Writing: Writing a Poem
Grammar/Language: Sensory Language
Listening/Speaking: Oral Reading
Collaboration: Literature Groups

Motivating STUDENTS

Literature Launchers: *Native American Storytelling*

Videodisc Side B, Segment 24 

Also available in VHS.

Selection Focus Transparency 66: Have students view the quote by Charles Lindbergh and discuss natural things that have inspired them.

Reading Focus: As an extension of the Reading Focus, have students in small groups examine whether their lists contain more natural objects or human-made objects.

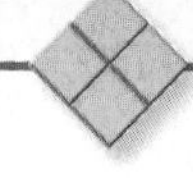

Before You Read

Birdfoot's Grampa* and *Miracles

MEET JOSEPH BRUCHAC

Joseph Bruchac (brōō′ shak) did not learn of his Native American ancestry until he was an adult. His grandfather, who raised him, kept it a secret. Now Bruchac proudly bears his Abenaki name, *Gahnegohheyoh,* which means "the good mind."

Joseph Bruchac was born in 1942. This poem was first published in 1978.

MEET WALT WHITMAN

Walt Whitman worked at everything from carpentry to teaching. He loved variety, not only in jobs, but also in the people and places of America. *Leaves of Grass,* his famous collection of poetry, celebrates the variety and vastness of this country.

Walt Whitman was born in New York in 1819 and died in 1892.

READING FOCUS

Do you ever stop to think about the beauty and the wonder in everyday life?

QuickWrite

Make a quick list of things in everyday life that you think are extraordinary or beautiful.

Setting a Purpose

Read these poems to find out how two poets express their reverence for life.

BUILDING BACKGROUND

Joseph Bruchac writes out of a long Native American tradition of viewing one's relationship to Earth in terms of family. Here are his words about that tradition.

"The Okanagan people of the Pacific Northwest speak of the Earth as Mother; the Sun as Father, and the animals as our brothers and sisters. This view of the world was held by the Navajo and the Abenaki, the Sioux and the Anishinabe, and most of the aboriginal people of this continent. They saw their role on this earth, not as rulers of Creation, but as beings entrusted with a special mission—to maintain the natural balance, to take care of our Mother, to be Keepers of the Earth."

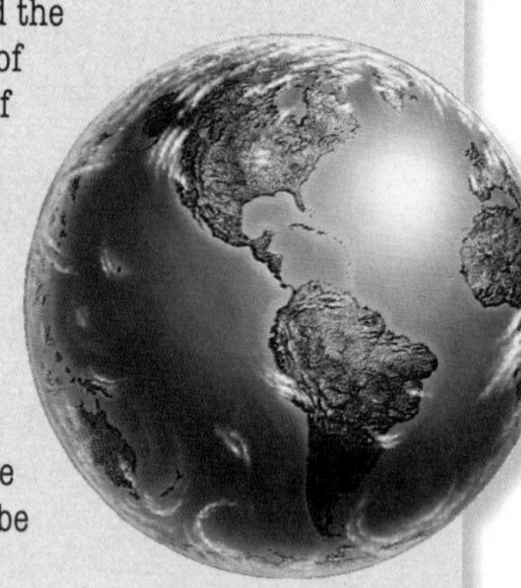

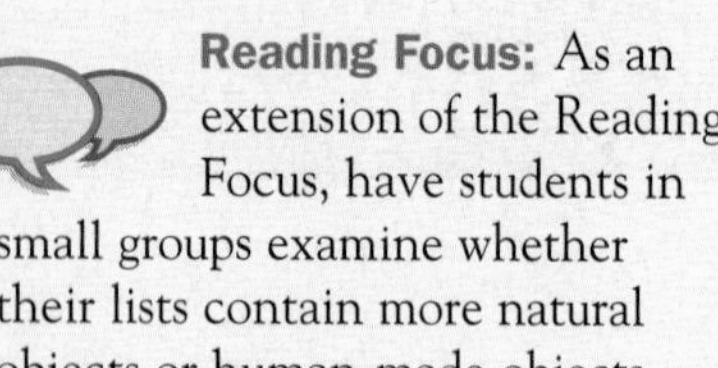

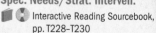

RESOURCE MANAGER

Teaching Tools and Resources
- Theme Eight Planning Guide,
- Literature Groups Sourcebook
- *inTIME* magazine, pp. 8-9

Essential Lesson Support

Lesson-Specific Instruction
- Selection Focus Transparency 66
- Literary Elements Transparency 66
- Active Reading Guide,* p. 66

Assessment
- Selection Quick Checks,* p. 66
- Sel. and Theme Assmt., pp. 113-114
- Testmaker: ExamView Pro
- Performance Assessment, p. 62

Systematic Language Instruction
- Gr. & Comp. Hdbk., L. 13.6

English Language Learners
- ELL Sourcebook, pp. 95-96
- Spanish Summaries, p. 66
- Audio Library*
- English, Yes!

Spec. Needs/Strat. Interven.

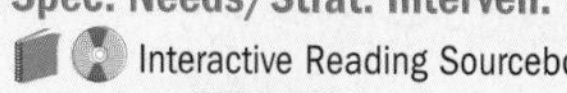

- Interactive Reading Sourcebook, pp. T228-T230
- Interactive Reading Workbook, p. 134

- Audio Library*

*Also available in Spanish

Birdfoot's Grampa

Joseph Bruchac

The old man
must have stopped our car
two dozen times to climb out
and gather into his hands
the small toads blinded
by our lights and leaping,
live drops of rain.

The rain was falling,
a mist about his white hair
and I kept saying
you can't save them all,
accept it, get back in
we've got places to go.

But, leathery hands full
of wet brown life,
knee deep in the summer
roadside grass,
he just smiled and said
they have places to go to
too.

Reading the Selection

A Active Reading Strategies

PREDICT Invite students to look at the title of this poem and the images on the page. Let a volunteer read the first stanza aloud. Then encourage students to predict what the conflict in the next two stanzas may be.

B Active Reading Strategies

EVALUATE After they read the second stanza, have students explain who Birdfoot is and who Grampa is. *(Grampa must be the old man who stops the car to pick up the blinded toads; Birdfoot, the man who wants his grandfather to get back in the car because they have places to go.)*

C Literary Elements

CHARACTERIZATION Encourage students to describe the differences between Birdfoot and his grandfather. *(Birdfoot is young and impatient. He doesn't care about the toads. Grampa is older, thoughtful, caring, and concerned about the toads.)*

Additional Resources

- ***Active Reading Guide,*** p. 66
- ***Audio Library***
- ***Spanish Audio Library***
- ***Spanish Summaries,*** p. 66

Teaching Support

Meeting Individual Needs: English Language Learners

Indirect Quotations Some English language learners may have difficulty understanding the indirect quotations in this poem and identifying the narrator.

Activity Ask volunteers to read the poem aloud, one stanza at a time. After they read the first stanza, encourage students to describe what has happened and who is telling the story. After students read aloud and discuss the second stanza, have them explain which lines tell what Birdfoot says to his grandfather. Finally, after the third stanza is discussed, have students explain which lines in this stanza are the grandfather's reply to Birdfoot.

Additional Resources

- ***English Language Learners Sourcebook,*** p. 96

Literature & Humanities

Have students examine the continuity of *The Sacred Circle*, in *Introducing Art*, page 122. Then have them listen to the song *Dance of All Beings*, on the *World of Music* CD 2, Track 25. Ask them to consider the different Native American views and their relationship to nature.

Active Reading Strategies

VISUALIZE Invite students to close their eyes while a volunteer reads aloud the poem's first fifteen lines. Encourage students to visualize each image. Discuss which images are most striking.

Active Reading Strategies

REVIEW Have students explain what Whitman thinks is a miracle. *(He thinks everything in life is a miracle.)*

Active Reading Strategies

EVALUATE Invite students to explain what the miracles in the final stanza have in common. *(All are related to the sea.)*

Thematic Focus

A Delicate Balance Invite students to explain how these two poems relate to the theme "A Delicate Balance." *(Both poems are about the delicate balance of nature.)*

FINE ART TRANSPARENCY 19

You may wish to use ***Fine Arts Transparency 19*** to enrich the development of theme concepts.

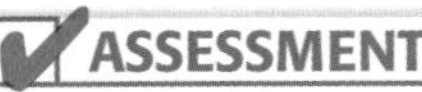

ASSESSMENT

Quick Checks, p. 66

Miracles

Walt Whitman

Why, who makes much of a miracle?
As to me I know of nothing else but miracles,
Whether I walk the streets of Manhattan,
Or dart my sight over the roofs of houses toward the sky,
Or wade with naked feet along the beach just in the edge of the water,
Or stand under trees in the woods,
Or talk by day with any one I love . . .
Or sit at table at dinner with the rest,
Or look at strangers opposite me riding in the car.
Or watch honey-bees busy around the hive of a summer forenoon,
Or animals feeding in the fields,
Or birds, or the wonderfulness of the sundown, or of stars shining so quiet and bright,
Or the exquisite° delicate thin curve of the new moon in spring;
These with the rest, one and all, are to me miracles,
The whole referring, yet each distinct and in its place.°

To me every hour of the light and dark is a miracle,
Every cubic inch of space is a miracle,
Every square yard of the surface of the earth is spread with the same,
Every foot of the interior swarms with the same.

To me the sea is a continual miracle,
The fishes that swim—the rocks—the motion of the waves—the ships with men in them,
What stranger miracles are there?

13 Something that is *exquisite* has a rare beauty, charm, or perfection.
15 This line suggests that all of these small, separate miracles are involved in, or refer to, some greater miracle.

784

Teaching Support

CONNECTING TO OTHER SELECTIONS
For a teaching strategy that connects "Miracles" to "Hurricanes," see the ***Theme Three Planning Guide***.

Reading *Minilesson*

Using Graphic Aids Some students may understand this poem better if they can visualize the images Whitman describes.

Activity Place a large sheet of butcher paper or mural paper on a bulletin board, table, or floor. Label it *Miracles.* Ask each student to draw one image from this poem on the paper. Encourage students to try to show the emotion and sense of awe Whitman feels about each of these images. When students have finished adding to the mural, read the poem aloud while listeners locate each image. **L2**

Additional Resources

Reading Skills Practice Workbook

Responding to Literature

PERSONAL RESPONSE

- Reread your QuickWrite from the **Reading Focus** on page 782. How did these two poems reinforce, or change, your own thoughts and feelings about the extraordinary nature of daily life?

Analyzing Literature

RECALL

1. In "Birdfoot's Grampa," why does the old man stop the car "two dozen times"?
2. List four events in "Miracles" that the speaker identifies as miracles relating to human beings and four relating to nature.
3. Give an example of imagery from each poem.

Brackets connect questions that are paired to develop higher-level thinking skills.

INTERPRET

4. What conflict takes place in "Birdfoot's Grampa"? How does it affect your feelings about the speaker or the old man?
5. How many of the five senses does Whitman include in his list of miracles? Give an example of each.

EVALUATE AND CONNECT

6. In "Birdfoot's Grampa," do you identify more with the speaker or the old man? Why?
7. What other miracles might be included in Whitman's list? Give at least three possibilities.
8. What are your favorite images from each of these poems? Explain why you like them.
9. Theme Connection What attitude toward life and nature do these poems convey?
10. Think of someone you know who would enjoy reading these poems. Why would the poems appeal to that person?

LITERARY ELEMENTS

Theme

The main idea behind a story, poem, novel, or play is usually expressed as a general statement called a **theme.** A theme usually states some truth, as the author sees it, about life or human nature. Sometimes a piece of writing has a **stated theme,** which is expressed directly. More often, a piece of writing has an **implied theme,** which the reader must infer from what the author presents. Sometimes the title of the piece hints at its theme. In poetry, the theme often becomes clear gradually through the combination of its imagery, word choice, and rhythm.

1. What is the theme of "Birdfoot's Grampa"? Is the theme stated directly or implied? Support your opinion with examples from the poem.
2. What is the theme of "Miracles"? How does the title of the poem relate to its theme?

- See **Literary Terms Handbook,** p. R11.

LITERARY ELEMENTS

1. The theme is that everything in nature has a purpose. The theme is implied. Grampa replies, "They have places to go to too."
2. The theme of "Miracles" is that everything in life is awe-inspiring. The concept is stated in the title.

Additional Resources

Literary Elements Transparency 66

Responding to the Selection

PERSONAL RESPONSE

Some students may say that Whitman expands their ideas about beauty. Others may say that Bruchac forces them to look at nature in a new way.

Analyzing Literature

1. The old man stops the car to pick up toads in the road and carry them to the tall grass beside the road.
2. Human miracles include the streets of Manhattan, roofs of houses, talking with loved ones, and eating dinner with friends. Nature's miracles include beaches, trees, honeybees, animals feeding, birds, sundown, stars, new moons, fish, rocks, and waves.
3. Examples of imagery include Grampa, the rain creating a "mist about his white hair," and the "delicate thin curve of the new moon in spring."
4. In "Birdfoot's Grampa" the old man wants to move toads from the road to safety. The young man doesn't want to waste time saving toads. This conflict may make students appreciate the way the old man takes time to think about other beings in nature.
5. Whitman includes sight: *sundown;* hearing: *stars shining so quiet;* touch: *wade with naked feet;* smell: *trees in the woods;* and taste: *sit at table at dinner.*
6. Students may identify with either character, depending on their personal beliefs.
7. Other possible miracles include laughter, flowers, and icicles.
8. Encourage students to explain why they like their chosen image.
9. The poems convey an attitude of appreciation of life and nature.
10. Students should explain why these poems would appeal to the person they choose.

Extending Your Response

Writing About Literature

Students' paragraphs should

- contain a topic sentence
- describe what the old man is like
- contain a sentence that succinctly wraps up the paragraph

Creative Writing

Poems or paragraphs should

- focus on one incident involving another person
- reveal a person's character by describing his or her actions
- contain sensory imagery

Literature Groups Before students meet, encourage them to jot down observations on how the two poems are alike and different. Then, in groups, have each member briefly describe one observation.

Listening and Speaking Encourage students to experiment with their voices to create varying effects. Encourage them to experiment with pauses.

Skill Minilesson

GRAMMAR AND LANGUAGE
• SENSORY LANGUAGE

Each sentence should appeal to at least two senses.

Additional Resources

- ***Grammar and Language Workbook,*** p. 117
- ***Grammar and Composition Handbook,*** Lesson 6.4
- ***Writer's Choice,*** Lesson 3.2

Extending Your Response

Writing About Literature

Characterization In "Birdfoot's Grampa," the poet packs a lot of information about the old man into very few words. Write a paragraph describing the old man as you picture him.

Creative Writing

Poem Write your own short poem or prose paragraph telling about a person. Focus on one incident that shows this person's character, as Joseph Bruchac does in "Birdfoot's Grampa."

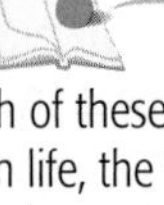

Literature Groups

Poet's Choice Although both of these poems deal with the beauty and wonder in life, the two poems are very different. Compare and contrast the two poems. Pick out examples from the poems that show how the poems are alike and how they are different.

Listening and Speaking

Appreciating Poetry Take turns reading these poems aloud to one another. Pay attention to how different readings affect your experience of each poem.

Reading Further

If you would like to read more by these poets, try these books:

The Girl Who Married the Moon by Joseph Bruchac

Walt Whitman: Poetry for Young People

Save your work for your portfolio.

Skill Minilesson

Reteach • Review

GRAMMAR AND LANGUAGE • SENSORY LANGUAGE

Joseph Bruchac's description of the old man's "leathery hands full of wet brown life" is a fine example of **sensory language**—language that appeals to the senses. Sensory language describes how something looks, sounds, feels, smells, or tastes.

PRACTICE Write a sentence about each of the following items. Try to use sensory language that appeals to at least two senses in each sentence.

1. a car
2. a dog
3. a tree
4. a banana
5. a beach

For more about sensory language and imagery, see **Literary Terms Handbook,** p. R10.

ASSESSMENT

- ***Quick Checks,*** p. 66
- ***Selection and Theme Assessment,*** pp. 113–114
- ***Performance Assessment,*** p. 62
- ***Testmaker: ExamView Pro***
- ***Interactive Tutor: Self-Assessment***

MEDIA Connection

MOVIE REVIEW

David Ansen reviews a film adaptation of Rudyard Kipling's *The Jungle Book.* One of the stories included in Kipling's book is "Rikki-tikki-tavi."

The Jungle Book

by David Ansen—*Newsweek*, January 16, 1995

Kipling purists may not cotton to Disney's new live-action version of *The Jungle Book*, but it's hard to think of anyone else who won't be enchanted. Jason Scott Lee's Mowgli, raised in the jungle by wild animals, uncontaminated by civilization, is no longer the boy Kipling imagined. He's sprouted into a buff young man whose best friends happen to be bears and wolves, but he's not unappreciative of the beauty of the English girl Kitty (Lena Headey), engaged to the dastardly Captain Boone (Cary Elwes). Director Stephen Sommers and his co-writers, Ronald Yanover and Mark D. Geldman, have imposed a taut, cliffhanging story structure upon Kipling's episodic stories, turning *The Jungle Book* into an action-packed love story with something for everyone: hidden treasures, death by quicksand, a Spielbergian lost temple, ecological mysticism, swinish colonialist villains, an irresistible supporting cast of cackling monkeys, a treacherous tiger, a loyal bear, and one very deadly serpent.

It's Lee's ingratiating innocence that holds it all together. He's a figure of the purest fantasy, and he plays Mowgli with a wide-eyed, silent-movie exuberance so disarming it compels belief (even as you wonder where in the overgrown jungle he gets his wardrobe).

Analyzing Media

1. Do you think you would like to see this movie? Why or why not?
2. What is your opinion of the kind of "action-packed love story" the reviewer describes? Use examples of movies you know in your answer.

MEDIA Connection

Objective

- To read and understand a movie review

Literature LINK

Rikki-tikki-tavi This review of *The Jungle Book* connects to the story "Rikki-tikki-tavi," pages 789–801.

Analyzing Media

1. Students who enjoy action, romance, and exotic locations might say they would like to see the movie. Other students may prefer more realistic movies.
2. Movies might include *Titanic, Star Wars, Indiana Jones.*

Additional Resources

Media Connections, p. 16

inTIME *inTIME* magazine

The movie mentioned in the review (*The Jungle Book*, 1994, 111 minutes, PG) is available for rental. The 1942 version (*Jungle Book*, 109 minutes, NR) is even better, and less violent. Be sure to preview any movies beforehand to determine if they are suitable for your class.

Teaching Support

Reading *Minilesson*

Identifying Author's Purpose Words and phrases from movie reviews are often used to advertise the movie and entice moviegoers.

Activity Have students work in groups to locate and read a review of a G- or PG-rated movie. Ask students to discuss the review and decide whether the reviewer's purpose was: 1) to present a balanced view of the film, 2) to encourage people to see the film, or 3) to discourage people from seeing the film. **L2**

Additional Resources

Reading Skills Practice Workbook

Movie Reviews Have students use a search engine to find reviews of movies they have seen. They might use the name of the movie and then add the word *review.*

Before Reading

Objectives

- To read and analyze a short story about the delicate balance between two types of predators
- To recognize anthropomorphism
- To write about how setting contributes to a story's effect

Skills

Reading/Thinking: Inferring; Using Graphic Aids; Drawing Conclusions; Identifying Bias; Evaluating
Writing: Writing from Another Point of View; Writing a News Article
Vocabulary: Definitions; Word Origins
Grammar/Language: Using Semicolons; Personal Pronouns
Listening/Speaking: Analyzing a Video; Readers Theater
Life Skills: Interviewing
Collaboration: Literature Groups

Motivating STUDENTS

Literature Launchers: *The Mongoose: A Snake's Deadly Enemy*

Videodisc Side B, Segment 22

Also available in VHS.

Selection Focus Transparency 67: Have students help create two lists on the board: animals that are often portrayed in stories as evil and animals that are often portrayed as good.

Reading Focus: As an extension of the Reading Focus, have students in small groups share facts about snakes found locally and around the world.

Before You Read

Rikki-tikki-tavi

MEET RUDYARD KIPLING

Shortly after writing "Rikki-tikki-tavi," Rudyard Kipling became involved in a family feud. After an argument with his brother-in-law that stopped just short of a fistfight, Kipling and his American wife left Vermont for England. Kipling lived the rest of his life in England and India. As a boy, and again as a young adult, he lived in India with his parents in bungalows like the one described in this story. In 1907 Kipling became the first British writer to win the Nobel Prize for Literature.

Rudyard Kipling was born in Bombay, India, in 1865 and died in England in 1936. This story was published in 1894.

READING FOCUS

What feelings do you have when you think about snakes?

Think/Pair/Share
Take a moment to jot down your response to this question. Then share your ideas with a partner.

Setting a Purpose
Read this story to find out what happens when a mongoose meets a snake.

BUILDING BACKGROUND

The Time and Place The story takes place in India during the late 1800s, a time when the country was ruled by the British. It was not unusual for snakes and other animals to find their way inside people's houses.

Did You Know? A mongoose is a small mammal of India and Africa, famous for its ability to kill snakes. Mongooses grow to an average length of only about sixteen inches, but their lightning speed makes them fearsome enemies of snakes.

VOCABULARY PREVIEW

scuttle (skut′ əl) *v.* to move with short, rapid steps; p. 789
cower (kou′ ər) *v.* to crouch down, as in fear or shame; p. 792
flinch (flinch) *v.* to draw back, as from something painful, dangerous, or unpleasant; p. 793
gait (gāt) *n.* a particular manner of moving on foot; p. 793
lunge (lunj) *v.* to make a sudden forward movement; charge; p. 794
fancy (fan′ sē) *v.* to picture mentally; imagine; p. 796
valiant (val′ yənt) *adj.* brave; courageous; p. 797
brood (brood) *n.* all of the young of an animal that are born or cared for at the same time; p. 799

788 THEME 8

RESOURCE MANAGER

Teaching Tools and Resources
- Theme Eight Planning Guide
- Literature Groups Sourcebook

Essential Lesson Support

Lesson-Specific Instruction
- Selection Focus Transparency 67
- Literary Elements Transparency 67
- Active Reading Guide,* p. 67
- Selection Vocabulary Practice, p. 48

Assessment
- Selection Quick Checks,* p. 67
- Sel. and Theme Assmt., pp. 115–116
- Testmaker: ExamView Pro
- Performance Assessment, p. 63

Systematic Language Instruction
- Gr. & Comp. Hdbk., L. 13.7
- Spelling Power, Lesson 30

English Language Learners
- ELL Sourcebook, pp. 97–98
- Spanish Summaries, p. 67
- Spanish Translations, pp. 199–211
-  Audio Library*
- English, Yes!

Spec. Needs/Strat. Interven.
- Interactive Reading Sourcebook, pp. T230–T233
- Interactive Reading Workbook, pp. 135–138
-  Audio Library*

*Also available in Spanish

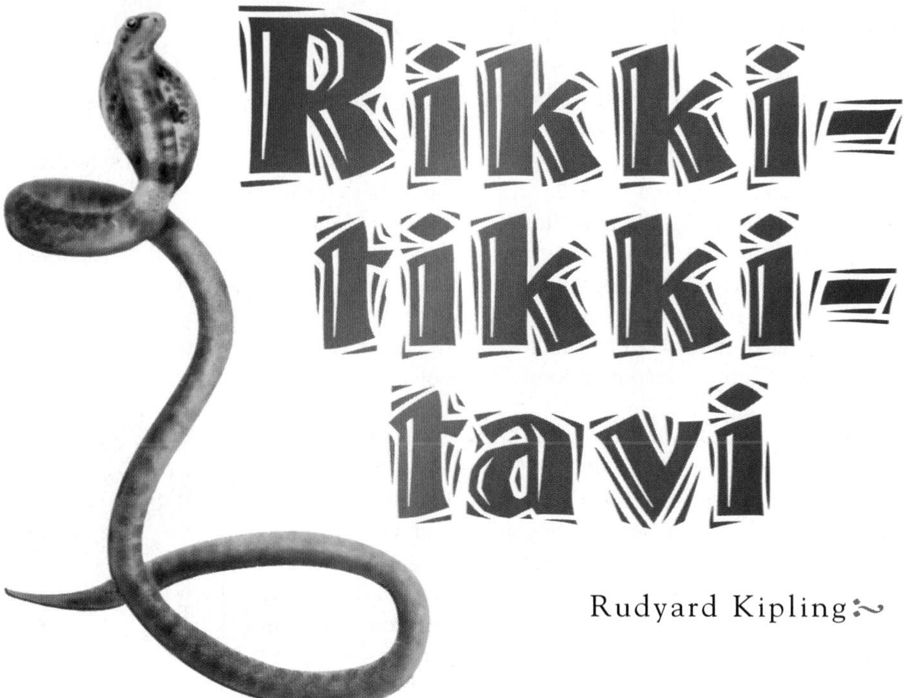

Rikki-tikki-tavi

Rudyard Kipling

This is the story of the great war that Rikki-tikki-tavi fought single-handed, through the bathrooms of the big bungalow in Segowlee cantonment.[1] Darzee, the tailorbird, helped him, and Chuchundra, the muskrat, who never comes out into the middle of the floor, but always creeps round by the wall, gave him advice; but Rikki-tikki did the real fighting.

He was a mongoose, rather like a little cat in his fur and his tail, but quite like a weasel in his head and his habits. His eyes and the end of his restless nose were pink; he could scratch himself anywhere he pleased, with any leg, front or back, that he chose to use; he could fluff up his tail till it looked like a bottle brush, and his war cry, as he scuttled through the long grass, was *"Rikk-tikk-tikki-tikki-tchk!"*

1. In India, a *cantonment* was a British military "town" where servicemen and their families lived in separate *bungalows,* or cottages.

Vocabulary

scuttle (skut′ əl) *v.* to move with short, rapid steps

Reading the Selection

SUMMARY

Rikki-tikki-tavi, a young mongoose moves into the territory of a pair of deadly cobras. Rikki-tikki kills Nag, the male cobra. Nagaina, the female cobra, blames Rikki-tikki's human friends for Nag's death; she corners the humans on their veranda. When Rikki-tikki battles Nagaina, he is dragged down a rat hole and presumed dead, but surprisingly, emerges victorious. From that day forward, no cobras dare enter the garden that Rikki-tikki-tavi guards.

Spanish Summaries, p. 67

A Active Reading Strategies

PREDICT Invite students to look at the title of this story and the illustrations. After volunteers read the first two paragraphs aloud, ask them to predict whom Rikki-tikki-tavi fights in the great war. Suggest that students periodically revisit their predictions to verify or revise them.

VOCABULARY Remind students to use context clues to unlock the meanings of new vocabulary words.

Additional Resources

- ***Active Reading Guide,*** p. 67
- ***Audio Library***
- ***Spanish Audio Library***

Teaching Support

CONNECTING TO OTHER SELECTIONS

The chart at the right shows three ways to connect "Rikki-tikki-tavi" to other selections in this book.

For specific teaching strategies, see the ***Theme Eight Planning Guide.***

Connection		Title
Life Skills: Problem Solving	→	"Beware of the Dog," p. 603
Thematic: Parents and Children	→	"Mother to Son," p. 342
Literary: Setting	→	"The Smallest Dragonboy," p. 683

B Literary Elements

POINT OF VIEW: *Narrator* Have students notice that the narrator reveals the thoughts of several of the characters.

C Active Reading Strategies

QUESTION Ask students to think what it might mean that Rikki-tikki likes the raw meat "immensely." *(It is a clue that mongooses are carnivores.)*

D Author's Craft

ANTHROPOMORPHISM Have students describe how Kipling makes Rikki-tikki-tavi seem like a person. *(The paragraph contains Rikki-tikki's thoughts, which seem like something a person might think. Rikki-tikki thinks about his family and why he wants to stay in the house.)*

E Active Reading Strategies

VISUALIZE Invite students to visualize this paragraph as you or a volunteer read it aloud. Encourage students to form mental images of Rikki-tikki-tavi nearly drowning in the bathtub, putting his nose in the ink, or burning his nose on a cigar.

Teaching Support

One day, a high summer flood washed him out of the burrow where he lived with his father and mother, and carried him, kicking and clucking, down a roadside ditch. He found a little wisp of grass floating there, and clung to it till he lost his senses. When he revived, he was lying in the hot sun on the middle of a garden path, very draggled[2] indeed, and a small boy was saying: "Here's a dead mongoose. Let's have a funeral."

"No," said his mother: "let's take him in and dry him. Perhaps he isn't really dead."

They took him into the house, and a big man picked him up between his finger and thumb and said he was not dead but half choked; so they wrapped him in cotton wool and warmed him, and he opened his eyes and sneezed.

"Now," said the big man (he was an Englishman who had just moved into the bungalow), "don't frighten him, and we'll see what he'll do."

B It is the hardest thing in the world to frighten a mongoose, because he is eaten up from nose to tail with curiosity. The motto of all the mongoose family is "Run and find out"; and Rikki-tikki was a true mongoose. He looked at the cotton wool, decided that it was not good to eat, ran all round the table, sat up and put his fur in order, scratched himself, and jumped on the small boy's shoulder.

"Don't be frightened, Teddy," said his father. "That's his way of making friends."

"Ouch! He's tickling under my chin," said Teddy.

Rikki-tikki looked down between the boy's collar and neck, snuffed at his ear, and climbed down to the floor, where he sat rubbing his nose.

"Good gracious," said Teddy's mother, "and that's a wild creature! I suppose he's so tame because we've been kind to him."

"All mongooses are like that," said her husband. "If Teddy doesn't pick him up by the tail, or try to put him in a cage, he'll run in and out of the house all day long. Let's give him something to eat."

C They gave him a little piece of raw meat. Rikki-tikki liked it immensely, and when it was finished he went out into the veranda and sat in the sunshine and fluffed up his fur to make it dry to the roots. Then he felt better.

Did You Know?
A *veranda* is a long porch, usually with a roof, along one or more sides of a house.

D "There are more things to find out about in this house," he said to himself, "than all my family could find out in all their lives. I shall certainly stay and find out."

E He spent all that day roaming over the house. He nearly drowned himself in the bathtubs, put his nose into the ink on a writing table, and burned it on the end of the big man's cigar, for he climbed up in the big man's lap to see how writing was done. At nightfall he ran into Teddy's nursery to watch how kerosene lamps[3] were lighted, and when Teddy went to bed Rikki-tikki climbed up too; but he was a restless companion, because he had to get up and attend to every noise all through the night and find out what made it.

2. *Draggled* means "wet and dirty."

3. A *kerosene lamp* burns a liquid fuel made from petroleum.

MEETING INDIVIDUAL NEEDS: ENGLISH LANGUAGE LEARNERS

Understanding Long Sentences For some English language learners, the length of the sentences in this story may make comprehension difficult. By breaking the sentences into smaller, more manageable units, students may find the story easier to understand.

Activity Have groups of students read this story together. Encourage students to stop whenever they see a comma or semicolon and summarize the action that has occurred up to that point. By discussing the action with other group members, students can discover whether their ideas about the events are accurate.

Additional Resources

English Language Learners Sourcebook, p. 97

Teddy's mother and father came in, the last thing, to look at their boy, and Rikki-tikki was awake on the pillow. "I don't like that," said Teddy's mother; "he may bite the child."

"He'll do no such thing," said the father. "Teddy's safer with that little beast than if he had a bloodhound to watch him. If a snake came into the nursery now—"

But Teddy's mother wouldn't think of anything so awful.

Early in the morning Rikki-tikki came to early breakfast in the veranda, riding on Teddy's shoulder, and they gave him banana and some boiled egg; and he sat on all their laps one after the other, because every well-brought-up mongoose always hopes to be a house mongoose someday and have rooms to run about in, and Rikki-tikki's mother (she used to live in the general's house at Segowlee) had carefully told Rikki what to do if ever he came across Englishmen.

Tent Hanging. Early 18th century, Mughal (Jaipur?). Cotton quilt embroidered in silk. Victoria and Albert Museum, London.

Viewing the artifact: How might the characters in "Rikki-tikki-tavi" have used a tent hanging? What do you think would have been its original use?

Then Rikki-tikki went out into the garden to see what was to be seen. It was a large garden, only half cultivated, with bushes as big as summer houses of roses, lime and orange trees, clumps of bamboos, and thickets of high grass. Rikki-tikki licked his lips. "This is a splendid hunting ground," he said, and his tail grew bottle-brushy at the thought of it, and he scuttled up and down the garden, snuffling here and there till he heard very sorrowful voices in a thornbush.

It was Darzee, the tailorbird, and his wife. They had made a beautiful nest by pulling two big leaves together and stitching them up the edges with fibers, and had

F Critical Thinking

INFERRING Have students finish the father's sentence for him. *(...the snake would kill Teddy.)* What might happen if a snake came into the nursery when Rikki-tikki-tavi was on the pillow? *(Rikki-tikki-tavi might attack and kill the snake.)*

G Literary Elements

ANTHROPOMORPHISM Ask students to describe the humanlike behaviors and thoughts of Rikki-tikki-tavi in this paragraph. *(Rikki-tikki is well-brought-up and has hopes for a better life. His mother has told him how to behave if he ever runs across English people.)*

VIEWING THE ARTIFACT

The Mughals invaded India in the sixteenth century, bringing the influence of Islamic art with them. Because Islam discourages the portrayal of human figures in art, their rugs and hangings made use of animals, geometrical figures, or floral motifs, usually repeated in a continuous pattern.

Viewing Response *The tent hanging might have been used for decoration. Originally, it might have been used as a partition or hung on the tent wall for decoration.*

Reading Minilesson

Using Graphic Aids Kipling gives the animals in this story human emotions and characteristics. On the board, begin a web for Rikki-tikki. Have students list human characteristics that they have noticed so far in Rikki-tikki. Add these ideas to the web on the board.

Rikki-tikki-tavi: *curious; restless; hopes to be a proper house mongoose; well-brought-up, knows proper etiquette*

Activity Have students create their own webs: one for Rikki-tikki-tavi and, later, one for Nag and Nagaina. On the web, ask students to keep track of the human emotions, characteristics, and thoughts that these animals display. **L2**

Additional Resources

Reading Skills Practice Workbook

H Author's Craft

DESCRIPTION Encourage students to identify phrases Kipling uses to make Nag seem evil. *(Phrases include "horrid cold sound," and "wicked snake's eyes.")*

Vo·cab·u·lar·y Skills

Word Origins The Portuguese navigator Vasco da Gama landed in India in 1498. There the Portuguese first saw a poisonous hooded snake, which Indians called *nag*. The Portuguese, however, called the snake *cobra de capello*, or "snake with the small cape, or hood." The English borrowed *cobra de capello* in the 1600s. By the 1800s, they had shortened the name to *cobra*.

I Literary Elements

FORESHADOWING Ask students what clues in this paragraph make them think that there will be conflict between Nag and Rikki-tikki. *(Rikki-tikki and Nag will probably have a fight. The paragraph says that a mongoose's business in life is to fight and eat snakes.)*

J Critical Thinking

DRAWING CONCLUSIONS Ask students whether a snake that eats birds is really more evil than a mongoose that eats snakes. *(Students may say that neither is more evil than the other. They are both using their instincts to survive.)*

filled the hollow with cotton and downy fluff. The nest swayed to and fro, as they sat on the brim and cried.

"What is the matter?" asked Rikki-tikki.

"We are very miserable," said Darzee. "One of our babies fell out of the nest yesterday, and Nag ate him."

"H'm!" said Rikki-tikki; "that is very sad—but I am a stranger here. Who is Nag?"

Darzee and his wife only cowered down in the nest without answering, for from the thick grass at the foot of the bush came a low hiss—a horrid cold sound that made Rikki-tikki jump back two clear feet. Then inch by inch out of the grass rose up the head and spread hood of Nag, the big black cobra, and he was five feet long from tongue to tail. When he had lifted one third of himself clear of the ground, he stayed balancing to and fro exactly as a dandelion tuft balances in the wind, and he looked at Rikki-tikki with the wicked snake's eyes that never change their expression, whatever the snake may be thinking of.

"Who is Nag?" he said. "*I* am Nag. The great god Brahm put his mark upon all our people when the first cobra spread his hood to keep the sun off Brahm as he slept. Look, and be afraid!"

He spread out his hood more than ever, and Rikki-tikki saw the spectacle mark on the back of it that looks exactly like the eye part of a hook-and-eye fastening. He was afraid for the minute; but it is impossible for a mongoose to stay frightened for any length of time, and though Rikki-tikki had never met a live cobra before, his mother had fed him on dead ones, and he knew that all a grown mongoose's business in life was to fight and eat snakes. Nag knew that too, and at the bottom of his cold heart he was afraid.

"Well," said Rikki-tikki, and his tail began to fluff up again, "marks or no marks, do you think it is right for you to eat fledglings[4] out of a nest?"

Nag was thinking to himself, and watching the least little movement in the grass behind Rikki-tikki. He knew that mongooses in the garden meant death sooner or later for him and his family, but he wanted to get Rikki-tikki off his guard. So he dropped his head a little and put it on one side.

"Let us talk," he said. "You eat eggs. Why should not I eat birds?"

"Behind you! Look behind you!" sang Darzee.

Rikki-tikki knew better than to waste time in staring. He jumped up in the air as high as he could go, and just under him whizzed by the head of Nagaina, Nag's wicked wife. She had crept up behind him as he was

4. Young birds that haven't yet grown the feathers needed to fly are called *fledglings.*

Vocabulary
cower (kou′ ər) *v.* to crouch down, as in fear or shame

Cobra

Teaching Support

SPECIAL NEEDS

Visually Impaired Visually-impaired students may have difficulty keeping track of the new vocabulary words introduced in the story.

Activity Have a proficient reader work with a visually-impaired student. Ask the proficient reader to read the story, pausing when he or she reads a word they do not understand. Together they can find the definitions or look them up in a dictionary and tape-record each of the vocabulary words along with its definition. The special-needs student can use the audiotape for future reference in the classroom or at home. **L2**

Additional Resources
Inclusion Strategies

K talking, to make an end of him; and he heard her savage hiss as the stroke missed. He came down almost across her back, and if he had been an old mongoose, he would have known that then was the time to break her back with one bite; but he was afraid of the terrible lashing return stroke of the cobra. He bit, indeed, but did not bite long enough, and he jumped clear of the whisking tail, leaving Nagaina torn and angry.

"Wicked, wicked Darzee!" said Nag, lashing up as high as he could reach toward the nest in the thornbush; but Darzee had built it out of the reach of snakes, and it only swayed to and fro.

Rikki-tikki felt his eyes growing red and hot (when a mongoose's eyes grow red, he is angry), and he sat back on his tail and hind legs like a little kangaroo, and looked all around him, and chattered with rage. But Nag and Nagaina had disappeared into the grass. When a snake misses its stroke, it never says anything or gives any sign of what it means to do next. Rikki-tikki did not care to follow them, for he did not feel sure that he could manage two snakes at once. So he trotted off to the gravel path near the house, and sat down to think. It was a serious matter for him.

If you read the old books of natural history, you will find they say that when the mongoose fights the snake and happens to get bitten, he runs off and eats some herb that cures him. That is not true. The victory is only a matter of quickness of eye and quickness of foot—snake's blow against mongoose's jump—and as no eye can follow the motion of a snake's head when it strikes, that makes things much more wonderful than any magic herb. Rikki-tikki knew he was a young mongoose, and it made him all the more pleased to think that he had managed to escape a blow from behind. It gave him confidence in himself, and when Teddy came running down the path, Rikki-tikki was ready to be petted.

But just as Teddy was stooping, something flinched a little in the dust, and a tiny voice said: "Be careful. I am death!" It was Karait, the dusty brown snakeling that lies for choice on the dusty earth; and his bite is as dangerous as the cobra's. But he is so small that nobody thinks of him, and so he does the more harm to people. L

Rikki-tikki's eyes grew red again, and he danced up to Karait with the peculiar rocking, swaying motion that he had inherited from his family. It looks very funny, but it is so perfectly balanced a gait that you can fly off from it at any angle you please; and in dealing with snakes this is an advantage. If Rikki-tikki had only known, he was doing a much more dangerous thing than fighting Nag, for Karait is so small, and can turn so quickly, that unless Rikki bit him close to the back of the head, he would get the return stroke in his eye or lip. But Rikki did not know: his eyes were all red, and he rocked back and forth, looking for a good place to hold. Karait struck out. Rikki jumped sideways and tried to run in, but the wicked little dusty gray head lashed within a fraction of his shoulder, and he had to jump over the body, and the head followed his heels close.

Vocabulary

flinch (flinch) *v.* to draw back, as from something painful, dangerous, or unpleasant

gait (gāt) *n.* a particular manner of moving on foot

K Author's Craft

CHARACTERIZATION Ask students how the author describes Nagaina and why. *(She is Nag's wicked wife, with a "savage hiss." Kipling does not seem to want the reader to have any sympathy for her.)*

FYI

Cobras and Kraits The *king cobra* of southern Asia is the largest poisonous snake in the world. It can reach sixteen feet in length, but its bite is not usually fatal. The *krait* (pronounced *krite*) is a small snake in Southeast Asia. Fifty percent of the people it bites die, even if antivenom is given.

L Active Reading Strategies

PREDICT Invite students to predict whether Karait will bite Teddy or Rikki-tikki. *(Students may think that since Karait is more dangerous than a cobra, Rikki-tikki may be harmed. Others may think that if Rikki-tikki can defeat Karait, he can defeat Nag and Nagaina.)*

MEETING INDIVIDUAL NEEDS: MULTIPLE MODES OF EXPRESSION

Spatial Some students may not be familiar with the many types of animals and plants mentioned in this story, such as *mongoose, cobra, tailorbird, bamboo.* To help students visualize these animals and plants, invite them to create an illustrated Plant and Animal Dictionary.

Activity Have students list as they read the names of any plants or animals they have never seen or would like to know more about. Then have students use a dictionary to look up these plants and animals and write their own definition for each. Encourage students to illustrate each plant or animal beside its entry. **L1**

M Active Reading Strategies

RESPOND Have students explain why they think Teddy's father continues to beat the dead snake. *(Snakes continue to move after they are dead. He wants to make certain that the snake is really dead.)*

N Active Reading Strategies

REVIEW Ask students to explain why Rikki-tikki-tavi's eyes occasionally get red and he goes off into a long war cry. *(His eyes get red when he is angry. Occasionally he also gets red eyes when he remembers how Nag and Nagaina tried to kill him.)*

O Literary Elements

AUTHOR'S PURPOSE Invite students to speculate why the author has Chuchundra say, "Those who kill snakes get killed by snakes." *(Kipling could be foreshadowing what is going to happen, or he could be trying to build suspense.)*

P Critical Thinking

INFERRING Encourage students to think about what Chua, the rat, has probably told Chuchundra. *(He has probably said that Nag is not in the garden where Rikki-tikki thinks he is. Perhaps Nag is planning to ambush Rikki-tikki or the family.)*

Rikki-tikki-tavi

Teddy shouted to the house: "Oh, look here! Our mongoose is killing a snake"; and Rikki-tikki heard a scream from Teddy's mother. His father ran out with a stick, but by the time he came up, Karait had lunged out once too far, and Rikki-tikki had sprung, jumped on the snake's back, dropped his head far between his forelegs, bitten as high up the back as he could get hold, and rolled away. That bite paralyzed Karait, and Rikki-tikki was just going to eat him up from the tail, after the custom of his family at dinner, when he remembered that a full meal makes a slow mongoose, and if he wanted all his strength and quickness ready, he must keep himself thin.

M He went away for a dust bath under the castor-oil bushes, while Teddy's father beat the dead Karait. "What is the use of that?" thought Rikki-tikki. "I have settled it all"; and then Teddy's mother picked him up from the dust and hugged him, crying that he had saved Teddy from death, and Teddy's father said that he was a providence,[5] and Teddy looked on with big scared eyes. Rikki-tikki was rather amused at all the fuss, which, of course, he did not understand. Teddy's mother might just as well have petted Teddy for playing in the dust. Rikki was thoroughly enjoying himself.

That night, at dinner, walking to and fro among the wineglasses on the table, he could have stuffed himself three times over with nice things; but he remembered Nag and Nagaina, and though it was very pleasant to be patted and petted by Teddy's mother, and to sit on Teddy's shoulder, his eyes would get red from time to time, and he would go off into his long war cry of *"Rikk-tikk-tikki-tikki-tchk!"* N

Teddy carried him off to bed and insisted on Rikki-tikki sleeping under his chin. Rikki-tikki was too well bred to bite or scratch, but as soon as Teddy was asleep he went off for his nightly walk round the house, and in the dark he ran up against Chuchundra, the muskrat, creeping round by the wall. Chuchundra is a broken-hearted little beast. He whimpers and cheeps all the night, trying to make up his mind to run into the middle of the room, but he never gets there.

"Don't kill me," said Chuchundra, almost weeping. "Rikki-tikki, don't kill me."

"Do you think a snake-killer kills muskrats?" said Rikki-tikki scornfully.

"Those who kill snakes get killed by snakes," said Chuchundra, more sorrowfully than ever. "And how am I to be sure that Nag won't mistake me for you some dark night?" O

"There's not the least danger," said Rikki-tikki; "but Nag is in the garden, and I know you don't go there."

"My cousin Chua, the rat, told me—" said Chuchundra, and then he stopped.

"Told you what?"

"H'sh! Nag is everywhere, Rikki-tikki. You should have talked to Chua in the garden." P

"I didn't—so you must tell me. Quick, Chuchundra, or I'll bite you!"

Chuchundra sat down and cried till the tears rolled off his whiskers. "I am a very

5. A *providence* (prov' ə dəns) is a blessing from God or nature.

Vocabulary
lunge (lunj) *v.* to make a sudden forward movement; charge

Teaching Support

MEETING INDIVIDUAL NEEDS — ADVANCED LEARNERS

Cobra vs. Mongoose The adversarial relationship between the deadly cobra and the fierce mongoose is one of the most fascinating in the animal world. Reading Kipling's story may raise many questions in students' minds about these creatures' habits and habitats.

Activity Interested students can work in pairs to list their questions, search a library database or the Internet to find sources of information, and summarize each relevant piece of research and cite its source properly on an index card. Then they can organize the cards in a sequence that will help them clearly present their most interesting findings in a written or oral report. Encourage them to include appropriate visuals. **L3**

poor man," he sobbed. "I never had spirit enough to run out into the middle of the room. H'sh! I mustn't tell you anything. Can't you *hear*, Rikki-tikki?"

Rikki-tikki listened. The house was as still as still, but he thought he could just catch the faintest *scratch-scratch* in the world—a noise as faint as that of a wasp walking on a windowpane—the dry scratch of a snake's scales on brickwork.

The house was as still as still, but he thought he could just catch the faintest scratch-scratch in the world—a noise as faint as that of a wasp walking on a windowpane—

"That's Nag or Nagaina," he said to himself; "and he is crawling into the bathroom sluice.[6] You're right, Chuchundra; I should have talked to Chua."

He stole off to Teddy's bathroom, but there was nothing there, and then to Teddy's mother's bathroom. At the bottom of the smooth plaster wall there was a brick pulled out to make a sluice for the bath water, and as Rikki-tikki stole in by the masonry curb where the bath is put, he heard Nag and Nagaina whispering together outside in the moonlight.

"When the house is emptied of people," said Nagaina to her husband, "*he* will have to go away, and then the garden will be our own again. Go in quietly, and remember that the big man who killed Karait is the first one to bite. Then come out and tell me, and we will hunt for Rikki-tikki together."

"But are you sure there is anything to be gained by killing the people?" said Nag.

"Everything. When there were no people in the bungalow, did we have any mongoose in the garden? So long as the bungalow is empty, we are king and queen of the garden; and remember that as soon as our eggs in the melon bed hatch (as they may tomorrow), our children will need room and quiet."

"I had not thought of that," said Nag. "I will go, but there is no need that we should hunt for Rikki-tikki afterward. I will kill the big man and his wife, and the child if I can, and come away quietly. Then the bungalow will be empty, and Rikki-tikki will go."

Rikki-tikki tingled all over with rage and hatred at this, and then Nag's head came through the sluice, and his five feet of cold body followed it. Angry as he was, Rikki-tikki was very frightened as he saw the size of the big cobra. Nag coiled himself up, raised his head, and looked into the bathroom in the dark, and Rikki could see his eyes glitter.

"Now, if I kill him there, Nagaina will know; and if I fight him on the open floor, the odds are in his favor. What am I to do?" said Rikki-tikki-tavi.

Nag waved to and fro, and then Rikki-tikki heard him drinking from the biggest water jar that was used to fill the bath. "That is good," said the snake. "Now, when Karait was killed, the big man had a stick. He may have that stick still, but when he comes in to bathe in the morning he will

6. Here, the *sluice* is a drainpipe.

Vo·cab·u·lar·y Skills

Etymology *Bungalow* is an Anglo-Indian variation of the Hindu word *bangala*. In India, it is a one-story house, usually with a wide porch.

Active Reading Strategies

REVIEW Invite students to explain what the cobras are planning and whether they think the plan will work. *(If the humans die, the house will be empty, so Rikki-tikki-tavi will leave. The cobras will have the garden back.)*

Critical Thinking

IDENTIFYING BIAS Have students discuss whether Nag and Nagaina are simply protecting their family the way any animal in the wild would. *(Students may say that the cobras are simply obeying their nature.)* Have students discuss how Kipling feels about cobras. *(He thinks that cobras are evil and that killing them off will give the story a happy ending.)*

Interdisciplinary Connection

Science How did Rikki-tikki-tavi know who his mother was? Konrad Lorenz (1893–1989) studied animal behavior, particularly how animal instinct and learned behavior worked together. He pioneered studies on how a young animal instinctively becomes attached to a parent.

Activity Interested students may wish to look into imprinting in more detail.

Although Lorenz did his experiments with goslings and ducklings, studies were replicated using mammals. Students could prepare a report, complete with visuals including diagrams, graphs, and photographs downloaded from a reliable Web site. **L3**

A DELICATE BALANCE 795

S Literary Elements

ANTHROPOMORPHISM Ask students to describe Rikki-tikki-tavi's human-like thoughts in this paragraph. *(He analyzes the situation much as a person would; he thinks about his strategy and where the best place to get a good hold is. He recognizes the consequences if he doesn't get a good hold in the proper place.)*

T Active Reading Strategies

QUESTION Ask students to discuss what has just happened here. What is the thunderclap and the red fire? *(The fight must have been noisy enough to wake up the Englishman, who shoots at the cobra. The thunderclap is the booming of the gun. The red fire is the bullet whizzing close to Rikki-tikki-tavi's fur.)*

U Literary Elements

HUMOR Have students explain what is funny or amusing about this situation. *(Rikki-tikki-tavi is probably badly bruised after the fight, but he clearly is not broken into forty pieces. His exaggerated evaluation creates humor.)*

Teaching Support

not have a stick. I shall wait here till he comes. Nagaina—do you hear me? I shall wait here in the cool till daytime."

There was no answer from outside, so Rikki-tikki knew Nagaina had gone away. Nag coiled himself down, coil by coil, round the bulge at the bottom of the water jar, and Rikki-tikki stayed still as death. After an hour he began to move, muscle by muscle, toward the jar. Nag was asleep, and Rikki-tikki looked at his big back, wondering which would be the best place for a good hold. "If I don't break his back at the first jump," said Rikki, "he can still fight; and if he fights—O Rikki!" He looked at the thickness of the neck below the hood, but that was too much for him; and a bite near the tail would only make Nag savage.

"It must be the head," he said at last; "the head above the hood; and when I am once there, I must not let go."

Then he jumped. The head was lying a little clear of the water jar, under the curve of it; and, as his teeth met, Rikki braced his back against the bulge of the red earthenware to hold down the head. This gave him just one second's purchase,[7] and he made the most of it. Then he was battered to and fro as a rat is shaken by a dog—to and fro on the floor, up and down, and round in great circles; but his eyes were red, and he held on as the body cartwhipped[8] over the floor, upsetting the tin dipper and the soap dish and the fleshbrush, and banged against the tin side of the bath. As he held, he closed his jaws tighter and tighter, for he made sure he would be banged to death, and, for the honor of his family, he preferred to be found with his teeth locked. He was dizzy, aching, and felt shaken to pieces when something went off like a thunderclap just behind him; a hot wind knocked him senseless, and red fire singed his fur. The big man had been wakened by the noise, and had fired both barrels of a shotgun into Nag just behind the hood.

Rikki-tikki held on with his eyes shut, for now he was quite sure he was dead; but the head did not move, and the big man picked him up and said: "It's the mongoose again, Alice; the little chap has saved *our* lives now." Then Teddy's mother came in with a very white face, and saw what was left of Nag, and Rikki-tikki dragged himself to Teddy's bedroom and spent half the rest of the night shaking himself tenderly to find out whether he really was broken into forty pieces, as he fancied.

When morning came he was very stiff, but well pleased with his doings. "Now I have Nagaina to settle with, and she will be worse than five Nags, and there's no knowing when the eggs she spoke of will hatch. Goodness! I must go and see Darzee," he said.

Without waiting for breakfast, Rikki-tikki ran to the thornbush where Darzee was singing a song of triumph at the top of his voice. The news of Nag's death was all over the garden, for the sweeper had thrown the body on the rubbish heap.

7. In this context, the *purchase* is an advantageous position for applying force.
8. Rikki's body is being thrown about like a whip *(cartwhipped)* as the cobra lashes.

Vocabulary
fancy (fan′ sē) *v.* to picture mentally; imagine

Listening and Speaking *Minilesson*

Analyzing a Video The story of Rikki-tikki-tavi has been re-created on film. Students may enjoy comparing a video version of this story with the print version.

Activity You may want to show the class the thirty-minute cartoon *Rikki-tikki-tavi,* created by renowned cartoonist Chuck Jones. As students view the video, have them take notes on how the two stories are similar and how they are different. After the viewing, divide the class into small groups. Have each group list similarities and differences between the two versions of the story. Finally, have each group decide which version they liked better and explain why. **L2**

"Oh, you stupid tuft of feathers!" said Rikki-tikki angrily. "Is this the time to sing?"

"Nag is dead—is dead—is dead!" sang Darzee. "The valiant Rikki-tikki caught him by the head and held fast. The big man brought the bang-stick, and Nag fell in two pieces! He will never eat my babies again."

"All that's true enough; but where's Nagaina?" said Rikki-tikki, looking carefully round him.

"Nagaina came to the bathroom sluice and called for Nag," Darzee went on; "and Nag came out on the end of a stick—the sweeper picked him up on the end of a stick and threw him upon the rubbish heap. Let us sing about the great, the red-eyed Rikki-tikki!" And Darzee filled his throat and sang.

"If I could get up to your nest, I'd roll all your babies out!" said Rikki-tikki. "You don't know when to do the right thing at the right time. You're safe enough in your nest there, but it's war for me down here. Stop singing a minute, Darzee."

"For the great, the beautiful Rikki-tikki's sake I will stop," said Darzee. "What is it, O Killer of the terrible Nag?"

"Where is Nagaina, for the third time?"

"On the rubbish heap by the stables, mourning for Nag. Great is Rikki-tikki with the white teeth."

"Bother my white teeth![9] Have you ever heard where she keeps her eggs?"

9. *Bother my white teeth* is a British way of saying, "Don't concern yourself with my teeth."

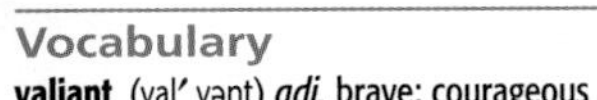

Vocabulary
valiant (val′ yənt) *adj.* brave; courageous

V Literary Elements

ANTHROPOMORPHISM Have students describe how this paragraph makes Rikki-tikki-tavi and Darzee seem like people. *(Rikki-tikki knows the fight is not over yet, so he is angry with Darzee for being so happy. Darzee is empty-headed and has no common sense. Rikki-tikki is more practical and needs to get answers from Darzee, who is too busy celebrating to answer his questions.)*

W Literary Elements

MOOD Ask students to discuss what they think the mood of this scene is. Do some find it comical? frantic? chaotic? Pairs of students might be interested in dramatizing this scene for the class.

X Active Reading Strategies

PREDICT Have students predict what Rikki-tikki will do if he finds out where Nagaina keeps her eggs. *(Rikki-tikki will destroy the eggs, so the garden will not be overrun by cobras.)*

Writing Minilesson

Writing from Another Point of View Invite students to try their hand at giving voice to one of the cobras' thoughts and concerns.

Activity Have students choose one dramatic scene involving Rikki-tikki-tavi and Nag or Nagaina. Invite students to work in pairs to rewrite this scene from the point of view of Nag or Nagaina. When students have finished, ask them to share their scenes with the rest of the class. Students can discuss whether this new perspective changes their ideas about the story. **L2**

Additional Resources

Writer's Choice, Lesson 4.5

Ⓨ Critical Thinking

EVALUATING Ask students to contrast Darzee and his wife. *(Darzee is foolish, unfocused, and opposed to destroying the eggs. His wife is sensible and sees the big picture: baby cobras mean danger to her young.)*

Ⓩ Literary Elements

ANTHROPOMORPHISM Have students describe the human qualities that Nagaina and Darzee's wife display here. *(Darzee's wife pretends; Nagaina blames, holds a grudge, and wants revenge.)*

FYI

Snake Facts Most reptiles abandon their eggs, which do not have to be kept warm all the time. Baby reptiles have an "egg tooth," which they use to break through the egg. The tooth falls off shortly after hatching. Snakes have no eyelids. Their eyes are protected by a permanent see-through covering. Snakes have internal ears.

Teaching Support

"In the melon bed, on the end nearest the wall, where the sun strikes nearly all day. She hid them there weeks ago."

"And you never thought it worthwhile to tell me? The end nearest the wall, you said?"

"Rikki-tikki, you are not going to eat her eggs?"

"Not eat exactly; no. Darzee, if you have a grain of sense you will fly off to the stables and pretend that your wing is broken, and let Nagaina chase you away to this bush! I must get to the melon bed, and if I went there now she'd see me."

Ⓨ Darzee was a featherbrained little fellow who could never hold more than one idea at a time in his head; and just because he knew that Nagaina's children were born in eggs like his own, he didn't think at first that it was fair to kill them. But his wife was a sensible bird, and she knew that cobras' eggs meant young cobras later on; so she flew off from the nest, and left Darzee to keep the babies warm, and continue his song about the death of Nag. Darzee was very like a man in some ways.

She fluttered in front of Nagaina by the rubbish heap and cried out, "Oh, my wing is broken! The boy in the house threw a stone at me and broke it." Then she fluttered more desperately than ever.

Ⓩ Nagaina lifted up her head and hissed, "You warned Rikki-tikki when I would have killed him. Indeed and truly, you've chosen a bad place to be lame in." And she moved toward Darzee's wife, slipping along over the dust.

"The boy broke it with a stone!" shrieked Darzee's wife.

"Well! It may be some consolation to you when you're dead to know that I shall settle accounts with the boy. My husband lies on the rubbish heap this morning, but before night the boy in the house will lie very still. What is the use of running away? I am sure to catch you. Little fool, look at me!"

Darzee's wife knew better than to do *that,* for a bird who looks at a snake's eyes gets so frightened that she cannot move. Darzee's wife fluttered on, piping sorrowfully, and never leaving the ground, and Nagaina quickened her pace.

Rikki-tikki heard them going up the path from the stables, and he raced for the end of the melon patch near the wall. There, in the warm litter about the melons, very cunningly hidden, he found twenty-five eggs, about the size of a bantam's eggs, but with whitish skin instead of shell.

Did You Know?
A *bantam* is a small breed of chicken.

"I was not a day too soon," he said; for he could see the baby cobras curled up inside the skin, and he knew that the minute they were hatched they could each kill a man or a mongoose. He bit off the tops of the eggs as fast as he could, taking care to crush the young cobras, and turned over the litter from time to time to see whether he had missed any. At last there were only three eggs left, and Rikki-tikki began to chuckle to himself, when he heard Darzee's wife screaming:

"Rikki-tikki, I led Nagaina toward the house, and she has gone into the veranda, and—oh, come quickly—she means killing!"

Rikki-tikki smashed two eggs, and tumbled backward down the melon bed

MEETING INDIVIDUAL NEEDS — ENGLISH LANGUAGE LEARNERS

Predators All over the world, some predators are seen as helpful to humans while others are seen as pests or enemies. Write the words *predator* and *prey* on the board. Have volunteers define each word.

Activity In mixed groups, have students list animals that are helpful to humans and animals that are seen as pests or dangerous enemies. Have students explain why those animals are enemies of humans. Finally, have each group draw a picture of one predator that is considered especially dangerous to people. Encourage groups to display their drawings for the rest of the class.

Additional Resources

English Language Learners Sourcebook, p. 98

with the third egg in his mouth, and scuttled to the veranda as hard as he could put foot to the ground. Teddy and his mother and father were there at early breakfast; but Rikki-tikki saw that they were not eating anything. They sat stone-still, and their faces were white. Nagaina was coiled up on the matting by Teddy's chair, within easy striking distance of Teddy's bare leg, and she was swaying to and fro singing a song of triumph.

"Look at your friends, Rikki-tikki. They are still and white; they are afraid. They dare not move, and if you come a step nearer I strike."

AA "Son of the big man that killed Nag," she hissed, "stay still. I am not ready yet. Wait a little. Keep very still, all you three. If you move I strike, and if you do not move I strike. Oh, foolish people, who killed my Nag!"

Teddy's eyes were fixed on his father, and all his father could do was to whisper, "Sit still, Teddy. You mustn't move. Teddy, keep still."

Then Rikki-tikki came up and cried: "Turn round, Nagaina; turn and fight!"

"All in good time," said she, without moving her eyes. "I will settle my account with *you* presently. Look at your friends, Rikki-tikki. They are still and white; they are afraid. They dare not move, and if you come a step nearer I strike."

"Look at your eggs," said Rikki-tikki, "in the melon bed near the wall. Go and look, Nagaina."

The big snake turned half round and saw the egg on the veranda. "Ah-h! Give it to me," she said.

Rikki-tikki put his paws one on each side of the egg, and his eyes were blood-red. "What price for a snake's egg? For a young cobra? For a young king cobra? For the last—the very last of the brood? The ants are eating all the others down by the melon bed." BB

Nagaina spun clear round, forgetting everything for the sake of the one egg; and Rikki-tikki saw Teddy's father shoot out a big hand, catch Teddy by the shoulder, and drag him across the little table with the teacups, safe and out of reach of Nagaina.

"Tricked! Tricked! Tricked! *Rikk-tck-tck!*" chuckled Rikki-tikki. "The boy is safe, and it was I—I—I that caught Nag by the hood last night in the bathroom." Then he began to jump up and down, all four feet together, his head close to the floor. "He threw me to and fro, but he could not shake me off. He was dead before the big man blew him in two. I did it. *Rikki-tikki-tck-tck!* Come then, Nagaina. Come and fight with me. You shall not be a widow long." CC

Nagaina saw that she had lost her chance of killing Teddy, and the egg lay between Rikki-tikki's paws. "Give me the egg, Rikki-tikki. Give me the last of my eggs, and I will go away and never come

Vocabulary

brood (brōōd) *n.* all of the young of an animal that are born or cared for at the same time

AA Author's Craft

ONOMATOPOEIA The word *hissed* replicates the sound it names. Nagaina adds, *"...stay still,"* thus prolonging the hissing and adding to the tension in the scene.

BB Literary Elements

ANTHROPOMORPHISM Ask your students to describe how Rikki-tikki feels here, and how his and Nagaina's reaction have human characteristics. *(Rikki-tikki-tavi is angry; his eyes are red. He is threatening Nagaina with destroying her egg, Nagaina reacts like any mother, by trying to protect her egg.)*

CC Active Reading Strategies

PREDICT Have students predict what will happen when Rikki and Nagaina fight. You may wish to share the following model to illustrate the thinking process involved in making predictions.

Model: I know this story is about Rikki-tikki-tavi's fight to survive. I don't think the war will be completely over until Nagaina and her babies are dead. If even one escapes, it will probably kill Rikki-tikki-tavi. I think he has to kill Nagaina before she kills him.

Life Skills Connection

Interviewing Ask students to interview someone who knows quite a bit about the characteristics of particular animals.

Activity Invite students to work in pairs to interview a bird watcher, a zookeeper, a veterinarian, or a pet owner to find out about the characteristics of two or more species of animals or two or more breeds of the same animal (such as two breeds of dogs). Have students list these characteristics and categorize each characteristic as one that 1) most humans will like; 2) most will dislike; or 3) most are neutral about. Can they make any assumptions about the animals' reputations among humans based on the characteristics they have listed? Have students share their ideas with the class. **L2**

back," she said, lowering her hood.

"Yes, you will go away, and you will never come back; for you will go to the rubbish heap with Nag. Fight, widow! The big man has gone for his gun! Fight!"

Rikki-tikki was bounding all round Nagaina, keeping just out of reach of her stroke, his little eyes like hot coals. Nagaina gathered herself together and flung out at him. Rikki-tikki jumped up and backward. Again and again and again she struck, and each time her head came with a whack on the matting of the veranda, and she gathered herself together like a watchspring. Then Rikki-tikki danced in a circle to get behind her, and Nagaina spun round to keep her head to his head, so that the rustle of her tail on the matting sounded like dry leaves blown along by the wind.

He had forgotten the egg. It still lay on the veranda, and Nagaina came nearer and nearer to it, till at last, while Rikki-tikki was drawing breath, she caught it in her mouth, turned to the veranda steps, and flew like an arrow down the path, with Rikki-tikki behind her. When the cobra runs for her life, she goes like a whiplash flicked across a horse's neck.

Rikki-tikki knew that he must catch her, or all the trouble would begin again. She headed straight for the long grass by the thornbush, and as he was running Rikki-tikki heard Darzee singing his foolish little song of triumph. But Darzee's wife was wiser. She flew off her nest as Nagaina came along, and flapped her wings about Nagaina's head. If Darzee had helped they might have turned her; but Nagaina only lowered her hood and went on. Still, the instant's delay brought Rikki-tikki up to her, and as she plunged into the rathole where she and Nag used to live, his little white teeth were clenched on her tail, and he went down with her—and very few mongooses, however wise and old they may be, care to follow a cobra into its hole. It was dark in the hole; and Rikki-tikki never knew when it might open out and give Nagaina room to turn and strike at him. He held on savagely and struck out his feet to act as brakes on the dark slope of the hot, moist earth.

. . . very few mongooses, however wise and old they may be, care to follow a cobra into its hole.

Then the grass by the mouth of the hole stopped waving, and Darzee said: "It is all over with Rikki-tikki! We must sing his death song. Valiant Rikki-tikki is dead. For Nagaina will surely kill him underground."

So he sang a very mournful song that he made up all on the spur of the minute, and just as he got to the most touching part the grass quivered again, and Rikki-tikki, covered with dirt, dragged himself out of the hole leg by leg, licking his whiskers. Darzee stopped with a little shout. Rikki-tikki shook some of the dust out of his fur and sneezed. "It is all over," he said. "The widow will never come out again." And the red ants that live between the grass stems heard him, and began to troop down one after another to see if he had spoken the truth.

DD Literary Elements

SIMILE Ask students to discuss the similes in these paragraphs. What do the two unlike things have in common? *(Examples include eyes/hot coals: red and glowing; tail rustle/dry leaves: sound.)*

EE Active Reading Strategies

QUESTION Invite students to explain what will happen if Rikki-tikki-tavi does not catch Nagaina. *(She and her baby will pose a constant danger.)*

FF Active Reading Strategies

RESPOND Encourage students to discuss why Kipling never explains what happens underground. *(He wants it to remain mysterious.)* Invite students to describe what they think happened underground. *(Rikki-tikki-tavi must somehow have bitten her and held on until she was dead.)*

FYI

The Mongoose Since mongooses are such fierce and destructive hunters, it is illegal to import them into this country. It is feared they will do great damage if they ever get loose. Even U.S. zoos are not allowed to import mongooses.

Teaching Support

Grammar and Language *Minilesson*

Using Semicolons If two main clauses are connected by *and, but,* or *or,* a comma precedes the conjunction: *All of the eggs were exposed, and only one survived.* However, if two main clauses do not each have an end mark and are not joined by a conjunction, a semicolon can be used as the connector: *All of the eggs were exposed; only one survived.*

Activity Write the following sentences on the board without semicolons. Ask students to punctuate them.

1. They are still and white; they are afraid.
2. His eyes at the end of his restless nose were pink; he could scratch himself anywhere he pleased; he could fluff up his tail till it looked like a bottlebrush.
3. You will go away, and you will never come back; you will go to the rubbish heap with Nag. **L2**

Additional Resources

- ***Grammar and Language Transparency 62***
- ***Grammar and Language Workbook,*** pp. 265–266
- ***Grammar and Composition Handbook,*** Lesson 13.5
- ***Writer's Choice,*** Lesson 20.5

Rikki-tikki curled himself up in the grass and slept where he was—slept and slept till it was late in the afternoon, for he had done a hard day's work.

"Now," he said, when he awoke, "I will go back to the house. Tell the coppersmith, Darzee, and he will tell the garden that Nagaina is dead."

The coppersmith is a bird who makes a noise exactly like the beating of a little hammer on a copper pot; and the reason he is always making it is because he is the town crier to every Indian garden, and tells all the news to everybody who cares to listen. As Rikki-tikki went up the path, he heard his "attention" notes like a tiny dinner gong; and then the steady "*Ding-dong-tock!* Nag is dead—*dong!* Nagaina is dead! *Ding-dong-tock!*" That set all the birds in the garden singing, and the frogs croaking, for Nag and Nagaina used to eat frogs as well as little birds.

When Rikki got to the house, Teddy and Teddy's mother (she still looked very white, for she had been fainting) and Teddy's father came out and almost cried over him; and that night he ate all that was given him till he could eat no more, and went to bed on Teddy's shoulder, where Teddy's mother saw him when she came to look late at night.

"He saved our lives and Teddy's life," she said to her husband. "Just think, he saved all our lives!"

Viewing the photograph: Did you imagine Darzee, the tailorbird, looking anything like this tailorbird? Why or why not?

Rikki-tikki woke up with a jump, for all mongooses are light sleepers. GG

"Oh, it's you," said he. "What are you bothering for? All the cobras are dead; and if they weren't, I'm here."

Rikki-tikki had a right to be proud of himself; but he did not grow too proud, and he kept that garden as a mongoose should keep it, with tooth and jump and spring and bite, till never a cobra dared show its head inside the walls.

GG Literary Elements

ANTHROPOMORPHISM Ask students for examples of human characteristics Kipling is using to portray Rikki-tikki. *(He is tired after the fight and needs to sleep to recover his energy; he is a little smug at having beaten a strong competitor; he now thinks he can take care of any cobras that might threaten the garden or the family.)*

VIEWING THE PHOTOGRAPH

The *tailorbird* is a warbler, a family of birds famous for its song. More than 100 species of warblers exist in Europe, Asia, Africa, and the Americas.

Viewing Response *Some students may have imagined Darzee as larger, or perhaps more comic in appearance.*

Thematic Focus

A Delicate Balance Have students explain how this story fits the theme "A Delicate Balance." *(The story is about the delicate balance in the natural world between animals that prey on one another, and other animals that help one another.)*

ASSESSMENT

Quick Checks, p. 67

REAL-WORLD CONNECTION

Review A review quickly highlights the main idea of a book, story, movie, or play. Reviews help people decide whether they want to read a book, see a movie, or go to a play. Explain to students that when they tell a friend about something they've seen or read, they are essentially providing a review.

Activity Invite students to work in pairs or groups to write a review of "Rikki-tikki-tavi." They might provide the review to groups that have not read the story, or send it to a friend or relative in a letter. **L2**

Responding to the Selection

PERSONAL RESPONSE

Some students may find the fight between Nagaina and Rikki-tikki-tavi the most exciting moment. Some may feel that the English family shares their attitude about snakes.

Analyzing Literature

1. Rikki-tikki-tavi lives in the house of a family from England.
2. Darzee, a tailorbird, relays important information to Rikki-tikki-tavi about when Nagaina is about to attack him and where she hides her eggs. Chuchundra, a muskrat, tells Rikki to listen to Nag crawling through the house. This information helps Rikki in his great war against the cobras.
3. The cobras think that if the people leave the house, Rikki-tikki-tavi will, too.
4. Rikki-tikki-tavi kills both Nag and Nagaina.
5. It provides the reader with a description of Rikki and his characteristics. Also, since the English family saved Rikki's life, it is only fitting that Rikki return the favor.
6. Darzee and Chuchundra are both cowardly. Rikki-tikki-tavi contrasts sharply with them.
7. Kipling presents Nagaina as a protective mother. She gives up on killing Teddy to get her last egg back.
8. Even though Rikki is a young, inexperienced mongoose, he figures out how to kill Nag in the bathroom and Nagaina in the rat hole.
9. If Rikki had been killed, then evil would have triumphed, and the ending of the story would not have been satisfactory.
10. Students may say they like stories of good versus evil because they know exactly whom to root for.

Active Reading and Critical Thinking

Responding to Literature

PERSONAL RESPONSE

- What moment in the story did you find the most exciting? Why?
- Look back at the notes you made in the **Reading Focus** on page 788. Do any of the characters in the story share your thoughts and feelings about snakes?

Analyzing Literature

RECALL

1. In whose house does Rikki live?
2. Who are Darzee and Chuchundra? How do they help Rikki in his "great war"?
3. Why do the cobras decide they have to kill the people in the house?
4. What finally happens to Nag and Nagaina?

Brackets connect questions that are paired to develop higher-level thinking skills.

INTERPRET

5. Why do you think Kipling starts the story with an account of the rescue of Rikki?
6. How does the author use Darzee and Chuchundra to call attention to Rikki's bravery?
7. Does Kipling present one of the cobras more sympathetically than the other? Use examples to support your answer.
8. How does Rikki's cleverness help protect the family?

EVALUATE AND CONNECT

9. For the **climax** of the story, Kipling could have chosen to have Rikki killed in Nagaina's hole. How would that change affect your response to the story?
10. "Rikki-tikki-tavi" is a story of "good versus evil." Do you like that kind of story, or do you prefer stories in which the characters are not so easy to classify? Why?

LITERARY ELEMENTS

Anthropomorphism

Kipling gives the animal characters in "Rikki-tikki-tavi" human emotions, characteristics, and intelligence. Authors use this technique, called **anthropomorphism,** to help readers feel a connection to characters who are not human. The conflict between Rikki-tikki-tavi and Nag is told through their actions, their words, and their thoughts.

1. How does the use of anthropomorphism contribute to the level of interest and suspense in the story?
2. How would your reaction to "Rikki-tikki-tavi" be changed if it were written as a newspaper story about a real fight between a snake and a mongoose?

- See **Literary Terms Handbook,** p. R1.

LITERARY ELEMENTS

1. It helps the readers know exactly what Rikki-tikki-tavi is thinking and planning. It makes the reader an active participant in the story.
2. If "Rikki-tikki-tavi" were written like a newspaper article about a fight, reactions might not be as sharp. Reporters would try to present the story from both sides.

Additional Resources

 ***Literary Elements Transparency 67***

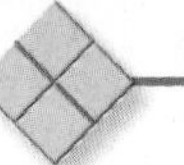

Literature and Writing

Writing About Literature

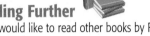

Setting The **setting** is the time and place in which a story takes place. Explain how the descriptions of the setting contribute to the story. What details help you to visualize the house, the garden, and the action between characters?

Creative Writing

News Article Imagine you have been assigned to write a news article about Rikki's heroics. Choose one character to interview. Then write a short article using quotations from your imaginary interview.

Extending Your Response

Literature Groups

A Fan of Snakes Robert Bakker wrote in *The Dinosaur Heresies,* "Whenever I read Kipling's 'Rikki-tikki-tavi,' I root for the snake. . . ." An authority on reptiles, Bakker thinks that Kipling is biased against snakes. Do you agree? Share your group's opinions with the class.

Performing

Readers Theater Prepare a readers theater presentation of the confrontation between Rikki and Nagaina on the veranda. Present it to a class of younger students.

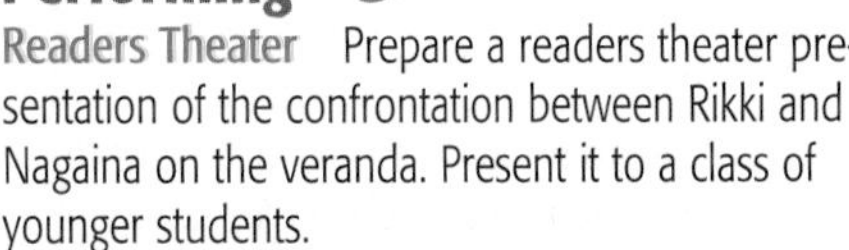

Interdisciplinary Activity

Science Not every snake is life-threatening to humans. Do some research on harmful and harmless snakes in your area. Use a variety of sources, such as books, magazines, the Internet, and other electronic resources. Make a two-column chart that identifies and illustrates the two categories of snakes you have researched.

Reading Further

If you would like to read other books by Rudyard Kipling, try these:

Kim

The Jungle Book

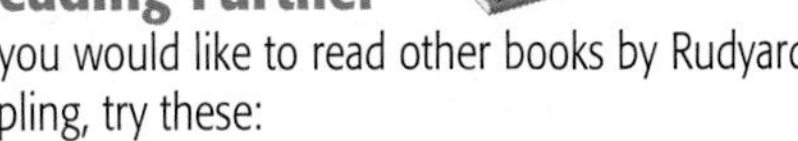

For warm and often hilarious stories about animals and the people who keep them, try this book of memoirs by country veterinarian James Herriot:

All Creatures Great and Small

Literature and Writing

Writing About Literature

Students' paragraphs should

- list specific descriptive details
- explain how the description affects their understanding of the story
- contain a clear topic sentence and conclusion

Creative Writing

Students' news articles should

- list *who, what, where, when,* and *why*
- contain quotations from one of the characters in the story
- contain an engaging hook, an intriguing title, and an appropriate conclusion

Extending Your Response

Literature Groups Encourage students to jot down story details that show a bias for or against snakes. Then, have each group come to a consensus about Kipling's attitude toward snakes.

Performing Ask students to experiment with dramatic pauses, yells, whispers, rapid speech, slow speech, rhythm, and evil, calm, and hysterical voices before they perform.

Interdisciplinary Activity Encourage students to consult a library computer catalog or an Internet search engine to find material on snakes.

ASSESSMENT

- ***Quick Checks,*** p. 67
- ***Selection and Theme Assessment,*** pp. 115–116
- ***Performance Assessment,*** p. 63
- ***Testmaker: ExamView Pro***
- ***Interactive Tutor: Self-Assessment***

Skill Minilessons

GRAMMAR AND LANGUAGE
PERSONAL PRONOUNS

1. He lived in a burrow with his father and mother.
2. After the flood, Rikki never saw them again.
3. They wanted everyone to fear them.
4. "When they are gone," Nagaina said to Nag, "the garden will belong to us."

READING AND THINKING
EVALUATING

Students' paragraphs should take a clear stand on Kipling's purpose for writing "Rikki-tikki-tavi." Then they should decide whether he has achieved his purpose. Students should use details from the story to support their ideas.

VOCABULARY
DICTIONARY SKILLS: DEFINITIONS

1. noun, 4
2. noun, 3
3. verb, 1
4. adjective, 1
5. verb, 2

Additional Resources

- ***Grammar and Language Workbook,*** pp. 103–104
- ***Grammar and Composition Handbook,*** Lesson 4.1
- ***Writer's Choice,*** Lesson 11.1
- ***Reading Skills Practice Workbook,*** pp. 119–120
- ***Vocabulary Practice,*** p. 48

Teaching Support

Skill Minilessons

Reteach • Review

GRAMMAR AND LANGUAGE • PERSONAL PRONOUNS

Personal pronouns refer to people or things. These pronouns have different forms depending on whether they are used in a sentence as subjects or as the objects of verbs or prepositions.

Singular subject pronouns: I, you, he, she, it

Plural subject pronouns: we, you, they

Singular object pronouns: me, you, him, her, it

Plural object pronouns: us, you, them

- For more about pronouns, see **Language Handbook,** p. R31.

PRACTICE Write each sentence, replacing each underlined word or phrase with a personal pronoun.

1. Rikki-tikki-tavi lived in a burrow with his father and mother.
2. After the flood, Rikki never saw his father and mother again.
3. Nag and Nagaina wanted everyone to fear Nag and Nagaina.
4. "When the people are gone," Nagaina said to Nag, "the garden will belong to Nag and Nagaina."

READING AND THINKING • EVALUATING

When you evaluate a piece of writing, one of the things you determine is whether or not the author has achieved his or her purpose.

- For more about evaluating what you read, see **Reading Handbook,** pp. R85–R99.

PRACTICE Was Kipling trying to entertain, to inform, or to persuade his audience with "Rikki-tikki-tavi"? Write a short paragraph stating the author's purpose and evaluating how well he achieved it. Use specific examples from the story to support your opinion.

VOCABULARY • DICTIONARY SKILLS: DEFINITIONS

When you see an unfamiliar word in your reading, the first thing you must do is decide how the word is being used. Is it a noun? a verb? an adjective or adverb? Then look at the **dictionary entry** to find the meanings that are given for the word as that part of speech. Use **context clues** to decide which meaning is the appropriate one.

fancy *n.* **1.** imagination, especially a playful imagination. **2.** something imagined; a mental image. **3.** a sudden wish or notion. **4.** a liking or fondness. *–adj.* **1.** decorated; not plain. **2.** showing expert skill: *fancy dancing.* **3.** of high quality and, therefore, more expensive: *a fancy brand of soup*. *–v.* **1.** to picture mentally; imagine. **2.** to have a liking for. **3.** to suppose; think without being sure: *I fancied she was about twelve.*

PRACTICE Review the dictionary definitions for the word *fancy.* Then decide which meaning of *fancy* is used in each sentence below. Write the part of speech (noun, adjective, or verb) and then the number of the appropriate definition.

1. I've always had a *fancy* for cats and dogs.
2. After reading "Rikki-tikki-tavi," I had a *fancy* to own a mongoose.
3. I could *fancy* myself feeding it and brushing its furry coat.
4. It wouldn't need a *fancy* collar and leash; plain ones would do.
5. My parents, however, didn't *fancy* the idea of another pet, especially a mongoose.

MEETING INDIVIDUAL NEEDS — MULTIPLE MODES OF EXPRESSION

Linguistic Students who learn best by listening, speaking, and writing may be interested in exploring the derivations of some words from this selection. For example, the verb *lunge* comes from the French *allonger,* which means "to lengthen." In the sport of fencing, *lunge* describes the action of extending one's sword to strike a blow at an opponent. The word was first introduced in English during the seventeenth century as *allonge* and was soon shortened to *lunge.*

Activity Invite students to search in dictionaries of word derivations at the library or online to gather information about the etymologies of vocabulary words from this selection. **L2**

Interdisciplinary Connection SCIENCE

Endangered Species

You've probably heard the slogan "Save the whales!" or read it on a bumper sticker. Do you know why this slogan began? It started as a protest from people who wanted to ban whale-hunting. Some types of whales are among the hundreds of endangered species. A species of animal or plant at risk of becoming extinct is called *endangered.*

Many people, such as naturalists who study the environment, believe it is important to save endangered species to maintain the balance of nature. Already, the passenger pigeon, dodo bird, and Labrador duck are extinct. Of course, dinosaurs are extinct too. However, dinosaurs did not disappear because of humans. Today, as the human population increases all over the planet, less space remains for other species to live in their natural habitats.

Species become endangered for many reasons. For example, the cutting down of forests destroys the natural habitats of forest animals. Some animals have been hunted to extinction or near extinction. Overfishing has endangered many fish species. Pesticides kill insects regarded by humans as pests, but they also endanger birds that depend on those insects for food. Pesticide-sprayed insects may also harm birds that feed on them.

Since the 1800s, people have been trying to protect wildlife with special programs. In 1973 the United States passed the Endangered Species Act. An important part of this law made it illegal for people in the United States to buy animals (or animal parts, such as furs) endangered anywhere in the world.

As of June 30, 1998, 350 animal species in the U.S. and another 521 elsewhere in the world were listed as endangered. A few are shown above.

ACTIVITY

Pick an endangered animal to "adopt." Learn everything you can about this animal. Then share with classmates a picture of your adopted animal and your ideas about why and how it should be protected.

Interdisciplinary Connection

Objective

- To understand basic conditions that affect endangered animal species

Teaching Strategies

You may wish to illustrate one of the points made in the text by connecting the situation of endangered species to consumer decisions. For example, bring in a piece of fruit bought at a grocery store. Explain that fruit growers often use pesticides to kill insects that eat the fruit. Birds eat the dead insects and are poisoned. Eventually, these birds could lose great numbers of their population, putting them at risk.

Ask students to come up with ways in which they can help break the cycle. One possibility is looking for fruits and vegetables grown organically. Another is to create and support sanctuaries where birds and other animals can thrive without threat of being poisoned.

Activity

Some students may choose animals that can be protected locally; others may share information on animals found in other parts of the world.

Teaching Support

MEETING INDIVIDUAL NEEDS

MULTIPLE MODES OF EXPRESSION

Bodily/Kinesthetic Bodily/kinesthetic learners will appreciate the chance to act out the drama of animals who experience loss of habitat.

Activity Designate each of the four corners of the classroom as a habitat: *jungle, forest, desert,* and *river.* Ask students to choose an animal indigenous to one of the habitats and go to that habitat. Label a series of index cards *Natural Disaster, Development, Pollution,* and *Poaching.* Hand the cards to different students and have them decide whether their animal can survive the threat or must flee to a different available habitat. Students can flee and go from habitat to habitat. When this is no longer possible, they must decide what to do to survive. **L2**

Before Reading

Objectives

- To read and analyze a short story about the balance between human and animal needs on a farm
- To recognize point of view in a first-person narrative
- To write about how the setting brings a story to life

Skills

Reading/Thinking: Using Graphic Aids; Logical Reasoning; Drawing Conclusions; Problem and Solution
Writing: Telling a Story from Another Point of View
Vocabulary: Unlocking Meaning
Grammar/Language: Apostrophes in Contractions; Consistent Verb Tenses
Listening/Speaking: Literature Groups
Collaboration: Literature Groups

Motivating STUDENTS

Literature Launchers: *A Conversation with Leslie Marmon Silko*

Videodisc Side B, Segment 23

Also available in VHS.

Selection Focus Transparency 68: Have students discuss the temperaments and reputations of different animals.

Reading Focus: To extend the Reading Focus, have students brainstorm to come up with English expressions that involve animals, e.g., *ponytail; stubborn as a mule, wily as a coyote,* and *to pig out.*

Before You Read

Uncle Tony's Goat

MEET LESLIE MARMON SILKO

Leslie Marmon Silko, who describes herself as Laguna, Pueblo, Mexican, and white, grew up on the Laguna Pueblo Reservation in New Mexico, listening to tales told by her female relatives. These stories gave Silko a sense of identity and inspired her writing. Silko's own stories explore her Pueblo heritage and the conflicts between traditional and modern ways. Silko decided to write "Uncle Tony's Goat" after a phone conversation with a friend, the poet Simon J. Ortiz, who told her a story about goats.

Leslie Marmon Silko was born in 1948. This story was first published in 1981.

READING FOCUS

Imagine meeting a large, unfamiliar animal. You feel the threat of its presence as it follows your movements with a watchful eye.

QuickWrite

How would such an experience make you feel? Jot down your response in a few sentences.

Setting a Purpose

Read this story to find out what one boy learns from his experience with a goat.

BUILDING BACKGROUND

The Time and Place The story is set on a small family farm in New Mexico.

Did You Know? Some people think goats are "garbage disposals" that chew tin cans and other trash. Actually, goats spend their days leisurely munching grass and weeds. Hardy animals, goats can live on sparse vegetation and produce milk even under extreme climatic conditions. Some types of goats are also valued for their wool, hides, and meat. Male goats are often called billy goats. A female goat is called a nanny or doe. A young goat is a kid.

VOCABULARY PREVIEW

compensate (kom′ pən sāt′) *v.* to make up for; balance in force, weight, or effect; p. 808
hostile (host′ əl) *adj.* feeling or showing dislike; unfriendly; p. 808
conspicuously (kən spik′ ū əs lē) *adv.* in a way that draws attention or is easily seen; p. 809

806 THEME 8

RESOURCE MANAGER

Teaching Tools and Resources
- Theme Eight Planning Guide
- Literature Groups Sourcebook

Essential Lesson Support

Lesson-Specific Instruction
- Selection Focus Transparency 68
- Literary Elements Transparency 68
- Active Reading Guide,* p. 68
- Selection Vocabulary Practice, p. 49

Assessment
- Selection Quick Checks,* p. 68
- Sel. and Theme Assmt., pp. 117–118
- Testmaker: ExamView Pro
- Performance Assessment, p. 64

Systematic Language Instruction
- Gr. & Comp. Hdbk., L. 13.8
- Vocabulary Power, Lesson 34

English Language Learners
- ELL Sourcebook, pp. 99–100
- Spanish Summaries, p. 68
- Audio Library*
- English, Yes!

Spec. Needs/Strat. Interven.
- Interactive Reading Sourcebook, pp. T234–T237
- Interactive Reading Workbook, pp. 139–140
- Audio Library*

*Also available in Spanish

Uncle Tony's Goat

Leslie Marmon Silko

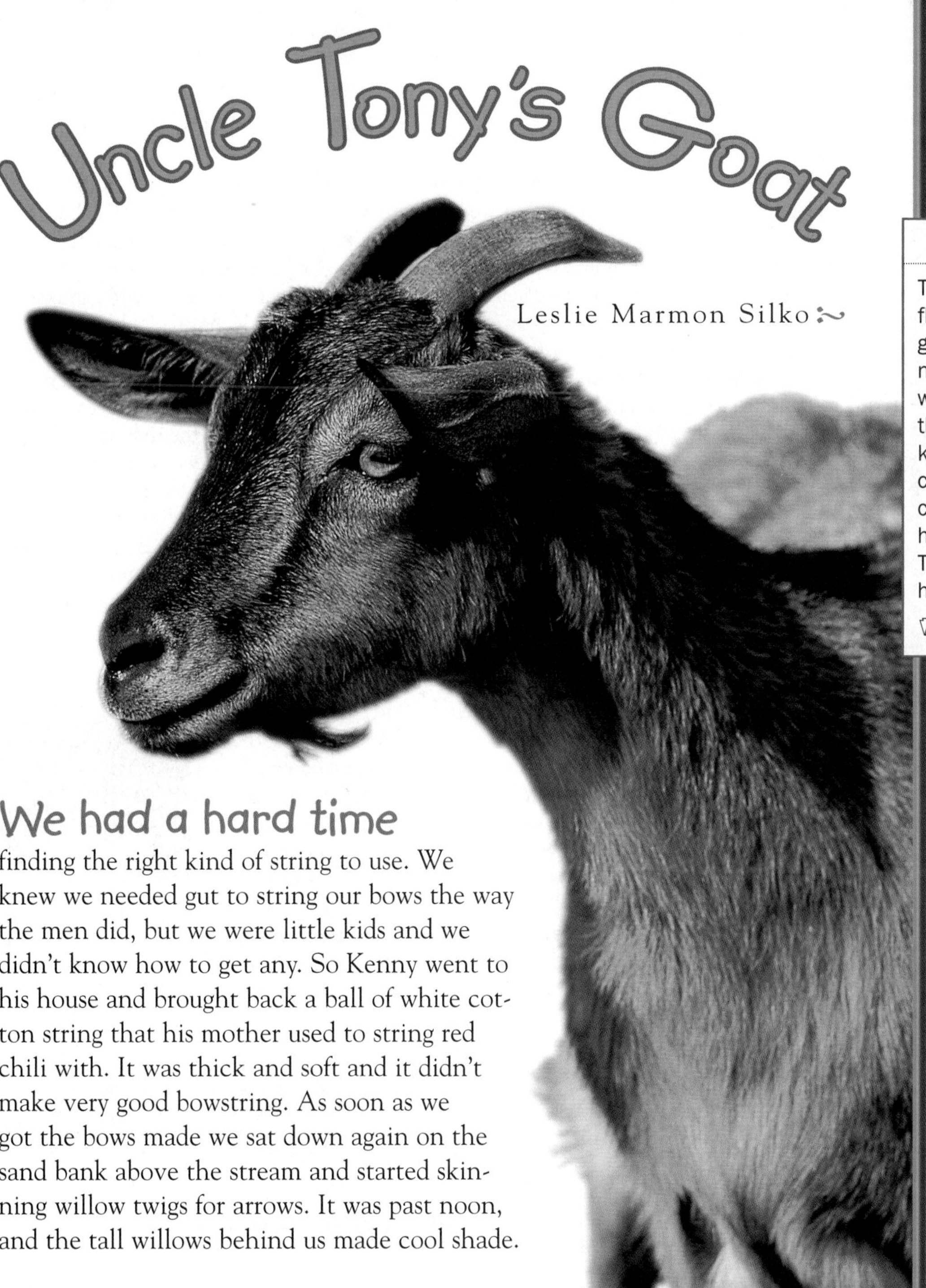

We had a hard time finding the right kind of string to use. We knew we needed gut to string our bows the way the men did, but we were little kids and we didn't know how to get any. So Kenny went to his house and brought back a ball of white cotton string that his mother used to string red chili with. It was thick and soft and it didn't make very good bowstring. As soon as we got the bows made we sat down again on the sand bank above the stream and started skinning willow twigs for arrows. It was past noon, and the tall willows behind us made cool shade.

Reading the Selection

SUMMARY

The narrator and his friends shoot flimsy bows and arrows at Uncle Tony's goats. Uncle Tony's big, black billy goat never forgets the incident. Much later, when the narrator is asked to chase the billy goat out of his pen, the goat knocks the narrator down and opens a cut above his eye. Uncle Tony knows he can't have an animal that harms humans and decides to kill the goat. The goat, sensing danger, jumps out of his pen and runs far away.

Spanish Summaries, p. 68

A Active Reading Strategies

PREDICT Ask a volunteer to read the title and the first paragraph aloud. Ask students to predict how the goat will interact with the narrator. Suggest that students periodically verify or revise their predictions.

VOCABULARY If you haven't previewed the selection vocabulary with students, stop and remind them to use context clues to unlock the meanings of new vocabulary words.

Additional Resources

- ***Active Reading Guide,*** p. 68
- ***Audio Library***
- ***Spanish Audio Library***

Teaching Support

CONNECTING TO OTHER SELECTIONS

The chart at the right shows three ways to connect "Uncle Tony's Goat" to other selections in this book.

For specific teaching strategies, see the ***Theme Eight Planning Guide.***

Connection		Title
Life Skills: Lifelong Learning	→	"Lob's Girl," p. 659
Thematic: Remembering	→	"Last Cover," p. 163
Literary: Narrative	→	"Atalanta," p. 718

B Literary Elements

NARRATOR: ***First-Person Narrative*** Ask students who is narrating the story and how they know. *(An older boy or man is telling about an incident that happened when he was younger. The narrator uses the pronouns we, I, and my, which show that the story is a first-person narrative.)*

C Critical Thinking

LOGICAL REASONING Have students explain whether the children's arrows are a threat to the goats. *(Possibly yes. However, the goats don't even seem to notice; the arrows do not take a direct path.)*

D Active Reading Strategies

QUESTION Have students explain why the billy goat takes the narrator into his memory. *(He doesn't want to forget who participated in the arrow shooting.)* Do students think goats can remember for a long time, hold a grudge, or plot revenge? *(Some may think goats can remember who has harmed them in the past.)*

There were lots of little minnows that day, flashing in the shallow water, swimming back and forth wildly like they weren't sure if they really wanted to go up or down the stream; it was a day for minnows that we were always hoping for—we could have filled our rusty coffee cans and old pickle jars full. But this was the first time for making bows and arrows, and the minnows weren't much different from the sand or the rocks now. B The secret is the arrows. The ones we made were crooked, and when we shot them they didn't go straight—they flew around in arcs and curves; so we crawled through the leaves and branches, deep into the willow groves, looking for the best, the straightest willow branches. But even after we skinned the sticky wet bark from them and whittled the knobs off, they still weren't straight. Finally we went ahead and made notches at the end of each arrow to hook in the bowstring, and we started practicing, thinking maybe we could learn to shoot the crooked arrows straight.

We left the river each of us with a handful of damp, yellow arrows and our fresh-skinned willow bows. We walked slowly and shot arrows at bushes, big rocks, and the juniper tree that grows by Pino's sheep pen. They were working better just like we had figured; they still didn't fly straight, but now we could compensate for that by the way we aimed them. We were going up to the church to shoot at the cats old Sister Julian kept outside the cloister.[1] We didn't want to hurt anything, just to have new kinds of things to shoot at.

1. Here, the *cloister* is a convent, the building in which nuns live.

But before we got to the church we went past the grassy hill where my uncle Tony's goats were grazing. A few of them were lying down chewing their cud[2] peacefully, and they didn't seem to notice us. The billy goat was lying down, but he was watching us closely like he already knew about little kids. His yellow goat eyes didn't blink, and he stared with a wide, hostile look. C The grazing goats made good deer for our bows. We shot all our arrows at the nanny goats and their kids; they skipped away from the careening[3] arrows and never lost the rhythm of their greedy chewing as they continued to nibble the weeds and grass on the hillside. D The billy goat was lying there watching us and taking us into his memory. As we ran down the road toward the church and Sister Julian's cats, I looked back, and my uncle Tony's billy goat was still watching me.

My uncle and my father were sitting on the bench outside the house when we walked by. It was September now, and the farming was almost over, except for bringing home the melons and a few pumpkins. They were mending ropes and bridles

Did You Know?
A *bridle* is the headgear for a horse. It includes the bit that fits in the horse's mouth and the reins the rider uses to guide the horse.

2. *Cud* is partially digested food brought back up from an animal's stomach for a second, more thorough, chewing.
3. *Careening* arrows would sway from side to side while moving, as if out of control.

Vocabulary
compensate (kom′ pən sāt′) *v.* to make up for; balance in force, weight, or effect
hostile (host′ əl) *adj.* feeling or showing dislike; unfriendly

Teaching Support

MEETING INDIVIDUAL NEEDS — ENGLISH LANGUAGE LEARNERS

Possessives English language learners may confuse possessives with plurals. To illustrate how possessives are formed, write the chart at right on the board. Use the examples to demonstrate word order and possession.

Activity Have students work in small groups to find other examples of possessives in the story to add to the chart. Then have students write five more possessives using the names of students in the group.

What	Whose It Is	This Is ______.
goat	Uncle Tony	Uncle Tony's goat
neck	the goat	the goat's neck

Additional Resources
English Language Learners Sourcebook, p. 99

and feeling the afternoon sun. We held our bows and arrows out in front of us so they could see them. My father smiled and kept braiding the strips of leather in his hand, but my uncle Tony put down the bridle and pieces of scrap leather he was working on and looked at each of us kids slowly. He was old, getting some white hair—he was my mother's oldest brother, the one that scolded us when we told lies or broke things.

E "You'd better not be shooting at things," he said, "only at rocks or trees. Something will get hurt. Maybe even one of you."

We all nodded in agreement and tried to hold the bows and arrows less conspicuously down at our sides; when he turned back to his work we hurried away before he took the bows away from us like he did the time we made the slingshot. He caught us shooting rocks at an old wrecked car; its windows were all busted out anyway, but he took the slingshot away. I always wondered what he did with it and with the knives we made ourselves out of tin cans. When I was much older I asked my mother, "What did he ever do with those knives and slingshots he took away from us?" She was kneading[4] bread on the kitchen table at the time and was probably busy thinking about the fire in the oven outside. "I don't know," she said; "you ought to ask him yourself." But I never did. I thought about it lots of times, but I never did. It would have been like getting caught all over again.

The goats were valuable. We got milk and meat from them. My uncle was careful to see that all the goats were treated properly; the worst scolding my older sister ever got was when my mother caught her and some of her friends chasing the newborn kids. My mother kept saying over and over again, "It's a good thing I saw you; what if your uncle had seen you?" and even though we kids were very young then, we understood very well what she meant.

The billy goat never forgot the bows and arrows, even after the bows had cracked and split and the crooked, whittled arrows were all lost. F This goat was big and black and important to my uncle Tony because he'd paid a lot to get him and because he wasn't an ordinary goat. Uncle Tony had bought him from a white man, and then he'd hauled him in the back of the pickup all the way from Quemado.[5] And my uncle was the only person who could touch this goat. If a stranger or one of us kids got too near him, the mane on the billy goat's neck would stand on end and the goat would rear up on his hind legs and dance forward trying to reach the person with his long, spiral horns. This billy goat smelled bad, and none of us cared if we couldn't pet him. But my uncle took good care of this goat. The goat would let Uncle Tony brush him with the horse brush and scratch him around the base of his horns. G Uncle Tony talked to the billy goat—in the morning when he unpenned the goats and in the evening when he gave them their hay and closed the gate for the night. I never paid too much attention to what he said to the billy goat; usually it was something like

4. The mother was pressing and squeezing, or *kneading,* bread dough.

5. *Quemado* (kā mä' dō)

Vocabulary

conspicuously (kən spik' ū əs lē) *adv.* in a way that draws attention or is easily seen

E Author's Craft

FORESHADOWING Ask students to note how the author is introducing the possibility of one of the children getting hurt if they shoot any arrows at the goats.

F Active Reading Strategies

EVALUATE Ask students to think about possible reasons the narrator would have for mentioning that the goat never forgot. You may wish to share the following model to illustrate the thinking process involved in evaluating.

Model: I know that the narrator is a character in the story. He is probably leading up to a dramatic scene with the goat later in the story. It will probably have to do with the incident of shooting arrows at the goats.

G Active Reading Strategies

RESPOND Invite students to describe Uncle Tony's feelings about the goat and how they differ from the narrator's attitude. *(Uncle Tony is grateful to the goat for what he provides and takes good care of him; the narrator treats the goat as a "thing" he can use to entertain himself, without a thought that the goat is a living creature.)*

Reading Minilesson

Using Graphic Aids As this story progresses, readers find out more and more about the narrator, Uncle Tony, and the billy goat.

Activity Invite students to begin a word web for each of these characters. At the end of the story, students can mark in color the character traits that they were most surprised to discover. **L2**

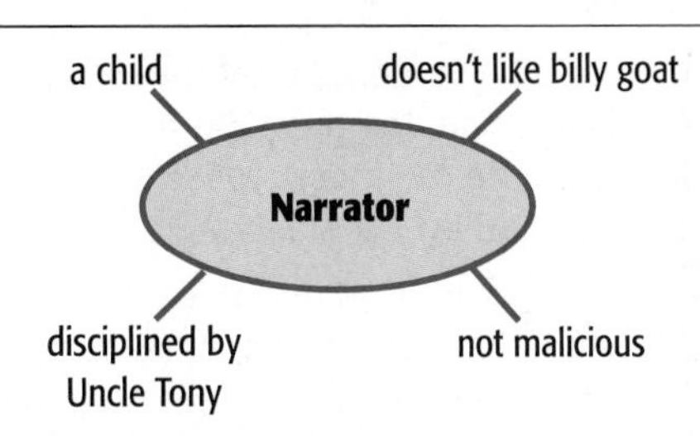

Additional Resources

Reading Skills Practice Workbook

VIEWING THE ART

Viewing Response *The story doesn't take place at night, so the art is different in that respect. The river doesn't look shady, like the riverbank where the narrator made bows and arrows. However, the hills look as if they could be the ones where the goats in the story graze, and the Southwest location is right for the story's setting.*

H Active Reading Strategies

EVALUATE Uncle Tony never says how he feels about the billy goat. What do students think Tony's actions show about his feelings? *(Uncle Tony thinks of the goat as more than just livestock. Uncle Tony treats the goat much like a pet.)*

I Active Reading Strategies

PREDICT Invite students to predict what may happen when the narrator tries to run the goats out of the pen. *(The females and young goats are docile and will do what the narrator wants, but the billy goat does not like the narrator. It may pose a problem, perhaps even hurt the narrator.)*

Crescent Moon Over the Southwest, 1990. Sherri Silverman. Pastel, 25¾ x 36 in. Private collection.

Viewing the painting: How is the scene in the painting similar to and different from the story's setting?

"Get up, big goat! You've slept long enough," or "Move over, big goat, and let the others have something to eat." I think Uncle Tony was proud of that billy goat.

We all had chores to do around home. My sister helped out around the house mostly, and I was supposed to carry water from the hydrant and bring in kindling. I helped my father look after the horses and pigs, and Uncle Tony milked the goats and fed them. One morning near the end of September I was out feeding the pigs their table scraps and pig mash;[6] I'd given the pigs their food, and I was watching them squeal and snap at each other as they crowded into the feed trough. Behind me I could hear the milk squirting into the eight-pound lard pail that Uncle Tony used for milking.

When he finished milking he noticed me standing there; he motioned toward the goats still inside the pen. "Run the rest of them out," he said as he untied the two milk goats and carried the milk to the house.

I was seven years old, and I understood that everyone, including my uncle, expected me to handle more chores; so I hurried over to the goat pen and swung the tall wire gate open. The does and kids

6. *Mash* is animal feed that consists of a mixture of ground grains.

Teaching Support

MEETING INDIVIDUAL NEEDS: MULTIPLE MODES OF EXPRESSION

Musical Students with strong musical abilities can use music to help them appreciate the mood, tone, and feelings generated by the story.

Activity Invite musical learners to imagine they are turning this story into a movie. As they read, have them stop whenever the action suggests to them a background song, a type of music, or a sound. Have them jot down a description of the music or sound, along with the emotions or mood it makes them feel. Students may find their notes useful when they complete the Responding to Literature activities on pages 813–815. Some students may want to tape-record music or sound effects to accompany a reading of an important scene from the story. **L2**

came prancing out. They trotted daintily past the pigpen and scattered out, intent on finding leaves and grass to eat. It wasn't until then I noticed that the billy goat hadn't come out of the little wooden shed inside the goat pen. I stood outside the pen and tried to look inside the wooden shelter, but it was still early and the morning sun left the inside of the shelter in deep shadow. I stood there for a while, hoping that he would come out by himself, but I realized that he'd recognized me and that he wouldn't come out. I understood right away what was happening and my fear of him was in my bowels and down my neck; I was shaking.

Finally my uncle came out of the house; it was time for breakfast. "What's wrong?" he called out from the door.

"The billy goat won't come out," I yelled back, hoping he would look disgusted and come do it himself.

"Get in there and get him out," he said as he went back into the house.

I looked around quickly for a stick or broom handle, or even a big rock, but I couldn't find anything. I walked into the pen slowly, concentrating on the darkness beyond the shed door; I circled to the back of the shed and kicked at the boards, hoping to make the billy goat run out. I put my eye up to a crack between the boards, and I could see he was standing up now and that his yellow eyes were on mine.

My mother was yelling at me to hurry up, and Uncle Tony was watching. I stepped around into the low doorway, and the goat charged toward me, feet first. I had dirt in my mouth and up my nose and there was blood running past my eye; my head ached. Uncle Tony carried me to the house; his face was stiff with anger, and I remembered what he'd always told us about animals; they won't bother you unless you bother them first. I didn't start to cry until my mother hugged me close and wiped my face with a damp wash rag. It was only a little cut above my eyebrow, and she sent me to school anyway with a Band-Aid on my forehead.

Uncle Tony locked the billy goat in the pen. He didn't say what he was going to do with the goat, but when he left with my father to haul firewood, he made sure the gate to the pen was wired tightly shut. He looked at the goat quietly and with sadness; he said something to the goat, but the yellow eyes stared past him.

"What's he going to do with the goat?" I asked my mother before I went to catch the school bus.

"He ought to get rid of it," she said. "We can't have that goat knocking people down for no good reason."

I didn't feel good at school. The teacher sent me to the nurse's office and the nurse made me lie down. Whenever I closed my eyes I could see the goat and my uncle, and I felt a stiffness in my throat and chest. I got off the school bus slowly, so the other kids would go ahead without me. I walked slowly and wished I could be away from home for a while. I could go over to Grandma's house, but she would ask me if my mother knew where I was and I would have to say no, and she would make me go home first to ask. So I walked very slowly, because I didn't want to see the black goat's hide hanging over the corral fence.

When I got to the house I didn't see a goat hide or the goat, but Uncle Tony was on his horse and my mother was standing

J Literary Elements

NARRATOR: ***Foreshadowing*** Invite students to explain how the narrator is presenting clues to prepare for what may happen between the goat and the boy. *(The goat has recognized the narrator as the person involved in the arrow-shooting incident. The goat does not like him and will not do what the boy wants. This foreshadows an unpleasant incident.)*

K Critical Thinking

DRAWING CONCLUSIONS Have students explain why Uncle Tony watches the narrator as he tries to get the goat out of the pen. *(Uncle Tony wants to see how the boy and the goat get along. Uncle Tony knows the goat is mean and probably recalls the arrow-shooting incident.)*

L Critical Thinking

DRAWING CONCLUSIONS Remind students that the narrator doesn't like the goat. Why might he feel sick at the thought of the goat's being killed? *(The narrator feels guilty because he believes he is responsible for the goat's fate. If he hadn't shot arrows at the goat, which he knew he wasn't supposed to do, the goat might not have misbehaved.)*

ADVANCED LEARNERS

Interview People who live on farms have many things to care for. In this story, the boy, who is only seven, feeds the pigs and helps look after the horses. Uncle Tony milks and feeds the goats. Invite students to find out more about daily life on a farm.

Activity Have students work in pairs to read about farm life or interview someone their age who lives and works on a farm in the region. Encourage students to find out what chores and activities must be done each day, and how chores and activities change, season by season. **L3**

Ⓜ Critical Thinking

DRAWING CONCLUSIONS Have students draw on story details and their prior knowledge of animal behavior to explain why the goat runs away on this day. *(Students may say that animal instinct is at work, and the goat somehow senses danger or threat.)*

Ⓝ Critical Thinking

DRAWING CONCLUSIONS Encourage students to explain why Uncle Tony's voice is strong and happy now that the goat is gone. *(He knows that the goat has escaped alive and he will not have to kill it. He also knows that the goat is gone for good, so it will not harm people.)*

Thematic Focus

A Delicate Balance Have students explain how this story fits the theme "A Delicate Balance." *(The story is about the balance between human needs and animal needs on a farm.)*

ASSESSMENT

Quick Checks, p. 68

Teaching Support

beside the horse holding a canteen and a flour sack bundle tied with brown string. I was frightened at what this meant. My uncle looked down at me from the saddle.

Ⓜ "The goat ran away," he said. "Jumped out of the pen somehow. I saw him just as he went over the hill beyond the river. He stopped at the top of the hill and he looked back this way."

Uncle Tony nodded at my mother and me and then he left; we watched his old roan gelding[7] splash across the stream and labor up the steep path beyond the river. Then they were over the top of the hill and gone.

Uncle Tony was gone for three days. He came home early on the morning of the fourth day, before we had eaten breakfast or fed the animals. He was glad to be home, he said, because he was getting too old for such long rides. He called me over and looked closely at the cut above my eye. It had scabbed over good, and I wasn't wearing a Band-Aid any more; he examined it very carefully before he let me go. He stirred some sugar into his coffee.

"That miserable goat," he said. "I followed him for three days. He was headed south, going straight to Quemado. I never could catch up to him." My uncle shook his head. "The first time I saw him he was already in the piñon forest, halfway into the mountains already. I could see him most of the time, off in the distance a mile or two. He would stop sometimes and look back." Uncle Tony paused and drank some more coffee. "I stopped at night. I had to. He stopped too, and in the morning we would start out again. The trail just gets higher and steeper. Yesterday morning there was frost on top of the blanket when I woke up and we were in the big pines and red oak leaves. I couldn't see him any more because the forest is too thick. So I turned around." Tony finished the cup of coffee. "He's probably in Quemado by now."

Did You Know?

Piñon (pin′ yun), a Spanish word, refers to any of several small pine trees found in Mexico and the southwestern United States.

I looked at him again, standing there by the door, ready to go milk the nanny goats.

"There wasn't ever a goat like that one," he said, "but if that's the way he's going to act, O.K. then. That stubborn goat was just too mean anyway."

He smiled at me and his voice was strong and happy when he said this. Ⓝ

7. *Roan* describes the horse's color, a reddish-brown mixed with gray or white. A *gelding* is a male horse that's been surgically "fixed" so that it cannot breed.

Grammar and Language *Minilesson*

Apostrophes in Contractions Write the following words on the board:

it is = it's   *he would = he'd*

The apostrophe has two primary uses: to signal a possession or to form a contraction. In a contraction, the apostrophe replaces one or more letters dropped when two words are combined into one.

Activity Have students add an apostrophe to each contraction they find and identify the words that were combined.

1. Its a good thing I saw you. *(It's, it is)*
2. Its eyes were yellow. *(no contraction)*
3. He wasnt an ordinary goat. *(wasn't, was not)*
4. Whats wrong? *(What's, What is)* **L2**

Additional Resources

- ***Grammar and Language Transparency 63***
- ***Grammar and Language Workbook,*** pp. 273–274
- ***Grammar and Composition Handbook,*** Lesson 13.7
- ***Writer's Choice,*** Lesson 20.7

Responding to Literature

PERSONAL RESPONSE

- Review your notes from the **Reading Focus** on page 806. How do your thoughts and feelings compare with those of the story's narrator?

Analyzing Literature

RECALL

1. What do Kenny and the narrator do when they encounter the goats on the hill? Why do you think they do that?
2. What is the billy goat's reaction to the boys' behavior?
3. What happens when the narrator attempts to run the goats from the pen?
4. What is the narrator afraid he will find when he returns from school? What happens instead?

Brackets connect questions that are paired to develop higher-level thinking skills.

INTERPRET

5. Why do you think the billy goat acts as he does when the narrator attempts to run the goats from the pen? Do you think Uncle Tony understands the goat's behavior? Why or why not?
6. Does the goat deserve to be killed as Uncle Tony seems to plan? Why or why not?
7. How does the narrator's attitude toward the goat change in the course of the story? Explain.
8. What do you think the narrator learned from his experience with Uncle Tony's goat?

EVALUATE AND CONNECT

9. Were you satisfied with the story's ending? Why or why not? Suggest two other possible endings for the story.
10. Theme Connection What does the story communicate to you about the relationship between humans and animals?

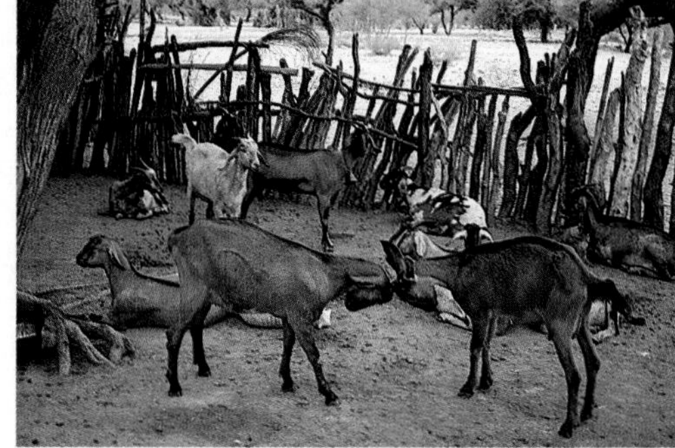

LITERARY ELEMENTS

Narrator

Narrative is a type of writing that tells a story. The person who tells the story is called the **narrator.** Because the narrator in "Uncle Tony's Goat" tells the events in his own words, using the pronoun *I,* this story is a **first-person narrative.** In a first-person narrative, all information about the story's characters and events comes from the narrator. A skillful reader must determine how the narrator's experience and opinions influence the telling of the story.

1. What affects the narrator's description of Uncle Tony?
2. If Uncle Tony were telling the story, how might he have described the goat?

- See **Literary Terms Handbook,** p. R7.

Responding to the Selection

PERSONAL RESPONSE

Students should use examples from the story to compare their thoughts and feelings with those of the narrator.

Analyzing Literature

1. They shoot arrows at the goats because they want to try out their arrows on moving targets.
2. The billy goat doesn't do anything at the time, but he remembers the incident and the boys involved.
3. All the goats except the billy goat leave the pen.
4. The narrator is afraid the billy goat will have been killed. Instead, he finds out that the goat has run away.
5. The goat remembers the arrow-shooting incident. He does not like the narrator and will not do what the narrator wants him to do. It seems that Uncle Tony understands that the goat does not like the narrator, which is why he watches to see what will happen.
6. Some students may say the goat deserves to be killed because he is dangerous to humans. Others may say the goat does not deserve to be killed because the narrator had picked on the goat.
7. The narrator dislikes the goat and is afraid of him. But later, when he thinks the goat will be killed, he is very unhappy because he knows he has at least partially caused the goat's behavior.
8. The narrator has learned that animals remember the way they are treated. Perhaps he will not tease animals again.
9. Other possible endings include Tony's killing the goat or the narrator's working with the goat until the goat trusts him.
10. *Example:* Both human needs and animal needs are important, but on a farm, the needs of humans must come first.

LITERARY ELEMENTS

1. The narrator's description is affected by his respect for Uncle Tony and by Uncle Tony's respect for his farm animals.
2. *Example:* He is stubborn, smart, and takes care of other goats in the herd.

Additional Resources

Literary Elements Transparency 68

Literature and Writing

Writing About Literature

Students' paragraphs should

- list specific details of setting
- describe techniques the author uses to bring the setting to life for readers
- use examples from the story

Creative Writing

Students' stories should

- be written from the goat's point of view
- describe the goat's thoughts about the narrator and Uncle Tony
- explain why the goat runs away

Extending Your Response

Art Activity Have students work together to create a story map that includes foreshadowing and share it with the class.

Literature Groups Have each member share one thought about how animals are portrayed in the two stories and discuss which method they prefer.

Learning for Life Encourage students to review the story if they have difficulty remembering the sequence of events.

Literature and Writing

Writing About Literature

Setting What is the setting of the story? How does the author bring the setting to life for her readers? Write a paragraph about the story's setting. Use examples and quotations from the story.

Creative Writing

Retelling the Story Rewrite the story as if the goat were narrating it. Be sure to include the goat's thoughts and feelings toward Uncle Tony, as well as his response to the boys' activities.

Extending Your Response

Art Activity

Story Map Leslie Marmon Silko uses foreshadowing when she offers her readers clues about what will occur next in the story. If you recognize these clues, you can predict what will happen. Reexamine the story. As a group, use chart paper to create a large story map that illustrates and charts the evidence foreshadowing the goat's attack on the narrator. Present your story map to the class.

interNET CONNECTION

Leslie Marmon Silko grew up on a pueblo in New Mexico. If you would like to learn more about the Pueblo people, type "Pueblo Indians" or "Anasazi" into a search engine to find some informative sites.

Literature Groups

Animal Portraits Compare the way animals are portrayed in "Rikki-tikki-tavi" and "Uncle Tony's Goat." Which animal portrait do you prefer? From which did you learn the most? Give reasons for your opinions.

Learning for Life

Incident Report Imagine you are Uncle Tony. Write a report for the police about your missing goat. Summarize the events that lead to the goat's escape. Also describe the goat and your nephew. Read your report to the class.

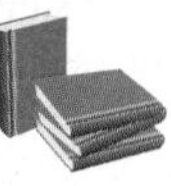

Reading Further

To learn more about the Pueblos and other Native Americans of the Southwest, try these books:

Mother Earth, Father Sky: Pueblo Indians of the American Southwest by David Lavender

Desert Dwellers: Native People of the American Southwest by Scott S. Warren

Save your work for your portfolio.

ASSESSMENT

- ***Quick Checks,*** p. 68
- ***Selection and Theme Assessment,*** pp. 117–118
- ***Performance Assessment,*** p. 64
- ***Testmaker: ExamView Pro***
- ***Interactive Tutor: Self-Assessment***

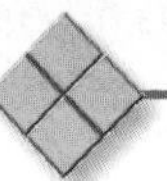

Skill Minilessons

Reteach · Review

GRAMMAR AND LANGUAGE • CONSISTENT VERB TENSES

It is important to keep the verb tenses consistent in your writing. If you jump from one tense to another, readers will be confused about when events take place.

CONFUSING: Uncle Tony **works** hard on the farm. The narrator **worked** on the farm too.

BETTER: Uncle Tony **works** hard on the farm. The narrator **works** on the farm too.

PRACTICE Write a paragraph summarizing the events in "Uncle Tony's Goat." Keep your verbs in the same tense unless you have a strong reason to change them. Exchange paragraphs with a partner and check for consistent verb tenses.

- For more about verb tense, see **Language Handbook,** pp. R15–R16.

READING AND THINKING • PROBLEM/SOLUTION

Most plots in fiction focus on one or more problems that the characters try to solve. Often, readers learn about characters by the way in which they respond to problems in their lives. In "Uncle Tony's Goat," there are a number of related problems. How do the different characters respond to the problems? How do they try to solve the problems?

PRACTICE Reread "Uncle Tony's Goat." Write a paragraph describing how two of the characters in the story respond to problems in their lives and how they finally solve them.

- To learn more about the problem/solution organization of text, see **Reading Handbook,** pp. R88–R89.

VOCABULARY • UNLOCKING MEANING

You can often use what you know about one word to figure out what another related word means. The narrator of "Uncle Tony's Goat" has the chore of gathering *kindling.* You know that *kindling* is small sticks or other material used to start a fire. You could use that information to figure out that the expression "kindled my anger" means "made me start to get angry."

PRACTICE Use what you know about the words on the left and familiar prefixes and suffixes to answer the questions.

1. *hostile* Hostilities are sure to occur during ______ .
   a. wars b. parties c. contests
2. *conspicuous* You might try to be inconspicuous to avoid being ______ .
   a. noticed b. alone c. neglected
3. *compensate* If your brother lost your jacket, what might he do to recompense you?
   a. apologize b. laugh c. buy you another

- For more about using word parts to unlock meaning, see **Reading Handbook,** pp. R73 and R79–R80.

Skill Minilessons

GRAMMAR AND LANGUAGE
CONSISTENT VERB TENSES

Students' paragraphs should
- accurately summarize the story
- use consistent verb tenses throughout
- switch verb tenses only for compelling reasons, such as to describe an incident that happened much earlier than the rest

READING AND THINKING
PROBLEM/SOLUTION

Students' paragraphs should
- describe the problems of two characters in the story
- explain how the two characters solve the problems
- contain a clear topic sentence and effective conclusion

VOCABULARY
UNLOCKING MEANING

1. a 2. a 3. c

Additional Resources

- ***Grammar and Language Workbook,*** pp. 83–84
- ***Grammar and Composition Handbook,*** Lesson 3.5
- ***Writer's Choice,*** Lesson 10.5
- ***Reading Skills Practice Workbook,*** pp. 121–122
- ***Vocabulary Practice,*** p. 49

Objective

- To recognize and apply strategies for forming possessive nouns and pronouns

Teaching Strategies

Before reading the problems and solutions on page 816, explain to students that they are in charge of proofreading signs that will be posted around town. Write the following texts on the board and ask students to make any necessary corrections: *Womens' Shoes* (Women's); *Rays Tire Shop* (Ray's); *Pet's Welcome* (Pets); *Dollys' Snack Shop* (Dolly's); *Eat at Joes'* (Joe's); *Teacher's Parking Lot* (Teachers').

Exercise

a. dresses'
b. sheep's
c. men's
d. class's
e. horns'
f. story's
g. James's
h. ours
i. ladies'
j. family's

Additional Resources

- ***Grammar and Language Workbook,*** pp. 65–66, 109–110
- ***Grammar and Composition Handbook,*** Lessons 2.3, 4.4
- ***Writer's Choice,*** Lessons 9.3, 11.4

Using Apostrophes to Show Possession

The **apostrophe** is used to show possession. Sometimes it is used alone, but it is usually combined with the letter *s.*

Problem 1 Singular, possessive nouns
Leslie Marmon Silkos story about the goat is humorous.

Solution Use an apostrophe and an *-s* to make a singular noun possessive, even if the noun ends in *-s.*
Leslie Marmon Silko's story about the goat is humorous.

Problem 2 Plural nouns ending in *-s*
Are your classmates responses the same as yours?

Solution If a plural noun ends in *-s,* make it possessive by adding only an apostrophe.
Are your classmates' responses the same as yours?

Problem 3 Plural nouns not ending in *-s*
Peoples ideas about goats have not changed much over time.

Solution If a plural noun does not end in *-s,* add an apostrophe and an *-s.*
People's ideas about goats have not changed much over time.

Problem 4 Possessive personal pronouns
The boys don't realize that the problem with the goat is their's.

Solution Apostrophes are not used in possessive pronouns, such as *yours* and *hers.*
The boys don't realize that the problem with the goat is theirs.

- For more about using apostrophes, see **Language Handbook,** pp. R40–R41.

EXERCISE

Write the possessive form of each word.

a. dresses
b. sheep
c. men
d. class
e. horns
f. story
g. James
h. our
i. ladies
j. family

Writing Minilesson

Writing a Tercet Explain that a tercet is a group of three lines that form a group. For example:

I like frogs' eyes,
Twinkling like starry skies,
Big and shiny, bright and wise.

Write a few tercets as a class. Encourage students to experiment with different line lengths and rhyming words.

Activity Have students work individually to write a tercet about something in nature. Ask that the tercet include at least one possessive noun formed with an apostrophe. **L2**

Additional Resources

- ***Writer's Choice,*** Lesson 3.6

LISTENING, SPEAKING, and VIEWING

Critical Viewing

How can you judge the accuracy of things you view on television, on film, or on the Internet? The following tips can help.

Critical Viewing Guidelines

Ask Why

- When you view a presentation, ask yourself about its purpose. Is it designed to entertain, to inform, or to persuade? Material should be accurate, but material intended to persuade may be one-sided.

Ask Who

- Who created the presentation? Is the creator an expert? Does he or she have a reputation for quality?

Ask When

- When was the presentation created? Older material may not be up-to-date. On the other hand, very new information may not yet have been reliably confirmed. Can you check key facts?

Ask How

- How is the material presented? Do you detect fuzzy thinking, sensationalism, one-sidedness, or other attempts to manipulate viewers?

Digital composite by John Lund/Tony Stone Images.

ACTIVITIES

1. On your own or with a partner, view a television commercial and use the Critical Viewing Guidelines to evaluate it. Make notes of your evaluation, and share your results with classmates.
2. Use the Critical Viewing Guidelines to evaluate a television program or video designed to inform. Write a paragraph explaining your evaluation.

LISTENING, SPEAKING, and VIEWING

Objective

- To recognize and apply strategies for critical viewing

Teaching Strategies

Point out to students that critical viewing is also important when they are using visual media during research for written or oral reports. Urge them to use the questions in the Critical Viewing Guidelines at such times. These and similar questions can also be adapted for application to ordinary reading materials.

Have students role-play two television spots: one a public service announcement urging viewers to take care of their bodies; the second an advertisement for a health club. Ask students to use their critical faculties and the guidelines on page 817 to discuss the differences between the two spots.

Activities

1. Some students may find that they already apply the critical viewing guidelines to their television watching, while others may be surprised by the results of their evaluation.
2. Students may wish to read their paragraphs aloud or share them in small groups.

Teaching Support

MEETING INDIVIDUAL NEEDS

ENGLISH LANGUAGE LEARNERS

Focus Groups Diverse cultural perspectives can provide all students with valuable insights into how an American television program might be perceived outside America.

Activity Have small groups of students choose a popular television program to analyze. Ask the groups to imagine they are living in a country where the only information they have about American culture comes from that television program. Have students view the program critically and use it to make assumptions about American life: What do Americans look like? How do they act? What is their family life like?

Additional Resources

 ***English Language Learners Sourcebook,*** p. 100

Before Reading

Objectives

- To read and enjoy a poem about the power of the natural world
- To understand and describe an extended metaphor
- To write about one's reaction to a poem

Skills

Reading/Thinking: Elaborating
Writing: Creating an Extended Metaphor
Listening/Speaking: Performing
Collaboration: Literature Groups

Motivating STUDENTS

Selection Focus Transparency 69: Have students discuss a construction project that is occurring locally. Who benefits? Who is harmed?

Reading Focus: As an extension of the Reading Focus, have students in small groups list forces of nature that change the earth suddenly and forces of nature that change the earth steadily over thousands of years.

Before You Read

Loo-Wit

MEET WENDY ROSE

Wendy Rose's mother was of Miwok descent, and her father was a full-blood Hopi. Her poems often reflect her personal search for tribal and personal identity. About her need to write, Rose once said, "Writing is just something that always has been and just is. For everything in this universe there is a song to accompany its existence; writing is another way of singing these songs. . . . Some people have tried to say I sing my songs because I'm half-Hopi; that's not true . . . I sing them because I hear them."

Wendy Rose was born in California in 1948.

READING FOCUS

Think about the extraordinary power of natural elements, such as a volcano, tornado, or the ocean tides. What words might describe that kind of power?

Sharing Ideas
Write down your ideas. Then share your thoughts in a small group discussion.

Setting a Purpose
Read this poem to discover how one poet describes a volcano.

BUILDING BACKGROUND

Loo-Wit is the Cowlitz Indian name for Mount St. Helens, the volcano that erupted in Washington in 1980. A volcano is a vent in the Earth from which molten rock and gas sometimes erupt. The molten rock that erupts, called lava, forms a hill or mountain around the vent. The lava sometimes flows out as liquid, or it may explode as solid particles. The fierce eruption of Mount St. Helens was the most violent volcanic event within the continental United States in recorded history.

RESOURCE MANAGER

Teaching Tools and Resources
- Theme Eight Planning Guide
- Literature Groups Sourcebook

Essential Lesson Support

Lesson-Specific Instruction
- Selection Focus Transparency 69
- Literary Elements Transparency 69
- Active Reading Guide,* p. 69
- *inTIME* magazine, pp. 12-13

Assessment
- Selection Quick Checks,* p. 69
- Sel. and Theme Assmt., pp. 119-120
- Testmaker: ExamView Pro
- Performance Assessment, p. 65

Systematic Language Instruction
- Gr. & Comp. Hdbk., L. 13.9

English Language Learners
- ELL Sourcebook, p. 101
- Spanish Summaries, p. 69
- Audio Library*
- English, Yes!

Spec. Needs/Strat. Interven.
- Interactive Reading Sourcebook, pp. T237-T239
- Interactive Reading Workbook, p. 141
- Audio Library*

*Also available in Spanish

Loo-Wit

Wendy Rose

The way they do
this old woman
no longer cares
what others think
but spits her black tobacco
any which way
stretching full length
from her bumpy bed.
Finally up
she sprinkles
ashes on the snow,
cold buttes°
promising nothing
but the walk
of winter.
Centuries of cedar
have bound her
to earth,
huckleberry ropes
lay prickly
on her neck.
Around her
machinery growls,
snarls and ploughs
great patches
of her skin.
She crouches
in the north,
her trembling
the source
of dawn.
Light appears
with the shudder
of her slopes,
the movement
of her arm.
Blackberries unravel,°
stones dislodge.°
It's not as if
they weren't warned.

She was sleeping
but she heard
the boot scrape,
the creaking floor,
felt the pull of the blanket
from her thin shoulder.
With one free hand
she finds her weapons
and raises them high;
clearing the twigs
from her throat
she sings, she sings,
shaking the sky
like a blanket about her
Loo-Wit sings and sings and sings!

12 *Buttes* (būts) are steep, isolated, flat-topped hills.

37 Here, *unravel* means "untangle; separate; come apart."
38 To *dislodge* is to move out of position.

Reading the Selection

A Active Reading Strategies

PREDICT Ask a volunteer to read the first sentence aloud. Have students suggest what the black tobacco is and what event is taking place. *(The black tobacco is volcanic ash spewing from Mount St. Helens.)*

Additional Resources

- ***Active Reading Guide,*** p. 69
- ***Audio Library***
- ***Spanish Audio Library***
- ***Spanish Summaries,*** p. 69

B Literary Elements

EXTENDED METAPHOR Mount St. Helens, or Loo-Wit, is described as a woman throughout this poem. Have students describe why Loo-Wit sings in the last stanza. *(Loo-Wit is angry at the scraping boots on her skin, the tearing off of her blanket of trees. She expresses her anger with her singing—a volcanic eruption.)*

Thematic Focus

A Delicate Balance Invite students to explain the delicate balance in this poem. *(The balance is between people and nature. Nature is stronger.)*

Teaching Support

Comparing selections

This selection is compared with "The Flower-Fed Buffaloes" on page 823. A lesson for teaching a comparison of the two selections appears on page 825.

ASSESSMENT

Quick Checks, p. 69

Responding to the Selection

PERSONAL RESPONSE

The poet demonstrates her connection by describing her understanding of Loo-Wit and treating her as a woman with emotions.

Analyzing Literature

1. The poet describes the volcano as an old woman who is upset at what is happening to her.
2. The metaphor helps readers understand that humans and nature are sometimes in conflict.
3. Loo-Wit is erupting. The author describes the volcanic eruption with words like "shaking the sky" and "singing."
4. The message is that humans are destructive and that nature fights back when things get bad.
5. Examples include "huckleberry ropes lay prickly on her neck"—huckleberries grow on the mountainsides; "the shudder of her slopes"—an earthquake that causes stones to dislodge; "the pull of the blanket from her thin shoulder"—removing trees or other vegetation blanketing the mountainside.
6. The poet uses the phrase *centuries of cedar* because it is less wordy and sounds melodious.
7. The poem relates to the theme because it shows what can happen when the balance of nature gets disturbed by humans. In this case, Loo-Wit fights back by creating a volcanic eruption.
8. Students should list elements of the poem that would appeal to the person they choose.

Active Reading and Critical Thinking

Responding to Literature

PERSONAL RESPONSE

- Could you feel the poet's connection to the subject of this poem? How would you describe her connection?

Analyzing Literature

RECALL AND INTERPRET

1. What metaphor does the poet use to describe the volcano?
2. How does the metaphor help you to understand the **theme** of the poem?
3. What is really happening in lines 50–55 of the poem?
4. What message about nature does the poem express?

EVALUATE AND CONNECT

5. In lines 5–6, the poet uses an image of an old woman who "spits her black tobacco." The poet's words are figurative, or metaphoric. She is really describing a volcano throwing out black ashes. That is the literal, or nonfigurative, meaning of the lines. Give three more examples of the poet's use of figurative language, explaining what each one means literally.
6. Find an example of **alliteration** in "Loo-Wit." (See **Literary Terms Handbook,** page R1.) Why do you think the poet uses this poetic device?
7. Theme Connection How is the poem related to the theme of "A Delicate Balance"? Explain.
8. Think of someone who would enjoy reading this poem. What about the poem would appeal to that person?

LITERARY ELEMENTS

Extended Metaphor

A **metaphor** is an **analogy**—a comparison of two basically different things that share, or can be said to share, one or more similarities. Like similes, metaphors create unique, unexpected images that bring a poem to life. In a metaphor, however, the comparison is stated directly, and the words *as* or *like* are not used. In a metaphor, one thing is not *like* another thing; it *is* another thing. In an **extended metaphor,** the comparison is extended through a long passage. In a poem, it may be carried throughout the entire piece. The comparison between an old woman and a volcano in "Loo-Wit" is an extended metaphor.

1. Describe how the poet first introduces the extended metaphor in "Loo-Wit."
2. Explain how the actions of the old woman in the poem mirror the actions of a volcano.

• See **Literary Terms Handbook,** p. R4.

LITERARY ELEMENTS

1. In lines 2–4 of "Loo-Wit," the poet writes, "this old woman/no longer cares/what others think."
2. She spits black tobacco (volcanic ash); her slopes shudder and her arm moves (an earthquake); she sings (erupts).

Additional Resources

Literary Elements Transparency 69

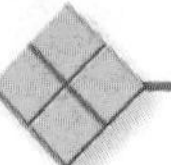

Extending Your Response

Writing About Literature

Analyzing Impressions In a paragraph or two, write about your own reaction as you read "Loo-Wit." First describe the poem's overall impact. Were you confused? challenged? intrigued? excited? Then give examples of how the poet's use of language helped to create the effect the poem had on you.

Literature Groups

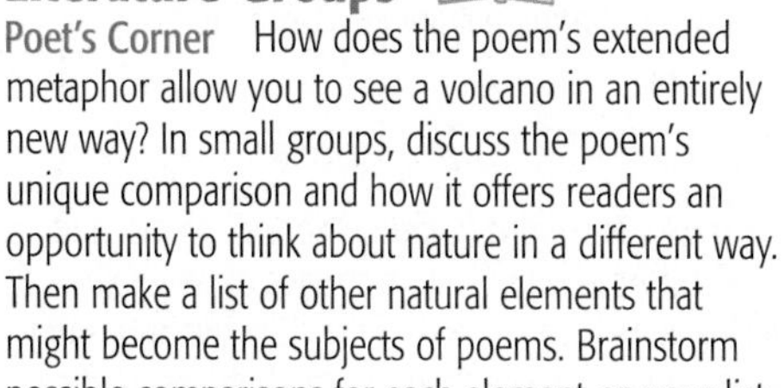

Poet's Corner How does the poem's extended metaphor allow you to see a volcano in an entirely new way? In small groups, discuss the poem's unique comparison and how it offers readers an opportunity to think about nature in a different way. Then make a list of other natural elements that might become the subjects of poems. Brainstorm possible comparisons for each element on your list.

Personal Writing

Extended Metaphor Using the notes you wrote for the **Reading Focus** on page 818, write your own extended metaphor. It can be a poem or a prose paragraph. Compare something in the natural world, such as a volcano or a hurricane, to something else, such as a train or an unruly student. Be creative in your comparison. Use sensory language and vivid imagery in your extended metaphor.

Performing

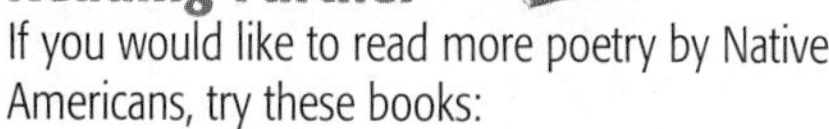

Role-Play Work with a partner. While one of you reads the poem aloud, the other will role-play the actions of the old woman described in the poem. Use props such as a blanket, a boot, twigs, stones, or chairs pushed together to make a "bumpy bed." Practice until you feel comfortable sharing your dramatization with your classmates.

Reading Further

If you would like to read more poetry by Native Americans, try these books:

In the Trail of the Wind: American Indian Poems and Ritual Orations by John Bierhorst

Rising Voices: Writings of Young Native Americans ed. by Arlene B. Hirschfelder

Save your work for your portfolio.

Skill Minilesson

Reteach · Review

READING AND THINKING • ELABORATING

What is the meaning of the poem "Loo-Wit"? You might respond in a simple sentence: *"Loo-Wit" is about the eruption of a volcano.* But a skillful thinker will consider a more elaborate response to the question. As you read, try to keep expanding, or elaborating your understanding of a poem by thinking about the different details and images that add rich texture to its meaning.

PRACTICE Reread "Loo-Wit." As you do, pay attention to the details that help you understand the rich texture of the meaning of the poem. In a short paragraph, elaborate on your understanding of the meaning of the poem.

- For more about main idea and details, see **Reading Handbook**, pp. R90–R91.

Extending Your Response

Writing About Literature

Students' paragraphs should
- contain a topic sentence that states how their feelings changed
- use examples from the poem
- contain a summarizing sentence

Literature Groups

Have students list natural events, such as hurricanes. In groups, have them make a combined list. Finally, have them identify comparisons.

Personal Writing

Students' poems or paragraphs should
- compare and contrast something in the natural world with something else
- help others see the subject in a new way

Performing Encourage students to experiment with their voices to create varying effects. Encourage them to experiment with movement as well.

Skill Minilesson

READING AND THINKING
- **ELABORATING**

Students' paragraphs should describe details that add additional layers of meaning and that deepen their understanding.

Additional Resources

Reading Skills Practice Workbook

ASSESSMENT

- ***Quick Checks,*** p. 69
- ***Selection and Theme Assessment,*** pp. 119–120
- ***Performance Assessment,*** p. 65
- ***Testmaker: ExamView Pro***
- ***Interactive Tutor: Self-Assessment***

Before Reading

Objectives

- To read and enjoy a poem about the delicate balance between machines and nature
- To recognize and appreciate alliteration

Skills

Reading/Thinking: Identifying Assumptions
Listening/Speaking: Performing
Collaboration: Literature Groups

Motivating STUDENTS

Selection Focus Transparency 70: Have students list ways in which trains helped and harmed the prairies and the West.

Reading Focus: As an extension of the Reading Focus, have students in small groups think about how the United States would be different if locomotives hadn't carried people westward in the 1800s.

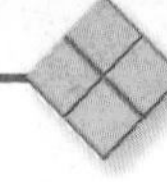

Before You Read

The Flower-Fed Buffaloes

MEET VACHEL LINDSAY

Vachel Lindsay earned the nickname the Vagabond Poet because as a young man he walked from Illinois to Colorado and New Mexico. Along the way, he performed his poems in return for food and shelter. Lindsay's sense of pride in his country is evident in the patriotic images, strong rhythms, and whimsical folklore found in his poetry. Like Walt Whitman, another poet who traveled widely and wrote about the full panorama of American life, Lindsay felt that poetry should touch upon every kind of human experience.

Vachel Lindsay was born in Springfield, Illinois, in 1879 and died in 1931.

READING FOCUS

Imagine the nineteenth-century landscape of the plains west of the Mississippi River. How do you think the locomotive changed that landscape?

Sharing Ideas

Jot down your ideas and then share them in a small-group discussion.

Setting a Purpose

Read this poem to find out how the speaker views the impact of the locomotive upon the natural environment.

BUILDING BACKGROUND

Did You Know? The word *buffalo* is commonly used to refer to the North American bison, a species of wild cattle. These majestic animals may weigh more than two thousand pounds each and stand more than six feet high. Bison once roamed freely throughout much of North America. There were more than 30 million bison in the grasslands west of the Mississippi River when white settlers first arrived. By the end of the nineteenth century, the bison population had been reduced to about five hundred, and many people feared their extinction. Today, the animals are raised on ranches and protected on refuges, and the bison population is increasing.

RESOURCE MANAGER

Teaching Tools and Resources
- Theme Eight Planning Guide
- Literature Groups Sourcebook

Essential Lesson Support

Lesson-Specific Instruction
- Selection Focus Transparency 70
- Literary Elements Transparency 70
- Active Reading Guide,* p. 70
- *inTIME* magazine, pp. 10–11, 16–17

Assessment
- Selection Quick Checks,* p. 70
- Sel. and Theme Assmt., pp. 119–120
- Testmaker: ExamView Pro
- Performance Assessment, p. 65

Systematic Language Instruction
- Gr. & Comp. Hdbk., L. 13.10
- Vocabulary Power, Lesson 35
- Spelling Power, Lesson 31

English Language Learners
- Spanish Summaries, p. 70
- Spanish Translations, p. 212
- Audio Library*
- English, Yes!

Spec. Needs/Strat. Interven.
- Interactive Reading Sourcebook, pp. T240–T241
- Interactive Reading Workbook, p. 142
- Audio Library*

*Also available in Spanish

The Flower-Fed Buffaloes

Vachel Lindsay

View in the 'Grand Detour', 1852. George Catlin. Oil on canvas, 11⅛ x 14¾ in. Thomas Gilcrease Institute of American History and Art, Tulsa, OK.

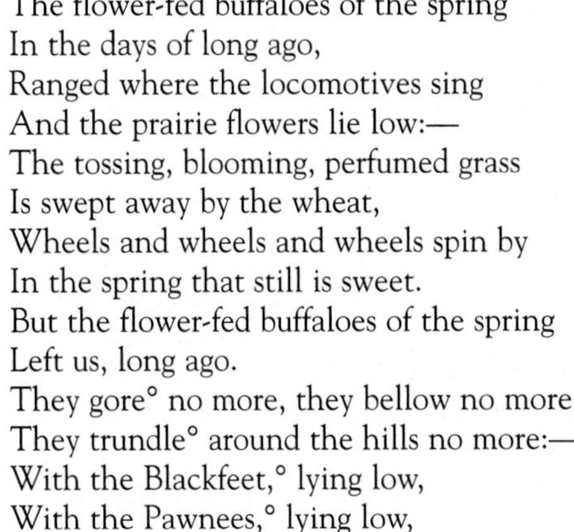

The flower-fed buffaloes of the spring
In the days of long ago,
Ranged where the locomotives sing
And the prairie flowers lie low:—
The tossing, blooming, perfumed grass
Is swept away by the wheat,
Wheels and wheels and wheels spin by
In the spring that still is sweet.
But the flower-fed buffaloes of the spring
Left us, long ago.
They gore° no more, they bellow no more,
They trundle° around the hills no more:—
With the Blackfeet,° lying low,
With the Pawnees,° lying low,
Lying low.

11 **gore:** to pierce with a horn, tusk, or sharp weapon.

12 **trundle:** to move or roll along on, or as if on, wheels.

13 The **Blackfeet** are Native Americans who lived east of the Rocky Mountains in what are now Montana and Saskatchewan, Canada. The homeland of the **Pawnees** was what is now west-central Nebraska.

Reading the Selection

A Active Reading Strategies

PREDICT Ask students to predict the conflict in the poem. *(The conflict may be between technological development and nature.)*

Additional Resources

- ***Active Reading Guide,*** p. 70
- ***Audio Library***
- ***Spanish Audio Library***
- ***Spanish Summaries,*** p. 70

B Literary Elements

ALLITERATION Have students list examples of alliteration from the first four lines of the poem. *(Examples: flower-fed, lie low.)*

C Critical Thinking

IDENTIFYING ASSUMPTIONS Ask how the poet feels about the extinction of the buffalo. *(The poet is sad to witness the end of a type of life.)*

Thematic Focus

A Delicate Balance Invite students to explain how this poem relates to the theme. *(The balance of nature has been upset by technology.)*

ASSESSMENT

- ***Quick Checks,*** p. 70

Teaching Support

Grammar and Language *Minilesson*

Using Hyphens Explain that hyphens are used in a compound adjective before a noun (as in "flower-fed buffaloes"), in some compound nouns ("father-in-law"), and in fractions ("two-thirds") and compound numbers ("forty-one").

Activity Ask students to supply hyphens where needed in the following.

1. great-grandmother
2. pitch-black night
3. junior high school
4. twenty-three
5. two-thirds **L2**

Additional Resources

- ***Grammar and Language Workbook,*** p. 275–276
- ***Grammar and Composition Handbook,*** Lesson 13.8
- ***Writer's Choice,*** Lesson 20.8

COMPARING *selections*

This selection is compared with "Loo-Wit" on page 819. A lesson for teaching a comparison of the two selections appears on page 825.

Responding to the Selection

PERSONAL RESPONSE

In their journals, students should describe the images, along with the feelings they evoke.

Analyzing Literature

1. The buffaloes ranged on the prairie. The wheat has swept away the prairie grass.
2. The wheels of trains spin by where the buffalo once roamed. The spring is still sweet.
3. The buffaloes left long ago. The Pawnee and the Blackfeet left with them.
4. The term *flower-fed* makes the buffalo seem peaceful and gentle. It maintains the harmonious and gentle mood of the poem.
5. Lindsay describes the buffalo as bellowing, trundling, goring, and feeding on flowers. The present has locomotives with "wheels and wheels and wheels" that spin by through massive wheat fields.
6. Lindsay uses *lying low* to mean that something is gone, suppressed, or near extinction.

Extending Your Response

Literature Groups Encourage group members to take turns, so that all the students have a chance to express their ideas.

Performing Encourage students to use their voices to create various effects. Students may want to speak softly, loudly, slowly, or quickly.

Active Reading and Critical Thinking

Responding to Literature

PERSONAL RESPONSE

- What images from the poem linger in your mind? Record them in your journal.

Analyzing Literature

RECALL AND INTERPRET

1. Where did the buffaloes range in the "days of long ago"? What has the wheat swept away?
2. What spins by now where the buffalo once roamed? What is still sweet?
3. When did the buffaloes leave? Who left with them?

EVALUATE AND CONNECT

4. How does the phrase "flower-fed" affect your image of the buffaloes? What effect does it have on the overall **mood** of the poem?
5. What comparisons does Lindsay make between the past and the present?
6. What meanings do you think Lindsay intended for the phrase "lying low"?

LITERARY ELEMENTS

Alliteration

Alliteration is the repetition of the same or very similar consonant sounds in words that are close together–most often, but not always, at the beginnings of words. In "The Flower-Fed Buffaloes," for example, the *f* sound is repeated in the words *flower* and *fed.* Poets use alliteration to emphasize particular words, to establish a mood, or to give their writing a musical tone.

1. Find and list three other examples of alliteration in "The Flower-Fed Buffaloes."
2. Find another poem that contains alliteration. Describe how alliteration affects the poem.

- See **Literary Terms Handbook**, p. R1.

Extending Your Response

Literature Groups

Theme Discussion Review your notes from the **Reading Focus** on page 822. Then, working in small groups, discuss the theme of "The Flower-Fed Buffaloes."

Performing

Poetry Reading Give your own reading of this poem. Listen to the sounds and rhythms of the poem as you practice reading aloud. When you are ready, read the poem aloud to the class.

Save your work for your portfolio.

LITERARY ELEMENTS

1. Examples of alliteration are: lie low; spring that still is sweet; wheels and wheels and wheels; left us, long ago
2. Paragraphs should use examples from the poem to support their ideas about alliteration.

Additional Resources

Literary Elements Transparency 70

ASSESSMENT

- ***Quick Checks,*** p. 70
- ***Selection and Theme Assessment,*** pp. 119–120
- ***Performance Assessment,*** p. 65
- ***Testmaker: ExamView Pro***
- ***Interactive Tutor: Self-Assessment***

824 THEME 8

Critical Thinking

COMPARING SELECTIONS

Loo-Wit and The Flower-Fed Buffaloes

COMPARE THEMES

View in the 'Grand Detour', 1852 (detail).

"Loo-Wit" and "The Flower-Fed Buffaloes" are poems that portray the power and beauty of nature. The theme of nature and its relationship to human beings and civilization plays an important role in both poems.

- How does "Loo-Wit" portray the force of nature? What role do humans play in the poem?
- How does "The Flower-Fed Buffaloes" portray the power and beauty of nature? What role do humans play in this poem?
- Compare and contrast how the relationship between nature and human beings is portrayed in these poems.

COMPARE POETIC LANGUAGE

Both poems are filled with sounds, imagery, and figurative language that help readers appreciate the total effect of the poem.

1. In small groups, talk about the total effect of each poem.
2. Pick out your favorite images, sounds, similes, or metaphors from each poem. Talk about each of your examples and why you chose them.
3. Share your thoughts and feelings with your classmates in a full-class forum.

COMPARE RESPONSES

Compare your overall feelings and attitudes about these poems. In one or two paragraphs, explain your thoughts and feelings as you answer the following questions:

- How are these poems alike? How are they different?
- Which poem do you prefer? Why?
- Which poem did you learn more from? What did you learn?

COMPARING selections

Objective

- To compare two poems that deal with the theme of nature and its relationship to civilization

COMPARE THEMES

- "Loo-Wit" portrays nature as something that can strike back at humans if they take advantage of it. Humans are destructive
- "The Flower-Fed Buffaloes" portrays nature as something that humans can destroy or change
- In "Loo-Wit" nature can defend itself, but in "Buffaloes," nature is at the mercy of civilization. In both poems, humans alter nature

COMPARE POETIC LANGUAGE

Student groups should

- allow each member to present reasons for liking a favorite image, sound, simile, or metaphor
- present the group's ideas in a full-class forum

COMPARE RESPONSES

Students' paragraphs should

- describe how the two poems are alike and different
- explain which poem the student prefers and why
- analyze which poem the student learned more from and describe what was learned

Additional Resources

 ***Literature Groups Sourcebook***

Teaching Support

PORTFOLIO OPTIONS

Select and Reflect Have students reflect on the paragraphs they wrote for the Compare Responses activity by asking themselves these questions:

- Do my paragraphs contain examples that show how the two poems are alike and different?
- Have I given careful thought to what I can learn from each poem?

Students should clip their reflections to their paragraphs and place them in their portfolios. **L1**

Additional Resources

Writing Assessment and Portfolio Management, pp. 38–45

Before Reading

Objectives

- To read and analyze an essay
- To identify the author's purpose
- To rewrite the essay from a different point of view

Skills

Reading/Thinking: Evaluating; Problem and Solution; Cause and Effect
Writing: Journal Entry
Vocabulary: Prefix *de-*
Grammar/Language: Run-on Sentences
Listening/Speaking: Literature Groups; Oral Report
Collaboration: Literature Groups

Motivating → STUDENTS

Selection Focus Transparency 71: Have students read and discuss the quote about the threat of extinction for some bird species.

Reading Focus: As an extension of the Reading Focus, invite students to work in small groups and create a dramatization of one of their humorous stories. Then have them perform it for the class.

Before You Read

Turkeys

MEET BAILEY WHITE

Not many first-grade teachers become famous radio celebrities or have books on the national bestseller list, but Bailey White is no ordinary first-grade teacher. She calls teaching first graders in her south Georgia town her "honorable job." After school she entertains listeners with her regular commentaries on National Public Radio's *All Things Considered*. White has written two collections of humorous autobiographical stories, *Mama Makes Up Her Mind* and *Sleeping at the Starlite Motel*.

Bailey White was born in 1948. This essay was published in 1993.

READING FOCUS

What amusing events do you remember from when you were a very young child? Choose one amusing event from that time in your life.

QuickWrite
Make a list of at least three details that you recall about that past event.

Setting a Purpose
Read this humorous essay to find out about the author's childhood experience with turkeys and ornithologists.

BUILDING BACKGROUND

The Time and Place It is the 1950s in a small town in southern Georgia.

Did You Know? An *ornithologist* is a scientist who studies birds. The ornithologists in this selection study birds native to the southeastern United States, including wild turkeys and several kinds of woodpeckers. The chuck-will's-widow, another bird mentioned in the essay, is shown here. These birds resemble whippoorwills but are somewhat larger.

VOCABULARY PREVIEW

domestic (də mes′ tik) *adj.* describes animals living with or near human beings and cared for by them; p. 828
degrade (di grād′) *v.* to lower in character or quality; make less pure; p. 828
demise (di mīz′) *n.* death; end; p. 828
sluggish (slug′ ish) *adj.* lacking energy or alertness; p. 828
elaborate (i lab′ ər it) *adj.* worked out carefully and thoroughly; detailed; complicated; p. 829
undertake (un′ dər tāk′) *v.* to enter into (a task); attempt; p. 829

RESOURCE MANAGER

Teaching Tools and Resources
- Theme Eight Planning Guide
- Literature Groups Sourcebook

Essential Lesson Support

Lesson-Specific Instruction
- Selection Focus Transparency 71
- Literary Elements Transparency 71
- Active Reading Guide,* p. 71
- Selection Vocabulary Practice, p. 50

Assessment
- Selection Quick Checks,* p. 71
- Sel. and Theme Assmt., pp. 121–122
- Testmaker: ExamView Pro
- Performance Assessment, p. 66

Systematic Language Instruction
- Gr. & Comp. Hdbk., L. 14.1–14.2
- Vocabulary Power, Lesson 36
- Spelling Power, Lesson 32

English Language Learners
- Spanish Summaries, p. 71
- Spanish Translations, pp. 213–214
- Audio Library*
- English, Yes!

Spec. Needs/Strat. Interven.
- Interactive Reading Sourcebook, pp. T242–T244
- Interactive Reading Workbook, pp. 143–144
- Audio Library*

*Also available in Spanish

TURKEYS

Bailey White

Something about my mother attracts ornithologists.[1] It all started years ago when a couple of them discovered she had a rare species of woodpecker coming to her bird feeder. They came in the house and sat around the window, exclaiming and taking pictures with big fancy cameras. But long after the red cockaded woodpeckers had gone to roost in their sticky little holes in the red hearts of our big old pine trees, and the chuck-will's-widows had started to sing their night chorus, the ornithologists were still there.

1. *Ornithologists* (ôr′ nə thol′ ə jists) are people who study birds or are experts on birds.

Reading the Selection

SUMMARY

When Bailey White was growing up, there were often ornithologists in and around her house, especially concerned with keeping wild and domestic turkeys from mixing. Once, when Bailey was in bed with a high fever, the ornithologists rescued turkey eggs and to keep them warm put them in her bed. She awoke with sixteen wild turkey chicks snuggling against her.

Spanish Summaries, p. 71

A Active Reading Strategies

CONNECT Have a volunteer read the first paragraph and discuss what the class knows about the different types of birds mentioned. Ask if any students have bird feeders, what kinds of birds come to them, and what they look like or what kinds of sound they make.

VOCABULARY If you haven't previewed the selection vocabulary with students, stop and remind them to use context clues to unlock the meanings of new vocabulary words.

Additional Resources

Active Reading Guide, p. 71
Audio Library
Spanish Audio Library

Teaching Support

CONNECTING TO OTHER SELECTIONS

The chart at the right shows three ways to connect "Turkeys" to other selections in this book.

For specific teaching strategies, see The ***Theme Eight Planning Guide***.

Connection		Title
Life Skills: Problem Solving	→	"Oh Broom, Get to Work," p. 383
Thematic: Challenges	→	"The Fish Crisis," p. 295
Literary: Humor	→	"Who's on First?" p. 555

Cultural Note

John James Audubon (1785–1851) was an American ornithologist and artist. During the early 1800s, he spent years traveling the country observing, studying, and drawing birds. The Audubon Society—an organization that seeks to protect birds—is named for him.

B Literary Elements

AUTHOR'S PURPOSE: *Setting* Ask students to think about the time and place the events take place. *(The events probably take place in the Carolina region in the 1950s.)*

C Literary Elements

AUTHOR'S PURPOSE What is Bailey White trying to convey to the readers in this paragraph? *(Bailey describes the demise and degradation of the birds, which upsets her, and she wants to share this information.)*

D Active Reading Strategies

PREDICT What text clues can help students predict why the ornithologists are interested in the girl's health? *(The "102 fever" is a context clue that might help them predict what the ornithologists' purpose might be.)*

There always seemed to be three or four of them wandering around our place, discussing the body fat of hummingbirds, telling cruel jokes about people who couldn't tell a pileated woodpecker from an ivory bill,[2] and staying for supper.

B In those days, during the 1950s, the big concern of ornithologists in our area was the wild turkey. They were rare, and the pure-strain wild turkeys had begun to interbreed with farmers' domestic stock. The species was being degraded. It was extinction by dilution,[3] and to the ornithologists it was just as tragic as the more dramatic demise of the passenger pigeon or the Carolina parakeet.[4]

C One ornithologist had devised a formula to compute the ratio of domestic to pure-strain wild turkey in an individual bird by comparing the angle of flight at takeoff and the rate of acceleration. And in those sad days, the turkeys were flying low and slow.[5]

It was during that time, the spring when I was six years old, that I caught the measles. I had a high fever, and my mother was worried about me. She kept the house quiet and dark and crept around silently, trying different methods of cooling me down.

Even the ornithologists stayed away—but not out of fear of the measles or respect for a household with sickness. The fact was, they had discovered a wild turkey nest. According to the formula, the hen was pure-strain wild—not a taint of the sluggish domestic bird in her blood—and the ornithologists were camping in the woods, protecting her nest from predators and taking pictures.

D One night our phone rang. It was one of the ornithologists. "Does your little girl still have measles?" he asked.

"Yes," said my mother. "She's very sick. Her temperature is 102."

"I'll be right over," said the ornithologist.

In five minutes a whole carload of them arrived. They marched solemnly into the house, carrying a cardboard box. "A hundred two, did you say? Where is she?" they asked my mother.

They crept into my room and set the box down on the bed. I was barely conscious, and when I opened my eyes, their worried faces hovering over me seemed to float out of the darkness like giant, glowing eggs.

2. The *cockaded woodpeckers* have red crests. The *chuck-will's-widows* are night-flying birds. The *pileated woodpecker* has a bright red crest on the top of its head. Ornithologists use the adjective *pileated* to describe any bird with a bright red crest. *Cockaded* indicates a small tuft of feathers on the top of the head; *ivory bill* refers to an ivory-colored bill.
3. After generations of interbreeding, the wild turkeys became less wild, a weakening *(dilution)* that could lead to their gradual dying out *(extinction)*.
4. Once common in the eastern United States, the *passenger pigeon* and the *Carolina parakeet* are now extinct.
5. Wild turkeys can fly, but domestic turkeys cannot. Their *low and slow* flight indicates that the wild birds have lost much of their pure strain.

Vocabulary

domestic (də mes′ tik) *adj.* describes animals living with or near human beings and cared for by them
degrade (di grād′) *v.* to lower in character or quality; make less pure
demise (di mīz′) *n.* death; end
sluggish (slug′ ish) *adj.* lacking energy or alertness

Teaching Support

MEETING INDIVIDUAL NEEDS — SPECIAL NEEDS

Learning Disabled Using a story frame helps learning-disabled students actively describe the story to themselves.

Activity Have students work in pairs to complete a story-frame chart for "Turkeys." **L1**

Characters	
Problem/Conflict	
Event 1	
Event 2	
Resolution	

Additional Resources

Inclusion Strategies

They snatched the covers off me and felt me all over. They consulted in whispers.

"Feels just right, I'd say."

"A hundred two—can't miss if we tuck them up close and she lies still."

I closed my eyes then, and after a while the ornithologists drifted away, their pale faces bobbing up and down on the black wave of fever.

The next morning I was better. For the first time in days I could think. The memory of the ornithologists with their whispered voices and their bony, cool hands was like a dream from another life. But when I pulled down the covers, there staring up at me with googly eyes and wide mouths, were sixteen fuzzy baby turkeys and the cracked chips and caps of sixteen brown speckled eggs.

E

I was a sensible child. I gently stretched myself out. The eggshells crackled, and the turkey babies fluttered and cheeped and snuggled against me. I laid my aching head back on the pillow and closed my eyes. "The ornithologists," I whispered. "The ornithologists have been here."

It seems the turkey hen had been so disturbed by the elaborate protective measures that had been undertaken in her behalf that she had abandoned her nest on the night the eggs were due to hatch. It was a cold night. The ornithologists, not having an incubator to hand, used their heads and came up with the next best thing.

F

The baby turkeys and I gained our strength together. When I was finally able to get out of bed and feebly creep around the house, the turkeys peeped and cheeped around my ankles, scrambling to keep up with me and tripping over their own big spraddle-toed[6] feet. When I went outside for the first time, the turkeys tumbled after me down the steps and scratched around in the yard while I sat in the sun.

Finally, in late summer, the day came when they were ready to fly for the first time as adult birds. The ornithologists gathered. I ran down the hill, and the turkeys ran too. Then, one by one, they took off. They flew high and fast. The ornithologists made V's with their thumbs and forefingers, measuring angles. They consulted their stopwatches and paced off distances. They scribbled in their tiny notebooks. Finally they looked at each other. They sighed. They smiled. They jumped up and down and hugged each other. "One hundred percent pure wild turkey!" they said.

Nearly forty years have passed since then. In many ways the world is a worse place now. But there's a vaccine for measles. And the woods where I live are full of pure wild turkeys. I like to think they are all descendants of those sixteen birds I saved from the vigilance of the ornithologists.

G

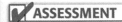

6. The toes of a *spraddle-toed* bird spread out in different directions.

Vocabulary

elaborate (i lab′ ər it) *adj.* worked out carefully and thoroughly; detailed; complicated

undertake (un′ dər tāk′) *v.* to enter into (a task); attempt

E Active Reading Strategies

VISUALIZE Have students visualize the scene of a six-year-old in bed with sixteen fuzzy baby turkeys and cracked chips and caps of eggshells around her. What do they think of the scene? *(Most students will recognize that this is a very humorous scene.)*

F Critical Thinking

EVALUATING What serious miscalculation do the ornithologists make and how could it have affected the outcome? *(They think that protecting the turkey hen from strangers would save the eggs, not realizing they also were "strangers" to the hen—they are surprised when she abandons her nest. If they had not thought quickly to use Bailey as the "incubator," all their hopes of a pure breed would have been dashed.)*

G Literary Elements

AUTHOR'S PURPOSE: ***Point of View*** Ask students to discuss Bailey's feelings for the ornithologists. Have them support their statements with examples from the essay. *(Bailey seems to have an admiration for the ornithologists even though she presents them with humor and shows how much they care about the birds.)*

Thematic Focus

A Delicate Balance Ask students how this selection relates to the theme. *(The ornithologists are trying to restore the balance of nature.)*

ASSESSMENT

Quick Checks, p. 71

Reading Minilesson

Problem and Solution Even though "Turkeys" is presented in a humorous tone, the author's purpose is to bring attention to the serious issue of bird extinction. She presents the reader with some basic survival problems birds face and presents some funny solutions.

Activity Have students work in small groups to discuss the story's main problems and how they were resolved. Suggest that students use a chart to keep track of the problems and their solutions. They can use the chart to help them answer the questions that follow the selection. **L2**

Additional Resources

Reading Skills Practice Workbook

Responding to the Selection

PERSONAL RESPONSE

Some students may think that it would be fun to have ornithologists and baby turkeys in the house. Others might object to having to share their backyard with sixteen turkeys.

Analyzing Literature

1. They discovered a rare species of woodpecker there.
2. They were breeding with domestic turkeys and losing the ability to fly.
3. "She kept the house quiet and dark and crept around silently, trying different methods of cooling me down."
4. Bailey's high body temperature would keep them warm enough to survive.
5. Yes. She describes in a humorous way the results of the "elaborate protective measures" taken on behalf of the mother turkey.
6. They took time to protect the mother and rescue the eggs, putting them in Bailey's bed.
7. Yes. She lets the ornithologists stay around her house and use her sick daughter's bed to save the birds.
8. Vigilance refers to the way they watched the mother turkey and eventually scared her away. Bailey provided a way to save the birds once the mother was gone.
9. She creates a mystery and says something funny all at once, which gives the story a lighthearted and humorous feeling.
10. Students' answers should rely on humor to explain the reasons for their responses.

Active Reading and Critical Thinking

Responding to Literature

PERSONAL RESPONSE

- Do you think you would have enjoyed living with Bailey White's family? Why or why not?

Analyzing Literature

RECALL

1. Why did the ornithologists first start coming to Bailey White's house?
2. Why were the scientists concerned about the wild turkeys?
3. Find and quote a passage that tells you something about Bailey White's mother.
4. Why did the ornithologists need Bailey to incubate the eggs?

Brackets connect questions that are paired to develop higher-level thinking skills.

INTERPRET

5. Do you think Bailey found the ornithologists amusing? Support your opinion.
6. In what ways does the author make clear the scientists' concern for wild turkeys?
7. Do you think Bailey's mother is a generous person? Why or why not?
8. The author says she saved the turkeys "from the vigilance of the ornithologists." What does she mean?

EVALUATE AND CONNECT

9. **Tone** is the attitude a writer expresses about his or her subject. How does White's first sentence help to set the tone of the story?
10. How would you react if a group of scientists barged into your bedroom when you were sick?

LITERARY ELEMENTS

Author's Purpose

The **author's purpose** is the writer's goal in writing a particular work. For example, the author of the humorous essay "Turkeys" probably wanted to **entertain** readers. An author's purpose in writing a newspaper editorial is probably to **persuade** readers of a viewpoint. The purpose of an encyclopedia article is usually to **inform.** Sometimes, especially in serious poetry, an author's purpose is to **express** an idea, a feeling, or a truth.

1. How well does Bailey White achieve her purpose of entertaining her readers? Support your opinion with examples from the selection.
2. What other purpose or purposes does White seem to have? How do you know?

- See **Literary Terms Handbook,** p. R2.

LITERARY ELEMENTS

1. She presents many funny scenes, such as putting the chicks into her bed, but she also makes it clear to the reader that these birds are facing extinction.
2. White's purpose is to educate people about endangered species. She cites and describes several examples.

Additional Resources

Literary Elements Transparency 71

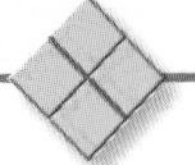

Extending Your Response

Personal Writing

Childhood Memories Look back at your QuickWrite list from the **Reading Focus** on page 826. Use the details on the list to write a journal entry about that humorous event in your life. Be sure to explain why that event has stayed in your memory. You may want to share your entry with your friends or family.

Literature Groups

Picture This Imagine that an article about young Bailey's adventures with the turkeys is going to appear in a wildlife magazine. Design a cover for the magazine that features a drawing and brief "teaser" to interest readers in the story. Post all the covers in the room. Discuss how they succeed at grabbing the attention of readers.

interNET CONNECTION

Did you know that Benjamin Franklin wanted to make the turkey, rather than the bald eagle, our national bird? To learn more about turkeys or other birds, type "birds," or the name of a type of bird, into a search engine.

Writing About Literature

Point of View "Turkeys" tells of an experience Bailey White had when she was six years old. The story is told from her point of view. Imagine how one of the ornithologists might remember the incident. Then write a brief summary of the story from the ornithologist's point of view.

Interdisciplinary Activity

Science Sharpen your own ornithological skills. Do some research on birds, using both print (books, magazines) and electronic (Internet sites, CD-ROMs, video tapes) resources. Then prepare a brief oral report for your class on how to tell the difference between a pileated woodpecker and an ivory-billed woodpecker–or between any other pair of birds common in your area. If you can, illustrate your report with photos or drawings of the birds. If appropriate, and you're a good whistler, you might also demonstrate how their songs differ.

Reading Further

Here are some more humorous autobiographies you might want to read

My Life and Hard Times by James Thurber

Growing Up by Russell Baker

For a hilarious memoir about an efficiency expert who tried to run his family (which included twelve children) like a factory, try

Cheaper by the Dozen by Frank B. Gilbreth and Ernestine Gilbreth Carey

Save your work for your portfolio.

Extending Your Response

Personal Writing

Students' journal entries should

- describe a humorous event in their lives from when they were very young
- explain why the event has stayed in their memories

Writing About Literature

Students' summaries should

- describe the events of the story
- be told from one of the ornithologists' point of view

Literature Groups Encourage students to make several sketches, trying to give a strong feeling about the characters and events in the story. Then have them create their cover and write the "teaser."

Interdisciplinary Activity Help students locate information in library reference books or on the Internet. Before they begin, you might have them list birds that are found in your area and identify the times of year they can observe specific types.

ASSESSMENT

- ***Quick Checks,*** p. 71
- ***Selection and Theme Assessment,*** pp. 121–122
- ***Performance Assessment,*** p. 66
- ***Testmaker: ExamView Pro***
- ***Interactive Tutor: Self-Assessment***

Before Reading

Objectives

- To read and analyze a poem
- To identify the effect of end-stopped rhymes
- To describe the effect of repetition in a poem

Skills

Reading/Thinking: Inferring
Writing: Poem
Grammar/Language: Mechanics: Semicolon, Colon
Listening/Speaking: Oral Reading; Choral Speaking
Collaboration: Listening and Speaking; Literature Groups

Motivating STUDENTS

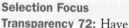

Selection Focus Transparency 72: Have students read and discuss the quote about how poems can have multiple meanings and evoke a range of feelings.

Reading Focus: As an extension of the Reading Focus, have students write a paragraph, using precise language and sensory imagery, about what it means to be a part of a family or group and share responsibilities.

Before You Read

The Pasture

MEET ROBERT FROST

Robert Frost worked as a mill worker, a shoemaker, a schoolteacher, a newspaper editor, and a farmer before he finally became a published poet. He lived most of his adult life on farms in Vermont and New Hampshire. "Three things have followed me," he wrote, "writing, teaching, and a little farming." His poems, inspired by the rural life and scenery of New England, are known for their plain language and natural rhythms.

Robert Frost was born in 1874 and died in 1963.

READING FOCUS

How do you feel about chores you're asked to do? Do you think it's possible to enjoy doing chores?

Sharing Ideas

Think about the questions above. Then share your thoughts in a small-group discussion. Does everyone feel the same way?

Setting a Purpose

Read this poem to discover how the speaker feels about his chores.

BUILDING BACKGROUND

Robert Frost, one of the most honored poets in America, won the Pulitzer Prize for Poetry four times. In 1961, when John F. Kennedy was elected president of the United States, Frost made history. At age eighty-seven, he became the first poet to read a poem at a presidential inauguration. His poem, "The Gift Outright," was heard by millions of people.

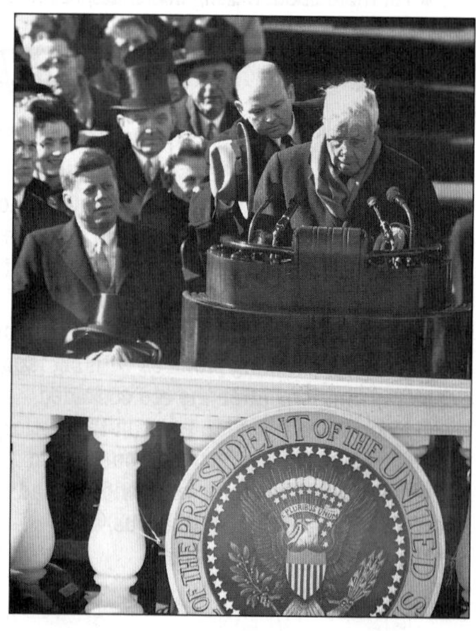

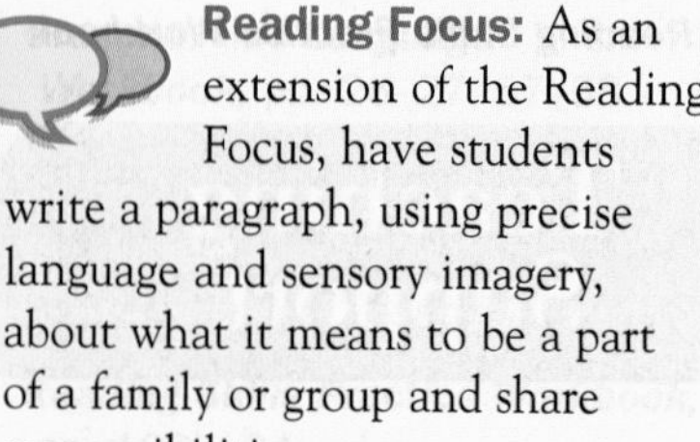

RESOURCE MANAGER

Teaching Tools and Resources
- Theme Eight Planning Guide
- Literature Groups Sourcebook

Essential Lesson Support

Lesson-Specific Instruction
- Selection Focus Transparency 72
- Literary Elements Transparency 72
- Active Reading Guide,* p. 72

Assessment
- Selection Quick Checks,* p. 72
- Sel. and Theme Assmt., p. 123
- Testmaker: ExamView Pro
- Performance Assessment, p. 67

Systematic Language Instruction
- Gr. & Comp. Hdbk., L. 14.3

English Language Learners
- Spanish Summaries, p. 72
- Spanish Translations, p. 215
- Audio Library*
- English, Yes!

Spec. Needs/Strat. Interven.
- Interactive Reading Sourcebook, pp. T244–T247
- Interactive Reading Workbook, p. 145
- Audio Library*

*Also available in Spanish

The Pasture

Robert Frost

I'm going out to clean the pasture spring;
I'll only stop to rake the leaves away
(And wait to watch the water clear, I may):
I sha'n't be gone long.—You come too.

I'm going out to fetch the little calf
That's standing by the mother. It's so young,
It totters when she licks it with her tongue.
I sha'n't be gone long.—You come too.

Autumn, 1958. Eric Sloane. Oil on Masonite, 26¾ x 21¾ in. Private collection. Would the title "You Come Too" be appropriate for this painting? Why or why not?

Reading the Selection

A Active Reading Strategies

VISUALIZE Encourage students to read each stanza carefully to picture as many details as possible.

Additional Resources

- ***Active Reading Guide,*** p. 72
- ***Audio Library***
- ***Spanish Audio Library***
- ***Spanish Summaries,*** p. 72

B Literary Elements

RHYTHM: *End-Stopped Lines* Help students see how Frost creates a natural pause at the end of each line. *(He also repeats the rhyme scheme in the second and third lines of each stanza: abbc/deec.)*

C Author's Craft

ASSONANCE Frost uses this technique by repeating the words *you* and *too* in the last line of each stanza.

Thematic Focus

A Delicate Balance Ask students how this poem relates to the theme "A Delicate Balance."

ASSESSMENT

- ***Quick Checks,*** p. 72

Teaching Support

Listening and Speaking Minilesson

Choral Speaking As performers, students must read critically, making a new language style and tone their own.

Activity Break the class into two groups for a choral reading of the poem. During rehearsal, encourage students to work on such vocal traits as musicality, dynamics, enunciation, and expressiveness to communicate meaning and engage listeners. Encourage them to use appropriate intonations (clued by punctuation) and reflect Frost's tone (clued by Frost's word choice and sentence construction). As one group performs, invite the other group to listen and enjoy the reading. L1

Literature & Humanities

Have students compare the poem with the painting *Crossing the Pasture,* in *Introducing Art,* page 68. Ask students which elements of the pasture each work might be celebrating.

Responding to the Selection

PERSONAL RESPONSE

Frost describes these chores in an inviting way and names jobs that are important to do; many students may think they would enjoy doing them.

Analyzing Literature

1. The speaker is going to clean the pasture spring. He will watch the water clear.
2. He must also fetch the little calf.
3. Most students will say that the speaker is an adult man or woman who lives on a farm and loves the pasture.
4. The poem is an invitation; repeating the last line reinforces its intent.
5. The speaker might be inviting a younger person, perhaps the speaker's child, though it could also be the reader.
6. They signify a pause. Omitting the pause would lessen the emphasis on the words "You come too."
7. An example of alliteration is: "And wait to watch the water clear, I may." The alliterations make the sound of the poem flow easily.
8. He describes the chore in a very caring way; his descriptions evoke a reverence for life and the land: "and wait to watch the water clear, I may;" "It's so young,/It totters when she licks it with her tongue."
9. He cares about them a great deal.
10. Students should name examples and explain why the chores might make them feel happy and satisfied.

Active Reading and Critical Thinking

Responding to Literature

PERSONAL RESPONSE

- Did the poem make you rethink the ideas that you shared in the **Reading Focus** on page 834? Explain.

Analyzing Literature

RECALL

1. What is the speaker going out to clean? What might he wait for?
2. What is the other chore the speaker is planning?

Brackets connect questions that are paired to develop higher-level thinking skills.

INTERPRET

3. Imagine and describe the speaker of "The Pasture."
4. Why do you think the poet ends both stanzas with the same line?

EVALUATE AND CONNECT

5. Whom do you think the speaker is inviting to "come too"?
6. What is the purpose of the dashes in lines 4 and 8? How would the poem sound different without the dashes?
7. Find an example of **alliteration** in the poem. (See **Literary Terms Handbook**, page R1.) How does this poetic device affect the way you read the poem aloud?
8. How does Frost make a common farm chore seem interesting? Use examples from the poem to explain your answer.
9. **Theme Connection** What can you infer from the second stanza about the speaker's attitude toward his farm animals?
10. **Personal Connection** What chores could you do that might make you feel happy and satisfied?

LITERARY ELEMENTS

Rhythm: End-Stopped Lines

When a pause occurs naturally at the end of a line of poetry, it is called an **end-stopped line.** The length of the stop, as you read or recite the poem, depends on the sense of the words and the kind of punctuation used. A period, question mark, exclamation point, colon, or semicolon generally call for a somewhat longer stop than a comma or dash. When a poet uses no punctuation at all, readers need to use the sense of the words to figure out whether lines are end-stopped. Because end-stops at every line can make a poem, especially a long one, seem monotonous, most poets generally avoid using them at every line.

1. Which lines in "The Pasture" are end-stopped? What punctuation marks does Frost use to indicate the pauses?
2. Read "The Pasture" out loud twice. First stop at the end of each line. Then pause only when the punctuation directs you to do so. Which reading makes the poem easier to understand?

- See **Literary Terms Handbook**, p. R9.

LITERARY ELEMENTS

1. Lines 1, 3, 4, 7, and 8 are end-stopped. Frost uses a semicolon, colon, and period to indicate the pauses.
2. The punctuation makes it easier to understand; stopping at the end of every line breaks up the connected thoughts.

Additional Resources

Literary Elements Transparency 72

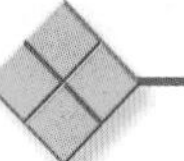

Extending Your Response

Writing About Literature

Mood The speaker in the poem seems to anticipate enjoying his chores. Write a paragraph describing the mood of the poem. How does the invitation at the end of each stanza contribute to the mood?

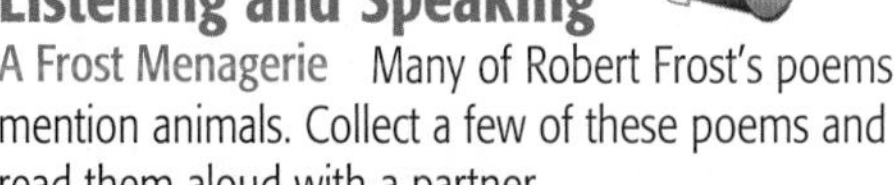

Listening and Speaking

A Frost Menagerie Many of Robert Frost's poems mention animals. Collect a few of these poems and read them aloud with a partner.

Creative Writing

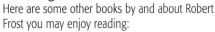

An Invitation Try to think about your own chores in a more interesting way. Write a poem inviting someone to join you as you go about your work.

Literature Groups

Pastoral Images The images in "The Pasture" are vivid and concrete. Draw a picture of the image created in one of the stanzas. Then compare your work with others and choose the drawing that best conveys the poet's vision of farm life.

Reading Further

Here are some other books by and about Robert Frost you may enjoy reading:

You Come, Too by Robert Frost

A Restless Spirit by Natalie S. Bober

Save your work for your portfolio.

Skill Minilesson

Reteach · Review

GRAMMAR AND LANGUAGE • MECHANICS: SEMICOLON, COLON

The semicolon and colon separate parts of a sentence that might otherwise be confused.

Rule 1: Use a semicolon to join parts of a compound sentence when a conjunction, such as *and, but,* or *or,* is not used.

Frost wrote poetry; he also worked a farm.

Rule 2: Use a colon to introduce a list of items that end a sentence. Use words such as *these* or *the following* to signal that a list is coming.

Try these books by Frost: *Birches; You Come, Too; Christmas Trees.*

PRACTICE Practice the rules by adding a semicolon or colon to each sentence.

1. This bicycle comes in the following colors red, blue, silver, and black.
2. Soccer clubs are very popular these clubs often play clubs from other cities.
3. We bought a new computer I'm eager to try it.
4. When you pack for the camping trip take these items flashlight, sleeping bag, warm clothes.

For more about semicolons and colons, see **Language Handbook**, pp. R38–R39.

Extending Your Response

Writing About Literature

Students' paragraphs should

- describe the mood of the poem
- explain how the end of each stanza contributes to the mood

Creative Writing

Students' poems should

- invite another person to join them as they work on a project or chore
- describe the work in terms that would convince someone to join in

Listening and Speaking Help students find other Frost poems. Tell them to read each poem more than once to see how new details emerge with each reading.

Literature Groups Have students take time to clearly visualize the scene before they begin drawing. When they compare images, discuss how the same words can evoke different impressions.

Skill Minilesson

GRAMMAR AND LANGUAGE

• **MECHANICS:** SEMICOLON, COLON

1. This bicycle comes in the following colors: red, blue, silver, and black.
2. Soccer clubs are very popular; these clubs often play clubs from other cities.
3. We bought a new computer; I'm eager to try it.
4. When you pack for the camping trip take these items: flashlight, sleeping bag, warm clothes.

Additional Resources

- ***Grammar and Language Workbook,*** pp. 265–266
- ***Grammar and Composition Handbook,*** Lesson 13.5
- ***Writers Choice,*** Lesson 20.5

ASSESSMENT

- ***Quick Checks,*** p. 72
- ***Selection and Theme Assessment,*** p. 123
- ***Performance Assessment,*** p. 67
- ***Testmaker: ExamView Pro***
- ***Interactive Tutor: Self-Assessment***

Objective

- To understand the elements of short forms of poetry

Teaching Strategies

Write the following lines on the board:

Yesterday, I bought
A cat at the pet shelter
On Main Street downtown.

Ask students to discuss whether they think these lines qualify as poetry or not. Some students might find something poetic in the lines, but many won't. After students have read the haiku poem on page 838, point out that the "poem" on the board has three lines, the appropriate number of syllables in each line, and an image from nature. Does that make it a haiku? Why or why not? *(No, it is a sentence broken up into lines and syllables, lacking interesting language, emotion, and imagery. It has the form of haiku, but not the content.)*

Refer students to the elements that make up the essence of haiku, described on pages 838–839: simplicity, depth, and a bond between human beings and the natural world.

Teaching Support

SHORT FORMS OF POETRY

Haiku, cinquains, and limericks are all short forms of poetry. Do you know this classic haiku?

> An old silent pond . . .
> A frog jumps into the pond,
> splash! Silence again.
>
> *–Matsuo Bashō*

Over three centuries old, this haiku was written in Japanese by Matsuo Bashō (mät sü′ ō bä′ shō), the poet who perfected the haiku form.

HAIKU

Haiku originated in Japan. A traditional haiku has only three lines made up of five syllables, seven syllables, and five syllables. Within this compact form, poets present simple images, often linked by unstated connections. It's left up to readers to discover, or to imagine, what the connections might be. What connections can you discover in the following haiku by an American writer?

> A balmy spring wind
> Reminding me of something
> I cannot recall
>
> *–Richard Wright*

Haiku are as striking for what they don't include as for what they do. Traditional haiku have no rhyme and no figures of speech. They usually include at least one nature image and one, often subtle, reference to a specific season of the year. (In the haiku by Bashō, the frog suggests summer.)

Translators of haiku sometimes maintain the traditions and sometimes alter them. In English translation, some haiku have fewer or more than seventeen syllables, and some even include rhyme:

> A morning-glory vine
> all blossoming, has thatched
> this hut of mine.
>
> *–Kobayashi Issa,*
> *translated by Harold G. Henderson*

MEETING INDIVIDUAL NEEDS

ENGLISH LANGUAGE LEARNERS

Translation A group translation project can give English language learners a chance to bring artistic works from their first language into class and practice explaining the words and images to others.

Activity Ask students to find a short poem written in their native language. Have students work in small groups to translate and illustrate these poems.

Make bilingual dictionaries available if possible. Each group can work on one or two poems, depending on how many non-English poems students have brought into class.

As poets of many eras and cultures work with haiku, they may change the form, adding new features, such as titles, or creating more modern images using figures of speech.

The New and the Old

Railroad tracks; a flight
of wild geese close above them
in the moonlit night.

–Shiki

What remains unchanged, despite any gulf of time or culture, is the essence of haiku: simplicity, depth, and a bond between human beings and the natural world.

CINQUAINS

Over time, haiku has influenced many forms of poetry, including one form called the **cinquain.** Invented by Adelaide Crapsey, the cinquain consists of five lines made up of two, four, six, eight, and two syllables, respectively. What elements of haiku do you recognize in the following cinquain?

A Warning

Just now,
Out of the strange
Still dusk . . . as strange, as still . . .
A white moth flew. Why am I grown
So cold?

–Adelaide Crapsey

Like haiku, the five-line, unrhymed cinquain uses imagery to suggest its real topic or theme and evoke emotion in the reader. In this case, the speaker suddenly, "just now," becomes aware of her own mortality. The theme of mortality is suggested by the time of day, dusk; by the short-lived white moth; and by the speaker's sensation of growing cold.

LIMERICKS

Another short poetic form is the **limerick.** While the haiku and cinquain usually suggest a more serious or delicate topic and tone, the limerick is *always* funny. Part of the fun of a limerick is its rhyme pattern.

No matter how grouchy you're feeling,
A smile is always quite healing;
It grows like a wreath
All around the front teeth,
Thus preventing the face from
congealing.

The limerick consists of five lines rhyming *aabba.* (See *rhyme* in **Literary Terms Handbook,** page R9.) Many limericks begin with some variation of the opening lines "There was a young lady of. . . ." or "There was a young man from. . . ."

The limerick's origin is unknown, but it may have come from an eighteenth-century Irish song. In the early twentieth century, the limerick became quite popular. Followers of the form made the verse more complicated by creating tongue twisters. How quickly can you read aloud this anonymous limerick?

A tutor who taught on the flute
Tried to teach two tooters to toot.
Said the two to the tutor,
"Is it harder to toot, or
To tutor two tooters to toot?"

Haiku Have students read aloud the haiku by Matsuo Bashō on page 838. Before reading the description of haiku that follows the poem, ask if they can deduce the elements of the form based on the haiku they have just read. You may want to prompt with questions such as: How many lines are there? How many syllables are in each line? What are the two most visual images in the poem? *(Many haiku poets juxtapose two contrasting images to create emotion in their poetry, as Bashō does in this haiku with the old silent pond and the lively frog.)*

Cinquains Point out to students the cyclical nature of the cinquain. Use "A Warning" as an example. The poem begins with two syllables, builds steadily in line length and dramatic tension, and then ends with two syllables. Students may find elements of haiku in the way Adelaide Crapsey contrasts the image of the "strange, still dusk" with the image of the white moth.

Limericks Have students practice writing quick limericks using their own names or regions. *(There once was a young girl named Anna...; An eager young student from Dallas...)* Encourage them to play with language and humor, but to keep the form and rhyme scheme of the limerick.

Technology

Poetry Table

Students can use a word processing program to create a six-column table of poetry elements as they read the poems in this unit. Ask students to insert the headings shown below. Students can use their tables as tools for study and review or as a valuable set of data for writing a comparison-and-contrast essay. **L2**

Title	Author	Type of Poem	Number of Lines/Syllables	Images	Emotion

Before Reading

Objectives

- To read and analyze five short poems
- To identify personification and explain how it contributes to a poem's power
- To explain how a poem's imagery supports its mood

Skills

Reading/Thinking: Comparing and Contrasting; Spatial Relationships
Writing: Haiku; Cinquain or Limerick
Vocabulary: Compound Words
Grammar/Language: Prepositional Phrases
Listening/Speaking: Reciting Haiku; Readers Theater
Collaboration: Literature Groups

Motivating → STUDENTS

Selection Focus Transparency 73: Have students look carefully at the photograph. Encourage them to study the structure of the snowflakes and notice how they are similar and different.

Reading Focus: As an extension of the Reading Focus, have students make a drawing of the object they described. Then have them write their description again and compare it with the first.

Before You Read

Short Poems

MEET THE POETS

Matsuo Bashō, who was born into the samurai, or warrior class, started writing poetry at the age of nine. Bashō taught poetry to many devoted students.

Bashō was probably born in 1644 and died in 1694.

Raymond R. Patterson was born in New York City. A former director of Black Poets Reading, Patterson also wrote a newspaper column on African American history.

Raymond R. Patterson was born in 1929.

Ann Atwood has been influenced by nature throughout her life. Many of her books and films fuse poetry with nature photography.

Ann Atwood was born in 1913.

Myra Cohn Livingston edited dozens of books of poetry for younger readers and taught the writing of poetry to both children and adults.

Myra Cohn Livingston was born in 1926 and died in 1996.

READING FOCUS

Have you ever heard the expression "Less is more"? Using as few words as possible, how would you describe an ordinary object, such as your locker or a chair?

QuickWrite

Jot down a few words describing an object you can see right now.

Setting a Purpose

Read these short poems first for enjoyment and then to become familiar with their forms.

BUILDING BACKGROUND

Did You Know? The seventeenth-century Japanese poet Matsuo Bashō is generally acknowledged as the innovator and master of the haiku form. One story about Bashō illustrates his approach to haiku. While walking one day, Bashō and a young student watched dragonflies darting through the fields. The student quickly made up a poem: "Red dragonflies! / Take off their wings, / and they are pepper pods!" Bashō responded, "No! That is not haiku. If you wish to make a haiku on the subject, you must say: "Red pepper pods! / Add wings to them, / and they are dragonflies!"

Matsuo Bashō

Raymond R. Patterson

Ann Atwood

Myra Cohn Livingston

RESOURCE MANAGER

Teaching Tools and Resources
- Theme Eight Planning Guide
- Literature Groups Sourcebook

Essential Lesson Support

Lesson-Specific Instruction
- Selection Focus Transparency 73
- Literary Elements Transparency 73
- Active Reading Guide,* p. 73

Assessment
- Selection Quick Checks,* p. 73
- Sel. and Theme Assmt., p. 124
- Testmaker: ExamView Pro
- Performance Assessment, p. 68

Systematic Language Instruction
- Gr. & Comp. Hdbk., L. 14.4–14.5
- Vocabulary Power, Unit 8 Review/Test
- Spelling Power, Unit 8 Review/Proofreading

English Language Learners
- Spanish Summaries, p. 73
- Spanish Translations, p. 216
- Audio Library*
- English, Yes!

Spec. Needs/Strat. Interven.
- Interactive Reading Sourcebook, pp. T247–T249
- Interactive Reading Workbook, p. 146
- Audio Library*

*Also available in Spanish

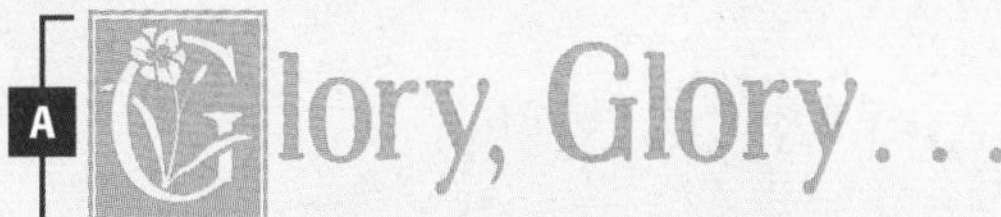

Glory, Glory...

Haiku by Raymond R. Patterson

Across Grandmother's knees
A kindly sun
Laid a yellow quilt.

Birds Circling at Dusk

Haiku by Ann Atwood

Birds circling at dusk.
The first night of my journey—
yet how far from home!

Bamboo Grove

Haiku by Matsuo Bashō

Song of the cuckoo:
in the grove of great bamboos,
moonlight seeping through.

Reading the Selection

A Literary Elements

PERSONIFICATION Have students note how the sun is personified in "Glory, Glory. . ." *(The sun places a yellow quilt across the grandmother's knee.)*

B Literary Elements

SYMBOL Ask students what the journey might symbolize in "Birds Circling at Dusk." *(The journey might be emotional—not just physical.)*

C Literary Elements

HAIKU This type of poetry has three lines and seventeen syllables. The first and third line have five syllables each; the middle line has seven syllables. Point out how the translator of Matsuo Bashō's haiku has maintained the same number of syllables.

Additional Resources

- ***Active Reading Guide,*** p. 73
- ***Audio Library***
- ***Spanish Audio Library***
- ***Spanish Summaries,*** p. 73

Teaching Support

MEETING INDIVIDUAL NEEDS — ADVANCED LEARNERS

Haiku Haiku is a challenge to write since it restricts expression to three lines and seventeen syllables.

Activity Have students work in pairs to write a three-line haiku. The first and third lines should have five syllables each and the middle line should have seven syllables. Have students write each line separately and count the syllables. Students may then illustrate their haiku on the same page to reinforce the imagery of the poem they created. **L3**

D Literary Elements

FIGURES OF SPEECH: *Personification* Draw out the subtlety of the T-shirt's personification. *(It "said something when it was new," probably with letters or symbols; "no one knows what you said..." implies that the shirt could speak.)*

E Literary Elements

RHYTHM AND RHYME Write the words *brighter* and *writer* on the board. Help students notice that these rhyming words end with an unstressed syllable. Explain that this is called a feminine rhyme. Rhyming on a stressed syllable is called a masculine rhyme. Feminine rhymes always consist of two or more syllables, while masculine rhymes consist of a single syllable. Have students find the masculine and feminine rhymes in the limerick. *(masculine: door, floor; feminine: Ealing, feeling, ceiling)*

Thematic Focus

A Delicate Balance Which of the poems most directly relate to the theme? *(The haiku, which contain images of nature—and often of nature in balance with itself and with the poet—most directly involve the theme.)* To enrich and extend the discussion, you might use ***Fine Art Transparency 6.*** Would a form other than poetry be as effective here?

ASSESSMENT

Quick Checks, p. 73

Teaching Support

T-Shirt

Cinquain by Myra Cohn Livingston

T-shirt,
you're my best thing
though you've faded so much
D no one knows what you said when you
were new.

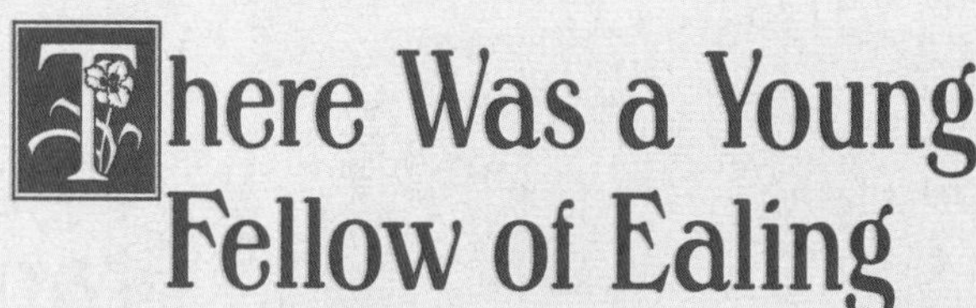

There Was a Young Fellow of Ealing

Anonymous Limerick

There was a young fellow of Ealing,
Endowed with such delicate feeling,
E When he read, on the door,
"Don't spit on the floor,"
He jumped up and spat on the ceiling.

Reading *Minilesson*

Comparing and Contrasting Haiku, cinquains, and limericks are distinct in many ways. The three haiku and the cinquain are fairly serious in tone, while the limerick is lighthearted and funny.

Activity After students have read the poems, have them work in small groups to fill in a chart comparing and contrasting these poetic elements: rhyme scheme, tone, imagery, and mood. L2

Characteristics	Haiku	Cinquain	Limerick
Rhyme scheme	none	none	a, a, b, b, a
Tone	serious	serious	funny
Imagery			
Mood			

Additional Resources

Reading Skills Practice Workbook

Responding to Literature

PERSONAL RESPONSE

- Which of the poems did you enjoy most? Explain why.

Analyzing Literature

RECALL

1. What are the **settings** of the three haiku?
2. In what condition is the T-shirt in the cinquain?
3. What funny event occurs in the limerick?

Brackets connect questions that are paired to develop higher-level thinking skills.

INTERPRET

4. In each haiku, what words or phrases provide clues to the time of day?
5. What might the T-shirt have said when it was new?
6. Why does the event make the limerick funny?

EVALUATE AND CONNECT

7. In your opinion, how does the Japanese poet Bashō feel about nature? Explain your answer.
8. In what ways are the three haiku similar and different?
9. Which poem do you think makes the most effective use of the least number of words? Why?
10. Which poem would you most like to share with another person? Explain why.

LITERARY ELEMENTS

Personification

Personification is a figure of speech in which an idea, object, or animal is given human form or human characteristics. The sentence *The impatient alarm clock shook me out of bed* is an example of personification. An object, an alarm clock, is described as though it were an impatient parent trying to get a sleepy child out of bed. Authors use personification to make their writing more vivid and to describe things in a way that people can imagine and understand.

1. Identify how personification is used in one of the poems.
2. Paraphrase the poem in one sentence without using personification. Do you think your image is as powerful as the poem's? Why or why not?
3. Using the photo at the left, write a short poem of your own using personification.

● See **Literary Terms Handbook**, p. R8.

LITERARY ELEMENTS

1. In "Glory, Glory. . ." the sun is shown placing a quilt on a woman's knees.
2. *Sunlight shone on Grandmother's knees.* The personification of the sun provides a more powerful description.
3. Students should use a figure of speech in which an animal, an object, or an idea is given human form or characteristics.

Additional Resources

Literary Elements Transparency 73

Responding to the Selection

PERSONAL RESPONSE

Encourage students to discuss imagery, form, content, and tone when they explain which poem they like best.

Analyzing Literature

1. The first setting is a relaxing sunny day. The next setting is dusk somewhere far from the speaker's home. The last is at night in a grove of bamboo trees.
2. The T-shirt is old and faded.
3. The young fellow jumped up and spat on the ceiling.
4. *Kindly sun* implies daytime; *dusk* indicates evening; *moonlight seeping through* indicates nighttime.
5. Students will probably suggest currently popular slogans or brands.
6. Because spitting on the ceiling would be much more difficult than spitting on the floor.
7. Most students will recognize that Bashō has a strong and intimate connection with nature; the entire poem focuses on images of the natural world.
8. All the poems include images of nature; the first two include the interaction between nature (personification) and humans; the third does not.
9. Most students will probably choose one of the haiku. (The first has the least number of words.)
10. Students should explain their choice.

Extending Your Response

Writing About Literature
Students' paragraphs should
- describe the mood of the poem
- explain how the imagery builds or supports the poem's mood

Listening and Speaking Before the students recite, have them read their poems two or three times.

Literature Groups As students discuss the poems, encourage them to list the details in each. Then have them make sketches and compare how each person's interpretation of a poem can be very different.

Performing Have students read slowly and clearly, making sure that their audience can understand their words.

Creative Writing
Students' poems should
- be short, possibly in the form of a cinquain or limerick
- create an image of a particular moment in time

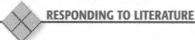

Extending Your Response

Writing About Literature

Imagery and Mood Choose one of the three haiku. Decide what mood the poem creates. Then think about the poem's imagery. Write a paragraph telling how the imagery builds or supports the poem's mood.

Listening and Speaking

Inspired by Nature Traditional haiku always contains an image from nature. With a partner, look around your classroom and out the window. Find a class pet or plant or a glimpse of the sky, a tree, an insect–any natural object or being–for inspiration. Collaborate with your partner to write a haiku about what you observe. Recite your haiku to the class.

Literature Groups

Snapshots If you think of a short poem as a snapshot of a moment, what would the snapshots look like from each of the five poems? Work with your group to discuss your ideas. Sketch them if you wish. Which snapshot contains the least detail and which contains the most? Compare your group's ideas with those of other groups.

Performing

Readers Theater Work with a small group to collect five or six short poems on a specific theme. Try to include a variety of short forms, such as haiku, cinquain, limerick, or any other short poem. Read your collection of poems aloud to the class. Have the class guess the theme of your collection and suggest a title for it.

Creative Writing

Short Poem Use one of the poems as a model for writing your own cinquain or limerick about the object you described in the **Reading Focus** on page 840.

Reading Further

If you wish to read more short poems, try these books:

O Sliver of Liver by Myra Cohn Livingston

Red Dragonfly on My Shoulder translated by Sylvia Cassedy and Kunihiro Suetake

Birds, Beasts, and the Third Thing by D. H. Lawrence

Save your work for your portfolio.

ASSESSMENT

- ***Quick Checks,*** p. 73
- ***Selection and Theme Assessment,*** p. 124
- ***Performance Assessment,*** p. 68
- ***Testmaker: ExamView Pro***
- ***Interactive Tutor: Self-Assessment***

Skill Minilessons

Reteach · Review

GRAMMAR AND LANGUAGE • PREPOSITIONAL PHRASES

A **preposition** is a word that relates a noun or a pronoun to some other word in the sentence. A **prepositional phrase** is a group of words that begins with a preposition and ends with a noun or pronoun, which is called the **object of the preposition.**

He jumped up and spat on the ceiling.

In this sentence, *on* is a preposition, and *on the ceiling* is the prepositional phrase. The object of the preposition is *ceiling*.

Commonly Used Prepositions			
about	before	for	on
above	behind	from	out
across	below	in	since
against	between	like	through
at	during	near	with

PRACTICE Write the prepositional phrase from each of the following sentences. Underline the preposition.

1. Haiku and cinquain are two short forms of poetry.
2. Centuries have passed since Bashō wrote his poems.
3. Within every classic haiku, there is one powerful image.
4. I'm looking for a startling image.
5. Across Grandmother's knees / A kindly sun / Laid a yellow quilt.

- For more about prepositional phrases, see **Language Handbook,** p. R30.

READING AND THINKING • SPATIAL RELATIONSHIPS/SPATIAL ORDER

Spatial relationships describe how things relate to one another in physical space. Matsuo Bashō's description of the "moonlight seeping *through*" helps readers imagine the image of the moonlight in the bamboo grove. Writers use words like *through, across, above, below, under,* and *next to* to help the reader understand the spatial order of the images in the poem and the relationship between the speaker and the things described.

PRACTICE Reread the three haiku and think about where the images the poets describe are in relationship to one another and to the speaker. Write a sentence or two about each poem using words that describe spatial relationships. Then underline those words.

- For more about spatial order, see **Reading Handbook,** p. R91.

VOCABULARY • COMPOUND WORDS

Moonlight is a common image in haiku. *Moonlight* is a **compound word,** a word made by joining two words to make a new word. Compound words can be spelled closed *(birthday),* hyphenated *(worn-out),* or open *(high school).* When writing compound words, remember to keep the original spelling of both words.

PRACTICE Combine words from both columns to make five compound words.

1. grand — berry
2. row — board
3. touch — mother
4. blue — down
5. card — boat

Skill Minilessons

GRAMMAR AND LANGUAGE
PREPOSITIONAL PHRASES

1. of poetry
2. since Basho wrote his poems
3. Within every classic haiku,
4. for a startling image
5. Across Grandmother's knees

READING AND THINKING
SPATIAL RELATIONSHIPS/SPATIAL ORDER

1. "Glory, Glory..." The sunlight is shining across the grandmother's knees.
2. "Birds Circling at Dusk" The birds are circling in the speaker's sight. The speaker is far from home.
3. "Bamboo Grove" The moonlight is seeping through a grove of trees; the cuckoo is in the grove.

VOCABULARY
COMPOUND WORDS

1. grandmother
2. rowboat
3. touchdown
4. blueberry
5. cardboard

Additional Resources

- ***Grammar and Language Workbook,*** pp. 141–142
- ***Grammar and Composition Handbook,*** Lesson 7.1
- ***Writer's Choice,*** Lesson 13.1
- ***Reading Skills Practice Workbook***
- ***Vocabulary Practice***

Writing WORKSHOP

Objectives

- To write a research report of approximately 500–700 words
- To plan, draft, revise, edit, and present a cause-and-effect essay
- To reflect on and assess the essay

GLENCOE TECHNOLOGY

WRITER'S ASSISTANT CD-ROM

Students can use Glencoe's templates and guidelines software for essay writing to aid them in working through the steps in the writing process in the lesson.

Teaching Strategies

PREWRITING

Select an Issue Have students create a list of issues that arise from common conflicts between people and nature. They may identify issues such as vegetarianism, animal rights, or the environment. Have them research a topic until they find a focus.

Research Causes and Effects Encourage students to contact organizations involved in the issue they have chosen. Special-interest groups and organizations often provide educational information free to the public.

Teaching Support

Writing WORKSHOP

Expository Writing: Research Report

In a national park, heavy smog damage causes officials to consider banning cars from the park. In a city, a decision about airport sites affects a rare animal's survival. Nature's way and people's way—how are they connected? Often we don't find out until they clash. By researching the causes and effects of a conflict, you can clarify your position on an issue and gain new insights as well.

Assignment: Follow the process explained in these pages to develop a research report exploring cause-and-effect relationships in an environmental issue.

- As you write your research report, refer to the **Writing Handbook,** pp. R55–R99.

EVALUATION RUBRIC

By the time you complete this Writing Workshop, you will have

- written a research report that examines the causes and effects of an environmental problem
- developed an introduction that captures attention and includes a position statement
- supported each cause and effect with accurate, convincing evidence
- documented sources accurately in a bibliography or a list of works cited
- created a conclusion that restates your position
- presented a research report that is free of errors in grammar, usage, and mechanics

The Writing Process

PREWRITING

PREWRITING TIP

Don't be fooled by coincidences. Remember that an event that came before another event hasn't necessarily caused it. Make sure a genuine cause-and-effect relationship exists. Don't forget that many events have multiple causes and effects.

Select an Issue

You may find issues in selections from this theme. For other ideas, watch television news and scan newspapers and magazines for environmental issues. Talk with parents and friends about issues affecting your community. You might also brainstorm a list of issues with your classmates. Use a computer to create an electronic database of environmental issues to research. Then choose one that you care about.

Research Causes and Effects

Before and during your research stage, pose relevant questions about your topic. What specific questions might you or your readers have? What are some causes and effects involved? As you research, try to find answers for these questions. Use Tips for Asking Research Questions in the **Reading Handbook,** page R100.

MEETING INDIVIDUAL NEEDS — ENGLISH LANGUAGE LEARNERS

Discussing the Issue After students have selected an issue for their cause-and-effect essay, have them form small discussion groups with other students who are writing about similar topics. Make sure the groups include English language learners as well as more-proficient speakers of English.

Activity Ask students to take turns talking about their topics and explaining the cause-and-effect relationships they plan to explore. Encourage them to share resources and information, to help each other create graphic organizers like the one shown on page 847, and to develop position statements.

Additional Resources

English Language Learners Sourcebook

Issue: Florida's manatees are endangered.

Causes	Effects
People go boating in waters where manatees live. Manatees don't know that propellers are dangerous.	Manatees are injured or killed in collisions with boats.
People build floodgates and canal locks.	Manatees drown or are crushed in floodgates and canal locks.
People put buoys and other foreign objects in the water.	Manatees become entangled in buoy lines and choke to death on foreign objects.

● Use a Variety of Sources

View nature programs, interview experts, or research your issue at the library or on the Internet. As you collect information, record your sources on **source cards** and make **note cards** for the information that you want to include in your report.

● Evaluate Your Sources

Make sure that your sources are accurate, that statements are supported by evidence, and that authors are unbiased. To evaluate information from television or the Internet, use critical viewing guidelines from **Listening, Speaking, and Viewing** on page 817.

● Customize for Audience and Purpose

Will you write for people who might take action, such as government officials? Or will you write to increase awareness among students? Decide which details will mean the most to your readers, and make those details stand out.

● Use Graphics

Forming a chain, causes lead to effects, which in turn become new causes, leading to further effects. Create a graphic similar to the one below to keep cause-and-effect relationships clear. Then write a position statement to set the direction of your draft.

Point: Accidents involving floodgates kill manatees.

Floodgate is opened to control flooding.	→	Water rushes in through floodgate.	→	Rushing water creates strong current.	→	Current pulls in slow-swimming manatees.	→	Held by current, manatees can't rise to surface to breathe.	→	Manatees drown.
Cause		**Effect/Cause**		**Effect/Cause**		**Effect/Cause**		**Effect/Cause**		**Effect/Cause**

Use a Variety of Sources Encourage students to use a variety of source types. Basic information may be most readily available in encyclopedias or online databases. However, personal interviews (their own or those found in books or other sources) can provide insights and details difficult to obtain from basic references. Documentary movies or videos can also provide valuable visual information not available elsewhere.

Customize for Audience and Purpose Point out to students that it is important to present information in a way that will engage their target audience. Readers will feel more receptive to a writer's point of view if it is balanced and draws on accurate, up-to-date information gathered from both sides of an issue.

Use Graphics Students may want to create their graphic organizers in pairs or groups. Encourage them to discuss whether the cause-and-effect chain makes sense. They should strive to make the links between the causes and their effects as strong and clear as they can.

Additional Resources

- ***Writing and Proofreading Practice,*** pp. 1–7, 57–63
- ***Writing and Proofreading Transparencies 1–6, 23–24, 39–40***
- ***Writer's Choice,*** Lesson 5.3

MEETING INDIVIDUAL NEEDS: MULTIPLE MODES OF EXPRESSION

Spatial Students who have strong spatial abilities can express their ideas by using images and pictures. Write a few common slogans on the board and ask students to talk about the kind of image or picture they would create to accompany the slogan. Slogans might be something like: *The Earth Is Your Mother; Keep Wildlife Wild; Think Globally, Act Locally.*

Activity Have students work in small groups to design posters advocating their position on the issue they have chosen. Students can use paint, collage, photographs, recycled materials, or anything else they can think of to get their point across. Encourage students to create a slogan from their position statement and include it on the poster. **L2**

DRAFTING

Start with an Anecdote Remind students that a story or anecdote that grabbed their attention will probably affect their readers the same way. A well-chosen story or anecdote can give the reader a glimpse into what possessed the writer to explore this particular topic to begin with.

Explain Connections Write this example on the board: *Run-off from cattle herds pollutes rivers and streams.* Ask students if they can answer the following questions after reading the statement: *What is run-off? Where does the run-off come from? What is the polluting substance?*

Writers should not assume that their readers know a lot about the subject matter. Connections need to be explained.

REVISING

Make Adjustments Suggest that students read their essays aloud to a partner and ask the partner to restate the cause-and-effect relationships described in the essay.

Check Documentation Remind students that accuracy is important when crediting sources. The spelling of authors' names, the URLs of Web sites, and the publication dates of periodicals are areas where citations most frequently go wrong. Suggest that students review these elements with particular care.

DRAFTING

DRAFTING TIP

Before you begin drafting the body of your report, look at the questions about your topic that you wrote in the prewritting stage and used to guide your research. Discard any questions that no longer seem relevant to your goal. Use the answers to the remaining questions to help you focus and shape your report.

Start with an Anecdote

A brief vivid story illustrating your issue can be a powerful opener. Put your position statement at the end of the introduction.

Explain Connections

Explain the causes and effects of your main points. Discuss multiple causes and effects and cause-and-effect chains. Include memorable details. You might conclude a restatement of your position or with a prediction about the future.

STUDENT MODEL • DRAFTING

Let's do our part to make sure that manatees continue to swim in the waters of Florida long after we are gone. When all is said and done, the future of the manatee is up to us.

Complete Student Model on pp. R114–R115.

REVISING

REVISING TIP

Some transitional words or phrases you can use to show cause and effect include *as a result of, because, so, therefore, consequently, this is why, the result is,* and *for this reason.*

Make Adjustments

This is the time to fine-tune. Look over your draft and consider possible improvements, using the **Rubric for Revising** as a guide.

Check Documentation

Refer to the **Writing Handbook** on pages R55-R59 or search the Internet for information about citing sources and creating a final list of works cited.

RUBRIC FOR REVISING

Your revised research report should have

- an introduction that includes an anecdote and ends with a position statement
- an explanation of causes and effects based on accurate, reliable evidence
- a conclusion that restates your position
- an accurate, correctly formatted bibliography or list of works cited

Your revised research report should be free of

- irrelevant information
- errors in documentation, grammar, usage, and mechanics

Teaching Support

Writing Minilesson

Developing Paragraphs As students work on revising their drafts, have them pay special attention to individual paragraphs within the essay. Remind them that their finished essay should reflect and support their position statement. Each paragraph contributes to this goal and should contain an identifiable topic sentence as well as supporting sentences.

Activity Ask students to work in pairs as they revise their drafts. Suggest that they exchange essays and read each other's work. Have them use note cards to identify and write down the topic sentence and supporting sentences in the paragraphs of their partner's essay. Afterward, encourage students to help each other add or delete information to improve their essays, paragraph by paragraph. Students can do this activity with the entire draft or focus on paragraphs they are having trouble with. **L2**

Additional Resources

Writer's Choice, Lesson 2.7

EDITING/PROOFREADING

Find and correct errors in grammar and mechanics. The **Proofreading Checklist** can help. Watch especially for incorrect use of apostrophes, as shown in the **Grammar Link** on page 816.

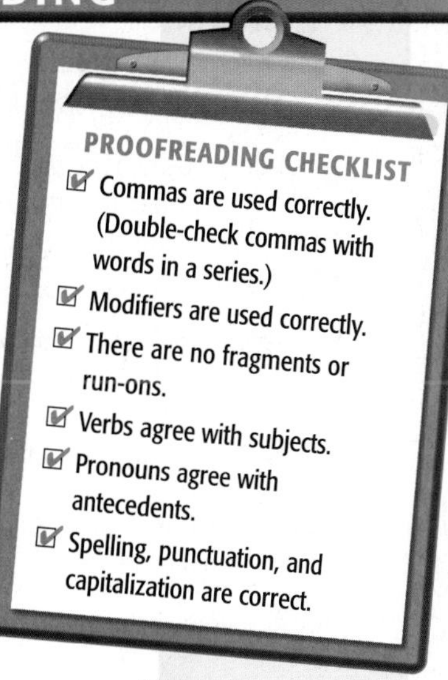

PROOFREADING CHECKLIST
Commas are used correctly. (Double-check commas with words in a series.)
Modifiers are used correctly.
There are no fragments or run-ons.
Verbs agree with subjects.
Pronouns agree with antecedents.
Spelling, punctuation, and capitalization are correct.

Grammar Hint

When you use commas with a series of words or phrases, be sure to put in all the commas—not just the first one:

Rain forests exist in Africa, South America, North America, and Southeast Asia.

STUDENT MODEL • EDITING/PROOFREADING

Manatees are gentle, playful intellent mammals.

Complete Student Model on pp. R114–115.

TECHNOLOGY TIP

Some word processing programs let you design graphics and insert them into your essay.

Complete Student Model

For a complete version of the model developed in this Workshop, see **Writing Workshop Models**, pp. R114–R115.

PUBLISHING/PRESENTING

Try creating graphic visual aids, such as graphs or cause-and-effect diagrams, to illustrate your ideas. Then share your writing with classmates. You and others who explored related issues might present your papers in a panel discussion.

PRESENTING TIP

For a panel discussion, make your visual aids poster-sized.

Reflecting

After thinking about the following questions, write your responses.

- Does your writing focus more on causes or on effects? Why?
- For what other classes might you write papers exploring cause-and-effect connections? What topics might you examine?

Save your work for your portfolio.

EDITING/PROOFREADING

Students may wish to edit and proofread their essays in a group. Encourage them to ask peers for help with grammar and punctuation questions. Suggest that students read their essays aloud if a sentence or paragraph doesn't seem right to them and ask for feedback from the group.

PUBLISHING/PRESENTING

Encourage students who have chosen conflicting sides of the same issue to present their essays in a debate format. In addition to creating graphic visual aids, students might want to take or describe a photograph they would use if they were to publish their essay in a magazine.

Reflecting

Portfolio Suggest that students ask themselves the following questions as they review their writing:

Does my cause-and-effect essay
- provide a clear position statement?
- present well-explained connections between cause and effect?
- engage the audience I targeted?

6+1 TRAITS™ OF WRITING

See the annotated **Writing Workshop Models** on pp. R103–R115 for additional help in evaluating student writing and in teaching the **6+1 Traits™ of effective writing.** Annotations and minilessons address and reinforce the **6+1 Traits™:** Ideas, Organization, Voice, Word Choice, Sentence Fluency, Conventions, and Presentation.

ASSESSMENT

Writing Assessment and Portfolio Management
- Writing Assessment, pp. 1–12, 35–37
- Portfolio Management, pp. 38–45

Theme Assessment

Objectives

- To offer a personal response to the selections in this theme
- To draw conclusions from information and ideas presented in reading sections
- To write a comparison of two selections
- To complete a self-evaluation, set a goal, and devise a plan for achieving the goal

Responding to the Theme

1. Students should provide evidence from the selections to support their opinions.
2. Accept all thoughtful observations and conclusions.
3. Allow time for students to share their policy statements, wildlife series, and multimedia presentations with classmates.

Analyzing Literature

Students' writing should include

- an introductory paragraph identifying the selections and elements chosen for comparison
- an analysis of how the selections illustrate the theme
- examples and details from the stories

Evaluate and Set Goals

Evaluate

Have students review their work and list activities they have completed for each task on this page. Suggest that they add other tasks as well, such as using desktop publishing software.

Have students use the rubric they developed in the first theme's evaluation to assess their work.

Set Goals

Have each student write the goal and the steps on a boxed equation graphic, using:
STEP 1 + STEP 2 + STEP 3 = GOAL

Discuss students' goals and plans in individual conferences.

A DELICATE BALANCE

Theme Assessment

Responding to the Theme

1. Which story, poem, or narrative in this theme helped you to better understand the relationships between humans and nature? Explain your answer.
2. What new ideas do you have about the following as a result of reading the literature in this theme?
   - people's attitudes and actions toward animals and nature
   - the importance of the relationship between nature and human beings
3. Present your theme project to the class.

Analyzing Literature

COMPARE SELECTIONS

Choose pieces from this unit to compare. You may compare the characters, settings, descriptions, or themes. You may compare how two pieces in different forms—such as a poem and a short story—illustrate the theme "A Delicate Balance." Support your ideas with quotations from the selections.

Evaluate and Set Goals

1. Which of the following tasks was most rewarding to you? Which was most difficult?
   - reading and thinking about the selections
   - doing independent writing
   - analyzing the selections in discussions
   - making presentations
   - performing dramatizations
2. Using the following scale, how would you assess your work in this theme? Give at least two reasons for your assessment.
   4 = outstanding   2 = fair
   3 = good   1 = weak
3. Based on what you found difficult in this theme, choose a goal to work toward to increase your understanding of literature next year.
   - Write down your goal and three steps you will take to try to reach it.
   - Next fall, meet with your teacher to review your goal and your plan for achieving it.

Build Your Portfolio

SELECT

Select two pieces of work you did during this theme to include in your portfolio. Use the following questions to help you decide.

- ✦ Which do you consider your best work?
- ✦ Which work "stretched" you the most?
- ✦ Which work did you enjoy the most?

REFLECT

Write some notes to accompany the work you selected. Use these questions to guide you.

- ✦ What do you like best about the piece?
- ✦ What did you learn from creating it?
- ✦ What might you do differently if you were beginning this piece again?

ASSESSMENT

Writing Assessment and Portfolio Management

- Writing Assessment, pp. 1–12
- Portfolio Management, pp. 38–45

GLENCOE TECHNOLOGY

MINDJOGGER VIDEOQUIZZES VIDEODISC

Use *MindJogger* to review the Theme 8 content.

Theme 8
Side B

Also available in VHS.

Reading on Your Own

If you have enjoyed the literature in this theme, you might also be interested in the following books.

The Call of the Wild

By Jack London Buck, a domestic dog, is taken from his home to serve as a sled dog during the Klondike gold rush. Amidst the wolves of the Far North, he begins to hear "the call of the wild."

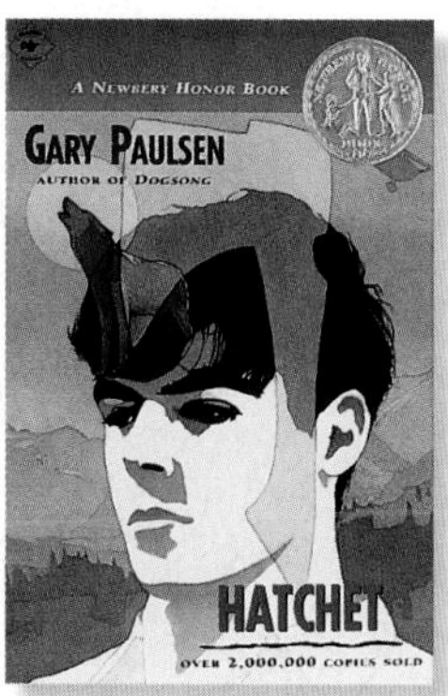

Hatchet

by Gary Paulsen
Brian, the only survivor of a plane crash in the Canadian wilderness, must try to stay alive with nothing more than the clothes on his back and a hatchet.

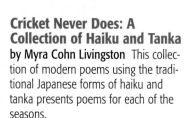

Cricket Never Does: A Collection of Haiku and Tanka

by Myra Cohn Livingston This collection of modern poems using the traditional Japanese forms of haiku and tanka presents poems for each of the seasons.

My Life with the Chimpanzees

by Jane Goodall The world's leading authority on chimpanzees describes her thirty years of living with and studying the chimpanzees of Tanzania.

Reading on Your Own

Tips for Independent Reading

Stress the importance of each student's spending at least thirty minutes a day in independent reading and suggest books, such as those shown here, related to this theme.

Reading Autobiography This form of literature more than any other offers the reader a personal connection with the writer. To make the connection, the writer, who is almost always the main character,

- tells the story in the first person
- reveals personal thoughts and feelings
- includes experiences and details that convey an intended theme

Practice Have small groups of students who have read autobiographical selections related to this theme discuss questions like these:

- What message about life or human nature does the story convey?
- Was it implied or directly stated?
- Which of the main character's experiences illustrate this theme?
- How does this theme relate to "A Delicate Balance"?
- What were the thoughts, feelings, fears, and joys revealed by the writer that helped you identify with him or her?

Glencoe Literature Library

The Call of the Wild and ***Hatchet*** are available in the *Glencoe Literature Library*. For a complete listing of the titles, see the **Glencoe Resources for Independent Reading** in the front of this book.

The *Glencoe Literature Library Study Guide* provides instructional support and student activities for works in the *Glencoe Literature Library*.

MEETING INDIVIDUAL NEEDS — SPECIAL NEEDS

You may wish to recommend *Cricket Never Does* by Myra Cohn Livingston for less-proficient readers. The limited scope, concrete imagery, and vivid language of these short poems may inspire and build the confidence of students who find reading long selections difficult. **L1**

The following books are rated for average readers **(L2)** or for students who need more challenging reading **(L3)**:

- *The Call of the Wild* by Jack London **L2**
- *Hatchet* by Gary Paulsen **L2**
- *My Life with the Chimpanzees* by Jane Goodall **L3**

Additional Resources

Inclusion Strategies

Standardized Test Practice

 **TEST-TAKING TIP**

From time to time, students will come across unfamiliar words. When a dictionary is not handy, they should try to use context clues to figure out the meaning of the word. Context clues in the surrounding sentences can often indicate what a word means. Try this example: *When it came to climbing mountains, Tim was a true neophyte. In fact, this was the first time he had ever tried climbing.*

Students will probably understand that neophyte means something like *beginner*. If this were a test question, they might even see the word *beginner* as one of the answer choices.

In cases where context clues do not help students determine a word's meaning, tell them to go back and substitute each answer choice in place of the unknown word in the original sentence. On tests, this will help students eliminate wrong answers.

The Princeton Review TEST-TAKING TIP

Remind students to read carefully. It only takes one word to change the meaning of a sentence or a test question, as in *Which of the following is not a FACT from the passage?* Missing the word *not* in the question can lead to an incorrect answer. Remind students to read carefully and to answer a question only after they are sure of what is being asked.

Standardized Test Practice

Read the following passage. Then read each question on page 853. Decide which is the best answer to each question. Mark the letter for that answer on your paper.

Why Have Flatbreads Always Been So Popular?

In many parts of the world, bread is not baked in the loaves that are commonly eaten in the United States. Instead, it is baked in thin sheets known as "flatbread." One of the most familiar types of flatbread is pita, which comes from the eastern Mediterranean. Pita bread is soft and is often used as a pocket of bread, into which meat or vegetables are placed to make a sandwich. Pita is gaining popularity and recognition as more people experiment with new types of baked goods. Many types of flatbread can be found in supermarkets and bakeries today.

The history of flatbread goes back several thousand years. It is one of the oldest known prepared foods. People have eaten flatbread wherever there was grain available because it is nourishing, it is easy to prepare, and it keeps well over time.

Many types of grain are used in the creation of flatbread, including rye, oats, corn, wheat, rice, and buckwheat. Sometimes vegetables are used as well; potatoes, chickpeas, and lentils add flavor and texture to the bread. Flatbreads can have unusual and distinctive tastes depending on the ingredients used. For example, "Sweet Armenian" bread is flavored with maleb, a black cherry pit. In Asia, a black onion seed, nigella, is added to the mixture. Ethiopians use teff flour for a unique molasses flavor. The additional ingredients often provide additional nutrients.

The way in which a flatbread is baked varies from place to place. No matter how it is done, flatbread is considered one of the world's great fast foods because of its rapid cooking time. This is an important quality in countries where fuel is scarce and needs to be conserved. In Asia, flatbread is baked in a tandoor. This barrel-shaped oven has hot coals in its center. The bread is slapped to the sides of the oven, and heat transfers rapidly from the oven sides to the bread. On the other hand, injeras (an Ethiopian sourdough), chapatis (an Indian bread), and tortillas (a Latin American bread) are often baked in a large, hot skillet over an open fire or on the flat surface of a wood-burning stove. Amazingly, Algerians and Tunisians can bake bread right on the fiery desert sand. Malaysians throw the dough up in the air over and over again until it becomes paper thin. Then they twist it and cook it on a griddle. The Hopi of North America made special piki stones that they used for baking flatbreads, a tradition that was passed down from generation to generation.

ENGLISH LANGUAGE LEARNERS

Sharing Recipes Sharing culinary treasures can be an interesting way of learning about new cultures. Ask students to name some of their family's favorite dishes. Invite them to give recipes for their preparation. Write each dish's name and its ingredients on the board in its native language. Have students share comments about the foods and name their ingredients using the English words for them.

Another important quality of flatbreads is that they are easy to store and preserve. In countries where the winters are long, people dry the bread after it is baked to help preserve a grain supply that needs to endure many cold months.

Flatbreads have varied ingredients and preparation techniques, and they can be used in many ways. Today we are rediscovering the nutritious, fast, and long-lasting flatbreads of many different cultures, enriching our own culinary offerings.

---

1 According to the passage, maleb and nigella can be used as ingredients in flatbreads to make them —
  A rise slowly
  B taste good
  C last longer
  D cook faster

2 Why did the author start the passage by mentioning pita bread?
  J To help readers recall what they already know about flatbreads
  K To show that pita bread is not as popular as other flatbreads
  L To persuade readers to eat pita bread
  M To describe how pita bread is used

3 Based on the information in the passage, you can predict that —
  A flatbreads will no longer be baked soon.
  B new ways of cooking flatbreads will continue to be found.
  C flatbreads will continue to be baked for a long time.
  D all breads will now be flatbreads.

4 After it is in the tandoor, the flatbread must then be —
  J cooked on a hot skillet.
  K thrown up into the air over and over.
  L twisted and cooked on a hot griddle.
  M slapped against the sides of the oven.

5 You would most likely find this article in —
  A a newspaper.
  B an almanac.
  C an encyclopedia.
  D an instruction manual.

6 The author provides evidence to suggest that —
  J pita bread is the most popular flatbread in the world.
  K flatbreads are more common in South America than in Central Asia.
  L flatbreads need many flavorings to make them tasty.
  M flatbreads have been popular for a long time throughout the world.

Answers and Analyses

1. B Students should find these two words as used in the passage. The third paragraph mentions that *maleb* is used for flavor. Items used for flavor are most likely there to make something taste good.

2. J The author states that "One of the most familiar types of flatbread is pita." Students should be able to find the context clue *familiar* within this sentence. The author is probably trying to begin the passage with the product that is most familiar to readers. Readers who do not know the word *flatbread* will realize what it is when they relate it to pita.

3. C Remind students that answers will always be supported by information within the passage. There is nothing in the text to support choice D. The last paragraph indicates that flatbreads are still popular, eliminating choice A. Choice B is a possibility, but the passage is about how flatbreads have not changed, which leaves C as the best possible choice.

4. M This is a fact stated in the passage. Students should find the word *tandoor* in the passage and reread that section.

5. C Students should be familiar with the kind of information in each of these references. Choices B and D can be eliminated immediately. Choice A is a possibility, but a text selection that provides general information on a specific subject is most likely to be found in an encyclopedia.

6. M Students should make sure that general statements are supported by evidence in the passage. Choice M paraphrases what is written in paragraph two.

Tested Objective

Item	Reading Objective
1	Use context clues to discover meaning
2	Identify and trace development of an author's point of view or perspective
3, 6	Assesses the accuracy and appropriateness of the author's evidence to support claims and assertions
4	Comprehension and analysis—locate and understand technical directions
5	Understand and analyze the differences among various categories of informational material

MORE PRACTICE

For additional practice, assign practice pages from one of the following standardized test resources available as part of Glencoe Literature.

Additional Resources
ITBS Preparation and Practice
SAT-9 Preparation and Practice
Terra Nova Preparation and Practice

Reference Section

Literary Terms Handbook

A

Act A major unit of a drama. A play may be subdivided into several acts. Many modern plays have two or three acts. A short play can be composed of one or more scenes but only one act—for example, Walter Hackett's adaptation of Mark Twain's *The Million-Pound Bank Note.*

See page 500.
See also SCENE.

Alliteration The repitition of consonant sounds, usually at the beginnings of words or syllables. Alliteration gives emphasis to words. For example, the following line from "The Highwayman," by Alfred Noyes, contains an example of alliteration:

Over the cobbles he clattered and clashed in the dark innyard. . . .

See page 824.

Allusion A reference in a work of literature to a well-known character, place, or situation in history, politics, or science or from another work of literature, music, or art. For example, the title of Borden Deal's "Antaeus" is an allusion to the name of the mighty wrestler from Greek mythology whose enormous strength came from his contact with the earth.

See page 357.

Analogy A comparison between two things, based on one or more elements that they share. Analogies can help the reader visualize an idea. In informational text, analogies are often used to explain something unfamiliar in terms of something known. For example, a science book might compare the flow of electricity to water moving through a hose. In literature, most analogies are expressed in metaphors or similes.

See also METAPHOR, SIMILE.

Anecdote A brief, entertaining story based on a single interesting or humorous incident or event. Anecdotes are frequently biographical and reveal some aspect of a person's character.

Antagonist A person or force that opposes the protagonist, or central character, in a story or a drama. The reader is generally meant not to sympathize with the antagonist. For example, Margot's entire class is her antagonist in "All Summer in a Day," by Ray Bradbury.

See also CONFLICT, PROTAGONIST.

Anthropomorphism Representing animals as if they had human emotions and intelligence. Fables and fairy tales often contain anthropomorphism. "Rikki-tikki-tavi," by Rudyard Kipling, is another example of this technique.

See page 802.

Aside In a play, a comment made by a character that is heard by the audience but not by the other characters onstage. The speaker turns to one side, or "aside," away from the other characters onstage. Asides are common in older plays—you will find many in Shakespeare's plays—but are infrequent in modern drama.

Assonance The repetition of vowel sounds, especially in a line of poetry. For example, the following line from "The Women's 400 Meters," by Lillian Morrison, contains an example of assonance:

they flex knees, drum heels and / shiver at the
starting line

See also RHYME, SOUND DEVICES.

LITERARY TERMS HANDBOOK R1

Author's purpose The intention of the writer. For example, the purpose of a story may be to entertain, to describe, to explain, to persuade, or a combination of these purposes. "A Crush," by Cynthia Rylant, both tells an entertaining story and describes.

See page 830.

Autobiography The story of a person's life written by that person. *Rosa Parks: My Story,* by Rosa Parks with Jim Haskins, is an example of autobiography.

See pages 62–63.
See also BIOGRAPHY, MEMOIR.

B

Ballad A short musical narrative song or poem. Folk ballads, which usually tell of an exciting or dramatic episode, were passed on by word of mouth for generations before being written down. Literary ballads are written in imitation of folk ballads. "Annabel Lee," by Edgar Allan Poe, is an example of a literary ballad.

See also NARRATIVE POETRY.

Biography The account of a person's life written by someone other than the subject. Biographies can be short or book-length. In "New Directions," Maya Angelou writes a biographical sketch of her grandmother.

See page 223.
See also AUTOBIOGRAPHY, MEMOIR.

C

Character A person in a literary work. (If a character is an animal, it displays human traits.) Characters who show varied and sometimes contradictory traits, such as the alternately stern and compassionate Mary in Dorothy M. Johnson's "Too Soon a Woman," are called **round.** Characters who reveal only one personality trait, like the flinty father in the same story, are called **flat.** A **stereotype** is a flat character of a familiar and often-repeated type. A **dynamic** character changes during the story. A **static** character remains primarily the same throughout the story.

See page 180.

Characterization The methods a writer uses to develop the personality of the character. In **direct characterization,** the narrator makes direct statements about a character's personality. In **indirect characterization,** the writer reveals a character's personality through the character's words and actions and through what other characters think and say about the character. These techniques are frequently blended, as in the characterization of Margot in Ray Bradbury's "All Summer in a Day."

See page 406.

Climax The point of greatest emotional intensity, interest, or suspense in a narrative. Usually the climax comes at the turning point in a story or drama, the point at which the resolution of the conflict becomes clear. The climax in O. Henry's "After Twenty Years" occurs when Bob discovers that the man he thinks is Jimmy Wells is actually someone else.

See page 550.

Comedy A type of drama that is humorous and has a happy ending. A heroic comedy focuses on the exploits of a larger-than-life hero. In American popular culture, comedy can take the form of a scripted performance involving one or more performers—either as a skit that is part of a variety show, as in vaudeville, or as a stand-up monologue. "Who's on First," by Bud Abbott and Lou Costello, is an example of a comedic skit with its roots in vaudeville.

See also HUMOR.

R2 LITERARY TERMS HANDBOOK

LITERARY TERMS HANDBOOK

Conflict The central struggle between opposing forces in a story or drama. An **external conflict** exists when a character struggles against some outside force, such as nature, society, fate, or another person–for example, the struggle of the two scientists with the Multivac computer in Isaac Asimov's "Key Item." An **internal conflict** exists within the mind of a character who is torn between opposing feelings or goals–as Antonio and Felix grapple with their desire for the championship and their reluctance to fight each other in "Amigo Brothers," by Piri Thomas.

See page 53.
See also ANTAGONIST, PLOT, PROTAGONIST.

Consonance A pleasing combination of sounds, especially in poetry. Consonance usually refers to the repetition of consonant sounds in stressed syllables. Notice, for example, the echoing *p* sounds in the following lines from "Slam, Dunk, & Hook," by Yusef Komunyakaa:

. . . Trouble / Was there slapping a blackjack /
Against an open palm. . . .

See also SOUND DEVICES.

D

Description Writing that seeks to convey the impression of a setting, a person, an animal, an object, or an event by appealing to the senses. Almost all writing, fiction and nonfiction, contains elements of description. The following example of descriptive writing comes from "Lob's Girl," by Joan Aiken:

Instinctively she shut her eyes and felt the sand being wiped off her face by something that seemed like a warm, rough, damp flannel. . . . It was a tongue. Its owner was a large and bouncy young Alsatian, or German shepherd, with topaz eyes, black-tipped prick ears, a thick, soft coat, and a bushy black-tipped tail.

See page 73.

Details Particular features of things used to make descriptions more accurate and vivid. Authors use details to help readers imagine the characters, scenes, and actions they describe, as in this description of a boy in Borden Deal's "Antaeus."

He was a stocky, robust kid with a shock of white hair, nothing sissy about him except his voice; he talked in this slow, gentle voice like you never heard before.

Dialect A variation of language spoken by a particular group, often within a particular region. Dialects differ from standard language because they may contain different pronunciations, forms, and meanings. There is an example of dialect in these lines from "Mother to Son" by Langston Hughes:

I'se been a-climbin' on,
And reachin' landin's,
And turnin' corners. . . .

See page 240.

Dialogue Conversation between characters in a literary work. The following lines from "Uncle Tony's Goat," by Leslie Marmon Silko, are an example of dialogue:

Finally my uncle came out of the house; it was time for breakfast. "What's wrong?" he called out from the door.

"The billy goat won't come out, " I yelled back. . . .

"Get in there and get him out," he said. . . .

See page 560.
See also MONOLOGUE.

Drama A story intended to be performed by actors on a stage or before movie or TV cameras. Most dramas before the modern period can be divided into two basic types: tragedy and comedy. The script of a drama includes dialogue (the words the actors speak) and stage directions (descriptions of the action and scenery). "The Monsters Are Due on Maple Street," by Rod Serling, is an example of a television drama.

See pages 500–501.
See also COMEDY, TRAGEDY.

LITERARY TERMS HANDBOOK R3

E

Essay A short piece of nonfiction writing on a single topic. The purpose of the essay is to communicate an idea or opinion. A **formal essay** is serious and impersonal. A **informal essay** entertains while it informs, usually in a light conversational style. "The Fish Crisis," by J. Madeleine Nash, is an example of a formal essay.

See page 396.

Exposition The part of the plot of a short story, novel, novella, or play in which the characters, setting, and situation are introduced.

Extended metaphor An implied comparison that continues through an entire poem. "Loo-Wit," by Wendy Rose, contains an extended metaphor.

See page 820.
See also METAPHOR.

F

Fable A short, simple tale that teaches a moral. The characters in a fable are often animals who speak and act like people. The moral, or lesson, of the fable is usually stated outright, as in "Anansi and His Visitor, Turtle."

See page 703.

Falling action In a play or story, the action that follows the climax.

See also PLOT.

Fantasy A form of literature that explores unreal worlds of the past, the present, or the future. "The Smallest Dragonboy," by Anne McCaffrey, is fantasy combined with science fiction.

See page 695.

Fiction A prose narrative in which situations and characters are invented by the writer. Some aspects of a fictional work may be based on fact or experience. Fiction includes short stories, novellas, and novels.

See also NOVEL, NOVELLA, SHORT STORY.

Figurative language Language used for descriptive effect, often to imply ideas indirectly. Expressions of figurative language are not literally true but express some truth beyond the literal level. Although it appears in all kinds of writing, figurative language is especially prominent in poetry, for example, in "The Courage That My Mother Had," by Edna St. Vincent Millay.

See page 343.
See also ANALOGY, FIGURE OF SPEECH, METAPHOR, PERSONIFICATION, SIMILE, SYMBOL.

Figure of speech Figurative language of a specific kind, such as **analogy, metaphor, simile,** or **personification.**

First-person narrative. See POINT OF VIEW.

Flashback An interruption in a chronological narrative that tells about something that happened before that point in the story or before the story began. A flashback gives readers information that helps to explain the main events of the story. Ray Bradbury uses a flashback to fill in details of Margot's life in "All Summer in a Day."

See page 613.

Folklore The traditional beliefs, customs, stories, songs, and dances of the ordinary people (the "folk") of a culture. Folklore is passed on by word of mouth and performance rather than in writing.

See also FOLKTALE, LEGEND, MYTH, ORAL TRADITION.

Folktale A traditional story passed down orally long before being written down. Generally the author of a folktale is anonymous. Folktales include animal stories, trickster stories, fairy tales, myths, legends, and tall tales. "Aunty Misery," by

LITERARY TERMS HANDBOOK

Judith Ortiz Cofer, is an example of a folktale retold by a modern author.

See page 599.
See also LEGEND, MYTH, ORAL TRADITION, TALL TALE.

Foreshadowing The use of clues by an author to prepare readers for events that will happen in a story. An example of foreshadowing is Daedalus's warning Icarus never to fly very low or very high in "Icarus and Daedalus," by Josephine Preston Peabody.

See page 248.

Free verse Poetry that has no fixed pattern of meter, rhyme, line length, or stanza arrangement. "Without Commercials," by Alice Walker, is an example of free verse.

See page 255.
See also RHYTHM.

G

Genre A literary or artistic category. The main literary genres are prose, poetry, and drama. Each of these is divided into smaller genres. For example: **Prose** includes fiction (such as novels, novellas, short stories, and folktales) and nonfiction (such as biography, autobiography, and essays). **Poetry** includes lyric poetry, dramatic poetry, and narrative poetry. **Drama** includes tragedy, comedy, historical drama, melodrama, and farce.

H

Haiku Originally a Japanese form of poetry that has three lines and seventeen syllables. The first and third lines have five syllables each; the middle line has seven syllables. "Birds Circling at Dusk," by Ann Atwood, is an example of haiku.

See page 838.

Hero A literary work's main character, usually one with admirable qualities. Although the word *hero* is applied only to males in traditional usage (the female form is *heroine*), the term now applies to both sexes. Prometheus is the hero of the myth of the same name as retold by Bernard Evslin.

See also LEGEND, MYTH, PROTAGONIST, TALL TALE.

Historical fiction A novel, novella, play, short story, or narrative poem that sets fictional characters against a historical backdrop and contains many details about the period in which it is set.

See also GENRE.

Humor The quality of a literary work that makes the characters and their situations seem funny, amusing, or ludicrous. Humorous writing can be as effective in nonfiction as in fiction, as shown in Merrill Markoe's "Dog Diaries."

See also COMEDY.

I

Idiom A figure of speech that belongs exclusively to a particular language, people, or region and whose meaning cannot be obtained, and might even appear ridiculous, by joining the meanings of the words composing it. You would be using an idiom if you said you *caught* a cold.

Imagery Language that emphasizes sensory impressions to help the reader of a literary work see, hear, feel, smell, and taste the scenes described in the work.

See page 336.
See also FIGURATIVE LANGUAGE.

Informational text One kind of nonfiction. This kind of writing conveys facts and information without introducing personal opinion. "Hurri-

LITERARY TERMS HANDBOOK R5

canes," by Patricia Lauber, is an example of informational text.

See page 312.

Irony A form of expression in which the intended meaning of the words used is the opposite of their literal meaning. *Verbal irony* occurs when a person says one thing and means another–for example, saying "Nice guy!" about someone you dislike. *Situational irony* occurs when the outcome of a situation is the opposite of what was expected.

See page 21.

L

Legend A traditional story, based on history or an actual hero, that is passed down orally. A legend is usually exaggerated and gains elements of fantasy over the years. Stories about Daniel Boone and Davy Crockett are American legends.

See page 732.

Limerick A light humorous poem with a regular metrical scheme and a rhyme scheme of *aabba.*

See page 839.
See also HUMOR, RHYME SCHEME.

Local color The fictional portrayal of a region's features or peculiarities and its inhabitants' distinctive ways of talking and behaving, usually as a way of adding a realistic flavor to a story. "Rip Van Winkle," by Washington Irving, is notable for its touches of local color.

Lyric The words of a song, usually with a regular rhyme scheme. "Time to Change" is an example of a lyric with a regular rhyme scheme and a **refrain.**

See also RHYME SCHEME.

Lyric poetry Poems, usually short, that express strong personal feelings about a subject or an event. Emily Dickinson's "I'm Nobody! Who are You?" is a lyric poem.

M

Main idea The most important idea expressed in a paragraph or an essay. It may or may not be directly stated. In "The Teacher Who Changed My Life," by Nicholas Gage, the main idea is expressed in the title.

See page 374.

Memoir A biographical or autobiographical narrative emphasizing the narrator's personal experience during a period or at an event. "The Teacher Who Changed My Life," by Nicholas Gage, is an example of a memoir.

See page 39.
See also AUTOBIOGRAPHY, BIOGRAPHY.

Metaphor A figure of speech that compares or equates seemingly unlike things. In contrast to a simile, a metaphor implies the comparison instead of stating it directly; hence, there is no use of connectives such as *like* or *as.* The following line from "The Highwayman," by Alfred Noyes, contains an example of metaphor:

The moon was a ghostly galleon tossed upon cloudy seas. . . .

See page 391.
See also FIGURE OF SPEECH, IMAGERY, SIMILE.

Meter A regular pattern of stressed and unstressed syllables that gives a line of poetry a predictable rhythm. For example, the meter is marked in the following lines from "The Courage That My Mother Had," by Edna St. Vincent Millay:

T̆he góld̆en bro̮óch m̆y móth̆er wóre
S̆he léft b̆ehínd f̆or mé t̆o weár. . . .

See page 631.
See also RHYTHM

Monologue A long speech by a single character in a play or a solo performance.

Mood The emotional quality or atmosphere of a story or poem.

See page 134.
See also SETTING.

Myth A traditional story of unknown authorship, often involving goddesses, gods, and heroes, that attempts to explain a natural phenomenon, a historic event, or the origin of a belief or custom. "Atalanta's Race," by Rex Warner, is a retelling of an ancient Greek myth.

See page 740.

N

Narration Writing or speech that tells a story. Narration is used in prose fiction and narrative poetry. Narration can also be an important element in biographies, autobiographies, and essays.

Narrative poetry Verse that tells a story. "The Highwayman," by Alfred Noyes, is an example of a narrative poem.

See page 232.

Narrator The person who tells a story. In some cases the narrator is a character in the story–for example, the narrator in "Uncle Tony's Goat," by Leslie Marmon Silko.

See page 813.
See also POINT OF VIEW.

Nonfiction Factual prose writing. Nonfiction deals with real people and experiences. Among the categories of nonfiction are biographies, autobiographies, and essays. Patricia Lauber's "Hurricanes: Big Winds and Big Damage" is an example of nonfiction.

See pages 290–291.
See also AUTOBIOGRAPHY, BIOGRAPHY, ESSAY, FICTION.

Novel A book-length fictional prose narrative. The novel has more scope than a short story in its presentation of plot, character, setting, and theme. Because novels are not subject to any limits in their presentation of these elements, they encompass a wide range of narratives.

See also FICTION

Novella A work of fiction shorter than a novel but longer than a short story. A novella usually has more characters, settings, and events and a more complex plot than a short story.

O

Onomatopoeia The use of a word or a phrase that actually imitates or suggests the sound of what it describes. The following lines from "The Women's 400 Meters," by Lillian Morrison, contain an example of onomatopoeia:

Bang! they're off / careening down the lanes / each chased by her own bright tiger.

See page 626.
See also SOUND DEVICES.

Oral tradition Stories, knowledge, customs, and beliefs passed by word of mouth from one generation to the next. "Racing the Great Bear," as retold by Joseph Bruchac, is an example of a story passed down through oral tradition among Native Americans.

See page 276.
See also FOLKLORE, FOLKTALE, LEGEND, MYTH.

P

Parallelism The use of a series of words, phrases, or sentences that have similar grammatical form. Parallelism emphasizes the items that

LITERARY TERMS HANDBOOK R7

are arranged in the similar structures. Gwendolyn Brooks uses parallelism in these lines from "Home.":

They watched his progress. He passed the Kennedy's, he passed the vacant lot, he passed Mrs. Blakemore's.

See also REPETITION.

Personification A figure of speech in which an animal, object, or idea is given human form or characteristics. The following lines from "old age sticks," by E. E. Cummings, contain examples of personification:

old age sticks / up Keep / Off / signs)& / youth yanks them / down. . . .

See page 843.
See also FIGURATIVE LANGUAGE, FIGURE OF SPEECH, METAPHOR.

Plot The sequence of events in a story, novel, or play. The plot begins with **exposition,** which introduces the story's characters, setting, and situation. The plot catches the reader's attention with a **narrative hook.** The **rising action** adds complications to the story's conflict, or problem, leading to the **climax,** or point of highest emotional pitch. The **falling action** is the logical result of the climax, and the **resolution** presents the final outcome.

See pages 144–145.

Plot twist An unexpected turn of events in a plot. The surprise ending in O. Henry's "After Twenty Years" is an example of a plot twist.

See page 550.

Poetry A form of literary expression that differs from prose in emphasizing the line as the unit of composition. Many other traditional characteristics of poetry—emotional, imaginative language; use of metaphor and simile; division into stanzas; rhyme; regular pattern of stress, or meter—apply to some poems.

See pages 616–617.

Point of view The relationship of the narrator, or storyteller, to the story. In a story with **first-person point of view,** the story is told by one of the characters, referred to as "I," as in "Too Soon a Woman," by Dorothy M. Johnson. The reader generally sees everything through that character's eyes. In a story with a **limited third-person point of view,** the narrator reveals the thoughts of only one character, but refers to that character as "he" or "she," as in "Broken Chain," by Gary Soto. In a story with an **omniscient point of view,** like "Amigo Brothers," by Piri Thomas, the narrator reveals the thoughts of several characters.

See page 62.

Props Theater slang (a shortened form of *properties*) for objects and elements of the scenery of a stage play or movie set.

Propaganda Speech, writing, or other attempts to influence ideas or opinions, often through the use of stereotypes, faulty generalizations, logical fallacies, and/or emotional language.

Prose Writing that is similar to everyday speech and language, as opposed to poetry. Its form is based on sentences and paragraphs without the patterns of rhyme, controlled line length, or meter found in much poetry. Fiction and nonfiction are the major categories of prose. Most modern drama is also written in prose.

See also DRAMA, ESSAY, FICTION, NONFICTION.

Protagonist The central character in a story, drama, or dramatic poem. Usually the action revolves around the protagonist, who is involved in the main conflict. For example, Keevan is the protagonist of "The Smallest Dragonboy," by Anne McCaffrey.

See page 144.
See ANTAGONIST, CONFLICT.

Pun A humorous play on two or more meanings of the same word or on two words with the same sound. Today puns often appear in adver-

LITERARY TERMS HANDBOOK

tising headlines and slogans–for example, "Our hotel rooms give you suite feelings."

See page 561.
See also HUMOR.

R

Refrain A line or lines repeated regularly, usually in a poem or song. This refrain appears at the end of each of the two stanzas of "The Pasture," by Robert Frost:

I sha'n't be gone long.—You come too.

Repetition The recurrence of sounds, words, phrases, lines, or stanzas in a speech or piece of writing. Repetition increases the feeling of unity in a work. When a line or stanza is repeated in a poem or song, it is called a refrain. The following lines from "the 1st," by Lucille Clifton, make use of repetition:

nothing about the emptied rooms
nothing about the emptied family

See also PARALLELISM, REFRAIN.

Resolution The part of a plot that concludes the falling action by revealing or suggesting the outcome of the conflict.

See page 456.

Rhyme The repetition of sounds at the ends of words that appear close to each other in a poem. **End rhyme** occurs at the ends of lines. **Internal rhyme** occurs within a single line. **Slant rhyme** occurs when words include sounds that are similar but not identical. Slant rhyme usually involves some variation of **consonance** (the repetition of consonant sounds) or **assonance** (the repetition of vowel sounds).The following lines from "The Cremation of Sam McGee" have both internal and end rhymes.

On a Christmas Day we were mushing our way
over the Dawson trail.
Talk of your cold! through the parka's fold it
stabbed like a driven nail.

See page 641.

Rhyme scheme The pattern of rhyme formed by the end rhyme in a poem. The rhyme scheme is designated by the assignment of a different letter of the alphabet to each new rhyme. For example, the opening stanza of "Annabel Lee," by Edgar Allan Poe, has a rhyme scheme of *ababcb.*

See page 262.

Rhythm The pattern created by the arrangement of stressed and unstressed syllables, especially in poetry. Rhythm gives poetry a musical quality that helps convey its meaning. Rhythm can be regular (with a predictable pattern or meter) or irregular, (as in free verse).

See page 631.
See also METER.

Rising action The part of a plot that adds complications to the problems in the story and increases reader interest.

See also FALLING ACTION, PLOT.

S

Scene A subdivision of an act in a play. Each scene takes place in a specific setting and time. An act may have one or more scenes.

See also ACT.

Science fiction Fiction dealing with the impact of real science or imaginary superscience on human or alien societies of the past, present, or future. Although science fiction is mainly a product of the twentieth century, nineteenth-century authors such as Mary Shelley, Jules Verne, and Robert Louis Stevenson were pioneers of the genre. Isaac Asimov's "Key Item" is an example of science fiction.

See page 467.

LITERARY TERMS HANDBOOK R9

Throughout this Language Handbook, you will find exercises and activities designed to give your students point-of-use practice in applying rules of grammar, usage, and mechanics.

Exercise

Sentence Fragments Direct the students to identify each of the following items as a sentence or a fragment. Then have them add words to each fragment to make it a sentence.

1. The boys standing in the corridor.
2. Suddenly dropped an armful of books.
3. No one moved.
4. Applauded each speaker as she or he rose to address the audience.
5. A small child started to cry.
6. When the banquet started.
7. At a table near the door.
8. An elaborate chandelier graced the entry.
9. Comfortable couches and overstuffed chairs.
10. The crystal glasses on the table sparkled.

Answers

Sample sentences are given.

1. F; The boys standing in the corridor waited for the dismissal bell.
2. F; The librarian suddenly dropped an armful of books.
3. sentence
4. F; The proud teacher applauded each speaker as she or he rose to address the audience.
5. sentence
6. F; Everyone took a seat when the banquet started.
7. F; John sat at a table near the door.
8. sentence
9. F; The reception area was furnished with comfortable couches and overstuffed chairs.
10. sentence

Language Handbook

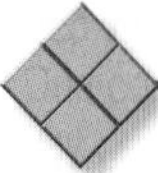

Troubleshooter

Use the Troubleshooter to recognize and correct common writing errors.

Sentence Fragment

A sentence fragment does not express a complete thought. It may lack a subject a predicate, or both.

Problem: Fragment that lacks a subject

The lion paced the floor of the cage. (Looked hungry.) *frag*

Solution: Add a subject to the fragment to make a complete sentence.

The lion paced the floor of the cage. He looked hungry.

Problem: Fragment that lacks a predicate

I'm painting my room. (The walls yellow.) *frag*

Solution: Add a predicate to make the sentence complete.

I'm painting my room. The walls are going to be yellow.

Problem: Fragment that lacks both a subject and a predicate

We walked around the reservoir. (Near the parkway.) *frag*

Solution: Combine the fragment with another sentence.

We walked around the reservoir near the parkway.

Rule of Thumb

You can use fragments when talking with friends or writing personal letters. Some writers use fragments to produce a special effect. Use complete sentences, however, for school or business writing.

Run-on Sentence

A run-on sentence is two or more sentences written incorrectly as one sentence.

Problem: Two main clauses separated only by a comma

Roller coasters make me dizzy, I don't enjoy them. *run-on*

Solution A: Replace the comma with a period or other end mark. Start the second sentence with a capital letter.

Roller coasters make me dizzy. I don't enjoy them.

Solution B: Replace the comma with a semicolon.

Roller coasters make me dizzy; I don't enjoy them.

Problem: Two main clauses with no punctuation between them

Acid rain is a worldwide problem there are no solutions in sight. *run-on*

Solution A: Separate the main clauses with a period or other end mark. Begin the second sentence with a capital letter.

Acid rain is a worldwide problem. There are no solutions in sight.

Solution B: Add a comma and a coordinating conjunction between the main clauses.

Acid rain is a worldwide problem, but there are no solutions in sight.

Problem: Two main clauses with no comma before the coordinating conjunction

Our chorus has been practicing all month but we still need another rehearsal. *run-on*

Solution: Add a comma before the coordinating conjunction.

Our chorus has been practicing all month, but we still need another rehearsal.

Exercise

Run-on Sentences Direct the students to correct the following run-on sentences.

1. The trip was long and boring naturally the small child became restless.
2. We picked apples and then we picked strawberries and we were tired.
3. Election day finally arrived and qualified voters flocked to the polling places.
4. The video game fascinated Ray he did not notice his father standing behind him.
5. Vacation was over tomorrow school would begin.
6. The spaghetti was overcooked and the meatballs were dried out.
7. Shelly embroidered the pillowcases she gave them to her mother.
8. The engineers set off the explosion and the old building crumbled in seconds.
9. I often enjoy a salad for lunch but in cold weather I prefer soup.
10. The article ran in the Sunday newspaper it was three pages long.

Possible Answers

1. The trip was long and boring. Naturally, the small child became restless.
2. We picked apples, and then we picked strawberries. We were tired.
3. Election day finally arrived, and qualified voters flocked to the polling places.
4. The video game fascinated Ray. He did not notice his father standing behind him.
5. Vacation was over. Tomorrow school would begin.
6. The spaghetti was overcooked, and the meatballs were dried out.
7. Shelly embroidered the pillowcases; she gave them to her mother.
8. The engineers set off the explosion, and the old building crumbled in seconds.
9. I often enjoy a salad for lunch, but in cold weather I prefer soup.
10. The article ran in the Sunday newspaper; it was three pages long.

Exercise

Subject-Verb Agreement

Direct the students to choose the correct word from the parentheses.

1. A bag of crispy red apples (make, makes) my mouth water.
2. The man in leather boots (look, looks) like a cowboy.
3. There (hang, hangs) my first pair of ballet slippers.
4. Each of the tourists (buy, buys) rugs and pottery.
5. Most of the people (react, reacts) calmly to the emergency.
6. Here (are, is) the puzzling facts about the woman's disappearance.
7. A collection of antique spoons (stand, stands) on the shelf.
8. Every one of the students (hand, hands) in the assignment on time.
9. Bales of cotton (fill, fills) the storehouse.
10. Here (come, comes) the athletes.

Answers

1. makes
2. looks
3. hangs
4. buys
5. react
6. are
7. stands
8. hands
9. fill
10. come

Lack of Subject-Verb Agreement

A singular subject calls for a singular form of the verb. A plural subject calls for a plural form of the verb.

Problem: A subject that is separated from the verb by an intervening prepositional phrase

The two policemen at the construction site (looks) bored. *agr*

The members of my baby-sitting club (is) saving money. *agr*

Solution: Make sure that the verb agrees with the subject of the sentence, not with the object of the preposition. The object of a preposition is never the subject.

The two policemen at the construction site look bored.

The members of my baby-sitting club are saving money.

Rule of Thumb

When subject and verb are separated by a prepositional phrase, check for agreement by reading the sentence without the prepositional phrase.

Problem: A sentence that begins with *here* or *there*

Here (come) the last bus to Pelham Heights. *agr*

There (is) my aunt and uncle. *agr*

Solution: In a sentence that begins with *here* or *there,* look for the subject after the verb. Make sure that the verb agrees with the subject.

Here comes the last bus to Pelham Heights.

There are my aunt and uncle.

Problem: An indefinite pronoun as the subject

Each of the candidates (are) qualified. *agr*

All of the problems on the test (was) hard. *agr*

Solution: Some indefinite pronouns are singular, some are plural, and some can be either singular or plural, depending on the noun they refer to. Determine whether the indefinite pronoun is singular or plural and make sure the verb agrees with it.

Each of the candidates is qualified.

All of the problems on the test were hard.

Problem: A compound subject that is joined by *and*

Fishing tackle and a life jacket (was) stowed in the boat. *agr*

Peanut butter and jelly (are) delicious. *agr*

Solution A: If the parts of a compound subject refer to different people or things, use a plural verb.

Fishing tackle and a life jacket were stowed in the boat.

Solution B: If the parts of a compound subject name one unit or if they refer to the same person or thing, use a singular verb.

Peanut butter and jelly is delicious.

Problem: A compound subject that is joined by *or* or *nor*

Either my aunt or my parents (plans) to attend parents' night. *agr*

Neither onions nor pepper (improve) the taste of this meatloaf. *agr*

Solution: Make the verb agree with the subject that is closer to it.

Either my aunt or my parents plan to attend parents' night.

Neither onions nor pepper improves the taste of this meatloaf.

Incorrect Verb Tense or Form

A verb has various tenses to show when the action takes place.

Problem: An incorrect or missing verb ending

The Parks Department (install) a new water fountain last week. *tense*

They have also (plant) flowers in all the flower beds. *tense*

Solution: To form the past tense and the part participle, add *-ed* to a regular verb.

The Parks Department installed a new water fountain last week.

They have also planted flowers in all the flower beds.

LANGUAGE HANDBOOK

Exercise

Subject-Verb Agreement/Verb Tense Direct the students to choose the correct word from the parentheses.

1. Peanut butter and jelly (make, makes) a delicious sandwich.
2. A dustpan and a broom (are, is) in the hall closet.
3. The owner and manager of the store (stay, stays) on the job until midnight.
4. Checkers or chess (keep, keeps) the retirees occupied for hours.
5. My friend and neighbor (own, owns) a new lawnmower.
6. My friend and her neighbor (come, comes) to visit on Fridays.
7. Your hat and coat (look, looks) brand new.
8. Jane (arrive, arrived) yesterday.
9. Either a pink blouse or a lavender one (complement, complements) your new suit.
10. Why have we (follow, followed) that car for five miles?

Answers

1. makes
2. are
3. stays
4. keeps
5. owns
6. come
7. look
8. arrived
9. complements
10. followed

Exercise

Verb Tense Direct the students to choose the correct word from the parentheses.

1. After you have (ate, eaten), be sure to clean up.
2. Peter (flew, flown) the plane all the way back to Newark.
3. No one (saw, seen) Edward at the game.
4. Marian (brung, brought) her puppet to school to demonstrate her hobby.
5. I have never (spoke, spoken) to a senator before today.
6. Kitty never (broke, broken) a promise to her mother.
7. Has anyone (forgot, forgotten) a set of house keys?
8. Everyone in the courtroom (rose, risen) when the judge entered.
9. The chorus (sang, sung) my favorite song.
10. Pam had (took, taken) a bite of my apple.

Answers

1. eaten
2. flew
3. saw
4. brought
5. spoken
6. broke
7. forgotten
8. rose
9. sang
10. taken

Problem: An improperly formed irregular verb

Wendell has standed in line for two hours. *tense*

I catched the fly ball and throwed it to first base. *tense*

Solution: Irregular verbs vary in their past and past participle forms. Look up the ones you are not sure of.

Wendell has stood in line for two hours.

I caught the fly ball and threw it to first base.

Problem: Confusion between the past form and the past participle

The cast for *The Music Man* has began rehearsals. *tense*

Solution: Use the past-participle form of an irregular verb, not its past form, when you use the auxiliary verb *have*.

The cast for *The Music Man* has begun rehearsals.

Problem: Improper use of the past participle

Our seventh grade drawn a mural for the wall of the cafeteria. *tense*

Solution: Add the auxiliary verb *have* to the past participle of an irregular verb to form a complete verb.

Our seventh grade has drawn a mural for the wall of the cafeteria.

Problem: Overuse of the passive voice

The mural was carried to the cafeteria by Alec and Juanita. *voice*
It was attached to the wall by Tania and Lee.

Solution: Change the verbs so that the subject of each sentence performs, rather than receives, the action of the verb.

Alec and Juanita carried the mural to the cafeteria. Tania and Lee attached it to the wall.

Incorrect Use of Pronouns

The noun that a pronoun refers to is called its **antecedent.** A pronoun must refer to its antecedent clearly. Subject pronouns refer to subjects in a sentence. Object pronouns refer to objects in a sentence.

Problem: A pronoun that could refer to more than one antecedent

Gary and Mike are coming, but he doesn't know the other kids. *ant*

Solution: Substitute a noun for the pronoun to make your sentence clearer.

Gary and Mike are coming, but Gary doesn't know the other kids.

Problem: A personal pronoun as a subject

Him and John were freezing after skating for three hours. *pro*

Lori and me decided not to audition for the musical. *pro*

Solution: Use a subject pronoun as the subject part of a sentence.

He and John were freezing after skating for three hours.

Lori and I decided not to audition for the musical.

Problem: A personal pronoun as an object

Ms. Wang asked Reggie and I to enter the science fair. *pro*

Ms. Wang helped he and I with the project. *pro*

Solution: Use an object pronoun as the object of a verb or a preposition.

Ms. Wang asked Reggie and me to enter the science fair.

Ms. Wang helped him and me with the project.

Rule of Thumb

When a pronoun is part of a compound subject or object, it is sometimes hard to choose the correct pronoun. Try saying the sentence with only the pronoun as the subject or object. That often makes the correct choice clear. For example, change *Dad gave Ronny and I a new basketball* to *Dad gave* I *a new basketball.* The pronoun *I* sounds wrong and should be changed to *me.*

Exercise

Pronoun Usage Direct the students to choose the right form of the pronoun from the parentheses.

1. Hannah and (she, her) practiced their piano duet.
2. My brother and (I, me) are both good swimmers.
3. Send an invitation to Janet and (he, him).
4. My cousins and (they, them) know one another.
5. Please give Sara and (I, me) a chance to perform.
6. (He, Him) and his friends have joined a writers' club.
7. That surprised Joanie and (I, me).
8. (Her, She) and Rick are cousins.
9. (Them, They) and (us, we) have an agreement.
10. Charlie and (he, him) will arrive later.

Answers

1. she
2. I
3. him
4. they
5. me
6. He
7. me
8. She
9. They, we
10. he

Exercise

Adjective Usage Direct the students to correct the errors in the use of adjectives in the following sentences.

1. The remake of the film is more good than the original.
2. If you try to make someone else feel comfortable at the party, you'll have a more better time yourself.
3. Your idea is the bestest I've heard so far.
4. Leaving questions unanswered is the baddest mistake you can make.
5. The acting in the play was worser than we had expected.
6. I have never seen Reva more happier than today.
7. Dan and I climbed the most highest mountain in the area.
8. The weather today will be more colder than yesterday.
9. Brigid's new hairdo makes her face look more thinner.
10. Last week we had the worsest storm of the season.

Answers

1. The remake of the film is better than the original.
2. If you try to make someone else feel comfortable at the party, you'll have a better time yourself.
3. Your idea is the best I've heard so far.
4. Leaving questions unanswered is the worst mistake you can make.
5. The acting in the play was worse than we had expected.
6. I have never seen Reva happier than today.
7. Dan and I climbed the highest mountain in the area.
8. The weather today will be colder than yesterday.
9. Brigid's new hairdo makes her face look thinner.
10. Last week we had the worst storm of the season.

Incorrect Use of Adjectives

Some adjectives have irregular forms: comparative forms for comparing two things and superlative forms for comparing more than two things.

Problem: Incorrect use of *good, better, best*

Their team is (more good) at softball than ours. *adj*

They have (more better) equipment too. *adj*

Solution: The comparative and superlative forms of *good* are *better* and *best.* Do not use *more* or *most* before irregular forms of comparative and superlative adjectives.

Their team is better at softball than ours.

They have better equipment too.

Problem: Incorrect use of *bad, worse, worst*

The flooding on East Street was the (baddest) I've seen. *adj*

Mike's basement was in (badder) shape than his garage. *adj*

Solution: The comparative and superlative forms of *bad* are *worse* and *worst.* Do not use *more* or *most* or the endings *-er* or *-est* with *bad.*

The flooding on East Street was the worst I've seen.

Mike's basement was in worse shape than his garage.

Problem: Incorrect use of comparative and superlative adjectives

The Appalachian Mountains are (more older) than the Rockies. *adj*

Mount Washington is the (most highest) of the Appalachians. *adj*

Solution: Do not use both *-er* and *more* or *-est* and *most* at the same time.

The Appalachian Mountains are older than the Rockies.

Mount Washington is the highest of the Appalachians.

Incorrect Use of Commas

Commas signal a pause between parts of a sentence and help to clarify meaning.

Problem: Missing commas in a series of three or more items

Sergio put mustard catsup and bean sprouts on his hot dog. *com*

Solution: If there are three or more items in a series, use a comma after each one, including the item preceding the conjunction.

Sergio put mustard, catsup, and bean sprouts on his hot dog.

Problem: Missing commas with direct quotations

"A little cold water" the swim coach said "won't hurt you." *com*

Solution: The first part of an interrupted quotation ends with a comma followed by quotation marks. The interrupting words are also followed by a comma.

"A little cold water," the swim coach said, "won't hurt you."

Problem: Missing commas with nonessential appositives

My sneakers a new pair are covered with mud. *com*

Solution: Determine whether the appositive is important to the meaning of the sentence. If it is not essential, set off the appositive with commas.

My sneakers, a new pair, are covered with mud.

Incorrect Use of Apostrophes

An apostrophe shows possession. It can also indicate missing letters in a contraction.

Problem: A singular possessive noun

A parrots toes are used for gripping. *poss*

The bus color was bright yellow. *poss*

Solution: Use an apostrophe and an *s* to form the possessive of a singular noun, even one that ends in *s*.

A parrot's toes are used for gripping.

The bus's color was bright yellow.

Exercise

Commas Direct students to insert commas where necessary in the following sentences.

1. Crackers peanut butter and apples were on the shopping list.
2. "Wearing the right swimsuit" said the coach "will improve your speed in the water."
3. The entire pep squad fifteen girls and three boys practiced every day.
4. We searched for the lost keys in coat pockets on shelves and even under the chairs.
5. Lauren asked "Is anyone walking home with you?"
6. Yesterday Mother gave me a gold chain an early birthday gift.
7. I've invited Jack my best friend to the concert.
8. Eggs sausage and cheese are the main ingredients in the dish.
9. "I waited for an hour" said Jean "but no train came."
10. The crowd clapped cheered and whistled after each performance in the skating competition.

Answers

1. Crackers, peanut butter, and apples were on the shopping list.
2. "Wearing the right swimsuit," said the coach, "will improve your speed in the water."
3. The entire pep squad, fifteen girls and three boys, practiced every day.
4. We searched for the lost keys in coat pockets, on shelves, and even under the chairs.
5. Lauren asked, "Is anyone walking home with you?"
6. Yesterday Mother gave me a gold chain, an early birthday gift.
7. I've invited Jack, my best friend, to the concert.
8. Eggs, sausage, and cheese are the main ingredients in the dish.
9. "I waited for an hour," said Jean, "but no train came."
10. The crowd clapped, cheered, and whistled after each performance in the skating competition.

Exercise

Apostrophes Direct the students to make four column on their papers. In the first column, they should list the words in the numbered list below. In the other three columns, they should list the singular possessive, the plural, and the plural possessive forms of each word.

1. teacher
2. woman
3. Smith
4. assistant
5. mouse
6. sheep
7. son
8. Diaz
9. actress
10. child

Answers

1. teacher's teachers teachers'
2. woman's women women's
3. Smith's Smiths Smiths'
4. assistant's assistants assistants'
5. mouse's mice mice's
6. sheep's sheep sheep's
7. son's sons sons'
8. Diaz's Diazes Diazes'
9. actress's actresses actresses'
10. child's children children's

Problem: A plural possessive noun ending in *s*

The visitors center closes at five o'clock. *poss*

The guide put several tourists luggage in one compartment. *poss*

Solution: Use an apostrophe alone to form the possessive of a plural noun that ends in *s.*

The visitors' center closes at five o'clock.

The guide put several tourists' luggage in one compartment.

Problem: A plural possessive noun not ending in *s*

The peoples applause gave courage to the young gymnast. *poss*

Solution: Use an apostrophe and an *s* to form the possessive of a plural noun that does not end in *s.*

The people's applause gave courage to the young gymnast.

Problem: A possessive personal pronoun

Jenny found the locker that was her's; she waited while her friends found their's. *poss*

Solution: Do not use an apostrophe with a possessive personal pronoun.

Jenny found the locker that was hers; she waited while her friends found theirs.

Incorrect Capitalization

Proper nouns, proper adjectives, and the first word of a sentence always begin with capital letters.

Problem: Words referring to ethnic groups, nationalities, and languages

Many canadians in the province of quebec speak french. *cap*

Solution: Capitalize proper nouns and adjectives that refer to ethnic groups, nationalities, and languages.

Many Canadians in the province of Quebec speak French.

Problem: A word that refers to a family member

Yesterday (aunt) Doreen asked me to baby-sit. *cap*

Don't forget to give (dad) a call. *cap*

Solution: Capitalize words that are used as part of or in place of a family member's name.

Yesterday Aunt Doreen asked me to baby-sit.

Don't forget to give Dad a call.

Rule of Thumb

Do not capitalize a word that identifies a family member when it is preceded by a possessive adjective: *My father bought a new car.*

Problem: The first word of a direct quotation

The judge declared, "(the) court is now in session." *cap*

Solution: Capitalize the first word in a direct quotation.

The judge declared, "The court is now in session."

Rule of Thumb

If you have difficulty with a rule of usage, try rewriting the rule in your own words. Check with your teacher to be sure you understand the rule.

Exercise

Capitalization Direct the students to correct the errors in capitalization in the following sentences.

1. Many american cities have names that date back to the time of spanish exploration.
2. Jan said, "the bookstore closes at 7:00 P.M."
3. We bought grandma a quilted robe.
4. We depended on uncle Tony for transportation.
5. My aunt teaches english to german immigrants.
6. "Watch closely," said the magician, "As I make your watch disappear."
7. My family is planning a trip to mexico.
8. Many Americans enjoy chinese and italian foods.
9. Ask dad if you can use the car.
10. Your Mother is a wonderful cook.

Answers

1. Many American cities have names that date back to the time of Spanish exploration.
2. Jan said, "The bookstore closes at 7:00 P.M."
3. We bought Grandma a quilted robe.
4. We depended on Uncle Tony for transportation.
5. My aunt teaches English to German immigrants.
6. "Watch closely," said the magician, "as I make your watch disappear."
7. My family is planning a trip to Mexico.
8. Many Americans enjoy Chinese and Italian foods.
9. Ask Dad if you can use the car.
10. Your mother is a wonderful cook.

Exercise

Troublesome Words Direct students to choose the correct word from the parentheses.

1. Do not (accept, except) a package on which the seal is broken.
2. What is meant by "the greenhouse (affect effect)"?
3. Have the package (all ready, already) when the messenger arrives.
4. Everyone (accept, except) Hal was on time.
5. (A lot, Alot) of my friends are going camping this weekend.
6. The tilt of Earth (affects, effects) the polar regions most dramatically.
7. Most of the tourists have (all ready, already) boarded the bus.
8. The presenters had to (accept, except) the award for the absent celebrity.
9. (I ain't, I'm not) leaving until my mother comes home.
10. The movie's special (affects, effects) were spectacular.

Answers

1. accept
2. effect
3. all ready
4. except
5. A lot
6. affects
7. already
8. accept
9. I'm not
10. effects

Troublesome Words

This section will help you choose between words and expressions that are often confusing or misused.

accept, except

Accept means "to receive." *Except* means "other than."

Phillip walked proudly to the stage to **accept** the award.

Everything fits in my suitcase **except** my sleeping bag.

affect, effect

Affect is a verb meaning "to cause a change in" or "to influence." *Effect* as a verb means "to bring about or accomplish." As a noun, *effect* means "result."

Bad weather will **affect** our plans for the weekend.

The new medicine **effected** an improvement in the patient's condition.

The gloomy weather had a bad **effect** on my mood.

ain't

Ain't is never used in formal speaking or writing unless you are quoting the exact words of a character or a real person. Instead of using *ain't,* say or write *am not, is not, are not;* or use contractions such as *I'm not, she isn't.*

The pizza **is not** going to arrive for another half hour.

The pizza **isn't** going to arrive for another half hour.

a lot

The expression *a lot* means "much" or "many" and should always be written as two words. Some authorities discourage its use in formal writing.

A lot of my friends are learning Spanish.

Many of my friends are learning Spanish.

all ready, already

All ready, written as two words, is a phrase that means "completely ready." *Already,* written as one word, is an adverb that means "before" or "by this time."

By the time the fireworks display was **all ready**, we had **already** arrived.

all right, alright

The expression *all right* should be written as two words. Some dictionaries do list the single word *alright* but usually not as a preferred spelling.

Tom hurt his ankle, but he will be **all right.**

all together, altogether

All together means "in a group." *Altogether* means "completely."

The Minutemen stood **all together** at the end of Lexington Green.

The rebel farmers were not **altogether** sure that they could fight the British soldiers.

among, between

Use *among* for three or more people, things, or groups. Use *between* for two people, things, or groups.

Mr. Kendall divided the jobs for the car wash **among** the team members.

Our soccer field lies **between** the gym and Main Street.

amount, number

Use *amount* with nouns that cannot be counted. Use *number* with nouns that can be counted.

This recipe calls for an unusual **amount** of pepper.

A record **number** of students attended last Saturday's book fair.

bad, badly

Bad is an adjective; it modifies a noun. *Badly* is an adverb; it modifies a verb, an adjective, or another adverb.

The **badly** burnt cookies left a **bad** smell in the kitchen.

Joseph **badly** wants to be on the track team.

beside, besides

Beside means "next to." *Besides* means "in addition to."

The zebra is grazing **beside** a wildebeest.

Besides the zoo, I like to visit the aquarium.

bring, take

Bring means "to carry from a distant place to a closer one." *Take* means "to carry from a nearby place to a more distant one."

Please **bring** a bag lunch and subway money to school tomorrow.

Don't forget to **take** your art projects home this afternoon.

LANGUAGE HANDBOOK

Exercise

Troublesome Words Direct the students to choose the correct word from the parentheses.

1. Many children have (all together, altogether) too much sugar in their diets.
2. Janet, are you feeling (all right, alright) this morning?
3. A small (amount, number) of people suffer from that rare disease.
4. Michael feels (bad, badly) about his mistake.
5. You should (bring, take) your poems with you to the poetry club meeting.
6. How many students (beside, besides) you have made the same mistake?
7. Divide the candy (among, between) the three children.
8. The commuters waited (all together, altogether) for the shuttle bus.
9. (Bring, Take) some of the leftover sandwiches home with you.
10. The cake requires only a small (amount, number) of butter.

Answers

1. altogether
2. all right
3. number
4. bad
5. bring
6. besides
7. among
8. all together
9. Take
10. amount

Exercise

Troublesome Words Direct the students to choose the correct word from the parentheses.

1. Eliza (can, may) swim as well as her brother.
2. The class will (choose, chose) a boy or girl to be a representative.
3. Many people (doesn't, don't) know their elected officials.
4. I can swim (farther, further) than my sister.
5. My baby brother speaks (good, well).
6. You (can, may) attend the game if your homework is finished.
7. That topic deserves (farther, further) investigation.
8. My aunt (choose, chose) to save her vacation days for an extended trip.
9. I feel (good, well) about my decision to run for class president.
10. Mary (doesn't, don't) come to club meetings any more.

Answers

1. can
2. choose
3. don't
4. farther
5. well
6. may
7. further
8. chose
9. good
10. doesn't

can, may

Can implies the ability to do something. *May* implies permission to do something.

You **may** take a later bus home if you **can** remember which bus to get on.

Rule of Thumb

Although *can* is sometimes used in place of *may* in informal speech, a distinction should be made when speaking and writing formally.

choose, chose

Choose means "to select." *Chose,* the past tense of *choose,* means "selected."

Dad helped me **choose** a birthday card for my grandmother.

Dad **chose** a card with a funny joke inside.

doesn't, don't

The subject of the contraction **doesn't** *(does not)* is the third-person singular (*he* or *she*). The subject of the contraction **don't** *(do not)* is *I, you, we,* or *they.*

Tanya **doesn't** have any tickets for the concert.

We **don't** need tickets if we stand in the back row.

farther, further

Farther refers to physical distance. *Further* refers to time or degree.

Our new apartment is **farther** away from the school.

I will not continue this argument **further.**

fewer, less

Fewer is used to refer to things or qualities that can be counted. *Less* is used to refer to things or qualities that cannot be counted. In addition, *less* is used with figures that are regarded as single amounts.

Fewer people were waiting in line after lunch.

There is **less** fat in this kind of peanut butter.

Try to spend **less** than ten dollars on a present. [The money is treated as a single sum, not as individual dollars.]

good, well

Good is often used as an adjective meaning "pleasing" or "able." *Well* may be used as an adverb of manner telling how ably something is done or as an adjective meaning "in good health."

That is a **good** haircut.

Marco writes **well.**

Because Ms. Rodriguez had a headache, she was not **well** enough to correct our tests.

in, into *In* means "inside." *Into* indicates a movement from outside toward the inside.	Refreshments will be sold **in** the lobby of the auditorium. The doors opened, and the eager crowd rushed **into** the auditorium.
it's, its Use an apostrophe to form the contraction of *it is.* The possessive of the personal pronoun *it* does not take an apostrophe.	**It's** hard to keep up with computer technology. The computer industry seems to change **its** products daily.
lay, lie *Lay* means "to place." *Lie* means "to recline."	I will **lay** my beach towel here on the warm sand. Help! I don't want to **lie** next to a hill of red ants!
learn, teach *Learn* means "to gain knowledge." *Teach* means "to give knowledge."	I don't **learn** very quickly. My uncle is **teaching** me how to juggle.
leave, let *Leave* means "to go away." *Let* means "to allow." With the word *alone,* you may use either *let* or *leave.*	Huang has to **leave** at eight o'clock. Mr. Davio **lets** the band practice in his basement. **Leave** me alone. **Let** me alone.
like, as Use *like,* a preposition, to introduce a prepositional phrase. Use *as,* a subordinating conjunction, to introduce a subordinate clause. Many authorities believe that *like* should not be used before a clause in formal English.	Andy sometimes acts **like** a clown. The detective looked carefully at the empty suitcase **as** she examined the room.

Rule of Thumb

As can be a preposition in cases like the following: *Jack went to the costume party as a giant pumpkin.*

Exercise

Troublesome Words Direct the students to choose the correct word from the parentheses.

1. The snake leaves (its, it's) old skin behind when it grows a new one.
2. Who (learned, taught) you how to string a bow?
3. The sparkling sun made the water look (as, like) gold.
4. The old cat likes to (lay, lie) in the sun.
5. The talking stopped when the teacher walked (in, into) the room.
6. Call me when (its, it's) time to go.
7. We had to wait for the doctor (as, like) I had expected.
8. Don't (leave, let) a stranger enter the house.
9. (Lay, Lie) your books on the hall table.
10. I will (leave, let) you in the minute you ring the doorbell.

Answers

1. its
2. taught
3. like
4. lie
5. into
6. it's
7. as
8. let
9. Lay
10. let

Exercise

Troublesome Words Direct the students to choose the correct word from the parentheses.

1. Put the money away carefully so you don't (loose, lose) it.
2. You should (raise, rise) all the window shades to the same height.
3. Ali is taller (than, then) his older brother.
4. (Set, Sit) the vase in the middle of the table.
5. The sailors met (their, there) families on shore.
6. My feet are (too, two) sore to walk any farther.
7. Where are the boys (who, whom) will carry the flags?
8. Who's, Whose) books are those?
9. Close the doors before the lab animals get (loose, lose)!
10. Stop, look, listen, and (than, then) cross the street.

Answers

1. lose
2. raise
3. than
4. Set
5. their
6. too
7. who
8. Whose
9. loose
10. then

loose, lose

Loose means "not firmly attached." *Lose* means "to misplace" or "to fail to win."

If you keep wiggling that **loose** tooth, you might **lose** it.

raise, rise

Raise means to "cause to move up." *Rise* means "to move upward."

Farmers in this part of Florida **raise** sugarcane.

The hot air balloon began to **rise** slowly in the morning sky.

set, sit

Set means "to place" or "to put." *Sit* means "to place oneself in a seated position."

I **set** the tips of my running shoes against the starting line.

After running the fifty-yard dash, I had to **sit** down and catch my breath.

than, then

Than introduces the second part of a comparison. *Then* means "at that time" or "after that."

I'd rather go to Disney World in the winter **than** in the summer.

The park is too crowded and hot **then.**

their, they're

Their is the possessive form of *they. They're* is the contraction of *they are.*

They're visiting Plymouth Plantation during **their** vacation.

to, too, two

To means "in the direction of." *Too* means "also" or "to an excessive degree." *Two* is the number after one.

I bought **two** tickets **to** the concert.

The music was **too** loud.

It's my favorite group **too.**

who, whom

Who is a subject pronoun. *Whom* is an object pronoun.

Who has finished the test already?

Mr. Russo is the man to **whom** we owe our thanks.

who's, whose

Who's is the contraction of *who is. Whose* is the possessive form of *who.*

Who's going to wake me up in the morning?

The policeman discovered **whose** car alarm was making so much noise.

Grammar Glossary

This glossary will help you quickly locate information on parts of speech and sentence structure.

A

Abstract noun. *See* Noun.

Action verb. *See* Verb.

Active voice. *See* Voice.

Adjective A word that modifies a noun or a pronoun. An adjective may answer one of these questions: *What kind? Which one? How many? How much?* (The *playful* dog splashed in the *cold* water.)

Many adjectives have different forms to indicate degree of comparison. *(bright, brighter, brightest)*

The comparative degree compares two persons, places, things, or ideas. *(worse, sadder)*

The superlative degree compares more than two persons, places, things, or ideas. *(worst, saddest)*

A predicate adjective always follows a linking verb. It describes the subject of the sentence. (Marathon running is *difficult.*)

A proper adjective is formed from a proper noun. It always begins with a capital letter. Most proper adjectives are formed by using the following endings: *-an, -ian, -ese, -ish. (Chin**ese**)*

A possessive noun (such as *poet's, classes'* or *Emerson's*) or possessive pronoun (*my, your, her, his, its, their*) functions as an adjective. It answers the question *Which one?*

A demonstrative adjective is a pronoun that answers the question *Which one?* (Jane read *that* book.)

Adverb A word that modifies a verb, an adjective, or another adverb. Adverbs answer the questions *How? When?* and *Where?* When modifying a verb, an adverb may appear in various positions in a sentence. (The van rocked *dangerously* on the bumpy road. *Gradually* we slowed down.)

When modifying an adjective or another adverb, an adverb appears directly before the modified word. (The driver stopped *quite* suddenly.) The negatives *no* and *not* and *-n't* (the contraction for *not*) are adverbs. (I could *not* see through the fog.) Other negative words, such as *nowhere, hardly,* and *never,* can function as adverbs of time, place, and degree. (She would *hardly* endorse such an idea.)

Some adverbs have various forms to indicate degree of comparison. *(loud, louder, loudest; sweetly, more sweetly, most sweetly)* Many adverbs are formed by adding *-ly* to adjectives. *(calmly)* However, not all words that end in *-ly* are adverbs. *(friendly)*

Antecedent. *See* Pronoun.

Appositive A noun placed next to another noun to identify it or add information about it. (My basketball coach, *Ms. Lopes,* called for a time out.)

Appositive phrase. *See* Phrase.

Article The adjectives *a, an,* and *the.*

A and *an* are indefinite articles. They refer to any one item of a group. (She bought *a* ticket.)

The is a definite article. It indicates that the noun is a specific person, place or thing. (She liked *the* movie.)

B C

Base form. *See* Verb tense.

Clause A group of words that has a subject and a predicate and that is used as part of a

Exercise

Adjectives and Adverbs Have the students identify all the adjectives and adverbs in each sentence and indicate which are adjectives *(adj.)* and which are adverbs *(adv.).* (Tell students not to include articles.)

1. The old horse stumbled over the rocky road.
2. The rowdy children ran upstairs when their stern father came in.
3. Beautiful flowers were placed in tall vases everywhere in the house.
4. Suddenly dark clouds covered the sun.
5. You can see that movie tomorrow.
6. A young clerk in a high, stiff collar waited patiently while two old ladies chose their groceries.
7. Thick undergrowth hindered the weary hikers from making rapid progress.
8. Fold a blank sheet of paper carefully in thirds.
9. The anxious mother tenderly hushed her fretful child.
10. The messenger delivered a bulky package yesterday.

Answers

1. *old,* adj.; *rocky,* adj.
2. *rowdy,* adj.; *upstairs,*, adv.; *their,* adj.; *stern,* adj.
3. *Beautiful,* adj.; *tall,* adj.; *everywhere,* adv.
4. *Suddenly,* adv.; *dark,* adj.
5. *that,* adj.; *tomorrow,* adv.
6. *young,* adj.; *high,* adj.; *stiff,* adj.; *patiently,* adv. *two,* adj.; *old,* adj. ; *their,* adj.
7. *Thick,* adj.; *weary,* adj.; *rapid,* adj.
8. *blank,* adj.; *carefully,* adv.
9. *anxious,* adj.; *tenderly,* adv.; *her,* adj.; *fretful,* adj.
10. *bulky,* adj.; *yesterday,* adv.

Exercise

Complements Have the students identify the underlined complement in each of the following sentences.

1. Annette chose a dramatic monologue for her audition.
2. The piano students gave their teacher a bouquet after the recital.
3. After the picnic, Amy felt sick.
4. Edward became the leader of the group.
5. I've answered every question they asked me.
6. Agnes lent Elaine a plaid skirt.
7. Talia was happy about her success as a writer.
8. The heart-shaped locket is an heirloom.
9. Tell your little brother a story at bedtime.
10. You should open the package immediately.

Answers

1. direct object
2. indirect object
3. predicate adjective
4. predicate noun
5. direct object
6. indirect object
7. predicate adjective
8. predicate noun
9. indirect object
10. direct object

sentence. Clauses fall into two categories: *main clauses,* which are also called *independent clauses,* and *subordinate clauses,* which are also called *dependent clauses.*

A **main clause** has a subject and a predicate and can stand alone as a sentence. There must be at least one main clause in every sentence. *(The water was cold.)*

A **subordinate clause** has a subject and a predicate, but it cannot stand alone as a sentence. A subordinate clause makes sense only when attached to a main clause. Many subordinate clauses begin with subordinating conjunctions or relative pronouns. (She returned the book *although she hadn't finished it.*) The best way to distinguish between a main clause and a subordinate clause is to see whether the clause can stand alone outside the sentence. Main clauses can stand alone; subordinate clauses cannot.

Collective noun. *See* Noun.

Common noun. *See* Noun.

Comparative degree. *See* Adjective; Adverb.

Complement A word or a phrase that completes the meaning of a verb. Three kinds of complements are *direct objects, indirect objects,* and *subject complements.*

A **direct object** answers the question *What?* or *Whom?* after an action verb. (He ate a *hamburger.* She mailed the *letter.*)

An **indirect object** answers the question *To whom? For whom? To what?* or *For what?* after an action verb. (Marcia gave the *baby* a bath.)

A **subject complement** follows a subject and a linking verb. It identifies or describes a subject. The two kinds of subject complements are *predicate nouns* and *predicate adjectives.*

A **predicate noun** is a noun that follows a linking verb and gives more information about the subject. (The first prize is a *medal.*)

A **predicate adjective** is an adjective that follows a linking verb and gives more information about the subject. (The day is *cloudy.* It looks *cold.*)

Complete predicate. *See* Predicate.

Complete subject. *See* Subject.

Complex sentence. *See* Sentence.

Compound predicate. *See* Predicate.

Compound preposition. *See* Preposition.

Compound sentence. *See* Sentence.

Compound subject. *See* Subject.

Conjunction A word that joins single words or groups of words.

A **coordinating conjunction** *(and, but, or, nor, for, yet)* joins words or groups of words that are equal in grammatical importance. (Pizza *and* spaghetti are the choices for lunch today.)

Correlative conjunctions *(both . . . and, just as . . . so, not only . . . but also, either . . . or, neither . . . nor)* are pairs of words used to connect words or phrases in a sentence. (Anna is *either* brilliant *or* very studious.)

A **subordinating conjunction** *(after, although, because, before, if, in order that, since, than, though, until, when, while)* joins a subordinate idea or clause to a main clause. (I read a book *while* I was waiting for you.)

Coordinating conjunction. *See* Conjunction.

Correlative conjunction. *See* Conjunction.

Declarative sentence. *See* Sentence.

Definite article. *See* Article.

Demonstrative. *See* Adjective; Pronoun.

Direct object. *See* Complement.

Exclamatory sentence. *See* Sentence.

Future tense. *See* Verb tense.

Gerund A verb form that is used as a noun. A gerund always ends in *-ing.* A gerund may function as a subject, an object of a verb, or an object of a preposition. (*Walking* is good exercise. I prefer *walking* to *running.*) One identification test is to replace the gerund or gerund phrase with the singular pronoun *it.* When you replace a gerund with *it,* the sentence still makes sense. Participles fail this test.

Gerund phrase. *See* Phrase.

Helping verb. *See* Verb.

Imperative sentence. *See* Sentence.

Indefinite article. *See* Article.

Indefinite pronoun. *See* Pronoun.

Indirect object. *See* Complement.

Infinitive A verb form that begins with the word *to.* An infinitive often functions as a noun in a sentence. The word *to* may also begin a prepositional phrase. However, when *to* precedes a verb, it is not a preposition but instead signals an infinitive. (*To achieve* a goal is very satisfying.)

Infinitive phrase. *See* Phrase.

Intensive pronoun. *See* Pronoun.

Interjection A word or phrase that expresses strong feeling. An interjection has no grammatical connection to other words in the sentence. Commas follow mild ones; exclamation points follow stronger ones. (*Oh no!* I left my subway pass at home! *Well,* we should leave anyway.)

Interrogative pronoun. *See* Pronoun.

Interrogative sentence. *See* Sentence.

Intransitive verb. *See* Verb.

Inverted order In most sentences in English, the subject comes before the predicate. In a sentence written in inverted order, the predicate comes before the subject. Some sentences are written in inverted order for variety or special emphasis. (In the middle of the park *grew a large oak tree.*) The subject generally follows the predicate in a sentence that begins with *there* or *here.* (*There* is a new girl in the class. *Here* come the clowns.) Questions, or interrogative sentences, are generally written in inverted order. Questions that begin with *who* or *what* follow normal word order.

Irregular verb. *See* Verb tense.

Linking verb. *See* Verb.

Main clause. *See* Clause.

Noun A word that names a person, a place, a thing, or an idea. The chart on page R30 shows the main types of nouns.

Number A noun, pronoun, or verb is singular in number if it refers to one, plural if it refers to more than one.

Object. *See* Complement.

Object pronoun. *See* Pronoun.

Participle A verb form that can function as an adjective. Present participles always end in *-ing.* Although past participles often end in *-ed,* they can take other forms as well. (I loved the actor's *engrossing* performance. Lori stared down the road with a *worried* expression on her face.)

Passive voice. *See* Voice.

Past tense. *See* Verb tense.

Perfect tenses. *See* Verb tense.

Personal pronoun. *See* Pronoun.

Activity
Infinitives and Participles

Direct the students to write ten original sentences, five of which should contain an infinitive or an infinitive phrase and five of which should contain a participle or a participial phrase. They should be prepared to identify the verbal in each sentence.

Examples

Alvin tried to skate backwards on the frozen lake. *infinitive phrase*

Turning to her father, Alma asked what she had done wrong. *participial phrase*

Exercise

Types of Nouns Direct the students to identify each noun in the following sentences as common, proper, abstract, concrete, collective, or compound. More than one category will apply to each noun.

1. A school of tropical fish darted through the seaweed.
2. Japanese and Norwegians are two peoples whose existence depends on fisheries.
3. Some restaurants have aquariums to provide a restful atmosphere.
4. A casual onlooker will often notice a group of diners looking intensely at a colorful aquarium.
5. Keeping tropical fish is an interesting hobby, but one that may be costly.

Answers

1. *school,* common, collective; *fish,* common, concrete; *seaweed,* common, concrete, compound
2. *Japanese,* proper, concrete; *Norwegians,* proper, concrete; *peoples,* common, concrete; *existence,* common, abstract; *fisheries,* common, concrete
3. *restaurants,* common, concrete; *aquariums,* common, concrete; *atmosphere,* common, abstract
4. *onlooker,* common, concrete, compound; *group,* common, concrete, collective; *diners,* common, concrete; *aquarium,* common, concrete
5. *fish,* common, concrete; *hobby,* common, abstract

Types of Nouns

Noun	Function	Examples
Abstract noun	Names an idea, a quality, or a characteristic	beauty, love
Collective noun	Names a group of people or things	audience, class
Common noun	Names a general, not a particular, type of a person, place, thing, or idea	writer, city, desk, fear
Compound noun	Is made up of two or more words	hairbrush, ice cream
Concrete noun	Names a thing that you can see or touch	pheasant, water
Possessive noun	Shows possession, ownership, or the relationship between two nouns	*Chris's* paper
Predicate noun	Follows a linking verb and gives information about the subject	The movie is a *comedy.*
Proper noun	Names a particular person, place, thing, or idea	Marco Polo, Chicago, Eiffel Tower

Phrase A group of words that acts in a sentence as a single part of speech.

An **appositive phrase** includes an appositive and other words that describe the appositive. Many appositives are set off by commas. (My next fish, *a striped bass,* was the biggest catch of the day.)

A **gerund phrase** includes a gerund and any complements and modifiers needed to complete its meaning. (*Watching the clock* doesn't make time move faster.)

An **infinitive phrase** includes an infinitive and any complements and modifiers. (I prefer *to wake up to music.*)

A **participial phrase** contains a participle and any modifiers necessary to complete its meaning. (*Huddled together in the damp cave,* the hikers waited for the storm to end.)

A **prepositional phrase** begins with a preposition and ends with a noun or a pronoun called the object of the preposition. A prepositional phrase can function as an adjective, modifying a noun or a pronoun. (Bach was a great composer *of the eighteenth century.*) A prepositional phrase may also function as an adverb when it modifies a verb, an adverb, or an adjective. (*Throughout his life,* Bach wrote sacred music.)

A **verb phrase** consists of one or more helping verbs followed by a main verb. (I *have been studying* all night.)

A **verbal phrase** contains a verbal plus any complements and modifiers. The three kinds of verbals are *participles, gerunds,* and *infinitives.*

Plural. *See* Number.

Possessive noun. *See* Noun.

Possessive pronoun. *See* Pronoun.

Predicate The verb or verb phrase and any modifiers that express the essential thought about the subject of a sentence.

A **simple predicate** is a verb or verb phrase that tells something about the subject. (The carpenter *left.*)

A **complete predicate** includes the simple predicate and any words that modify or complete it. (The carpenter *left very early.* The carpenter *built a beautiful cabinet.*)

A **compound predicate** has two or more verbs or verb phrases that are joined by a conjunction and share the same subject. (The receiver *caught the pass and headed for the end zone.*)

Predicate adjective. *See* Adjective; Complement.

Predicate noun. *See* Complement; Noun.

Preposition A word that shows the relationship of a noun or pronoun to some other word in the sentence. Prepositions include *about, above, across, among, as, behind, below, beyond, but, by, down, during, except, for, from, into, like, near, of, on, outside, over, since, through, to, under, until, with.* (We skated *across* the ice.)

A compound preposition is made up of more than one word. Compound prepositions include *according to, across from, ahead of, as to, because of, by means of, in addition to, in spite of, on account of.* (*Because of* our late start, we had to park at a distance from the rink.)

Prepositional phrase. *See* Phrase.

Present tense. *See* Verb tense.

Progressive form. *See* Verb tense.

Pronoun A word that takes the place of a noun, a group of words acting as a noun, or another pronoun. The word or group of words that a pronoun refers to is called its antecedent. (In the following sentence, *girls* is the antecedent of *they. When the girls camped on the mountain, they slept well.*)

A demonstrative pronoun points out specific persons, places, things, or ideas. *(this, that, these, those)*

An indefinite pronoun refers to persons, places, or things in a more general way than a noun does. *(all, another, any, both, each, either, enough, everything, few, many, most, much, neither, nobody, none, one, other, others, plenty, several, some)*

An intensive pronoun adds emphasis to another noun or pronoun. If an intensive pronoun is omitted, the meaning of the sentence will be the same. (The mayor *himself* gave the diplomas to the graduates.)

An interrogative pronoun is used to form questions. *(Who? Whom? Whose? What? Which?)*

A personal pronoun refers to a specific person or thing. The form of the personal pronoun depends on its use in the sentence. The chart on this page shows the forms of the various personal pronouns.

A reflexive pronoun reflects back to a noun or pronoun used earlier in the sentence, indicating that the same person or thing is involved. (We congratulated *ourselves* on winning the pennant.)

A relative pronoun is used to begin a subordinate clause. *(who, whose, whomever, that, what, whom, whoever, whomever, whichever, whatever)*

Proper adjective. *See* Adjective.

Proper noun. *See* Noun.

Reflexive pronoun. *See* Pronoun.

Regular verb. *See* Verb tense.

Relative pronoun. *See* Pronoun.

Personal Pronouns		
Singular Pronouns	**Plural Pronouns**	**Use in Sentence**
I, you, she, he, it	we, you, they	subject or predicate nominative
me, you, her, him, it	us, you, them	direct object, indirect object, or object of a preposition
my, your, her, his, its	our, your, their	possessive used before nouns (*our* car)
mine, yours, hers, his, its	ours, yours, theirs	possessive used alone (The car is *ours*.)

Exercise

Types of Pronouns Direct the students to identify each underlined pronoun as demonstrative, indefinite, intensive, interrogative, personal, possessive, reflexive, or relative. (Not all pronouns are underlined.)

1. I like shoes like yours.
2. How much did those cost you?
3. I told myself you wouldn't mind answering my question.
4. None of the other girls would respond.
5. What seems to be their problem?
6. Mona is a person who is trustworthy.
7. Mrs. Blaine herself agrees with that.
8. Both of my cousins blame themselves for the misunderstanding.
9. That makes me feel better.
10. Do you yourself agree with me?

Answers

1. *I,* personal; *yours,* possessive
2. *those,* demonstrative
3. *myself,* reflexive
4. *None,* indefinite
5. *What,* interrogative
6. *who,* relative
7. *herself,* intensive; *that,* demonstrative
8. *Both,* indefinite; *themselves,* reflexive
9. *That,* demonstrative
10. *yourself,* intensive

Exercise

Types of Sentences Direct students to identify each sentence as simple, compound, complex, or compound-complex.

1. The koala and the kiwi are native to Australia.
2. Koalas, mammals that feed only on eucalyptus leaves, are sometimes referred to as koala bears.
3. Australia is an island, but it is also considered a continent.
4. Because Australia is in the Southern Hemisphere, its seasons are the opposite of those in the United States.
5. Australia was once a penal colony; people who could not pay their debts in England were sent there.

Answers

1. simple
2. complex
3. compound
4. complex
5. compound-complex

S

Sentence A group of words expressing a complete thought. Every sentence has a subject and a predicate. *See also* Clause; Predicate; Subject.

A **simple sentence** has only one main clause and no subordinate clauses. A simple sentence may contain a compound subject or a compound predicate or both. The subject and the predicate can be expanded with adjectives, adverbs, prepositional phrases, appositives, and verbal phrases. As long as the sentence has only one main clause, however, it remains a simple sentence. *(Doreen swam and snorkled. Doreen and David swam and snorkled. Students in grades seven and eight will plant a vegetable garden this spring and sell vegetables next fall.)*

A **compound sentence** has two or more main clauses. Each main clause of a compound sentence has its own subject and predicate, and these main clauses are usually joined by a comma and a coordinating conjunction. *(The spacecraft landed on Mars, and a special camera took pictures of rocks.)* A semicolon can also be used to join the main clauses in a compound sentence. *(The play ended late; we missed the last bus home.)*

A **complex sentence** has one main clause and one or more subordinate clauses. *(I'll be glad when this day is over.)*

The chart on this page shows the kinds of sentences by function.

Simple predicate. *See* Predicate; Sentence; Subject.

Subject The part of a sentence that tells what the sentence is about.

A **simple subject** is the main noun or pronoun. (*Leaves* covered the yard.)

A **complete subject** includes the simple subject and any words that modify it. (*Wet leaves from the old maple tree* covered the front yard.)

A **compound subject** has two or more subjects that are joined by a conjunction. The subjects share the same verb. (*Lee, Kim, and Andrew* won prizes in the spelling bee.)

Subordinate clause. *See* Clause.

Subordinating conjunction. *See* Conjunction.

Superlative degree. *See* Adjective; Adverb.

T V

Tense. *See* Verb tense.

Transitive verb. *See* Verb.

Verb A word that expresses action or a state of being and is necessary to make a statement. *(sing, is, had)*

An **action verb** names an action and tells what a subject does. Action verbs can express either physical or mental action. (He *plays* the piano. Linda *prefers* this movie.)

Types of Sentences

Sentence Type	Function	Ends with . . .	Examples
Declarative sentence	Makes a statement	A period	The red kangaroo lives in Australia.
Exclamatory sentence	Expresses strong emotion	An exclamation point	How loud that thunder is!
Imperative sentence	Gives a command or makes a request	A period or an exclamation point	Please leave a message.
Interrogative sentence	Asks a question	A question mark	When does the movie begin?

A helping verb helps the main verb tell about an action or make a statement. (Naomi *is* playing the lead in the spring musical.) The forms of *be* and *have* are the most common helping verbs. *(am, is, are, was, were, being, been; has, have, had, having)* Other helping verbs are *can, could; do, does, did; may, might; must; shall, should; will, would.* Helping verbs are also called auxiliary verbs.

A transitive verb is an action verb that is followed by a direct object that answers the question *What?* or *Whom?* (The Pony Express rider *delivered* the mail.)

An intransitive verb is an action verb that is *not* followed by a direct object. (The horse *ran* across the field.) A dictionary will indicate whether a verb is transitive or intransitive.

A linking verb links, or connects, the subject of a sentence with a noun or an adjective that identifies or describes the subject. The predicate tells what the subject is or is like. (The Lincoln Memorial *is* a national monument. The Lincoln Memorial *is* huge.) A linking verb does not show action. *To be* in all its forms is the most common linking verb. *(am, is, are, was, were, will be, been, being)* Other linking verbs are *appear, become, feel, grow, look, remain, seem, sound, smell, stay, taste.*

Verb phrase. *See* Phrase.

Verb tense The tense of a verb indicates when the action or state of being occurs. All the verb tenses are formed from the four principal parts of a verb: a base form *(freeze),* a present participle *(freezing),* a simple past form *(froze),* and a past participle *(frozen).*

A regular verb forms its simple past and past participle by adding *-ed* to the base form. (*help, helped, helped*)

A verb that forms its past and past participle in some other way is called an irregular verb. *(begin, began, begun; am, is, are, was, were, been; win, won, won)*

In addition to present, past, and future tenses, there are three perfect tenses.

The present perfect tense expresses an action or condition that occurred at some indefinite time in the past. This tense also shows an action or condition that began in the past and continues into the present. (Naomi *has played* important roles in school plays every year.)

The past perfect tense indicates that one past action or condition began *and* ended before another past action started. (The guests *had called* us before they heard about the storm.)

The future perfect tense indicates that one future action or condition will begin *and* end before another future event starts. Use *will have* or *shall have* with the past participle of a verb. (By the time you are finally ready, the bus *will have left.*)

Each tense has a progressive form that expresses a continuing action. To make the progressive forms, use the appropriate tense of the verb *be* with the present participle of the main verb. (Maria *will be working.*)

Verbal A verb form that functions in a sentence as a noun, an adjective, or an adverb. The three kinds of verbals are *participles, gerunds,* and *infinitives.*

Voice The voice of a verb shows whether the subject performs the action or receives the action of the verb.

A verb is in the active voice if the subject of the sentence performs the action. (The dog chased the boy.) The verb is in the passive voice if the subject of the sentence receives the action of the verb. (The boy was chased by the dog.)

LANGUAGE HANDBOOK

Exercise

Types and Tenses of Verbs

Direct students to identify each verb as transitive, intransitive, or linking. Then have them indicate the tense of the verb.

Example

Sam is starting his project.
is starting: transitive, present progressive

1. The gymnasts practiced for months before the competition.
2. By the time they are ready, many months will have passed.
3. No one was expecting such stellar performances.
4. Champion routines on the still rings had been hard to achieve.
5. Coaches and parents will be giving the athletes their enthusiastic support.

Answer

1. *practiced:* intransitive, past
2. *are:* linking, present; *will have passed:* intransitive, future perfect
3. *was expecting:* transitive, past progressive
4. *had been:* linking, past perfect
5. *will be giving:* transitive, future progressive

Exercise

Capitalization Have students correct errors in capitalization in the following sentences.

1. The team won the championship. The captain accepted the trophy.
2. Ally announced, "prizes will be awarded tomorrow."
3. "No one believed," said Jeff, "That our principal had been a rock star."
4. When did robert e. lee surrender?
5. My mother consulted dr. Chang about the problem.
6. My brother plans to become a Doctor.
7. "no one answered the doorbell," said Sue. "maybe they're not at home."
8. Alan explained that the eclipse would take place on Tuesday.
9. Bea ended the letter with the phrase "Sincerely Yours."
10. During much of the 1930s, f.d.r. was president.

Answers

1. correct
2. Ally announced, "Prizes will be awarded tomorrow."
3. "No one believed," said Jeff, "that our principal had been a rock star."
4. When did Robert E. Lee surrender?
5. My mother consulted Dr. Chang about the problem.
6. My brother plans to become a doctor.
7. "No one answered the doorbell," said Sue. "Maybe they're not at home."
8. correct
9. Bea ended the letter with the phrase "Sincerely yours."
10. During much of the 1930s, F.D.R. was president.

Mechanics

This section will help you use correct capitalization, punctuation, and abbreviations in your writing.

Capitalization

Capitalizing Sentences, Quotations, and Salutations

Rule	Example
A capital letter appears at the beginning of a sentence.	**A**nother gust of wind shook the house.
Capitalize the first word when quoting the exact words of a speaker.	Sabrina said, "**T**he lights might go out."
When a quoted sentence is interrupted by explanatory words, such as *she said,* do not begin the second part of the sentence with a capital letter.	"There's a rainbow," exclaimed Jeffrey, "**o**ver the whole beach."
When the second part of a quotation is a new sentence, put a period after the explanatory words; begin the new part with a capital letter.	"Please come inside," Justin said. "**W**ipe your feet."
Do not capitalize an indirect quotation.	Jo said that **t**he storm was getting worse.
Capitalize the first word in the salutation and the closing of a letter. Capitalize the title and the name of the person addressed.	**D**ear **D**r. **M**enino **D**ear **E**ditor **S**incerely

Capitalizing Names and Titles of People

Rule	Example	
Capitalize the names of people and the initials that stand for their names.	**M**alcolm **X** **R**obert **E**. **L**ee	**J. F. K.** **Q**ueen **E**lizabeth I
Capitalize a title or an abbreviation of a title when it comes before a person's name or when it is used in direct address.	**D**r. **S**alinas "Your patient, **D**octor, is waiting."	
Do not capitalize a title that follows or is a substitute for a person's name.	Marcia Salinas is a good **d**octor. He asked to speak to the **d**octor.	

Rule	Example	
Capitalize the names and the abbreviations of academic degrees that follow a person's name. Capitalize *Jr.* and *Sr.*	Marcia Salinas, **M.D.** Donald Bruns **S**r.	Raoul Tobias, **A**ttorney Ann Lee, **P**h.**D.**
Capitalize words that show family relationships when used as titles or as substitutes for a person's name.	We saw **U**ncle Carlos. She read a book about **M**other **T**eresa.	
Do not capitalize words that show family relationships when they follow a possessive noun or pronoun.	Jason's **b**rother will give us a ride. I forgot my **m**other's phone number.	
Always capitalize the pronoun *I*.	After **I** clean my room, **I**'m going swimming.	

Capitalizing Names of Places

Rule of Thumb

Do not capitalize articles and prepositions in proper nouns: *the Rock of Gibraltar, the Statue of Liberty.*

Rule	Example	
Capitalize the names of cities, counties, states, countries, and continents.	**S**t. **L**ouis, **M**issouri **A**ustralia	**M**arin **C**ounty **S**outh **A**merica
Capitalize the names of bodies of water and other geographical features.	the **G**reat **L**akes the **D**ust **B**owl	**C**ape **C**od
Capitalize the names of sections of a country and regions of the world.	**E**ast **A**sia the **P**acific **R**im	**N**ew **E**ngland the **M**idwest
Capitalize compass points when they refer to a specific section of a country.	the **N**orthwest the **S**outh	
Do not capitalize compass points when they indicate direction.	Canada is **n**orth of the United States.	
Do not capitalize adjectives indicating direction.	**w**estern Utah	
Capitalize the names of streets and highways.	**D**orchester **A**venue	**R**oute 22
Capitalize the names of buildings, bridges, monuments, and other structures.	**W**orld **T**rade **C**enter **C**hesapeake **B**ay **B**ridge	

LANGUAGE HANDBOOK

Exercise

Capitalization Have the students state a rule to tell why each underlined word or word group is or is not capitalized.

1. Marty grew up in Omaha, Nebraska.
2. The family enjoyed summer vacations on Cape Cod.
3. Evanston is located north of Chicago.
4. Have you been to the top of the Empire State Building?
5. We took a historic trip along old Route 66.
6. Mandy enjoyed living in the South.
7. The fall colors in New England are beautiful.
8. When will Aunt Julia arrive?
9. My aunt took me to Kennedy Center.
10. The artist painted landscapes of western New York State.

Answers

1. Capitalize the names of cities and states.
2. Capitalize the names of geographic features.
3. Do not capitalize compass points when they indicate direction.
4. Capitalize the names of buildings.
5. Capitalize the names of highways.
6. Capitalize compass points when they refer to a section of the country.
7. Capitalize the names of sections of the country.
8. Capitalize words that show family relationships when used as titles.
9. Do not capitalize the names of family relationships when they are proceeded by a possessive pronoun.
10. Do not capitalize adjectives indicating direction.

Exercise

Capitalization Have students correct the errors in capitalization in the following sentences.

1. My brother studies japanese and latin.
2. Hot dogs and apple pie are two popular american foods.
3. My family is saving for a european tour in the summer.
4. Everyone joined in the chorus of "Take me out to the ball game."
5. The fireworks on the fourth of July were spectacular.
6. The flowers we planted in november will not bloom until Spring.
7. My oldest sister is a Girl scout leader.
8. The children filled their bowls with Crunchy Delight Cereal.
9. The New York giants play their games in New Jersey.
10. The book's title was The Stranger inside.

Answers

1. My brother studies Japanese and Latin.
2. Hot dogs and apple pie are two popular American foods.
3. My family is saving for a European tour in the summer.
4. Everyone joined in the chorus of "Take Me Out to the Ball Game."
5. The fireworks on the Fourth of July were spectacular.
6. The flowers we planted in November will not bloom until spring.
7. My oldest sister is a Girl Scout leader.
8. The children filled their bowls with Crunchy Delight cereal.
9. The New York Giants play their games in New Jersey.
10. The book's title was *The Stranger Inside.*

Capitalizing Other Proper Nouns and Adjectives

Rule	Example
Capitalize the names of clubs, organizations, businesses, institutions, and political parties.	**H**ouston **O**ilers the **F**ood and **D**rug **A**dministration **B**oys and **G**irls **C**lub
Capitalize brand names but not the nouns following them.	**Z**ippo energy bar
Capitalize the names of days of the week, months, and holidays.	**S**aturday **J**une **T**hanksgiving **D**ay
Do not capitalize the names of seasons.	**w**inter, **s**pring, **s**ummer, **f**all
Capitalize the first word, the last word, and all important words in the title of a book, play, short story, poem, essay, article, film, television series, song, magazine, newspaper, and chapter of a book.	***T**he **C**all of the **W**ild* ***W**orld **B**ook **E**ncyclopedia* "**J**ingle **B**ells" **S**tar **W**ars **C**hapter 12
Capitalize the names of ethnic groups, nationalities, and languages.	**L**atino **J**apanese **E**uropean **S**panish
Capitalize proper adjectives that are formed from the names of ethnic groups and nationalities.	**S**hetland pony **J**ewish holiday

Punctuation

Using the Period and Other End Marks

Rule	Example
Use a period at the end of a declarative sentence.	My great-grandfather fought in the Mexican Revolution**.**
Use a period at the end of an imperative sentence that does not express strong feeling.	Please set the table**.**
Use a question mark at the end of an interrogative sentence.	How did your sneakers get so muddy**?**
Use an exclamation point at the end of an exclamatory sentence or a strong imperative.	How exciting the play was**!** Watch out**!**

Using Commas

Rule	Example
Use commas to separate three or more items in a series.	The canary eats bird seed, fruit, and suet.
Use commas to show a pause after an introductory word and to set off names used in direct address.	Yes, I offered to take care of her canary this weekend. Please, Stella, can I borrow your nail polish?
Use a comma after two or more introductory prepositional phrases or when the comma is needed to make the meaning clear. A comma is not needed after a single short prepositional phrase, but it is acceptable to use one.	From the back of the balcony, we had a lousy view of the stage. After the movie we walked home. (no comma needed)
Use a comma after an introductory participle and an introductory participial phrase.	Whistling and moaning, the wind shook the little house.
Use commas to set off words that interrupt the flow of thought in a sentence.	Tomorrow, I think, our projects are due.
Use a comma after conjunctive adverbs such as *however, moreover, furthermore, nevertheless,* and *therefore.*	The skating rink is crowded on Saturday; however, it's the only time I can go.
Use commas to set off an appositive if it is not essential to the meaning of a sentence.	Ben Wagner, a resident of Pittsfield, won the first round in the golf tournament.
Use a comma before a conjunction (*and, or, but, nor, so, yet*) that joins main clauses.	We can buy our tickets now, or we can take a chance on buying them just before the show.
Use a comma after an introductory adverb clause.	Because I stayed up so late, I'm sleepy this morning.
In most cases, do not use a comma with an adverb clause that comes at the end of a sentence.	The picnic will be canceled unless the weather clears.
Use a comma or a pair of commas to set off an adjective clause that is not essential to the meaning of a sentence.	Tracy, who just moved here from Florida, has never seen snow before.
Do not use a comma or pair of commas to set off an essential clause from the rest of the sentence.	Anyone who signs up this month will get a discount.

LANGUAGE HANDBOOK

Exercise

Commas Have students supply commas where they are needed in the following sentences.

1. Donald are these books yours?
2. Judy Garland a famous singer and actress was Liza Minelli's mother.
3. In the middle of the night we heard a loud crash.
4. The right answer I believe is choice B.
5. If only a few people come to the first performance the play will be canceled.
6. The Smith brothers who moved here from California are excellent musicians.
7. The day was overcast; however our picnic went on as planned.
8. The menu featured Portuguese eggs French toast and Belgian waffles.
9. Our guide explained the museum exhibits and we were all impressed by her in-depth knowledge.
10. Having no place to land the plane circled the area for an hour.

Answers

1. Donald, are these books yours?
2. Judy Garland, a famous singer and actress, was Liza Minelli's mother.
3. In the middle of the night, we heard a loud crash.
4. The right answer, I believe, is choice B.
5. If only a few people come to the first performance, the play will be canceled.
6. The Smith brothers, who moved here from California, are excellent musicians.
7. The day was overcast; however, our picnic went on as planned.
8. The menu featured Portuguese eggs, French toast, and Belgian waffles.
9. Our guide explained the museum exhibits, and we were all impressed by her in-depth knowledge.
10. Having no place to land, the plane circled the area for an hour.

Exercise

Commas and Semicolons

Direct students to supply commas and semicolons where they are needed, or delete them if unneeded, in the following sentences.

1. The earthquake on January 20 2001 caused enormous damage.
2. We visited Akron Ohio on our trip from New York to Chicago.
3. "The best remedy for a cold" said Kay "is plenty of rest."
4. The verdict was in the defendant was not guilty.
5. We purchased beans, tomatoes, and broccoli no tomatoes were available.
6. For some workers days were long and boring.
7. Joseph Kalb Ph.D. is the chair of the university's math department.
8. Sign the letter "Sincerely yours Brenda."
9. The city had record snowfalls in December, 2000.
10. Stand tall never slouch.

Answers

1. The earthquake on January 20, 2001, caused enormous damage.
2. We visited Akron, Ohio, on our trip from New York to Chicago.
3. "The best remedy for a cold," said Kay, "is plenty of rest."
4. The verdict was in; the defendant was not guilty.
5. We purchased beans, potatoes, and broccoli; no tomatoes were available.
6. For some workers, days were long and boring.
7. Joseph Kalb, Ph.D., is the chair of the university's math department.
8. Sign the letter "Sincerely yours, Brenda."
9. The city had record snowfalls in December 2000.
10. Stand tall; never slouch.

Rule	Example
Use commas before and after the year when it is used with both the month and the day. If only the month and the year are given, do not use a comma.	On January 2, 1985, my parents moved to Dallas, Texas. I was born in May 1985.
Use commas before and after the name of a state or a country when it is used with the name of a city. Do not use a comma after the state if it is used with a ZIP code.	The area code for Concord, New Hampshire, is 603. Please forward my mail to 6 Madison Lane, Topsham, ME 04086
Use a comma or a pair of commas to set off an abbreviated title or degree following a person's name.	The infirmary was founded by Elizabeth Blackwell, M.D., the first woman in the United States to earn a medical degree.
Use a pair of commas to set off *too* in the middle of a sentence when *too* means "also."	We, too, bought groceries, from the new online supermarket.
Use a comma or commas to set off a direct quotation.	"My nose," exclaimed Pinocchio, "is growing longer!"
Use a comma after the salutation of a friendly letter and after the closing of both a friendly letter and a business letter.	Dear Gary, Sincerely, Best regards,
Use a comma when necessary to prevent misreading of a sentence.	In math, solutions always elude me.

Using Semicolons and Colons

Rule	Example
Use a semicolon to join the parts of a compound sentence when a coordinating conjunction, such as *and, or, nor,* or *but,* is not used.	Don't be late for the dress rehearsal; it begins at seven o'clock sharp.
Use a semicolon to join parts of a compound sentence when the main clauses are long and are subdivided by commas. Use a semicolon even if these clauses are already joined by a coordinating conjunction.	In the gray light of early morning, on a remote airstrip in the desert, two pilots prepared to fly on a dangerous mission; but accompanying them were a television camera crew, three newspaper reporters, and a congressman from their home state of Nebraska.

Rule	Example
Use a semicolon to separate main clauses joined by a conjunctive adverb. Be sure to use a comma after the conjunctive adverb.	We've been climbing all morning; therefore, we need a rest.
Use a colon to introduce a list of items that ends a sentence. Use words such as *these, the following,* or *as follows* to signal that a list is coming.	Remember to bring the following items: a backpack, a bag lunch, sunscreen, and insect repellent.
Do not use a colon to introduce a list preceded by a verb or preposition.	Remember to bring a backpack, a bag lunch, sunscreen, and insect repellent. (No colon is used after *bring.*)
Use a colon to separate the hour and the minutes when you write the time of day.	My Spanish class starts at 9:15.
Use a colon after the salutation of a business letter.	Dear Dr. Coulombe: Director of the Personnel Dept.:

Using Quotation Marks and Italics

Rule	Example
Use quotation marks before and after a direct quotation.	"Curiouser and curiouser," said Alice.
Use quotation marks with both parts of a divided quotation.	"This gymnastics trick," explained Amanda, "took me three months to learn."
Use a comma or commas to separate a phrase such as *she said* from the quotation itself. Place the comma that precedes the phrase inside the closing quotation marks.	"I will be late," said the cable technician, "for my appointment."
Place a period that ends a quotation inside the closing quotation marks.	Scott said, "Thanks for letting me borrow your camping tent."
Place a question mark or an exclamation point inside the quotation marks when it is part of the quotation.	"Why is the door of your snake's cage open?" asked my mother.

Activity

Semicolons, Colons, and Quotation Marks Have students write original sentences to illustrate the rules on this page. Then direct the students to exchange papers with a partner. Partners should correct the papers they receive and discuss the corrections with one another. Monitor the students' activity and resolve questions that arise. You may wish to have a few students write sentences on the board.

Exercise

Quotation Marks, Italics, and Apostrophes Have the students correct the punctuation in the following sentences.

1. Blanche asked, "What topic have you chosen for your report"?
2. What an exciting short story we enjoyed when we read "The Most Dangerous Game."
3. Angelas painting was exhibited in the school entrance.
4. The boys bicycles are parked on the outside rack.
5. Is this math book your's?
6. Jane and Bobs mother took us to the skating rink.
7. Someones camera was lying on the park bench.
8. The president arrived in Air Force One.
9. The latest issue of Time has an article entitled What Next for the Space Program?
10. My favorite poem is The Highwayman.

Answers

1. Blanche asked, "What topic have you chosen for your report?"
2. What an exciting short story we enjoyed when we read "The Most Dangerous Game"!
3. Angela's painting was exhibited in the school entrance.
4. The boys' bicycles are parked on the outside rack.
5. Is this math book yours?
6. Jane and Bob's mother took us to the skating rink.
7. Someone's camera was lying on the park bench.
8. The president arrived in *Air Force One.*
9. The latest issue of *Time* has an article entitled "What Next for the Space Program?"
10. My favorite poem is "The Highwayman."

Rule	Example
Place a question mark or an exclamation point outside the quotation marks when it is part of the entire sentence.	How I love "The Pit and the Pendulum"**!**
Use quotation marks for the title of a short story, essay, poem, song, magazine or newspaper article, or book chapter.	short story: **"**The Necklace**"** poem: **"**The Fish**"** article: **"**Fifty Things to Make from Bottlecaps**"**
Use italics or underlining for the title of a book, play, film, television series, magazine, newspaper, or work of art.	book: *To Kill a Mockingbird* magazine: *The New Republic* painting: *Sunflowers*
Use italics or underlining for the names of ships, trains, airplanes, and spacecraft.	ship: *Mayflower* airplane: *Air Force One*

Using Apostrophes

Rule	Example
Use an apostrophe and an *s ('s)* to form the possessive of a singular noun.	my brother**'s** rock collection Chris**'s** hat
Use an apostrophe and an *s ('s)* to form the possessive of a plural noun that does not end in *s.*	the geese**'s** feathers the oxen**'s** domestication

Rule of Thumb

If a thing is owned jointly by two or more individuals, only the last name should show possession: *Mom and Dad's car.* If the ownership is not joint, each name should show possession: *Mom's and Dad's parents are coming for Thanksgiving.*

Rule	Example
Use an apostrophe alone to form the possessive of a plural noun that ends in *s.*	the animal**s'** habitat the instrument**s'** sound
Use an apostrophe and an *s ('s)* to form the possessive of an indefinite pronoun.	everyone**'s** homework someone**'s** homework
Do not use an apostrophe in a possessive pronoun.	The dog knocked over **its** dish. **Yours** is the best entry in the contest. One of these drawings must be **hers.**

Rule	Example
Use an apostrophe to replace letters that have been omitted in a contraction.	it + is = **it's** can + not = **can't** I + have = **I've**
Use an apostrophe to form the plural of a letter, a figure, or a word that is used as itself.	Write three ***7's.*** The word is spelled with two ***m's.*** The sentence contains three ***and's.***
Use an apostrophe to show missing numbers in a year.	the class of **'02**

Using Hyphens, Dashes, and Parentheses	
Rule	**Example**
Use a hyphen to show the division of a word at the end of a line. Always divide the word between its syllables. **Rule of Thumb** One-letter divisions (for example, *e-lectric*) are not permissible. Avoid dividing personal names if possible.	With the new recycling pro- gram, more residents are recycling their trash.
Use a hyphen in a number written as a compound word.	He sold forty-six ice creams in one hour.
Use a hyphen in a fraction.	We won the vote by a two-thirds majority. Two-thirds of the votes have been counted.
Use a hyphen or hyphens in certain compound nouns.	great-grandmother merry-go-round
Hyphenate a compound modifier only when it precedes the word it modifies.	A well-known musician visited our school. The story was well written.
Use a hyphen after the prefixes *all-*, *ex-*, and *self-* when they are joined to a noun or adjective.	all-star ex-president self-conscious
Use a hyphen to separate a prefix from a word that begins with a capital letter.	un-American mid-January

Exercise

Hyphens, Dashes, and Parentheses Have the students supply hyphens, dashes, or parentheses where they are needed in the following sentences.

1. The new pillow was very uncomfortable.
2. The child even before her second birthday could count to ninety-nine.
3. The recipe calls for two thirds cup of raisins.
4. The coupons we'd collected dozens of them expired in mid-January.
5. The tots enjoyed their ride on the merry go round.
6. After the inauguration of the new officers, the expresident of the club gave a speech.
7. Three fourths of the students plan to attend the concert.
8. The hyperactive overly active boy was difficult to control.
9. The cost of the trip was all inclusive.
10. We saw the much talked about movie.

Answers

1. The new pillow was very uncomfortable.
2. The child—even before her second birthday—could count to ninety-nine.
3. The recipe calls for two-thirds cup of raisins.
4. The coupons—we'd collected dozens of them—expired in mid-January.
5. The tots enjoyed their rides on the merry-go-round.
6. After the inauguration of the new officers, the ex-president of the club gave a speech.
7. Three-fourths of the students plan to attend the concert.
8. The hyperactive (overly active) boy was difficult to control.
9. The cost of the trip was all-inclusive.
10. We saw the much-talked-about movie.

Exercise

Dashes, Parentheses, and Abbreviations Direct students to state the rules that answer the following questions. Ask them write sentences illustrating the rules they give for items 1, 2, and 3.

1. When are dashes used in a sentence?
2. How do you set off words that define or explain a word in a sentence?
3. How should you write abbreviations that are pronounced as words?
4. When should you abbreviate days and months?
5. When may you abbreviate street names and state names?
6. What units of measure require the use of periods?
7. When do you use the abbreviations A.M. and P.M.?
8. Give an example of a title that is abbreviated before a person's name.
9. How would you correct the following sentence? *Annette lives on Seneca Ave. in Brooklyn, N. Y.*
10. Why do you use a period in 2 in. but not in 5 *cm?*

Answers

1. Use dashes to show a sudden break or a change in thought or speech.
2. Use parentheses to set off words that define or explain a word in a sentence.
3. Abbreviations that are pronounced as words should be written with capital letters and without periods.
4. Abbreviate days and months only in charts and lists.
5. Abbreviate street names and state names only on envelopes.
6. Use periods after abbreviations of English measures.
7. Use the abbreviations A.M. and P.M. with exact times.
8. *Mr., Mrs., Ms.,* and *Dr.* are abbreviated before a person's name.
9. Annette lives on Seneca Avenue in Brooklyn, New York.
10. Use a period after an abbreviation of an English unit of measure *(in.)* but not after an abbreviation of a metric unit *(cm).*

LANGUAGE HANDBOOK

Rule	Example
Use a dash or dashes to show a sudden break or change in thought or speech.	Daniel—he's kind of a pest—is my youngest cousin.
Use parentheses to set off words that define or helpfully explain a word in a sentence.	The transverse flute **(*transverse* means "sideways")** is a wind instrument.

Abbreviations

Rule	Example
Abbreviate the titles *Mr., Mrs., Ms.,* and *Dr.* before a person's name. Also abbreviate professional or academic degree that follows a name. The titles *Jr.* and *Sr.* are *not* preceded by a comma.	**Dr.** Stanley Livingston (doctor) Luisa Mendez, **M.A.** (Master of Arts) Martin Luther King Jr.
Use capital letters and no periods with abbreviations that are pronounced letter by letter or as words. Exceptions are *U.S.* and *Washington, D.C.,* which do use periods.	**NAACP** National Association for the Advancement of Colored People **UFO** unidentified flying object **MADD** Mothers Against Driving Drunk
With exact times, use *A.M.* (*ante meridiem,* "before noon") and *P.M.* (*post meridiem,* "after noon"). For years, use *B.C.* (before Christ) and, sometimes, *A.D.* (*anno Domini,* "in the year of the lord," after Christ).	8:15 **A.M.** 6:55 **P.M.** 5000 **B.C.** **A.D.** 235
Abbreviate days and months only in charts and lists.	School will be closed on **Mon., Sept.** 3 **Wed., Nov.** 11 **Thurs., Nov.** 27
In scientific writing, abbreviate units of measure. Use periods with English units but not with metric units.	inch(es) **in.** meter(s) **m** yard(s) **yd.** milliliter(s) **ml**
On envelopes only, abbreviate street names and state names. In general text, spell out street names and state names.	Ms. Karen Holmes 347 Grandville **St.** Tilton, **NH** 03276 Karen lives on Grandville **Street** in Tilton, **New Hampshire.**

Writing Numbers	
Rule	**Example**
In charts and tables, always write numbers as numerals. Other rules apply to numbers not in charts or tables.	Student Test Scores Student · Test **1** · Test **2** · Test **3** Lai, W. · **82** · **89** · **94** Ostos, A. · **78** · **90** · **86**
Spell out a number that is expressed in one or two words.	We carried enough supplies for **twenty-three** days.
Use a numeral for a number of more than two words.	The tallest mountain in Mexico rises **17,520** feet.
Spell out a number that begins a sentence or reword the sentence so that it does not begin with a number.	**One hundred forty-three** days later the baby elephant was born. The baby elephant was born **143** days later.
Write a very large number as a numeral followed by the word *million* or *billion.*	There are **15 million** people living in or near Mexico City.
Related numbers should be written in the same way. If one number must be written as a numeral, use numerals for all the numbers.	There are **365** days in the year, but only **52** weekends.
Spell out an ordinal number. (*first, second*)	Welcome to our **fifteenth** annual convention.
Use words to express the time of day unless you are writing the exact time or using the abbreviation *A.M.* or *P.M.*	My guitar lesson is at **five o'clock**. It ends by 5:45 **P.M.**
Use numerals to express dates, house and street numbers, apartment and room numbers, telephone numbers, page numbers, amounts of money of more than two words, and percentages. Write out the word *percent.*	August **5, 1999** **9** Davio Dr. Apartment **9F** **24 percent**

Exercise

Writing Numbers Have students correct the number references in the following sentences.

1. We will meet tomorrow morning at 6 o'clock.
2. The check is valid for one hundred twenty-five days.
3. The commercial reached twenty-five million viewers each week.
4. The bell rang promptly at eight forty-five A.M.
5. We bought the computer at a fifteen percent discount.
6. The 2nd annual picnic was a great success.
7. Marge lives in Apartment Seven A.
8. The information you need is on page thirty.
9. Two-hundred-twenty students took part in the walkathon.
10. The tower was 555 feet high, not counting its twelve-foot base.

Answers

1. We will meet tomorrow morning at six o'clock.
2. The check is valid for 125 days.
3. The commercial reached 25 million viewers each week.
4. The bell rang promptly at 8:45 A.M.
5. We bought the computer at a 15 percent discount.
6. The second annual picnic was a great success.
7. Marge lives in Apartment 7A.
8. The information you need is on page 30.
9. Two hundred twenty students took part in the walkathon.
10. The tower was 555 feet high, not counting its 12-foot base.

Exercise

Spelling Dictate the following words. Direct students to refer to the rules on page R44 if they have trouble spelling the words.

1. preparation
2. dividend
3. deceive
4. leisure
5. stately
6. smiling
7. believable
8. continuous
9. likely
10. nimbly

Spelling

The following rules, examples, and exceptions can help you master the spelling of many words.

Spelling *ie* and *ei*

Put *i* before *e* except when both letters follow *c* or when the letters are pronounced as *a.*

believe	**sieve**	**weight**
receive	**relieve**	**neighborhood**

It is helpful to memorize exceptions to this rule. Exceptions include the following words: *species, science, weird, either, seize, leisure,* and *protein.*

Spelling unstressed vowels

Notice the vowel sound in the second syllable of the word *op-p_-site.* This is the unstressed vowel sound; dictionary respellings use the schwa symbol (ə) to indicate it. Because any vowel can be used to spell this sound, you might find yourself uncertain about which vowel to use. To spell words with unstressed vowels, try thinking of a related word in which the syllable containing the vowel sound is stressed.

Unknown Spelling	Related Word	Word Spelled Correctly
opp_site	oppose	opposite
observ_nt	observation	observant
res_dent	reside	resident

Suffixes and the silent e

Many English words end in a silent *e.* Keep the *e* when adding a suffix that begins with a consonant. Drop the silent *e* when adding a suffix beginning with a vowel. When adding the suffix *-ly* to a word that ends in *le,* drop the *le.*

wise + ly = wisely
skate + ing = skating
gentle + ly = gently
noise + y = noisy

There are exceptions to the rule, including the following:

awe + ful = awful
true + ly = truly
dye + ing = dyeing
judge + ment = judgment
mile + age = mileage

Suffixes and the final *y*

When you are adding a suffix to a word ending with a vowel + *y*, keep the *y*. For a word ending with a consonant + *y*, change the *y* to *i* unless the suffix begins with *i*. To avoid having two *i*'s together, keep the *y*.

enjoy + ment = enjoyment	**merry + ment = merriment**
display + ed = displayed	**lazy + ness= laziness**
play + ful = playful	**worry + ing = worrying**

Note: Some words have alternate spellings:

sly + er = slyer *or* slier
shy + est = shyest *or* shiest

Adding prefixes

When you add a prefix to a word, do not change the spelling of the word.

un + done = undone	**re + schedule = reschedule**
il + legible = illegible	**semi + sweet = semisweet**

Doubling the final consonant

Double the final consonant in a one-syllable word that ends with a single consonant preceded by a single vowel. Double the final consonant of a word that has an accent on the last syllable if the accent stays there after the suffix is added.

sit + ing = sitting	**rub + ing = rubbing**
commit + ed = committed	**confer + ed = conferred**

Do not double the final consonant if the accent is not on the last syllable or if the accent moves when the suffix is added.

cancel + ing = canceling	**refer + ent = referent**
travel + ed = traveled	**defer + ence = deference**

Do not double the final consonant if the word ends in two consonants or if the suffix begins with a consonant.

climb + er = climber	**nervous + ness = nervousness**
import + ance = importance	**star + dom = stardom**

When adding *-ly* to a word that ends in *ll*, drop one *l*.

dull + ly = dully	**full + ly = fully**

Exercise

Spelling Direct the students to write the following words as you dictate them. Check the work by having the students spell the words aloud. Ask for volunteers to identify the spelling rule that the word follows.

1. annoyed
2. repayment
3. appliance
4. knitting
5. occurred
6. wrapping
7. unraveled
8. dully
9. starring
10. consumable

Exercise

Spelling: Forming Plurals

Have students write the plural form of each of the following words.

1. glass
2. stereo
3. family
4. sheaf
5. tomato
6. pulley
7. dairy
8. trio
9. reflex
10. ranch

Answers

1. glasses
2. stereos
3. families
4. sheaves
5. tomatoes
6. pulleys
7. dairies
8. trios
9. reflexes
10. ranches

Forming Plurals

GENERAL RULES FOR PLURALS		
If the noun ends in	**Rule**	**Example**
s, ch, sh, x, or *z*	add *-es*	loss, losses latch, latches bush, bushes box, boxes quiz, quizzes
a consonant + *y*	change *y* to *i* and add *-es*	ferry, ferries baby, babies worry, worries
a vowel + *y*	add *-s*	chimney, chimneys monkey, monkeys toy, toys
a vowel + *o*	add *-s*	cameo, cameos radio, radios rodeo, rodeos
a consonant + *o*	add *-es* but sometimes add *-s*	potato, potatoes echo, echoes photo, photos solo, solos
f or *ff*	add *-s* but sometimes change *f* to *v* and add *-es*	proof, proofs bluff, bluffs sheaf, sheaves thief, thieves hoof, hooves
lf	change *f* to *v* and add *-es*	calf, calves half, halves loaf, loaves
fe	change *f* to *v* and add *-s*	knife, knives life, lives

SPECIAL RULES FOR PLURALS	
Rule	**Example**
To form the plural of most proper names and one-word compound nouns, follow the general rules for plurals.	Jones, Joneses Hatch, Hatches workbook, workbooks
To form the plural of a hyphenated compound noun or a compound noun of more than one word, make the most important word plural.	mother-in-law, mothers-in-law credit card, credit cards district attorney, district attorneys
Some nouns have irregular plural forms and do not follow any rules.	man, men foot, feet tooth, teeth
Some nouns have the same singular and plural forms	deer, deer species, species sheep, sheep

Forming compound words

When forming a compound word, keep the original spelling of both words.

home + work = homework
scare + crow = scarecrow
pea + nut = peanut

LANGUAGE HANDBOOK

Exercise

Spelling: Forming Plurals

Have students write the plural form of each of the following words.

1. mouse
2. moose
3. goose
4. shrimp
5. shoelace
6. James
7. attorney-at-law
8. woman
9. ox
10. maid of honor

Answers

1. mice
2. moose
3. geese
4. shrimp
5. shoelaces
6. Jameses
7. attorneys-at-law
8. women
9. oxen
10. maids of honor

Writing Handbook

The Writing Process

The writing process consists of five stages: prewriting, drafting, revising, editing/proofreading, and publishing/presenting. By following the stages in order, you can turn your ideas into polished pieces of writing. Most writers take their writing through all five stages, repeating stages as necessary.

The Writing Process

Prewriting

Prewriting is the process of gathering and organizing your ideas. It begins whenever you start to consider what you will write about or what will interest your readers. Try keeping a small notebook with you for several days and using it to jot down possible topics. Consult the chart below for tips on using the prewriting techniques of listing, questioning, and clustering.

Listing	Questioning	Clustering
List as many ideas as you can–whatever comes into your head on a particular topic. Later you can go back over the list and circle the ideas you like best. Eventually you'll hit on an idea you can use.	Ask yourself questions related to your audience. *What do my friends already know about my topic? What would they find most interesting about my topic? What words would I need to explain to my audience?*	Write your topic in the middle of a piece of paper. Organize related ideas around the topic in a cluster of circles, with lines showing how the ideas are related. Clustering can help you decide which part of a topic to write about.

R48 WRITING HANDBOOK

WRITING HANDBOOK

When you have selected your topic, organize your ideas around the topic. Identify your main ideas and supporting ideas. Each main idea needs examples or facts to support it. Then write a plan for what you want to say. The plan might be an organized list or outline. It does not have to use complete sentences.

Drafting

Drafting is the stage that turns your list into sentences and paragraphs. Use your prewriting notes to remember what you want to say. Begin by writing an introduction that gets the reader's attention. Move ahead through the topic, paragraph by paragraph. Let your words flow. This is the time to express yourself or try out a new idea. Don't worry about mistakes in spelling and grammar; you can correct them later. If you get stuck, try one of the tips below.

Tips for drafting

- Work on the easiest part first. You don't have to begin at the beginning.
- Make a diagram, sketch, or drawing of the topic.
- Focus on just one sentence or paragraph at a time.
- Freewrite your thoughts and images. You can organize them later.
- Pretend that you are writing to a friend.
- Ask more questions about your topic.
- Speak your ideas into a tape recorder.
- Take a break. Take a walk or listen to music. Return to your writing later.

Revising

The goal of revising is to make your writing clearer and more interesting. When you revise, look at the whole piece of writing. Ask whether the parts go together smoothly and whether anything should be added or deleted. You may see a way to organize the draft more effectively. Some writers make several revisions before they are satisfied.

- ☑ **Did I stick to my topic?**
- ☑ **Did I accomplish my purpose?**
- ☑ **Did I keep my audience in mind?**
- ☑ **Does my main idea come across clearly?**
- ☑ **Do all the details support the main idea?**
- ☑ **Did I give the right amount of information?**
- ☑ **Did I use transition words such as *first, then* and *next* to make my sentences flow smoothly?**

WRITING HANDBOOK R49

WRITING HANDBOOK

Tips for revising

- Step back. If you have the time, set your draft aside for a while. When you look at it again, you may see it from a new point of view. You may notice that some information is missing or that part of the paper is disorganized.
- Read your paper aloud. Listen carefully to the way it sounds. You may notice repetitive or unclear sections that can be improved.
- Have a writing conference with a peer reviewer, one of your friends or classmates. A second opinion helps. Your reader can offer a fresh point of view.

Peer review

You can direct peer responses in one or more of the following ways.

- Ask readers to tell you what they have read in their own words. If you do not hear your ideas restated, revise your writing for clarity.
- Ask readers to tell you the part they liked best and why. You may want to expand those parts.
- Repeat in your own words what the readers have told you. Ask the readers if you have understood their suggestions.
- Discuss your writing with your readers. Listen to their suggestions carefully.

As you confer, make notes of your reviewers' comments. Then revise your draft, using your own judgment and including what is helpful from your reviewers' comments.

Editing/Proofreading

When you are satisfied with the changes you've made, edit your revised draft. Replace dull, vague words with lively verbs and precise adjectives. Vary the length of your sentences. Take time to correct errors in spelling, grammar, capitalization, and punctuation. Refer to the Proofreading Checklist on page R51 or on the inside back cover of this book.

Editing for style

Use the following checklist to help you improve the style of your writing. Try to make your writing as interesting and as effective as possible.

- ☑ **Have I used the right words?**
- ☑ **Is the tone of my writing appropriate?**
- ☑ **Have I made clear connections between ideas?**
- ☑ **Do my sentences and paragraphs flow smoothly?**
- ☑ **Does the ending sum up what I'm saying clearly and effectively?**

R50 WRITING HANDBOOK

Proofreading

Use this proofreading checklist to help you check for errors in your writing , and use the proofreading symbols in the chart below to mark places that need corrections.

- ☑ **Have I avoided run-on sentences and sentence fragments and punctuated sentences correctly?**
- ☑ **Have I used every word correctly, including plurals, possessives, and frequently confused words?**
- ☑ **Do verbs and subjects agree? Are verb tenses correct?**
- ☑ **Do pronouns refer clearly to their antecedents and agree with them in person, number, and gender?**
- ☑ **Have I used adverb and adjective forms and modifying phrases correctly?**
- ☑ **Have I spelled every word correctly, and checked the unfamiliar ones in a dictionary?**

Proofreading Symbols		
⊙	Lieut Brown	Insert a period.
∧	No one came the party.	Insert a letter or a word.
≡	I enjoyed paris.	Capitalize a letter.
/	The Class ran a bake sale.	Make a capital letter lowercase.
⁀ ‿	The campers are home sick.	Close up a space.
(sp)	They visited N.Y. (sp)	Spell out.
∧ ∧	Sue please come I need your help.	Insert a comma or a semicolon.
∾	He enjoyed feild day.	Transpose the position of letters or words.
#	alltogether	Insert a space.
ℊ	We went to to Boston.	Delete letters or words.
∨ ∨ ∨	She asked, Whos coming?	Insert quotation marks or an apostrophe.
/ = /	mid January	Insert a hyphen.
¶	"Where?" asked Karl. "Over there," said Ray.	Begin a new paragraph.

WRITING HANDBOOK

Publishing/Presenting

Now your writing is ready for an audience. You may consider adding graphics (such as photographs, diagrams, or charts) to your paper. Make a clean, neat copy, and add your name and date. Check that the paper has a title. If you wish, enclose the paper in a folder or binder to give it a professional look. Hand it in to your teacher or share it in one of the ways described below. When the paper is returned, keep it in your writing portfolio.

Ideas for presenting

- Oral presentation Almost any writing can be shared aloud by an individual or a group. Try including music or slides.
- Class book A collection of class writing is a good contribution to the school library.
- Newspaper Some schools have a school newspaper. Local newspapers often publish student writing, especially if it is about local people and events.
- Literary magazine Magazines such as *Cricket* and *Stone Soup* publish student writing. Some schools have a literary magazine that publishes student writing once or twice a year.
- Bulletin board A rotating display of student writing is an effective way to see what your classmates have written. Illustrations and photographs add interest.
- Multimedia presentation Use computer software that allows you to combine text with sound and visuals (such as photos, drawings, maps, and animation or movie files). A multimedia presentation can be kept on a computer's hard drive, added to a local network, or recorded onto a disk, CD, or DVD.

Some writing, such as journal writing, is private and not intended for an audience. However, even if you don't share your paper, don't throw it away. It may contain ideas that you can use later.

Writing Modes

There are four different types, or modes, of writing—expository, descriptive, narrative, and persuasive. Each mode has its own purpose and characteristics.

Expository Writing

Expository writing communicates knowledge. It provides and explains information; it may also give general directions or step-by-step instructions for an activity. Use the checklist at the right to help you improve your expository writing.

- ☑ Is the opening paragraph interesting?
- ☑ Are my explanations accurate and complete? Is information clear and easy to read?
- ☑ Is information presented in a logical order?
- ☑ Does each paragraph have a main idea? Does all the information in the paragraph support the main idea?
- ☑ Does my essay have an introduction, a body, and a conclusion?
- ☑ Have I defined any unfamiliar terms?
- ☑ Are my comparisons clear and logical?

Kinds of expository writing

Expository writing covers a wide range of styles. The chart below describes some of the possibilities.

Kinds of Expository Writing	Examples
General instructions on how to do something	Explain how to train for a cross-country race, how to arrange a surprise party, or how to clean up your room more efficiently.
Compare-and-contrast essay	Compare two athletes or two sports, two fictional characters, two books or movies, two places, or two kinds of vacations.
Step-by-step directions	Give directions for building a model plane, making lemon meringue pie, or drawing on a computer screen.
Information and explanation	Explain what causes sunspots, how plants grow in the desert, or why camels have humps.
A report or essay	Write a book report, a report on the Buddhist religion, or a report on a new wildlife center.

WRITING HANDBOOK R53

Descriptive Writing

Descriptive writing can make a person, place, or thing come to life. The scene described may be as unfamiliar and far away as the bottom of the sea or as familiar and close as the gym locker room. By presenting details that awaken the reader's senses, descriptive writing can help your readers see the world more clearly. The checklist at the right can help you improve your descriptive writing.

- ☑ **Does my introduction identify the person or place that will be described?**
- ☑ **Are my details vivid? Are nouns and adjectives precise?**
- ☑ **Do all the details contribute to the same impression?**
- ☑ **Is it clear why this place or person is special?**
- ☑ **Are transitions clear? Do the paragraphs follow a logical order?**
- ☑ **Does each paragraph contain a main idea?**
- ☑ **Have I communicated a definite impression or mood?**

Narrative Writing

Narrative writing tells a story, either real or fictional. It answers the question *What happened?* A well-written narrative holds the reader's attention by presenting interesting characters in a carefully ordered series of events. You can get some tips on improving your narrative writing from the checklist at the right.

- ☑ **Does my first sentence get the reader's attention?**
- ☑ **Are the characters and setting described in enough detail?**
- ☑ **Do the characters speak and behave realistically?**
- ☑ **Are the events narrated in an order clear enough for the reader to follow?**
- ☑ **Are there places where dialogue should be added?**
- ☑ **Does the story have a satisfactory conclusion?**

Persuasive Writing

Persuasive writing presents an opinion. Its goal is to make readers feel or think a certain way about a situation or an idea. The writer includes facts and opinions often designed to urge readers to take action. Good persuasive writing appeals to the readers' common sense and to their emotions. Check the list at the right for ways to make your persuasive writing more effective.

- ☑ **Is my main idea expressed in a clear statement?**
- ☑ **Have I presented good reasons to support my point of view?**
- ☑ **Have I supported my reasons with facts and opinions?**
- ☑ **Have I taken account of the opposing points of view?**
- ☑ **Have I addressed the interests of my audience?**
- ☑ **Have I ended with a strong closing statement?**

Research Report Writing

When you write a research report, you explore a topic by gathering factual information from several resources. Through your research, you develop a point of view or draw a conclusion. This point of view or conclusion becomes the main idea, or thesis statement, of your report.

Select a Topic

Because a research report usually takes time to prepare and write, your choice of topic is especially important. Follow these guidelines.

- Brainstorm to make a list of possible topics. Choose a topic that is neither too narrow nor too broad for the length of paper you will write.
- Select a topic that genuinely interests you.
- Be sure you can find information on your topic from several sources.

Do Research

Start by reading general information about your topic in an encyclopedia. Then look for answers to specific questions in other sources. The catalog in a library can tell you what books are available on your topic. Online databases such as the *Reader's Guide to Periodical Literature* can help you locate magazine and newspaper articles. Current research on your topic may be found on electronic sources such as CD-ROMs or the Internet. If you need help in finding or using any of these resources, ask the librarian.

Be aware that anyone can post information on the Internet. Make sure that the information you use comes from a reputable source. Being a critical reader is an important part of being a good researcher. Stay focused on your topic as you do your research and be sure you have enough facts to support the statements you will make in your report.

Make Source Cards

In a research report, you must document the source of your information. To keep track of your sources, write the author, title, publication information, and location of each source on a separate index card. Give each source card a number and write that number in the upper right-hand corner. These cards will be useful for preparing your documentation.

WRITING HANDBOOK

WRITING HANDBOOK R55

Take Notes

PRACTICE

Rubric

Students should

- select a topic suitable for a research report of about 750 words
- use the library or the Internet to find three sources of information on the chosen topic
- create a source card for each source
- fill out a note card with one useful bit of information from each source
- follow the forms of the sample source and note cards in their textbook

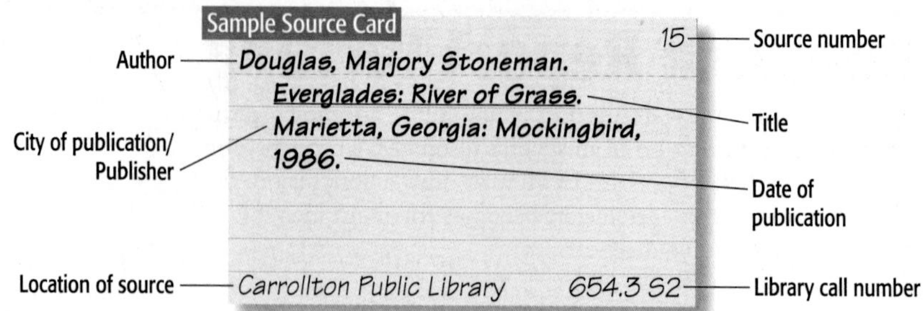

Take Notes

As you read, you encounter many new facts and ideas. Taking notes will help you keep track of information and focus on the topic. Here are some helpful suggestions:

- Use a new card for each important piece of information. Separate cards will help you to organize your notes effectively.
- At the top of each card, write a key word or phrase that tells you about the information. Also, write the number of the source you used.
- Write only details and ideas that relate to your topic.
- Summarize information in your own words.
- Record a phrase or a quotation only when the words are especially interesting or come from an important source. Enclose all quotations in quotation marks to make clear that the words belong to someone else.

This sample note card shows information to include.

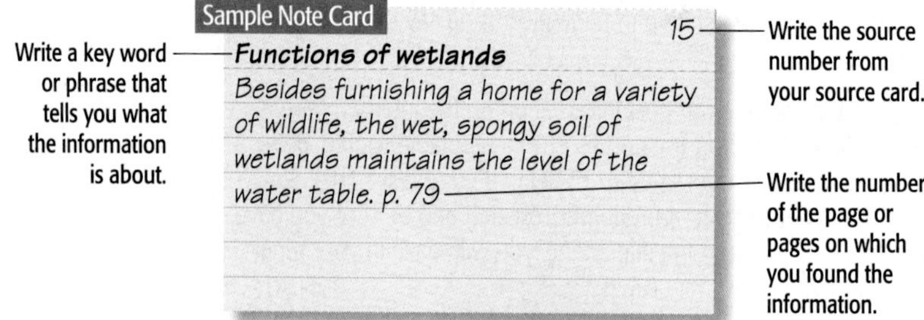

Sample Note Card
15
Write the source number from your source card.
Write a key word or phrase that tells you what the information is about.
Functions of wetlands
Besides furnishing a home for a variety of wildlife, the wet, spongy soil of wetlands maintains the level of the water table. p. 79
Write the number of the page or pages on which you found the information.

PRACTICE

Think of a topic you might use for a research report of about 750 words.

1. Use the library or the Internet to find three sources of information on your topic. Try to get a variety of sources—for example, a book, a periodical, a Web site. Make a source card for each source.

continued

PRACTICE

2. Find one useful bit of information from each source and fill out a note card with that information. Follow the form of the sample card above.

Develop Your Thesis

As you begin researching and learning about your topic, stay focussed on the overall point you want to make. Write down a thesis statement and keep it in mind as you continue your research. The thesis will help you determine what information is important. However, be prepared to change your thesis if the information you find does not support it.

Write an Outline

When you finish taking notes, organize the information in an outline. Write down the main ideas that you want to cover. Write your thesis statement at the beginning of your outline. Then list the supporting details. Follow an outline form like the one below.

Sample Outline

Everglades National Park is a beautiful but endangered animal habitat.

I. Special aspects of the Everglades
   A. Characteristics of wetlands
   B. Endangered birds and animals
II. Pressures on the Everglades
   A. Florida agriculture
   B. Carelessness of visitors
III. How to protect the Everglades
   A. Change agricultural practices
   B. Educate visitors who come to the park
      1. Mandatory video on safety for individuals and environment
      2. Instructional reminders posted throughout the park

The thesis statement identifies your topic and the overall point you will make.

If you have subtopics under a main topic, there must be at least two. They must relate directly to your main topic.

If you wish to divide a subtopic, you must have at least two divisions. Each must relate to the subtopic above it.

WRITING HANDBOOK

WRITING HANDBOOK R57

Document Your Information

You must document, or credit, the sources of all the information you use in your report. There are two common ways to document information.

Footnotes

To document with footnotes, place a number at the end of the information you are documenting. Number your notes consecutively, beginning with number 1. These numbers should be slightly raised and should come after any punctuation. The documentation information itself goes at the bottom of the page, with a matching number.

In-text number for note:

The Declaration of Independence was read in public for the first time on July 6, 1776.[3]

Footnote at bottom of page:

[3] John Smith, The Declaration of Independence (New York: DI, 2001) 221.

Parenthetical Documentation

In this method, you give the source for your information in parentheses at the end of the sentence where the information appears. You do not need to give all the details of the source. Just provide enough information for your readers to identify it. Here are the basic rules to follow.

- Usually it is enough to give the author's last name and the number of the page where you found the information.

  The declaration was first read in public by militia colonel John Nixon (Smith 222).

- If you mention the author's name in the sentence, you do not need to repeat it in the parentheses.

  According to Smith, the reading was greeted with wild applause (224).

- If your source does not identify a particular author, as in a newspaper or encyclopedia article, give the first word or two of the title of the piece.

  The anniversary of the reading was commemorated by a parade and fireworks ("Reading Celebrated").

Full information on your sources goes in a list at the end of your paper.

R58 WRITING HANDBOOK

Works Cited or Bibliography

At the end of your paper, list all the sources of information that you used in preparing your report. Arrange them alphabetically by the author's last name (or by the first word in the title if no author is mentioned) as shown below. Title this list *Works Cited.* (Use the term *bibliography* if all your sources are printed media, such as books, magazines, or newspapers.)

Works Cited

Newspaper article — Bertram, Jeffrey. "African Bees: Fact or Myth?" *Orlando Sentinel* 18 Aug. 1999: D2.

Magazine article — Gore, Rick. "Neanderthals." National Geographic. (January 1996): 2–35.

Book with one author — Gould, Stephen J. The Panda's Thumb. New York: Norton, 1982.

Book with two authors — McNeill, John Robert, and Paul Kennedy. *Something New Under the Sun: An Environmental History of the Twentieth-Century World*. New York: Norton, 2000.

Book with three or more authors — Quirk, Randolph, et al. *An Old English Grammar*. DeKalb, IL: Northern Illinois UP, 1994.

Online article — "Governor Chiles Vetoes Anti-Everglades Bills–5/13/98." Friends of the Everglades. May 1998. 26 Aug 1998 <http://www.everglades.org/pressrel_may28.htm>.

Encyclopedia — "Neanderthal Man." The Columbia Encyclopedia. 5th ed. New York: Columbia UP, 1993.

Interview — Pabst, Laura. Personal interview. 11 March 1998.

Video Recording — Kubrick, Stanley, dir. *2001: A Space Odyssey*. 1968. DVD. Warner, 1999.

Indent all but the first line of each item.

Include page numbers for a magazine article but not for a book, unless the book is a collection of essays by various authors.

Et al means "and others"

Include the name of the site (in italics), the date it was created or revised, and the date you accessed it.

PRACTICE

Think of a good topic for a research paper. Then look for five sources of information about that topic. Your sources should include one book, one encyclopedia article, two magazine articles, and one online article. Using the proper format, prepare a list of works cited for your five sources.

Works Cited or Bibliography

PRACTICE

Rubric

Students should

- choose a topic suitable for a research paper
- find five sources of information on the topic, including a book, an encyclopedia article, an online article, and two magazine articles
- prepare a list of works cited for the five sources
- follow correct bibliographic formats

Business Writing

BUSINESS LETTERS

Direct students to the writing model on pages R106–R107 for an example of the block style for business letters. Have them compare that style with the modified block style shown here and ask them to identify the differences. *(In the block style, all text, including the heading and closing, begins at the left margin, and a line space is used between paragraphs in place of paragraph indentation.)*

Business Writing

Two standard formats for business letters are block style and modified block style. In block style, all the sections and paragraphs of the letter begin at the left-hand margin. In modified block style (as shown below), the heading and closing are indented to the right and each paragraph is indented.

10 Pullman Lane
Cromwell, CT 06416
January 16, 2001

— In the heading, write your address and the date on separate lines.

Mr. Philip Fornaro
Principal
Cromwell School
179 West Maple Street
Cromwell, CT 06416

— In the inside address, write the name and address of the person to whom you are sending the letter.

Dear Mr. Fornaro:

— Use a colon after the greeting.

My friends and I in the seventh grade at Brimmer Middle School feel that there is not enough to do in Cromwell during the winter vacation week. Some students can afford to go away for vacation. Many families, however, cannot afford to go away, or the parents have to work.

— In your introduction, say who you are and why you are writing.

I would like to suggest that you keep the Brimmer Middle School gym open during the vacation week. If the gym were open, the basketball teams could practice. The fencing club could meet. We could meet our friends there instead of going to the mall.

— In the body of your letter, provide details concerning your request.

Thanks for listening to my request. I hope you will think it over.

— Conclude by restating your purpose and thanking the person you are writing to.

Sincerely,
Kim Goodwin
Kim Goodwin

— In the closing, use *Sincerely, Sincerely yours,* or *Yours truly* followed by a comma. Include both your signature and your printed or typed name.

General guidelines

Follow these guidelines when writing a business letter.

- Use correct business-letter form, as shown on page R60. Whether you write, type, or use a word processor, use 8½-by-11-inch white or off-white paper. Be sure your letter is neat and clean.
- Use Standard English. Check your spelling carefully.
- Be polite, even if you are making a complaint or expressing a negative opinion.
- Be brief and to the point. State your reason for writing within the first two or three sentences.
- Include all necessary information.
- If you are making a request, be specific. Make sure what you are asking is reasonable. Express your appreciation at the end of the letter.
- Be considerate. Request only information you cannot get another way.
- When expressing an opinion or a complaint, state your reasons clearly and logically. Avoid emotional language.
- When requesting an interview, make it easy for the interviewee to meet with you. Suggest a few dates.

Writing a Memo

A memo, or memorandum, is a brief, efficient way of communicating information to another person or group of people. It begins with a header that provides basic information. A memo does not have a formal closing.

TO: *Brimmer Banner* staff
FROM: Terry Glinski
SUBJECT: Winter issue
DATE: January 18, 2002

Articles for the winter issue of the *Brimmer Banner* are due by February 1. Please see Terry about your assignment as soon as possible! The following articles or features have not yet been assigned:

Cafeteria Mess: Who Is Responsible?
Teacher Profile: Mr. Jinks, Ms. Magee
Sports roundup

WRITING HANDBOOK

WRITING HANDBOOK R61

Communications Skills Handbook

Using a Computer for Writing

Using a computer with a word processing program to write offers advantages at every stage of the writing process.

Prewriting

A computer can help you gather and organize ideas and information.

Brainstorming

While brainstorming for topics or details, you can dim the computer screen and do "invisible writing." Some writers find that this technique allows their ideas to flow more freely.

Researching

CD-ROMs are disks that store large amounts of text, graphics, and sounds. If your computer has a CD-ROM drive, you can use a CD-ROM encyclopedia to find not only text and pictures, but also sound, animated cartoons or graphics, and live-action video clips.

If you have a modem and are connected with an online service, you can access material from an online encyclopedia, magazine, or Web site.

Outlining

Some word processing programs offer an outlining feature that automatically indents headings and uses various type styles for main headings and subheadings.

Drafting/Revising

Most word processing programs make it easy to do the following:

- *insert* new text at any point in your document
- *delete* or *copy* text
- *move* text from one position to another
- *undo* a change or series of changes you just made
- *save* each draft or revision of your document
- *print* copies of your work-in-progress for others to read

R62 COMMUNICATIONS SKILLS HANDBOOK

Editing/Proofreading

You can edit and proofread directly on the computer, or you can mark your changes on a printout, or hard copy and then input the changes on screen. The following word processing features are helpful:

- Grammar checker The computer finds possible errors in grammar and suggests revisions.
- Spelling checker The computer finds misspellings and suggests corrections.
- Thesaurus If you want to replace an inappropriate or overused word, you can highlight the word and the computer will suggest synonyms.
- Search and replace If you want to change or correct something that occurs several times in your document, the computer can quickly make the change throughout the document.

Rule of Thumb: The grammar checker, spelling checker, and thesaurus cannot replace your own careful reading and judgment. Because English grammar is so complex, the suggestions that the grammar checker makes may not be appropriate. The spelling checker will not tell you that you have typed *brake* when you meant *break,* for example, because both are valid words. The thesaurus may offer you several synonyms for a word, but you need to consider the connotations of each before deciding which fits your context.

Presenting

The computer allows you to enhance the readability, attractiveness, and visual interest of your document in many ways.

Formatting your text

The computer gives you a variety of options for the layout and appearance of your text. You can easily add or change the following elements:

- margin width
- number of columns
- type size and style
- page numbering
- header or footer (information such as a title that appears at the top or bottom of every page)

Visual aids

Some word processing programs have graphic functions that allow you to create graphs, charts, and diagrams. Collections of photos, clip art, and pictures you can copy and paste into your document are also available.

COMMUNICATIONS SKILLS HANDBOOK R63

Study and Test-Taking Skills

Study Skills

Good study skills grow out of good habits. Try making the following suggestions part of your daily school routine. Write down each subject and each assignment daily in an assignment notebook. For each assignment, set a study goal. Decide how long it will take you to meet each goal. Divide long assignments into smaller tasks.

Tips for good study habits

- Keep an assignment notebook. Keep it up to date.
- Keep your notes for each course together in one place.
- Find a good place to study. Choose a place that has as few distractions as possible. Try to study in the same place each day.
- Try to study at the same time each day.
- Don't study one subject too long. If you haven't finished after thirty minutes, switch to another subject.
- Take notes on your reading. Keep your notes in one place.

Taking Tests

How well you perform on a test is not a matter of chance. Some specific strategies can help you answer test questions. This section of the handbook will show how to improve your test-taking skills.

Tips for preparing for tests

Here are some useful suggestions:

- Gather information about the test. When will it be given? How long will it take? Exactly what material will it cover?
- Review material from your textbook, class notes, homework, quizzes, and handouts. Review the study questions at the end of each section of a textbook. Try to define terms in boldface type.
- Make up some sample questions and answer them. As you skim selections, try to predict what may be asked.
- Draw charts and cluster or Venn diagrams to help you remember information and to picture how one piece of information relates to another.
- Give yourself plenty of time to study. Avoid cramming for a test. Several short review sessions are more effective than one long one.
- In addition to studying alone, study with a partner or small group. Quiz one another on topics you think the test will cover.

R64 COMMUNICATIONS SKILLS HANDBOOK

Tips for using test time

Try following these steps:

- Read all directions carefully. Understanding the directions can prevent mistakes.
- Ask for help if you have a question.
- Answer the easier items first. By skipping the hard items, you will have time to answer all the easy ones.
- In the time that is left, return to the items you skipped. Answer them as best you can. If you won't be penalized for doing so, guess at an answer.
- If possible, save some time at the end to check your answers.

Taking objective tests

An objective test is a test of factual information. The answers to the questions are either right or wrong. You are asked to recall information, not to present your ideas. Objective test questions include true-or-false items, multiple-choice items, fill-in-the-blanks statements, short-answer items, and matching items. At the beginning of an objective test, scan the number of items. Then budget your time.

Multiple-choice items Multiple-choice questions ask you to answer a question or complete a sentence. They are the kind of question you will encounter most often on objective tests. Read all the choices before answering. Pick the best response.

What is a peninsula?
(a) a range of mountains
(b) a circle around the moon
(c) a body of land surrounded by water on three sides

Correct answer: (c)

- Read the question carefully. Be sure that you understand it.
- Read all the answers before selecting one. Reading all of the responses is especially important when one of the choices is "all of the above" or "none of the above."
- Eliminate responses that are clearly incorrect. Focus on the responses that might be correct.
- Look for absolute words, such as *never, always, all, none.* Most generalizations have exceptions. Absolute statements are often incorrect. (Note: This tip applies to true-or-false items also.)

COMMUNICATIONS SKILLS HANDBOOK

COMMUNICATIONS SKILLS HANDBOOK R65

Answering essay questions

Essay questions ask you to think about what you have learned and to write about it in one or more paragraphs. Some tests present a choice of essay questions. If a test has both an objective part and an essay part, answer the objective questions first but leave yourself enough time to work on the essay.

Read the essay question carefully. What does it ask you to do? Discuss? Explain? Define? Summarize? Compare and contrast? These key words tell what kind of information you must give in your answer.

Key Verbs in Essay Questions	
Argue	Give your opinion and supporting reasons.
Compare and contrast	Discuss likenesses and differences.
Define	Give details that show exactly what something is like.
Demonstrate	Give examples to support a point.
Describe	Present a picture with words.
Discuss	Show detailed information on a particular subject.
Explain	Give reasons.
Identify	Give specific characteristics.
List (also outline, trace)	Give details, give steps in order, give a time sequence.
Summarize	Give a short overview of the most important ideas or events.

Tips for answering essay questions

Consider the following suggestions:

- Read the question or questions carefully. Determine the kind of information required by the question.
- Plan your time. Do not spend too much time on one part of the essay.
- Make a list of what you want to cover.
- If you have time, make revisions and proofreading corrections.

Taking standardized tests

Standardized tests are taken by large groups of students. Your performance on the test is compared with the performance of other students at your grade level. There are many kinds of standardized tests. Some measure your progress in such subjects as English, math, and science, while others measure how well you think. Standardized tests can show how you learn and what you do best.

Preparing for standardized tests

There is no way to know exactly what information will be on a standardized test or even what topics will be covered. The best preparation is to do the best you can in your daily schoolwork. However, you can learn the *kinds* of questions that will appear on a standardized test. Some general tips will also help.

Tips for taking standardized tests

You may find the following suggestions helpful:

- Get enough sleep the night before the test. Eat a healthful breakfast.
- Arrive early for the test. Try to relax.
- Listen carefully to all test directions. Ask questions if you don't understand the directions.
- Complete easy questions first. Leave harder items for the end.
- Be sure your answers are in the right place on the answer sheet.
- If points are not subtracted for wrong answers, guess at answers that you aren't sure of.

Analogies Analogy items test your understanding of the relationships between things or ideas. On standardized tests, analogies are written in an abbreviated format, as shown below.

man : woman :: buck : doe

The symbol *:* means "is to"; the symbol *::* means "as."

This chart shows some word relationships you may find in analogy tests.

Relationship	Definition	Example
Synonyms	Two words have a similar meaning.	huge : gigantic :: scared : afraid
Antonyms	Two words have opposite meanings.	bright : dull :: far : near
Use	Words name a user and something used.	farmer : tractor :: writer : computer
Cause-Effect	Words name a cause and its effect.	tickle : laugh :: polish : shine
Category	Words name a category and an item in it.	fish : tuna :: building : house
Description	Words name an item and a characteristic of it.	knife : sharp :: joke : funny

COMMUNICATIONS SKILLS HANDBOOK R67

COMMUNICATIONS SKILLS HANDBOOK

Listening, Speaking, and Viewing Skills

Listening Effectively

A large part of the school day is spent either listening or speaking to others. By becoming a better listener and speaker, you will know more about what is expected of you and understand more about your audience.

Listening to instructions in class

Some of the most important listening in the school day involves listening to instructions. Use the following checklist to help you.

- Make sure you understand what you are listening for. Are you receiving instructions for homework or for a test? What you listen for depends upon the type of instructions being given.
- Think about what you are hearing and keep your eyes on the speaker. This will help you stay focused on the important points.
- Listen for key words or word clues. Examples of word clues are phrases such as *above all, most important,* or *the three basic parts.* These clues help you identify important points that you should remember.
- Take notes on what you hear. Write down only the most important parts of the instructions.
- If you don't understand something, ask questions. Then if you're still unsure about the instructions, repeat them aloud to your teacher to receive correction on any key points that you may have missed.

Interpreting nonverbal clues

Understanding nonverbal clues is part of effective listening. Nonverbal clues are everything you notice about a speaker *except* what the speaker says. As you listen, ask yourself these questions:

- Where and how is the speaker standing?
- Are some words spoken with more emphasis than others?
- Is a word, phrase, or sentence repeated?
- Does the speaker make eye contact?
- Does he or she smile or look angry?
- What message is sent by the speaker's gestures and facial expression?

R68 COMMUNICATIONS SKILLS HANDBOOK

PRACTICE

Work with a partner to practice listening to instructions. Each of you should find a set of directions for using a simple device—for example, a mechanical tool, a telephone answering machine, or a VCR. Study the instructions carefully. If you can bring the device to class, ask your partner to try to use it by following your step-by-step instructions. If you cannot have the device in class, ask your partner to explain the directions back to you. Then change roles and listen as your partner gives you a set of directions.

Speaking Effectively

- Speak slowly, clearly, and in a normal tone of voice. Raise your voice a bit or use gestures to stress important points.
- Pause a few seconds after making an important point.
- Use words that help your audience picture what you're talking about. Visual aids such as pictures, graphs, charts, and maps can also help make your information clear.
- Stay in contact with your audience. Make sure your eyes move from person to person in the group you're addressing.

Speaking informally

Most oral communication is informal. When you speak casually with your friends, family, and neighbors, you use informal speech. Human relationships depend on this form of communication.

- Be courteous. Listen until the other person has finished speaking.
- Speak in a relaxed and spontaneous manner.
- Make eye contact with your listeners.
- Do not monopolize a conversation.
- When telling a story, show enthusiasm.
- When giving an announcement or directions, speak clearly and slowly. Check that your listeners understand the information.

Presenting an oral report

The steps in preparing an oral report are similar to the steps in the writing process, except that an additional step—*practicing*—is added before *presenting*. (See the chart on the following page.) Complete each step carefully and you can be confident of presenting an effective oral report.

Listening Effectively: Interpreting nonverbal clues

PRACTICE

Rubric

Students should

- locate a set of directions for using a simple device
- learn the directions
- give the directions orally to a partner, who will either perform a task on the device or repeat the directions back to the speaker
- switch roles as the partner gives a new set of oral directions to follow
- discuss with the partner any problems in understanding the directions and ways of improving them

Speaking Effectively: Presenting an oral report

PRACTICE

Rubric

Students should

- plan a report for fifth graders on adjusting to middle school conditions
- include lively descriptions and examples in the report
- use vocal techniques and body language effectively
- accept feedback from a partner on how to improve the presentation
- switch roles with the partner to listen to and critique his or her presentation

Steps in Preparing an Oral Report	
Prewriting	Determine your purpose and audience. Decide on a topic and narrow it.
Drafting	Make an outline. Fill in the supporting details. Write the report.
Revising and editing	Review your draft. Check the organization of ideas and details. Reword unclear statements.
Practicing	Practice the report aloud in front of a family member. Time the report. Ask for and accept advice.
Presenting	Relax in front of your audience. Make eye contact with your audience. Speak slowly and clearly.

PRACTICE

Pretend that you have been invited to give an oral report to a group of fifth graders. Your report will tell them what to expect and how to adjust to new conditions when they enter middle school. As you plan your report, keep your purpose and your audience in mind. Include lively descriptions and examples to back up your suggestions and hold your audience's attention. As you practice giving your report, be sure to give attention to your body language as well as your vocal projection. Ask a partner to listen to your report and give you feedback on how to improve your performance. Do the same for your partner after listening to his or her report.

Viewing Effectively

Critical viewing means thinking about what you see while watching a TV program, newscast, film, or video. It requires paying attention to what you hear and see and deciding whether information is true, false, or exaggerated. If the information *seems* to be true, try to determine whether it is based on a fact or an opinion.

Fact versus opinion

A fact is something that can be proved. An opinion is what someone *believes* is true. Opinions are based on feelings and experiences and cannot be proved.

Television commercials, political speeches, and even the evening news contain both facts and opinions. They use emotional words and actions to persuade the viewer to agree with a particular point of view. They may also use faulty reasoning, such as linking an effect with the wrong cause. Think through what is being said. The speaker may seem sincere, but do his or her reasons make sense? Are the reasons based on facts or on unfair generalizations?

Commercials contain both obvious and hidden messages. Just as you need to discover the author's purpose when you read a writer's words, you must be aware of the purpose of nonverbal attempts to persuade you. What does the message sender want, and how is the sender trying to influence you? For example, a magazine or TV ad picturing a group of happy teenagers playing volleyball on a sunny beach expresses a positive feeling. The advertiser hopes viewers will transfer that positive feeling to the product being advertised–perhaps a soft drink or a brand of beachwear. This technique, called **transfer,** is one of several propaganda techniques regularly used by advertisers to influence consumers. Following are a few other common techniques.

Testimonial–Famous and admired people recommend or praise a product, a policy, or a course of action even though they probably have no professional knowledge or expertise to back up their opinion.

Bandwagon–People are urged to follow the crowd ("get on the bandwagon") by buying a product, voting for a candidate, or whatever else the advertiser wants them to do.

Glittering generalities–The advertiser uses positive, good-sounding words (for example, *all-American* or *medically proven*) to impress people.

PRACTICE

Think of a television commercial that you have seen often or watch a new one and take notes as you watch it. Then analyze the commercial.

- What is the purpose behind the ad?
- What is expressed in written or spoken words?
- What is expressed nonverbally (in music or sound effects as well as in pictures and actions)?
- What methods does the advertiser use to persuade viewers?
- What questions would you ask the advertiser if you could?
- How effective is the commercial? Why?

Working in Groups

Working in a group is an opportunity to learn from others. Whether you are planning a group project (such as a class trip) or solving a math

Viewing Effectively: Fact versus opinion

PRACTICE

Rubric

Students should

- select a television commercial
- identify the purpose of the commercial
- identify the methods used by the advertiser to persuade viewers
- distinguish between and analyze the verbal and nonverbal methods of persuasion
- evaluate the effectiveness of the commercial

problem, each person in a group brings specific strengths and interests to the task. When a task is large, such as planting a garden, a group provides the necessary energy and talent to get the job done.

Small groups vary in size according to the nature of the task. Three to five students is a good size for most small-group tasks. Your teacher may assign you to a group, or you may be asked to form your own group. Don't work with your best friend if you are likely to chat too much. Successful groups often have a mix of student abilities and interests.

Individual role assignments give everyone in a group something to do. One student, the group recorder, may take notes. Another may lead the discussion, and another report the results to the rest of the class.

Roles for a Small Group	
Reviewer	Reads or reviews the assignment and makes sure everyone understands it
Recorder 1 (of the process)	Takes notes on the discussion
Recorder 2 (of the results)	Takes notes on the final results
Reporter	Reports results to the rest of the class
Discussion leader	Asks questions to get the discussion going; keeps the group focused
Facilitator	Helps the group resolve disagreements and reach a compromise

For a small group of three or four students, some of these roles can be combined. Your teacher may assign a role to each student in your group. Or you may be asked to choose your own role.

Tips for working in groups

- Review the group assignment and goal. Be sure that everyone in the group understands the assignment.
- Review the amount of time allotted for the task. Decide how your group will organize its time.
- Check that all the group members understand their roles in the group.
- When a question arises, try to solve it as a group before asking a teacher for help.
- Listen to other points of view. Take turns during a discussion.
- When it is your turn to talk, address the subject and help the project move forward.

R72 COMMUNICATIONS SKILLS HANDBOOK

Reading Handbook

The Reading Process

As reading materials get more difficult, you'll need to use a variety of active reading strategies to understand texts. This handbook is designed to help you find and use the tools you'll need before, during, and after reading.

Word Identification

Word identification skills are a necessary building block for understanding what you read. They prepare you to deal with unknown words you'll encounter as you read.

Look before, at, and after a new word. Use the other words and sentences around an unknown word to help you make an educated guess about what that word might be. Think about the following questions as you try to read new words.

- What other word would make sense in this sentence?
- Can I sound this new word out?
- Can I figure out this word from its place in the sentence?

Using letter-sound cues

One way to figure out a new word is to try to sound it out. Use the following tips when sounding out new words.

- Look at the beginning of the word. What letter or group of letters makes up the beginning sound or beginning syllable of the word?

  Example: In the word *coagulate, co-* rhymes with *so.*

- Look at the end of the word. What letter or group of letters makes up the ending sound or syllable? Knowing how a word begins and ends will help you take a better guess at the whole word.

  Example: In the word *coagulate, late* is a word you know.

- Look at the middle of the word. What are the sounds of the letters and groups of letters within the word? Is there a word you already know inside the new word? Is the middle of the word similar to other words you know? What vowel or vowel pattern is represented in each syllable?

READING HANDBOOK R73

READING HANDBOOK

Example: In the word *coagulate,* the syllable *ag* has the same vowel sound as *bag* and the syllable *u* is pronounced like the letter *u.* Now try pronouncing the whole word: *co ag u late.*

Using language structure cues

Word order, or **syntax,** helps you make sense of a sentence, so looking at the position of a new word in a sentence can help you identify a word. For instance, look at the following nonsense sentence.

The drazzy lurds miffled the bonkee blams.

Your experience with English sentence patterns and parts of speech tells you that the action word, or verb, in this sentence is *miffled.* Who did the *miffling?*–the *lurds*. What kind of *lurds* were they?–*drazzy.* Whom did they *miffle?*–the *blams.* What kind of blams were they?–*bonkee.* Even though you do not know word meanings in the nonsense sentence, you can make some sense of the entire sentence by using syntax.

Using context clues

When you read on your own, you can often figure out the meaning of a new word by looking at its **context,** the words and sentences that surround it. For instance, look at the following example.

The area suffered an earthquake followed by a flood. After such *cataclysms,* it took some time to return to normal.

You can see from the first sentence that *cataclysms* refers to both an earthquake and a flood. It is a general word for violent change in the forces of nature. The context provides examples of the unknown word.

Tips for Using Context

- Look before, at, and after the unknown word for
  - –a synonym or definition of the unknown word in a sentence
    To avoid a collision, the car ***swerved,*** *or* ***turned aside.***
  - –a clue to what the word is like or not like
    Like a human top, *the little dancer* ***pirouetted*** *gracefully.*
  - –a general topic associated with the word
    The ***gardener*** *shoveled* ***mulch*** *onto all the flower beds.*
  - –a description or action associated with the word
    The seamstress used ***pinking shears*** *to* ***trim*** *the seams of the dress.*
- Connect what you know with what the author has written.
- Predict a possible meaning.
- Apply the meaning in the sentence.
- Try again if your guess does not make sense.

R74 READING HANDBOOK

Using word parts to read new words

Knowing word parts can help you sound out unknown words. It can also help you discover word meanings or enable you to change a word's meaning.

- Roots The base part of a word is called its root. If you know a root within a new word, start from there to sound out the rest of the word. The root can also give you a hint about the word's meaning. Some roots, mainly those that came from Anglo-Saxon, are familiar words. For example, the roots *dear* and *mark* can be found in such longer words as *endearing* and *remarkable*. Other roots are less familiar borrowings from Greek and Latin. For example, *spectator* contains the Latin root *spec*, which means "to look at."
- Prefixes A prefix is added to the beginning of a word. it changes the meaning of the word. For example, *semi-* means "half," so *semicircle* means "half circle."
- Suffixes A suffix can be added to the end of a word to change how the word is used in a sentence. For example, fear (a noun or a verb) becomes an adjective when the suffix *-ful* (meaning "full of") is added. *Fearful* means "full of fear."

Using reference materials

When looking at or around an unknown word does not help you identify it, dictionaries, glossaries, and other reference sources can be useful tools.

A **dictionary** provides the pronunciation and literal meaning or meanings of a word. It may also give other forms of the word, its part of speech, alternate spellings, examples, synonyms, origins, and other useful information. Look at the dictionary entry below.

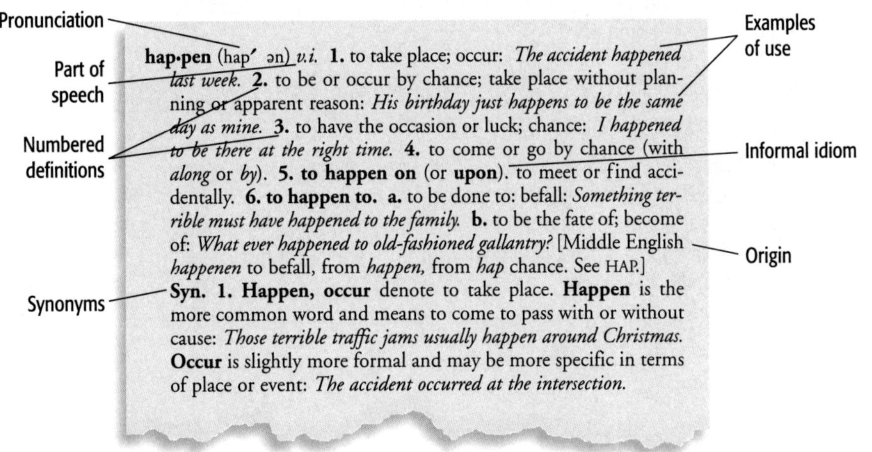

hap·pen (hap′ ən) *v.i.* **1.** to take place; occur: *The accident happened last week.* **2.** to be or occur by chance; take place without planning or apparent reason: *His birthday just happens to be the same day as mine.* **3.** to have the occasion or luck; chance: *I happened to be there at the right time.* **4.** to come or go by chance (with *along* or *by*). **5. to happen on** (or **upon**). to meet or find accidentally. **6. to happen to. a.** to be done to: befall: *Something terrible must have happened to the family.* **b.** to be the fate of; become of: *What ever happened to old-fashioned gallantry?* [Middle English *happenen* to befall, from *happen,* from *hap* chance. See HAP.]
Syn. 1. Happen, occur denote to take place. **Happen** is the more common word and means to come to pass with or without cause: *Those terrible traffic jams usually happen around Christmas.* **Occur** is slightly more formal and may be more specific in terms of place or event: *The accident occurred at the intersection.*

READING HANDBOOK R75

A **glossary** is a condensed dictionary within a specific text. It provides an alphabetical listing of words used within that text, together with their definitions and other information necessary to understand the words as they appear in the text. Look at the example below.

A

abolitionist a person who favors doing away with slavery (p. 416)

abstain to not take part in some activity, such as voting (p. 440)

adobe a sun-dried mud brick used to build the homes of Native Americans (p. 31)

affirmative action an active effort to improve educational and employment opportunities for minority groups and women (p. 887)

affluence the state of having much wealth (p. 808)

airlift a system of transporting food and supplies by aircraft into an area otherwise impossible to reach (p. 777)

A **thesaurus** is a dictionary of synonyms. It can be especially useful for choosing precise, descriptive language. Some thesauruses are available on CD-ROM and on the Internet.

Reading Fluency

Becoming an accomplished reader is like learning a sports skill or a musical instrument: the more you practice, the better you will be. The more you read aloud, the less attention you will need to pay to sounding words out and the more attention you can give to understanding the meaning in a selection.

Tips for Becoming a Fluent Reader

- Develop a good sight vocabulary.
- Practice reading aloud on independent level materials.
- Begin with a short interesting passage.
- Reread the same passage aloud at least three times.
- As your reading sounds smoother, move on to a longer or slightly more difficult passage.

READING HANDBOOK

Reading in appropriate level materials

How do you decide if something is too easy, too hard, or just right for you to read? If you want to develop into a smooth, fluent reader, it is important to read regularly in materials that are easy for you. However, it is also important to grow as a strategic reader. To do that, you will want to read materials that are challenging but manageable.

To decide what level of reading material is right for each reading task, look at the following chart:

Reading Level	Definition/Criteria	When to Use
Independent level	No more than 5 difficult words per 100 words read	• On your own, anytime • To practice smooth reading
Instructional level	No more than 10 difficult words per 100 words read	• With support from teacher, parent, or other more experienced reader • To challenge yourself
Beyond instructional level	More than 10 difficult words per 100 words read	• As material read to you by someone else • To develop new vocabulary through listening

Adjusting reading rate—skimming, scanning, and careful reading

It is important to adjust your reading speed to suit your purposes and the task you face. When you read something for enjoyment, you might read quickly. If you want to refresh your memory of a passage or get a quick impression of new material, skim the selection. **Skimming** is reading quickly over a piece of writing to find its main idea or to get a general overview of it. When you need to find a particular piece or type of information, scan the selection. In **scanning,** you run your eyes quickly over the material, looking only for key words or phrases that have to do with the information you seek.

When you read a chapter of a textbook filled with new concepts, when you follow complex written directions, or when you study for a test, read slowly, take notes, make a graphic organizer, and even reread passages in order to remember them later.

Look at the following models.

READING HANDBOOK R77

READING HANDBOOK

> It was a perfect day at Bowen Lake. At noon the woods and the lake were warm in the sun. Seated on a rock at the top of a hill, the boy watched the scene below him. The lake was a mirror of glass, occasionally broken by a leaping fish or a swooping bird. Far across the lake, he could sometimes see a canoe gliding by. He felt at peace with himself and the world, absorbed in the magic of being alone with nature.

> Osmosis is the tendency of a liquid, usually water, to flow through a semipermeable membrane that blocks the transport of salts or other solutes through it. Osmosis is a fundamental effect in all biological systems. When two volumes of liquid are separated by a semipermeable membrane, water will flow from the side of low solute concentration to the side of high solute concentration.

Which paragraph could you read more quickly? Why? What would you do to be sure you remembered the information in each paragraph?

Reading aloud

Reading out loud, alone or with others, can make a writer's work come to life and can be an enjoyable way of sharing a selection. Reading a complicated paragraph aloud can also be a powerful aid to understanding. Here are some suggestions for reading aloud:

- First read the selection silently a number of times.
- Think about the best way to make the main ideas understandable to your listeners.
- Use pauses to separate complete thoughts and be sure you observe all punctuation marks.
- Read carefully and clearly. Vary your speed and volume to reflect the important ideas in a passage.
- Use a lively voice. Emphasize important words and phrases to make the meaning clear.
- Practice difficult words and phrases until you've mastered them.
- Practice in front of another person, if possible, or use a tape recorder to hear how you sound.

Reading silently

Be sure to avoid distractions or interruptions when you read silently.

Tips for Sustained Silent Reading

- Be sure you're comfortable but not too comfortable.
- Check your concentration regularly by asking yourself **questions** about the selection.
- **Summarize** what you've read from time to time.
- Use a **study guide** or **story map** while reading difficult passages.
- Make a **graphic organizer,** if necessary, to understand and remember important concepts or a sequence of events.
- Take regular breaks when you need them and vary your reading rate with the demands of the text.

PRACTICE

With a partner, choose a selection from your text. Read the selection silently, adjusting your speed to the difficulty of the text. When both of you have finished, take turns asking questions to check your comprehension. Finally, choose a small section of the passage and take turns reading it aloud. Exchange suggestions about your oral reading.

Reading a Variety of Texts

Learn to read a wide range of materials for a variety of purposes. Throughout this textbook, you can read both classic and contemporary writing. From "Rip Van Winkle" to "The Scholarship Jacket," you will see how a variety of selections broadens your knowledge and deepens your appreciation of people and cultures.

Reading varied sources

Strategic readers take advantage of a variety of sources for information and for entertainment. For instance, to create a detailed and interesting portrait of a famous writer from your hometown or state, you might refer to sources like those listed below.

- **Encyclopedias** provide a basic foundation of information.
- **Letters, memos, speeches, newspapers,** and **magazines** add valuable information as well as personal perspectives.
- **Databases, library indexes,** and **Internet sites** often supply or lead you to interesting information.
- **Fiction, poems, plays,** and **anthologies,** (collections of literature), provide excellent opportunities to read for pleasure as well as to explore the ideas of a writer in a particular time.

Reading Fluency: Reading silently

PRACTICE

Rubric

Students should

- with a partner, select a selection to read
- read the selection silently
- take turns with the partner asking each other questions to check comprehension of the selection
- take turns with the partner reading a portion of the selection aloud
- critique each other's oral reading

Reading a Variety of Texts: Reading for various purposes

PRACTICE

Rubric

Students should

- choose a topic of interest and read about it in at least three sources
- make a presentation to the class in one of the following ways
  - a short written report
  - a speech
  - a demonstration
  - an attempt to persuade classmates
- explain to the class the purpose of the presentation and make an evaluation of each source

Reading for various purposes

Active reading begins with thinking about a reason for reading. You may find that you have more than one purpose or that your purposes overlap. For instance, you might enjoy reading an intense and thrilling mystery for entertainment and, at the same time, discover how police detectives work. The reading strategies you use to guide you through a text will depend on your purposes.

When your purpose for reading is

- **to be informed,** read slowly, take notes, construct a graphic organizer, reread, and review difficult sections.
- **to be entertained,** read at a faster rate.
- **to appreciate a writer's craft,** read carefully to admire how well others write and to determine how they do so.
- **to discover models for your own writing,** look at other writers' works to help stimulate your own ideas.
- **to take action,** read carefully so you can correctly complete forms, make recommendations, and write responses.

PRACTICE

Choose a topic that interests you and read about it in at least three sources. Decide on an action to take as a result of your reading. You may write a short report, give a speech, demonstrate how something works, or try to persuade your classmates to believe or do something. Make a short presentation to your class, explaining your purpose for reading and the value of each of your sources.

Vocabulary Development

Having a good vocabulary means more than just knowing the meanings of isolated words. It means knowing the larger concepts that surround those words. The best way to build a good vocabulary is to read widely, listen carefully, and participate actively in discussions in which new words and concepts are used.

Listening

Books that may be just a little too hard for you to read on your own are often excellent choices as selections to be read aloud to you. They provide a good way to learn new vocabulary. "Read-alouds" also give you a model for your own future oral reading. As you hear new words, try to pay attention to their **context**–the words and ideas surrounding the unknown words. Try to guess what meaning would make sense for new words. Many times you will guess accurately if you pay careful attention.

Using experience and prior knowledge

Because of your life experiences, you know certain things and understand the meanings of certain words and ideas. Those experiences, called **prior knowledge,** help you determine word meanings. For instance, if you have had experience using computers, you'll understand the following sentence.

She needed to clean her mouse to make her cursor move.

Sometimes you'll need to look beyond the exact meaning of words in a selection and consider some of the following variations of language.

- Idioms An expression that has a meaning apart from the literal meaning of the words is called an idiom. If a comedian's jokes *bring down the house,* it means that he or she has made the audience applaud or laugh loudly. When someone is *stretching a point,* he or she is making an exception. In each case, combine the words with prior knowledge to interpret what the expression means.
- Multiple meanings Words can have more than one meaning, so check the context to be sure the meaning you have chosen makes sense. Look at these examples:
  *The organ **stops** were jammed, so the organist had to **stop** playing.*
  *Jay **spoke** to his dad about the loose **spoke** on his bicycle wheel.*
- Figurative language Writers sometimes make comparisons by using figurative language, such as analogies, similes, and metaphors. An **analogy** is a comparison between two things or ideas, one of which is usually less familiar to most readers or listeners. An analogy concentrates on those characteristics that are in some way similar. For example, you could make an analogy between a phone call and an e-mail: Both are means of communicating over a distance, both use ordinary language, and both carry messages electronically over wires or via satellites. Similes and metaphors are forms of analogy that are found frequently in literature. A **simile** uses the word *like* or *as* to make a comparison between two unlike things. A **metaphor** states that one thing *is* another.
  Simile: *Snow **like** small white feathers floated down from the sky.*
  Metaphor: *Her eyes were stars that sparkled at the good news.*

PRACTICE

1. List at least three idioms with which you are familiar. Tell what each idiom really means.
2. Use a dictionary, if necessary, to find a word that has at least three very different meanings. Write a sentence demonstrating each of the meanings.

continued

Vocabulary Development: Using experience and prior knowledge

PRACTICE

Rubric

Students should demonstrate a familiarity with and ability to use idioms, multiple-meaning words, analogies, similes, and metaphors by

1. listing and defining three idioms
2. using a dictionary to find a word with at least three meanings and writing a sentence demonstrating each meaning
3. writing an analogy to explain a topic or process to someone unfamiliar with it
4. creating a simile to help describe a person and turning that simile into a metaphor

READING HANDBOOK

3. Write an analogy you might use to explain some topic or process you know quite well to someone who was unfamiliar with it. (For example, explain the use of an electronic keyboard by making an analogy with a piano.)
4. Create a simile you might use in a description of a person you know. Then turn that simile into a metaphor.

Clarifying meanings with reference aids

Sometimes meanings of words and phrases can remain unclear even after using context clues, drawing on your personal background, and listening carefully. In that case, look to other reference aids to help clarify the meanings and usage of difficult terms.

- **Thesauruses** and books of synonyms can clarify a word by listing other words that have similar meanings.
- **Dictionaries** will often be able to clear up word meanings because they provide a variety of definitions for a word and examples of each definition in a sentence. You can often find the meaning of an idiom by looking in a dictionary under the main word in the phrase. Look at the idioms listed under the word *time*.

against time. in an effort to finish within or before a certain time: *Police were working against time in their search for the hidden bomb.*
ahead of time. before the time due or expected; early: *She arrived at the appointed place ahead of time.*
at the same time. however; nevertheless.
at times. sometimes; occasionally.
behind the times. old-fashioned.
for the time being. for the present; temporarily.
from time to time. now and then; occasionally.
in good time. **a.** at the proper time; within reasonable time. **b.** when or sooner than expected; quickly.
in no time. almost instantly; very rapidly.
in time. **a.** before it is too late. *Do you think we can get there in time for the first act?* **b.** in the course of time; eventually: *In time, all this will be forgotten.* **c.** in the correct or corresponding rhythm or tempo: *to clap in time to music.*
on time. **a.** at the correct or appointed time; punctual or punctually. **b.** payable in installments over time.
time after time. repeatedly. Also, **time and again.**
time out of mind. longer than can be remembered.
to keep time. to record time, as a clock.
to make time. **a.** to move rapidly, as in attempting to recover lost time. **b.** *Slang.* to progress in gaining favor or acceptance, as in carrying on a flirtation.

R82 READING HANDBOOK

READING HANDBOOK

- **Software** for a computer will often include reference materials that can clarify meanings and usage for difficult words.

Using word parts to determine meaning

Another way to determine the meaning of a word is to take the word itself apart. If you understand the meaning of the **base,** or **root** part, of a word and also know the meanings of key syllables added either to the beginning or end of the base, you can usually figure out what a word means.

Word Part	Definition	Example
Root or base	the most basic part of a word	*ced* means "go"
Prefix	a syllable used before a root word to add to or change its meaning	*pre-* means "before" *precede* means "go before"
Suffix	a syllable used after a root word to change its meaning or its use	*-ous* means "full of" *joyous* means "full of joy"

Roots English contains many words based on roots from Anglo-Saxon (the earliest form of our language, also known as Old English) and from ancient languages like Greek and Latin. Familiarity with some of these roots can help you to determine meanings, pronunciations, and spellings in English. Look at the following examples.

Root	Meaning	Example
astro (Greek)	star	astronaut, astronomy, asterisk
fare (Anglo-Saxon)	go; feed	farewell, welfare
vid (Latin)	see	video, evidence
hydr (Greek)	water	hydrant, dehydrate

Affixes These syllables are added to a base word either at its beginning (as a prefix) or its end (as a suffix). For example, *unusually* is made up of the word *usual* and the affixes *un-* and *-ly*. The prefix *un-* means "not." The suffix *-ly* means "in a particular manner." If you put them together, unusually means "not in the usual manner."

Suppose you come across an unfamiliar word like *hydroelectrification* in your reading. You can see that the root *electr* (as in electricity) is within the word. If you know that *hydro* means "water" and *-fication* means "making" or "producing," you can figure out that *hydroelectrification* refers to the production of electricity by using water as a power source–at a dam site, for example.

READING HANDBOOK R83

Vocabulary Development: Using word parts to determine meaning

PRACTICE

English learners and students reading below level may be asked to work on this activity with a partner or in small groups. Advanced learners should be able to work on their own or help others who need assistance.

Rubric

Students should

- use a dictionary to find the meaning of each listed word part
- create a chart listing each root, its meaning, and two modern English examples of words using the root
- use a dictionary to make sure each modern English word listed is actually derived from the Greek, Latin, or Old English root

Example:

Root	Meaning	Example
like	similar, pleased with	likely, likeness, likable
reck	care, regard	reckon, reckless, recklessness
demos	people	democracy, democrat, demographic
meter	measure	thermometer, metric, metronome
aud	to hear	audience, audible, audition
man	hand	manage, manifest, emancipate

PRACTICE

Following are some additional Old English (Anglo-Saxon), Greek, and Latin word parts. Use a dictionary to find the meaning of each one. Then make a chart similar to the second chart on page R83, giving at least two examples of modern English words based on each. Check the words in a dictionary that gives etymologies, or word histories, to make sure they are really based on the word part. Compare your chart with those of others in your class.

like–from Old English (ge)*lik*
reck–from Old English *reccan*
demos–from Greek *demos*
meter–from Greek *metron*
aud–from Latin *audire*
man–from Latin *manus*

Using word meanings across subjects

Have you ever learned a new word and then noticed it in many places and across many subjects? The word may not mean exactly the same thing in each place, but you can often use what you know about a word's meaning to help you interpret its meaning in a different context. Look at the following example from two subjects:

Social studies: *Altitude is one of the* ***factors*** *affecting climate.*

Math: *The numbers 2 and 3 are* ***factors*** *of 6.*

A factor is something that contributes to something else, so in geography, altitude causes a climate to be warmer or cooler. In math, a factor is a number that can be multiplied by another number to produce a product.

When you learn vocabulary across subject areas, you may learn

- new meanings for a word you know
- new words for a concept or idea you know about
- new words for a completely new concept or idea

Listening to news stories and current events is a good way to increase your vocabulary. Actively discuss ideas as well as new vocabulary that you hear in news reports. Friends, teachers, and parents will have their own ideas about the subtle meanings of words, so careful listening will add to your vocabulary development. Look at the model below. Can you figure out the meaning of the italicized word in the first sentence of this news report?

> The President pledged to continue with his economic *agenda*, beginning with the reform of the Social Security Administration.

What strategies did you use to determine that *agenda* means "plan"? How could you use the word in another context?

PRACTICE

Find a science or social studies textbook that includes a list of key vocabulary at the beginning of a chapter. Use prior knowledge or word parts to predict what the words might mean. Then read the passages in which the words are located and use syntax or context to check or further refine the meanings you predicted.

Determining denotation and connotation

Determining special meanings of words is an important aid to understanding. Look at these two ways to distinguish between word meanings:

- Denotation A **denotation** expresses the literal, or dictionary, meaning of a word. A word may have more than one denotation, but all of its denotations will be listed in the dictionary.
- Connotation When a word has an implied meaning or association in addition to its dictionary meaning, it has a **connotation.** You may say that flowers have a *fragrance* but that garbage has a *stench.* Both words have a denotation that means "smell," but *fragrance* has a pleasant connotation, while the word *stench* connotes something unpleasant.

Understanding historical influences on words

In addition to giving you word spellings, pronunciations, and meanings, a dictionary will give you the historical background of a word. Many English words have Greek, Latin, or Anglo-Saxon origins. The Earl of Sandwich devised a way of eating meat between two pieces of bread so he would not have to interrupt his card game for meals. Did you realize that the word *sandwich* originated from this historical fact? Or that the *martial* in *martial arts* recalls the name of Mars, the Roman god of warfare?

Comprehension

The main job you have in reading is to understand what you have read. Using the best strategies at the right times will improve your understanding of what you are reading.

Previewing

Before you begin to read, it's helpful to **preview** a selection.

- **Look** at the title and the illustrations that are included.

Vocabulary Development: Using word meanings across subjects

PRACTICE

If students lack access to a science or social studies textbook of their own, try to make several available for their use. Look for texts that regularly list subject-matter vocabulary at the beginning of each lesson or chapter. Ask students to take turns identifying and giving their definitions for one of the words they found and, as appropriate, explaining how they determined the meaning of a previously unknown word.

Have the class as a whole discuss words that are difficult to define solely from their structure or from their context. Point out that textbooks in math, science, and social studies are likely to have glossaries that will help students by defining words that they may not be able to fully understand on their own.

- **Read** the headings, subheadings, and anything in bold letters.
- **Skim** the passage; that is, take a quick look at the whole thing.
- **Decide** what the author's purpose might be for writing.
- **Predict** what the selection will be about.
- **Set a purpose** for your own reading.

Using knowledge and experience to understand

Reading is an interactive process between you and a writer. Even the youngest child has a body of information and personal experiences that are important and uniquely his or her own. When you use your own knowledge and experience and combine it with the words on a page, you create meaning in a selection. Drawing on this personal background is called **activating prior knowledge.** As you read, ask yourself

- What do I know about this **topic?**
- Have I been to places similar to the **setting** described by this writer?
- What **experiences** have I had that compare or contrast with what I am reading?
- What **characters** from life or literature remind me of the characters or narrator in the selection?

Establishing and adjusting purposes for reading

Think about these possible purposes that you might have for reading:

- to find out something
- to understand a process or an idea
- to interpret a writer's work and create meaning in a passage
- to enjoy a selection or be entertained by a story
- to solve problems or to perform a task

Each purpose allows for different active reading strategies. To find information for a report, you might skim an entire passage until you find the section you're looking for and then read more slowly. To understand new information, you might read slowly from beginning to end or even reread passages that are unclear. To simply enjoy a piece of good writing, you may allow yourself to read quickly or slow yourself down to appreciate something beautifully written.

It's also important to be able to adjust your purposes as well as your strategies to get the most out of your reading.

Making and verifying predictions

As you read, take educated guesses about story events and outcomes. **Make predictions** before and during your reading. Using your prior knowledge and the information you have gathered in your preview, predict what you will learn or what might happen in a selection. Then, as you read, **adjust your prediction.** Finally, **verify your prediction.** Whether your original prediction is precisely accurate does not matter, but careful predictions and later verifications or adjustments based on your reading increase your understanding of a selection.

Monitoring and modifying reading strategies

No matter what your purposes for reading, your most important task is to understand what you have read. Ask yourself questions as you read. Monitor or check your understanding using the following strategies.

- **Summarize** what you read by answering *who, what, where, when, why,* and *how.*
- **Clarify** what you don't understand by careful rereading.
- **Question** important ideas and story elements.
- **Predict** what will happen next.
- **Evaluate** what you have read so far.

You might practice a strategy once or twice in an easy entertaining selection or after every paragraph in a nonfiction passage.

Tips for Monitoring Understanding

- **Reread.** If silently rereading a passage several times does not help, read it aloud. Observe punctuation marks and slow your rate.
- **Map out the main thoughts or ideas.** A graphic organizer like a story map or Venn diagram can help get your thoughts on track.
- **Look for context clues.** Often a writer will include an example or a definition of a difficult word or idea somewhere in the surrounding sentences. Synonyms or antonyms also provide clues.
- **Ask questions.** Teachers, parents, and other classmates can shed light on difficult passages.
- **Write comments** as well as questions on another piece of paper for later review or discussion.
- **Use reference aids.** Sometimes looking up one word is all it takes to clear up a difficult passage. Dictionaries, glossaries, thesauruses, and encyclopedias provide access to most information.

Visualizing

Creating pictures in your mind as you read is a powerful aid to understanding. According to your imagination and the text, what do characters look like? Can you picture the steps in a process when you read nonfiction? If you can visualize what you read, selections will be more vivid, and you'll recall them better later on. Be sure, though, that what you picture is accurately based on information from the text.

READING HANDBOOK

Comprehension: Visualizing

PRACTICE

Rubric

As you read a piece of literature to students, they should

- for fiction, draw a character, setting, or action from the text description
- for nonfiction, draw a place or thing described or diagram the steps in a process
- compare drawings with a partner and discuss similarities and differences
- examine the text you read to verify information or adjust their drawings

PRACTICE

During a time when your teacher is reading aloud to you, either from a piece of fiction or nonfiction, try sketching what you're hearing. If the selection is fiction, draw a character, setting, or action, from the text description. If the selection is nonfiction, see if you can draw the steps in a process or make a small diagram of the place or thing described. Compare your sketch with a partner's and talk about similarities and differences. Go back to the text to adjust or verify your information.

Constructing graphic organizers

Graphic organizers help you organize what you're reading so you can sort ideas out, clear up difficult passages, and remember important ideas in a selection. Look at the following examples of good graphic organizers and notice how they are used.

Web You can show a main idea and supporting details by using a web. Put the main idea in the middle circle and the supporting details in the surrounding circles. Notice how you might include other circles branching off from the detail circles. Use those for further information about your details.

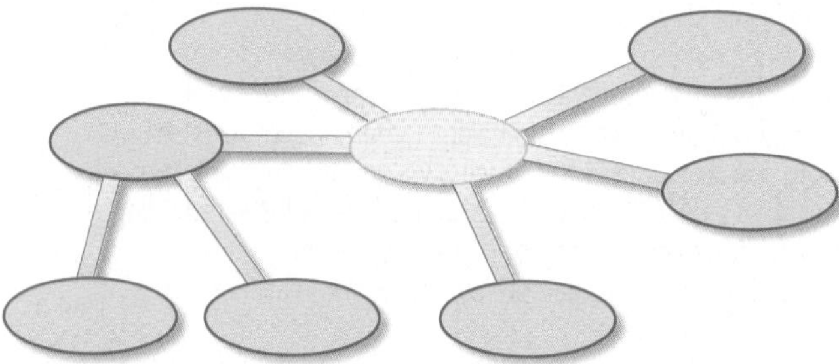

Flowchart When you want to keep track of events in a time order or show a cause-and-effect relationship between events, use a flowchart. Arrange your ideas or events in the boxes, putting them in their logical order. Then draw arrows between the boxes to show how one idea or event flows into another.

READING HANDBOOK

Venn diagram To look at the similarities and differences between two ideas, characters, or events, use a Venn diagram. The outer portions of each circle will show how two items contrast, or are different. Use the overlapping portion of the circles to show how they are the same.

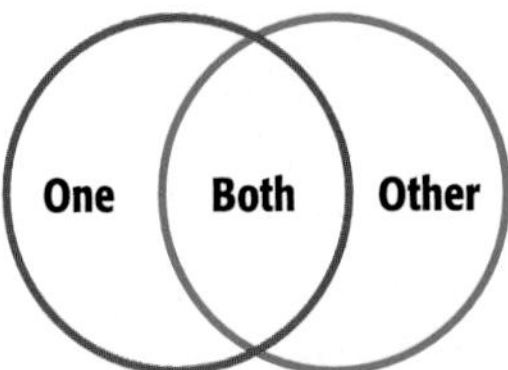

Using text structures

Writers organize their ideas in a variety of ways, depending on their topic and their purpose for writing. When you find that pattern of organization or **text structure** within a selection, it's easier to locate and recall a writer's ideas. Here are four ways that writers structure or organize text, together with word clues that characterize those text structures.

Kind of Organization	Purpose	Clues
Comparison and contrast	To determine similar-ities and differences	Words and phrases such as *similarly, on the other hand, in contrast to, but, however*
Cause and effect	To explore the reasons for something and to examine the results of events or actions	Words and phrases such as *so, because, as a result*
Chronological order	To present events in time order	Words and phrases such as *first, next, then, later, finally*
Problem/Solution	To examine how conflicts or obstacles are overcome	Words and phrases such as *need, attempt, help, obstruction*

Writers might use one text structure within another, but it is usually possible to figure out one main pattern of organization that will focus your attention on the important ideas in a selection. Look for **signal words,** the clues that lead you to the text structure. Read the two models on the following page.

READING HANDBOOK R89

Melissa carefully planned her experiment in baking. One Saturday morning, when everyone in the family had left for the day, she took out the recipe she had tucked away. First, she assembled the ingredients she would need for butterscotch cookies and carefully adjusted the oven to the required temperature. Next, she sprayed two baking sheets with nonstick vegetable oil. Then she prepared the batter and dropped it by teaspoonfuls onto the baking sheets. After setting the timer, she went into the living room to watch TV.

For twelve hours, the snow fell steadily throughout the city. An army of snowplows and salt trucks were ready to roll, but because of the heavy snow, plowed streets were clogged an hour after they had been cleared. As soon as the snow stopped, subzero temperatures set in, causing the salting operation to have minimal results. Because of the difficulty in traveling, many plants and offices were closed. School was cancelled as well. The entire city was at a standstill.

What is the basic text structure of the first model? Of the second? Explain how you determined your answers.

Determining main ideas and supporting details

The most important idea in a paragraph or passage is called the **main idea.** The examples or ideas that further explain the main idea are called **supporting details.** Some main ideas are clearly stated in sentences within a passage. Other times, without directly stating a main idea, an author will suggest it by providing a variety of clues.

Often the main idea will be the first sentence of a paragraph, but a main idea might be anywhere, even in the last sentence of a passage.

A selection can have a number of main ideas in it. Each paragraph may contain a main idea, as in most nonfiction, or entire passages can have a main idea, as in both fiction and nonfiction.

When you need to find the main idea, ask yourself these questions:

- What is each sentence about?
- Is there one sentence that tells about the whole passage or that is more important than the others?

- If the main idea is not directly stated, what main idea do the supporting details point out?

Finding the main ideas will help you understand a selection. Look at the following model.

Main idea — **Hibernation is important for the survival of animals like the bear.** By going into hibernation—a dormant, sleep-like state—the bear can bypass winter. Bears would find it extremely difficult to find enough food when the temperatures grow cold. During hibernation the bear cuddles up in a cave or in a hollowed-out tree, safe from the dangers of winter. In order to survive this long period of inactivity, the bear must build up its body weight by accumulating fat. — Supporting details

Sequencing

The order in which thoughts are arranged is called **sequence.** A good sequence is one that is logical, given the ideas in a selection. Here are three common forms of sequencing.

- **Chronological order**–time order
- **Spatial order**–the order in which things would be arranged within a certain space–for example, left to right, top to bottom, clockwise, foreground to background.
- **Order of importance**–going from most important to least important or the other way around

Recognizing the sequence of something is important when you have to follow **directions.** If you fail to follow steps in a certain order, you may not be able to accomplish your task.

Paraphrasing

When you retell something using your own words, you are **paraphrasing.** You might paraphrase just the main ideas of a selection, or you might retell an entire story in your own words. Paraphrasing is a useful strategy for reviewing and for checking comprehension.

Original text: *The key to developing a healthy eating plan you can live with–one that you can easily incorporate into your daily life–is to discover your personal obstacles to healthy eating and then to make one or two small changes at a time.*

Paraphrase: *To make healthy eating a regular part of your daily routine, change your unhealthy eating habits gradually.*

Comprehension: Summarizing

PRACTICE

Rubric

Students should

- read (or reread) "The Teacher Who Changed My Life"
- list the main ideas of the selection
- list the supporting details under each main idea
- write a one-paragraph summary of the selection
- include in the summary only the main ideas and the most important details
- avoid errors in grammar, usage, or mechanics

The summary of Gage's personal narrative on page 368 of this Teacher's Edition can serve as an example of the kind of brief summary students should produce.

Summarizing

When you **summarize,** you relate the main ideas of a selection in a logical sequence and in your own words. To create a good summary, include all the main ideas and only essential supporting details.

A good summary can be easily understood by someone who has not read the whole selection. Look at the following model and summary.

> The Dead Sea is not dead. It is not a sea either. Even though the water of the Dead Sea is too salty for fish and other animals to live there, some microscopic organisms that use the sun to photosynthesize, and others from which petroleum can be made make the waters of the Dead Sea their home. This body of water is not a sea but is instead a salt lake. It has the lowest elevation of any place on Earth. The water contains more salt and other minerals than any other body of water.
>
> **Summary:** The Dead Sea, a salt lake, is the saltiest body of water in the world and the lowest place on Earth. Even though fish and other animals cannot live there, microscopic plants call the Dead Sea home.

PRACTICE

Read "The Teacher Who Changed My Life" on page 368 of this book. On separate paper, list the main ideas in the selection. Under each main idea, list the supporting details that explain it. Use this information to write a one-paragraph summary of what you have read.

Drawing inferences

Writers don't always directly state what they want you to understand in a selection. By providing clues and interesting details, they suggest certain information. Whenever you combine those clues with your own background and knowledge, you are drawing an inference. An **inference** involves using your reason and experience to come up with an idea based on what an author implies or suggests. In reading, you **infer** when you use context clues and your own knowledge to figure out what an author is suggesting. The following active reading behaviors are examples of drawing an inference.

- Predicting When you guess what a story will be about or what will happen next, you are drawing an inference.

READING HANDBOOK

- Drawing conclusions A conclusion is a general statement you can make and explain with reasoning or with supporting details from a selection.
- Generalizing When you draw an inference that can apply to more than one item or group, you are making a generalization.

Classifying

When you **classify**, you place things into categories according to certain characteristics they share. For example, the selections in this book could be classified into fiction and nonfiction or into poetry and prose, or they could be put into more specific categories such as short stories, essays, articles, and narrative poems.

Finding similarities and differences across texts

As your reading takes you across a variety of sources, **compare and contrast** the things you've read. When you look for similarities and differences in your reading selections, you'll gain a better understanding of all the material you've read. Ask yourself in what ways sources might be alike or different. What is included in one selection that might be left out of another? Why might that be?

Here are some of the ways in which you can compare and contrast writers' works:

- Scope Take a broad look at each selection. How would you compare the time periods covered? How much information is given in each nonfiction selection? How many characters and settings are involved in fiction pieces? How extended is the entire selection?
- Treatment Look at how each writer presents important ideas. Who tells the story? Is the narrator's attitude serious or funny? How would you compare the writers' purposes? Styles?
- Organization Compare selections in terms of how writers arrange their thoughts. Is a writer using chronological order? Comparing and contrasting? Cause and effect? Problem and solution?

When you look for similarities and differences in what you've read, you'll learn to read more critically and get more out of each selection.

Distinguishing fact from opinion

When deciding whether to believe what a writer has written, you need to distinguish between fact and opinion. A **fact** is a statement that can be proved with supporting information. An **opinion,** on the other hand, is what a writer believes on the basis of his or her personal viewpoint. Writers can support their opinions with facts, but an opinion cannot be proved. Look at the following examples of fact and opinion.

READING HANDBOOK R93

Fact: *New York State produces fruits and other agricultural products.*
Opinion: *New York is a wonderful place for a vacation.*

When interpreting something you read, be sure that you distinguish between statements of fact and statements of opinion.

Answering questions

Often you'll need to answer questions about selections you've read. Look at the chart below to help you find the answers.

Type of Question	What Is It?	Example	How to Find the Answer
Literal	Has a definite answer	What color was Snow White's hair?	Look for direct statement in text.
Interpretive	Answer based on text and prior knowledge	Why was Snow White a threat to the queen?	Use text information and/or prior knowledge.
Open-ended	No right or wrong answer	Is Snow White a role model for girls today?	Use personal background and opinions.

You may find various types of questions on a test.

Tips for Answering Test Questions

- True-or-false questions If any part of a true or false question is false, the correct answer is "false."
- Short answer Use complete sentences so your responses will be clear. Try to put your thoughts in logical sequence.
- Multiple choice First read all the responses. Eliminate the answers you know are incorrect. Choose the best remaining answer.

Representing text information

After reading various sources, you may want to reproduce what you have learned in a visual way, perhaps to present it to your class or to show the teacher that you have understood it.

- Outlines An **outline** is helpful if you are organizing information for a report. Roman numerals, together with uppercase and lowercase letters, show the basic structure of the report. Look at the following sample model of a topic outline.

R94 READING HANDBOOK

READING HANDBOOK

Each main topic is one of the big ideas of your subject. Suppose that your subject is surfing. The first main topic could be the history of surfing.

If you have subtopics under a main topic, there must be at least two. They must relate directly to the main topic.

I. Main topic
   A. First subtopic
      1. Division of a subtopic
      2. Division of a subtopic
   B. Second subtopic

If you wish to divide a subtopic, you must have at least two divisions. Each division must relate to the subtopic above it.

- Time lines A time line shows the chronological order of events over a period of time. Use a line to document the amount of time you want to cover. Add events above or below the line to show the order in which they occurred. Look at the example below.

The title shows the subject of the time line. It also may include the dates covered.

Space between events shows the amount of time that passed between them. Which two events came closest together?

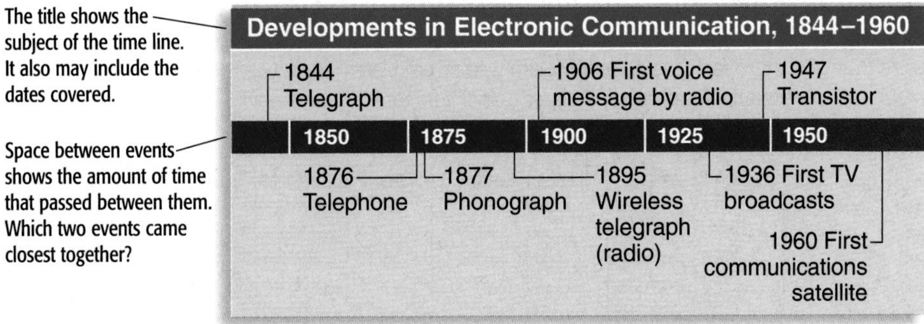

- Graphic organizers Word webs, flowcharts, Venn diagrams, and other kinds of graphic organizers can help you present information in a visual way so that both you and your audience can easily see, understand, and remember what is presented.

Using study strategies

If you're preparing for a quiz or test or getting ready for a class presentation, you'll want to use a study strategy that helps you organize and remember the material you've read. Here are some useful strategies.

- Using story maps A **story map** can help you sort out important literary elements in works of fiction. Look at the model on the following page to see how a story map works as a tool for review.

READING HANDBOOK R95

STORY MAP

Characters	Setting
Plot Conflict (problem)	**Plot** Resolution (solution)

- Using KWL **KWL** is a good way to keep track of what you are learning when you read informational text. Make three columns on a page. Label the first column *What I Know,* the second column *What I Want to Know,* and the third column *What I Learned.* Before reading, list the things you already know about a topic in the first column. List your questions in the second column. When you've finished reading, record what you've learned in the third column. You can add more columns to record places where you found information and places to look for more.

KWL

What I Know	What I Want to Know	What I Learned	Where I Got Information
			Where I Can Get More

- Using SQ3R A useful study strategy for studying subject areas like science or social studies is **SQ3R.** This stands for **s**urvey, **q**uestion, **r**ead, **r**ecord, and **r**eview. Here's how it works.
  1. **Survey** Take a quick look over the entire selection you need to study. Notice anything boldfaced. Look at headings, subheadings, or pictures.
  2. **Question** Think of a number of questions you'll want to answer as you read.
  3. **Read** Read the selection carefully. Vary your reading rate as you encounter easy or difficult passages.
  4. **Record** Take notes about important ideas. Record your comments and additional questions that come up as you read.
  5. **Review** When you've finished reading, go back over the text once again to be sure you've understood important ideas. Add any other information you'll need to remember.

- Creating and using study guides Your teacher may provide you with a guide to focus your attention on important vocabulary and ideas, or you may create your own using end-of-chapter questions.

PRACTICE

Select a chapter from your social studies or science text. Use SQ3R as you read the material. Have a classmate quiz you by using end-of-chapter questions to see how well you remember what you studied.

Literary Response

Whenever you share your thoughts and feelings about something you've read, you are responding to a text. You have your own learning style, so you will want to respond in ways that are comfortable for you. Some students learn best when speaking and writing, while others enjoy moving around or creating something artistic. Your responses can take a variety of forms. You can offer an observation, draw a connection to your life or to another work you've read, or question a character's actions or motives.

Tips for Responding to and Interpreting Literature

- **Discuss** what you have read and share your views in active classroom discussions or at home.
- **Keep a journal** about what you read. Record your thoughts and feelings. Write down your impressions of a selection as well as questions you might have about it.
- **Take part in dramatizations, oral interpretations,** and **readers theater.** These activities can allow you to present characters through actions and dialogue and give you the opportunity to use your voice, facial expressions, and body language to convey meaning.
- **Tape record or videotape** your oral readings or dramatizations.

Supporting responses and interpretations

Whether you respond with your mind or with your emotions, you need to support your responses by going back to the text itself. Make sure you provide details from the author's work to back up your thoughts and feelings. It is not enough to say, "I really liked the main character." You must show what you liked about him or her. Look for specific descriptions and information. Ask yourself questions like these:

- What is interesting about this story's setting?
- What do I like or dislike about this character?

READING HANDBOOK

Comprehension: Using SQ3R

PRACTICE

Rubric

Students should

- select a chapter from a social studies or science text
- use the SQ3R method to study the chapter
- successfully answer end-of-chapter questions selected by a classmate

- How is the overall theme or idea expressed?
- What specific details account for my views about this selection?
- How have my own experiences and prior knowledge influenced my feelings in this selection?

Whenever you make a connection or compare and contrast themes, ideas, and issues across texts, you need to support your thoughts with the writer's own words. If you can't provide adequate text proofs, you may need to rethink your response.

Identifying the purpose of a text

Authors have a variety of reasons for writing. They may simply want to **entertain** you. They may want to **inform** you about a topic. They may feel the need to **express** thoughts and emotions through a narrative or biographical essay. They also may want to **influence** your thinking so that you believe something or are motivated to act in a certain way. How can you tell what a writer's purpose is? To identify the purposes of different types of texts, use the following tips.

Tips for Identifying the Purpose of a Text

- **Look at word choices.** Authors select words according to the words connotations, which carry emotional or implied meanings, as well as their denotations, or dictionary meanings. For example, a writer's opinion of a character described as *bold* and *adventurous* is different from that of a character described as *weird* and *reckless.*
- **Consider the intended audience.** Most selections are written with an audience in mind. A speech at a pep rally might have a different purpose from one given before a committee of student council members.
- **Look at the structure of the text.** Writers use patterns of organization to clearly present their messages. Figuring out whether a writer has used chronological order, comparison-and-contrast structure, or cause-and-effect structure can help you determine his or her purpose.

Comparing elements across genres

Have you ever seen a movie or a television program that was based on a book you have read? How were they similar? How were they different? If you read the book *Sarah Plain and Tall* and then saw the made-for-TV movie, you might have noticed that some scenes were left out of the movie in order to make the story fit into a particular time frame. Some characters in movies are not represented precisely as they are described in books. As you look to see how the same story may vary across genres, look at similarities and differences in the following story elements:

R98 READING HANDBOOK

- **Characters** Are all characters represented? Are some characters combined?
- **Settings** Is the setting presented similarly in each work? What differences affect the story as a whole?
- **Plot** How is the plot adjusted to fit the strengths and limitations of the genre?
- **Themes or ideas** Are important ideas well developed?
- **Author's point of view** Does the author's attitude affect how the story is told?
- **Author's purpose** Why is the author telling this story?
- **Author's style** What format and word choices are used?

Analyzing inductive and deductive reasoning

As you think about works you've read, ask yourself whether the reasoning behind an author's ideas are logical. Here are two kinds of logical reasoning writers use.

Inductive reasoning When you consider a certain number of examples a writer gives you or see a particular number of cases to illustrate a point or an idea, you may be able to arrive at a **generalization–** a conclusion or general statement–by using **inductive reasoning.** For instance, if the tulips your class planted on the shady side of your school building did not grow, there is never grass on that side of the building, and a bush planted there last year still has no leaves, you can inductively reason that the shady side of your school building may not be the best place to plant things. This logic moves from the **specific** to the **general.**

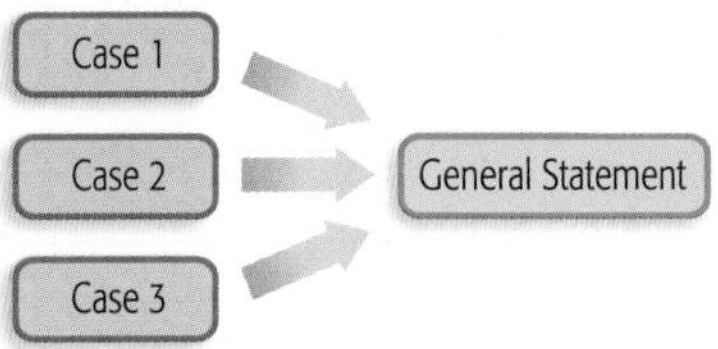

Deductive reasoning When you take a general statement and apply it through reasoning to a number of specific situations, you are using **deductive reasoning.** For example, you know that plants do not grow well in shady places. Therefore, you can deductively reason that it might not be wise to plant tulips or expect grass to grow well on the shady side of a building. This logic moves from the **general** to the **specific.** The diagram on the following page illustrates deductive reasoning.

READING HANDBOOK

READING HANDBOOK R99

READING HANDBOOK

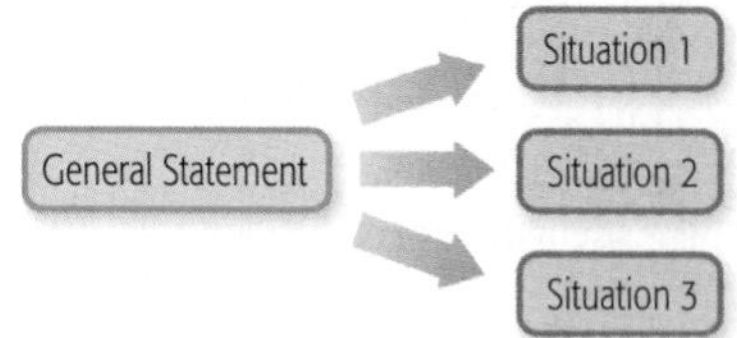

Inquiry and Research

Whenever you read to learn, you'll need to come up with interesting and useful questions. As you read in a variety of sources, you will think of new questions or revise your originial questions to take into account new information. When you ask important questions and carefully research thorough answers, you will draw conclusions about your topic. The process may lead you to other interesting questions and areas for further study.

Forming and revising questions

Finding an interesting and relevant question or topic is an important first step in doing research and deserves your careful attention.

Tips for Asking Research Questions

- Think of a question or topic that interests you.
- Choose a question that helps you focus on one main idea.
- Be sure the question is not too broad or too narrow.
  Too broad: *What can cause mummification?*
  Better: *Why did the Egyptians mummify the remains of their Pharaohs?*

Using text organizers

Once you've found an interesting question to investigate, the next step is to locate information and organize it. Textbooks, references, magazines, and other sources use a variety of ways to help you find what you need quickly and efficiently.

- **Tables of contents** Look at a table of contents first to see whether a resource offers information you need.
- **Indexes** An index, found in the back of a book, is a detailed, alphabetical listing of all people, places, events, and topics mentioned in the book.
- **Headings and subheadings** The headings often identify the information that follows.
- **Graphic features** Photos, maps, graphs, and other graphic features can convey a large amount of information at a glance.

R100 READING HANDBOOK

READING HANDBOOK

Using multiple sources for research

The research you do will be more interesting and balanced when you include various types of sources. To find the most recent information, it may be necessary to use sources other than books. The following are some helpful resources for conducting research.

- Print resources: textbooks, magazines, reference books, and other specialized references
- Nonprint information: films, videos, and recorded interviews
- Electronic texts: CD-ROM encyclopedias and the Internet
- Experts: people who are specialists on the topic you have chosen

Interpreting graphic aids

When you're researching a topic, be sure to read and interpret the graphic aids included. **Graphic aids** let you see information at a glance.

Reading a map Maps are flat representations of land. A **compass rose** allows you to determine direction. A **legend** explains the map's symbols, and a **scale** shows you how the size of the map relates to the actual distances covered. Look at the map below.

Compass rose

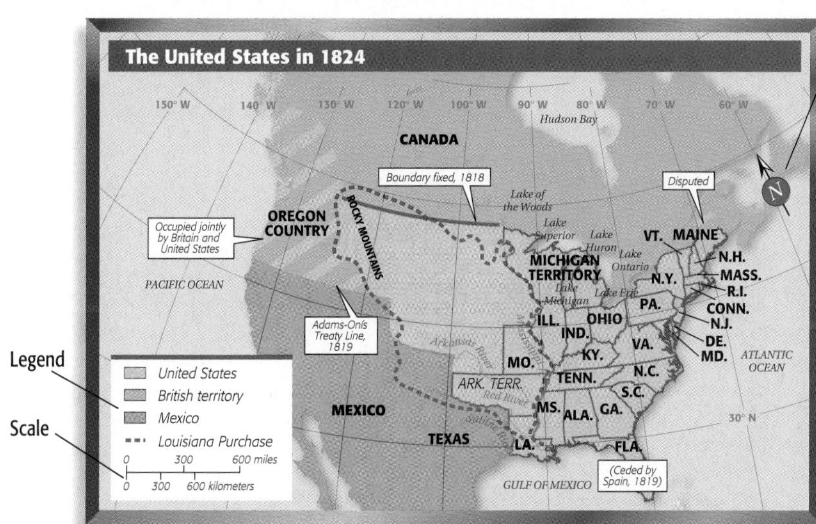

Reading a graph Graphs show information pictorially. Graphs can use circles, dots, bars, or lines. Look at the title and the labels on the bar graphs on the following page, which compare types of crops produced in the South. Next, look at the labels along the bottom of the graphs. Each bar represents a decade. The numbers along the side represent millions of pounds, bales, or bushels. Can you interpret the information?

READING HANDBOOK R101

Inquiry and Research: Interpreting graphic aids

PRACTICE

Rubric

Students should

- find an example of a chart, table, or graph in a newspaper or newsmagazine
- explain the graphic aid to the class
- analyze for the class the information presented in the graphic

You may wish to have students arrange their graphics in a class bulletin-board display, categorizing them according to type—for example, tables, graphs (bar, line, circle, picture), charts (organization, sequence).

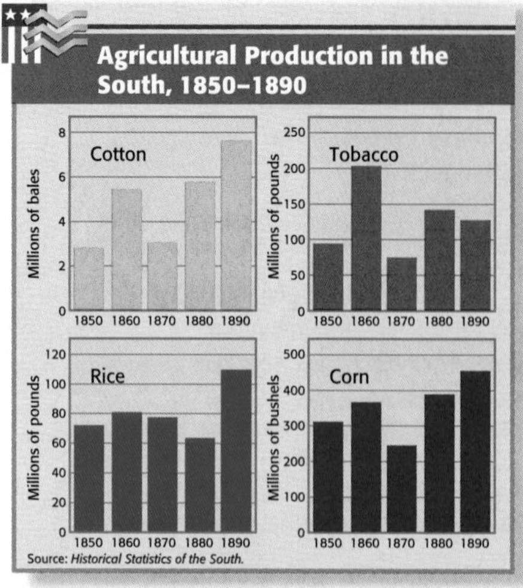

Reading a table A table allows you to compare numbers or facts by putting them into categories. Look at the table below. Read the title first. You can read the table to find just one piece of information—for instance, how much per gallon gasoline cost in 1973—or you can compare the consumption of gasoline across the years. What other information can you gather from this table?

Gasoline Consumption and Prices

Year	Consumption (billions of gallons)	Cost per Gallon		
		Reg.	Prem.	No lead
1973	110.5	$.40	.45	NA
1974	106.3	.53	.57	.55
1975	109.0	.57	.61	.60
1976	115.7	.59	.64	.61
1977	119.6	.62	.67	.66
1978	125.1	.63	.69	.67
1979	122.1	.86	.92	.90
1980	115.0	1.19	1.28	1.25

Source: *Statistical Abstract of the United States.*

PRACTICE

Look in a current newspaper or newsmagazine to find an example of a chart, table, or graph. Explain the graphic aid to the class and briefly analyze the information presented.

R102 READING HANDBOOK

Writing Workshop Models

The following Writing Workshop Models are complete versions of the student models developed in the Writing Workshops at the end of each theme in this book. Use these models as examples of how one student might have responded to the assignments in the Writing Workshops.

Theme 1, pages 104–107

Narrative Writing: Autobiographical Anecdote

A Hard Lesson

A Muddy water surged past our feet. A storm had turned our irrigation canal into a rushing river. It was exciting to a couple of nine-year-olds like my friend Ray and me. It was also exciting to me that Ray, who was much bigger than me, was my friend. I was having fun, but I was also a little afraid. My mother had warned us not to go near the canal. I reminded Ray that we would get in trouble if our parents found out where we were. He just laughed. Ray was never afraid of anything. As we played alongside the canal, he struck a goofy pose. "Look!" he laughed. "I'm a surfer!" He stretched out his arms and swayed back and forth on the slippery bank. Suddenly I heard a loud splash. It took me a second to realize what had happened. Then it hit me. Ray had lost his balance and slipped into the water! I fell to my belly, reached out, and grabbed his hand just as the current caught him.

"Hold on!" I screamed. Ray struggled to keep his head above the swirling brown water. "Help me!" he cried. I felt the pull of the current, and I tightened my grip. I looked at Ray's face, and I saw fear in his eyes. I was shocked. Ray, the biggest boy in the fourth grade, was afraid! Now it was up to me, the smallest boy in the fourth grade, to save him. I wanted to run back to the house to get help, but I knew that I couldn't let go. I was Ray's best hope, his only hope.

B Churning water swooshed in my ears, and the musty odor of flood water filled my nose. Again and again, I tried to pull Ray onto the bank. Again and again, I failed. I was losing my tug-of-war with the current. The water was just too strong.

Ray called out in a hoarse voice, "I'm cold! I can't hold on much longer!" I had to do something fast. Out of the corner of my eye, I saw a large tree branch sticking out from the bank into the water. I called out to Ray, "Over there! To your right! Grab that branch!" I pulled him toward it with all my might. Finally, my hand ached so much that I just gave up. I relaxed my grip, and Ray was gone.

C A knot of fear rose in my stomach. I pushed myself up from the slimy mud and scrambled to the branch. Ray was nowhere in sight. I called out his name over and over, but he did not answer. I have never felt smaller or more alone.

Suddenly I saw something rise out of the current. At first I thought it was a piece of wood. I held onto the branch and leaned over the water for a better look. Could it be? Yes! It was a hand! It was Ray's hand! I leaned over as far as I could, grabbed his wrist, and pulled him in.

continued

Writing Minilesson

Focus on Sentence Style and Variety Have students review the dialogue in "A Hard Lesson." Ask them to identify techniques the writer uses to create realistic conversation between the two characters. *(Characters use fragments and short sentences and do not always answer each other immediately. Exclamation points indicate excitement, fear, or anger on the part of the characters.)*

Activity Ask students to write a brief dialogue similar to a conversation they have recently had with a friend or family member. Encourage them to imitate the sentence structure in "A Hard Lesson" to make the dialogue realistic and interesting.

Teaching the Writing Workshop Models

Use the annotated writing models on pages R103–R115 as teaching tools to show how students might apply the **6+1Traits™ of Writing:** Ideas, Organization, Voice, Word Choice, Sentence Fluency, Conventions, and Presentation. The model for each Writing Workshop meets the criteria listed in the Evaluation Rubric and Rubric for Revising. The annotations point out a few of each model's strongest features.

As they read "A Hard Lesson," invite students to comment on the autobiographical anecdote, using the criteria in the Writing Workshop rubrics on pages 104 and 106.

A Literary Elements

Foreshadowing The opening foreshadows the anecdote's central conflict. Have students discuss how foreshadowing affects their reading of the piece. *(It captures readers' interest and creates suspense.)*

B Word Choice

Precise Language The writer employs precise verbs and adjectives. Ask students to list examples of precise language and to discuss how these words add to the anecdote. *(Examples: The verb* swooshed *and the adjectives* churning *and* musty *describe the water vividly and contribute to the setting.)*

C Voice

Tone By using an intimate tone, the writer creates a personal voice. Have students examine their own drafts to determine what tone they have created and to decide whether the tone is appropriate. *(Students should show an understanding of the tone they convey in their drafts.)*

D Ideas and Content

THEME Ask students to discuss why the essay's final paragraph is effective. *(The paragraph states the theme of the anecdote and provides a sense of closure. The writer tells readers what the experience meant to him and how it changed him.)*

Ray crawled onto the bank, shivering. "Why did you let go?" he asked.

"I couldn't help it!" I cried.

"Thanks to you I almost drowned," Ray said accusingly.

I was angry, and I let him know it. "Hey, it's not my fault that you were showing off and fell in! If it hadn't been for me, you would have drowned! Whose idea was it to go to the canal, anyway? I told you that we should stay away!" Angry tears rolled down my face.

"What a baby!" he sneered. "Why don't you run home to Mama?"

I had heard him say things like that to other boys many times, and it had always made me laugh. Now he was being mean to me, and I wasn't laughing. We walked home our separate ways.

D That day I learned a hard lesson. I realized that Ray was not really my friend at all. He had just been using me to make himself feel important. All the times that I had laughed at his mean comments and dangerous behavior I had helped make him the center of attention. In return, Ray had made me feel big. I was embarrassed about being so small for my age, and Ray had somehow made me feel bigger. After I helped save his life, I realized that I did not need him to feel big. I already was, at least inside. From that moment on, I walked a little taller, and I walked without him.

Expository Writing: Compare-and-Contrast Essay

Little Boxes

A Ernie, in the short story "The Crush" by Cynthia Rylant, and Katie in "The Birthday Box" by Jane Yolen both suffer the tragedy of their mothers' deaths. Although Ernie and the daughter are different people from very different backgrounds, they both eventually find the strength to rebuild their lives. For each, the key is a cardboard box.

Ernie is thirty-three years old and mentally disabled. All his life, his mother has been overprotective of him. While she is still alive, Ernie's box is delivered by mistake to their home. The box is plain and full of seed packages. He doesn't know what the seed packages are or what to do with them. He just likes to look at the pretty flowers on the covers of the packages. After his mother's sudden death, Ernie is moved to a group home. He takes his beloved box with him.

B At first, Ernie cries for his mother, but he stops after a few weeks. He begins to observe life around him. He learns how to garden and eventually experiences the joy and reward of watching plants grow. He likes to see the physical results of his work, but he can't stand to plant seeds from his box. Finally Ernie falls in love with a lonely woman named Dolores. This experience gives him the courage to plant his own seeds and separate himself from his beloved box. He welcomes the life that grows from the seeds he has planted outside the group home. In fact, he uses the seeds to share his newfound love with Dolores by secretly leaving her flowers every Wednesday.

C Katie's situation in "The Birthday Box" is both similar to and different from Ernie's. She's only ten, which is a lot younger than Ernie. She's bright and talented and likes to write. Her mother doesn't die suddenly, but rather after a long, painful battle with cancer. On the day her mother dies, she gives Katie a beautifully decorated box. In contrast to Ernie's box, this box is empty. "It's you," Katie's mother tells her. But Katie doesn't understand why there's nothing inside the box. When she moves in with her father, she takes the empty box with her, but she throws it in the closet.

Unlike Ernie, Katie takes a long time to accept her mother's death. She feels nothing but emptiness and anger. She stops writing, and she cries at every occasion that reminds her of her mother. She can't stand her half-brothers, stepmother, or father. Her box sits in her closet as far from her as possible.

Finally, on the first anniversary of the death of her mother, Katie stops crying and discovers the meaning of her mother's dying words. She realizes that "It's you" isn't about the box; it is about her. She and the box are alike. Both are sturdy and pretty on the outside. Both need to be filled up before they will be complete.

D Ernie and the daughter are two very different characters, but each learns a lesson from a box. Ernie finds the strength and courage he needs to rebuild his life when he gives up the contents of his box. Katie finds her courage and strength by accepting the challenge to fill her box with her writing and by making her own sweet memories.

WRITING WORKSHOP MODELS

As they read "Little Boxes," invite students to comment on the compare-and-contrast essay, using the criteria in the Writing Workshop rubrics on pages 208 and 210.

A Organization

Thesis Statement Ask students how the writer uses comparison and contrast in the thesis. *(The thesis is based on a comparison of two characters. Possible thesis: Katie and Ernie, two very different characters, receive boxes that give them strength to enjoy life after the deaths of their mothers.)*

B Literary Elements

Characterization The writer develops Ernie's character by revealing details about his actions. Ask students how details from the story illustrate changes in Ernie's character. *(Possible answer: The writer uses Ernie's learning to garden as evidence of his growth as a person who learns how to express his love.)*

C Word Choice

Similarities and Differences
Carefully chosen words (for example, *both, similar to, different from, only,* and *younger*) highlight similarities and differences between Ernie and Katie. Have students list examples of words in the essay that signal comparison or contrast and then examine their own drafts for places where they might use such words to compare and contrast characters or ideas.

D Ideas and Content

Conclusion Ask students how the conclusion expresses the essay's main idea and completes the essay. *(While the body of the essay illustrates many of the differences between the two characters, the conclusion emphasizes the similarity of their experiences and restates the writer's thesis.)*

Writing Minilesson

Focus on Organization Point out to students that the writer of "Little Boxes" uses a subject-by-subject organizational pattern based on characters, focusing first on Ernie and then on Katie. Ask students why they think the writer chose this form of organization over feature-by-feature organization.

Activity Have students prepare both a subject-by-subject outline (based on characters) and a feature-by-feature outline (based on events) for their compare-and-contrast essays. Then ask them to decide which pattern would work best in their own essays.

As they read "No Curfew," invite students to comment on the letter to the editor, using the criteria in the Writing Workshop rubrics on pages 316 and 318.

A Ideas and Content

Introduction The letter's first paragraph starts with a question. The writer then presents a response to the question. Ask students what is effective about this opening. *(Opening the letter with a question will engage the readers' interest, and the following answer to the question clearly states the writer's position on the subject.)*

B Organization

Enumeration The writer uses enumeration as an organizing technique, beginning his major arguments with the words *first, second,* and *final.* Ask students to identify the writer's main arguments. *(The curfew (1) would affect the wrong people, (2) would be unfair to good kids and their parents, and (3) would be hard on the police.)*

C Voice

Paragraph Structure This paragraph combines two effective techniques. It presents an argument in favor of the curfew and then uses a personal example—the writer's sister—to refute that argument. Ask students how the paragraph advances the writer's argument. *(Addressing possible counterarguments and using an example to provide concrete evidence can make an argument more convincing.)*

Theme 3, pages 316–319

Persuasive Writing: Editorial

2461 Valley Drive
Fairview, California 94085
January 3, 2002

Editor
Fairview Herald
400 East Main Street
Fairview, California 94085

Dear Editor:

A Will setting a curfew of 10 P.M. for kids under the age of sixteen really make our town a better place? The editorial in last week's *Herald* makes it sound as if a curfew would be good for our town, but I disagree. A curfew would not stop the real troublemakers; it would just make life harder for kids, their parents, and the police.

B My first argument against a curfew is that it would affect the wrong people. If you read the crime reports in the *Herald,* you will see that older teenagers and adults cause more crime than younger people do. About the worst crime that young people commit is spraying graffiti on buildings and signs. I would never say that graffiti isn't a problem; it is. I hate the sight of it. But there are better ways to stop graffiti than a curfew. Instead, stores should keep spray paint and large marking pens in locked glass cases. That way taggers could not steal paint and pens, which is what they do now.

My second argument against a curfew is that it is unfair to all the good kids and their parents. The editorial makes it sound as if most teenagers are on the streets at night, but they aren't. Fairview is a quiet town. I don't know anyone my age who is allowed to be out late at night, especially on school nights. Our parents already set curfews for us. In fact, we took a poll in my English class about how late our parents let us stay out, and not one of the twenty-three students polled was allowed out alone after 9:30 P.M. without a good reason.

C Some adults may think that there is no good reason for young people to be out past 10 P.M., but that is not true. For example, my fifteen-year-old sister is sometimes out late because the neighbors that she babysits for do not always get home on time. Should my sister get in trouble just for doing her job? Should my parents get in trouble just because my sister walks the block home at 10:15 rather than 9:59?

My final argument against a curfew is that it would be hard on the police. They have enough to do without tracking down tardy teenagers. Besides, if police see a kid out after 10 P.M., wouldn't it be hard for them to know how old the kid is just by looking at him or her? Do we really want to ask the police to guess the age of every teenager on the street after 10 P.M.?

continued

A curfew would not solve our problems; it would just cause new ones. Most of the parents and kids in this town are good, responsible people. Let's trust them to make their own decisions. Curfews should be a personal matter between parents and their children, not a public matter between children and the town.

D

Sincerely,

Daniel Anslow

Daniel Anslow, grade 7

WRITING WORKSHOP MODELS

WRITING WORKSHOP MODELS

D Conventions

Complimentary Closing The writer follows conventions for a business letter by including a formal closing, followed by his name. Ask students what other conventions the writer follows. *(heading, inside address, salutation followed by a colon, block letter style)*

Writing Minilesson

Focus on Ideas and Content The writer of "No Curfew" uses logical arguments and presents specific facts and examples to support them. Have students summarize the arguments the writer uses to convince readers to oppose a curfew.

Activity Have students evaluate the arguments in their own letters to the editor. Ask them to divide a sheet of paper into two columns. In one column, they should list arguments they are presenting to persuade readers to agree with their opinions. In the other column, they should list the facts and/or examples that support each argument.

As they read "My Favorite Place," invite students to comment on the description, using the criteria in the Writing Workshop rubrics on pages 420 and 422.

A Organization

Spatial Order The writer describes the setting by using spatial order. Ask students to discuss how this organization helps them visualize the setting. *(Spatial order gives the reader a sense of perspective by showing how parts of the scene stand in relation to one another and how those parts make up the whole.)*

B Word Choice

Present Tense Verbs Although describing a past event, the writer chooses to use the present tense. Ask students how this affects the reader's experience. *(The present tense allows the reader to experience details with more immediacy. The senses of touch, sight, and sound seem more vivid.)*

C Voice

Tone The writer uses a personal and confiding tone. Have students discuss how this tone influences them as they read the description. *(A personal and confiding tone draws the reader in and leads to a more participatory experience.)*

D Literary Elements

Mood Details create a particular mood or atmosphere. Ask students to describe the mood and to discuss the details that contribute to it. *(Example: The mood is both hopeful and sad. The "weather-beaten rocks" imply endurance; the wind's rustling sounds like sighing—perhaps implying that the world is weary; the dried plants appear dead but lead the speaker to hope for spring.)*

Theme 4, pages 420–423

Descriptive Writing: A Photo in Words

My Favorite Place

It is near and yet so far away. It belongs to someone else now, and yet it will always belong to me. It is where I grew up, and it is still my favorite place in all the world. When I close my eyes, I can see it perfectly. It is fall. I am eight years old, and the school bus is pulling up to the gravel road that leads to the house. From the window of the bus, I can see the golden meadow, the big white house with the red roof, and the trees that circle the hidden pond. Behind them are the mountains that tower over everything like giants. **A**

I jump out of the bus and run through the meadow. The dry grass is almost as tall as I am. It tickles my arms, and I can feel the hard, dry ground under my feet. I stretch my neck to see over the grass, and the house seems to get bigger and bigger. Finally I reach it. I pull open the big blue door, take off my backpack full of books, and throw it on the floor. Then I yell out to my mother to let her know that I am home. I do not need to tell her where I am going because she already knows. The pond is my special place. **B**

Every day after school, the peaceful pond calls to me. When I am near it, my eyes gaze on beauty and my mind roams free. For a little while, I forget about the arithmetic problems that I have to do, the spelling words that I have to memorize, and the books that I am supposed to read. I am just another animal that lives near the pond. **C**

The pond is deep in the woods behind the house. As I run through the woods, I kick my sneakers through bright piles of leaves, and the leaves rustle, crackle, and crunch. I plop down in the middle of a pile, and I sink into a colorful blanket of yellow, red, and orange. As I lie on my back looking up, the late afternoon sunlight makes the leaves high above me look as if they are on fire. I daydream for a while, and then I make my way to the pond.

There it is, in the distance. The sunlight filters through the tall branches of the maples, casting hopeful shadows across the clear blue water. It seems as if nothing can go wrong here. It is quiet and peaceful. I walk over to the weather-beaten rocks and lean against them. The wind rustles through the tall grass, and it makes me think that the whole world is sighing. I see that the wild roses and raspberries that grow around the pond are dry and brown. They look dead now, but I know that they will come back to life in the spring. The tall grass will stand through the winter and protect them. The thought is comforting. **D**

If I lie still, deer may walk up to the water. One time I saw the big dark shape of a buck. Ducks sometimes stop at the pond before moving on. Other birds move among the branches and leaves. Two squirrels chase each other up the trunk of a tree. People have left the pond alone, giving privacy to the animals and me.

About three years ago my family and I moved away from my childhood home. My father got tired of the long drive to work, and my parents bought us a house closer to town. However, I still visit the pond in my mind. I just close my eyes, and I see the gentle blue water, the tall trees, and the big white house with the red roof near the foot of the mountain.

Writing Minilesson

Focus on Word Choice The writer of "My Favorite Place" helps readers experience the pond and the area surrounding it by using words and phrases that appeal to the senses of sight, touch, and hearing. Ask students to give examples of the sensory language.

Activity Have students list what they see, hear, feel, smell, and maybe even taste when they are near the person or place they are describing in their own descriptive essays. Then ask students to write down vivid, precise words and phrases that will communicate these sensations to readers.

Theme 5, pages 530–533

Expository Writing: Definition Essay

True Courage

A Are you courageous? According to *Webster's Dictionary,* if you have the "mental or moral strength to venture, persevere, and withstand danger, fear, or difficulty," you are. A courageous person, then, is someone who can face a difficult or dangerous situation without fear. Three people who showed this mental or moral strength are Stacy Allison, Lou Gehrig, and Rosa Parks. Although the challenges they faced were different, their responses to challenge were similar. Their actions define what courage truly is.

B For Stacy Allison, courage came one step at a time. In 1987 Allison tried to climb to the top of Mount Everest, the tallest mountain in the world. She and three other experienced climbers had spent two years carefully planning the climb. When they were two-thirds of the way up the mountain, they ran into trouble. A heavy snowstorm hit the area, and they had to wait it out. At 25,500 feet above sea level, the air is very thin. Climbers can survive for only a week or two. After several days of waiting, one of the men in the group was too weak to go on. Allison and her group had to turn back. After such a disappointing defeat, most people would give up their dream, but Allison was not like most people. The next year she found the strength to venture to Mount Everest again. In the face of countless dangers and difficulties, she persevered. Her courage paid off. She is the first American woman to climb to the top of Mount Everest.

Baseball great Lou Gehrig had another kind of mountain to climb. C In 1939 he found out that he had a deadly disease called ALS. At the time, Gehrig was at the top of his game. He was the best first baseman in all of baseball. He had been the captain of the legendary Yankee teams of the 1920s and had played with Babe Ruth. He had a lifetime batting average of .340 and had batted in almost 2,000 runs. What he is most remembered for today, however, is not his ability to play the game of baseball but the game of life. The Yankees honored him by making July 4, 1939, Lou Gehrig Day at Yankee Stadium. He was expected to appear before a crowd of 60,000 fans to make a speech. That may not seem like much, but he was so weak he had to have support just to stand up. The master of ceremonies knew how weak Gehrig was and had told the crowd that Gehrig would not speak. The fans chanted, "We want Lou! We want Lou!" anyway. Gehrig mustered up the strength to give what would become the most famous speech in the history of baseball. Although he knew that he would die soon, he told the crowd that he thought he was the luckiest man on the face of the Earth to have played with the Yankees. A little less than two years later he was gone, but his courage will never be forgotten.

D Neither will the courage of Rosa Parks. To me, she is the most courageous person of all. On December 1, 1955, she made history when she refused to give up her seat on a bus to a white person. The law in Montgomery, Alabama, at the time said that African Americans had to sit at the back of buses and had to give up their seats if white people were left standing. Parks bravely challenged the law and was arrested. Unlike Allison, Parks did not plan to make history. Unlike Gehrig, she was not already famous and admired. She was just an ordinary working woman who found the moral strength to challenge an unfair law. Her courage inspired the Montgomery bus boycott, a key event in the Civil Rights movement of the 1950s. Rosa Parks's case went all the way to the Supreme Court, where the Court finally ruled that segregated buses were unconstitutional. Parks showed great moral strength. She ventured into unknown territory, persevered, and withstood danger, fear, and difficulty. In the process, she made

continued

WRITING WORKSHOP MODELS

As they read "True Courage," invite students to comment on the definition essay, using the criteria in the Writing Workshop rubrics on pages 530 and 532.

A Literary Elements

Point of View In the introduction, the writer uses the second person (*you*). Ask students what effect this technique may have on the reader. *(The reader may feel a direct connection with the writer and become more interested in the essay.)*

B Organization

Comparisons This definition essay uses comparison-contrast organization. Point out to students that there are two ways to organize a comparison-contrast essay: (1) by feature (responses to courage) and (2) by subject (the courageous people). Ask students to identify the type of organization in this essay. *(by subject)*

C Voice

Awareness of Audience and Purpose Because the essay is written for a general audience—for people interested in courage, not for experts in mountain climbing, baseball, or civil rights—the writer includes general information the reader may need to know. For example, the writer describes the disease ALS as "deadly," Gehrig as an excellent first baseman, and the Yankees of the 1920s as "legendary." Have students point out other passages in the essay that give the reader general information. *(Examples: The writer refers to Mount Everest as "the tallest mountain in the world"; explains that at 25,500 feet above sea level, the air is thin and climbing is dangerous; summarizes the Montgomery bus law.)*

D Word Choice

Precise Verbs The writer uses verbs in this paragraph that precisely portray the actions of Parks. *Refused [to],* for example, is more precise

continued

than *did not.* Other precise verbs include *challenged, persevered, and withstood.* Have students work with partners to examine the verbs in their own essays. Ask partners to place check marks above verbs that seem vague, understated, overstated, or otherwise inaccurate. Students should revise their own essays by replacing imprecise verbs with precise ones.

life better for thousands of other people. She stands as an everlasting example of what courage can do.

Stacy Allison, Lou Gehrig, and Rosa Parks had the mental and moral strength to persevere. Instead of giving in to difficulty or fear, they managed to overcome their challenges with dignity. Do you have what it takes to be courageous? If you follow their examples, I think that you will find that you do.

Writing Minilesson

Focus on Organization In each paragraph and almost every sentence of "True Courage," the writer explains or illustrates his or her definition of courage. As students revise their own definition essays, they should ask themselves "Does each paragraph and sentence connect directly to the main point (that is, to my definition of a personal quality)?" Any extraneous material—no matter how interesting—only misleads, distracts, or confuses readers.

Activity Have students work in groups to find and remove information that strays from the main point of the paper, which is to define a personal quality. Each writer should then decide whether additional examples, comparisons, or other support needs to be added to replace what was removed.

Theme 6, pages 644–647

Narrative Writing: Short Story

In a Kingdom by the Sea

A "I think you're crazy."

"Maybe I am," I replied. "But I'm going on anyway. Remember your promise."

"I said I'd take you there and give you the key. Just don't expect me to go in with you."

B Randolf had finally admitted to me that his family had been wrong to separate his sister Annabel and me when we were in love. Annabel had died of a broken heart after they'd torn us apart, but even then his family scorned me. The family refused to let me come to the funeral, so I had never seen my beloved's resting-place. I had hounded Randolf for months before he had finally agreed to take me to Annabel's secret tomb.

I looked at the young man walking beside me. It was dark, but I could see his pale face, his straight dark hair, and his deep brown eyes. He reminded me so much of his sister that it hurt. I had thought of her every day since her death. And thinking of Annabel now made me even more determined to continue our strange journey.

We walked in silence for five more minutes. Then her brother stopped.

"Listen!" he said sharply. In the distance, I could hear the sound of waves breaking. "The sea. We're almost there."

"You can leave me then," I said. "Give me the key."

"No. I've gone this far. I guess I can take you to the tomb."

He led the way across a rocky field. Sometimes we tripped on stones that stuck up through the earth. It was misty too. Sometimes we had to stop because we could not see more than a few yards ahead of us. But we kept going when the mist swirled away. The sound of the sea grew louder and louder.

Suddenly the moon broke through the clouds, and we could see clearly for the first time that night. It was an awesome sight. We were standing on the edge of a cliff. Below us the gray sea pounded on the rocks.

Her brother put his hand on my shoulder and pointed. At first I could not make out what he wanted me to see. Then I knew. In the dark, I saw what looked like a huge square boulder perched on the highest point of the cliff, but the moonlight revealed a barred window and a narrow dark door. This was the sepulcher, the tomb of my beloved Annabel Lee. This was where I had longed to be since she had died mysteriously five years before. Ever since that day I had wanted to see her once more.

I began stumbling over the rocks towards the gray tomb. I could hear Randolf panting behind me. The building grew larger and darker as we approached. Why had her relatives buried her in such a deserted and gloomy place, I wondered.

Soon we were at the door. I pounded on it, as if someone would let me in. It made a deep hollow sound.

Her brother drew up beside me. I could hear him fishing in his pocket for the key.

"One last time," he said, "let me try to persuade you not to go in. What you see could destroy you."

"I must go in," I replied. "I can't come this far and not see her."

He handed me a huge rusty key as big as my hand.

"Good luck," he said as he walked slowly away.

C At first the key would not turn. Then I grabbed it with both hands and twisted hard. The old lock finally squeaked open, and I threw my weight against the iron door. It moved with a groan, and I stepped inside the sepulcher.

I had to wait for my eyes to get used to the darkness. Gradually I could see a beam of moon-

continued

WRITING WORKSHOP MODELS

WRITING WORKSHOP MODELS

As they read "In a Kingdom by the Sea," invite students to comment on the short story, using the criteria in the Writing Workshop rubrics on pages 644 and 646.

A Conventions

Paragraphing The writer begins a new paragraph whenever the speaker in the dialogue changes. Explain to students that this convention is particularly helpful to the reader when, as happens here, a speaker is not always identified. Then ask students to identify other points in the story where the speaker changes.

B Organization

Background Events This paragraph supplies the reader with necessary background information. It introduces a character (Randolf) and explains what has brought the narrator and Randolf together (an agreement to see Annabel's tomb). Ask students to describe the difference in verb tense between the background and the rest of the story. *(The background is in past perfect tense; the rest of the story is predominantly in simple past tense.)*

C Ideas and Content

Sensory Details The writer enlivens the story with memorable description. Details such as the lock squeaking open, the door moving "with a groan," and the "beam of moonlight falling from a high window onto a long wooden box" help make the story seem more real. Have students point to other sensory details that make the story come to life. *(Possible answers: the "stones that stuck up through the earth"; "the gray sea [that] pounded on the rocks"; the "huge rusty key")*

D **Literary Elements**

Suspense The writer imbues this paragraph with a feeling of suspense—uncertainty and dread about what is going to happen next. Have students discuss the techniques the writer uses to create this suspense. *(Examples: The repetition of the word* door *reflects the urgency of the narrator; the narrator's unanswered questions add to the reader's uncertainty; vivid adjectives, such as* terrified, *reflect the narrator's fear.)*

C light falling from a high window onto a long wooden box resting on a table.

It was her coffin.

I walked slowly towards the table, not knowing what I would find.

There was a stale, damp smell. Even though it was cold, I could feel sweat on my forehead. Would the lid open, or did it need a key too?

I grasped the cover and lifted. It moved easily.

Inside there was-nothing! The coffin was empty.

I gasped and staggered backwards. Was this a joke? Where had they put her? Was she still alive?

The door—I had to find the door. Groping through the dark, I tripped over an object on the floor and fell down. I reached out and touched something that made my heart leap. Annabel Lee lay on the floor. She had died there. Had they buried her alive? Is that what Randolf had tried to tell me? Terrified, I stumbled to my feet. In the darkness, I searched for the door. I was desperate to get out of this tomb, this nightmare! **D**

But when I found the door, I realized my nightmare had just begun. The door was locked from the outside. My rusty key was useless. Randolf had promised to let me enter the tomb, but he hadn't promised to let me out of it. In despair, I sank to the floor. I would spend the rest of my life with my Annabel Lee after all.

Writing Minilesson

Sentence Style & Variety In speech people often use short sentences or fragments. Point out that the writer of "In a Kingdom by the Sea" imitates this speaking style in the dialogue.

Activity Ask students to listen to a conversation between classmates at lunch or in the hall and to record the conversation as accurately as possible. Then have students rewrite the dialogue, making fragments into complete sentences and short sentences into longer ones. Have them compare the two dialogues and decide which dialogue sounds more realistic.

Theme 7, pages 760–763

Expository Writing: Book Review

Acorns for Dinner

A
B
Imagine eating this for dinner: "A mound of sort of fluffy mashed cattail tubers, mushrooms, and dogtooth violet bulbs, smothered in gravy thickened with acorn powder." Now imagine that you are eating out of turtle shells and sitting in a hollowed-out tree trunk. The cook is a teenaged boy named Sam Gribley. He is the hero of *My Side of the Mountain,* a novel by Jean Craighead George.

C
At the beginning of the novel, Sam lives in New York City with his mother, father, and eight brothers and sisters. He is not unhappy, but he wants to get away from the crowds and live off the land, so he runs away from home and goes to a forest that was once his great-grandfather's farm in the Catskill Mountains. All Sam has with him is an ax, a pocketknife, a ball of cord, and $40, but he lives up on his mountain for a whole year. During that time, he learns how to find food and stay warm, even in the winter. He does not want to leave, and in the end he does not have to. Instead, his family moves up to the mountain with him.

The main character is Sam, who tells his own story. The first-person narrative point-of-view makes the story easy to read and personal. If it had been told in the third person, it would not have seemed so real and immediate. The other main characters are mostly animals. Frightful goes everywhere with Sam. She is a falcon that Sam caught and trained when she was a baby bird. Frightful rides on Sam's shoulder and catches rabbits and pheasants for him to eat. There is also a weasel called the Baron. He is not really a pet because he is always attacking Sam, but Sam seems to like him. Finally, there is a raccoon called Jessie Coon James, who steals food and helps Sam find clams in the stream.

At first Sam is all alone with the animals. Then he begins to meet people. One person is a college English teacher called Bando. He gets lost in the woods the first summer, and he returns for Christmas dinner. Sam's father comes for Christmas too, so there are three people crowded into Sam's "house" in the hollowed-out tree. There is a hiker called Aaron, who writes music based on the bird songs he hears. There are also two boys from the village who begin to spend time with Sam.

The book does not really have a plot. It is just about Sam's struggle to survive. But there is a conflict in Sam's mind. Part of him wants to stay in the woods forever, away from the city. "People live too close together," he tells one of the boys who come to visit. But Sam also enjoys company. He looks forward to Bando's Christmas visit, and he loves showing the boys around his mountain. In the end, he gives his visitors so much information about himself that the newspapers print stories about "the wild boy" living on the mountain. Finally Sam realizes that he wants to be found.

D
I enjoyed reading *My Side of the Mountain.* I liked hearing about all the weird food Sam ate, even if I did not want to eat it myself. I also thought it was interesting that Sam wanted to be with people and did not want to be with people. I feel like that sometimes too. But I think there was something unbelievable about Sam's character. He did not even think about his mother and eight brothers and sisters for a whole year. They did not know where he was and must have been worried. Why didn't Sam write to them? He was happy to see them at the end. Sam's attitude toward his family did not seem realistic.

My Side of the Mountain is never boring. It teaches interesting facts about plants and animals, and it has some good nature drawings by the author. If you would like to know what it's like to train a falcon, eat clams rolled up in grape leaves, or make your own clothes out of deerskin, this is the book for you.

WRITING WORKSHOP MODELS

As they read "Acorns for Dinner," invite students to comment on the book review, using the criteria in the Writing Workshop rubrics on pages 760 and 762.

A Organization

Introduction The writer draws the reader in with a provocative quotation from the novel. Have students discuss why this technique is well suited for the opening of a book review. *(The technique focuses the reader on the book itself.)*

B Sentence Style and Variety

Imperative Sentences Most sentences in expository writing are declarative. Here, however, the writer begins the book review with two imperative sentences, both of which use the verb *imagine.* Explain to students that the sentences invite the reader's participation. Encourage them to try various sentence types in their own book reviews.

C Organization

Avoiding Extended Plot Summaries The writer confines his summary of the plot to the second paragraph. Advise students to avoid retelling the story in detail and to leave room in their reviews to examine various aspects of their books. Then ask students what aspects of the novel are discussed in the next three paragraphs. *(main characters, secondary characters, themes)*

D Voice

Sincerity The writer engages the reader in this paragraph by giving straightforward opinions. Have students discuss why the writer's straightforward opinions seem sincere. *(The writer uses first-person point of view, adds personal information ["I feel like that sometimes too"], and includes both positive and negative reactions.)*

Writing Minilesson

Ideas and Content Even though the writer of "Acorns for Dinner" strongly recommends *My Side of the Mountain* to readers, he or she discusses the book's weaknesses as well as its strengths. Ask students to share some of the strengths and weaknesses of the books they are reviewing.

Activity If students are reviewing a book they like, have them write down its weaknesses. If they are reviewing a book they dislike, have them write down its strengths. Then ask students to talk with classmates about ways to incorporate analysis of weaknesses into a positive book review and discussion of strengths into a negative one.

As they read "The Endangered Manatee," invite students to comment on the research report using the criteria in the Writing Workshop rubrics on pages 846 and 848.

A Ideas and Content

Facts and Statistics The writer effectively elaborates on the topic sentence of the paragraph ("Manatees still live . . .") with a statistic and some facts. The statistic tells precisely how many manatees are left. The facts recall legislation meant to protect the manatee. Ask students to explain what makes this elaboration effective. *(The statistics should help students realize that relatively few manatees remain; the dates of the legislation may suggest that new measures are called for.)*

B Organization

Transition Sentences The first sentence of this paragraph asks a question that follows logically from the preceding paragraph: Why are the manatees dying off? Have students find other transition sentences in the report. Ask them which transition sentence functions most like the one in this paragraph. *(The first sentence of the second, fourth, fifth, and sixth paragraphs are transitions sentences. The last of these sentences, like the one in the third paragraph, asks a question that follows logically from the preceding argument.)*

C Sentence Style and Variety

Repetition Several sentences in this paragraph make cross-references to preceding sentences by means of key words—*accidents, walls, pull(ed).* The writer's repeated use of these key words helps the reader follow along. Encourage students to use this technique in their own research reports.

Theme 8, pages 846–849

Expository Writing: Research Report

The Endangered Manatee

When Christopher Columbus sailed to the New World, he saw many things that seemed strange to him. One of the strangest was three unusual-looking mermaids. He wrote in his journal that they were "not so beautiful as they are painted, since in some ways they have a face like a man" (Ellis 88). If you saw what he saw, you might agree. The creatures were grayish-brown, had hairy snouts and probably weighed about a thousand pounds each. Of course, the creatures that Columbus wrote about were not mermaids at all. Scientists believe that the creatures were actually West Indian manatees. Long ago superstitious sailors who were unfamiliar with manatees sometimes mistook the gentle water mammals for mermaids.

A Manatees still live in the warm waters in and around Florida, but they may not be there much longer. As of July 2000, there were only about 2,400 manatees left (Sawicki 6). Even though the manatee is protected by the Marine Mammal Protection Act of 1972, the Endangered Species Act of 1973, and the Florida Manatee Sanctuary Act of 1978, it is dying off. The disappearance of the manatee should concern us all. In the long run, anything that upsets the balance of nature is harmful to us too. Besides, we owe it to future generations to protect our waters and the animals that call it home.

B The manatee has no natural enemies, so what is killing off the gentle giant? Sadly, the answer is people. More than 90 percent of the people who live in Florida live within ten miles of the coast, and more than 800 more people join them each day (Koeppel 68). Many of those people enjoy boating. Though boating is fun for people, it can be harmful to manatees. In fact, the chief cause of manatee deaths in recent years has been collisions with boats ("Manatee Mortality Statistics"). Manatees eat plants that grow deep in the water, but like other water mammals they must surface to breathe. When they surface, they sometimes swim into the path of an oncoming motorboat. Because they are slow swimmers, they cannot quickly get out of the way. Even if they could, they might not know when a motorboat is headed their way. Scientists believe that manatees cannot hear low-frequency sounds like those made by motors. As a result, manatees are often hit and killed by boats or injured by boat propellers. In fact, the Mote Marine Laboratory in Sarasota, Florida, estimates that 80 percent of Florida's manatees have been hit at least once by marine craft (Koeppel 68).

C Collisions with boats are not the manatee's only problem. Many manatees are killed in accidents with floodgates and canal locks. Accidents involving these structures are the second leading cause of manatee deaths ("Manatee"). To understand why these accidents occur, you must know what flood gates and canal locks look like and what they do. Picture large underwater walls that can be raised and lowered or opened and closed to control water levels. When those walls are opened, water comes rushing in and creates a strong current. That current is strong enough to pull in just about anything around it, including slow-moving manatees. Some manatees drown when they get pulled in by the current and cannot get to the surface of the water to breathe. Other manatees get caught between the gates and are crushed or trapped and drowned (Clark 37).

Other objects that people put in the water also cause problems for manatees. Florida's rivers and bays contain many small buoys, floating objects that fishermen place on the water to warn boaters that crab traps are below. The fishermen attach the traps to the buoys with wires or strong plastic lines that can become entangled around a manatee's flippers. When the manatee struggles to free

continued

itself, it can become injured. All too often, the injury becomes infected, and the manatee dies (Clark 35). Manatees have also been known to choke to death on fishhooks and on garbage that has been thrown in the water.

What can we do to protect manatees from accidental deaths? Concerned citizens say that we should demand that the laws protecting endangered species be strictly enforced. According to Judith Vallee of Save the Manatee, a group that works to protect manatees, enforcement of those laws is currently "pathetic" (Sawicki 6). Another way that we can protect manatees is to avoid boating in waters where manatees are known to live. Naturally, many boaters do not want to give up their hobby, but soon they may not have to. Edmund Gerstein of Florida Atlantic University is working to develop a sort of warning alarm for manatees. The device sends out high-frequency sounds that manatees can hear (Eliot xxxii). When these devices are available, boaters should be required to attach them to their watercraft, and fishermen should be required to attach them to their buoys. The devices should also be attached to floodgates and canal locks. Finally we should be careful to recycle our garbage to help keep it out of our oceans and other waterways.

Thousands of years before you and I were born, manatees lived in the waters in and around the area we know as the state of Florida. Let's do our part to make sure that manatees continue to swim there long after we are gone. When all is said and done, the future of the manatee is up to us. **D**

Works Cited

Clark, Margaret Goff. *The Vanishing Manatee*. New York: Cobblehill, 1990.

Eliot, John L. "Deaf to Danger: Manatees Can't Hear Boats." *National Geographic* 197:2 (Feb. 2000): xxxii.

Ellis, Richard. *Monsters of the Sea*. New York: Knopf, 1994.

Koeppel, Dan. "Kiss of the Manatee." *Travel Holiday*. 182:1 (Feb. 1999): 66-69.

"Manatee Mortality Statistics." Save the Manatee Club. 12 Feb. 2001 <www.savethemanatee.org/mort.htm>.

Sawicki, Stephen. "Manatee Protectors Turn to the Courts." *Animals* 133:4 (July 2000): 6.

E

WRITING WORKSHOP MODELS

D Organization

Conclusion The report's conclusion both returns to the theme of the manatee's long history and calls the reader to action. Ask students why these two facets to the conclusion fit well together. *(The reader may be convinced that the manatee is endangered. But without a reminder of the manatee's long history, the reader may not be persuaded to help save the manatee from extinction.)*

E Conventions

Works Cited Go over the works listed and have students identify the type of source each item refers to. *(They are, in order, book, article, book, article, online source, article.)* Then have them discuss the significant differences among the citations. *(For example, volume and page numbers in periodical references, URLs in online sources, quotation marks for titles of articles and underscoring—or italics—for titles of books and magazines.)* Suggest to students that they carefully proofread the formats of the entries in their own works-cited lists.

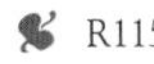

Writing Minilesson

Focus on Conventions The sources used for "The Endangered Manatee" are cited correctly in both the internal references and the works-cited list. For example, the source of each fact cited is placed in parentheses immediately following the fact's appearance in the text. In the works-cited list, all but the first line of each item is indented. Direct students to study the rules for source citation on pages R58–R59.

Activity Have students proofread the internal references and the works-cited lists in their own research reports and make necessary revisions to ensure that all items are accurate and conform to the rules for source citation.

WRITING WORKSHOP MODELS R115

Glossary

This glossary lists the vocabulary words found in the selections in this book. The definitions given are for the words as they are used in the selections; you may wish to consult a dictionary for other meanings of these words. The key below is a guide to the pronunciation symbols used in the entries.

a	at	**ō**	hope	**ng**	sing
ā	ape	**ô**	fork, all	**th**	thin
ä	father	**oo**	wood, put	**th**	this
e	end	**o͞o**	fool	**zh**	treasure
ē	me	**oi**	oil	**ə**	ago, taken, pencil, lemon, circus
i	it	**ou**	out	**′**	indicates primary stress
ī	ice	**u**	up	**′**	indicates secondary stress
o	hot	**ū**	use		

A

absurdity (ab sur′ də tē) *n.* the state of being ridiculous, senseless, or irrational; p. 567

accede (ək sēd′) *v.* to give in; go along with; p. 677

acutely (ə kūt′ lē) *adv.* sharply and with intensity; p. 493

aggrieved (ə grēvd′) *adj.* feeling wronged, as by an insult or unfair treatment; p. 666

agility (ə jil′ə tē) *n.* quickness and ease in motion or thought; p. 282

agitated (aj′ ə tāt′ ed) *adj.* 1. upset; disturbed; p. 36. 2. excited, nervous, stirred up; p. 667

agony (ag′ ə nē) *n.* great pain and suffering of the mind or body; p. 745

amplify (am′ plə fī′) *v.* to increase; extend; p. 300

anguished (ang′ gwisht) *adj.* having or showing extreme mental or physical suffering; p. 286

antagonism (an tag′ ə niz′ əm) *n.* hostility; p. 511

anticipation (an tis′ə pā′ shən) *n.* a feeling of excited expectation; p. 390

appalling (ə pô′ ling) *adj.* shocking; horrifying; p. 79

apparatus (ap′ ə rat′ əs) *n.* something created or invented for a particular purpose; p. 465

aptitude (ap′ tə to͞od′) *n.* a natural ability; talent; p. 743

aroma (ə rō′ mə) *n.* a pleasant smell; odor; p. 708

artful (ärt′ fəl) *adj.* done with skill or cleverness; p. 565

ascertain (as′ ər tān′) *v.* to find out with certainty; determine; p. 413

assess (ə ses′) *v.* to determine the meaning or importance of; analyze; p. 222

authoritarian (ə thôr′ ə tār′ ē ən) *adj.* having or expecting complete obedience to authority; p. 369

avert (ə vurt′) *v.* to keep from happening; prevent; p. 401

R116 GLOSSARY

avidly (av′ id lē) *adv.* eagerly; enthusiastically; p. 372
awe (ô) *n.* wonder combined with respect; p. 351

B

balmy (bä′ mē) *adj.* mild; soothing; p. 222
barrage (bə räzh′) *n.* a heavy concentration or great outpouring, as of words; p. 119
barren (bar′ ən) *adj.* having little or no plant life; bare; empty; p. 753
benefactor (ben′ ə fak′ tər) *n.* one who gives financial assistance; p. 584
bewildered (bi wil′ dərd) *adj.* very confused; p. 118
bleak (blēk) *adj.* cheerless; depressing; p. 164
boycott (boi′ kot) *n.* an organized protest in which the participants refuse to buy, sell, or use a product or service; p. 90
bravado (brə vä′ dō) *n.* a false show of bravery; p. 353
brink (bringk) *n.* the point at which something may begin; p. 282
brood (bro͞od) *n.* all of the young of an animal that are born or cared for at the same time; p. 799

C

casually (kazh′ o͞o əl lē) *adv.* in a relaxed, informal way; p. 362
chaotic (kā ot′ ik) *adj.* confused and disorganized; in great disorder; p. 8
charismatic (kar′ iz mat′ ik) *adj.* having personal qualities that enable one to inspire loyalty and devotion; p. 283
claim (klām) *v.* to ask for or demand possession of one's right to something; p. 721
clamor (klam′ ər) *n.* a loud, continuous noise; uproar; p. 79
clan (klan) *n.* a group of families descended from a common ancestor; p. 270
coincidence (kō in′ si dəns) *n.* an accidental occurrence of events, ideas, or circumstances at the same time, without one causing the other; p. 452
collaborator (kə lab′ ə rā′ tər) *n.* one who works or cooperates with another; p. 415
collective (kə lek′ tiv) *adj.* having to do with a group of persons or things; common; shared; p. 677
colossal (kə los′ əl) *adj.* extraordinarily or awesomely large; p. 754
commencement (kə mens′ mənt) *n.* a beginning; start; graduation ceremonies; p. 9
compact (kəm pakt′) *adj.* occupying a relatively small space or area; tightly packed; p. 306
compensate (kom′ pən sāt′) *v.* to make up for; balance in force, weight, or effect; p. 808
competent (kom′ pət ənt) *adj.* having enough ability for the purpose; capable; p. 577
comply (kəm plī′) *v.* to go along with a request; p. 86
comprehend (kom′ pri hend′) *v.* to grasp mentally; understand fully; p. 413
concede (kən sēd′) *v.* to admit to be true or proper; p. 221
conceive (kən sēv′) *v.* to form an image or idea of; p. 577
condemn (kən dem′) *v.* to express strong disapproval of; criticize sharply; p. 715
confront (kən frunt′) *v.* to come face to face with; stand facing; p. 416
consecutive (kən sek′ yə tiv) *adj.* following one after another in order without interruption; p. 27
consequence (kon′ sə kwens′) *n.* importance; significance; p. 464
consolation (kon′ sə lā shən) *n.* a comfort; p. 373
conspicuously (kən spik′ ū əs lē) *adv.* in a way that draws attention or is easily seen; p. 809
contemplate (kon′ təm plāt′) *v.* to give intense attention to; consider carefully; p. 296
converge (kən vurj′) *v.* to come together at a place; p. 299

GLOSSARY

GLOSSARY R117

cordially (kôr′ jəl lē) *adv.* in a genuinely warm and friendly way; p. 752
correspond (kôr ə spond′) *v.* to communicate by exchanging letters; p. 567
cower (kou′ ər) *v.* to crouch down, as in fear or shame; p. 792
culprit (kul′ prit) *n.* one guilty of some offense; p. 405
cunning (kun′ ing) *adj.* crafty; sly; p. 390
cynically (sin′ ə kəl lē) *adv.* in a way that shows doubt or disbelief; doubtfully; p. 547

D

deception (di sep′ shən) *n.* that which fools or misleads; p. 125
decree (di krē′) *n.* an official rule, order, or decision; p. 743
defiant (di fī′ ənt) *adj.* showing bold resistance to authority or an opponent; p. 511
degrade (di grād′) *v.* to lower in character or quality; make less pure; p. 828
delectable (di lek′ tə bəl) *adj.* highly pleasing or delightful, especially to the taste; delicious; p. 389
demise (di mīz′) *n.* death; end; p. 828
depleted (di plēt′ id) *adj.* greatly reduced in amount; p. 296
desolation (des′ ə lā′ shən) *n.* sadness; loneliness; p. 689
despair (di spār′) *n.* complete loss of hope; desperation; p. 708
desperation (des′ pə rā′ shən) *n.* distress caused by great need or loss of hope; p. 50
destine (des′ tin) *v.* to determine beforehand; p. 400
devastating (dev′ əs tāt ing) *adj.* causing great pain, damage, or destruction; overwhelming; p. 434
devise (di vīz′) *v.* to think out; invent; plan; p. 384
diligently (dil′ ə jənt lē) *adv.* in a way that shows great attention, care, and effort; p. 301
discern (di surn′) *v.* to detect or recognize; p. 492
discreetly (dis krēt′ lē) *adv.* in a manner showing good judgment; cautiously; p. 155
discrepancy (dis krep′ ən sē) *n.* a lack of agreement, as between facts; p. 28
dismally (diz′ məl lē) *adv.* in a gloomy, cheerless way; p. 567
dismay (dis mā′) *n.* a feeling of alarm or uneasiness; p. 453
dispense (dis pens′) *v.* to give out in portions; p. 385
distinct (dis tingkt′) *adj.* different in quality or kind; p. 285
divulge (di vulj′) *v.* to make known; give away; p. 38
domestic (də mes′ tik) *adj.* describes animals living with or near human beings and cared for by them; p. 828

E

eccentric (ik sen′ trik) *adj.* not usual or normal in behavior; peculiar; p. 578
ecology (ē kol′ ə jē) *n.* the relationship of living things to their environment and to each other; p. 309
ecstatic (ek stat′ ik) *adj.* overwhelmed with joy; p. 371
efficient (i fish′ ənt) *adj.* producing a desired effect with a minimum of effort or waste; p. 677
elaborate (i lab′ ər it) *adj.* worked out carefully and thoroughly; detailed; complicated; p. 829
elicit (i lis′ it) *v.* to draw forth or bring out; p. 29
eloquent (el′ ə kwənt) *adj.* expressive, effective, and stirring in speech or writing; p. 29
embrace (em brās′) *v.* to hug or hold in the arms, especially as a sign of love or affection; p. 275
emerge (i murj′) *v.* to come out; p. 52
emphatic (em fat′ ik) *adj.* strongly expressive; forceful; p. 361
endeavor (en dev′ ər) *n.* a serious attempt to accomplish something; undertaking; p. 404
endure (en door′) *v.* to put up with; undergo, as pain, stress, or other hardship; p. 238

R118 GLOSSARY

enticing (en tīs′ ing) *adj.* offering pleasure or reward; p. 684

enviable (en′ vē ə bəl) *adj.* good enough to be highly desired; p. 685

envious (en′ vē əs) *adj.* having resentment over, and a wish to possess for oneself, something possessed by another; p. 716

esteem (es tēm′) *n.* favorable opinion; high regard; p. 29

etiquette (et′ i kit) *n.* the rules of good manners and polite behavior; p. 414

evacuate (i vak′ ū āt′) *v.* to leave or clear an area; p. 307

evading (i vād′ ing) *adj.* escaping or avoiding; p. 440

eventually (i ven′ cho͞o ə lē) *adv.* in the end; finally; p. 153

exasperation (ig zas′ pə rā′ shən) *n.* anger or great irritation; p. 689

excavated (eks′ kə vāt′ əd) *adj.* uncovered or removed by digging; unearthed; p. 119

excess (ek′ ses) *adj.* more than usual or necessary; p. 149

exotic (ig zot′ ik) *adj.* strangely attractive; foreign; p. 8

explicit (eks plis′ it) *adj.* clearly expressed; p. 524

exploit (iks ploit′) *v.* to use or develop for profit, often in a selfish, unjust, or unfair way; p. 299

extricate (eks′ trə kāt′) *v.* to release from entanglement or difficulty; set free; p. 404

F

faltering (fôl′ tər ing) *adj.* shaky because of uncertainty; p. 199

fanciful (fan′ si fəl) *adj.* showing imagination in design or construction; imaginative; p. 753

fancy (fan′ sē) *v.* to picture mentally; imagine; p. 795

fixed (fikst) *adj.* steadily directed and unchanging; p. 708

flail (flāl) *v.* to wave or swing, especially swiftly or violently; p. 440

fleetest (flēt′ əst) *adj.* swiftest; fastest; p. 719

flinch (flinch) *v.* to draw back, as from something painful, dangerous, or unpleasant; p. 793

flourishing (flur′ ish ing) *adj.* growing or developing successfully; doing very well; p. 354

formidable (for′ mi də bəl) *adj.* causing fear or dread by reason of size, strength, or power; p. 69

fortitude (fôr tə to͞od′) *n.* firm courage or strength of mind in the face of pain or danger; p. 401

frail (frāl) *adj.* lacking in strength; weak; p. 463

frenzy (fren′ zē) *n.* a state of intense excitement or disturbance; p. 246

frustration (frus trā′ shən) *n.* disappointment or irritation at being kept from doing or achieving something; p. 777

G

gait (gāt) *n.* a particular manner of moving on foot; p. 793

gaunt (gônt) *adj.* looking like skin and bones; p. 237

giddy (gid′ dē) *adj.* dizzy or light-headed; p. 604

gnarled (närld) *adj.* rough, twisted, and knotty, as a tree trunk or branches; p. 702

grim (grim) *adj.* fierce; severe; stern; forbidding; p. 237

grimace (grim′ əs) *v.* to twist the face, as in pain or displeasure; p. 79

grudging (gruj′ ing) *adj.* given or allowed unwillingly or resentfully; p. 236

gruffly (gruf′ lē) *adv.* in a rough, stern manner; p. 239

H

habitual (hə bich′ o͞o əl) *adj.* done by habit; p. 565

haggard (hag′ ərd) *adj.* looking worn as a result of grief, worry, or illness; p. 666

hallowed (hal′ ōd) *adj.* regarded as sacred or holy; p. 717

GLOSSARY

GLOSSARY R119

hardy (här′ dē) *adj.* able to endure hardship; strong and healthy; p. 155

hindrance (hin′ drəns) *n.* something that holds back progress or movement; obstacle; p. 30

hostile (host′ əl) *adj.* feeling or showing dislike; unfriendly; p. 808

hover (huv′ ər) *v.* to remain as if suspended in the air over a particular spot; p. 745

humility (hū mil′ ə tē) *n.* the quality of being humble or modest; p. 744

hurtle (hurt′ əl) *v.* to move rapidly, especially with much force; p. 664

I

illuminated (i lo͞o′ mə nāt id) *adj.* lit up; p. 152

immobilize (i mō′ bə līz′) *v.* to make unable to move; fix in place; p. 119

impetuous (im pech′ o͞o əs) *adj.* marked by force or violent action; p. 494

impose (im pōz′) *v.* to apply legally; enforce; p. 100

impoverished (im pov′ ər isht) *adj.* reduced to poverty; made very poor; p. 370

improbable (im prob′ ə bəl) *adj.* not likely; p. 151

improvise (im′ prə vīz′) *v.* to invent, compose, or do without much preparation; p. 438

impulse (im′ puls) *n.* an internal force that causes one to act without thinking; p. 50

impunity (im pū′ nə tē) *n.* freedom from punishment, harm, or bad effects; p. 187

incessantly (in ses′ ənt lē) *adv.* endlessly; constantly; p. 188

incomprehensible (in′ kom prē hen′ sə bəl) *adj.* not understandable; p. 191

inconvenience (in′ kən vēn′ yəns) *v.* to cause someone difficulty, bother, or hassle; p. 93

incredulous (in krej′ ə ləs) *adj.* unwilling or unable to believe something; p. 170

incriminate (in krim′ ə nāt′) *v.* to show the guilt of; p. 515

indifferent (in dif′ ər ənt) *adj.* having or showing a lack of feeling, concern, or care; p. 385

indignity (in dig′ nə tē) *n.* an offense against one's pride or dignity; humiliation; p. 94

indiscriminately (in′ dis krim′ ə nit lē) *adv.* in a way that does not pay attention to differences; carelessly; p. 300

inert (i nurt′) *adj.* without power to move or act; p. 352

inevitably (i nev′ ə tə blē) *adv.* in a way that cannot be avoided or prevented; p. 7

infantile (in′ fən tīl′) *adj.* like an infant; childish; p. 413

infinite (in′ fə nit) *adj.* boundless; limitless; extremely great; p. 177

initial (i nish′ əl) *adj.* at the beginning; first; p. 7

initiative (i nish′ ə tiv) *n.* the action of taking the first step; p. 476

insistent (in sis′ tənt) *adj.* demanding attention or notice; p. 176

insolently (in′ sə lənt lē) *adv.* in a boldly rude manner; p. 544

instill (in stil′) *v.* to put in gradually, little by little; p. 510

instinct (in′ stingkt) *n.* a way of knowing, behaving, or reacting that comes naturally rather than through learning; p. 167

intact (in takt′) *adj.* undamaged and whole; p. 597

intellectual (int′ əl ek′ cho͞o əl) *adj.* appealing to or involving mental ability; p. 608

intense (in tens′) *adj.* of a very high degree; very strong; p. 610

intently (in tent′ lē) *adv.* in a firmly focused way; with concentration; p. 154

intimidated (in tim′ ə dāt′ əd) *adj.* made timid or fearful; bullied; p. 510

intricate (in′ tri kit) *adj.* full of complicated detail; p. 565

intrusion (in tro͞o′ zhən) *n.* a sudden interruption; p. 384

invalid (in′ və lid) *n.* one who is disabled by disease or injury; p. 165

invariably (in vār′ ē ə blē) *adv.* without exception; p. 194

ironically (ī ron′ i kəl ē) *adv.* in a way that is different from what would be expected; p. 6

J

jeer (jēr) *v.* to make fun of (someone or something) rudely and openly; p. 684
jest (jest) *v.* to speak or act in a playful manner; joke; p. 596
jubilant (jo͞o′ bə lənt) *adj.* filled with great joy and excitement; high-spirited; p. 721
juncture (jungk′ chər) *n.* a critical point of time; p. 36

K

keen (kēn) *adj.* highly sensitive; sharp; p. 272

L

laden (lād′ ən) *adj.* loaded; weighed down; burdened; p. 386
lapse (laps) *n.* a slipping or falling away; p. 548
legitimate (li jit′ ə mit) *adj.* that which follows the rules; lawful; p. 517
lolling (lol′ ing) *adj.* hanging down loosely; drooping; p. 246
loom (lo͞om) *v.* to appear to the mind as threatening; p. 222
lunge (lunj) *v.* to make a sudden forward movement; charge; p. 794

M

malicious (mə lish′ əs) *adj.* having or showing a desire to harm another; p. 484
maneuver (mə no͞o′ vər) *v.* to move or handle skillfully, as into a position or toward a goal; p. 68
meek (mēk) *adj.* patient and mild in manner; gentle; p. 389
menace (men′ əs) *n.* a threat or danger; p. 68
merge (murj) *v.* to join together so as to become one; unite; p. 7
meticulously (mi tik′ yə ləs lē) *adv.* in a way that shows careful attention to details; p. 221
mobilize (mō′ bə līz′) *v.* to become prepared, as for war or an emergency; p. 91
moderately (mod′ ər it lē) *adv.* neither too great nor too small; within limits; p. 568
mortified (môr′ tə fīd′) *adj.* greatly embarrassed; p. 370
murky (mur′ kē) *adj.* dark; not clear; p. 414
muse (mūz) *v.* to think or reflect; p. 190
muster (mus′ tər) *v.* to find and gather together; collect; p. 453

N

naive (nä ēv′) *adj.* simple in nature; childlike; p. 37
narrative (nar′ ə tiv) *n.* story; storytelling; p. 37
negotiate (ni gō′ shē āt′) *v.* to discuss in order to bring about an agreement; p. 97
nimble (nim′ bəl) *adj.* light and quick in movement; p. 439
novelty (nov′ əl tē) *n.* anything new and unusual; p. 595
nurture (nur′ chər) *v.* to care for and help grow; p. 356

O

obligation (ob′ lə gā′ shən) *n.* a sense of duty; responsibility; p. 474
obligingly (ə blī′ jing lē) *adv.* helpfully; agreeably; p. 244
obnoxious (ob nok′ shəs) *adj.* annoying and disagreeable; p. 69
obscure (əb skyoor′) *adj.* difficult to understand; p. 350
obsessed (əb sesd′) *adj.* overly concentrated or focused on a single emotion or idea; p. 118
obsession (əb sesh′ ən) *n.* a single emotion or idea that occupies or troubles the mind; p. 414
obstinate (ob′ stə nit) *adj.* stubborn; difficult to overcome or control; p. 361
omen (ō′ mən) *n.* a sign or event thought to foretell good or bad fortune; p. 774
ominous (om′ ə nəs) *adj.* threatening harm or evil; p. 222

GLOSSARY R121

oppression (ə presh′ ən) *n.* the act of controlling or governing by the cruel and unjust use of force or authority; p. 95

overtake (ō′ vər tāk′) *v.* to catch up with or to reach and then pass; p. 708

P

painstaking (pānz′ tā′ king) *adj.* requiring close, careful labor or attention; p. 123

parched (pärcht) *adj.* severely in need of moisture; very dry; p. 717

passive (pas′ iv) *adj.* not participating or active; p. 166

perilous (per′ ə ləs) *adj.* dangerous; risky; p. 403

perpetual (pər pech′ o͞o əl) *adj.* constant; unceasing; p. 437

perplexity (pər plek′ sə tē) *n.* doubt or uncertainty; puzzlement; p. 194

perseverance (pur′ sə vēr′ əns) *n.* continuation despite difficulty; determination; p. 187

persistently (pər sis′ tənt lē) *adv.* repeatedly; p. 70

perspective (pər spek′ tiv) *n.* point of view; p. 370

pinnacle (pin′ ə kəl) *n.* a high point, or peak; p. 285

pious (pī′ əs) *adj.* having either genuine or pretended religious devotion; p. 385

plummet (plum′ it) *v.* to fall or drop straight downward; plunge; p. 296

podium (pō′ dē əm) *n.* a small, raised platform or stand with a slanted shelf for holding a speaker's papers; p. 728

pompous (pom′ pəs) *adj.* showing an exaggerated sense of self-importance; p. 385

portly (pôrt′ lē) *adj.* having a stout but dignified appearance; p. 369

possessively (pə zes′ iv lē) *adv.* in a way that shows ownership or control; p. 361

potion (pō′ shən) *n.* a drink, especially of a liquid that is supposed to have magical powers; p. 702

pounce (pouns) *v.* to swoop down, spring, or leap suddenly in attack; p. 729

precise (pri sīs′) *adj.* strictly accurate or clearly defined; exact; p. 605

predator (pred′ ə tər) *n.* an animal, such as a lion or hawk, that kills other animals for food; p. 125

prejudice (prej′ ə dis) *n.* an unfavorable opinion or judgment formed unfairly; p. 524

premonition (prē′ mə nish′ ən) *n.* a feeling that something is about to happen; warning or sign; p. 400

primly (prim′ lē) *adv.* in a formal and proper manner; p. 548

principle (prin′ sə pəl) *n.* a basic law, truth, or belief; rule of personal conduct; p. 354

proposition (prop′ ə zish′ ən) *n.* something offered for consideration; proposal; p. 573

prosperous (pros′ pər əs) *adj.* having wealth or good fortune; successful; p. 592

pursue (pər so͞o′) *v.* to chase; p. 273

Q

quavering (kwā′ vər ing) *adj.* trembling or shaking; p. 484

quench (kwench) *v.* to satisfy or put an end to a need or desire; p. 739

R

rash (rash) *adj.* done without thought or preparation; reckless; p. 738

raucous (rô′ kəs) *adj.* loud and rough-sounding; p. 544

ravenous (rav′ ə nəs) *adj.* extremely hungry; p. 390

rebuke (ri būk′) *n.* an expression of sharp criticism or disapproval; p. 578

reel (rēl) *v.* to turn or seem to turn round and round; whirl; p. 739

reflective (ri flek′ tiv) *adj.* showing serious and careful thinking; thoughtful; p. 507

R122 GLOSSARY

GLOSSARY

reformation (ref′ ər mā′ shən) *n.* a change for the better; improvement; p. 547

regretfully (ri gret′ fəl lē) *adv.* in a way that shows sorrow, distress, or disappointment; p. 774

reluctantly (ri luk′ tənt lē) *adv.* unwillingly; p. 247

replenish (ri plen′ ish) *v.* to provide a new supply; p. 687

resigned (ri zīnd′) *adj.* giving in without resistance; p. 88

resilient (ri zil′ yənt) *adj.* capable of springing back into shape or position after being bent, stretched, or compressed; p. 465

resolute (rez′ ə lo͞ot′) *adj.* determined; stubborn; p. 348

resourceful (ri sôrs′ fəl) *adj.* capable or skillful in dealing with new or difficult situations; p. 727

retrieve (ri trēv′) *v.* to locate and bring back; recover; fetch; p. 50

ritual (rich′ o͞o əl) *n.* an established form of doing something; ceremony; p. 37

robust (rō bust′) *adj.* strong and full of energy; p. 341

S

sanction (sangk′ shən) *v.* to give support or encouragement to; approve; p. 168

sanctuary (sangk′ cho͞o er′ ē) *n.* a place of safety or protection; p. 170

saunter (sôn′ tər) *v.* to walk in a relaxed way; p. 246

savor (sā′ vər) *v.* to take great delight in; p. 239

scavenger (skav′ in jər) *n.* an animal, such as a hyena or vulture, that feeds on dead, decaying animals; p. 125

scurry (skur′ ē) *v.* to run or move briskly or in an agitated way; p. 774

scuttle (skut′ əl) *v.* to move with short, rapid steps; p. 789

secretive (sē′ kri tiv) *adj.* keeping one's thoughts and feelings to oneself; p. 663

sedately (si dāt′ lē) *adv.* in a quiet, restrained style or manner; calmly; p. 239

sensation (sen sā′ shən) *n.* a cause of excitement or great interest; a wonder; p. 754

shrewd (shro͞od) *adj.* sharp, clever, and practical; p. 584

simultaneously (sī′ məl tā′ nē əs lē) *adv.* at the same time; p. 546

sinewy (sin′ ū ē) *adj.* physically tough, or powerful; p. 274

singularity (sing′ gyə lar′ ə tē) *n.* that which is remarkable or out of the ordinary; unusualness; p. 191

skimpy (skim′ pē) *adj.* lacking in quantity, fullness, or size; barely enough or not quite enough; p. 236

slither (sli<u>th</u>′ ər) *v.* to move along with a sliding or gliding motion, as a snake; p. 246

sluggish (slug′ ish) *adj.* lacking energy, liveliness, or alertness; p. 828

soberly (sō′ bər lē) *adv.* very seriously; p. 476

solemnly (sol′ əm lē) *adv.* seriously; p. 546

somberly (som′ bər lē) *adv.* in a gloomy manner; p. 490

sorcerer (sor′ sər ər) *n.* a person who practices magic with the aid of evil spirits; p. 701

spare (spār) *v.* to treat with mercy; hold back from harming or injuring; p. 274

spasm (spaz′ əm) *n.* a sudden uncontrollable tightening of a muscle; p. 243

specify (spes′ ə fī′) *v.* to state or describe in detail; p. 7

speculation (spek′ yə lā′ shən) *n.* the act of forming an opinion or conclusion based on guesswork; p. 150

spendthrift (spend′ thrift′) *n.* one who spends money generously or wastefully; p. 594

spite (spīt) *n.* a desire to hurt or annoy another person; p. 744

squander (skwon′ dər) *v.* to spend or use in a reckless or wasteful manner; p. 593

staccato (stə kä′ tō) *adj.* made of short, sharp sounds or movements; p. 362

staple (stā′ pəl) *adj.* important; main; p. 38

GLOSSARY R123

GLOSSARY

stark (stärk) *adv.* completely; harshly or grimly; p. 177

subsidize (sub′ sə dīz′) *v.* to aid or support with a contribution of money; p. 301

subtle (sut′ əl) *adj.* not open or direct; not obvious; p. 178

succeed (sək sēd′) *v.* to come or happen after in time, place, or order; p. 666

sufficient (sə fish′ ənt) *adj.* adequate; enough; p. 677

sullen (sul′ ən) *adj.* stubbornly withdrawn or gloomy; sulky; p. 45

surge (surj) *v.* to rise or increase suddenly; move with a violent swelling motion, as waves; p. 441

surly (sur′ le) *adj.* rude and bad tempered; gruff; p. 164

swagger (swag′ ər) *v.* to walk or behave in a bold, rude, or overly proud way; p. 45

T

tact (takt) *n.* the ability to handle people or situations without causing displeasure or resentment; p. 370

taunt (tônt) *v.* to make fun of in a scornful, insulting way; p. 701

taut (tôt) *adj.* stretched tight; p. 150

tentatively (ten′ tə tiv lē) *adv.* hesitantly; uncertainly; p. 492

therapy (ther′ ə pē) *n.* treatment of an injury, disease, or mental disorder; p. 676

tumultuously (too mul′ chōō əs lē) *adv.* in a wildly excited, confused, or disturbed way; p. 465

U

ultimately (ul′ tə mit lē) *adv.* in the end; finally; p. 369

uncanny (un kan′ ē) *adj.* so strange as to cause fear or wonder; weird; p. 404

uncommitted (un′ kə mit′ id) *adj.* not having or showing a particular opinion, view, or course of action; p. 474

undermine (un′ dər mīn′) *v.* to weaken, wear away, or destroy slowly; p. 298

undertake (un′ dər tāk′) *v.* to enter into (a task); attempt; p. 829

undulating (un′ jə lāt′ ing) *adj.* moving in waves; rippling; p. 603

unique (ū nēk′) *adj.* highly uncommon; rare; one-of-a-kind; p. 309

unpalatable (un pal′ ə tə bəl) *adj.* not agreeable to the taste, mind, or feelings; unacceptable; p. 222

V

vaguely (vāg′ lē) *adv.* in a way that is not clear, exact, or definite; p. 7

vainly (vān′ lē) *adv.* without success; uselessly; p. 739

valiant (val′ yənt) *adj.* brave; courageous; p. 797

validity (və lid′ ə tē) *n.* state of being supported by facts; truth; p. 511

veer (vēr) *v.* to shift or change direction; p. 737

venture (ven′ chər) *v.* to do something in spite of possible risk or danger; p. 152

vigor (vig′ ər) *n.* strength and energy; p. 246

vile (vīl) *adj.* very bad; unpleasant; foul; p. 455

vital (vīt′ əl) *adj.* of primary importance; essential; p. 464

W

wary (wār′ ē) *adj.* cautious; on the alert; p. 437

waver (wā′ vər) *v.* to become unsteady; p. 738

wholeheartedly (hōl′ här′ tid lē) *adv.* completely; sincerely; enthusiastically; p. 68

wily (wī′ lē) *adj.* full of tricks; crafty; sly; p. 170

wince (wins) *v.* to draw back slightly, as in pain; p. 48

withdrawn (with drôn′) *adj.* shy, reserved, or unsociable; p. 454

woe (wō) *n.* great sadness or suffering; great trouble or misfortune; p. 474

R124 GLOSSARY

Spanish Glossary

A

absurdity/absurdo *s.* cualidad de disparatado o ridículo; irracional; p. 567
accede/acceder *v.* aceptar; consentir; p. 677
acutely/agudamente *adv.* de modo punzante e intenso; p. 493
aggrieved/apesadumbrado *adj.* afligido o apenado, por ejemplo por un insulto o un trato injusto; p. 666
agility/agilidad *s.* rapidez y ligereza de movimiento o pensamiento; p. 282
agitated/agitado *adj.* 1. molesto; turbado; p. 36. 2. excitado; nervioso; trastornado; p. 667
agony/agonía *s.* gran dolor y sufrimiento mental o físico; p. 745
amplify/ampliar *v.* aumentar; extender; p. 300
anguished/angustiado *adj.* que siente o demuestra un gran sufrimiento mental o físico; p. 286
antagonism/antagonismo *s.* hostilidad; p. 511
anticipation/anticipación *s.* expectación; sensación de esperar algo con interés o ilusión; p. 390
appalling/pasmoso *adj.* impactante; horrorizante; p. 79
apparatus/aparato *s.* algo creado o inventado con un fin particular; p. 465
aptitude/aptitud *s.* habilidad natural; talento; p. 743
aroma/aroma *s.* olor agradable; fragancia; p. 708
artful/habilidoso *adj.* hecho con habilidad o ingenio; p. 565
ascertain/averiguar *v.* cerciorarse; comprobar; p. 413
assess/evaluar *v.* determinar el significado o la importancia de algo; analizar; p. 222
authoritarian/autoritario *adj.* que tiene o exige total obediencia a la autoridad; dominante; p. 369
avert/prevenir *v.* impedir que ocurra; evitar; p. 401
avidly/ávidamente *adv.* de modo intenso; ansiosamente; con mucho ánimo; p. 372
awe/veneración *s.* admiración combinada con respeto; p. 351

B

balmy/suave *adj.* balsámico; calmante; p. 222
barrage/descarga *s.* concentración o efusión grande, como de palabras; p. 119
barren/yermo *adj.* que tiene poca o ninguna vegetación; árido; vacío; p. 753
benefactor/benefactor *s.* quien brinda ayuda financiera; p. 584
bewildered/perplejo *adj.* muy confundido; p. 118
bleak/sombrío *adj.* triste; deprimente; p. 164
boycott/boicot *s.* protesta organizada en la que los participantes se niegan a comprar, vender o usar un producto o servicio; p. 90
bravado/bravuconería *s.* falsa demostración de valentía; p. 353
brink/margen *s.* borde; a punto de; p. 282
brood/camada *s.* crías de un animal que nacen a un mismo tiempo; p. 799

C

casually/casualmente *adv.* de modo informal o imprevisto; p. 362
chaotic/caótico *adj.* confuso y desorganizado; muy desarreglado; p. 8
charismatic/carismático *adj.* con cualidades personales que inspiran lealtad y admiración; p. 283
claim/reclamar *v.* solicitar o exigir la posesión o el derecho de algo; p. 721

SPANISH GLOSSARY R125

clamor/algarabía *s.* ruido fuerte y continuo; griterío; p. 79
clan/clan *s.* grupo de familias descendientes de un antepasado común; p. 270
coincidence/coincidencia *s.* acontecimientos, circunstancias o ideas que ocurren al mismo tiempo por accidente; casualidad; p. 452
collaborator/colaborador *s.* alguien que trabaja o coopera con otro; p. 415
collective/colectivo *adj.* relativo a un grupo de personas o cosas; común; compartido; p. 677
colossal/colosal *adj.* extraordinaria o asombrosamente grande; p. 754
commencement/comienzo *s.* principio; ceremonia de graduación; p. 9
compact/compacto *adj.* que ocupa un espacio o área relativamente pequeño; macizo; p. 306
compensate/compensar *v.* dar algo a cambio; equilibrar en fuerza, peso o efecto; p. 808
competent/competente *adj.* que tiene suficiente habilidad para un fin concreto; capaz; p. 577
comply/acatar *v.* aceptar una solicitud; cumplir con algo; p. 86
comprehend/comprender *v.* captar mentalmente; entender por completo; p. 413
concede/conceder *v.* admitir que algo es cierto o apropiado; p. 221
conceive/concebir *v.* formarse una imagen o idea de algo; p. 577
condemn/condenar *v.* expresar total desacuerdo; criticar agudamente; p. 715
confront/confrontar *v.* encontrarse cara a cara; enfrentar; p. 416
consecutive/consecutivo *adj.* seguido uno de otro en orden y sin interrupción; p. 27
consequence/consecuencia *s.* importancia; significación; p. 464
consolation/consolación *s.* aliento; alivio; p. 373
conspicuously/conspicuamente *adv.* de modo que capta atención o notoriedad; p. 809
contemplate/contemplar *v.* prestar gran atención a algo; considerar cuidadosamente; p. 296
converge/converger *v.* reunirse en un lugar; p. 299
cordially/cordialmente *adv.* de modo cálido y amistoso; p. 752
correspond/cartearse *v.* comunicarse mediante cartas; p. 567
cower/encogerse *v.* agacharse, como cuando se siente miedo o vergüenza; p. 792
culprit/culpable *s.* el que ha cometido una ofensa; p. 405
cunning/astuto *adj.* vivo; engañoso; p. 390
cynically/cínicamente *adv.* de un modo que muestra duda o incertidumbre; dudosamente; p. 547

D

deception/engaño *s.* mentira o enredo; p. 125
decree/decreto *s.* regla, orden o decisión oficial; p. 743
defiant/desafiante *adj.* que se enfrenta atrevidamente a la autoridad o a un oponente; p. 511
degrade/degradar *v.* rebajar las características o la calidad; hacer menos puro; p. 828
delectable/deleitable *adj.* muy placentero o agradable, especialmente al gusto; delicioso; p. 389
demise/defunción *s.* muerte; fin; p. 828
depleted/disminuido *adj.* muy reducido en cantidad; p. 296
desolation/desolación *s.* tristeza; soledad; p. 689
despair/desesperanza *s.* pérdida total de la esperanza; desesperación; desconsuelo; p. 708
desperation/desesperación *s.* angustia causada por una gran necesidad o pérdida de la esperanza; p. 50
destine/destinar *v.* determinar con anticipación; asignar; p. 400
devastating/devastador *adj.* que causa gran dolor, daño o destrucción; abrumador; p. 434
devise/ingeniar *v.* pensar; inventar; planear; p. 384
diligently/diligentemente *adv.* de modo que muestra gran atención, cuidado y esfuerzo; p. 301

R126 SPANISH GLOSSARY

discern/discernir *v.* distinguir o reconocer; p. 492
discreetly/discretamente *adv.* de un modo sensato y cuidadoso; p. 155
discrepancy/discrepancia *s.* desacuerdo, como cuando dos hechos no concuerdan; p. 28
dismally/desconsoladamente *adv.* de un modo melancólico y triste; p. 567
dismay/consternación *s.* sentimiento de alarma o intranquilidad; p. 453
dispense/dispensar *v.* dar en porciones; distribuir; p. 385
distinct/distinto *adj.* diferente en calidad o tipo; p. 285
divulge/divulgar *v.* dar a conocer; emitir; p. 38
domestic/doméstico *adj.* relativo a los animales que conviven con los seres humanos; p. 828

E

eccentric/excéntrico *adj.* que no es común o normal en su comportamiento; peculiar; p. 578
ecology/ecología *s.* relación de los seres vivientes entre sí y con su medio ambiente; p. 309
ecstatic/extasiado *adj.* encantado; lleno de júbilo; p. 371
efficient/eficiente *adj.* que produce un efecto deseado con un mínimo de esfuerzo o gasto; p. 677
elaborate/elaborado *adj.* hecho con cuidado y esmero; detallado; complicado; p. 829
elicit/sacar *v.* revelar; p. 29
eloquent/elocuente *adj.* expresivo, efectivo y conmovedor, ya sea al hablar o escribir; p. 29
embrace/abrazar *v.* estrechar entre los brazos en demostración de amor o afecto; p. 275
emerge/emerger *v.* salir; surgir; brotar; p. 52
emphatic/enfático *adj.* que se expresa con intensidad o fuerza; p. 361
endeavor/empeño *s.* deseo intenso de hacer o lograr algo y tesón para alcanzarlo; p. 404
endure/soportar *v.* resistir o aguantar algo, como por ejemplo dolor, tensión u otra dificultad; p. 238
enticing/tentador *adj.* que ofrece placer o recompensa; p. 684
enviable/envidiable *adj.* suficientemente bueno como para que se desee mucho; ansiado; p. 685
envious/envidioso *adj.* que siente resentimiento por la suerte ajena o desearía algo que le pertenece a otra persona; p. 716
esteem/estima *s.* opinión favorable; aprecio; p. 29
etiquette/etiqueta *s.* normas de buenos modales y buena educación; p. 414
evacuate/evacuar *v.* despejar o limpiar un área; p. 307
evading/evasivo *adj.* que evita o escapa; p. 440
eventually/con el tiempo *adv.* al final; por último; p. 153
exasperation/exasperación *s.* rabia o gran irritación; p. 689
excavated/excavado *adj.* desenterrado o descubierto al cavar; p. 119
excess/exceso *adj.* más de lo usual o de lo necesario; p. 149
exotic/exótico *adj.* que tiene un atractivo extraño; foráneo; p. 8
explicit/explícito *adj.* expresado claramente; p. 524
exploit/explotar *v.* usar o aprovechar, a menudo de manera egoísta o injusta; p. 299
extricate/desembrollar *v.* sacar de un problema o dificultad; p. 404

F

faltering/titubeante *adj.* que muestra inseguridad, duda o vacilación; p. 199
fanciful/fantástico *adj.* con un diseño o construcción imaginativo y atrayente; p. 753
fancy/idear *v.* visualizar; imaginar; p. 795
fixed/fijo *adj.* asegurado; que no cambia; p. 708
flail/zarandear *v.* agitar o sacudir, especialmente de modo rápido o brusco; p. 440
fleetest/apresurado *adj.* el más rápido; el más veloz; p. 719

SPANISH GLOSSARY

SPANISH GLOSSARY

SPANISH GLOSSARY  R127

flinch/recular *v.* retroceder o echarse hacia atrás, ya sea por algo doloroso, peligroso o desagradable; p. 793

flourishing/floreciente *adj.* que crece o se desarrolla con éxito; que progresa; p. 354

formidable/formidable *adj.* que causa temor o asombro debido a su tamaño, fuerza o poder; p. 69

fortitude/fortaleza *s.* valor y tranquilidad ante el sufrimiento o el peligro; p. 401

frail/frágil *adj.* que carece de fuerza; débil; p. 463

frenzy/frenesí *s.* estado de intenso entusiasmo o enojo; p. 246

frustration/frustración *s.* desilusión o irritación por no poder hacer o alcanzar algo; p. 777

G

gait/andadura *s.* modo particular de caminar; p. 793

gaunt/esquelético *adj.* excesivamente flaco; p. 237

giddy/aturdido *adj.* mareado o atontado; p. 604

gnarled/retorcido *adj.* torcido y nudoso, como el tronco o las ramas de un árbol; p. 702

grim/severo *adj.* estricto; austero; inflexible; p. 237

grimace/hacer muecas *v.* hacer gestos con la cara, como cuando se siente dolor o desagrado; p. 79

grudging/de mala gana *adj.* que se da o permite sin querer o con resentimiento; p. 236

gruffly/rudamente *adv.* de modo severo o grosero; p. 239

H

habitual/habitual *adj.* que se hace por hábito o costumbre; p. 565

haggard/demacrado *adj.* de aspecto enfermizo o cansado debido a una pena, preocupación o enfermedad; p. 666

hallowed/sagrado *adj.* que se considera santificado o bendito; p. 717

hardy/resistente *adj.* capaz de soportar dificultades; fuerte y saludable; p. 155

hindrance/estorbo *s.* algo que impide el progreso o movimiento; obstáculo; p. 30

hostile/hostil *adj.* que siente o muestra antipatía o desagrado; p. 808

hover/revolotear *v.* permanecer en un sitio como si estuviera suspendido del aire; p. 745

humility/humildad *s.* cualidad de ser humilde o modesto; p. 744

hurtle/precipitarse *v.* moverse rápidamente, especialmente con fuerza o ansiedad; p. 664

I

illuminated/iluminado *adj.* encendido; p. 152

immobilize/inmovilizar *v.* impedir que se mueva; fijar en un sitio; p. 119

impetuous/impetuoso *adj.* que actúa con fuerza o violencia; p. 494

impose/imponer *v.* llevar a cabo legalmente; aplicar; p. 100

impoverished/empobrecido *adj.* reducido a la pobreza; arruinado; p. 370

improbable/improbable *adj.* que no es probable; incierto; p. 151

improvise/improvisar *v.* inventar, componer o hacer sin mucha preparación; p. 438

impulse/impulso *s.* fuerza interna que obliga a actuar sin pensar; p. 50

impunity/impunidad *s.* exención de castigo, perjuicio o consecuencias negativas; p. 187

incessantly/incesantemente *adv.* de modo constante; sin parar; p. 188

incomprehensible/incomprensible *adj.* que no se entiende; p. 191

inconvenience/estorbar *v.* causar molestias o dificultades a alguien; p. 93

incredulous/incrédulo *adj.* que no quiere o no puede creer en algo; p. 170

incriminate/incriminar *v.* demostrar culpabilidad; p. 515

indifferent/indiferente *adj.* que no demuestra interés, sentimiento o preocupación; p. 385

R128 SPANISH GLOSSARY

SPANISH GLOSSARY

indignity/oprobio *s.* ofensa contra el orgullo o dignidad; humillación; p. 94

indiscriminately/indiscriminadamente *adv.* de un modo que no presta atención a las diferencias; sin hacer distinciones; p. 300

inert/inerte *adj.* incapaz de moverse o actuar; p. 352

inevitably/inevitablemente *adv.* de un modo que no se puede evitar o prevenir; p. 7

infantile/infantil *adj.* como lo haría un niño; pueril; p. 413

infinite/infinito *adj.* sin fronteras; ilimitado; inmenso; p. 177

initial/inicial *adj.* al comienzo; lo primero; p. 7

initiative/iniciativa *s.* acción de dar el primer paso o iniciar una acción; p. 476

insistent/insistente *adj.* que exige atención a toda costa; p. 176

insolently/insolentemente *adv.* de modo atrevido o rudo; p. 544

instill/instilar *v.* verter gradualmente o poco a poco; p. 510

instinct/instinto *s.* modo natural de saber, comportarse o reaccionar que no se ha aprendido; p. 167

intact/intacto *adj.* que no se ha dañado; que está completo; p. 597

intellectual/intelectual *adj.* relativo a la habilidad mental o a la inteligencia; p. 608

intense/intenso *adj.* acentuado o potente; muy fuerte; p. 610

intently/resueltamente *adv.* de un modo firme y decidido; con concentración; p. 154

intimidated/intimidado *adj.* atemorizado o asustado; p. 510

intricate/intrincado *adj.* con muchos detalles complicados; p. 565

intrusion/intrusión *s.* interrupción repentina; p. 384

invalid/inválido *s.* alguien que está incapacitado debido a una enfermedad o herida; p. 165

invariably/invariablemente *adv.* sin excepción; p. 194

ironically/irónicamente *adv.* de un modo diferente al que se espera; p. 6

J

jeer/mofarse *v.* burlarse de algo o alguien de manera brusca y abierta; p. 684

jest/chancear *v.* hablar o actuar de manera jocosa; bromear; p. 596

jubilant/jubiloso *adj.* que está muy contento o emocionado; p. 721

juncture/coyuntura *s.* momento o punto crítico; p. 36

K

keen/agudo *adj.* muy sensible; despierto; p. 272

L

laden/cargado *adj.* abrumado; agobiado; atiborrado; p. 386

lapse/traspié *s.* caída o resbalón; p. 548

legitimate/legítimo *adj.* que sigue las reglas; legal; p. 517

lolling/oscilante *adj.* que cuelga flojamente; colgante; p. 246

loom/vislumbrarse *v.* que surge en la mente como algo temible; p. 222

lunge/arremeter *v.* moverse repentinamente hacia adelante; atacar; p. 794

M

malicious/malicioso *adj.* que tiene o muestra el deseo de perjudicar a alguien; p. 484

maneuver/maniobrar *v.* desempeñarse con destreza, por ejemplo para obtener un cargo o alcanzar una meta; p. 68

meek/apacible *adj.* paciente y tranquilo; gentil; p. 389

menace/amenaza *s.* peligro o riesgo; p. 68

merge/fusionar *v.* unir; agrupar; p. 7

SPANISH GLOSSARY R129

meticulously/meticulosamente *adv.* de un modo que muestra mucha atención a los detalles; p. 221

mobilize/movilizar *v.* prepararse, como para una guerra o emergencia; p. 91

moderately/moderadamente *adv.* ni mucho ni poco; dentro de los límites; p. 568

mortified/mortificado *adj.* muy avergonzado; p. 370

murky/lóbrego *adj.* obscuro o sombrío; p. 414

muse/meditar *v.* pensar o reflexionar; p. 190

muster/congregar *v.* buscar y reunir; agrupar; p. 453

N

naive/ingenuo *adj.* simple por naturaleza; infantil; p. 37

narrative/narración *s.* cuento; relato; p. 37

negotiate/negociar *v.* discutir con el fin de llegar a un acuerdo; p. 97

nimble/ágil *adj.* ligero y rápido de movimiento; p. 439

novelty/novedad *s.* algo nuevo e inusual; p. 595

nurture/criar *v.* cuidar y ayudar a crecer; p. 356

O

obligation/obligación *s.* sentido del deber; responsabilidad; p. 474

obligingly/servicialmente *adv.* que muestra el deseo de ser útil o servir; cortésmente; p. 244

obnoxious/odioso *adj.* molesto y desagradable; p. 69

obscure/confuso *adj.* difícil de entender; p. 350

obsessed/obsesionado *adj.* demasiado concentrado o dedicado a una sola emoción o idea; p. 118

obsession/obsesión *s.* emoción o idea fija que ocupa la mente; p. 414

obstinate/obstinado *adj.* terco; difícil de controlar o superar; p. 361

omen/presagio *s.* suceso visto como señal de buena o mala suerte; p. 774

ominous/ominoso *adj.* algo que anuncia temor o daño; p. 222

oppression/opresión *s.* acto de controlar o gobernar mediante el uso cruel e injusto de la fuerza o autoridad; p. 95

overtake/alcanzar *v.* dar alcance y rebasar; p. 708

P

painstaking/esmerado *adj.* que requiere de mucha atención o trabajo; p. 123

parched/reseco *adj.* que necesita humedad con urgencia; muy seco; p. 717

passive/pasivo *adj.* que no participa ni es activo; p. 166

perilous/peligroso *adj.* azaroso; arriesgado; p. 403

perpetual/perpetuo *adj.* constante; incesante; p. 437

perplexity/perplejidad *s.* duda o incertidumbre; aturdimiento; p. 194

perseverance/perseverancia *s.* voluntad para continuar haciendo algo aunque sea difícil; determinación; p. 187

persistently/persistentemente *adv.* repetidamente; una y otra vez; p. 70

perspective/perspectiva *s.* punto de vista; p. 370

pinnacle/pináculo *s.* cumbre o cima; punto más alto; p. 285

pious/piadoso *adj.* que tiene o finge devoción religiosa; p. 385

plummet/desplomarse *v.* caer verticalmente; derrumbarse; p. 296

podium/podio *s.* plataforma pequeña con una repisa para sostener los papeles de la persona que habla; p. 728

pompous/pomposo *adj.* que muestra exagerado orgullo o vanidad; p. 385

portly/corpulento *adj.* que tiene una figura robusta y respetable; p. 369

possessively/posesivamente *adv.* de un modo que muestra control o posesión sobre algo o alguien; p. 361

potion/poción *s.* bebida, especialmente referente a líquidos con poderes mágicos; p. 702

R130 SPANISH GLOSSARY

pounce/abalanzarse *v.* saltar o caer encima de repente con intención de atacar; embestir; p. 729
precise/preciso *adj.* muy claro o definido; exacto; p. 605
predator/depredador *s.* animal, tal como el león o el halcón, que mata a otros animales para alimentarse; p. 125
prejudice/prejuicio *s.* opinión o juicio desfavorable sin bases justas; p. 524
premonition/premonición *s.* sensación de que algo está por ocurrir; señal o advertencia; p. 400
primly/formalmente *adv.* de modo formal y apropiado; p. 548
principle/principio *s.* ley, verdad o creencia básica; norma de conducta personal; p. 354
proposition/proposición *s.* algo que se ofrece o propone; propuesta; oferta; p. 573
prosperous/próspero *adj.* que tiene riquezas o buena suerte; exitoso; acaudalado; p. 592
pursue/perseguir *v.* dar caza; p. 273

Q

quavering/trémulo *adj.* tembloroso; p. 484
quench/aplacar *v.* satisfacer o mitigar una necesidad o deseo; p. 739

R

rash/apresurado *adj.* hecho a la carrera sin pensarlo ni prepararlo; p. 738
raucous/estridente *adj.* sonido fuerte y áspero; p. 544
ravenous/hambriento *adj.* con mucha hambre; p. 390
rebuke/reproche *s.* expresión severa de crítica o desacuerdo; p. 578
reel/remolinar *v.* dar vueltas o parecer como si diera vueltas; girar; p. 739
reflective/reflexivo *adj.* que piensa seria y cuidadosamente; pensativo; p. 507
reformation/reforma *s.* cambio positivo; mejora; p. 547
regretfully/lamentablemente *adv.* de un modo que muestra pesar o desilusión; p. 774
reluctantly/a regañadientes *adv.* sin querer; de mala gana; p. 247
replenish/reabastecer *v.* dar nuevo suministro; volver a llenar; p. 687
resigned/resignado *adj.* que cede o acepta sin oponer resistencia; p. 88
resilient/flexible *adj.* capaz de volver a su forma o posición original después de que se dobla, estira o comprime; p. 465
resolute/resuelto *adj.* determinado; decidido; p. 348
resourceful/recursivo *adj.* hábil para enfrentarse a situaciones nuevas o difíciles; p. 727
retrieve/recobrar *v.* localizar y traer de nuevo; recuperar; p. 50
ritual/ritual *s.* forma establecida de hacer algo; ceremonia; p. 37
robust/robusto *adj.* fuerte y lleno de energía; p. 341

S

sanction/ratificar *v.* respaldar o aprobar algo; p. 168
sanctuary/santuario *s.* lugar de resguardo o protección; p. 170
saunter/deambular *v.* caminar tranquilamente; pasearse; p. 246
savor/saborear *v.* gozar de algo con gran placer; p. 239
scavenger/carroñero *s.* animal que se alimenta de cadáveres descompuestos de animales, como por ejemplo las hienas o los buitres; p. 125
scurry/escurrirse *v.* correr o moverse rápida o agitadamente; p. 774
scuttle/apresurarse *v.* caminar con pasos rápidos y cortos; p. 789
secretive/reservado *adj.* que no expresa sus pensamientos o emociones; p. 663
sedately/sosegadamente *adv.* de modo tranquilo y silencioso; calmadamente; p. 239

SPANISH GLOSSARY

SPANISH GLOSSARY R131

sensation/sensación *s.* motivo de asombro o gran interés; maravilla; p. 754

shrewd/sagaz *adj.* astuto, listo y práctico; p. 584

simultaneously/simultáneamente *adv.* al mismo tiempo; p. 546

sinewy/vigoroso *adj.* físicamente fuerte o poderoso; p. 274

singularity/singularidad *s.* cualidad de notorio o fuera de lo ordinario; peculiaridad; p. 191

skimpy/escaso *adj.* de poca cantidad o tamaño; incompleto; insuficiente o que apenas alcanza; p. 236

slither/deslizarse *v.* avanzar resbalándose como una serpiente; p. 246

sluggish/flojo *adj.* sin energía, vitalidad o ánimo; p. 828

soberly/severamente *adv.* muy seriamente; p. 476

solemnly/solemnemente *adv.* seriamente; p. 546

somberly/lúgubremente *adv.* de modo sombrío o tétrico; p. 490

sorcerer/hechicero *s.* persona que practica la magia con la ayuda de espíritus malignos; p. 701

spare/perdonar *v.* tener misericordia de alguien; desistir de hacerle daño; p. 274

spasm/espasmo *s.* tirantez repentina e incontrolable de un músculo; p. 243

specify/especificar *v.* establecer o describir en detalle; p. 7

speculation/especulación *s.* acto de formarse una opinión o conclusión basándose en suposiciones; p. 150

spendthrift/derrochador *s.* aquél que gasta dinero de modo generoso o que lo desperdicia; p. 150

spite/rencor *s.* deseo de herir o molestar a otra persona; p. 744

squander/malgastar *v.* gastar o usar de forma imprudente o innecesaria; p. 593

staccato/entrecortado *adj.* hecho de ruidos o movimientos cortos y agudos; p. 362

staple/principal *adj.* importante; prominente; p. 38

stark/absolutamente *adv.* completamente; rígida o severamente; p. 177

subsidize/subsidiar *v.* ayudar o respaldar con dinero; p. 301

subtle/sutil *adj.* que no es abierto o directo; que no es obvio; p. 178

succeed/seguir *v.* ocurrir después, ya sea en tiempo, orden o lugar; p. 666

sufficient/suficiente *adj.* adecuado; bastante; p. 677

sullen/hosco *adj.* malhumorado, retraído o sombrío; resentido; p. 45

surge/surgir *v.* elevarse de repente; moverse con agitación violenta, como el oleaje; p. 441

surly/arisco *adj.* rudo y de malhumor; hosco; p. 164

swagger/contonearse *v.* caminar o comportarse de modo altanero, brusco o demasiado orgulloso; p. 45

T

tact/tacto *s.* habilidad para manejar situaciones o personas sin causar desagrado ni herir sentimientos; p. 370

taunt/mofarse *v.* burlarse de manera despreciativa e insultante; p. 701

taut/tirante *adj.* tenso; estirado; p. 150

tentatively/tentativamente *adv.* de modo dudoso; inciertamente; posiblemente; p. 492

therapy/terapia *s.* tratamiento de una herida, enfermedad o desorden mental; p. 676

tumultuously/tumultosamente *adv.* de un modo agitado o confuso; p. 465

U

ultimately/por último *adv.* al final; finalmente; p. 369

uncanny/extraño *adj.* que produce asombro; misterioso; p. 404

uncommitted/imparcial *adj.* que no demuestra una opinión o punto de vista particular o definido; p. 474

R132 SPANISH GLOSSARY

undermine/socavar *v.* debilitar, desgastar o destruir lentamente; p. 298

undertake/emprender *v.* iniciar una labor o proyecto; intentar; acometer; p. 829

undulating/ondulante *adj.* que se mueve como las olas; fluctuante; p. 603

unique/único *adj.* muy particular; raro; singular; p. 309

unpalatable/desagradable *adj.* que no es agradable al gusto, la mente o los sentidos; inaceptable; p. 222

V

vaguely/vagamente *adv.* de un modo que no es claro, exacto o definido; p. 7

vainly/vanamente *adv.* sin éxito; ineficaz; p. 739

valiant/valiente *adj.* intrépido; valeroso; p. 797

validity/validez *s.* condición de ser apoyado por los hechos; verdad; p. 511

veer/virar *v.* girar o cambiar de dirección; p. 737

venture/aventurarse *v.* hacer algo a pesar de los posibles riesgos o peligros; p. 152

vigor/vigor *s.* fortaleza y energía; p. 246

vile/vil *adj.* muy malo; perverso; desagradable; p. 455

vital/vital *adj.* de enorme importancia; esencial; p. 464

W

wary/cauteloso *adj.* cuidadoso; prudente; p. 437

waver/tambalear *v.* perder el equilibrio; p. 738

wholeheartedly/sinceramente *adv.* francamente; con gusto; p. 68

wily/taimado *adj.* hipócrita; engañoso; p. 170

wince/recular *v.* retroceder ligeramente, como cuando se siente dolor; p. 48

withdrawn/retraído *adj.* tímido, reservado o poco sociable; p. 454

woe/aflicción *s.* gran tristeza o sufrimiento; gran preocupación o desdicha; p. 474

Index of Skills

References beginning with R refer to handbook pages.

Literary Concepts

R134 INDEX OF SKILLS

INDEX OF SKILLS

INDEX OF SKILLS

Reading and Thinking

R136 INDEX OF SKILLS

INDEX OF SKILLS

INDEX OF SKILLS R137

INDEX OF SKILLS

Grammar and Language

R138 INDEX OF SKILLS

INDEX OF SKILLS

INDEX OF SKILLS R139

INDEX OF SKILLS

R140 INDEX OF SKILLS

INDEX OF SKILLS

Vocabulary

Writing

INDEX OF SKILLS R141

INDEX OF SKILLS

R142 INDEX OF SKILLS

INDEX OF SKILLS

Listening, Speaking, and Viewing

INDEX OF SKILLS R143

INDEX OF SKILLS

Research and Study Skills

Media and Technology

R144 INDEX OF SKILLS

Interdisciplinary Studies

INDEX OF SKILLS

INDEX OF SKILLS R145

INDEX OF SKILLS

R146 INDEX OF SKILLS

Index of Authors and Titles

INDEX OF AUTHORS AND TITLES R147

INDEX OF AUTHORS AND TITLES

R148 INDEX OF AUTHORS AND TITLES

INDEX OF AUTHORS AND TITLES

INDEX OF AUTHORS AND TITLES R149

Index of Art and Artists

R150 INDEX OF ART AND ARTISTS

INDEX OF ART AND ARTISTS

INDEX OF ART AND ARTISTS R151

Acknowledgments

(Continued from page iv)

Literature

Theme 1

"Names/Nombres" Copyright © 1985 by Julia Alvarez. First published in *Nuestro,* March 1985. Reprinted by permission of Susan Bergholz Literary Services, New York. All rights reserved.

"One" from *When I Dance,* copyright © 1991, 1988 by James Berry, reprinted by permission of Harcourt Brace & Company.
"One" from *When I Dance,* copyright © 1991, 1988 by James Berry. Reprinted by permission of The Peters Fraser Dunlop Group Limited on behalf of the author.

"I'm Nobody! Who are you?" reprinted by permission of the publishers and the Trustees of Amherst College from *The Poems of Emily Dickinson,* Thomas H. Johnson, ed., Cambridge, Mass.: The Belknap Press of Harvard University Press, Copyright © 1951, 1955, 1979, 1983 by the President and Fellows of Harvard College.

"Face It" reprinted with the permission of Margaret K. McElderry Books, an imprint of Simon & Schuster Children's Publishing Division from *A Suitcase of Seaweed and Other Poems* by Janet S. Wong. Copyright © 1996 Janet S. Wong.

"Almost Ready" from *Slow Dance Heart Break Blues* by Arnold Adoff. Copyright © 1995 by Arnold Adoff. Reprinted by permission of Lothrop, Lee & Shepard Books, a division of HarperCollins Publishers.

"Heroes" by Erma Bombeck, reprinted by permission of the Aaron Priest Literary Agency, Inc.

Foreword by Ron Rapaport from *Covering the Bases* by Benedict Cosgrove, © 1997, published by Chronicle Books, San Francisco.

"Strong Men Weep" by Shirley Povitch. Copyright © 1939 The Washington Post. Reprinted with permission.

Reprinted with the permission of Simon & Schuster from *Wait Till Next Year* by Doris Kearns Goodwin. Copyright © 1997 by Blithedale Productions.

"Broken Chain" from *Baseball in April and Other Stories,* copyright © 1990 by Gary Soto, reprinted by permission of Harcourt Brace & Company.

"Without Commercials" from *Horses Make a Landscape Look More Beautiful,* copyright © 1984 by Alice Walker, reprinted by permission of Harcourt Brace & Company.

From *Barrio Boy* by Ernesto Galarza. Copyright © 1971 by the University of Notre Dame Press: Notre Dame, Indiana. Reprinted by permission of the publisher.

"Fish Cheeks" Copyright © 1987 by Amy Tan. First appeared in *Seventeen* Magazine. Reprinted by permission of Amy Tan and the Sandra Dijkstra Literary Agency.

From *Rosa Parks: My Story* by Rosa Parks with Jim Haskins. Copyright © 1992 by Rosa Parks. Used by permission of Dial Books for Young Readers, a division of Penguin Putnam Inc.

Theme 2

"Hollywood and the Pits," copyright © 1992 by Cherylene Lee. Reprinted by permission of Bret Adams Ltd.

"Time to Change" by Raymond Bloodworth, Chris Welch and Billy Meshel. Copyright © 1971 by Famous Music Corporation. Reprinted by permission.

"Growing Pains" from *Hey World, Here I Am!* Copyright © 1986 by Jean Little. Used by permission of HarperCollins Publishers.
"Growing Pains" from *Hey World, Here I Am!* by Jean Little used by permission of Kids Can Press Ltd., Toronto. Copyright © 1986 by Jean Little. Available in the U.S. from HarperCollins.

"NBA's Sister Act" by Steve Wulf. Copyright © 1997 Time Inc. Reprinted by permission.

Yusef Komunyakaa, "Slam, Dunk and Hook" from *Magic City,* © 1992 by Yusef Komunyakaa, Wesleyan University Press by permission of the University Press of New England.

"A Crush" from *A Couple of Kooks and Other Stories About Love* by Cynthia Rylant. Copyright © 1990 by Cynthia Rylant. Reprinted by permission of Orchard Books, New York.

"Last Cover" from *The Best Nature Stories of Paul Annixter.* Copyright © 1974 by Jane and Paul Annixter. Reprinted by permission of Lawrence Hill Books, an imprint of Chicago Review Press, Inc.

"Birthday Box" by Jane Yolen. Copyright © 1995 by Jane Yolen. First appeared in *Birthday Surprises: Ten Great Stories to Unwrap,* published by HarperCollins Publishers. Reprinted by permission of Curtis Brown, Ltd.

"There Is No Word for Goodbye" by Mary TallMountain. Copyright © 1994 TallMountain Estate, previously published in *Light on the Tent Wall,* LA:AISC, 1990. Reprinted by permission of the TallMountain Circle.

"old age sticks," copyright © 1958, 1986, 1991 by the Trustees for the E. E. Cummings Trust, from *Complete Poems: 1904–1962* by E. E. Cummings. Edited by George J. Firmage. Reprinted by permission of Liveright Publishing Corporation.

Theme 3

"New Directions" from *Wouldn't Take Nothing For My Journey Now* by Maya Angelou. Copyright © 1993 by Maya Angelou. Reprinted by permission of Random House, Inc.

"Too Soon a Woman" by Dorothy M. Johnson. Copyright © 1953 and renewed © 1981 by Dorothy M. Johnson. By permission of McIntosh and Otis, Inc.

"A Boy and His Dog" from *Paradise Café and Other Stories* by Martha Brooks. Copyright © 1988 by Martha Brooks. By permission of Little, Brown and Company.
"A Boy and His Dog" by Martha Brooks, from *Paradise Café and Other Stories* (Thistledown Press Ltd., 1988).

"The Women's 400 Meters" from *The Sidewalk Racer and Other Poems of Sports and Motion* by Lillian Morrison. Copyright © 1968, 1977 Lillian Morrison. Used by permission of Marian Reiner for the author.

ACKNOWLEDGMENTS

"A Poem (for langston hughes)", copyright © 1995 by Nikki Giovanni, from *The Selected Poems of Nikki Giovanni.*

"Dreams" from *Collected Poems* by Langston Hughes. Copyright © 1994 by the Estate of Langston Hughes. Reprinted by permission of Alfred A. Knopf, Inc., a division of Random House, Inc.

"Racing the Great Bear" from *Flying with the Eagle, Racing the Great Bear.* Copyright © 1993 by Joseph Bruchac. Reprinted by permission of Bridgewater Books, an imprint of Troll Communications, L.L.C.

"Blown Away" from *Beyond the Limits* by Stacy Allison. Copyright © 1993 by Stacy Allison and Peter Carlin. By permission of Little, Brown and Company.

"Fish Crisis" by J. Madeline Nash. Copyright © 1997 Time Inc. Reprinted by permission.

"Americans Continue to Worry About the Decline of the Oceans" a SeaWeb Ocean Update, February 1998. © 1998 SeaWeb.

"There aren't many of us left . . ." (cartoon). The *Washington Post* National Weekly Edition, December 8, 1997. Reprinted by permission of Scott Bateman.

"Big Winds and Big Damage" from *Hurricanes* by Patricia Lauber. Copyright © 1996 by Patricia Lauber. Reprinted by permission of Scholastic, Inc.

Theme 4

"Bums in the Attic" from *The House on Mango Street.* Copyright © 1984 by Sandra Cisneros. Published by Vintage Books, a division of Random House, Inc., and in hardcover by Alfred A. Knopf, a division of Random House, Inc. Reprinted by permission of Susan Bergholz Literary Services, New York. All rights reserved.

"En un Barrio de Los Angeles/In a Neighborhood in Los Angeles" from *Body in Flames: Cuerpo en Llamas* by Francisco Alarcon, © 1990, published by Chronicle Books, San Francisco.

"The Courage That My Mother Had" by Edna St. Vincent Millay. From *Collected Poems,* HarperCollins. Copyright © 1954, 1982 by Norma Millay Ellis. All rights reserved. Used by permission of Elizabeth Barnett, literary executor.

"Mother to Son" from *Collected Poems* by Langston Hughes. Copyright © 1994 by the Estate of Langston Hughes. Reprinted by permission of Alfred A. Knopf, Inc., a divison of Random House, Inc.

"Kids from Chicago's Cabrini Green Learn Urban Farming in Arkansas" by Paisley Dodds. *Associated Press,* August 19, 1997. Reprinted by permission of Associated Press.

"Home" from the novel *Maud Martha* by Gwendolyn Brooks. Copyright © 1991 by Gwendolyn Brooks Blakely. Published by Third World Press, Chicago. Reprinted by permission of The Estate of Gwendolyn Brooks.

"the 1st" copyright © 1969 by Lucille Clifton. First appeared in *Good Times,* published by Random House. Reprinted by permission of Curtis Brown, Ltd.

"The Teacher Who Changed My Life" by Nicholas Gage. Reprinted with permission of the author and *Parade,* copyright © 1989.

"How I Learned English" by Gregory Djanikian, from *Falling Deeply into America,* Carnegie-Mellon University Press, 1989. Reprinted by permission of Gregory Djanikian.

"Oh Broom, Get to Work" reprinted with the permission of Simon & Schuster Books for Young Readers, an imprint of Simon & Schuster Children's Publishing Division from *The Invisible Thread* by Yoshiko Uchida. Copyright © 1991 by Yoshiko Uchida.

"The Night the Bed Fell," copyright © 1933 by James Thurber. Copyright © renewed 1961 by Hellen Thurber and Rosemary A. Thurber. Reprinted by arrangement with Rosemary A. Thurber and the Barbara Hogenson Agency.

"Dog Diaries" from *What the Dogs Have Taught Me* by Merrill Markoe. Copyright © 1992 by Merrill Markoe. Used by permission of Viking Penguin, a division of Penguin Putnam Inc.

Theme 5

"Amigo Brothers" from *Stories from the Barrio* by Piri Thomas. Copyright © 1978 by Piri Thomas. Reprinted by permission of the author.

"The Face of Venus" from *Views of the Solar System.* Copyright © Calvin J. Hamilton. Reprinted by permission.

"All Summer in a Day" by Ray Bradbury. Reprinted by permission of Don Congdon Associates, Inc. Copyright © 1954, renewed 1982 by Ray Bradbury.

"The Bird Like No Other" from *The Richer, The Poorer,* by Dorothy West. Copyright © 1995 by Dorothy West. Used by permission of Doubleday, a division of Random House, Inc.

"The Old Demon" by Pearl S. Buck. Reprinted by permission of Harold Ober Associates Inc. Copyright © 1939 by Pearl S. Buck. Copyright renewed 1966 by Pearl S. Buck.

"The Boy and His Grandfather" by Rudolfo Anaya, from *Cuentos: Tales from the Hispanic Southwest.* Copyright © 1980 by the Museum of New Mexico Press.

"The Monsters Are Due On Maple Street" by Rod Serling. Reprinted by permission of The Rod Serling Trust. All rights reserved. © 1960 Rod Serling; © 1988 by Carolyn Serling, Jodi Serling and Anne Serling.

Theme 6

"Charles" from *The Lottery* by Shirley Jackson. Copyright © 1948, 1949 by Shirley Jackson, and copyright renewed © 1976 by Laurence Hyman, Barry Hyman, Mrs. Sarah Webster and Mrs. Joanne Schnurer. Reprinted by permission of Farrar, Straus & Giroux, Inc.

"No News" retold by Connie Regan-Blake and Barbara Freeman. Reprinted by permission of Connie Regan-Blake and Folktellers.

"Who's on First?" by Bud Abbott and Lou Costello reprinted by permission of TCA Television Corp., The Estate of Bud Abbott Jr. and Hi Neighbor.

"The Million-Pound Bank Note" reprinted by permission from *Radio Plays for Young People,* by Walter Hackett. Copyright © 1950 by Walter Hackett. Publishers: Plays, Inc., Boston, MA.

"The Force of Luck" by Rudolfo A. Anaya, from *Cuentos.* Copyright © 1980 by the Museum of New Mexico Press. Reprinted by permission.

"Beware of Dog" from *Over to You,* copyright © 1946 by Roald Dahl. Reprinted by permission of the Estate of Roald Dahl and the Watkins/Loomis Agency.

ACKNOWLEDGMENTS R153

ACKNOWLEDGMENTS

Excerpted from *Martha Black,* edited by Flo Whyard, Copyright © 1976, 1980, 1986 and 1988. Reprinted with permission of Alaska Northwest Books™.

Theme 7

Excerpt from "Seizure-Alert Dog Is Girl's Lifeline" by Sarah Christie, from *Dog Fancy,* June 1997. Reprinted by permission of the author.

"Lob's Girl" from *A Whisper in the Night* by Joan Aiken. Copyright © 1984 by Joan Aiken. Used by permission of Bantam Doubleday Dell Books for Young Readers, a division of Random House, Inc. "Lob's Girl," copyright © Joan Aiken Enterprises Ltd., 1984. Reprinted by permission of A. M. Heath.

"Key Item" from *Buy Jupiter and Other Stories* by Isaac Asimov. Copyright © 1975 by Isaac Asimov. Used by permission of Doubleday, a division of Random House, Inc.

"The Smallest Dragonboy" by Anne McCaffrey. Reprinted by permission of Checkerboard Press.

"Aunty Misery: A Folktale from Puerto Rico" by Judith Ortiz Cofer. Reprinted by permission of the author.

"Strawberries," a traditional Cherokee story retold by Gayle Ross. Reprinted by permission of the author.

"Atalanta's Race" from *Men and Gods* by Rex Warner. Copyright © 1950 by MacGibbon & Kee. Reprinted by permission of Michigan State University Press.

"Atalanta" by Betty Miles. Copyright © 1973 Free To Be Foundation, Inc.

Cat and Rat: The Legend of the Chinese Zodiac by Ed Young. Copyright © 1995 by Ed Young. Reprinted by permission of Henry Holt and Company, Inc.

"Prometheus" from *Heroes, Gods and Monsters of Greek Myths* by Bernard Evslin. Copyright © 1966, 1977 by Scholastic, Inc. Reprinted by permission of Scholastic, Inc.

"First Battle Interlude from Paul Bunyan" from *The Complete Works of W. H. Auden: Libretti.* Reprinted by permission of Faber & Faber.

The Bunyans by Audrey Wood, illustrated by David Shannon. Text copyright © 1996 by Audrey Wood, illustrations copyright © 1996 by David Shannon. All rights reserved. Reprinted by permission of Scholastic, Inc. Published by The Blue Sky Press, an imprint of Scholastic, Inc.

"Brer Rabbit and Brer Lion" from *The Tales of Uncle Remus* by Julius Lester. Copyright © 1987 by Julius Lester. Used by permission of Dial Books for Young Readers, a division of Penguin Putnam Inc.

Theme 8

"We Are All One" from *The Rainbow People* by Laurence Yep. Copyright © 1989 by Laurence Yep. Used by permission of HarperCollins Publishers.

"See Robby Run" by Edie Scher. Reprinted by permission of Runner's World Magazine. Copyrighted 1998, Rodale Press, Inc., all rights reserved.

"Birdfoot's Grampa" from *Entering Onondaga,* copyright © 1975 by Joseph Bruchac. Reprinted by permission of Barbara S. Kouts.

"The Jungle Book" review by David Ansen, from *Newsweek,* January 16, 1995. Copyright © 1995 Newsweek, Inc. All rights reserved. Reprinted by permission.

"Uncle Tony's Goat" Copyright © 1981 by Leslie Marmon Silko. Reprinted from *Storyteller* by Leslie Marmon Silko, published by Seaver Books, New York, New York.

"Loo-Wit" copyright © 1985 by Wendy Rose. Reprinted by permission of West End Press.

"The Flower-Fed Buffaloes," from *Going to the Stars* by Vachel Lindsay. Copyright 1926 by D. Appleton & Co., renewed 1954 by Elizabeth C. Lindsay. A Hawthorn Book. Used by permission of Dutton's Children's Books, a division of Penguin Putnam Inc.

"Turkeys" from B. White, *Mama Makes Up Her Mind,* © 1993 by Bailey White. Reprinted by permission of Addison-Wesley Longman, Inc.

Reprinted with the permission of Atheneum Books for Young Readers, an imprint of Simon & Schuster Children's Publishing division from *Haiku-Vision* by Ann Atwood. Copyright © 1977 Ann Atwood.

"Bamboo Grove" from *An Introduction to Haiku* by Harold G. Henderson. Copyright © 1958 by Harold G. Henderson. Used by permission of Doubleday, a division of Random House, Inc.

"Glory, Glory," from *26 Ways of Looking at a Black Man and Other Poems* by Raymond R. Patterson. Copyright © 1969 by Raymond R. Patterson. Reprinted by permission of the author.

"T-Shirt" from *O Sliver of Liver* by Myra Cohn Livingston. Copyright © 1979 by Myra Cohn Livingston. Used by permission of Marian Reiner.

"There was a young fellow of ealing . . ." from *Peter Pauper's Limerick Book.* Reprinted by permission of Peter Pauper Press, Inc.

Maps

Ortelius Design, Inc.

Photography

Abbreviation key: **AH**=Aaron Haupt Photography; **AR**=Art Resource, New York; **BAL**=Bridgeman Art Library, London/New York; **CB**=Corbis/Bettmann; **CI**=Christie's Images; **LPBC/AH**=book provided by Little Professor Book Company. Photo by AH; **LOC**=Library of Congress; **PR**=Photo Researchers; **SIS**=Stock Illustration Source; **SS**=SuperStock; **TSI**=Tony Stone Images; **TSM**=The Stock Market.

Cover (guitar)Doug Martin, (painting)*The Guitar Player,* 1897. Pierre Auguste Renoir. Oil on canvas. Musée des Beaux Arts, Lyon, France/SS; **vii** (t to b)Bob Fitch/Black Star, Millport Conservancy, SS, SS, Bill Angresano, Photofest, Scholastic, Inc., Jeff & Alexa Henry/Peter Arnold, Inc.; **viii** Printed by permission of the Norman Rockwell Family Trust ©1954 the Norman Rockwell Family; **ix** (l)Rich Brommer, (r)The Grand Design/SS; **x** (t)Amanita Pictures, (b)Stuart Kingston Gallery; **xi** Annie Leibovitz/Contact Press Images; **xii** Reproduced by permission of the IDB; **xiii** (t)Ken Chernus/FPG, (b)Glencoe photo; **xiv** Larry Hamill; **xv** Mark Burnett; **xvi** (t)Jason Hawkes/TSI, (b)Mark Burnett; **xvii** (l)Imperial War Museum, (r)Kactus Foto, Santiago, Chile/SS; **xviii** Dan Bosler/TSI; **xix** Wally Findlay Galleries, New York/SS; **xx** Jeff Lynch/Mendola Ltd./TSM; **xxi** (t)The Newark Museum/AR, (b)UPI/CB; **xxii** (l)Jade Albert/FPG, (r)Sid and Diana Avery Trust; **xxiii** John Lund/TSI; **1** Printed by permission of the Norman Rockwell Family Trust ©1954 the Norman Rockwell Family; **2** Drawing by Chas. Addams, ©1977 The New Yorker Magazine, Inc.; **3** (t)Lisa Quinones/Black Star, (cl)Al Rendon/CB, (cr)Eric Lars/Black Star, (b)Fred Ward/

R154 ACKNOWLEDGMENTS

ACKNOWLEDGMENTS

Black Star; **4** Theo Westernberger/Gamma Liaison; **5** Schalkwijk/AR; **6** Chuck Pefley/TSI; **7** Robert Van Der Hilst/TSI; **8** CI; **9, 10** Mark Burnett; **13** (tl)courtesy Harper Collins, (r)Trustees of Amherst College, (bl)CB; **14–15** Diana Ong/SS; **16** Joseph T. Collins/PR; **18** (t)courtesy Simon & Schuster, (b)Virginia Hamilton Adoff; **19** Mark Burnett; **20** SS; **22** AR; **24** AP/Wide World; **25** (l)courtesy Benedict Cosgrove, (r)courtesy *The Washington Post;* **26** UPI/CB; **27** FPG; **28** Photo File; **31** UPI/CB; **32, 33** Mark Burnett; **34** (l)AP Photo/Steve Herbert, (r)FPG; **35** Mark Burnett; **36** CB; **37** UPI/CB; **38, 39** FPG; **40** CB; **41, 42** Photofest; **43** (l)courtesy Gary Soto, (r)Walter Bibikow/FPG; **44** Mark Gottlieb/FPG; **46** Richard Laird/FPG; **47** Alan & Sandy Carey/PR; **49** Mark Burnett; **51** Phoebe Beasley; **53** John D. Wibberley; **54** Mark Gottlieb/FPG; **58** (t)Adam Scull/Globe Photos, (b)Chris Brown/Stock Boston; **64** AH; **66** Courtesy Stanford University News Service; **67** CI; **68** FPG; **69** City of Sacramento Archives and Museum Collection Center; **70** Rich Brommer; **74** City of Sacramento Archives and Museum Collection Center; **76** (l)Andrea Renault/Globe Photos, (r)FoodPix; **77** Mark Burnett; **78** Courtesy Dr. Michael Sullivan, St. Catherine's College, Oxford, England; **80** Flip Nicklin/Minden Pictures; **82** (t)E.R. Degginger/PR, (cl)Geoff Butler, (cr)courtesy John Scott & Son Haggis, Fife, Scotland, (b)Kelvin Aitken/Peter Arnold, Inc.; **84** Bob Fitch/Black Star; **85** Brian Lanker; **86** The publisher wishes to thank The National Association for the Advancement of Colored People for authorizing the use of this photograph; **88** AP/Wide World Photos; **92, 95** Dan Weiner, courtesy Sandra Weiner; **98, 99** AP/Wide World Photos; **100** National Museum of American Art, Washington DC/AR; **101** AP/Wide World Photos; **102** CB; **105** Mark Burnett; **109** (br)Mark Burnett, (others)AH; **112–113** The Grand Design/SS; **115** (t)Ray Ellis/PR, (b)Rafael Macia/PR; **116, 120** Courtesy Cherylene Lee; **117** Ken Biggs/TSI; **119** Tom McHugh/PR; **123** Greg Vaughn/Tom Stack & Associates; **124,126** Natural History Museum of Los Angeles County/Tom McHugh/PR; **127, 130** Tom McHugh/PR; **128** Amanita Pictures; **131** Photofest; **132** (l)courtesy Penguin Books, Toronto, (r)Rick Rusing/TSI; **135** Jeffrey Myers/FPG; **136** DUOMO/Darren Carroll; **137** (l)Tony Getsug, (r)David Madison/TSI; **139** Carl Schneider/Gamma Liaison; **140** Glencoe photo; **146–147** Mark Burnett; **148** (l)courtesy Blue Sky Press, (r)LPI/FPG; **149** Mark Burnett; **150** Hulton Getty/TSI; **152, 153** Mark Burnett; **154** O.K. Harris Works of Art, New York; **157** Derek Fell; **158** Amanita Pictures; **163** Gene Frazier; **165** Museum of American Art, Philadelphia; **168** John W. Warden/SS; **172** Alvin E. Staffan; **174** (t)Jason Stemple, (bl)University of Fairbanks AK, (br)Amanita Pictures; **175–176** Mark Steinmetz; **178** SS; **179** John Bigelow Taylor, New York/Thaw Collection, Fenimore House Museum, Cooperstown NY; **180** Geoff Butler; **184** FPG; **185** The Millport Conservancy; **186** Glencoe photo; **188** The Millport Conservancy; **190** Stuart Kingston Gallery; **193, 195** The Millport Conservancy; **196** National Gallery of Art, Washington DC; **201, 202, 203** Stuart Kingston Gallery; **204** CB; **205** SS; **207** Stuart Kingston Gallery; **213** AH; **216–217** Annie Leibovitz/Contact Press Images; **219** Ray Pfortner/Peter Arnold, Inc.; **220** Thomas Lau/Outline; **221** James Selkin/Gamma Liaison; **222** Mark Burnett; **223** Private collection/Christian Pierre/SS; **226** (t)*Harper's Weekly*/CB, (c)CI, (b)courtesy Pinkie Gardner; **229** The Metropolitan Museum of Art, New York; **231** Elizabeth Barakah Hodges/SS; **232** Royal Albert Memorial Museum, Exeter, England/BAL/SS; **234** Mansfield Library Archives, University of MT, Missoula; **235** The Brooklyn Museum: Polhemus Fund; **236** Bob Daemmrich/The Image Works; **240** Ed Reschke/Peter Arnold, Inc.; **242** (l)courtesy Martha Brooks, (r)Kent Knudson/Stock Boston; **243** Glencoe photo; **245** Oldham Art Gallery, Manchester, England/BAL/SS; **249** (t)Ed Reschke/Peter Arnold, Inc., (b)Mark Burnett; **252–253** Spencer Rowell/FPG; **254** Blair Seitz/PR; **255** Jim Cummins/FPG; **256** Glencoe photo; **258** (t)Barron Claiborne/Outline, (bl)LOC/Corbis, (br)Sherry Suris/PR; **259** Glencoe photo; **261** National Portrait Gallery, Smithsonian Institution/AR; **262** William J. Weber; **263** Doug Martin; **266** (t)James Firmiss, *The Wonderful Skunk & Opossum Web Site v. 4,* (b)David M. Dennis; **267** (l)courtesy Joseph Bruchac, (r)courtesy the British Museum; **268–269** CI; **270** Courtesy The NY State Museum, Albany; **271** Newberry Library, Chicago/SS; **272, 273, 274** CI; **275** Catherine Gehm; **276** Glencoe photo; **279** (tr)Larry Moore/SIS, (others)Glencoe photo; **280** Courtesy Stacy Allison; **281** Nova Online/Gamma Liaison; **282** Tom McHugh/PR; **284, 286** Nova Online/Gamma Liaison; **292–293** Jeff Greenberg/PR; **294** Time, Inc.; **295** Matt Johnson/Alaska Stock; **297** Vanessa Vick/PR; **298** ©1997 Time, Inc. Reprinted by permission; **301** Rondi/Tani Church/PR; **302** Glencoe photo; **303** Richard Ellis/PR; **304** Scott Bateman; **305** Courtesy Scholastic, Inc.; **307** Len Kaufman/Black Star; **308** Ben Van Hook/Black Star; **310** Larry Lipsky/Tom Stack & Associates; **311** Steven Jaffe/Reuters/CB; **312** Bill Hoyt/Panoramic Images; **321** (b)Mark Burnett; (others)AH; **324–325** Reproduced by permission of the IDB; **326** The Cartoon Bank; **328** (t)M. Toussaint/Gamma Liaison, (b)LPBC/AH; **329** Vic Huber/Corbis Los Angeles; **332** (tl br)SS, (tr)Hans Blohm/Masterfile, (bl)Chris Salvo/FPG, (inset)AH; **333** Annie Valva/Chronicle Books; **334–335** Comstock; **340** LOC/Corbis; **341** SS; **342** Armistad Research Center, Tulane University; **343** Bob Daemmrich/TSI; **345** Danny Johnston/AP/Wide World Photos; **346** Babs H. Deal/AP/Wide World Photos; **347** Glencoe photo; **348** SS; **348–356** (grass) Glencoe photo; **349** Private Collection. Courtesy Tibor de Nagy Gallery, New York; **352** Photograph ©1997 The Museum of Modern Art, New York. Inter-American Fund; **357** Alan & Linda Detrick/PR; **358** Renato Rotolo/Gamma Liaison; **360** (t)UPI/CB, (bl)Gerardo Somoza/Outline, (br)Butler Institute of American Art, Youngstown OH; **361** Fisk University Art Gallery; **363** Hunter Museum of American Art, Chattanooga TN; **367** Allen/Gamma Liaison; **368** Eddie Adams; **371, 372** Courtesy Nicholas Gage; **373** J. Noelker/The Image Works; **374** Courtesy Nicholas Gage; **376** (t)Tommy Leonardi, (b)Print Collection, Miriam and Ira D. Wallach Division of Arts, Prints and Photographs. The New York Public Library. Astor, Lennox and Tilden Foundation; **377** Glencoe photo; **378** Ken Chernus/FPG; **379** John Goodman/FPG; **380** (t)courtesy Nicholas Gage, (b)Glencoe photo; **382** (l)courtesy McMillan, (r)Mark Burnett; **383** Courtesy Mr. and Mrs. Jay Peter Moffat; **384** Glencoe photo; **386** Mark Burnett; **387** Tomomi Saito/Dunq/PR; **388, 389** From *Ananse's Feast: An Ashanti Tale* by Tolowa M. Mollel. Jacket illustration ©1997 by Andrew Glass. Reprinted by permission of Clarion Books/Houghton Mifflin Company. All rights reserved; **390** Bonnie Sue/PR; **391** Mark Burnett; **398** (l)CB, (r)©1933 by James Thurber. ©Renewed 1960 by James Thurber. Reprinted by arrangement with Rosemary A. Thurber and the Barbara Hogenson Agency; **401, 402** ©1933 by James Thurber. ©Renewed 1960 by James Thurber. Reprinted by arrangement with Rosemary A. Thurber and the Barbara Hogenson Agency; **403** Carey/The Image Works; **405, 407** ©1933 by James Thurber. ©Renewed 1960 by James Thurber. Reprinted by arrangement with Rosemary A. Thurber and the Barbara Hogenson Agency; **410** Michael Ferguson/Globe Photos; **411** Mark Steinmetz; **412** Courtesy Rodrigue Studio; **414** Sandy Skoglund/SS; **416** Mark Steinmetz; **418** Stephanie Rausser/FPG; **421** Sid and Diana Avery Trust; **425** (br)Mark Burnett, (others)AH; **428–429** Larry Hamill; **431** Glencoe photo; **432** Courtesy Piri Thomas; **433** Spencer/Jones/FPG; **435** Bill Angresano; **439** Fratelli Alinari/SS; **442** CI; **444** (l)Photographs and Prints Division, Schomburg Center for Research in Black Culture. The New York Public Library. Astor, Lenox and Tilden Foundations, (r)Milwaukee Art Museum; **445** M. Angelo/Corbis Los Angeles; **447** Mark Burnett; **448** (t)Arthur Tilley/FPG, (b)Jade Albert/FPG; **449** (t)Larry Moore/SIS, (b)Rosanne Olson/TSI; **450** Bob Daemmrich/The Image Works; **451** Mark Burnett; **453** Walter H. Hodge/Peter Arnold, Inc.; **454** Gerald Peters Gallery, Sante Fe NM; **456** Mark Burnett; **457** Bob Daemmrich/Stock Boston; **459** Jack Zehrt/FPG; **460** Satelight/Gamma Liaison; **461** Jeffrey Myers/FPG; **462–463** AR; **464** SS; **465** Glencoe photo; **466** Jeffrey Myers/FPG; **467** Freeman Patterson/Masterfile; **468** Glencoe photo; **471** (t)FPG, (b)Vincent Frye; **473, 475** SS; **477** Stella Jones Gallery, New Orleans LA; **478** Louise Freshman Brown/SS; **482** (t)Wide World Photo, (b)Miriam Berkley; **483** National Gallery of Canada; **486** Courtesy Dr. Michael Sullivan, St. Catherine's College, Oxford, England; **488–489** The Metropolitan Museum of Art, New York.

ACKNOWLEDGMENTS R155

ACKNOWLEDGMENTS

Photograph by Malcolm Varon; **492** Private collection/Bonnie Kwan Huo/SS; **494** Mark Burnett; **495** Bjorn Bolstad/Peter Arnold, Inc.; **496** Jim Cummins/FPG; **497** AP/Wide World Photos; **500** Masterfile; **502–503** Geoff Butler; **504** UPI/CB; **507** Fine Arts Museums of San Francisco; **508** FPG; **513** E.T. Archive, London/SS; **514–515** Yale University Art Gallery; **520** Peter Jacobs, New York; **525** Photofest; **526** FPG; **528** CBS Photo Archive; **530** Bob Fitch/Black Star; **531** (t)courtesy Stacy Allison, (b)CB; **535** (br)Lawrence Migdale, (others)AH; **538–539** Jason Hawkes/TSI; **540** Photofest; **543** (t)Lawrence J. Hyman, courtesy Bantam Books, (bl)courtesy Barbara Freeman, (br)Laura Dwight/Peter Arnold, Inc.; **544** Amanita Pictures; **545** Hulton Getty/TSI; **548–549** From the Permanent Collection of the Museum of American Folk Art; **551** Julianne Fringado, age 5; **554** (t)CB, (b)Culver Pictures; **555** CB; **557** Mark Burnett; **560** Photofest/Jagarts; **564** CB; **565** Doug Martin; **566–567** San Diego Museum of Art; **569** Whitney Museum of American Art, New York; **571** (t)Larry Moore/SIS, (b)Lawrence Migdale; **572** (l)AP/Wide World Photos, (r)Photofest; **578** CI; **585** Christopher Wood Gallery, London/BAL/SS; **588** Photofest/Jagarts; **590** (l)Miriam Berkley, (r)Kathy Plunkett Versluys/FPG; **591, 594** CI/SS; **598** Schalkwijk/AR; **601** G. Randall/FPG, (inset)Christian Michaels/FPG; **602** (l)Horst Tappe/Camera Press London, (r)Salamander Picture Library; **607** A.K.G. Berlin/SS; **609** Imperial War Museum; **610** Geoff Butler; **611** CI; **612** Charly Herscovici/AR; **614** Salamander Picture Library; **616** The Newark Museum/AR; **618–619** Lawrence Migdale; **620** (t)AP/Wide World Photos, (b)Farrell Grehan/FPG; **621** Hermann Eisenheiss/PR; **623** James Wyeth; **626** Richard Pasley/Viesti Associates; **628** (t)FPG, (b)CB; **629** The Metropolitan Museum of Art, New York. Photograph by Geoffrey Clements; **630** J.H. Robinson/PR; **631** Peter Jacobs, New York; **632** National Museum of American Art, Washington DC/AR; **634** Culver Pictures; **635** UPI/CB; **636–637** Courtesy Rockwell Kent Legacies; **638–640** NSPI/Mauritius/Nawrocki; **641** SS; **642** Collection of The Museum of African American Art, Los Angeles CA. Palmer C. Hayden Collection, Gift of Marian A. Hayden; **649** (br)Mark Burnett, (others)AH; **652–635** Kactus Foto, Santiago, Chile/SS; **654** The New Yorker Magazine, Inc.; **655** Icon Images; **656, 657** Mark Hertzberg/*Racine Journal Times;* **658** Rod Delroy; **659** CI; **660** Franz Gorski/Peter Arnold, Inc.; **663** Onne Van Der Wal/Stock Newport; **665** Peter Henschel/FPG; **669** John Chard/TSI; **670** Lawrence Migdale/PR; **674** (l)Peter C. Jones/Alex Gotfryd/CB, (r)Jonathan Elderfield/Gamma Liaison; **678** Dan Piraro/Universal Press Syndicate; **679** Paul Shambroom/PR; **680** Glencoe photo; **681** Alex Bartel/Science Photo Library/PR; **682** (l)Tara Heinemann/Camera Press London, (r)Werner Forman/AR; **686** Roy Calne/SS; **693, 695** CI; **696** Private collection/Greg Larson/SS; **698** Roy Calne/SS; **699** Mark Burnett; **700** Miriam Berkley; **701** Glencoe photo; **703** Charles Benes/FPG; **704** Schalkwijk/AR; **706** (l)courtesy Gayle Ross, (r)Newberry Library, SS; **707** (t)Michael P. Gadomski/PR, (b)Miyoko Komine/Photonica; **709** (t)G. Peter Jemison, (b)Miyoko Komine/Photonica; **710** Larry Hamill; **713** Glencoe photo; **714** Melanie Carr/The Viesti Collection; **715** Gianni Dagli/CB; **716, 718–719** Dan Bosler/TSI; **720** T. Zimmerman/FPG; **722** Amanita Pictures; **723** Arthur Tilley/FPG; **725** (l)courtesy Henry Holt and Co., Inc., (r)Dennis Cox/FPG; **726 through 731** Reprinted by permission of Henry Holt and Co., Inc.; **733** Vanessa Vick/PR; **736** Courtesy Radcliffe College Archives; **737** (t)Glencoe photo, (r)Art Montes de Oca/FPG; **738** Giradon/AR; **740** S. Brookens/TSM; **742** (l)courtesy Mrs. Bernard Evslin, (r)Museo Gregoriano Etrusco Vaticano/AR; **743** Japack/Corbis Los Angeles; **744** (t)Gianni Dagli Oriti/Corbis, (b)Japack/Corbis Los Angeles; **745** Japack/Corbis Los Angeles; **747** Giradon/AR; **749** (t)courtesy Audrey Wood, (b)Milan Sabatini/courtesy Julius Lester; **750 through 753** Reprinted by permission of Scholastic, Inc.; **755, 756** Private collection/Christian Pierre/SS; **758** ©Walt Disney Productions; **761** Mark Burnett; **765** (br)Mark Burnett, (others)AH; **768** Wally Findlay Galleries, New York/SS; **770** The Cartoon Bank; **772** (l)courtesy Scholastic, Inc., (r)CB; **773** Scott Camazine/PR; **774** Larry West/FPG; **775** C. Allan Morgan/Peter Arnold, Inc.; **776** Free Library, Philadelphia, PA/A.K.G., Berlin/SS; **778** CI; **782** (t)courtesy Joseph Bruchac, (bl)FPG, (br)Jeff Lynch/Mendola, Ltd./TSM; **783** Michael P. Gadomski/PR; **784** Richard Price/FPG; **786** John Cancalosi/Peter Arnold, Inc.; **787** Photofest; **788** (l)FPG, (r)Len Rue/Stock Boston; **789** Keith H. Murakham/Tom Stack & Associates; **790** Stafford Cliff and Suzanne Slesin; **791** Victoria & Albert Museum, London/AR; **792** B.N.S. Deo–TCL/Masterfile; **797** Nigel Dennis/PR; **798** Telegraph Colour Library/FPG; **801** R. Dev/PR; **802** PR; **803** Gunter Ziesler/Peter Arnold, Inc.; **805** (t)Steven Walker/Peter Arnold, Inc., (cl)John Cancalosi/Peter Arnold, Inc., (cr)Jeff Lepore/PR, (bl)Steve Kaufman/Peter Arnold, Inc., (br)Doug Cheeseman/Peter Arnold, Inc.; **806** (l)courtesy Arcade Publishing/photo by Arb, (r)Janet Adams; **807** Jim Strawser from Grant Heilman; **808** C. Blair; **810** Private collection/Sherrie Silverman/SS; **812** David M. Dennis; **813** C. Allan Morgan/Peter Arnold, Inc.; **817** (t)Larry Moore/SIS, (b)John Lund/TSI; **818** (l)courtesy Jane Katz, (r)Gary Rosenquist/Earth Images; **819** Carmona Photography/FPG; **820** Bios (A. Compost)/Peter Arnold, Inc.; **822** (l)FPG, (r)Fred Bruemmer/Peter Arnold, Inc.; **823** Thomas Gilcrease Institute of American History & Art; **824** Jeff & Alexa Henry/Peter Arnold, Inc.; **826** (l)courtesy Alfred A. Knopf/Spencer, (r)reprinted by permission of Houghton Mifflin Company. All rights reserved; **827** Tom Vezo/The Wildlife Collection; **828** Tim Davis/PR; **830** Lynn M. Stone; **834** (l)E.O. Hoppe/Corbis, (r)UPI/CB; **835** CI; **837** Alan & Sandy Carey/PR; **838** Color Box/FPG; **840** (tl)Tenri University/Japan, (tr)Lynn Saville, (bl)courtesy Scribner's, (br)AP Photo/Marilyn Sanders; **841** G. Buttner/Naturbild/OKAPIA/PR; **842** Mark Burnett; **843** Mike Dobel/Masterfile; **844** Hans Pfletschinger/Peter Arnold, Inc.; **847** Fred Bavendam/Peter Arnold, Inc.; **851** (br)Geoff Butler, (others)AH.

R156 ACKNOWLEDGMENTS